Volume 1 • 2009

WHAT DO I READ NEXT?

A Reader's Guide to Current Genre Fiction

- Fantasy
- Popular Fiction
- Romance
- Horror
- Mystery
- Science Fiction
- Historical
- Inspirational

ISSN 1052-2212

Volume 1 • 2009

WHAT DO I READ NEXT?

A Reader's Guide
to Current
Genre Fiction

- Fantasy
- Popular Fiction
- Romance
- Horror
- Mystery
- Science Fiction
- Historical
- Inspirational

DANIEL S. BURT

DON D'AMMASSA

NATALIE DANFORD

JIM HUANG

KRISTIN RAMSDELL

GALE
CENGAGE Learning™

Detroit • New York • San Francisco • New Haven, Conn • Waterville, Maine • London

GALE
CENGAGE Learning™

What Do I Read Next 2009, Volume 1

Project Editor: Dana Ferguson

Editorial: Michelle Kazensky, Hazel Rumney, Marie Toft

Editorial Support Services: Tom Potts

Composition and Electronic Prepress: Gary Leach, Evi Seoud

Product Design: John Watkins

Manufacturing: Rita Wimberley

For product information and technology assistance, contact us at **Gale Customer Support, 1-800-877-4253.**
For permission to use material from this text or product, submit all requests online at **www.cengage.com/permissions.**
Further permissions questions can be emailed to **permissionrequest@cengage.com**

Gale
27500 Drake Rd.
Farmington Hills, MI, 48331-3535

LIBRARY OF CONGRESS CONTROL NUMBER 82-15700

ISBN-13: 978-1-4144-2216-9
ISBN-10: 1-4144-2216-4

ISSN: 1052-2212

Printed in the United States of America
1 2 3 4 5 6 7 13 12 11 10 09

Contents

Introduction

Thousands of books are published each year intended for devoted fans of genre fiction. Dragons, outlaws, lovers, murderers, monsters, and aliens abound on our own world or on other worlds, throughout time—all featured in the pages of fantasy, western, romance, mystery, horror, science fiction, historical, inspirational, and popular fiction. Given the huge variety of titles available each year, added to the numbers from previous years, readers can be forgiven if they're stumped by the question "What do I read next?" And that's where this book comes in.

Designed as a tool to assist in the exploration of genre fiction, *What Do I Read Next?* guides the reader to both current and classic recommendations in eight widely read genres: Mystery, Romance, Western, Fantasy, Horror, Science Fiction, Historical, Inspirational, and Popular Fiction. *What Do I Read Next?* allows readers quick and easy access to specific data on recent titles in these popular genres. Plus, each entry provides alternate reading selections, thus coming to the rescue of librarians and booksellers, who are often unfamiliar with a genre, yet must answer the question frequently posed by their patrons and customers, "What do I read next?"

Details on Titles

Volume 1 of this year's edition of *What Do I Read Next?* contains entries for titles published primarily in the last half of 2008 and the first half of 2009. These entries are divided into sections for Mystery, Romance, Fantasy, Horror, Science Fiction, Historical, Inspirational, and Popular Fiction. Experts in each field compile the entries for their respective genres. The experts also discuss topics relevant to their genres in essays that appear at the beginning of each section.

The criteria for inclusion of specific titles vary somewhat from genre to genre. In genres such as Romance and Mystery, where large numbers of titles are published each year, the inclusion criteria are more selective, with the experts attempting to select the recently published books that they consider best. In genres such as Horror, where the amount of new material is relatively small, a broader range of titles is represented, including many titles published by small or independent houses and some young adult books.

The entries are listed alphabetically by main author in each genre section. Most provide the following information:

- **Author or editor's** name and real name if a pseudonym is used. Co-authors, co-editors, and illustrators are also listed where applicable.
- **Book title.**
- **Date and place of publication; name of publisher.**
- **Series name.**
- **Story type:** Specific categories within each genre, identified by the compiling expert. Definitions of these types are listed in the "Key to Genre Terms" section.
- **Subject(s):** Gives the subject matter covered by the title.
- **Major character(s):** Names and brief descriptions of up to three characters featured in the title.
- **Time period(s):** Tells when the story takes place.
- **Locale(s):** Tells where the story takes place.
- **What the book is about:** A brief plot summary.
- **Where it's reviewed:** Citations to reviews of the book, including the source of the review, date of the source, and the page on which the review appears. Reviews are included from genre-specific sources such as *Locus* and *Affaire de Coeur*, as well as more general reviewing sources such as *Booklist* and *Publishers* Weekly.
- **Other books by the author:** Titles and publication dates of other books the author has written, useful for those wanting to read more by a particular author.
- **Other books you might like:** Titles by other authors written on a similar theme or in a similar style. These titles further the reader's exploration of the genre.

Indexes Answer Readers' Questions

The nine indexes in *What Do I Read Next?* used separately or in conjunction with each other, create many pathways to the featured titles, answering general questions or locating specific titles. For example:

"Are there any new Maisie Dobbs books?"
    The SERIES INDEX lists entries by the name of the series of which they are a part.

"I like Regency Romances. Can you recommend any new ones?"

The GENRE INDEX breaks each genre into story types or more specialized areas. In the Romance genre for example, there is a story type heading "Regency." For the definitions of story types, see the "Key to Genre Terms."

"I'm looking for a story set in Paris."

The GEOGRAPHIC INDEX lists titles by their locale. This can help readers pinpoint an area in which they may have a particular interest, such as their home town, another country, or even Cyberspace.

"Do you know of any science fiction stories set during the 22nd century?"

The TIME PERIOD INDEX is a chronological listing of the time settings in which the main entry titles take place.

"What books are available that feature teachers?"

The CHARACTER DESCRIPTION INDEX identifies the major characters by occupation (e.g. Accountant, Editor, Librarian) or persona (e.g. Cyborg, Noble woman, Stowaway).

"Has anyone written any new books with Sherlock Holmes in them?"

The CHARACTER NAME INDEX lists the major characters named in the entries. This can help readers who remember some information about a book, but not an author or title.

"What has Laurell K. Hamilton written recently?"

The AUTHOR INDEX contains the names of all authors featured in the entries and those listed under "Other books you might like."

The TITLE INDEX includes all main entry titles and all titles recommended under "Other books by the author" and "Other books you might like" in one alphabetical listing. Thus a reader can find a specific title, new or old, then go to that entry to find out what new titles are similar.

"I'm interested in books that depict military life."

The SUBJECT INDEX is an alphabetical listing of all the subjects covered by the main entry titles.

The indexes can also be used together to narrow down or broaden choices. A reader interested in Mysteries set in New York during the 19th century would consult the TIME PERIOD INDEX and GEOGRAPHIC INDEX to see which titles appear in both. Time Travel is a common theme in Science Fiction but occasionally appears in other genres such as Fantasy and Romance. Searching for this theme in other genres would enable a reader to cross over into previously unknown realms of reading experiences. And with the AUTHOR and TITLE indexes, which include all books listed under "Other books by the author" and "Other books you might like," it is easy to compile an extensive list of recommended reading, beginning with a recently published title or a classic from the past.

Also Available Online

The entries in this book can also be found online in Gale's new *Books & Authors* database. This electronic product encompasses over 140,000 books, including genre fiction, mainstream fiction, and nonfiction. All the books included in the online version are recommended by librarians or other experts, award winners, or appear on bestseller lists. The user-friendly functionality allows users to refine their searching by using several criteria, while making it easy to identify similar titles for further research and reading. *Books & Authors* is updated with new information several times a year. For more information about *Books & Authors*, please visit Gale online at gale.cengage.com.

Suggestions Are Welcome

The editors welcome any comments and suggestions for enhancing and improving *What Do I Read Next?* Please address correspondence to the Editor, *What Do I Read Next?*, at the following address:

Gale, Cengage Learning

27500 Drake Rd.

Farmington Hills, MI 48331-3535

Phone: 248-699-GALE

Toll-free: 800-347-GALE

Fax: 248-699-8054

About the Genre Experts

Daniel S. Burt (Historical Fiction) Burt is a writer and college professor who has taught undergraduate courses at Trinity College and graduate literature courses at Wesleyan University, where he was a dean for nine years. He is the author of *The Chronology of American Literature* (Houghton Mifflin, 2004), *What Historical Novel Do I Read Next?* Volumes 1-3 (Gale, 1997-2003), *The Novel 100* (Facts on File, 2003), *The Literary 100* (Facts on File, 2001), *The Biography Book* (Greenwood/Oryx, 2001), *Drama 100* (Facts on File, 2007). He is the academic director for an annual series of educationally-based workshops held in Ireland (www.discoverytours.ws). When not teaching and traveling to Ireland, he lives with his wife on Cape Cod, Massachusetts.

Don D'Ammassa (Science Fiction, Horror, and Fantasy) D'Ammassa was the book reviewer for *Science Fiction Chronicle* for almost thirty years. He has had fiction published in fantastic magazines and anthologies and has contributed essays to a variety of reference books dealing with fantastic literature. D'Ammassa is the author of the novels *Blood Beast* (Windsor, 1988), *Servants of Chaos* (Leisure, 2002), *Scarab* (Five Star, 2004), *Haven* (Five Star, 2004), *Narcissus* (Five Star, 2007), and the nonfiction works *Encyclopedia of Science Fiction* (Facts on File, 2005), the *Encyclopedia of Fantasy and Horror* (Facts on File, 2006), and the *Encyclopedia of Adventure Fiction* (Facts on File, 2008).

Natalie Danford (Popular Fiction) Danford is the author of *Inheritance*, a novel published by St. Martin's Press. She is also coeditor of the annual *Best New American Voices* anthology series, which introduces emerging writers. An experienced freelance writer and book critic, Natalie has published articles and reviews in *People, The Los Angeles Times, Salon,* and many other publications.

Jim Huang (Mystery Fiction) Huang has sold mystery books for 20 years, including stints in Boston, Kalamazoo, Michigan, and now Carmel, Indiana, where he and his wife own The Mystery Company, a bookstore devoted to the genre. From 1982 through 2005, Huang edited and published The Drood Review, a mystery book review newsletter. He has edited reference books for mystery lov-ers, including *100 Favorite Mysteries of the Century* (winner of the Anthony and Agatha Awards for best nonfiction of 2000), *They Died in Vain: Overlooked, Underappreciated and Forgotten Mystery Novels* (winner of the Agatha, Anthony and Macavity Awards for best nonfiction of 2002) and *Mystery Muses: 100 Classics That Inspire Today's Mystery Writers* (a nominee for the Agatha Award for best nonfiction of 2006), the latter co-edited with Austin Lugar. Since 2000, he has volunteered as the Program Director for Magna Cum Murder, a festival for mystery lovers that takes place each October in Muncie, Indiana. He is the co-chair of the 2009 Boucheron, the World Mystery Convention scheduled for Indianapolis in October 2009. In 2006, Huang was elected to the board of Sisters in Crime, an international organization devoted to combating discrimination against women in the mystery genre; he is the first "brother" to serve on the board in this organization's 20 year history. Huang lives with his wife, Jennie Jacobson, and their two daughters in Carmel.

Kristin Ramsdell (Romance Fiction) Ramsdell is a librarian at California State University, East Bay and is a nationally known speaker and consultant on the subject of romance fiction. Besides writing articles about the romance genre, she writes a romance review column for *Library Journal* and is the author of *Romance Fiction: A Guide to the Genre* (Libraries Unlimited, 1999) and its predecessor, *Happily Ever After: A Guide to Reading Interests in Romance Fiction* (Libraries Unlimited, 1987). She was named Librarian of the Year by Romance Writers of America in 1996 and received in 2007 the Melinda Helfer Fairy Godmother Award from *Romantic Times* Magazine.

Contributors

John Charles (Romance Fiction) Charles, a reference librarian and retrospective fiction selector for the Scottsdale Public Library, was named 2002 Librarian of the Year by the Romance Writers of America. Charles reviews books for *Library Journal, Booklist,* the *Chicago Tribune,* and *VOYA(Voice of Youth Advocates)* and co-authors VOYA's annual "Clueless: Adult Mysteries with Young Adult Appeal" column. John Charles is co-author of *The Mystery*

Readers' Advisory: The Librarian's Clues to Murder and Mayhem (ALA, 2001). Along with co-author Shelley Mosley, Charles has twice been the recipient of the Romance Writers of America's Veritas Award.

Shelley Mosley (Romance Fiction) Retired library manager Shelley Mosley has co-authored several non-fiction books: The Suffragists in Literature for Youth; Romance Today: An A-to-Z Guide to Contemporary Ameri-

can Romance Writers; The Complete Idiot's Guide to the Ultimate Reading List;and Crash Course in Library Supervision. With John Charles, she has won two Romance Writers of America's Veritas awards. Mosley, Romance Writers of America's 2001 Librarian of the Year, reviews books for both Booklist and Library Journal. She also writes romantic comedies with Deborah Mazoyer under the pen name Deborah Shelley. Their novels have been published by Kensington and, most recently, Avalon Books.

Key to Genre Terms

The following is a list of terms used to classify the story type of each novel included in What Do I Read Next? along with brief definitions of the terms. To find books that fall under a particular story type heading, see the Genre Index.

Action/Adventure ❚ Minimal detection; not usually espionage, but can contain rogue police or out of control spies.

Adult ❚ Fiction dealing with adult characters and mature, developed ideas.

Adventure ❚ The character(s) must face a series of obstacles, which may include monsters, conflict with other travelers, war, interference by supernatural elements, interference by nature, and so on.

Alternate History ❚ A story dealing with how society might have evolved if a specific historical event had happened differently, e.g., if the South had won the American Civil War.

Alternate Intelligence ❚ Story featuring an entity with a sense of identity and able to self-determine goals and actions. The natural or manufactured entity results from a synergy, generally unpredictable, of individual elements. This subgenre frequently involves a computer-type intelligence.

Alternate Universe ❚ More accurately, in most cases, alternate history, in which the South won the Civil War, the Nazis triumphed, etc. The idea is a venerable one in SF.

Alternate World ❚ The story starts out in the everyday world, but the main character is transported to an alternate/parallel world by supernatural means.

Amateur Detective ❚ Detective work is performed by a non-professional rather than by police or a private detective.

Americana ❚ A romance set in the present that features themes that are particularly American; often focuses on small-town life.

Ancient Evil Unleashed ❚ The evils may take familiar forms, like vampires undead for centuries, or malevolent ancient gods released from bondage by careless humans, or ancient prophecies wreaking havoc on today's world. The so-called *Cthulhu Mythos* originated by H.P. Lovecraft, in which *Cthulhu* is prominent among a pantheon of ancient evil gods, is a specific variation of this.

Anthology ❚ A collection of short stories by different authors, usually sharing a common theme.

Apocalyptic Horror ❚ Traditionally, horrors that signal or presage the end of the world, or the world of the characters, and the establishment of a new, possibly very sinister order.

Arts ❚ Fiction that incorporates some aspect of the arts, whether it be music, painting, drama, etc.

Biblical Fiction ❚ Novels that take their plots or characters from the Bible.

Black Magic ❚ Magic directed toward malevolent ends, as distinct from white magic, which is directed toward benevolent ends. Witchcraft is commonly thought of as a black art. Voodoo consists of mysterious rites and practices, including sorcery, magic and conjuration, and often has evil goals.

Carnival-Circus Horror ❚ Derived from its setting, especially the freakish world of the sideshow, in which the distorted or horrific is the norm and is sometimes used as a distorting mirror to reveal hidden selves.

Chase ❚ A traditional Western in which the action of the plot is based on some form of pursuit.

Child-in-Peril ❚ The innocence of childhood is often used to heighten the intensity and unpredictability of evil.

Collection ❚ A book of short stories by a single author.

Coming-of-Age ❚ A story in which the primary character is a young person, usually a teenager. The growth of maturity is chronicled.

Contemporary ❚ A story set in the present.

Contemporary/Exotic ❚ Set in the present but with an especially unusual or exotic setting, e.g., the tent of a desert sheik or a boat on the Amazon.

Contemporary/Fantasy ❚ A contemporary story that makes use of fantasy or supernatural elements.

Contemporary/Innocent ❚ Story set in the present that contains little or no sex.

Contemporary/Mainstream ❚ A story set in the present that would be more properly categorized as general fiction rather than a work in a specific genre.

Contemporary Realism ❚ An accurate representation of characters, settings, ideas, themes in the present day. Not idealistic in nature.

Curse ❚ Words said when someone wishes evil or harm on someone or something, such as a witch's or prophet's curse.

Cyberpunk ❚ Usually applied to the stories by a group of writers who became prominent in the mid-1980s, such as

William Gibson and his *Necromancer* (1984). The "cyber" is derived from cybernetics, nominally the study of control and communications in machines. These books also feature a downbeat, punk sensibility reminiscent of the hardboiled school of detective fiction writers.

Disaster ❚ A tale recounting some event or events seriously disruptive of the social fabric but not as serious as a holocaust.

Domestic ❚ Fiction relating to household and family matters. Concerned with psychological and emotional needs of family members.

Doppelganger ❚ A double or alter ego, popularized in the works of E.T.A. Hoffmann, Edgar Allan Poe, and Robert Louis Stevenson.

Dystopian ❚ The antonym of utopian, sometimes called anti-utopian, in which traditionally positive utopian themes are treated satirically or ironically and the mood is downbeat or satiric.

End of the World ❚ A story that concerns the last events following some sort of disaster.

Erotic Horror ❚ Sexuality and horror are often argued to be inextricably linked, as in Bram Stoker's *Dracula* and Sheridan Le Fanu's "Carmilla," although others have argued that they are antithetical. Sexuality became increasingly explicit in the 1980s, sometimes verging on the pornographic, as in Brett Easton Ellis' *American Psycho*.

Espionage ❚ Involving the CIA, KGB, or other organizations whose main focus is the collection of information from the other side. Can be either violent or quiet.

Espionage Thriller ❚ Plot contains a high level of action and suspense relating to espionage.

Ethnic ❚ A work in which the ethnic background of the characters is integral to the story. Usually the focus is on an American ethnic minority group (e.g., African American, Asian American, Native American, Latino) and the two main characters are members of this group.

Evil Children ❚ The presumed innocence of a child is replaced with adult-like malevolence and cunning, contradicting the reader's usual expectations.

Family Saga ❚ Stories focusing on the problems or concerns of a family; estrangement and reunion are common themes.

Fantasy ❚ A story that contains some fantasy or supernatural elements.

Femme Fatale ❚ A seductress for whom men abandon careers, families, and responsibilities and who feels no pity or compunction in return; a common figure in history and literature.

First Contact ❚ Any story about the initial meeting or communication of humans with extraterrestrials or aliens. The term may take its name from the eponymous 1945 story by Murray Leinster.

Future Shock ❚ A journalistic term derived from Alvin Toffler's 1970 book and which refers to the alleged disorientation resulting from rapid technological change.

Futuristic ❚ A story with a science fiction setting. Often these stories are set on other planets, aboard spaceships or space stations, or on Earth in an imaginary future or, in some cases, past.

Gay/Lesbian Fiction ❚ Stories portraying homosexual characters or themes.

Generation Starship ❚ If pseudoscientific explanations involving faster-than-light drives are rejected, then the time required for interstellar travel will encompass many human generations.

Genetic Manipulation ❚ Sometimes called genetic engineering, this assumes that the knowledge exists to shape creatures, human or otherwise, using genetic means, as in *Brave New World* (1932).

Ghost Story ❚ The spirits of the dead, who can be benevolent, as in Charles Dickens, or malevolent, as in the tales of M.R. James.

Gothic ❚ A story with a strong mystery suspense plot that emphasizes mood, atmosphere, and/or supernatural or paranormal elements. Unexplained events, ancient family secrets, and a general feeling of impending doom often characterize these tales. These stories are most often set in the past.

Gothic Family Chronicle ❚ A story often covering several generations of a family, many of whose members are typically evil, perverted, or loathsome, and in which family violence is common. The family may live in a decaying mansion suggestive of those in 18th century Gothic novels.

Hard Science Fiction ❚ Stories in which the author adheres with varying degrees of rigor to scientific principles believed to be true at the time of writing, principles derived from hard (physical, biological) rather than soft (social) sciences.

Haunted House ❚ Literally, a house visited by ghosts, usually with evil intentions in horror fiction, but sometimes the subject of comedy.

Historical ❚ Set in an earlier time frame than the present.

Historical/American Civil War ❚ Set during the American Civil War, 1861-1865.

Historical/American Revolution ❚ Set during the American Revolutionary period.

Historical/American West ❚ Set in the Western portion of the United States, usually during the second half of the 19th century. Stories often involve the hardships of pioneer life (Indian raids, range wars, climatic disasters, etc.) and the main characters (most often the hero) can be of Native American extraction.

Historical/American West Coast ❚ Set in the American Far West (California, Oregon, Washington, or Alaska). Stories often focus on the Gold Rush and the tension between Spanish Land Grant families and immigrants from the Pacific Rim, usually China.

Historical/Americana ❚ A story dealing with themes unique to the American experience.

Historical/Ancient Egypt ❚ A novel set during the time of the pharaohs from the fourth century B.C. to the first century A.D. and the absorption of Egypt into the Roman Empire.

Historical/Ancient Greece ▌ Set during the flowering of the ancient Greek civilization, particularly during the age of Pericles in the 5th century B.C.

Historical/Ancient Rome ▌ Covering the history of Rome from its founding and the Roman Republic before Augustus through the decline and fall of the Roman Empire in the fifth century.

Historical/Antebellum American South ▌ Set in the American Old South (prior to the Civil War).

Historical/Canadian West ▌ Set in the western or frontier portions of Canada, usually during the 19th century. Stories most often revolve around the hardships of frontier life.

Historical/Colonial America ▌ Set in America before the American Revolution, 1620-1775. Stories featuring the Jamestown Colony, the Salem Witch Trials, and the French and Indian Wars are especially popular.

Historical/Depression Era ▌ Set mainly in America during the period of economic hardship brought on by the 1929 Stock Market Crash that continued throughout the 1930s.

Historical/Edwardian ▌ Set during the reign of Edward VII of England, 1901-1910.

Historical/Eighteenth Century ▌ A work of fiction set during the eighteenth century.

Historical/Elizabethan ▌ A novel set during the reign of Elizabeth I of England (1558-1603). There is some overlap with the last part of the Historical Renaissance category but the emphasis is British.

Historical/Exotic ▌ Setting is an unusual or exotic place.

Historical/Fantasy ▌ A historical work that makes use of fantasy or supernatural elements.

Historical/French Revolution ▌ Set during the French Revolution, 1789-1795.

Historical/Georgian ▌ Set during the reigns of the first three "Georges" of England. Roughly corresponds to the 18th century. Stories often focus on the Jacobite Rebellions and the escapades of Bonnie Prince Charlie.

Historical/Mainstream ▌ Historical fiction that would be more properly categorized as fiction rather than a specific genre.

Historical/Medieval ▌ Set during the Middle Ages, approximately the fifth through the fifteenth centuries. Stories feature battles, raids, crusades, and court intrigues; plotlines associated with the Battle of Hastings (1066) are especially popular.

Historical/Napoleonic Wars ▌ Set between 1803-1815 during the wars waged by and against France under Napoleon Bonaparte.

Historical/Post-American Civil War ▌ Set in the years following the Civil War/War Between the States, generally from 1865 into the 1870s.

Historical/Post-American Revolution ▌ Set in the years immediately following the Civil War, 1865-1870s.

Historical/Post-French Revolution ▌ Set during the years immediately following the French Revolution; stories usually take place in France or England.

Historical/Pre-History ▌ Set in the years before the Middle Ages.

Historical/Regency ▌ A novel that is set during the Regency period (1811-1820).

Historical/Renaissance ▌ Novel set in the years of the Renaissance in Europe, generally lasting from the 14th through the 17th centuries.

Historical/Roaring Twenties ▌ Usually has an American setting and takes place in the 1920s.

Historical/Russian Revolution ▌ These stories are set around and during the 1917 Russian Revolution.

Historical/Seventeenth Century ▌ A work of fiction set during the 17th century. Stories of this type often center around the clashes between the Royalists and the Cromwellians and the Restoration.

Historical/Tudor Period ▌ A novel set during the Tudor dynasty in England (1485-1603). Roughly corresponds to the Renaissance, but the emphasis is British. Overlaps with the Elizabethan period, which is marked by the reign of Elizabeth Tudor.

Historical/Victorian ▌ Set during the reign of Queen Victoria, 1837-1901. This designation does not include works with a predominately American setting.

Historical/Victorian America ▌ Set in America, usually the Eastern part, during the Victorian Period, 1837-1901.

Historical/War of 1812 ▌ Set during the British-U.S. conflict which lasted from 1812 to 1814.

Historical/World War I ▌ Set during the First World War, 1914-1918.

Historical/World War II ▌ Set in the years of the Second World War, 1939-1945.

Holiday Themes ▌ Fiction that focuses on or is set during a particular holiday or holiday season (e.g., Christmas, Valentine's Day, Mardi Gras).

Horror ▌ Refers to stories in which interest in the events, the intellectual puzzle characteristic of much of SF, is subordinated to a feeling of terror or horror by the reader, which could result from a variety of causes, including a disaster or an invasion of earth.

Humor ▌ Story with an amusing story line.

Immortality ▌ Usually includes extreme longevity, resulting from fountains of youth, elixirs, or something with a pseudoscientific basis.

Indian Culture ▌ These novels center on the lives, customs, and cultures of characters who are American Indians or who lived among the Indians.

Indian Wars ▌ Often traditional Westerns, these stories are set during the period of the Indian wars and rely on this warfare for plots, characters, and themes.

Inspirational ▌ A novel with an uplifting, often Christian theme, and usually considered "innocent."

Invasion of Earth ▌ An extremely common theme, often paralleling historical events and reflecting fears of the time. Most invasions are depicted as malign, only occasionally benign.

Legal ▌ Main focus is on a lawyer, though it does not always involve courtroom action.

Legend ▮ A story based on a legend, myth, or fairy tale that has been rewritten.

Lesbian/Contemporary ▮ A story with lesbian protagonists set in the present.

Lesbian/Historical ▮ Historical fiction with lesbian protagonists.

Light Fantasy ▮ There is a great deal of humor throughout the story and it is almost guaranteed to have a happy ending.

Literary ▮ Relates to the nature and knowledge of literature; can be applied to setting or characters.

Lost Colony ▮ Stories centering around a colony on another world that loses contact with or is abandoned by its parent civilization and the type of society that evolves under those conditions. Conflict usually arises when contact is re-established between the colony and its home world.

Magic Conflict ▮ The main conflict of the story stems from magical interference. Protagonists may be caught in the middle of a conflict between sorcerers or may themselves be engaged in conflict with other sorcerers.

Magic Realism ▮ A style of prose fiction writing in which the author blends the realism of describing ordinary places and incidents with fantastic, dreamlike, or mythical events and does not differentiate between the real and the magical.

Man Alone ▮ A lone man, alienated from the society that would normally support him, faces overwhelming dangers.

Medical ▮ Stories in which medical themes are dominant.

Military ▮ Stories have a military theme; may deal with life in the armed forces or military battles.

Modern ▮ Reflection of the present time period.

Mountain Man ▮ Any story in which the principal characters are mountain men and women, living in mountain areas remote from civilization and depending upon their own resourcefulness for survival.

Multicultural ▮ A romance in which the ethnic background of the characters is integral to the story.

Mystery ▮ Usually a story where a crime occurs or a puzzle must be solved.

Mystical ▮ Fiction dealing with spiritual elements. Miraculous or supernatural characteristics of events, characters, settings, and themes.

Nature in Revolt ▮ Tales in which normally docile plants or animals suddenly turn against humankind, sometimes transformed (giant crabs resulting from radioactivity, predatory rats, plagues, blobs that threaten London or Miami, etc.).

Occult ▮ An adjective suggesting fiction based on a mystical or secret doctrine, but sometimes referring to supernatural fiction generally. Implies that there is a reality beyond the perceived world that only adepts can penetrate.

Paranormal ▮ Novel contains supernatural elements. Story may include ghosts, UFOs, aliens, demons, and haunted houses among other unexplained phenomenon.

Parody ▮ A narrative that follows the form of the original but usually changes its sense to nonsense, thus making fun of the original or its ideas.

Police Procedural ▮ A story in which the action is centered around a police officer.

Political ▮ The novel deals with political issues that are skewed by the use and presence of fantastic elements.

Possession ▮ Domination, usually of humans, by evil spirits, demons, aliens, or other agencies in which one's own volition is replaced by an outside force.

Post-Disaster ▮ Story set in a much degraded environment, frequently involving a reduction in population and the resulting loss of access to processes, resources, technology, etc.

Post-Holocaust ▮ The events following a world-wide disaster, often the result of human folly rather than natural events (collision with a meteor, etc.).

Post-Nuclear Holocaust ▮ The events following a world-wide nuclear disaster.

Private Detective ▮ Usually detection, involving a professional for hire.

Psychic Powers ▮ Parapsychological or paranormal powers.

Psychological ▮ Fiction dealing with mental or emotional responses.

Psychological Suspense ▮ Tales in which the psychological exploration and quirks of characters generate suspense and plot.

Quest ▮ The central characters are on a journey filled with dangers to reach some worthwhile goal.

Ranch Life ▮ The basic cowboy story, in which the plot and characters are inextricably bound up in the workings of a ranch.

Reanimated Dead ▮ These can take many forms, such as mummies and zombies (often the result of Voodoo).

Regency ▮ A light romance involving the British upper classes, set during the Regency Period, 1811-1820. During this time, the Prince of Wales acted as Prince Regent because of the incapacity of his father, George III. In 1820, "Prinny" became George IV. These stories, in the style of Jane Austen, are essentially comedies of manners and the emphasis is on language, wit, and style. Georgette Heyer set the standard for the modern version of this genre. This designation is also given to stories of similar type that may not fit precisely within the Regency time period.

Reincarnation ▮ A tale in which the horror arises in connection with the reincarnation of one of the characters.

Religious ▮ Religion of any sort plays a primary role in the plot.

Revenge ▮ A character who has suffered an unjust loss returns to take vengeance. This is one of the most common traditional themes.

Robot Fiction ▮ From the Jewish Golem to the traditional clanking bucket of bolts to the human-like android, robots in various guises have been among us for centuries. The term comes from Karl Capek's play, *R.U.R.*, which stands for Rossum's Universal Robots. Robots are often surrogates for humans and may be treated seriously or comically.

Romance ▌ Stories involving love affairs and love stories; deals with the emotional attachments of the characters.

Romantic Suspense ▌ Romance with a strong mystery suspense plot. This is a broad category including works in the tradition of Mary Stewart, as well as the newer women-in-jeopardy tales by writers such as Mary Higgins Clark. These stories usually have contemporary settings but some are also set in the past.

Saga ▌ A multi-generational story that usually centers around one particular family and its trials, tribulations, successes, and loves.

Satanism ▌ Suggests worship of evil rather than benevolent gods, the antithesis of conventional theism, whether Christianity or other religions. Evil demons are Satan writ small and usually lack the awful majesty of their parent.

Satire ▌ Fiction written in a sarcastic and ironic way to ridicule human vices or follies; usually using an exaggeration of characteristics to stress a point.

Science Fantasy ▌ A somewhat vague term in which there are "rational" elements from SF and "magical" or "fanciful" elements from fantasy, which hopefully cohere in a plausible story.

Science Fiction ▌ Although the story has been classified in another genre, there are strong elements of science fiction.

Serial Killer ▌ A multiple murderer, going back to Bluebeard and up to Ed Gein, who inspired Robert Bloch's *Psycho*.

Series ▌ A number of books united either by continuing characters and situations or by a common theme. Series books may appear under a single author's name or each book in the series may be by a different author.

Small Town Horror ▌ The coziness and intimacy of a small community is disrupted by some sort of horrific happening, suggesting an unjustified placidity and complacency on the part of the citizens.

Space Colony ▌ A permanent space station, usually orbiting Earth but in principal located in deep space or near other planets or stars.

Space Opera ▌ Intergalactic adventures; westerns in space; a specialized form of the genre type Adventure.

Supernatural Vengeance ▌ Punishment inflicted by God or a godlike creature, whether justly or capriciously.

Sword and Sorcery ▌ Often a muscle-bound swordsman, who is innocent of thought and common sense, up against evil sorcerers and sorceresses, who naturally lose in the end because they are evil.

Techno-Horror ▌ Suggests a catastrophe with horrific elements resulting from a scientific miscalculation or technological hubris; Victor Frankenstein's unnamed monster or a plague resulting from a laboratory mishap.

Techno-Thriller ▌ Stories in which a technological development, such as an invention, is linked to a series of suspenseful (thrilling) events.

Theological ▌ Stories in which religion or religious belief plays an important role.

Time Travel ▌ A story in which characters from one time are transported either literally or in spirit to another time period. The time shifts are usually between the present and another historical period.

Traditional ▌ Traditional stories may deal with virtually any time period or situation, but they are related by shared conventions of setting and characterization.

Trail Drive ▌ Any story in which a cattle drive (or, more rarely, a drive of sheep or horses) is a major plot component.

UFO ▌ Unidentified Flying Objects, literally, although sometimes used more generally to refer to any object of mysterious origin or intent.

Urban ▌ Stories set in large cities; usually the tone of the novel is gritty and realistic and may involve issues such as drugs and gangs.

Utopia ▌ A large, often influential, story type that takes its name from Thomas More's 1516 book. Usually refers to a society considered better by the author, even if not perfect. Aldous Huxley's *Island* (1962) is a utopia, whereas his more famous *Brave New World* (1932) is a dark twin, a dystopia.

Vampire Story ▌ Based on mythical bloodsucking creatures possessing supernatural powers and various forms, both animal and human. The concept can be traced far back in history, long before Bram Stoker's famous novel, *Dracula*.

Wagon Train ▌ A book that deals with wagon trains traveling across the American West.

Werewolf Story ▌ Were is Old English for man, suggesting the ancient lineage of a creature that once dominated a world in which witches and sorcerers were equally feared. Sometimes used to refer to any shape shifter, whether wolves or other animals.

Wild Talents ▌ The phrase comes from Charles Fort's writings and usually refers to parapsychological powers such a telepathy, psychokinesis, and precognition, collectively called psychic or psi phenomena.

Witchcraft ▌ Characters either profess to be or are stigmatized as witches or warlocks, and practitioners of magic associated with witchcraft. This can include black magic or white magic (e.g., Wicca).

Young Adult ▌ A marketing term for publishers; one or more of the central characters is a teenager often testing his or her skills against adversity to achieve a greater degree of maturity and self-awareness. A category used by librarians to shelve books of likely appeal to teenage readers.

Young Readers ▌ A novel with characters, plot, and vocabulary primarily aimed at juveniles.

Award Winners

Mystery Awards
by Jim Huang

The Anthony

The Anthony Awards for books published in 2007 were presented at Bouchercon, the World Mystery Convention, in October 2008 in Baltimore, Maryland. The award, like the convention itself, is named for the late mystery editor, reviewer and writer Anthony Boucher. Nominations and final voting are by the members of the convention.

Best Novel: *What the Dead Know* by Laura Lippman.

Best First Novel: *In the Woods* by Tana French.

Best Paperback Original: *Arthur Conan Doyle: A Life in Letters* by Jon Lellenberg, Daniel Stashower and Charles Foley

Best Short Story: "Hardly Knew Her" by Laura Lippman.

Best Critical/Non-Fiction Work: *Arthur Conan Doyle: A Life in Letters* by Jon Lellenberg, Daniel Stashower, and Charles Foley.

The Barry

This award is named for the late fan reviewer Barry Gardner. Voting is by subscribers to *Deadly Pleasures* and to *Mystery News*. The winners were announced at Bouchercon in Baltimore, Maryland in October 2008, honoring books published the year prior.

Best Novel: *What the Dead Know* by Laura Lippman.

Best First Novel: *In the Woods* by Tana French.

Best Paperback Original: *Queenpin* by Megan Abbott.

Best British Mystery Novel: *Damnation Falls* by Edward Wright.

Best Thriller: *The Watchman* by Robert Crais.

Best Short Story: "The Problem of the Summer Snowman" by Edward D. Hoch.

The Hammett

The Hammett is given by the North American Branch of the International Association of Crime Writers, with nominees chosen by the organization's nominating committee. Final selection is done by a rotating panel of outside judges. The 2008 award, for books published in 2007, was presented at the New Atlantic Independent Booksellers Association trade show in Baltimore in September 2008.

Winner: *The Outlander* by Gil Adamson.

The Macavity

Named for T.S. Eliot's *Old Possum's Book of Practical Cats* mystery cat, the Macavity is nominated and voted on by members of Mystery Readers International. The winners were announced at Bouchercon in Baltimore, Maryland, in October 2008, honoring books published the year prior.

Best Novel: *What the Dead Know* by Laura Lippman.

Best First Novel: *In the Woods* by Tana French.

Best Short Story: "Please Watch Your Step" by Rhys Bowen.

Best Non-Fiction: *The Essential Mystery Lists: For Readers, Collectors, and Librarians* by Roger Sobin.

The Nero

The Nero Wolfe Award is annually presented to an author for literary excellence in the mystery genre by the Wolfe Pack, the Nero Wolfe Society. It is presented at the Black Orchid Banquet, traditionally held in December in New York City.

Winner: *Anatomy of Fear* by Jonathan Santlofer.

The Shamus

Nominations and final voting are by members of the Private Eye Writers of America. The 2008 awards, for books published in 2007, were presented at the PWA's banquet in October 2008 held during, but not as part of, Bouchercon.

Best Novel: *Soul Patch* by Reed Farrel Coleman.

Best First Novel: *Big City, Bad Blood* by Sean Chercover.

Best Paperback Original: *Songs of Innocence* by Richard Aleas.

Best Short Story: "Hungry Enough" by Cornelia Read.

The Eye (for Lifetime Achievement): Joe Gores.

The Hammer (Recognizing a Private Eye Character): Bill Pronzini's The Nameless Detective.

Romance Awards
by Kristin Ramsdell

As romance fiction has attained increased recognition as a legitimate literary genre, various publications, organizations, and groups have developed to support the interests of its writers and readers. As part of this mission, a number of these offer awards to recognize the accomplishments of the practitioners. Some awards are juried and are presented for excellence in quality and style of writing; others are based on popularity and are selected by the readers. Usually awards are given for a particular work by a particular writer; however, some awards are presented for a body of work produced over a number of years (a type of career award) and others are given for various types of contributions to romance fiction in general. The included categories may change over time to reflect the changing nature of the genre. The Romance Writers of America and the *Romantic Times* are the sponsors of most of the awards listed below.

Romance Writers of America Awards

A number of awards for excellence in romance fiction writing are presented by the Romance Writers of America at the annual RWA conference in July. The awards presented in 2008 are listed in volume 2 of *What Do I Read Next? 2008*. The winners of the awards to be presented at the 2009 Conference in Washington, D.C., were not available as of this writing.

Romantic Times Bookclub Reviewer's Choice Awards

Presented by *Romantic Times Bookclub Magazine* for outstanding romances published in the previous year. Selection is done by the *RT* romance reviewers. Categories may vary from year to year. The awards for books published in 2007 were published in volume 2 of *What Do I Read Next? 2008*. The awards for books published in 2008 will be presented at RT's Annual Booklovers Convention in Orlando, Florida, and are not available as of this writing.

Awards information courtesy of the Romance Writers of America and the Romantic Times Publishing Group.

Fantastic Fiction Awards
by Don D'Ammassa

Several organizations present awards for science fiction, fantasy, and horror fiction, usually on an annual basis, sometimes with open balloting, sometimes confining the final decision to a group of judges. These awards typically cover short fiction of varying lengths, dramatic presentations, and other categories in addition to those involving a specific book as shown below. Since these awards are all presented retroactively, the individual titles below will have been covered in earlier editions of *What Do I Read Next?*.

Hugo Awards

The Hugo Awards, named in honor of Hugo Gernsback for his pioneering work in creating science fiction magazines, are presented at the World Science Fiction convention which takes place annually on a rotating regional schedule. This year's convention took place in Denver, Colorado. This is the fantastic fiction's oldest award originating in 1953. Anyone who purchases a membership is entitled to nominate and vote. The nominees for 2009 include the following titles:

Best Novel: *Little Brother* by Cory Doctorow, *The Graveyard Book* by Neil Gaiman, *Zoe's Tale* by John Scalzi, *Anathem* by Neal Stephenson, and *Saturn's Children* by Charles Stross.

Best Related Book: *The Vorkosigan Companion: The Universe of Lois McMaster Bujold* edited by Lillian Stewart Carl and John Helfers, *Spectrum 15: The Best in Contemporary Fantastic Art* edited by Cathy and Arnie Fenner, *What It Is We Do When We Read Science Fiction* by Paul Kincaid, *Rhetorics of Fantasy* by Farah Mendlesohn, and *Your Hate Mail Will be Graded: A Decade of Whatever, 1998-2008* by John Scalzi.

Locus Poll

The news magazines *Locus* conducts an annual poll of its readers to choose the most popular in many categories. Those involving book length works are listed below:

Best Science Fiction Novel: *The Yiddish Policemen's Union* by Michael Chabon.

Best Fantasy Novel: *Making Money* by Terry Pratchett.

Best First Novel: *Heart-Shaped Box* by Joe Hill.

Best Young Adult Book: *Un Lun Dun* by China Mieville.

Best Anthology: *The New Space Opera* edited by Gardner Dozois and Jonathan Strahan.

Best Collection: *The Winds of Marble Arch and Other Stories* by Connie Willis.

Best Non-Fiction Book: *Breakfast in the Ruins: Science Fiction in the Last Millennium* by Barry Malzberg.

Nebula Awards

The Nebula Awards are presented by the Science Fiction and Fantasy Writers of America at their annual meeting. Only full members are entitled to vote for the final selection. This year's meeting was held in New York City. The award has been presented annually since 1965. The winners for 2008 are as follows:

Best Novel: *Powers* by Ursula K. le Guin.

Runners-up: *Little Brother* by Cory Doctorow, *Cauldron* by Jack McDevitt, *Brasyl* by Ian McDonald, *Making Money* by Terry Pratchett, and *Superpowers* by David J. Schwartz.

World Fantasy Awards

Readers nominate a list of potential winners for this annual award but the final decision is made by a panel of judges. This year's awards were presented at the World Fantasy Convention in Calgary, Alberta:

Best Novel: *Ysabeau* by Guy Gavriel Kay.

Runners-up: *Territory* by Emma Bull, *Fangland,/i>* by John Marks, *Gospel of the Knife* by Will Shetterly, and *The Servants* by Michael Marshall Smith

Best Anthology: *Inferno: New Tales of Terror and the Supernatural* edited by Ellen Datlow.

Runners-up: *Five Strokes to Midnight* edited by Gary A. Braunbeck and Hank Schwaeble, *Wizards: Magical Tales from the Masters of Modern Fantasy* edited by Jack Dann and Gardner Dozois, *The Coyote Road: Trickster Tales* edited by Ellen Datlow and Terri Windling, and *Logorrhea: Good Words Make Good Stories* edited by John Klima.

Best Collection: *Tiny Deaths* by Robert Shearman.

Runners-up: *Plots and Misadventures* by Stephen Gallagher, *Portable Childhoods* by Ellen Klages, *The Secret Files of the Diogenes Club* by Kim Newman, *Hart & Boot and Other Stories* by Tim Lucas, and *Dagger Key and Other Stories* by Lucius Shepard.

Bram Stoker Awards

This award is presented by the Horror Writers of America at their annual meeting. All members can nominate but only full members can vote on the final ballot. The award is named after the author of *Dracula* and has been presented since 1987. Additional ballots and awards will be announced later in the year from the International Horror Guild, the World Fantasy Awards, and the Locus Poll. This year's winners are as follows:

Best Novel: *The Missing* by Sarah Langan

Best First Novel: *The Heart Shaped Box* by Joe Hill

Best Collection: *Proverbs for Monsters* by Michael A. Arnzen, and *5 Stories* by Peter Straub (Tie).

Best Anthology: *Five Strokes to Midnight* edited by Gary Braunbeck and Hank Schwaeble

Best Non-Fiction: *The Cryptopedia: A Dictionary of the Weird, Strange, & Downright Bizarre* by Jonathan Maberry and David F. Kramer.

International Horror Guild Awards

This award is presented at the annual World Horror Convention. The winner is selected by a panel of judges.

Best Novel: *The Terror* by Dan Simmons.

Runners-up: *Grin of the Dark* by Ramsey Campbell, *Generation Loss* by Elizabeth Hand, *The Missing* by Sarah Langan, and *Season of the Witch* by Natasha Mostert.

Best Collection: *Dagger Key and Other Stories* by Lucius Shepard.

Runners-up: *The Imago Sequence and Other Stories* by Laird Barron, *Plots and Misadventures* by Stephen Gallagher, *Shadows of Kith and Kin* by Joe R. Lansdale, and *Masques of Satan* by Reggie Oliver.

Non-Fiction: *Mario Bava: All the Colors of Dark* by Tim Lucas.

Runners-up: *Warnings to the Curious: A Sheaf of Criticism on M.R. James* by Rosemary Pardoe and S.T. Joshi, *Frankenstein: A Cultural History* by Susan Tyler, and *The Science of Stephen King* by Bob Weinberg and Lois M. Gresh.

Inspirational Fiction Awards

The Christy Awards

In 1999 several Christian publishers launched an award to recognize the good work being published in the area of Christian fiction. The Christy Award is named in honor of the most famous novel of Catherine Marshall, one of the pioneers of Christian fiction. Publishers submit novels they feel are most deserving of the honor of an award. Those novels are then judged by a panel of seven judges. There are currently nine categories for submission, including one for young adult novels. The 2009 finalists are listed below.

Contemporary Romance: *Beyond the Night* by Marlo Schalesky, *Finding Stefanie* by Susan May Warren, and *Zora and Nicky: A Novel in Black and White* by Claudia Mair Burney.

Contemporary (Stand Alone): *Dogwood* by Chris Fabry, *Embrace Me* by Lisa Samson, and *Tuesday Night at the Blue Moon* by Debbie Fuller Thomas.

Contemporary (Series, Sequels and Novellas): *Sisterchicks Go Brit!* by Robin Jones Gunn, *Summer Snow* by Nicole Baart, and *You Had Me at Good-by* by Tracey Bateman.

First Novel: *Blue Hole Back Home* by Joy Jordan-Lake, *Rain Song* by Alice J. Wisler, and *Safe at Home* by Richard Doster.

Historical: *Shadow of Colossus* by T.L. Higle, *Until We Reach Home* by Lynn Austink and *Washington's Lady* by Nancy Moser.

Historical Romance: *Calico Canyon* by Mary Connealy, *From a Distance* by Tamera Alexander, and *The Moon in the Mango Tree* by Pamela Binnings Ewen.

Suspense: *By Reason of Insanity* by Randy Singer, *The Rook* by Steven James, and *Winter Haven* by Athol Dickso.

Visionary: *The Battle for Vast Dominion* by George Bryan Polivka, *Shade* by John B. Olson, and *Vanish* by Tom Pawlik.

Young Adult: *The Fruit of My Lipstick* by Shelley Adin, *I Have Seen Him in the Watchfires* by Cathy Gohlke, and *On the Edge of the Dark Sea of Darkness* by Andrew Peterson.

ECPA Christian Book Awards

The Evangelical Christian Publishers Association revised its Gold Medallion Book Awards in 2006, eliminating several categories. They retained the fiction awards. The awards are now known as the ECPA Christian Book Awards.

Winner: *The Shape of Mercy* by Susan Meissner.

Finalists: *Less Than Dead* by Tim Downs, *The Outsider* by Ann H. Gabhart, *Riven* by Jerry B. Jenkins, *Home Another Way* by Christa Parrish.

Popular Fiction Awards
by Natalie Danford

Man Booker Prize

Great Britain's major literary prize is awarded annually to the author of a full-length novel. The prize was established in 1968 by Booker PLC, an international food company, and the Book Trust and Publishers Association. The Man Group took over sponsorship for the prize in 2002

2008 Winner: *The White Tiger* by Aravind Adiga.

Finalists: *The Secret Scripture* by Sebastian Barry, *Sea of Poppies* by Amitav Ghosh, *The Clothes on Their Backs* by Linda Grant, *The Northern Clemency* by Philip Hensher, and *A Fraction of the Whole* by Hamish Hamilton.

Medal for Distinguished Contributions to American Letters

This award is sponsored by the National Book Foundation and is given out annually to an author whose total body of work has made a significant contribution to American literature.

2008 Winner: Maxine Hong Kingston.

National Book Award for Fiction

The National Book Award for Fiction, sponsored by the National Book Foundation, was established in 1950. The award is given out each year for a work judged to be commendable. Nominees are submitted by publishers and the winner is determined by a panel of independent judges.

2008 Winner: *Shadow Country* by Peter Matthiessen.

Finalists: *The Lazarus Project* by Aleksandar Hemon, *Telex from Cuba* by Rachel Kushner, *Home* by Marilynne Robinson, and *The End* by Salvatore Scibona.

Nobel Prize for Literature

The prize is awarded by the Swedish Academy. The selection is based on a writer's total body of work.

2008 Winner: Jean-Marie Gustave Le Clezio.

The Mystery Genre in 2008
by
Jim Huang

When we survey the landscape of the mystery genre, it's far easier to see what's changing than it is to see what's staying the same. The book industry is in flux right now, as is every other industry in the most challenging economic climate since the Great Depression. Of course the challenges we face in the book business are different because while most consumer products pretty much stay the same—toilet paper will always be toilet paper—we can't even be confident that most titles will continue to be available as text printed on sheets of paper that are bound between covers. If Amazon has its way—and given its power in the marketplace, it's hard to bet against them—we'll all be wirelessly downloading texts to our Kindles, reading proprietary pixels on proprietary screens.

We may not know where books are going, but chatter about change seems to take all the air out of the room. It's as if once we finish (if we ever finish) talking through the pros and cons of print on demand, the disappearing mass market paperback, brick and mortar versus buying over the internet, the coolness of being able to download electronic books anytime anyplace anywhere, the decline and death of book reviews in magazines and newspapers, cutbacks among publishers that are curtailing if not eliminating author tours, the digitization of the vast holdings of university libraries and distribution of these texts, and every other issue that the business faces|POonce we talk about all this, we have trouble marshalling the energy to talk about books and authors, and about the stability and commonality that binds us together in this genre.

This is still a young genre. We are barely a century past the first appearances of the original iconic detective figure, Sherlock Holmes. In 2009 we are celebrating the 150th anniversary of the birth of Sir Arthur Conan Doyle and the 75th anniversary of the founding of the Baker Street Irregulars, the society for Sherlock Holmes enthusiasts. The BSI and its scion societies throughout the United States and across the world are engaging and lively groups, and they're fully invested in celebrating these anniversaries through a variety of events this year. Still, 150 is not that big a number.

In 2008 we lost a number of our genre's greatest stars, writers whose contributions were as significant as Doyle's, whose characters and books are just as familiar. Among the mystery writers who died last year were Phyllis Whitney, who for decades defined romantic suspense; Gregory Mcdonald, a master of wise-cracking dialogue in his series of Fletch and Flynn novels; Michael Crichton, the first bestselling author of medical and scientific thrillers; Hillary Waugh, creator of the police procedural novel (predating Ed McBain by several years); Edward D. Hoch, master of the short story who published in every issue of Ellery Queen's Mystery Magazine for more than thirty years; George C. Chesbro, author of a series of wild and wonderful novels featuring dwarf-circus-acrobat-turned-professor-of-criminology Dr. Robert Frederickson—that description of the protagonist says it all; hardboiled poet James Crumley, accurately described in Wikipedia as a cross between Raymond Chandler and Hunter S. Thompson; Tony Hillerman, who was once told to leave the Indian stuff out of the manuscript he was shopping but instead stuck to his guns and cemented the place of ethnography in our genre; and, on the last day of the year, Donald Westlake, the versatile and brilliant author of two series featuring thieves, the Dortmunder and Parker novels (the latter published under the pseudonym Richard Stark). At the beginning of 2009 we lost John Mortimer, creator of the beloved Horace Rumple and his wife, She Who Must Be Obeyed.

The passing of all these great mystery writers in 2008 is all the more remarkable when we realize how many of these writers were true, first-generation pioneers, among the earliest if not the first to push out the boundaries of the mystery novel in their own distinctive and exciting directions. The genre clearly does have its boundaries, perhaps not as rigid as those laid down by Father Ronald Knox eighty years ago in his Ten Commandments for mystery writers, but nevertheless quite real. At the same time, mystery lovers are delighted to see writers do new things. Knox's rules were violated from the time they were codified and published, and many those violations are among our most celebrated books. As mystery lovers, we are accustomed to hearing folks outside the genre dismiss mysteries as being all the same. But our greatest authors have always considered the rules to be more like guidelines, and it's impossible to think about the novels of folks such as Whitney, Crichton, Crumley, Hillerman and Westlake as cut from the same mold.

So when we talk about stability and commonality in the context of our genre, we do so against a backdrop of chaos and change in the book business itself; with a nod to the loss of some of this genre's pioneers, many of whom were still publishing at or near their deaths; and with a recognition of both the genre's boundaries and our enthusiasm for writers who push out the limits. The landscape of the genre continues to renew and refresh itself, growing and changing in ways that nevertheless leave it a recognizable place that is comfortable and challenging—usually both at the same time.

Every mystery lover ought to revisit Knox's rules from time to time. Though they are dated and routinely violated, their spirit continues to be relevant, and they give us a framework to consider where we are as a genre. On the Thrilling Detective website, one of the genre's greatest resources (located at www.thrillingdetective. com,) you can find this version of the Knox's Decalogue:

1. The criminal must be someone mentioned in the early part of the story, but must not be anyone whose thoughts the reader has been allowed to follow.

2. All supernatural or preternatural agencies are ruled out as a matter of course.

3. Not more than one secret room or passage is allowable.

4. No hitherto undiscovered poisons may be used, nor any appliance which will need a long scientific explanation at the end.

5. No Chinaman must figure in the story.

6. No accident must ever help the detective, nor must he ever have an unaccountable intuition which proves to be right.

7. The detective must not himself commit the crime.

8. The detective must not light on any clues which are not instantly produced for the inspection of the reader.

9. The stupid friend of the detective, the Watson, must not conceal any thoughts which pass through his mind; his intelligence must be slightly, but very slightly, below that of the average reader.

10. Twin brothers, and doubles generally, must not appear unless we have been duly prepared for them.

Of Knox and his rules, Thrilling Detective's creator, Kevin Burton Smith, writes "I think he was mostly joking." It's easy to argue this both ways. On one hand, at the time Knox codified these rules in 1929, Agatha Christie had already violated rules one and seven three

years earlier, in what is still considered one of her finest works. More recently, bestselling thriller writer Harlan Coben has also violated the very same rules in a novel that earned widespread praise, demonstrating that writers are still interesting in breaking the rules. (For the benefit of those who've not yet read these books, I won't mention titles here.)

On the other hand, if we look at the spirit of the rules rather than the specifics, they're much harder to dismiss. We may not be able to defend or even take seriously a prohibition against Chinamen, but it's easy to see that as a whole, the rules are all about fair play, a plea for the writers of detective stories to give readers of detectives stories afair chance at solving the mysteries. This is especially clear in Knox's definition of the detective story, which, he writes: "must have as its main interest the unraveling of a mystery; a mystery whose elements are clearly presented to the reader at an early stage in the proceedings, and whose nature is such as to arouse curiosity, a curiosity which is gratified at the end."

It's still true that most mysteries fit this mold, that the heart of the genre as represented in the great majority of new mystery titles would be recognizable to readers of Knox's era, especially in the latest entries in sturdy series by writers such as Donna Andrews, Linda Barnes, M.C. Beaton, Jan Brogan, Barbara Cleverly, William Kent Krueger, Stuart MacBride, Archer Mayor, Daniel Silva and Will Thomas, to name just ten diverse examples from the latter months of 2008.

The same can be said for international and ethnographic mysteries, segments of the genre that didn't exist in Knox's time but that would not have seemed foreign to Knox and his contemporaries. The explosion of international mysteries in translation continues unabated; Stieg Larsson's *The Girl With the Dragon Tattoo*, translated from the Swedish, was among the most talked about new books of 2008. We also were also treated to new mysteries set in Laos (Colin Cotterill's *Curse of the Pogo Stock*, fifth in this amazing series), Mongolia (Michael Walters' *Shadow Walker*), in Gaza (Matt Benyon Rees' *A Grave in Gaza*) and South Africa (Michael Stanley's *A Carrion Death*), among other exotic destinations. In various ways, these skillful writers use the familiar conventions and practices of the detective story to introduce armchair travelers to out-of-the-way places. You might even find a Chinaman or two, especially in fine novels by Henry Chang and Peter May.

But it's also in this spirit that we can see that the paranormal mystery isn't necessarily the oxymoron it appears to be at first glance. Mysteries are, of course, the most rational of stories, predicted on the abilities of great intellects to apply deductive reasoning, not "unaccountable intuition." A century ago, the genre grew up in an era that saw the growing application of science and technology throughout society. Detective fiction was caught up in this wave, evidenced by the popularity of Sherlock Holmes' ratiocination and of a detective known as The Thinking Machine, introduced by Jacques Futrelle in 1905.

As an Old School reader, I generally side with Knox in believing that "supernatural or preternatural agencies are ruled out as a matter of course." But there's no denying the prevalence and popularity of today's mysteries featuring witches, vampires, ESP and other paranormal phenomena. In the two paranormal series that I enjoy most, Nancy Atherton's wonderful Aunt Dimity novels and Alice Kimberly's frothy Haunted Bookshop series, ghosts are present, but they don't do a whole lot more than add in knowledge that the spirits acquired during their lifetimes (i.e. they're a shortcut against more research) and information that might be acquired by any sidekick. The ghosts also serve as support for the series heroines. Kimberly's ghost, Jack Shephard, does take a few somewhat more active steps in aid of Penelope Thornton-McClure's investigations. Still, despite the presence of ghosts in both Kimberly's and Atherton's series, these books more or less honor Knox's spirit.

In fact, what's really going on in these paranormal mysteries is part of a larger, long-term trend in the genre away from stories about detectives solving a case toward stories about detectives. There's still "curiosity" involved, so Knox's requirement that the mystery arouse curiosity is addressed. But in mysteries that are more about detectives, our curiosity isn't always "gratified at the end." Recent paranormal series by Madelyn Alt (launched in 2006), Shirley Damsgaard (2005) and Casey Daniels (2006) are as much about heroines discovering, embracing and exploring their psychic/paranormal powers as they are about solving crimes. Crime presents a question that can be answered in the course of a novel. But the former, the exploration of paranormal phenomena, is unlikely to achieve closure. Still, readers seem not to mind, as long as the journey is entertaining.

An even more extreme example of this trend away from solving cases and towards watching the detectives is found in Lisa Lutz's Spellman series: *The Spellman Files* (2007), *Curse of the Spellmans* (2008) and *Revenge of the Spellmans* (2009). These books offer everything one might ask for in a detective novel: an engaging private eye narrator with a distinct perspective and unique voice, truly witty banter, PI tradecraft that's both well-executed and well-described, and clever plotting that keeps readers on our toes‌—everything, that is, apart from real cases for our detective to solve. Izzy Spellman spends her time dealing with her parents, both private eyes; her younger sister, also a private eye; and her brother, who isn't a private eye, having turned respectable. Sure, there are minor mysteries that Izzy is asked to solve, but these are essentially incidental. Just when you think that she's about to become involved in a real investigation on behalf of a client, she ends up embroiled in another family investigation melodrama, as the Spellmans turn their detective prowess against each other.

Still, the Spellman books are great fun; it's hard to complain when we're laughing so often. Lutz's books have earned award nominations from the Independent Mystery Booksellers Association (a 2008 Dilys nomination for *The Spellman Files*) and from the Mystery Writers of America (a 2009 Edgar nomination for *Curse of the Spellmans*). The latter is especially surprising, as the MWA rarely notices comic novels; Lutz' Edgar nomination for this book tells us that she's achieved something special.

In Knox's formulation and the mysteries that adhere rigidly to it, the mystery plot is something apart from the detective, a problem that's brought from the outside for the investigation and resolution. But writers and readers know that in the best mysteries, plot and character are part and parcel of the same thing. Sean Chercover, winner of a 2008 Shamus Award and a 2009 Dilys Award, has summed this up by saying "plot is character in motion." We see this most clearly in Laura Lippman's extraordinary short story collection, *Hardly Knew Her*, which offers seventeen little gems of character in motion. The protagonists of these stories are cold and calculating, and stop short of nothing including murder, to achieve their goals. You might say that they are amoral, and at times you may be right ("The Crack Cocaine Diet"). But in other stories, especially the two featuring suburban soccer mom/call girl and madam Heloise Lewis ("One True Love" and "Scratch a Woman"), Lippman paints a much more nuanced portrait.

It's no surprise to be able to label a new book by Laura Lippman "outstanding." She has already proven herself to be among the top writers in our genre; she won 2008 Anthony, Barry and Macavity Awards for her novel *What the Dead Know*. But *Hardly Knew Her* is nevertheless a revelation, including some of the darkest, most noir writing Lippman has published. In story after story, Lippman creates vivid, memorable characters, then puts them in motion through plots in which each of the stunning twists is perfectly in keeping with the character's nature. These are stories about crime, but the true mysteries lie in these characters' hearts. Lippman has already been honored with a 2008 Anthony Award for the collection's title story, "Hardly Knew Her," and she is a nominee for a 2009 Edgar Award for "Scratch a Woman."

In an afterword, Lippman writes that "Scratch a Woman" is an homage to James M. Cain, and it's an engrossing example of how today's writers rework the elements and themes of genre classics. In what has to be the most remarkable new mystery "novel" of 2008, Pierre Bayard takes this exercise even further. *Sherlock Holmes Was Wrong* is a thorough re-examination of the case originally investigated by Sherlock Holmes on Dartmoor over a century earlier. Bayard examines the record of Holmes' original investigation as narrated by Holmes' first chronicler Dr. John Watson and published under the byline Arthur Conan Doyle. Bayard looks not only the account of the Baskerville case but at the entire Holmes canon, isolating the elements of Holmes' methods and identifying instances where the method leaves open the possibility of various conclusions if not outright mistakes. He then lays out a theory of "detective criticism," not just an examination of a text but an intervention that allows him to conclude that Sherlock Holmes was wrong.

It's hard, at first, to know what to make of *Sherlock Holmes Was Wrong*. The book itself is billed as "part intellectual entertainment, part love letter to crime novels, and part crime novel in itself." In dissecting Holmes and *The Hound of the Baskervilles*, Bayard certainly appears to be in earnest, and his methodical, point-by-point dissection of Watson's narrative is lively, provocative and often convincing. Is the book a novel? Pierre Bayard is, we are told, a psychoanalyst and French literary theorist, but it seems just as easy to see him as a (fictional) protagonist in an intellectual melodrama, just another Watson figure chronicling a Sherlock Holmes adventure. Indeed, Bayard himself encourages us to break down the barrier between fiction and reality. He writes of his certainty that there is a "great permeability between fiction and reality. There is no point in trying to patrol the borders between these worlds, for passages between them occur constantly, in both directions. Not only|POcan we inhabit one fictional world or another, but the inhabitants of that world also at times come to live in ours."

Sherlock Holmes devotees at the Baker Street Irregulars have never hesitated to treat the Great Detective as a historical figure, engaging in a great game of scholarship and speculation. Bayard's remarkable conclusions, which readers may accept or discard, result from a ruthlessly logical process of good, old-fashioned ratiocination, Holmes' own methods turned against himself.

Father Knox would be proud.

Recommended Titles

Sherlock Holmes Was Wrong by Pierre Bayard

Teaser by Jan Brogan

Trigger City by Sean Chercover

The Victoria Vanishes by Christopher Fowler

Hell Hole by Chris Grabenstein

Hail to the Chef by Julie Hyzy

Envy the Night by Michael Koryta

Red Knife by William Kent Krueger

Hardly Knew Her by Laura Lippman

Third Strike by Zoe Sharp

Veil of Lies by Jeri Westerson

Mystery Titles

MADELYN ALT

No Rest for the Wiccan

(New York: Berkley, 2008)

Story type: Paranormal; Amateur Detective
Series: Maggie O'Neill. Book 4
Subject(s): Witches and Witchcraft; Family
Major character(s): Maggie O'Neill, Empath, Detective—
   Amateur; Melanie Craven, Spouse; Felicity "Liss"
   Dow, Store Owner, Witch
Time period(s): 2000s
Locale(s): Stony Mill, Indiana

Summary: One hot summer in the small Indiana town of
Stony Mill, Margaret Mary-Catherine O'Neill, known as
Maggie, gets roped into helping her pregnant and bedridden sister Melanie. Maggie recently discovered her
abilities as an empath and is familiar with things of a
mystical nature. When Mel unknowingly invites a dark
spirit into the house via a Ouija board, Maggie calls on
her boss Felicity "Liss" Dow for help. Felicity owns
Enchantments, an antique store and witch emporium.
After helping Mel, Maggie finds her services needed by
Libby Turner. Libby's husband Joel just died and Libby
wants to make sure his spirit isn't hanging around. Maggie agrees to help, but discovers that there's more to
Joel's death than the police realize.

Other books by the same author:
Hex Marks the Spot, 2007
A Charmed Death, 2006
The Trouble with Magic, 2006

Other books you might like:
Shirley Damsgaard, *Charmed to Death*, 2006
Casey Daniels, *Don of the Dead*, 2006
Yasmine Galenorn, *Ghost of a Chance*, 2003
Alice Kimberly, *The Ghost and Mrs. McClure*, 2004

DONNA ANDREWS

Six Geese A-Slaying

(New York: St. Martin's, 2008)

Story type: Amateur Detective
Series: Meg Langslow. Book 10

Subject(s): Christmas; Family
Major character(s): Meg Langslow, Artisan, Detective—
   Amateur
Time period(s): 2000s
Locale(s): Caerphilly, Virginia

Summary: Meg Langslow is once again caught in an
organizational nightmare as she tries to plan the town
Christmas parade, loosely based on "The Twelve Days
of Christmas." The parade begins at her house and ends
at the local college, where Santa will hear the wishes of
all of Caerphilly's children. Unfortunately Meg's nephew
Eric comes up to her and asks "What's wrong with
Santa?" Someone has driven a stake through the grouchy
Santa's heart. It's up to Meg to find out whodunit.

Where it's reviewed:
Booklist, December 1, 2008, page 32
Deadly Pleasures, Fall 2008, page 49
Mystery News, December/January 2009, page 16
Mystery Scene, Holiday 2008, page 78
Publishers Weekly, September 29, 2008, page 63

Other books by the same author:
Cockatiels at Seven, 2008
The Penguin Who Knew Too Much, 2007
Owls Well That Ends Well, 2005
Murder with Puffins, 2000
Murder with Peacocks, 1997

Other books you might like:
Marian Babson, *The Twelve Deaths of Christmas*, 1979
Parnell Hall, *A Puzzle in a Pear Tree*, 2002
Ngaio Marsh, *Tied up in Tinsel*, 1972
Denise Swanson, *Murder of a Barbie and Ken*, 2003

MAUREEN ASH

Death of a Squire

(New York: Berkley, 2008)

Story type: Historical/Medieval
Series: Bascot de Marins. Book 2
Subject(s): Knights and Knighthood; Crusades
Major character(s): Bascot de Marins, Knight
Time period(s): 11th century (1200)
Locale(s): Lincoln, England

Summary: After spending eight years in captivity in the Holy Land, Templar Bascot de Marins escaped and is now resting in the town of Lincoln. When a young, infamous squire is found hanging dead from a tree, Bascot is asked by Lincoln Castle castellan Lady Nicolaa de la Haye to find out who murdered the boy and why. Was it poachers in the woods? Outlaws? Conspirators closing a blabbing mouth? The angry family of a milkmaid? The clock is ticking, for he must discover the murderer before King John and the King of Scotland meet for the first time within the castle's walls. The situation becomes more personal when Bascot's mute servant boy, Gianni, goes missing.

Other books by the same author:
The Alehouse Murders, 2007

Other books you might like:
Michael Jecks, *The Last Templar*, 1995
Bernard Knight, *The Awful Secret*, 2000
Edward Marston, *The Foxes of Warwick*, 1999
Sharan Newman, *To Wear the White Cloak*, 2000

SARAH ATWELL

Pane of Death

(New York: Berkley, 2008)

Story type: Amateur Detective
Series: Emmeline Dowell. Book 2
Subject(s): Art; Computers
Major character(s): Emmeline Dowell, Art Dealer, Detective—Amateur; Matt Lundgren, Police Officer, Boyfriend (of Emmeline); Cameron Dowell, Computer Expert
Time period(s): 2000s
Locale(s): Tucson, Arizona

Summary: Glassblower Emmeline Dowell makes a living and a home for herself among the artists of Tucson's Warehouse District. Her business is successful and she hopes that her recent run-ins with murders won't affect it. But she's in for a disappointment when she finds software mogul Peter Ferguson dead in his own home after being invited to work on his multimillion-dollar stained glass collection. Now the glass is missing and Em is a suspect in the murder, thanks to her jealous colleague, Maddy Sheffield. She hopes she can clear her name and repair her almost-shattered relationship with Police Chief Matt Lundgren before the real killer gets away for good.

Other books by the same author:
Through a Glass, Deadly, 2008

Other books you might like:
Donna Andrews, *Crouching Buzzard, Leaping Loon*, 2003
Sheila Connolly, *One Bad Apple*, 2008
Melissa Glazer, *A Fatal Slip*, 2008
Jayne Ann Krentz, *Sharp Edges*, 1998

KATHLEEN BACUS

Anchors Aweigh

(New York: Lovespell, 2008)

Story type: Amateur Detective
Series: Tressa Jayne Turner. Book 6
Subject(s): Cruise Ships; Relationships
Major character(s): Tressa Jayne "Calamity Jayne" Turner, Journalist, Detective—Amateur; Rick Townsend, Ranger; Manny DeMarco, Biker, Consultant
Time period(s): 2000s
Locale(s): At Sea; Montego Bay, Jamaica; Cayman Islands

Summary: Now that her Grandma Hannah is married, Tressa Jayne Turner, aka Calamity Jayne, is joining the newlyweds and their families on a weeklong Caribbean cruise. Tressa is looking forward to the all-you-can-eat buffets and spending time with "Ranger" Rick Townsend, who just may be The One. Tressa's dreams are shattered by the news that it's a weight-loss cruise. The arrival of biker bad boy Manny DeMarco also worries Tressa. Manny and Tressa recently faked an engagement to please his aunt Mo, who has a bad heart. As Tressa struggles with the two men courting her, she also manages to overhear a conversation: one of the newlyweds on board plans to leave the ship as a widower. Now, Tressa has just one week to find a killer before he strikes.

Other books by the same author:
Fiance at Her Fingertips, 2008
Calamity Jayne Goes to College, 2007
Calamity Jayne Heads West, 2007
Calamity Jayne Rides Again, 2006
Ghouls Just Want to Have Fun, 2006

Other books you might like:
Lori Avocato, *Deep Sea Dead*, 2006
Candy Calvert, *Mai Tai to Murder*, 2007
Janet Evanovich, *Seven Up*, 2001
Jane Heller, *Princess Charming*, 1997

DEB BAKER

Ding Dong Dead

(New York: Berkley, 2008)

Story type: Amateur Detective
Series: Gretchen Birch. Book 4
Subject(s): Dolls and Dollhouses; Museums
Major character(s): Gretchen Birch, Artist, Detective—Amateur; Caroline Birch, Writer; Matt Albright, Detective—Police, Divorced Person
Time period(s): 2000s
Locale(s): Phoenix, Arizona

Summary: Doll restoration artist Gretchen Birch has her hands full with her business and with directing a fundraising play for a new doll museum in Phoenix, the World of Dolls. Gretchen's date with new boyfriend Matt Albright, a police detective, is interrupted when

Matt has to visit a crime scene: a woman's body has been found in a local cemetery. A note near the body states, "Die, Dolly, Die." Gretchen's mother Caroline discovers that she has a connection to the dead woman. Soon after, a truck pushes Caroline's car into traffic causing a horrible accident. When Gretchen finds a note on her car just like the one in the cemetery, she begins to worry that the killer may be targeting the Birch women.

Other books by the same author:
Dolly Departed, 2008
Murder Talks Turkey, 2008
Goodbye Dolly, 2007
Murder Grins and Bears It, 2007
Dolled Up for Murder, 2006

Other books you might like:
Barbara Allan, *Antiques Roadkill*, 2006
Nancy Cohen, *Hair Raiser*, 2000
Jeanne M. Dams, *Malice in Miniature*, 1998
John J. Lamb, *The False-Hearted Teddy*, 2007

7

SAM BAKER

Deadly Beautiful

(New York: Ballantine, 2008)

Story type: Amateur Detective
Series: Annie Anderson. Book 2
Subject(s): Missing Persons; Models, Fashion
Major character(s): Annie Anderson, Journalist, Detective—Amateur; Luella "Lou" McCartney, Critic; Scarlett Ulrich, Model
Time period(s): 2000s; 1980s
Locale(s): New York, New York; London, England; Tokyo, Japan

Summary: While attending Fashion Week in New York, fashion critic Lou McCartney receives a phone call from her estranged father, wealthy businessman Rufus Ulrich. Lou's half-sister, 18-year-old model Scarlett, is missing in Tokyo. Upset, Lou turns to her friend, fashion journalist Annie Anderson, for help. A former investigative reporter, Annie has experience finding people. Earning a trip to Tokyo by promising her editor an exclusive story on Scarlett, Annie is determined to find out what happened to the young model. Annie learns that several tall, blond Western women have been murdered recently. As Annie searches for Scarlett, she discovers that Scarlett's unhappy life and relationship with her father may be the real reason behind her disappearance.

Where it's reviewed:
Booklist, June 1, 2008, page 49
Mystery Scene, Fall 2008, page 73
Publishers Weekly, June 9, 2008, page 32

Other books by the same author:
Fashion Victim, 2005

Other books you might like:
Sujata Massey, *The Floating Girl*, 2000
Tara Moss, *Fetish*, 2005
Magdalen Nabb, *Property of Blood*, 2001
S.J. Rozan, *Mandarin Plaid*, 1996

8

SANDRA BALZO

Bean There, Done That

(New York: Severn House, 2008)

Story type: Amateur Detective
Series: Maggy Thorsen. Book 3
Subject(s): Restaurants; Family Relations
Major character(s): Maggy Thorsen, Store Owner (coffee shop), Detective—Amateur; Sarah Kingston, Real Estate Agent, Detective—Amateur; Jake Pavlik, Police Officer
Time period(s): 2000s
Locale(s): Milwaukee, Wisconsin

Summary: When Maggy Thorsen, owner of Uncommon Grounds, suburban Milwaukee's premier coffee shop, is asked by her ex-husband Ted's new wife to help her prove that Ted has been cheating on her, she is at first outraged, and then intrigued. Was Ted having affairs during his and Maggy's marriage long before he met the lovely Rachel? But then Rachel turns up in Lake Michigan—very dead. Did Ted kill her? Why? Ted insists he is innocent. He turns to Maggy for help. Maggy's new man, Sheriff Jake Pavlik, tells her to stay out of the fray. But her best friend, Sarah, is right there to help her get into things. So of course, Maggy finds herself in the thick of the action. When Ted disappears, Maggy thinks she knows where he is. Maggy and Sarah take off in pursuit.

Where it's reviewed:
Booklist, September 1, 2008, page 52
Deadly Pleasures, Fall 2008, page 52
Publishers Weekly, July 21, 2008, page 145

Other books by the same author:
Grounds for Murder, 2007
Uncommon Grounds, 2004

Other books you might like:
Cleo Coyle, *Espresso Shot*, 2008
Diane Mott Davidson, *The Grilling Season*, 1997
Jimmie Ruth Evans, *Flamingo Fatale*, 2005
Rosemary Harris, *Pushing Up Daisies*, 2008

9

RAY BANKS

Sucker Punch

(Boston: Houghton Mifflin Harcourt, 2009)

Story type: Amateur Detective
Series: Cal Innes. Book 2
Subject(s): Sports/Boxing; Drugs
Major character(s): Callum "Cal" Innes, Convict, Detective—Amateur; Liam Wooley, Sports Figure, Teenager; Nelson Byrne, Coach
Time period(s): 2000s
Locale(s): Manchester, England; Los Angeles, California; Palm Desert, California

Summary: In Manchester, England, former private investigator and ex-con Cal Innes works as a caretaker at the Lad's Club, a local boxing gym. Club owner Paulo Gray asks Innes to accompany Liam Wooley to Los Angeles. Wooley, only 17 years old, has been invited to participate in an amateur boxing competition and Gray wants Innes to look after the young boxer. Shortly after their arrival in Los Angeles, Innes meets Nelson Byrne, a former boxer, who offers to train Wooley. Just before his final bout in the competition, Wooley goes missing. As Innes searches for him, he learns that Byrne isn't who he says he is and may be responsible for Wooley's disappearance.

Where it's reviewed:
Booklist, December 1, 2008, page 33
Mystery Scene, Winter 2009, page 69
Publishers Weekly, November 17, 2008, page 39

Other books by the same author:
Gun, 2008
Saturday's Child, 2008
The Big Blind, 2004

Other books you might like:
Ed Gorman, *Blood Game*, 1989
Steve Monroe, *'57 Chicago*, 2001
Eddie Muller, *The Distance*, 2002
Tom Schreck, *TKO*, 2008

10

CHRISTINE BARBER

The Replacement Child

(New York: St. Martin's, 2008)

Story type: Police Procedural; Amateur Detective
Subject(s): Drugs; Journalism
Major character(s): Lucy Newroe, Journalist, Detective—Amateur; Gil Montoya, Detective—Police
Time period(s): 2000s
Locale(s): Santa Fe, New Mexico

Summary: It is late at night, and newspaper city editor Lucy Newroe is working on a story when the "Scanner Lady" calls to say she has picked up a report on the police scanner of a possible dead body found. But when a reporter tries to track down the story, he finds nothing. The next day, Detective Sergeant Gilbert Montoya hears of the death of a fellow officer's sister, Melissa Baca, an apparent homicide victim. Montoya is assigned to be liaison on the case between the family and the state police, who are conducting the official investigation. Melissa, a young teacher, had an excellent reputation, but as Montoya and others investigate, they find odd things in her life, particularly in the area of illegal drugs.

Where it's reviewed:
Booklist, October 1, 2008, page 30
Mystery News, October/November 2008, page 28
Publishers Weekly, August 18, 2008, page 47

Other books you might like:
Tony Hillerman, *Dance Hall of the Dead*, 1973
Michael McGarrity, *Tularosa*, 1996
Walter Satterthwait, *Wall of Glass*, 1987
Aimee Thurlo, *Blackening Song*, 1995
David Thurlo, co-author

11

LINWOOD BARCLAY

Too Close to Home

(New York: Bantam, 2008)

Story type: Revenge; Amateur Detective
Subject(s): Family Problems; Secrets
Major character(s): Jim Cutter, Businessman, Detective—Amateur; Derek Cutter, Teenager, Crime Suspect; Randall Finley, Government Official
Time period(s): 2000s
Locale(s): Promise Falls, New York

Summary: When 17-year-old Derek Cutter's next door neighbors, the Langleys, leave for a week's vacation, Derek sees this as the perfect opportunity to use their house as a quiet getaway for him and his girlfriend Penny. After hiding in the basement for some time, Derek is surprised when the Langleys return. As he hides behind a couch, Derek hears voices upstairs and then three gunshots. When the police arrest Derek for the murders, his father Jim knows Derek is innocent and sets out to find the truth. Jim believes that the murders are somehow connected to a novel that Derek found on an old computer that is almost identical to the novel written by local author Conrad Chase.

Where it's reviewed:
Booklist, July 1, 2008, page 45
Library Journal, July 15, 2008, page 58
Publishers Weekly, August 11, 2008, page 28

Other books by the same author:
No Time for Goodbye, 2007
Stone Rain, 2007
Lone Wolf, 2006
Bad Guys, 2005
Bad Move, 2004

Other books you might like:
Harlan Coben, *The Innocent*, 2005
Thomas H. Cook, *Red Leaves*, 2005
Laura Lippman, *To the Power of Three*, 2005
Donald E. Westlake, *The Hook*, 2000

12

LINDA BARNES

Lie Down with the Devil

(New York: St. Martin's, 2008)

Story type: Private Detective
Series: Carlotta Carlyle. Book 12
Subject(s): Organized Crime; Marriage
Major character(s): Carlotta Carlyle, Detective—Private, Taxi Driver; Joseph Mooney, Detective—Police; Sam Gianelli, Boyfriend (of Carlotta)
Time period(s): 2000s
Locale(s): Boston, Massachusetts; Cape Cod, Massachusetts

Summary: Carlotta's boyfriend, Sam Gianelli, has taken off for parts unknown, and Carlotta isn't sure whether his disappearance is mob related or not. Meanwhile, she's asked by her assistant, Roz, to help out Jessica Franklin, who wants Carlotta to make sure her fiance is faithful before they marry. Carlotta is annoyed with herself when she loses the boyfriend's trail, but confused when Jessica not only turns up dead, but is found to have introduced herself under an assumed name. Sam appears to be connected to the murder, and Carlotta is suspect number one. She teams up with her old boss, Joseph Mooney, now retired from the force, to help her solve the case. The trail takes them out to Cape Cod, where a Native American tribe is working to secure some land.

Where it's reviewed:
Booklist, May 1, 2008, page 36
Mystery Scene, Fall 2008, page 71
Publishers Weekly, June 9, 2008, page 35

Other books by the same author:
Heart of the World, 2006
Deep Pockets, 2004
The Big Dig, 2000
Flash Point, 1999
Cold Case, 1997

Other books you might like:
Laura Lippman, *By a Spider's Thread*, 2004
Sujata Massey, *The Typhoon Lover*, 2005
Marcia Muller, *Cyanide Wells*, 2003
S.J. Rozan, *Reflecting the Sky*, 2001

13

JOE BARONE

The Body in the Record Room
(New York: St. Martin's, 2008)

Story type: Amateur Detective
Subject(s): Mental Illness
Major character(s): Roy Rogers, Mentally Ill Person, Detective—Amateur; Harry, Mentally Ill Person
Time period(s): 1950s (1954)
Locale(s): Sunrise, Missouri

Summary: It's 1954 and Roy Rogers is a patient at Sunrise Mental Hospital. That's not his actual name, of course—he is a patient who admires the real Rogers and has adopted his name. Roy is not considered dangerous and so has the freedom of the mental institution, which is actually a very large farm. One evening he finds the body of a stranger in the hospital records room. He decides he needs to hide it, so he and his friend, Harry, go out later that night and bury the body, dressed as a priest, in a horse stall. But a note that Roy finds in the man's pocket leads him to do his own investigating, and he and Harry find information linking this man's death to a murder that happened 20 years before.

Where it's reviewed:
Booklist, September 15, 2008, page 27
Mystery News, February/March 2009, page 12
Publishers Weekly, August 25, 2008, page 54

Other books you might like:
Barbara D'Amato, *Death of a Thousand Cuts*, 2004
G.H. Ephron, *Delusion*, 2002
John Katzenbach, *The Madman's Tale*, 2004
Sue Walker, *The Reunion*, 2004

14

BEVERLY BARTON

Cold Hearted
(New York: Zebra, 2008)

Story type: Romantic Suspense; Private Detective
Subject(s): Relationships; Serial Killers
Major character(s): Rick Carson, Detective—Private; Jordan Price, Widow(er); Devon Markham, Assistant, Homosexual
Time period(s): 2000s
Locale(s): Priceville, Georgia; Trenton, Georgia; Knoxville, Tennessee

Summary: Ryan Price hires the Powell Private Security and Investigation Agency to prove that his brother, Senator Dan Price, did not commit suicide. Private investigator Rick Carson is picked to head the case. Rick's first inclination is to believe that Jordan, Dan's widow, is the most likely suspect. Twenty years younger than her late husband, Jordan didn't shed a tear during Dan's funeral. Also, Jordan stands to inherit one-third of Dan's estate; this isn't the first time Jordan has benefited from a loved one's death. Jordan has buried a fiance and two husbands, including Dan. Just as Rick is ready to accept that Jordan is guilty, he discovers that she is the victim of a demented killer.

Where it's reviewed:
Publishers Weekly, June 16, 2008, page 38

Other books by the same author:
The Murder Game, 2008
A Time to Die, 2007
Amnesia, 2007
Close Enough to Kill, 2006
Killing Her Softly, 2005

Other books you might like:
Harlan Coben, *Tell No One*, 2001
Lisa Gardner, *The Perfect Husband*, 1998
Lisa Jackson, *Final Scream*, 2005
Patricia MacDonald, *Secret Admirer*, 1995

15

LOUIS BAYARD

The Black Tower
(New York: Morrow, 2008)

Story type: Historical/Post-French Revolution
Subject(s): Kings, Queens, Rulers, etc.; Identity, Concealed
Major character(s): Hector Carpentier, Doctor, Student; Eugene Francois Vidocq, Historical Figure, Detective—Police; Charles Rapskeller, Gardener

Time period(s): 1810s (1818)

Locale(s): Paris, France; Saint-Cloud, France; Saint-Denis, France

Summary: In 1818, Parisian medical student Hector Carpentier is questioned by the famous police detective Eugene Vidocq. Founder of the newly formed investigative force, the Brigade de Surete, Vidocq is looking into the death of Chretien Leblanc. A piece of paper bearing Carpenter's name was found on Leblanc's body when he died. While questioning Carpentier, Vidocq learns that it was actually Carpentier's father Leblanc was seeking. Many years ago, the elder Carpentier was the physician for the Dauphin of France, Louis-Charles. Louis-Charles was the son of the executed King Louis XVI, and had supposedly died two years after his parents went to the guillotine. Vidocq and Carpentier soon realize that Leblanc died because he learned that a simple gardener named Charles Rapskeller may actually be Louis XVII, King of France.

Where it's reviewed:

Booklist, August 1, 2008, page 43

Entertainment Weekly, August 22, 2008, page 127

Library Journal, August 15, 2008, page 61

Mystery News, October/November 2008, page 23

Publishers Weekly, July 21, 2008, page 140

Other books by the same author:

The Pale Blue Eye, 2006

Mr. Timothy, 2003

Endangered Species, 2001

Fool's Errand, 1999

Other books you might like:

John Dickson Carr, *Captain Cut-Throat*, 1955

Ann Dukthas, *The Prince Lost to Time*, 1995

Vincent McConnor, *I Am Vidocq*, 1985

Charles O'Brien, *Mute Witness*, 2001

16

PIERRE BAYARD

Sherlock Holmes Was Wrong

(New York: Bloomsbury, 2008)

Story type: Mystery; Literary

Subject(s): Detection; Literature

Major character(s): Sherlock Holmes, Detective—Private (consulting); Pierre Bayard, Professor

Time period(s): 1900s (1901); 2000s

Locale(s): Dartmoor, England; Paris, France

Summary: In France, literary theorist Pierre Bayard reopens the case of the Hound of the Baskervilles, originally investigated by Sherlock Holmes on Dartmoor over a century earlier. Bayard examines the record of Holmes' original investigation as narrated by Holmes' chronicler Dr. John Watson and published under the byline Arthur Conan Doyle. Bayard looks not only at the account of the Baskerville case but at the entire Holmes canon, isolating the elements of Holmes' methods and identifying instances where the method leaves open the possibility of various conclusions—if not outright mistakes. He then lays out a theory of "detective criti-

cism," not just an examination of a text but an intervention that allows him to conclude that Sherlock Holmes was wrong.

Where it's reviewed:

Mystery Scene, Holiday 2008, page 67

Publishers Weekly, September 1, 2008, page 45

Other books by the same author:

Who Killed Roger Ackroyd?, 2001

Other books you might like:

Arthur Conan Doyle, *The Hound of the Baskervilles*, 1902

Laurie R. King, *The Beekeeper's Apprentice*, 1994

Vincent Starrett, *The Private Life of Sherlock Holmes*, 1933

Carlos Ruiz Zafon, *The Shadow of the Wind*, 2004

17

M.C. BEATON   (Pseudonym of Marion Chesney)

A Spoonful of Poison

(New York: St. Martin's, 2008)

Story type: Private Detective; Humor

Series: Agatha Raisin. Book 19

Subject(s): Cooks and Cooking; Country Life

Major character(s): Agatha Raisin, Detective—Private; Toni Gilmour, Assistant; George Selby, Religious

Time period(s): 2000s

Locale(s): Costwolds, England

Summary: Agatha Raisin is looking for some respite from her busy detective agency, and decides to take weekends off. However, when handsome widower and vicar George Selby asks for her help in planning the village fete to raise money for the church roof, she can hardly refuse. The fete begins well and ends badly when one elderly woman dies after throwing herself off the church tower. It turns out the jam for the fete has been laced with LSD, and the Vicar hires Agatha and her sidekick Toni to solve the case, which appears to have local roots.

Where it's reviewed:

Booklist, September 15, 2008, page 31

Deadly Pleasures, Fall 2008, page 51

Other books by the same author:

Kissing Christmas Goodbye, 2007

Love, Lies and Liquor, 2006

Agatha Raisin and the Day the Floods Came, 2002

Agatha Raisin and the Fairies of Fryfam, 2000

Agatha Raisin and the Wizard of Evesham, 1999

Other books you might like:

Simon Brett, *The Witness at the Wedding*, 2005

Dicey Deere, *The Irish Village Murder*, 2004

Ellen Hart, *An Intimate Ghost*, 2004

Ann Purser, *Weeping on Wednesday*, 2003

18

LARRY BEINHART

Salvation Boulevard

(New York: Nation, 2008)

Story type: Private Detective
Subject(s): Legal Thriller; Religion
Major character(s): Carl Van Wagener, Detective—Private; Emmanuel "Manny" Goldfarb, Lawyer; Paul Plowright, Religious
Time period(s): 2000s
Locale(s): Davis

Summary: When Nathaniel MacLeod, a philosophy and religion professor, is murdered, one of his Persian students, Ahmad Nazami, confesses to the murder and is arrested. Nazami's lawyer, Manny Goldfarb, calls in private investigator Carl Van Wagener to help him with the case. Nazami claims that he didn't kill Professor MacLeod, and the only reason he signed the confession was because he was tortured and forced to sign it. Agreeing to look into Nazami's case, Van Wagener soon finds himself at odds with his wife and his church. Van Wagener is a born-again Christian who takes his faith very seriously, as does his wife Gwen. Both Gwen and their pastor, Paul Plowright, pressure Van Wagener to drop the case.

Where it's reviewed:
Booklist, August 1, 2008, page 47
Publishers Weekly, July 28, 2008, page 51

Other books by the same author:
Wag the Dog, 2005
The Librarian, 2004
American Hero, 1993
Foreign Exchange, 1991
You Get What You Pay For, 1988

Other books you might like:
Alex Berenson, *The Faithful Spy*, 2007
John Connolly, *The Black Angel*, 2005
Dan Fesperman, *The Prisoner of Guantanamo*, 2006
Robert Littell, *Vicious Circle*, 2006

19

RICHARD BELZER
MICHAEL BLACK , Co-Author

I Am Not a Cop!

(New York: Simon & Schuster, 2008)

Story type: Amateur Detective
Subject(s): Actors and Actresses; Missing Persons
Major character(s): Richard Belzer, Actor, Detective—Amateur; Rudy Markovich, Immigrant, Friend (of Richard); Anna Katrina Doskeav, Spy
Time period(s): 2000s
Locale(s): New York, New York (Brighton Beach)

Summary: While his wife Harlee is away, actor Richard Belzer, known for his role as Detective John Munch on *Law & Order: Special Victims Unit*, goes to Brighton Beach to meet an old friend for dinner. Rudy Markovich, a Russian immigrant, is the medical examiner for New York. When the two make plans to meet at a boxing match the next evening, Belzer begins to worry about his friend when Rudy doesn't show up. Detective Max Kaminsky informs Belzer that Rudy's car was found near the river, a bullet hole in the door and Rudy's coat still inside, soaked with blood. Belzer believes that since he plays a police detective on television, he can investigate Rudy's disappearance on his own.

Where it's reviewed:
Booklist, September 1, 2008, page 55
Library Journal, September 15, 2008, page 43
Mystery News, October/November 2008, page 20
Publishers Weekly, August 18, 2008, page 38

Other books you might like:
Steve Allen, *Murder on the Glitter Box*, 1989
Ed Koch, *Murder at City Hall*, 1995
Joan Rivers, *Murder at the Academy Awards*, 2009
George Sanders, *Crime on My Hands*, 1944

20

JAMES R. BENN

Blood Alone

(New York: Soho Press, 2008)

Story type: Historical/World War II
Series: Billy Boyle. Book 3
Subject(s): Armed Forces; Crime and Criminals
Major character(s): Billy Boyle, Police Officer, Military Personnel; Piotr Augustus Kazimierz, Military Personnel, Nobleman; Enrico Sciafani, Doctor
Time period(s): 1940s (1943)
Locale(s): Gela, Italy; Agrigento, Italy; Vittoria, Italy

Summary: In 1943, Lieutenant Billy Boyle is a special investigator for General Dwight Eisenhower, or "Uncle Ike" as Billy refers to him. But upon waking in a field hospital in Sicily, Billy can't remember any of this. He's suffering from psychogenic amnesia due to a traumatic event. As bits and pieces of his memory return, Billy is reunited with fellow officer and friend Piotr Augustus Kazimierz. He learns that the yellow silk handkerchief that he's been carrying around is actually a message he was sent to Sicily to deliver. The handkerchief belongs to mobster Lucky Luciano, and it gives Billy the credibility needed when he meets Sicilian Mafia boss Don Calogero to ask for the Don's help in stopping local soldiers from fighting American troops. Unfortunately for Billy, others know of his mission and will try to stop him from completing it.

Where it's reviewed:
Booklist, August 1, 2008, page 41
Deadly Pleasures, Fall 2008, page 51
Mystery News, October/November 2008, page 14
Publishers Weekly, June 23, 2008, page 40

Other books by the same author:
The First Wave, 2007
Billy Boyle, 2006
Desperate Ground, 2004

Other books you might like:
Margery Allingham, *Traitor's Purse*, 1941
Max Allan Collins, *The Million-Dollar Wound*, 1986
John Gardner, *Troubled Midnight*, 2006
John Lawton, *Bluffing Mr. Churchill*, 2004

21

IRA BERKOWITZ

Old Flame

(New York: Three Rivers, 2008)

Story type: Police Procedural
Series: Jackson Steeg. Book 2
Subject(s): Family; Law Enforcement
Major character(s): Jackson Steeg, Detective—Homicide (retired); Arne Jensen, Detective—Homicide; Pete Toal, Detective—Homocide
Time period(s): 2000s
Locale(s): New York, New York; Seaside, New York; Dobbs Ferry, New York

Summary: Former New York cop Jackson Steeg is still dealing with the results of a shootout that left a pimp dead and bullet damage in his own lung. When Steeg's ex-wife's current husband, Tony Ferris, is beaten to death outside a trendy restaurant, Steeg's former mother-in-law asks Steeg to find out who killed him. As he begins to investigate, Steeg discovers that Ferris' death may be linked to millions of dollars in construction contracts and that the detective in charge of the case, Pete Toal, doesn't seem that interested in finding the killer. Meanwhile, Steeg is also trying to help an old friend, Danny Reno, who embezzled money from a deadly Israeli mobster.

Where it's reviewed:
Booklist, October 15, 2008, page 26
Library Journal, November 1, 2008, page 47
Mystery Scene, Holiday 2008, page 77
Publishers Weekly, September 22, 2008, page 41

Other books by the same author:
Family Matters, 2006

Other books you might like:
Gabriel Cohen, *The Graving Dock*, 2007
Reed Farrel Coleman, *The James Deans*, 2005
S.J. Rozan, *In This Rain*, 2006
Charlie Stella, *Shakedown*, 2006

22

WILLIAM BERNHARDT

Nemesis: The Final Case of Eliot Ness

(New York: Ballantine, 2009)

Story type: Historical/Depression Era
Subject(s): Serial Killers; Law Enforcement
Major character(s): Eliot Ness, Government Official; Peter Merylo, Detective—Homicide; Francis Sweeney, Doctor
Time period(s): 1930s; 1950s (1957)
Locale(s): Coudersport, Pennsylvania; Cleveland, Ohio; Newburgh Heights, Ohio

Summary: In 1935, treasury agent Eliot Ness, known for taking down gangster Al Capone, is appointed Safety Director in Cleveland, Ohio. Ness begins to clean up the city by clearing out crooked cops from the police force. Then Ness targets illegal gambling establishments. When dismembered bodies start appearing in the city, Ness is forced to take charge of the investigation himself. Homicide detective Peter Merylo has been on the case since the first body was discovered, and now finds himself reporting to Ness. When Ness discovers the truth about the killings, he has to battle with not only a serial killer but also with the politicians who run the city.

Where it's reviewed:
Booklist, November 15, 2008, page 20
Mystery News, February/March 2009, page 15
Publishers Weekly, November 24, 2008, page 38

Other books by the same author:
Capitol Conspiracy, 2008
Capitol Threat, 2007
Strip Search, 2007
Capitol Murder, 2006
Dark Eye, 2005

Other books you might like:
Howard Browne, *Pork City*, 1988
Max Allan Collins, *Butcher's Dozen*, 1988
John Peyton Cooke, *Torsos*, 1993
Steve Thayer, *Saint Mudd*, 1988

23

CORDELIA FRANCES BIDDLE

Deception's Daughter

(New York: St. Martin's, 2008)

Story type: Historical/Post-American Revolution; Amateur Detective
Series: Martha Beale. Book 2
Subject(s): Kidnapping; Parenthood
Major character(s): Martha Beale, Heiress, Detective— Amateur; Thomas Kelman, Political Figure; Georgine Crowther, Parent
Time period(s): 19th century (1842)
Locale(s): Philadelphia, Pennsylvania

Summary: When wealthy, engaged, young Dora Crowther disappears, an apparent kidnap victim, Thomas Kelman is dispatched by the mayor of Philadelphia to investigate. Because the Crowthers are of a different class than he is, he calls on his friend and almost girlfriend, Martha Beale, to help out. Although she has just lost her father and is trying to raise two adopted children, Martha agrees. With the excellent combination of compassion and practicality on her side and because she is of the same class as the Crowthers, she is able to help Thomas unravel the web of deception around the case, which is intensified by the disappearance of Dora's fiancee.

Where it's reviewed:
Booklist, July 1, 2008, page 42
Library Journal, April 1, 2008, page 55
Publishers Weekly, May 12, 2008, page 38
School Library Journal, February 1, 2009, page 129

Other books by the same author:
The Conjurer, 2007

Other books you might like:
Cynthia Peale, *Murder at Bertram's Bower*, 2001
Anne Perry, *A Sudden, Fearful Death*, 1993
P.B. Ryan, *A Death on Beacon Hill*, 2004
Victoria Thompson, *Murder on Marble Row*, 2004

24

LISA BLACK

Takeover

(New York: Morrow, 2008)

Story type: Psychological Suspense
Subject(s): Hostages; Law Enforcement
Major character(s): Theresa MacLean, Scientist, Fiance(e) (of Paul); Christopher Cavanaugh, Police Officer; Paul Cleary, Fiance(e) (of Theresa)
Time period(s): 2000s
Locale(s): Cleveland, Ohio

Summary: When Mark Ludlow, a banking executive in Cleveland, is murdered, forensic scientist Theresa Ma- cLean is called in to assist with the investigation. Also on the case are homicide detective Paul Cleary, There- sa's fiance, and Paul's partner Frank Patrick, Theresa's cousin. Just hours after Ludlow's body is discovered, Paul walks into a hostage situation at the Federal Reserve Bank where Ludlow worked. Theresa is horrified to learn that Paul is a hostage and hurries to the scene. Hostage negotiator Chris Cavanaugh arrives to begin the negotia- tions, but has little luck in dealing with the two men inside the bank. When Paul is shot, Theresa offers to trade herself for him as a hostage. Once inside, Theresa gains a clearer picture of the robbers' intentions.

Where it's reviewed:
Library Journal, July 15, 2008, page 58
Mystery News, October/November 2008, page 28
Mystery Scene, Fall 2008, page 67
Publishers Weekly, July 7, 2008, page 37

Other books you might like:
Elizabeth Becka, *Unknown Means*, 2007
Robert Crais, *Hostage*, 2001
Jeffery Deaver, *A Maiden's Grave*, 1995
Tess Gerritsen, *Vanish*, 2005

25

ANNETTE BLAIR

A Veiled Deception

(New York: Berkley, 2009)

Story type: Amateur Detective
Subject(s): Weddings; Psychic Powers

Major character(s): Madeira "Maddie" Cutler, Designer, Detective—Amateur; Nick Jaconetti, FBI Agent; Lyt- ton Werner, Detective—Police
Time period(s): 2000s
Locale(s): Mystick Falls, Connecticut; Wickford, Rhode Island; New Orleans, Louisiana

Summary: New York fashion designer Madeira "Maddie" Cutler has come home to Mystick Falls, Connecticut, to help with her youngest sister Sherry's wedding. Arriving in time for Sherry and Justin's engagement party, Mad- die learns that Justin's old flame, Jasmine Updike, is at the party acting like she is the bride-to-be. Shortly after, Maddie discovers Jasmine's body lying on the floor, Sherry's veil wrapped tightly around her neck. Detective Sergeant Lytton Werner, a former classmate of Maddie's, considers Sherry to be the prime suspect in Jasmine's murder. Determined to clear her sister's name, Maddie begins her own investigation. Meanwhile, Maddie's visit home forces her to take a look at her life and question whether or not New York is the right place for her.

Other books by the same author:
Gone with the Witch, 2008
Sex and the Psychic Witch, 2007
My Favorite Witch, 2006
The Scot, the Witch and the Wardrobe, 2006
The Butterfly Garden, 2005

Other books you might like:
Lorna Barrett, *Murder Is Binding*, 2008
JoAnna Carl, *The Chocolate Cat Caper*, 2002
Yasmine Galenorn, *One Hex of a Wedding*, 2006
Alice Kimberly, *The Ghost and Mrs. McClure*, 2004

26

LAWRENCE BLOCK

Hit and Run

(New York: Morrow, 2008)

Story type: Action/Adventure
Series: John Keller. Book 4
Subject(s): Political Thriller; Crime and Criminals
Major character(s): John Keller, Criminal
Time period(s): 2000s
Locale(s): Des Moines, Iowa; Indiana; New York, New York

Summary: Though a pretty normal guy most of the time, John Keller is a hit man. He's in Des Moines to do his final job, asked by a mysterious man with hairy ears to choose a particular type of gun and wait for his signal. Keller agrees up to a point, but he's not naive. The African American governor of Ohio is assassinated in Des Moines. Sure enough, Keller has been set up to take the fall, presumably by Hairy Ears. Keller then happens to see an article about the murder of Dorthea Harbison— his friend Dot—who had total access to his retirement fund. Everything he has—money, apartment, his stamp collection, and even his identity—is gone. His efforts to clear his name and secure a new identity take him from Iowa to Indiana to New York and ultimately to New Orleans.

Where it's reviewed:
Booklist, February 15, 2008, page 4
Deadly Pleasures, Summer 2008, page 50
Mystery News, June/July 2008, page 22
Mystery Scene, Summer 2008, page 84
Publishers Weekly, May 5, 2008, page 46

Other books by the same author:
Hit List, 2000
Hit Man, 1998
When the Sacred Ginmill Closes, 1986
Eight Million Ways to Die, 1982
Burglars Can't Be Choosers, 1977

Other books you might like:
Lee Child, *Bad Luck and Trouble*, 2007
Barry Eisler, *The Last Assassin*, 2006
Robert B. Parker, *A Savage Place*, 1981
Greg Rucka, *Patriot Acts*, 2007

27

LAWRENCE BLOCK

One Night Stands and Lost Weekends

(New York: Harper, 2008)

Story type: Collection
Subject(s): Detection; Violence

Summary: Originally published in magazines between 1958 and 1962 and reprinted by Crippen & Landru in two volumes in 1999 and 2001, this collection of 25 short stories and three novellas showcases Lawrence Block's earliest works. The short stories focus mainly on tough guys, sex, and violence; "Nor Iron Bars a Cage" is Block's only story in the science fiction genre. The three novellas, featuring private detective Ed London, are classic hardboiled tales. Set in New York, "The Naked and the Deadly" has London investigating a blackmail case. Client Rhona Blake asks London to pay off a blackmailer, but London discovers that there's more to the case than Rhona is telling him.

Where it's reviewed:
Booklist, October 15, 2008, page 26
Library Journal, September 1, 2008, page 102
Publishers Weekly, September 29, 2008, page 59

Other books by the same author:
A Diet of Treacle, 2008
Lucky at Cards, 2007
Hit Parade, 2006
All the Flowers Are Dying, 2005
The Burglar on the Prowl, 2004

Other books you might like:
Donald Hamilton, *Night Walker*, 1954
Richard S. Prather, *Gat Heat*, 1967
Mickey Spillane, *Vengeance Is Mine*, 1951
Donald E. Westlake, *Somebody Owes Me Money*, 1969

STEPHANIE BOND

3 Men and a Body

(Don Mills, Ontario: Mira, 2008)

Story type: Amateur Detective
Series: Body Movers. Book 3
Subject(s): Relationships; Suspense
Major character(s): Carlotta Wren, Saleswoman, Detective—Amateur; Wesley Wren, Gambler; Cooper Craft, Doctor
Time period(s): 2000s
Locale(s): Atlanta, Georgia; Daytona Beach, Florida; Boca Raton, Florida

Summary: Cooper Craft, Carlotta Wren's brother's boss, asks if she would like to accompany him on a body retrieval in Florida. Carlotta loves the idea of a vacation, but any romantic intentions Cooper may have had are dampened when her brother Wesley tags along. However, Carlotta has an ulterior motive for wanting to go to Florida. Detective Jack Terry informed Carlotta that her father's fingerprints were found at a motel in Daytona Beach. Randolph Wren has been a fugitive for ten years now, leaving Carlotta to raise Wesley. When Cooper, Carlotta, and Wesley arrive in Boca Raton to pick up the body of socialite Kiki Deerling, they find that they're not the only ones who want to claim Kiki's body. Kiki supposedly died of an asthma attack, but someone wants to make sure her family never sees her body and learns the truth.

Other books by the same author:
4 Bodies and a Funeral, 2009 (Body Movers. Book 4)
2 Bodies for the Price of 1, 2007 (Body Movers. Book 2)
Body Movers, 2006 (Body Movers. Book 1)
Finding Your Mojo, 2006
In Deep Voodoo, 2005
My Favorite Mistake, 2005

Other books you might like:
Kathleen Bacus, *Anchors Aweigh*, 2008
Tim Cockey, *The Hearse You Came in On*, 2000
Wendy Roberts, *The Remains of the Dead*, 2007
Sarah Strohmeyer, *Bubbles Ablaze*, 2003

29

MICHAEL BOWEN

Shoot the Lawyer Twice

(Scottsdale: Poisoned Pen, 2008)

Story type: Amateur Detective
Series: Rep and Melissa Pennyworth. Book 4
Subject(s): Law; Universities and Colleges
Major character(s): Rep Pennyworth, Lawyer; Melissa Pennyworth, Professor, Detective—Amateur; Tereska Bleifert, Student—College
Time period(s): 2000s
Locale(s): Milwaukee, Wisconsin; Chicago, Illinois

Summary: College student Jimmy Clevenger shows up at

a Fourth of July party on Carolyn Hoeckstra's boat. Carolyn claims that Jimmy threatened to rape her. She jumps off her boat and swims to shore. Then she files charges against Clevenger. Rep Pennyworth is hired to defend Clevenger, who is charged in Wisconsin with piracy. While Rep deals with what he considers to be a frivolous lawsuit that has gotten out of control, his wife Melissa, an English professor, is stuck between two quarreling colleagues. When one of them is murdered, Melissa searches for the truth while trying to protect a young college student named Tereska Bleifert.

Where it's reviewed:
Booklist, September 1, 2008, page 57
Deadly Pleasures, Fall 2008, page 48
Publishers Weekly, August 11, 2008, page 32

Other books by the same author:
Putting Lipstick on a Pig, 2006
Unforced Error, 2004
Screen Scam, 2001
Collateral Damage, 1999
Worst Case Scenario, 1996

Other books you might like:
Ruth Dudley Edwards, *Murdering Americans*, 2007
John Mortimer, *Rumpole Misbehaves*, 2007
S.J. Rozan, *Mandarin Plaid*, 1996
David J. Walker, *The End of Emerald Woods*, 2000

30

GYLES BRANDRETH

Oscar Wilde and a Game Called Murder

(New York: Simon & Schuster, 2008)

Story type: Historical/Victorian
Series: Oscar Wilde. Book 2
Subject(s): Murder; Authors and Writers
Major character(s): Oscar Wilde, Historical Figure, Writer; Robert Sherard, Writer; Alphonse Byrd, Hotel Worker, Magician
Time period(s): 1890s (1892)
Locale(s): London, England; Eastbourne, England; Beachy Head, England

Summary: In 1892, Oscar Wilde is enjoying the success of his newest play, *Lady Windermere's Fan*. One Sunday in London at a meeting of the Socrates Club, a supper club Wilde created, he invites the attendees to play a game of murder. They must each write down the name of someone they'd like to murder. The names of the "victims" are then drawn out of a bag and read by club secretary, Alphonse Byrd, the night-manager of the Cadogan Hotel. The next day Wilde and his friend Robert Sherard are shocked to learn that the first murder "victim" from the night before, Elizabeth Scott-Rivers, has been found burned to death. When more deaths occur in the order the names were read that fateful night, Wilde enlists the aid of Sherard and their friend Arthur Conan Doyle to discover who took their game of murder a little too seriously.

Where it's reviewed:
Booklist, August 1, 2008, page 46
Mystery News, October/November 2008, page 26
Publishers Weekly, July 7, 2008, page 40

Other books by the same author:
Oscar Wilde and a Death of No Importance, 2007

Other books you might like:
Anne Perry, *Half Moon Street*, 2000
James Reese, *The Dracula Dossier*, 2008
Roberta Rogow, *The Problem of the Evil Editor*, 2000
Walter Satterthwait, *Wilde West*, 1991

31

JAN BROGAN

Teaser

(New York: St. Martin's, 2008)

Story type: Amateur Detective
Series: Hallie Ahern. Book 3
Subject(s): Journalism; Computers
Major character(s): Hallie Ahern, Journalist, Detective—Amateur; Matt Cavanaugh, Lawyer
Time period(s): 2000s
Locale(s): Providence, Rhode Island

Summary: Reporter Hallie Ahern is trolling on social networking sites when she comes across a provocative video of two teenage girls. She's stunned to see what appears to be kiddie porn, out in the open. She finds a screen name for one of the girls and sends her a message, setting up a meeting. Then she pitches the story idea to her editor, pointing out the potential appeal of the story to the newspaper's online readership. Ahern knows that in today's newspaper business, there's nothing that the publisher values more than drawing traffic to the paper's Web site. The girl fails to show for their meeting, but Ahern links her to a local Catholic school where she finds a friend who tells her more about the video operation.

Where it's reviewed:
Booklist, November 15, 2008, page 21
Library Journal, December 15, 2008, page 98
Publishers Weekly, October 6, 2008, page 38

Other books by the same author:
Yesterday's Fatal, 2007
A Confidential Source, 2005
Final Copy, 2001

Other books you might like:
Michael Connelly, *The Scarecrow*, 2009
Libby Fischer Hellmann, *Easy Innocence*, 2008
Laura Lippman, *To the Power of Three*, 2005
Archer Mayor, *Chat*, 2007

32

P.J. BROOKE (Pseudonym of Philip O'Brien and Jane Brooke)

Blood Wedding

(New York: Soho, 2008)

Story type: Police Procedural
Series: Inspector Max Romero. Book 2

Subject(s): Muslims; Terrorism
Major character(s): Max Romero, Detective—Homicide; Hassan Khan, Student, Assistant; Vicente Gonzalez, Police Officer
Time period(s): 1940s (1947); 2000s
Locale(s): Diva, Spain; Granada, Spain; Capa, Spain

Summary: British Muslim graduate student Leila Mahfouz is living in Diva, Spain, with her father Ahmed while she works on her thesis focusing on the Spanish Civil War. When Leila's body is discovered lying in a ditch, Sub-Inspector Max Romero from nearby Granada is called in to assist with the investigation. Max is the police liaison to the Muslim community and is acquainted with both Leila and Ahmed. The local police officer in charge of the case, Vicente Gonzalez, immediately decides that another British Muslim graduate student, Hassan Khan, killed Leila. Hassan and Leila were seeing each other, but he broke off their relationship the day she died. While Max tries to conduct an investigation, free from Gonzalez's corruption, he also has to deal with an anti-terrorism unit from Madrid that wants his help.

Where it's reviewed:
Booklist, November 15, 2008, page 19
Publishers Weekly, October 13, 2008, page 40

Other books you might like:
Alex Carr, *The Prince of Bagram Prison*, 2008
Charles Cumming, *The Spanish Game*, 2008
Rebecca Pawel, *The Summer Snow*, 2006
Robert Wilson, *The Hidden Assassins*, 2006

33

CARL BROOKINS

The Case of the Deceiving Don

(Waterville, ME: Five Star, 2008)

Story type: Private Detective
Series: Sean Sean. Book 2
Subject(s): Crime and Criminals; Retirement
Major character(s): Sean Sean, Detective—Private; Catherine Mckerney, Masseuse, Businesswoman; Ricardo Simon, Detective—Homicide
Time period(s): 2000s
Locale(s): Roseville, Minnesota; St. Paul, Minnesota; Minneapolis, Minnesota

Summary: Minnesota private detective Sean Sean is returning home one afternoon when a nearby nursing home resident's wheelchair explodes just outside Sean's house. Roseville police inform Sean that the dead man's name was Augustus Molinaro, but Sean soon learns that he was actually "Greasy Gus" Molinaro, a crime boss with Mob connections. Sean begins to investigate the case on his own, but then two mysterious men hire him to find Molinaro's killer. Sean soon finds himself a target when someone takes a shot at him while he's in his office. Unsure if it is Molinaro's killer or the person in a silver-blue Audi who keeps following him, Sean doesn't let the threat stop him from seeking the company of his sweetheart, Catherine Mckerney.

Other books by the same author:
Bloody Halls, 2008
Old Silver, 2005
The Case of the Greedy Lawyers, 2005
A Superior Mystery, 2002
Inner Passages, 2000

Other books you might like:
David Housewright, *Practice to Deceive*, 1998
Stuart M. Kaminsky, *Denial*, 2005
John Lutz, *Spark*, 1993
Ronald Tierney, *Asphalt Moon*, 2007

34

RITA MAE BROWN

Santa Clawed

(New York: Bantam, 2008)

Story type: Holiday Themes; Amateur Detective
Series: Mrs. Murphy. Book 17
Subject(s): Animals/Cats; Religion
Major character(s): Mary Minor "Harry" Haristeen, Farmer, Detective—Amateur; Cynthia Cooper, Police Officer; Mrs. Murphy, Animal (cat), Detective—Amateur
Time period(s): 2000s
Locale(s): Crozet, Virginia; Waynesboro, Virginia; Charlottesville, Virginia

Summary: While picking out their Christmas tree, Mary Minor "Harry" Haristeen and her husband discover the body of Christopher Hewitt, a monk at the nearby Brothers of Love monastery. Someone cut Brother Christopher's throat and placed an obol under his tongue. In Greek mythology, an obol was used to pay the ferryman to deliver the dead across the River Styx to the underworld. Both Harry and Cynthia Cooper, Crozet's sheriff's deputy, wonder if the killer placed the Greek coin under Brother Christopher's tongue as a symbol of his sin; Christopher had joined the Brothers of Love after being convicted of insider trading. When more deaths occur in the small Virginia town, Harry herself is placed in danger after her crafty pets, including tiger cat Mrs. Murphy, alert her to a box of money hidden on her property.

Where it's reviewed:
Booklist, October 1, 2008, page 30
Library Journal, October 15, 2008, page 54
Mystery News, December/January 2009, page 16
Publishers Weekly, September 15, 2008, page 49

Other books by the same author:
The Purrfect Murder, 2008
Puss 'n Cahoots, 2007
Sour Puss, 2006
Cat's Eyewitness, 2005
Whisker of Evil, 2004

Other books you might like:
Lydia Adamson, *A Cat on Jingle Bell Rock*, 1997
Donna Andrews, *Six Geese A-Slaying*, 2008
Carole Nelson Douglas, *Cat in a Golden Garland*, 1997
Shirley Rousseau Murphy, *Cat Deck the Halls*, 2007

35

DON BRUNS

Stuff Dreams Are Made Of

(Ipswich, MA: Oceanview, 2008)

Story type: Amateur Detective
Series: Skip Moore and James Lessor. Book 2
Subject(s): Catering Business; Evangelism
Major character(s): Skip Moore, Salesman, Detective—
Amateur; James Lessor, Detective—Amateur,
Businessman; Thomas LeRoy, Businessman,
Criminal
Time period(s): 2000s
Locale(s): Carol City, Florida; South Beach, Florida;
Miami, Florida

Summary: Working on his next get-rich-quick scheme,
entrepreneur James Lessor convinces his best friend,
Skip Moore, that they will make some quick cash by
cooking and serving food at a church revival near Miami,
Florida. The revival, led by the charismatic Reverend
Preston Cashdollar, draws thousands of attendees. While
James and Skip rake in the money, they also become
suspicious of Reverend Cashdollar and his true
intentions. Unfortunately, James and Skip become the
targets of someone in the reverend's organization when
they start to question whether Cashdollar had anything
to do with the murders of a senator and a Miami talk
show host.

Where it's reviewed:
Booklist, July 1, 2008, page 44
Mystery News, August/September 2008, page 21

Other books by the same author:
St. Barts Breakdown, 2008
Stuff to Die For, 2007
South Beach Shakedown, 2006
Barbados Heat, 2003
Jamaica Blue, 2002

Other books you might like:
Jerome Doolittle, *Head Lock*, 1993
Jerrilyn Farmer, *Immaculate Reception*, 1999
Richard Hoyt, *Snake Eyes*, 1995
Richard Stark, *Comeback*, 1997

36

DECLAN BURKE

The Big O

(Orlando: Harcourt, 2008)

Story type: Domestic
Subject(s): Crime and Criminals; Kidnapping
Major character(s): Karen King, Receptionist, Criminal;
Ray Brogan, Kidnapper, Artist; Francis Dolan, Doc-
tor
Time period(s): 2000s
Locale(s): Larkhill Mews, England

Summary: Armed robber and doctor's office receptionist
Karen King's life is about to become very complicated.
Karen's ex, Rossi Callaghan, is being released from
prison. Karen knows that Rossi will come looking for
her. However, Karen just met Ray Brogan who is pretty
intimidating himself. Ray is a professional kidnapper
who is trying to get out of the business. Ray's boss gives
him one last job, to kidnap Margaret Dolan. Frank,
Margaret's soon-to-be ex-husband, wants Margaret
kidnapped so that he can collect the insurance money.
The only problem is that Margaret is a friend of Karen's.
When Ray tells Karen about the job, they convince
Margaret to go ahead with the kidnapping so they can
double-cross Frank and take the money themselves.

Where it's reviewed:
Booklist, September 1, 2008, page 52
Publishers Weekly, July 21, 2008, page 139

Other books by the same author:
Eight Ball Boogie, 2004

Other books you might like:
Roberta Kray, *The Debt*, 2006
Jay MacLarty, *Bagman*, 2004
Rick Riordan, *Cold Springs*, 2003
Joe Schreiber, *Chasing the Dead*, 2006

37

ELIZABETH KANE BUZZELLI

Dead Dancing Women

(Woodbury, MN: Midnight Ink, 2008)

Story type: Amateur Detective
Series: Emily Kincaid. Book 1
Subject(s): Small Town Life
Major character(s): Emily Kincaid, Journalist, Detective—
Amateur; Dolly Wakowski, Police Officer; Flora Coy,
Aged Person
Time period(s): 2000s
Locale(s): Leetsville, Michigan; Traverse City, Michigan

Summary: Journalist and would-be mystery author Emily
Kincaid moved to northern Michigan after divorcing her
husband, in hopes of working on her writing. While
Emily has enjoyed the peace and quiet of living in the
woods outside Leetsville, her quiet is disturbed when she
discovers a severed head in her trashcan. Emily calls the
police, and Deputy Dolly Wakowski is the first on the
scene. When the case is handed over to the state police,
Emily and Deputy Dolly team up to solve the case on
their own. They soon learn that the victim, Ruby Poet,
belonged to Women of the Moon, a group of older
women who loved nature and celebrated by dancing and
singing around a bonfire in the woods. Now, someone is
determined to put an end to the women's festivities by
killing them one by one.

Where it's reviewed:
Booklist, September 15, 2008, page 28
Library Journal, September 1, 2008, page 100

Other books you might like:
Doug Allyn, *Black Water*, 1996
Kathleen Hills, *Witch Cradle*, 2006
Henry Kisor, *Cache of Corpses*, 2007
William Kent Krueger, *Copper River*, 2006

38

CHELSEA CAIN

Sweetheart

(New York: St. Martin's, 2008)

Story type: Serial Killer
Series: Archie Sheridan and Gretchen Lowell. Book 2
Subject(s): Psychological Thriller; Journalism
Major character(s): Archie Sheridan, Detective—Homicide; Gretchen Lowell, Serial Killer; Susan Ward, Journalist, Writer
Time period(s): 2000s
Locale(s): Portland, Oregon; Salem, Oregon

Summary: Portland, Oregon, police detective Archie Sheridan has never fully recovered from being kidnapped and tortured by serial killer Gretchen Lowell. Attempting to put his obsession with Gretchen behind him, Archie tries to focus on his family and his work. When the body of a young woman is discovered in a local park, Archie can't help but remember that this park is also where he found Gretchen's first victim. Journalist Susan Ward is also interested in Archie's case, and helps the police uncover the dead woman's identity. However, Archie is soon distracted from the case when he learns that Gretchen has escaped from police custody. When his phone rings shortly thereafter, Archie isn't surprised to hear Gretchen's voice on the other end. Concealing his plans, Archie puts his own life at risk to recapture the deadly beauty.

Where it's reviewed:
Booklist, July 1, 2008, page 6
Entertainment Weekly, September 12, 2008, page 141
Library Journal, August 15, 2008, page 64
Mystery News, October/November 2008, page 19
Publishers Weekly, July 21, 2008, page 138

Other books by the same author:
Heartsick, 2007
Confessions of a Teen Sleuth: A Parody, 2005

Other books you might like:
Joy Fielding, *Charley's Web*, 2008
Brian Freeman, *Stalked*, 2008
Thomas Harris, *The Silence of the Lambs*, 1988
Thomas Perry, *Nightlife*, 2006

39

BILL CAMERON

Chasing Smoke

(Madison, WI: Bleak House, 2008)

Story type: Police Procedural
Subject(s): Cancer; Suicide
Major character(s): Thomas "Skin" Kadash, Detective—Homicide; Susan Mulvaney, Detective—Homicide; Tobias Hern, Doctor
Time period(s): 2000s
Locale(s): Portland, Oregon

Summary: Homicide detective Thomas "Skin" Kadash is on leave in Portland, Oregon, while he undergoes treatment for bladder cancer. Skin's former partner, Detective Susan Mulvaney, asks him to come to the scene of an apparent suicide, Raymond Orwoll. When Skin finds a prescription bottle with Dr. Tobias Hern's name on it, he realizes why Susan asked for his help. Dr. Hern is the oncologist who is treating Skin. Orwoll isn't the first patient of Dr. Hern's to kill himself. Skin learns that four men, all with cancer, recently killed themselves. Not convinced that the deaths were suicides, Skin begins an unofficial investigation as he deals with the pain and the reality of his illness.

Where it's reviewed:
Booklist, November 15, 2008, page 19
Library Journal, October 1, 2008, page 46
Publishers Weekly, October 6, 2008, page 38

Other books by the same author:
Lost Dog, 2007

Other books you might like:
Robert Greer, *Heat Shock*, 2003
T. Jefferson Parker, *The Blue Hour*, 1999
Mark Schorr, *Borderline*, 2006
Marcia Talley, *Sing It to Her Bones*, 1999

40

STEPHEN J. CANNELL

At First Sight

(New York: Vanguard, 2008)

Story type: Psychological
Subject(s): Marriage; Stalking
Major character(s): Charles "Chick" Best Jr., Businessman, Murderer; Paige Ellis, Teacher, Artist; Robert Butler, Detective—Homicide
Time period(s): 2000s
Locale(s): Lahaina, Hawaii; Los Angeles, California; Charlotte, North Carolina

Summary: Dot-com millionaire Chick Best is vacationing in Hawaii with his trophy wife Evelyn and their 16-year-old daughter Melissa, worrying about the fact that money has just about run out. Lounging around the pool, Chick spots Paige Ellis. Paige, a painter and kindergarten teacher from Charlotte, North Carolina, is on Maui with her husband Chandler. From the moment Chick sees Paige, he becomes obsessed with her. After returning from Hawaii, Chick detours after a disastrous business meeting in New York and drives to Charlotte where he runs down Chandler outside a drugstore. Deciding that his wife Evelyn is an obstacle in his relationship with Paige, Chick kills her too. When Paige flies to Los Angeles to console Chick after Evelyn's death, Paige eventually discovers that Chick has more in mind than friendship.

Where it's reviewed:
Booklist, July 1, 2008, page 5
Publishers Weekly, May 26, 2008, page 35

Other books by the same author:
Three Shirt Deal, 2008
White Sister, 2006
Cold Hit, 2005
Vertical Coffin, 2004
Runaway Heart, 2003

Other books you might like:
James M. Cain, *Double Indemnity*, 1943
Carl Hiaasen, *Skinny Dip*, 2004
Donald E. Westlake, *The Ax*, 1997
Stuart Woods, *Santa Fe Dead*, 2008

41

JOANNA CARL (Pseudonym of Eve K. Sandstrom)

The Chocolate Snowman Murders

(New York: Obsidian, 2008)

Story type: Amateur Detective
Series: Chocoholic Mysteries. Book 8
Subject(s): Carnivals; Secrets
Major character(s): Lee McKinney Woodyard, Business-
    woman, Detective—Amateur; Joe Woodyard,
    Lawyer, Spouse (of Lee); Mozelle French, Volunteer
Time period(s): 2000s
Locale(s): Warner Pier, Michigan; Grand Rapids,
    Michigan

Summary: Lee Woodyard, business manager of TenHuis
Chocolade in Warner Pier, Michigan, reluctantly agrees
to volunteer for the town's annual WinterFest. Her
husband Joe is chosen to pick up Fletcher Mendenhall,
the judge for the festival's art exhibit. When a meeting
delays Joe, Lee finds herself making the trip to the Grand
Rapids airport. On the way back to Warner Pier, an
inebriated Fletcher tries to put the moves on her.
Disgusted with his behavior, Lee leaves Fletcher at a
motel outside of town. Joe finds Fletcher's body the next
morning, his head bashed in. Joe and Lee become murder
suspects and must find the killer in the midst of the
festivities before more dead bodies turn up.

Where it's reviewed:
Library Journal, October 15, 2008, page 54
Publishers Weekly, August 18, 2008, page 47

Other books by the same author:
The Chocolate Jewel Case, 2007
The Chocolate Bridal Bash, 2006
The Chocolate Mouse Trap, 2005
The Chocolate Puppy Puzzle, 2004
The Chocolate Frog Frame-Up, 2003

Other books you might like:
Laura Childs, *The Theodosia Browning Series*, 2001-
Jo Dereske, *Cut and Dry*, 1997
Joanne Fluke, *Blueberry Muffin Murder*, 2002
Lise McClendon, *Nordic Nights*, 1999

42

DONIS CASEY

The Sky Took Him

(Scottsdale: Poisoned Pen, 2009)

Story type: Historical/World War I; Amateur Detective
Series: Alafair Tucker. Book 4
Subject(s): Family; Secrets
Major character(s): Alafair Tucker, Farmer, Detective—
    Amateur; Martha Tucker, Secretary; Buck Collins,
    Businessman
Time period(s): 1910s (1915)
Locale(s): Enid, Oklahoma; Boynton, Oklahoma; Garber,
    Oklahoma

Summary: In 1915, farmer's wife Alafair Tucker receives
a letter from her sister Ruth Ann asking her to come to
Enid, Oklahoma. Ruth Ann's husband Lester is dying
and Ruth Ann wants her family with her. Alafair's eldest
daughter Martha and youngest daughter Grace are accompanying Alafair on her journey. Ruth Ann's son-in-
law Kenneth Crawford is away on an ill-timed business
trip and has not contacted his wife Olivia in several
days. When Kenneth's body is discovered in a family-
owned freezer, the town believes that businessman Buck
Collins had something to do with it. Alafair doesn't
believe that Buck is guilty and decides to investigate
Kenneth's death herself.

Where it's reviewed:
Mystery News, December/January 2009, page 17
Publishers Weekly, December 8, 2008, page 48

Other books by the same author:
The Drop Edge of Yonder, 2007
Hornswoggled, 2006
The Old Buzzard Had It Coming, 2005

Other books you might like:
Cordelia Frances Biddle, *Deception's Daughter*, 2008
Karen Rose Cercone, *Steel Ashes*, 1997
Fred Harris, *Coyote Revenge*, 1999
Clyde Linsley, *Saving Lousia*, 2003

43

C.S. CHALLINOR

Christmas Is Murder

(Woodbury, MN: Midnight Ink, 2008)

Story type: Holiday Themes
Series: Rex Graves. Book 1
Subject(s): Christmas
Major character(s): Reginald "Rex" Graves, Lawyer,
    Widow(er); Helen D'Arcy, Counselor; Dahlia Smith-
    ings, Hotel Owner
Time period(s): 2000s
Locale(s): Edinburgh, Scotland; Swanmere, England

Summary: When Scottish barrister Rex Graves receives an
invitation to spend Christmas at Swanmere Manor, he
expects that he'll have to solve a series of murders before
sitting down to Christmas dinner. Upon arrival, Rex
learns that one of the guests, elderly Henry Lawdry, died
the day before. After discovering Rex's profession, medic
Charley Perkins informs Rex that Henry did not die a
natural death; he was poisoned. Rex tells Dahlia Smith-
ings, owner of Swanmere Manor and a friend of his
mother's, that he would like to quietly investigate
Henry's death. When more deaths occur, Rex has to
work quickly to find the killer, all the while hoping it's
not Helen D'Arcy, a young school counselor that Rex
has taken a liking to.

Where it's reviewed:
Booklist, September 15, 2008, page 27
Deadly Pleasures, Summer 2008, page 44

Other books you might like:
Agatha Christie, *Hercule Poirot's Christmas*, 1939
Joan Coggin, *Dancing with Death*, 2004
Cyril Hare, *An English Murder*, 1951
Anne Perry, *A Christmas Journey*, 2003

44

HENRY CHANG

Year of the Dog

(New York: Soho, 2008)

Story type: Police Procedural
Series: Jack Yu. Book 2
Subject(s): Illegal Immigrants; Chinese Americans
Major character(s): Jack Yu, Detective—Police; Tat Louie, Gang Member; Ah Por, Psychic (fortune teller)
Time period(s): 2000s
Locale(s): New York, New York

Summary: Homicide detective Jack Yu's turf is New York's Chinatown, a locale as foreign to outsiders as Shanghai. Yu grew up in Chinatown and easily moves through it discovering things a non-Chinese American police officer couldn't. He deals with the murder/suicide of a Taiwanese family, gang warfare that makes New York politicos nervous, a series of warehouse burglaries, and the murder of a Chinese American honor student working for his family's restaurant. The investigation encompasses Chinese mobsters, murder, extortion, illegal betting, slavery, credit card scams, and busing Chinese laborers across the country to work cheaply in restaurants and on construction projects. Yu relies on modern police methods, but he also visits an aged fortune teller to help him solve crimes.

Where it's reviewed:
Booklist, November 15, 2008, page 22
Entertainment Weekly, October 31, 2008, page 66
Publishers Weekly, September 8, 2008, page 39

Other books by the same author:
Chinatown Beat, 2006

Other books you might like:
Leslie Glass, *Stealing Time*, 1999
Dan Mahoney, *The Two Chinatowns*, 2001
S.J. Rozan, *A Bitter Feast*, 1998
Victoria Thompson, *Murder in Chinatown*, 2007

45

SEAN CHERCOVER

Trigger City

(New York: Morrow, 2008)

Story type: Private Detective
Series: Ray Dudgeon. Book 2
Subject(s): Conspiracies; Business
Major character(s): Ray Dudgeon, Detective—Private; Isaac Richmond, Military Personnel (retired)
Time period(s): 2000s
Locale(s): Chicago, Illinois

Summary: Ray Dudgeon has a shoulder injury and needs lots of money to get it fixed. When retired Colonel Isaac Richmond asks Ray to look into the death of his shy and unassuming daughter—an offer that comes with a $50,000 check—Ray can hardly refuse. Richmond's daughter was shot and killed by Steven Zhang, a disgruntled co-worker who then killed himself. Ray visits Steven's wife. Finding her terrified, he realizes that the case is not as simple as he had originally thought. He and his assistant Vince must unravel many layers to figure out what really happened, layers that lead to the war in Iraq and a conspiracy they could not have anticipated.

Where it's reviewed:
Deadly Pleasures, Fall 2008, page 57
Library Journal, October 15, 2008, page 52
Publishers Weekly, August 25, 2008, page 50

Other books by the same author:
Big City, Bad Blood, 2007

Other books you might like:
Robert Crais, *Indigo Slam*, 1997
Loren D. Estleman, *Sweet Women Lie*, 1990
Michael Koryta, *A Welcome Grave*, 2007
Robert B. Parker, *A Savage Place*, 1981

46

LAURA CHILDS (Pseudonym of Gerry Schmitt)

Death Swatch

(New York: Berkley, 2008)

Story type: Amateur Detective
Series: Carmela Bertrand. Book 6
Subject(s): Treasure, Buried; Crafts
Major character(s): Carmela Bertrand, Businesswoman, Detective—Amateur; Ava Grieux, Businesswoman; Edgar Babcock, Detective—Homicide
Time period(s): 2000s
Locale(s): New Orleans, Louisiana

Summary: It's Mardi Gras time in New Orleans again. Memory Mine scrapbook store owner Carmela Bertrand is attending a Mardi Gras party hosted by local businessman Jekyl Hardy in his swanky French Quarter apartment. Soon after meeting Jekyl's neighbor, float designer Archie Baudier, Carmela is shocked to find Archie on Jekyl's balcony with a barbed wire garrote around his throat. Not content to leave the detecting to the police, Carmela and Ava Grieux, a close friend and owner of the Juju Voodoo shop, decide to do some sleuthing of their own, much to the dismay of police lieutenant Edgar Babcock. Learning of Archie's interest in the missing treasure of pirate Jean Lafitte, Carmela and Ava discover that Archie may have found the treasure and been killed because of it.

Where it's reviewed:
Booklist, September 1, 2008, page 53
Publishers Weekly, July 21, 2008, page 145

Mystery

Other books by the same author:
Frill Kill, 2007
Motif for Murder, 2006
Bound for Murder, 2004
Photo Finished, 2004
Keepsake Crimes, 2003

Other books you might like:
Barbara Colley, *Married to the Mop*, 2006
Mary Anna Evans, *Findings*, 2008
Mary Ellen Hughes, *Paper-Thin Alibi*, 2008
Joanna Campbell Slan, *Paper, Scissors, Death*, 2008

47

LAURA CHILDS (Pseudonym of Gerry Schmitt)

Eggs in Purgatory

(New York: Berkley, 2008)

Story type: Amateur Detective
Series: Cackleberry Club. Book 1
Subject(s): Small Town Life; Women
Major character(s): Suzanne Deitz, Businesswoman,
    Detective—Amateur; Toni Garrett, Waiter/Waitress;
    Vern Manchester, Real Estate Agent
Time period(s): 2000s
Locale(s): Kindred, Midwest

Summary: After Suzanne, Toni, and Petra all lose their
husbands, in very different ways, Suzanne opens up the
Cackleberry Club in her hometown of Kindred. When
Bobby Waite, Suzanne's lawyer, is murdered in the alley
behind the cozy little cafe, Suzanne decides to investigate
the murder herself. While Suzanne makes a few inquiries into Bobby's murder, she also becomes aware of a
possible scandal involving her late husband Walter and a
multi-million dollar kickback from a construction
contract. Sifting through Walter's papers, Suzanne finds
no evidence of the missing money. When Suzanne does
find a link between Bobby's murder and a young woman
who has run away from a nearby religious cult, Suzanne
finds her own life in danger.

Other books by the same author:
Death Swatch, 2008
The Silver Needle Murder, 2008
Dragonwell Dead, 2007
Frill Kill, 2007
Motif for Murder, 2006

Other books you might like:
Lynn Bulock, *Love the Sinner*, 2005
Diane Mott Davidson, *Dark Tort*, 2006
Jimmie Ruth Evans, *Flamingo Fatale*, 2005
Kathleen Taylor, *Foreign Body*, 2001

48

ANN CLEEVES

White Nights

(New York: St. Martin's, 2008)

Story type: Police Procedural
Series: Jimmy Perez. Book 2

Subject(s): Artists and Art; Blackmail
Major character(s): Jimmy Perez, Detective—Police,
    Divorced Person; Fran Hunter, Artist, Single Parent;
    Kenny Thomson, Farmer
Time period(s): 2000s
Locale(s): Lerwick, Scotland; Biddista, Scotland; Hudder-
    sfield, England

Summary: During an art exhibit in the small village of
Biddista in the Shetland Islands, police inspector Jimmy
Perez is looking forward to his date with Fran Hunter,
one of the artists whose work is being featured that
evening. Jimmy's date is interrupted, however, by a
mysterious man who bursts into tears at the sight of a
painting by the wealthy Bella Sinclair, the other artist in
the exhibit. When Jimmy tries to question the man, he
claims to have amnesia and has no idea why the painting
affected him. Before Perez can ask any more questions,
the man runs off. The next day, crofter Kenny Thomson
discovers the man's body hanging in a shed. As Perez
investigates the murder, he starts to uncover some village secrets that may have led someone to murder.

Where it's reviewed:
Booklist, July 1, 2008, page 45
Publishers Weekly, July 7, 2008, page 37

Other books by the same author:
Hidden Depths, 2007
Raven Black, 2007
Telling Tales, 2005
Burial of Ghosts, 2003
The Sleeping and the Dead, 2001

Other books you might like:
S.J. Bolton, *Sacrifice*, 2008
Stephen Booth, *Black Dog*, 2000
Jeanne M. Dams, *Holy Terror in the Hebrides*, 1997
Louise Penny, *Still Life*, 2006

49

BARBARA CLEVERLY

Bright Hair about the Bone

(New York: Delta, 2008)

Story type: Historical
Series: Laetitia Talbot Mystery. Book 2
Subject(s): Archaeology; Religion
Major character(s): Laetitia Talbot, Archaeologist; William
    Gunning, Veteran, Bodyguard; Edmond d'Aubec,
    Nobleman, Businessman
Time period(s): 1920s
Locale(s): Fontigny Sainte-Reine, France; Cambridge,
    England

Summary: A coded message from her late godfather
Daniel Thorndon sends British archaeologist Laetitia
Talbot to the Burgundy region of France where Daniel
was stabbed to death while researching religious artifacts.
Determined to find out what happened, Laetitia travels to
the village of Fontigny Sainte-Reine with Great War
veteran William Gunning as her personal bodyguard.
Working under the name Stella St. Clair, Laetitia
volunteers at an archaeological dig that was part of
Daniel's research. When a local nobleman, Edmond

d'Aubec, meets Laetitia he informs her that he was working with Daniel. Struggling with her attraction to Edmond, Laetitia continues Daniel's research and soon learns that the killer is someone she has grown fond of.

Where it's reviewed:
Booklist, September 15, 2008, page 27
Publishers Weekly, August 4, 2008, page 47

Other books by the same author:
Folly Du Jour, 2008
The Tomb of Zeus, 2007
Tug of War, 2007
The Bee's Kiss, 2006
The Palace Tiger, 2005

Other books you might like:
Tasha Alexander, *A Poisoned Season*, 2007
Clare Langley-Hawthorne, *Consequences of Sin*, 2006
Elizabeth Peters, *Tomb of the Golden Bird*, 2006
Deanna Raybourn, *Silent in the Sanctuary*, 2008

50

BARBARA CLEVERLY

Folly Du Jour

(New York: Soho, 2008)

Story type: Historical/Roaring Twenties; Police Procedural
Series: Joe Sandilands. Book 7
Subject(s): Actors and Actresses; Serial Killers
Major character(s): Joe Sandilands, Police Officer; George Jardine, Crime Suspect; Georges Simenon, Journalist
Time period(s): 1920s (1926)
Locale(s): Paris, France

Summary: Sir George Jardine is at the Folies Bergere in Paris, and he sees someone he knows, Sir Stanley Somerton, slumped over in his box. Sir George goes to help, and finds Sir Stanley's throat slit. The usherette thinks Sir George is the killer, and he is arrested. Luckily his friend, Commander Joe Sandilands of Scotland Yard, is in Paris for an Interpol conference. Sandilands and French Inspector Bonnefoye are able to get him released. The pathologist points out that the killing is similar to several others, and with the help of reporter Georges Simenon, Sandilands is able to track down an elusive killer.

Where it's reviewed:
Booklist, May 1, 2008, page 30
Mystery News, October/November 2008, page 15
Mystery Scene, Fall 2008, page 70
Publishers Weekly, May 26, 2008, page 40

Other books by the same author:
Tug of War, 2007
The Palace Tiger, 2005
The Damascened Blade, 2004
Ragtime in Simla, 2003

Other books you might like:
Cara Black, *Murder in the Bastille*, 2003
Howard Engel, *Murder on Montparnasse*, 1999
Alan Furst, *The World at Night*, 1996
Georges Simenon, *The Madman of Bergerac*, 1940

51

JEFFREY COHEN

It Happened One Knife

(New York: Berkley, 2008)

Story type: Amateur Detective
Series: Elliot Freed. Book 2
Subject(s): Movie Industry; Comedians

Summary: Elliot Freed owns a movie theater named Comedy Tonight that only shows classic and modern comedies. Elliot is excited because his favorite comedy team, Lillis & Townes, will reunite for a special screening of their classic film *Cracked Ice*. At the screening, Harry Lillis gives Elliot a clue to a famous Hollywood mystery. Lillis says that Les Townes murdered his wife and then burned down their house. Elliot doesn't want to believe one of his legends is a murderer so he begins investigating this cold case. At the same time one of the ushers of Comedy Tonight is ready to screen his independent film, but the only copy of the movie has gone missing. Suspecting foul play, he blames Elliot.

Where it's reviewed:
Deadly Pleasures, Fall 2008, page 51

Other books by the same author:
Some Like It Hot-Buttered, 2007
As Dog Is My Witness, 2005
A Farewell to Legs, 2003
For Whom the Minivan Rolls, 2002

Other books you might like:
Loren D. Estleman, *Frames*, 2008
Terence Faherty, *Kill Me Again*, 1996
Ron Goulart, *Elementary, My Dear Groucho*, 1999
Stuart M. Kaminsky, *Bullet for a Star*, 1977

52

MICHAEL CONNELLY

The Brass Verdict

(New York: Little, Brown, 2008)

Story type: Legal; Police Procedural
Series: Mickey Haller. Book 2
Subject(s): Legal Thriller; Movie Industry
Major character(s): Mickey Haller, Lawyer; Harry Bosch, Detective—Homicide; Walter Elliot, Producer
Time period(s): 1990s (1992); 2000s (2007)
Locale(s): Los Angeles, California

Summary: Defense attorney Mickey Haller is recovering from surgery when he is notified that famed criminal attorney Jerry Vincent has just been murdered—and he has been named to take over Vincent's cases. Notable among these is that of Walter Elliot, a movie producer who has been charged with the murder of his wife and her lover. As Haller investigates the details of the case, he finds gaps in the police account of the day of the murder. He becomes convinced that Elliot is innocent, but as the case goes to trial, he doesn't understand why Elliott is so confident he will get off. Meanwhile, Detective Harry Bosch is trying to find Vincent's killer, and he and Haller keep bumping heads over the case, especially when Haller thinks the killer is now after him.

Where it's reviewed:
Booklist, August 1, 2008, page 5
Library Journal, September 1, 2008, page 114
Mystery Scene, Fall 2008, page 72
Publishers Weekly, November 24, 2008, page 52

Other books by the same author:
The Overlook, 2007
Echo Park, 2006
The Closers, 2005
The Lincoln Lawyer, 2005
The Narrows, 2004

Other books you might like:
Robert Crais, *Chasing Darkness*, 2008
John Lescroart, *Betrayal*, 2007
Steve Martini, *Double Tap*, 2005
Brad Meltzer, *Dead Even*, 1998

53

PATRICIA CORNWELL

Scarpetta

(New York: Putnam, 2008)

Story type: Medical; Police Procedural
Series: Kay Scarpetta. Book 16
Subject(s): Stalking; Dwarves
Major character(s): Kay Scarpetta, Doctor; Benton Wesley, Psychologist; Oscar Bane, Crime Suspect
Time period(s): 2000s
Locale(s): New York, New York

Summary: Dr. Kay Scarpetta is summoned from her new practice in Boston to New York's Bellevue Hospital to examine a patient of psychologist Benton Wesley. Oscar Bane is suspected but not yet accused of murdering his girlfriend, Terri Bridges. Both are afflicted with dwarfism. Bane tells Scarpetta that he didn't kill her, though he saw her body, and that "people are after" him. Meanwhile, NYPD is working the murder case under the direction of Jaime Berger with a new detective, Mike Morales, in charge. Pete Marino, now working for Berger, and Lucy, living in New York, also join in. What does Terri's murder have to do with a vicious gossip column that has attacked Scarpetta? Is Bane innocent? Then, there is a copycat murder.

Where it's reviewed:
Booklist, December 1, 2008, page 5
Publishers Weekly, November 24, 2008, page 40

Other books by the same author:
Book of the Dead, 2007
Predator, 2005
Trace, 2004
Blow Fly, 2003
The Last Precinct, 2000

Other books you might like:
Jefferson Bass, *Carved in Bone*, 2006
Simon Beckett, *The Chemistry of Death*, 2006
Barbara D'Amato, *White Male Infant*, 2002
Kathy Reichs, *Break No Bones*, 2006

54

COLIN COTTERILL

Curse of the Pogo Stick

(New York: Soho, 2008)

Story type: Political; Mystical
Series: Siri Paiboun. Book 5
Subject(s): Kidnapping; Political Movements
Major character(s): Siri Paiboun, Doctor; Dtui, Nurse
Time period(s): 1970s (1977)
Locale(s): Laos

Summary: Dr. Siri Paiboun, the national coroner of Laos, is at a boring Party meeting in the north of Laos when he discovers the body of a comrade in the audience. His superior is more upset with Dr. Siri's disturbing the meeting than he is with the news of the death itself. He informs Dr. Siri that they will be driving back to Vientiane instead of flying. Though assured the trip is perfectly safe, Dr. Siri is not surprised when their caravan is ambushed and he is kidnapped by Hmong villagers. At the same time, back in Vientiane, a booby-trapped corpse is delivered to the morgue. Observant Nurse Dtui is able to save the life of the substitute coroner by recognizing the incision where the home-made bomb was implanted, but who is behind the deed, obviously directed at Dr. Siri?

Where it's reviewed:
Booklist, May 1, 2008, page 26
Deadly Pleasures, Summer 2008, page 47
Mystery News, August/September 2008, page 22
Publishers Weekly, May 5, 2008, page 47

Other books by the same author:
Anarchy and Old Dogs, 2007
Disco for the Departed, 2006
Thirty-Three Teeth, 2005
The Coroner's Lunch, 2004

Other books you might like:
James D. Doss, *Snake Dreams*, 2008
Christopher Fowler, *The Victoria Vanishes*, 2008
Naomi Hirahara, *The Mas Arai Series*, 2004 -
Eliot Pattison, *Bone Mountain*, 2002

55

MICHAEL COX

The Glass of Time

(New York: Norton, 2008)

Story type: Historical/Victorian
Subject(s): Identity, Concealed; Family
Major character(s): Esperanza Gorst, Orphan, Servant; Emily Grace Duport, Noblewoman, Widow(er); Montagu Wraxall, Lawyer, Aged Person
Time period(s): 1870s; 1880s
Locale(s): Evenwood, England; London, England; Paris, France

Summary: When 19-year-old Esperanza Gorst is informed by her guardian, Madame de l'Orme, that she must leave her home in France and travel to England to become a lady's maid, she has no idea of her role in an intricate plan that seeks to right a past injustice. Esperanza is employed by Lady Emily Duport, the 26th Baroness of Tansor. Esperanza is told that she will receive three letters from Madame de l'Orme that will explain the Great Task, her ultimate goal. Although Lady Emily can be a difficult employer at times, Esperanza soon gains her affection, and catches the eye of both Duport sons, Perseus and Randolph. Just as Esperanza and Perseus reveal their attraction for one another, the third and final letter outlining Esperanza's Great Task arrives. The information it contains throws Esperanza's life upside down and forces her to choose between duty and love.

Where it's reviewed:
Booklist, August 1, 2008, page 6
Deadly Pleasures, Fall 2008, page 57
Library Journal, September 1, 2008, page 114
Publishers Weekly, August 18, 2008, page 39

Other books by the same author:
The Meaning of Night, 2006

Other books you might like:
Jonathan Barnes, *The Somnambulist*, 2008
Betsy Tobin, *Bone House*, 2001
Sarah Waters, *Fingersmith*, 2002
Carlos Ruiz Zafon, *The Shadow of the Wind*, 2004

56

CLEO COYLE   (Pseudonym of Alice Alfonsi and Marc Cerasini)

Espresso Shot

(New York: Berkley, 2008)

Story type: Amateur Detective
Series: Clare Cosi. Book 7
Subject(s): Weddings
Major character(s): Clare Cosi, Businesswoman; Matteo "Matt" Allegro, Businessman, Bridegroom; Mike Quinn, Detective—Police
Time period(s): 2000s
Locale(s): New York, New York

Summary: Clare Cosi is the manager of the popular New York coffeehouse The Village Blend. She has her hands full when she is asked to create a gourmet coffee and dessert bar for an upcoming wedding reception at the Metropolitan Museum of Art. If the stress of catering such a high profile event weren't enough, the wedding is that of Matteo Allegro, Clare's ex-husband. While Clare and Matt are still friends and business partners, Matt's fiancee, Breanne Summour, is convinced that Clare wants Matt back. Unfortunately, Breanne has bigger problems to worry about than losing her fiance. Someone is trying to kill her. When a Breanne look-alike stripper is killed shortly after Matt's bachelor party, Matt begs Clare to look after his soon-to-be bride. Putting her sleuthing skills to work, Clare attempts to discover who wants Breanne dead.

Where it's reviewed:
Library Journal, September 1, 2008, page 98
Publishers Weekly, August 11, 2008, page 32

Other books by the same author:
French Pressed, 2008
Decaffeinated Corpse, 2007
Murder Most Frothy, 2006
Latte Trouble, 2005
Through the Grinder, 2004

Other books you might like:
Sandra Balzo, *Grounds for Murder*, 2007
M.C. Beaton, *Love, Lies and Liquor*, 2006
JoAnna Carl, *The Chocolate Bridal Bash*, 2006
Laura Childs, *The Silver Needle Murder*, 2008

57

ROBERT CRAIS

Chasing Darkness

(New York: Simon & Schuster, 2008)

Story type: Private Detective
Series: Elvis Cole. Book 12
Subject(s): Arson; Serial Killers
Major character(s): Elvis Cole, Detective—Private; Joe Pike, Detective—Private; Yvonne Bennett, Prostitute
Time period(s): 2000s
Locale(s): Laurel Canyon, California; Los Angeles, California

Summary: As a fire rages through Laurel Canyon, police officers go from house to house, evacuating residents. At one house they sense something is wrong. Inside is a dead man, an apparent suicide, holding photos of seven women, photographed moments after being killed. The police are delighted to have cleared a serial killer case; Elvis Cole, who worked on the dead man's defense three years before, isn't so sure. Cole had found evidence that got the man acquitted and goes to work trying to find the real killer of the seven women, including prostitute Yvonne Bennett, whose photograph the dead man was holding along with the others.

Where it's reviewed:
Booklist, June 1, 2008, page 5
Deadly Pleasures, Summer 2008, page 50
Entertainment Weekly, July 11, 2008, page 77
Publishers Weekly, May 19, 2008, page 31

Other books by the same author:
The Forgotten Man, 2005
The Last Detective, 2003
L.A. Requiem, 1999
Indigo Slam, 1997
Sunset Express, 1996

Other books you might like:
Michael Connelly, *Angel's Flight*, 1998
Jonathon King, *A Visible Darkness*, 2003
Michael Koryta, *Sorrow's Anthem*, 2006
Dennis Lehane, *A Drink Before the War*, 1994

58

MICHAEL CRAVEN

Body Copy
(New York: Harper, 2009)

Story type: Private Detective
Subject(s): Business; Sports/Surfing
Major character(s): Donald Tremaine, Detective—Private; Nina Aldeen, Professor; John Lopez, Police Officer
Time period(s): 2000s
Locale(s): Malibu, California; Los Angeles, California; Atlanta, Georgia

Summary: Fifteen years ago, Donald Tremaine was the top professional surfer in the world. Having left the sport at the top of his career, Tremaine is now a private detective in Malibu, California. Tremaine's newest client is Nina Aldeen, a UCLA professor. Aldeen wants Tremaine to find out who killed her uncle, Roger Gale. Gale, an advertising tycoon, was killed a year ago and the police still haven't figured out who did it. Tremaine interviews Gale's employees and family, and comes up with nothing. Tracking down the police detective who originally worked the case, Tremaine realizes that the late ad exec had a lot of secrets, and one of them killed him.

Where it's reviewed:
Publishers Weekly, November 24, 2008, page 40

Other books you might like:
Richard Barre, *Burning Moon*, 2003
Jeff Shelby, *Killer Swell*, 2005
Jill Sorenson, *Crash Into Me*, 2009
Don Winslow, *The Dawn Patrol*, 2008

59

DEBORAH CROMBIE

Where Memories Lie
(New York: Morrow, 2008)

Story type: Police Procedural
Series: Gemma James and Duncan Kincaid. Book 12
Subject(s): Nazis; World War II
Major character(s): Gemma James, Detective—Police; Duncan Kincaid, Detective—Police; Erika Rosenthal, Historian (retired)
Time period(s): 2000s; 1950s (1952)
Locale(s): London, England; Leyton, England

Summary: A diamond brooch in an auction catalog brings back memories for retired historian Dr. Erika Rosenthal. The brooch was created by Erika's late father Jakob and given to Erika as she and her husband David fled Nazi Germany. Stolen during their journey to England, the brooch has now mysteriously surfaced. Erika believes the brooch is somehow connected to David's death in 1952, and calls on her neighbor Detective Inspector Gemma James for help. Unfortunately, the first person Gemma questions at the auction house, clerk Kristin Cahill, is the victim of a hit-and-run soon afterwards. When more deaths occur, Gemma looks to her partner, Scotland

Yard Superintendent Duncan Kincaid, for help in finding answers.

Where it's reviewed:
Mystery News, August/September 2008, page 17
Publishers Weekly, June 2, 2008, page 32

Other books by the same author:
Water Like a Stone, 2006
In a Dark House, 2004
Now May You Weep, 2003
And Justice There Is None, 2002
A Finer End, 2001

Other books you might like:
Elizabeth George, *A Place of Hiding*, 2003
P.D. James, *Original Sin*, 1994
Peter Robinson, *Close to Home*, 2003
S.J. Rozan, *The Shanghai Moon*, 2009

60

JEANNE M. DAMS

Indigo Christmas
(McKinleyville, CA: Perserverance, 2008)

Story type: Historical/Victorian America; Amateur Detective
Series: Hilda Johansson. Book 6
Subject(s): Babies; Christmas
Major character(s): Hilda Johansson Cavanaugh, Housewife, Detective—Amateur; Patrick Cavanaugh, Businessman, Spouse (of Hilda); Norah O'Neill, Servant, Friend (of Hilda)
Time period(s): 1900s (1904)
Locale(s): South Bend, Indiana

Summary: While former maid Hilda Johansson is delighted to be married at last to longtime beau Patrick Cavanaugh, she is struggling with her change in social status. Once a maid to the wealthy Studebaker family, Hilda now has her own household—servants included—thanks to her husband's status as a partner in the family dry goods store. When her dear friend Norah, who still works for the Studebakers, gives birth at the Cavanaugh's home, Hilda finds a purpose in both helping Norah through a difficult birth and helping to prove that Norah's husband Sean is innocent of a murder. Hilda also works to help form a local boys club with some of the other well-to-do ladies in town. The ladies plan a Christmas party for the boys.

Where it's reviewed:
Booklist, August 1, 2008, page 43
Publishers Weekly, June 30, 2008, page 165

Other books by the same author:
Crimson Snow, 2005
Silence Is Golden, 2002
Green Grow the Victims, 2001
Red, White, and Blue Murder, 2001
A Death in Lacquer Red, 1999

Other books you might like:
Dianne Day, *The Bohemian Murders*, 1997
Cynthia Peale, *Murder at Bertram's Bower*, 2001
P.B. Ryan, *Murder on Black Friday*, 2005
Victoria Thompson, *Murder in Gramercy Park*, 2001

61

JOHN DARNTON

Black and White and Dead All Over

(New York: Knopf, 2008)

Story type: Police Procedural
Subject(s): Newspapers; Revenge
Major character(s): Jude Hurley, Journalist; Priscilla Bollingsworth, Detective—Homicide, Divorced Person; Francis O'Donnell, Journalist
Time period(s): 2000s
Locale(s): New York, New York

Summary: When the body of *New York Globe* assistant managing editor Theodore Ratnoff is found in the newsroom, an editor's spike stuck deep in his chest, the police soon realize that they have plenty of suspects to choose from. Ratnoff was known for being a tyrant. Investigative reporter Jude Hurley is assigned to cover the story of Ratnoff's murder. Hurley finds himself teaming up with homicide detective Priscilla Bollingsworth, a young woman who comes from a wealthy family. When two other murders occur, Hurley and Bollingsworth wonder why someone is killing off the *Globe*'s employees.

Where it's reviewed:
Booklist, June 1, 2008, page 47
Library Journal, June 15, 2008, page 57
Mystery News, October/November 2008, page 21
The New York Times Book Review, August 3, 2008, page 9
Publishers Weekly, May 19, 2008, page 31

Other books by the same author:
The Darwin Conspiracy, 2005
Mind Catcher, 2002
The Experiment, 1999
Neanderthal, 1969

Other books you might like:
Michael Connelly, *The Scarecrow*, 2009
Leonard Downie Jr., *The Rules of the Game*, 2009
Richard Hoyt, *30 for a Harry*, 1981
Keith Peterson, *The Rain*, 1988

62

DAVID STUART DAVIES

Without Conscience

(New York: St. Martin's, 2008)

Story type: Historical/World War II; Private Detective
Series: Johnny Hawke. Book 2
Subject(s): World War II; Orphans
Major character(s): Johnny Hawke, Detective—Private; Harryboy Jenkins, Criminal; Peter Blake, Orphan, Child
Time period(s): 1940s (1942)
Locale(s): London, England

Summary: Sandra Riley hires London private eye Johnny Hawke because she believes her husband Walter is being unfaithful to her. Almost immediately, Hawke discovers that Walter, who works at the War Office, is a cross-dresser. Hawke is inclined to give Walter his privacy, but he's killed in a burglary that Hawke witnesses. Sandra asks Hawke to find the killer. The killer is Harryboy Jenkins, a man without conscience who has ensnared Rachel Howells, a woman he picks up in a bar, in a dangerous rampage. Meanwhile, young Peter Blake, an evacuee in the countryside, runs away from his adopted family, making his way back to London. He's looking for the one man whom, he believes, cares for him: Johnny Hawke.

Where it's reviewed:
Booklist, November 1, 2008, page 28
Library Journal, October 1, 2008, page 46
Publishers Weekly, September 15, 2008, page 48

Other books by the same author:
Forests of the Night, 2007

Other books you might like:
Christopher Fowler, *Full Dark House*, 2004
John Gardner, *Bottled Spider*, 2002
Pip Granger, *Trouble in Paradise*, 2004
John Lawton, *Black Out*, 1995

63

PABLO DE SANTIS

The Paris Enigma

(New York: HarperCollins, 2008)

Story type: Historical
Subject(s): Detection; Competition
Major character(s): Sigmundo Salvatrio, Assistant; Renato Craig, Detective—Private; Viktor Arzaky, Detective—Private
Time period(s): 1880s
Locale(s): Buenos Aires, Argentina; Montevideo, Uruguay; Paris, France

Summary: In 1888, Sigmundo Salvatrio answers an ad in a Buenos Aires newspaper. The ad, placed by famous private detective Renato Craig, announces Craig's intent to open a small academy for those interested in learning his detection techniques. Although Salvatrio isn't Craig's best student, he is chosen to be his acolyte, or assistant. Craig is also one of the founders of The Twelve, a group of the finest detectives in the world. When Craig is unable to attend a meeting of The Twelve in Paris during the 1889 World's Fair, he sends Salvatrio in his place. Soon after Salvatrio's arrival in Paris, one of The Twelve, Louis Darbon, falls to his death from the Eiffel Tower. Salvatrio is given the opportunity to work on the case when he teams up with the group's other founder, Polish detective Viktor Arzaky.

Where it's reviewed:
Mystery Scene, Holiday 2008, page 68
Publishers Weekly, September 15, 2008, page 44

Other books by the same author:
Transilvania Express, 1995

Other books you might like:
Oliver Bleys, *The Ghost in the Eiffel Tower*, 2003
Claude Izner, *Murder on the Eiffel Tower*, 2008
Guillermo Martinez, *The Book of Murder*, 2008
Carlos Ruiz Zafon, *The Shadow of the Wind*, 2004

64

JEFFERY DEAVER

The Bodies Left Behind

(New York: Simon & Schuster, 2008)

Story type: Police Procedural
Subject(s): Wilderness; Identity, Concealed
Major character(s): Kristen Brynn McKenzie, Police Officer; Michelle Alison Kepler, Paralegal; Terrance Hart, Consultant
Time period(s): 2000s
Locale(s): Humboldt, Wisconsin; Milwaukee, Wisconsin; Green Bay, Wisconsin

Summary: Off-duty police deputy Brynn McKenzie receives a request to check out an aborted 911 call. She has no idea of the horrific scene she's about to walk into. Arriving at a weekend home on Lake Mondac, Brynn finds the bodies of the owners, Emma and Steven Feldman, lying in a pool of blood. After Brynn enters the house, she realizes that the killers are still inside. Brynn tries to escape from them in the remote Wisconsin wilderness. She find Michelle, a young paralegal, who was staying with the Feldmans for the weekend. When Brynn finally makes it to safety, she tries to learn why the Feldmans were murdered. This leads her to the true identity of their weekend houseguest.

Where it's reviewed:
Booklist, September 15, 2008, page 4
Mystery News, February/March 2009, page 10
Mystery Scene, Holiday 2008, page 79
Publishers Weekly, September 15, 2008, page 42

Other books by the same author:
The Broken Window, 2008
The Sleeping Doll, 2007
The Cold Moon, 2006
The Twelfth Card, 2005
Garden of Beasts, 2004

Other books you might like:
Greg Iles, *24 Hours*, 2000
Michael Koryta, *Envy the Night*, 2008
William Kent Krueger, *Boundary Waters*, 1999
Richard Matheson, *Hunted Past Reason*, 2002

65

JAMES D. DOSS

Snake Dreams

(New York: St. Martin's, 2008)

Story type: Police Procedural; Indian Culture
Series: Charlie Moon. Book 13

Subject(s): Abuse; Runaways
Major character(s): Charlie Moon, Investigator, Rancher; Nancy Yazzi, Teenager; Daisy Perika, Shaman, Relative (aunt of Charlie)
Time period(s): 2000s
Locale(s): Granite Creek, Colorado

Summary: Charlie Moon's aunt, Shaman Daisy Perika, gets a message from beyond: Nancy Yazzi's dead mother is worried because Nancy has been left behind with her abusive husband. Nancy comes to stay with Daisy and attend the 16th birthday party of her ward, Sarah. The news that Nancy's stepfather has been murdered comes during the party. Nancy's missing boyfriend is the main suspect. Nancy goes on a rampage, stealing Sarah's birthday present, and forcing Charlie to postpone proposing to his girlfriend, FBI agent Lila McTeague, so that he can concentrate on solving the crime with a little help from his Aunt Daisy.

Where it's reviewed:
Mystery News, December/January 2009, page 14
Publishers Weekly, September 15, 2008, page 49

Other books by the same author:
Three Sisters, 2007
Stone Butterfly, 2006
The Shaman's Bones, 1997
The Shaman Laughs, 1995
The Shaman Sings, 1994

Other books you might like:
Margaret Coel, *The Girl with the Braided Hair*, 2007
Tony Hillerman, *Listening Woman*, 1978
William Kent Krueger, *Red Knife*, 2008
Aimee Thurlo, *Turquoise Girl*, 2007

66

JANET EVANOVICH

Plum Spooky

(New York: St. Martin's, 2009)

Story type: Amateur Detective; Humor
Series: Stephanie Plum Between the Numbers. Book 4
Subject(s): Animals/Monkeys; Scientific Experiments
Major character(s): Stephanie Plum, Bounty Hunter, Detective—Amateur; Martin Munch, Criminal; John Diesel, Bounty Hunter
Time period(s): 2000s
Locale(s): Trenton, New Jersey ("The Burg"); Pine Barrens, New Jersey

Summary: Bail bondswoman Stephanie Plum has her hands full. First, she finds herself baby-sitting Carl the monkey while his owner is on her honeymoon. Next she is stymied by a skip, Martin Munch, who should have been easy to find, but isn't. Third, she finds Diesel camping out in her apartment. Diesel always brings trouble. This time he's looking for Wulf Grimoire, who is his cousin, Munch's new business partner, and a very weird and dangerous person. Munch and Wulf are planning some kind of disastrous experiment with scientific equipment Munch stole from his workplace. Stephanie's and Diesel's search for the two troublemakers takes them to and from and back to the mysterious Pine Barrens, where strange things happen and even stranger people live.

Where it's reviewed:
Booklist, December 15, 2008, page 4
Mystery News, February/March 2009, page 17

Other books by the same author:
Fearless Fourteen, 2008
Plum Lucky, 2008
Lean Mean Thirteen, 2007
Plum Lovin', 2007
Twelve Sharp, 2006

Other books you might like:
Linwood Barclay, *Bad Guys*, 2005
Rhys Bowen, *Her Royal Spyness*, 2007
Chris Grabenstein, *Tilt a Whirl*, 2005
Lisa Lutz, *The Spellman Files*, 2007

CLYDE FORD

Precious Cargo
(New York: Vanguard, 2008)

Story type: Private Detective
Series: Charlie Noble. Book 2
Subject(s): Prostitution; Boats and Boating
Major character(s): Charles Noble, Detective—Private, Widow(er); Dan Ravenheart "Raven" Washington, Diver, Artisan; Maria Delarosa, Activist
Time period(s): 2000s
Locale(s): Fairhaven, Washington; Bellingham, Washington; Mount Vernon, Washington

Summary: When Marvin and Angela Baynes pull up the body of a young Hispanic woman on their anchor just off the San Juan Islands, they hire private investigator Charlie Noble to find out who the woman was. Charlie engages the services of a diver nicknamed Raven, a Native American and former SEAL, to search the area where the Bayneses found the body. Charlie and Raven find two more bodies, also Hispanic females. As Charlie tries to discover the identities of the dead women, an activist named Maria Delarosa approaches Charlie with information. She knows who the women are and is able to give Charlie enough information to lead him into the dangerous world of human trafficking and prostitution.

Where it's reviewed:
Booklist, September 15, 2008, page 30

Other books by the same author:
Deuce's Wild, 2006
Red Herring, 2005
The Long Mile, 2005

Other books you might like:
Doug Allyn, *Black Water*, 1996
Linda Greenlaw, *Fisherman's Bend*, 2008
Merry Jones, *The River Killings*, 2006
Randy Wayne White, *Twelve Mile Limit*, 2002

CHRISTOPHER FOWLER

The Victoria Vanishes
(New York: Bantam, 2008)

Story type: Police Procedural
Series: Peculiar Crimes Unit. Book 6
Subject(s): Serial Killers; Saloons; Conspiracies
Major character(s): Arthur Bryant, Detective—Police; John May, Detective—Police; Janice Longbright, Detective—Police
Time period(s): 2000s
Locale(s): London, England

Summary: Middle-aged ladies are dropping dead in London pubs, and the Peculiar Crimes Unit is alerted. Senior Detective Arthur Bryant saw the latest victim alive outside a pub before her death—except that the pub does not exist. When he returns to investigate, he discovers that it had been torn down years ago and a shop exists on the site. Is his memory succumbing to age? Meanwhile, his partner and close friend, Senior Detective John May, has a secret of his own: a tumor on his heart that will soon require serious surgery. When the PCU tracks down the murderer, the Home Office declares the case closed, but Bryant and May disagree. Is there more to this case than appears on the surface?

Where it's reviewed:
Booklist, October 1, 2008, page 30
Mystery News, October/November 2008, page 22
Publishers Weekly, August 25, 2008, page 54

Other books by the same author:
White Corridor, 2007
Ten Second Staircase, 2006
Seventy-Seven Clocks, 2005
The Water Room, 2004
Full Dark House, 2003

Other books you might like:
Colin Cotterill, *The Coroner's Lunch*, 2004
Barry Maitland, *No Trace*, 2006
Will Thomas, *Some Danger Involved*, 2004
Jacqueline Winspear, *Maisie Dobbs*, 2003

TANA FRENCH

The Likeness
(New York: Viking, 2008)

Story type: Police Procedural
Series: Cassie Maddox. Book 2
Subject(s): College Life; Role Playing
Major character(s): Cassie Maddox, Detective—Police; Sam O'Neill, Detective—Police; Frank Mackey, Detective—Police
Time period(s): 2000s
Locale(s): Glenskahey, Ireland

Summary: When Dublin Murder Squad detective Cassie Maddox was working undercover, her cover name was

Lexie Madison. Now, Cassie is called in on a case where the dead girl is Cassie's double, and the victim's name is Lexie Madison. Cassie had thought Lexie a figment of her imagination. Cassie agrees to infiltrate Lexie's tight living arrangement with four other graduate students who are disliked by the surrounding villagers. Once undercover, Cassie wears a microphone (which sometimes gets turned off at opportune moments), as she is drawn more closely into Lexie's friendships.

Where it's reviewed:
Booklist, May 1, 2008, page 38
Library Journal, July 15, 2008, page 48
Mystery Scene, Summer 2008, page 86
Publishers Weekly, May 19, 2008, page 32

Other books by the same author:
In the Woods, 2007

Other books you might like:
Julia Wallis Martin, *A Likeness in Stone*, 1997
Ruth Rendell, *A Judgement in Stone*, 1977
Minette Walters, *The Dark Room*, 1995
Laura Wilson, *A Little Death*, 1999

70

DAVID FULMER

Lost River

(Boston: Houghton Mifflin Harcourt, 2009)

Story type: Historical
Series: Valentin St. Cyr Mystery. Book 4
Subject(s): Prostitution
Major character(s): Valentin St. Cyr, Detective—Private; Justine Mancarre, Model, Girlfriend (of Valentin); Evelyne Dallencort, Socialite
Time period(s): 1910s (1913)
Locale(s): New Orleans, Louisiana; Jackson, Louisiana

Summary: Former New Orleans police officer turned detective Valentin St. Cyr used to work as a fixer for Tom Anderson, the "King of Storyville," in the city's red-light district. Valentin left, hoping to start a better life for himself and his girlfriend, Justine Mancarre. When bodies start appearing in some of the more expensive bordellos in Storyville, madam Mary Jane Parker convinces Valentin to return and find the killer. Justine, a former sporting girl, isn't happy that Valentin has returned to Storyville and finds herself flirting with a mysterious young man. While Valentin tracks down a killer, a high-society matron plans to remove Tom Anderson and become the "Queen of Storyville."

Where it's reviewed:
Booklist, November 15, 2008, page 20
Library Journal, November 1, 2008, page 46
Publishers Weekly, October 6, 2008, page 38

Other books by the same author:
The Blue Door, 2008
The Dying Crapshooter's Blues, 2008
Jass, 2006
Rampart Street, 2006
Chasing the Devil's Tail, 2001

Other books you might like:
John Dickson Carr, *Papa La-bas*, 1968
Barbara Hambly, *Die upon a Kiss*, 2001
Robert Skinner, *Skin Deep, Blood Red*, 1997
Penn Williamson, *Mortal Sins*, 2000

71

LEIGHTON GAGE

Buried Strangers

(New York: Soho, 2009)

Story type: Police Procedural
Series: Mario Silva. Book 2
Subject(s): Missing Persons; Murder
Major character(s): Mario Silva, Detective—Police; Arnaldo Nunes, Detective—Police; Hector Costa, Detective—Police
Time period(s): 2000s
Locale(s): Brasilia, Brazil; Sao Paulo, Brazil

Summary: When a large group of bodies is discovered illegally buried near a park in Sao Paulo, Chief Inspector Mario Silva and his assistant Arnaldo Nunes fly from Brasilia to take charge of the case. They work with Silva's nephew, Hector Costa, who is already in Sao Paulo. Autopsies show that the victims, who were buried in small groups, were families. The breastbone of each body was sawn in two, suggesting that the murderer was after organs, probably the heart. The trail is a long and twisting one, involving missing persons, emigration to the United States, two desperate parents with an infant who needs a new heart, and corruption at every level in the city police.

Where it's reviewed:
Booklist, December 1, 2008, page 28
Mystery Scene, Winter 2009, page 60
Publishers Weekly, November 10, 2008, page 34

Other books by the same author:
Blood of the Wicked, 2008

Other books you might like:
Andrea Camilleri, *The Shape of Water*, 2002
Ruth Francisco, *Confessions of a Deathmaiden*, 2003
Luiz Alfredo Garcia-Roza, *The Silence of the Rain*, 2002
Michael Stanley, *A Carrion Death*, 2008

72

JOHN GALLIGAN

The Clinch Knot

(Madison, WI: Bleak House, 2008)

Story type: Amateur Detective
Series: Ned Oglivie. Book 3
Subject(s): Fishing; Friendship
Major character(s): Ned "Dog" Oglivie, Fisherman, Detective—Amateur; D'Ontario Sneed, Friend (of Dog), Crime Suspect; Aretha Sneed, Fire Fighter, Mother (of D'Ontario)

Time period(s): 2000s

Locale(s): Livingston, Montana; Seattle, Washington

Summary: Ned Oglivie, known as "Dog," is a self-proclaimed trout bum and drunk. A former security expert, Dog now spends his time fly fishing in Montana. When Dog's friend D'Ontario Sneed finds love with Livingston local Jesse Ringer, Dog begins to feel like a third wheel and plans to leave town. After a run-in with a couple of skinheads who don't like the fact that D'Ontario is black and Jesse is white, Dog learns that Jesse has been shot to death and D'Ontario is unconscious nearby with a gun lying next to him. The police arrest D'Ontario for Jesse's murder, but Dog doesn't believe that his friend is guilty and teams up with D'Ontario's mother Aretha to prove his innocence.

Where it's reviewed:

Booklist, August 1, 2008, page 41

Mystery Scene, Fall 2008, page 72

Publishers Weekly, July 28, 2008, page 55

Other books by the same author:

The Blood Knot, 2005

The Nail Knot, 2005

Red Sky, Red Dragonfly, 2001

Other books you might like:

Steve Hamilton, *Blood Is the Sky*, 2003

Richard Hugo, *Death and the Good Life*, 1991

William G. Tapply, *Bitch Creek*, 2004

Jim Tenuto, *Blood Atonement*, 2005

73

MEG GARDINER

The Dirty Secrets Club

(New York: Dutton, 2008)

Story type: Psychological Suspense

Series: Jo Beckett. Book 1

Subject(s): Suicide; Revenge

Major character(s): Johanna "Jo" Beckett, Doctor, Widow(er); Amy Tang, Police Officer; Gabriel Quintana, Health Care Professional, Student

Time period(s): 2000s

Locale(s): San Francisco, California; Palo Alto, California

Summary: Forensic psychiatrist Jo Beckett is called to an accident scene one late night when a woman drives her car off a highway overpass in San Francisco. Police identify the woman as Assistant U.S. Attorney Callie Harding. A witness claims that Callie drove her car off the bridge on purpose, committing suicide. Jo's job is to determine the psychological well-being of the victim before the crash. Finding the words "dirty" and "pray" written in lipstick on Callie's legs leads Jo to the Dirty Secrets Club, an exclusive group of people with some nasty little secrets. Assisting Lieutenant Amy Tang in the investigation, Jo discovers that someone is killing off the members of the club one by one.

Where it's reviewed:

Booklist, May 1, 2008, page 26

Deadly Pleasures, Summer 2008, page 48

Mystery News, June/July 2008, page 33

Mystery Scene, Summer 2008, page 73

Publishers Weekly, March 24, 2008, page 49

Other books by the same author:

Kill Chain, 2006

Crosscut, 2005

Jericho Point, 2004

Mission Canyon, 2003

China Lake, 2002

Other books you might like:

Brian Freeman, *Stalked*, 2008

Sarah Lovett, *Acquired Motives*, 1996

M.J. Rose, *The Delilah Complex*, 2006

Anna Salter, *Prison Blues*, 2002

74

JOHN GARDNER

Moriarty

(Orlando: Harcourt, 2008)

Story type: Historical/Victorian

Series: Professor Moriarty. Book 3

Subject(s): Crime and Criminals; Secrets

Major character(s): James Moriarty, Organized Crime Figure, Professor; Sally Hodges, Madam; Jack "Idle Jack" Idell, Organized Crime Figure, Nobleman

Time period(s): 1900s

Locale(s): London, England; Oxford, England; Steventon, England

Summary: After surviving the struggle with his archnemesis Sherlock Holmes at the top of Reichenbach Falls in Switzerland, criminal mastermind Professor James Moriarty is returning to London. Spending time in the United States building a criminal empire after his struggle with Holmes, Moriarty learns that his London criminal underground has virtually disappeared. His former employees have left to work under the gentleman criminal Idle Jack, aka Sir Jordan Jack Idell. While Moriarty intends to reestablish his criminal society in London, his appearance has another purpose. He intends to discover the identity of a traitor within his private guard. As Moriarty carries out his plans, Sal Hodges, the mother of his son, is forced to reveal a shocking secret to Moriarty.

Where it's reviewed:

Booklist, November 15, 2008, page 21

Publishers Weekly, September 29, 2008, page 62

Other books by the same author:

No Human Enemy, 2008

Troubled Midnight, 2006

License Renewed, 1981

The Revenge of Moriarty, 1975

The Return of Moriarty, 1974

Other books you might like:

John R. King, *The Shadow of Reichenbach Falls*, 2008

Laurie R. King, *The Beekeeper's Apprentice*, 1994

Michael Kurland, *The Great Game*, 2001

David Pirie, *The Night Calls*, 2003

75

BRENT GHELFI

Volk's Shadow

(New York: Henry Holt, 2008)

Story type: Espionage Thriller
Series: Alexei Volkovoy. Book 2
Subject(s): Russians; Organized Crime
Major character(s): Alexei "Volk" Volkovoy, Military Personnel (investigator), Organized Crime Figure; Valya Novaskaya, Mercenary, Military Personnel (former); Golko Kachan, Military Personnel, Investigator
Time period(s): 2000s
Locale(s): Moscow, Russia; Vladimir, Russia; Tindi, Russia

Summary: After being injured during a terrorist attack on an American oil company's headquarters in Moscow, Russian military investigator Alexei "Volk" Volkovoy is given a new assignment by his boss, the General. The General is tracking down missing Imperial Faberge eggs, five of which disappeared during the revolution. One of the General's agents, Captain Dubinin, had located one of the Imperial eggs, but was killed before he could deliver it to the General. Now, the General wants Volk to investigate Dubinin's death and recover the egg. Meanwhile, Volk is also looking into the abduction of a young girl, Galina, who may have been kidnapped by a former soldier named Semerko.

Where it's reviewed:
Booklist, May 1, 2008, page 45
Library Journal, June 15, 2008, page 56
Mystery News, August/September 2008, page 20
Publishers Weekly, May 12, 2008, page 35

Other books by the same author:
Volk's Game, 2007

Other books you might like:
Anna Blundy, *Vodka Neat*, 2008
Boris Riskin, *Scrambled Eggs*, 2005
David Rosenbaum, *Sasha's Trick*, 1995
Thomas Swan, *The Final Faberge*, 1999

76

PAUL GOLDSTEIN

A Patent Lie

(New York: Doubleday, 2008)

Story type: Legal
Series: Michael Seeley. Book 2
Subject(s): Biotechnology; Trials
Major character(s): Michael Seeley, Lawyer, Divorced Person; Leonard Seeley, Doctor; Lily Warren, Scientist
Time period(s): 2000s
Locale(s): Buffalo, New York; San Francisco, California; Atherton, California

Summary: Lawyer Michael Seeley left a high-powered New York law firm to open up his own practice in Buffalo. Michael isn't thrilled when his estranged brother Leonard comes to him for help. Leonard is the chief medical officer for Vaxtek, a small biotech company in San Francisco. Vaxtek is currently engaged in a patent infringement lawsuit against St. Gall, a large Swiss pharmaceutical company, over an AIDS vaccine. Bob Pearsall, the head lawyer for Vaxtek, recently threw himself in front of an oncoming train, and Leonard wants Michael to take over the case. Michael reluctantly agrees, but soon discovers that even Leonard is involved in a cover-up.

Where it's reviewed:
Booklist, June 1, 2008, page 51
Publishers Weekly, April 21, 2008, page 30

Other books by the same author:
Order of Proof, 2008
Errors and Omissions, 2006

Other books you might like:
April Christofferson, *Patent to Kill*, 2003
Barry Eisler, *Fault Line*, 2009
Patrick Reinken, *Judgment Day*, 1996

77

DOLORES GORDON-SMITH

Mad about the Boy?

(New York: Soho, 2008)

Story type: Historical/Roaring Twenties
Series: Jack Haldean. Book 2
Subject(s): Country Life; Russians
Major character(s): Jack Haldean, Writer, Veteran; Arthur Stanton, Veteran, Crime Suspect; Malcolm Smith-Fennimore, Banker, Veteran
Time period(s): 1920s (1923)
Locale(s): London, England; Stanmore Parry, England; Cranston, England

Summary: While attending his aunt and uncle's anniversary party at their country home in Sussex in 1923, writer and World War I veteran Jack Haldean finds himself investigating two deaths that occur at the estate. First, Tim Preston, a friend of Jack's, commits suicide during a fireworks display. Tim's suicide note blames his death on money problems. Then, Lord Victor Lyvenden is murdered. Arthur Stanton, also a friend of Jack's who is still shell-shocked from the war and who is completely smitten with Jack's cousin Isabelle, is found with Lord Lyvenden's body. While all evidence points to Arthur being guilty, Isabelle refuses to believe that Arthur is capable of murder. While Jack tries to find out who killed Lord Lyvenden and whether Tim's death was really a suicide, he also begins to suspect that Isabelle's fiance, Malcolm Smith-Fennimore, has something to do with all of this.

Where it's reviewed:
Deadly Pleasures, Fall 2008, page 54
Mystery Scene, Summer 2008, page 82
Publishers Weekly, May 5, 2008, page 47

Other books by the same author:
A Fete Worse than Death, 2007

Other books you might like:
Barbara Cleverly, *The Tomb of Zeus*, 2007
Carola Dunn, *The Winter Garden Mystery*, 1995
Catriona McPherson, *After the Armistice Ball*, 2005
David Roberts, *Sweet Poison*, 2001

78

CHRIS GRABENSTEIN

Hell Hole

(New York: St. Martin's, 2008)

Story type: Police Procedural
Series: Ceepak and Boyle. Book 4
Subject(s): Veterans; Suicide
Major character(s): John Ceepak, Police Officer; Danny
  Boyle, Police Officer; Dale Dixon, Military Personnel
Time period(s): 2000s
Locale(s): Sea Haven, New Jersey

Summary: When John Ceepak's partner Danny Boyle gets
called in on a noise complaint, he gets more than he
bargained for. The Iraq War vets partying in the noisy
house get a call that one of their brother soldiers has
committed suicide in a rest stop men's room on the
Garden State Parkway. The team investigating the crime
is somewhat slapdash, but Boyle manages to take some
photos of the scene that convince both himself and
Ceepak that the death is not a suicide. They agree to
look into it on behalf of the soldiers, one of whom is the
son of an ambitious senator.

Where it's reviewed:
Booklist, May 1, 2008, page 34
Mystery Scene, Fall 2008, page 66
Publishers Weekly, April 21, 2008, page 30

Other books by the same author:
Hell for the Holidays, 2007
Whack a Mole, 2007
Mad Mouse, 2006
Slay Ride, 2006
Tilt a Whirl, 2005

Other books you might like:
Tim Cockey, *Hearse of a Different Color*, 2001
Tom Corcoran, *Octopus Alibi*, 2003
Mark de Castrique, *Blackman's Coffin*, 2008
Carl Hiaasen, *Tourist Season*, 1986

79

C.S. GRAHAM (Pseudonym of Steven Harris and Candice Proctor)

The Archangel Project

(New York: Harper, 2008)

Story type: Espionage Thriller
Subject(s): Parapsychology; Terrorism
Major character(s): October "Tobie" Guinness, Veteran,
  Linguist; James "Jax" Alexander, Spy; Lance Palmer,
  Veteran, Mercenary

Time period(s): 2000s
Locale(s): New Orleans, Louisiana; Washington, District
  of Columbia; Dallas, Texas

Summary: October "Tobie" Guinness is an Iraq War
veteran who was given a psychological discharge after
she claimed to have visions. Returning to the States, Tobie enrolled in Tulane University and began working
with Dr. Henry Youngblood on a government-sponsored
remote viewing project. Tobie is a remote viewer, meaning that she has the ability to gather information on an
unseen target from miles away. When Youngblood is
murdered, because of the information gained during one
of his sessions with Tobie, Tobie has to go on the run to
avoid the same fate. With no other choice, Tobie puts
her trust in CIA agent Jax Alexander, who was sent to
New Orleans to investigate Youngblood's murder. Working together, Jax and Tobie discover a plot to assassinate
a high-ranking government official.

Where it's reviewed:
Publishers Weekly, June 2, 2008, page 33

Other books you might like:
Robert Doherty, *Psychic Warrior*, 2000
James Rollins, *The Last Oracle*, 2008
Billy Dee Williams, *PSI/Net*, 1999
  Rob MacGregor, co-author

80

SARAH GRAVES

A Face at the Window

(New York: Bantam, 2009)

Story type: Amateur Detective
Series: Jacobia Tiptree. Book 12
Subject(s): Kidnapping; Suspense
Major character(s): Jacobia "Jake" Tiptree, Carpenter,
  Detective—Amateur; Ozzie Campbell, Construction
  Worker, Murderer; Helen Nevelson, Teenager,
  Babysitter
Time period(s): 2000s
Locale(s): Eastport, Maine

Summary: Home repair maven Jacobia "Jake" Tiptree approaches the police in her home of Eastport, Maine, with
her concerns after giving a victim statement in the
prosecution of Ozzie Campbell. Over 30 years ago,
Campbell became obsessed with Jake's mother and killed
her. Campbell has disappeared just weeks before he is to
go on trial for the 30-year-old crime. Jake is worried that
Campbell might try to come after her. Jake is also spending the week looking after Lee, the daughter of her best
friend Ellie White. Jake leaves Lee with babysitter Helen
Nevelson; both Lee and Helen are kidnapped. Jake finds
that she has to confront the man who killed her mother
in order to save Lee's life.

Where it's reviewed:
Booklist, December 1, 2008, page 29
Mystery News, February/March 2009, page 9
Publishers Weekly, October 13, 2008, page 39

Other books by the same author:
The Book of Old Houses, 2007
Trap Door, 2006
Nail Biter, 2005
Mallets Aforethought, 2004
Tool and Die, 2004

Other books you might like:
JoAnna Carl, *The Chocolate Bridal Bash*, 2006
Kate Flora, *Liberty or Death*, 2003
Leslie Meier, *Tippy-Toe Murder*, 1994
Valerie Wolzien, *Murder in the Forecast*, 2001

81

LINDA GREENLAW
Fisherman's Bend
(New York: Hyperion, 2008)

Story type: Action/Adventure
Series: Jane Bunker. Book 2
Subject(s): Missing Persons; Drugs
Major character(s): Jane Bunker, Insurance Investigator, Police Officer; Cal Dunham, Fisherman; Parker Alley, Fisherman
Time period(s): 2000s
Locale(s): Green Haven, Maine; Cobble Harbor, Maine; At Sea

Summary: Former Miami police detective Jane Bunker now lives in the small town of Green Haven, Maine. Working as a marine insurance investigator and a deputy sheriff for Knox County, Jane is on her way home after looking into a case of vandalism aboard a research vessel when she and her friend Cal, a fisherman, discover a boat floating adrift. Jane and Cal's worst suspicions are confirmed when no one is found onboard the vessel. Its owner, Parker Alley, is assumed to be dead. As Jane looks into Alley's life, she discovers that the fisherman was involved in heroin smuggling. The deeper Jane digs into the case, the more she is convinced that Alley faked his disappearance because of his illegal activities.

Where it's reviewed:
Booklist, June 1, 2008, page 49
Deadly Pleasures, Summer 2008, page 45
Mystery Scene, Summer 2008, page 82
Publishers Weekly, May 5, 2008, page 47

Other books by the same author:
Slipknot, 2007

Other books you might like:
J.S. Borthwick, *Bodies of Water*, 1990
Archer Mayor, *The Catch*, 2008
Dana Stabenow, *Killing Grounds*, 1998
William G. Tapply, *Nervous Water*, 2005

82

ROBERT GREER
Blackbird, Farewell
(Berkeley, CA: Frog, 2008)

Story type: Private Detective
Series: C.J. Floyd. Book 7

Subject(s): Sports/Basketball; Cheating; Cooks and Cooking
Major character(s): C.J. Floyd, Detective—Private; Damion Madrid, Friend (of C.J.); Flora Jean Benson, Detective—Private, Parent (mother of Damion); Annie Capshaw, Divorced Person, Detective—Amateur; Eve DeCateur, Friend (of Annie); Jim MacDonald, Restaurateur, Boyfriend (of Annie)
Time period(s): 2000s; 2000s
Locale(s): Denver, Colorado; Arlington, Virginia

Summary: Shandell Bird (a.k.a. Blackbird) has everything going for him. He's the number two pick in the NBA draft. His product endorsements promise to give him lots more money. Then a threatening phone call leads him to his old basketball court, where he and a reporter are shot to death. Blackbird's college roommate, Damion Madrid, decides to find out who killed his friend and why. He has three weeks until he starts medical school. His friend and mentor, CJ Floyd, is away from Denver, in Hawaii on his honeymoon. As Damion discovers new things about Blackbird, he soon finds himself in over his head, and his life is threatened as well. Helped by his attorney mother, CJ's partner Flora Jean Benson and others, Damion works through a maze of information until CJ returns to help close the case. Annie Capshaw has left the safety of her job at the bank and is now working at her boyfriend Jim's restaurant, Bellywasher's, in Old Town Alexandria, Virginia. She thinks it's the first day of the rest of her life, until Jacques fails to show up for a cooking class that he's teaching together with Jim. Then Jacques's assistant Greg is murdered. Determined to discover the fate of her friend and also why anyone would want to kill kind, unassuming Greg, Annie dives into her favorite hobby: amateur detection. With help from her boyfriend, her ex, her best friend, and her best friend's ex, Annie hopes to solve this new mystery before anyone else cooks his last meal.

Where it's reviewed:
Booklist, September 1, 2008, page 40
Mystery Scene, Holiday 2008, page 64
Publishers Weekly, August 18, 2008, page 47
School Library Journal, December 1, 2008, page 156

Other books by the same author:
Dead Men Don't Get the Munchies, 2007
Murder on the Menu, 2007
The Mongoose Deception, 2007
Cooking Up Murder, 2006
The Fourth Perspective, 2006
Resurrecting Langston Blue, 2005
Heat Shock, 2003
The Devil's Backbone, 1998

Other books you might like:
Sammi Carter, *Goody Goody Gunshots*, 2008
Stephen L. Carter, *The Emperor of Ocean Park*, 2002
Harlan Coben, *Fade Away*, 1996
John Corrigan, *Out of Bounds*, 2006
Isis Crawford, *A Catered Murder*, 2003
Krista Davis, *The Diva Runs out of Thyme*, 2008
John Feinstein, *Winter Games*, 1995
Jacqueline Girdner, *Fat-Free and Fatal*, 1993

83

KATHRYN MILLER HAINES

The Winter of Her Discontent
(New York: Harper, 2008)

Story type: Historical/World War II; Amateur Detective
Series: Rosie Winter. Book 2
Subject(s): Actors and Actresses; Crime and Criminals
Major character(s): Rosie Winter, Actress, Detective—Amateur; Jayne Hamilton, Actress, Dancer; Vinnie Garvaggio, Criminal
Time period(s): 1940s (1943)
Locale(s): New York, New York

Summary: In 1943, Rosie Winter is an actress trying to make a name for herself on Broadway. When Rosie learns that Al, a mob-enforcer friend who once came to her rescue, has been arrested for murder, Rosie is determined to prove Al's innocence. Al is suspected of killing Paulette Monroe, a well-known actress. To learn more about Paulette, Rosie and Jayne Hamilton, Rosie's best friend and roommate, audition for parts in the musical in which Paulette had recently been cast. Rosie and Jayne learn that many people are mourning Paulette, including two husbands, a fiance, and a boyfriend. As Rosie continues her investigation, she also tries to learn what happened to her ex-boyfriend Jack, a soldier who's missing in action.

Where it's reviewed:
Booklist, May 1, 2008, page 45
Mystery Scene, Summer 2008, page 85
Publishers Weekly, April 7, 2008, page 45

Other books by the same author:
The War Against Miss Winter, 2007

Other books you might like:
Hal Glatzer, *Too Dead to Swing*, 2004
M.T. Jefferson, *A Victory Dance Murder*, 2000
Lise McClendon, *One O'Clock Jump*, 2001
Sandra Scoppettone, *This Dame for Hire*, 2005

84

DAVID HANDLER

The Sour Cherry Surprise
(New York: St. Martin's, 2008)

Story type: Police Procedural
Series: Berger and Mitry. Book 6
Subject(s): Small Town Life; Family Problems; Drugs
Major character(s): Des Mitry, Detective—Police; Mitch Berger, Critic; Molly Proctor, Child
Time period(s): 2000s
Locale(s): Dorset, Connecticut; New York, New York; California

Summary: Des Mitry and Mitch Berger have broken up. Des is back with her ex-husband, and is struggling with black-out spells. Mitch is in New York City, considering a California TV movie critic job. He has lost weight and feels terrible. Both become involved when a neighbor, young Molly Proctor, finds her family falling apart. Molly's mom has kicked her dad out of the house and now seems totally unconnected to reality. Then her dad is found murdered. Did her mom's new and distinctly unfriendly boyfriend do it? Why are strangers from the EPA wandering around the woods near her home? Molly is a smart kid. She knows something is going on, but what?

Where it's reviewed:
Booklist, August 1, 2008, page 48
Deadly Pleasures, Fall 2008, page 54
Mystery News, August/September 2008, page 26
Publishers Weekly, May 5, 2008, page 47

Other books by the same author:
The Sweet Golden Parachute, 2006
The Burnt Orange Sunrise, 2004
The Bright Silver Star, 2003
The Hot Pink Farmhouse, 2002
The Cold Blue Blood, 2001

Other books you might like:
Margaret Maron, *Death's Half Acre*, 2008
Sarah R. Shaber, *Shell Game*, 2007
Ray Sipherd, *Dance of the Scarecrows*, 1996
David J. Walker, *The End of Emerald Woods*, 2000

85

SOPHIE HANNAH

Hurting Distance
(New York: Soho, 2008)

Story type: Police Procedural
Series: Waterhouse and Zailer. Book 2
Subject(s): Missing Persons; Rape
Major character(s): Simon Waterhouse, Detective—Police; Charlie Zailer, Detective—Police; Naomi Jenkins, Businesswoman
Time period(s): 2000s
Locale(s): Spilling, England; Spain; Scotland

Summary: Businesswoman Naomi Jenkins has been having an affair with a married man, Robert Haworth, for the past year. Every Thursday they meet at a motel for a few hours, until one Thursday when Robert doesn't show up. Worried, Naomi goes to his home in Spilling and encounters Robert's wife, Juliet. Naomi believes that Juliet may have harmed Robert and she goes to the local police. Detective Constable Simon Waterhouse and Detective Sergeant Charlie Zailer meet with Naomi, but believe that Robert had probably tired of his mistress. When the police don't believe that Robert may be missing, Naomi tells them that he raped her three years ago. While Naomi's accusations are false, this information puts Waterhouse and Zailer on the trail of a serial rapist.

Where it's reviewed:
Booklist, August 1, 2008, page 43
Publishers Weekly, August 4, 2008, page 45

Other books by the same author:
The Point of Rescue, 2008
Little Face, 2007
The Superpower of Love, 2002
Cordial and Corrosive, 2000
Gripless, 1999

Other books you might like:
Frances Fyfield, *Without Consent*, 1997
Karin Slaughter, *Blindsighted*, 2001
Louise Ure, *Forcing Amaryllis*, 2005
Minette Walters, *Acid Row*, 2002

86

CORA HARRISON

A Secret and Unlawful Killing

(New York: St. Martin's, 2008)

Story type: Historical/Medieval
Series: Burren Mysteries. Book 2
Subject(s): Kings, Queens, Rulers, etc.; Law
Major character(s): Brehon Mara, Judge
Time period(s): 16th century (1509)
Locale(s): Kingdom of the Burren, Ireland

Summary: The unpopular steward of the MacNamara clan, Ragnall MacNamara, has raised taxes and is traveling all over the countryside collecting goods. When everyone gathers in the Burren for Michaelmas, MacNamara is found dead. By custom, the guilty party admits to his or her deed, but when no one does, Brehon (or Judge) Mara must sift through the facts of the case to determine the guilty party, a quest made more urgent by a second murder. Each chapter is prefaced with premises of established law that Mara must take into account, as she uses logic and deduction to solve the case.

Where it's reviewed:
Booklist, September 1, 2008, page 57
Mystery News, December/January 2009, page 18
Publishers Weekly, July 14, 2008, page 46

Other books by the same author:
My Lady Judge, 2007

Other books you might like:
Michael Jecks, *The Abbot's Gibbet*, 1998
Candace Robb, *The Cross Legged Knight*, 2002
Caroline Roe, *Cure for a Charlatan*, 1999
Peter Tremayne, *The Haunted Abbot*, 2002

87

CAROLYN HART

Ghost at Work

(New York: Morrow, 2008)

Story type: Amateur Detective; Ghost Story
Series: Bailey Ruth. Book 1
Subject(s): Ghosts; Heaven
Major character(s): Bailey Ruth Raeburn, Spirit, Detective—Amateur; Kathleen Abbott, Friend (of Bailey), Spouse
Time period(s): 2000s
Locale(s): Adelaide, Oklahoma

Summary: When Bailey Ruth and her husband are killed in a boating accident, Bailey joins Heaven's Department of Good Intentions, where she's able to help people on earth in her ghostly form. Her fussbudget supervisor, Wiggins, gives her a set of rules to follow, such as not letting people know she's a ghost, but that proves difficult for her. When her old friend Kathleen Abbott, the rector's wife, finds a dead body on her porch, Bailey Ruth is determined to find the culprit so her old friend won't be accused of the crime. The victim was widely disliked, which makes things even trickier for Bailey Ruth.

Where it's reviewed:
Booklist, September 15, 2008, page 28
Publishers Weekly, September 8, 2008, page 38

Other books by the same author:
Engaged to Die, 2003
Sugarplum Dead, 2000
Death in Paradise, 1998
Yankee Doodle Dead, 1998
Scandal in Fair Haven, 1994

Other books you might like:
Nancy Atherton, *Aunt Dimity and the Duke*, 1994
Mignon F. Ballard, *Angel at Troublesome Creek*, 1999
Casey Daniels, *Don of the Dead*, 2006
Mary Stanton, *Defending Angels*, 2008

88

JOHN HARVEY

Cold in Hand

(Orlando: Harcourt, 2008)

Story type: Police Procedural
Series: Charlie Resnick. Book 11
Subject(s): Law Enforcement; Crime and Criminals
Major character(s): Charlie Resnick, Detective—Police; Lynn Kellogg, Detective—Homicide; Viktor Zoukas, Businessman
Time period(s): 2000s
Locale(s): Nottingham, England; London, England; Constanta, Romania

Summary: On her way home from conducting a hostage negotiation, Detective Inspector Lynn Kellogg is called to the scene of a disturbance. As two girls circle each other with knives, Kellogg steps between them and grabs one of the girls, young Kelly Brent, just as shots are fired. One hits Kellogg, the other kills Brent. Detective Inspector Charlie Resnick, Kellogg's boyfriend, is assigned to look into the shooting when Brent's father accuses Kellogg of using his daughter as a human shield. After her recovery, Kellogg is assigned a case that involves human trafficking. Albanian businessman Viktor Zoukas is accused of bringing women from Eastern Europe to England and selling them off. If this isn't enough for Kellogg to deal with, the Serious and Organised Crime Agency is also keeping a close eye on her and her current case.

Where it's reviewed:
Booklist, July 1, 2008, page 5
Mystery Scene, Fall 2008, page 75

Other books by the same author:
Last Rites, 1998
Still Water, 1997
Easy Meat, 1996
Living Proof, 1995
Cold Light, 1994

Other books you might like:
Mark Billingham, *Buried*, 2007
Bill James, *In Good Hands*, 2000
Ian Rankin, *Fleshmarket Alley*, 2005
Stella Shepherd, *Embers of Death*, 1997

89

MICHAEL HARVEY

The Fifth Floor

(New York: Knopf, 2008)

Story type: Private Detective
Series: Michael Kelly. Book 2
Subject(s): Abuse; Conspiracies
Major character(s): Michael Kelly, Detective—Private;
    Janet Woods, Abuse Victim, Spouse (of Johnny);
    Johnny Woods, Political Figure, Spouse (of Janet)
Time period(s): 2000s; 19th century (1871)
Locale(s): Chicago, Illinois

Summary: Michael Kelly, ex-cop turned P.I., is asked by
former flame Janet Woods to tail her husband, Johnny,
who's been abusing her. Kelly tails Johnny to a murder
scene—one that seems to shock both of them equally.
Interestingly, the scene ties the Great Chicago Fire of
1871 to the mayor's office, and a long-ago land and
power grab with repercussions in the present world of
Chicago politics. The story turns on the storied "Fifth
Floor" of city hall where the mayor works. Meanwhile,
Janet's daughter is still terrified for her mother, and
Michael's own love life is taking a beating.

Where it's reviewed:
Publishers Weekly, June 9, 2008, page 30

Other books by the same author:
The Chicago Way, 2007

Other books you might like:
Michael A. Black, *Windy City Knights*, 2004
C.J. Box, *Blue Heaven*, 2008
Sean Chercover, *Trigger City*, 2008
Loren D. Estleman, *Gas City*, 2008

90

STEVEN F. HAVILL

The Fourth Time Is Murder

(New York: St. Martin's, 2008)

Story type: Police Procedural
Series: Estelle Reyes-Guzman. Book 6
Subject(s): Family Relations; Traffic Accidents
Major character(s): Estelle Reyes-Guzman, Police Officer;

Robert Torrez, Police Officer; Bill Gastner, Police
Officer
Time period(s): 2000s
Locale(s): Posadas County, New Mexico

Summary: A seemingly straightforward one-vehicle accident turns questionable for Undersheriff Estelle Reyes-
Guzman when she sees the body of the driver. For one
thing, there is a boot print on the driver's hand, definitely
made after he was thrown out of his vehicle. Who was
there to make it? Later that same night, the handgun of
one of the Posadas deputies goes off accidentally. No
one is hit, but neither Estelle nor former Sheriff Bill
Gastner think the deputy is entirely at fault. Meanwhile,
a national reporter is coming to town to do a story on
Estelle and her precocious pianist son, Francisco.

Where it's reviewed:
Booklist, December 1, 2008, page 29
Mystery News, December/January 2009, page 17
Publishers Weekly, September 15, 2008, page 48

Other books by the same author:
Final Payment, 2007
Statute of Limitations, 2006
A Discount for Death, 2003
Scavengers, 2002

Other books you might like:
J.A. Jance, *Dead Wrong*, 2006
Craig Johnson, *The Cold Dish*, 2005
Michael McGarrity, *Death Song*, 2008
Aimee Thurlo, *Coyote's Wife*, 2008
    David Thurlo, co-author

91

MO HAYDER

Ritual

(New York: Atlantic Monthly, 2008)

Story type: Police Procedural
Series: Jack Caffery. Book 3
Subject(s): Missing Persons; Drugs
Major character(s): Jack Caffery, Detective—Police;
    Phoebe "Flea" Marley, Diver, Police Officer; Tommy
    Baines, Convict
Time period(s): 2000s
Locale(s): Bristol, England; Bath, England; Nailsea,
    England

Summary: Police diver Sergeant Phoebe "Flea" Marley
recovers a severed hand at the bottom of a harbor in
Bristol, England. She believes that the hand was cut off
while the victim was still alive. Investigating the case is
Detective Inspector Jack Caffery, a man who is obsessed
with the disappearance of his younger brother Ewan
when they were children. Inquiries lead Jack to believe
that the severed hand was used in a muthi ritual, a form
of African witchcraft that uses body parts in a ceremony.
Meanwhile, Flea tries taking Ibogaine, a legal hal-
lucinogenic drug from Africa, in an attempt to communicate with her parents, whose tragic deaths two years
ago still haunt Flea.

Where it's reviewed:
Booklist, August 1, 2008, page 47
Library Journal, July 15, 2008, page 50
Mystery News, October/November 2008, page 10
Publishers Weekly, July 14, 2008, page 42

Other books by the same author:
Pig Island, 2007
Tokyo, 2004
The Treatment, 2001
Birdman, 1999

Other books you might like:
Doug Allyn, *Icewater Mansions*, 1995
Heather Graham, *The Vision*, 2006
Michael Gruber, *Tropic of Night*, 2003
Douglas Preston, *Riptide*, 1998
    Lincoln Child, co-author

92

PETER HELTON

Rainstone Fall

(New York: Soho, 2008)

Story type: Private Detective
Series: Chris Honeysett. Book 3
Subject(s): Artists and Art; Blackmail
Major character(s): Chris Honeysett, Artist, Detective—
    Private; Annis Jordan, Artist; Tim Bigwood, Consult-
    ant
Time period(s): 2000s
Locale(s): Bath, England; Swainswick, England

Summary: Painter Chris Honeysett lives and works in the
English town of Bath where he also operates a small
detective agency, Aqua Investigations. While working on
a surveillance job for an insurance company, Chris is approached by two teens, Cairn and Heather, who want to
hire Chris to find a man named Albert whom they believe
is going to be murdered. Chris doesn't take the conversation seriously until his car is stolen and a dead body is
found inside. Before Chris can find out if the body in his
car is the mysterious Albert, he receives a call from a
kidnapper demanding that Chris and his associates, fellow artist Annis Jordan and safe-cracker Tim Bigwood,
complete a series of thefts. If they don't, a young boy
will be killed.

Where it's reviewed:
Publishers Weekly, July 7, 2008, page 41

Other books by the same author:
Slim Chance, 2006
Headcase, 2005

Other books you might like:
Simon Brett, *Dead Room Farce*, 1998
Christopher Fowler, *Ten Second Staircase*, 2006
Morag Joss, *Funeral Music*, 2005
Peter Lovesey, *Bloodhounds*, 1996

93

JOSEPH HEYWOOD

Death Roe

(Guilford, CT: Lyons, 2008)

Story type: Police Procedural
Series: Grady Service. Book 6
Subject(s): Wildlife Conservation; Food
Major character(s): Grady Service, Game Warden; Dani
    Denninger, Game Warden; Zhenya Leukonovich,
    Agent
Time period(s): 2000s
Locale(s): Michigan; New York, New York; Florida

Summary: Grady Service, Conservation Officer with the
Michigan Department of Natural Resources, is given
confidential information about a statewide effort to
harvest Michigan salmon eggs (legally and illegally) and
mix them with New York eggs (declared unfit for human
consumption by the FDA) to sell as caviar. Grady soon
finds out that this could be a very big case. With
representatives from the state of New York and the IRS,
he and others from the DNR stage a raid on a plant they
believe is behind the illegal blending of eggs. Grady
finds himself working as part of a large interstate network
trying to bring a far-flung group of criminals to justice,
work that will take him to several states and to Costa
Rica.

Other books by the same author:
Strike Dog, 2007
Running Dark, 2005
Chasing a Blond Moon, 2003
Blue Wolf in Green Fire, 2002
Ice Hunter, 2001

Other books you might like:
C.J. Box, *Free Fire*, 2007
Steve Hamilton, *North of Nowhere*, 2002
Kirk Russell, *Night Game*, 2004
Randy Wayne White, *Black Widow*, 2008

94

REGINALD HILL

The Price of Butcher's Meat

(New York: Harper, 2008)

Story type: Police Procedural
Series: Dalziel and Pascoe. Book 23
Subject(s): Healing; Murder
Major character(s): Andrew "Andy" Dalziel, Detective—
    Police; Peter Pascoe, Detective—Police; Charlotte
    Heywood, Student—College
Time period(s): 2000s
Locale(s): Willingden, England; Sandytown, England

Summary: Still recovering from his injuries sustained during a bombing in Yorkshire, Detective Superintendent
Andy Dalziel decides to spend a few weeks recuperating
at a convalescent home in the seaside village of
Sandytown. Dalziel's quiet recovery is interrupted by the
death of Lady Daphne Denham. Lady Denham's body

was found during a pig roast in Sandytown. Not able to keep away from a murder case, Dalziel teams up with another newcomer to the village, Charlotte Heywood, who is researching the alternative therapies the clinic offers. Detective Chief Inspector Peter Pascoe arrives on the scene to begin the official investigation only to find a familiar face from his past, Franny Roote.

Where it's reviewed:
Library Journal, September 1, 2008, page 103
Publishers Weekly, September 8, 2008, page 38

Other books by the same author:
Death Comes for the Fat Man, 2007
Good Morning, Midnight, 2004
Death's Jest Book, 2003
Dialogues of the Dead, 2002
Arms and the Women, 1999

Other books you might like:
Simon Brett, *Death on the Downs*, 2001
P.D. James, *The Private Patient*, 2008
Peter Lovesey, *The House Sitter*, 2003
Peter Robinson, *Close to Home*, 2003

95

VICTORIA HOUSTON

Dead Hot Shot

(Madison, WI: Bleak House, 2008)

Story type: Police Procedural
Series: Lewellyn Ferris. Book 9
Subject(s): Small Town Life; Inheritance
Major character(s): Paul Osborne, Dentist (retired), Widow(er); Lewellyn "Lew" Ferris, Police Officer; Frances Dark Sky, Teenager, Indian
Time period(s): 2000s
Locale(s): Loon Lake, Wisconsin

Summary: On Thanksgiving Day, the body of socialite Nolan Reece is found by her husband when it washes up on shore near their Loon Lake, Wisconsin, home. Police chief Lewellyn "Lew" Ferris calls in deputy coroner Paul Osborne, who's also Lew's boyfriend, along with fishing guide and expert tracker Ray Pradt to aid her in the investigation. Discovering that the overbearing Nolan was universally disliked, Lew and Paul soon determine that Nolan's death was not accidental. Grumpy grocery store owner Mildred Taggert becomes the next victim when she's shot near her home. The arrival of forensic expert and former investigative reporter Gina Palmer, who's looking into several cases of credit card theft in the area, puts an unexpected twist on the murder cases.

Where it's reviewed:
Publishers Weekly, May 19, 2008, page 38

Other books by the same author:
Dead Madonna, 2007
Dead Boogie, 2006
Dead Jitterbug, 2005
Dead Hot Mama, 2004
Dead Frenzy, 2003

Other books you might like:
Paula Gosling, *A Few Dying Words*, 1994
Mary Logue, *Maiden Rock*, 2007
William G. Tapply, *Close to the Bone*, 1996
Charlene Weir, *A Cold Christmas*, 2001

96

CHARLIE HUSTON

Every Last Drop

(New York: Del Rey, 2008)

Story type: Vampire Story
Series: Joe Pitt. Book 4
Subject(s): Vampires; Fantasy
Major character(s): Joe Pitt, Detective—Private, Vampire; Dexter Predo, Vampire; Amanda Horde, Scientist
Time period(s): 2000s
Locale(s): New York, New York

Summary: Forced into exile in the Bronx, vampire and private detective Joe Pitt is roaming the streets one late night when he's attacked and kidnapped. Dexter Predo, head of the Coalition Clan of vampires, wants to question Joe about a new Clan in New York. Scientist Amanda Horde has formed the Cure Clan; she is attempting to find a cure for the Vyrus, the disease that creates vampires and causes them to crave blood. Predo wants Joe to infiltrate this new Clan to find its weak spot. As Joe moves between the Clans, he discovers that someone is trying to control the vampires' blood source and start a war between the Clans.

Where it's reviewed:
Booklist, September 15, 2008, page 28
Publishers Weekly, July 28, 2008, page 56

Other books by the same author:
Half the Blood of Brooklyn, 2007
A Dangerous Man, 2006
No Dominion, 2006
Already Dead, 2005
Six Bad Things, 2005

Other books you might like:
Mario Acevedo, *X-Rated Bloodsuckers*, 2007
Jim Butcher, *Death Masks*, 2003
P.N. Elrod, *A Chill in the Blood*, 1998
Tanya Huff, *Blood Trail*, 1992

97

NOEL HYND

Conspiracy in Kiev

(Grand Rapids, MI: Zondervan, 2008)

Story type: Espionage Thriller
Series: Russian Trilogy. Book 1
Subject(s): Conspiracies; Russians
Major character(s): Alexandra "Alex" LaDuca, Government Official (U.S. Treasury Agent); Yuri Federov, Organized Crime Figure, Businessman; Gian Antonio Rizzo, Police Officer

Time period(s): 2000s
Locale(s): Washington, District of Columbia; Kiev, Ukraine; Rome, Italy

Summary: FBI Special Agent Alexandra "Alex" LaDuca is currently on assignment with a Treasury Department agency that investigates international financial fraud. When Alex's fiance, Secret Service Agent Robert Timmons, tells Alex that she has been chosen to go undercover to Kiev during an upcoming presidential visit to the Ukrainian city, she is not thrilled with the idea of going back out into the field. However, Alex's financial knowledge and experience, combined with her skills with foreign languages, make her the ideal candidate for the job. Alex's assignment is to question Russian businessman Yuri Federov, who owes the U.S. government two million dollars in back taxes. Alex is told to get close to Federov and try to find out about his illegal business dealings.

Other books by the same author:
The Enemy Within, 2006
The Lost Boy, 1999
Rage of Spirits, 1997
The Prodigy, 1997

Other books you might like:
Brian Freemantle, *Triple Cross*, 2004
Stuart M. Kaminsky, *People Who Walk in Darkness*, 2008
Martin Cruz Smith, *Wolves Eat Dogs*, 2004
Robin White, *Siberian Light*, 1997

98

JULIE HYZY

Hail to the Chef

(New York: Berkley, 2008)

Story type: Amateur Detective
Series: Olivia Paras. Book 2
Subject(s): Cooks and Cooking; Presidents
Major character(s): Olivia "Ollie" Paras, Cook, Detective—Amateur
Time period(s): 2000s
Locale(s): Washington, District of Columbia

Summary: The First Lady appears to be trying to set up White House chef Ollie Paras with her nephew Sean. Before Ollie and Sean have a chance to say anything more than hello, Secret Service whisks everyone into the bunker: there's a bomb threat. The threat is lifted, but the White House remains on a heightened state of alert as Ollie prepares for Thanksgiving and the rest of the holiday season. The season is marred by Sean's death, an apparent suicide, and by the death of a White House electrician, an apparent accident. Though she has plenty to worry about in the kitchen, Ollie also asks questions about both deaths and she is threatened on the way home from work.

Other books by the same author:
State of the Onion, 2008
Deadly Interest, 2006
Deadly Blessings, 2005
Artistic License, 2004

Other books you might like:
Miranda Bliss, *Cooking Up Trouble*, 2006
Diane Mott Davidson, *Dark Tort*, 2006
Phyllis Richman, *The Butter Did It*, 1997
Elliott Roosevelt, *Murder in the East Room*, 1993

99

CLAUDE IZNER   (Pseudonym of Liliane Korb and Laurence Lefevre)

Murder on the Eiffel Tower

(New York: St. Martin's Minotaur, 2008)

Story type: Historical; Amateur Detective
Series: Victor Legris. Book 1
Subject(s): Books and Reading
Major character(s): Victor Legris, Store Owner, Detective—Amateur; Kenji Mori, Businessman; Tasha Kherson, Artist
Time period(s): 1880s (1889)
Locale(s): Paris, France

Summary: In 1889, Parisians are excited to visit the newly opened Eiffel Tower. Bookseller Victor Legris is one of the many visitors to the tower. Legris is meeting a journalist friend who is celebrating the success of his new newspaper, *Le Passe-partout*. Also attending the celebration is Kenji Mori, Legris's business partner, and Tasha Kherson, a Russian artist. Eugenie Patinot is on the tower, too. Unfortunately, her visit is cut short when she keels over dead after apparently being stung by a bee. When several other deaths occur, also involving bee stings, Legris's curiosity leads him to suspect foul play and he begins to investigate the strange deaths.

Where it's reviewed:
Booklist, August 1, 2008, page 44
Library Journal, August 15, 2008, page 57
Mystery News, October/November 2008, page 23
Mystery Scene, Fall 2008, page 76
Publishers Weekly, June 30, 2008, page 158

Other books you might like:
Boris Akunin, *Murder on the Leviathan*, 2004
Oliver Bleys, *The Ghost in the Eiffel Tower*, 2003
Richard Crabbe, *Suspension*, 2000
Pablo De Santis, *The Paris Enigma*, 2008

100

ALAN JACOBSON

The 7th Victim

(New York: Vanguard, 2008)

Story type: Serial Killer; Police Procedural
Subject(s): Family Problems; Psychological Thriller
Major character(s): Karen Vail, FBI Agent; Roberto Hernandez, Detective—Police; Paul Bledsoe, Detective—Homicide
Time period(s): 2000s
Locale(s): Aquia, Virginia; Vienna, Virginia; New York, New York

Summary: Special Agent Karen Vail is the first woman to become a profiler with the FBI. Currently, Vail is assigned to the Dead Eyes task force. An extremely brutal killer, Dead Eyes plunges knives into the victims' eyes after killing them. When Vail is suspended after attacking her abusive soon-to-be ex-husband, she relies on two other members of the task force, homicide detective Paul Bledsoe and police detective Roberto Hernandez, to keep her up to date with the case. After visiting her mother, Vail learns a dark family secret. Unfortunately, Vail soon discovers that her family's secret may be the key to unraveling the identity of the Dead Eyes killer.

Where it's reviewed:
Booklist, October 1, 2008, page 26
Deadly Pleasures, Fall 2008, page 45
Library Journal, September 15, 2008, page 44
Publishers Weekly, September 15, 2008, page 43

Other books by the same author:
The Hunted, 2001
False Accusations, 1998

Other books you might like:
Chelsea Cain, *Heartsick*, 2007
Lisa Gardner, *The Next Accident*, 2001
Val McDermid, *Killing the Shadows*, 2001
Erica Spindler, *All Fall Down*, 2000

101

P.D. JAMES

The Private Patient

(New York: Knopf, 2008)

Story type: Police Procedural
Series: Adam Dalgliesh. Book 14
Subject(s): Journalism; Hospitals
Major character(s): Adam Dalgliesh, Detective—Police, Writer; Kate Miskin, Detective—Police; Francis Benton-Smith, Detective—Police
Time period(s): 2000s
Locale(s): London, England; Stoke Cheverell, England; Droughton Cross, England

Summary: Investigative journalist Rhoda Gradwyn checks herself into Cheverell Manor, a private clinic in Dorset, to have plastic surgeon Dr. George Chandler-Powell remove a facial scar she received as a child. The day after her surgery, Gradwyn is murdered in her room. Commander Adam Dalgliesh, Detective Inspector Kate Miskin, and Sergeant Francis Benton-Smith are summoned from London to conduct the investigation into Gradwyn's death. The Special Investigation Squad discovers several suspects at Cheverell Manor, including a friend of Gradwyn's who stands to inherit from Gradwyn. Suspecting that her career of ferreting out unpleasant facts may have been behind Gradwyn's murder, Dalgliesh and his team research the backgrounds of the staff at the manor.

Where it's reviewed:
Booklist, September 15, 2008, page 5
Library Journal, October 15, 2008, page 63
Publishers Weekly, September 22, 2008, page 42

Other books by the same author:
The Lighthouse, 2005
The Murder Room, 2003
Death in Holy Orders, 2001
A Certain Justice, 1997
Original Sin, 1994

Other books you might like:
Sarah Caudwell, *The Sibyl in Her Grave*, 2000
Deborah Crombie, *Dreaming of the Bones*, 1997
Elizabeth George, *A Traitor to Memory*, 2001
Minette Walters, *The Dark Room*, 1996

102

J.A. JANCE

Cruel Intent

(New York: Touchstone, 2008)

Story type: Amateur Detective
Series: Alison Reynolds. Book 4
Subject(s): Internet; Serial Killers
Major character(s): Alison "Ali" Reynolds, Journalist (former); Dave Holman, Detective—Homicide; Bryan Forester, Contractor, Crime Suspect
Time period(s): 2000s
Locale(s): Sedona, Arizona; Phoenix, Arizona; Cottonwood, Arizona

Summary: Former television newscaster Ali Reynolds is now living in Sedona, Arizona, and occupies her time overseeing the remodeling of an old mansion. When Morgan Forester, the wife of Ali's contractor Bryan, is brutally murdered, the police believe that Bryan killed her. Although Detective Dave Holman warns Ali about involving herself in the case and being too friendly with a murder suspect, Ali can't seem to help herself. When Ali learns that Morgan was cheating on Bryan using a Web Site called singleheart.com, Ali decides to check out the Web Site. Unfortunately, Morgan's killer is monitoring the Web Site. Putting herself in danger, Ali tries to find Morgan's killer with the help of a computer expert.

Where it's reviewed:
Booklist, October 1, 2008, page 27
Mystery News, December/January 2009, page 29
Mystery Scene, Holiday 2008, page 67
Publishers Weekly, September 29, 2008, page 59

Other books by the same author:
Damage Control, 2008
Hand of Evil, 2007
Web of Evil, 2007
Dead Wrong, 2006
Edge of Evil, 2006

Other books you might like:
Jan Brogan, *Teaser*, 2008
Alafair Burke, *Dead Connection*, 2007
Michael Connelly, *The Scarecrow*, 2009
Hank Phillippi Ryan, *Face Time*, 2007

103

DANIEL JUDSON

The Water's Edge

(New York: St. Martin's, 2008)

Story type: Amateur Detective
Subject(s): Organized Crime
Major character(s): Jake Bechet, Businessman, Detective—Amateur; Tommy Miller, Detective—Private (former), Landlord; Kay Barton, Friend
Time period(s): 2000s
Locale(s): Hampton Bays, New York; Southampton, New York; East Hampton, New York

Summary: Jake Bechet is a former professional boxer who now lives and works in Hampton Bays, New York. When Jake learns about the brutal murder of two men, whose bodies were found hanging from a bridge between Southampton and Hampton Bays, he suspects that someone from his unsavory past may be involved. Jake was once an enforcer for the South American Castello crime family. Jorge Castello, the current head of the family, pressures Jake into finding out who committed the murders. Also investigating the case is former private investigator Tommy Miller. Tommy is drawn to the case after learning that his ex-girlfriend Abby was involved with one of the dead men.

Where it's reviewed:
Booklist, April 1, 2008, page 33
Deadly Pleasures, Summer 2008, page 50
Mystery News, June/July 2008, page 22
Mystery Scene, Summer 2008, page 86
Publishers Weekly, April 7, 2008, page 44

Other books by the same author:
The Darkest Place, 2006
The Bone Orchard, 2002
The Poisoned Rose, 2002

Other books you might like:
Gabriel Cohen, *The Graving Dock*, 2007
Chuck Hogan, *The Killing Moon*, 2007
Chris Knopf, *Head Wounds*, 2008
Michael Koryta, *Envy the Night*, 2008

104

LARRY KARP

The King of Ragtime

(Scottsdale: Poisoned Pen, 2008)

Story type: Historical
Series: Ragtime. Book 2
Subject(s): Music and Musicians; Illness
Major character(s): Scott Joplin, Musician, Composer; Martin Niederhoffer, Accountant, Musician; Eleanor Stark "Nell" Stanley, Musician
Time period(s): 1910s (1916)
Locale(s): New York, New York; St. Louis, Missouri

Summary: In 1916, ragtime musician and composer Scott Joplin is trying to sell a musical drama he's written. Joplin's health is deteriorating. Hoping to provide for his wife Lottie after he's gone, he approaches producer Irving Berlin to ask if Berlin will buy his work. The day after Joplin and Berlin meet, Martin Niederhoffer, a piano student of Joplin's, walks into his office to find Joplin standing over the bloody body of Sid Altman, another employee of Berlin's, with a razor blade in his hand. Hurrying Joplin away from the murder scene, Niederhoffer and Joplin look to fellow musician Nell Stanley for help in clearing their names. Calling on her father, John Stark, an old friend of Joplin's, Stark and Stanley try to discover the killer's identity to help their dying friend.

Where it's reviewed:
Booklist, September 1, 2008, page 55
Publishers Weekly, June 30, 2008, page 164

Other books by the same author:
The Ragtime Kid, 2006
First Do No Harm, 2004
The Midnight Special, 2001
The Music Box Murders, 1999

Other books you might like:
Ace Atkins, *Crossroad Blues*, 1998
Barbara Cleverly, *Ragtime in Simla*, 2003
Grace F. Edwards, *A Toast Before Dying*, 1998
David Fulmer, *Jass*, 2005

105

ALEX KAVA

Exposed

(Don Mills, Ontario: Mira, 2008)

Story type: Psychological Suspense
Series: Maggie O'Dell. Book 6
Subject(s): Diseases; Terrorism
Major character(s): Maggie O'Dell, FBI Agent; R.J. Tully, FBI Agent; Benjamin Platt, Doctor, Military Personnel
Time period(s): 2000s
Locale(s): Quantico, Virginia; Elk Grove, Virginia; Newburgh Heights, Virginia

Summary: When FBI agent Maggie O'Dell and her boss Assistant Director Cunningham discover an anonymous, threatening note, they race to Elk Grove, Virginia, expecting to find a bomb. What they find, however, is a mother and child who are both highly contagious with an unknown virus. O'Dell and Cunningham are taken to an Army isolation facility while Dr. Benjamin Platt tries to figure out what they have been exposed to. Meanwhile, O'Dell's partner, R.J. Tully, investigates several other reports of virus exposure across the country. After O'Dell is released from isolation, she and Tully discover that the killer has been sending the virus through the mail. An admirer of criminal masterminds, the killer uses snippets of quotes and clues from criminals such as the Unabomber and the Anthrax Killer. A clue from Tully's past causes him to realize who the killer might be.

Where it's reviewed:
Publishers Weekly, August 25, 2008, page 49

Other books by the same author:
Whitewash, 2007
A Necessary Evil, 2006
One False Move, 2004
At the Stroke of Madness, 2003
The Soul Catcher, 2002

Other books you might like:
Stephen J. Cannell, *The Devil's Workshop*, 1999
Jan Coffey, *The Deadliest Strain*, 2008
Daniel Kalla, *Pandemic*, 2005
Joshua Spanogle, *Isolation Ward*, 2006

106

SHARON KAYE

Black Market Truth

(Las Vegas: Parmenides, 2008)

Story type: Action/Adventure
Series: Dana McCarter. Book 1
Subject(s): Philosophy; Religion
Major character(s): Dana McCarter, Historian, Adoptee; Domenico Conti, Detective—Homicide; Giuseppe Torelli, Religious
Time period(s): 2000s
Locale(s): Rome, Italy; New York, New York; Moscow, Russia

Summary: Vatican police inspector Domenico Conti is called in to investigate a break-in at St. Paul's Basilica. A guard has been killed, and St. Paul's sarcophagus has been destroyed. Conti learns that five ancient scrolls rested within the sarcophagus. He is ordered by Cardinal Giuseppe Torelli to find and retrieve the stolen scrolls. Conti's search leads him to New York, and to Dr. Dana McCarter. McCarter is the new director of the Advanced Institute for the Study of Antiquity at NYU. McCarter has already seen one of the scrolls; a mysterious man named Turk Selenka brought one of them to the Institute to be inspected by McCarter for authenticity. McCarter joins forces with Conti in hopes of finding the other scrolls. Unfortunately, they are not the only ones looking.

Other books you might like:
Jennifer Lee Carrell, *Interred with Their Bones*, 2007
Margaret Doody, *Aristotle Detective*, 1978
Lyn Hamilton, *The Xibala Murders*, 1997
Philip Kerr, *A Philosophical Investigation*, 1993

107

JONATHAN KELLERMAN

Bones

(New York: Ballantine, 2008)

Story type: Psychological Suspense
Series: Alex Delaware. Book 23
Subject(s): Police Procedural; Family
Major character(s): Alex Delaware, Psychologist, Consultant; Milo Sturgis, Detective—Homicide; Travis Huck, Steward

Time period(s): 2000s
Locale(s): Marina del Ray, California; Los Angeles, California; Pacific Palisades, California

Summary: When several bodies are discovered in a protected marshland near Marina del Ray, homicide detective Milo Sturgis calls in LAPD psychological consultant Alex Delaware. The first body discovered is that of Selena Bass, a music teacher. As Sturgis and Delaware look into Bass's private life, they discover that the young woman taught Kelvin Vander, the son of wealthy businessman Simon Vander. When they pay a visit to the Vander home, Sturgis and Delaware meet Travis Huck, the estate's manager. Later, Sturgis learns of Huck's criminal past. So when Huck disappears, he becomes a prime suspect in Selena's murder. When Huck finally does turn up, the information he gives Sturgis and Delaware lead them to a murderer within the Vander family.

Where it's reviewed:
Booklist, September 15, 2008, page 5
Mystery Scene, Holiday 2008, page 75
Publishers Weekly, September 8, 2008, page 37

Other books by the same author:
Compulsion, 2008
Obsession, 2007
Gone, 2006
Rage, 2005
Therapy, 2004

Other books you might like:
Keith Ablow, *Compulsion*, 2002
Andrew Klavan, *Man and Wife*, 2003
Martin J. Smith, *Shadow Image*, 1998
Stephen White, *Harm's Way*, 1996

108

ALICE KIMBERLY (Pseudonym of Alice Alfonsi and Marc Cerasini)

The Ghost and the Haunted Mansion

(New York: Berkley, 2009)

Story type: Amateur Detective
Series: Haunted Bookshop. Book 5
Subject(s): Ghosts; Inheritance
Major character(s): Penelope "Pen" Thornton-McClure, Store Owner, Detective—Amateur; Jack Shepard, Spirit, Detective—Private; Seymour Tarnish, Postal Worker
Time period(s): 2000s; 1940s (1947)
Locale(s): New York, New York; Quindicott, Rhode Island; Millstone, Rhode Island

Summary: When bookstore owner Penelope Thornton-McClure discovers the body of Quindicott recluse Miss Timothea Todd, she calls the police who immediately question local mailman Seymour Tarnish. Seymour is quickly found innocent and is also revealed to be the heir to Miss Todd's estate. Pen and her aunt are involved in an auto accident in Seymour's van: someone tampered with the brakes. Pen begins to worry that Seymour may be in danger because of the inheritance. As she tries to figure out who killed Miss Todd, Pen receives help from her ghost, 1940s private investigator Jack Shepard. When Jack seems to disappear, Pen is forced to protect Seymour and solve the case on her own.

Other books by the same author:
The Ghost and the Femme Fatale, 2008
The Ghost and the Dead Man's Library, 2006
The Ghost and the Dead Deb, 2005
The Ghost and Mrs. McClure, 2004

Other books you might like:
Madelyn Alt, *The Trouble with Magic*, 2006
Nancy Atherton, *Aunt Dimity Beats the Devil*, 2000
Lorna Barrett, *Murder Is Binding*, 2008
Jeanne M. Dams, *Killing Cassidy*, 2000

109

JOHN R. KING

The Shadow of Reichenbach Falls

(New York: Forge, 2008)

Story type: Historical/Victorian
Subject(s): Crime and Criminals; Memory Loss
Major character(s): Thomas Carnacki, Student—College, Detective—Private; Anna Schmidt, Young Woman; Sherlock Holmes, Detective—Private, Amnesiac
Time period(s): 1890s (1891); 1880s
Locale(s): Bern, Switzerland; London, England; Paris, France

Summary: Thomas Carnacki is a down-and-out Cambridge student who has travelled to the Swiss town of Meiringen. Starving, he spots a young woman with a basket full of food, and after striking up a conversation Thomas learns that her name is Anna Schmidt and she is going to Reichenbach Falls for a picnic. Thomas accompanies Anna to the Falls, where they are shocked to witness two men locked in a struggle. When one of the men is pushed over the edge, Thomas and Anna rescue him from the raging waters below. Unfortunately, the victim has suffered amnesia and has no idea why someone is trying to kill him. As they try to help the man recover his identity, they are drawn into a dangerous confrontation between criminal mastermind Professor James Moriarty and his nemesis, Sherlock Holmes.

Where it's reviewed:
Mystery News, August/September 2008, page 13
Publishers Weekly, May 5, 2008, page 47

Other books you might like:
John Gardner, *Moriarty*, 2008
William Hope Hodgson, *Carnacki, the Ghost Finder*, 1913
H.R. Knight, *What Rough Beast*, 2005
Michael Kurland, *The Great Game*, 2001

110

NATSUO KIRINO

Real World

(New York: Knopf, 2008)

Story type: Psychological Suspense
Subject(s): Teen Relationships; Death
Major character(s): Toshiko "Toshi" Yamanaka, Student—High School; Ryo, Student—High School, Murderer; Kiyomi "Yuzan" Kaibara, Student—High School, Lesbian
Time period(s): 2000s
Locale(s): Tokyo, Japan; Karuizawa, Japan

Summary: The brutal murder of a housewife shocks the residents of the Suginami-ku suburb of Tokyo one hot summer day. Toshi Yamanaka, a high school senior, is on her way to school when she sees her neighbor, a teenager she has nicknamed "Worm," leave his house with a smile on his face. That evening, Toshi learns that Worm's mother has been murdered. When the police question her, Toshi realizes that Worm is a suspect in the murder. Having stolen Toshi's bike and cell phone while she was in school, Worm begins calling the numbers on her phone, connecting with three of her friends. The girls begin to compete for Worm's time and affection, which leads to a deadly conclusion.

Where it's reviewed:
Booklist, July 1, 2008, page 43
Library Journal, May 1, 2008, page 56
Publishers Weekly, May 5, 2008, page 45

Other books by the same author:
What Remains, 2008
Grotesque, 2007
Out, 2003

Other books you might like:
Hitomi Kanehara, *Snakes and Earrings*, 2005
Yu Miri, *Gold Rush*, 2002
Miyuki Miyabe, *The Devil's Whisper*, 2007
Ryu Murakami, *Piercing*, 2007

111

DEAN R. KOONTZ

Your Heart Belongs to Me

(New York: Bantam, 2008)

Story type: Psychological Suspense
Subject(s): Transplants; Supernatural
Major character(s): Ryan Perry, Businessman, Wealthy; Samantha Reach, Writer, Journalist; Violet, Spy
Time period(s): 2000s
Locale(s): Newport Coast, California; Las Vegas, Nevada; Denver, Colorado

Summary: Ryan Perry is a 34-year-old millionaire who made a fortune after creating an online social-networking site. After selling his company, Ryan now spends his days surfing and enjoying the company of his journalist girlfriend Samantha Reach. When Ryan begins to experience chest pain, his doctor informs him that he has an enlarged heart and has one year to live unless he has a heart transplant. Ryan soon learns that a heart has been found for him and he rushes to China for the emergency surgery. One year later, Ryan is trying to reconnect with Samantha when he is approached by a Chinese woman in a parking lot. The mysterious woman stabs Ryan and tells him, "Your heart belongs to me." Ryan's subsequent search for information about his heart's donor leads to a terrifying conclusion.

Where it's reviewed:
Booklist, November 15, 2008, page 5
Publishers Weekly, October 27, 2008, page 35

Other books by the same author:
The Darkest Evening of the Year, 2007
The Good Guy, 2007
The Husband, 2006
Velocity, 2005
Life Expectancy, 2004

Other books you might like:
Sandra Brown, *Charade*, 1994
Edna Buchanan, *Pulse*, 1998
Michael Connelly, *Blood Work*, 1998
Gayle Lynds, *Mesmerized*, 2001

112

MICHAEL KORYTA

Envy the Night

(New York: St. Martin's, 2008)

Story type: Revenge
Subject(s): Fathers and Sons; Crime and Criminals
Major character(s): Frank Temple III, Student—College; Grady Morgan, FBI Agent; Nora Stafford, Mechanic
Time period(s): 2000s
Locale(s): Willow Flowage, Wisconsin

Summary: Frank Temple III is leaving his fifth college in seven years. The writing teacher with whom he was eager to work turns out to be interested in only one thing: a memoir about Frank Temple II, a federal marshal who had a shadow career as a hit man. Betrayed by Devin Matteson, Frank Temple II chose suicide over jail. Frank Temple III learns that Matteson is headed for the small Wisconsin town where his father had a cabin. At loose ends after leaving school, Temple III also heads for Wisconsin, seeking revenge. FBI agent Grady Morgan is concerned when he hears that Frank is on the move. In Wisconsin, Frank is disturbed by the presence of some dangerous men. He also finds Nora Stafford, an auto mechanic who gets caught up in the crossfire.

Where it's reviewed:
Booklist, July 1, 2008, page 42
Publishers Weekly, June 2, 2008, page 28

Other books by the same author:
A Welcome Grave, 2007
Sorrow's Anthem, 2006
Tonight I Said Goodbye, 2005

Other books you might like:
Jeffery Deaver, *The Bodies Left Behind*, 2008
William Kent Krueger, *Boundary Waters*, 1999
James Sallis, *Cripple Creek*, 2006
Edward Wright, *Damnation Falls*, 2008

113

JULIE KRAMER

Stalking Susan

(New York: Doubleday, 2008)

Story type: Amateur Detective; Serial Killer
Series: Riley Spartz. Book 1
Subject(s): Television; Serial Killers
Major character(s): Riley Spartz, Journalist, Detective—Amateur; Nick Garnett, Security Officer; Brent Redding, Widow(er)
Time period(s): 2000s
Locale(s): Minneapolis, Minnesota

Summary: Riley Spartz is a television reporter in Minneapolis/St. Paul. She gets a tip from Nick Garnett, a former top Minneapolis homicide detective who now works as head of corporate security for the Mall of America. Garnett has discovered that two women named Susan died exactly one year apart, on November 19, 1991 and November 19, 1992. Soon Riley finds other Susans who died on other November 19ths, and she discovers that two of the victims have a raincoat in common. The novel is punctuated with references to classic mysteries, and Nick and Riley trade movie quotes whenever they meet. Riley pursues the Susan story, anticipating a boost in her station's ratings. She also finds time to report on veterinarians and a pet cremation scam.

Where it's reviewed:
Booklist, June 1, 2008, page 54
Deadly Pleasures, Summer 2008, page 46
Library Journal, July 15, 2008, page 58
Publishers Weekly, May 19, 2008, page 34

Other books you might like:
Jan Brogan, *Yesterday's News*, 2007
Mary Jane Clark, *Hide Yourself Away*, 2004
Kelly Lange, *Graveyard Shift*, 2005
Hank Phillippi Ryan, *Face Time*, 2007

114

WILLIAM KENT KRUEGER

Red Knife

(New York: Atria, 2008)

Story type: Private Detective
Series: Cork O'Connor. Book 8
Subject(s): Gangs; Racial Conflict
Major character(s): Cork O'Connor, Detective—Private; Annie O'Connor, Student—High School; Buck Reinhart, Crime Suspect
Time period(s): 2000s

Locale(s): Aurora, Minnesota

Summary: Trouble arrives in the quiet town of Aurora, Minnesota, when Alex Kingbird and his wife, Rayette, are killed execution-style. Alex was head of the Red Boyz, the Iron Lake Ojibwe Reservation's gang of young men searching for meaning and identity. Blame for their deaths falls on Buck Reinhardt, an older Anglo who has been accusing the Red Boyz in the death of his daughter from a drug overdose. However, Reinhardt appears to have an alibi for the shooting. With his Ojibwe ties, Cork O'Connor is pulled into the case by Anglos and the Ojibwe as a private investigator. As Cork searches for clues and tries to calm tensions between whites and Ojibwe, he and his family become targets of an evil that grows greater and greater.

Where it's reviewed:
Booklist, August 1, 2008, page 47
Deadly Pleasures, Summer 2008, page 38
Mystery News, October/November 2008, page 17
Publishers Weekly, July 14, 2008, page 45

Other books by the same author:
Thunder Bay, 2007
Copper River, 2006
Mercy Falls, 2005
Blood Hollow, 2004
Purgatory Ridge, 2001

Other books you might like:
C.J. Box, *Free Fire*, 2007
Steven F. Havill, *Final Payment*, 2007
Craig Johnson, *Another Man's Moccasins*, 2008
Michael McGarrity, *Nothing but Trouble*, 2005

115

VICKI LANE

In a Dark Season

(New York: Dell, 2008)

Story type: Amateur Detective
Series: Elizabeth Goodweather. Book 4
Subject(s): Appalachia; Suicide
Major character(s): Elizabeth Goodweather, Farmer, Widow(er); Phillip Hawkins, Teacher, Veteran; Nola Barrett, Aged Person
Time period(s): 2000s (2006); 1860s
Locale(s): Hot Springs, North Carolina; Ransom, North Carolina; Dewell Hill, North Carolina

Summary: Elizabeth Goodweather and her husband Sam moved to the small North Carolina town of Hot Springs several years ago. Today, Elizabeth is a widow who owns Full Circle Farm. As she and her boyfriend, former police detective Phillip Hawkins, are driving past the old house at Gudger's Stand, Elizabeth catches a glimpse of someone standing on the porch railing. Approaching the house, Elizabeth realizes that the person standing on the railing is her new friend Nola Barrett. Elizabeth tries to talk her down, but Nola jumps, trying to end her life. When Nola's niece puts her in a nursing home to recover from her injuries, Elizabeth tries to discover what made her friend so desperate. Elizabeth's inquiries lead to the discovery of an 11-year-old rape case that was never

reported, and to Nola's role in the cover-up.

Where it's reviewed:
Mystery News, August/September 2008, page 27

Other books by the same author:
Old Wounds, 2007
Art's Blood, 2006
Signs in the Blood, 2005

Other books you might like:
Sallie Bissell, *A Darker Justice*, 2002
Charlaine Harris, *A Secret Rage*, 1984
Barbara Neely, *Blanche Passes Go*, 2000
Kathryn R. Wall, *Bishop's Reach*, 2006

116

WARD LARSEN

Stealing Trinity

(Ipswich, MA: Oceanview, 2008)

Story type: Historical/World War II
Subject(s): Nazis; Spies
Major character(s): Alexander Braun, Military Personnel, Spy; Michael Thatcher, Military Personnel, Widow(er); Lydia Cole Murray, Heiress
Time period(s): 1940s (1945)
Locale(s): Berlin, Germany; Newport, Rhode Island; Los Alamos, New Mexico

Summary: In the final days of World War II, a small group of high-ranking Nazi officers attempt to ensure the future of the Third Reich. A spy has been planted in a top-secret government project in America. Captain Alexander Braun is chosen to make contact with the undercover agent, known as "Die Wespe." All Braun knows of this top-secret project is that it will change the way future wars are fought. In England, Major Michael Thatcher is interrogating a German prisoner who worked for a Nazi officer. The prisoner gives Thatcher Braun's name and the phrase "the Manhattan Project." Thatcher heads for the States, where his search for Braun leads him to heiress Lydia Cole, who knew Braun before the war. Together, Thatcher and Cole try to stop Braun from meeting with Die Wespe and selling off America's nuclear secrets to the Russians.

Where it's reviewed:
Booklist, September 1, 2008, page 57
Library Journal, August 15, 2008, page 69
Publishers Weekly, August 18, 2008, page 41

Other books by the same author:
The Perfect Assassin, 2006

Other books you might like:
John Altman, *A Gathering of Spies*, 2000
Joseph Kanon, *Los Alamos*, 1997
Peter Millar, *Stealing Thunder*, 1999
Martin Cruz Smith, *Stallion Gate*, 1986

117

ASA LARSSON

The Black Path

(New York: Delta, 2008)

Story type: Police Procedural
Series: Rebecka Martinsson. Book 3
Subject(s): Miners and Mining; Industry and Trade
Major character(s): Rebecka Martinsson, Lawyer; Anna-Maria Mella, Police Officer; Mauri Kallis, Businessman
Time period(s): 2000s; 1980s
Locale(s): Abisko, Sweden; Kiruna, Sweden; Stockholm, Sweden

Summary: On an early spring night in northern Sweden, the body of a woman is discovered by a fisherman. Police inspector Anna-Maria Mella and her colleague Sven-Erik Stalnacke are called to Tornetrask to investigate. Identifying the body as Inna Wattrang, the head of information for Kallis Mining, Mella soon learns that Wattrang was severely tortured before she was murdered. Wanting to learn more about Kallis Mining before she meets with its owner Mauri Kallis, Mella turns to attorney Rebecka Martinsson for help in sifting through information about the company. Although Martinsson is happy to help Mella with the investigation, she is still recovering herself from a previous case. Investigating both Kallis and Wattrang's brother, Diddi, Mella soon learns that Kallis Mining's business dealings may be the cause of Wattrang's death.

Where it's reviewed:
Booklist, June 1, 2008, page 47
Mystery News, August/September 2008, page 23
Publishers Weekly, June 23, 2008, page 35

Other books by the same author:
The Blood Spilt, 2007
Sun Storm, 2006

Other books you might like:
Kjell Eriksson, *The Princess of Burundi*, 2006
Stieg Larsson, *The Girl with the Dragon Tattoo*, 2008
Yrsa Sigurdardottir, *Last Rituals*, 2007
Helen Tursten, *The Torso*, 2006

118

STIEG LARSSON

The Girl with the Dragon Tattoo

(New York: Knopf, 2008)

Story type: Amateur Detective
Subject(s): Missing Persons; Journalism
Major character(s): Carl Mikael Blomkvist, Journalist, Detective—Amateur; Lisbeth Salander, Researcher, Computer Expert; Henrik Vanger, Industrialist (retired), Aged Person
Time period(s): 2000s
Locale(s): Stockholm, Sweden; Hedeby Island, Sweden; Melbourne, Australia

Summary: After Swedish journalist Mikael Blomkvist is

convicted of libel in a lawsuit involving a shady financier, he receives an unusual offer from retired industrialist Henrik Vanger. Vanger wants to hire Blomkvist to find out what really happened to his great-niece Harriet who disappeared almost 40 years ago. In 1966, Harriet vanished from the family estate on Hedeby Island in Sweden. The police searched the island for days, but found no trace of the missing teen. Vanger believes that Harriet was murdered all those years ago, possibly by someone in the Vanger family. Assisting Blomkvist in his search is 24-year-old Lisbeth Salander, a freelance researcher and expert computer hacker. As Blomkvist and Salander look into Harriet's disappearance, they stumble upon a horrifying Vanger family secret that finally explains what happened to Harriet.

Where it's reviewed:
Booklist, August 1, 2008, page 5
Deadly Pleasures, Fall 2008, page 26
Entertainment Weekly, October 10, 2008, page 77
Mystery Scene, Fall 2008, page 69
Publishers Weekly, July 14, 2008, page 40

Other books you might like:
Mari Jungstedt, *Unspoken*, 2007
Asa Larsson, *The Black Path*, 2008
Henning Mankell, *One Step Behind*, 1997
Hakan Nesser, *The Mind's Eye*, 2008

119

JOYCE LAVENE
JIM LAVENE , Co-Author

The Telltale Turtle

(Woodbury, MN: Midnight Ink, 2008)

Story type: Amateur Detective
Subject(s): Psychic Powers; Animals
Major character(s): Mary Catherine Roberts, Radio Personality, Psychic; Charlie Dowd, Detective—Private; Colin Jamison, Radio Personality, Crime Suspect
Time period(s): 2000s
Locale(s): Wilmington, North Carolina

Summary: On her way home after finishing another episode of her popular radio talk show, pet psychic Mary Catherine Roberts hears the plaintive cry of an animal in distress. When her driver Danny pulls up to an old brick mansion, he and Mary Catherine discover a small wounded turtle named Tommy. The body of Tommy's owner, wealthy socialite Ferndelle Jamison, is lying nearby. Colin Jamison, the dead woman's nephew, is the station manager at WRSC in Wilmington, North Carolina, where Mary Catherine does her pet psychic show. When Colin is suspected of murdering his aunt, Mary Catherine teams up with private investigator Charlie Dowd to try and find the real killer.

Where it's reviewed:
Booklist, September 15, 2008, page 31

Other books by the same author:
Hooked Up, 2008
Wicked Weaves, 2008
Perfect Poison, 2008
Poisoned Petals, 2007
Swapping Paint, 2007

Other books you might like:
Barbara Block, *Blowing Smoke*, 2001
Melissa Cleary, *First Pedigree Murder*, 1994
Christine T. Jorgensen, *Curl Up and Die*, 1997
Victoria Laurie, *Abby Cooper, Psychic Eye*, 2004

120

JOYCE LAVENE
JIM LAVENE , Co-Author

Wicked Weaves

(New York: Berkley, 2008)

Story type: Amateur Detective
Series: Renaissance Faire. Book 1
Subject(s): Fairs; Family Problems
Major character(s): Jessie Morton, Professor, Detective—
    Amateur; Mary Shift, Artisan, Businesswoman;
    Chase Manhattan, Lawyer, Consultant
Time period(s): 2000s
Locale(s): Myrtle Beach, South Carolina; Columbia,
    South Carolina

Summary: Jessie Morton, assistant professor at the
University of South Carolina, spends her summers
researching medieval crafts at the Renaissance Faire Village in Myrtle Beach. This summer, Jessie is apprentic-
ing for Mary Shift, a traditional Gullah basket weaver.
The body of Mary's estranged husband Joshua is
discovered just steps away from Mary's store in the village, Wicked Weaves. The police take Mary in for
questioning. Joshua was strangled with a piece of Mary's
unique basket weave. Jessie teams up with the village
bailiff, lawyer Chase Manhattan, to uncover more about
Mary's past, which Jessie believes will help them catch
the killer.

Where it's reviewed:
Mystery News, December/January 2009, page 15
Publishers Weekly, July 21, 2008, page 147

Other books by the same author:
Hooked Up, 2008
The Telltale Turtle, 2008
Perfect Poison, 2008
Poisoned Petals, 2007
Swapping Paint, 2007

Other books you might like:
Nancy Atherton, *Aunt Dimity Slays the Dragon*, 2009
Joan Hess, *Damsels in Distress*, 2007
Dean James, *Baked to Death*, 2005
Mary Monica Pulver, *Murder at the War*, 1987

121

JOHN LAWTON

Second Violin

(New York: Atlantic Monthly, 2008)

Story type: Historical/World War II
Series: Frederick Troy. Book 6
Subject(s): Internment; Rabbis
Major character(s): Frederick Troy, Detective—Police;
    Rod Troy, Journalist; Josef Hummel, Tailor
Time period(s): 1930s; 1940s (1940)
Locale(s): London, England; Vienna, Austria; Isle of
    Man, England

Summary: In 1938, after reporting on the violence of Kri-
stallnacht, journalist Rod Troy is sent back to England
by the German government. Rod's younger brother, Frederick, has just been assigned to Scotland Yard's Murder
Squad and is investigating the murders of several London
rabbis. Frederick learns that seven East End rabbis had
written to newspaper editors and called for the arrest of
Nazi sympathizers. Now, someone seems to be killing
off the rabbis one by one. Meanwhile, Rod, who was
born in Austria before the Troy family settled in England,
is sent to an internment camp on the Isle of Man in a
program that incarcerates immigrants.

Where it's reviewed:
Library Journal, October 1, 2008, page 48
Mystery News, December/January 2009, page 23
Publishers Weekly, September 15, 2008, page 43

Other books by the same author:
A Little White Death, 2006
Flesh Wounds, 2005
Bluffing Mr. Churchill, 2004
Old Flames, 2003
Sweet Sunday, 2002

Other books you might like:
Marshall Browne, *The Eye of the Abyss*, 2003
Jack Gerson, *Death Squad London*, 1990
Jo Walton, *Farthing*, 2006
Jacqueline Winspear, *An Incomplete Revenge*, 2008

122

KATHRYN LILLEY

A Killer Workout

(New York: Obsidian, 2008)

Story type: Amateur Detective
Series: Fat City. Book 2
Subject(s): Weight Control; Journalism
Major character(s): Kate Gallagher, Journalist, Detective—
    Amateur; Riley Matthews, Businessman; Jonathan
    Reed, Detective—Homicide
Time period(s): 2000s
Locale(s): Durham, North Carolina; Maggie Hollow,
    North Carolina; Atlanta, Georgia

Summary: After Channel Twelve investigative reporter
Kate Gallagher's on-air ratings start to drop when she

puts on some weight, she decides to spend a week at a weight-loss boot camp outside Durham, North Carolina, called Body Blast. The camp's owner, Riley Matthews, is an old friend of Kate's from Boston and is only too happy to have her as his guest. Kate's focus shifts from weight-loss to murder, however, when her Body Blast roommate Marnie Taylor is found dead the next morning. Riley informs Kate that this isn't the first suspicious death they've had at the camp. Worried, Riley asks her to look into the deaths. Kate agrees to help, but starts asking questions that may result in her own death.

Other books by the same author:
Dying to Be Thin, 2007

Other books you might like:
Joan Hess, *A Diet to Die For*, 1989
Bonnie Hearn Hill, *Killer Body*, 2004
Karen MacInerney, *Murder Most Maine*, 2008
G.A. McKevett, *Cereal Killer*, 2004

123

LAURA LIPPMAN

Hardly Knew Her

(New York: Morrow, 2008)

Story type: Mystery; Collection
Subject(s): Mystery and Detective Stories; Crime and Criminals
Time period(s): 2000s
Summary: This collection of 17 stories includes some of the darkest, most noir fiction Lippman has published. Two stories feature Heloise Lewis, call girl and madam who has moved from the streets of Baltimore out to the suburbs in order to provide a better life for her young son. Her soccer-mom identity is threatened in "One True Love" when a client recognizes her on the sidelines of a soccer game. This story won a 2008 Anthony Award for best short story. A follow-up story, "Scratch a Woman," is an homage to James M. Cain; this story is published for the first time in this collection. Two stories feature Lippman's series character, Baltimore private investigator Tess Monaghan, including "The Accidental Detective," written in the form of a magazine profile.

Where it's reviewed:
Booklist, September 1, 2008, page 55
Deadly Pleasures, Fall 2008, page 50
Library Journal, September 1, 2008, page 124
Mystery News, February/March 2009, page 19
Mystery Scene, Holiday 2008, page 70

Other books by the same author:
What the Dead Know, 2007
No Good Deeds, 2006
To the Power of Three, 2005
By a Spider's Thread, 2004
Baltimore Blues, 1997

Other books you might like:
James M. Cain, *Double Indemnity*, 1943
Patricia Highsmith, *The Selected Stories of Patricia Highsmith*, 2001
Joyce Carol Oates, *The Museum of Dr. Moses*, 2007
Cornell Woolrich, *Rear Window and Other Stories*, 1994

124

ANN LITTLEWOOD

Night Kill

(Scottsdale: Poisoned Pen, 2008)

Story type: Amateur Detective
Subject(s): Zoos; Suspense
Major character(s): Iris Oakley, Zoo Keeper, Detective—Amateur; Denny Stellar, Zoo Keeper; Neal Dawson, Veterinarian
Time period(s): 2000s
Locale(s): Vancouver, Washington; Portland, Oregon; Los Angeles, California

Summary: Fed up with her husband Rick's drinking, zookeeper Iris Oakley walks out on him. A week later at a party, Iris learns that Rick has quit drinking and wants to reconcile. Thrilled, Iris goes to work the next morning only to find her co-workers huddled around the feline exhibit. Iris is taken aside and informed that Rick's body was found in the lion habitat, reeking of alcohol. Not willing to believe that her husband was so careless, or that he'd broken his promise to her about his drinking, Iris starts to question her colleagues, trying to find out the truth about Rick's death. When Iris experiences a couple of near-death "accidents," she starts to understand that Rick's killer is willing to kill again to keep his secret.

Where it's reviewed:
Booklist, August 1, 2008, page 46
Library Journal, August 15, 2008, page 58
Publishers Weekly, July 7, 2008, page 41

Other books you might like:
Edie Claire, *Never Sorry*, 1999
Alison Glen, *Trunk Show*, 1995
Mary Willis Walker, *Zero at the Bone*, 1991
Betty Webb, *The Anteater of Death*, 2008

125

BILL LOEHFELM

Fresh Kills

(New York: Putnam, 2008)

Story type: Psychological
Subject(s): Fathers; Death
Major character(s): John "Junior" Sanders Jr., Saloon Keeper/Owner; Julia Sanders, Artist, Lesbian; Nathaniel Waters, Detective—Homicide
Time period(s): 2000s
Locale(s): New York, New York; Eltingville, New York

Summary: New York bartender John "Junior" Sanders is surprised to see Detective Carlo Purvis on his doorstep. Childhood friends, Junior and Carlo had a falling out several years ago. When Carlo informs Junior that his father, John Sr., has been shot and killed outside a neighborhood deli, Junior's first reaction is indifference. John Sr. beat his son frequently when Junior was a child. When Junior's sister Julia arrives for the funeral, Junior is forced to confront his feelings for his father and their past. This sets Junior off on a search for his father's killer, which damages Junior's relationship with Julia, and with his high school sweetheart, Molly Francis.

Where it's reviewed:
Booklist, August 1, 2008, page 42
Entertainment Weekly, August 22, 2008, page 128
Library Journal, October 15, 2008, page 103
Mystery News, October/November 2008, page 19
Publishers Weekly, July 7, 2008, page 40

Other books you might like:
Con Lehane, *What Goes Around Comes Around*, 2005
Rick Riordan, *Big Red Tequila*, 1997
S.J. Rozan, *Absent Friends*, 2004
Carolyn Wheat, *Fresh Kills*, 1995

126

MARY LOGUE

Point No Point

(Madison, WI: Bleak House, 2008)

Story type: Police Procedural
Series: Claire Watkins. Book 7
Subject(s): Marriage; Parenthood
Major character(s): Claire Watkins, Police Officer; Meg Watkins, Teenager, Student—High School; Rich Haggard, Farmer
Time period(s): 2000s
Locale(s): Pepin County, Wisconsin

Summary: Deputy Sheriff Claire Watkins is called in when a man's body is found drowned in the Mississippi River in her jurisdiction. Claire's boyfriend Rich Haggard gets a phone call from his friend Chet Baker. When Rich gets to Chet's house, he finds Chet's wife shot to death. Chet is lying on the bed next to her, crying. Rich calls Claire, who hands off the drowning case to another officer to investigate the shooting. Rich is unhappy that Claire is in "cop" mode, and this drives a wedge into their relationship. Meanwhile, Claire's 16-year-old daughter Meg is experimenting with her boyfriend.

Where it's reviewed:
Deadly Pleasures, Fall 2008, page 46
Library Journal, November 1, 2008, page 47
Publishers Weekly, September 2, 2008, page 41

Other books by the same author:
Maiden Rock, 2007
Poison Heart, 2005
Bone Harvest, 2004
Glare Ice, 2001
Blood Country, 1999

Other books you might like:
Kate Flora, *Chosen for Death*, 1994
Ellen Hart, *The Iron Girl*, 2005
William Kent Krueger, *Thunder Bay*, 2007
Julia Spencer-Fleming, *Out of the Deep I Cry*, 2004

127

SHEILA LOWE

Written in Blood

(New York: Obsidian, 2008)

Story type: Amateur Detective
Series: Claudia Rose. Book 2
Subject(s): Schools/Boarding Schools; Family Problems
Major character(s): Claudia Rose, Consultant (graphologist), Detective—Amateur; Paige Sorensen, Widow(er); Annabelle Giordano, Teenager
Time period(s): 2000s
Locale(s): Playa del Reina, California; Los Angeles, California; Las Vegas, Nevada

Summary: After suffering a stroke, Torg Sorensen died and left his young wife Paige the bulk of his estate and the Sorensen Academy, a school for young girls. Torg's children are claiming that the signature on his will is a forgery, so Paige hires handwriting expert Claudia Rose. Claudia is able to authenticate Torg's signature, helping Paige win the case and allowing her to stay on as headmistress of the school. Claudia also volunteers to examine the handwriting of a troubled student at the school, Annabelle Giordano. As time goes by, Claudia and Annabelle form a tenuous friendship. When both Paige and Annabelle are reported missing, Claudia puts her own life in danger as she searches for her friends.

Where it's reviewed:
Mystery News, October/November 2008, page 27

Other books by the same author:
Poison Pen, 2007

Other books you might like:
Kate Flora, *Stalking Death*, 2008
Marion Moore Hill, *Deadly Will*, 2006
Jodi Larsen, *At First Sight*, 2001
Fiona Mountain, *Pale as the Dead*, 2004

128

JOHN LUTZ

Night Kills

(New York: Pinnacle, 2008)

Story type: Police Procedural
Series: Frank Quinn. Book 3
Subject(s): Serial Killers; Dating (Social Customs)
Major character(s): Frank Quinn, Detective—Homicide (retired), Aged Person; Jill Clark, Unemployed; Harley Renz, Police Officer (commissioner)
Time period(s): 2000s
Locale(s): New York, New York; New Jersey; Mexico City, Mexico

Summary: After the dismembered bodies of two women are discovered in New York, Police Commissioner Harley Renz asks retired homicide detective Frank Quinn and his team to investigate. Both women were shot in the heart with the same gun, and both women were sexually penetrated with a long, lubricated stake, their bodies dumped for others to find. Quinn's associates, Larry

Fedderman and Pearl Kasner, help Quinn try to identify the killer. Quinn also receives information from Jill Clark, a temp who has recently joined e-bliss.org, an on-line dating service. Jill is warned that the service has a much more sinister intent than simply matching up lonely people.

Other books by the same author:
In for the Kill, 2007
Chill of Night, 2006
Fear the Night, 2005
Darker than Night, 2004
The Night Caller, 2001

Other books you might like:
Alafair Burke, *Dead Connection*, 2007
Edward Dee, *Nightbird*, 1999
Dan Mahoney, *Black and White*, 1999
J.D. Robb, *Holiday for Death*, 1998

129

STUART MACBRIDE

Flesh House

(New York: St. Martin's, 2008)

Story type: Police Procedural; Serial Killer
Series: Logan McRae. Book 4
Subject(s): Missing Persons; Serial Killers
Major character(s): Logan McRae, Detective—Homicide; Heather Inglis, Housewife; David Insch, Detective—Homicide
Time period(s): 2000s
Locale(s): Aberdeen, Scotland

Summary: It started in 1987 with a missing mother and two other missing parents, and a suspect arrested for carving the bodies of the parents into meat. Called the Flesher by the press, the man charged with the crime was imprisoned. Twenty years later, human remains packaged as meat products are found and traced back to a particular butcher shop. What connection does this store have with Kenneth Wiseman, the man known as the Flesher who was freed from jail when his case was overthrown? As more people go missing, Heather Inglis arrives home one evening to find her husband uncon-scious; she is kidnapped. Detective Inspector David In-sch, the man who originally arrested Wiseman, is convinced Wiseman is the murderer. Logan McRae works with a large team of investigators, carefully piec-ing together evidence and information as more and more crimes occur in a terrified city.

Where it's reviewed:
Booklist, August 1, 2008, page 7
Library Journal, August 15, 2008, page 58
Mystery News, December/January 2009, page 19
Mystery Scene, Holiday 2008, page 73
Publishers Weekly, August 4, 2008, page 45

Other books by the same author:
Bloodshot, 2007
Dying Light, 2006
Cold Granite, 2005

Other books you might like:
Stephen Booth, *Scared to Live*, 2008
Denise Mina, *Field of Blood*, 2005
Ian Rankin, *Fleshmarket Alley*, 2004
Peter Robinson, *Friend of the Devil*, 2007

130

KAREN MACINERNEY

Murder Most Maine

(Woodbury, MN: Midnight Ink, 2008)

Story type: Amateur Detective
Series: Natalie Barnes. Book 3
Subject(s): Hotels and Motels; Weight Control
Major character(s): Natalie Barnes, Innkeeper, Detective—Amateur; John Quinton, Police Officer
Time period(s): 2000s
Locale(s): Cranberry Island, Maine

Summary: It's Natalie Barnes' second year as proprietor of the Gray Whale Inn on Cranberry Island off the coast of Maine. As an old skeleton is found in a lighthouse, Natalie is preparing to host a weight loss retreat, includ-ing handsome trainer Dirk DeLeon. Natalie comes across a guest, a magazine reporter, snooping in Dirk's room. She uses her passkey to check the room, and finds client files that detail Dirk's extensive use of questionable supplements. The next day, the group goes out for a walk and finds Dirk dead on the trail. A newspaper ac-count suggests that the death was the result of poison and that he might have been poisoned at the inn. Na-talie's boyfriend, John Quinton, is suspected.

Where it's reviewed:
Library Journal, November 1, 2008, page 47
Mystery News, December/January 2009, page 27
Publishers Weekly, September 22, 2008, page 42

Other books by the same author:
Dead and Berried, 2007
Murder on the Rocks, 2006

Other books you might like:
Philip R. Craig, *Death on a Vineyard Beach*, 1997
G.A. McKevett, *Cereal Killer*, 2004
Leslie Meier, *Star Spangled Murder*, 2004
Cynthia Riggs, *Deadly Nightshade*, 2001

131

SERENA MACKESY

Hold My Hand

(New York: Soho, 2008)

Story type: Haunted House
Subject(s): Single Parent Families; Evacuees
Major character(s): Bridget Sweeny, Housekeeper, Single Parent; Kieran Fletcher, Divorced Person, Bully; Lily Rickett, Spirit, Child
Time period(s): 2000s; 1940s
Locale(s): London, England; Meneglos, England; Wade-bridge, England

Summary: When single mom Bridget Sweeny is offered the live-in housekeeper position at a remote Cornish hotel, she jumps at the chance to leave London. Moving herself and her six-year-old daughter Yasmin to Rospet-roc House in Meneglos, Bridget hopes that her abusive ex-husband Kieran won't be able to find them. As Bridget settles into her new job, Yasmin begins to make new friends, including a girl named Lily. An evacuee during World War II, nine-year-old Lily disappeared from the house where Bridget and Yasmin now live. Now, Lily's ghost still haunts the old house. When Kieran tracks Bridget down, Lily intervenes and handles the situation herself.

Where it's reviewed:
Booklist, September 15, 2008, page 29
Mystery News, October/November 2008, page 9
Mystery Scene, Holiday 2008, page 73
Publishers Weekly, September 15, 2008, page 48

Other books by the same author:
Simply Heaven, 2004
The Temp, 2003
Virtue, 2000

Other books you might like:
Veronica Black, *My Name Is Polly Winter*, 1993
Deborah Grabien, *Cruel Sister*, 2006
Carol O'Connell, *Judas Child*, 1998
Betsy Thornton, *Ghost Towns*, 2002

132

KAREN MAITLAND

Company of Liars

(New York: Delacorte, 2008)

Story type: Historical/Medieval
Subject(s): Plague; Middle Ages
Major character(s): Camelot, Peddler; Narigorm, Psychic; Osmond, Artist
Time period(s): 14th century (1348)
Locale(s): England

Summary: On Midsummer's Day 1348 at the fair in Kilmington, a traveler called Camelot sees a girl being beaten. The old man breaks up the fight and learns that the girl, Narigorm, is a diviner. The man says he is on a journey to Saint John Shorne's shrine at North Marston, where he believes there's money to be made: Camelot trades in fake relics. He also believes that the journey will keep him ahead of the plague, which is rapidly advancing across the country. Before long, Camelot collects a band of fellow travelers: Narigorm, a storyteller with a swan's wing instead of an arm, a musician and his curious apprentice, a painter and his wife, and others—nine in all. As the group journeys across the land, they face harsh conditions, including death and murder. They also tell stories about how they came to be on this road, stories that may or may not be true.

Where it's reviewed:
Booklist, September 1, 2008, page 41
Library Journal, August 15, 2008, page 70
Mystery News, October/November 2008, page 23
Mystery Scene, Holiday 2008, page 70
Publishers Weekly, August 25, 2008, page 49

Other books you might like:
Ariana Franklin, *Mistress of the Art of Death*, 2007
C.L. Grace, *Saintly Murders*, 2001
Candace Robb, *The Nun's Tale*, 1995
Caroline Roe, *Remedy for Treason*, 1998

133

TIM MALEENY

Greasing the Pinata

(Scottsdale: Poisoned Pen, 2008)

Story type: Private Detective
Series: Cape Weathers. Book 3
Subject(s): Missing Persons; Crime and Criminals
Major character(s): Cape Weathers, Detective—Private; Sally Mei, Criminal (assassin); Oscar Garcia, Detective—Police
Time period(s): 2000s
Locale(s): San Francisco, California; Puerto Vallarta, Mexico

Summary: Private detective Cape Weathers is in Puerto Vallarta on the trail of a missing former California state senator and his son. They are both found dead on a resort's golf course, missing body parts. At least that's the story being peddled by Mexican police inspector Oscar Garcia, but Cape isn't convinced that the case is over. Indeed, when Cape reports back to his client, the dead men's estranged daughter and sister Rebecca, she asks him to continue his investigation and find out what was going on. The senator resigned his seat suddenly and disappeared from public view a few months earlier, ostensibly to spend more time with his family. Rebecca hasn't seen him for ten years.

Where it's reviewed:
Booklist, December 1, 2008, page 33
Deadly Pleasures, Fall 2008, page 49
Library Journal, October 1, 2008, page 48
Mystery News, February/March 2009, page 16
Publishers Weekly, September 1, 2008, page 38

Other books by the same author:
Beating the Babushka, 2007
Stealing the Dragon, 2007

Other books you might like:
Mark Coggins, *Runoff*, 2007
Robert Crais, *Sunset Express*, 1997
Forrest DeVoe Jr., *Into the Volcano*, 2006
Tom Schreck, *On the Ropes*, 2007

134

G.M. MALLIET

Death of a Cozy Writer

(Woodbury, MN: Midnight Ink, 2008)

Story type: Police Procedural
Series: Arthur St. Just. Book 1
Subject(s): Inheritance; Family Relations
Major character(s): Arthur St. Just, Detective—Police;

Violet Mildenhall Winthrop, Widow(er); Adrian Beauclerk-Fisk, Writer, Nobleman

Time period(s): 2000s

Locale(s): London, England; Newton Coombe, England; Cambridge, England

Summary: After receiving wedding announcements, the children of famed British mystery writer Sir Adrian Beauclerk-Fisk make their way to his estate, Waverly Court, in Cambridgeshire. Sir Adrian is a tyrant and takes pleasure in tormenting his children Ruthven, George, Sarah, and Albert. The four of them have every intention of talking their father out of marrying Violet Mildenhall Winthrop, a widow whose previous husband was mysteriously bludgeoned to death. Their plans change, however, when Ruthven's body is discovered in the cellar. Detective Chief Inspector Arthur St. Just is called in to investigate and soon discovers that several family members had motives to kill off the heir to the Beauclerk-Fisk fortune.

Where it's reviewed:
Deadly Pleasures, Fall 2008, page 53
Library Journal, May 1, 2008, page 45
Mystery Scene, Summer 2008, page 73
Publishers Weekly, May 19, 2008, page 39

Other books you might like:
James Anderson, *The Affair of the 39 Cufflinks*, 2003
Nancy Atherton, *Aunt Dimity Takes a Holiday*, 2003
P.D. James, *Unnatural Causes*, 1967
Rett MacPherson, *A Misty Mourning*, 2000

135

MARGARET MARON

Death's Half Acre

(New York: Grand Central, 2008)

Story type: Amateur Detective
Series: Deborah Knott. Book 14
Subject(s): Real Estate; Fathers and Daughters
Major character(s): Deborah Knott, Judge, Detective—Amateur; Dwight Bryant, Police Officer; Kezzie Knott, Aged Person, Bootlegger
Time period(s): 2000s
Locale(s): Dobbs, North Carolina; Durham, North Carolina

Summary: When Colleton County commissioner Candace Bradshaw is found dead in her home, her suicide note claims responsibility for several corrupt business deals. However, forensics declares Candace's death was a murder, and sheriff's deputy Dwight Bryant begins an investigation. Deborah Knott, Dwight's wife and a judge in Colleton County, becomes involved after learning that Candace had a file containing information about both Deborah and Deborah's father, Kezzie. Several years ago, Kezzie pulled some strings to get Deborah a seat on the bench. Now, Deborah is afraid this information will become public if she doesn't get her hands on the file. At the same time, she is suspicious of her father's recent activities. A former bootlegger, Kezzie appears to be running a scam on a controversial local preacher.

Where it's reviewed:
Booklist, May 1, 2008, page 30
Deadly Pleasures, Summer 2008, page 39
Mystery News, October/November 2008, page 27
Mystery Scene, Fall 2008, page 73
Publishers Weekly, June 9, 2008, page 34

Other books by the same author:
Hard Row, 2007
Winter's Child, 2006
Rituals of the Season, 2005
High Country Fall, 2004
Slow Dollar, 2002

Other books you might like:
Sallie Bissell, *A Darker Justice*, 2002
John Hart, *Down River*, 2007
Vicki Lane, *Old Wounds*, 2007
Justin Scott, *McMansion*, 2007

136

ANDREW MARTIN

Murder at Deviation Junction

(Boston, MA: Mariner, 2009)

Story type: Historical/Edwardian; Police Procedural
Series: Jim Stringer. Book 4
Subject(s): Railroads
Major character(s): Jim Stringer, Detective—Police; Stephen Bowman, Journalist; Ernest Shillito, Detective—Police
Time period(s): 1900s (1909)
Locale(s): Middlesbrough, England; York, England; Inverness, Scotland

Summary: In December 1909, North Eastern Railway detective Jim Stringer is traveling to York after failing to arrest Donald Clegg, a Middlesbrough footballer accused of assault. Traveling with Stringer are his wife Lydia and their young son Harry. Stringer is worried that his failure will impact his upcoming promotion, which will allow the Stringers to hire a nurse for the sickly Harry. When the body of photographer Paul Peters is discovered in the snow on the railroad tracks, Stringer finds himself investigating the young man's death. Stringer is able to recover one of Peters' cameras, stolen shortly before his death, and believes that the killer is in one of the last photographs Peters took.

Where it's reviewed:
Booklist, December 15, 2008, page 26
Library Journal, January 15, 2009, page 64
Publishers Weekly, November 17, 2008, page 46

Other books by the same author:
The Lost Luggage Porter, 2008
The Blackpool Highflyer, 2007
The Necropolis Railway, 2007

Other books you might like:
Steve Hockensmith, *On the Wrong Track*, 2007
Edward Marston, *The Railway Detective*, 2004
Larry Millett, *Sherlock Holmes and the Red Demon*, 1996
Robin Paige, *Death on the Lizard*, 2006

137

ESTEBAN MARTIN
ANDREU CARRANZA , Co-Author

The Gaudi Key
(New York: Morrow, 2008)

Story type: Religious
Subject(s): Secrets; Christianity
Major character(s): Maria Givell, Art Historian; Miguel, Scientist, Professor; Alvaro Climent, Businessman
Time period(s): 2000s (2006); 1920s (1926)
Locale(s): Barcelona, Spain; Reus, Spain; Africa

Summary: In a nursing home in Barcelona, 92-year-old Juan Givell passes on a secret to his beloved granddaughter Maria. As a child, Juan was apprenticed to the famous architect Antonio Gaudi. Juan tells Maria that Gaudi was also the Grand Master of an ancient religious organization known as the Knights of Moriah. The Knights are entrusted with the task of guarding a sacred relic. When Gaudi died in 1926, Juan was trained to be the next Grand Master. Now that Juan's health is deteriorating, he knows it is time to pass on the relic to Maria. He uses a series of puzzles to guide her to it. Aiding Maria in her search is her boyfriend Miguel, a mathematician who will have to protect both of them from a satanic cult that wants to stop the Knights of Moriah from carrying out its mission.

Where it's reviewed:
Booklist, September 1, 2008, page 55
Publishers Weekly, June 2, 2008, page 28

Other books you might like:
Steve Berry, *The Templar Legacy*, 2006
Dan Brown, *The Da Vinci Code*, 2003
Ian Caldwell, *The Rule of Four*, 2004
    Duston Thomason, co-author
Kate Mosse, *Labyrinth*, 2006

138

GUILLERMO MARTINEZ

The Book of Murder
(New York: Viking, 2008)

Story type: Psychological Suspense
Subject(s): Authors and Writers; Revenge
Major character(s): Luciana B., Secretary (typist); Kloster, Writer; Unnamed Character, Narrator
Time period(s): 2000s
Locale(s): Buenos Aires, Argentina

Summary: Ten years ago, Luciana worked for a month for a young writer—the unnamed narrator of this novel—who had broken his wrist. Unable to type, he dictated his new book to Luciana, who usually worked for another writer, a reclusive figure known only as Kloster. At the end of the month, the writer did not expect to hear from her again. Over ten years, the young writer's career stalls while Kloster becomes a bestselling mystery writer. Out of the blue, Luciana gets in touch with the writer, pleading for help. She believes that Kloster has been system-

atically murdering people close to her and that he intends to kill her. The writer listens to her story, and tries to turn it into a narrative that makes sense. Then he goes to Kloster to hear his side of the story.

Where it's reviewed:
Booklist, August 1, 2008, page 41
Publishers Weekly, July 28, 2008, page 51

Other books by the same author:
The Oxford Murders, 2005

Other books you might like:
Patricia Carlon, *The Souvenir*, 1996
Minette Walters, *The Sculptress*, 1993
Donald E. Westlake, *The Hook*, 2000
Carlos Ruiz Zafon, *The Shadow of the Wind*, 2004

139

AMANDA MATETSKY

Dial Me for Murder
(New York: Berkley, 2008)

Story type: Historical
Series: Paige Turner. Book 5
Subject(s): Crime and Criminals; Prostitution
Major character(s): Paige Turner, Journalist, Writer; Dan Street, Detective—Homicide; Sabrina Stanhope, Madam
Time period(s): 1950s (1955)
Locale(s): New York, New York

Summary: In 1955 New York, Paige Turner isn't finding it easy to be the only female investigative reporter for true crime magazine Daring Detective. When the murder of beautiful secretary Victoria Pratt is splashed all over the newspapers, Paige is determined to grab the story for herself. She receives a mysterious phone call that leads her to a posh Gramercy Park apartment. Paige learns more about the case when wealthy Sabrina Stanhope hires her to solve Victoria's murder. It turns out that Victoria was a secretary by day and a high-priced call girl by night. As her madam, Sabrina wants Victoria's killer found, but doesn't want to expose her business or her wealthy clients to scandal.

Other books by the same author:
Murder on a Hot Tin Roof, 2006
How to Marry a Murderer, 2005
Murder Is a Girl's Best Friend, 2004
Murderers Prefer Blondes, 2003

Other books you might like:
Megan Abbott, *Die a Little*, 2005
Carolyn Hart, *Letter from Home*, 2003
M.T. Jefferson, *The Victory Dance Murder*, 2002
Lise McClendon, *One O'Clock Jump*, 2001

140

PETER MAY

Snakehead
(Scottsdale: Poisoned Pen, 2009)

Story type: Police Procedural
Series: Li Yan and Margaret Campbell. Book 4

Subject(s): Illegal Immigrants; Diseases
Major character(s): Margaret Campbell, Doctor; Li Yan, Detective—Police; Felipe Mendez, Professor
Time period(s): 2000s
Locale(s): Houston, Texas; Washington, District of Columbia; Frederick, Maryland

Summary: In Texas, a sheriff's deputy discovers an abandoned truck outside a Mexican restaurant. The truck contains 98 illegal Chinese immigrants, and all of them are dead. Houston pathologist and medical examiner Margaret Campbell is called in to determine why the immigrants died. Working with Air Force Major Steve Cardiff, a fellow pathologist, Margaret discovers that all of the immigrants were injected with something shortly after arriving in the States. Meanwhile, Beijing detective Li Yan, currently working at the Chinese Embassy in Washington, DC, is sent to Houston to investigate the case. There, Li comes face to face with Margaret, his former lover who left him in China. Together they uncover a plot to infect America with a deadly flu virus.

Other books by the same author:
The Killing Room, 2008
The Critic, 2007
The Fourth Sacrifice, 2007
Extraordinary People, 2006
The Firemaker, 2005

Other books you might like:
Beverly Connor, *One Grave Too Many*, 2003
Val Davis, *Return of the Spanish Lady*, 2001
S.J. Rozan, *A Bitter Feast*, 1998
Lisa See, *Flower Net*, 1997

141

ARCHER MAYOR

The Catch

(New York: St. Martin's, 2008)

Story type: Police Procedural
Series: Joe Gunther. Book 19
Subject(s): Police Procedural; Drugs
Major character(s): Joe Gunther, Detective—Police; Sammie Martens, Detective—Police
Time period(s): 2000s
Locale(s): Rockland, Maine; Vermont; Boston, Massachusetts

Summary: Joe Gunther, the field force commander of the Vermont Bureau of Investigation, learns that a police officer has been killed in the line of duty, shot along a Vermont highway during a traffic stop. The killing is captured (in part) by a camera mounted in the officer's car, but Gunther quickly realizes that the case is much more complex that it first appears. At the same time, a drug kingpin is shot to death in Rockland, Maine. The connections between the two incidents aren't immediately apparent, but Gunther methodically tracks a web of links, including one that takes him and his team to a rooftop shootout in Boston's Dorchester neighborhood and another to his girlfriend's family, her father lost at sea and her brother, recently released from prison on a drug charge.

Where it's reviewed:
Booklist, September 1, 2008, page 53
Library Journal, August 15, 2008, page 57
Publishers Weekly, June 23, 2008, page 40

Other books by the same author:
Chat, 2007
The Second Mouse, 2006
Bellows Falls, 1997
The Skeleton's Knee, 1993
Open Season, 1988

Other books you might like:
Kate Flora, *The Angel of Knowlton Park*, 2008
Steve Hamilton, *A Stolen Season*, 2007
Donald Harstad, *The Carl Houseman Series*, 1998-
William G. Tapply, *Cutter's Run*, 1998

142

BRIAN MCGILLOWAY

Borderlands

(New York: St. Martin's, 2008)

Story type: Police Procedural
Subject(s): Drugs; Orphans
Major character(s): Benedict "Ben" Devlin, Detective—Homicide; Angela Cashell, Teenager; Caroline Williams, Detective—Police
Time period(s): 2000s
Locale(s): Ireland; Ireland, Northern

Summary: Benedict Devlin is an inspector with the Irish Garda, working along the boundary between Ireland and Northern Ireland in an area known as the borderlands. When a teenaged girl's dead body is found there, she is claimed by the Garda since she was a resident of Lifford in Ireland. Angela Cashell was no more than 16; what had happened to her? Though her father, Johnny, the local troublemaker, thinks he knows the killer, Detective Benedict Devlin is not so sure. As he and his team investigate, more and more odd things keep turning up, including another murder. Then another teen is found dead while in police custody. Are all these deaths related? Ben not only has these investigations to cope with, but the appearance of an old flame has his wife upset—and his former girlfriend's family seems to be involved in the crimes.

Where it's reviewed:
Booklist, July 1, 2008, page 41
Mystery News, December/January 2009, page 13
Mystery Scene, Fall 2008, page 75
Publishers Weekly, June 30, 2008, page 164

Other books you might like:
Stephen Booth, *Black Dog*, 2000
John Brady, *A Stone of the Heart*, 1988
Ken Bruen, *Once Were Cops*, 2008
Barry Maitland, *No Trace*, 2006

143

ROSE MELIKAN

The Blackstone Key

(New York: Simon & Schuster, 2008)

Story type: Historical/Georgian; Amateur Detective
Subject(s): Espionage; Inheritance
Major character(s): Mary Finch, Teacher, Detective—Amateur; Robert Holland, Military Personnel; Paul Deprez, Businessman, Spy
Time period(s): 18th century (1795)
Locale(s): Woodbridge, England; Lindham, England; London, England

Summary: In 1795, 20-year-old Mary Finch is surprised to receive a letter from her uncle Edward. Edward and his younger brother Richard, Mary's father, had a falling out many years ago. Mary is delighted that Edward is now reaching out to her, and asking her to visit him at his estate, the White Ladies, near Lindham, England. Upon arriving at the White Ladies, Mary discovers that Edward died recently. Just as Mary learns that she is Edward's sole heir, she also uncovers a traitorous plot involving secret codes, smugglers, and spies. As Mary tries to uncover a traitor, she relies on her new friend Captain Robert Holland, an artillery man who has secrets of his own.

Where it's reviewed:
Booklist, July 1, 2008, page 41
Deadly Pleasures, Fall 2008, page 58
Library Journal, June 1, 2008, page 83
Mystery News, August/September 2008, page 19
Mystery Scene, Fall 2008, page 77

Other books you might like:
Bruce Alexander, *Death of a Colonial*, 1999
C.S. Harris, *When Gods Die*, 2006
Kate Ross, *A Broken Vessel*, 1994
Lauren Willig, *The Masque of the Black Tulip*, 2006

144

BRAD MELTZER

The Book of Lies

(New York: Grand Central, 2008)

Story type: Action/Adventure
Subject(s): Conspiracies; Biblical Fiction
Major character(s): Cal Harper, Volunteer; Mitchell Siegel, Businessman
Time period(s): 2000s
Locale(s): Fort Lauderdale, Florida

Summary: Cal Harper works with the homeless as a volunteer in Fort Lauderdale. He meets a vagrant who turns out to be his long-lost father Lloyd. Cal and Lloyd are attacked by an assassin wielding a mysterious weapon with a past: that same gun was used in the 1932 murder of Mitchell Siegel, the father of Superman creator Jerry Siegel. All of this ties back to the very first murder of all time: Cain killing Abel. The chase involves a federal agent, a mysterious woman, a divine book that contains the secrets to immortality, and a dangerous group called The Leadership that will do anything to protect its secrets.

Where it's reviewed:
Booklist, July 1, 2008, page 5
Entertainment Weekly, September 5, 2008, page 81
Library Journal, August 1, 2008, page 70
Publishers Weekly, July 28, 2008, page 50

Other books by the same author:
The Book of Fate, 2006
The Zero Game, 2004
The Millionaires, 2002
The First Counsel, 2001
Dead Even, 1998

Other books you might like:
David Baldacci, *Saving Faith*, 1999
Dan Brown, *Angels and Demons*, 2003
Elizabeth Kostova, *The Historian*, 2005
James Rollins, *Map of Bones*, 2005

145

JOHN RAMSEY MILLER

The Last Day

(New York: Bantam Dell, 2009)

Story type: Domestic
Subject(s): Stalking; Grief
Major character(s): Natasha McCarty, Doctor; Ward McCarty, Businessman; Alice Palmer, Student—College
Time period(s): 2000s
Locale(s): Concord, North Carolina; Dillworth, North Carolina; Charlotte, North Carolina

Summary: Pediatric surgeon Natasha McCarty and her husband Ward, a successful North Carolina businessman, are still grieving over the death of their young son Barney. One year ago, Barney was accidently electrocuted. Now, both Natasha and Ward notice that Barney's things are being moved around their home. Natasha suspects that someone is drugging them; her hands have begun to shake and Ward is becoming increasingly forgetful. At work, someone sabotages Ward's computer server, sending pornographic images to their customers' e-mail addresses. As Natasha and Ward try to figure out who is destroying their lives, a man who calls himself the Watcher is stalking the McCartys and has every intention of ending their lives.

Other books by the same author:
Smoke and Mirrors, 2008
Too Far Gone, 2006
Side by Side, 2005
Upside Down, 2005
Inside Out, 2004

Other books you might like:
Linwood Barclay, *No Time for Goodbye*, 2007
Harlan Coben, *No Second Chance*, 2003
Jeffery Deaver, *The Bodies Left Behind*, 2008
Andrew Klavan, *Don't Say a Word*, 1991

146

KAYE MORGAN

Sinister Sudoku

(New York: Berkley, 2008)

Story type: Amateur Detective
Series: Liza Kelly. Book 3
Subject(s): Games; Prisoners and Prisons
Major character(s): Liza Kelly, Writer, Detective—
Amateur; Kevin Shepard, Innkeeper; Ted Everard,
Detective—Police
Time period(s): 2000s
Locale(s): Maiden's Bay, Oregon; Portland, Oregon; Otis,
Oregon

Summary: Sudoku columnist Liza Kelly has been teaching
a small class of prisoners at the Seacoast Correctional
Facility as part of an experimental program. While her
students are interested in any sort of distraction, Chris
Dalen proves to be exceptional at Sudoku puzzles. Chris
has spent several years in jail after stealing a valuable
painting. On the day Chris is released from prison, Liza
runs into him at the Killamook Inn where she's having
dinner with boyfriend Kevin Shepard. A snowstorm traps
Liza at the inn, and after arriving in her room Liza
discovers Chris's body stuffed under her mattress. State
police detective Ted Everard arrives to investigate the
murder and Liza is determined to help, even though
Everard says he doesn't want assistance from an amateur.

Where it's reviewed:
Mystery News, October/November 2008, page 27

Other books by the same author:
Murder by Numbers, 2008
Death by Sudoku, 2007

Other books you might like:
Peter Abrahams, *End of Story*, 2006
Nero Blanc, *Wrapped Up in Crosswords*, 2004
Shelley Freydont, *The Sudoku Murder*, 2007
Parnell Hall, *The Sudoku Puzzle Murders*, 2008

147

DAVID MORRELL

The Spy Who Came for Christmas

(New York: Vanguard, 2008)

Story type: Holiday Themes
Subject(s): Espionage; Russians
Major character(s): Paul Kagan, Spy; Andrei, Organized
Crime Figure; Meredith Brody, Abuse Victim
Time period(s): 2000s
Locale(s): Santa Fe, New Mexico

Summary: On a snowy Christmas Eve in Santa Fe, New
Mexico, an injured man stumbles through the crowds
and tries desperately to stay hidden. His name is Paul
Kagan, a spy for the United States government. Tucked
away beneath Kagan's coat is an infant, the son of
prominent Middle Eastern doctor Ahmed Hassan. Kagan
has been working undercover for months trying to
infiltrate the Russian mafia in the US. After Kagan and

his Russian associates kidnapped Hassan's son, Kagan
grabbed the baby and ran. Now, Kagan is being hunted
by one of his former colleagues, Andrei, and takes refuge
in a nearby home. Inside, Meredith Brody is recovering
after a beating from her alcoholic husband Ted, while
her 12-year-old son Cole stands by, determined to protect
his mother.

Where it's reviewed:
Booklist, September 15, 2008, page 31
Library Journal, October 15, 2008, page 54
Mystery Scene, Holiday 2008, page 68
Publishers Weekly, November 24, 2008, page 51

Other books by the same author:
The Chosen, 2008
Scavenger, 2007
Creepers, 2005
The Protector, 2003
Long Lost, 2002

Other books you might like:
Ken Follett, *Whiteout*, 2004
Chris Grabenstein, *Slay Ride*, 2006
Heather Graham, *The Last Noel*, 2007
Carol O'Connell, *Judas Child*, 1998

148

MARCIA MULLER

Burn Out

(New York: Grand Central, 2008)

Story type: Private Detective
Series: Sharon McCone. Book 25
Subject(s): Family; Native Americans
Major character(s): Sharon McCone, Detective—Private,
Businesswoman; Kristen Lark, Police Officer; Amy
Perez, Teenager
Time period(s): 2000s
Locale(s): Vernon, California; Carson City, Nevada; San
Francisco, California

Summary: San Francisco private investigator Sharon Mc-
Cone has left the city to recuperate at her husband's
ranch near Yosemite in California. After facing several
life-or-death situations in her line of work, McCone is
uncertain about what she wants to do with her future.
Although she is determined not to investigate anything
while on her vacation, McCone can't help but look into
the murder of Hayley Perez, the niece of her ranch
manager Ramon Perez. McCone witnessed the abuse of
Hayley's sister Amy and learns that she disappeared
soon after. When Hayley and Amy's alcoholic mother,
Miri, dies from an apparent suicide, McCone discovers
that a dark secret from the family's past may be the key
to uncovering the killer's identity.

Where it's reviewed:
Booklist, August 1, 2008, page 6
Deadly Pleasures, Fall 2008, page 51
Library Journal, August 15, 2008, page 58
Mystery Scene, Fall 2008, page 74
Publishers Weekly, July 7, 2008, page 40

Other books by the same author:
The Ever-Running Man, 2007
The Dangerous Hour, 2004
Cyanide Wells, 2003
Dead Midnight, 2002
Listen to the Silence, 2000

Other books you might like:
Linda Barnes, *Heart of the World*, 2006
Mike Doogan, *Skeleton Lake*, 2008
Stephen Greenleaf, *Strawberry Sunday*, 1999
Sara Paretsky, *Fire Sale*, 2005

149

KATHERINE NEVILLE

The Fire

(New York: Ballantine, 2008)

Story type: Mystery; Saga
Subject(s): Games; Treasure
Major character(s): Alexandra Solarin, Genius, Sports
  Figure (chess); Haidee, Teenager
Time period(s): 1820s (1822); 2000s
Locale(s): Colorado; Albania; Morocco

Summary: In 2003, chess genius Alexandra Solarin is
called home to Colorado for her mother's birthday—
which she finds odd, as her mother usually doesn't
celebrate her birthday. Her mother is Cat Velis, who appeared in Neville's 1989 first novel, *The Eight*. When
Alexandra arrives at home, she discovers that her mother
is actually missing. Her disappearance seems to be tied
to the reappearance of a chess set that once belonged to
Charlemagne, a set Alexandra's parents thought they had
scattered years ago. In 1822, young Haidee, daughter of
a sultan, must make her own dangerous journey to find
the pieces of this same chess set. Both women travel
around the world on their quests.

Where it's reviewed:
Booklist, September 1, 2008, page 53
Library Journal, September 1, 2008, page 120
Publishers Weekly, August 4, 2008, page 44

Other books by the same author:
The Magic Circle, 1998
A Calculated Risk, 1992
The Eight, 1988

Other books you might like:
Steve Berry, *The Romanov Prophecy*, 2004
Dan Brown, *The Da Vinci Code*, 2003
Greg Iles, *Footprints of God*, 2003
Arturo Perez-Reverte, *The Flanders Panel*, 2004

150

GARY NEWMAN

The Ruffian on the Stair

(New York: Soho, 2008)

Story type: Amateur Detective
Subject(s): Artists and Art; Victorian Period

Major character(s): Sebastian "Seb" Rolvenden, Writer,
  Detective—Amateur; Leah Rooney, Professor; Patri-
  cia Hague, Professor
Time period(s): 2000s
Locale(s): London, England; Wivenhoe, England;
  Colchester, England

Summary: When freelance writer Sebastian Rolvenden
receives some papers that belonged to his grandfather,
he discovers a family secret. A notebook reveals that
Seb's grandfather, also named Sebastian, had lived a
somewhat seedy life in his youth. Making the acquaintance of an Impressionist painter named Julian Rawbeck,
the elder Sebastian wrote of how he awoke after a night
of drink and drugs in 1899 to find himself lying near
Julian's bloody body. Sebastian fled the room and
returned home to his fiancee Cecily, became a vicar and
lived on the isle of Jersey. After reading the notebook
and learning that Julian Rawbeck disappeared in 1899,
Seb becomes obsessed with finding out what happened
to him.

Where it's reviewed:
Booklist, September 15, 2008, page 30
Publishers Weekly, August 25, 2008, page 54

Other books you might like:
Janet Gleeson, *The Serpent in the Garden*, 2005
Greg Iles, *Dead Sleep*, 2001
Nicholas Kilmer, *Dirty Linen*, 1999
Sarah Stewart Taylor, *O' Artful Death*, 2003

151

KAREN E. OLSON

Shot Girl

(New York: Obsidian, 2008)

Story type: Amateur Detective
Series: Annie Seymour. Book 4
Subject(s): Journalism; Stalking
Major character(s): Annie Seymour, Journalist, Detec-
  tive—Amateur; Tom Behr, Detective—Police; Vinny
  DeLucia, Detective—Private
Time period(s): 2000s
Locale(s): New Haven, Connecticut

Summary: In New Haven, Connecticut, journalist Annie
Seymour attends a colleague's bachelorette party and
runs into her ex-husband Ralph. A former reporter who
was caught fabricating stories, Ralph is now the manager
of a strip club. After hearing gunshots outside the club,
Annie discovers Ralph's body lying on the sidewalk.
When Detective Tom Behr discovers Annie's relationship to the recently deceased Ralph, and finds a gun in
her car, he takes Annie in for questioning. After the
police determine that Ralph died of a heart attack, Annie
is released. As Annie looks into who may have wanted
to shoot Ralph, she is stalked by someone from her past.

Where it's reviewed:
Mystery News, December/January 2009, page 27

Other books by the same author:
Dead of the Day, 2007
Secondhand Smoke, 2006
Sacred Cows, 2005

Other books you might like:
Jan Brogan, *Final Copy*, 2001
Cleo Coyle, *Espresso Shot*, 2008
Diane Mott Davidson, *Double Shot*, 2004
Edward Wright, *Damnation Falls*, 2008

152

P.J. PARRISH (Pseudonym of Kristy Montee and Kelly Nichols)

South of Hell

(New York: Pocket, 2008)

Story type: Private Detective
Series: Louis Kincaid. Book 9
Subject(s): Missing Persons; Family Problems
Major character(s): Joe Frye, Police Officer; Louis
   Kincaid, Detective—Private; Jake Shockey, Police
   Officer (retired)
Time period(s): 2000s
Locale(s): Ann Arbor, Michigan; Hell, Michigan; Florida

Summary: Private detective Louis Kincaid gets a mysterious call from Ann Arbor, Michigan, where he first worked as a police officer in the 1980s. A retired police officer, Jake Shockey, is looking into the case of Jean Brandt. Brandt's husband reported her missing from their Michigan farmhouse in 1981. Shockey claims Louis overlooked some vital evidence the first time around. The Brandts' daughter, only five at the time of the disappearance, has been plagued by memories of a violent killing. Intrigued and needing a paycheck, Louis heads to Ann Arbor, where the old case proves to be more complicated than it had first appeared. Along with Joe Frye, Kincaid's girlfriend, they work together to solve the case.

Other books by the same author:
A Thousand Bones, 2007
Island of Bones, 2004
Thicker than Water, 2003
Dead of Winter, 2001
Dark of the Moon, 1999

Other books you might like:
K.J. Erickson, *The Last Witness*, 2003
Tess Gerritsen, *Vanish*, 2005
Steve Hamilton, *Blood Is the Sky*, 2003
Karin Slaughter, *Indelible*, 2004

153

MICHAEL PEARCE

A Dead Man in Barcelona

(New York: Soho, 2008)

Story type: Historical; Police Procedural
Series: Sandor Seymour. Book 5
Subject(s): Riots; Family
Major character(s): Sandor Seymour, Detective—Police;
   Chantale de Lissac, Girlfriend (of Sandor); Leila
   Lockhart, Widow(er), Businesswoman
Time period(s): 1910s (1912)

Locale(s): Barcelona, Spain; Gibraltar, Spain; Tarragona,
   Spain

Summary: After receiving a tip about a British businessman who's been killed in Barcelona, Scotland Yard detective Sandor Seymour is sent to Spain to investigate. Two years earlier, in 1910, Sam Lockhart was involved in the riots known as "Tragic Week" after troops refused to serve in Spanish Morocco. Lockhart was arrested and thrown in jail. Later, Lockhart was found dead in his cell. A well-thought of and influential businessman, Seymour begins to think that Lockhart's death may have been political. Seymour's assignment allows him to reconnect with Chantale de Lissac, a half-French, half-Arab woman whom Seymour hopes to marry. Chantale's Arab background and people skills help Seymour understand the passion behind whoever killed Lockhart.

Where it's reviewed:
Mystery News, February/March 2009, page 25
Publishers Weekly, October 6, 2008, page 38

Other books by the same author:
A Dead Man in Tangier, 2007
A Dead Man in Athens, 2006
A Dead Man in Istanbul, 2005
The Point in the Market, 2005
A Dead Man in Trieste, 2004

Other books you might like:
Barbara Cleverly, *Tug of War*, 2007
David Dickinson, *Death on the Nevskii Prospekt*, 2006
David Roberts, *Bones of the Buried*, 2001
C.J. Sansom, *Winter in Madrid*, 2008

154

THOMAS PERRY

Runner

(Boston: Houghton Mifflin Harcourt, 2009)

Story type: Chase
Series: Jane Whitefield. Book 6
Subject(s): Missing Persons; Family Problems; Babies
Major character(s): Jane Whitefield, Rescuer, Guide;
   Christine Monahan, Young Woman; Richard Beale,
   Businessman
Time period(s): 2000s
Locale(s): Buffalo, New York; Minneapolis, Minnesota;
   San Diego, California

Summary: Jane Whitefield has been living a quiet life for the past five years as a surgeon's wife, hoping to start a family. When young, pregnant Christine Monahan comes to her for help in running from people trying to hurt her, Jane takes her on with mixed feelings—reluctance to go back to her old job of helping hunted people disappear, but eagerness to help someone in trouble. Pregnant by the brutal Richard Beale, Christine is being hunted by Beale's thugs. If he doesn't find her and present her and her baby to his wealthy parents, he will be disinherited. Jane moves Christine across the country, until she thinks they have shaken the pursuers. But Christine is young and does not always act wisely. Soon Beale's thugs uncover her whereabouts.

Where it's reviewed:
Booklist, December 1, 2008, page 4
Deadly Pleasures, Fall 2008, page 56
Mystery Scene, Winter 2009, page 62
Publishers Weekly, November 17, 2008, page 41

Other books by the same author:
Blood Money, 1999
The Face-Changers, 1998
Shadow Woman, 1997
Dance for the Dead, 1996
The Butcher's Boy, 1982

Other books you might like:
Lee Child, *Echo Burning*, 2001
Michael Connelly, *The Scarecrow*, 2009
Andrew Gross, *The Blue Zone*, 2008
Bill Pronzini, *The Other Side of Silence*, 2008

155

ELIZABETH PETERS

The Laughter of Dead Kings

(New York: Morrow, 2008)

Story type: Amateur Detective; Arts
Series: Vicky Bliss. Book 6
Subject(s): Mummies; Archaeology
Major character(s): Vicky Bliss, Art Historian, Detective—
   Amateur; John Tregarth, Antiques Dealer; Anton Z.
   Schmidt, Museum Curator
Time period(s): 2000s
Locale(s): Munich, Germany; London, England; Egypt

Summary: Life is fairly quiet for art historian Vicky Bliss these days. She is living and working in Munich at the National Museum under Schmidt, her indulgent boss, and seeing her longtime flame, John Tregarth, when she can get to London to visit him. One evening, John arrives unannounced. A few moments later, so does an old friend from Egypt, who informs them that a most valuable antiquity has been stolen from its secure location near Luxor, Egypt. Though John is now a respectable antiques dealer, his history has been a bit questionable, and certain persons think he might be responsible. When he is hired by the Egyptian secretary general to find the missing antiquity, he realizes that he has no choice, except that finding a stolen mummy is easier said than done.

Where it's reviewed:
Booklist, June 1, 2008, page 6
Library Journal, July 15, 2008, page 51
Mystery News, October/November 2008, page 16
Publishers Weekly, July 7, 2008, page 36

Other books by the same author:
Tomb of the Golden Bird, 2006
The Serpent on the Crown, 2005
Guardian of the Horizon, 2004
Children of the Storm, 2003
Night Train to Memphis, 1994

Other books you might like:
Jennifer Lee Carrell, *Interred with Their Bones*, 2007
Barbara Cleverly, *The Tomb of Zeus*, 2007
Lyn Hamilton, *The African Quest*, 2001
Iain Pears, *The Titian Committee*, 1991

156

CAROLINE PETIT

Deep Night

(New York: Soho, 2008)

Story type: Historical/World War II
Series: Leah Kolbe. Book 2
Subject(s): Espionage; China; War
Major character(s): Leah Kolbe, Businesswoman, Spy;
   Tokai Ito, Businessman; Stephen Albemarle,
   Diplomat, Spy
Time period(s): 1940s
Locale(s): Hong Kong, China; Macao

Summary: Hong Kong antiques dealer Leah Kolbe has just accepted a marriage proposal from her longtime boyfriend Jonathan Hawatyne when the Japanese bomb Pearl Harbor. Jonathan, a volunteer in the military, is called into service, leaving Leah alone. After Hong Kong surrenders to the Japanese, Leah flees the city and makes her way to Macao. When Leah goes to the British Embassy on Macau for help, she is hired by the consul, Stephen Albemarle, to be his assistant. Leah puts herself in great danger after agreeing to spy on Japanese businessman Tokai Ito, and even becomes his mistress to gain information about his family's manufacturing plants, but she may be sacrificing her future with Jonathan.

Where it's reviewed:
Booklist, November 15, 2008, page 20
Library Journal, December 15, 2008, page 118
Mystery News, December/January 2009, page 15
Publishers Weekly, October 6, 2008, page 36

Other books by the same author:
The Fat Man's Daughter, 2005

Other books you might like:
Holly Baxter, *Tears of the Dragon*, 2007
Lyn Hamilton, *The Chinese Alchemist*, 2007
Mo Hayder, *The Devil of Nanking*, 2005
S.J. Rozan, *The Shanghai Moon*, 2009

157

DONALD PFARRER

A Common Ordinary Murder

(New York: Random House, 2008)

Story type: Police Procedural
Subject(s): Marriage; Faith; Missing Persons
Major character(s): Steven McCord, Police Officer,
   Veteran; Nora McCord, Civil Servant; Lindy Alden,
   Nurse
Time period(s): 1980s (1985)
Locale(s): Midwest

Summary: After 20 years as a police officer, 42-year-old Steven McCord feels like he needs a change. Instead of trying to get a promotion to captain, like his wife wants him to, McCord takes night classes to become a lawyer. His profession isn't the only thing in his life McCord is thinking of changing. Tempted by the lovely Lindy Alden, a young nurse, McCord considers betraying his devoted wife Nora. As McCord suffers a mid-life crisis, he's also overseeing a murder case. Charles Carden, a World War II veteran, was recently discovered in his home, his throat slashed. As the investigation continues, McCord believes that Carden's daughter, Marie, who was arriving for a visit the night her father was killed, may have been abducted by the killers.

Where it's reviewed:
Booklist, May 1, 2008, page 24
Mystery News, December/January 2009, page 25
Publishers Weekly, June 9, 2008, page 30

Other books by the same author:
The Fearless Man: A Novel of Vietnam, 2004
Temple and Shipman, 1999
Neverlight, 1982

Other books you might like:
Michael Collins, *Lost Souls*, 2004
Donald Harstad, *Eleven Days*, 1998
John Hart, *Down River*, 2007
Steven Sidor, *Skin River*, 2004

158

MARTHA POWERS

Conspiracy of Silence

(Ipswich, MA: Oceanview, 2008)

Story type: Amateur Detective
Subject(s): Adoption; Identity, Concealed
Major character(s): Clare Prentice, Journalist, Adoptee; Nathan Hanssen, Writer, Widow(er); Jake Jorgenson, Artist
Time period(s): 2000s
Locale(s): Grand Rapids, Minnesota; Bemidji, Minnesota; Deer River, Minnesota

Summary: When Chicago journalist Clare Prentice learns that she was adopted as a young child, she is completely shocked. Rose, the woman Clare believed to be her mother, died recently. She never once mentioned anything about Clare being adopted. Curious about her birth parents, Clare follows a clue to Grand Rapids, Minnesota, to find out more. While she's there, Clare's editor gives her the assignment of interviewing reclusive writer Nathan Hanssen. Clare quickly finds out that her birth mother, Lily, was murdered, and that Jimmy, Clare's father, confessed to the crime. As Clare tries to dig up more about her family, she becomes the target of a killer who wants to silence her.

Where it's reviewed:
Publishers Weekly, September 1, 2008, page 36

Other books by the same author:
Death Angel, 2006
Bleeding Heart, 2000
Sunflower, 1998
False Pretenses, 1991
The Runaway Heart, 1990

Other books you might like:
Barbara D'Amato, *White Male Infant*, 2002
Kate Flora, *Chosen for Death*, 1994
Patricia MacDonald, *Mother's Day*, 1994
Ralph McInerny, *Blood Ties*, 2005

159

BILL PRONZINI

The Other Side of Silence

(New York: Walker, 2008)

Story type: Psychological Suspense
Subject(s): Family Relations; Loneliness
Major character(s): Rick Fallon, Security Officer, Divorced Person; Casey Dunbar, Crime Victim, Parent
Time period(s): 2000s
Locale(s): Death Valley; Las Vegas, Nevada; Laughlin, Nevada

Summary: After his wife leaves him and files for divorce, Rick Fallon loads up his Jeep and heads for Death Valley. A loner, Fallon finds peace in the desert. In Warm Springs Canyon, he comes across a crippled Toyota Camry. He finds what appears to be a suicide note and photographs of a young boy. He searches the area and, through pure luck, finds Casey Dunbar, still barely alive. He gets her out of the desert and on the road to recovery, learning that her husband kidnapped their son and hired a thug to beat and rape Casey. Fallon sets out to find the boy for her, a trail that takes him to Las Vegas and beyond.

Where it's reviewed:
Booklist, September 1, 2008, page 56
Deadly Pleasures, Fall 2008, page 56
Publishers Weekly, August 4, 2008, page 46

Other books by the same author:
Fever, 2008
The Alias Man, 2004
A Wasteland of Strangers, 1997
Blue Lonesome, 1995
Hoodwink, 1981

Other books you might like:
Lee Child, *Echo Burning*, 2001
Michael Connelly, *The Scarecrow*, 2009
Thomas Perry, *Runner*, 2009
Minette Walters, *The Dark Room*, 1996

Mystery

160

ANDREW PYPER

The Killing Circle

(New York: St. Martin's, 2008)

Story type: Psychological Suspense
Subject(s): Writing; Missing Persons
Major character(s): Patrick Rush, Writer; Sam Rush, Child; Angela Whitmore, Writer
Time period(s): 2000s
Locale(s): Toronto, Ontario, Canada

Summary: Journalist Patrick Rush is still grieving the loss of his wife to cancer when he decides to join a writers' circle in order to try fiction. When a member of the group is killed in a car accident (according to an account in a small town newspaper), Patrick takes parts of the story she had shared with the group, a story about a serial killer named the Sandman, and completes it, becoming a bestselling novelist. But then the "dead" writer turns up at a book signing. She tells him that she has felt that she was being watched, something that Patrick and others in the group have also felt. Another member of the group is found murdered. Patrick senses that he and his son Sam are being followed, and that Sam is in danger. Then there are the scary emails Patrick begins receiving from the real Sandman.

Where it's reviewed:
Booklist, August 1, 2008, page 44
Publishers Weekly, July 7, 2008, page 38

Other books by the same author:
The Wildfire Season, 2006
The Trade Mission, 2002
Lost Girls, 2000

Other books you might like:
Peter Abrahams, *End of Story*, 2006
Peter Lovesey, *The Circle*, 2005
Val McDermid, *Killing the Shadows*, 2001
Donald E. Westlake, *The Hook*, 2000

161

FREDERICK RAMSAY

Stranger Room

(Scottsdale: Poisoned Pen, 2008)

Story type: Police Procedural
Series: Ike Schwartz. Book 4
Subject(s): Family; Civil War
Major character(s): Isaac "Ike" Schwartz, Police Officer; Karl Hedrick, FBI Agent, Police Officer; Jonathan Lydell IV, Writer
Time period(s): 1860s (1864); 2000s
Locale(s): Picketsville, Virginia; Bolton, Virginia

Summary: Jonathan Lydell IV comes from an old Southern family and still occupies the same Virginia mansion that his ancestors lived in during the Civil War. When freelance writer Anton Grotz, a lodger in Lydell's home, is found dead in his room, Picketsville sheriff Ike Schwartz is called in to investigate. Grotz was staying in the stranger room of Lydell's mansion. In the days of stagecoach travel, homeowners would rent out a stranger room to overnight guests; the room was connected to the house, but had a private door so the guests wouldn't disturb the homeowners. Schwartz knows the history of the Lydell house and is aware of a similar murder that occurred in the same room in 1864. As Schwartz and his deputy, FBI agent Karl Hedrick, investigate Grotz's death, they discover that the previous murder is key to solving this one.

Where it's reviewed:
Booklist, May 1, 2008, page 42
Library Journal, July 15, 2008, page 48
Mystery News, October/November 2008, page 16
Mystery Scene, Fall 2008, page 66
Publishers Weekly, June 9, 2008, page 34

Other books by the same author:
Buffalo Mountain, 2007
Judas: The Gospel of Betrayal, 2007
Impulse, 2006
Secrets, 2005
Artscape, 2004

Other books you might like:
Michael Bowen, *Collateral Damage*, 1999
Tom Dyja, *The Moon in Our Hands*, 2005
Ronald Levitsky, *The Love That Kills*, 1991
Peter Lovesey, *Bloodhounds*, 1996

162

IAN RANKIN

Exit Music

(New York: Little, Brown, 2008)

Story type: Police Procedural
Series: Inspector Rebus. Book 17
Subject(s): Murder; Retirement
Major character(s): John Rebus, Detective—Homicide; Siobhan Clarke, Detective—Homicide; Morris Gerald Cafferty, Criminal
Time period(s): 2000s (2006)
Locale(s): Edinburgh, Scotland

Summary: Days before Detective Inspector John Rebus is scheduled to retire, he is tying up some loose ends when he and Detective Sergeant Siobhan Clarke are ordered to investigate the death of a Russian poet. Alexander Todorov was living in exile in Edinburgh. What at first appears to be a random mugging that turned violent soon becomes more complicated when Rebus and Clarke learn that several Russian businessmen are in town negotiating with Scottish politicians and bankers. One of the Scottish businessmen dealing with the Russians is Big Ger Cafferty, a local criminal and Rebus' long-time nemesis. Rebus is determined to close the case before his own time runs out.

Where it's reviewed:
Booklist, August 1, 2008, page 6
Entertainment Weekly, September 26, 2008, page 97
Library Journal, August 15, 2008, page 58
Publishers Weekly, July 7, 2008, page 35

Other books by the same author:
The Naming of the Dead, 2007
Fleshmarket Alley, 2005
A Question of Blood, 2004
Resurrection Men, 2003
The Falls, 2001

Other books you might like:
K.C. Constantine, *Cranks and Shadows*, 1995
John Harvey, *Cold in Hand*, 2008
Stuart MacBride, *Cold Granite*, 2005
Denise Mina, *Deception*, 2004

163

JAMES REESE

The Dracula Dossier

(New York: Morrow, 2008)

Story type: Historical/Victorian
Subject(s): Serial Killers; Authors and Writers
Major character(s): Bram Stoker, Writer, Businessman; Thomas Hall Caine, Writer; Francis Tumblety, Doctor
Time period(s): 2000s (2007); 1880s (1888)
Locale(s): London, England; New York, New York; Edinburgh, Scotland

Summary: When a letter arrives at a New York publishing house in 2007, it promises a tale of real-life horror and suspense written by author Bram Stoker in 1888. Before he wrote *Dracula*, Stoker was the manager of the Lyceum Theatre Company in London, which was headed by the famous actor Henry Irving. At a party one day, Stoker is encouraged by Lady Jane Wilde, mother of Oscar Wilde, to attend a meeting of the Order of the Golden Dawn. It is at this meeting that Stoker witnesses a horrifying ritual involving an unethical American doctor, Francis Tumblety. Soon after, Stoker spies Tumblety in the Whitechapel district of London. When the murders of several prostitutes occur shortly thereafter, Stoker and several of his friends attempt to track down Tumblety, whom they believe may be Jack the Ripper.

Where it's reviewed:
Booklist, September 15, 2008, page 24
Library Journal, September 15, 2008, page 47
Publishers Weekly, August 18, 2008, page 38

Other books by the same author:
The Witchery, 2006
The Book of Spirits, 2005
The Book of Shadows, 2002

Other books you might like:
Gyles Brandreth, *Oscar Wilde and a Game Called Murder*, 2008
Edward B. Hanna, *The Whitechapel Horrors*, 1992
Anne Perry, *The Whitechapel Conspiracy*, 2001
Robert J. Randisi, *Curtains of Blood*, 2002

164

STELLA RIMINGTON

Illegal Action

(New York: Knopf, 2008)

Story type: Espionage
Series: Liz Carlyle. Book 3
Subject(s): Russians; Espionage
Major character(s): Elizabeth Carlyle, Spy; Nikita Brunovsky, Businessman; Greta Darnshof, Editor
Time period(s): 2000s
Locale(s): London, England; Paris, France; Cork, Ireland

Summary: MI5 agent Liz Carlyle isn't thrilled to be transferred from Counter-Terrorism to the Counter-Espionage branch of operations. Believing it to be a demotion of sorts, Liz is surprised to learn of all the foreign spies operating in London, having thought that espionage ended with the Cold War. Liz is assigned to a case involving a plot to kill Nikita Brunovsky, a Russian billionaire living in London who has been openly criticizing Vladimir Putin. Going undercover as an art student studying some of the works in Brunovsky's home, Liz soon becomes the target of the traitor in Brunovsky's entourage. She has to work quickly to uncover the identity of the traitor after she is attacked herself.

Where it's reviewed:
Booklist, May 1, 2008, page 35
Entertainment Weekly, July 11, 2008, page 77
Mystery News, October/November 2008, page 21
Publishers Weekly, May 12, 2008, page 36

Other books by the same author:
Secret Asset, 2007
At Risk, 2005

Other books you might like:
Gavin Lyall, *The Crocus List*, 1985
Francine Mathews, *The Cutout*, 2001
Greg Rucka, *A Gentleman's Game*, 2004
Daniel Silva, *Moscow Rules*, 2008

165

WENDY ROBERTS

Devil May Ride

(New York: Obsidian, 2008)

Story type: Paranormal
Series: Ghost Dusters. Book 2
Subject(s): Ghosts; Cults
Major character(s): Sadie Novak, Businesswoman, Psychic; Zack Bowman, Worker; Scott Reed, Journalist
Time period(s): 2000s
Locale(s): Seattle, Washington; Kirkland, Washington; Redmond, Oregon

Summary: Sadie Novak, medium and owner of the trauma cleaning company Scene-2-Clean, becomes the target of a Seattle biker gang when she discovers a large amount of cash hidden in a wall during a cleaning job. On the same day, she and employee Zack Bowman discover a newborn baby boy in the remains of a meth lab. The baby's mother, now a ghostly spirit, tells Sadie that she gave her baby willingly to a dark ritual. After her brother Brian committed suicide six years ago, Sadie learned that she could see and communicate with the dead. Sadie learns that since she interrupted the ritual, the Witigo cultists will need another baby, and Sadie's pregnant sister Dawn is due any day now.

Where it's reviewed:
Mystery News, February/March 2009, page 11

Other books by the same author:
The Remains of the Dead, 2007
Dating Can Be Deadly, 2005

Other books you might like:
Madelyn Alt, *The Trouble with Magic*, 2006
Charlie Huston, *The Mystic Arts of Erasing All Signs of Death*, 2009
Alice Kimberly, *The Ghost and Mrs. McClure*, 2004
Victoria Laurie, *What's a Ghoul to Do?*, 2007

166

PRISCILLA ROYAL

Forsaken Soul

(Scottsdale: Poisoned Pen, 2008)

Story type: Historical/Medieval
Series: Prioress Eleanor. Book 5
Subject(s): Religion; Monasticism

Summary: During the summer of 1273, Eleanor, the head of Tyndal Priory, is besieged with problems. Sister Juliana, the new anchoress who lives in religious seclusion and dispenses advice, has refused to be waited on by women. She requests that a monk keep her company. Ralf the Crowner, a friend of Eleanor's, has returned to Tyndal a widower with a newborn child to care for. Eleanor is also battling her own feelings for one of the monks at the priory, Brother Thomas. When Martin the Cooper is poisoned at the local inn while upstairs with his whore, Ivetta, Eleanor offers her assistance to track down the murderer. As Ralf soon discovers, Martin was fiercely disliked in Tyndal and many people had reason to want him dead.

Where it's reviewed:
Publishers Weekly, June 2, 2008, page 31

Other books by the same author:
Justice for the Damned, 2007
Sorrow Without End, 2006
Tyrant of the Mind, 2004
Wine of Violence, 2003

Other books you might like:
Margaret Frazer, *The Maiden's Tale*, 1998
Paul L. Moorcraft, *The Anchoress of Shere*, 2002
Sharan Newman, *Death Comes As Epiphany*, 1994
Peter Tremayne, *The Haunted Abbot*, 2004

167

SANDRA RUTTAN

The Frailty of Flesh

(New York: Leisure, 2008)

Story type: Police Procedural
Series: Nolan, Hart and Tain Mysteries. Book 2
Subject(s): Missing Persons; Family
Major character(s): Ashlyn Hart, Police Officer; Tain, Police Officer; Craig Nolan, Police Officer
Time period(s): 2000s
Locale(s): Port Moody, British Columbia, Canada; Vancouver, British Columbia, Canada; Coquitlam, British Columbia, Canada

Summary: Royal Canadian Mounted Police constables Hart and Tain are called to a park in Port Moody, near Vancouver, when the body of a young boy is discovered. Four-year-old Jeffrey Reimer was beaten to death. Jeffrey's older brother, 11-year-old Christopher, is a witness and tells the police that their 16-year-old sister Shannon is the one who committed the horrific crime. Now, Shannon has disappeared and her friends tell the police that she wanted to run away. When Hart and Tain take Christopher home and inform his parents about Jeffrey, the Reimers act coldly and impede the investigation at every turn. Meanwhile, Hart's boyfriend, Constable Craig Nolan, is given the difficult assignment of reviewing evidence from an old murder case, a case on which his father had worked.

Other books by the same author:
What Burns Within, 2008
Suspicious Circumstances, 2007

Other books you might like:
Elisabeth Bowers, *No Forwarding Address*, 1981
Laurence Gough, *Memory Lane*, 1996
Irvine Welsh, *Crime*, 2008
Laurali R. Wright, *Strangers Among Us*, 1996

168

MARCUS SAKEY

Good People

(New York: Dutton, 2008)

Story type: Psychological Suspense
Subject(s): Infertility; Money
Major character(s): Tom Reed, Spouse; Anna Reed, Spouse
Time period(s): 2000s
Locale(s): Chicago, Illinois

Summary: Tom and Anna Reed are overextended. Both have good jobs and they own a brownstone in downtown Chicago, part of which they rent out. But Anna's prolonged infertility treatments are taking a toll both on their bank account and their marriage. One night they smell something burning in their tenant's apartment. They are forced to break in. They find not only a dead tenant but also $400,000 in cash, which seems like the answer to their prayers. It's far from it, of course, as

Tom and Anna have to discover their true priorities as they fight for their lives.

Where it's reviewed:
Deadly Pleasures, Summer 2008, page 53
Entertainment Weekly, August 15, 2008, page 69
Mystery News, October/November 2008, page 11
Mystery Scene, Fall 2008, page 79
Publishers Weekly, June 16, 2008, page 31

Other books by the same author:
At the City's Edge, 2008
The Blade Itself, 2007

Other books you might like:
Harlan Coben, *Gone for Good*, 2002
Michael Connelly, *Void Moon*, 1999
Michael Koryta, *Envy the Night*, 2008
Scott Smith, *A Simple Plan*, 1993

169

BART SCHNEIDER

The Man in the Blizzard

(New York: Three Rivers, 2008)

Story type: Private Detective
Subject(s): Music and Musicians; Neo-Nazis
Major character(s): August "Augie" Boyer, Detective—Private, Drug Addict; Bobby Sabbatini, Detective—Police; Elizabeth Odegard, Musician
Time period(s): 2000s
Locale(s): St. Paul, Minnesota; Minneapolis, Minnesota; Woodbury, Minnesota

Summary: Shortly before the Republican National Convention comes to the Twin Cities, violinist Elizabeth Odegard hires Augie Boyer to find out if her husband Perry is engaged in illegal business practices. Augie, a private investigator who spends his time smoking weed and memorizing poetry, agrees to take on Elizabeth's case, but is suspicious of her actions. Augie discovers that Perry is dealing in rare violins that were stolen by the Nazis in World War II. As Augie investigates Perry and Elizabeth's uncle, a Neo-Nazi named Frederick Kunz, he uncovers an assassination plot that is supposed to take place during a protest rally at which Augie's daughter, a radical singer known as Minnesota Rose, is performing.

Where it's reviewed:
Booklist, August 1, 2008, page 44
Library Journal, July 15, 2008, page 67
Publishers Weekly, June 23, 2008, page 36

Other books by the same author:
Beautiful Inez, 2005
Secret Love, 2001
Blue Bossa, 1998

Other books you might like:
Reggie Nadelson, *Red Hook*, 2006
Roger L. Simon, *The Big Fix*, 1973
Domenic Stansberry, *The Ancient Rain*, 2008
Richard Thompson, *Fiddle Game*, 2008

170

DEBORAH SHARP

Mama Does Time

(Woodbury, MN: Midnight Ink, 2008)

Story type: Amateur Detective
Series: Mace Bauer. Book 1
Subject(s): Mothers and Daughters; Identity, Concealed
Major character(s): Mason "Mace" Bauer, Animal Lover, Detective—Amateur; Carlos Martinez, Detective—Police, Widow(er); Emma Jean Valentine, Receptionist
Time period(s): 2000s
Locale(s): Himmarshee, Florida

Summary: After receiving a phone call from her mother Rosalee, Mace Bauer rushes to the police station in Himmarshee, Florida. Mace learns that a body was discovered in the trunk of her mother's car. Detective Carlos Martinez, a new addition to the Himmarshee P.D. believes that Rosalee is guilty of murder and throws her in jail. Mace decides that the only way she can prove Rosalee's innocence is to find the real killer. The victim was Jim Albert, aka Jimmy "the Weasel" Albrizio, a New York mobster. Mace believes her mother's boyfriend, Salvatore Provenza, who's also a New Yorker, is involved in Albrizio's death. To complicate matters, Mace's ex, a cowboy named Jeb Ennis, has returned to town and it looks like he has a motive to kill Albrizio as well.

Where it's reviewed:
Deadly Pleasures, Fall 2008, page 50
Mystery News, February/March 2009, page 11
Mystery Scene, Fall 2008, page 68

Other books you might like:
Nora Charles, *Hurricane Homicide*, 2006
Anne George, *Murder Makes Waves*, 1998
Rita Lakin, *Getting Old Is Murder*, 2005
Mary Saums, *Thistle and Twigg*, 2008

171

ZOE SHARP

Third Strike

(New York: St. Martin's, 2008)

Story type: Action/Adventure
Series: Charlie Fox. Book 7
Subject(s): Fathers and Daughters; Conspiracies
Major character(s): Charlie Fox, Bodyguard; Richard Foxcroft, Doctor; Sean Meyer, Bodyguard
Time period(s): 2000s
Locale(s): New York, New York

Summary: Bodyguard Charlie Fox's father, Richard Foxcroft, has never approved of her profession, and the two are estranged. When Charlie one day turns on the television and sees her father, a prominent surgeon in the U.K., admit to a drinking problem and medical negligence that resulted in a death, she knows that despite their problems she can't let him go down. Besides, she suspects he's being set up by the government. When she calls home, even her mother is behaving strangely. Helped by her boss and boyfriend Sean Meyer, the quest to clear her father's name takes the pair all over Manhattan and Brooklyn.

Where it's reviewed:
Booklist, September 15, 2008, page 31
Deadly Pleasures, Fall 2008, page 52
Mystery News, February/March 2009, page 26
Publishers Weekly, August 11, 2008, page 27

Other books by the same author:
Road Kill, 2005
First Drop, 2004
Hard Knocks, 2003
Riot Act, 2002
Killer Instinct, 2001

Other books you might like:
Lee Child, *The Enemy*, 2004
Robert Crais, *L.A. Requiem*, 1999
Barry Eisler, *Killing Rain*, 2005
Greg Rucka, *Keeper*, 1996

172

RICK SHEFCHIK

Green Monster

(Scottsdale: Poisoned Pen, 2008)

Story type: Private Detective
Series: Sam Skarda. Book 2
Subject(s): Sports/Baseball; Blackmail
Major character(s): Sam Skarda, Detective—Private; Louis Kenwood, Businessman, Wealthy; Heather Canby, Assistant
Time period(s): 2000s
Locale(s): Boston, Massachusetts; Los Angeles, California; Caracas, Venezuela

Summary: Boston Red Sox owner Louis Kenwood is still riding high a few years after the Red Sox ended their 86-year losing streak by winning the 2004 World Series. That is, until Kenwood receives a letter claiming that their 2004 victory was fixed. The letter demands $50 million, or this information will be released to the public. Kenwood, fearful of the public's reaction to this blatant lie, hires private investigator Sam Skarda to track down the blackmailer. With the help of Kenwood's executive assistant Heather Canby, Skarda finds two baseball players who performed questionably during the World Series and could be the potential blackmailers. What Skarda and Canby find, however, is a tale of gambling and kidnapping, and a missing son who's returned from the dead.

Where it's reviewed:
Booklist, July 1, 2008, page 42
Mystery News, October/November 2008, page 21
Mystery Scene, Fall 2008, page 75
Publishers Weekly, July 21, 2008, page 145

Other books by the same author:
Amen Corner, 2007

Other books you might like:
Crabbe Evers, *Fear in Fenway*, 1993
Robert B. Parker, *Mortal Stakes*, 1975
Mary-Ann Tirone Smith, *Dirty Water*, 2008
  Jere Smith, co-author
Troy Soos, *Murder at Fenway Park*, 1994

173

LYNN SHOLES
JOE MOORE , Co-Author

The 731 Legacy

(Woodbury, MN: Midnight Ink, 2008)

Story type: Theological
Series: Cotten Stone. Book 4
Subject(s): Biological Warfare; Suspense
Major character(s): Cotten Stone, Journalist; John Tyler, Religious, Archaeologist; Chung Moon Jung, Scientist
Time period(s): 2000s
Locale(s): New York, New York; Pyongyang, Korea, North; Rome, Italy

Summary: A dying man staggers into the Satellite News Network lobby in New York and asks to speak to senior investigative correspondent Cotten Stone. Cotten arrives just in time to hear the man's final words: "Black Needles." Tracking down others who have recently died in a similar way, Cotten learns that Black Needles was the code name for a Japanese biochemical warfare project during World War II. Trying to discover who is responsible for unleashing Black Needles today, Cotten is distracted when the unrequited love of her life, Cardinal John Tyler, contracts the deadly virus. To save John's life, Cotten must face an evil enemy, the Son of the Dawn, who wants Cotten because the blood of angels flows through her body.

Other books by the same author:
The Hades Project, 2007
Last Secret, 2006
The Grail Conspiracy, 2005

Other books you might like:
John Case, *The First Horseman*, 1998
Tim Downs, *Plague Maker*, 2006
Chuck Hogan, *The Blood Artists*, 1998
Daniel Kalla, *Pandemic*, 2005

174

JEFFREY M. SIGER

Murder in Mykonos

(Scottsdale: Poisoned Pen, 2009)

Story type: Police Procedural
Subject(s): Serial Killers; Missing Persons
Major character(s): Andreas Kaldis, Police Officer; Annika Vanden Haag, Tourist; Tassos Stamatos, Detective—Homicide
Time period(s): 2000s

Locale(s): Mykonos, Greece; Syros, Greece; Delos, Greece

Summary: Former Athens homicide detective Andreas Kaldis isn't happy about his promotion to chief of police on the island of Mykonos. To Kaldis, it feels like a punishment, being forced to police an island of tourists and rich party-goers. Not long after Kaldis' arrival, the mutilated body of a woman is discovered in a church. Kaldis calls in the homicide unit and teams up with veteran investigator Tassos Stamatos. An investigation of the church reveals several more bodies and Kaldis and Stamatos realize that a serial killer has been murdering women on Mykonos for several years now. Meanwhile, Dutch tourist Annika Vanden Haag is missing and Kaldis and Stamatos realize that Annika fits the profile of the serial killer's victims.

Where it's reviewed:
Booklist, November 15, 2008, page 21
Library Journal, November 1, 2008, page 47
Publishers Weekly, September 29, 2008, page 62

Other books you might like:
Paris Aristides, *The Viper's Kiss*, 2001
Robert Goddard, *Into the Blue*, 1991
Helen MacInnes, *The Double Image*, 1966
Mary Stewart, *The Moonspinners*, 1962

175

DANIEL SILVA

Moscow Rules

(New York: Putnam, 2008)

Story type: Espionage Thriller
Series: Gabriel Allon. Book 8
Subject(s): Terrorism; Artists and Art
Major character(s): Gabriel Allon, Spy, Artist; Elena Kharkov, Spouse (of Ivan); Ivan Kharkov, Criminal
Time period(s): 2000s
Locale(s): Jerusalem, Israel; Moscow, Russia; Saint-Tropez, France

Summary: In Umbria, Gabriel Allon's honeymoon with his new wife Chiara is interrupted when he is asked to go to Rome to meet with an informer. Just as the meeting is about to take place, the informant, Russian newspaperman Boris Ostrovsky, drops dead. Gabriel learns that Ostrovsky had a message for him regarding possible terrorist attacks on the West and Israel. Ostrovsky's source was Elena Kharkov, whose husband Ivan plans on selling weapons to al-Qaeda. When Gabriel discovers that Elena collects paintings by Mary Cassatt, he lures Elena to an English estate with a rare Cassatt painting and asks for her help. Elena agrees to smuggle out information on Ivan's business dealings, but when she is caught she has to rely on Gabriel to rescue her.

Where it's reviewed:
Booklist, June 1, 2008, page 8
Library Journal, July 15, 2008, page 68
Publishers Weekly, May 26, 2008, page 37

Other books by the same author:
The Secret Servant, 2007
The Messenger, 2006
Prince of Fire, 2005
A Death in Vienna, 2004
The Confessor, 2003

Other books you might like:
Anna Blundy, *Vodka Neat*, 2008
Brian Freemantle, *Bomb Grade*, 1996
Brent Ghelfi, *Volk's Shadow*, 2008
Gerald Seymour, *Traitor's Kiss*, 2006

176

SHELIA SIMONSON

Buffalo Bill's Defunct

(McKinleyville, CA: Perseverance, 2008)

Story type: Police Procedural
Subject(s): Native Americans
Major character(s): Margaret "Meg" McLean, Librarian, Police Officer; Robert Neill, Detective—Police; Carol Tichnor, Store Owner
Time period(s): 2000s
Locale(s): Klalo, Washington

Summary: Meg McLean is the new head librarian in the small Washington town of Klalo. As Meg is moving into her new home, she discovers a Native American artifact in her garage. Unfortunately, when the police arrive on the scene, they discover a dead body. Meg's next-door neighbor, sheriff's investigator Rob Neill, is in charge of the investigation, and is familiar with the petroglyph Meg found. Ten years ago, Rob bungled a case involving stolen artifacts similar to this one. This time Rob intends to get it right. Recognizing Meg's research skills, Rob deputizes Meg so that she can help him with the investigation. When two other murders occur, Rob soon realizes that there is more to this case than the looting of artifacts.

Where it's reviewed:
Publishers Weekly, July 21, 2008, page 146

Other books by the same author:
Malarkey, 1997
Meadowlark, 1996
Mudlark, 1993
Skylark, 1992
Larkspur, 1990

Other books you might like:
Margaret Coel, *The Drowning Man*, 2006
Micah S. Hackler, *Legend of the Dead*, 1995
Mary Morgan, *Deeper Waters*, 2002
Naomi Stokes, *The Tree People*, 1995

177

JOANNA CAMPBELL SLAN

Paper, Scissors, Death

(Woodbury, MN: Midnight Ink, 2008)

Story type: Amateur Detective
Subject(s): Crafts; Mothers and Daughters

Major character(s): Kiki Lowenstein, Artisan; Chad Detweiler, Detective—Police
Time period(s): 2000s
Locale(s): St. Louis, Missouri

Summary: When quiet, mousy Kiki Lowenstein is informed that her husband George has been found dead, she knows there is more going on than meets the eye. Concerned about how her daughter, Anya, is coping with her dad's death, she finds herself in a battle with George's mother over who can take better care of the 11-year-old. As she continues to investigate as best she can, she finds herself depending more and more on attractive Detective Detweiler who is leading the investigation into George's death. As Kiki tries to turn her scrapbooking hobby into a source of income, someone breaks into her house. She soon finds herself under arrest, charged with the murder of George's girlfriend.

Where it's reviewed:
Booklist, September 1, 2008, page 56
Mystery News, October/November 2008, page 28

Other books you might like:
Laura Childs, *Keepsake Crimes*, 2003
Mary Ellen Hughes, *Paper-Thin Alibi*, 2008
Cathy Pickens, *Hush My Mouth*, 2008
Sharon Short, *Death of a Domestic Diva*, 2003

178

MARY-ANN TIRONE SMITH
JERE SMITH , Co-Author

Dirty Water

(Kingston, RI: Hall of Fame, 2008)

Story type: Police Procedural
Subject(s): Sports/Baseball; Illegal Immigrants
Major character(s): Rocky Patel, Detective—Homicide; Marty Flanagan, Police Officer; George Sanchez, Real Estate Agent
Time period(s): 2000s
Locale(s): Boston, Massachusetts; Bristol, Connecticut; Newport Beach, California

Summary: As members of the Red Sox change in the clubhouse at Fenway Park, the sound of crying alerts them to the presence of an abandoned baby. After he is taken to the hospital, the nurses name the baby Ted Williams, and a search begins for his identity. Shortly after the discovery of baby Ted, the body of Cinthia Sanchez is discovered, beaten and drowned, in a Boston park. After learning of Cinthia's death, the Sanchez family inquires about Cinthia's son Arturo and the police realize that baby Ted is actually Arturo Sanchez. Homicide detective Rocky Patel is given the job of discovering who killed Cinthia and why Arturo was kidnapped. Rocky receives help from an unexpected source when an anonymous Red Sox blogger discusses details about the case on his Web Site.

Where it's reviewed:
Booklist, September 1, 2008, page 40
Publishers Weekly, September 1, 2008, page 39

Other books you might like:
Peter Abrahams, *The Fan*, 1995
Crabbe Evers, *Fear in Fenway*, 1993
Rick Shefchik, *Green Monster*, 2008
Troy Soos, *Murder at Fenway Park*, 1994

179

MEHMET MURAT SOMER

The Kiss Murder

(New York: Penguin, 2008)

Story type: Amateur Detective
Series: Hop-Ciki-Yaya. Book 2
Subject(s): Homosexuality/Lesbianism; Secrets
Major character(s): Unnamed Character, Homosexual, Computer Expert; Sofya, Entertainer; Huseyin, Taxi Driver
Time period(s): 2000s
Locale(s): Istanbul, Turkey

Summary: Computer consultant by day, drag queen by night is the life of the transvestite who owns part of an Istanbul nightclub. An Audrey Hepburn look-alike, she plays hostess to the underworld criminals who frequent the club. When one of her "girls," an older performer named Buse, asks for help, the unnamed hostess agrees to listen to her story. Buse apparently had an affair with a prominent Turkish businessman, and has the letters and photos to prove it. Blackmailers want the mementos from Buse's relationship, and are willing to kill to get it. When Buse turns up dead, the blackmailers target the nightclub hostess. Determined to find out who killed Buse, she turns to Huseyin, a taxi driver who is infatuated with her, and Sofya, a rival, for help.

Where it's reviewed:
Mystery Scene, Holiday 2008, page 72
Publishers Weekly, October 27, 2008, page 36

Other books by the same author:
The Prophet Murders, 2008

Other books you might like:
Jason Goodwin, *The Snake Stone*, 2007
Donna Leon, *Dressed for Death*, 1994
    published as *The Anonymous Venetian* in the UK
Barbara Nadel, *Belshazzar's Daughter*, 2003
Michael Pearce, *A Dead Man in Istanbul*, 2005

180

JILL SORENSON

Crash Into Me

(New York: Bantam, 2009)

Story type: Romantic Suspense
Subject(s): Law Enforcement; Family
Major character(s): Sonora "Sonny" Vasquez, FBI Agent; Benjamin Fortune, Sports Figure, Crime Suspect; James Matthews, Teenager
Time period(s): 2000s

Locale(s): San Diego, California; Quantico, Virginia; Tijuana, Mexico

Summary: FBI Special Agent Sonny Vasquez goes undercover in the beach community of La Jolla, California, to catch a killer. Young women are turning up dead, and the evidence points to famed professional surfer Ben Fortune as the killer. Ben's wife Olivia was killed a few years ago and now the police wonder if that was the start of Ben's career as a murderer. When Sonny saves Ben's daughter Carly from drowning, she and Ben are immediately attracted to each other. Sonny tries to stay focused on her assignment, but soon finds herself falling in love with Ben. When the body of Carly's best friend Lisette is discovered, the police question Ben, and Sonny worries that she may be involved with a killer.

Where it's reviewed:
Publishers Weekly, December 15, 2008, page 40

Other books by the same author:
Dangerous to Touch, 2008

Other books you might like:
Michael Craven, *Body Copy*, 2009
Karen Robards, *Beachcomber*, 2003
Jeff Shelby, *Killer Swell*, 2005
Don Winslow, *The Dawn Patrol*, 2008

181

MICKEY SPILLANE
MAX ALLAN COLLINS , Co-Author

The Goliath Bone

(Orlando: Harcourt, 2008)

Story type: Private Detective
Series: Mike Hammer. Book 14
Subject(s): Archaeology; Marriage
Major character(s): Mike Hammer, Detective—Private, Fiance(e) (of Velda); Velda Sterling, Secretary, Fiance(e) (of Mike); Charlene Hurley, Professor
Time period(s): 2000s
Locale(s): New York, New York; Marathon, Florida

Summary: As private investigator Mike Hammer is leaving a bar one snowy New York night, he walks into a situation involving Middle Eastern terrorists. Hammer spots a gunman going after Matthew Hurley and Jenna Sheffield, two New York University graduate students who've just picked up a very important package. After rescuing them, Hammer learns that the package contains a huge femur bone belonging to the biblical Goliath. Matthew and Jenna hire Hammer and his fiancee Velda Sterling to protect them. Hammer soon discovers that everyone is interested in Goliath's bone, from Hollywood to Islamic terrorists, and some of them are willing to kill to get it. This novel was completed by Max Allan Collins after Spillane's death in 2006.

Where it's reviewed:
Booklist, September 1, 2008, page 5
Deadly Pleasures, Fall 2008, page 47
Library Journal, October 1, 2008, page 48
Mystery News, December/January 2009, page 20
Mystery Scene, Holiday 2008, page 74

Other books by the same author:
Black Alley, 1996
The Girl Hunters, 1962
Vengeance Is Mine, 1950
I the Jury, 1947

Other books you might like:
J.A. Konrath, *Dirty Martini*, 2007
Bill Napier, *Splintered Icon*, 2005
James Rollins, *Map of Bones*, 2005
Andrew Vachss, *Another Life*, 2008

182

PATRICIA SPRINKLE

Daughter of Deceit

(New York: Avon, 2008)

Story type: Amateur Detective
Series: Katharine Murray. Book 3
Subject(s): Genealogy; Secrets
Major character(s): Katharine Murray, Genealogist, Detective—Amateur; Bara Holcomb Weidenauer, Socialite; Murdoch Payne, Cousin
Time period(s): 2000s
Locale(s): Atlanta, Georgia

Summary: Katharine Murray is busy putting her treasured Atlanta home back together after vandals almost destroyed it months ago. When Katharine meets socialite Bara Holcomb Weidenauer, she gets talked into researching some old military medals of Bara's late father Winnie, who served in World War II. Bara's been going through a rough period in her life. Her husband Foley is divorcing her and trying to take Bara for everything she has. So when Foley is murdered, the police naturally suspect Bara. Katharine believes that Bara is innocent, and that the key to proving that lies in the history of Bara's family.

Where it's reviewed:
Mystery News, December/January 2009, page 27

Other books by the same author:
What Are You Wearing to Die?, 2008
Guess Who's Coming to Die?, 2007
Sins of the Father, 2007
Death on the Family Tree, 2006
Did You Declare the Corpse?, 2006

Other books you might like:
Anne George, *Murder Runs in the Family*, 1997
Rett MacPherson, *Thicker than Water*, 2005
Celestine Sibley, *A Plague of Kinfolks*, 1995
Kathy Hogan Trocheck, *Homemade Sin*, 1994

183

J.B. STANLEY

Stiffs and Swine

(Woodbury, MN: Midnight Ink, 2008)

Story type: Amateur Detective
Series: Supper Club. Book 4

Subject(s): Food; Contests
Major character(s): James Henry, Librarian, Detective—Amateur; Lucy Hanover, Police Officer, Detective—Amateur; Gillian O'Malley, Businesswoman, Widow(er)
Time period(s): 2000s
Locale(s): Quincy's Gap, Virginia; Hudsonville, Virginia

Summary: Known as the "Flab Five," the members of a supper club in Quincy's Gap, Virginia, are also well-known for their amateur sleuthing skills. When the supper club members are invited to be guest judges at a nearby barbecue contest in Hudsonville, they are only too happy to say yes. There, they meet contestant Jimmy Lang, an obnoxious ex-felon. When Jimmy dies of propane poisoning, one of the club members, Gillian O'Malley, is arrested for the murder. The other members, librarian James, sheriff's deputy Lucy, mailman Bennett, and teacher Lindy, work together to find Jimmy's killer. The situation becomes more complicated when James' girlfriend, Murphy Alistair, a newspaper reporter, arrives in Hudsonville.

Where it's reviewed:
Booklist, October 15, 2008, page 28

Other books by the same author:
Chili Con Corpses, 2008
A Deadly Dealer, 2007
Fit to Die, 2007
A Fatal Appraisal, 2006
Carbs and Cadavers, 2006

Other books you might like:
John J. Lamb, *The Mournful Teddy*, 2006
Laura Levine, *The PMS Murder*, 2006
Kathryn Lilley, *Dying to Be Thin*, 2007
Lou Jane Temple, *Revenge of the Barbeque Queens*, 1997

184

MARY STANTON

Defending Angels

(New York: Berkley, 2008)

Story type: Paranormal; Amateur Detective
Series: Beaufort and Company. Book 1
Subject(s): Angels; Law
Major character(s): Brianna Winston-Beaufort, Lawyer, Detective—Amateur; Antonia Winston-Beaufort, Student—College; Gabriel Striker, Detective—Private
Time period(s): 2000s
Locale(s): Savannah, Georgia

Summary: Lawyer Bree Winston-Beaufort has moved to Savannah after inheriting her late uncle Franklin's law practice. Bree receives a mysterious phone call from billionaire Benjamin Skinner. Thinking that the call is a prank, Bree calls Skinner's home only to be told that he died that afternoon. When Bree seeks out her law school mentor, Professor Armand Cianquino, for answers, she receives one she does not expect. Cianquino informs Bree that she will be practicing Celestial Law and representing clients, such as Benjamin Skinner, in Celestial Court. Not only does Bree have to find out who

killed Skinner, but she also has to plead his case in Celestial Court, where Skinner is on trial for greed.

Where it's reviewed:
Publishers Weekly, October 13, 2008, page 41

Other books you might like:
Nancy Atherton, *Aunt Dimity's Christmas*, 1999
Mignon F. Ballard, *Angel at Troublesome Creek*, 1999
Casey Daniels, *Tombs of Endearment*, 2007
Alice Kimberly, *The Ghost and Mrs. McClure*, 2004

185

JAMES SWAIN

The Night Stalker

(New York: Ballantine, 2008)

Story type: Private Detective
Series: Jack Carpenter. Book 2
Subject(s): Serial Killers; Fathers and Sons
Major character(s): Jack Carpenter, Detective—Private; Abb Grimes, Prisoner; Ron Cheeks, Detective—Police
Time period(s): 2000s
Locale(s): Starke, Florida; Fort Lauderdale, Florida; Dania, Florida

Summary: Ex-cop Jack Carpenter now works as a private detective, specializing in finding missing children in Florida. Jack's current client is death row inmate Abb Grimes, a convicted serial killer who's asked Jack to find his abducted grandson, three-year-old Sampson. Jack discovers that Sampson's mother, Heather Rinker, is a childhood friend of his daughter Jessie's. Agreeing to take the case, Jack learns that the main suspect is Sampson's father Jed. Although the police believe that Jed may be continuing Abb's legacy of violence, Jack doesn't believe that the young man is guilty. His search for Sampson leads to an Internet chat group that gives tips for would-be child abusers. The grisly murder of Abb's lawyer forces Jack to work quickly to find Sampson and clear Jed's name.

Where it's reviewed:
Booklist, October 1, 2008, page 28
Mystery News, December/January 2009, page 21
Publishers Weekly, August 18, 2008, page 41

Other books by the same author:
Midnight Rambler, 2007
Deadman's Bluff, 2006
Deadman's Poker, 2006
Mr. Lucky, 2005
Loaded Dice, 2004

Other books you might like:
Lisa Miscione, *The Darkness Gathers*, 2003
Mark Nykanen, *Search Angel*, 2005
Nancy Pickard, *The Whole Truth*, 2000
John Shannon, *The Concrete River*, 1996

186

MARCIA TALLEY

Dead Man Dancing

(New York: Severn House, 2008)

Story type: Amateur Detective
Series: Hannah Ives. Book 7
Subject(s): Dancing; Marriage
Major character(s): Hannah Ives, Detective—Amateur, Survivor (of cancer); Ruth, Relative (sister of Hannah), Fiance(e) (of Hutch); Hutch, Fiance(e) (of Ruth), Dancer
Time period(s): 2000s
Locale(s): Annapolis, Maryland

Summary: Hannah's sister Ruth is engaged to Hutch, a skilled ballroom dancer. Ruth wants to be able to keep up with him at their wedding, so she signs up for dance lessons and convices Hannah to as well. When they get to their first lesson, it's apparent the instructor and Hutch are old friends. However, Hutch and Ruth dance so well that the studio encourages them to audition for a television dancing show. Ruth is attacked, forcing Hutch to find a new partner. Someone is killed on the night of the competition. Hannah steps in to find the killer and help save her sister's marriage.

Where it's reviewed:
Booklist, October 1, 2008, page 27
Mystery News, February/March 2009, page 28

Other books by the same author:
Through the Darkness, 2006
This Enemy Town, 2005
In Death's Shadow, 2004
Unbreathed Memories, 2000
Sing It to Her Bones, 1999

Other books you might like:
Heather Graham, *Dead on the Dance Floor*, 2004
Jane Haddam, *Skeleton Key*, 2000
Nancy Pickard, *But I Wouldn't Want to Die There*, 1993
Kathy Hogan Trocheck, *Midnight Clear*, 1998

187

HEATHER TERRELL

The Map Thief

(New York: Ballantine, 2008)

Story type: Adventure
Series: Mara Coyne. Book 2
Subject(s): Archaeology; Historical
Major character(s): Mara Coyne, Lawyer; Ben Coleman, Archaeologist; Ma Zhi, Cartographer
Time period(s): 2000s; 15th century
Locale(s): New York, New York; Xi'an, China; Lisbon, Portugal

Summary: In the 1420s, Ma Zhi is chosen to be a cartographer on a sea voyage around the world. Even though all records of the trip are to be destroyed, Chinese Admiral Zheng He had Zhi create a map of the expedition's findings. Today, wealthy art collector Richard Tobias hires Mara Coyne to find Zhi's map. Tobias is funding an archaeology dig in China, headed by Ben Coleman. Coleman found the map, but it was stolen from the site. Mara, whose firm recovers stolen art, understands why the ancient map is so valuable; it would be the first map in history to correctly portray the entire world. Mara teams up with Ben to identify the thief and recover the map before it makes its way into the hands of an unethical collector and is lost forever.

Where it's reviewed:
Booklist, June 1, 2008, page 51
Library Journal, July 15, 2008, page 68
Publishers Weekly, April 28, 2008, page 109

Other books by the same author:
The Chrysalis, 2007

Other books you might like:
Lyn Hamilton, *The Chinese Alchemist*, 2007
James Rollins, *Map of Bones*, 2005
S.J. Rozan, *The Shanghai Moon*, 2009
Lisa See, *Dragon Bones*, 2003

188

TERRI THAYER

Old Maid's Puzzle

(Woodbury, MN: Midnight Ink, 2008)

Story type: Amateur Detective
Series: Dewey Pellicano. Book 2
Subject(s): Quilts; Friendship
Major character(s): Dewey Pellicano, Store Owner, Detective—Amateur; Buster Healy, Detective—Homicide; Gussie Johnston, Aged Person, Widow(er)
Time period(s): 2000s
Locale(s): San Jose, California

Summary: Dewey Pellicano inherited her mother's quilt shop, Quilter Paradiso, and has spent the last few months trying to make the store her own. This isn't easy, especially with Dewey's sister-in-law acting like she's in charge of the family business. During an evening quilting class, Dewey is informed by the police that a body was found in the alley behind her store. The police question everyone in Quilter Paradiso, and Dewey discovers that the police believe the victim, Frank Bascomb, was poisoned. With Dewey trying to prepare her store for its 20th anniversary sale, the last thing she needs is a murder scaring off customers. As Dewey begins to unravel the threads of the mystery, what she discovers leads her to one of her mother's old friends.

Other books by the same author:
Stamped Out, 2008
Wild Goose Chase, 2008

Other books you might like:
JoAnna Carl, *The Chocolate Bridal Bash*, 2006
Mary Daheim, *The Alpine Quilt*, 2005
Monica Ferris, *Crewel World*, 1999
Earlene Fowler, *Fool's Puzzle*, 1994

189

JOHAN THEORIN

Echoes from the Dead

(New York: Delacorte, 2008)

Story type: Amateur Detective
Subject(s): Missing Persons; Suspense
Major character(s): Julia Davidsson, Nurse, Detective—Amateur; Gerlof Davidsson, Aged Person; Nils Kant, Crime Suspect
Time period(s): 1970s (1972); 1990s
Locale(s): Marnas, Sweden; Stenvik, Sweden; Gothenburg, Sweden

Summary: In the summer of 1972, five-year-old Jens Davidsson goes missing on the Swedish island of Oland. Jens slipped out of the house while his grandmother slept, and his mother Julia and grandfather Gerlof were away. No trace of Jens was ever found, until now. Twenty years later, Gerlof receives a child's sandal in the mail, Jens' sandal. Julia returns to Stenvik and hopes that she will finally find the answers she desperately needs regarding her son's disappearance. Gerlof believes that Nils Kant may have something to do with Jens' disappearance. A local man who killed two German soldiers on the island during World War II, Nils has become a frightful figure who supposedly roams Oland at night.

Where it's reviewed:
Booklist, October 1, 2008, page 28
Deadly Pleasures, Fall 2008, page 43
Library Journal, November 1, 2008, page 48
Mystery News, December/January 2009, page 22
Mystery Scene, Holiday 2008, page 71

Other books you might like:
Arnaldur Indridason, *Jar City*, 2004
Stieg Larsson, *The Girl with the Dragon Tattoo*, 2008
Henning Mankell, *Before the Frost*, 2005
Jo Nesbo, *The Redbreast*, 2007

190

WILL THOMAS

The Black Hand

(New York: Touchstone, 2008)

Story type: Private Detective; Historical/Victorian
Series: Barker and Llewelyn. Book 5
Subject(s): Gangs; Organized Crime
Major character(s): Cyrus Barker, Detective—Private; Thomas Llewelyn, Detective—Private
Time period(s): 1880s (1885)
Locale(s): London, England

Summary: When two Italian assassins are found dead and stuffed in a barrel in the Thames, Cyrus Barker, private enquiry agent, and his apprentice, Thomas Llewelyn, are called to the scene. Accompanying the bodies to the morgue, the two find another corpse, that of Sir Alan Bledsoe, the director of the East and West India docks. All three have been murdered by a Sicilian criminal society calling itself the Mafia. Members of the Mafia are trying to take over the docks and force out the other crime gangs in the East End of London. The government enlists Barker's help in resolving the crimes, but it seems whoever is masterminding the Mafia knows exactly what Barker is up to. Soon both Barker and Thomas receive the notorious Black Hand notes, threatening their lives.

Where it's reviewed:
Booklist, May 1, 2008, page 18
Deadly Pleasures, Summer 2008, page 57
Mystery News, October/November 2008, page 18
Mystery Scene, Summer 2008, page 80
Publishers Weekly, May 26, 2008, page 41

Other books by the same author:
The Hellfire Conspiracy, 2007
The Limehouse Text, 2006
To Kingdom Come, 2005
Some Danger Involved, 2004

Other books you might like:
Bruce Alexander, *The Color of Death*, 2000
Maureen Jennings, *Except the Dying*, 1997
Laurie R. King, *The Beekeeper's Apprentice*, 1994
Anne Perry, *Buckingham Palace Gardens*, 2008

191

AIMEE THURLO
DAVID THURLO , Co-Author

Coyote's Wife

(New York: Forge, 2008)

Story type: Police Procedural; Indian Culture
Series: Ella Clah. Book 13
Subject(s): Cultural Conflict; Technology
Major character(s): Ella Clah, Detective—Police; Justine Goodluck, Detective—Police
Time period(s): 2000s
Locale(s): New Mexico

Summary: When a worker for a technology company planning to bring satellite phone service to the Navajo Reservation dies in a wood-cutting accident, there are just enough things off-kilter to make Ella Clah and her cousin Justine, detectives with the Navajo Tribal Police, suspect that the death was not an accident. StarTalk, the satellite phone company, has been experiencing vandalism, and growing hostility from traditional Navajos toward the company results in additional bad feelings. When a powerful member of the tribe, who is also the mother-in-law of the head of the phone company, is attacked, Ella has her hands full. She is also coping with family issues: her daughter, Dawn, has received a scholarship to an excellent boarding school off the reservation.

Where it's reviewed:
Booklist, September 1, 2008, page 53
Publishers Weekly, July 14, 2008, page 45

Other books by the same author:
Turquoise Girl, 2007
Mourning Dove, 2006
White Thunder, 2005
Wind Spirit, 2004
Tracking Bear, 2003

Other books you might like:
Margaret Coel, *Blood Memory*, 2008
James D. Doss, *Snake Dreams*, 2008
Steven F. Havill, *The Fourth Time Is Murder*, H2008
Kirk Mitchell, *Cry Dance*, 1999

192

MARGARET TRUMAN

Murder Inside the Beltway

(New York: Ballantine, 2008)

Story type: Police Procedural
Series: Capital Crimes. Book 24
Subject(s): Prostitution; Political Thriller
Major character(s): Matthew Jackson, Detective—Homicide; Mary Hall, Detective—Homicide; Jerrold "Jerry" Rollins, Lawyer
Time period(s): 2000s
Locale(s): Washington, District of Columbia

Summary: Homicide detectives Walter Hatcher, Matt Jackson, and Mary Hall are investigating the death of Rosalie Curzon, a Washington, DC, call girl. Without her clients' knowledge, Rosalie videotaped her encounters. After recognizing several people on one of Rosalie's videotapes, the detectives wonder if one of Rosalie's high-powered clients killed her. As the police continue their investigation, Jackson and Hall become involved in a kidnapping case. Samantha, the seven-year-old daughter of Jerry Rollins, was kidnapped after a family outing. Rollins is a political advisor to presidential candidate Robert Colgate. When the kidnappers request a particular videotape as the ransom, Jackson and Hall realize that the kidnapping is connected to Rosalie's murder.

Where it's reviewed:
Mystery News, December/January 2009, page 29
Publishers Weekly, September 22, 2008, page 39

Other books by the same author:
Murder on K Street, 2007
Murder at the Opera, 2006
Murder at the Washington Tribune, 2005
Murder at Union Station, 2004
Murder at Ford's Theatre, 2002

Other books you might like:
James Grippando, *The Abduction*, 1998
Brad Meltzer, *The Tenth Justice*, 1997
Michele Mitchell, *Our Girl in Washington*, 2006
George P. Pelecanos, *Hell to Pay*, 2002

193

ELAINE VIETS

Murder with All the Trimmings

(New York: Obsidian, 2008)

Story type: Holiday Themes; Amateur Detective
Series: Josie Marcus. Book 4
Subject(s): Shopping; Parent and Child

Major character(s): Josie Marcus, Detective—Amateur, Consultant (mystery shopper); Nathan "Nate" Weekler, Convict; Doreen, Businesswoman
Time period(s): 2000s
Locale(s): St. Louis, Missouri; Maplewood, Missouri

Summary: Josie Marcus is a single mom in St. Louis who supports herself and her nine-year-old daughter Amelia with her income as a mystery shopper. When Josie is assigned to rate two year-round Christmas stores, she is dismayed. One of the Christmas stores is owned by Doreen, Josie's boyfriend Mike's ex-girlfriend. Doreen is also the mother of his surly teenage daughter Heather. As if Josie didn't have enough to deal with, her ex-boyfriend Nate unexpectedly shows up on her doorstep. Josie had told Amelia that her father was dead, instead of explaining that Nate was in jail for dealing drugs. Josie now has to handle her daughter's anger at being lied to. When Nate falls ill and dies after eating a chocolate cake from one of the Christmas stores, Josie needs to discover who poisoned Nate and why.

Other books by the same author:
Clubbed to Death, 2008
An Accessory to Murder, 2007
Murder with Reservations, 2007
High Heels Are Murder, 2006
Murder Unleashed, 2006

Other books you might like:
Donna Andrews, *Six Geese A-Slaying*, 2008
Jennifer Apodaca, *Ninja Soccer Moms*, 2004
Linda Barnes, *Heart of the World*, 2006
Joan Hess, *Death by the Light of the Moon*, 1992

194

MICHAEL WALTERS

The Shadow Walker

(New York: Berkley, 2008)

Story type: Police Procedural
Series: Inspector Nergui. Book 1
Subject(s): Serial Killers; Kidnapping
Major character(s): Inspector Nergui, Police Officer, Spy; Drew McLeish, Detective—Police; Doripalam, Police Officer
Time period(s): 2000s
Locale(s): Ulan Baatar, Mongolia; Dalanzadgad, Mongolia

Summary: In Ulan Baatar, Mongolia, a serial killer is littering the streets with bodies. When a British citizen, geologist Ian Ransom, is brutally killed, the Mongolian government allows a British detective, Chief Inspector Drew McLeish, to assist in the investigation. Working with Nergui, the former head of the Serious Crimes Team and currently a part of the Ministry of Justice and Internal Affairs, and Nergui's successor Doripalam, McLeish is quickly brought up to speed. Shortly after McLeish's arrival another victim is found; this time it is a police officer. After McLeish and Nergui travel into Mongolia's interior, they begin to see a connection between the murders and Mongolia's large supply of natural resources. When McLeish is kidnapped, Nergui and Doripalam have to work quickly to uncover the serial killer's identity before McLeish becomes his next victim.

Where it's reviewed:
Booklist, July 1, 2008, page 43
Library Journal, July 15, 2008, page 48
Publishers Weekly, June 16, 2008, page 35

Other books you might like:
James Church, *A Corpse in the Koryo*, 2006
Colin Cotterill, *The Coroner's Lunch*, 2004
Eliot Pattison, *The Skull Mantra*, 1999
Qiu Xiaolong, *Death of a Red Heroine*, 2002

195

BETTY WEBB

The Anteater of Death

(Scottsdale: Poisoned Pen, 2008)

Story type: Amateur Detective
Series: Gunn Zoo Mystery. Book 1
Subject(s): Zoos; Relationships
Major character(s): Theodora "Teddy" Bentley, Zoo Keeper, Detective—Amateur; Joe Rejas, Police Officer, Widow(er); Jeanette Gunn-Harrill, Socialite, Widow(er)
Time period(s): 2000s
Locale(s): Gunn Landing, California; San Sebastian, California

Summary: After a late-night fundraiser at the Gunn Landing Zoo in California, the body of wealthy real-estate broker Grayson Harrill is discovered in the giant anteater exhibit, his skin ripped from his body. Zookeeper Theodora "Teddy" Bentley discovers Grayson's body and defends the anteater, Lucy, when it is believed that Lucy killed Grayson. When a bullet is found in Grayson's body, Sheriff Joe Rejas, Teddy's former high school sweetheart, enlists her help in questioning the zoo staff. Someone becomes uncomfortable with Teddy's sleuthing, however, and a violent attack sends Teddy to the hospital. Determined to continue with her investigation, Teddy learns that the wealthy of Gunn Landing are keeping some deadly secrets.

Where it's reviewed:
Booklist, November 1, 2008, page 26
Library Journal, October 1, 2008, page 48
Mystery News, December/January 2009, page 29
Mystery Scene, Holiday 2008, page 68
Publishers Weekly, September 22, 2008, page 41

Other books by the same author:
Desert Cut, 2008
Desert Run, 2006
Desert Shadows, 2004
Desert Wives, 2003
Desert Noir, 2001

Other books you might like:
Edie Claire, *Never Sorry*, 1999
Alison Glen, *Trunk Show*, 1995
Ann Littlewood, *Night Kill*, 2008
Mary Willis Walker, *Zero at the Bone*, 1991

196

MELINDA WELLS   (Pseudonym of Linda Palmer)

Death Takes the Cake

(New York: Berkley, 2009)

Story type: Amateur Detective
Series: Della Cooks. Book 2
Subject(s): Cooks and Cooking; Competition
Major character(s): Della Carmichael, Cook, Detective—Amateur; Nicholas D'Martino, Journalist; Addison Jordan, Television
Time period(s): 2000s
Locale(s): Santa Monica, California; Los Angeles, California

Summary: As a way to boost the ratings for her cable television cooking show, Della Carmichael agrees to take part in a cake-baking competition. While the winner will receive $25,000, Della is reluctant to participate when she learns that the competition is being sponsored by the Reggi-Mixx Cake Company. Not only do Reggi-Mixx cake mixes taste terrible, but Della also knows the owner of the company, Regina Davis, from college. Della helped prove that Regina was a thief, stealing money out of other girls' dorm rooms. When Della arrives at the cooking site late one evening, she discovers Regina's body, her head lying in a bowl of cake batter. Della begins to investigate Regina's death with the help of her new love interest, crime reporter Nicholas D'Martino.

Other books by the same author:
Killer Mousse, 2008

Other books you might like:
Sandra Balzo, *Grounds for Murder*, 2007
Diane Mott Davidson, *Tough Cookie*, 2000
Jerrilyn Farmer, *Mumbo Gumbo*, 2003
Joanne Fluke, *Strawberry Shortcake Murder*, 2001

197

JERI WESTERSON

Veil of Lies

(New York: St. Martin's, 2008)

Story type: Historical/Medieval
Series: Crispin Guest. Book 1
Subject(s): Knights and Knighthood
Major character(s): Crispin Guest, Knight (tarnished)
Time period(s): 14th century (1384)
Locale(s): London, England

Summary: Crispin Guest plotted against Richard II. As a result, he's lost everything—his rank, his honor, his patron and his home. Nicholas Walcote, the richest mercer in London, summons Guest and asks him to determine whether his wife is faithful. That evening, Guest follows Philippa Walcote and witnesses an unusual tryst. When he returns the next morning to report to Nicholas Walcote, he finds the man dead inside a locked room. Unwilling to trust the sheriff, Philippa hires Guest to find a missing relic, a scrap of cloth that was used to wipe tears from Christ's face on his way to the cross.

It's said that anyone in the presence of the relic must tell the truth. Guest does not trust Philippa, but he needs the money, so he accepts the job. Others are also on the trail of the relic, including enemies of England.

Where it's reviewed:
Booklist, October 1, 2008, page 30
Library Journal, October 1, 2008, page 48
Mystery News, December/January 2009, page 18
Mystery Scene, Holiday 2008, page 69
Publishers Weekly, September 1, 2008, page 38

Other books you might like:
Michael Clynes, *The Relic Murders*, 1996
    Pseudonym of Paul Doherty
Ariana Franklin, *Grave Goods*, 2009
Susanna Gregory, *A Bone of Contention*, 1997
Karen Maitland, *Company of Liars*, 2008

198

DARRYL WIMBERLEY

Kaleidoscope

(New Milford, CT: Toby, 2008)

Story type: Historical/Roaring Twenties
Subject(s): Carnivals; Money
Major character(s): Jack Romaine, Gambler, Widow(er);
    Arno Becker, Murderer; Oliver Bladehorn, Organized
    Crime Figure
Time period(s): 1920s (1929)
Locale(s): Cincinnati, Ohio; Tampa, Florida

Summary: In 1929, gambler Jack Romaine is unable to pay off his debts and is forced to work for Cincinnati gangster Oliver Bladehorn. Bladehorn tells Romaine that he'll pay off his debts if Romaine will recover some stolen property for him. Romaine is supposed to meet Sally Price, who knows where the stolen goods are, but arrives too late at the workhouse where she was released. When Sally is killed, a lead sends Romaine to an off-season camp for carnies outside Tampa, Florida. Romaine gets a job at the camp and inquires about a man named Alex Goodman, his only lead in the case. Everyone clams up at the mention of Alex's name. Unfortunately, a killer named Arno Becker is also looking for Bladehorn's property. Becker has no qualms about killing whomever he must to find it.

Where it's reviewed:
Library Journal, August 15, 2008, page 77
Mystery News, October/November 2008, page 11
Publishers Weekly, July 14, 2008, page 47

Other books by the same author:
Pepperfish Keys, 2007
The King of Colored Town, 2007
Dead Man's Bay, 2001
Strawman's Hammock, 2001

Other books you might like:
Robert Edmond Alter, *Carny Kill*, 1966
Loren D. Estleman, *Whiskey River*, 1990
Craig Holden, *The Jazz Bird*, 2002
Cathie John, *Little Mexico*, 2000

199

DAVE ZELTSERMAN

Small Crimes

(New York: Serpent's Tail, 2008)

Story type: Psychological Suspense
Subject(s): Law Enforcement; Organized Crime
Major character(s): Joe Denton, Police Officer (former),
    Addict; Dan Pleasant, Police Officer
Time period(s): 2000s
Locale(s): Bradley, Vermont

Summary: Joe Denton readily admits that he is a crooked cop, cocaine user, and gambling degenerate. He has just been released from jail after serving seven years for arson, attempted murder, and maiming District Attorney Phil Coakley. Those actions occurred when Denton was destroying incriminating evidence. His former boss, Sheriff Dan Pleasant, tells Denton that he now has to "take care of" either mobster Manny Vessey or Coakley because Vessey is about to confess to a litany of crimes that will implicate Pleasant, Denton, and many other law officers. Denton doesn't want to kill either man. Instead of leaving town, he tries to find other means of silencing Vessey. His actions bring serious harm to several innocent people.

Where it's reviewed:
Booklist, August 1, 2008, page 47
Publishers Weekly, August 11, 2008, page 29

Other books by the same author:
Bad Thoughts, 2007
Fast Lane, 2004

Other books you might like:
James M. Cain, *Double Indemnity*, 1936
Massimo Carlotto, *The Goodbye Kiss*, 2006
Jim Thompson, *The Killer Inside Me*, 1952
Charles Willeford, *Miami Blues*, 1984

Romance Fiction in Review
by
Kristin Ramsdell

"Romance has been elegantly defined as the offspring of fiction and love."

—Benjamin Disraeli

"Love is life. And if you miss love, you miss life."

—Leo Buscaglia

Buscaglia might not have been talking about fiction when he made that statement, but he couldn't have captured the heart of the romance genre more succinctly if he'd tried. The idea that love relationships are the most important things in life and that love really can conquer all—at least to some degree—is at the center of every romance; and while the stories can take many forms and are becoming increasingly diverse, the belief in the power and importance of love still underlies them all.

Diversity, in content and style, as well as in method of delivery, is currently a driving force within romance. Not only does the genre continue to make room for stories that range across the board, including everything from the comfortably traditional to the dangerously edgy, but the delivery systems are evolving as well, and romances are now reaching readers in an increasing variety of audio and e-book formats (some complete with visual or video enhancements), as well as in the more traditional print. However, as inclusive, all-encompassing, and adaptable as the romance genre is, it is still the love story and its satisfactory resolution that accounts for the basic appeal of the genre.

At the moment, we are in the midst of an economic downturn, in many respects unlike anything experienced since the Great Depression of the 1930s. Everything is being affected and the publishing industry is no exception. One only has to look at some of the industry blogs or online newsletters and take note of the cuts, layoffs, and various restructurings to see how bad things have gotten. The 2008 preliminary statistics (see statistics section below) highlight this decline. How this will affect the romance genre remains to be seen; however, people often look for temporary escape during hard times (e.g., consider the popularity of musical comedy films and historical romances during the 30s and early 40s),

and providing hopeful, optimistic, love-filled stories, where a safe and happy ending is assured, is something that the romance genre does better than any other. And the readers know it.

A Genre Overview

As usual, romance has continued to evolve in both expected and unexpected ways, retaining and refining popular themes and series, while also taking a riskier path and experimenting with edgier ideas and formats. Although each subgenre changes and develops in its own way, there are a few trends that stretch across the entire romance genre and cannot be limited to one particular subgenre.

One of these genre-spanning trends is humor and for some years it has infected subgenres across the board. Slapstick or subtle, magical or mundane, lighthearted or laced with danger, humor adds charm and a sense of comic relief to romance of all types. MaryJanice Davidson's paranormal romp *Fish out of Water*, Jayne Castle's quirky psychic Futuristic *Dark Light*, and Holly Jacob's small town heartwarmer *Once upon a Thanksgiving*, are some of the many current examples.

Hot books are still, well, hot; and except for the Inspirationals and a few traditionally sweet lines, all subgenres have seen a gradual increase in sensuality levels and sexual explicitness in recent years. Style, tone, and language vary greatly and can range from the discreetly sensual to those that border on pure erotica. Incidentally, erotica, which is not romance because the focus is on the sex rather than the romantic relationship between the protagonists, remains popular but demand appears to be leveling off.

Diversity of all kinds continues to be reflected within the genre; and while there are lines that are devoted to specific groups, often defined by ethnicity or age, romances, in general, are increasingly including characters of a wide variety of ethnicities, sexualities, ages, and religious persuasions as a matter of course. Generally seen as recognition of the diversity of the United

States as a whole, this also may be thought of as the romance genre's coming of age.

Although there are various paranormal or fantasy subgenres, it is worth noting that many supernatural elements and characters slide across the boundaries of other romance subgenres, and while they might not be strictly considered as hardcore "Paranormal," they might appeal to readers who enjoy a bit of fantasy with their romance. Heather Graham's Flynn Brothers series, Cait London's Psychic Sisters Series, and Shari Anton's Magic series are only some that might qualify.

Series and linked books of all kinds remain popular, and although series may be getting shorter according to some sources, trilogies are still all the rage. In fact, nearly half of the books in this latest volume are connected to a series in some way. Cathy Maxwell's *A Seduction at Christmas*, first in her Scandals and Seductions series; Annette Mahon's *Holiday Dreams*, second in her Matchmaker Quilt series; and Debbie Macomber *8 Sandpiper Way*, the eighth in her Cedar Cove series are three examples of the many that exist.

Format, also, cuts across all romance subgenres and does not discriminate among types. E-books and downloadable audio books of romances of all varieties, especially those by popular authors, are currently available, and seem to be on the increase.

Finally, all things domestic are taking center stage as books on knitting (e.g., *Casting Spells* by Barbara Bretton) and cooking (e.g., *Marry-Me Christmas* by Shirley Jump, *Talk of the Town* by Sherrill Bodine, *All that Matters* by Stef Ann Holm, *Delicious* by Sherry Thomas), sometimes complete with instructions and recipes, are attracting fans.

Subgenres In Depth

Although we don't have official statistics yet, a quick look at the current crop of titles confirms that, as in the past, contemporary romance continues to claim the major portion of the market, accounting for about half the titles published each year. Although this is largely due to the popular Harlequin and Silhouette contemporary series, most other romance publishers contribute to this group as well. Limited only by time period—the present— Contemporaries range widely in theme, setting, style, and sensuality levels. Settings can be a little glitzy and high-powered (e.g., Leanne Banks' *Billionaire's Marriage Bargain*, Stephanie Bond's *No Peeking*), slightly exotic (e.g., Annette Mahon's Hawaii-set *Holiday Dreams* or Gail Barrett's Peruvian adventure, *To Protect a Princess*), or filled with small-town or rural ambience (e.g., Deborah Shelley's *Marriage 101*, Sherryl Woods' *Welcome to Serenity*). Characters range from single parents, craftsmen, and librarians, to corporate moguls, celebrity concierges, and adventurers. Sports figures continue to be popular and titles such as Gemma Bruce's *The Man for Me* (baseball), Pamela Britton's *On the Move* (NASCAR racing), Marie Force's *Line of Scrimmage*, and Deirdre Martin's *Power Play* (hockey) are a few relevant examples. Children and families continue to attract readers, and Barbara McMahon's *Parents in Training*, Maureen Child's *High-Society Secret Pregnancy*, and Karen Rose Smith's *The Daddy Verdict* are examples of the popular "unexpected baby" plot pattern. In addition, while plenty of upbeat, urban-set romances still exist, the larger chicklit genre's popularity is slipping a bit. Sassy, charming, sweet, steamy, adventurous, or serious, this current batch of Contemporaries has something for everyone and should appeal to most fans.

Historicals, second only to the Contemporaries, continue to grow in popularity. Although all time periods and settings are theoretically possible and the current group of romances includes settings as diverse as Ancient Egypt (e.g., Constance O'Bsnyon's *Daughter of Egypt*) and World War I France (Danielle Steel's *A Good Woman*), the most popular setting by far remains the British Regency period of the early nineteenth century. Authors such as Julia Quinn, Jo Goodman, Suzanne Enoch, Stephanie Laurens, and Liz Carlyle are only a few of the growing number of popular writers who specialize in this time period. Victorian, Georgian, and Medieval periods also have their fans, and the American West is once again attracting interest. Like the other subgenres, Historicals display a wide range of sensuality levels; however, the Historical trend is definitely toward the hotter end of the scale.

Romantic Suspense remains a perennial reader favorite, and stories as varied as Shannon McKenna's sexy, action-oriented adventure, *Ultimate Weapon*; Heather Graham's taut, paranormal Flynn Brothers trilogy; and Karen Harper's chilling, child-focused thriller, *The Hiding Place* share the limelight with Penny McCall's lighter, fast-paced *Ace is Wild*. Although crimes and mysteries of all types abound, arson was popular this time around with Trish Milburn's *Firefighter in the Family* and Jill Shalvis' *Flashback* being two examples. Although most Romantic Suspense novels are set in modern times, some, such as Mary Lennox's *Sword of Shadows*, take place in the past. In addition, mystery and suspense elements can be found in many of the other subgenres, and very often paranormal romances will have strong suspense or mystery plotlines. As always, Romantic Suspense continues to serve as a launching pad for romance writers attempting to break into the larger general Mystery/Suspense Genre.

The Alternative Realities subgenres, especially the Paranormal and Fantasy groups with their surfeit of witches, faeries, dragons, vampires, werewolves, and other shapechangers, are more popular than ever. The genre is evolving, however, and while "vamps" are still the current supernatural creature of choice, others are edging their way in, such as shape-shifting fairies in J.D. Warren's *Crate and Peril*, psychic triplets in Cait London's *For Her Eyes Only*, and demons in Pamela Palmer's *Dark Deceiver*. Futuristics (e.g., Jayne Castle's *Dark Light* and Robin D. Owens' *Heart Fate*), Speculative Fiction (Eve Kenin's *Hidden*), and other creative forms of the subgenre are beginning to make inroads, however, they are still a niche market and are less abundant than their paranormal siblings. "Half-breeds" of various types, usually mixed with humans, are also increasing; Virginia Kantra's *Sea Fever* (half selkie/half human), Jennifer Ashley's *Immortals: The Redeeming* (half human/half demon), and Barbara Bretton's *Casting Spells* (half human/half sorceress) are a few examples.

Multicultural Romance continues to sparkle, not only in imprints dedicated to particular cultures and ethnicities (e.g. Harlequin's Kimani and Kensington's Dafina lines), but also across the romance genre as a whole as characters of various ethnicities, races, and backgrounds regularly populate romances released as part of publishers' general lines. *For All We Know*, a contemporary story focusing on AIDS in children by Sandra Kitt; *Cafe au Lait*, a tropical vacation romance by Liane Spicer; Nicole Foster's *The Bridesmaid's Turn*; Kathryn Albright's Western Historical, *the Rebel and the Lady*; Olivia Gates' Middle Eastern Contemporary, *The Desert King*; and Annette Mahon's *Holiday Dreams* are several relevant titles included in this issue of *What Do I Read Next?*.

Inspirationals, although apparently lessening in popularity somewhat, remain popular with their core readership and are holding their own as a niche market. Reflecting conservative Christian values, these usually sweet stories can be either historical (usually set in the American West) or contemporary and are published primarily by religious publishing houses, Harlequin's Steeple Hill imprint, and, to a lesser degree, through the Christian fiction lines of some mainstream commercial houses. Janet Tronstad's *Snowbound in Dry Creek*, Lisa Wingate's *Word Gets Around*, and Tracie Peterson's *A Promise to Believe In* are examples of the subgenre.

Finally, series and linked books continue to be popular, as a simple glance through this volume's romances will show. Almost half of the books included are parts of series. This trend remains on a roll and because editors still like them and writers are still producing them, it doesn't show signs of ending anytime soon.

A Few Preliminary Statistics

Although as of this writing the 2008 statistics for romance publishing have not been tallied and are not yet available, we do have some preliminary numbers for the publishing industry as a whole, which might provide a hint of what's to come. According to the Association of American Publishers (AAP) in a March 31, 2009, press release (www.publishers.org/main/IndustryStats/IndStats/2008/2008_Stats.htm), total net book sales for 2008 are estimated at $24.8 billion, representing a drop of 2.8% from the year before. Adult hard covers fell by a whopping 13%, but adult trade paperbacks rose by 3.6%, to account for $2.43 billion and $2.36 billion in sales, respectively. However, mass-market totals fell by 3%, for total sales of $1.1 billion. Book club and mail-order sales also declined to $600 million, a loss of 3.4%. The breakdown by format was especially interesting with audio book sales plummeting by 21% to $172 million in sales and e-books rocketing up by an amazing 68.4% to $113 million. Although e-books still account for only a fraction of total book sales, this spike in sales does reflect the growing acceptance and popularity of the format.

As mentioned above, most of the figures for romance aren't available yet; however, Harlequin's early reports show increases in 2008 revenues and operating profits of 2.2% and 11.2% respectively, providing some hope that the romance genre may possibly buck the downward trend 'News Briefs.' *Publishers Weekly* 256 (March 2, 2009): 4-9. Finally, an interesting bit of romance data on the e-book front: major e-book retailer Fictionwise reported that 50% of all its sales in 2008 were romances! (*Wall Street Journal*, March 6, 2009, B4.)

Other romance news

Although numerous romance-related conferences, workshops, and retreats are held each year, by far the most important is the annual Romance Writers of America conference held in July. The 2008 conference was held in San Francisco, California, and was preceded by the Librarians' Day Pre-conference. Both events boasted a wealth of excellent presentations and stellar speakers. Speakers for the main conference included: Theresa Behenna, Opening Session; Victoria Alexander, Keynote; Connie Brockway, Awards Luncheon; and Suzanne Brockmann, Awards Ceremony Emcee. Librarians' Day, a traditionally well-attended event that targets local librarians and booksellers, also had its share of romance luminaries. Historical romance writer Stephanie Laurens was the featured luncheon speaker and best-selling authors Debbie Macomber, Jo Beverley, Jodi Thomas, Caridad Pineiro, and several other authors, editors, and librarians gave presentations as well. Plans are already in the works for the 2009 RWA Conference and Librarians' Day Event, Which will be held in Washington, D.C. Librarians interested in attending the one-day pre-conference should consult www.rwanational.org/cs/overview_librarians for further details.

Several other relevant conference presentations took place in 2008, one at the Public Library Association biennial conference and one at the Popular Culture Association annual conference; however, because these were mentioned in Volume 1 of WDIRN 2008, the details will not be repeated here.

RWA has once again chosen a Librarian of the Year, and this year the award goes to Deborah Schneider of the King County Library System, King County, Washington. The award will be presented at the 2009 RWA Conference Awards Luncheon on July 17.

The Academic Grant Committee of RWA considered a vastly increased number of proposals this year and awarded its latest research grant to Catherine Roach of the University of Alabama for her work, "Book Lovers: Love, Desire, and Fantasy in Popular Culture Romance Narratives." For more information on her research project and that of past recipients, see www.rwanational.org/cs/academic_research_grant/past_recipients on the RWA web site.

Future Trends

So what comes next? Actually, it's anybody's guess because, as we all have recently learned, it takes very little to throw the best-laid plans and suppositions off course. Nevertheless, the current trends might give us a few hints; so with the past as a guide, let's take a look at what might be down the road for romance.

Technology, with its ever-increasing role in everyday life, will continue to impact the genre in exponentially increasing ways. The current technology—e-books, audio and video downloads, blogs, wikis, twitter, etc.—are being adopted, used, and expanded upon for both content delivery and marketing purposes at an ever increasing rate and are in danger of becoming old hat, although I believe e-books and downloads are here to stay for the moment. (I did hear someone say recently that blogs were "so last year," which does put things into a weird kind of perspective.) Every week someone comes out with a new bit of technology or a new way to make use of an existing one (e.g., books delivered in short, 70-word installments to cell phones in China), so while it's impossible to predict the next innovation, it makes sense to be ready for anything—because it will happen.

Given the overall mood of the country, there may be an increase in historical novels, romantic comedy, and other upbeat stories that provide some distraction from the more dismal present. There might also be an increase in novels set during the Thirties (ala some of Dorothy Garlock's classics) with an emphasis on successfully coming through a similar crisis. On the other hand, I doubt that stockbrokers, mortgage bankers, and other financial types (unless they are special, in some way) will be hero or heroine material for some time to come.

Although the field is getting crowded, all things magical, fantastic, paranormal, and otherworldly will still be in; however, there will be more variety, more experimentation, and more creative world-building, and stories may become more speculative

Stories, in general, will continue to reflect the growing diversity of our population, and though the dedicated multicultural lines will probably continue, romances from all publishers will become more multicultural across the board.

Contemporaries and Romantic Suspense will continue to shine, and Historicals, especially Regencies (although I wonder when that star will begin to lose its luster), and Westerns will gain readership. Inspirationals will slip a bit, but because they have a guaranteed niche market, they will hold up.

Chicklit, as a separate type, may wane a bit, but some of its sassier, carefree, funny elements have already shown up in contemporary romances, and this should continue.

Sex is still selling, and although there seems to be less of a push to ramp everything up to the steamiest, it's unlikely that romances will suddenly revert to the chastity standards of the 1950s. There are all levels of sensuality available at the moment, and that seems likely to remain.

Finally, trilogies and other linked books will continue strong. As with sagas, soap operas, and the current prime-time TV series, readers apparently enjoy the worlds that writers create and enjoy revisiting them in subsequent books.

Will any of this happen? Given the current economic uncertainty, the perennial volatility of the publishing world, and the ways in which technology is altering the publishing landscape, it's hard to say. As always, there are no guarantees but one - at the very least, 2009 should be an interesting year.

Romance in Review

Booklist (www.ala.org/ala/booklist/booklist.htm), *Library Journal* (www.libraryjournal.com), and to a lesser extent *Publishers Weekly* (www.publishersweekly.com) continue their coverage of the romance genre, as do a number of newspapers across the country. *Library Journal* publishes a regular bimonthly romance review column with occasional additional mini-columns; *Booklist* has a separate romance fiction category in each issue, as do the other genres; and *Publishers Weekly* includes a limited number of romances in its general mass market or fiction review sections. All three provide online review coverage to varying degrees. Many of these journal and newspaper reviews are picked up by various indexing services, such as EbscoHosts' Academic Search Premier and InfoTrac's Expanded Academic ASAP, or bookseller's web sites, such as Amazon.com. and Barnes & Noble.

Although coverage of the romance genre by mainstream sources has improved over the years, the most comprehensive coverage still is provided by the genre-specific publications, with *Romantic Times Bookclub Magazine* (www.romantictimes.com) being one of the best. Many of these print publications have a web presence as well; and reviews, as well as other materials, may also be available online. Purely online romance reviews sites continue to grow in popularity; and while most of them, like any web source—or any review, for that matter, need to be viewed with a critical eye, they are important and are certainly worth checking out. All About Romance (www.likesbooks.com/), Romance Reviews Today (www.romrevtoday.com), The Romance Reader (www.theromancereader.com), Romance in Color (www.romanceincolor.com), and Speculative Romance Online (www.specromonline.com/are some of the many currently available. Online lists, such as RRA-L (Romance Readers Anonymous) (est. 1992), remain useful forums for romance readers to discuss the genre and share their views and recommendations. Log on to http://groups.yahoo.com/group/rra-l to subscribe. Fiction-L is another list of interest to readers and librarians that, while not specifically devoted to romance, does focus on the genre on a regular basis. For more information see their website (www.webrary.org/rs/flbklistmenu.html). Blogs, wikis, and similar sites are increasing exponentially and can also be a source of opinions, if not formal reviews, and can include everything from Romancing the Blog (www.romancingtheblog.com), a site that provides links to a number of authors' blogs, to Smart Bitches Love Trashy Books (www.smartbitches trashybooks.com/), a trendy, currently popular site that dishes out forthright commentary with earthy language and snarky flair. Finally, those interested in the academic side of the genre may be interested in the Romance Scholar listserv (mailman.depaul.edu/mailman/listinfo/romancescholar), as well as the Romance Wiki www.romancewiki.com, an active site useful to readers, writers, and scholars alike.

Recommendations for Romance

Reading tastes vary greatly. What makes a book appeal to one person may make another reject it. By the same token, two people may like the same book for totally different reasons. Obviously, reading is a highly subjective and personal undertaking. For this reason, the recommended readings attached to each entry have tried to cast as broad a net as was reasonably possible. Suggested titles have been chosen on the basis of similarity to the main entry in one or more of the following areas: historical time period, geographic setting, theme, character types, plot pattern or premise, writing style, or overall mood or "feel." All suggestions may not appeal to the same person, but it is hoped that at least one would appeal to most.

Because romance reading tastes do vary so widely and readers (and writers) often apply vastly differing criteria in determining what makes a romance good, bad, or exceptional, I cannot claim that the following list of recommendations consists solely of the "best" romance novels of the year. (In fact many of these received no awards or special recognition at all.) It is simply a selection of books that the romance contributors, John Charles, Shelley Mosley, Sandra Van Winkle, and I found particularly interesting; perhaps some of these will appeal to you, too.

Seduction of a Proper Gentleman by Victoria Alexander

Fiance at Her Fingertips by Kathleen Bacus

Don't Let It Be True by Jo Barrett

My Lord and Spymaster by Joanna Bourne

The Way Home by Jean Brashear

Hot Flash by Kathy Carmichael

A Virgin River Christmas by Robyn Carr

Dark Light by Jayne Castle

The Private Concierge by Suzanne Forster

Leaving Whiskey Bend by Dorothy Garlock

In Bed with the Devil by Lorraine Heath

The Real Enemy by Kathy Herman

When the Duke Returns by Eloisa James

Hidden by Eve Kenin

A Wallflower Chistmas by Lisa Kleypas

Come the Night by Susan Krinard

Stand by Your Hitman by Leslie Langrty

A Bride for His Convenience by Edith Layton

The Mistress Diaries by Julianne MacLean

Breach of Trust by Diann Mills

Heart Fate by Robin D. Owens

Behind the Shadows by Patricia Potter

The Edge of Impropriety by Pam Rosenthal

His Wicked Sins by Eve Silver

Delicious by Sherry Thomas

Christmas Spirit by Rebecca York

For Further Reference

Publisher Websites and Book Clubs

In addition to going to the general websites of online book suppliers such as Amazon.com and traditional bookstores such as Borders and Barnes & Noble, readers can now order books in print and/or e-book, and in some cases downloadable audio, formats directly from a number of individual publishers' websites. Many of these websites also feature reviews, information on any subscription book clubs the publisher has, and ways for readers to connect with each other. Several of these (e.g., Avalon, Five Star) target the library market and have standing order plans available. Services vary from website to website; several of the more popular are listed below.

Publishers

Avalon Books. www.avalonbooks.com/

Barbour Publishing (Heartsong Presents). www.barbourbooks.com (See Heartsong Presents book club information below).

Cerridwen Press. www.jasminejade.com/

Ellora's Cave. www.ellorascave.com/

Five Star. www.galegroup.com/fivestar/

HarperCollins/Avon Books. www.harpercollins.com (choose Avon Romance in the Categories menu box)

Dorchester Publishing (Leisure and Love Spell). www.dorchesterpub.com. See website for book club information.

Harlequin Books (Harlequin, Silhouette, Spice, MIRA, Red Dress Ink, Luna, HQN, Steeple Hill, Kimani Press, Worldwide Library). eharlequin.com

Kensington Books (Zebra, Dafina, Brava, Strapless, Aphrodisia, Urban Soul, Pinnacle). www.kensingtonbooks. com. (choose Books or Advanced Search to get to the romance links).

Medallion Press. www.medallionpress.com

Penguin Group. (Berkley, Putnam, Signet, NAL, Jove, Plume, Dutton, Onyx) us.penguingroup.com (choose Romance under the Special Interests pull-down menu).

Red Sage Publishing. www.eredsage.com

Simon and Schuster (Pocket) www.simonsays.com (Choose Categories and then choose the link for Romance).

Sourcebooks, Inc. (Sourcebooks Casablanca) www. sourcebooks.com (Choose the link in the left-hand column for Romance).

Tom Doherty Associates. (Tor Paranormal Romance) us. macmillan.com/TorForge.aspx (choose Books and then Romance on the dropdown menu).

Selected Book Clubs and Mail Order Services

Dorchester Book Clubs. Provides Love Spell and Leisure romance titles, as well as those of several other fiction genres, on a monthly subscription basis. Check the website for club options and subscription information. http://www.dorchesterpub.com/Dorch/BookClub.cfm

Harlequin Romance Book Clubs. Provides books in the Harlequin and Silhouette series on a monthly subscription basis. Check the website for series descriptions and price information: http://www.bookclubdeals.com/harlequin-book-club_pro54.html

Harlequin Romance Ebook Clubs. Provides Harlequin and Silhouette series romances in eBook format on a monthly subscription basis. Check the website for more information: http://www.bookclubdeals.com/index.php?action=2&idm=902

Heartsong Presents. Provides contemporary and historical Christian romances, published by Barbour Publishing Company on a subscription basis. Check the website for titles, price, and subscription information: http://www.heartsongpresents.com

Rhapsody Book Club. Rhapsody provides romances from a variety of sources on a subscription basis. Check the website, phone, or write for more information: http://www.rhapsodybookclub.com

Conferences

Numerous conferences are held each year for writers and readers of romance fiction. Two of the more important national ones are listed below. For a more complete listing, particularly of regional or local conferences designed primarily for romance writers, consult the *Romance Writers' Report*, a monthly publication of The Romance Writers of America or visit their website www.rwanational.org.

The Annual RT Book Lovers Convention is sponsored by *Romantic Times Book Club Magazine*. The 25th Annual RT Book Lovers Convention was held on April 16-20, 2008, in Pittsburgh, Pennsylvania. (This organization also sponsors a number of romance-related tours for readers and writers.) The 26th Annual Book Lovers Convention is scheduled to be held April 22-26, 2009, in Orlando, Florida.

The RWA Annual Conference is sponsored by Romance Writers of America and usually held in July. The 2008 Conference was held July 30-August 2 in San Francisco, California. The 2009 conference is scheduled for July 15-18th in Washington, D.C. This "working" conference is aimed at romance writers, editor, librarians, and other romance professionals, rather than fans and readers.

Romance Titles

200

SARAH ABBOT (Pseudonym of Sarah Shupe)

Destiny Bay

(New York: Love Spell, 2008)

Story type: Romantic Suspense; Contemporary
Subject(s): Psychological Thriller; Small Town Life; Stalking
Major character(s): Abrielle Lancaster, Television Personality (host of "Write Away"); Ryan Brannigan, Landlord, Fisherman
Time period(s): 2000s
Locale(s): St. Celeste Island, Maine

Summary: Abrielle "Abby" Lancaster travels to St. Celeste Island, Maine, for answers about her mother's hidden past. What happened nearly 30 years ago in this tiny fishing village that scarred her mother so badly that she ultimately committed suicide? The locals are downright unfriendly and seem to be carrying a long-standing grudge for some reason against Abby and her mother. Abby's bags are barely unpacked before she finds she's being stalked by a menacing, deranged figure with evil intent. She gets little sympathy from the townsfolk, who would prefer that she simply leave. Undaunted, Abby is determined to get what she came for, and ultimately, that would include her handsome landlord, Ryan Brannigan, who has a strong emotional link to Abby's past—and her future. First novel.

Where it's reviewed:
Romantic Times, September 2008, page 79

Other books you might like:
Sandra Brown, *French Silk*, 1992
Catherine Coulter, *The Cove*, 1996
Merline Lovelace, *After Midnight*, 2003
Elizabeth Lowell, *Amber Beach*, 1997
Nora Roberts, *Angels Fall*, 2006

201

CHERRY ADAIR

Night Shadow

(New York: Ballantine, 2008)

Story type: Contemporary; Romantic Suspense
Series: T-FLAC. Book 14

Subject(s): Terrorism; Spies; Espionage
Major character(s): Alexis "Lexi" Stone, Spy (T-FLAC operative), Psychic; Alex Stone, Spy (T-FLAC operative), Psychic
Time period(s): 2000s
Locale(s): Earth

Summary: Lexi and Alex Stone (no relation) are working together, but Lexi is supposed to make sure that Alex isn't turning rogue and Alex is supposed to be sure that newby Lexi is doing well in the field. However, evil is afoot and its up to Lexi and Alex to discover what the terrorists are up to. When they do, they will need all the help they can get.

Where it's reviewed:
Romantic Times, December 2008, page 60

Other books by the same author:
Night Fall, 2008 (T-Flac. Book 12)
Night Secrets, 2008 (T-Flac. Book 13)
White Heat, 2007 (T-Flac. Book 11)
Edge of Darkness, 2006 (T-Flac. Book 10)
Edge of Fear, 2006 (T-Flac. Book 9)

Other books you might like:
Suzanne Brockmann, *Hot Target*, 2005
Suzanne Brockmann, *Over the Edge*, 2001
Christina Dodd, *Almost Like Being in Love*, 2004
Cindy Gerard, *To the Brink*, 2006
Merline Lovelace, *The Middle Sin*, 2005

202

G.A. AIKEN (Pseudonym of Shelly Laurenston)

About a Dragon

(New York: Zebra, 2008)

Story type: Historical/Fantasy; Historical/Medieval
Series: Dragon Kin. Book 2
Subject(s): Dragons; Magic
Major character(s): Talaith, Witch; Briec the Mighty, Mythical Creature (dragon)
Time period(s): Indeterminate Past
Locale(s): Fictional Country

Summary: When her husband finally convinces everyone in the village that she is a witch, Talaith thinks she might end up being burned at the stake until a dragon shows up and rescues her. The dragon turns out to be Briec the

Mighty, the arrogantly sexy warrior, who had earlier tried to claim Talaith as his own. According to dragon law, now that he has rescued her, Talaith belongs to him, but Briec soon discovers that Talaith doesn't follow any laws but her own.

Where it's reviewed:
Romantic Times, December 2008, page 83

Other books by the same author:
Dragon Actually, 2008

Other books you might like:
Shana Abe, *The Smoke Thief*, 2005
Jo Beverley, *Dragon Lovers*, 2007
Claire Delacroix, *The Sorceress*, 1994
Teresa Medeiros, *The Bride and the Beast*, 2001
Tina St. John, *Heart of the Hunter*, 2005

203

KATHRYN ALBRIGHT

The Rebel and the Lady

(Toronto: Harlequin, 2008)

Story type: Historical/American West; Americana
Subject(s): American History; Mexicans; War
Major character(s): Victoria Torrez, Noblewoman, Patriot; Jake Dumont, Drifter, Gunfighter (the Alamo)
Time period(s): 1830s (1836)
Locale(s): San Antonio de Bejar, Texas (Southern Texas Territory); San Jacinto, Texas (Southern Texas Territory)

Summary: During the Texas war for independence, with Santa Anna's army practically at their doorstep, the Torrez family must make hasty plans to flee their Texas Territory ranch. With no time to spare, beautiful Victoria Torrez is spirited away to San Antonio de Bejar to stay with cousins there. Jake Dumont, a drifter on a quest to find his younger brother who has joined the army, happens to also be in San Antonio, and he becomes smitten by young Victoria. The war is not his concern, but before long, Mexican troops are advancing on the town, and the locals must take cover in the Alamo mission, where heroism and deception collide. Fateful history is made, and Jake realizes he cares far more than he could have imagined.

Where it's reviewed:
Romantic Times, September 2008, page 52

Other books by the same author:
The Angel and the Outlaw, 2007

Other books you might like:
Leigh Greenwood, *Scarlet Sunset, Silver Nights*, 2005
Gail Link, *Luck of the Draw*, 2006
Maureen McKade, *A Reason to Believe*, 2007
Linda Lael Miller, *One Wish*, 2000
Maggie Osborne, *The Promise of Jenny Jones*, 1997

204

VICTORIA ALEXANDER (Pseudonym of Cheryl Griffin)

Seduction of a Proper Gentleman

(New York: Avon, 2008)

Story type: Historical/Victorian
Series: Last Man Standing. Book 4
Subject(s): Marriage; Seduction; Memory Loss
Major character(s): Kathleen MacDavid MacDav, Gentlewoman, Amnesiac; Oliver Leighton, Nobleman (Earl of Norcroft)
Time period(s): 1850s (1854)
Locale(s): England

Summary: On her way to break an ancient family curse by convincing he Earl of Norcroft to marry her, Kathleen MacDavid falls off the train platform and loses her memory. She ends up on the estate and as she struggles to regain her memory, she and the earl begin to fall for each other. Unfortunately, things might change drastically once she recovers her memory, which is happening. Brilliant dialogue, memorable characters, and clever plotting are plusses.

Where it's reviewed:
Library Journal, June 15, 2008, page 50
Romantic Times, September 2008, page 44

Other books by the same author:
A Little Bit Wicked, 2007 (Last Man Standing. Book 1)
Secrets of a Proper Lady, 2007 (Last Man Standing. Book 3)
What a Lady Wants, 2007 (Last Man Standing. Book 2)
When We Meet Again, 2005
Love with the Proper Husband, 2003

Other books you might like:
Mary Balogh, *Deceived*, 1993
Laura Lee Guhrke, *And Then He Kissed Her*, 2007
Candice Hern, *In the Thrill of the Night*, 2006
Eloisa James, *Duchess by Night*, 2003
Sabrina Jeffries, *Never Seduce a Scoundrel*, 2006

205

LOUISE ALLEN (Pseudonym of Melanie Hilton)

The Shocking Lord Standon

(Toronto: Harlequin, 2008)

Story type: Historical/Regency
Series: Those Scandalous Ravenhursts. Book 3
Subject(s): Identity, Concealed; Scandal; Seduction
Major character(s): Jessica Gifford, Governess; Gareth Morant, Nobleman (Earl of Standon)
Time period(s): 1810s (1816)
Locale(s): England

Summary: After Gareth Morant, the Earl of Standon, helps her escape from one of London's most scandalous brothels with her reputation intact, Jessica Gifford realizes she owes him. So when Gareth asks for Jessica's help with his own problem, Jessica, of course, has no choice but to agree. The only way Gareth can get out of his engagement to Maude Templeton is by ruining his reputation with scandal. So Gareth convinces Jessica to take on the role of his new, mysterious mistress, the scandalous, widowed Francesca Carleton. The only problem with Gareth's plan is that he never expected to fall in love with his new "mistress!"

Where it's reviewed:
Romantic Times, September 2008, page 51

Other books by the same author:
No Place for a Lady, 2008
The Dangerous Mr. Ryder, 2008
The Outrageous Lady Felsham, 2008
A Most Unconventional Courtship, 2007
Virgin Slave, Barbarian King, 2007

Other books you might like:
Elizabeth Boyle, *Love Letters from a Duke*, 2007
Liz Carlyle, *Never Lie to a Lady*, 2007
Jacquie D'Alessandro, *Whirlwind Affair*, 2002
Candice Hern, *Her Scandalous Affair*, 2004
Julia London, *The Dangers of Deceiving a Viscount*, 2007

206

LIZ ALLISON
WENDY ETHERINGTON , Co-Author
BRENDA JACKSON , Co-Author
MARISA CARROLL , Co-Author
JEAN BRASHEAR , Co-Author

A NASCAR Holiday 3

(Don Mills, Ontario: HQN, 2008)

Story type: Contemporary; Holiday Themes
Subject(s): Sports/Auto Racing
Time period(s): 2000s
Locale(s): United States; Bahamas

Summary: This anthology of sweet holiday romances adds another to Harlequin's growing NASCAR series and features a delightful collection of racing heroes and heroines who can tame them. Included are "Have a Beachy Little Christmas" by Liz Allison and Wendy Etherington, "Winning the Race" by Brenda Jackson, "All They Want for Christmas" by Marisa Carroll, and "A Family for Christmas" by Jean Brashear. The last two novellas are family focused while the first two are more couples oriented. A good anthology with something for everyone.

Where it's reviewed:
Library Journal, October 15, 2008, page 49
Romantic Times, November 2008, page 90

Other books you might like:
Helen Brenna, *Peak Performance*, 2008
Pamela Britton, *In the Groove*, 2006
Pamela Britton, *A NASCAR Holiday 2*, 2007
    anthology
Marisa Carroll, *Forbidden Attraction*, 2008
Kimberly Raye, *A NASCAR Holiday*, 2006
    anthology

207

SHARI ANTON   (Pseudonym of Sharon Antoniewicz)

Magic in His Kiss

(New York: Forever, 2008)

Story type: Historical/Medieval; Paranormal
Series: Magic. Book 3
Subject(s): Marriage; Psychic Powers; Magic
Major character(s): Nicole de Leon, Psychic, Ward (of the king); Rhodri ap Daffyd, Warrior, Minstrel (bard)
Time period(s): 12th century (1153)
Locale(s): Wales; England

Summary: A virtual prisoner and ward of King Stephen, seer Nicole de Leon, knows she will be forced to marry whomever the King chooses. However, her Welsh uncle is out to foil Stephen's plans and sends bard and warrior Rhodri ap Daffyd to kidnap her, if need be, and bring her home. Although of different social classes, Nicole and Rhodri are attracted to each other, creating another layer of tension in this action-filled tale of politics, history, and war that is laced with psychic magic. This is the final volume in Anton's Magic trilogy featuring the psychically gifted de Leon sisters.

Where it's reviewed:
Booklist, July 2008, page 47
Library Journal, June 15, 2008, page 51
Romantic Times, July 2008, page 39

Other books by the same author:
Twilight Magic, 2006 (Magic. Book 2)
At Her Service, 2005
Midnight Magic, 2005 (Magic. Book 1)
Once a Bride, 2004
The Ideal Husband, 2003

Other books you might like:
Juliana Garnett, *The Baron*, 1999
Madeline Hunter, *By Possession*, 2000
Margaret Moore, *My Lord's Desire*, 2007
Margaret Moore, *The Notorious Knight*, 2007
Tina St. John, *White Lion's Lady*, 2001

208

JENNIFER ASHLEY

Immortals: The Redeeming

(New York: Love Spell, 2008)

Story type: Paranormal; Contemporary
Series: Immortals. Book 5
Subject(s): Magic; Crime and Criminals; Redemption
Major character(s): Samantha, Supernatural Being (half demon, half human), Police Officer (Los Angeles Police Department); Tain, Immortal, Supernatural Being (chameleon)
Time period(s): 2000s
Locale(s): Los Angeles, California; Venice Beach, California

Summary: Someone or something is killing demon women in Los Angeles and the LAPD Paranormal Division is on

Romance

the case. Samantha, a half demon, half human police detective, is working undercover at a Venice Beach nightclub looking for leads when a demon attack erupts. Amid the confusion, Tain, the youngest of the Immortal warriors, suddenly appears in the crowd and quells the uprising, protecting Samantha. She recognizes Tain, having met him "one year, four months, and one week" prior—but who's counting? Samantha had helped Tain's brothers free him from the clutches of a sadistic demon who had tortured Tain to the brink of insanity. Now back in Samantha's life, Tain realizes she's exactly what he needs, and he soon discovers she has a mutual demon need for him.

Where it's reviewed:
Romantic Times, September 2008, page 98

Other books by the same author:
Highland Ever After, 2008 (Nvengaria. Book 3)
Immortals: The Calling, 2007 (Immortals. Book 1)
Immortals: The Gathering, 2007 (Immortals. Book 4)
Penelope and Prince Charming, 2006 (Nvengaria. Book 1)
The Mad Bad Duke, 2006 (Nvengaria. Book 2)

Other books you might like:
Joy Nash, *Immortals: The Crossing*, 2008
Pamela Palmer, *Dark Deceiver*, 2008
Robin T. Popp, *Immortals: The Haunting*, 2008
J.D. Warren, *Crate and Peril*, 2008
Elissa Wilds, *Between Light and Dark*, 2008

209

HEIDI ASHWORTH

Miss Delacorte Speaks Her Mind

(New York: Avalon, 2008)

Story type: Regency
Subject(s): Courtship; Family; Gardens and Gardening
Major character(s): Ginerva "Ginny" Delacorte, Gentlewoman; Anthony Crenshaw, Nobleman
Time period(s): 1810s
Locale(s): England

Summary: When his grandmother, the dowager Duchess of Marcross, insists that someone must see that her prized roses are all right, Anthony Crenshaw not only finds himself traveling through the countryside but stuck with the company of Miss Ginerva Delacorte as well. Any hope the two might have for a quick trip are dashed when they not only are robbed by highwaymen, but are later forced to stay with a neighbor while Ginny's maid recuperates from an illness. The more time the two spend together, though, the less thrilled both Ginny and Anthony are about the idea of their trip coming to an end.

Where it's reviewed:
Booklist, November 1, 2008, page 29

Other books you might like:
Louise Bergin, *A Worthy Opponent*, 2004
Diane Farr, *Fair Game*, 1999
Candice Hern, *A Garden Folly*, 1997
Regina Scott, *Utterly Devoted*, 2002
Rhonda Woodward, *Moonlight and Mischief*, 2004

210

KATHLEEN BACUS

Anchors Aweigh

(New York: Love Spell, 2008)

Story type: Humor; Amateur Detective
Series: Tressa Jayne Turner. Book 6
Subject(s): Cruise Ships; Family Relations; Humor
Major character(s): Tressa Jayne "Calamity Jayne" Turner, Journalist, Detective—Amateur; Rick Townsend, Ranger; Manny DeMarco, Biker, Consultant
Time period(s): 2000s
Locale(s): At Sea

Summary: For trouble-magnet Tressa "Calamity Jayne" Turner, even a luxurious, week-long ocean cruise can result in a major fiasco. This particular voyage, meant to celebrate her grandmother's recent nuptials, turns into a juggling act between two potential onboard lovers. Add to this a murder plot, and beef-addict Tressa's panic over the ship's healthy cuisine, and the stage is set for yet another "Calamity Jayne" disaster.

Where it's reviewed:
Romantic Times, November 2008, page 55

Other books by the same author:
Fiance at Her Fingertips, 2008
Calamity Jayne Goes to College, 2007 (Tressa Jayne Turner. Book 4)
Calamity Jayne Heads West, 2007 (Tressa Jayne Turner. Book 5)
Calamity Jayne Rides Again, 2006 (Tressa Jayne Turner. Book 2)
Ghouls Just Want to Have Fun, 2006 (Tressa Jayne Turner. Book 3)

Other books you might like:
Sue Jaffarian, *Thugs and Kisses*, 2008
    Odelia Grey. Book 3
Leslie Langtry, *Stand by Your Hitman*, 2008
    Greatest Hits. Book 3
Lisa Lutz, *The Spellman Files*, 2007
    Spellman. Book 1
Claire Matturro, *Bone Valley*, 2007
    Lilly Belle Cleary. Book 2
Sarah Strohmeyer, *Bubbles All the Way*, 2006
    Bubbles Yablonsky. Book 3

211

KATHLEEN BACUS

Fiance at Her Fingertips

(New York: Love Spell, 2008)

Story type: Humor; Paranormal
Subject(s): Magic; Humor; Family Relations
Major character(s): Debra Daniels, Counselor (crime victims); Logan Tyler Alexander, Lawyer, Mythical Creature
Time period(s): 2000s
Locale(s): Springfield, Illinois

Summary: Debra Daniels is tired of her mother's match-making efforts and the blind dates from hell resulting from them. Even her dad has gone to the dark side, joining her mother in her Cupid-esque activities. On a visit to a novelty shop, Debra discovers the answer to her problems: Fiance-at-Your-Fingertips. This boxed set, complete with a full profile of "Lawyer Logan," her fictitious mystery man, as well as a set of lifelike photographs, provides just enough evidence for Debra to convince her parents that she's romantically involved. Then one day, the unimaginable happens. Logan shows up at Debra's door, making her realize that the kit she bought to fool her parents actually fooled her, because it was a box of magic just waiting to happen.

Other books by the same author:

Anchors Aweigh, 2008 (Tressa Jayne Turner. Book 6)

Calamity Jayne Goes to College, 2007 (Tressa Jayne Turner. Book 4)

Calamity Jayne Heads West, 2007 (Tressa Jayne Turner. Book 5)

Calamity Jayne Rides Again, 2006 (Tressa Jayne Turner. Book 2)

Ghouls Just Want to Have Fun, 2006 (Tressa Jayne Turner. Book 3)

Other books you might like:

Annette Blair, *The Scot, the Witch and the Wardrobe*, 2006
    Accidental Witch. Book 3

Angie Fox, *The Accidental Demon Slayer*, 2008

Judi McCoy, *Making over Mr. Right*, 2008
    Goddess. Book 3

Jenna McKnight, *A Greek God at the Ladies' Club*, 2003

Vicki Lewis Thompson, *Wild and Hexy*, 2008
    Hex. Book 2

212

NINA BANGS

Eternal Pleasure

(New York: Leisure, 2008)

Story type: Contemporary/Fantasy
Subject(s): Magic; Mythology
Major character(s): Kelly Maloy, Student—Graduate; Ty Endeka, Warrior, Immortal
Time period(s): 2000s
Locale(s): Houston, Texas

Summary: Kelly Maloy thought driving sexy Ty Endeka around Houston would be an easy part-time job. Then Kelly discovers Ty is an immortal warrior: one of an alliance of 11 who have been summoned by Kelly's employer to battle those trying to end the world. Now Kelly realizes she should have asked for more money!

Where it's reviewed:
Booklist, June 1, 2008, page 55
Romantic Times, July 2008, page 96

Other books by the same author:

One Bite Stand, 2008
Wicked Fantasy, 2007
A Taste of Darkness, 2006
Wicked Pleasure, 2006
Wicked Nights, 2005

Other books you might like:

Kresley Cole, *No Rest for the Wicked*, 2006
Christine Feehan, *Dark Prince*, 1999
Sherrilyn Kenyon, *Dance with the Devil*, 2003
Katie MacAlister, *Sex, Lies, and Vampires*, 2003

213

LEANNE BANKS

Billionaire's Marriage Bargain

(New York: Silhouette, 2008)

Story type: Contemporary
Series: Billionaire's Club. Book 2
Subject(s): Wealth; Independence; Family
Major character(s): Mallory James, Heiress, Philanthropist (charity volunteer); Alex Megalos, Wealthy (billionaire), Businessman (Megalos-De Luca Resorts Intl.)
Time period(s): 2000s
Locale(s): Las Vegas, Nevada

Summary: Mallory James' overprotective father, Edwin, would like nothing more than to see his daughter married and settled down, but Mallory has goals and aspirations that are far from domestic. Alex Megalos, a business associate of Edwin's, volunteers to be the one to tame Mallory, and he pursues her with a passion. When potentially embarrassing photographs of the couple turn up on the Internet, Alex marries Mallory to defuse a scandal. It isn't long before Mallory discovers her marriage to Alex may be nothing more than a business arrangement orchestrated by her father. Where's the love in that?

Where it's reviewed:
Romantic Times, August 2008, page 110

Other books by the same author:

Blackmailed into a Fake Engagement, 2009
Trouble in High Heels, 2009
Bedded by the Billionaire, 2008 (Billionaire's Club. Book 1)
Footloose, 2006
Underfoot, 2006

Other books you might like:

Maureen Child, *Falling for King's Fortune*, 2008
Jennifer Lewis, *Prince of Midtown*, 2008
Yvonne Lyndsay, *Claiming His Runaway Bride*, 2008
Maxine Sullivan, *Mistress and a Million Dollars*, 2008
Laura Wright, *Front Page Engagement*, 2008

214

GAIL BARRETT

To Protect a Princess

(New York: Silhouette, 2008)

Story type: Contemporary; Adventure
Subject(s): Archaeology; Gypsies; Secrets
Major character(s): Dara Adams, Gypsy (Roma), Royalty (Roma princess); Logan Burke, Drifter, Gypsy (half Roma)
Time period(s): 2000s
Locale(s): Peru (Quillacocha Ruins)

Summary: Dara Adams (Adara Adamovich) is in Peru on a quest to find the legendary Roma dagger, a priceless relic of her Roma Gypsy heritage that disappeared long ago. Her research leads her to the royal tomb at the Quillacocha Ruins, and she enlists the help of a reluctant drifter, Logan Burke, to guide her there. Many have lost their lives searching for the dagger, and it appears that Dara and Logan could be next, as a sniper for the ruthless Order of the Black Crescent Moon is hot on their trail in a race to find the dagger.

Where it's reviewed:
Romantic Times, November 2008, page 118

Other books by the same author:
Heart of a Thief, 2008
Facing the Fire, 2006
Where He Belongs, 2005

Other books you might like:
S.K. McClafferty, *Nothing to Lose*, 2006
Michelle Perry, *In Enemy Hands*, 2006
Sharon Silva, *Spirit Dancer*, 2004
Colleen Thompson, *The Salt Maiden*, 2007
Debra Webb, *Nameless*, 2008

215

BEVERLY BARTON (Pseudonym of Beverly Beaver)

Dying for You

(Don Mills, Ontario: HQN, 2008)

Story type: Romantic Suspense; Contemporary
Series: Protectors
Subject(s): Kidnapping; Murder; Sexual Assault
Major character(s): Lucie Evans, Bodyguard, Security Officer (security expert); Sawyer McNamara, Businessman, Security Officer (security expert)
Time period(s): 2000s
Locale(s): Atlanta, Georgia; Chattanooga, Tennessee; San Luis, South America

Summary: Lucie Evans loves her boss, Sawyer McNamara, who runs the Dundee Private Security and Investigation Agency, and who is totally oblivious to her feelings. Sawyer assigns Lucie to be a bodyguard for a washed-up television celebrity. When the has-been tries to rape Lucie, Sawyer pooh-poohs the attack, saying Lucie can take care of herself. Sawyer's offhand reaction to her brutal attack is the last blow to Lucie's unrequited love, and she quits her job. When she becomes a personal

bodyguard to a wealthy South American heiress, Lucie gets kidnapped by mistake. Suddenly, Sawyer realizes what Lucie means to him, and he won't rest until she's safe.

Where it's reviewed:
Romantic Times, December 2008, page 61

Other books by the same author:
A Time to Die, 2007
Close Enough to Kill, 2006
Dangerous Deception, 2006
Killing Her Softly, 2005
The Last to Die, 2004

Other books you might like:
Lindsay McKenna, *Dangerous Prey*, 2008
Carla Neggers, *Cold Pursuit*, 2008
Patricia Potter, *Behind the Shadows*, 2008
Tara Taylor Quinn, *At Close Range*, 2008
Maureen Smith, *No One but You*, 2008

216

ELIZABETH BEVARLY

Ready and Willing

(New York: Berkley Sensation, 2008)

Story type: Contemporary; Paranormal
Series: Kentucky. Book 2
Subject(s): Business; Fashion Design; Ghosts
Major character(s): Audrey Fine Magill, Designer (hats); Nathaniel Summerfield, Businessman; Silas Leyton Summerfield, Sea Captain
Time period(s): 2000s
Locale(s): Louisville, Kentucky

Summary: Audrey Fine Magill has enough to do with trying to open her own hat shop before Derby week without being a messenger for the dead. But when Audrey purchases a painting of Captain Silas Leyton Summerfield, she not only has his ghost haunting her home but also demanding that Audrey contact his descendant, businessman Nathaniel Summerfield, and convince him not to go through with the most lucrative deal in his career. Silas knows that if Nathaniel completes the deal, he will lose his soul forever, but for Audrey, finding a way to convince "dollars and cents" Nathaniel of that fact without him thinking she is nuts won't be easy!

Where it's reviewed:
Romantic Times, November 2008, page 90

Other books by the same author:
Fast and Loose, 2008
Flirting with Trouble, 2008
Overnight Male, 2008
Married to His Business, 2007
My Only Vice, 2006

Other books you might like:
Kristine Grayson, *Utterly Charming*, 2000
Lynn Kurland, *A Garden in the Rain*, 2003
Judi McCoy, *Almost a Goddess*, 2006
Hope Tarr, *The Haunting*, 2007

217

LAWANA BLACKWELL

The Jewel of Gresham Green

(Bloomington, MN: Bethany House, 2008)

Story type: Inspirational; Historical/Victorian
Series: Gresham Chronicles. Book 4
Subject(s): Working Mothers; Writing; Faith
Major character(s): Jewel Libby, Single Parent, Unemployed; Philip Hollis, Doctor (successful surgeon)
Time period(s): 1880s (1884)
Locale(s): Birmingham, England; Gresham Green, England

Summary: Single mother Jewel Libby has a backbreaking job sewing corsets 60 hours a week in a Dickensian factory; no one to keep her young daughter; and a pedophile landlord. Her life is an extreme contrast to that of Adela Phelps, a 26-year-old "spinster" who lives with her family in the Gresham Green vicarage. Unfortunately, Adela's rambunctious nieces and nephews make it nearly impossible for her to work in the house. To get the solitude she needs to write, Adela moves to a forest cottage. Jewel, concerned for the safely of her daughter, flees Birmingham, seeking sanctuary in Gresham Green, and when her path crosses those of Adela and her brother, Philip, survival suddenly seems like a possibility.

Where it's reviewed:
Booklist, August 1, 2008, page 36
Romantic Times, August 2008, page 62

Other books by the same author:
The Dowry of Miss Lydia Clark, 2008 (Gresham Chronicles. Book 3)
The Courtship of the Vicar's Daughter, 2007 (Gresham Chronicles. Book 2)
The Widow of Larkspur Inn, 2007 (Gresham Chronicles. Book 1)

Other books you might like:
Linore Rose Burkard, *Before the Season Ends*, 2008
Cathy Marie Hake, *Whirlwind*, 2008
Jill Marie Landis, *Homecoming*, 2008
Ruth Axtell Morren, *The Making of a Gentleman*, 2008
Janet Oke, *Love's Abiding Joy*, 2003
Love Comes Softly. Book 4

218

MARY BLAYNEY

Lover's Kiss

(New York: Bantam, 2008)

Story type: Historical/Regency
Subject(s): Family; Secrets
Major character(s): Olivia Pennistan, Gentlewoman; Michael Garrett, Military Personnel (former soldier)
Time period(s): 1810s (1816)
Locale(s): England

Summary: While riding through the forests of Derbyshire on his way home from war, Michael Garrett stumbles across a woman nearly frozen to death in the snow. After finding shelter for them both, Michael later discovers the lady is Olivia Pennistan and she is running from two men who had abducted her. The choices of work for an ex-soldier are limited, but Michael never expected his next job would be to become Olivia's bodyguard, nor that he would fall in love with his new employer.

Where it's reviewed:
Romantic Times, November 2008, page 45

Other books by the same author:
The Captain's Mermaid, 2004
The Pleasure of His Company, 2003
His Heart's Delight, 2002
His Last Lover, 2002

Other books you might like:
Mary Balogh, *Slightly Scandalous*, 2003
Liz Carlyle, *No True Gentleman*, 2002
Gaelen Foley, *The Devil Takes a Bride*, 2004
Jo Goodman, *All I Ever Needed*, 2003
Kathryn Smith, *Elusive Passion*, 2001

219

MARY BLAYNEY

Traitor's Kiss

(New York: Bantam, 2008)

Story type: Historical/Regency
Subject(s): Espionage; Secrets
Major character(s): Charlotte Parnell, Widow(er); Gabriel Pennistan, Nobleman, Scientist
Time period(s): 1810s (1813)
Locale(s): France; England

Summary: Gabriel Pennistan is certain it is just a matter of time before he is executed until a beguiling and beautiful Frenchwoman turns up at his jail cell. The woman reluctantly gives Gabriel her name, Charlotte Parnell, but she refuses to divulge much more of her plan to get him out of the country and back to England. Working as an amateur spy for the Duke of Wellington has given Gabriel quite a bit of experience, and he is determined to use those skills to find out everything about the mysterious and seductive Charlotte.

Where it's reviewed:
Romantic Times, November 2008, page 45

Other books by the same author:
The Captain's Mermaid, 2004
The Pleasure of His Company, 2003
His Heart's Delight, 2002
His Last Lover, 2002

Other books you might like:
Nita Abrams, *The Spy's Reward*, 2006
Jo Beverley, *The Rogue's Return*, 2006
Sabrina Jeffries, *Beware a Scot's Revenge*, 2007
Lynn Kerstan, *The Golden Leopard*, 2002
Sari Robins, *More than a Scandal*, 2005

220

SHERRILL BODINE

Talk of the Town

(New York: Forever, 2008)

Story type: Contemporary; Humor
Subject(s): Newspapers; Work; Journalism
Major character(s): Rebecca Covington, Journalist (columnist); David Sumner, Businessman (newspaper CEO)
Time period(s): 2000s
Locale(s): Chicago, Illinois

Summary: Threatened by dismissal after an item in her gossip column angers a powerful politician, Rebecca Covington temporarily accepts an assignment as a recipe columnist—and she doesn't know how to cook! Furious, because she feels it's really a matter of age discrimination, she plans to fight to get her old job back; however, when she meets the gorgeous new CEO, David Sumner, their sizzling mutual attraction promises to cause unexpected problems for them both. Plenty of humor infuses this lively, sexy story that features mature protagonists.

Where it's reviewed:
Romantic Times, December 2008, page 76

Other books you might like:
Jennifer Crusie, *Welcome to Temptation*, 2000
Rachel Gibson, *True Confessions*, 2001
Karen Hawkins, *Talk of the Town*, 2008
Kristan Higgins, *To Good to Be True*, 2009
Shirley Jump, *Pretty Bad*, 2007

221

STEPHANIE BOND (Pseudonym of Stephanie Bond Hauck)

No Peeking

(Toronto: Harlequin, 2008)

Story type: Contemporary; Holiday Themes
Subject(s): Christmas; Humor; Sexual Behavior
Major character(s): Violet Summerlin, Consultant (personal concierge), Businesswoman (Summerlin at Your Service); Dominick Burns, Businessman, Sports Figure (extreme sports)
Time period(s): 2000s
Locale(s): Atlanta, Georgia; Miami, Florida

Summary: Violet Summerlin's thriving personal concierge business leaves her little time for fun—or for romance. However, when sexy Dominick Burns accidentally finds a letter Violet had written years earlier for a college sexuality class describing her sexual fantasies, he sees a challenge and sets out to fulfill her every dream. A business trip to Miami over the Christmas holidays to check out an extreme sports company sets the stage for a series of funny, sexy adventures that end up with them both getting more than they had expected.

Where it's reviewed:
Library Journal, December 2008, page 106
Romantic Times, December 2008, page 100

Other books by the same author:
Body Movers: 2 Bodies for the Price of 1, 2007 (Body Movers. Book 2)
Body Movers, 2006 (Body Movers. Book 1)
Finding Your Mojo, 2006
I Think I Love You, 2005
In Deep Voodoo, 2005

Other books you might like:
Barbara Dunlop, *The Billionaire Who Bought Christmas*, 2007
Anne Eames, *Christmas Elopement*, 1996
Lori Foster, *Jingle Bell Rock*, 2003 anthology
Lori Foster, *The Night before Christmas*, 2005 anthology
Elda Minger, *Christmas with Eve*, 1996

222

JOANNA BOURNE

My Lord and Spymaster

(New York: Berkley Sensation, 2008)

Story type: Historical/Regency
Subject(s): Espionage; Secrets
Major character(s): Jess Whitby, Businesswoman, Thief; Sebastian Kennett, Sea Captain, Spy
Time period(s): 1810s
Locale(s): England

Summary: After her father is falsely imprisoned as the infamous traitor "Cinq," Jess Whitby uses her former skills as a pickpocket to try and plant evidence on the person she believes is really responsible: Captain Sebastian Kennett. Jess' plan takes an unexpected turn, though, when Sebastian saves her and brings her back to his ship. What Jess doesn't know is that Sebastian is really working for the government, and once he realizes what Jess is doing, he decides to help her.

Where it's reviewed:
Romantic Times, July 2008, page 36

Other books by the same author:
The Spymaster's Lady, 2008

Other books you might like:
Nita Abrams, *The Spy's Reward*, 2006
Elizabeth Boyle, *Brazen Temptress*, 1999
Liz Carlyle, *Never Lie to a Lady*, 2007
Lynn Kerstan, *Dangerous Deceptions*, 2004
Amanda Quick, *Deception*, 2003

223

ELIZABETH BOYLE

Tempted by the Night

(New York: Avon, 2008)

Story type: Historical/Fantasy; Historical/Regency
Subject(s): Animals/Dogs; Family; Magic
Major character(s): Hermoine Marlowe, Gentlewoman

Thomas, Nobleman (Earl of Rockhurst)
Time period(s): 1810s (1810)
Locale(s): London, England
Summary: When Lady Hermoine Marlowe wishes that there was some way she could follow the Earl of Rockhurst, around to prove that he is not a wicked rake, she has no idea her wish will come true. Fortunately for her, Hermoine just happens to have a very unique ring that, unbeknownst to its owners, can grant wishes. Now every night as soon as the sun sets, Hermoine turns invisible, which allows her to track Rockhursts nightly wanderings. However, it is really quite difficult to get the man of your dreams to fall in love with you if he doesn't even know you are there!

Where it's reviewed:
Booklist, September 15, 2008, page 43
Romantic Times, September 2008, page 44

Other books by the same author:
Love Letters from a Duke, 2007
His Mistress by Morning, 2006
Something about Emmaline, 2005
This Rake of Mine, 2005
It Takes a Hero, 2004

Other books you might like:
Jo Beverley, *Forbidden Magic*, 1998
Susan Carroll, *The Night Drifter*, 1999
Teresa Medeiros, *After Midnight*, 2005
Mary Jo Putney, *The Marriage Spell*, 2006

224

JEAN BRASHEAR
The Way Home
(Toronto: Harlequin, 2008)

Story type: Contemporary
Subject(s): Memory Loss; Marriage; Healing
Major character(s): Bella Parker, Amnesiac, Gardener; James Parker, Businessman, Spouse (of Bella)
Time period(s): 2000s
Locale(s): Lucky Draw, Colorado; Parker's Ridge, Alabama

Summary: After more than 30 years of marriage, James Parker cheats on his wife, Bella. Distraught, Bella leaves James—and Alabama—but never reaches her destination. In Colorado, her car's stolen, and she's beaten and left for dead. Suffering from amnesia, Bella's taken in and cared for by "Dr. Sam," who begins to love her. Then James learns where Bella is. When James arrives at Dr. Sam's house, Bella not only doesn't recognize her husband, she's afraid of him. Determined to have his wife back, James hopes that once Bella's memory returns, she'll decide to forgive him, and that her time in Colorado hasn't made her fall in love with another man.

Where it's reviewed:
Romantic Times, July 2008, page 112

Other books by the same author:
Return to West Texas, 2007
Sweet Mercy, 2006
Coming Home, 2005
Forgiveness, 2005
Most Wanted, 2004

Other books you might like:
Carrie Alexander, *Nobody's Hero*, 2008
Elizabeth Ashtree, *The Child Comes First*, 2008
Melinda Curtis, *Marriage between Friends*, 2008
Roz Denny Fox, *More than a Memory*, 2008
Tara Taylor Quinn, *Trusting Ryan*, 2008

225

BARBARA BRETTON
Casting Spells
(New York: Berkley, 2008)

Story type: Paranormal; Contemporary
Subject(s): Magic; Murder; Small Town Life
Major character(s): Chloe Hobbs, Businesswoman, Store Owner (Sticks and Strings); Luke MacKenzie, Detective—Police
Time period(s): 2000s
Locale(s): Sugar Maple, Vermont

Summary: Chloe Hobbs, the daughter of a sorceress and a human, owns Sugar Maple's award-winning yarn and knitting shop. Sugar Maple, a crime-free, picturesque, small town has a supernatural citizenry of werewolves, vampires, sprites, and warlocks. The only reason they're not detected by outsiders is a protective spell provided by Chloe's ancestors. Now, however, there's been a murder. The populace of Sugar Maple decides Chloe needs a paranormal mate to find her inner magick; but after she meets police detective Luke MacKenzie, a human investigating the homicide, she only has eyes for him, and without her magical powers, the small town faces certain destruction.

Where it's reviewed:
Booklist, November 1, 2008, page 29
Publisher's Weekly, September 15, 2008, page 43
Romantic Times, November 2008, page 98

Other books by the same author:
Just Desserts, 2008
Just Like Heaven, 2007
Someone Like You, 2005
Chances Are, 2004
Girls of Summer, 2003

Other books you might like:
Amanda Ashley, *Night's Master*, 2008
Jennifer Ashley, *Immortals: The Redeeming*, 2008
Meljean Brook, *Demon Bound*, 2008
Susan Krinard, *Chasing Midnight*, 2007
Robin T. Popp, *Immortals: The Haunting*, 2008

226

TERRI BRISBIN (Pseudonym of Theresa S. Brisbin)
Possessed by the Highlander
(Toronto: Harlequin, 2008)

Story type: Historical/Medieval
Subject(s): Scandal; Marriage

Major character(s): Marian Robertson, Noblewoman (laird's sister); Sir Duncan MacLerie, Diplomat ("The Peacemaker"), Nobleman
Time period(s): 14th century
Locale(s): Scotland

Summary: On his way to negotiate with the new Laird Robertson, Duncan MacLerie rescues Marian "Mara" Robertson from a man's unwanted advances not realizing that she is the Robertson Harlot, the dishonored sister of the laird he is on his way to see. Duncan is attracted to her and her young daughter, but she resists, not wanting to harm his reputation. However, the Laird notices Duncan's interest, and anxious to see his sister married, he arranges for Duncan to be drugged and found with Mara so they will be forced to wed. Politics and scandal enliven this sweet romance of two people who must lay the past to rest in order to find true happiness. This title contains links to Brisbin's earlier Highlander books about the Clan MacLerie.

Where it's reviewed:
Romantic Times, August 2008, page 48

Other books by the same author:
Surrender to the Highlander, 2008
The Earl's Secret, 2007
Taming the Highlander, 2006
The Maid of Lorne, 2006
The Duchess's Next Husband, 2005

Other books you might like:
Juliana Garnett, *The Laird*, 2002
Hannah Howell, *Highland Promise*, 1999
Paula Quinn, *A Highlander Never Surrenders*, 2008
Amanda Scott, *Highland Princess*, 2004
Lyn Stone, *The Highland Wife*, 2001

227

PAMELA BRITTON

On the Move

(Don Mills, Ontario: HQN, 2008)

Story type: Contemporary
Series: NASCAR
Subject(s): Literacy; Secrets; Sports/Auto Racing
Major character(s): Vicki VanCleef, Public Relations; Brandon Burke, Sports Figure (NASCAR driver)
Time period(s): 2000s
Locale(s): New York, New York (Manhattan); North Carolina

Summary: Vicki VanCleef's job description at Sports Services, Inc., a prominent sports agency, is to tame NASCAR bad boy Brandon Burke. However, making him behave in public seems like an unreachable goal. Then Vicki learns Brandon's darkest secret, and suddenly, she knows the real cause of his angry outbursts. She just doesn't know whether or not she can help him solve his problems. If she doesn't, he's going to spin more out of control.and he won't have a career to salvage. Neither will she.

Where it's reviewed:
Romantic Times, September 2008, page 91

Other books by the same author:
To the Limit, 2007 (NASCAR)
Total Control, 2007 (NASCAR)
In the Groove, 2006 (NASCAR)
On the Edge, 2006 (NASCAR)
Dangerous Curves, 2005 (NASCAR)

Other books you might like:
Ken Casper, *Speed Bumps*, 2007
    NASCAR
Marie Force, *Line of Scrimmage*, 2008
Susan Elizabeth Phillips, *Heaven, Texas*, 1995
Nancy Warren, *Turn Two*, 2007
    NASCAR
Pat White, *Ring around My Heart*, 2004

228

CAROLYN BROWN

The Dove

(New York: Avalon, 2008)

Story type: Historical/American West; Americana
Subject(s): Family Problems; Forgiveness; American West
Major character(s): Katy Lynn Logan, Saloon Keeper/Owner (of The Soiled Dove); Joshua Carter, Religious (Southern Baptist preacher)
Time period(s): 1890s (1898); 1900s (1905)
Locale(s): Spanish Fort, Texas

Summary: It's bad enough that Joshua Carter is forced to break up with his first love, Katy Lynn Logan, at her father's funeral. Josh's overbearing, fire-and-brimstone father goes so far as to pay Katy, the "soiled dove," to never see his son again. For five years Katy keeps her part of the bargain. Then time and curiosity bring Joshua back to Spanish 11b Fort, Texas, where he discovers he has seriously underestimated Katy's potential, as well as the depth of his feelings for her.

Other books by the same author:
To Commit, 2008 (Broken Roads. Book 2)
Evening Star, 2007 (Drifters and Dreamers. Book 3)
Sweet Tilly, 2007 (Drifters and Dreamers. Book 2)
Morning Glory, 2007 (Drifters and Dreamers. Book 1)
To Trust, 2007 (Broken Roads. Book 1)

Other books you might like:
Judith French, *The Taming of Shaw MacCade*, 2001
Leigh Greenwood, *A Texan's Honor*, 2006
Merline Lovelace, *The Colonel's Daughter*, 2002
Nan Ryan, *A Lifetime of Heaven*, 1994
Cheryl St. John, *The Preacher's Daughter*, 2007

229

GEMMA BRUCE

The Man for Me

(New York: Brava, 2008)

Story type: Contemporary
Subject(s): Sports/Baseball; Family

Major character(s): Jess Green, Young Woman, Journalist (*Sports Today*); Tommy Bainbridge, Sports Figure (major league pitcher), Philanthropist
Time period(s): 2000s
Locale(s): Gilbeytown, Pennsylvania

Summary: Sportswriter J.T. "Jess" Green is on assignment in Gilbeytown, Pennsylvania, to cover a story on the local amateur team, the Gilbeytown Beavers, and to get the scoop on their hometown hero, major league pitcher Tommy Bainbridge. Rumors are flying about Tommy's possible retirement from baseball, and J.T. wants the story. After she wins his trust, and his heart, he reveals to her his plans to develop a stadium for his community. Small town politics and dirty dealings threaten to derail the project, and ruin Tommy's reputation. It doesn't help when a doctored photo of J.T. turns up in a tabloid, with the headline "Reporter Caught in Locker Room Orgy." They're playing hardball in Gilbeytown.

Other books by the same author:
Who Wants to Be a Sex Goddess?, 2007
Who Loves Ya, Baby?, 2005
Who's Been Sleeping in My Bed?, 2005

Other books you might like:
Erica DeQuaya, *Hunks of Hockey*, 2008
Marie Force, *Line of Scrimmage*, 2008
Rachel Gibson, *See Jane Score*, 2008
Liana Laverentz, *Thin Ice*, 2007
Deirdre Martin, *Power Play*, 2008

230

EMILY BRYANT (Pseudonym of Diana Groe)

Pleasuring the Pirate
(New York: Leisure Books, 2008)

Story type: Historical; Humor
Subject(s): Pirates; Courtship; Humor
Major character(s): Jacquelyn "Mistress Jack" Wren, Steward (estate manager), Young Woman; Gabriel "Cornish Dragon" Drake, Nobleman, Pirate
Time period(s): 1720s (1720)
Locale(s): Cornwall, England

Summary: After being pardoned by the king, the dread pirate captain The Cornish Dragon wants to settle down into a respectable life and raise a family. Now known by his real name instead of his terrifying moniker, Lord Gabriel Drake is ready to take his rightful place among the nobility. The problem is, he lacks the charm and polish to fit in. Jacquelyn Wren, a wannabe warrior and well-known courtesan's daughter, is also looking for respectability, and managing Gabriel's estate gives her a chance at propriety. Gabriel wants "Mistress Jack" to do more than take care of his property—he wants her to teach him proper manners and acceptable courting techniques.

Where it's reviewed:
Romantic Times, August 2008, page 43

Other books by the same author:
Vexing the Viscount, 2009
Distracting the Duchess, 2008

Other books you might like:
Jennifer Ashley, *The Pirate Next Door*, 2003
Kinley MacGregor, *A Pirate of Her Own*, 1999
Connie Mason, *The Pirate Prince*, 2004
Linda Lael Miller, *Pirates*, 1995
Jade Parker, *To Catch a Pirate*, 2007

231

SHIRLEE BUSBEE

Seduction Becomes Her
(New York: Zebra, 2008)

Story type: Historical/Regency
Subject(s): Inheritance; Secrets; Marriage
Major character(s): Daphne Beaumont, Gentlewoman; Charles Weston, Nobleman
Time period(s): 19th century
Locale(s): Cornwall, England

Summary: As a result of their brother's lucky inheritance, Daphne Beaumont is able to take her two young siblings from a difficult life in London to live in Cornwall. However, it is not quite the luxurious estate they had expected. At the same time Charles Weston is on his way to Cornwall to find some answers about the death of his half-brother, never realizing that a rock slide will trap him with Daphne—and that in order to avoid scandal he will need to offer marriage. The key, however, will be in convincing Daphne to marry him! Busbee is one of the original Avon Ladies who set the historical romance subgenre aflame in the Seventies.

Where it's reviewed:
Romantic Times, July 2008, page 36

Other books by the same author:
Scandal Becomes Her, 2009
Surrender Becomes Her, 2009
Coming Home, 2003
At Long Last, 2000
Lady Vixen, 1980

Other books you might like:
Catherine Coulter, *The Offer*, 1997
Suzanne Enoch, *After the Kiss*, 2008
Lisa Kleypas, *Seduce Me at Sunrise*, 2008
Edith Layton, *The Chance*, 2000
Anne Mallory, *Three Nights of Sin*, 2008

232

LISA CACH
GEMMA HALLIDAY , Co-Author
MELANIE JACKSON , Co-Author

These Boots Were Made for Strutting
(New York: Love Spell, 2008)

Story type: Paranormal; Anthology
Subject(s): Magic; Romance; Anthology
Time period(s): 2000s

Locale(s): United States

Summary: In Lisa Cach's "A Rose by Any Other Name," landscaper Kelsey Safire finds her inner goddess—and love with Jack Lovgren—thanks to her magic shoes from Hiheelia. "So I Dated an Axe Murderer" by Gemma Halliday features another pair of enchanted footwear from Hiheelia that takes plain-Jane web designer Kya Bader to a more glamorous existence. In Melanie Jackson's "And They Danced," the final story of the anthology, Faith finds romance through a pair of killer dancing shoes.

Other books you might like:
Lisa Cach, *Have Glass Slippers, Will Travel*, 2005
Gemma Halliday, *Killer in High Heels*, 2007
Melanie Jackson, *A Curious Affair*, 2008

233

STELLA CAMERON

Cypress Nights

(Don Mills, Ontario: Mira, 2008)

Story type: Contemporary; Romantic Suspense
Series: Bayou. Book 10
Subject(s): Murder; Small Town Life; Serial Killers
Major character(s): Bleu Laveau, Teacher; Roche Savage, Doctor (psychiatrist)
Time period(s): 2000s
Locale(s): Toussaint, Louisiana

Summary: Someone apparently has an issue with the new school that is being planned in Toussaint and is killing supporters to make his point. Anxious to find the killer, psychiatrist Roche Savage and teacher Bleu Laveau join forces and find themselves drawing closer to each other in the process. Characters from Cameron's earlier Bayou novels reappear and add to the depth of this chilling mystery.

Where it's reviewed:
Romantic Times, August 2008, page 67

Other books by the same author:
Cold Day in Hell, 2007 (Bayou. Book 9)
Target, 2007 (Bayou. Book 8)
A Marked Man, 2006 (Bayou. Book 7)
Body of Evidence, 2006 (Bayou. Book 6)
A Grave Mistake, 2005 (Bayou. Book 5)

Other books you might like:
Sandra Brown, *Fat Tuesday*, 1998
Linda Howard, *After the Night*, 1995
Karen Robards, *Bait*, 2005
Katherine Sutcliffe, *Bad Moon Rising*, 2003
Joanna Wayne, *Mystic Isle*, 2002

234

CANDACE CAMP

The Wedding Challenge

(Don Mills, Ontario: HQN, 2008)

Story type: Historical/Regency
Series: Matchmaker. Book 3

Subject(s): Trust; Revenge; Family Relations
Major character(s): Calandra, Noblewoman, Wealthy; Richard, Nobleman (Earl of Bromwell)
Time period(s): 1800s
Locale(s): London, England

Summary: Lady Calandra, "Callie," has been through five Seasons, but she still doesn't have a husband. Every man who's wooed her has been found short by her powerful, formidable brother, the Duke of Rochford. However, Rochford recognizes his sister's need for a suitable spouse, so he hires Francesca Haughston, matchmaker to the aristocracy, a woman he trusts, to help his sister find a man he deems worthy. Unfortunately, Richard, Earl of Bromwell, wins Callie's heart, and as far as Rochford is concerned, she couldn't have picked a worse match. Unbeknownst to Callie, Richard and Rochford hate each other, and Richard's immediate goal is to exact revenge any way he can, even at Callie's expense.

Where it's reviewed:
Publishers Weekly, June 16, 2008, page 37
Romantic Times, September 2008, page 47

Other books by the same author:
The Courtship Dance, 2009 (Matchmaker. Book 4)
The Bridal Quest, 2008 (Matchmaker. Book 2)
A Dangerous Man, 2007
The Marriage Wager, 2007 (Matchmaker. Book 1)
No Other Love, 2001

Other books you might like:
Claudia Dain, *The Courtesan's Daughter*, 2007
Christina Dodd, *The Prince Kidnaps a Bride*, 2006
Suzanne Enoch, *The Rake*, 2002
Lisa Kleypas, *Mine Till Midnight*, 2007
Stephanie Laurens, *Beyond Seduction*, 2007

235

LIZ CARLYLE (Pseudonym of Susan Woodhouse)

Never Romance a Rake

(New York: Pocket Star, 2008)

Story type: Historical/Regency
Series: Never|PO. Book 3
Subject(s): Gambling; Mystery; Secrets
Major character(s): Camille Marchand, Noblewoman, Bastard Daughter; Kieran Neville, Nobleman (Baron Rothewell), Rake
Time period(s): 1820s
Locale(s): England

Summary: A cynical, notorious rake haunted by the past and a beautiful half-French emigre strike a bargain of necessity when Camille Marchand's vile father wagers her hand in a card game, and Kieran, Baron Rothewell, saves her from a man more dissolute than he by cheating to win the game. Camille needs to marry and have a child in order to claim her inheritance, and Kieran has reasons of his own for the match. However, neither expects to fall in love or have to deal with those who will do anything to keep them from being happy. Laced with mystery, this highly sensual romance is third in a trilogy linked by those involved in the Neville Shipping Company.

Where it's reviewed:
Romantic Times, August 2008, page 38

Other books by the same author:
Never Deceive a Duke, 2007
Never Lie to a Lady, 2007
Three Little Secrets, 2006
Two Little Lies, 2006
One Little Sin, 2005

Other books you might like:
Jo Beverley, *To Rescue a Rogue*, 2006
Gayle Callen, *Never Trust a Scoundrel*, 2008
Eloisa James, *Midnight Pleasures*, 2000
Sabrina Jeffries, *A Dangerous Love*, 2000
Mary Jo Putney, *One Perfect Rose*, 1997

236

ROBYN CARR

A Virgin River Christmas

(Don Mills, Ontario: Mira, 2008)

Story type: Contemporary; Holiday Themes
Series: Virgin River. Book 4
Subject(s): Small Town Life; Christmas
Major character(s): Marcie Sullivan, Widow(er); Ian Buchanan, Military Personnel (Iraq veteran), Recluse
Time period(s): 2000s
Locale(s): Virgin River, California

Summary: A woman on a mission to thank the man who saved her husband's life in Iraq (even though he died later) finds the vet, depressed and alone, in a cabin in the Northern California mountains. Fate and the flu keep Marcie Sullivan in Ian Buchanan's cabin, and as they spend time together, they both find closure as well as love in this touching, poignant story of love and loss and renewal.

Where it's reviewed:
Library Journal, October 15, 2008, page 49
Romantic Times, November 2008, page 85

Other books by the same author:
Paradise Valley, 2009 (Virgin River. Book 7)
Temptation Ridge, 2009 (Virgin River. Book 6)
Second Chance Pass, 2009 (Virgin River. Book 5)
Virgin River, 2007 (Virgin River. Book 1)
Never Too Late, 2006

Other books you might like:
Judy Duarte, *Her Best Christmas Ever*, 2008
Debbie Macomber, *A Cedar Cove Christmas*, 2008
Fern Michaels, *Comfort and Joy*, 2007
    anthology
Linda Lael Miller, *A McKettrick Christmas*, 2008
Lisa Plumley, *Home for the Holidays*, 2008

237

KATHRYN CASKIE

To Sin with a Stranger

(New York: Avon, 2008)

Story type: Historical/Regency
Series: Sinclair Family. Book 1
Subject(s): Family; Seduction; Sports/Boxing
Major character(s): Isobel Carington, Gentlewoman; Sterling Sinclair, Nobleman (Marquess of Blackburn)
Time period(s): 1810s
Locale(s): London, England; Scotland

Summary: When a feisty Isobel Carington tries to break up his bout with an Irish prize fighter, Sterling Sinclair, the Marquess of Blackburn, is first amused and then annoyed, since Sterling is counting on the purse he will win to help support his siblings. Once Sterling learns that the *ton* is now wagering as to whether he will marry Isobel, Sterling realizes it is the perfect opportunity to earn even more money. All he has to do is convince Isobel, who would rather give him a few good punches herself than become his new wife!

Where it's reviewed:
Romantic Times, December 2008, page 41

Other books by the same author:
How to Propose to a Prince, 2008
How to Engage an Earl, 2007
How to Seduce a Duke, 2006
Love Is in the Heir, 2006
A Lady's Guide to Rakes, 2005

Other books you might like:
Jessica Benson, *Much Obliged*, 2001
Jacquie D'Alessandro, *Whirlwind Affair*, 2002
Suzanne Enoch, *The Rake*, 2002
Karen Hawkins, *How to Treat a Lady*, 2003
Eloisa James, *The Taming of the Duke*, 2006

238

KEN CASPER

A Lady's Luck

(New York: Silhouette, 2008)

Story type: Romantic Suspense; Contemporary
Series: Thoroughbred Legacy. Book 8
Subject(s): Horse Racing; Dishonesty; Family
Major character(s): Devon Hunter, Noblewoman, Teacher (Briar Hills Academy); Brent Preston, Equestrian (race horse, Leopold's Legacy), Businessman (Quest Stables)
Time period(s): 2000s
Locale(s): Louisville, Kentucky; London, England

Summary: When Brent Preston's champion race horse, Leopold's Legacy, fails a DNA test, revealing that the horse's sire is not the one named on the registration papers, the prospects of lucrative stud fees, along with the reputation of Quest Stables, are ruined. Brent travels to England to see Nolan Hunter, owner of Apollo's Ice,

Romance

the intended sire of Leopold's Legacy, to see what went wrong. It seems there are a lot of unanswered questions surrounding Apollo's Ice, including why several witnesses to the live insemination have turned up dead or missing. For Brent, the only bright spot in the trip is meeting Nolan's sister, Devon Hunter. Brent is quite taken with the beautiful schoolteacher, but realizes he has a difficult decision to make. In order to clear his own family's name, he will have to ruin the reputation of Devon's.

Other books by the same author:
Hitting the Brakes, 2008 (Harlequin NASCAR. Book 23)
Running on Empty, 2008 (Harlequin NASCAR. Book 28)
Miles Apart, 2007 (Harlequin NASCAR. Book 14)
Speed Bumps, 2007 (Harlequin NASCAR. Book 5)
Upstairs at Miss Hattie's, 2007

Other books you might like:
Barbara Dunlop, *Millions to Spare*, 2008
Patricia Guthrie, *In the Arms of the Enemy*, 2007
Tami Hoag, *Dark Horse*, 2004
Maggie Price, *Who's Cheatin' Who?*, 2008
Joanne Rock, *Something to Talk About*, 2008

239

CARLA CASSIDY (Pseudonym of Carla Bracale)

Broken Pieces

(New York: Signet Eclipse, 2008)

Story type: Contemporary; Romantic Suspense
Subject(s): Abuse; Murder; Suspense
Major character(s): Mariah Sayers, Single Parent; Jack Taylor, Veterinarian
Time period(s): 2000s
Locale(s): Plains Point, Missouri

Summary: Raped and impregnated as a teen and literally abandoned by her conservative parents, Mariah Sayers flees to Chicago to make a new life for herself and her baby. Now, sixteen years later, her parents are dead and their house is hers, so Mariah and daughter Kelsey go back to tiny Plains Point, Missouri, to sell the house and lay some old ghosts. However, when brutal attacks against women begin again, Mariah fears the worst and is faced with some life-changing decisions. Chilling suspense is laced with sexy romance as she reconnects with classmate Jack Taylor, now a gorgeous veterinarian.

Where it's reviewed:
Romantic Times, September 2008, page 78

Other books by the same author:
Last Gasp, 2009
Every Move You Make, 2008
Without a Sound, 2006
The Perfect Family, 2005
Trace Evidence, 2003

Other books you might like:
Beverly Barton, *After Dark*, 2000
Beverly Barton, *The Fifth Victim*, 2003
Karen Rose, *I'm Watching You*, 2004
Tina Wainscott, *Unforgivable*, 2001
Karen Young, *Never Tell*, 2005

240

JAYNE CASTLE (Pseudonym of Jayne Ann Krentz)

Dark Light

(New York: Jove, 2008)

Story type: Futuristic; Paranormal
Series: Harmony. Book 5
Subject(s): Psychic Powers; Mystery; Marriage
Major character(s): Sierra McIntyre, Psychic, Journalist (investigative reporter); John Fontana, Psychic, Businessman (ghost hunter guild boss)
Time period(s): Indeterminate Future
Locale(s): Harmony, Fictional Country

Summary: There's some kind of conspiracy going on within the Ghost Hunters Guild and the new guild boss, John Fontana, needs answers. His solution comes in the form of reporter Sierra McIntyre, who is on the trail of a story about drugs and ghost hunters who disappear into the mysterious, energy-riddled tunnels, and who has the contacts that he needs. So he proposes! Of course, it's only a ruse to keep her safe, until they fall in love. Plenty of danger, psychic and otherwise, fills the pages of this lively, funny, sexy romp that nicely continues Castle's growing futuristic Harmony series.

Where it's reviewed:
Library Journal, August 2008, page 59
Romantic Times, August 2008, page 100

Other books by the same author:
Silver Master, 2007 (Harmony. Book 4)
Ghost Hunter, 2006 (Harmony. Book 4)
After Glow, 2004 (Harmony. Book 2)
After Dark, 2000 (Harmony. Book 1)
Orchid, 1998

Other books you might like:
Anne Avery, *All's Fair*, 1994
Susan Grant, *Your Planet or Mine?*, 2006
Dara Joy, *Ritual of Proof*, 2001
Robin D. Owens, *Heart Fate*, 2008
Robin D. Owens, *Heart Thief*, 2003

241

JANET CHAPMAN

The Man Must Marry

(New York: Pocket Star, 2008)

Story type: Contemporary
Series: Sinclair Brothers. Book 1
Subject(s): Marriage; Inheritance
Major character(s): Willamina Kent, Businesswoman

(casket maker), Heiress (shipping company); Sam Sinclair, Businessman (shipping company)

Time period(s): 2000s
Locale(s): New York, New York; At Sea; Maine

Summary: Reluctantly agreeing to help dying shipping mogul Abram Sinclair by going to New York to vote his proxy and choose which of his three beloved grandsons will succeed him as CEO, Maine-based casket maker Willa Kent is faced with an even greater dilemma when Abram dies and leaves everything to her. There's a catch, of course—she must marry one of the grandsons within three months or the company will be sold to his arch rival. Angry and needing time to sort things out, Willa sets sail for Maine; but when Sam Sinclair, the grandson who has sparked her interest and fury from the start, joins her aboard ship—with ultimately mutually satisfactory results.

Where it's reviewed:
Romantic Times, November 2008, page 88

Other books by the same author:
Moonlight Warrior, 2009 (Midnight Bay. Book 1)
Stranger in Her Bed, 2007 (Logger. Book 2)
The Seduction of His Wife, 2006 (Logger. Book 1)
The Dangerous Protector, 2005 (Foster Sisters. Book 2)
The Seductive Imposter, 2004 (Foster Sisters. Book 1)

Other books you might like:
Jill Barnett, *Carried Away*, 1996
Barbara Bretton, *At Last*, 2000

Kimberly Cates, *Lighthouse Cove*, 2002
Marcia Evanick, *Christmas on Conrad Street*, 2002
    Misty Harbor. Book 2
Allison Leigh, *The Bride and the Bargain*, 2008

242

ROWENA CHERRY

Knight's Fork

(New York: Love Spell, 2008)

Story type: Fantasy; Futuristic
Subject(s): Fantasy; Murder; Sexual Behavior
Major character(s): Electra Djerroldina, Royalty (Queen of Volnoth); Djarrhett Raven Perseus Pendra Djames, Royalty (prince), Knight
Time period(s): 1990s (1994)
Locale(s): Mythical Place

Summary: Caught in an interstellar chess game of gallantry and deception, virtuous knight "Rhett" is trapped in a Knight's Fork, when he becomes the target of Imperial Princess and barbarian Queen Electra Djerroldina, who desires his semen to produce an heir. Her Mate, the King of Volnoth, is unable to do so, but being promised to him, she is forced to pursue other, more creative measures of conception.

Where it's reviewed:
Romantic Times, October 2008, page 107

Other books by the same author:
Insufficient Mating Material, 2007
Forced Mate, 2004
Mating Net, 2004

Other books you might like:
G.A. Aiken, *Dragon Actually*, 2008
Christine Feehan, *Dark Curse*, 2008
Angela Knight, *Warrior: The Time Hunters*, 2008
Robin D. Owens, *Heart Fate*, 2008
C.L. Wilson, *King of Sword and Sky*, 2008

243

MAUREEN CHILD (Pseudonym of Ann Carberry)

Bedeviled

(New York: Signet, 2009)

Story type: Paranormal; Humor
Subject(s): Fairies; Quest; Demons
Major character(s): Maggie Donovan, Artist, Warrior (novice); Culhane, Mythical Creature (faery), Warrior
Time period(s): 2000s
Locale(s): Castle Bay, California; Otherworld, Mythical Place

Summary: Artist Maggie Donovan is forced to support herself by painting holiday scenes on store windows. Except for baby-sitting her mouthy 12-year-old niece, Maggie's life is pretty dull. However, Fate has some surprises in store for her. Maggie has been chosen to overthrow Mab, the evil Faery queen, and Faery warrior Culhane is supposed to help her do it. At first, Maggie is unconvinced, but when she sees her worthless fiance eaten by a demon, and then discovers she can float through the air, Maggie believes. Bezel, the constantly grouchy pixie, is given the task of training her. With Baranca demons disguised as humans at every turn, Maggie finds the road to her destiny more dangerous—and exciting—than she could ever possibly have imagined.

Where it's reviewed:
Romantic Times, January 2009, page 98

Other books by the same author:
A Fiend in Need, 2008
Bargaining for the King's Baby, 2008 (Kings of California. Book 1)
Marrying for King's Millions, 2008 (Kings of California. Book 2)
Falling for King's Fortune, 2008 (Kings of California. Book 3)
High-Society Secret Pregnancy, 2008

Other books you might like:
MaryJanice Davidson, *Undead and Unpopular*, 2007
Angie Fox, *The Accidental Demon Slayer*, 2008
Katie MacAlister, *Up in Smoke*, 2008
    Silver Dragons. Book 2
Stephanie Rowe, *Date Me Baby, One More Time*, 2006
Vicki Lewis Thompson, *Wild and Hexy*, 2008
    Hex. Book 2

Romance (side tab)

244

MAUREEN CHILD (Pseudonym of Ann Carberry)

High-Society Secret Pregnancy

(New York: Silhouette, 2008)

Story type: Contemporary
Series: Park Avenue Scandals
Subject(s): Scandal; Pregnancy; Wealth
Major character(s): Julia Prentice, Wealthy, Socialite; Max Rolland, Wealthy
Time period(s): 2000s
Locale(s): New York, New York (Manhattan)

Summary: After a passionate one-night stand with wealthy Max Rolland, socialite Julia Prentice finds herself pregnant. At first, Max denies that the baby is his. However, once he's convinced that he is indeed the father, he agrees to marry Julia, but only for one year.

Where it's reviewed:
Romantic Times, July 2008, page 113

Other books by the same author:
Bargaining for the King's Baby, 2008 (Kings of California. Book 1)
Falling for King's Fortune, 2008 (Kings of California. Book 3)
Marrying for King's Millions, 2008 (Kings of California. Book 2)
Captured by the Billionaire, 2007
Reasons for Revenge, 2007

Other books you might like:
Leanne Banks, *Billionaires Marriage Bargain*, 2008
Jan Colley, *Billionaire's Favorite Fantasy*, 2008
Sara Orwig, *Wed to the Texan*, 2008
Maxine Sullivan, *The CEO Takes a Wife*, 2008
Laura Wright, *Front Page Engagement*, 2008

245

PAMELA CLARE

Untamed

(New York: Leisure, 2008)

Story type: Historical/Georgian
Series: MacKinnon's Rangers. Book 2
Subject(s): French and Indian War; Friendship; Secrets
Major character(s): Amalie Chavenet, Gentlewoman; Morgan MacKinnon, Military Personnel (British Army major)
Time period(s): 1750s
Locale(s): Canada

Summary: After being captured by the French, a severely wounded Major Morgan MacKinnon knows he has only two options: escape and return to the Rangers or die trying. What Morgan did not count upon was falling in love with Amalie Chavenet, the Frenchwoman who nursed him back to health. Now Morgan has two choices: betray the men with whom he has fought for years by staying with the French or betray the woman he now loves.

Where it's reviewed:
Publishers Weekly, October 27, 2008, page 38
Romantic Times, December 2008, page 42

Other books by the same author:
Unlawful Contact, 2008
Hard Evidence, 2006
Surrender, 2006
Extreme Exposure, 2005
Ride the Fire, 2005

Other books you might like:
Jo Beverley, *The Rogue's Return*, 2006
May McGoldrick, *The Rebel*, 2002
Kerrelyn Sparks, *For Love or Country*, 2002
Jeane Westin, *Lady Merry's Dashing Champion*, 2007

246

KRESLEY COLE

Dark Desires after Dusk

(New York: Pocket Books, 2008)

Story type: Contemporary/Fantasy; Paranormal
Series: Immortals after Dark. Book 5
Subject(s): Magic; Seduction
Major character(s): Holly Ashwin, Mythical Creature (Valkyrie), Professor; Cadeon Woede, Demon
Time period(s): 2000s
Locale(s): New Orleans, Louisiana; United States

Summary: When a band of demons capture her, Professor Holly Ashwin's anger—and a lightning bolt—turn her into a Valkyrie, which gives her the power to kill them, but she still needs the help of mercenary demon Cadeon Woede. In order to help restore his brother Rydstrom to his throne as Demon King, Cadeon must first kill Omert the Deathless, and to do so he needs a special sword. The only way Cadeon can get the weapon he needs though is by trading Holly's life for it.

Other books by the same author:
Dark Needs at Nights Edge, 2008
If You Deceive, 2007
Wicked Deeds on a Winter's Night, 2007
If You Desire, 2007
A Hunger Like No Other, 2006

Other books you might like:
Lara Adrian, *Kiss of Midnight*, 2007
Christine Feehan, *The Twilight Before Christmas*, 2003
Sherrilyn Kenyon, *Night Pleasures*, 2002
Michelle Rowen, *Bitten and Smitten*, 2006
Gena Showalter, *Awaken Me Darkly*, 2005

247

KATHLEEN CREIGHTON

Daredevil's Run

(New York: Silhouette, 2008)

Story type: Romantic Suspense; Contemporary
Series: Taken. Book 2

Subject(s): Family Relations; Physically Handicapped; Sports/White Water Rafting

Major character(s): Alex Penny, Businesswoman (Penny Tours); Matt Pearson, Handicapped (paraplegic), Adventurer

Time period(s): 2000s

Locale(s): Wofford Heights, California

Summary: The last time Alex Penny saw her old lover and business partner, Matt Pearson, he was recovering from a terrible rock climbing accident that cost him the use of his legs. Matt had ended their relationship back then so that Alex could move on. But now, five years later, he's ready to get back into the game, and finds that Alex is still available too. She has mixed emotions about booking Matt on a white water rafting excursion—guilt about the day he fell, and doubts about his ability to handle this physically demanding trek. To make things worse, someone is sabotaging the expedition. Alex and Matt learn a lot about each other as they match wits with the elements and their perceived limitations.

Where it's reviewed:
Romantic Times, August 2008, page 111

Other books by the same author:
Danger Signals, 2008 (Taken. Book 1)
Lazlo's Last Stand, 2007
Secret Agent Sam, 2005
An Order of Protection, 2004
The Top Gun's Return, 2003

Other books you might like:
Carla Cassidy, *Natural-Born Protector*, 2008
Diana Duncan, *Midnight Hero*, 2005
Marie Farrarella, *Colton's Secret Service*, 2008
Sharron McClellan, *Mercenary's Honor*, 2008
Marilyn Pappano, *Intimate Enemy*, 2008

▮**248**▮

JANET DAILEY

Searching for Santa

(New York: Zebra, 2008)

Story type: Contemporary; Holiday Themes

Subject(s): Christmas; Ranch Life; Competition

Major character(s): Casey Gilmore, Rancher; Flint McAllister, Rancher (ranch manager)

Time period(s): 2000s

Locale(s): Nebraska (Anchor Bar Ranch)

Summary: Unhappy when the bank decides that the Anchor Bar needs an outsider to manage things while her father recovers from a hip replacement, Casey Gilmore is determined to show Flint McAllister, and everyone else, that she can run the ranch on her own. However, she doesn't count on falling in love with the man she is determined to get rid of in this sweet, holiday-filled romance. This is an updated version of *Boss Man from Ogallala* (1980), the Nebraska title in Dailey's Americana series.

Where it's reviewed:
Romantic Times, October 2008, page 92

Other books by the same author:
Lone Calder Star, 2005 (Calder. Book 9)
Calder Promise, 2004 (Calder. Book 8)
Shifting Calder Wind, 2003
Scrooge Wore Spurs, 2002
A Capital Holiday, 2001

Other books you might like:
Millie Criswell, *A Western Family Christmas*, 2001 anthology
Theresa Hill, *Twelve Days*, 2000
Linda Howard, *Christmas Kisses*, 1996 anthology
Debbie Macomber, *Return to Promise*, 2000
Diana Palmer, *Lone Star Christmas*, 1997 includes two stories, one by Joan Johnston

▮**249**▮

B.J. DANIELS (Pseudonym of Barbara Heinlein)

Montana Royalty

(Toronto: Harlequin, 2008)

Story type: Romantic Suspense; Contemporary

Series: Whitehorse, Montana. Book 7

Subject(s): Kings, Queens, Rulers, etc.; Jealousy; Ranch Life

Major character(s): Rory Buchanan, Rancher; Devlin Barrow, Bastard Son (of King Roland Wycliffe II), Equestrian (groom at Stanwood stables)

Time period(s): 2000s

Locale(s): Whitehorse, Montana

Summary: Rory Buchanan is tired of her wealthy neighbors' repeated attempts to buy her ranch—it's not for sale. The royal Wycliffes have already marred the Montana scenery with the construction of their replica of Stanwood castle outside the town of Whitehorse. Rory suspects that the Peeping Tom who has been prowling about her property is someone from the castle as well. But when Rory rescues a Stanwood groom (Devlin) who'd been thrown from his saddle during a severe thunderstorm, everything changes. Soaking wet, and stranded for the night in a drafty line shack, they share a single horse blanket for warmth, and things get mighty cozy in the dark. In the morning, Rory regrets fraternizing with the enemy, and Devlin can't remember what happened, since he'd been drugged and expected to die in the storm. Fate brings them back together when Devlin is framed for a royal murder, and a now-pregnant Rory comes face to face with the vindictive Peeping Tom.

Where it's reviewed:
Romantic Times, September 2008, page 112

Other books by the same author:
Matchmaking with a Mission, 2008 (Whitehorse, Montana. Book 5)
Second Chance Cowboy, 2008 (Whitehorse, Montana. Book 6)
Classified Christmas, 2007 (Whitehorse, Montana. Book 4)
The Mystery Man of Whitehorse, 2007 (Whitehorse, Montana. Book 3)
The New Deputy in Town, 2007 (Whitehorse, Montana. Book 2)

Other books you might like:
Mallory Kane, *Solving the Mysterious Stranger*, 2008
Dana Marton, *Sheik Protector*, 2008
Dani Sinclair, *Bodyguard to the Bride*, 2008
Patricia Thayer, *Texas Ranger Takes a Bride*, 2008
Donna Young, *Secret Agent, Secret Father*, 2008

250

MARYJANICE DAVIDSON (Pseudonym of MaryJanice Alongi)

Fish out of Water

(New York: Jove, 2008)

Story type: Humor; Paranormal
Series: Fred the Mermaid. Book 3
Subject(s): Mermaids; Humor; Family Relations
Major character(s): Fredrika Bimm, Mythical Creature (half mermaid, half human), Scientist (marine biologist); Thomas Pearson, Scientist (marine biologist), Doctor (medical)
Time period(s): 2000s
Locale(s): Sanibel Island, Florida; Atlantic Ocean; Undersea Environment/Habitat

Summary: Marine biologist Fredrika "Fred" Bimm is a hybrid. Her mother is human, and her father a merman. Distrusted by the Undersea Folks because of her father's treachery and treated as a sideshow by humans, Fred fits in with neither culture. Even her love life is confused. Should she choose Prince Artur, merman royal, or Thomas Pearson, her colleague and former lover? And how should she handle the evil father she's just met? There's lots of fun and adventure as Fred goes from one world to the other.

Where it's reviewed:
Romantic Times, December 2008, page 84

Other books by the same author:
Dead over Heels, 2008 (collection by Davidson)
Undead and Unworthy, 2008 (Queen Betsy. Book 7)
The Royal Mess, 2007
Undead and Uneasy, 2007 (Queen Betsy. Book 6)
Undead and Unpopular, 2007 (Queen Betsy. Book 5)

Other books you might like:
Charlaine Harris, *From Dead to Worse*, 2008
    Southern Vampire Mysteries. Book 8
Sandra Hill, *Viking Unchained*, 2008
Katie MacAlister, *Playing with Fire*, 2008

Silver Dragons. Book 1
Judi McCoy, *Making over Mr. Right*, 2008
    Goddess. Book 3
Minda Webber, *The Reinvented Miss Bluebeard*, 2007

251

MARYJANICE DAVIDSON
SUSAN GRANT , Co-Author
GENA SHOWALTER , Co-Author
P.C. CAST , Co-Author

Mysteria Lane

(New York: Berkley Sensation, 2008)

Story type: Paranormal; Contemporary
Subject(s): Magic; Paranormal; Anthology
Time period(s): 2000s
Locale(s): Mysteria, Colorado

Summary: Returning to the small Colorado town of Mysteria, where everything paranormal and magical is normal, the same four authors who penned the quartet of novellas in the original *Mysteria* (2006) deliver four steamy stories that introduce new magical misfits, reprise a few older ones, and set the sparks flying. The anthology gets off to a roaring start when a misadventure with a magic wishing well turns one of the infamous Desdaine triplets into a fierce warrior and ages her by 12 years in MaryJanice Davidson's "Disdaining Trouble"; a demon who yearns to be human is sent on a deadly mission in Susan Grant's "The Nanny from Hell"; a creative witch with a magical pen writes her own version of lovely revenge in Gena Showalter's "A Tawdry Affair"; and a vegetarian teacher's unpredictable magic drops her into a romantic painting along with a sexy vampire in P.C. Cast's "It's in His Kiss."

Where it's reviewed:
Romantic Times, October 2008, page 100

Other books by the same author:
Mysteria, 2006 (anthology by the same authors)

Other books you might like:
P.C. Cast, *Goddess of the Rose*, 2006
Christine Feehan, *Dangerous Tides*, 2006
Julie Kenner, *Aphrodite's Flame*, 2004
Katie MacAlister, *You Slay Me*, 2004
Gena Showalter, *Awaken Me Darkly*, 2005

252

AUTUMN DAWN

No Words Alone

(New York: Love Spell, 2008)

Story type: Futuristic; Romantic Suspense
Subject(s): Aliens; Loyalty; Love
Major character(s): Xera Harrisdaughter, Military Personnel (Galactic Explorer lieutenant), Linguist (ship's interpreter); Ryven Atarus, Military Personnel (Scorpio ship commander), Nobleman (Lord of the High Family)

Time period(s): Indeterminate Future
Locale(s): Planet—Imaginary

Summary: After crash-landing together on a desolate planet in the Scorpio constellation, Lieutenant Xera Harrisdaughter and the surviving Galactic Explorers are taken captive by Scorpio Commander Ryven Atarus, who is Lord of the Scorpio High Family. Ryven is fascinated by Xera, a human woman of rank, beauty, intelligence, and courage—with amazing blue eyes. When a Scorpio rescue ship arrives, Ryven brings Xera along back to his planet, Rsik, intending her to become the ambassador to the humans. But Ryven also has a personal interest in Xera—he's fallen in love with her. Although Scorpio men do not express their emotions with words, Ryven's persuasive kisses speak volumes.

Where it's reviewed:
Romantic Times, October 2008, page 84

Other books by the same author:
Beast Warriors, 2006
Dark Lands, 2006
Ride the Stars, 2005
Something Wild, 2005
Teasing Danger, 2003

Other books you might like:
Marilynn Byerly, *Star-Crossed*, 2000
Susan Grant, *My Favorite Earthling*, 2007
Susan Kearney, *The Quest*, 2006
Kat Martin, *Season of Strangers*, 2008
Gena Showalter, *The Nymph King*, 2005

253

GERALYN DAWSON   (Pseudonym of Geralyn Dawson Williams)

Always Look Twice

(New York: Signet Eclipse, 2008)

Story type: Contemporary; Romantic Suspense
Series: Callahan Brothers. Book 3
Subject(s): Murder; Interpersonal Relations; Marriage
Major character(s): Annabelle Monroe, Investigator—Private, Military Personnel (former special ops); Mark Callahan, Military Personnel (former special ops)
Time period(s): 2000s
Locale(s): United States

Summary: Partners in the military as part of a special ops unit, married, and then divorced, Matt Callahan and P.I. Annabelle Monroe reluctantly join forces when someone starts killing the members of their former unit, "the Fixers." This passionate, danger-filled story moves along at a fast clip as the pair learn to deal with the fact that their love has never died and find a killer before he does any more damage. Third in the Holy Terrors or Callahan Brothers Series.

Where it's reviewed:
Booklist, September 15, 2008, page 36

Other books by the same author:
The Loner, 2008
Never Say Never, 2007 (Callahan Brothers. Book 2)
Give Him the Slip, 2006 (Callahan Brothers. Book 1)
My Long Tall Texas Heartthrob, 2004
My Big Old Texas Heartache, 2003

Other books you might like:
Cherry Adair, *Dare Me*, 2005 anthology
Suzanne Brockmann, *Flashpoint*, 2004
Cindy Gerard, *To the Brink*, 2006
Cindy Gerard, *To the Edge*, 2005
Cindy Gerard, *Under the Wire*, 2006

254

KATHRYNN DENNIS

Shadow Rider

(New York: Zebra, 2008)

Story type: Historical/Medieval; Mystical
Subject(s): Castles; Knights and Knighthood; Animals/Horses
Major character(s): Sybilla Corbuc, Servant, Midwife (horses); Sir Guy of Warwick, Knight, Avenger
Time period(s): 14th century
Locale(s): Balwin Forest, England; Cornbury, England

Summary: Sybilla Corbuc has a knack for horses, but a woman engaged in midwifery, and assisting with the birth of a colt, is deemed an abomination to the church. Just as she's about to be imprisoned for her offense, a nobleman, Sir Guy of Warwick, offers to purchase her as his servant. Considering the alternative, Sybilla reluctantly agrees and travels with Sir Guy to his castle, along with the newborn colt, Regalo. At first Sybilla and Sir Guy deny the intense feelings growing between them, but as time passes, and trouble brews in the kingdom, they are ultimately drawn together with the common purpose of avenging the past, and to stop Lord Harmon.

Where it's reviewed:
Romantic Times, October 2008, page 50

Other books by the same author:
Dark Rider, 2007

Other books you might like:
Sarah Brophy, *Dark Heart*, 2008
Diana Cosby, *His Captive*, 2007
Deborah MacGillivray, *A Restless Knight*, 2006
Paula Quinn, *Laird of the Mist*, 2007
Gerri Russell, *Warrior's Bride*, 2007

255

HELENKAY DIMON

Hot as Hell

(New York: Brava, 2008)

Story type: Contemporary; Romantic Suspense
Subject(s): Mystery; Murder

Major character(s): Alexa Stuart, Businesswoman (Stuart Enterprises); Noah Paxton, Security Officer (security expert)

Time period(s): 2000s

Locale(s): Utah

Summary: At a Utah spa to figure out if her former fiance is taking money from her family's company, Lexy Stuart is startled to find not only the object of her sleuthing, security expert Noah Paxton, at the same resort, but a dead body in her hotel room. Sorting it all out isn't easy, especially when she doesn't trust Noah but is drawn to him, just the same. Passion reigns supreme in this romance where the desert setting is as hot as the sex.

Where it's reviewed:
Romantic Times, November 2008, page 88

Other books by the same author:
It's Hotter in Hawaii, 2009
Your Mouth Drives Me Crazy, 2009
Hard as Nails, 2008
Right Here, Right Now, 2008
Viva Las Bad Boys, 2006

Other books you might like:
Lori Foster, *When Good Things Happen to Bad Boys*, 2006
    anthology
Donna Kauffman, *To All a Good Night*, 2008
    anthology
Barbara Keaton, *One in a Million*, 2008
Erin McCarthy, *Flat-Out Sexy*, 2008

256

CHRISTINA DODD

Into the Flame

(New York: signet, 2009)

Story type: Contemporary; Fantasy

Series: Darkness Chosen. Book 4

Subject(s): Magic; Good and Evil

Major character(s): Firebird Wilder, Single Parent; Doug Black, Police Officer, Supernatural Being (shape changer)

Time period(s): 2000s

Locale(s): United States

Summary: Picking up where *Into the Shadow* leaves off, this final book in the series focuses on the relationship of Firebird Wilder, who suddenly learns she is not the Wilder's biological child and Doug Black, her shape-changing college sweetheart, who learns that he is a Wilder. Secrets unfold, questions are answered, and the prophecy plays itself out as the pieces finally all fall into place in this action-packed, violent conclusion to the series.

Where it's reviewed:
Romantic Times, August 2008, page 92

Other books by the same author:
Storm of Shadows, 2009 (Chosen. Book 2)
Storm of Visions, 2009 (Chosen. Book 1)
Into the Shadow, 2008 (Darkness Chosen. Book 3)
Scent of Darkness, 2007 (Darkness Chosen. Book 1)
Touch of Darkness, 2007 (Darkness Chosen. Book 2)

Other books you might like:
Christine Feehan, *Dark Curse*, 2008
    Carpathian. Book 16
Sherrilyn Kenyon, *Acheron*, 2008
    Dark-Hunter. Book 12
Sherrilyn Kenyon, *Unleash the Night*, 2005
J.R. Ward, *Lover Enshrined*, 2008
    Black Dagger Brotherhood. Book 6
Christine Warren, *Walk on the Wild Side*, 2008

257

CHRISTINA DODD

Into the Shadow

(New York: Signet, 2008)

Story type: Contemporary; Fantasy

Series: Darkness Chosen. Book 3

Subject(s): Magic; Devil; Good and Evil

Major character(s): Karen Sonnet, Businesswoman (adventure resorts); Adrik Wilder, Supernatural Being (shape shifter), Warlord

Time period(s): 2000s

Locale(s): Nepal

Summary: Warlord of a band of mercenaries operating near the border between Tibet and Nepal, Adrik has given in to the evil side of his cursed family's nature—or so he thinks. Karen Sonnet, in Nepal supervising the building of one of her family's adventure hotels, knows him only as a secret lover who comes to her at night, until he rescues her from a disaster on Mount Anaya—and then keeps her. Separated when danger threatens, Karen returns home, breaks with her stepfather, and sets out to carve a new life for herself. But Warlord has promised to find her again, and when he does, the danger only increases. This is the third in Dodd's chilling series of a family trying to undo the curse resulting from an ancestor's deal with the devil centuries earlier.

Where it's reviewed:
Romantic Times, July 2008, page 98

Other books by the same author:
Storm of Shadows, 2009 (Chosen. Book 2)
Storm of Visions, 2009 (Chosen. Book 1)
Into the Flame, 2008 (Darkness Chosen. Book 4)
Scent of Darkness, 2007 (Darkness Chosen. Book 1)
Touch of Darkness, 2007 (Darkness Chosen. Book 2)

Other books you might like:
Christine Feehan, *Dark Guardian*, 2002
L.L. Foster, *Servant: The Awakening*, 2007
Lori Handeland, *Dark Moon*, 2005
Sherrilyn Kenyon, *Unleash the Night*, 2005
J.R. Ward, *Lover Awakened*, 2006
    Black Dagger Brotherhood. Book 3

258

SHANNON DRAKE (Pseudonym of Heather Graham Pozzessere)

The Pirate Bride

(Don Mills, Ontario: HQN, 2008)

Story type: Historical/Georgian
Subject(s): Pirates; Identity, Concealed; Adventure and Adventurers
Major character(s): Captain Red Robert, Pirate, Imposter (cross-dressing heroine); Logan Haggerty, Sea Captain, Laird
Time period(s): 1710s (1716); 17th century (1689)
Locale(s): Caribbean; At Sea; Scotland

Summary: Roaming the seas in search of Blair Colm, the ruthless villain who sold her as a child into indentured servitude in the American Colonies, Roberta, known to most as the feared pirate Captain Red Robert, gains an unexpected ally when she captures merchant sea captain Logan Haggerty, who is also on Colm's trail. However, before they find their quarry, a storm strands them on a secluded island; and by the time they are rescued, they have become more than allies in their search for their nemesis. Romance, passion, and plenty of bloody action keep the pace moving in this swashbuckling adventure that sees wrongs avenged and lovers nicely aligned.

Where it's reviewed:
Romantic Times, November 2008, page 49.

Other books by the same author:
Blood Red, 2007
The Seance, 2007
The Dead Room, 2007
Suspicious, 2005
Dead on the Dance Floor, 2004.

Other books you might like:
Marsha Canham, *The Iron Rose*, 2003
Jane Feather, *The Least Likely Bride*, 2000
Sabrina Jeffries, *The Pirate Lord*, 1998
Kinley MacGregor, *Master of Seduction*, 2000
Kinley MacGregor, *A Pirate of Her Own*, 1999

259

LAURA DREWRY

Dancing with the Devil

(New York: Leisure Books, 2008)

Story type: Paranormal; Historical/Americana
Subject(s): Humor; Devil; Forgiveness
Major character(s): Rhea, Widow(er); Deacon, Demon (former), Mythical Creature (son of Satan)
Time period(s): 1880s (1882)
Locale(s): Penance, Texas

Summary: Rhea welcomes her supposedly dead husband, Deacon, home by shooting him. Theoretically, it shouldn't have hurt him. He is, after all, already deceased, not to mention the son of Satan. But now he's human, and the shot does injure him. As a guilty Rhea

nurses him back to health, she wonders if Deacon is indeed a new man, and if she should take a huge risk by letting him back into her life.

Where it's reviewed:
Romantic Times, December 2008, page 48

Other books by the same author:
The Devil's Daughter, 2008
Charming Jo, 2006
Here Comes the Bride, 2005

Other books you might like:
MaryJanice Davidson, *Undead and Unworthy*, 2008
    Queen Betsy. Book 7
Angie Fox, *The Accidental Demon Slayer*, 2008
Victoria Laurie, *Demons Are a Ghoul's Best Friend*, 2008
Katie MacAlister, *You Slay Me*, 2004
    Aisling Grey Guardian. Book 1
Stephanie Rowe, *He Loves Me, He Loves Me Hot*, 2007
    Immortally Sexy. Book 3

260

JUDY DUARTE

Her Best Christmas Ever

(Toronto: Harlequin, 2008)

Story type: Contemporary; Holiday Themes
Subject(s): Holidays; Ranch Life; Family
Major character(s): Connie Montoya, Cook, Parent (new baby); Greg Clayton, Musician (country singing star)
Time period(s): 2000s
Locale(s): Texas (Rocking C Ranch)

Summary: Stranded at the family ranch by flooding rain, country singer Greg Clayton ends up doing something totally unexpected—he delivers the baby of the family cook, young, attractive Connie Montoya. In the weeks that follow, Greg and Connie are drawn to each other, but with their different life styles and the fact that Connie is hiding from her brutal ex-boyfriend, a future together seems dim. Memorable secondary characters fill the pages of this touching, family-centered romance that features most of the major winter holidays.

Where it's reviewed:
Library Journal, October 25, 2008, page 49
Romantic Times, December 2008, page 107

Other books by the same author:
A Real Live Cowboy, 2009
In Love with the Bronc Rider, 2008
Romancing the Cowboy, 2008
Once upon a Pregnancy, 2008
Mulberry Park, 2008

Other books you might like:
Robyn Carr, *A Virgin River Christmas*, 2008
Debbie Macomber, *A Cedar Cove Christmas*, 2008
Fern Michaels, *Silver Bells*, 2008
    anthology
Linda Lael Miller, *A McKettrick Christmas*, 2008
Lisa Plumley, *Home for the Holidays*, 2008

261

CASSIE EDWARDS

Savage Abandon

(New York: Leisure, 2008)

Story type: Indian Culture; Mystical
Series: Savage. Book 30
Subject(s): Indians of North America; Shamanism; Love
Major character(s): Mia Collins, Captive; Wolf Hawk, Chieftan (leader of the Bird Clan), Mythical Creature (shapeshifter)
Time period(s): 1840s (1840)
Locale(s): Rush River, Minnesota

Summary: While navigating up Minnesota's Rush River with her parents, Mia Collins loses her mother to a warrior's arrow, and the shock of seeing his wife killed before his eyes causes Mia's father to suffer a heart attack. Weakened and grieving, the two turn about, and head for home. When they come ashore for the night, their scow is stolen by a pair of fleeing fur trappers, who are responsible for the deaths of two young Bird Clan braves. The last thing Mia or her dying father needs is to be confronted by angry warriors accusing them of the killings. The stress proves fatal for Mia's father, and she finds herself alone and captive. The clan's leader, Wolf Hawk, admires Mia's spirit and believes her claim of innocence. Compassion turns to passion as Wolf Hawk realizes he's finally found his Lady Hawk.

Where it's reviewed:
Romantic Times, September 2008, page 52

Other books by the same author:
Savage Flames, 2008 (Savage. Book 31)
Savage Glory, 2007 (Savage. Book 27)
Savage Skies, 2007 (Savage. Book 29)
Savage Intrigue, 2007 (Savage. Book 28)
Savage Quest, 2007 (Savage. Book 26)

Other books you might like:
Madeline Baker, *Under a Prairie Moon*, 1998
Karen Kay, *Red Hawk's Woman*, 2007
Jill Marie Landis, *Homecoming*, 2008
Kate Lyon, *Hope's Captive*, 2006
Diane Davis White, *Moon of the Falling Leaves*, 2008

262

SUZANNE ENOCH

After the Kiss

(New York: Avon, 2008)

Story type: Historical/Regency
Series: Notorious Gentlemen. Book 1
Subject(s): Blackmail; Animals/Horses; Robbers and Outlaws
Major character(s): Lady Isabel "Tibby" Chalsey, Noblewoman; Sullivan James Waring, Thief (Mayfair Marauder), Horse Trainer (horse breeder)
Time period(s): 1810s (1813)
Locale(s): England

Summary: Caught in the act of stealing a painting that actually belongs to him, horse breeder Sullivan Waring, aka the Mayfair Marauder, steals a most memorable kiss from lovely Lady Isabel Chalsey and escapes—only to realize that he no longer is wearing his mask! She recognizes him when she and her brother are looking at horses, but instead of accusing him, she blackmails him into training an unbroken mare for her to ride—even though she is afraid of horses. Lively banter and plenty of sexual tension add to this enjoyable story that is second in Enoch's series about three gentlemen with secret, dangerous lives.

Where it's reviewed:
Romantic Times, July 2008, page 34

Other books by the same author:
Always a Scoundrel, 2009 (Notorious Gentlemen. Book 3)
Before the Scandal, 2008 (Notorious Gentlemen. Book 2)
By Love Undone, 2008
Sins of a Duke, 2007
Twice the Temptation, 2007

Other books you might like:
Jo Beverley, *Tempting Fortune*, 1994
Candice Hern, *Her Scandalous Affair*, 2005
Eloisa James, *Duchess by Night*, 2008
Sabrina Jeffries, *One Night with a Prince*, 2005
Julia London, *Highlander Unbound*, 2004

263

SUZANNE ENOCH

Before the Scandal

(New York: Avon, 2008)

Story type: Historical/Regency
Series: Notorious Gentlemen. Book 2
Subject(s): Robbers and Outlaws; Family Problems; Trust
Major character(s): Alyse Donnelly, Noblewoman, Orphan; Phineas Bromley, Military Personnel (lieutenant colonel), Highwayman
Time period(s): 1800s
Locale(s): London, England

Summary: When Lieutenant Colonel Phineas Bromley of the First Royal Dragoons hears that his brother is gravely ill, he goes home on emergency leave. He comes back to a dismal shadow of the estate he loved. His brother is better, but in a wheelchair. Alyse, the love of his youth, is orphaned and indentured to an embittered, acrimonious aunt. The houses around the estate are burned to the ground, and everything else is damaged by floods. Phineas' family is in real danger of losing their estate. So Phineas decides to put his skills as an equestrian, a crack shot, and a swordsman to use—he becomes a highwayman.

Where it's reviewed:
Booklist, July 1, 2008, page 45
Romantic Times, August 2008, page 38

Other books by the same author:
After the Kiss, 2008 (Notorious Gentlemen. Book 1)
By Love Undone, 2008
Sins of a Duke, 2007
Twice the Temptation, 2007
Something Sinful, 2006

Other books you might like:
Candace Camp, *No Other Love*, 2001
Mary Ellen Dennis, *The Landlord's Black-Eyed Daughter*, 2007
Valerie King, *Highwayman*, 2001
Ruth Ryan Langan, *The Sea Nymph*, 2001
Dawn MacTavish, *The Marsh Hawk*, 2007

264

JANET EVANOVICH

Fearless Fourteen

(New York: St. Martin's Press, 2008)

Story type: Humor; Romantic Suspense
Series: Stephanie Plum. Book 14
Subject(s): Humor; Kidnapping; Crime and Criminals
Major character(s): Stephanie Plum, Bounty Hunter, Detective—Amateur; Joe Morelli, Detective—Police; Carlos "Ranger" Manoso, Bounty Hunter
Time period(s): 2000s
Locale(s): Trenton, New Jersey (Chambersburg, a.k.a. "The Burg")

Summary: Stephanie Plum, bounty hunter, is back in action when Joe Morelli's cousin, Loretta, a single mom, is arrested for a liquor store robbery. There's no one to take care of Loretta's delinquent son, Mario, except Stephanie. Loretta's released, and then kidnapped. To top everything off, Carlos "Ranger" Manoso and Stephanie are assigned to baby-sit and guard a difficult pop diva. Life is never dull when Stephanie Plum's around.

Where it's reviewed:
Publishers Weekly, August 25, 2008, page 70

Other books by the same author:
Lean Mean Thirteen, 2007 (Stephanie Plum. Book 13)
Twelve Sharp, 2006 (Stephanie Plum. Book 12)
Eleven on Top, 2005 (Stephanie Plum. Book 11)
Ten Big Ones, 2004 (Stephanie Plum. Book 10)
To the Nines, 2003 (Stephanie Plum. Book 9)

Other books you might like:
Kathleen Bacus, *Calamity Jayne*, 2006
Tressa Jayne Turner. Book 1
Liz Evans, *Cue the Easter Bunny*, 2007
Sue Jaffarian, *Thugs and Kisses*, 2008
Odelia Grey. Book 3
Lisa Lutz, *The Spellman Files*, 2007
Spellman. Book 1
Sarah Strohmeyer, *Bubbles All the Way*, 2006
Bubbles Yablonsky. Book 3

265

JANE FEATHER
SABRINA JEFFRIES , Co-Author
JULIA LONDON , Co-Author

Snowy Night with a Stranger

(New York: Pocket Books, 2008)

Story type: Anthology; Historical/Regency
Subject(s): Christmas; Travel; Weather
Time period(s): 1810s

Summary: Wintry weather brings romance in this trio of historical novellas. In Feather's "Holiday Gamble," a snowstorm and a band of highwaymen has Ned Vasey, Viscount Alleton, seeking refuge at Lord Roger Selby's home, where he meets the nobleman's intriguing and mysterious ward, Georgina. In Jeffries' "When Sparks Fly," after a coaching accident leaves them stranded, Eleanor Bancroft finds herself and her charges the unexpected and unwelcome guests of Martin Thorncliff, the "Black Baron," but when Eleanor breaks through the baron's cold front, she finds herself falling in love with him. In London's "A Snowy Night with a Highlander," when Fiona Haines sets out to find her missing brother, Laird Duncan Buchanan agrees to be her guide, but once Fiona discovers his real identity, will she still want his help?

Where it's reviewed:
Romantic Times, November 2008, page 48

Other books you might like:
Nicola Cornick, *Christmas Wedding Belles*, 2007
Sabrina Jeffries, *The School for Heiresses*, 2007
Stephanie Laurens, *Hero Come Back*, 2005
Deborah Simmons, *Love Match*, 2002

266

CHRISTINE FEEHAN

Turbulent Sea

(New York: Jove, 2008)

Story type: Contemporary; Paranormal
Series: Drake Sisters. Book 6
Subject(s): Witches and Witchcraft; Psychic Powers
Major character(s): Joley Drake, Singer, Witch; Ilya Prakenskii, Bodyguard
Time period(s): 2000s
Locale(s): United States

Summary: Singing star Joley Drake is concerned that her band is beginning to attract the wrong kinds of people, dangerous people, They are picking up stalkers and disappearance of a teenager and then a murder confirms it. Threatened, Joley turns for help to the only man who can save her, Russian bodyguard Ilya Prakenskii, a man who has attracted and repelled he from the very first. Secrets, magic, and very real danger abound in this story of Feehan's fabulous Drake sisters.

Where it's reviewed:
Romantic Times, August 2008, page 88

Other books by the same author:
Hidden Currents, 2009 (Drake Sisters. Book 7)
Dangerous Tides, 2006 (Drake Sisters. Book 4)
Magic in the Wind, 2005 (Drake Sisters. Book 1)
Oceans of Fire, 2005 (Drake Sisters. Book 3)
The Twilight Before Christmas, 2003 (Drake Sisters. Book 2)

Other books you might like:
Susan Carroll, *The Silver Rose*, 2006
Ruth Ryan Langan, *The Knight and the Seer*, 2003
Mary Jo Putney, *Kiss of Fate*, 2008
Nora Roberts, *Dance upon the Air*, 2001
Nora Roberts, *Face the Fire*, 2002

267

MARIE FERRARELLA

Colton's Secret Service

(New York: Silhouette, 2008)

Story type: Romantic Suspense; Contemporary
Series: Colton's: Family First
Subject(s): Family Relations; Small Town Life; Secrets
Major character(s): Georgeann Grady Colton, Single Parent; Nick Sheffield, Government Official (secret service agent)
Time period(s): 2000s
Locale(s): Esperanza, Texas

Summary: Secret Service agent Nick Sheffield is sent to the small town of Esperanza, Texas, to investigate threats made against Senator Joe Colton, a presidential hopeful. He suspects Georgeann Grady, a professional rodeo competitor and single parent of five-year-old Emma. However, Georgeann has a secret, one that blindsides even the ultra-observant Nick.

Where it's reviewed:
Romantic Times, September 2008, page 118

Other books by the same author:
A Doctor's Secret, 2008
Protecting His Witness, 2008
Cavanaugh Heat, 2008
Secret Agent Affair, 2008
Her Sworn Protector, 2007

Other books you might like:
Kylie Brandt, *Terms of Surrender*, 2008
Carla Cassidy, *Natural-Born Protector*, 2008
Merline Lovelace, *Undercover Wife*, 2008
Sharron McClellan, *Mercenary's Honor*, 2008
Marilyn Pappano, *Intimate Enemy*, 2008

268

DONNA FLETCHER

Under the Highlander's Spell

(New York: Avon, 2008)

Story type: Historical/Medieval
Series: Sinclare Brothers. Book 2

Subject(s): Magic; Superstition; Witches and Witchcraft
Major character(s): Zia Black, Healer; Altair Sinclare, Warrior, Nobleman
Time period(s): 16th century
Locale(s): Scotland

Summary: Miraculously rescued by Altair Sinclare and his men just seconds from being burned as a witch, healer Zia agrees to take Altair to his brother Ronan, whom she healed when he was wounded. However, when they reach Zia's home, Ronan has gone and enemies are on the prowl in this adventurous, mystical romance that is second in Fletcher's Scotland-set series about the Sinclare brothers.

Where it's reviewed:
Romantic Times, October 2008, page 48

Other books by the same author:
Return of the Rogue, 2008
The Highlander's Bride, 2007
Irish Hope, 2006
The Bewitching Twin, 2006
Taken by Storm, 2006

Other books you might like:
Lois Greiman, *The Warrior Bride*, 2002
Hannah Howell, *Highland Wolf*, 2008
Karyn Monk, *Once a Warrior*, 1997
Karyn Monk, *The Witch and the Warrior*, 1998
Amanda Scott, *Border Wedding*, 2008

269

MARIE FORCE

Line of Scrimmage

(Naperville, IL: Sourcebooks Casablanca, 2008)

Story type: Contemporary; Humor
Subject(s): Divorce; Sports/Football; Trust
Major character(s): Susannah Sanderson, Spouse; Ryan Sanderson, Sports Figure (football superstar)
Time period(s): 2000s
Locale(s): Denver, Colorado

Summary: Susannah Sanderson is finally ready for her wedding to Henry Merrill, a dull man with a domineering mother. He's the exact opposite of football superstar Ryan Sanderson, her soon-to-be-ex-husband. However, Ryan doesn't consider their marriage over yet. He has ten days before their divorce is final to convince Susannah that he's the right man for her, and to make his point, he moves back into their house.

Where it's reviewed:
Booklist, September 15, 2008, page 36
Publishers Weekly, July 28, 2008, page 57

Other books you might like:
Bella Andre, *Game for Anything*, 2008
Kate Angell, *Strike Zone*, 2008
Pamela Britton, *On the Move*, 2008
   NASCAR
Susan Elizabeth Phillips, *Heaven, Texas*, 1995
Pat White, *Ring around My Heart*, 2004

270

SUZANNE FORSTER

The Private Concierge

(Don Mills, Ontario: Mira, 2008)

Story type: Contemporary; Romantic Suspense
Subject(s): Murder; Scandal; Suspense
Major character(s): Lane Chandler, Businesswoman (The Private Concierge); Rick Bayless, Police Officer (former)
Time period(s): 2000s
Locale(s): Los Angeles, California

Summary: Lane Chandler has struggled to build her personal service company, The Private Concierge, up to the point where her clients are some of the best know celebrities in country. Now it's on the brink of ruin when her clients begin falling victim to scandal and murder. Someone is out to bring her down and she needs help to catch the culprit. Ex-cop Rick Bayless takes an interest because of the murder of an old friend, but he also remembers Lane when she was a fifteen-year-old accused of prostitution, and is suspicious of her now. Wariness wars with sizzling sexual attraction in this hard-hitting, well-plotted thriller.

Where it's reviewed:
Romantic Times, October 2008, page 80

Other books by the same author:
The Arrangement, 2007
Decadent, 2006
Tease, 2006
While She Was Sleeping, 2003
Angel Face, 2001

Other books you might like:
Beverly Barton, *Dying for You*, 2008
Shannon K. Butcher, *No Escape*, 2008
Heather Graham, *Deadly Night*, 2008
Shannon McKenna, *Ultimate Weapon*, 2008
Karen Robards, *To Trust a Stranger*, 2001

271

L.L. FOSTER (Pseudonym of Lori Foster)

Servant: The Acceptance

(New York: Jove, 2008)

Story type: Urban; Paranormal
Series: Servant. Book 2
Subject(s): Trust; Murder; Paranormal
Major character(s): Gabrielle Cody, Psychic, Hunter (avenger); Luther Cross, Detective—Police
Time period(s): 2000s
Locale(s): United States

Summary: Gabrielle Cody, gifted with the ability to sense evil demons and destroy them, is on another mission—this time she is protecting prostitutes from someone who is out to kill them, and avenging them. Because of her calling and its dangers, Gaby avoids close relationships; however, Detective Luther Cross is a hard man to ignore.

Violent, chilling, and fast-paced, this creative urban fantasy is second in Foster's well-conceived series.

Where it's reviewed:
Romantic Times, September 2008, page 106

Other books by the same author:
Servant: The Awakening, 2007 (Servant. Book 1)

Other books you might like:
Christine Feehan, *Mind Game*, 2004
Sherrilyn Kenyon, *Unleash the Night*, 2006
Jade Lee, *Seduced by Crimson*, 2006
Liz Maverick, *Crimson Rogue*, 2006
J.R. Ward, *Dark Lover*, 2005

272

LORI FOSTER
DEIRDRE MARTIN, Co-Author
JACQUIE D'ALESSANDRO, Co-Author
PENNY MCCALL, Co-Author

Double the Pleasure

(New York: Berkley, 2008)

Story type: Contemporary; Anthology
Time period(s): 2000s

Summary: Identical twins switch places in Lori Foster's steamy tale "Deuces Wild" leading Christy Nash to believe that the new love of her life is her neighbor, Hart Winston, when it's really his brother, Dexter. Deirdre Martin's "Luck of the Irish," an Irish love story set in New York City, pairs feisty Maggie O'Brien with stubborn Brendan Kelly. In Jacquie D'Alessandro's "Your Room or Mine?" newly promoted Jack Walker inherits a department|POand an unwanted consultant. Penny McCall's "Double the Danger" is filled with suspense from the moment country doctor Abigail West finds that the body she's supposed to autopsy is her former lover. But this FBI agent is not really dead.

Other books you might like:
Jacquie D'Alessandro, *Sleepless at Midnight*, 2007
    Mayhem in Mayfair. Book 1
Lori Foster, *Hard to Handle*, 2008
    SBC Fighters. Book 3
Deirdre Martin, *Power Play*, 2008
Penny McCall, *Ace Is Wild*, 2008

273

NICOLE FOSTER (Pseudonym of Danette Fertig-Thompson and Annette Chartier-Warren)

The Bridesmaid's Turn

(New York: Silhouette, 2008)

Story type: Contemporary
Series: Brothers of Rancho Pintada. Book 5
Subject(s): Weddings; Family Relations; Brothers
Major character(s): Aria Charez, Young Woman; Cruz Declan, Military Personnel (captain)
Time period(s): 2000s

Locale(s): Rancho Pintada

Summary: Cruz Declan doesn't meet his father, Jed Garrett, and four adult brothers until he attends a family wedding at Rancho Pintada. He also meets, and falls for, bridesmaid Aria Charez. But Cruz is confused. He doesn't know why, after 35 years, the family wants to meet him, and he certainly hadn't bargained for Aria.

Where it's reviewed:
Romantic Times, September 2008, page 118

Other books by the same author:
The Cowboy's Lady, 2008 (Brothers of Rancho Pintada. Book 4)
The Rancher's Second Chance, 2007 (Brothers of Rancho Pintada. Book 2)
What Makes a Family?, 2007 (Brothers of Rancho Pintada. Book 3)
Sawyer's Special Delivery, 2005 (Brothers of Rancho Pintada. Book 1)
Hallie's Hero, 2003

Other books you might like:
Stella Bagwell, *Hitched to the Horseman*, 2008
Susan Crosby, *The Rancher's Surprise Marriage*, 2008
Linda Lael Miller, *A Stone Creek Christmas*, 2008
Diana Palmer, *Heart of Stone*, 2008
Karen Rose Smith, *The Daddy Verdict*, 2008

274

ANGIE FOX

The Accidental Demon Slayer

(New York: Love Spell, 2008)

Story type: Paranormal; Humor
Subject(s): Witches and Witchcraft; Humor; Family Relations
Major character(s): Lizzie Brown, Witch (novice), Warrior (novice demon slayer); Dimitri Kallinikos, Mythical Creature (griffin), Warrior
Time period(s): 2000s
Locale(s): Atlanta, Georgia; Red Skull

Summary: Lizzie Brown leads a ho-hum life until the day she turns 30 when all hell breaks loose. Literally. Lizzie's Harley-riding grandmother shows up at her door and announces that she's a witch. A biker witch, to be specific. Lizzie's dog, Pirate, begins to speak. To top everything off, a murderous demon shows up in her toilet. Suddenly, Lizzie is thrust into her destiny, that of the Promised One, the Exalted Demon Slayer of Dalea. Fortunately, fate includes her protector, Dimitri Kallinikos, a movie-star handsome, shape-shifting griffin. Unfortunately, it also includes Vlad, the biggest, baddest demon of them all—and the dictate to kill him might very well end up to be a suicide mission.

Where it's reviewed:
Booklist, August 1, 2008, page 49
Romantic Times, August 2008, page 100

Other books you might like:
Annette Blair, *Gone with the Witch*, 2008
Triplet Witch. Book 2
Katie MacAlister, *Up in Smoke*, 2008

Silver Dragons. Book 2
Stephanie Rowe, *Sex and the Immortal Bad Boy*, 2008
Immortally Sexy. Book 4
Kerrelyn Sparks, *Be Still My Vampire Heart*, 2007
Love at Stake. Book 3
Minda Webber, *Bustin'*, 2007

275

DOROTHY GARLOCK

Leaving Whiskey Bend

(New York: Grand Central, 2008)

Story type: Historical/American West
Subject(s): Abuse; Family Relations; Ranch Life
Major character(s): Hallie Wolcott, Teacher; Eli Morgan, Military Personnel (former general), Rancher
Time period(s): 1890s (1890)
Locale(s): Bison City, Colorado; Whiskey Bend, Colorado

Summary: When Mary Sinclair is abused, teacher Hallie Wolcott and widow Pearl Parsons rescue her and together they leave Whiskey Bend. With no particular destination in mind other than to get as far away from Whiskey Bend as they can, they travel until a driving rainstorm slows them down and the distraught Mary throws herself into the raging river. Rescued by former Army general Eli Morgan and his uncle, the three women are taken to the ranch and welcomed into a rather dysfunctional family. Romance develops between Hallie and Eli, but problems remain, including the fact that someone is out to kill Eli and the villain who abused Mary is out for vengeance. Gritty, realistic, violent, but ultimately salutary, this story is classic Garlock.

Where it's reviewed:
Romantic Times, November 2008, page 50

Other books by the same author:
A Week from Sunday, 2007
On Tall Pine Lake, 2007
Train from Marietta, 2006
River Rising, 2005
Song of the Road, 2004

Other books you might like:
Catherine Anderson, *Keegan's Lady*, 1996
Megan Chance, *The Way Home*, 1997
Maggie Osborne, *Shotgun Wedding*, 2003
Patricia Potter, *Defiant*, 1995
Bobbi Smith, *Tessa*, 2000

276

WHITNEY GASKELL

Good Luck

(New York: Bantam, 2008)

Story type: Contemporary
Subject(s): Lottery; Secrets; Scandal
Major character(s): Lucy Parker, Teacher; Mal, Teacher (tennis instructor)

Time period(s): 2000s
Locale(s): Ocean Falls, Florida; Palm Beach, Florida
Summary: Teacher Lucy Parker fails the wealthiest student at an elite preparatory school. For revenge, the teen accuses her of making sexual advances toward him. Since his father is one of the institution's major financial backers, the principal accepts the student's allegations, and Lucy is fired. Within hours, Lucy's car breaks down, and once she gets home, she discovers her boyfriend having sex with a hot blonde. That day, though, Lucy buys a lottery ticket, and she wins more than $34 million. Lucy's luck spins back and forth. She becomes rich, but someone leaks the story of her student's accusations, and she's an instant pariah. Lucy takes the money and runs to Palm Beach, where she changes her identity and her hair color, but has no idea how long her masquerade can last.

Where it's reviewed:
Booklist, October 1, 2008, page 24
Publishers Weekly, August 11, 2008, page 27

Other books by the same author:
Mommy Tracked, 2007
Testing Katie, 2006
She, Myself, and I, 2005
True Love (and Other Lies), 2004
Pushing 30, 2003

Other books you might like:
Pete Hautman, *Mrs. Million*, 2000
Susan Kearney, *Kiss Me Deadly*, 2007
    lottery winning and murder
K. Reid, *Powerball 310*, 2006
G. Edward Warren, *The Lottery Winner*, 2005
Patricia Wood, *Lottery*, 2008

277

DIANE GASTON (Pseudonym of Diane Perkins)

Scandalizing the Ton

(Toronto: Harlequin, 2008)

Story type: Historical/Regency
Subject(s): Newspapers; Scandal
Major character(s): Lydia Wexin, Noblewoman, Widow(er); Adrian Pomroy, Nobleman (Viscount Cavanley)
Time period(s): 1810s (1818)
Locale(s): London, England

Summary: While out shopping one day, Lady Lydia Wexin is saved from a particularly annoying journalist, who is determined to get the real story about the *ton*'s most scandalous widow, by Adrian Pomroy, Viscount Cavanley. After Adrian takes Lydia home, the two find themselves tempted into indulging in an unexpected night of passion. When Lydia later discovers she is pregnant, it only adds to the scandal surrounding her since now everyone wants to know who is responsible for her new condition: her late husband or her mysterious new lover.

Where it's reviewed:
Booklist, October 15, 2008, page 28
Romantic Times, October 2008, page 52

Other books by the same author:
The Vanishing Viscountess, 2008
Innocence and Impropriety, 2007
A Reputable Rake, 2006
The Wagering Widow, 2006
The Mysterious Miss M, 2005

Other books you might like:
Mary Balogh, *Slightly Tempted*, 2004
Christina Dodd, *Scandalous Again*, 2003
Diane Farr, *Under a Lucky Star*, 2004
Brenda Hiatt, *Scandalous Virtue*, 1999
Kathryn Smith, *A Game of Scandal*, 2002

278

OLIVIA GATES

The Desert King

(New York: Silhouette, 2008)

Story type: Contemporary; Multicultural
Series: Throne of Judar. Book 3
Subject(s): Middle East; Kings, Queens, Rulers, etc.; Trust
Major character(s): Aliyah Morgan, Royalty (princess of Zohayd); Kamal Aal Masood, Royalty (king of Judar)
Time period(s): 2000s
Locale(s): Judar, Fictional Country (country in Middle East)

Summary: Kamal ben Hareth ben Essan Ed-Deen Aal Masood becomes king of Judar after his two older brothers choose love over ruling their kingdom. Kamal won't choose love—after his passionate affair with Aliyah Morgan, he knows that women can't be trusted. However, things spin out of control for the monarch when, because of an agreement made a generation ago, he has to wed the princess of Zohayd. When that woman turns out to be Aliyah, a battle royal begins.

Where it's reviewed:
Romantic Times, September 2008, page 116

Other books by the same author:
The Desert Lord's Baby, 2008 (Throne of Judar. Book 1)
The Desert Lord's Bride, 2008 (Throne of Judar. Book 2)
Radical Cure, 2006 (Dr. Calista St. James. Book 2)
Strong Medicine, 2005 (Dr. Calista St. James. Book 1)

Other books you might like:
Michelle Celmer, *An Affair with the Princess*, 2008
Maureen Child, *Baby Bonanza*, 2008
Joan Hohl, *The M.D.'s Mistress*, 2008
Leslie LaFoy, *The Money Man's Seduction*, 2008
Jennifer Lewis, *Prince of Midtown*, 2008

279

GEORGINA GENTRY (Pseudonym of Lynn Murphy)

To Seduce a Texan

(New York: Zebra, 2009)

Story type: Historical/American West; Humor
Subject(s): Kidnapping; Inheritance; Self-Perception
Major character(s): Rosemary Burke, Heiress; Waco McClain, Military Personnel, Outlaw
Time period(s): 1860s (1864)
Locale(s): Red River, Texas; Prairie View, Kansas

Summary: Thanks to her mother's running commentary, heiress Rosemary Burke feels fat and frumpy. Home from a year-long tour of Europe, Rosemary discovers that her stepfather, who killed her mother, plans to marry, and then kill her, too. Fate intervenes when Confederate officer Waco McClain kidnaps Rosemary for a ransom that will fund the Southern cause. Much to his surprise, Waco finds the pampered rich girl to be full of spunk and courage. He even admires her sturdy stature, one of the traits that makes him irresistible to his captive.

Where it's reviewed:
Romantic Times, January 2009, page 48

Other books by the same author:
To Wed a Texan, 2008
To Love a Texan, 2007
To Tease a Texan, 2006
To Tempt a Texan, 2005
To Tame a Rebel, 2004

Other books you might like:
Lori Copeland, *Promise Me Today*, 1992
    Sisters of Mercy Flats. Book 1
Geralyn Dawson, *Her Outlaw*, 2007
    Bad Luck Brides. Book 3
Kathleen Kane, *Catch a Fallen Angel*, 2000
    humorous paranormal western
Nancy J. Parra, *A Wanted Man*, 2002
Allie Shaw, *The Impossible Bride*, 2002

280

COLLEEN GLEASON

When Twilight Burns

(New York: Signet Eclipse, 2008)

Story type: Historical/Fantasy; Historical/Regency
Series: Gardella Vampire Chronicles. Book 3
Subject(s): Murder; Vampires
Major character(s): Victoria Gardella Grantworth de Lacy, Noblewoman, Vampire Hunter; Sebastian Vioget, Vampire Hunter; Max Pesaro, Vampire Hunter
Time period(s): 1810s
Locale(s): London, England

Summary: After engaging in a deadly battle with vampires in Italy, Victoria Gardella Grantworth de Lacy has finally returned home to London. Any plans Victoria might have to rest and recuperate have to be put on hold when evidence of a new breed of vampires—ones who can walk in the sunlight-is discovered in London. Now Victoria not only has to figure out a way to fight vampires both during the day and at night; she has to find a way to clear her own name when she is framed for their murders.

Where it's reviewed:
Romantic Times, August 2008, page 38

Other books by the same author:
Rises the Night, 2008
The Rest Falls Away, 2007
A Whisper of Rosemary, 2002

Other books you might like:
Susan Carroll, *The Bride Finder*, 1998
Teresa Medeiros, *After Midnight*, 2005
Amanda Quick, *Deception*, 1993
Jaclyn Reding, *White Mist*, 2000
Susan Squires, *Sacrament*, 2002

281

JANE GOODGER

Marry Christmas

(New York: Zebra, 2008)

Story type: Historical/Victorian
Subject(s): Marriage; Inheritance; Change
Major character(s): Elizabeth Cummings, Heiress, Socialite (American); Randall Blackmore, Nobleman (Duke of Bellingham)
Time period(s): 1890s (1892)
Locale(s): Newport, Rhode Island; England

Summary: Cruelly bullied by her selfish mother, wealthy Elizabeth Cummings agrees to wed Randall Blackmore Duke of Bellingham, even though she loves another, or so she thinks. Since it's a marriage of convenience for them both—Randall needs her money, Elizabeth's mother wants her to have the title—they come to an understanding. Love comes to them both, eventually, but not before jealousy, miscommunication, and an old suitor's despicable behavior cause a serious rift between them.

Where it's reviewed:
Romantic Times, October 2008, page 52

Other books by the same author:
Gifts from the Sea, 2001
The Perfect Wife, 2000
Into the Wild Wind, 1999
Dancing with Sin, 1998
Anything for Love, 1997

Other books you might like:
Elizabeth Boyle, *No Marriage of Convenience*, 2000
Eloisa James, *Duchess in Love*, 2002
Edith Layton, *A Bride for His Convenience*, 2008
Julianne MacLean, *To Marry the Duke*, 2003
Patricia Rice, *All a Woman Wants*, 2001

282

JO GOODMAN (Pseudonym of Joanne Dobrzanski)

The Price of Desire

(New York: Zebra, 2008)

Story type: Historical/Regency
Subject(s): Gambling; Conduct of Life; Scandal
Major character(s): Olivia Cole, Gentlewoman; Griffin Wright-Jones, Nobleman (Viscount Breckenridge), Businessman (gaming hell owner)
Time period(s): 1820s (1823)
Locale(s): England

Summary: When her irresponsible brother "gives" her as collateral to Viscount Breckenridge, the owner of a gaming hell, until he can pay his debt, Olivia Cole is drawn into a dangerous, shadowy world and into the life of a man who intrigues her far more than he should and has a definite agenda of his own. Passion flares between them as they are swept up in a malevolent web of betrayal, death, deceit, and abuse that must be sorted out and dealt with before they can find happiness. Readers should be aware that this rather dark story includes issues of child abuse.

Where it's reviewed:
Romantic Times, September 2008, page 51

Other books by the same author:
If His Kiss Is Wicked, 2007
One Forbidden Evening, 2006
A Season to Be Sinful, 2005
Everything I Ever Wanted, 2003
Let Me Be the One, 2002

Other books you might like:
Mary Balogh, *One Night for Love*, 1999
Elizabeth Boyle, *Tempted by the Night*, 2008
Liz Carlyle, *A Woman of Virtue*, 2001
Lynn Kerstan, *Dangerous Deceptions*, 2004
Lynn Kerstan, *Heart of the Tiger*, 2003

283

LINDA GOODNIGHT

Winning the Single Mom's Heart

(Toronto: Harlequin, 2008)

Story type: Contemporary
Subject(s): Widows/Widowers; Doctors; Twins
Major character(s): Natalie Thompson, Baker (Wedding Belles wedding planner), Single Parent (of twin daughters); Cooper Sullivan, Doctor (pediatric cardiologist)
Time period(s): 2000s
Locale(s): Boston, Massachusetts

Summary: Widowed single mom Natalie Thompson, self-proclaimed "cake fairy" for The Wedding Belles wedding planning agency, has her hands full. She works full time while raising her twin eight-year-old daughters, Rose and Lily. Natalie is still recovering from the tragic death of her husband two years before, and though she's struggling, she's determined to make it on her own. Then a chance reunion with Cooper Sullivan, an old college friend, changes everything. Cooper, now an accomplished pediatric cardiologist, would like nothing more than to be with Natalie and her girls, but the memory of Natalie's late husband has him second-guessing his motives. Rebellious Rose complicates matters by doing her worst to keep Natalie and Cooper apart.

Where it's reviewed:
Romantic Times, July 2008, page 110

Other books by the same author:
A Time to Heal, 2008
The Millionaire's Nanny Arrangement, 2008
Married under the Mistletoe, 2006
Sometimes When We Kiss, 2006
Prince Incognito, 2006

Other books you might like:
Caroline Andersen, *The Tycoon's Instant Family*, 2006
Judy Christenberry, *The Rancher's Inherited Family*, 2008
Shirley Jump, *Sweetheart Lost and Found*, 2008
Susan Mallery, *Sweet Spot*, 2008
Trish Milburn, *A Firefighter in the Family*, 2008

284

ANNE GRACIE

His Captive Lady

(New York: Berkley Sensation, 2008)

Story type: Historical/Regency
Series: Devil Riders. Book 2
Subject(s): Scandal; Change; Marriage
Major character(s): Helen "Nell" Freymore, Noblewoman (daughter of an earl); Harry Morant, Military Personnel (former Devil Rider), Bastard Son (of an earl)
Time period(s): 1810s (1817)
Locale(s): England

Summary: Returning from war, all Harry Morant, the natural son of an earl, wants to do is breed horses, and he has found the perfect place to do it, Firmin Court. But Firmin Court is also the former home of Lady Helen Freymore, the destitute daughter of a late, profligate earl, and when Harry meets Nell, there is only one thought in his mind—marriage. A protective hero who still struggles with childhood rejection issues and a heroine with dark secrets of her own find love, happiness, and vindication in this heartwarming romance that nicely continues the Devil Riders series.

Where it's reviewed:
Romantic Times, September 2008, page 46

Other books by the same author:
The Stolen Princess, 2008 (Devil Riders. Book 1)
The Perfect Kiss, 2007 (Merridew. Book 4)
The Perfect Stranger, 2006 (Merridew. Book 3)
The Perfect Rake, 2005 (Merridew. Book 1)
The Perfect Waltz, 2005 (Merridew. Book 2)

Other books you might like:
Mary Balogh, *Simply Love*, 2006

Miss Martin's School for Girls. Book 2
Jo Beverley, *A Lady's Secret*, 2008
Sophia Nash, *A Dangerous Beauty*, 2007
Julia Quinn, *The Lost Duke of Wyndham*, 2008
Julia Quinn, *Mr. Cavendish, I Presume*, 2008

285

HEATHER GRAHAM (Pseudonym of Heather Graham Pozzessere)

Deadly Gift

(Don Mills, Ontario: MIRA, 2008)

Story type: Contemporary; Romantic Suspense
Series: Flynn Brothers. Book 3
Subject(s): Family Problems; Paranormal; Murder
Major character(s): Caer Cavannaugh, Nurse, Mythical Creature; Zach Flynn, Detective—Private
Time period(s): 2000s
Locale(s): Dublin, Ireland; Newport, Rhode Island

Summary: Assigned to accompany recovering Sean O'Riley from a Dublin hospital to his home in Rhode Island, "nurse" Caer Cavannaugh knows his life is in danger and that she must protect him at all costs. P.I. Zach Flynn has been called in, as well, because one of Sean's partners has turned up missing. However, Zach doesn't know Caer's role, and while he is attracted to her, he thinks she's hiding something—and she is. In this cast of quirky characters there are plenty of suspects to go around, and while the ultimate ending of the story is never really in doubt, there are any number of surprises that are sure to please fans. This tense, romantic suspense is a satisfying end to the Flynn Brothers Trilogy.

Where it's reviewed:
Romantic Times, December 2008, page 60

Other books by the same author:
The Death Dealer, 2009
Deadly Harvest, 2008 (Flynn Brothers. Book 2)
Deadly Night, 2008 (Flynn Brothers. Book 1)
The Dead Room, 2007
The Seance, 2007

Other books you might like:
Stella Cameron, *Breathless*, 1994
Catherine Coulter, *The Cove*, 1996
Kay Hooper, *Haunting Rachel*, 1998
Elizabeth Lowell, *Moving Target*, 2001
Nora Roberts, *Carolina Moon*, 2000

286

HEATHER GRAHAM (Pseudonym of Heather Graham Pozzessere)

Deadly Harvest

(Don Mills, Ontario: MIRA, 2008)

Story type: Contemporary; Romantic Suspense
Series: Flynn Brothers. Book 2
Subject(s): Serial Killers; Paranormal; Suspense
Major character(s): Rowenna Cavanaugh, Psychic, Consultant (occult expert); Jeremy Flynn, Detective—Private, Musician
Time period(s): 2000s
Locale(s): Salem, Massachusetts; New Orleans, Louisiana

Summary: Called to Salem, Massachusetts, to investigate the bizarre disappearance of the wife of an old friend, P.I. Jeremy Flynn finds himself working with psychic Rowenna Cavanaugh, with whom he has a budding romantic relationship, to find the real killer. Rowenna's frightening, recurring dreams of crows, cornfields, and bloody scarecrows convince her that something evil is afoot—and then they find a real bloody scarecrow, and the investigation takes on a different tone. The old Harvest Man legend adds a touch of the occult to this chilling tale.

Where it's reviewed:
Romantic Times, November 2008, page 61

Other books by the same author:
The Death Dealer, 2009
Deadly Gift, 2008 (Flynn Brothers. Book 3)
Deadly Night, 2008 (Flynn Brothers. Book 1)
The Dead Room, 2007
The Seance, 2007

Other books you might like:
Shannon Drake, *The Awakening*, 2003
Nora Roberts, *Blood Brothers*, 2007
    Sign of Seven. Book 1
Nora Roberts, *The Hollow*, 2008
    Sign of Seven. Book 2
Nora Roberts, *The Pagan Stone*, 2008
    Sign of Seven. Book 3
Patricia Simpson, *The Dark Lord*, 2004

287

HEATHER GRAHAM (Pseudonym of Heather Graham Pozzessere)

Deadly Night

(Don Mills, Ontario: MIRA, 2008)

Story type: Contemporary; Romantic Suspense
Series: Flynn Brothers. Book 1
Subject(s): Serial Killers; Legends; Paranormal
Major character(s): Kendall Montgomery, Businesswoman (cafe and gift shop owner), Psychic (reluctant); Aidan Flynn, Detective—Private, Heir
Time period(s): 1860s (1863); 2000s
Locale(s): New Orleans, Louisiana

Summary: When a relative they never knew about dies and leaves them a crumbling, haunted plantation along the Mississippi River, the three Flynn brothers, partners in their own private investigation agency, arrive in New Orleans to consider their options. When P.I. Aidan Flynn discovers a human bone in the old slave quarters, and other bones turn up along the river, he and psychic Kendall Montgomery are drawn into a current serial killer investigation that involves a number of old, unsolved cases, as well. Old legends, ghostly apparitions, and psychic premonitions add chills to this first book in the suspenseful paranormal trilogy about the three Flynn brothers.

Where it's reviewed:
Romantic Times, October 2008, page 80

Other books by the same author:
The Death Dealer, 2009
Deadly Gift, 2008 (Flynn Brothers. Book 3)
Deadly Harvest, 2008 (Flynn Brothers. Book 2)
The Dead Room, 2007
The Seance, 2007

Other books you might like:
Stella Cameron, *A Marked Man*, 2006
Karen Robards, *Ghost Moon*, 2000
Karen Robards, *Wait Until Dark*, 2001
  anthology
JoAnn Ross, *No Safe Place*, 2007
Tina Wainscott, *Unforgivable*, 2001

288

PATRICIA GRASSO

Enticing the Prince

(New York: Zebra, 2008)

Story type: Historical/Regency
Series: Kazanov Brothers
Subject(s): Revenge; Seduction; Scandal
Major character(s): Katerina Pavlova Garibaldi, Noble-woman (Contessa de Salerno), Jeweler; Drako Kazanov, Royalty (prince)
Time period(s): 1820s (1821)
Locale(s): England

Summary: Seeking revenge for her family's ruin, Katerina Pavlova Garibaldi, brilliant jeweler and woman of mystery, targets Prince Drako Kazanov as the culprit. However, when she comes to know—and love—him, she realizes he is not the one she's after. Now they must unmask the real villain before they become victims themselves.

Where it's reviewed:
Romantic Times, November 2008, page 52

Other books by the same author:
Tempting the Prince, 2007 (Kazanov Brothers)
Pleasuring the Prince, 2006 (Kazanov Brothers)
Seducing the Prince, 2005 (Kazanov Brothers)
To Catch a Countess, 2004
To Love a Princess, 2004

Other books you might like:
Mary Balogh, *Thief of Dreams*, 1998
Jane Feather, *Almost a Bride*, 2005
Lynn Kerstan, *Heart of the Tiger*, 2003
Lynn Kerstan, *The Silver Lion*, 2003
Lisa Kleypas, *Lady Sophia's Lover*, 2002

289

LAURA LEE GUHRKE

Secret Desires of a Gentleman

(New York: Avon, 2008)

Story type: Historical/Victorian
Series: Girl Bachelors. Book 3

Subject(s): Cooks and Cooking; Family
Major character(s): Maria Martingale, Cook (pastry chef); Phillip Hawthorne, Nobleman (Marquess of Kayne)
Time period(s): 1890s (1895)
Locale(s): London, England

Summary: For months Maria Martingale has been searching for the perfect location for her pastry shop, and now she has finally found it. The only problem is that her new shop is right next door to the temporary home of Phillip Hawthorne, the Marquess of Kayne. Twelve years ago, Phillip prevented Maria from eloping with his brother Lawrence by bribing her to leave, but now that Maria is back in London, Phillip is certain she will ruin Lawrence's engagement to an American heiress. What Phillip didn't expect was that he would be the one to find Maria too delicious to resist.

Where it's reviewed:
Romantic Times, October 2008, page 48

Other books by the same author:
And Then He Kissed Her, 2007
The Wicked Ways of a Duke, 2007
She's No Princess, 2006
The Marriage Bed, 2005
His Every Kiss, 2004

Other books you might like:
Adele Ashworth, *The Duke's Indiscretion*, 2007
Robyn DeHart, *Deliciously Wicked*, 2007
Deborah Hale, *Highland Rogue*, 2004
Lisa Kleypas, *Lady Sophia's Lover*, 2002
Sherry Thomas, *Private Arrangements*, 2008

290

BARBARA HANNAY

Adopted: Outback Baby

(Toronto: Harlequin, 2008)

Story type: Contemporary
Subject(s): Adoption; Forgiveness; Family Relations
Major character(s): Nell Ruthven, Artist (quilts); Jacob Tucker, Rancher
Time period(s): 1980s; 2000s
Locale(s): Half Moon, Australia

Summary: Young lovers Nell Ruthven and Jacob Tucker are forced apart by her father, and Tegan, the baby girl resulting from that union, is given up for adoption. Twenty years pass, and Tegan dies, but not before giving birth to a son. Now, Nell and Jacob have another chance at life together as they raise their grandson.

Where it's reviewed:
Romantic Times, July 2008, page 111

Other books by the same author:
Blind Date with the Boss, 2008
The Bridesmaid's Best Man, 2008
In the Heart of the Outback, 2007
Needed: Her Mr. Right, 2007
The Mirrabrook Marriage, 2005

Other books you might like:
Claire Baxter, *Pregnant: Father Wanted*, 2008
Barbara Dunlop, *Overheated*, 2008
Linda Goodnight, *The Millionaire's Nanny Arrangement*, 2008
Marion Lennox, *Wanted: Royal Wife and Mother*, 2008
Raye Morgan, *The Prince's Secret Bride*, 2008

291

KAREN HARPER

The Hiding Place

(Don Mills, Ontario: MIRA, 2008)

Story type: Contemporary; Romantic Suspense
Subject(s): Murder; Children; Change
Major character(s): Tara Kinsale, Detective—Private (seeks missing children), Guardian; Nick MacMahon, Guardian, Animal Trainer (dogs)
Time period(s): 2000s
Locale(s): Colorado

Summary: Waking from an 11-month coma, Tara Kinsale-Lohan learns that her best friend has been murdered and she is now the guardian for her young daughter, Claire; that her husband has divorced her and has remarried; and that she might have had a baby while she was unconscious. To top it off, Nick MacMahon, Claire's uncle, is back from the Middle East and plans to assume guardianship of Claire. Claire is still emotionally fragile, so Tara gladly agrees to stay and help for the time being. Her mysterious pregnancy, however, puzzles her, and as she begins to sort things out, the truth that emerges is nothing like what she could have imagined. Danger, deception, and love are part of this chilling thriller.

Where it's reviewed:
Romantic Times, November 2008, page 66

Other books by the same author:
Below the Surface, 2008
Hurricane, 2006
The Falls, 2006
Dark Angel, 2005 (Maplecreek. Book 3)
Dark Harvest, 2004 (Maplecreek. Book 2)

Other books you might like:
Jasmine Cresswell, *The Refuge*, 2000
Jasmine Cresswell, *Secret Sins*, 1997
Heather Graham, *Tall, Dark, and Deadly*, 1999
Dinah McCall, *Chase the Moon*, 1997
Karen Robards, *Maggie's Child*, 1994

292

JESSICA HART

Newlyweds of Convenience

(Toronto: Harlequin, 2008)

Story type: Contemporary
Subject(s): Inheritance; Castles; Trust
Major character(s): Mallory Hunter McIver, Interior Decorator; Torr McIver, Businessman (wealthy), Heir (run-down Scottish castle)
Time period(s): 2000s
Locale(s): Ellsborough; Scotland (Kincaillie, a Highlands castle)

Summary: When interior designer Mallory Hunter works her magic on wealthy Torr McIver's fabulous house, she has no idea that she'll end up marrying this stern, forbidding businessman, and this will be her home. Mallory's partner and lover, Steve, has scammed her, leaving her with a mountain of debts, and marriage to Torr is the only way out for Mallory. Torr and Mallory have an agreement—their relationship will have no emotions; Torr will cover her debts; Mallory will keep their house beautiful; and when he needs a hostess for business meals and get-togethers, Mallory will make him look good. After a disastrous wedding night, their five platonic months together have been polite, but cold. Then Torr moves them to Kincaille, a decaying castle in the Scottish Highlands that he's inherited, and suddenly, as they renovate it and turn it into a home, the standoffish spouse turns into someone Mallory could really fall for.

Where it's reviewed:
Romantic Times, July 2008, page 110

Other books by the same author:
Last-Minute Proposal, 2008
Promoted: To Wife and Mother, 2008
Appointment at the Altar, 2007
Barefoot Bride, 2007
Outback Boss, 2007

Other books you might like:
Jennie Adams, *The Boss's Unconventional Assistant*, 2008
Donna Alward, *Falling for Mr. Dark and Dangerous*, 2008
Judy Christenberry, *The Rancher's Inherited Family*, 2008
Susan Meier, *Millionaire Dad, Nanny Needed!*, 2008
Raye Morgan, *The Prince's Secret Bride*, 2008

293

KAREN HAWKINS

Talk of the Town

(New York: Pocket, 2008)

Story type: Contemporary
Subject(s): Family; Murder
Major character(s): Roxanne Lynne "Roxie" Treymayne, Divorced Person; Nick Sheppard, Police Officer
Time period(s): 2000s
Locale(s): Raleigh, North Carolina; Glory, North Carolina

Summary: After divorcing her cheating husband, a new and improved Roxie Treymayne has plans for a totally different future for herself, but those plans take an unexpected detour when Roxie's mother falls ill. Forced into returning home, Roxie can't believe the first person she meets is an old romantic fling: Nick Sheppard, Glory's sheriff. Roxie is more than willing to pick up where the two of them left off; but based on their past, Nick is certain any new romantic relationship with Roxie will be just another mistake waiting to happen.

Where it's reviewed:
Romantic Times, December 2008, page 76

Other books by the same author:
To Catch a Highlander, 2008
How to Abduct a Highland Lord, 2007
To Scotland with Love, 2007
Her Master and Commander, 2006
Her Officer and Gentleman, 2006

Other books you might like:
Elizabeth Bevarly, *Her Man Friday*, 1999
Jennifer Crusie, *Tell Me Lies*, 1998
Jennifer Greene, *Where Is He Now?*, 2003
Luanne Jones, *The Dixie Belle's Guide to Love*, 2002
Susan Elizabeth Phillips, *Aint She Sweet?*, 2004

294

LORRAINE HEATH (Pseudonym of Jan Nowasky)

In Bed with the Devil

(New York: Avon, 2008)

Story type: Historical/Victorian
Series: Scoundrels of St. James. Book 1
Subject(s): Murder; Conduct of Life; Social Classes
Major character(s): Lady Catherine Mabry, Noblewoman (daughter of a duke); Lucian Langdon, Nobleman (Earl of Claybourne)
Time period(s): 1850s (1851)
Locale(s): London, England

Summary: Claimed as the long-lost grandson of the Earl of Claybourne and rescued by the Earl, along with his fellow street urchins, when he was fourteen and accused of murder, Lucian Langdon, the Earl of Claybourne, also known as the Devil Earl, is still viewed with suspicion by much of polite society. However, Lady Catherine Mabry needs his help to free her friend from an abusive marriage—and so they strike an outrageous bargain. Catherine will teach the woman Lucian wants to marry how to behave as a countess, and Lucian will get rid of her friend's husband. Naturally, things don't evolve as planned in this emotionally rich story that is darker than Heath's normal fare, but every bit as captivating.

Where it's reviewed:
Romantic Times, January 2008, page 35

Other books by the same author:
Between the Devil and Desire, 2008
A Duke of Her Own, 2006
Promise Me Forever, 2006
As an Earl Desires, 2005
An Invitation to Seduction, 2004

Other books you might like:
Julie Garwood, *For the Roses*, 1995
    Victorian American setting
Jo Goodman, *A Season to Be Sinful*, 2005
    Compass Club. Book 4
Johanna Lindsey, *A Loving Scoundrel*, 2004
Kat Martin, *Innocence Undone*, 1997
Rachelle Morgan, *A Scandalous Lady*, 2003

295

SHIRL HENKE

Pale Moon Stalker

(New York: Leisure, 2008)

Story type: Historical/American West; Indian Culture
Series: Wild West. Book 2
Subject(s): Marriage; Inheritance; Revenge
Major character(s): Sky Eyes Brewster, Indian (Ehanktonwon Sioux), Widow(er); Maxwell Stanhope, Bounty Hunter, Nobleman (Baron Ruxton)
Time period(s): 1800s (1884)
Locale(s): Bismarck, South Dakota; London, England; Denver, Colorado

Summary: After Sky Eyes Brewster's preacher husband is murdered, she seeks to hire Max Stanhope, an English nobleman known as "The Limey," to hunt down the killer. Her timing couldn't be better. As it happens, Max, an accomplished bounty hunter, has just learned his uncle has died, and he stands to gain a sizable inheritance if he returns to England with a wife. Max isn't interested in receiving his uncle's title or estate; he just wants to keep the family's fortune out of the hands of his unscrupulous drunkard cousin. Max and Sky Eyes strike a bargain to fulfill each other's particular need, by marrying for convenience and then separating when their deal is completed. The trouble is, while attempting to pull off a convincing "marriage," they end up falling in love.

Where it's reviewed:
Romantic Times, November 2008, page 50

Other books by the same author:
The River Nymph, 2008 (Wild West. Book 1)
Rebel Baron, 2004 (American Lords. Book 2)
Texas Viscount, 2004 (American Lords. Book 3)
Yankee Earl, 2003 (American Lords. Book 1)
Wicked Angel, 2001 (Blackthorne. Book 2)

Other books you might like:
Kathryn Albright, *The Rebel and the Lady*, 2008
R.B. Conroy, *The Heart of a Gunman*, 2007
B.J. Daniels, *Montana Royalty*, 2008
Julie Garwood, *For the Roses*, 1996
Linda Lael Miller, *High Country Bride*, 2002

296

VIRGINIA HENLEY

The Decadent Duke

(New York: Signet, 2008)

Story type: Historical/Georgian
Subject(s): Family Relations; Mothers and Daughters; Brothers
Major character(s): Georgina Gordon, Noblewoman; John Russell, Nobleman (duke's brother)
Time period(s): 1800s
Locale(s): London, England

Summary: Lady Georgina Gordon has four sisters, all wed into powerful, wealthy families. Now her mother expects her to do even better for herself. Unfortunately, her mother's choice for a perfect son-in-law is the dreadfully dull Francis Russell, Duke of Bedford. Georgina's got another man in mind—the duke's younger brother, the notorious rake John Russell.

Where it's reviewed:
Romantic Times, November 2008, page 45

Other books by the same author:
Tempted, 2008
Notorious, 2007
Infamous, 2006
Unmasked, 2005
Undone, 2003

Other books you might like:
Candace Camp, *The Wedding Challenge*, 2008
Suzanne Enoch, *Reforming a Rake*, 2000
    With This Ring. Book 1
Lynn Kerstan, *Dangerous Passions*, 2005
Anne Mallory, *The Bride Price*, 2008
Maya Rodale, *The Rogue and the Rival*, 2008

297

STEF ANN HOLM

All That Matters

(Don Mills, Ontario: HQN, 2008)

Story type: Contemporary
Subject(s): Stalking; Romance; Small Town Life
Major character(s): Chloe Lawson, Baker, Divorced
    Person; John Moretti, Lawyer, Single Parent
Time period(s): 2000s
Locale(s): Boise, Idaho

Summary: Just as Chloe's bakery is taking off, she is notified that a large supermarket chain, Garretson's, is moving into the shopping center and will be taking her space, as well. Determined to fight, she connects with John Moretti, an attorney and single father with two teenagers, and is surprised when he comes to her with an huge offer from Garretson's to leave before her lease is up. Principle wars with pragmatism as the action heats up in this sweetly romantic story that includes a possible stalker and some violence and reintroduces readers to the engaging Moretti family. Links to *All the Right Angles*.

Where it's reviewed:
Romantic Times, November 2008, page 88

Other books by the same author:
All the Right Angles, 2007
Lucy Gets Her Life Back, 2006
Undressed, 2003
Hearts, 2001
Honey, 2000

Other books you might like:
Laura Castoro, *Icing on the Cake*, 2007
Millie Criswell, *The Trouble with Mary*, 2001
Barbara Freethy, *The Sweetest Thing*, 1999
Debbie Macomber, *6 Rainier Drive*, 2006

Cedar Cove. Book 6
Susan Wiggs, *The Winter Lodge*, 2007

298

HANNAH HOWELL
ADRIENNE BASSO , Co-Author
EVE SILVER , Co-Author

Nature of The Beast

(New York: Kensington, 2008)

Story type: Paranormal; Vampire Story
Subject(s): Vampires; Love; Revenge

Summary: A common thread of valiant vampires ties this anthology together. Vampires are being unjustly hunted in Hannah Howell's "Dark Hero," set in 16th-century Scotland; a vampire lord gets sweet revenge in Adrienne Basso's "Bride of the Beast," set in 13th-century Wales; and a vampire doctor is wrongly accused in Eve Silver's 19th-century London tale, "Kiss of the Vampire."

Where it's reviewed:
Romantic Times, September 2008, page 49

Other books you might like:
Kresley Cole, *A Hunger Like No Other*, 2006
Joy Nash, *Immortals: The Crossing*, 2008
Sara Reinke, *Dark Thirst*, 2007
Gena Showalter, *The Darkest Night*, 2008
Dawn Thompson, *The Brotherhood*, 2007

299

ELIZABETH HOYT (Pseudonym of Nancy M. Finney)

To Seduce a Sinner

(New York: Forever, 2008)

Story type: Historical/Georgian
Series: Four Soldiers. Book 2
Subject(s): Marriage; Secrets; Seduction
Major character(s): Melisande Fleming, Gentlewoman;
    Jasper Renshaw, Nobleman (Viscount Vale)
Time period(s): 1760s (1765)
Locale(s): England

Summary: After her cousin jilts Jasper Renshaw, Viscount Vale, Melisande Fleming offers to marry Jasper herself. At first Jasper is surprised by Melisande's proposal, but since he needs a wife and has already lost two fiancees, Jasper accepts. At first their marriage is supposed to be simply one of convenience, but when both Jasper and and Melisande find themselves falling in love with each other, nothing about their new marriage becomes convenient.

Where it's reviewed:
Booklist, November 1, 2008, page 30
Romantic Times, November 2008, page 47

Other books by the same author:
To Taste Temptation, 2008
The Leopard Prince, 2007
The Serpent Prince, 2007
The Raven Prince, 2006

Other books you might like:
Jo Beverley, *Devilish*, 2000
Liz Carlyle, *The Devil You Know*, 2003
Madeline Hunter, *Rules of Seduction*, 2006
Eloisa James, *Desperate Duchesses*, 2007
Karen Ranney, *To Love a Scottish Lord*, 2003

300

HOLLY JACOBS   (Pseudonym of Holly Fuhrmann)

Everything but a Bride

(New York: Avalon, 2008)

Story type: Contemporary; Humor
Series: Everything but|PO. Book 2
Subject(s): Weddings; Superstition; Friendship
Major character(s): Callie Smith, Businesswoman (Salo Construction); Noah Salo, Businessman (Salo Construction)
Time period(s): 2000s
Locale(s): Erie, Pennsylvania

Summary: When Callie's stepsister Julianna bails on her wedding to Noah Salo, Callie, Noah's longtime friend, agrees to go with him, platonically, on the honeymoon so the reservations don't go to waste. Of course, they soon discover that they are more than friends; but will their love break the Salo family wedding curse, or not? Charming, funny, and heartwarming, this story nicely continues Jacobs' series about the Salo wedding curse.

Where it's reviewed:
Booklist, July 1, 2008, page 45
Library Journal, August 2008, page 60

Other books by the same author:
Everything but the Groom, 2007
Laugh Lines, 2007
The House on Briar Hill Road, 2007
Night Calls, 2006
Love Handles, 2005

Other books you might like:
Judith Arnold, *The Wrong Bride*, 1999
Kimberly Cates, *A Perfect Match*, 2007
Millie Criswell, *No Strings Attached*, 2005
Shirley Jump, *Simply the Best*, 2008
Christie Ridgway, *This Perfect Kiss*, 2001

301

HOLLY JACOBS   (Pseudonym of Holly Fuhrmann)

Once upon a Christmas

(Toronto: Harlequin, 2008)

Story type: Contemporary
Series: American Dads. Book 2
Subject(s): Family; Schools; Family Relations
Major character(s): Michelle Hamilton, Guardian; Daniel McLean, Businessman (house restoration), Carpenter; Brandon Hamilton, Teenager
Time period(s): 2000s

Locale(s): Erie, Pennsylvania

Summary: Raising her nephew, Brandon, is the most important thing in Michelle Hamilton's life, so when Brandon says he wants to find his father, her protective antennae go on full alert. After all, his mother, Michelle's free-spirited sister, flitted from man to man and was not noted for her selectivity. Brandon charges ahead; and when he finds some of his mother's papers that lead him to Daniel McLean, the scene is set for a wonderfully romantic, heartwarming story that makes good use of the holiday season. Characters that continue from the previous volume in the series add to the small town charm of this engaging series.

Where it's reviewed:
Romantic Times, December 2008, page 100

Other books by the same author:
Everything but a Wedding, 2009
Once upon a Valentine, 2009 (American Dads. Book 3)
Everything but a Bride, 2008
Once upon a Thanksgiving, 2008 (American Dads. Book 1)
Everything but the Groom, 2007

Other books you might like:
Marcia Evanick, *Christmas on Conrad Street*, 2002
Marcia Evanick, *Mistletoe Bay*, 2007
Jill Marie Landis, *Heat Wave*, 2004
   Twilight Cove. Book 2
Linda Lael Miller, *Montana Creeds: Tyler*, 2009
   Montana Creeds. Book 3
Karyn Witmer, *A Simple Gift*, 2006

302

HOLLY JACOBS   (Pseudonym of Holly Fuhrmann)

Once upon a Thanksgiving

(Toronto: Harlequin, 2008)

Story type: Contemporary
Series: American Dads. Book 1
Subject(s): Family; Trust; Schools
Major character(s): Samantha Williams, Single Parent, Nurse; Harry Remington, Principal
Time period(s): 2000s
Locale(s): Erie, Pennsylvania

Summary: Volunteered to take charge of the school Thanksgiving pageant after she missed a PTA meeting, Samantha Williams, single mom to four active grade-schoolers and an RN besides, has her hands full. Not surprisingly, a new relationship is the last thing on her mind; but when the new temporary school principal turns out to be an old classmate from grade school, they strike up a comfortable friendship that soon turns into something else. This sweet, charming, funny story is first in Jacobs' trilogy that focuses on three single PTA moms, the holiday events they are in charge of, and the loving relationships that they each, eventually, find.

Where it's reviewed:
Romantic Times, October 2008, page 116

Other books by the same author:
Everything but a Wedding, 2009
Everything but a Bride, 2008
Once upon a Christmas, 2008
Everything but the Groom, 2007
The House on Briar Hill Road, 2007

Other books you might like:
Kimberly Cates, *Lighthouse Cove*, 2002
Marcia Evanick, *Mistletoe Bay*, 2007
Linda Lael Miller, *Montana Creeds: Logan*, 2009
Karen White, *After the Rain*, 2003
Ruth Wind, *Beautiful Stranger*, 2000
　　more serious

303

ARLENE JAMES (Pseudonym of Deborah Rather)

His Small-Town Girl

(Toronto: Steeple Hill, 2008)

Story type: Contemporary; Inspirational
Series: Eden, Oklahoma. Book 1
Subject(s): Faith; Family Relations; Small Town Life
Major character(s): Charlotte Jefford, Hotel Owner (Heavenly Arms); Tyler Aldrich, Wealthy, Businessman
Time period(s): 2000s
Locale(s): Eden, Oklahoma

Summary: When Tyler Aldrich's $100,000 car runs out of gas, he finds himself stranded in Eden, Oklahoma, where the sidewalks are rolled up at 6:00 p.m. However, it's after six, and the only place open is the Heavenly Arms motel, owned and operated by Charlotte Jefford. Taking pity on this lonely traveler, and knowing how limited his choices are for supper, Charlotte invites Tyler to eat with her. Against all odds, the dynamic executive and the reserved small-town girl find themselves attracted to each other, but unsure of their future, since their lives are so very different. Fortunately, Charlotte's faith serves as a guide as this odd couple begin their challenging journey to true love.

Where it's reviewed:
Romantic Times, June 2008, page 125

Other books by the same author:
A Mommy in Mind, 2007 (Tiny Blessings. Book 3)
When Love Comes Home, 2007
A Family to Share, 2006
A Love So Strong, 2006
Butterfly Summer, 2006 (Davis Landing. Book 1)

Other books you might like:
Debra Clopton, *The Cowboy Takes a Bride*, 2008
Dana Corbit, *Homecoming at Hickory Ridge*, 2008
Marta Perry, *Mission: Motherhood*, 2008
Janet Tronstad, *A Heart for the Dropped Stitches*, 2008
Lenora Worth, *Long Star Secret*, 2008

304

ELOISA JAMES (Pseudonym of Mary Bly)

When the Duke Returns

(New York: Avon 2008)

Story type: Historical/Georgian
Series: Desperate Duchesses. Book 4
Subject(s): Family; Marriage; Seduction
Major character(s): Isidore Jermyn, Noblewoman (Duchess of Cosway); Simeon Jermyn, Nobleman (Duke of Cosway)
Time period(s): 1780s (1784)
Locale(s): England

Summary: Isidore, the Duchess of Cosway, met her husband, Simeon Jermyn, for the first time 11 years after their wedding. After their marriage by proxy, Simeon left England to travel around the world, but now he is finally ready to return home to take up his responsibilities as duke. Simeon is more than willing to give Isidore an annulment so the two of them can go their own ways, but he did not count on the fact that once Isidore finally meets her husband, she isn't about to give him up.

Where it's reviewed:
Booklist, December 1, 2008, page 35
Library Journal, December 2008, page 106
Romantic Times, December 2008, page 41

Other books by the same author:
Duchess by Night, 2008
An Affair Before Christmas, 2007
Desperate Duchesses, 2007
Pleasure for Pleasure, 2006
The Taming of the Duke, 2006

Other books you might like:
Connie Brockway, *My Seduction*, 2004
Christina Dodd, *Scandalous Again*, 2003
Elizabeth Hoyt, *The Raven Prince*, 2006
Lauren Royal, *Amber*, 2001

305

TARA JANZEN

Loose and Easy

(New York: Dell, 2008)

Story type: Contemporary; Romantic Suspense
Series: Steele Street—Loose. Book 4
Subject(s): Art; Crime and Criminals; Suspense
Major character(s): Esme Alden, Investigator—Private (art recovery expert); Johnny Ramos, Military Personnel (special defense forces), Government Official (special operative)
Time period(s): 2000s
Locale(s): Denver, Colorado

Summary: Posing as a hooker is part of Esme Alden's plan to retrieve some stolen art and save her father from debt-collecting thugs; but when high school friend Johnny Ramos, special defense forces operative, sees her, he interferes and nearly ruins the whole plan. As things become more dangerous, they join forces, a move that may help them bring down the criminals, but may put their hearts in danger, as well.

Where it's reviewed:
Romantic Times, September 2008, page 76

Other books by the same author:
Breaking Loose, 2009 (Steele Street—Loose. Book 4)
Cutting Loose, 2007 (Steele Street—Loose. Book 3)
On the Loose, 2007 (Steele Street—Loose. Book 1)
Crazy Love, 2006 (Steele. Book 5)
Crazy Sweet, 2006 (Steele. Book 6)

Other books you might like:
Suzanne Brockmann, *Breaking Point*, 2005
Cindy Gerard, *To the Brink*, 2006
JoAnn Ross, *Crossfire*, 2008
Christina Skye, *Code Name: Baby*, 2005
Christina Skye, *To Catch a Thief*, 2008

306

CAROLYN JEWEL

My Wicked Enemy

(New York: Forever, 2008)

Story type: Paranormal; Fantasy
Subject(s): Witches and Witchcraft; Paranormal; Demons
Major character(s): Carson Philips, Witch, Orphan; Nikodemus, Demon
Time period(s): 2000s
Locale(s): San Francisco, California

Summary: Raised by the powerful and evil sorcerer Alvaro Magellan, orphaned witch Carson Philips eventually realizes the full extent of Magellan's evil and flees. Warlord Nikodemus finds her wandering in San Francisco, and although he suspects her at first of being in league with Magellan, he soon realizes she is on Magellan's hit list and needs protection. This creative paranormal is chilling and fast-paced.

Where it's reviewed:
Romantic Times, August 2008, page 94

Other books by the same author:
My Forbidden Desire, 2009
Scandal, 2009
A Darker Crimson, 2005 (Crimson City. Book 4)
The Spare, 2004
Lord Ruin, 2002

Other books you might like:
L.L. Foster, *Servant: The Acceptance*, 2008
   Servant. Book 2
L.L. Foster, *Servant: The Awakening*, 2007
   Servant. Book 1
Sherrilyn Kenyon, *Unleash the Night*, 2006
Marjorie M. Liu, *A Taste of Crimson*, 2005
   Crimson City. Book 2
Liz Maverick, *Shards of Crimson*, 2007
   Crimson City

307

IRIS JOHANSEN

The Treasure

(New York: Bantam, 2008)

Story type: Historical/Medieval
Subject(s): Good and Evil; Adventure and Adventurers; Treasure
Major character(s): Lady Selene Ware, Noblewoman; Kadar Ben Arnaud, Criminal (former assassin)
Time period(s): 12th century (1190s)
Locale(s): Scotland; Middle East

Summary: Picking up where *Lion's Bride* left off, Lady Selene Ware follows reformed assassin Kadar Ben Arnaud when he is called back to Syria by the assassin leader, Sinan, only to be captured in order to insure Kadar's obedience. However, when Kadar learns that Sinan is dead and the one who really summoned him is the power-crazed, evil Nasim, the adventure moves into high gear as the two are sent on a deadly quest for a powerful artifact that could destroy them both. This exotic, sexy, Medieval adventure features a number of paranormal elements and is a classic battle between good and evil. It also ties up any loose ends from *Lion's Bride* and is Johansen's first historical romance since 1996.

Where it's reviewed:
Library Journal, October 15, 2008, page 51
Romantic Times, December 2008, page 41

Other books by the same author:
Dark Summer, 2008
Quicksand, 2008
Silent Thunder, 2008
Pandora's Daughter, 2007
Lion's Bride, 1996

Other books you might like:
Patricia Grasso, *Desert Eden*, 1993
   later time period
Julia Ross, *Night of Sin*, 2005
   later time period
Tina St. John, *Black Lion's Bride*, 2002
Bertrice Small, *The Love Slave*, 1995
Katherine Sutcliffe, *Notorious*, 2000
   later time period

308

ALISSA JOHNSON

As Luck Would Have It

(New York: Leisure, 2008)

Story type: Historical/Regency
Subject(s): Espionage; Seduction
Major character(s): Sophie Everton, Gentlewoman, Spy; Alexander Durmant, Nobleman (Duke of Rockeforte), Spy
Time period(s): 1810s (1811)
Locale(s): England

Summary: Sophie Everton has no other choice; she will

just have to become a spy! Fortunately for Sophie, working for the Prince Regent pays well. All Sophie has to do is subtly discover if any of her cousin Lord Loudor's friends might be spying for Napoleon, and she will receive the money she desperately needs to keep her family's estate. What Sophie doesn't know is that she isn't the only one doing a bit of spying. Alexander Durmant, Duke of Rockeforte, has been given the task of seducing Sophie.

Where it's reviewed:
Romantic Times, October 2008, page 52

Other books you might like:
Celeste Bradley, *Seducing the Spy*, 2006
Shana Galen, *Blackthorne's Bride*, 2007
Sabrina Jeffries, *Never Seduce a Scoundrel*, 2006
Jenna Petersen, *Desire Never Dies*, 2007
Sari Robins, *When Seducing a Spy*, 2007

309

SOPHIE JORDAN (Pseudonym of Sherie Kohler)

Surrender to Me

(New York: Avon, 2008)

Story type: Historical/Regency
Subject(s): Marriage; Murder
Major character(s): Lady Astrid, Noblewoman (Duchess of Derring); Griffin Shaw, Heir—Lost, Landowner (Texas)
Time period(s): 1810s
Locale(s): Scotland; England

Summary: Accosted by highwaymen while on her way to stop her long-absent husband from making a bigamous marriage in Scotland, Lady Astrid, Duchess of Derring, is rescued by the sharp-shooting skills of Griffin Shaw, a Texan in Scotland to ferret out some family secrets. She thinks she'll never see him again, but when her wayward husband is murdered and she ends up as the prime suspect, Astrid is rescued once again by the sexy American. More adventures follow and it is some time before the well-matched pair can come to terms with their feelings for each other in this lively, romantic tale.

Where it's reviewed:
Romantic Times, August 2008, page 44

Other books by the same author:
Sins of a Wicked Duke, 2009
One Night with You, 2007
Too Wicked to Tame, 2007
Once upon a Wedding Night, 2006

Other books you might like:
Arnette Lamb, *Beguiled*, 1996
Johanna Lindsey, *The Heir*, 2000
Cathy Maxwell, *The Marriage Contract*, 2001
Patricia Potter, *The Marshall and the Heiress*, 1996
Jean Ewing Ross, *Flowers under Ice*, 1999

310

SHIRLEY JUMP

Marry-Me Christmas

(Toronto: Harlequin, 2008)

Story type: Contemporary; Holiday Themes
Series: Bride for All Seasons. Book 4
Subject(s): Marriage; Christmas; Cooks and Cooking
Major character(s): Samantha Barnett, Baker, Businesswoman (bakery owner); Flynn MacGregor, Journalist (food writer)
Time period(s): 2000s
Locale(s): Riverbend, Indiana

Summary: Sent to a small Indiana town to interview the baker who bakes cookies that, reputedly, make people fall in love, journalist Flynn MacGregor wants to get the interview and leave. Unfortunately, neither the weather nor baker Samantha Barnett cooperates, leaving him in the last place he wants to spend Christmas—a cheerful, caring town that reminds him of the home he never had. Both Sam and Flynn have secrets to hide and trust issues that need to be overcome in this sweet, delectable confection that overflows with Holiday charm.

Where it's reviewed:
Romantic Times, December 2008, page 103

Other books by the same author:
Sweetheart Lost and Found, 2008 (Wedding Planners. Book 1)
Pretty Bad, 2007
Rescued by Mr. Right, 2006
The Bachelor Preferred Pastry, 2006
The Angel Craved Lobster, 2005

Other books you might like:
Janet Dailey, *Mistletoe and Molly*, 2007
Marcia Evanick, *A Berry Merry Christmas*, 2004
    Misty Harbor. Book 4
Marcia Evanick, *Mistletoe Bay*, 2007
Kristin Hardy, *Her Christmas Surprise*, 2007
Debbie Macomber, *When Christmas Comes*, 2004

311

SHIRLEY JUMP

Simply the Best

(New York: Zebra, 2008)

Story type: Contemporary
Subject(s): Friendship; Romance; Love
Major character(s): Alexandra "Alex" Kenner, Journalist; Mack Douglas, Carpenter
Time period(s): 2000s
Locale(s): Boston, Massachusetts

Summary: Alex and Mack have been best friends since grade school, sharing romantic ups and downs and just being there for each other; but when Alex moves into her grandmother's crumbling house in order to fix it up for her and Mack agrees to help, things take a much more interesting and romantic turn. Funny, heartwarming, and charming, this is one more in Jump's series of feel-good romances.

Where it's reviewed:
Romantic Times, December 2008, page 79

Other books by the same author:
Sweetheart Lost and Found, 2008 (Wedding Planners. Book 1)
Pretty Bad, 2007
Rescued by Mr. Right, 2006
The Angel Craved Lobster, 2005
The Bride Wore Chocolate, 2004

Other books you might like:
Elizabeth Bevarly, *Indecent Suggestion*, 2005
Millie Criswell, *No Strings Attached*, 2005
Dee Holmes, *Coming Home*, 2003
Susan Elizabeth Phillips, *Dream a Little Dream*, 1998
Christie Ridgway, *This Perfect Kiss*, 2001

312

JULIA JUSTISS (Pseudonym of Janet Justiss)

A Most Unconventional Match

(Toronto: Harlequin, 2008)

Story type: Historical/Regency
Subject(s): Business; Family; Courtship
Major character(s): Elizabeth Lowery, Artist, Widow(er);
   Hal Waterman, Gentleman
Time period(s): 1820s (1820)
Locale(s): London, England

Summary: Hal Waterman has so far successfully escaped his mother's matchmaking schemes, and instead, much to his mother's disdain, concentrated all of his time and effort on business. Now the one woman Hal ever loved, Elizabeth Lowery, is back in his life. At first Hal reluctantly helps Elizabeth sort out her late husband's tangled finances, but as the two spend more time together, Hal finds himself thinking less about business and more about a way to win Elizabeth's love.

Where it's reviewed:
Romantic Times, July 2008, page 40

Other books by the same author:
Rogue's Lady, 2007
The Untamed Heiress, 2006
The Courtesan, 2005
Wicked Wager, 2003
For My Lady's Honor, 2002

Other books you might like:
Jo Beverley, *To Rescue a Rogue*, 2006
Loretta Chase, *Not Quite a Lady*, 2007
Diane Gaston, *The Wagering Widow*, 2006
Candice Hern, *Just One of Those Flings*, 2006
Julia London, *The Hazards of Hunting a Duke*, 2006

313

JULIA JUSTISS
ANNIE BURROWS , Co-Author
TERRI BRISBIN , Co-Author

One Candlelight Christmas

(Toronto: Harlequin, 2008)

Story type: Historical/Regency; Anthology
Subject(s): Christmas
Time period(s): 1810s

Summary: The Christmas season brings romance to three different couples in this trio of novellas. In Justis' "Christmas Wedding Wish," after her fiance dies in India, Meredyth Wellingford has resigned herself to life as a spinster, but when a party of guests arrives at her family's estate for the holidays, Meredyth finds herself rethinking the idea of romance after meeting Allen Mansfell. In Burrows' "The Rake's Secret Son," Nell Tillotson thought her husband Carleton was dead until he turns up on her doorstep one cold December day, and Nell must choose between taking Carleton back or cutting him out of her life forever. In Brisbin's "Blame It on the Mistletoe," despite her best efforts, it seems as if Julia Fairchild finds herself always caught under the mistletoe with Iain MacLerie.

Where it's reviewed:
Romantic Times, November 2008, page 77

Other books you might like:
Mary Balogh, *A Regency Christmas Feast*, 1996
Elisabeth Fairchild, *A Regency Christmas Present*, 1999
Amanda McCabe, *Regency Christmas Magic*, 2004
Elizabeth Rolls, *Mistletoe Kisses*, 2006

314

VIRGINIA KANTRA

Sea Fever

(New York: Berkley Sensation, 2008)

Story type: Contemporary; Paranormal
Series: Children of the Sea. Book 2
Subject(s): Mythology; Mystery; Paranormal
Major character(s): Regina Barone, Caterer (daughter of
   restaurant owner), Single Parent; Dylan Hunter,
   Mythical Creature (selkie)
Time period(s): 2000s
Locale(s): World's End, Maine (island)

Summary: Feeling sorry for herself because the last eligible bachelor on the tiny Maine island where she lives has just gotten married, caterer and single mom Regina Barone wanders off to the beach with a bottle of Proseco to keep her company. She isn't alone for long, though; and when Dylan Hunter, the sexy, newly returned brother of the groom, joins her, things take an impulsive, passionate turn—a circumstance that Dylan, who has chosen the selkie half of his heritage, soon uses to his advantage when he is sent back to the island by the prince of the mer to discover why the demons are so interested in World's End. Then Regina becomes a target

Romance

and it's up to Dylan to keep her safe as the struggle against the demons becomes increasingly fierce.

Where it's reviewed:
Romantic Times, August 2008, page 90

Other books by the same author:
Sea Lord, 2009 (Children of the Sea. Book 3)
Sea Witch, 2008 (Children of the Sea. Book 1)
Home before Midnight, 2006
Close Up, 2005
Her Beautiful Assassin, 2003

Other books you might like:
Christina Dodd, *A Well-Favored Gentleman*, 1994
    historical selkie lore
Christine Feehan, *Turbulent Sea*, 2008
    Drake Sisters. Book 6
Melanie Jackson, *The Selkie*, 2003
Deborah Smith, *Alice at Heart*, 2002
    merfolk
Natale Stenzel, *The Druid Made Me Do It*, 2008

315

VIRGINIA KANTRA

Sea Witch

(New York: Berkley Sensation, 2008)

Story type: Contemporary; Paranormal
Series: Children of the Sea. Book 1
Subject(s): Mythology; Mystery; Paranormal
Major character(s): Margred, Mythical Creature (selkie); Caleb Hunter, Police Officer (chief of police), Military Personnel (Iraq veteran)
Time period(s): 2000s
Locale(s): World's End, Maine (island)

Summary: With her mate long dead and in need of sex, Margred comes ashore on World's End, a tiny island off the coast of Maine in search of a man to satisfy her needs temporarily. Being a selkie, she's not looking human love and commitment; however, her growing feelings for sexy police chief Caleb Hunter, plus the fact that she is afraid that her selkie pelt was destroyed during a fiery demon attack and without it she can't return to the sea, are beginning to cause her to question what her future holds. Selkie lore adds a mystical touch to this tale of murder, mystery, and romance that the first of three stories of the Hunter siblings, children of a selkie mother and a human father.

Where it's reviewed:
Romantic Times, July 2008, page 101

Other books by the same author:
Sea Lord, 2009 (Children of the Sea. Book 3)
Sea Fever, 2008 (Children of the Sea. Book 2)
Home before Midnight, 2006
Close Up, 2005
Her Beautiful Assassin, 2003

Other books you might like:
Christina Dodd, *A Well-Favored Gentleman*, 1994
    historical selkie lore
Christine Feehan, *Oceans of Fire*, 2005

Drake Sisters
Melanie Jackson, *The Selkie*, 2003
Nora Roberts, *Face the Fire*, 2002
    Three Sisters Island. Book 3
Deborah Smith, *Alice at Heart*, 2002
    merfolk

316

DONNA KAUFFMAN
JILL SHALVIS , Co-Author
HELENKAY DIMON , Co-Author

To All a Good Night

(New York: Brava, 2008)

Story type: Contemporary; Holiday Themes
Subject(s): Anthology; Christmas
Time period(s): 2000s
Locale(s): United States

Summary: This steamy trilogy of super-sensual novellas is perfect for stocking-stuffing this holiday season. Included are: Donna Kauffman's pet-focused "Unleashed"; Jill Shalvis's slightly scientific "Finding Mr. Right"; and HelenKay Dimon's legally oriented "Can You Hand Me the Tape?" This is a unique, sexy collection.

Where it's reviewed:
Romantic Times, December 2008, page 77

Other books you might like:
HelenKay Dimon, *Hot as Hell*, 2008
Lori Foster, *Jingle Bell Rock*, 2003
    anthology
Donna Kauffman, *Merry Christmas, Baby*, 2004
    anthology
Elda Minger, *Christmas with Eve*, 1996
Jill Shalvis, *Strong and Sexy*, 2008
    Sky High Air. Book 2

317

EVE KENIN (Pseudonym of Eve Silver)

Hidden

(New York: Love Spell, 2008)

Story type: Futuristic; Paranormal
Subject(s): Plague; Identity, Concealed; Revenge
Major character(s): Tatiana, Thief (retrieval expert); Tristan, Scientist
Time period(s): 2090s (2093)
Locale(s): Arctic (Northern Waste)

Summary: On a mission to find a plague that could destroy the world and also stop a madman and his minion, Tatiana, who is physically and mentally gifted with numerous talents, warily joins forces with an enigmatic stranger, Tristan, and together they find the lab where the plague has been created. Danger stalks them, but so does passion, and it takes all of their combined efforts to stop the plague and bring the villain to justice. Secrets, violence, and a good sense of time and place add to this fast-paced story that is linked to *Driven*.

Where it's reviewed:
Library Journal, June 15, 2008, page 51
Romantic Times, July 2008, page 95

Other books by the same author:
Driven, 2007

Other books you might like:
Susan Grant, *Moonstruck*, 2008
Susan Grant, *The Scarlet Empress*, 2004
Susan Kearney, *The Quest*, 2006
Susan Krinard, *Kinsman's Oath*, 2004
Susan Squires, *Body Electric*, 2002

318

KATHRYNE KENNEDY

Double Enchantment

(New York: Love Spell, 2008)

Story type: Historical/Fantasy; Historical/Victorian
Series: Relics of Merlin. Book 2
Subject(s): Family; Magic
Major character(s): Jasmina Karlyle, Noblewoman, Sorceress; Sterling Thorn, Nobleman, Sorcerer (shapeshifter)
Time period(s): 1840s (1848)
Locale(s): England

Summary: In order to return a brooch that her mother "borrowed" from a friend, Jasmina Karlyle casts a spell to create a double of herself. Instead of staying home as she was supposed to, Jasmina's new "twin" Jaz goes out into to society and creates a storm of gossip with her scandalous behavior. When Sterling Thorn meets the lovely and mysterious Jaz at a ball, he finds himself falling in love with her, until, that is, he meets the real thing in the form of Jasmina.

Where it's reviewed:
Romantic Times, September 2008, page 52

Other books by the same author:
Enchanting the Lady, 2008
Beneath the Thirteen Moons, 2005

Other books you might like:
Shana Abe, *The Smoke Thief*, 2005
Naomi Bellis, *Step into Darkness*, 2006
Susan Carroll, *The Bride Finder*, 1998
Tracy Fobes, *Forbidden Garden*, 2000
Colleen Shannon, *Catspell*, 2006

319

SANDRA KITT

For All We Know

(Toronto: Kimani Arabesque, 2008)

Story type: Contemporary; Multicultural
Subject(s): AIDS (Disease); African Americans; Survival
Major character(s): Michaela Landry, Professor; Cooper

"Smith" Townsend, Religious (pastor), Contractor
Time period(s): 2000s
Locale(s): Memphis, Tennessee

Summary: In Memphis house-sitting for her godparents, academic Michaela Landry discovers a runaway boy in her shed and becomes involved in his life in ways she would never have imagined. AIDS, and the social ramifications of the disease, as well as the misconceptions about it, are key to this heartwarming, sometimes almost inspirational, novel that pairs a D.C. academic with a Tennessee activist preacher and makes it work. Part of a series of books (Novels of Hope) that highlights the activities of St. Jude's Children's Research Hospital.

Where it's reviewed:
Library Journal, August 2008, page 60

Other books by the same author:
Celluloid Memories, 2007
Back in Your Arms, 2006
The Next Best Thing, 2005
Southern Comfort, 2004
She's the One, 2001

Other books you might like:
Gwynne Forster, *What Matters Most*, 2008
Kristin Hannah, *Summer Island*, 2001
Frances Ray, *The Way You Love Me*, 2008
Barbara Samuel, *No Place Like Home*, 2002
Simona Taylor, *Wonderful and Wild*, 2004

320

LISA KLEYPAS

A Wallflower Christmas

(New York: St. Martin's Press, 2008)

Story type: Historical/Regency; Holiday Themes
Subject(s): Christmas; Courtship; Marriage
Major character(s): Hannah Appleton, Companion; Rafe Bowman, Businessman; Natalie Blandford, Noblewoman
Time period(s): 1840s (1845)
Locale(s): England

Summary: Reluctantly agreeing to consider an engagement to a young English aristocrat, American businessman and rake Rafe Bowman comes to England to meet his intended, Lady Natalie Blandford. However, it is not the lovely debutante who makes his heart beat faster but her no-nonsense cousin and companion, Hannah. Charming, witty, sensual, and filled with characters from earlier books in the Wallflower series, this holiday-linked romance adds to the series but stands on its own as well.

Where it's reviewed:
Library Journal, October 15, 2008, page 50
Publishers Weekly, August 18, 2008, page 40
Romantic Times, October 2008, page 50

Other books by the same author:
Blue-Eyed Devil, 2008
Devil in Winter, 2006 (Wallflower. Book 3)
Scandal in Spring, 2006 (Wallflower. Book 4)
It Happened One Autumn, 2005 (Wallflower. Book 2)
Secrets of a Summer Night, 2004 (Wallflower. Book 1)

Other books you might like:
Mary Balogh, *Simply Perfect*, 2008
    Miss Martins School for Girls. Book 4
Christina Dodd, *Rules of Attraction*, 2001
Eloisa James, *An Affair Before Christmas*, 2007
    Desperate Duchesses. Book 2
Stephanie Laurens, *All about Love*, 2001
Sherry Thomas, *Delicious*, 2008

321

DEIDRE KNIGHT

Red Fire

(New York: Signet Eclipse, 2008)

Story type: Paranormal
Series: Gods of Midnight. Book 1
Subject(s): Demons; Magic
Major character(s): Shay Angel, Hunter (demon hunter); Ajax Petrakos, Warrior
Time period(s): 2000s
Locale(s): Savannah, Georgia; England

Summary: After the battle of Thermopylae, Ajax Petrakos and six other of his fellow Spartan warriors were given the chance to become immortal warriors in order to continue their fight against evil. For centuries Ajax successfully battled demons, but now his worst enemy has appeared in Savannah. Once Ajax arrives he discovers not only is Sable waiting to destroy him, but the woman for whom he has searched thousands of years: his one true love, Shay Angel.

Where it's reviewed:
Romantic Times, October 2008, page 100

Other books by the same author:
Parallel Desire, 2007
Parallel Seduction, 2007
Parallel Attraction, 2006
Parallel Heat, 2006

Other books you might like:
Lara Adrian, *Kiss of Midnight*, 2007
Kresley Cole, *No Rest for the Wicked*, 2006
Christina Dodd, *Scent of Darkness*, 2007
Karen Marie Moning, *Darkfever*, 2006
Gena Showalter, *Awaken Me Darkly*, 2005

322

SUSAN KRINARD

Come the Night

(Don Mills, Ontario: HQN, 2008)

Story type: Paranormal; Werewolf Story
Subject(s): Werewolves; Social Classes; Murder
Major character(s): Gillian Maitland, Werewolf; Ross Kavanaugh, Werewolf, Police Officer
Time period(s): 2000s
Locale(s): New York, New York; England

Summary: Shocked to lean he has a son by Gillian Mait-land, the woman he wanted to marry years earlier but couldn't because his werewolf blood wasn't pure enough for he father, New York cop Ross Kavanaugh goes to England determined to prove his worth. A rash of murders in which Ross is implicated cause a few problems for them both in this romantic, suspenseful werewolf tale.

Where it's reviewed:
Romantic Times, October 2008, page 46

Other books by the same author:
Dark of the Moon, 2008
Kinsman's Oath, 2004
To Catch a Wolf, 2003
The Forest Lord, 2002
Touch of the Wolf, 1999

Other books you might like:
Lori Handeland, *Blue Moon*, 2004
Tracy Jones, *Scent of the Wolf*, 2004
Sherrilyn Kenyon, *Unleash the Night*, 2006
Angela Knight, *Master of the Moon*, 2005
Rebecca York, *Killing Moon*, 2003
    Moon. Book 1

323

LESLIE LANGTRY (Pseudonym of Leslie Thompson)

Stand by Your Hitman

(New York: Making It, 2008)

Story type: Humor; Romantic Suspense
Series: Greatest Hits. Book 3
Subject(s): Humor; Television; Murder
Major character(s): Mississippi "Missi" Bombay, Criminal (assassin), Inventor (murderous devices); Lex Danby, Saloon Keeper/Owner (bartender), Widow(er)
Time period(s): 2000s
Locale(s): Costa Rica; Toronto, Canada; Santa Muerta, South America (island off coast of S. America)

Summary: Missi Bombay is a genius when it comes to inventing weapons. No one appreciates her creations, such as Jell-O Bullets, more than her family members. It's not just a matter of familial pride—the Bombays have been assassins for centuries, and Missi's work benefits them all. Now the family council has an assignment for her: Lex Danby. Much to Missi's dismay, she has to go on the Canadian reality show *Survival* to get to him.

Where it's reviewed:
Romantic Times, September 2008, page 84

Other books by the same author:
Guns Will Keep Us Together, 2008 (Greatest Hits. Book 2)
'Scuse Me While I Kill This Guy, 2007 (Greatest Hits. Book 1)

Other books you might like:
Kathleen Bacus, *Anchors Aweigh*, 2008
    Tressa Jayne Turner. Book 6
Meg Cabot, *Size 14 Is Not Fat, Either*, 2006

Heather Wells. Book 2
Toni Causey, *Bobbie Fayes (Kinda, Sorta, Not Exactly) Family Jewels*, 2008
Liz Evans, *Cue the Easter Bunny*, 2007
Lisa Lutz, *The Spellman Files*, 2007
  Spellman. Book 1

324

STEPHANIE LAURENS

The Edge of Desire

(New York: Avon, 2008)

Story type: Historical/Regency
Series: Bastion Club. Book 8
Subject(s): Family; Murder
Major character(s): Letitia Randall, Gentlewoman, Widow(er); Christian Michael Allardyce, Nobleman (Marquess of Dearne)
Time period(s): 1810s (1816)
Locale(s): England

Summary: Letitia Vaux promised Christian Allardyce she would wait for him until he returned home from fighting Napoleon, but four years later, while Christian was still in France, Letitia married George Randall. Now eight years later, Christian suddenly receives a note from Letitia asking for his help. Letitia's husband has been murdered and everyone believes Letitia's brother Justin is the killer, even though she knows he is not a murderer. Christian is more than willing to help Letitia find the real killer, but he has his price: he wants romantic revenge on the woman who rejected him.

Where it's reviewed:
Romantic Times, September 2008, page 44

Other books by the same author:
Where the Heart Leads, 2008
Beyond Seduction, 2007
The Taste of Innocence, 2007
To Distraction, 2006
What Price Love?, 2006

Other books you might like:
Jo Beverley, *To Rescue a Rogue*, 2006
Liz Carlyle, *Never Deceive a Duke*, 2007
Sabrina Jeffries, *Never Seduce a Scoundrel*, 2006
Lynn Kerstan, *Dangerous Deceptions*, 2004
Julia London, *The Dangers of Deceiving a Viscount*, 2007

325

STEPHANIE LAURENS
MARY BALOGH , Co-Author
JACQUIE D'ALESSANDRO , Co-Author
CANDICE HERN , Co-Author

It Happened One Night

(New York: Avon, 2008)

Story type: Historical/Regency; Anthology
Subject(s): Reunions; Interpersonal Relations

Time period(s): 19th century
Locale(s): England

Summary: Four authors join forces to produce an anthology based on the premise of a hero and heroine who haven't seen each other for more than ten years suddenly encountering each other at the same roadside inn and reassessing their former relationships. Misunderstandings, family interference, and immaturity are part of the problems in this lively, well-written anthology that does an exceptional job of showing that style, tone, and imagination are more important than a simple plot premise. Included are "The Fall of Rogue Gerrard" by Stephanie Laurens, "Spellbound" by Mary Balogh, "Only You" by Jacquie D'Alessandro, and "From This Moment On" by Candice Hern.

Where it's reviewed:
Library Journal, October 15, 2008, page 51
Romantic Times, October 2008, page 48

Other books you might like:
Mary Balogh, *Under the Mistletoe*, 2003
  anthology
Cheryl Bolen, *One Golden Ring*, 2005
Nicola Cornick, *Christmas Wedding Belles*, 2007
  anthology
Jo Ann Ferguson, *A Christmas Bride*, 2000
Elizabeth Rolls, *Mistletoe Kisses*, 2006
  anthology

326

JADE LEE (Pseudonym of Katherine Grill)

The Dragon Earl

(New York: Leisure, 2008)

Story type: Historical/Regency
Subject(s): Family; Marriage
Major character(s): Evelyn Stanton, Gentlewoman; Jacob Cato, Religious (monk), Nobleman (Earl of Warhaven)
Time period(s): 1810s
Locale(s): England

Summary: When a Chinese monk interrupts Evelyn Stanton's wedding and declares he is her rightful fiancé, Evelyn is certain the man is crazy. Then Evelyn discovers she really was once engaged to the monk since he is Jacob Cato, the long-lost heir to the Earl of Warhaven. Now after spending years in China, Jacob has returned to England not only to come terms with his past but to also reclaim the woman he loves.

Where it's reviewed:
Romantic Times, September 2008, page 46

Other books by the same author:
Dragonborn, 2008
The Tao of Sex, 2008
Cornered Tigress, 2007
Tempted Tigress, 2007
Burning Tigress, 2006

Romance

Other books you might like:
Elizabeth Boyle, *This Rake of Mine*, 2005
Kathryn Caskie, *Love Is in the Heir*, 2006
Eloisa James, *The Taming of the Duke*, 2006
Stephanie Laurens, *Scandal's Bride*, 1999
Maya Rodale, *The Heir and the Spare*, 2007

327

LORA LEIGH
ERIN MCCARTHY , Co-Author
NALINI SINGH , Co-Author
LINDA WINSTEAD JONES , Co-Author

The Magical Christmas Cat
(New York: Berkley Sensation, 2008)

Story type: Paranormal; Holiday Themes
Subject(s): Christmas; Animals/Cats; Magic
Time period(s): 21st century
Locale(s): United States

Summary: This quartet of sizzlingly hot Holiday novellas by some of the genre's more popular writers features paranormal stories that focus on felines of various types. All these novellas, except for the one by Jones, are spin-offs from the authors' previous stories or existing series. Included are "Stroke of Enticement" by Nalini Singh, a charming romance linked to her Psy-Changeling series; "Christmas Bree" by Erin McCarthy, a magical match-making story featuring the Murphy sisters; "Sweet Dreams" by Linda Winstead Jones, a relatively sweet love story focusing on a small jade cat figurine from a mysterious admirer; and "Christmas Heat" by Lora Leigh, a fast-paced, suspenseful story featuring Leigh's popular Breeds series.

Where it's reviewed:
Romantic Times, October 2008, page 105

Other books you might like:
Carly Alexander, *The Secret Life of Mrs. Claus*, 2005
MaryJanice Davidson, *Undead and Unreturnable*, 2005
Christine Feehan, *The Shadows of Christmas Past*, 2004
  anthology
Kim Harrison, *Holidays Are Hell*, 2007
  anthology
Maggie Shayne, *An Enchanted Season*, 2007
  similar anthology

328

MARY LENNOX (Pseudonym of Mary Glazer)

Lord of Shadows
(Waterville, ME: Five Star 2008)

Story type: Historical/Victorian; Romantic Suspense
Subject(s): Spies; Victorian Period; Espionage
Major character(s): Caroline Berring, Noblewoman; Devlin Carmichael, Nobleman (Marquess of Headleymoor), Spy
Time period(s): 1840s (1843)
Locale(s): England

Summary: In an effort to redeem Lady Caroline Berring's undeserved "love child" reputation and bolster her standing with the *ton* so his friend can make an offer for her, Devlin Carmichael, Marquess of Headleymoor, finds himself attracted to the lady in spite of his good intentions. However, Devlin is more than he seems, and his other persona as a British spy is so dangerous that it could doom any relationship between them. A strong, determined heroine and a hero caught between two worlds strive to make their love last in this lively, intricately plotted Victorian that gives readers a taste of some of the darker side of the period, as well

Where it's reviewed:
Booklist, July 2008, page 47

Other books by the same author:
My Lord Beast, 2005

Other books you might like:
Candace Camp, *Secrets of the Heart*, 2003
  earlier time period
Lynn Kerstan, *The Golden Leopard*, 2002
Anne Mallory, *The Bride Price*, 2008
Elizabeth Thornton, *Dangerous to Hold*, 1996
  earlier time period

329

JULIE LETO

Phantom's Touch
(New York: Signet Eclipse, 2008)

Story type: Contemporary; Fantasy
Series: Phantom. Book 2
Subject(s): Magic; Movie Industry
Major character(s): Lauren Cole, Actress; Aiden Forsyth, Nobleman, Military Personnel (soldier); Ross Marchand, Producer (movie)
Time period(s): 2000s
Locale(s): Hollywood, California

Summary: Lauren Cole got everything she wanted from her ex-husband, movie producer Ross Marchand, except the antique sword he bought for her and now refuses to give up. So Lauren decides to "borrow" the sword to help her with the action scenes for her latest "Athena" film. What Lauren didn't expect was that once she had the sword, she would somehow release Aiden Forsyth, who had been imprisoned inside the weapon more than 200 years earlier by an evil sorcerer.

Where it's reviewed:
Romantic Times, December 2008, page 86

Other books by the same author:
Phantom Pleasures, 2008
Stripped, 2007
Dirty Little Secrets, 2006
The Domino Effect, 2006
Making Waves, 2005

Other books you might like:
Cherry Adair, *Edge of Danger*, 2006
Sandy Blair, *A Highlander for Christmas*, 2007
Christine Feehan, *The Twilight Before Christmas*, 2003
Sherrilyn Kenyon, *Fantasy Lover*, 2002
Christina Skye, *Christmas Knight*, 1998

Romance

330

CAIT LONDON (Pseudonym of Lois Kleinsasser)

For Her Eyes Only

(New York: Avon, 2008)

Story type: Paranormal; Romantic Suspense
Series: Psychic Sisters. Book 3
Subject(s): Psychic Powers; Triplets; Revenge
Major character(s): Leona Aisling Chablis, Psychic (clairvoyant), Store Owner (Timeless Vintage); Owen Shaw, Investor (real estate), Financier (former investment broker)
Time period(s): 2000s
Locale(s): Lexington, Kentucky

Summary: When the Viking Thorgood bested Borg and won the hand of the powerful psychic Aisling, Borg vowed vengeance and cursed their family forever. Now, centuries later, Leona, the eldest of the psychic Aisling triplets and a reluctant clairvoyant, knows that Borg's descendant is hunting for them and will stop at nothing to destroy them. Then Owen Shaw and his troubled, psychic sister, Janice, come to town and Leona is soon caught up in solving Janice's issues which end up being tied closely to her family's own. While definitely Leona and Owen's story, this novel reprises other characters, solves the mystery, and ties up any lingering loose threads.

Where it's reviewed:
Romantic Times, October 2008, page 81

Other books by the same author:
A Stranger's Touch, 2008 (Psychic Sisters. Book 2)
At the Edge, 2007 (Psychic Sisters. Book 1)
Flashback, 2005
Hidden Secrets, 2005
With Her Last Breath, 2003

Other books you might like:
Christine Feehan, *Magic in the Wind*, 2005
    expanded version of a short story in the 2003
    anthology *Lover Beware*.
Virginia Kantra, *Sea Witch*, 2008
    Children of the Sea. Book 1
Jayne Ann Krentz, *Running Hot*, 2009
    Arcane Society. Book 5
Nora Roberts, *Face the Fire*, 2002
    Three Sisters Island. Book 3
Nora Roberts, *The Pagan Stone*, 2008
    Sign of Seven. Book 3

331

JULIE ANNE LONG

Like No Other Lover

(New York: Avon, 2008)

Story type: Historical/Regency
Series: Pennyroyal Green. Book 2
Subject(s): Marriage; Scandal
Major character(s): Cynthia Brightly, Gentlewoman; Miles

Redmond, Nobleman, Scientist (entomologist)
Time period(s): 1810s
Locale(s): England

Summary: At a house party at the Redmond estate Cynthia Brightly has one goal in mind—to find a suitable husband before word of the scandal surrounding her name filters out of London. Things are taken out of her hands, however, when her host Miles Redmond offers her his silence and help in exchange for a kiss. Although he is supposed to be wooing another, Miles can't help his growing feelings for Cynthia, nor can she ignore him. Bugs, insects, and spiders have a part to play in this funny, lively romance that continues Long's stories of the Eversea and Redmond families.

Where it's reviewed:
Library Journal, October 15, 2008, page 51
Romantic Times, November 2008, page 52

Other books by the same author:
The Perils of Pleasure, 2008
The Secret to Seduction, 2007
Beauty and the Spy, 2006
Ways to be Wicked, 2006
To Love a Thief, 2005

Other books you might like:
Connie Brockway, *So Enchanting*, 2009
    a dash of magic
Liz Carlyle, *A Woman Scorned*, 2000
Eloisa James, *Kiss Me, Annabel*, 2005
Tracy Anne Warren, *The Accidental Mistress*, 2007
Christine Wells, *Scandal's Daughter*, 2007

332

MERLINE LOVELACE
LORI DEVOTI , Co-Author

Holiday with a Vampire II

(New York: Silhouette, 2008)

Story type: Contemporary; Paranormal
Subject(s): Vampires; Christmas; Redemption
Time period(s): 2000s
Locale(s): United States

Summary: Vampires are front and center in this unusual pair of Christmas romances from two the genre's most popular writers. A vampire on the way to her clan's annual conclave and a police officer end up spending Christmas together in an isolated cabin with life-changing results in Merline Lovelace's "A Christmas Kiss"; and a vampire falls in love with the woman he had planned to use to avenge himself on his adoptive family in Lori Devoti's mesmerizing "The Vampire Who Stole Christmas." Halloween meets Christmas in this intriguing duet of redeeming vampire tales.

Where it's reviewed:
Library Journal, December 2008, page 107
Romantic Times, December 2008, page 106

Other books you might like:
Maureen Child, *Holiday with a Vampire*, 2007

anthology with Caridad Pineiro
MaryJanice Davidson, *Undead and Unreturnable*, 2005
Christine Feehan, *The Shadows of Christmas Past*, 2004
Kim Harrison, *Holidays Are Hell*, 2007
    anthology
Maggie Shayne, *An Enchanted Season*, 2007

333

KATIE MACALISTER (Pseudonym of Marthe Arends)

Up in Smoke

(New York: Signet, 2008)

Story type: Humor; Paranormal
Series: Silver Dragons. Book 2
Subject(s): Dragons; Humor; Demons
Major character(s): Mayling, Mythical Creature (doppelganger); Gabriel, Mythical Creature (Silver Dragon)
Time period(s): 2000s
Locale(s): Mythical Place

Summary: Mayling is not only a doppelganger, but thanks to destiny, she's also the mate of Gabriel, who's a Silver Dragon. Regrettably, Mayling was created to serve as the consort of the Demon Lord Magoth, an egotistical fiend straight from the Underworld. Although Gabriel, the leader of the Silver Dragons, the wyvern of his sept, is a very powerful being, he advises Mayling to continue with the consort process. Mayling isn't happy about Gabriel's decision, especially since Magoth is so capriciously evil, and Gabriel could take him on if he really wanted. Or so she thinks.

Where it's reviewed:
Booklist, October 1, 2008, page 31
Romantic Times, October 2008, page 100

Other books by the same author:
Playing with Fire, 2008 (Silver Dragons. Book 1)
Zen and the Art of Vampires, 2008
Holy Smokes, 2007 (Aisling Grey, Guardian. Book 4)
Last of the Red-Hot Vampires, 2007 (Dark Ones. Book 5)
Light My Fire, 2006 (Aisling Grey, Guardian. Book 3)

Other books you might like:
Angie Fox, *The Accidental Demon Slayer*, 2008
Tara Hallaway, *Romancing the Dead*, 2008
    Garnet Lacey. Book 3
Stephanie Rowe, *Date Me Baby, One More Time*, 2006
    Immortally Sexy. Book 1
Vicki Lewis Thompson, *Over Hexed*, 2007
Minda Webber, *The Daughters Grimm*, 2008

334

JULIANNE MACLEAN

The Mistress Diaries

(New York: Avon, 2008)

Story type: Historical/Victorian
Series: Pembroke Place. Book 2

Subject(s): Lovers; Conduct of Life; Family Relations
Major character(s): Cassandra Montrose, Widow(er), Noblewoman (Lady Colchester); Vincent Sinclair, Nobleman (Duke of Pembroke's son), Rake
Time period(s): 1870s (1873-1874)
Locale(s): England

Summary: When an abandoned night of passion with Lord Vincent Sinclair results in a daughter, young widow Cassandra Montrose, Lady Colchester, shunned by her family and then diagnosed with consumption, has no choice but to take her baby to the father, hoping that he will care for her. Things change, however, when Cassandra learns that she is not dying after all and that Vincent wants to be involved with his daughter's life, even though he is about to marry another to insure his inheritance. Refusing to be his mistress, Cassandra agrees to a platonic arrangement—which ends up being far more difficult to maintain than either of them had expected.

Where it's reviewed:
Library Journal, August 2008, page 60
Romantic Times, August 2008, page 44

Other books by the same author:
In My Wildest Fantasies, 2007 (Pembroke Palace. Book 1)
Surrender to a Scoundrel, 2007
Portrait of a Lover, 2006
Love According to Lily, 2005
An Affair Most Wicked, 2004

Other books you might like:
Mary Balogh, *Simply Love*, 2006
    Miss Martin's School for Girls. Book 2
Mary Balogh, *Simply Perfect*, 2008
    Miss Martin's School for Girls. Book 4
Lisa Kleypas, *Lady Sophia's Lover*, 2002
Lisa Kleypas, *Where Dreams Begin*, 2000
Jacquelin Navin, *The Heiress of Hyde Park*, 2004
    Mayfair Brides. Book 2

335

DEBBIE MACOMBER

8 Sandpiper Way

(Don Mills, Ontario: MIRA, 2008)

Story type: Contemporary
Series: Cedar Cove. Book 8
Subject(s): Relationships; Trust; Secrets
Major character(s): Emily Flemming, Housewife; Dave Flemming, Religious (pastor)
Time period(s): 2000s
Locale(s): Cedar Cove, Washington

Summary: Woven into the patchwork of other Cedar Cove family tribulations is Pastor Dave Flemming, who finds himself accused of infidelity. His wife, Emily, discovers a pair of diamond earrings in his jacket pocket. A few more suspicious events have her convinced he's seeing another woman. The good news is he's not an adulterer. The bad news is, he may be a jewel thief. Seems the pastor's old criminal record has returned to haunt him.

Where it's reviewed:
Romantic Times, September 2008, page 55

Other books by the same author:
Twenty Wishes, 2008 (Blossom Street. Book 4)
74 Seaside Avenue, 2007 (Cedar Cove. Book 7)
Back on Blossom Street, 2007 (Blossom Street. Book 3)
6 Rainier Drive, 2006 (Cedar Cove. Book 6)
50 Harbor Street, 2005 (Cedar Cove. Book 5)

Other books you might like:
Melody Carlson, *All I Have to Give*, 2008
Judy Christenberry, *The Cowboy's Secret Son*, 2007
Kathryn Cushman, *Waiting for Daybreak*, 2008
Kathleen Eagle, *The Last Good Man*, 2000
Karen Kingsbury, *Sunset*, 2008

336

DEBBIE MACOMBER

A Cedar Cove Christmas

(Don Mills, Ontario: Mira, 2008)

Story type: Contemporary; Holiday Themes
Series: Cedar Cove. Book 9
Subject(s): Small Town Life; Christmas
Major character(s): Mary Jo Wyse, Young Woman; Mack McAfee, Health Care Professional (paramedic)
Time period(s): 2000s
Locale(s): Cedar Cove, Washington

Summary: In a story highly reminiscent of the First Christmas, Mary Jo Wyse comes to Cedar Cove to warn the father of her soon-to-be-born-baby that her brothers (the three Wyse men) are on the warpath. Finding the only hotel sold out, Mary Jo ends up in an apartment above the stable housing the Christmas pageant animals, and when she goes into early labor, paramedic and firefighter Mack McAfee delivers her baby. Heartwarming, sweet, and satisfying, this story is wonderfully predictable and adds another tale to Macomber's growing Cedar Cove series.

Where it's reviewed:
Library Journal, October 15, 2008, page 50
Romantic Times, October 2008, page 59

Other books by the same author:
Where Angels Go, 2007
6 Rainier Drive, 2006 (Cedar Cove. Book 5)
There's Something about Christmas, 2005
The Snow Bride, 2003
The Christmas Basket, 2002

Other books you might like:
Robyn Carr, *A Virgin River Christmas*, 2008
Judy Duarte, *Her Best Christmas Ever*, 2008
Fern Michaels, *Sliver Bells*, 2008
    anthology
Lisa Plumley, *Home for the Holidays*, 2008
Sherryl Woods, *Welcome to Serenity*, 2008

337

MICHELLE MADDOX (Pseudonym of Michelle Rouillard)

Countdown

(New York: Love Spell, 2008)

Story type: Futuristic
Subject(s): Competition; Television
Major character(s): Kira Jordan, Thief; Rogan Ellis, Murderer
Time period(s): Indeterminate Future
Locale(s): Fictional Country

Summary: Waking up chained in a dark room with the man who murdered her family is not Kira Jordan's idea of a good day. It turns out, though, that both Kira and Rogan Ellis have been chosen as "contestants" in a private reality show called "Countdown." Now if both Kira and Rogan can survive the six increasingly difficult levels of the show, they will earn their freedom, unless, of course, they kill each other first!

Where it's reviewed:
Booklist, July 2008, page 45

Other books you might like:
Susan Grant, *Moonstruck*, 2008
Eve Kenin, *Driven*, 2007
Jade Lee, *Seduced by Crimson*, 2005
Liz Maverick, *Crimson City*, 2005
Gena Showalter, *Awaken Me Darkly*, 2005

338

ANNETTE MAHON

Holiday Dreams

(New York: Avalon, 2008)

Story type: Contemporary; Multicultural
Series: Matchmaker Quilt. Book 2
Subject(s): Holidays; Quilts; Interpersonal Relations
Major character(s): Momi Kanahele, Librarian (children's); Rick Mahoney, Landlord (apartment manager), Businessman (apartment owner)
Time period(s): 2000s
Locale(s): Kona, Hawaii

Summary: Although she had always believed in the powers of the special quilt that was supposed to bring true love to the woman who currently possessed it, librarian Momi Kanahele has a hard time believing that her difficult apartment manager, Rick Mahoney, might be the one, in spite of the chemistry that flickers between them. After all, Momi doesn't even like him, or so she thinks! A hero with secret wounds finds love in the arms of a warm, generous heroine and learns to embrace the holidays in the process. A sweet romance with a good amount of sexual tension.

Where it's reviewed:
Library Journal, October 15, 2008, page 50

Other books by the same author:
The Secret Correspondence, 2008 (Secret. Book 6)
Dolphin Dreams, 2007 (Matchmaker Quilt. Book 1)
An Ominous Death, 2006
The Secret Wish, 2006 (Secret. Book 5)
The Secret Beau, 2004 (Secret. Book 4)

Other books you might like:
Geraldine Burrows, *Stranger in Paradise*, 2003
Colleen Coble, *Black Sands*, 2005
   inspirational and suspense elements
Colleen Coble, *Distant Echoes*, 2005
   inspirational and suspense elements
Jill Marie Landis, *Glass Beach*, 1996
   historical Hawaii
Shirley Marks, *Honeymoon Husband*, 2007

339

SUSAN MALLERY   (Pseudonym of Susan Macias Redmond)

Sweet Spot

(Don Mills, Ontario: HQN, 2008)

Story type: Contemporary
Series: Bakery Sisters. Book 2
Subject(s): Family Relations; Sisters; Twins
Major character(s): Nicole Keyes, Baker; Eric Hawkins, Coach
Time period(s): 2000s
Locale(s): Seattle, Washington

Summary: Nicole Keyes, who has always been the "responsible" daughter, is fed up with thinking about everyone except herself. Discovering her husband having sex with her younger sister makes her declaration of independence that much easier, but fate won't let Nicole shirk her responsibilities. As Nicole recovers from major surgery, her estranged twin shows up on her doorstep. Nicole's world gets even crazier when a foster child steals donuts from her bakery, and the teen's coach, Eric Hawkins, convinces Nicole to let the boy work off his offense.

Where it's reviewed:
Romantic Times, August 2008, page 80

Other books by the same author:
Accidentally Yours, 2008
Sweet Trouble, 2008 (Bakery Sisters. Book 3)
Sweet Talk, 2008 (Bakery Sisters. Book 1)
Sizzling, 2007 (Buchanans. Book 3)
Tempting, 2007

Other books you might like:
Judith Arnold, *Blooming All Over*, 2004
Barbara Bretton, *Just Desserts*, 2008
Stef Ann Holm, *All That Matters*, 2008
Jennifer O'Connell, *Dress Rehearsal*, 2007
Christine Son, *Off the Menu*, 2008

340

SUSAN MALLERY   (Pseudonym of Susan Macias Redmond)

Sweet Trouble

(Don Mills, Ontario: HQN, 2008)

Story type: Contemporary
Series: Bakery Sisters. Book 3
Subject(s): Sisters; Trust; Child Custody

Major character(s): Jesse Keyes, Single Parent, Baker; Matthew Fenner, Businessman (computer game company owner), Computer Expert
Time period(s): 2000s
Locale(s): Seattle, Washington

Summary: When she fled from Seattle five years earlier, Jesse Keyes was pregnant, devastated, and alone. Now, after five years in Spokane, she has gotten her life back on track and returns to Seattle with her four-year-old son, Gabriel, to make amends for the past and to introduce Gabe to his father. A vindictive hero and a strong heroine clash in this story that delves deeply into the past and focuses on trust, forgiveness, and relationship issues between Matt and Jesse, as well as between Jesse and her sister Nicole. This story nicely completes Mallery's entertaining Bakery Sisters trilogy.

Where it's reviewed:
Library Journal, August 2008, page 60
Romantic Times, September 2008, page 90

Other books by the same author:
Accidentally Yours, 2008
Sweet Talk, 2008 (Bakery Sisters. Book 1)
Sweet Spot, 2008 (Bakery Sisters. Book 2)
Sizzling, 2007 (Buchanans. Book 3)
Tempting, 2007 (Buchanans Book 4)

Other books you might like:
Barbara Bretton, *Just Desserts*, 2008
Laura Castoro, *Icing on the Cake*, 2007
Hailey North, *Not the Marrying Kind*, 2007
Susan Elizabeth Phillips, *Ain't She Sweet?*, 2004
Susan Wiggs, *Snowfall at Willow Lake*, 2008

341

ANNE MALLORY   (Pseudonym of Anne Hearn)

The Bride Price

(New York: Avon, 2008)

Story type: Historical/Regency
Subject(s): Marriage; Competition; Revenge
Major character(s): Carolyn Martin, Gentlewoman, Companion; Sebastien Deville, Bastard Son (of the Duke of Grandien), Rake; Lady Sarah Pims, Noblewoman
Time period(s): 1820s (1822)
Locale(s): London, England

Summary: The King is sponsoring a contest for all third and illegitimate sons and the winner will get a fortune, a title, lands, and a suitable bride! It's just the thing that Sebastien Deville, the illegitimate son of the Duke of Grandien and well-known rake, has been waiting for and he's determined to win and reclaim his mother's lands. He cares little about the bride, Lady Sarah Pims, but when he meets her protective cousin, Caroline Martin, he suddenly finds himself attracted to the wrong woman. Outside manipulation by the Duke make things difficult, and the tension and the attraction sparks between Caroline and Sebastien from the start in this romance with an unusual premise.

Where it's reviewed:
Romantic Times, November 2008, page 47

Other books by the same author:
Three Nights of Sin, 2008
What Isabella Desires, 2007
The Earl of Her Dreams, 2006
The Viscount's Wicked Ways, 2006
Daring the Duke, 2005

Other books you might like:
Mary Balogh, *No Man's Mistress*, 2001
Mary Balogh, *One Night for Love*, 1999
Candice Hern, *The Bride Sale*, 2002
Lynn Kerstan, *Heart of the Tiger*, 2003
    darker
Kathryn Smith, *A Seductive Offer*, 2002

342

MARIANNE MANCUSI

Razor Girl

(New York: Love Spell, 2008)

Story type: Paranormal; Future Shock
Subject(s): Medical Thriller; Apocalypse; Underground Resistance Movements
Major character(s): Molly Anderson, Survivor, Heroine; Chase Griffen, Survivor, Hero
Time period(s): 2030s (2030)
Locale(s): Monroeville, South Carolina; Orlando, Florida (Disney World)

Summary: High school classmates Molly Anderson and Chase Griffen make a horrifying discovery. A government-sponsored AIDS vaccine has gone terribly wrong, turning ordinary townsfolk into grotesque, blood-thirsty, pus-oozing zombies. Molly is forced to move underground into the family bunker, not knowing what would become of her friends. After six years in hiding, Molly emerges into a hostile world populated with unspeakable evil. She discovers that only a handful of normal people remain, and among them is Chase. Together, the small group of survivors claws their way to Florida, aided by Molly's surgically implanted cybernetic razors, to join Molly's medical-researcher dad working underground at Disney World. She wonders what gave him the foresight to arm her for this journey years before. Had he known?

Where it's reviewed:
Romantic Times, September 2008, page 103

Other books by the same author:
News Blues, 2008
A Hoboken Hipster in Sherwood Forest, 2007
Moongazer, 2007
What, No Roses?, 2006
A Connecticut Fashionista in King Arthur's Court, 2005

Other books you might like:
Lori Handeland, *Blue Moon*, 2004
Colby Hodge, *Star Shadows*, 2007
A.J. Menden, *Phenomenal Girl 5*, 2008
Pamela Palmer, *Dark Deceiver*, 2008
J.D. Robb, *Naked in Death*, 1995

343

DEB MARLOWE

An Improper Aristocrat

(Toronto: Harlequin, 2008)

Story type: Historical/Regency
Subject(s): Archaeology; Family; Treasure
Major character(s): Chione Latimer, Gentlewoman, Writer; Niall "Trey" Stafford, Nobleman (Earl of Treyford)
Time period(s): 1820s (1820)
Locale(s): Egypt; England

Summary: While in Egypt, the Earl of Treyford promises his dying partner, Richard Latimer, he would deliver the man's scarab pendant to his sister, and that he would also protect her from any danger. After Trey arrives in England and finally tracks Chione Latimer down, though, the annoying woman refuses to take possession of the pendant. Chione wants nothing to do with the family relic that sent her brother off on a foolish treasure hunt for the Pharoah's Lost Jewel, but when it turns out that the legend might be more fact than fiction, Chione realizes she needs Trey's help.

Where it's reviewed:
Romantic Times, December 2008, page 48

Other books by the same author:
Scandalous Lord, Rebellious Miss, 2008

Other books you might like:
Connie Brockway, *As You Desire*, 1997
Loretta Chase, *Lord Perfect*, 2006
Kathryn Greyle, *Miss Woodley's Experiment*, 2002
Sabrina Jeffries, *Only a Duke Will Do*, 2006
Amanda Quick, *Deception*, 1993

344

DEIRDRE MARTIN

Power Play

(New York: Berkley Sensation, 2008)

Story type: Contemporary; Humor
Series: New York Blades. Book 8
Subject(s): Sports/Hockey; Actors and Actresses; Family
Major character(s): Monica Geary, Actress (daytime drama); Eric Mitchell, Sports Figure (hockey player)
Time period(s): 2000s
Locale(s): New York, New York

Summary: Monica Geary, a popular daytime television leading lady, and Eric Mitchell, a midseason replacement on the New York Blades hockey team, each need a publicity boost. Monica's agent devises a ploy guaranteed to attract the paparazzi, by fixing up Monica and Eric in a high-profile, pretend romance. Strictly business. Having met, Monica can't stand self-absorbed lady's man Eric, and he has no intention of giving up his "horndog" ways for any woman. Still, they play the loving couple for the cameras, until things heat up for real.

Where it's reviewed:
Romantic Times, October 2008, page 92

Other books by the same author:
Just a Taste, 2008 (New York Blades. Book 7)
Chasing Stanley, 2007 (New York Blades. Book 6)
Hot Ticket, 2006 (New York Blades. Book 5)
The Penalty Box, 2006 (New York Blades. Book 4)
Total Rush, 2005 (New York Blades. Book 3)

Other books you might like:
Erica DeQuaya, *Hunks of Hockey*, 2008
Rachel Gibson, *See Jane Score*, 2008
Liana Laverentz, *Thin Ice*, 2007
Carly Phillips, *Hot Property*, 2008
Angela Steed, *1080 Kiss*, 2007

345

KAT MARTIN

Season of Strangers

(Don Mills, Ontario: MIRA, 2008)

Story type: Contemporary; UFO
Subject(s): Aliens; Family Problems; Love
Major character(s): Julie Ferris, Real Estate Agent (Donovan Real Estate); Patrick Donovan, Heir, Addict; Valenden Zarkazian, Alien (Torillian), Scientist (human research)
Time period(s): 2000s
Locale(s): Malibu Beach, California; Beverly Hills, California

Summary: Valenden "Val" Zarkazian, a Torillian alien, takes on the body and mind of Patrick Donovan, a spoiled real estate heir, whose heart fails suddenly from a lifestyle of excess and addiction. As "Patrick," Val hopes to be able to study more closely his human subject, Julie Ferris. Julie's past relationship with Patrick was rocky, but now, following his heart attack and seemingly miraculous recovery, Patrick appears to have reinvented himself. When she becomes convinced Patrick's playboy days are over, she finds herself falling for him. At first, Val is careful to conceal his true identity from Julie, as he experiences Earth and humanity first-hand with her. However, there's no way he could have prepared himself for the power of love, or the pain of leaving.

Where it's reviewed:
Romantic Times, June 2008, page 111

Other books by the same author:
Heart of Fire, 2008 (Heart. Book 2)
Heart of Honor, 2007 (Heart. Book 1)
The Summit, 2007
Scent of Roses, 2006
The Handmaiden's Necklace, 2006

Other books you might like:
Karen Kelley, *The Bad Boys Guide to the Galaxy*, 2008
Robin D. Owens, *Heart Dance*, 2007
J.D. Robb, *Out of This World*, 2001
Robin L. Rotham, *Alien Overnight*, 2007
Gena Showalter, *Playing with Fire*, 2006

346

LIZ MAVERICK (Pseudonym of Elizabeth Edelstein)

Irreversible

(New York: Love Spell, 2008)

Story type: Time Travel; Science Fiction
Subject(s): Brainwashing; Memory Loss; Technology
Major character(s): Katherine "Kitty" Gibbs, Captive (psychological experimentation), Amnesiac (drug-induced); Walter Q. Sheffield, Technician (time anomaly specialist), Time Traveler (traversing temporal wires); Leonardo Kaysar, Kidnapper
Time period(s): Indeterminate Future
Locale(s): Fictional City

Summary: Time anomaly specialist Walter "Q" Sheffield has been hired to penetrate the temporal barrier that separates two realities—the one from which Leonardo Kaysar kidnapped Katherine Gibbs, and the one where she is being forced to live in Kaysar's mindless time-loop experiment. By keeping her in a drug-induced amnesia, Kitty's captors are able to manipulate her into believing their weekly ruse, then wipe her memory clean every Sunday to begin again. After infiltrating Kaysar's world, "Q" is able to blend in and gain access to Kitty, but her weekly brainwashing makes it difficult for him to leave any lasting impression, until he finds his way into her heart.

Where it's reviewed:
Romantic Times, October 2008, page 102

Other books by the same author:
Wired, 2007
Crimson Rogue, 2006 (Crimson City. Book 6)
Crimson City, 2005 (Crimson City. Book 1)
Adventures of an Ice Princess, 2004
The Shadow Runners, 2004 (2176. Book 3)

Other books you might like:
Eve Kenin, *Hidden*, 2008
Michele Lang, *Netherwood*, 2008
Michelle Maddox, *Countdown*, 2008
Marianne Mancusi, *Razor Girl*, 2008
A.J. Menden, *Phenomenal Girl 5*, 2008

347

CATHY MAXWELL

A Seduction at Christmas

(New York: Avon, 2008)

Story type: Historical/Regency
Series: Scandals and Seductions. Book 1
Subject(s): Murder; Seduction; Scandal
Major character(s): Fiona Lachlan, Gentlewoman (impoverished), Orphan; Dominic Lynsted, Nobleman (Duke of Holborn)
Time period(s): 1800s (1800; 1809)
Locale(s): Greece; England

Summary: Thinking to earn a bit of money and do a friend a favor by drugging Lord Belkins' wine, Fiona Lachlan arrives at his room only to find the lord missing and be grabbed by a shocked Duke of Holborn, instead. Fiona looks remarkably like the woman in a vision he at Delphi, and since this has sent him on his current quest to retrieve a family ring, Dominic is not about to let her go. A team of assassins—plus a goblet of drugged wine—soon have things in an uproar, and they end up joining forces to escape being killed. Attracted to each other, Fiona and Dominic work together to solve the mystery and find the missing ring in this sexy, action-packed romance.

Where it's reviewed:
Library Journal, October 15, 2008, page 50
Romantic Times, November 2008, page 45

Other books by the same author:
In the Highlander's Bed, 2008
Bedding the Heiress, 2007
In the Bed of a Duke, 2006
The Price of Indiscretion, 2005
The Temptation of a Proper Governess, 2004

Other books you might like:
Connie Brockway, *My Surrender*, 2005
　　Rose Hunters. Book 3
Liz Carlyle, *No True Gentleman*, 2002
Elizabeth Hoyt, *To Seduce a Sinner*, 2008
Amanda Quick, *With This Ring*, 1998
　　more humorous
Elizabeth Thornton, *Dangerous to Hold*, 1996

348

PENNY MCCALL (Pseudonym of Penny McCusker)

Ace Is Wild

(New York: Berkley Sensation, 2008)

Story type: Contemporary; Romantic Suspense
Subject(s): Humor; Psychic Powers; Mystery
Major character(s): Vivienne "Vivi" Foster, Psychic; Daniel "Ace" Pierce, Lawyer (U.S. Attorney), FBI Agent (former)
Time period(s): 2000s
Locale(s): Boston, Massachusetts

Summary: Shocked and angered when psychic Vivi Foster drags him off stage and whisks him away at gun point from a charity event in order to save his live, federal prosecutor Daniel Pierce isn't about to believe her story. However, soon they both are running for their lives—and into love at the same time in this lively, funny, fast-paced romance.

Where it's reviewed:
Romantic Times, August 2008, page 67

Other books by the same author:
Packing Heat, 2009
All Jacked Up, 2007
Tag, You're It, 2007

Other books you might like:
Kathleen Bacus, *Calamity Jayne*, 2006
Charlotte Douglas, *Pelican Bay*, 2005
Janet Evanovich, *Seven Up*, 2001
Kasey Michaels, *Maggie Needs an Alibi*, 2002
Christina Skye, *Code Name: Baby*, 2005

349

SHANNON MCKENNA

Ultimate Weapon

(New York: Brava, 2008)

Story type: Contemporary; Romantic Suspense
Subject(s): Organized Crime; Murder; Revenge
Major character(s): Tamara Steele, Artisan (Wearable Weaponry), Single Parent (adopted daughter); Valery Janos, Organized Crime Figure, Avenger
Time period(s): 2000s
Locale(s): Portland, Oregon; Budapest, Hungary; Paris, France

Summary: Professional assassin Valery Janos hoped he was through with the PSS, a ruthless crime syndicate with a dark agenda. Instead, they force him into the most critical assignment of his life. They're holding his longtime mentor and father figure captive, and will subject the man to torture and certain death if Val fails to deliver Tamara Steele to lecherous crime boss Daddy Novak. Novak blames Tamara for the death of his son. Val has no choice but to cooperate. What he doesn't count on is falling in love with Tamara and her adopted daughter. Val realizes that despite Tamara's obvious ability to take care of herself, she's no match for Novak, who will stop at nothing to get his hands on her.

Where it's reviewed:
Romantic Times, November 2008, page 61

Other books by the same author:
Extreme Danger, 2008
Hot Night, 2008
All about Men, 2007
Edge of Midnight, 2007 (McCloud Brothers. Book 4)
Out of Control, 2006 (McCloud Brothers. Book 3)

Other books you might like:
Shannon K. Butcher, *No Control*, 2008
Jessica Hall, *Heat of the Moment*, 2004
Lora Leigh, *Killer Secrets*, 2008
Cheyenne McCray, *Moving Target*, 2008
JoAnn Ross, *No Safe Place*, 2007

350

BARBARA MCMAHON

Parents in Training

(Toronto: Harlequin, 2008)

Story type: Contemporary; Romance
Subject(s): Pregnancy; Family Problems; Love
Major character(s): Annalise Fulton, Real Estate Agent; Dominic Fulton, Computer Expert
Time period(s): 2000s
Locale(s): Washington, District of Columbia

Summary: Annalise and Dominic Fulton have it all; lucrative careers, money, travel, a posh Washington D.C. flat within spitting distance to the Capital Mall—and now, they're about to have a baby, too. The problem is Dominic does not want to have children. He's experienced first-hand what unplanned family responsibilities can do to a man, and to a relationship. While Annalise adjusts to the surprise pregnancy and looks forward to motherhood, stubborn Dominic suggests a trial separation. He's not about to diminish his lifestyle for anyone, but once he gets a taste of life without his Annalise, his priorities change.

Where it's reviewed:
Romantic Times, July 2008, page 100

Other books by the same author:
A Pregnancy Promise, 2008
Rescued by the Sheikh, 2008
The Boss's Little Miracle, 2007
The Forbidden Brother, 2007
The Nanny and The Sheikh, 2007

Other books you might like:
Kara Lennox, *The Pregnancy Surprise*, 2008
Susan Meier, *Her Pregnancy Surprise*, 2007
Raye Morgan, *The Boss's Pregnancy Proposal*, 2007
Elizabeth Sinclair, *The Pregnancy Clause*, 2000
Linda Randall Wisdom, *Pregnancy Countdown*, 2003

351

A.J. MENDEN (Pseudonym of Amy Mendenhall)

Phenomenal Girl 5
(New York: Love Spell, 2008)

Story type: Contemporary; Reincarnation
Subject(s): Magic; Demons; Supernatural
Major character(s): Lainey Livingston, Apprentice (partner to the Reincarnist), Sorceress (Phenomenal Girl 5); Robert Elliot, Reincarnated Person (the Reincarnist), Teacher (magic arts); Wesley Charles, Reincarnated Person (the Reincarnist), Avenger (dragon conqueror)
Time period(s): 2000s
Locale(s): Corvo City, Mythical Place

Summary: Lainey Livingston, a.k.a. Phenomenal Girl 5, has a lot to learn about crime fighting and magic. Ever since she was little, Lainey was groomed to one day become the apprentice of Robert Elliot, the Reincarnist. Elliot is a distinguished, brooding, 40-something magician, who has lived many previous lives, and retains the collected knowledge from each of them. When Elliot takes Lainey under his wing to develop her skills and tutor her in the magic arts, they fall in love, only to be tragically parted in a battle. When Robert dies and re-emerges as a new Reincarnist, 20-something Wesley Charles, he has no immediate memory of his previous life, or his love for Lainey. Now, broken-hearted, it's Lainey's turn to guide this virtual stranger as he adjusts to being the new Reincarnist—while evil prepares its final apocalyptic assault.

Where it's reviewed:
Romantic Times, November 2008, page 98

Other books you might like:
Eve Kenin, *Hidden*, 2008
Michele Lang, *Netherwood*, 2008
Michelle Maddox, *Countdown*, 2008
Marianne Mancusi, *Razor Girl*, 2008
Liz Maverick, *Irreversible*, 2008

352

CHRISTINE MERRILL

The Mistletoe Wager
(Toronto: Harlequin, 2008)

Story type: Historical/Regency
Subject(s): Christmas; Marriage
Major character(s): Elise Pennyngton, Noblewoman (Countess of Anneslea); Harry Pennyngton, Nobleman (Earl of Anneslea); Nicholas Tremaine, Lover (of Elise)
Time period(s): 1810s
Locale(s): England

Summary: In order to win back his estranged wife Elise, Harry Pennyngton, the Earl of Anneslea offers Elise's new lover, Nicholas Tremaine, a proposal: if Harry can't get Nicholas, who hates the whole holiday season, to wish him a Merry Christmas by Twelfth Night, Harry will grant Elise the divorce she wants. Harry knows how much Elise loves Christmas, and he is certain that once she hears that Nicholas doesn't have any Christmas spirit, she will dump him. What Harry didn't plan on was that Nicholas would bring Elise along with him as his guest to Harry's holiday houseparty in the country!

Where it's reviewed:
Romantic Times, December 2008, page 45

Other books by the same author:
An Unladylike Offer, 2007
The Inconvenient Duchess, 2006

Other books you might like:
Louise Allen, *The Earl's Intended Wife*, 2006
Terri Brisbin, *The Earl's Secret*, 2007
Diane Gaston, *The Wagering Widow*, 2006
Candice Hern, *Lady Be Bad*, 2007
Michelle Styles, *A Christmas Wedding Wager*, 2007

353

FERN MICHAELS
JOANN ROSS , Co-Author
MARY BURTON , Co-Author
JUDY DUARTE , Co-Author

Silver Bells
(New York: Zebra, 2008)

Story type: Contemporary; Holiday Themes
Subject(s): Christmas; Anthology; Small Town Life
Time period(s): 2000s
Locale(s): United States

Summary: A touch of mystery and small town ambiance adds to the holiday charm of these four novellas from four of romance's most popular writers. Include are: "Silver Bells" by Fern Michaels, the story of a Hollywood star who goes home for the holidays and discovers love; "Dear Santa." by JoAnn Ross, in which a jaded mystery author finds the spirit of Christmas when her car breaks down near Santa's Village; "Christmas Past" by Mary Burton, in which a woman uncovers a killer's identity and puts the past to rest; and "A Mulberry Park Christmas" by Judy Duarte, a romantic story of rekindled love.

Where it's reviewed:
Library Journal, October 15, 2008, page 50

Other books you might like:
Robyn Carr, *A Virgin River Christmas*, 1008
Judy Duarte, *Her Best Christmas Ever*, 2008
Annette Mahon, *Holiday Dreams*, 2008
Lisa Plumley, *Home for the Holidays*, 2008
Sherryl Woods, *Welcome to Serenity*, 2008

354

TRISH MILBURN

Firefighter in the Family
(Toronto: Harlequin, 2008)

Story type: Contemporary; Romantic Suspense
Subject(s): Arson; Family Problems; Forgiveness
Major character(s): Miranda Cooke, Investigator (state arson investigator); Zac Parker, Saloon Keeper/Owner (The Beach Bum)
Time period(s): 2000s
Locale(s): Horizon Beach, Florida

Summary: State arson investigator Miranda "Randi" Cooke returns to her hometown to inspect the scene of a suspicious fire and to gather clues to the identity of the arsonist. One of the initial suspects is Zak Parker, a former firefighter and old beau of Randi's who now runs a local watering hole. Zac had been accused of arson in a different case years ago, a claim that ultimately proved to be false, but he never recovered from the stigma. Now he's named again in this fire, but Randi suspects Zac is being set up. Her investigation is complicated by threats of violence, the bad blood that runs between her brothers and Zac, and her own guilt about causing her father's career-ending injury. Thank goodness for the surf, the sunsets, and Zac.

Where it's reviewed:
Romantic Times, September 2008, page 110

Other books by the same author:
Heartbreak River, 2009
Her Very Own Family, 2009

Other books you might like:
Jo Davis, *Trial by Fire*, 2008
Kate Hardy, *The Firefighter's Fiance*, 2006
Sammie Jo Moresca, *Smolder*, 2008
Alison Roberts, *The Firefighter's Baby*, 2005
JoAnn Ross, *Blaze*, 2005

355

LINDA LAEL MILLER

A McKettrick Christmas
(Don Mills, Ontario: HQN, 2008)

Story type: Historical/American West; Holiday Themes
Series: McKettrick. Book 10

Subject(s): Christmas; Family; Disasters
Major character(s): Lizzie McKettrick, Teacher; Morgan Shane, Doctor
Time period(s): 1890s (1896)
Locale(s): Arizona

Summary: On her way home to the Triple M ranch with a potential fiance and the exciting news that she is going to be the new local teacher, Lizzie McKettrick is trapped aboard the train when an avalanche covers the tracks. She works with attractive Dr. Morgan Shane to help a fascinating assortment of passengers, keeping them comfortable and optimistic, even though it looks as though they'll be spending Christmas on a train that is dangerously perched on the edge of a ledge. They are eventually rescued by the McKettrick men, and everything works out in perfectly magical holiday fashion, thanks to a little angelic help from a mysterious peddler.

Where it's reviewed:
Library Journal, October 15, 2008, page 50
Romantic Times, November 2008, page 50

Other books by the same author:
A Stone Creek Christmas, 2008
A Wanted Man, 2008
The Rustler, 2008
Deadly Deceptions, 2008
The McKettrick Way, 2007 (McKettrick. Book 9)

Other books you might like:
Millie Criswell, *A Western Family Christmas*, 2001
    anthology
Debbie Macomber, *A Cedar Cove Christmas*, 2008
Debbie Macomber, *Return to Promise*, 2000
Diana Palmer, *Lone Star Christmas*, 1997
    two stories, one by Joan Johnston
Cheryl St. John, *Christmas Gold*, 2002
    anthology

356

MARGARET MOORE (Pseudonym of Margaret Wilkins)

A Lover's Kiss
(Toronto: Harlequin, 2008)

Story type: Historical/Regency
Subject(s): Family; Law
Major character(s): Juliette Bergerine, Seamstress; Douglas Drury, Lawyer (barrister)
Time period(s): 1810s (1819)
Locale(s): London, England

Summary: After Juliette Bergerine rescues Douglas Drury by throwing potatoes at the band of men trying to beat him up, she quickly comes to regret that decision. Not only does Douglas seem rudely ungrateful for her help, but soon after their meeting, Juliette finds her own life in danger from one of Douglas's old enemies. When Juliette is forced into taking refuge with Douglas, she somehow finds herself falling in love with the infuriating man!

Where it's reviewed:
Romantic Times, August 2008, page 46

Other books by the same author:
Knave's Honor, 2008
My Lord's Desire, 2007
The Notorious Knight, 2007
Hers to Command, 2006
Hers to Desire, 2006

Other books you might like:
Pamela Britton, *Scandal*, 2004
Jacquie D'Alessandro, *Not Quite a Gentleman*, 2005
Lynn Kerstan, *The Silver Lion*, 2003
Stephanie Laurens, *What Price Love?*, 2006
Amanda Quick, *Deception*, 1993

357

RAYE MORGAN (Pseudonym of Helen Conrad)

The Prince's Secret Bride

(Toronto: Harlequin, 2008)

Story type: Alternate History; Family Saga
Series: Royals of Montenevada. Book 1
Subject(s): Kings, Queens, Rulers, etc.; Memory Loss; Love
Major character(s): Marie "Marisa" DuBonnet, Amnesiac, Businesswoman (DuBonnet Chocolatier); Nico Montenevada, Royalty (prince)
Time period(s): 2000s
Locale(s): MYP

Summary: Marie DuBonnet is confused. She senses that something terrible has happened, but she can't recall what it is. She doesn't remember her own name, or how she came to be alone on Gonglia Bridge in the middle of the night, with a head injury. And to top it off, she discovers that, apparently, she is also pregnant. Fortune smiles on Marie when Prince Nico of the Royal House of Montenevada rescues her in her vulnerable state, and insists that she stay at his castle until she can recover her memory. With the Montenevada princes, Nico, Dane, and Mychale, recently returned from exile, the last thing the fragile kingdom needs is a scandal, and a young pregnant woman living at the castle is mighty tempting fodder for the tabloids. Plus, no one can be sure that "Marisa's" convenient amnesia is real. This much is certain—whoever she is, Prince Nico will do anything to protect her and the child she carries.

Where it's reviewed:
Romantic Times, August 2008, page 108

Other books by the same author:
Abby and the Playboy Prince, 2008 (The Royals of Montenevada. Book 2)
Found: His Royal Baby, 2008 (The Royals of Montenevada. Book 3)
Bride by Royal Appointment, 2008 (Royal House of Niroli. Book 7)
The Boss's Double Trouble Twins, 2007 (Nine to Five. Book 31)
The Boss's Pregnancy Proposal, 2007

Other books you might like:
B.J. Daniels, *Montana Royalty*, 2008
Susan Meier, *Her Pregnancy Surprise*, 2007
Elizabeth Sinclair, *The Pregnancy Clause*, 2000
Patricia Thayer, *Texas Ranger Takes a Bride*, 2008
Linda Randall Wisdom, *Pregnancy Countdown*, 2003

358

SARAH MORGAN

The Rebel Doctor's Bride

(Toronto: Harlequin, 2008)

Story type: Contemporary; Medical
Subject(s): Shyness; Small Town Life; Redemption
Major character(s): Flora Harris, Nurse; Connor MacNeil, Doctor (surgeon), Rebel (troubled youth)
Time period(s): 2000s
Locale(s): Glenmore Island, Scotland

Summary: When bad boy Connor MacNeil returns to Glenmore Island to join his cousin's medical practice, he is met with snubs and rejection from the locals. Even though his days of juvenile mayhem are long over, the close-knit islanders still carry a grudge. Shy bookworm Flora Harris, a former schoolmate and quite possibly the only girl Connor hadn't kissed, is the clinic's capable nurse. With everyone in town clearly avoiding him, Flora senses that Connor could use a friend, and before long, their quiet conversations turn into a secret romance. Connor manages to redeem himself among the townsfolk when he performs a heroic rescue at the pier, but the real buzz around the island is learning the identity of Connor's latest female conquest. No one would ever suspect quiet, boring Flora.

Other books by the same author:
The Vasquez Baby, 2009
Italian Doctor, Sleigh-Bell Bride, 2008
The Vasquez Mistress, 2008
The Prince's Waitress Wife, 2008
The Sicilian Doctor's Mistress, 2008 (Mediterranean Doctors. Book 3)

Other books you might like:
Amy Andrews, *Top-Notch Surgeon, Pregnant Nurse*, 2008
Ken Casper, *A Lady's Luck*, 2008
Lilian Darcy, *A Proposal Worth Waiting For*, 2008
Kate Hardy, *The Spanish Doctor's Love Child*, 2008
Molly O'Keefe, *Worth Fighting For*, 2008

359

JOY NASH

Immortals: The Crossing

(New York: Love Spell, 2008)

Story type: Fantasy; Paranormal
Series: Immortals. Book 6
Subject(s): Magic; Paranormal; Hell
Major character(s): Artemis Black, Witch; Manannan Mac

Lir, Royalty (Prince of Annwyn), Deity (Celtic demigod)

Time period(s): 2000s
Locale(s): Scotland; Hell

Summary: Heart-throb musician Manannan Mac Lir has more important matters to attend to than touring and groupies. As the Guardian of Celtic Magical Creatures in the Human World, he sets out to find Artemis Black, a witch who is raiding inland faerie villages, and casting death spells to steal the faeries' life essence. She believes her motive is justified, because her son is being held for ransom by a demon in hell, who will release the boy in exchange for the essence she harvests. Mac, who is longing for a more meaningful relationship in his life, falls for Artemis, and risks it all when he follows her to the underworld to help save Zander.

Where it's reviewed:
Booklist, October 1, 2008, page 30
Romantic Times, October 2008, page 108

Other books by the same author:
Deep Magic, 2008 (Druids of Avalon. Book 2)
Immortals: The Awakening, 2007 (Immortals. Book 3)
The Grail King, 2006 (Druids of Avalon. Book 1)
Celtic Fire, 2005
Crystal Shadows, 2005

Other books you might like:
Shana Abe, *The Smoke Thief*, 2005
Jude Deveraux, *A Knight in Shining Armor*, 1989
Candace Havens, *Charmed and Dangerous*, 2005
Sherrilyn Kenyon, *Acheron*, 2008
C.L. Wilson, *King of Sword and Sky*, 2008

360

BRENDA NOVAK

Trust Me

(Don Mills, Ontario: MIRA, 2008)

Story type: Romantic Suspense; Contemporary
Series: Last Stand Trilogy. Book 1
Subject(s): Abuse; Self-Reliance; Stalking
Major character(s): Skye Kellerman, Abuse Victim, Businesswoman (owns a self-defense company); David Willis, Detective—Police (Sacramento P.D.), Divorced Person; Oliver Burke, Convict
Time period(s): 2000s
Locale(s): Sacramento, California; Sherman Island, California (Sacramento River Delta)

Summary: Skye Kellerman's sadistic attacker, Dr. Oliver Burke, is up for early parole after serving only three years of his ten-year sentence—and he's intent on revenge. David Willis, the detective on the original Kellerman case, is frustrated by his inability to produce conclusive evidence that would have put Burke away for good. He's also achingly aware of his long-resisted, mutual attraction with Skye, who's on his mind more than he'd like to admit. But now that her life is once again in imminent danger, they're spending a lot more time together searching for answers, and not just about the case. Meanwhile, David's manipulative, jealous ex-wife is pushing him for reconciliation.

Where it's reviewed:
Romantic Times, June 2008, page 81

Other books by the same author:
Stop Me, 2008 (Last Stand. Book 2)
Watch Me, 2008 (Last Stand. Book 3)
Dead Giveaway, 2007 (Stillwater. Book 2)
Dead Right, 2007 (Stillwater. Book 3)
Dead Silence, 2006 (Stillwater. Book 1)

Other books you might like:
Sarah Abbot, *Destiny Bay*, 2008
Laura Griffin, *One Last Breath*, 2007
Shannon McKenna, *Ultimate Weapon*, 2008
Marilyn Pappano, *Intimate Enemy*, 2008
E.C. Sheedy, *Over Her Dead Body*, 2005

361

BRENDA NOVAK

Watch Me

(Don Mills, Ontario: MIRA, 2008)

Story type: Contemporary; Romantic Suspense
Series: Last Stand Trilogy. Book 3
Subject(s): Murder; Suspense; Mystery
Major character(s): Sheridan Kohl, Social Worker (for The Last Stand); Cain Granger, Government Official (wildlife resources agent)
Time period(s): 2000s
Locale(s): Whiterock, Tennessee

Summary: When Sheridan Kohl returns to Tennessee to check out some new information she has about someone who shot her 12 years ago—and killed Jason Wyatt, the boy she was with—she is attacked, but rescued by Cain Granger, Jasons brother, and together they work to solve the mystery, catch the killer, and fall in love, as well.

Where it's reviewed:
Romantic Times, August 2008, page 66

Other books by the same author:
Stop Me, 2008 (Last Stand Trilogy. Book 2)
Trust Me, 2008 (Last Stand Trilogy. Book 1)
Dead Giveaway, 2007 (Stillwater. Book 2)
Dead Right, 2007 (Stillwater. Book 3)
Every Waking Moment, 2005

Other books you might like:
Beverly Barton, *After Dark*, 2000
Allison Brennan, *See No Evil*, 2007
Heather Graham Pozzessere, *Slow Burn*, 1994
Karen Rose, *Scream for Me*, 2008
Antoinette Stockenberg, *Keepsake*, 1999

362

CONSTANCE O'BANYON (Pseudonym of Evelyn Gee)

Daughter of Egypt

(New York: Leisure, 2008)

Story type: Historical/Ancient Egypt
Subject(s): Identity, Concealed; Trust; Adoption

Major character(s): Thalia, Orphan, Royalty (secret); Ashtyn, Nobleman (count), Military Personnel (commander)

Time period(s): 36 B.C.; 44 B.C.

Locale(s): Rome, Italy; Bal Forea, Fictional Country (an island kingdom)

Summary: Count Ashtyn, a.k.a. "The Destroyer," has been searching for his betrothed. Thalia, a young princess deserted in Rome, went from street urchin to happy adoptee, never knowing who she really is. Ashtyn has been promised Thalia, the granddaughter of the aged King Melik, as his bride, and he's determined to claim her as his own. After meeting his intended, Ashtyn's resolved to win her love, but first, he has to get Thalia to trust him.

Where it's reviewed:
Romantic Times, July 2008, page 40

Other books by the same author:
Desert Prince, 2008
Lord of the Nile, 2007
Sword of Rome, 2007
Hawk's Pledge, 2006
Hawk's Pursuit, 2006

Other books you might like:
Margaret George, *The Memoirs of Cleopatra: A Novel*, 1998
Merline Lovelace, *Lady of the Upper Kingdom*, 1996
Michelle Moran, *The Heretic Queen*, 2008
Michelle Moran, *Nefertiti*, 2008
Irene Roberts, *Kingdom of the Sun*, 2002

363

MOLLY O'KEEFE (Pseudonym of Molly Fader)

Worth Fighting For

(Toronto: Harlequin, 2008)

Story type: Contemporary

Series: Mitchells of Riverview Inn. Book 3

Subject(s): Family Relations; Hotels and Motels; Gardens and Gardening

Major character(s): Daphne Larson, Gardener (Athens Organics), Divorced Person; Jonah Closky, Businessman (real estate developer)

Time period(s): 2000s

Locale(s): Athens, New Jersey; New York, New York

Summary: Successful New Jersey real estate developer Jonah Closky doesn't need family in his life—or so he thinks. Abandoned by his father as a child, Jonah is filled with anger and resentment toward the man, so he can't understand his mother's renewed interest in seeing him again. Grudgingly, overprotective Jonah accompanies her to his father's country hotel, the Riverview Inn, for a long overdue reunion with his father and estranged brothers. His plans for a short stay are extended after he meets captivating Daphne Larson, a local organic gardener and the inn's produce supplier. Like Jonah, Daphne is no stranger to abandonment, and her trust issues are just as acute. However, shes willing to risk heartbreak one last time following a Cinderella night in New York with Jonah.

Where it's reviewed:
Romantic Times, August 2008, page 109

Other books by the same author:
A Man Worth Keeping, 2008 (Mitchells of Riverview Inn. Book 2)
The Son Between Them, 2008
Baby Makes Three, 2007 (Mitchells of Riverview Inn. Book 1)
Undercover Protector, 2007
His Best Friend's Baby, 2006

Other books you might like:
Ken Casper, *A Lady's Luck*, 2008
Lori Foster, *Treat Her Right*, 2008
Linda Goodnight, *Winning the Single Mom's Heart*, 2008
Myrna MacKenzie, *The Heir's Convenient Wife*, 2008
Susan Mallery, *Irresistible*, 2006

364

SARA ORWIG

Wed to the Texan

(New York: Silhouette, 2008)

Story type: Contemporary

Series: Platinum Grooms. Book 3

Subject(s): Inheritance; Courtship; Trust

Major character(s): Emily Carlisle, Secretary; Jake Thorne, Wealthy (tycoon), Heir

Time period(s): 2000s

Locale(s): Dallas, Texas

Summary: In order to claim his inheritance, Jake Thorne has to be married. Unfortunately, he isn't. So he proposes to the most accessible woman in his life—his secretary, Emily Carlisle. Emily, who's in love with Jake, says yes. But when she discovers the real reason for their marriage, Emily doesn't hesitate to let him know how she feels, and Jake realizes he needs to woo her properly for her to remain his wife.

Where it's reviewed:
Romantic Times, August 2008, page 110

Other books by the same author:
Pregnant at the Wedding, 2008 (Platinum Grooms. Book 1)
Seduced by the Enemy, 2008 (Platinum Grooms. Book 2)
Seduced by the Wealthy Playboy, 2007
Revenge of the Second Son, 2006
Scandals from the Third Bride, 2006

Other books you might like:
Maureen Child, *Baby Bonanza*, 2008
Olivia Gates, *The Desert King*, 2008
Jennifer Lewis, *Prince of Midtown*, 2008
Catherine Mann, *His Expectant Ex*, 2008
Emilie Rose, *Wed by Deception*, 2008

365

ROBIN D. OWENS

Heart Fate

(New York: Berkley Sensation, 2008)

Story type: Futuristic
Series: Celta. Book 7
Subject(s): Psychic Powers; Marriage; Cultures and Customs
Major character(s): Lahsin Burdock Yew, Runaway, Noblewoman; Tinne Holly, Nobleman, Businessman (fencing salon owner)
Time period(s): Indeterminate Future
Locale(s): Celta, Planet—Imaginary

Summary: Married to an older man when she was just 14, Lahsin Burdock Yew, about to come of age psychically and legally, runs from her controlling husband and family and takes refuge in a magical garden, the Healing Grove. Found by the man who is destined to be her true love or HeartMate, Tinne Holly, Lahsin survives her passage into adulthood with Tinne's help. This is an emotionally rich, well-paced story with characters readers will care about.

Where it's reviewed:
Library Journal, August 2008, page 59
Romantic Times, September 2008, page 98

Other books by the same author:
Heart Dance, 2007 (Celta. Book 6)
Heart Quest, 2006 (Celta. Book 5)
Heart Choice, 2005 (Celta. Book 4)
Heart Duel, 2004 (Celta. Book 3)
Heart Thief, 2003 (Celta. Book 2)

Other books you might like:
Lois McMaster Bujold, *Shards of Honor*, 1986
Jayne Castle, *Silver Master*, 2007
Susan Grant, *Moonstruck*, 2008
Susan Grant, *The Star Princess*, 2003
Susan Krinard, *Kinsman's Oath*, 2004

366

PAMELA PALMER (Pseudonym of Pamela Poulsen)

Dark Deceiver

(New York: Silhouette, 2008)

Story type: Contemporary; Paranormal
Series: Missives from the Dark. Book 2
Subject(s): Good and Evil; Underground Resistance Movements; Mysticism
Major character(s): Autumn McGinn, Young Woman, Human; Kade Smith, Demon (The Punisher, Kaderil the Dark), Immortal (Esri)
Time period(s): 2000s
Locale(s): Washington, District of Columbia

Summary: Kaderil the Dark, a cruel Esri henchman known as "The Punisher" assumes the identity of Kade Smith to infiltrate a group of Esri resistance fighters in Washington D.C. Kaderil's mission among the humans is to recover the hidden "draggon stone" a mystical key that will unlock the portal separating the realms of Earth and Esria, unleashing certain annihilation on all humankind. His plan becomes far more complicated when he encounters Autumn McGinn, a young freedom fighter who proves to be more clever—and problematic—than Kade had anticipated. She stirs long forgotten emotions in him that weaken his resolve to search and destroy, and that test his loyalty between these two very different worlds.

Where it's reviewed:
Romantic Times, June 2008, page 85

Other books by the same author:
The Dark Gate, 2007 (Missives from the Dark. Book 1)

Other books you might like:
Jayne Castle, *Silver Master*, 2007
Deborah Cooke, *Kiss of Fury*, 2008
Colby Hodge, *Star Shadows*, 2007
Deidre Knight, *Parallel Seduction*, 2007
Patti O'Shea, *In the Midnight Hour*, 2007

367

MARILYN PAPPANO

Intimate Enemy

(New York: Silhouette, 2008)

Story type: Romantic Suspense; Contemporary
Subject(s): Stalking; Jealousy; Love
Major character(s): Jamie Munroe, Lawyer, Survivor (knife attack); Russ Calloway, Businessman (Calloway Construction), Divorced Person
Time period(s): 2000s
Locale(s): Copper Lake, Georgia

Summary: Someone is stalking lawyer Jamie Munroe. It began innocently at first, but her secret admirer is becoming increasingly dangerous. As the threats and attacks escalate, Jamie needs protection, and she is taken into hiding by construction contractor Russ Calloway, a man no one would ever suspect of helping her. After all, Jamie had represented Russ's ex-wife in his very bitter, very expensive divorce—the same woman he had dumped Jamie to marry. He absolutely hates Jamie—doesn't he? Now, the time they spend together in Russ's secluded country lodge forces them to confront their past, and before long, old passions reignite. Except now, as they become closer, the stalker resorts to even more vicious and brazen tactics. Who is this deranged person who seems to know their every move?

Where it's reviewed:
Romantic Times, September 2008, page 117

Other books by the same author:
Forbidden Stranger, 2008
More than a Hero, 2008
One Stormy Night, 2007
Somebody's Hero, 2007
The Bluest Eyes in Texas, 2005

Other books you might like:
Laura Griffin, *One Last Breath*, 2007
Susan Kearney, *Kiss Me Deadly*, 2007

Brenda Novak, *Trust Me*, 2008
Tara Taylor Quinn, *In Plain Sight*, 2006
Colleen Thompson, *Triple Exposure*, 2008

368

TRACIE PETERSON

A Promise to Believe In

(Bloomington, MN: Bethany House, 2008)

Story type: Inspirational; Historical/American West
Series: Brides of Gallatin County. Book 1
Subject(s): Sisters; Family Problems; Guilt
Major character(s): Gwen Gallatin, Innkeeper, Orphan; Hank Bishop, Hero, Wealthy
Time period(s): 1870s (1879)
Locale(s): Montana (Montana Territory)

Summary: With their mother dead and their father accidentally killed in a drunken shoot-out, the Gallatin sisters are left to run the family hotel. It's not easy being women in the untamed Montana territory. To make matters worse, oldest sister Gwen, whose groom, Harvey, died from measles ten days after their wedding, believes she's been cursed by God, and that's why they're in this predicament. Hank Bishop, a man claiming to be Harvey's brother, has shown up at the sisters' door, but the siblings aren't sure he can be trusted. Besides, they have their hands full fending off Rafe Reynolds, owner of the adjacent saloon/bordello, who covets the Gallatin property, and will stop at nothing to get it.

Where it's reviewed:
Booklist, September 15, 2008, page 38
Romantic Times, September 2008, page 63

Other books by the same author:
A Lady of Hidden Intent, 2008 (Ladies of Liberty. Book 2)
A Lady of Secret Devotion, 2008 (Ladies of Liberty. Book 3)
A Lady of High Regard, 2007 (Ladies of Liberty. Book 1)
Where My Heart Belongs, 2007
Whispers of Winter, 2006

Other books you might like:
Lynn Austin, *Until We Reach Home*, 2008
Tracey Bateman, *Dangerous Heart*, 2008
    Westward Hearts. Book 3
Deeanne Gist, *Deep in the Heart of Trouble*, 2008
Lauraine Snelling, *Rebecca's Reward*, 2008
    Daughter of Blessings. Book 4
Stephanie Grace Whitson, *Unbridled Dreams*, 2008

369

ANDREA PICKENS (Pseudonym of Andrea DaRif)

The Scarlet Spy

(New York: Forever, 2008)

Story type: Historical/Regency
Series: Merlin's Maidens. Book 3

Subject(s): Espionage; Secrets; Seduction
Major character(s): Sofia, Spy, Imposter; Deverill Osborne, Nobleman
Time period(s): 1810s
Locale(s): London, England

Summary: When it comes to playing the part of a lady, no one is better than Sofia. Thus it is only logical that Sofia would take on Mrs. Merlin's latest assignment: infiltrating the *ton* to find out if there is any connection between the opium-related death of a young nobleman and a secret society known as the Scarlet Knights. Disguised as the widowed Contessa Sofia Constanza Bingham della Silveri, Sofia arrives in London determined to complete her assignment, but she quickly finds herself matching wits with sexy Lord Deverill Osborne, who is determined to discover all of her secrets.

Where it's reviewed:
Booklist, September 15, 2008, page 43
Romantic Times, October 2008, page 50

Other books by the same author:
Seduced by a Spy, 2008
The Spy Wore Silk, 2007
A Stroke of Luck, 2003
The Banished Bride, 2002
The Storybook Hero, 2002

Other books you might like:
Celeste Bradley, *The Pretender*, 2003
Gaelen Foley, *The Duke*, 2000
Karen Hawkins, *Her Master and Commander*, 2006
Lynn Kerstan, *Dangerous Deceptions*, 2004
Jenna Petersen, *From London with Love*, 2006

370

LISA PLUMLEY

Home for the Holidays

(New York: Zebra, 2008)

Story type: Contemporary; Holiday Themes
Subject(s): Christmas; Small Town Life; Change
Major character(s): Rachel Porter, Unemployed (celebrity stylist); Reno Wright, Sports Figure (former NFL player), Store Owner (sporting goods)
Time period(s): 2000s
Locale(s): Los Angeles, California; Kismet, Michigan

Summary: When a self-inflicted career disaster sends high-flying celebrity stylist Rachel Porter home to tiny Kismet, Michigan, for the holidays, she has every intention of returning to Hollywood once the scandalous storm has blown over. However, former NFL star Reno Wright proves to be an attraction she can't resist; and when love becomes part of the scene, Rachel begins to look at her hometown in a new light. Ambition and attitude war with core values and desires in this funny, touching romance that features a lovely secondary romance as well.

Where it's reviewed:
Library Journal, October 15, 2008, page 50
Romantic Times, October 2008, page 94

Other books by the same author:
Let's Misbehave, 2007
Mad about Max, 2006
The Rascal, 2006
The Scoundrel, 2006
Once upon a Christmas, 2005

Other books you might like:
Judith Arnold, *'Tis the Season*, 2000
Jude Deveraux, *The Blessing*, 1998
Kathleen Long, *Cherry on Top*, 2005
Susan Elizabeth Phillips, *Ain't She Sweet?*, 2004
Gina Wilkins, *Seductively Yours*, 2000

371

ROBIN T. POPP

Immortals: The Haunting

(New York: Love Spell, 2008)

Story type: Contemporary; Paranormal
Series: Immortals. Book 7
Subject(s): Demons; Magic; Shamanism
Major character(s): Mia Groves, Mythical Creature (wood nymph), Journalist (*New York Voice*); Nicholas Blackhawk, Mythical Creature (chameleon), Bodyguard (Blackhawk Securities)
Time period(s): 2000s
Locale(s): New York, New York

Summary: Strange and terrifying things are happening to investigative reporter and wood nymph Mia Groves, and she's unable to determine if they're real, or just more traumatic stress hallucinations. She seeks the help of a shaman sleep walker, bodyguard Nicholas Blackhawk, hoping he can relieve her of the visions she's been experiencing, and help her regain her lost mystical power. Mia soon discovers her troubles aren't in her mind, they're very real—from the dark figure that's trying to kill her for her explosive political article, to the mirrored underworld portals in her apartment complex. At least her dreams are sweet, when a phantom lover begins visiting her sleep.

Where it's reviewed:
Romantic Times, November 2008, page 102

Other books by the same author:
Immortals: The Darkening, 2007 (Immortals. Book 2)
Lord of the Night, 2007 (Night Slayer. Book 4)
Tempted in the Night, 2007 (Night Slayer. Book 3)
Seduced by the Night, 2006 (Night Slayer. Book 2)
Out of the Night, 2005 (Night Slayer. Book 1)

Other books you might like:
Jennifer Ashley, *Immortals: The Calling*, 2007
Elizabeth Guest, *Night Life*, 2007
Joy Nash, *Immortals: The Awakening*, 2007
Pamela Palmer, *Dark Deceiver*, 2008
J.D. Warren, *Crate and Peril*, 2008

372

PATRICIA POTTER

Behind the Shadows

(New York: Berkley Sensation, 2008)

Story type: Contemporary; Romantic Suspense
Subject(s): Identity; Secrets
Major character(s): Kira Douglas, Journalist (newspaper reporter); Chris Burke, Investigator—Private; Max Payton, Lawyer
Time period(s): 2000s
Locale(s): Atlanta, Georgia

Summary: Stunned when she couldn't donate a kidney to her mother because her blood proved she wasn't her mother's daughter, Kira Douglas realizes the switch was made at birth and is determined to find out who she really is. P.I. Chris Burke lends a hand and learns that heiress Leigh Howard might be the one. Leigh's attorney, Max Payton, isn't so sure, however, but when someone tries to kill Kira, he reconsiders. Chilling and filled with twists and turns, this is an intriguing tale of romantic suspense.

Where it's reviewed:
Romantic Times, December 2008, page 61

Other books by the same author:
Catch a Shadow, 2008
Beloved Warrior, 2007
Beloved Stranger, 2006
Tempting the Devil, 2006
Beloved Imposter, 2004

Other books you might like:
Jasmine Cresswell, *Secret Sins*, 1997
Barbara Freethy, *Silent Run*, 2006
Eileen Goudge, *Thorns of Truth*, 1998
Mary Alice Monroe, *The Four Seasons*, 2001
Jean Stone, *Ivy Secrets*, 1996

373

JULIA QUINN   (Pseudonym of Julie Cotler Pottinger)

Mr. Cavendish, I Presume

(New York: Avon, 2008)

Story type: Historical/Regency
Subject(s): Identity; Inheritance; Family Relations
Major character(s): Amelia Willoughby, Noblewoman; Thomas Cavendish, Nobleman
Time period(s): 1810s
Locale(s): England

Summary: When a man who ends up being the "real" Duke of Wyndham shows up, Thomas Cavendish, the current Duke of Wyndham, has a problem. Not only has his entire life been turned upside down, but the woman he loves will probably be marrying the new duke! Closely linked to the companion novel, *The Lost Duke of Wyndham*, this story parallels the action of its predecessor from a different perspective and fills in any remaining details with flair and accuracy.

Where it's reviewed:
Library Journal, August 2008, page 60
Romantic Times, October 2008, page 46

Other books by the same author:
The Lost Duke of Wyndham, 2008 (companion to this title)
The Secret Diaries of Miss Miranda Cheever, 2007
On the Way to the Wedding, 2006
The Further Observations of Lady Whistledown, 2003
Romancing Mr. Bridgerton, 2002

Other books you might like:
Alexandra Bassett, *His Chosen Bride*, 2005
Jo Beverley, *The Dragon's Bride*, 2001
Jo Beverley, *A Most Unsuitable Man*, 2005
Cheryl Bolen, *One Golden Ring*, 2005
Eloisa James, *Kiss Me, Annabel*, 2005

374

GAIL RANSTROM

Unlacing Lilly

(Toronto: Harlequin, 2008)

Story type: Historical/Regency
Subject(s): Revenge; Kidnapping; Kings, Queens, Rulers, etc.
Major character(s): Lillian O'Roarke, Young Woman; Devlin Ferrell, Bastard Son (son of the Duke of Rutherford), Businessman
Time period(s): 1820s (1821)

Summary: Wanting only a better life for her mother and sisters, common-born Lilly O'Roarke agrees to marry the spoiled and unscrupulous heir of the Duke of Rutherford. Meanwhile, Devlin Farrell, a local businessman and the champion of the poor in Whitechapel, has an old score to settle with the Rutherfords. When he overhears the marriage proposal, he devises a plot that will spoil the wedding, embarrass the deceitful Rutherford clan, and save Lilly from a lifetime of hurt. The plot becomes far more complicated than Devlin intends when he kidnaps Lilly on her wedding day while she's wearing the valuable Rutherford sapphires, which she is promptly accused of stealing. Devlin must now hide her from the Rutherfords, and the authorities, and to top it off, he's fallen in love with her. It seems everyone wants Lilly O'Roarke.

Where it's reviewed:
Romantic Times, September 2008, page 51

Other books by the same author:
Lord Libertine, 2007
Indiscretions, 2006
The Courtesan's Courtship, 2006
The Missing Heir, 2005
The Rake's Revenge, 2004

Other books you might like:
Victoria Alexander, *Seduction of a Proper Gentleman*, 2008
Julie Beard, *Very Truly Yours*, 2001
Candace Camp, *So Wild a Heart*, 2002

B.J. Daniels, *Montana Royalty*, 2008
Elizabeth Thornton, *The Perfect Princess*, 2001

375

KIMBERLY RAYE

Slippery When Wet

(New York: Love Spell, 2008)

Story type: Humor; Contemporary
Subject(s): Sports/Auto Racing; Family Problems; Self-Acceptance
Major character(s): Jaycee Anderson, Sports Figure (NASCAR driver), Businesswoman (Race Chicks, Inc.); Rory Canyon, Sports Figure (NASCAR driver), Businessman (Xtreme Racing); Riley Vaughn, Businesswoman (Race Chicks, Inc.)
Time period(s): 2000s
Locale(s): Dallas, Texas

Summary: Half-sisters Riley Vaughn and Jaycee Anderson, owners of the NASCAR racing team Race Chicks, Inc., face losing their corporate sponsor unless Riley can find a way to soften Jaycee's crude tomboy image, and fast. Rory Canyon, a fellow driver and long-time friend of Jaycee's, has always had a secret crush on her. But now, seeing her suddenly morph from sweats to stilettos is almost more than he can take. No matter how hard he tries to maintain his competitive focus, he can't get Jaycee out of his head. Rory suspects Jaycee is just doing this to distract him, and Jaycee wonders if Rory's sudden interest in her is merely meant to throw her off balance. Whatever it is, it's working.

Where it's reviewed:
Romantic Times, December 2008, page 80

Other books by the same author:
Drop Dead Gorgeous, 2008
Just One Bite, 2008 (Dead End Dating. Book 4)
Dead Sexy, 2007
Your Coffin or Mine?, 2007 (Dead End Dating. Book 3)
Dead End Dating, 2007 (Dead End Dating. Book 1)

Other books you might like:
Jean Brashear, *Extreme Caution*, 2008
Pamela Britton, *Total Control*, 2007
Marisa Carroll, *Victory Lane*, 2008
Ken Casper, *Running on Empty*, 2008
Michele Dunaway, *Out of Line*, 2008

376

PATRICIA RICE

Mystic Rider

(New York: Signet Eclipse, 2008)

Story type: Historical/Fantasy; Historical/French Revolution
Series: Mystic Isle. Book 2
Subject(s): Magic; Music and Musicians
Major character(s): Chantal Deveau, Musician; Ian Olympus, Warrior (Sky Rider)

Time period(s): 1790s (1791)
Locale(s): Mystic Isle, Fictional Country; Paris, France

Summary: Not only does Ian Olympus' vision tell him where to locate the Mystic Isle of Aelynn's magical Chalice of Plenty, it also tells him the woman who owns the chalice is his soul mate. Chantal Deveau has no idea her silver bell was Ian's missing relic, so of course when he turns up at her door, Chantal thinks he is crazy. Now the fate of Ian's country not only rests on his ability to convince Chantal to give him the chalice, but his own romantic future depends on him convincing Chantal that they are soul mates.

Where it's reviewed:
Romantic Times, July 2008, page 34

Other books by the same author:
Mystic Guardian, 2007
Magic Man, 2006
Much Ado about Magic, 2005
This Magic Moment, 2004
The Trouble with Magic, 2003

Other books you might like:
Shana Abe, *The Smoke Thief*, 2005
Naomi Bellis, *Step into Darkness*, 2006
Tracy Fobes, *My Enchanted Enemy*, 2002
Margo Maguire, *A Warrior's Taking*, 2007
Susan Spencer Paul, *Touch of Night*, 2005

377

ALIX RICKLOFF

Lost in You

(New York: Zebra, 2008)

Story type: Historical/Fantasy; Historical/Regency
Subject(s): Fairies; Magic; Treasure
Major character(s): Ellery Reskeen, Gentlewoman; Conor Bligh, Mythical Creature (fairy), Warrior
Time period(s): 1810s (1815)
Locale(s): England

Summary: When Ellery Reskeen lets a wounded man into her home late one night, she refuses to believe Conor Bligh's tales of evil *fey*, magical relics, and dangerous hunters known as *Keun Marow*, until the hellish creatures try to kill her themselves. Now the only one Ellery can trust to help her is Conor, especially once Ellery discovers she has magical powers that a demon lord will stop at nothing to possess.

Where it's reviewed:
Romantic Times, August 2008, page 47

Other books you might like:
Naomi Bellis, *Step into Darkness*, 2006
Sarah Gabriel, *To Wed a Highland Bride*, 2007
Karen Harbaugh, *Dark Enchantment*, 2004
Teresa Medeiros, *After Midnight*, 2005
Mary Jo Putney, *The Marriage Spell*, 2006

378

J.D. ROBB
MARY BLAYNEY , Co-Author

RUTH RYAN LANGAN , Co-Author
MARY KAY MCCOMAS , Co-Author

Suite 606

(New York: Berkley, 2008)

Story type: Paranormal; Anthology
Subject(s): Mystery; Paranormal; Magic
Time period(s): Indeterminate
Locale(s): United States; England

Summary: In the same mode as their anthology *Dead of Night*, this latest quartet of paranormal novellas is both heartwarming and frightening as it makes good use of myth, magic, and dashes of evil to help their heroes and heroines find love. Included are: "Ritual in Death" by J.D. Robb, "Love Endures" by Mary Blayney, "Cold Case" by Ruth Ryan Langan, and "Wayward Wizard" by Mary Kay McComas.

Where it's reviewed:
Romantic Times, November 2008, page 104

Other books you might like:
Amanda Ashley, *Midnight Pleasures*, 2003
    paranormal anthology
Jo Beverley, *Faery Magic*, 1998
    fantasy anthology
Jo Beverley, *Irresistible Forces*, 2004
    fantasy anthology
Nora Roberts, *Once upon a Midnight*, 2003
    fantasy anthology
Nora Roberts, *Once upon a Rose*, 2001
    fantasy anthology

379

ELISABETH ROSE (Pseudonym of Elisabeth Hoorweg)

Coming Home

(New York: Avalon, 2008)

Story type: Contemporary
Subject(s): Reunions; Music and Musicians; Change
Major character(s): Libby McNeill, Musician (former cellist), Companion; Charles Hogarth, Architect
Time period(s): 2000s
Locale(s): Sydney, Australia

Summary: When her world-class career as a cellist is put on hold because of a repetitive stress injury, Libby McNeill returns to Sydney in search of a job. By chance she encounters Charles Hogarth, a man she'd met briefly years earlier in Vienna when he lived in the apartment below her and complained about her practicing, and they renew their platonic acquaintance. Things change drastically, however, when his great-aunt, who lives with him, hires Libby as a live-in companion, and they see each other on a daily basis. A sweet romance that has a definite Australian feel.

Where it's reviewed:
Booklist, November 1, 2008, page 29

Other books by the same author:
The Right Chord, 2007

Other books you might like:

Faith E.W. Garner, *When Someday Comes*, 1995
Barbara McMahon, *The Substitute Wife*, 2002
Bernadette Pruitt, *A Christmas Wish*, 1996
Allison Rushby, *The Dairy Queen*, Don Mills
     Australia with a chicklit flair
Diane Tyrrel, *On Winding Hill Road*, 2005
     gothic elements

380

PAM ROSENTHAL

The Edge of Impropriety

(New York: Signet Eclipse, 2008)

Story type: Historical/Regency
Subject(s): Scandal; Conduct of Life; Authors and Writers
Major character(s): Marina Wyatt, Writer, Noblewoman
     (Countess of Gorham); Jasper Hedges, Antiquarian,
     Scholar
Time period(s): 1810s (1818); 1820s (1829)
Locale(s): Lake Como, Italy; England

Summary: A noted writer of popular romance novels,
Marina Wyatt, the widowed Countess of Gorham, makes
good use of her scandalous reputation to help her book
sales. However, when a young nobleman declares himself
smitten, his scholarly uncle arrives to rescue him from
Marina's wiles and falls under her spell himself.
Rosenthal's tale is witty, passionate, and exceptionally
well-written.

Where it's reviewed:
Booklist, November 1, 2008, page 29
Library Journal, October 15, 2008, page 51
Romantic Times, November 2008, page 51

Other books by the same author:
The Slightest Provocation, 2006
The Bookseller's Daughter, 2004
Almost a Gentleman, 2003

Other books you might like:
Liz Carlyle, *A Woman of Virtue*, 2001
Brenda Hiatt, *Scandalous Virtue*, 1999
Eloisa James, *Desperate Duchesses*, 2007
Eloisa James, *The Taming of the Duke*, 2006
Julia Ross, *The Seduction*, 2002

381

CANDACE SAMS

Electra Galaxy's Mr. Interstellar Feller

(New York: Love Spell, 2008)

Story type: Humor; Paranormal
Subject(s): Beauty Contests; Aliens; Smuggling
Major character(s): Sagan Carter, Police Officer; Keir
     Trask, Alien (Oceanun), Police Officer
Time period(s): Indeterminate Future
Locale(s): Los Angeles, California

Summary: The women of Los Angeles—and the rest of
the universe—have worked themselves into a frenzy. It's
time for Electra Galaxy's Mr. Interstellar Feller pageant,
and sexy males from all over the galaxy will be
competing. Oceanun Keir Trask is one of the contestants,
but not of his own free will. As an extraterrestrial law
enforcer, he's on the trail of intergalactic weapons smugglers, and participating in the contest is his cover. Sagan
Carter, an Earthling police officer, is managing the case.
She's supposed to be managing Keir, too, but the stubborn alien is busy trying to control her while he breaks
up the smuggling ring.

Where it's reviewed:
Romantic Times, July 2008, page 98

Other books by the same author:
Goblin Moon, 2008
Stone Heart, 2008
Gryphon's Quest, 2007
Tales of the Order: The Gazing Globe, 2007
The Craftsman, 2006

Other books you might like:
Kathleen Bacus, *Fiance at Her Fingertips*, 2008
Judi McCoy, *Wanted: One Perfect Man*, 2004
     Starlight. Book 1
Jenna McKnight, *A Date on Cloud Nine*, 2004
Stephanie Rowe, *Sex and the Immortal Bad Boy*, 2007
     Immortally Sexy. Book 4
Natale Stenzel, *The Druid Made Me Do It*, 2008

382

CHARLENE SANDS (Pseudonym of Charlene Swink)

Five Star Cowboy

(New York: Silhouette, 2008)

Story type: Contemporary
Series: Suite Secrets. Book 1
Subject(s): Hotels and Motels; Family; Courtship
Major character(s): Julia Lowell, Advertising (Los Angeles
     marketing firm), Hotel Worker (marketing V.P.);
     Trent Tyler, Hotel Owner (Tempest West Hotel),
     Cowboy
Time period(s): 2000s
Locale(s): Crimson Canyon, Arizona

Summary: Cowboy hotelier Trent Tyler seeks to hire Julia
Lowell to develop a marketing strategy that will rescue
his faltering Arizona hotel. Being between jobs at the
time of Trent's offer, Julia agrees to take the position. At
first, Trent and Julia pick up their torrid relationship
right where they left off a few months before, at Trent's
brother Evan's wedding. They can't get enough of each
other. Then Julia discovers that Trent had interfered with
her previous job prospect, to ensure that she'd remain
unemployed, and available to accept his offer. Feeling
betrayed and manipulated, Julia decides that Trent's only
love is his business, and he's just using her to attract
customers, and warm his bed. Trent gets a wake-up call
when Julia announces that she's quitting, and leaving the
Tempest West.

Where it's reviewed:
Romantic Times, August 2008, page 110

Other books by the same author:
Do Not Disturb Until Christmas, 2008
Taming the Texan, 2008
The Corporate Raider's Revenge, 2008
Between the CEO's Sheets, 2007
Bodine's Bounty, 2007

Other books you might like:
Caroline Anderson, *The Single Mom and the Tycoon*, 2008
Ally Blake, *Hired: The Boss's Bride*, 2008
Liz Fielding, *The Tycoon's Takeover*, 2002
Jessica Hart, *Last-Minute Proposal*, 2008
Leigh Michaels, *The Tycoon's Proposal*, 2006

383

LYNSAY SANDS

The Rogue Hunter

(New York: Avon, 2008)

Story type: Contemporary; Vampire Story
Series: Argeneau Family. Book 10
Subject(s): Vampires; Humor
Major character(s): Samantha Willan, Lawyer, Vacationer; Garrett Mortimer, Vampire Hunter, Vampire
Time period(s): 2000s
Locale(s): Ontario, Canada (rural cottage area)

Summary: On vacation with her two sisters and looking forward to a little R & R, frazzled attorney Samantha Willan is attracted to her sexy neighbor, little realizing that he has a secret that is beyond her wildest imaginings. A rogue hunter (a "good" vampire who hunts the "bad" vampires who prey on humans instead of satisfying their blood lust through more acceptable means) finds his life mate where he least expects it in this sensual addition to Sands' memorable Argeneau family of vampirism

Where it's reviewed:
Romantic Times, October 2008, page 102

Other books by the same author:
The Immortal Hunter, 2009
The Accidental Vampire, 2008
Vampire Interrupted, 2008
Vampires Are Forever, 2008
Bite Me If You Can, 2007

Other books you might like:
MaryJanice Davidson, *Undead and Unwed*, 2004
Christine Feehan, *Dark Symphony*, 2003
Katie MacAlister, *Sex and the Single Vampire*, 2004
Jennifer Rardin, *Another One Bites the Dust*, 2008
Michelle Rowan, *Lady and the Vamp*, 2008

384

AMANDA SCOTT (Pseudonym of Lynne Scott-Drennan)

Border Lass

(New York: Forever, 2008)

Story type: Historical/Medieval
Subject(s): Politics; Marriage

Major character(s): Lady Amalie Murray, Noblewoman; Sir Garth Napier, Knight, Nobleman (Lord of Westruther)
Time period(s): 14th century (1389-1390)
Locale(s): Scotland

Summary: When young noblewoman Amalie Murray accidentally overhears a dangerous, treasonous plot, Sir Garth Napier saves her from discovery and then realizes he needs to protect her from the villain who wants to take over the kingdom. The protagonists clash beautifully in this lively medieval that is definitely up to Scott's exceptional standard. Accurate historical detain and characters add depth to this fast-paced historical that is passionate, romantic, and will draw in fans and keep them reading. Follows *Border Wedding*.

Where it's reviewed:
Romantic Times, September 2008, page 46

Other books by the same author:
Border Wedding, 2008
Knight's Treasure, 2007
Lady's Choice, 2006
Lord of the Isles, 2005
Prince of Danger, 2005

Other books you might like:
Terri Brisbin, *Taming the Highlander*, 2006
Elizabeth English, *The Border Bride*, 2001
Hannah Howell, *Highland Barbarian*, 2006
Susan King, *Laird of the Wind*, 1998
Lyn Stone, *The Highland Wife*, 2001

385

JILL SHALVIS

Flashback

(Toronto: Harlequin, 2008)

Story type: Contemporary; Romantic Suspense
Subject(s): Arson; Family; Love
Major character(s): Mackenzie Stafford, Actress (soap opera); soap opera Aidan Donnelly, Fire Fighter
Time period(s): 2000s
Locale(s): Santa Rey, California

Summary: Following the death of her fire fighter brother in a suspicious blaze, Mackenzie Stafford returns to Santa Rey to clear his name. She refuses to believe the claims that he was a serial arsonist, and she won't leave town until she finds the truth. While searching for clues on board her brother's boat, a mysterious explosion and fire erupt, engulfing the vessel. The Santa Rey fire department responds to the scene, and Mackenzie is pulled to safety by none other than her old flame, Aidan Donnelly, now a member of the department. Mackenzie has no intention of rekindling their old relationship. He'd broken her heart years ago. That was then, though, and everyone deserves a second chance.

Where it's reviewed:
Romantic Times, August 2008, page 104

Other books by the same author:
Flashpoint, 2008
Superb and Sexy, 2008 (Sky High Air. Book 3)

Smart and Sexy, 2007 (Sky High Air. Book 1)
Strong and Sexy, 2007 (Sky High Air. Book 2)
The Trouble with Paradise, 2007

Other books you might like:
Jo Davis, *Trial by Fire*, 2008
Kate Hardy, *The Firefighter's Fiance*, 2006
Sammie Jo Moresca, *Smolder*, 2008
Alison Roberts, *The Firefighter's Baby*, 2005
JoAnn Ross, *Blaze*, 2005

386

MAGGIE SHAYNE (Pseudonym of Margaret Benson)

Angel's Pain

(Don Mills, Ontario: Mira, 2008)

Story type: Contemporary; Paranormal
Series: Wings in the Night. Book 15
Subject(s): Vampires; Revenge; Mental Telepathy
Major character(s): Briar, Vampire; Reaper, Vampire
Time period(s): 2000s
Locale(s): United States

Summary: Out for revenge on the brutally sadistic vampire Gregor, Briar, a vampire herself, links up with Reaper and his band who have the same agenda as she does. Gregor, of course, has his own nefarious ideas, and the result is a violent, romantic, adventurous tale that fans of Shayne's legendary Wings in the Night series will welcome.

Where it's reviewed:
Romantic Times, October 2008, page 101

Other books by the same author:
Lover's Bite, 2008 (Wings in the Night. Book 14)
Demon's Kiss, 2007 (Wings in the Night. Book 13)
Prince of Twilight, 2006 (Wings in the Night. Book 12)
Blue Twilight, 2005 (Wings in the Night. Book 11)
Edge of Twilight, 2004 (Wings in the Night. Book 10)

Other books you might like:
Lara Adrian, *Kiss of Midnight*, 2007
MaryJanice Davidson, *Undead and Unwed*, 2004
Christine Feehan, *Lover Beware*, 2003
   anthology
Sherrilyn Kenyon, *Dead after Dark*, 2008
   anthology
Lynsay Sands, *The Rogue Hunter*, 2009
   Argeneau Family. Book 10

387

DEBORAH SHELLEY (Pseudonym of Shelley Mosley and Deborah Mazoyer)

Marriage 101

(New York: Avalon, 2008)

Story type: Contemporary; Humor
Subject(s): Schools/High Schools; Divorce; Family Relations
Major character(s): Rachel Levin, Teacher (high school);

Danny Ricucci, Coach (high school), Musician (pianist)
Time period(s): 2000s
Locale(s): Los Libros, California

Summary: New teacher Rachel Levin is an academic expert in human relationships. She knows everything there is to know about relationships—except what it's like to actually be in one. Coach Danny Ricucci thinks there's a divorce gene in his family. For generations, all of the Ricucci marriages have failed. All, that is, but his oldest sisters—and she's married to the church. Danny's so certain that the tendency toward doomed relationships is hereditary that he's decided never to wed. Together, Rachel and Danny discover that there's more to love than scholarly studies, and that sometimes, genes are overrated.

Where it's reviewed:
Booklist, May 1, 2008, page 74
Library Journal, June 15, 2008, page 51

Other books by the same author:
My Favorite Flavor, 2000
One Starry Night, 2000
It's in His Kiss, 1999
Talk about Love, 1999

Other books you might like:
Carolyn Hughey, *Cupid's Web*, 2008
Cheryl Kushner, *He Said, She Said*, 2005
Cathie Linz, *Big Girls Don't Cry*, 2007
Tanya Michaels, *Not Quite as Advertised*, 2004
Kelley St. John, *To Catch a Cheat*, 2007

388

EVE SILVER

His Wicked Sins

(New York: Zebra, 2008)

Story type: Historical/Regency; Gothic
Subject(s): Murder; Serial Killers; Schools/Boarding Schools
Major character(s): Elizabeth "Beth" Canham, Teacher; Griffin Fairfax, Gentleman, Single Parent
Time period(s): 1820s (1828)
Locale(s): Yorkshire, England

Summary: Beth Canham arrives in the remote northern Yorkshire village of Burndale to accept a teaching position at Burndale Academy only to discover that two of the school's former teachers had been murdered. Before long, she is being stalked by the same person. In true gothic fashion, she begins to think the handsome, brooding hero, Griffin Fairfax, might be the guilty party. Atmospheric, chilling, and mysterious, this well-crafted story is reminiscent of the popular Gothics of the 1960s, but is brought up to date with steamy sensuality and more graphic violence.

Where it's reviewed:
Library Journal, August 2008, page 60
Romantic Times, August 2008, page 47

Other books by the same author:
Demon's Hunger, 2008 (Compact of Sorcerers)

Dark Prince, 2007
Demon's Kiss, 2007 (Compact of Sorcerers)
His Dark Kiss, 2006
Dark Desires, 2005

Other books you might like:
Victoria Holt, *Mistress of Mellyn*, 1960
    a modern classic
Evelyn Rogers, *Devil in the Dark*, 2001
Jennifer St. Giles, *The Mistress of Trevelyan*, 2004
Colleen Shannon, *The Trelayne Inheritance*, 2002
Karen White, *Whispers of Goodbye*, 2001

389

ELIZABETH SINCLAIR

Angel Unaware

(St. Charles, IL: Medallion, 2008)

Story type: Contemporary; Fantasy
Subject(s): Angels; Christmas; Fantasy
Major character(s): Dora DeAngelo, Angel, Child-Care
    Giver (Nanny); Tony Falcone, Guardian (of young
    niece), Businessman (construction company owner);
    Penny, Child
Time period(s): 2000s
Locale(s): New York (upstate New York)

Summary: Sent to Earth to help bachelor Tony Falcone
become a father and bond with his orphaned niece and
give six-year-old Penny the home she deserves, reluctant
angel Dora DeAngelo becomes Penny's nanny. She only
has until midnight on Christmas Eve to accomplish this,
and it won't be easy. Falling in love and becoming mortal
are not part of the bargain for Dora, even though she
longs to be human; however, miracles can happen,
especially when it's Christmas. This is a sweet, charming holiday read.

Where it's reviewed:
Publishers Weekly, October 13, 2008, page 42
Romantic Times, December 2008, page 83

Other books by the same author:
Burning Secrets, 2009
Into the Mist, 2008
Touched by Fire, 2007
Baptism in Fire, 2006
Eye of the Dream, 2006

Other books you might like:
Mary Balogh, *Angel Christmas*, 1994
    anthology
Heather Graham, *Angel's Touch*, 1995
Teresa Hill, *Twelve Days*, 2000
Debbie Macomber, *Where Angels Go*, 2007
    Christmas angels
Judi McCoy, *Heaven Sent*, 2003

390

SUSAN SIZEMORE
ERIN MCCARTHY , Co-Author

CHRIS MARIE GREEN , Co-Author
MELJEAN BROOK , Co-Author

First Blood

(New York: Berkley, 2008)

Story type: Paranormal; Anthology
Subject(s): Vampires; Werewolves; Demons
Time period(s): 2000s
Locale(s): United States

Summary: This lively quartet of paranormal novellas
includes stories that are linked to other works by these
authors. Included are: "Cave Canem" by Suzanne
Sizemore, in which a pair of hellhound pups are stolen
and need to be retrieved; "Russian Roulette" by Erin Mc-
Carthy, in which a vampire slayer turned vampire needs
to be kept safe; "Double the Bite" by Chris Marie Green,
in which one vampire twin's love for a mortal cop causes
jealousy problems; and "Thicker than Blood" by Meljean
Brook, in which a woman-turned-vampire reconnects
with her mortal love with ultimately positive results.
Although these stories will be most enjoyed by fans of
the authors' series, each novella does stand on its own.

Where it's reviewed:
Romantic Times, August 2008, page 92

Other books you might like:
Gerry Bartlett, *Real Vampires Have Curves*, 2008
    Glory St. Clair. Book 1
Meljean Brook, *Demon Bound*, 2008
    Guardians. Book 7
Chris Marie Green, *Night Rising*, 2007
    Vampire Babylon. Book 1
Erin McCarthy, *Bit the Jackpot*, 2008
    Vegas Vampires. Book 2
Erin McCarthy, *Sucker Bet*, 2008
    Vegas Vampires. Book 4

391

CHRISTINA SKYE (Pseudonym of Roberta Helmer)

To Catch a Thief

(Don Mills, Ontario: HQN, 2008)

Story type: Contemporary; Romantic Suspense
Subject(s): Art; Paranormal; Crime and Criminals
Major character(s): Nell Macinnes, Art Historian (art
    expert), Mountaineer; Dakota Smith, Military Person-
    nel (Navy S.E.A.L.)
Time period(s): 2000s
Locale(s): Scotland; San Francisco, California

Summary: Assigned to keep an eye on art expert Nell MacInnes, who is suspected of having something to do with
a stolen sketch by Leonardo da Vinci, navy S.E.A.L.
Dakota Smith first encounters her when he helps her
rescue some stranded teenagers from a mountain top on
the Isle of Skye. Attracted to her but suspicious because
of her art thief father's reputation, Dakota is drawn
further into the mystery when he keeps Nell from being
kidnapped and her father, newly released from prison
and trying to avoid his old ties and keep Nell safe, sends
her off to Draycott Abbey for help. Terrorist elements,

sizzling passion, and a dash of the paranormal add to this action-packed thriller that combines characters from two of Skye's popular series.

Where it's reviewed:
Booklist, August 2008, page 50
Romantic Times, September 2008, page 75

Other books by the same author:
Code Name: Bikini, 2007
Code Name: Blondie, 2006
Code Name: Baby, 2005
Code Name: Nanny, 2004
Code Name: Princess, 2004

Other books you might like:
Suzanne Brockmann, *Bodyguard*, 1999
Suzanne Enoch, *Don't Look Down*, 2002
    more humorous
Tara Janzen, *Loose and Easy*, 2008
Joyce Lamb, *Relative Strangers*, 2002
Marjorie M. Liu, *Shadow Touch*, 2006

392

DEANN SMALLWOOD

Montana Star

(New York: Avalon, 2008)

Story type: Historical/American West
Subject(s): Ranch Life; Mail Order Brides; Doctors
Major character(s): Aries Burnett, Doctor, Mail Order Bride; Jarrett McCabe, Rancher
Time period(s): 19th century
Locale(s): Montana

Summary: When her father dies leaving mountains of debt, Aries Burnett, trained as a doctor but not certified because of her gender, agrees to become a mail order bride and takes her young brother and heads for Montana. Things aren't quite as they seem, and when Aries arrives and learns that the person who placed the ad is the younger brother of the intended bridegroom, who knows nothing of this plan and is furious when he finds out, the situation explodes predictably. Jarrett wants her to leave, Aries is determined to stay, and love eventually wins out in this sweet Western romance that is Smallwood's debut novel for Avalon.

Where it's reviewed:
Booklist, September 15, 2008, page 38

Other books you might like:
Carolyn Brown, *Emma's Folly*, 2002
Carolyn Brown, *Willow*, 2003
Christine Bush, *Love, Julie*, 2006
Jill Marie Landis, *Rose*, 1990
Nancy J. Parra, *The Lovin' Kind*, 2006

393

KAREN ROSE SMITH

The Daddy Verdict

(New York: Silhouette, 2008)

Story type: Contemporary
Series: Darling Daddies. Book 3

Subject(s): Pregnancy; Family Relations; Love
Major character(s): Sierra Girard, Store Owner (Beaded For You); Ben Barclay, Lawyer (assistant district attorney)
Time period(s): 2000s
Locale(s): Albuquerque, New Mexico

Summary: Assistant District Attorney Ben Barclay thinks like a lawyer, so when Sierra Girard announces to him that she is pregnant with his child, his first reaction is to do the right thing and request a paternity test. It appears that the evening of passion they shared six weeks before has resulted in a baby, and they must now prepare for parenthood. They marry out of presumed obligation, though neither will admit that they feel the same madly intense attraction that drew them together in the first place. When Sierra finally confronts Ben about the lack of intimacy in their marriage, ooh baby!

Where it's reviewed:
Romantic Times, September 2008, page 118

Other books by the same author:
Her Mr. Right?, 2008
The Daddy Plan, 2008 (Darling Daddies. Book 2)
The Daddy Dilemma, 2008 (Darling Daddies. Book 1)
The Bracelet, 2007
Take a Chance on Me, 2004

Other books you might like:
Kara Lennox, *The Pregnancy Surprise*, 2008
Barbara McMahon, *Parents in Training*, 2008
Raye Morgan, *The Boss's Pregnancy Proposal*, 2007
Teresa Southwick, *Expecting the Doctor's Baby*, 2008
Linda Randall Wisdom, *Pregnancy Countdown*, 2003

394

KATHRYN SMITH

Let the Night Begin

(New York: Avon, 2008)

Story type: Vampire Story; Historical/Victorian
Series: Brotherhood of the Blood. Book 4
Subject(s): Marriage; Secrets; Vampires
Major character(s): Olivia Gavin, Vampire; Reign Gavin, Vampire
Time period(s): 1890s (1899)
Locale(s): England

Summary: The last time Olivia Gavin saw her husband, Reign, was on their wedding night when Olivia tried to kill him. Of course, Olivia had a very good reason for trying to eliminate her new spouse, since Reign betrayed her trust by turning her into a vampire. Now 30 years later, the only one who can help Olivia with a dangerous problem is Reign, but his assistance has a steep price: Reign wants his wife back!

Where it's reviewed:
Romantic Times, July 2008, page 36

Other books by the same author:
Night of the Huntress, 2007
Taken by the Night, 2007
Be Mine Tonight, 2006
In the Night, 2005

Romance

Still in My Heart, 2005

Other books you might like:
Tracy Fobes, *The Forbidden Garden*, 2000
Karen Harbaugh, *Dark Enchantment*, 2004
Teresa Medeiros, *After Midnight*, 2005
Amanda Quick, *Wait Until Midnight*, 2005
Colleen Shannon, *The Trelayne Inheritance*, 2002

395

LAURAINE SNELLING
JILLIAN HART , Co-Author

Yuletide Treasure

(New York: Steeple Hill, 2008)

Story type: Holiday Themes; Inspirational
Subject(s): Christmas; Love; Family
Locale(s): United States

Summary: These two heartwarming historical novellas from two favorite inspirational authors are linked by unexpected love and the magic of Christmas. A young, not especially beautiful woman who spends her time bringing the holiday spirit to others, finds love when she visits a woodcarver's shop to buy a treasured nutcracker and meets his grandson in Lauraine Snelling's "The Finest Gift." A tough bounty hunter agrees to find a young girl's mother and finds love where he least expects it in Jillian Hart's "A Blessed Season."

Where it's reviewed:
Romantic Times, November 2008, page 74

Other books you might like:
Millie Criswell, *A Western Family Christmas*, 2001
   anthology
Carolyn Davidson, *One Christmas Wish*, 2000
   anthology
Carolyn Davidson, *One Starry Christmas*, 2004
   anthology
Linda Lael Miller, *Springwater Christmas*, 1999
   Springwater Seasons. Book 6
Catherine Palmer, *A Victorian Christmas Quilt*, 1998

396

TERESA SOUTHWICK

Expecting the Doctor's Baby

(New York: Silhouette, 2008)

Story type: Contemporary; Medical
Series: Men of Mercy Medical. Book 3
Subject(s): Criticism; Family Problems; Pregnancy
Major character(s): Samantha Ryan, Counselor, Adoptee; Mitch Tenney, Doctor (emergency room), Divorced Person
Time period(s): 2000s
Locale(s): Las Vegas, Nevada

Summary: Doctor Mitch Tenney needs to work on his bedside manner. A tough childhood compounded later by a painful divorce, have left him brusque, outspoken, and intolerant—traits not well suited for an emergency room doctor. In one final attempt to salvage his job, Mercy Medical Center hires a consulting firm to get at the heart of Mitch's troublesome behavior. Samantha "Sam" Ryan, the adopted daughter of the hospital's administrator, becomes Mitch's relationship coach, and before long their affiliation becomes far more than professional. While Mitch's attitude improves immensely with Sam in his life, problems escalate in the Ryan family when she becomes pregnant with Mitch's child.

Where it's reviewed:
Romantic Times, September 2008, page 118

Other books by the same author:
Marrying the Virgin Nanny, 2009
The Millionaire and the M.D., 2008 (Men of Mercy Medical. Book 2)
When a Hero Comes Along, 2008 (Men of Mercy Medical. Book 2)
The Sheikh's Contract Bride, 2007 (Brothers of Bha'Khar. Book 1)
The Sheikh's Reluctant Bride, 2007 (Brothers of Bha'Khar. Book 2)

Other books you might like:
Lucy Clark, *The Surgeon's Secret*, 2001
Lynn Marshall, *Single Dad, Nurse Bride*, 2008
Joanna Neil, *Emergency at Valley Hospital*, 2003
Alison Roberts, *The Recovery Assignment*, 2004
Leeanne Marie Stephenson, *A Prescription for Love*, 2007

397

KERRELYN SPARKS

All I Want for Christmas Is a Vampire

(New York: Avon, 2008)

Story type: Paranormal; Vampire Story
Series: Love at Stake. Book 5
Subject(s): Vampires; Christmas
Major character(s): Toni Davis, Bodyguard, Guardian; Ian MacPhie, Vampire
Time period(s): 2000s
Locale(s): New York, New York

Summary: Turned into a vampire at 15 and looking like a teenager for 500 years has not been easy for Ian MacPhie. Now, thanks to a special drug, he has physically aged twelve years, and is looking for romance. However, he only wants to date another vampire—until he meets Toni, a gorgeous human who has been hired to guard his household of vampires while they are asleep and vulnerable. This is funny, sexy paranormal with a gentle dusting of holiday charm.

Where it's reviewed:
Library Journal, October 15, 2008, page 50
Romantic Times, November 2008, page 100

Other books by the same author:
Secret Life of a Vampire, 2009 (Love at Stake. Book 6)
The Undead Next Door, 2008 (Love at Stake. Book 4)

Be Still My Vampire Heart, 2007 (Love at Stake. Book 3)

Vamps and the City, 2006 (Love at Stake. Book 2)

How to Marry a Millionaire Vampire, 2005 (Love at Stake. Book 1)

Other books you might like:

Maureen Child, *Holiday with a Vampire*, 2007
anthology with Caridad Pineiro

Christine Feehan, *The Shadows of Christmas Past*, 2004

Kim Harrison, *Holidays Are Hell*, 2007
paranormal anthology

Merline Lovelace, *Holiday with a Vampire II*, 2008
anthology with Lori Devoti

Lynsay Sands, *Bite Me If You Can*, 2007

398

LIANE SPICER (Pseudonym of Charmaine Rousseau)

Cafe au Lait

(New York: Leisure, 2008)

Story type: Contemporary; Multicultural

Subject(s): African Americans; Romance; Vacations

Major character(s): Shari Zamore, Teacher; Michael Chancery, Businessman, Wealthy

Time period(s): 2000s

Locale(s): Port of Spain, Trinidad and Tobago

Summary: London school teacher Shari Zamore decides to take a much needed sabbatical to the tropics, to visit relatives, relax, and do some long-overdue soul-searching. On her flight to Trinidad and Tobago, she meets a very handsome, but rather surly passenger, Michael Chancery, who looks somehow familiar to her. It seems no matter where on the island Shari's cousin, Wanda, and her club scene entourage take her, the mysterious Michael shows up, too. In time, the enchantment of the islands works its magic on the two, and Shari becomes pregnant, but trouble brews in paradise when Michael's complicated past catches up with him.

Where it's reviewed:

Romantic Times, September 2008, page 92

Other books you might like:

Rochelle Alers, *Taken by Storm*, 2008

E. Lynn Harris, *Just Too Good to Be True*, 2008

Brenda Jackson, *Irresistible Forces*, 2008

Kayla Perrin, *Everlasting Love*, 1998

Kimberla Lawson Roby, *One in a Million*, 2008

399

CHERYL ST. JOHN (Pseudonym of Cheryl Ludwigs)

Her Montana Man

(Toronto: Harlequin, 2008)

Story type: Historical/American West

Subject(s): American West; Abuse

Major character(s): Eliza Jane Sutherland, Gentlewoman,

Care Giver; Jonas Black, Hotel Owner, Saloon Keeper/Owner

Time period(s): 1880s (1885)

Locale(s): Silver Bend, Montana

Summary: Giving up her accounting job at her father's brick factory in order to help her dying sister and young nephew was not easy for Eliza Jane Sutherland, but she loved her sister and her nephew. However, when she realizes that her slimy brother-in-law only married her sister for her share of the brick company and is making inappropriate advances, she realizes that she needs help—and it comes in the form of sexy Sheriff Jonas Black. Kidnappings and assorted adventures—as well as love—follow in this lively, romantic Western romance.

Where it's reviewed:

Romantic Times, December 2008, page 48

Other books by the same author:

The Preacher's Wife, 2009

The Lawman's Bride, 2007

The Preacher's Daughter, 2007

The Bounty Hunter, 2005

Other books you might like:

Catherine Anderson, *Keegan's Lady*, 1996

Catherine Anderson, *Simply Love*, 1997

Christine Bush, *Love, Julie*, 2006
sweeter

Cathy Maxwell, *Wild West Brides*, 2002
anthology

Bobbi Smith, *Tessa*, 2000

400

KELLEY ST. JOHN

Live and Yearn

(Toronto: Harlequin, 2008)

Story type: Contemporary; Paranormal

Series: Sixth Sense

Subject(s): Ghosts; Dreams and Nightmares; Automobile Accidents

Major character(s): Nanette Vicknair, Young Woman; Charles Roussel, Government Official (parish president)

Time period(s): 2000s

Locale(s): St. Charles Parish, Louisiana (Vicknair Plantation)

Summary: The Vicknair cousins are doing more than just restoring the family plantation after Hurricane Katrina—they're helping ghosts cross over to the other side. During all of this activity, normal and paranormal, Nanette Vicknair has to deal with parish president Charles Roussel. Then Charles has a car accident, and, as his spirit hovers between worlds, he finds he can visit Nanette in her dreams and seduce her.

Where it's reviewed:

Romantic Times, September 2008, page 110

Other books by the same author:

Bed on Arrival, 2008

Fire in the Blood, 2008

Ghosts and Roses, 2007

Shiver and Spice, 2007
Kiss and Dwell, 2007

Other books you might like:
Karen Foley, _Overnight Sensation_, 2008
Cindy Myers, _At Her Pleasure_, 2008
Debbi Rawlins, _Do Not Disturb_, 2008
Jamie Sobrato, _Seducing a S.E.A.L._, 2008
Tawny Weber, _Risque Business_, 2008

401

DANIELLE STEEL

A Good Woman

(New York: Delacorte, 2008)

Story type: Historical/Americana
Subject(s): Rape; Secrets; World War I
Major character(s): Annabelle Worthington, Socialite, Health Care Professional; Josiah Millbank, Homosexual (closet)
Time period(s): 1900s
Locale(s): New York, New York; France (battle front, WWI); Newport, Rhode Island

Summary: When Annabelle Worthington gets the flu, she can't go on the family vacation. Regrettably, the Worthingtons are sailing on the _Titanic_. Annabelle's brother and father drown, sending her mother, Consuelo, into a deep depression. Annabelle marries Josiah Millbank, a man old enough to be her father, but he has a shocking secret. He divorces her, ironically making Annabelle an outcast. She escapes society's scorn by fleeing to war-torn France, where she puts her medical skills to good use on the front. Even though fate has more tragedies in store for Annabelle, she holds on tight to her courage and pride.

Where it's reviewed:
Booklist, September 1, 2008, page 5
Publishers Weekly, October 20, 2008, page 8

Other books by the same author:
Honor Thyself, 2008
Rogue, 2008
Amazing Grace, 2007
Sisters, 2007
Coming Out, 2006

Other books you might like:
Sebastian Faulks, _Birdsong_, 1997
Belva Plain, _Random Winds_, 1980
Christina Schwarz, _Drowning Ruth_, 2001
LaVyrle Spencer, _Years_, 1986
Jacqueline Winspear, _Maisie Dobbs_, 2003

402

NATALE STENZEL

The Druid Made Me Do It

(New York: Love Spell, 2008)

Story type: Humor; Paranormal
Subject(s): Healing; Mythology; Humor

Major character(s): Janelle Corrington, Doctor, Guardian (of Robin Goodfellow); Robin "Kane" Goodfellow, Mythical Creature (puca)
Time period(s): 2000s
Locale(s): United States

Summary: Dr. Janelle Corrington has a one-night stand with an incredibly sexy man named Kane. For her, it's love at first sight, but Kane disappears the next morning. After all, he is Faerie King Oberon's son; his real name is Robin Goodfellow; and he's best known as a puca who uses his magic to seduce women. But Oberon isn't thrilled when, eight years later, Robin punishes his brother for a crime he didn't commit. Oberon appoints the jilted Janelle to be Robin's guardian. Part of Robin's sentence is to make it up to everyone he's ever hurt. During his period of atonement, Robin, who has never been in love, falls for the dedicated doctor, and begins to know how very fragile a heart can be.

Where it's reviewed:
Romantic Times, August 2008, page 90

Other books by the same author:
Pandora's Box, 2008
Seeking Miss Scarlet, 2005
All Shook Up, 2004
Pop-Up Dating, 2004
Forget Prince Charming, 2003

Other books you might like:
Kathleen Bacus, _Fiance at Her Fingertips_, 2008
Angie Fox, _The Accidental Demon Slayer_, 2008
Judi McCoy, _One Night with a Goddess_, 2007
  Goddess. Book 2
Vicki Lewis Thompson, _Over Hexed_, 2007
  Hex. Book 1
Minda Webber, _The Reinvented Miss Bluebeard_, 2007

403

ANNE STUART
TINA LEONARD , Co-Author
MARION LENNOX , Co-Author

Christmas Getaway

(Toronto: Harlequin, 2008)

Story type: Contemporary; Holiday Themes
Subject(s): Christmas; Mystery; Suspense
Time period(s): 2000s
Locale(s): United States; Australia

Summary: Mystery, escape, adventure, passion, and a dash of violence add zing to this appealing collection of Holiday getaway novellas. Included are: "Claus and Effect" by Anne Stuart, a story of a desperate cop who kidnaps a doctor in the hope that she can clear him of a crime ; "Caught at Christmas" by Tina Leonard, which involves a maid of honor taken into protective custody by the bride's Texas Ranger brother to keep her safe; and "Candy Canes and Crossfire" by Marion Lennox, in which bullets at her wedding send her packing to an isolated cabin only to find it already occupied by a man and three kids! This is a funny, action-packed anthology.

Where it's reviewed:
Romantic Times, November 2008, page 88

Other books you might like:
Cherry Adair, *Red Hot Santa*, 2005
 anthology
Jennifer Crusie, *Santa Baby*, 2006
 anthology
Claudia Dain, *Silent Night*, 2004
 anthology
Christine Feehan, *The Shadows of Christmas Past*, 2004
 two holiday novellas, one by Susan Sizemore
J.D. Robb, *Silent Night*, 1998
 anthology

404

CATHY GILLEN THACKER

The Inherited Twins

(Toronto: Harlequin, 2008)

Story type: Contemporary
Series: Made in Texas. Book 1
Subject(s): Hotels and Motels; Grief; Children
Major character(s): Claire Olander, Businesswoman (Red
 Sage Guest Ranch Retreat); Heath McPherson,
 Banker (trust administrator), Divorced Person
Time period(s): 2000s
Locale(s): Summit, Texas

Summary: Following the tragic deaths of her sister and
brother-in-law, struggling guest ranch owner Claire Olander inherits their 4-year-old orphaned twins. The
administrator of the twins' trust fund, Heath McPherson,
is burdened with the task of telling Claire that her guest
ranch must turn a profit soon, or she will be forced to
sell the twins' share of the property. Oil prospectors and
investment companies are already sniffing about, but
their purchase offers don't appeal to Claire, who is
determined to preserve the ranch, intact, and keep it in
the family. When Heath finds that he's falling in love
with Claire, he questions his ability to remain impartial
in managing the children's financial affairs, while pursu-
ing a future with Claire.

Where it's reviewed:
Romantic Times, October 2008, page 116

Other books by the same author:
A Baby in the Bunkhouse, 2008 (Made in Texas. Book
 2)
From Texas, with Love, 2008 (McCabes: Next
 Generation. Book 6)
The Rancher's Family Thanksgiving, 2008 (Texas
 Legacies: Carrigans. Book 2)
The Gentleman Rancher, 2008 (Texas Legacies:
 Carrigans. Book 4)
Hannah's Baby, 2008 (Made in Texas. Book 3)

Other books you might like:
Laura Marie Altom, *A Daddy for Christmas*, 2008
Caroline Andersen, *The Tycoon's Instant Family*, 2006

Judy Christenberry, *The Rancher's Inherited Family*,
 2008
Tanya Michaels, *Mistletoe Baby*, 2008
Marin Thomas, *The Cowboy and the Angel*, 2008

405

PATRICIA THAYER (Pseudonym of Patricia Wright)

Texas Ranger Takes a Bride

(Toronto: Harlequin, 2008)

Story type: Contemporary; Ranch Life
Series: Western Weddings. Book 2
Subject(s): Fathers and Sons; Reunions; Love
Major character(s): Mallory Kendrick Hagan, Widow(er),
 Businesswoman; Chase Landon, Lawman (Texas
 Ranger), Parent (father of Ryan); Ryan Hagan, Child
 (of Mallory and Chase)
Time period(s): 2000s
Locale(s): Texas

Summary: Texas Ranger Chase Landon is called to rescue
kidnapped members of the Kendrick family, including
8-year-old Ryan, the son of his former love, Mallory
(Kendrick) Hagan. Chase had left Mallory behind years
before when he first began his Ranger training. He'd
returned for her a few months later, only to find she had
married another, and was out of his life for good. But
now, when Chase rescues the kidnapped boy, he is
stunned by the obvious resemblance and realizes that
Ryan is his son. Mallory had always intended to tell
Chase about his child but the timing was never right.
Well, how about now?

Where it's reviewed:
Romantic Times, September 2008, page 114

Other books by the same author:
Wedding Bells at Wandering Creek Ranch, 2008
 (Western Weddings. Book 5)
A Mother for the Tycoon's Child, 2007 (Rocky
 Mountain Brides. Book 2)
Raising the Rancher's Family, 2007 (Rocky Mountain
 Brides. Book 1)
The Rancher's Doorstep Baby, 2007 (Western
 Weddings. Book 3)
Coming Home to the Cowboy, 2006 (Brides of Bella
 Lucia. Book 1)

Other books you might like:
Judy Christenberry, *The Rancher's Inherited Family*,
 2008
Melissa James, *The Bridegroom's Secret*, 2008
Cathy Gillen Thacker, *The Inherited Twins*, 2008
Rebecca Winters, *Crazy about Her Spanish Boss*, 2008
Trish Wylie, *The Millionaire's Proposal*, 2008

406

MIA THERMOPOLIS (Pseudonym of Meg Cabot)

Ransom My Heart

(New York: Avon, 2009)

Story type: Historical/Medieval; Humor
Subject(s): Humor; Middle Ages; Kidnapping

Major character(s): Finnula Crais, Kidnapper, Outlaw (poacher); Hugo Fitzstephen, Nobleman (Earl of Stephensgate), Captive
Time period(s): 13th century (1291)
Locale(s): Stephensgate, Mythical Place

Summary: Finnula Crais is the best archer in her village. She uses her skills to bag illegal game in Hugo Fitzstephen, Earl of Stephensgate's forest, and then share the meat with those less fortunate. When one of Finnula's many sisters announces her engagement, the family doesn't have enough money to provide a proper dowry. Finnula decides to kidnap Sir Hugo, who's coming home from the Crusades with riches and other spoils from the war. Then every thing goes wildly awry when Finnula falls in love with her captive. A hilarious romp through the Middle Ages.

Where it's reviewed:
Romantic Times, January 2009, page 46

Other books you might like:
Sandy Blair, *A Thief in a Kilt*, 2006
Christina Dodd, *Rules of Surrender*, 2000
Julie Garwood, *Guardian Angel*, 1990
Teresa Medeiros, *The Bride and the Beast*, 2001
Amanda Quick, *Desire*, 1994

407

JODI THOMAS (Pseudonym of Jodi Koumalats)

Tall, Dark, and Texan
(New York: Jove, 2008)

Story type: Historical/American West
Series: Whispering Mountain. Book 3
Subject(s): Ranch Life; Marriage; Secrets
Major character(s): Jessica Anne Barton, Widow(er), Single Parent; Teagen McMurray, Rancher
Time period(s): 1850s (1856)
Locale(s): Texas

Summary: With no place to go except Whispering Mountain Ranch, Jessie Barton takes her three girls and heads to Texas and prays that Teagen McMurray, a man who had done business with her late husband's Chicago bookstore for several years, will be as kind as his letters sound. Reluctantly, he takes them in, and when Jessie's former in-laws threaten to take the children, they agree to marry. Love grows slowly between them as they work together to keep the ranch from greedy villains and their family safe in this heartwarming Western romance.

Where it's reviewed:
Booklist, December 1, 2008, page 36
Romantic Times, November 2008, page 48

Other books by the same author:
Texas Princess, 2007 (Whispering Mountain. Book 2)
Texas Rain, 2006 (Whispering Mountain. Book 1)
The Texan's Reward, 2005
The Texan's Luck, 2004
When a Texan Gambles, 2003

Other books you might like:
Catherine Anderson, *Keegan's Lady*, 1996
Dorothy Garlock, *Sweetwater*, 1998

Lorraine Heath, *Texas Glory*, 1998
Linda Lael Miller, *Springwater*, 1999
LaVyrle Spencer, *The Gamble*, 1987

408

MELODY THOMAS

Passion and Pleasure in London
(New York: Avon, 2008)

Story type: Historical/Victorian
Subject(s): Family; Secrets
Major character(s): Winter Ashburn, Gentlewoman, Thief; Rory Jameson, Gentleman
Time period(s): 1870s (1877)
Locale(s): England

Summary: Summoned home by his dying grandfather, Rory Jameson plans on refusing his inheritance, but on the way there, Rory is injured trying to retrieve his wallet after a thief steals it at an inn. Winter Ashburn tries to help the less fortunate locals by "borrowing" from those with more money, but now she sees that her methods have consequences. Winter takes a wounded Rory back to her cottage to recuperate, but the more time they spend together, the more Winter finds herself falling in love with the "enemy."

Where it's reviewed:
Romantic Times, September 2008, page 46

Other books by the same author:
Sin and Scandal in England, 2007
Wild and Wicked in Scotland, 2007
Angel in My Bed, 2006
A Match Made in Scandal, 2005
Must Have Been the Moonlight, 2004

Other books you might like:
Adele Ashworth, *Duke of Scandal*, 2006
Robyn DeHart, *Deliciously Wicked*, 2006
Judith Ivory, *The Indiscretion*, 2001
Lisa Kleypas, *Mine Till Midnight*, 2007
Amanda Quick, *Wait Until Midnight*, 2005

409

SHERRY THOMAS

Delicious
(New York: Bantam, 2008)

Story type: Historical/Victorian
Subject(s): Scandal; Cooks and Cooking; Seduction
Major character(s): Verity Durant, Cook (exceptional chef); Stuart Somerset, Political Figure, Heir
Time period(s): 1890s (1892); 1880s (1882)
Locale(s): England

Summary: A noted chef with a slightly scandalous reputation fears that her secrets are going to be exposed now that her employer and protector has died and his bastard brother has inherited his estate. Things are complicated by the fact that Verity and Stuart also shared an anonymous affair years ago, and it's only a matter of time before he makes the connection. Food, delicious and seductive, is at the heart of this exquisite Cinderella story.

Where it's reviewed:
Library Journal, August 2008, page 60
Publishers Weekly, June 16, 2008, page 38
Romantic Times, August 2008, page 40

Other books by the same author:
Private Arrangements, 2008

Other books you might like:
Gayle Callen, *Never Trust a Scoundrel*, 2008
Jo Goodman, *Magically Delicious Kisses*, 2002
    anthology
Judith Ivory, *Sleeping Beauty*, 1998
Susan King, *Waking the Princess*, 2003
Julia London, *The Secret Lover*, 2002

410

COLLEEN THOMPSON

Triple Exposure

(New York: Leisure, 2008)

Story type: Romantic Suspense; Contemporary
Subject(s): Rape; Small Town Life; Redemption
Major character(s): Rachel Copeland, Photographer (photography teacher), Abuse Victim (drugged and raped); Zeke Pike, Artisan (furniture craftsman), Recluse (fugitive from justice)
Time period(s): 2000s
Locale(s): Marfa, Texas

Summary: Rachel Copeland has returned to the small Texas town of Marfa, hoping to start her life over and escape the sensationalist publicity of her high profile assault trial. In a moment of self-defense, Rachel had shot and killed an attacker whose celebrity mother now seems intent on revenge. Rachel takes refuge in her photography, which leads to a close friendship with a local recluse, Zeke Pike, whose handcrafted furniture is as intricate as his mysterious past. When one of Rachel's photos of Zeke catches the attention of a local art society and gets published, Zeke's cover is blown. After that, no one is sure whose stalker is whose, but life in sleepy little Marfa becomes an exercise in survival.

Where it's reviewed:
Romantic Times, August 2008, page 69

Other books by the same author:
Head On, 2007
The Salt Maiden, 2007
Heat Lightning, 2006
The Deadliest Denial, 2006
Fade the Heat, 2005

Other books you might like:
Sarah Abbot, *Destiny Bay*, 2008
Gail Barrett, *To Protect a Princess*, 2008
Kathleen Creighton, *Daredevil's Run*, 2008
Brenda Novak, *Trust Me*, 2008
Marilyn Pappano, *Intimate Enemy*, 2008

411

JANET TRONSTAD

Calico Christmas at Dry Creek

(New York: Steeple Hill, 2008)

Story type: Historical/American West; Inspirational
Series: Dry Creek Historical. Book 1
Subject(s): Christmas; Small Town Life; Prejudice
Major character(s): Elizabeth O'Brien, Widow(er); Jake Hargrove, Trapper (former), Guardian (of nieces)
Time period(s): 1870s (1879)
Locale(s): Montana Territory, Montana

Summary: The Montana Territory is a harsh place and Jake Hargrove needs help. His infant niece needs a wet nurse and the only option is Elizabeth Collins, a woman who still grieving the deaths of her husband and baby and would, at the moment, prefer to die as well. Elizabeth can't resist the baby, however, and she agrees to a marriage in name only, little realizing that it will eventually become one in fact. Prejudice (the baby and her sister are part-Lakota) is only one of the issues dealt with in the sweet inspirational romance that is the first in Tronstad's new Dry Creek Historical series.

Where it's reviewed:
Romantic Times, November 2008, page 119

Other books by the same author:
A Dry Creek Courtship, 2008
Snowbound in Dry Creek, 2008 (Dry Creek. Book 14)
Dry Creek Sweethearts, 2008
A Heart for the Dropped Stitches, 2008
A Dropped Stitches Christmas, 2007

Other books you might like:
Carolyn Davidson, *The Magic of Christmas*, 2008
    anthology
Jillian Hart, *High Plains Wife*, 2003
Robin Lee Hatcher, *Promise Me Spring*, 1991
    not inspirational
Kerri Mountain, *The Parson's Christmas Gift*, 2008
Lauraine Snelling, *Yuletide Treasure*, 2008
    anthology with Jillian Hart

412

JANET TRONSTAD

Snowbound in Dry Creek

(New York: Steeple Hill, 2008)

Story type: Contemporary; Inspirational
Series: Dry Creek. Book 14
Subject(s): Small Town Life; Weather; Change
Major character(s): Jenny Collins, Widow(er), Single Parent; Zach "Lightning" Lucas, Rodeo Rider, Postal Worker (temporary mail carrier)
Time period(s): 2000s
Locale(s): Dry Creek, Montana

Summary: A rodeo star who reluctantly agrees to make the last mail delivery before Christmas—dressed as Santa, no less—in exchange for veterinary care for his sick horse finds himself snowbound over the with a young widow and her two children. This sweetly inspirational romance features likable characters, a classic plot, and plenty of down-home holiday charm, and is a "refreshed version" of *Stranded with Santa*, first published in 2002.

Where it's reviewed:
Romantic Times, October 2008, page 123

Other books by the same author:
A Dry Creek Courtship, 2008
Calico Christmas at Dry Creek, 2008
Dry Creek Sweethearts, 2008
A Heart for the Dropped Stitch, 2008
A Dropped Stitches Christmas, 2007

Other books you might like:
Margaret Daley, *A Texan Thanksgiving*, 2008
Jillian Hart, *His Holiday Heart*, 2008
Susan Horicks, *More than a Cowboy*, 2008
Annie Jones, *Somebody's Santa*, 2008
Brenda Minton, *His Little Cowgirl*, 2008

413

J.D. WARREN   (Pseudonym of Vance Briceland)

Crate and Peril

(New York: Love Spell, 2008)

Story type: Paranormal; Contemporary
Series: World of the Storm Ravens. Book 2
Subject(s): Supernatural; Conspiracies; Devil
Major character(s): Samantha Dorringer, Investigator (fairie invasion); Corydonais, Immortal (shapeshifter), Royalty (Circle of the Copper Crown)
Time period(s): 2000s
Locale(s): Venice, California

Summary: Shapeshifting fairies are infiltrating Venice, California, and blending in with the humans. Samantha Dorringer is investigating this paranormal activity, and she is well aware that not all fairies, like the Kinland Peri, are dangerous. She would know, because her lover, Corydonais, is himself a Peri, of the valiant Order of the Storm Ravens. However, members of a rival Peri death cult, the Order of the Crow, are also here, and with wicked intent. Samantha, Cor, and the Storm Ravens must stop the cult before they can procure a half-human demon child to perpetuate their evil existence.

Where it's reviewed:
Romantic Times, October 2008, page 107

Other books by the same author:
Bedlam, Bath and Beyond, 2008 (World of the Storm Ravens. Book 1)

Other books you might like:
Ilona Andrews, *Magic Burns*, 2008
P.C. Cast, *Goddess of the Rose*, 2006
Yasmine Galenorn, *Witchling*, 2006
Michelle Pillow, *Faery Queen*, 2007
Eileen Wilks, *Night Season*, 2008

414

MINDA WEBBER

The Daughters Grimm

(New York: Love Spell, 2008)

Story type: Humor; Fantasy
Subject(s): Humor; Sisters; Fairy Tales
Major character(s): Greta Grimm, Young Woman; Rae Grimm, Young Woman; Fen Shortz, Nobleman (baron), Single Parent (unruly children)
Time period(s): 1780s (1786)
Locale(s): Cornwall, England; Wolfach, Germany (edge of the Black Forest)

Summary: Greta and Rae Grimm, doomed to a life of spinsterhood in Cornwall, are sent to live with their aunt in Prussia, where young men are said to be in great supply. Greta, who believes in magic and fairy tales, is thrilled to be going to a place so near the legendary Black Forest. Rae, on the other hand, is forced by circumstance to marry the Baron Fen Schortz and mother his brood of hellions. As Rae battles her newly acquired brats, Greta decides to look for vampires. Each sister discovers that the path to true love can be downright treacherous.

Where it's reviewed:
Romantic Times, July 2008, page 45

Other books by the same author:
Bustin', 2007
The Reinvented Miss Bluebeard, 2007
The Reluctant Miss Helsing, 2006
The Remarkable Miss Frankenstein, 2005

Other books you might like:
Maureen Child, *Bedeviled*, 2009
Angie Fox, *The Accidental Demon Slayer*, 2008
Katie MacAlister, *Up in Smoke*, 2008
    Silver Dragons. Book 2
Judi McCoy, *One Night with a Goddess*, 2007
    Goddess. Book 2
Vicki Lewis Thompson, *Over Hexed*, 2007
    Hex. Book 1

415

TAWNY WEBER

Risque Business

(Toronto: Harlequin, 2008)

Story type: Contemporary
Subject(s): Books and Reading; Competition; Writing
Major character(s): Delaney Madison "D.M." Conner, Critic, Professor; Nick Angel, Writer
Time period(s): 2000s
Locale(s): California

Summary: Only her closest friend knows that professor D.M. Conner is also popular fiction critic Delaney Madison, and that is exactly how Delaney wants it; especially since she is competing to become the next assistant head of the English department at Santa Rosita

College. But when Delaney criticizes best-selling thriller writer Nick Angel's sexy suspense books for their lack of emotional content, he challenges her to a literary competition. If Delaney wins, Nick agrees to write more "emotion" into the love scenes of his next book, but if Nick wins, Delaney has to admit that his readers simply want a sexy story.

Where it's reviewed:
Romantic Times, September 2008, page 110

Other books by the same author:
Does She Dare, 2008
Double Dare, 2007

Other books you might like:
Stephanie Bond, *It Takes a Rebel*, 2000
Julie Kenner, *Nobody Does It Better*, 2000
Isabel Sharpe, *What Have I Done for Me Lately?*, 2006
Hope Tarr, *Strokes of Midnight*, 2007
Cathy Yardley, *Working It*, 2003

416

CHRISTINE WELLS

The Dangerous Duke

(New York: Berkley Sensation, 2008)

Story type: Historical/Regency
Subject(s): Diaries; Family; Politics
Major character(s): Kate Fairchild, Gentlewoman, Widow(er); Maxwell Brooke, Nobleman (Duke of Lyle); Stephen Holt, Relative (brother of Kate)
Time period(s): 1810s (1817)
Locale(s): England

Summary: Maxwell Brooke, the newly inherited Duke of Lyle, believes Lady Kate Fairchild's brother Stephen Holt knows something about the arsonists who killed several members of his family. When jailing Holt does nothing to loosen his tongue, Maxwell takes Kate captive, intending to use her to pressure her brother into talking. As a counter-measure Kate threatens to publish her scandalous diary if Maxwell doesn't release Stephen. But Kate's plans to publish her diary threaten to derail the careers of several powerful politicians, and now Kate finds that she needs Maxwell's protection herself.

Where it's reviewed:
Romantic Times, September 2008, page 46

Other books by the same author:
Scandal's Daughter, 2008

Other books you might like:
Jo Beverley, *Lady Beware*, 2007
Liz Carlyle, *A Deal with the Devil*, 2004
Sabrina Jeffries, *Never Seduce a Scoundrel*, 2006
Sophia Nash, *A Dangerous Beauty*, 2007
Sari Robins, *More than a Scandal*, 2005

417

DIANE WHITESIDE

Bond of Darkness

(New York: Berkley Sensation, 2008)

Story type: Contemporary; Paranormal
Series: Texas Vampires. Book 3
Subject(s): Vampires; Murder; Sexual Behavior
Major character(s): Stephanie Reynolds, Police Officer (Texas Ranger); Ethan Templeton, Vampire
Time period(s): 2000s; 1900s (1927)
Locale(s): New Orleans, Louisiana

Summary: Texas Ranger Stephanie Reynolds is on the trail of a vicious killer she suspects is a vampire. She's no stranger to night stalkers since her lover and occasional partner in crime fighting, Ethan Templeton, is also a vampire, so she understands their ways. She's met her match with the murderous Devol and his evil cohorts, who have a penchant for stalking and killing women. When Stepanie's own life becomes threatened, Templeton must intervene, despite probable dire consequences.

Where it's reviewed:
Romantic Times, October 2008, page 109

Other books by the same author:
Bond of Fire, 2008 (Texas Vampires. Book 2)
The Northern Devil, 2007 (Devil. Book 4)
Bond of Blood, 2006 (Texas Vampires. Book 1)
The Southern Devil, 2006 (Devil. Book 3)
The Hunter's Prey, 2006

Other books you might like:
Kresley Cole, *Dark Needs at Night's Edge*, 2008
Delilah Devlin, *Into the Darkness*, 2007
Sharon Page, *Blood Rose*, 2007
Gena Showalter, *The Darkest Night*, 2008
J.R. Ward, *Lover Enshrined*, 2008

418

ELISSA WILDS

Between Light and Dark

(New York: Love Spell, 2008)

Story type: Paranormal; Contemporary
Subject(s): Good and Evil; Wicca; Love
Major character(s): Laurell Pittman, Witch (Earth Balancer's chosen mother); Axiom, Deity (Gray Balancer of Light Realm)
Time period(s): 2000s
Locale(s): Lake Geneva, Wisconsin

Summary: Laurell Pittman doesn't know it yet, but she's been chosen by the Divine Council of the Light Realm to be the human mother of the Earth Balancer, the one who will protect the equilibrium of good and evil on the Earth. The supernatural being chosen to father this child is Axiom, a gentlemanly but irresistible "Gray" deity who possesses the forces of both dark and light magic. Ultimately, Axiom hopes to earn his way onto the elite Divine Council by accepting this assignment, but he hadn't counted on falling in love with Laurell, the mother of his child, and this changes everything.

Where it's reviewed:
Romantic Times, November 2008, page 105

Other books you might like:
Rowena Cherry, *Knight's Fork*, 2008
Christine Feehan, *Dark Prince*, 2005
Yasmine Galenorn, *Witchling*, 2006
Pamela Palmer, *Dark Deceiver*, 2008
J.D. Warren, *Crate and Peril*, 2008

419

C.L. WILSON

King of Sword and Sky

(New York: Leisure, 2008)

Story type: Fantasy; Paranormal
Series: Tairen Soul. Book 3
Subject(s): Fairies; Magic; Supernatural
Major character(s): Ellysetta Baristani, Healer, Royalty (queen consort); Rain Tairen Soul, Immortal, Royalty (king of the Tairen Soul)
Time period(s): 2000s
Locale(s): Mythical Place

Summary: Deception is at work within the realm of the Fading Lands. Rain Tairen Soul, king of a rare "Fey" race of flying feline beings, confronts his enemies and prepares for war. Meanwhile, his true mate, Ellysetta Baristani, is also preparing. She's learning to harness and unleash her powerful magic to help save the Tairen from extinction.

Where it's reviewed:
Romantic Times, October 2008, page 75

Other books by the same author:
Queen of Song and Souls, 2009 (Tairen Soul. Book 4)
Lady of Light and Shadows, 2007 (Tairen Soul. Book 2)
Lord of the Fading Lands, 2007 (Tairen Soul. Book 1)

Other books you might like:
Rowena Cherry, *Knight's Fork*, 2008
Dave Duncan, *Sky of Swords: A Tale of the King's Blades*, 2001
Christine Feehan, *Dark Prince*, 2005
Karen Marie Moning, *Faefever*, 2008
Joy Nash, *Immortals: The Crossing*, 2008

420

LISA WINGATE

Word Gets Around

(Bloomington, MN: Bethany House, 2009)

Story type: Contemporary; Inspirational
Series: Daily, Texas. Book 2
Subject(s): Movie Industry; Small Town Life; Family Relations
Major character(s): Lauren Eldridge, Teacher (university teaching assistant); Nathaniel Heath, Writer

Time period(s): 2000s
Locale(s): Daily, Texas; Malibu, California

Summary: Justin Shay, Hollywood megastar, decides to make his next movie, a western, in Daily, Texas, and the little town throws out the red carpet. At her dad's request, Lauren Eldridge leaves her teaching assistant job at Kansas State University to help with the horses on the set. Even though he knows the script is horrible, Justin's best friend from their foster care days, writer Nathaniel Heath, joins him on the venture. Justin's girlfriend, Amber Anderson, just off a singing tour, comes along for the trek to her hometown. Hollywood meets small town America, and the results have a profound effect on everyone.

Other books by the same author:
The Summer Kitchen, 2009
A Month of Summer, 2008 (Blue Sky Hills. Book 1)
Talk of the Town, 2008 (Daily, Texas. Book 1)
A Thousand Voices, 2007 (Tending Roses. Book 5)
Drenched in Light, 2006

Other books you might like:
Tracey Bateman, *That's (Not Exactly) Amore*, 2008
Rachel Hauck, *Love Starts with Elle*, 2008
Beth Pattillo, *Heavens to Betsy*, 2005
Emilie Richards, *Sister's Choice*, 2008
Kathryn Springer, *The Prince Charming List*, 2008

421

SHERRYL WOODS

Welcome to Serenity

(Don Mills, Ontario: Mira, 2008)

Story type: Contemporary; Americana
Series: Sweet Magnolias. Book 4
Subject(s): Small Town Life; Christmas; Family
Major character(s): Jeanette Brioche, Businesswoman (beauty expert); Tom McDonald, Government Official (city manager)
Time period(s): 2000s
Locale(s): Serenity, South Carolina

Summary: Christmas-averse Jeanette Brioche is co-opted into working on the Christmas festival with an equally Holiday-challenged new city manager, Tom McDonald, only to find they have a lot more in common than they'd thought in this heartwarming, Christmas-infused romantic charmer that will please series fans. Many characters from Woods' earlier Sweet Magnolias books are reprised in this sweet story.

Where it's reviewed:
Library Journal, October 15, 2008, page 51
Romantic Times, December 2008, page 78

Other books by the same author:
Seaview Inn, 2008
A Slice of Heaven, 2007 (Sweet Magnolias. Book 2)
Mending Fences, 2007
Stealing Home, 2007 (Sweet Magnolias. Book 1)
Feels Like Family, 2007 (Sweet Magnolias. Book 3)

Other books you might like:
Robyn Carr, *A Virgin River Christmas*, 2008
Judy Duarte, *Her Best Christmas Ever*, 2008
Debbie Macomber, *A Cedar Cove Christmas*, 2008
Linda Lael Miller, *A McKettrick Christmas*, 2008
Lisa Plumley, *Home for the Holidays*, 2008

422

REBECCA YORK (Pseudonym of Ruth Glick)

Christmas Spirit

(Toronto: Harlequin, 2008)

Story type: Contemporary; Holiday Themes
Subject(s): Paranormal; Ghosts; Murder
Major character(s): Chelsea Caldwell, Psychic (sees ghosts), Artist (painter); Michael Bryant, Journalist
Time period(s): 2000s
Locale(s): Jenkins Cove, Maryland

Summary: On a hunt to unmask frauds who pretend to see ghosts, Michael Bryant focuses on Chelsea Caldwell, a woman who runs a B & B and also sees ghosts. However, Chelsea's abilities are real and before long both she and Michael are involved in a deadly mystery, complete with dead bodies, that threatens to see them both dead.

Where it's reviewed:
Romantic Times, October 2008, page 117

Other books by the same author:
Ghost Moon, 2008
Beyond Fearless, 2007
New Moon, 2007
Shadow of the Moon, 2006
Killing Moon, 2003

Other books you might like:
Linda Anderson, *The Secrets of Sadie Maynard*, 1999
Christine Feehan, *Lover Beware*, 2003
    anthology
Linda Howard, *Dream Man*, 1995
Jayne Ann Krentz, *Sizzle and Burn*, 2008
Maggie Shayne, *Destiny*, 2001

423

DONNA YOUNG

A Bodyguard for Christmas

(Toronto: Harlequin, 2008)

Story type: Contemporary; Romantic Suspense
Subject(s): Mystery; Espionage; Murder
Major character(s): Regina Menlow, Store Owner (book store); Jordon Beck, Spy, Government Official (special agent)
Time period(s): 2000s
Locale(s): United States

Summary: Honoring his British Ambassador dad's last wish and also trying to find out who killed him, M16 agent Jordan Beck rescues bookstore owner Regina Menlow when her store is set ablaze by someone after the journal left in her care by Jordan's late father. Now Jordan is honor bound to keep her safe; and like it or not, Regina has acquired a tempting, but infuriating, bodyguard just in time for Christmas. Espionage, terrorism, and betrayal are all part of this fast-paced thriller that is linked to other books in her Labyrinth series that feature members of an elite special ops division of the CIA.

Where it's reviewed:
Romantic Times, December 2008, page 101

Other books by the same author:
Secret Agent, Secret Father, 2008
Bodyguard Confessions, 2007
The Bodyguard Contract, 2007
Engaging Bodyguard, 2006
Bodyguard Rescue, 2005

Other books you might like:
Suzanne Brockmann, *Bodyguard*, 1999
Suzanne Brockmann, *Identity Unknown*, 2000
Rita Herron, *Silent Night Sanctuary*, 2008
Dana Marton, *Tall, Dark, and Lethal*, 2008
Cassie Miles, *Christmas Crime in Colorado*, 2008

The Year in Fantasy: 2008
by
Don D'Ammassa

Modern fantasy has remained fairly monolithic for the past decade, consisting primarily of High Fantasy—castles, kings and queens, dragons, and sorcerers—usually arranged in trilogies, and almost always with a medieval style setting, though not in our historical past. There have always been exceptions, of course, perhaps most notably writers such as Jim Butcher and Simon R. Green, who have fathered extended series of fantasies set in the contemporary world. The occasional historical fantasy has provided some variation, and sword and sorcery thrives after a fashion in the world of gaming tie-ins, chiefly from Wizards of the Coast and in Black Library's Warhammer series.

This year saw a dramatic change in the mix, the seeds of which had begun to emerge over the past two or three years. The most significant is the rise of paranormal romances using fantasy themes, almost always set in the contemporary world or one close to it. The boundaries of this new form are ill defined and range from the occasionally humorous other world adventures as in T.A. Pratt's novels set in the city of Felport to the more realistic world depicted by Kat Richardson, Charlaine Harris, Devon Monk, and others. Many of these involve vampires and other supernatural creatures and could also be read as horror novels. Although trilogies still appear, most series have become much longer or even open ended. In fact, almost every fantasy novel published during 2008 was part of a series. Fantasy has become very successful for young adults and children as well, and part of this is no doubt carryover from the very popular Harry Potter novels by J. K. Rowling. Many of these are written with a degree of sophistication missing from much other fiction targeted at this age group, and like Rowling's novels, many of them have also found an appreciative audience among adults.

One of the best fantasy novels for younger readers this year was *Inkdeath* by Cornelia Funke, the concluding volume in a trilogy that opened with *Inkheart* in 2003 and continued with *Inkspell* in 2005. The first volume will be appearing as a motion picture in 2009. The premise is that a fantasy world created by a writer has become real and the protagonists find themselves caught up in it. The concept of characters trapped inside a book is not new—L. Sprague de Camp and Fletcher Pratt wrote the Harold Shea series with a similar premise during the 1940s—but Funke gives the concept her own twist. The series is quite complex, with more than one hundred characters, but the results are worth rising to the challenge. Bruce Coville also concludes a trilogy this year, one which began with *In the Land of the Unicorns* in 1994, and continued in *Song of the Wanderer* in 2001. *Dark Whispers* consists of two parallel quest stories that will converge to reveal not only the fate of the main characters but finally explain the source of the animosity between the people of Coville's magical realm and the unicorns who share their land.

A third exceptional children's fantasy is *Lamplighter* by D.M. Cornish, sequel to last year's *Foundlling*. The protagonist is an orphan in a world that vaguely resembles Victorian England. He is taken in by the lamplighters whose job is to provide the illumination that protects people from the creatures who live in darkness. The arrival of the first girl to enter their order upsets everyone involved. Witty prose and an inventive imagination are evident here. A concluding volume will follow. One other notable young adult fantasy novel appeared in 2008, one with dark themes and a sexual subtext that is likely to make it controversial. Margo Lanagan's *Tender Morsels* features a protagonist who has been raped and molested by her father and who has fled their pre-industrial civilization into a closed universe where she and her baby can live a life of peace and tranquility. Unfortunately, the barrier protecting her is not absolute and visitors from the other reality will cause fresh heartbreak and pain.

Urban fantasy was well represented, led by T.A. Pratt's *Dead Reign*, third in an ongoing series set in the mythical city of Felport and featuring Marsha Mason, the city's chief magician, who in this adventure has to outwit Death in physical form, a manifestation of the Lord of the Underworld who takes over the city. Mason responds by invading Hell in this witty, often humorous, and very clever adventure story. Newcomer Devon Monk opens a rather different series with *Magic to the Bone*, set in a fantasy version of Portland, Oregon. The protagonist has a rare talent. Exposed to the results of a curse, she can psychically backtrack to its origin and find out who is responsible. An abused child appears to have been cursed by his own father, but the truth turns out to be much more complicated. Monk has developed an unusual magic system for his fantasy world which suggests that everything has consequences, and shifting those to another party can be more appalling than the act itself.

Perhaps the best single fantasy novel of the year was *Knights of the Cornerstone* by James P. Blaylock, his first book in several years. The protagonist visits his aunt and uncle in a remote community in northern California and finds himself caught up in the battle between two forces for control of certain sacred artifacts. As always, Blaylock introduces his fantastic elements in such a matter of fact manner that the reader is willing to accept even the most outrageous events. The best quasi-historical fantasy this year was *Swiftly* by Adam Roberts, set in an alternate world where Gulliver's adventures actually happened. When war breaks out between England and France, the Lilliputians and Brobdingnabians choose opposite sides. The novel is clever and inventive.

High fantasy may have been in decline, but that doesn't mean that no one was writing fine stories in that form. Dennis L. McKiernan has been chronicling events in his mythical world of Mithgar for several years. *City of Jade* is probably his best single book, although familiarity with some of the earlier volumes would make the plot of this intricate novel somewhat less dense. It is cast as a kind of retelling of Jason and the Argonauts, describing the mustering of a crew for a ship bound to explore remote regions of a magical world. Episodic in structure, it has a strong central story to bind it together. Kage Baker returns with a sequel to *The Anvil of the World*. *The House of the Stag* follows a young man from youth to adult as he deals with his half-human heritage, survives a stint as a gladiator, and matures into a more thoughtful person. The novel deals with matters of conscience and faith as well as providing high adventure and even moments of genuine humor. Baker's already enviable reputation as a science fiction writer is likely to widen to include fantasy as well.

Several of the very best of the year's fantasy novels draw upon some elements of high fantasy, but set them in far more original worlds, some where the very laws of nature are different, others closely resembling our own. Alan Campbell returns to the world of 2007's *Scar Night* for *Iron Angel*, set in a surreal future city which is the battleground between the ruler of a league of mystical wizards and a pantheon of godlike beings. The novel's vivid settings and bizarre juxtapositions of events is complex and rewards close attention, although it ends disappointingly with a cliffhanger setting up the next and perhaps final volume in the series. An even more original

world is revealed in Jay Lake's *Escapement*, sequel to *Mainspring*. Lake mixes a quasi-Victorian civilization usually associated with the Steampunk movement to a unique world, one operated through elaborate and oversized mechanisms. In both of these novels, the setting is so fascinating in its own right that it tends at times to overshadow the characters and conflicts that advance the plot.

Sarah A. Hoyt has been writing first-rate historical fantasy for a few years now. She switched to a more contemporary setting for *Draw One in the Dark* last year, and this year she followed up with a sequel, *Gentleman Takes a Chance*. It resembles paranormal fantasy in that the magical creatures—in this case people who can assume a variety of animal forms—are living secretly among us. The protagonist is a were-panther who finds herself torn between two worlds, and unable to devote time to resolving that conflict because of a series of murders. Because all of the victims were shape shifters, members of that community decide to act on their own, even if that means open warfare between the two species.

British writer Robert V.S. Redick's *The Red Wolf Conspiracy* also borrows from high fantasy, but most of the story is set aboard a vast sea going vessel, centuries old, which is engaged on a mission to negotiate a peace between two rival kingdoms. The ship is a self-contained world in itself, with internal conflicts, long hidden secrets, and even a small tribe with a separate culture within a culture. This was easily the best first fantasy novel of the year. Holly Phillips' *The Engine's Child* is also set at sea because it takes place on a world almost completely covered with water. The protagonist is a relative innocent who gets caught up in the struggle among various secretive groups to gain certain ends, including the development of a technology that will allow its owners to locate the rare spots of solid land. Although the main character is not an admirable person, the world she inhabits is fascinating and the prose is smooth and entertaining.

Richard Morgan is the author of several highly praised science fiction novels, and *The Steel Remains* was his first foray into fantasy. Morgan also borrows from high fantasy; his protagonist is a wizened veteran of a magical war who has fallen on hard times and lives in his own memories. He and two companions embark on what appears to be a typical fantasy quest, but their adventures are transformed by a kind of gritty realism and intensity rarely found in such adventure stories. Patricia A. McKillip, on the other hand, has carved out a small niche for herself, a brand of fantasy that might include high adventure but which has characters who are familiar-seeming people rather than heroic figures. In *The Bell at Sealey Head* , a small town in a rural otherworld is troubled by the pealing of a phantom bell that no one can see. There is also a delightful mansion full of unexpected magic and unusual events. A mysterious visitor and a dying woman will contribute to the solution of the mystery.

Although traditional sword and sorcery has not produced a notable novel in some time, 2008 also saw a new, multi-volume reissue of Michael Moorcock's classic "Elric" stories. These novels and short stories feature one of the earliest fantasy anti-heroes. Elric is in a sense possessed by his own sword, which compels him to spill blood so that it can devour human souls. His exploits changed tone over the years from high adventure to more intellectual struggles. The series has become nearly as popular as Robert E. Howard's Conan tales and a series of movies based on them is currently being developed.

Recommended Titles

The titles listed below reflect the dramatic changes that appear to be transforming contemporary fantasy. Although there was considerable short fantasy fiction this year, there was only one collection that stood out. Some of the titles listed below are from the first half of the year and were covered in second volume of *What Do I Read Next? 2008.*

The House of the Stag by Kage Baker

The Knights of the Cornerstone by James P. Blaylock

Iron Angel by Alan Campbell

The Lamplighter by D.M. Cornish

Dark Whispers by Bruce Coville

Inkdeath by Cornelia Funke

The Gentleman Takes a Chance by Sarah A. Hoyt

Escapement by Jay Lake

Tender Morsels by Margo Lanagan

City of Jade by Dennis L. McKiernan

The Bell at Sealey Head by Patricia A. McKillip

Magic to the Bone by Devon Monk

The Steel Remains by Richard K. Morgan

The Engine's Child by Holly Phillips

The Red Wolf Conspiracy by Robert V.S. Redick

Swiftly by Adam Roberts

Fantasy Titles

JOAN AIKEN

The Serial Garden

(Easthampton, MA: Big Mouth House, 2008)

Story type: Collection
Subject(s): Short Stories

Summary: These two dozen stories all feature the Armitage family, who have weird and wacky adventures in their house. They are among the author's earliest work and four of them have not previously appeared in print. The family deals with a book of magic incantations, a visit by the Furies, wizards, and gateways to wondrous other worlds.

Other books by the same author:
The Cockatrice Boys, 1996
Is, 1992
The Moon's Revenge, 1987
The Stolen Lake, 1981
The Whispering Mountain, 1968

Other books you might like:
Edward Eager, *Seven Day Magic*, 1962
Norton Juster, *The Phantom Tollbooth*, 1961
E. Nesbit, *Wet Magic*, 1913
Andre Norton, *Steel Magic*, 1965
Mary Norton, *The Borrowers*, 1952

PIERS ANTHONY

Two to the Fifth

(New York: Tor, 2008)

Story type: Humor; Magic Conflict
Series: Xanth
Subject(s): Humor; Quest
Major character(s): Cyrus, Cyborg; Ragna Roc, Mythical Creature, Ruler; Don, Robot
Time period(s): Indeterminate
Locale(s): Alternate Universe

Summary: Cyrus the Cyborg wants to become a playwright rather than follow the paths suggested for him by his parents. He visits the greatest sorcerer in Xanth for help, only to discover that the entire land is menaced by the magical powers of Ragna Roc. Cyrus becomes the focus of a group of people whose combined powers might be able to overcome the evil sorcery that holds them in check.

Other books by the same author:
Air Apparent, 2007
Pet Peeve, 2005
Currant Events, 2004
Cube Route, 2003
Havoc, 2003

Other books you might like:
John DeChancie, *Castle Murders*, 1991
Esther Friesner, *Majyk by Hook or Crook*, 1994
Craig Shaw Gardner, *A Difficulty with Dwarves*, 1987
Andrew Harman, *The Scrying Game*, 1996
Terry Pratchett, *Equal Rites*, 1987

CATHERINE ASARO

The Night Bird

(Don Mills, Ontario: Luna, 2008)

Story type: Romance; Sword and Sorcery
Series: Lost Continent. Book 4
Subject(s): Romance; Magic
Major character(s): Allegra, Prisoner; Markus Onyx, Warrior; Cobalt, Ruler
Time period(s): Indeterminate
Locale(s): Alternate Universe

Summary: Allegra lives in a society where women acknowledge no masters, but she is carried off by a group of barbaric invaders, one of whom becomes fascinated with her. Although his manners are crude and insensitive, she finds herself falling in love with him.

Other books by the same author:
The Fire Opal, 2007
Alpha, 2006
The Dawn Star, 2006
The Misted Cliffs, 2005
The Charmed Sphere, 2004

Other books you might like:
Lynn Abbey, *Beneath the Web*, 1994
Suzy McKee Charnas, *The Furies*, 1994
Maggie Furey, *Harp of Winds*, 1994
Sharon Green, *The Hidden Realms*, 1993
Elizabeth Vaughan, *Warlord*, 2007

427

KAGE BAKER

The House of the Stag

(New York: Tor, 2008)

Story type: Sword and Sorcery; Magic Conflict
Subject(s): Magic; Revenge
Major character(s): Gard, Mythical Creature, Slave; Kdwyr, Nobleman; Quickfire, Businessman
Time period(s): Indeterminate
Locale(s): Alternate Universe

Summary: The Yendri people were not martial by nature and they were easily conquered by the Riders. Gard is the only Yendri to fight back, in part because he is part demon as well as part human. He is disgraced among his own people, enslaved, but eventually regains his freedom and finds a new maturity.

Where it's reviewed:
Booklist, September 15, 2008, page 32
Library Journal, September 15, 2008, page 48
Publishers Weekly, July 28, 2008, page 56

Other books by the same author:
Gods and Pawns, 2007
The Sons of Heaven, 2007
The Machine Child, 2006
The Children of the Company, 2005
The Anvil of the World, 2003

Other books you might like:
Sara Douglass, *Enchanter*, 2001
Barbara Hambly, *Stranger at the Wedding*, 1994
Elizabeth Haydon, *Elegy for a Lost Star*, 2004
Dennis L. McKiernan, *Into the Forge*, 1997
Lawrence Watt-Evans, *The Wizard Lord*, 2006

428

ELIZABETH BEAR

Hell and Earth

(New York: Roc, 2008)

Story type: Historical; Magic Conflict
Series: Promethean Age. Book 4
Subject(s): Fairies; Magic
Major character(s): Elizabeth, Ruler; Kit Marley, Writer; William Shakespeare, Writer
Time period(s): 16th century
Locale(s): England; Mythical Place

Summary: Elizabethan England is actually ruled by the Prometheus Club through Queen Elizabeth, who employs Shakespeare and others to imbue their plays with magi-cal words that help direct the nation. Kit Marley is an agent of the throne who is able to travel to the parallel world of Faerie, where he hopes to enlist aid against a plot to undermine the throne.

Where it's reviewed:
Booklist, August 1, 2008, page 53
Publishers Weekly, June 23, 2008, page 41

Other books by the same author:
Ink and Steel, 2008
New Amsterdam, 2007
The Chains That You Refuse, 2007
Whiskey and Water, 2007
Blood and Iron, 2006

Other books you might like:
Sara Douglass, *The Nameless Day*, 2000
Sarah A. Hoyt, *All Night Awake*, 2002
Mercedes Lackey, *Any Less Than Kind*, 2008
   Roberta Gellis, co-author
Judith Tarr, *House of War*, 2003
Chelsea Quinn Yarbro, *A Mortal Glamour*, 1985

429

GALEN BECKETT

The Magicians and Mrs. Quent

(New York: Bantam, 2008)

Story type: Alternate World; Mystery
Subject(s): Magic; Secrets
Major character(s): Ivy Lockwell, Worker; Dashton Rafferdy, Government Official; Eldyn Garritt, Businessman
Time period(s): Indeterminate
Locale(s): Alternate Universe

Summary: Altania is a magical world that bears a strong similarity to late Victorian England. Ivy Lockwell is the strongest personality among three sisters who are worried about their father's obsessive reclusiveness. Ivy takes a job working for the mysterious Mr. Quent and discovers that her world is far more complex, dangerous, and exciting than she had ever suspected. First novel.

Where it's reviewed:
Library Journal, July 1, 2008, page 72
Locus, August 2008, page 27
Publishers Weekly, June 2, 2008, page 33

Other books you might like:
Jonathan Barnes, *The Somnambulist*, 2007
Susanna Clarke, *Jonathan Strange and Mr. Norrell*, 2004
Gordon Dahlquist, *The Glass Books of the Dream Eaters*, 2006
Jeffrey Ford, *The Portrait of Mrs. Charbuque*, 2002
Paula Volsky, *Illusion*, 1991

430

JAMES P. BLAYLOCK

The Knights of the Cornerstone
(New York: Ace, 2008)

Story type: Contemporary; Magic Conflict
Subject(s): Secrets; Legends
Major character(s): Calvin Bryson, Wealthy; Al Lymon, Aged Person, Knight; Bob Postum, Aged Person, Criminal
Time period(s): 2000s
Locale(s): New Cyprus, California

Summary: Calvin Bryson visits his aunt and uncle in a remote California town and finds himself in the middle of a battle for control of a magical religious artifact. The entire town belongs to the Knights of the Cornerstone, a modern day version of the Knights Templar. Opposed to them is a criminal organization led by Bob Postum, who is willing to commit murder to achieve his goals.

Where it's reviewed:
Locus, November 2008, page 19
Publishers Weekly, October 13, 2008, page 41

Other books by the same author:
The Rainy Season, 1999
Lord Kelvin's Machine, 1992
The Paper Grail, 1991
The Stone Giant, 1989
Land of Dreams, 1987

Other books you might like:
Jonathan Carroll, *Bones of the Moon*, 1987
Charles De Lint, *Greenmantle*, 1988
Richard Grant, *In the Land of Winter*, 1997
Tim Powers, *Three Days to Never*, 2006
Gene Wolfe, *Castleview*, 1990

431

PATRICIA BRIGGS

Cry Wolf
(New York: Ace, 2008)

Story type: Romance; Werewolf Story
Series: Alpha and Omega. Book 1
Subject(s): Werewolves
Major character(s): Anna Latham, Werewolf; Charles Cornick, Werewolf; Bran Cornick, Leader
Time period(s): 2000s
Locale(s): Montana

Summary: Anna Latham became a werewolf after surviving an attack. For her own protection and the safety of those around her, a pack of similar shapechangers takes her to a remote community where she can learn to control her new nature. There she becomes involved in romance and a search for a rogue werewolf who could jeopardize their secret society.

Other books by the same author:
Iron Kissed, 2008
Blood Bound, 2007

Moon Called, 2006
Raven's Shadow, 2004
Dragon Blood, 2003

Other books you might like:
Ilona Andrews, *Magic Bites*, 2007
Charles De Lint, *Wolf Moon*, 1988
Yasmine Galenorn, *Changeling*, 2007
Sarah A. Hoyt, *Draw One in the Dark*, 2006
Pat Murphy, *Nadya*, 1996

432

TERRY BROOKS

The Gypsy Morph
(New York: Del Rey, 2008)

Story type: Disaster; Magic Conflict
Series: Genesis of Shannara. Book 3
Subject(s): Disasters; Magic
Major character(s): Angel Perez, Knight; Kirisin Bellorus, Mythical Creature (elf); Hawk, Teenager
Time period(s): Indeterminate
Locale(s): Alternate Universe

Summary: The old world of rational thought and science has given way to a new type of existence in which magic is restored to the Earth and creatures thought to be legendary are proven to be real. New nations rise and wars are begun, and a handful of people possess knowledge and abilities which could affect the outcome and the future of the world.

Where it's reviewed:
Booklist, June 1, 2008, page 6
Library Journal, August 1, 2008, page 74

Other books by the same author:
The Elves of Cintra, 2007
Armageddon's Children, 2006
The Heritage of Shannara, 2003
Antrax, 2001
Ilse Witch, 2000

Other books you might like:
Joan Aiken, *The Cockatrice Boys*, 1996
Peter Dickinson, *The Changes*, 1975
Larry Niven, *The Magic Goes Away*, 1978
Madeline Robins, *The Stone War*, 1999
John Shirley, *Demons*, 2002

433

JIM BUTCHER

Princeps' Fury
(New York: Ace, 2008)

Story type: Sword and Sorcery; Magic Conflict
Series: Codex Alera. Book 5
Subject(s): Magic; War
Major character(s): Tavi, Ruler; Isana, Noblewoman; Ehren, Warrior
Time period(s): Indeterminate

Locale(s): Alternate Universe

Summary: An officer in the army of Alera, Tavi has distinguished himself and has now been proclaimed as heir to the throne. Unfortunately, there may be no throne to inherit. Despite having made peace with their immediate enemy, the savage Vord are still on the move, and for the first time in its history, Alera teeters on the edge of collapse.

Where it's reviewed:
Publishers Weekly, October 27, 2008, page 37

Other books by the same author:
Small Favor, 2008
Captain's Fury, 2007
Cursor's Fury, 2006
Academ's Fury, 2005
Furies of Calderon, 2004

Other books you might like:
Dave Duncan, *The Cutting Edge*, 1992
Jennifer Fallon, *Harshini*, 2005
Raymond Feist, *Exile's Return*, 2004
David Gemmell, *The Hawk Eternal*, 1996
L.E. Modesitt Jr., *The Death of Chaos*, 1995

434

RICHARD LEE BYERS

Undead

(Renton, WA: Wizards of the Coast, 2008)

Story type: Sword and Sorcery; Magic Conflict
Series: Haunted Lands. Book 2
Subject(s): Magic; Quest
Major character(s): Szass Tam, Sorcerer; Bareris, Warrior; Tammith, Vampire
Time period(s): Indeterminate
Locale(s): Alternate Universe

Summary: A battle between two factions of wizards has gotten out of hand. They raised armies of the undead to battle one another, and now they are so numerous that they seem destined to take over the world. An archmage, a warrior, and an ambivalent vampire are among those caught up in the battle to restore the old way of life.

Other books by the same author:
The Enemy Within, 2007
Unclean, 2007
The Rite, 2005
The Rage, 2003
The Shattered Mask, 2001

Other books you might like:
Mark Acres, *Dark Divide*, 1991
Glen Cook, *Reap the East Wind*, 1987
Christie Golden, *Dance of the Dead*, 1992
Steve Perry, *Conan the Defiant*, 1987
Lawrence Watt-Evans, *Touched by the Gods*, 1997

435

RACHEL CAINE

Gale Force

(New York: Roc, 2008)

Story type: Magic Conflict; Contemporary
Series: Weather Warden. Book 7
Subject(s): Magic; Legends
Major character(s): Joanne Baldwin, Sorceress; David, Mythical Creature (djinn); Rahel, Mythical Creature (djinn)
Time period(s): 2000s
Locale(s): Florida

Summary: Joanne Baldwin's magic control of the weather is tested again when a supernaturally devised earthquake hits Florida. Her attempts to discover who is responsible and prevent another disaster is complicated by her impending marriage to a djinn and the persistence of a curious reporter who wants to uncover her secrets.

Where it's reviewed:
Locus, August 2008, page 27

Other books by the same author:
Thin Air, 2007
Firestorm, 2006
Chill Factor, 2004
Heat Stroke, 2004
Ill Wind, 2003

Other books you might like:
Patricia Briggs, *Moon Called*, 2006
Karen Chance, *Midnight's Daughter*, 2008
Kat Richardson, *Greywalker*, 2006
Jeanne C. Stein, *Legacy*, 2008
Anton Strout, *Dead to Me*, 2008

436

KRISTIN CASHORE

Graceling

(New York: Harcourt, 2008)

Story type: Young Adult; Magic Conflict
Subject(s): Psychic Powers; Secrets
Major character(s): Katsa, Teenager; Po, Royalty; Leck, Ruler
Time period(s): Indeterminate
Locale(s): Alternate Universe

Summary: A handful of people in a fantastic world are born with unusual powers. This first novel follows the adventures of four of these characters, one adult and three children. Each has a unique ability which makes them dangerous or capable of other extreme attributes. A young girl who is ashamed of her gift makes common cause with others against an evil king.

Where it's reviewed:
Booklist, October 1, 2008, page 42
Locus, September 2008, page 27
Publishers Weekly, July 21, 2008, page 160

Other books you might like:
Bruce Coville, *Dark Whispers*, 2008
Diana Wynne Jones, *Drowned Ammet*, 1977
Vivian Vande Velde, *The Conjurer Princess*, 1997
Jane Yolen, *The Magic Three of Solatia*, 1974
Mary Frances Zambreno, *A Plague of Sorcerers*, 1991

437

MARK CHADBOURN

The Burning Man

(London: Gollancz, 2008)

Story type: Contemporary; Magic Conflict
Series: Kingdom of the Serpent. Book 2
Subject(s): Magic; Quest
Major character(s): Jack Churchill, Time Traveler; Ryan Veitch, Warrior; Niamh, Deity
Time period(s): 2000s
Locale(s): England

Summary: Jack Churchill has traveled through time and space at the will of the gods, but now he is back in the contemporary world. There he discovers that the vast majority of the population has fallen under a spell which can only be lifted if he and his few allies secure a number of mystical artifacts, and avoid those determined to stop them.

Other books by the same author:
Jack of Ravens, 2006
The Hounds of Avalon, 2005
Queen of Sinister, 2004
The Devil in Green, 2002
Darkest Hour, 2000

Other books you might like:
Joan Aiken, *The Cockatrice Boys*, 1996
Peter Dickinson, *The Changes*, 1975
Simon R. Green, *Agents of Light and Darkness*, 2003
Katherine Kurtz, *St. Patrick's Gargoyle*, 2001
Madeline Robins, *The Stone War*, 1999

438

DEBORAH CHESTER

The Crown

(New York: Ace, 2008)

Story type: Sword and Sorcery; Magic Conflict
Series: Sword. Book 4
Subject(s): Magic; Quest
Major character(s): Lea E'non, Royalty; Shadrael, Nobleman; Caelan, Ruler
Time period(s): Indeterminate
Locale(s): Alternate Universe

Summary: Lord Shadrael has kidnapped the emperor's sister at the bidding of priests who have promised to restore his soul. A bond between the two has grown, and they escape together when the priests renege on their promise, surviving in a hostile and terrifying wilderness.

Other books by the same author:
The King Imperilled, 2005
The Queen's Knight, 2004
The Queen's Gambit, 2002
The Chalice, 2001
The Ring, 2000

Other books you might like:
David Gemmell, *The Swords of Light and Day*, 2004
Simon R. Green, *Blue Moon Rising*, 1991
Barbara Hambly, *Icefalcon's Quest*, 1998
Michael Moorcock, *The Vanishing Tower*, 1977
Jennifer Roberson, *Sword Sworn*, 2002

439

DAVID B. COE

The Horseman's Gambit

(New York: Tor, 20089)

Story type: Sword and Sorcery; Magic Conflict
Series: Blood of the Southlands. Book 2
Subject(s): Magic; Plague
Major character(s): Grinsa jal Arriet, Sorcerer; Q'Daer, Sorcerer; Tirnya Onjaef, Military Personnel
Time period(s): Indeterminate
Locale(s): Alternate Universe

Summary: Someone has set loose a plague that specifically targets those people who use magic. This leaves the Qirsi people seriously weakened and unable to defend themselves when neighboring peoples attempt to seize disputed lands. They gather their forces anyway and the entire world seems poised on the brink of war.

Where it's reviewed:
Publishers Weekly, November 10, 2008, page 35

Other books by the same author:
The Sorcerers' Plague, 2007
Weavers of War, 2007
Shapers of Darkness, 2005
Bonds of Vengeance, 2004
Seeds of Betrayal, 2003

Other books you might like:
David Gemmell, *Ghost King*, 1988
Sharon Green, *Convergence*, 1996
Barbara Hambly, *Mother of Winter*, 1996
Mindy L. Klasky, *The Glasswright's Master*, 2004
Jennifer Roberson, *Children of the Lion*, 2001

440

D.M. CORNISH

Lamplighter

(New York: Putnam, 2008)

Story type: Young Adult; Magic Conflict
Series: Monster Blood Tattoo. Book 2
Subject(s): Monsters; Magic
Major character(s): Rossamunde Bookchild, Child, Orphan; Grindrod, Worker; Threnody, Child, Student

Fantasy

Time period(s): Indeterminate
Locale(s): Alternate Universe

Summary: Rossamunde has been apprenticed to the lamp-lighters, whose job is to make sure that the roads are well lit and safe from monsters. When another apprentice appears, a young girl named Threnody, Rossamunde becomes involved with her and her mission to hunt monsters. The adventure is light-hearted and punctuated by clever humor.

Where it's reviewed:
Booklist, October 1, 2008, page 58
Kliatt, May 2008, page 8

Other books by the same author:
Foundling, 2007

Other books you might like:
Bruce Coville, *The Dragonslayers*, 1994
Diana Wynne Jones, *The Dark Lord of Derkholm*, 1998
Norton Juster, *The Phantom Tollbooth*, 1961
Philip Pullman, *The Golden Compass*, 1997
Rick Riordan, *The Battle of the Labyrinth*, 2008

441

BRUCE COVILLE

Dark Whispers

(New York: Scholastic, 2008)

Story type: Young Adult; Quest
Series: Unicorn Chronicles. Book 3
Subject(s): Secrets; Quest
Major character(s): Cara Diana Hunter, Teenager; Lightfoot, Mythical Creature (unicorn); Ian Hunter, Rescuer
Time period(s): Indeterminate
Locale(s): Alternate Universe; India

Summary: While her father is searching for his wife, who has been imprisoned somewhere in India, Cara Hunter travels to an alternate reality accompanied by an intelligent unicorn. There she seeks to uncover the secret behind a long-standing war between the unicorns and the delvers, and learns even more than she had hoped.

Where it's reviewed:
Booklist, September 1, 2008, page 90

Other books by the same author:
Odds Are Good, 2006
The Dragon of Doom, 2004
Juliet Dove, Goddess of Love, 2003
A Glory of Unicorns, 1998
Into the Land of the Unicorns, 1994

Other books you might like:
Peter S. Beagle, *The Last Unicorn*, 1968
Steven R. Boyett, *Ariel*, 1983
Terry Brooks, *The Black Unicorn*, 1987
Mary Brown, *The Unlikely Ones*, 1986
Elizabeth Ann Scarborough, *The Unicorn Creed*, 1983

442

DAVID DRAKE

The Gods Return

(New York: Tor, 2008)

Story type: Sword and Sorcery; Magic Conflict
Series: Crown of the Isles. Book 3
Subject(s): Magic; Disasters
Major character(s): Garric, Ruler; Cashel, Warrior; Liane, Royalty
Time period(s): Indeterminate
Locale(s): Alternate Universe

Summary: A magic world has been physically altered so that most of its various islands have been united into a single continent under a unified ruler. The change also drove the old gods out of the world, but a pantheon of new ones appear, and these are even less benevolent than their predecessors. The newly crowned king must battle the gods themselves to protect his people.

Where it's reviewed:
Booklist, September 1, 2008, page 60
Publishers Weekly, September 1, 2008, page 39

Other books by the same author:
The Mirror of Worlds, 2007
The Fortress of Glass, 2006
Master of the Cauldron, 2004
Goddess of the Ice Realm, 2003
Mistress of the Catacombs, 2001

Other books you might like:
Poul Anderson, *The War of the Gods*, 1997
Jacqueline Carey, *Godslayer*, 2005
Lin Carter, *Thongor Against the Gods*, 1967
Simon R. Green, *The God Killer*, 1991
R.A. Salvatore, *The Demon Awakens*, 1996

443

DAVE DUNCAN

Ill Met in the Arena

(New York: Tor, 2008)

Story type: Psychic Powers; Coming-of-Age
Subject(s): Coming-of-Age; Psychic Powers
Major character(s): Quirt, Nobleman, Sports Figure; Humate, Sports Figure; Hyla, Psychic
Time period(s): Indeterminate
Locale(s): Alternate Universe

Summary: In a world where women have psychic powers, men have superhuman strength and can teleport themselves from place to place. Quirt is a mysterious, older man who enters the gladiatorial contests. Humate is a talented younger contestant whose curiosity about Quirt will lead to secrets revealed and a quest for vengeance.

Where it's reviewed:
Booklist, July 1, 2008, page 79
Publishers Weekly, June 2, 2008, page 33

Fantasy

Other books by the same author:
The Alchemist's Code, 2008
Mother of Lies, 2007
The Alchemist's Apprentice, 2007
Children of Chaos, 2006
Impossible Odds, 2003

Other books you might like:
L. Sprague de Camp, *The Goblin Tower*, 1968
Sara Douglass, *Beyond the Hanging Wall*, 2003
David Gemmell, *Midnight Falcon*, 1999
Barbara Hambly, *Sisters of the Raven*, 2002
Lawrence Watt-Evans, *The Misenchanted Sword*, 1985

444

STEVEN ERIKSON

Toll the Hounds

(New York: Tor, 2008)

Story type: Sword and Sorcery; Magic Conflict
Series: Malazan Book of the Fallen. Book 8
Subject(s): Disasters; Magic
Major character(s): Anomander Rake, Ruler; Karsa Orlong, Warrior; Iskaral Pust, Religious
Time period(s): Indeterminate
Locale(s): Alternate Universe

Summary: Anomander Rake seems secure in his rule until a rash of portents and unusual events suggest that a magical force is about to take a hand in mundane affairs. Threats of war arise, assassins undertake difficult tasks, and contending interests arise to battle for control of the future of the world.

Where it's reviewed:
Booklist, August 1, 2008, page 54
Publishers Weekly, July 28, 2008, page 57

Other books by the same author:
Reaper's Gale, 2008
Midnight Tides, 2007
The Bonehunters, 2007
House of Chains, 2006
Memories of Ice, 2005

Other books you might like:
Dave Duncan, *Impossible Odds*, 2003
David Eddings, *Pawn of Prophecy*, 1982
David Gemmell, *The King Beyond the Gate*, 1985
L.E. Modesitt Jr., *Scion of Cyador*, 2000
Brandon Sanderson, *Mistborn*, 2006

445

CHRIS EVANS

A Darkness Forged in Fire

(New York: Pocket, 2008)

Story type: Sword and Sorcery; Magic Conflict
Series: Iron Elves. Book 1
Subject(s): Quest; Magic

Major character(s): Konowa Swift Dragon, Military Personnel, Mythical Creature (elf); Visyna Tekoy, Noblewoman; Yimt Arkhorn, Royalty
Time period(s): Indeterminate
Locale(s): Alternate Universe

Summary: Konowa was an honored soldier at one time, but his reputation has been sullied by charges of murder and debauchery. He has become a recluse when a noblewoman is dispatched from the throne insisting that he take up a new set of duties and help her address a magical threat to the future of the kingdom. First novel.

Where it's reviewed:
Booklist, July 1, 2008, page 48
Library Journal, July 1, 2008, page 70

Other books you might like:
Mary Gentle, *Carthage Ascendant*, 2000
Ian R. MacLeod, *The House of Storms*, 2005
China Mieville, *Iron Council*, 2004
Michael Moorcock, *The Fortress of the Pearl*, 1989
Michael Swanwick, *The Dragons of Babel*, 2008

446

DAVID FARLAND

The Wyrmling Horde

(New York: Tor, 2008)

Story type: Sword and Sorcery; Magic Conflict
Series: Runelords. Book 7
Subject(s): Magic; Adventure and Adventurers
Major character(s): Fallion Orden, Warrior, Prisoner; Vulgnash, Knight; Talon, Orphan
Time period(s): Indeterminate
Locale(s): Alternate Universe

Summary: Fallion Orden has been captured by Lord Despair, an evil sorcerer who has taken advantage of the merging of two realities to raise an army with which he plans to conquer the universe. Only Fallion can undo the binding of worlds and restore a more stable life, and only if his various allies can find and free him.

Where it's reviewed:
Library Journal, September 15, 2008, page 48
Publishers Weekly, July 28, 2008, page 56

Other books by the same author:
Worldbinder, 2007
Sons of the Oak, 2006
The Lair of Bones, 2003
Wizardborn, 2001
The Runelords, 1998

Other books you might like:
James Barclay, *Cry of the Newborn*, 2005
Dave Duncan, *Children of Chaos*, 2006
Raymond Feist, *A Darkness at Sethanon*, 1986
Maggie Furey, *The Heart of Myrial*, 1999
Tad Williams, *River of Blue Fire*, 1998

447

CHARLIE FLETCHER

Ironhand

(New York: Hyperion, 2008)

Story type: Young Adult; Contemporary
Series: Stoneheart. Book 2
Subject(s): Secrets; Magic
Major character(s): George Chapman, Child; Edie Laemmel, Child; Gunner, Mythical Creature
Time period(s): 2000s
Locale(s): London, England

Summary: George Chapman has discovered that the various statues in London are actually living creatures involved in a secret battle that will affect the fate of humanity. When his friend Edie and his protector, the Gunner, are kidnapped by the enemy statues, George must find a way to rescue them by relying on his own resources.

Where it's reviewed:
Booklist, September 1, 2008, page 120
School Library Journal, June 2008, page 140

Other books by the same author:
Stoneheart, 2007

Other books you might like:
Piers Anthony, *Geis of the Gargoyle*, 1995
Margot Benary-Isbert, *The Wicked Enchantment*, 1955
Richard A. Knaak, *Frostwing*, 1995
Katherine Kurtz, *St. Patrick's Gargoyle*, 2001
Vickie Taylor, *Carved in Stone*, 2005

448

LYNN FLEWELLING

Shadows Return

(New York: Bantam, 2008)

Story type: Sword and Sorcery; Magic Conflict
Series: Nightrunners. Book 4
Subject(s): Magic; Secrets
Major character(s): Seregil, Spy; Alec, Spy; Thero, Wizard
Time period(s): Indeterminate
Locale(s): Alternate Universe

Summary: Two professional spies are engaged on a mission for their ruler when they are taken captive and sold separately into slavery. One of them has a valuable heritage that his new owner hopes to magically exploit in order to enhance his own powers.

Where it's reviewed:
Locus, June 2008, page 27

Other books by the same author:
The Oracle's Queen, 2006
Hidden Warrior, 2003
The Bone Twin's Doll, 2001
Traitor's Moon, 1999
Stalking Darkness, 1997

Other books you might like:

James Barclay, *Dawnthief*, 1999
Simon R. Green, *Beyond the Blue Moon*, 2000
Fritz Leiber, *The First Book of Lankhmar*, 2001
Andrew J. Offutt, *The Ironlords*, 1979
Jennifer Roberson, *Sword Sworn*, 2002

449

KATE FORSYTH

The Gypsy Crown

(New York: Hyperion, 2008)

Story type: Young Adult; Historical
Subject(s): Gypsies; Magic
Major character(s): Emilia Finch, Teenager, Gypsy; Luka, Teenager, Gypsy; Spurgeon, Religious
Time period(s): 17th century (1658)
Locale(s): England

Summary: Emilia and Luka are two young gypsies who escape capture when their family is arrested in 17th century England and charged with a murder they didn't commit. Despite Luka's skepticism, Emilia is determined to acquire the charms from several gypsy families in order to evoke an ancient magic and rescue her family.

Where it's reviewed:
Booklist, April 15, 2008, page 53

Other books by the same author:
The Heart of Stars, 2007
The Shining City, 2006
The Starthorn Tree, 2005
The Fathomless Caves, 2002
The Forbidden Land, 2001

Other books you might like:
Poul Anderson, *The Demon of Scattery*, 1979
    Mildred Downey Broxon, co-author
Steven Brust, *Gypsy*, 1992
    Megan Lindholm, co-author
Nancy Springer, *Larque on the Wing*, 1994
Vivian Vande Velde, *A Well-Timed Enchantment*, 1996
Jane Yolen, *Sister Light, Sister Dark*, 1988

450

DIANA PHARAOH FRANCIS

The Black Ship

(New York: Roc, 2008)

Story type: Sword and Sorcery; Magic Conflict
Series: Crosspointe. Book 2
Subject(s): Magic; Sea Stories
Major character(s): Thorn, Slave, Sailor; Plusby, Sailor; Crabbel, Sailor
Time period(s): Indeterminate
Locale(s): Alternate Universe

Summary: Thorn is a skilled pilot, one of the few who can successfully navigate across the ocean. When he is stripped of his guild membership and impressed into the crew of another ship, it appears that his luck has reached bottom. Then he discovers that his new ship is cursed, both magically and by the presence of a saboteur on board.

Other books by the same author:
The Cipher, 2007
Path of Blood, 2006
Path of Honor, 2004
Path of Fate, 2003

Other books you might like:
Hannes Bok, *The Sorcerer's Ship*, 1969
Allan Cole, *The Far Kingdoms*, 1993
　　Chris Bunch, co-author
Robin Hobb, *Ship of Destiny*, 2000
China Mieville, *The Scar*, 2002
Robert V.S. Redick, *The Red Wolf Conspiracy*, 2008

451

GREGORY FROST

Lord Tophet

(New York: Del Rey, 2008)

Story type: Mystery; Magic Conflict
Series: Shadowbridge. Book 2
Subject(s): Secrets; Magic
Major character(s): Leodora, Entertainer; Soter, Businessman; Diverus, Entertainer, Musician
Time period(s): Indeterminate
Locale(s): Alternate Universe

Summary: Leodora lives in a magical world that consists entirely of a system of interconnected bridges. Her success as an entertainer attracts the unwanted attention of a demigod who dispatches some of his minions to kill her. She discovers as well that this was the fate that destroyed her father many years earlier.

Where it's reviewed:
Booklist, August 1, 2008, page 54
Library Journal, July 1, 2008, page 70
Locus, July 2008, page 60
Publishers Weekly, May 26, 2008, page 42

Other books by the same author:
Shadowbridge, 2007
Fitcher's Brides, 2002
Remscela, 1988
Tain, 1986
Lyrec, 1984

Other books you might like:
Iain Banks, *The Bridge*, 1986
Neal Barrett Jr., *The Treachery of Kings*, 2001
Mary Gentle, *Architecture of Desire*, 1991
Ian R. MacLeod, *The House of Storms*, 2005
Paula Volsky, *The Grand Ellipse*, 2000

452

CORNELIA FUNKE

Inkdeath

(New York: Chicken House, 2008)

Story type: Young Adult; Magic Conflict
Series: Inkheart. Book 3
Subject(s): Quest; Magic
Major character(s): Meggie Folchart, Child; Mortimer Folchart, Artisan; Adderhead, Ruler
Time period(s): Indeterminate
Locale(s): Alternate Universe

Summary: Meggie and her father have fallen into the world created by a book of fairy tales. They have had various adventures there as they help rebels fight against a cruel ruler, Adderhead. The situation grows more desperate in the final volume as the characters are no longer under the control of the book's author and chaos threatens to overwhelm their magical world.

Where it's reviewed:
Booklist, November 1, 2008, page 34
Owl, November 2008, page 38
Publishers Weekly, September 22, 2008, page 59

Other books by the same author:
Igraine the Brave, 2007
When Santa Fell to Earth, 2006
Inkspell, 2005
Dragon Rider, 2004
Inkheart, 2003

Other books you might like:
K.A. Applegate, *Search for Senna*, 1999
Bruce Coville, *Dark Whispers*, 2007
Alan Garner, *The Weirdstone of Brisingamen*, 1960
Norton Juster, *The Phantom Tollbooth*, 1961
Rick Riordan, *The Lightning Thief*, 2005

453

YASMINE GALENORN

Dragon Wytch

(New York: Berkley, 2008)

Story type: Contemporary; Magic Conflict
Series: D'Artigo Sisters. Book 4
Subject(s): Magic; Mystery
Major character(s): Delilah D'Artigo, Mythical Creature; Menolly D'Artigo, Vampire; Camille D'Artigo, Witch
Time period(s): 2000s
Locale(s): Seattle, Washington

Summary: Three sisters, each with a different supernatural talent, operate as a detective agency specializing in unusual cases and unusual clients. They are engaged in solving a handful of what appear to be small, unrelated problems when they become aware that an ancient, dark, and secretive force is stirring and preparing to change everything.

Fantasy

Where it's reviewed:
Locus, June 2008, page 27

Other books by the same author:
Changeling, 2007
Darkling, 2007
A Harvest of Bones, 2005
Legend of the Jade Dragon, 2004
Ghost of a Chance, 2003

Other books you might like:
Patricia Briggs, *Blood Bound*, 2007
Rachel Caine, *Gale Force*, 2008
Karen Chance, *Midnight's Daughter*, 2008
Kat Richardson, *Underground*, 2008
Jeanne C. Stein, *Legacy*, 2008

454

FELIX GILMAN

Thunderer

(New York: Bantam, 2008)

Story type: Quest; Magic Conflict
Series: Ararat. Book 1
Subject(s): Magic; Quest
Major character(s): Arjun, Traveller; Jack Sheppard, Teenager; Ilona, Noblewoman
Time period(s): Indeterminate
Locale(s): Alternate Universe

Summary: Arjun is a young man traveling the world in search of the answer to a religious question. He arrives in the immense city of Ararat just as portents suggest that major changes are about to transform the world. His arrival will inadvertently precipitate a crisis that could have disastrous consequences. First novel.

Where it's reviewed:
Booklist, December 1, 2007, page 30
Library Journal, December 1, 2007, page 104

Other books you might like:
Iain Banks, *The Bridge*, 1986
Gregory Frost, *Lord Tophet*, 2008
China Mieville, *Perdido Street Station*, 2001
Brandon Sanderson, *Elantris*, 2005
Jeff Vandermeer, *Veniss Underground*, 2005

455

ALISON GOODMAN

Eon: Dragoneye Reborn

(New York: Viking, 2008)

Story type: Coming-of-Age; Magic Conflict
Series: Eon. Book 1
Subject(s): Magic; Coming-of-Age
Major character(s): Eona, Warrior, Student; Ido, Nobleman; Tyron, Nobleman
Time period(s): Indeterminate
Locale(s): Alternate Universe

Summary: Eon appears to be an ambitious young man

who wants to become one of the few who are able to connect with the dragons who provide enormous power in the kingdom. However, Eon is actually Eona, a young woman disguised as a boy so that she can penetrate a clique from which her gender is excluded.

Where it's reviewed:
Locus, November 2008, page 25

Other books by the same author:
Killing the Rabbit, 2007
Singing the Dogstar Blues, 2003

Other books you might like:
Lynn Abbey, *Daughter of the Bright Moon*, 1979
Jennifer Fallon, *Medalon*, 2004
Naomi Kritzer, *Fires of the Faithful*, 2002
Tamora Pierce, *Emperor Mage*, 1995
Jo Walton, *The King's Peace*, 2000

456

MARTIN H. GREENBERG , Editor
JANET DEAVER-PACK , Co-Editor

Catopolis

(New York: DAW, 2008)

Story type: Anthology
Subject(s): Short Stories; Animals/Cats

Summary: All 17 of the original fantasy stories in this anthology involve cats. Thematically they range from humorous to adventure to near horror. The contributors include Esther Friesner, Jean Rabe, Elaine Cunningham, Janny Wurts, Ed Greenwood, and others.

Other books by the same author:
All Hell Breaking Loose, 2005
Children of the Night, 1999
Black Cats and Broken Mirrors, 1998 (John Helfers, co-editor)
Celebrity Vampires, 1995
Back from the Dead, 1991 (Charles G. Waugh, co-editor)

Other books you might like:
Elizabeth Boyer, *Keeper of the Cats*, 1995
Diane Duane, *The Book of Night with Moon*, 1997
Esther Friesner, *Majyk by Accident*, 1993
Ursula K. Le Guin, *Catwings*, 1988
Tad Williams, *Tailchaser's Song*, 1985

457

ED GREENWOOD

Dark Vengeance

(New York: Tor, 2008)

Story type: Sword and Sorcery; Magic Conflict
Series: Niflheim. Book 2
Subject(s): Revenge; Magic
Major character(s): Orivon Firefist, Slave; Luelldar, Mythical Creature (elf); Taerel, Mythical Creature (elf)

Time period(s): Indeterminate
Locale(s): Alternate Universe

Summary: Orivon Firefist was a human captive of the elves who served as a slave for much of his childhood. He gains his freedom as an adult, but has learned to hate the people who abused him. Although he is free to make a life for himself, he decides that it is more important to strike back at the cave-dwelling elves so that they cannot take more human slaves.

Where it's reviewed:
Booklist, August 1, 2008, page 54
Library Journal, August 1, 2008, page 75
Publishers Weekly, July 21, 2008, page 147

Other books by the same author:
Dark Warrior Rising, 2007
The Silent House, 2004
The Dragon's Doom, 2003
A Dragon's Ascension, 2002
Hand of Fire, 2002

Other books you might like:
David B. Coe, *The Sorcerers' Plague*, 2007
David Gemmell, *The Hawk Eternal*, 1996
Dennis L. McKiernan, *The Dark Tide*, 1984
R.A. Salvatore, *The Demon Awakens*, 1996
Lawrence Watt-Evans, *Dragon Weather*, 1999

458

LAURELL HAMILTON

Swallowing Darkness

(New York: Ballantine, 2008)

Story type: Magic Conflict; Romance
Series: Meredith Gentry. Book 7
Subject(s): Legends; Erotica
Major character(s): Meredith Gentry, Royalty; Taranis, Mythical Creature (fairy); Doyle, Mythical Creature (shapeshifter)
Time period(s): 2000s
Locale(s): Alternate Universe

Summary: In order to legitimize her claim to the throne of Faery, Meredith Gentry must prove her ability to become pregnant and produce an heir. She is locked in a battle with her uncle, Taranis, who seeks to separate her from her friends and neutralize her growing power.

Where it's reviewed:
Publishers Weekly, September 29, 2008, page 63

Other books by the same author:
Mistral's Kiss, 2006
Strange Candy, 2006
A Stroke of Midnight, 2005
Seduced by Moonlight, 2004
A Kiss of Shadows, 2000

Other books you might like:
Patricia Briggs, *Cry Wolf*, 2008
Sherrilyn Kenyon, *Acheron*, 2008
Karen Marie Moning, *Darkfever*, 2006
Sarban, *Ringstones*, 1961
Maggie Shayne, *Destiny*, 2001

459

CORY J. HERNDON
SCOTT MCGOUGH , Co-Author

Morningtide

(Renton, WA: Wizards of the Coast, 2008)

Story type: Magic Conflict; Sword and Sorcery
Series: Magic the Gathering
Subject(s): Magic; Quest
Major character(s): Ashling, Religious; Rhys, Mythical Creature (elf); Maralen, Mythical Creature (elf)
Time period(s): Indeterminate
Locale(s): Alternate Universe

Summary: A young woman battles to control a power she never wanted in the first place. An exiled elf flees his enemies, who are determined to track him down and punish him for killing another of their kind. The fate of the two will lead them together and to an unusual resolution of their differing problems.

Other books by the same author:
Dissension, 2006
Guildpact, 2006
Ravnica, 2005
The Fifth Dawn, 2004

Other books you might like:
Lynn Abbey, *Planeswalker*, 1998
Clayton Emery, *Johan*, 2001
J. Robert King, *Onslaught*, 2002
Jess Lebow, *The Darksteel Eye*, 2001
Robert E. Vardeman, *Dark Legacy*, 1996

460

SARAH A. HOYT

Gentleman Takes a Chance

(New York: Baen, 2008)

Story type: Contemporary; Legend
Series: Kyrie Smith. Book 2
Subject(s): Magic; Legends
Major character(s): Kyrie Smith, Mythical Creature (shapeshifter); Tom Ormson, Mythical Creature (shapeshifter); Rafiel Thrall, Police Officer, Mythical Creature (shapeshifter)
Time period(s): 2000s
Locale(s): Goldport, Colorado

Summary: Kyrie Smith is one of the many varied shapechangers that live secretly among the human race. She can change into a panther, her boyfriend can become a dragon, and others of her acquaintance can assume other forms. When someone starts killing shapechangers, she is reluctantly dragged into the investigation and into danger.

Where it's reviewed:
Library Journal, October 15, 2008, page 60
Locus, October 2008, page 25

Other books by the same author:
Heart and Soul, 2008

Fantasy

Heart of Light, 2008
Soul of Fire, 2008
Draw One in the Dark, 2006
Any Man So Daring, 2003

Other books you might like:
Ilona Andrews, *Magic Bites*, 2007
Doranna Durgin, *Changespell*, 1997
Constance O'Day-Flannery, *Shifting Love*, 2004
Stephanie Rowe, *Must Love Dragons*, 2006
Sharon Shinn, *The Thirteenth House*, 2006

461

SARAH A. HOYT

Heart and Soul

(New York: Bantam, 2008)

Story type: Alternate World; Quest
Series: Nigel Oldhall. Book 3
Subject(s): Alternate History; Quest
Major character(s): Nigel Oldhall, Adventurer, Explorer;
    Red Jade, Royalty; Wen, Ruler
Time period(s): 19th century
Locale(s): Alternate Universe; Africa

Summary: Nigel Oldhall believes he is near the end of his quest to return a set of magical jewels to their rightful owners in India. Unfortunately, he is attacked and captured by Chinese pirates including a shapeshifting princess who wants to restore her family's dominance in Asia.

Where it's reviewed:
Publishers Weekly, September 29, 2008, page 64

Other books by the same author:
Gentleman Takes a Chance, 2008
Heart of Light, 2008
Soul of Fire, 2008
Draw One in the Dark, 2006
Any Man So Daring, 2003

Other books you might like:
Jonathan Barnes, *The Somnambulist*, 2007
James P. Blaylock, *Homunculus*, 1986
Gordon Dahlquist, *The Glass Books of the Dream
    Eaters*, 2006
Barbara Hambly, *Bride of the Rat God*, 1994
S.M. Peters, *Whitechapel Gods*, 2008

462

SARAH A. HOYT

Soul of Fire

(New York: Bantam, 2008)

Story type: Historical; Magic Conflict
Subject(s): Mystery; Magic
Major character(s): Peter Farewell, Mythical Creature
    (shapechanger), Explorer; Sofie Warington, Teenager,
    Fugitive; Lalita, Servant
Time period(s): 19th century

Locale(s): Alternate Universe; India

Summary: Peter Farewell is a shapechanger who travels to British India in an alternate Victorian world in search of a magical ruby. He meets a young woman who has fled there to avoid a forced marriage and their two lives become intertwined. Within her dowry is the very gem which Farewell is seeking.

Other books by the same author:
Heart of Light, 2008
Draw One in the Dark, 2006
Any Man So Daring, 2003
All Night Awake, 2002
Ill Met by Moonlight, 2001

Other books you might like:
Jonathan Barnes, *The Somnambulist*, 2007
Esther Friesner, *Druid's Blood*, 1988
Barbara Hambly, *Bride of the Rat God*, 1994
Jane Lindskold, *The Buried Pyramid*, 2004
S.M. Peters, *Whitechapel Gods*, 2008

463

JALEIGH JOHNSON

Mistshore

(Renton, WA: Wizards of the Coast, 2008)

Story type: Sword and Sorcery; Magic Conflict
Series: Forgotten Realms
Subject(s): Magic; Secrets
Major character(s): Icelin, Sorceress; Kredaron, Business-
    man; Cerest Elenithil, Worker
Time period(s): Indeterminate
Locale(s): Alternate Universe

Summary: Icelin has been living a secret life, hiding her magical powers and concealing the secrets of her past from even her friends. Her enemies have not forgotten her, however, and unless she comes to terms with her abilities and learns to use them, it is her friends who will suffer.

Other books by the same author:
The Howling Delve, 2007

Other books you might like:
Troy Denning, *Beyond the High Road*, 1999
Ed Greenwood, *Cloak of Shadows*, 1995
Richard A. Knaak, *Reavers of the Blood Sea*, 1999
Thomas M. Reid, *The Emerald Scepter*, 2005
Steven E. Schend, *Blackstaff Tower*, 2008

464

PAUL KEARNEY

The Ten Thousand

(Nottingham, United Kingdom: Solaris, 2008)

Story type: Sword and Sorcery; Magic Conflict
Subject(s): Magic; War

Major character(s): Rictus, Warrior; Jason, Warrior; Sinon, Warrior
Time period(s): Indeterminate
Locale(s): Alternate Universe

Summary: The king of a major nation in an alternate universe faces an unusual challenge. His brother has decided to seize the throne and to that end he has recruited an army from among the Macht, a legendary race of super-warriors who normally hold themselves aloof from the rest of the world.

Other books by the same author:
This Forsaken Earth, 2006
The Mark of Ran, 2005
Ships from the West, 2002
The Second Empire, 2000
The Heretic Kings, 1996

Other books you might like:
David B. Coe, *Rules of Ascension*, 2002
Jennifer Fallon, *The Lion of Senet*, 2002
David Gemmell, *The Hawk Eternal*, 1996
R.A. Salvatore, *Ascendance*, 2001
Elizabeth Vaughan, *Warprize*, 2005

465

SYLVIA KELSO

The Red Country

(Waterville, ME: Five Star, 2008)

Story type: Sword and Sorcery; Magic Conflict
Series: Rihannar Chronicles. Book 3
Subject(s): Magic; Legends
Major character(s): Sellithar, Royalty; Zam, Wizard; Kastir, Military Personnel
Time period(s): Indeterminate
Locale(s): Alternate Universe

Summary: The princess Sellithar ascends the throne of Everran, but her plan to reform the government is disrupted when civil war breaks out and some of her allies become her enemies. She has a vision in which she learns that the solution involves a journey, which leads her to a reclusive wizard. Although he prefers not to involve himself in worldly affairs, she convinces him that the future of their world depends on his cooperation.

Other books by the same author:
Amberlight, 2007
The Moving Water, 2007
Everran's Bane, 2005

Other books you might like:
Jacqueline Carey, *Kushiel's Dart*, 2001
Jennifer Fallon, *Harshini*, 2005
Raymond Feist, *Prince of the Blood*, 1989
Barbara Hambly, *Mother of Winter*, 1996
Jennifer Roberson, *Daughter of the Lion*, 1989

466

MERCEDES LACKEY
ROBERTA GELLIS , Co-Author

And Less than Kind

(New York: Baen, 2008)

Story type: Alternate History; Magic Conflict
Series: Elizabeth. Book 4
Subject(s): Magic; Historical
Major character(s): Elizabeth Tudor, Ruler; Vidal Dhu, Mythical Creature (elf); Denoriel, Mythical Creature (elf)
Time period(s): 15th century
Locale(s): England

Summary: In an alternate version of 15th century England, Elizabeth Tudor's ascension to the throne is opposed not only by her human enemies but by an evil elf lord. Fortunately, she has allies from both races as well, but the conflict between the two threatens to turn England into a secretive battleground where she may well lose her life.

Other books by the same author:
By Slanderous Tongues, 2007 (Roberta Gellis, co-author)
Aerie, 2006
Ill Met by Moonlight, 2005 (Roberta Gellis, co-author)
Alta, 2004
This Scepter'd Isle, 2004 (Roberta Gellis, co-author)

Other books you might like:
Lynn Abbey, *Unicorn and Dragon*, 1987
Gael Baudino, *Strands of Starlight*, 1989
Sara Douglass, *The Crippled Angel*, 2005
Sarah A. Hoyt, *All Night Awake*, 2002
Judith Tarr, *Pride of Kings*, 2001

467

MERCEDES LACKEY

Foundation

(New York: DAW, 2008)

Story type: Sword and Sorcery; Coming-of-Age
Series: Collegium Chronicles. Book 1
Subject(s): Magic; Coming-of-Age
Major character(s): Mags, Apprentice, Slave; Cole Pieters, Businessman; Dallen, Mythical Creature
Time period(s): Indeterminate
Locale(s): Alternate Universe

Summary: A young orphan who was impressed into virtual slave labor at a mine is taken away by a party of nobles who want to train him to be a Herald in service to the throne. The training system is undergoing considerable turmoil, however, and there is intrigue as well as education to be found within its walls. This series is a continuation of the Valdemar sequence.

Where it's reviewed:
Locus, September 2008, page 27

Other books by the same author:
The Snow Queen, 2008
Reserved for the Cat, 2007
The Wizard of London, 2005
Take a Thief, 2001
The Serpent's Shadow, 2001

Other books you might like:
R. Scott Bakker, *The Darkness That Comes Before*, 2004
Jennifer Fallon, *Eye of the Labyrinth*, 2002
Barbara Hambly, *Icefalcon's Quest*, 1998
L.E. Modesitt Jr., *Legacies*, 2002
Jennifer Roberson, *A Pride of Princes*, 1988

468

MERCEDES LACKEY
JAMES MALLORY , Co-Author

The Phoenix Endangered

(New York: Tor, 2008)

Story type: Sword and Sorcery; Magic Conflict
Series: Enduring Flame. Book 2
Subject(s): Quest; Magic
Major character(s): Tiercel, Wizard; Bisochim, Wizard, Leader; Shaiara, Leader
Time period(s): Indeterminate
Locale(s): Alternate Universe

Summary: An evil wizard has become the leader of a savage army, which has driven many of the peaceable tribes off their traditional land. One tribe seeks a possibly mystical oasis where they may find the power to resist the onslaught, while elsewhere a good magician seeks other methods of resistance.

Where it's reviewed:
Booklist, September 15, 2008, page 32
Library Journal, August 1, 2008, page 75
Publishers Weekly, July 14, 2008, page 49

Other books by the same author:
The Phoenix Unchained, 2007 (James Mallory, co-author)
When Darkness Falls, 2006 (James Mallory, co-author)
The Wizard of London, 2005
To Light a Candle, 2004 (James Mallory, co-author)
The Outstretched Shadow, 2003 (James Mallory, co-author)

Other books you might like:
Jennifer Fallon, *Treason Keep*, 2004
Raymond Feist, *Talon of the Silver Hawk*, 2003
David Gemmell, *Hero in the Shadows*, 2000
Barbara Hambly, *The Armies of Daylight*, 1983
John Marco, *The Jackal of Nar*, 1999

469

MERCEDES LACKEY

The Snow Queen

(Don Mills, Ontario: Luna, 2008)

Story type: Romance; Legend
Series: Five Hundred Kingdoms. Book 4
Subject(s): Legends; Romance
Major character(s): Aleksia, Sorceress; Kay, Teenager; Icehart, Mythical Creature
Time period(s): Indeterminate
Locale(s): Alternate Universe

Summary: Aleksia has become the Snow Queen and in that role she hopes to mentor young Kay, who in turn is pursued by Gerda, the young woman who has fallen in love with him. Aleksia is distracted when someone impersonating her begins using evil magic, and is forced to track down the imposter to restore her own reputation.

Other books by the same author:
Fortune's Fool, 2007
Aerie, 2006
Alta, 2004
The Fairy Godmother, 2004
Exile's Valor, 2003

Other books you might like:
Pamela Dean, *Tam Lin*, 1991
Robin McKinley, *Beauty*, 1978
Ursula Synge, *Swan's Wing*, 1984
Patricia C. Wrede, *Snow White and Rose Red*, 1989
Jane Yolen, *Briar Rose*, 1992

470

MARGO LANAGAN

Tender Morsels

(New York: Knopf, 2008)

Story type: Young Adult; Magic Conflict
Subject(s): Magic; Secrets
Major character(s): Liga, Teenager; Branza, Child; Urdda, Child
Time period(s): Indeterminate
Locale(s): Alternate Universe

Summary: A young woman and her two children are able to escape from the cruelties of their world by entering a special realm designed for them. Unfortunately the border between the two realities loses its integrity and creatures and emotions from the old world begin to infiltrate and change their lives and their reality.

Where it's reviewed:
Booklist, August 1, 2008, page 69
Horn Book Magazine, September-October 2008, page 590
Publishers Weekly, September 8, 2008, page 51

Other books by the same author:
Red Spikes, 2007
White Time, 2006

Black Juice, 2005
The Tankermen, 1998
Touching Earth Lightly, 1998

Other books you might like:
Ursula K. Le Guin, *Powers*, 2007
Patricia A. McKillip, *In the Forests of Serre*, 2003
Robin McKinley, *Rose Daughter*, 1997
Nancy Springer, *Chains of Gold*, 1986
Lawrence Watt-Evans, *The Rebirth of Wonder*, 1992

471

MIKE LEE

Nagash the Sorcerer

(Nottingham, United Kingdom: Black Library, 2008)

Story type: Sword and Sorcery; Magic Conflict
Series: Warhammer
Subject(s): Magic; Quest
Major character(s): Nagash, Ruler, Religious; Rakh-amn-
Hotep, Ruler, Religious; Neferem, Ruler
Time period(s): Indeterminate
Locale(s): Alternate Universe

Summary: Nagash the priest-king has decided that his
reign should last forever. In order to accomplish that, he
must become immortal and invulnerable. To that end, he
conceives a plan that will give him the power to rule not
only the living but even the dead. First novel.

Other books you might like:
Robert Earl, *The Corrupted*, 2006
Aaron Rosenberg, *Night of the Daemon*, 2007
Gav Thorpe, *The Heart of Chaos*, 2004
Lawrence Watt-Evans, *Touched by the Gods*, 1997
C.L. Werner, *Palace of the Plague Lord*, 2007

472

JOHN LEVITT

New Tricks

(New York: Ace, 2008)

Story type: Contemporary; Vampire Story
Series: Mason. Book 2
Subject(s): Magic; Vampires
Major character(s): Mason, Investigator; Louie, Animal
(dog); Victor, Investigator
Time period(s): 2000s
Locale(s): San Francisco, California

Summary: Mason used to work as an enforcer preventing
people from using magical powers in unauthorized ways.
He retired, but he has to come out of retirement when
his ex-girlfriend turns up mentally scarred by a failed attempt at possession.

Other books by the same author:
Dog Days, 2007

Other books you might like:
Jim Butcher, *Small Favor*, 2008
Marc Del Franco, *Unquiet Dreams*, 2008

Kat Richardson, *Greywalker*, 2006
S. Andrew Swann, *The Dwarves of Whiskey Island*,
2005
Rob Thurman, *Madhouse*, 2008

473

JANE LINDSKOLD

Thirteen Orphans

(New York: Tor, 2008)

Story type: Contemporary; Alternate World
Subject(s): Magic; Secrets
Major character(s): Brenda Morris, Student; Pearl Bright,
Expatriate, Orphan; Gaheris Morris, Orphan
Time period(s): 2000s
Locale(s): California

Summary: A college student discovers that what she
believed to be her family's past is actually false. Her
father and several others are exiles from an alternate
reality where magic works. They sought refuge from
their enemies in this world, but their enemies have found
them.

Where it's reviewed:
Booklist, September 15, 2008, page 33
Library Journal, August 1, 2008, page 76
Publishers Weekly, September 15, 2008, page 49

Other books by the same author:
Wolf Blood, 2007
Wolf Hunting, 2006
Child of a Rainless Year, 2005
The Buried Pyramid, 2004
Wolf Captured, 2004

Other books you might like:
Lynn Abbey, *Jerlayne*, 1999
Emma Bull, *War for the Oaks*, 1987
Esther Friesner, *New York by Knight*, 1986
Paul Park, *A Princess of Roumania*, 2005
Roger Zelazny, *Nine Princes in Amber*, 1970

474

DENISE LITTLE , Editor

Enchantment Place

(New York: DAW, 2008)

Story type: Anthology
Subject(s): Short Stories

Summary: This is a collection of 17 original fantasy short
stories with a common setting, a shopping mall that
caters to supernatural and mythological creatures like
fairies and vampires. The contributors include Esther
Friesner, Sarah Hoyt, Susan Sizemore, Diane Duane, and
Kristine Kathryn Rusch. The stories are predominantly
light adventure and humor.

Other books by the same author:
The Magic Toybox, 2006
The Magic Shop, 2004

Familiars, 2002
A Constellation of Cats, 2001
Creature Fantastic, 2001

Other books you might like:
Diane Duane, *To Visit the Queen*, 1999
Esther Friesner, *Elf Defense*, 1988
Sarah A. Hoyt, *Crawling Between Heaven and Earth*, 2002
Kristine Kathryn Rusch, *Fantasy Life*, 2003
Susan Sizemore, *The Autumn Lord*, 1996

475

DENISE LITTLE , Editor

Witch High

(New York: DAW, 2008)

Story type: Anthology
Subject(s): Short Stories; Witches and Witchcraft

Summary: The 14 original fantasy stories in this anthology all share a common element. There is a school where the special needs of young witches and warlocks are addressed. Although they may have some advantages, the students here are also subject to some unusual problems of adjustment, and survival.

Other books by the same author:
Enchantment Place, 2008
Hags, Sirens, and Other Bad Girls of Fantasy, 2006
Familiars, 2002
A Constellation of Cats, 2001
Creature Fantastic, 2001

Other books you might like:
Brenda Jordan, *The Brentwood Witches*, 1987
Fritz Leiber, *Conjure Wife*, 1952
J.K. Rowling, *Harry Potter and the Sorcerer's Stone*, 1997
Vivian Vande Velde, *Magic Can Be Murder*, 2000
Mary Frances Zambreno, *Journeyman Wizard*, 1994

476

JOHN R. LITTLE

Miranda

(Anaheim, CA: Bad Moon, 2008)

Story type: Literary; Time Travel
Subject(s): Time Travel
Major character(s): Michael Johnson, Worker; Miranda, Young Woman; Doof, Animal (dog)
Time period(s): 20th century
Locale(s): United States

Summary: Michael Johnson lives a very different life. His first memory is of dying and he has been living his life backwards ever since. Michael fears that except for his dog he will have no companions because of his odd relationship to time, but then he meets Miranda.

Other books by the same author:

Placeholders, 2007

Other books you might like:
Philip K. Dick, *Counter Clock World*, 1967
Lord Dunsany, *The Charwoman's Shadow*, 1926
Ursula K. Le Guin, *Powers*, 2007
Bentley Little, *The Ignored*, 1997
Robert Nathan, *Portrait of Jennie*, 1940

477

MARJORIE M. LIU

The Iron Hunt

(New York: Ace, 2008)

Story type: Contemporary; Magic Conflict
Subject(s): Magic; Romance
Major character(s): Maxine Kiss, Hunter; Grant Cooperon, Investigator; Zee, Mythical Creature
Time period(s): 2000s
Locale(s): United States

Summary: Maxine Kiss has tattoos all over her body, but they serve more than a decorative purpose. When needed, the tattoos disengage and become magical creatures that help her in her battles against demonic invasions into our world. Her efforts to protect the human race become complicated when she finds romance.

Where it's reviewed:
Magazine of Fantasy & Science Fiction, October 2008, page 38
Publishers Weekly, May 26, 2008, page 44

Other books by the same author:
Soul Song, 2007
Eye of Heaven, 2006
The Red Heart of Jade, 2006
Dark Mirror, 2005
Tiger Eye, 2005

Other books you might like:
Yasmine Galenorn, *Changeling*, 2007
Laurell Hamilton, *Blood Noir*, 2008
Kat Richardson, *Greywalker*, 2006
Anton Strout, *Dead to Me*, 2008
Rob Thurman, *Madhouse*, 2008

478

NATHAN LONG

Elfslayer

(Nottingham, United Kingdom: Black Library, 2008)

Story type: Sword and Sorcery; Magic Conflict
Series: Warhammer
Subject(s): Magic; Quest
Major character(s): Gotrek, Mythical Creature, Warrior; Felix Jaeger, Warrior; Max Schreiber, Wizard
Time period(s): Indeterminate
Locale(s): Alternate Universe

Summary: Two heroes, one human and one dwarf, team

up with a wizard to battle a horde of evil elves. They are initially taken prisoner aboard an oversized floating fortress, but win their freedom and fight their way through legions of their enemies.

Other books by the same author:
Manslayer, 2007
Orcslayer, 2006
Tainted Blood, 2006
The Broken Lance, 2005
Valnir's Bane, 2004

Other books you might like:
Dan Abnett, *Fell Cargo*, 2006
Robert Earl, *Ancient Blood*, 2008
Richard A. Knaak, *The Black Talon*, 2008
Nick Kyme, *Oathbreaker*, 2008
Mike Lee, *Nagash the Sorcerer*, 2008

479

VIOLETTE MALAN

The Soldier King

(New York: DAW, 2008)

Story type: Sword and Sorcery; Military
Series: Dhulyn and Parno. Book 2
Subject(s): Magic; Psychic Powers
Major character(s): Dhulyn Wolfshead, Military Personnel; Parno Lionsmane, Military Personnel; Edmir, Ruler
Time period(s): Indeterminate
Locale(s): Alternate Universe

Summary: A band of mercenaries hires on to participate in a war, which is successfully concluded with the capture of the leader of the opposition. The rules of war guarantee the prisoner's safe conduct, but when their employers refuse to honor that tradition, two members of the organization decide that their honor is more important than obedience to their employer.

Where it's reviewed:
Locus, October 2008, page 25

Other books by the same author:
The Mirror Prince, 2007
The Sleeping God, 2007

Other books you might like:
Glen Cook, *The Black Company*, 1984
Simon R. Green, *Blue Moon Rising*, 1991
Paul Kearney, *The Ten Thousand*, 2008
Stan Nicholls, *Bodyguard of Lightning*, 1998
David Sherman, *Onslaught*, 2002

480

JOHN MARCO , Editor
MARTIN H. GREENBERG , Co-Editor

Imaginary Friends

(New York: DAW, 2008)

Story type: Anthology
Subject(s): Short Stories

Summary: None of the 13 stories in this collection have been previously published. The common theme is the imaginary friend, a common phenomenon in childhood. The companions range from dragons to humans to animated toys. A few stories have darker elements but most are light adventures. The contributors include Fiona Patton, Rick Hautala, Juliet McKenna, Kristine Kathryn Rusch, Tim Waggoner, and others.

Other books by the same author:
Army of the Fantastic, 2007 (Martin H. Greenberg, co-editor)
The Sword of Angels, 2005
The Devil's Armor, 2003
The Eyes of God, 2002
The Grand Design, 2000

Other books you might like:
Rick Hautala, *Beyond the Shroud*, 1996
Juliet E. McKenna, *The Gambler's Fortune*, 2000
Fiona Patton, *The Silver Lake*, 2005
Kristine Kathryn Rusch, *Fantasy Life*, 2003
Tim Waggoner, *Like Death*, 2005

481

JULIET MARILLIER

Heir to Sevenwaters

(New York: Roc, 2008)

Story type: Mystery; Quest
Series: Sevenwaters. Book 4
Subject(s): Magic; Quest
Major character(s): Clodagh, Noblewoman; Cathal, Bodyguard; Mac Dara, Royalty
Time period(s): Indeterminate
Locale(s): Alternate Universe

Summary: Clodagh is charged with taking care of her infant brother, so it is her responsibility when the family discovers one morning that the child has been replaced by a changeling. Accompanied by a guardsman whom she dislikes, she travels into a magical other world to reclaim her brother.

Where it's reviewed:
Library Journal, October 15, 2008, page 60
Publishers Weekly, September 8, 2008, page 39

Other books by the same author:
The Well of Shades, 2007
Blade of Fortriu, 2006
The Dark Mirror, 2005
Child of the Prophecy, 2002
Daughter of the Forest, 2000

Other books you might like:
Elizabeth Haydon, *Rhapsody*, 1989
Patricia A. McKillip, *Ombria in Shadow*, 2002
Jennifer Roberson, *Karavans*, 2006
Sharon Shinn, *Fortune and Fate*, 2008
Lawrence Watt-Evans, *Taking Flight*, 1993

Fantasy

482

A. LEE MARTINEZ

Too Many Curses

(New York: Tor, 2008)

Story type: Humor
Subject(s): Humor; Magic
Major character(s): Margle, Wizard; Nessy, Housekeeper; Thedeus, Knight
Time period(s): Indeterminate
Locale(s): Alternate Universe

Summary: Margle the Wizard cursed a number of people and unpeople during his lifetime, and most of them are kept in his castle, transformed and harmless. His housekeeper is at ease among them until Margle dies unexpectedly. The various curses begin to wear off and some of the most powerful and evil of his enemies regain the power to act.

Where it's reviewed:
Booklist, September 1, 2008, page 60
Library Journal, September 15, 2008, page 48
Publishers Weekly, July 21, 2008, page 147

Other books by the same author:
The Automatic Detective, 2008
A Nameless Witch, 2007
In the Company of Ogres, 2006
Gil's All Fright Diner, 2005

Other books you might like:
John DeChancie, *Castle Dreams*, 1992
Esther Friesner, *Gnome Man's Land*, 1991
Craig Shaw Gardner, *A Difficulty with Dwarves*, 1987
Tom Holt, *Nothing but Blue Skies*, 2001
Terry Pratchett, *Monstrous Regiment*, 2003

483

JAMES MAXEY

Dragonforge

(Nottingham, United Kingdom: Solaris, 2008)

Story type: Sword and Sorcery; Magic Conflict
Series: Dragon Age. Book 2
Subject(s): Magic; Legends
Major character(s): Bitterwood, Hunter; Graxen, Mythical Creature (dragon); Pet, Rebel, Warrior
Time period(s): Indeterminate
Locale(s): Alternate Universe

Summary: Although the evil king has been overthrown and killed, there is still no peace in the land. Despite the fact that not all dragons supported the tyrant, a group of fanatics has raised an army in order to destroy them all. Only a handful of humans and dragons are convinced that it is possible for the two races to live in harmony.

Other books by the same author:
Bitterwood, 2007

Other books you might like:
Mark Acres, *Dragon War*, 1994

Robin Wayne Bailey, *Triumph of the Dragon*, 1995
Carol Dennis, *Dragon's Pawn*, 1987
Barbara Hambly, *Dragonsbane*, 1985
Carl Miller, *Dragonbound*, 1988

484

DENNIS L. MCKIERNAN

City of Jade

(New York: Roc, 2008)

Story type: Sword and Sorcery; Quest
Series: Mithgar
Subject(s): Quest; Magic
Major character(s): Aravan, Sea Captain, Explorer; Aylis, Explorer, Psychic; Binkton, Artisan
Time period(s): Indeterminate
Locale(s): Alternate Universe

Summary: There have been stories of the fabulous city of jade for generations but few believe it to be a real place. One exception is Captain Aravan, who gathers a crew of humans and dwarves and sets out to find the lost city, encountering various dangers along the way before finally achieving his goal.

Where it's reviewed:
Booklist, September 1, 2008, page 60
Library Journal, September 15, 2008, page 49
Publishers Weekly, August 18, 2008, page 49

Other books by the same author:
Once upon a Summer Day, 2005
Red Slippers, 2004
Silver Wolf, Black Falcon, 2000
The Iron Tower, 2000
Voyage of the Fox Rider, 1993

Other books you might like:
Hannes Bok, *The Sorcerer's Ship*, 1969
Diana Pharaoh Francis, *The Black Ship*, 2008
China Mieville, *The Scar*, 2002
Mel Odom, *The Sea Devil's Eye*, 2000
Robert V.S. Redick, *The Red Wolf Conspiracy*, 2008

485

PATRICIA A. MCKILLIP

The Bell at Sealey Head

(New York: Ace, 2008)

Story type: Light Fantasy; Legend
Subject(s): Magic; Legends
Major character(s): Raven Sproule, Farmer; Judd Cauley, Innkeeper; Gwyneth Blair, Businesswoman
Time period(s): Indeterminate
Locale(s): Alternate Universe

Summary: The town of Sealey Head is a quiet place most of the time, but occasionally magical bells sound that can only be heard by the local residents and a few outsiders. From time to time, ghostly figures from another age can interact with the world of the living.

Where it's reviewed:
Booklist, September 1, 2008, page 59
Library Journal, September 15, 2008, page 49

Other books by the same author:
Solstice Wood, 2006
Harrowing the Dragon, 2005
Alphabet of Thorn, 2004
In the Forests of Serre, 2003
Ombria in Shadow, 2002

Other books you might like:
Diane Duane, *Stealing the Elf-King's Roses*, 2002
Phyllis Ann Karr, *At Amberleaf Fair*, 1986
Robin McKinley, *The Hero and the Crown*, 1984
Sharon Shinn, *Summers at Castle Auburn*, 2001
Sheri S. Tepper, *The Revenants*, 1984

486

SUZANNE MCLEOD

The Sweet Scent of Blood
(London: Gollancz, 2008)

Story type: Contemporary; Vampire Story
Series: Spellcrackers. Book 1
Subject(s): Magic; Vampires
Major character(s): Genevieve Taylor, Mythical Creature (sidhe); October, Vampire; Stella Raynham, Witch
Time period(s): 2000s
Locale(s): London, England

Summary: Genny Taylor is a sidhe, a magical creature who passes as a human and works for an organization of witches in a version of London where vampires and goblins are accepted citizens, even celebrities. Although most vampires adhere to the rules, she must take action when someone crosses the line. First novel.

Other books you might like:
Patricia Briggs, *Blood Bound*, 2007
Yasmine Galenorn, *Darkling*, 2007
Kat Richardson, *Underground*, 2008
Maggie Shayne, *Angel's Pain*, 2008
Rob Thurman, *Madhouse*, 2008

487

GRAHAM MCNEILL

Heldenhammer
(Nottingham, United Kingdom: Black Library, 2008)

Story type: Sword and Sorcery; Magic Conflict
Series: Warhammer
Subject(s): Magic; Quest
Major character(s): Sigmar Heldenhammer, Royalty, Warrior; Cuthwin, Teenager; Wolfgart, Warrior
Time period(s): Indeterminate
Locale(s): Alternate Universe

Summary: This is the first of three novels chronicling the career of a recurring character in the Warhammer series. Sigmar Heldenhammer is the son of a king but he must prove himself a powerful warrior and an effective leader before he can take the throne. As a young man he proves his worthiness in a series of violent encounters.

Other books by the same author:
Defenders of Ulthuan, 2008
Guardians of the Forest, 2005
Ursun's Teeth, 2004
The Ambassador, 2003
Storm of Iron, 2002

Other books you might like:
Lin Carter, *Quest of Kadji*, 1971
Jennifer Fallon, *Warlord*, 2007
Maggie Furey, *Aurian*, 1994
Anthony Reynolds, *Knight Errant*, 2008
C.L. Werner, *Runefang*, 2008

488

L.E. MODESITT JR.

The Lord Protector's Daughter
(New York: Tor, 2008)

Story type: Sword and Sorcery; Magic Conflict
Series: Corean Chronicles. Book 7
Subject(s): Magic; Mystery
Major character(s): Mykella, Noblewoman; Rachylana, Noblewoman; Cheleyza, Criminal
Time period(s): Indeterminate
Locale(s): Alternate Universe

Summary: Mykella is the oldest daughter of a wealthy government official. She discovers that someone is embezzling family funds and is determined to identify the thief. A messenger tells her that she must visit a remote site and acquire a magical power, but before she can do so, someone makes several attempts to kill members of the family.

Where it's reviewed:
Publishers Weekly, September 22, 2008, page 43

Other books by the same author:
Mage-Guard of Hamor, 2008
Natural Ordermage, 2007
Ordermaster, 2005
Scepters, 2004
Legacies, 2002

Other books you might like:
Lynn Abbey, *Rifkind's Challenge*, 2006
Stephen R. Donaldson, *The Mirror of Her Dreams*, 1986
Maggie Furey, *Aurian*, 1994
Elizabeth Haydon, *Prophecy*, 2000
Mindy L. Klasky, *The Glasswright's Apprentice*, 2000

489

DEVON MONK

Magic to the Bone
(New York: Roc, 2008)

Story type: Contemporary; Magic Conflict
Subject(s): Magic; Secrets

Fantasy

Major character(s): Allison Beckstrom, Investigator; Zayvion Jones, Wizard; Dane Lanister, Criminal
Time period(s): 2000s
Locale(s): Portland, Oregon; Alternate Universe

Summary: Allie Beckstrom is a Hound. She hunts down people who have used magic to shift their own metaphysical debts to others. She is investigating the plight of a young boy who appears to have been victimized by her own father when she encounters a mysterious man whom she is simultaneously drawn to and repelled by. First novel.

Where it's reviewed:
Publishers Weekly, September 22, 2008, page 44

Other books you might like:
Marie Brennan, *Doppelganger*, 2006
Karen Chance, *Embrace the Night*, 2006
Yasmine Galenorn, *Dragon Wytch*, 2008
Suzanne McLeod, *The Sweet Scent of Blood*, 2008
Kat Richardson, *Greywalker*, 2006

490

MICHAEL MOORCOCK

Elric: The Sleeping Sorceress

(New York: Del Rey, 2008)

Story type: Collection; Sword and Sorcery
Subject(s): Short Stories

Summary: This is the third collection in a new compilation of the Elric stories. This volume includes two complete short novels, *The Sleeping Sorceress* and *Elric of Melnibone*, as well as essays, illustrations, and other related materials.

Other books by the same author:
Elric: Stealer of Souls, 2008
Elric: To Rescue Tanelorn, 2008
The White Wolf's Son, 2005
The Skrayling Tree, 2003
The Dreamthief's Daughter, 2001

Other books you might like:
Lin Carter, *The Wizard of Zao*, 1978
John Jakes, *The Fortunes of Brak*, 1980
Andrew J. Offutt, *Shadows out of Hell*, 1980
David C. Smith, *The Sorcerer's Shadow*, 1978
Karl Edward Wagner, *Death Angel's Shadow*, 1973

491

MICHAEL MOORCOCK

Elric: To Rescue Tanelorn

(New York: Del Rey, 2008)

Story type: Collection; Sword and Sorcery
Subject(s): Short Stories

Summary: This is the second volume in a new compilation of the Elric stories, blending some of the original stories from the 1960s with some of the more recent additions to the saga. Included are well-known stories including "The Singing Citadel" and "The Eternal Champion."

Other books by the same author:
Elric: Stealer of Souls, 2008
Elric: The Sleeping Sorceress, 2008
The White Wolf's Son, 2005
The Skrayling Tree, 2003
The Dreamthief's Daughter, 2001

Other books you might like:
Lin Carter, *Kesrick*, 1982
John Jakes, *Brak the Barbarian*, 1968
Andrew J. Offutt, *The Ironlords*, 1979
David C. Smith, *The Ghost Army*, 1983
Karl Edward Wagner, *Bloodstone*, 1975

492

RICHARD K. MORGAN

The Steel Remains

(London: Gollancz, 2008)

Story type: Sword and Sorcery; Magic Conflict
Subject(s): Magic; Mystery
Major character(s): Ringil Eskiath, Warrior; Egar, Leader; Archeth, Government Official
Time period(s): Indeterminate
Locale(s): Alternate Universe

Summary: Rumors of supernatural appearances bring turmoil to a land still recovering from a long and brutal war. Three veterans of the earlier conflict—a dissolute and outcast soldier, a government adviser, and the leader of a nomad clan—will all face this new threat in their separate ways, but will eventually be brought together.

Other books by the same author:
Thirteen, 2007
Black Man, 2006
Market Forces, 2004
Broken Angels, 2003
Altered Carbon, 2002

Other books you might like:
Steven Erikson, *Toll the Hounds*, 2008
David Farland, *The Wyrmling Horde*, 2008
Raymond Feist, *Exile's Return*, 2004
China Mieville, *Iron Council*, 2004
R.A. Salvatore, *The Ancient*, 2008

493

ANDRE NORTON
SASHA MILLER , Co-Author

The Knight of the Red Beard

(New York: Tor, 2008)

Story type: Sword and Sorcery; Magic Conflict
Series: Book of the Oak. Book 5
Subject(s): Magic; Secrets

Major character(s): Elin, Teenager; Mikkel, Child; Ashen, Ruler
Time period(s): Indeterminate
Locale(s): Alternate Universe

Summary: This is the concluding volume in a series created by the late Andre Norton. Ashen and Gaurin have assumed the throne and restored stability to their kingdom. Unfortunately, two of their children decide to explore the world on their own and both become enmeshed in plots that could undo much of the work done by their parents.

Where it's reviewed:
Library Journal, October 15, 2008, page 60
Publishers Weekly, August 4, 2008, page 49

Other books by the same author:
Dragon Blade, 2005 (Sasha Miller, co-author)
Three Hands for Scorpio, 2005
A Crown Disowned, 2002 (Sasha Miller, co-author)
Knight or Knave, 2001 (Sasha Miller, co-author)
To the King a Daughter, 2000 (Sasha Miller, co-author)

Other books you might like:
Dave Duncan, *Children of Chaos*, 2006
Jennifer Fallon, *Lord of the Shadows*, 2003
Dennis L. McKiernan, *Once upon an Autumn Eve*, 2006
Sasha Miller, *Ladylord*, 2006
Sharon Shinn, *Mystic and Rider*, 2005

494

RICHARD PARKS

The Long Look

(Waterville, ME: Five Star, 2008)

Story type: Sword and Sorcery; Magic Conflict
Subject(s): Magic; Humor
Major character(s): Tymon the Black, Wizard; Athesa, Noblewoman; Vor, Nobleman
Time period(s): Indeterminate
Locale(s): Alternate Universe

Summary: Tymon the Black has the reputation of being the most evil wizard in the world because from time to time he does things that seem terrible, including arranging for apparently innocent people to die. His secret is that he has the ability to foresee the future, and sometimes takes steps necessary to avoid even greater tragedies. His latest effort, however, appears to have backfired and he is desperate to correct the situation.

Where it's reviewed:
Booklist, September 1, 2008, page 60
Library Journal, August 1, 2008, page 76
Locus, September 2008, page 19
Publishers Weekly, July 14, 2008, page 49

Other books by the same author:
Worshipping Small Gods, 2007
The Ogre's Wife, 2002

Other books you might like:
Piers Anthony, *Air Apparent*, 2007
Robert Lynn Asprin, *M.Y.T.H. Inc. in Action*, 1990
John DeChancie, *Castle Spellbound*, 1992

Simon R. Green, *Down Among the Dead Men*, 1993
J. Calvin Pierce, *The Sorceress of Ambermere*, 1992

495

FIONA PATTON

The Golden Tower

(New York: DAW, 2008)

Story type: Sword and Sorcery; Coming-of-Age
Series: Warriors of Estavia. Book 2
Subject(s): Coming-of-Age; Magic
Major character(s): Graize, Teenager; Spar, Psychic; Brax, Warrior
Time period(s): Indeterminate
Locale(s): Alternate Universe

Summary: The city of Anavatan is protected from human and inhuman enemies by a magical shield. A prophecy contends that a group of children will be born who will alter the future of both the city and the existence of the gods themselves, and the crisis seems to be rushing toward them before the children have matured enough to deal with it.

Other books by the same author:
The Silver Lake, 2005
The Golden Sword, 2001
The Granite Shield, 1999
The Painter Knight, 1998
The Stone Prince, 1997

Other books you might like:
Dave Duncan, *Children of Chaos*, 2006
Maggie Furey, *The Heart of Myrial*, 1999
David Gemmell, *Knights of Dark Renown*, 1989
Sharon Green, *Convergence*, 1996
Elizabeth Haydon, *Prophecy*, 2000

496

HOLLY PHILLIPS

The Engine's Child

(New York: Del Rey, 2008)

Story type: Quest; Alternate World
Subject(s): Magic; Quest
Major character(s): Ghar, Nobleman; Moth, Apprentice; Vashmarna, Noblewoman
Time period(s): Indeterminate
Locale(s): Alternate Universe

Summary: The original world of a magical people was damaged and they fled to an alternate one, although some among their number wish to return. Two members of the aristocracy and one humble novice will each in their separate ways affect the future of two worlds and the peoples who live in them.

Where it's reviewed:
Library Journal, August 1, 2008, page 76
Publishers Weekly, September 1, 2008, page 40

Other books by the same author:
In the Palace of Repose, 2006
The Burning Girl, 2006

Other books you might like:
Dave Duncan, *Children of Chaos*, 2006
Raymond Feist, *Magician*, 1982
Gregory Frost, *Lord Tophet*, 2008
Mary Gentle, *Rats and Gargoyles*, 1990
China Mieville, *The Scar*, 2002

497

TAMORA PIERCE

The Melting Stones

(New York: Scholastic, 2008)

Story type: Young Adult; Disaster
Subject(s): Secrets; Magic
Major character(s): Rosethorn, Magician; Evvy, Apprentice; Luvo, Mythical Creature
Time period(s): Indeterminate
Locale(s): Alternate Universe

Summary: The magician Rosethorn has been summoned to a remote island which is threatened by the sudden death of many plants and animals. His apprentice, Evvy, is able to communicate with a spirit of the land and discovers that a dormant volcano is about to become active and is the source of all the problems that face them.

Where it's reviewed:
Kliatt, November 2008, page 16

Other books by the same author:
Terrier, 2006
Shatterglass, 2004
Lady Knight, 2002
The Magic Steps, 2001
Briar's Book, 2000

Other books you might like:
Susan Cooper, *Mandrake*, 1964
Peter Dickinson, *The Changes*, 1975
Peni R. Griffin, *Hobkin*, 1992
Mollie Hunter, *The Walking Stones*, 1970
Ursula K. Le Guin, *A Wizard of Earthsea*, 1968

498

T.A. PRATT

Dead Reign

(New York: Bantam, 2008)

Story type: Humor; Magic Conflict
Series: Marla Mason. Book 3
Subject(s): Humor; Magic
Major character(s): Marla Mason, Sorceress; Death, Mythical Creature; Rondeau, Investigator
Time period(s): Indeterminate
Locale(s): Alternate Universe

Summary: Marla Mason is supposed to watch over all magical events in the city of Felport, but she may be out of her league when Death himself leaves the underworld to spend some time in her city. She and her partner Rondeau appear to be powerless to stop him as he wreaks havoc among her people.

Where it's reviewed:
Publishers Weekly, September 15, 2008, page 51

Other books by the same author:
Poison Sleep, 2008
Blood Engines, 2007

Other books you might like:
Jim Butcher, *Small Favor*, 2008
Simon R. Green, *The God Killer*, 1991
Tanya Huff, *Blood Price*, 1993
Terry Pratchett, *Mort*, 1987
Rob Thurman, *Madhouse*, 2008

499

GUILLAUME PREVOST

The Gate of Days

(New York: Scholastic, 2008)

Story type: Young Adult; Time Travel
Series: Book of Time. Book 2
Subject(s): Quest; Magic
Major character(s): Sam Faulkner, Teenager, Time Traveler; Vlad Tepes, Nobleman; Lily, Teenager
Time period(s): Indeterminate Past
Locale(s): Earth

Summary: A set of magic coins enables Sam Faulkner to travel through time and space. He uses them to escape the castle of Vlad Tepes and find a way to rescue his father, who is marooned in the 15th century. Aided only by his cousin Lily, he has to keep one step ahead of his enemies.

Where it's reviewed:
Kliatt, November 2008, page 17

Other books by the same author:
The Book of Time, 2007

Other books you might like:
Margaret Anderson, *In the Keep of Time*, 1977
Barbara Bartholomew, *The Time Keeper*, 1985
John Bellairs, *The Trolley to Yesterday*, 1989
Ann Downer, *Hatching Magic*, 2003
Andre Norton, *Red Hart Magic*, 1976

500

PHILIP REEVE

Here Lies Arthur

(New York: Scholastic, 2008)

Story type: Young Adult; Legend
Subject(s): Orphans; Legends; Arthurian Legends
Major character(s): Gwyna, Teenager; Myrrdin, Musician; Arthur, Nobleman
Time period(s): Indeterminate Past
Locale(s): England

Summary: An orphan girl joins a traveling bard who is secretly in the service of young Arthur, who will one day become king of all Britain. They use illusion and other devices to further the career of the man they admire, and to maneuver his enemies into defeat.

Where it's reviewed:
Horn Book Magazine, November-December 2008, page 713
Kliatt, November 2008, page 17
Publishers Weekly, October 6, 2008, page 55

Other books by the same author:
A Darkling Plain, 2007
Larklight, 2007
Infernal Engines, 2005
Predator's Gold, 2004
Mortal Engines, 2002

Other books you might like:
Barbara Benedict, *Enchantress*, 1996
Nancy Springer, *I Am Mordred*, 1998
Rosemary Sutcliff, *Sword at Sunset*, 1963
T.H. White, *The Once and Future King*, 1958
Jane Yolen, *Sword of the Rightful King*, 2003

501

MIKE RESNICK

Stalking the Vampire

(Amherst, NY: Pyr, 2008)

Story type: Humor; Vampire Story
Series: John Justin Mallory. Book 2
Subject(s): Humor; Vampires
Major character(s): John Justin Mallory, Detective— Private; Winnifred Carruthers, Detective—Private; Aristotle Draconis, Vampire
Time period(s): Indeterminate
Locale(s): Alternate Universe

Summary: John Justin Mallory is just beginning to adjust to life in an alternate world where magic works when the arrival of a European vampire in America sets off a string of comedic disasters. Mallory's partner's nephew is on the verge of becoming a vampire himself when he is murdered, and the various helpers Mallory enlists in his investigation do more harm than good.

Where it's reviewed:
Booklist, July 1, 2008, page 50

Other books by the same author:
Dragon America, 2005
The Amulet of Power, 2004
Lucifer Jones, 1992
Stalking the Unicorn, 1987
Adventures, 1985

Other books you might like:
MaryJanice Davidson, *Undead and Unwed*, 2004
Lionel Fenn, *The Mark of the Moderately Vicious Vampire*, 1992
Esther Friesner, *Demon Blues*, 1989
Craig Shaw Gardner, *Bride of the Slime Monster*, 1990
Terry Pratchett, *Good Omens*, 1990

Neil Gaiman, co-author

502

ANTHONY REYNOLDS

Knight Errant

(Nottingham, United Kingdom: Black Library, 2008)

Story type: Sword and Sorcery; Magic Conflict
Series: Warhammer
Subject(s): Magic; Quest
Major character(s): Bertelis, Nobleman, Warrior; Calard, Nobleman, Warrior; Gunther, Warrior
Time period(s): Indeterminate
Locale(s): Alternate Universe

Summary: When the king of Bretonne dies, his two unproven sons, Bertelis and Calard, are left to lead a distinguished order of knights into battle against a horde of invading goblins. Unfortunately, despite their early successes, the war turns against them when they discover the real force behind the attack.

Other books by the same author:
Empire in Chaos, 2008
Dark Apostle, 2007
Mark of Chaos, 2006

Other books you might like:
Jennifer Fallon, *Harshini*, 2005
Barbara Hambly, *Dragonshadow*, 1999
John Marco, *The Jackal of Nar*, 1999
Graham McNeill, *Heldenhammer*, 2008
C.L. Werner, *Runefang*, 2008

503

KAT RICHARDSON

Underground

(New York: Roc, 2008)

Story type: Contemporary; Mystery
Series: Harper Blaine. Book 3
Subject(s): Magic; Secrets
Major character(s): Harper Blaine, Detective—Private; Will Novak, Worker; Quinton, Investigator
Time period(s): 2000s
Locale(s): Seattle, Washington

Summary: Harper Blaine was briefly dead and after her resuscitation, she found she had the ability to see the supernatural creatures that are invisible to most of the rest of the world. Her latest investigation begins when an old friend tells her that there are zombies in the sewers and that he may be implicated in their deaths.

Where it's reviewed:
Booklist, August 1, 2008, page 53
Locus, August 2008, page 27

Other books by the same author:
Poltergeist, 2007
Greywalker, 2006

Other books you might like:
Marie Brennan, *Doppelganger*, 2006
Yasmine Galenorn, *Dragon Wytch*, 2008
Laura Anne Gilman, *Burning Bridges*, 2007
Charlaine Harris, *From Dead to Worse*, 2008
Rob Thurman, *Moonshine*, 2007

504

RICK RIORDAN

The Battle of the Labyrinth

(New York: Hyperion, 2008)

Story type: Young Adult; Legend
Series: Olympians. Book 4
Subject(s): Magic; Legends
Major character(s): Percy Jackson, Teenager; Annabeth
  Chase, Teenager; Kronos, Deity
Time period(s): 2000s
Locale(s): United States; Mythical Place

Summary: A group of teenagers at a summer camp get involved in a war between the gods of ancient Greece. Kronos and his forces are outmaneuvering the more benevolent gods and among the sites to be attacked is the camp itself, so Percy Jackson and his friends must form an alliance with other demigods and thwart the plot of conquest.

Where it's reviewed:
Booklist, October 1, 2008, page 58

Other books by the same author:
The Titan's Curse, 2007
The Sea of Monsters, 2006
The Lightning Thief, 2005

Other books you might like:
K.A. Applegate, *Gateway to the Gods*, 2000
Tom Holt, *Valhalla*, 2000
David Lee Jones, *Zeus and Co.*, 1993
Robert Sheckley, *Godshome*, 1999
Thorne Smith, *The Night Life of the Gods*, 1931

505

JENNIFER ROBERSON

Guinevere's Truth and Other Stories

(Waterville, ME: Five Star, 2008)

Story type: Collection
Subject(s): Short Stories

Summary: Jennifer Roberson provides short adventure stories drawn from a variety of fantasy traditions, from alternate worlds where magic works to historical settings in the time of King Arthur. Some of the stories are related to her various novels. All 20 appearing in this collection have been previously published.

Where it's reviewed:
Publishers Weekly, September 22, 2008, page 42

Other books by the same author:
Deepwood, 2007
Karavans, 2006
Sword Sworn, 2002
Shapechanger's Song, 2001
The Lion Throne, 2001

Other books you might like:
Barbara Hambly, *Icefalcon's Quest*, 1998
Nancy Kress, *The Prince of Morning Bells*, 1981
Mercedes Lackey, *Foundation*, 2008
Patricia A. McKillip, *Harrowing the Dragon*, 2005
Judith Tarr, *Bring Down the Sun*, 2008

506

EMILY RODDA

Deltora Quest

(New York: Scholastic, 2008)

Story type: Young Adult; Collection
Subject(s): Quest; Magic

Summary: This is the omnibus edition of all eight of the Deltora Quest novels. A magical land is menaced by an evil presence which threatens to conquer the world. A group of young people set out on a quest to find a series of magical artifacts which, if all gathered together, will provide a defense capable of defeating their enemy.

Other books by the same author:
The Key to Rondo, 2008
Rowan and the Keeper of the Crystal, 2002
Rowan and the Travelers, 2001
Finders Keepers, 1991
Pigs Might Fly, 1986

Other books you might like:
Bruce Coville, *Dark Whispers*, 2007
Alan Garner, *The Moon of Gomrath*, 1963
William Nicholson, *Seeker*, 2006
Rick Riordan, *The Lightning Thief*, 2005
Jane Yolen, *White Jenna*, 1989

507

DENISE ROSSETTI

The Flame and the Shadow

(New York: Ace, 2008)

Story type: Sword and Sorcery; Magic Conflict
Subject(s): Magic; Quest
Major character(s): Grayson, Mercenary, Sorcerer; Cenda,
  Witch; Shad, Mythical Creature
Time period(s): Indeterminate
Locale(s): Alternate Universe

Summary: Grayson is a sorcerer who has traveled among the worlds and who is secretly subject to the dark passions of the entity known as Shad. His life changes direction when he meets Cenda, a witch suffering from grief at the loss of her child, and the romance that sparks between them will change the future of worlds. First novel.

Other books you might like:
Jacqueline Carey, *Kushiel's Mercy*, 2008
Jennifer Fallon, *Eye of the Labyrinth*, 2002
Maggie Furey, *Aurian*, 1994
Marjorie M. Liu, *The Wild Road*, 2008
Elizabeth Vaughan, *Dagger-Star*, 2007

▮508▮

BRIAN RUCKLEY

Bloodheir

(London: Gollancz, 2008)

Story type: Sword and Sorcery; Magic Conflict
Series: Godless World. Book 2
Subject(s): Magic; Psychic Powers
Major character(s): Orisian oc Lannis-Haig, Leader; Kanin oc Horin-Gyre, Leader; Mordyn Jerain, Government Official
Time period(s): Indeterminate
Locale(s): Alternate Universe

Summary: A war between two clans has spread and threatens a much wider conflict. Orisian is one of the few survivors of a clan that was attacked and nearly wiped out. As the clans begin squabbling among themselves, a powerful sorcerer invokes magical powers in a bid to elevate himself to a dominant position.

Other books by the same author:
Winterbirth, 2007

Other books you might like:
Jennifer Fallon, *Harshini*, 2005
John Marco, *The Devil's Armor*, 2003
George R.R. Martin, *A Game of Thrones*, 1996
L.E. Modesitt Jr., *The Death of Chaos*, 1995
R.A. Salvatore, *Bastion of Darkness*, 2000

▮509▮

MICHELLE SAGARA

Cast in Fury

(Don Mills, Ontario: Luna, 2008)

Story type: Romance; Mystery
Series: Chronicles of Elantra. Book 4
Subject(s): Romance; Psychic Powers
Major character(s): Kaylin Neva, Sorceress, Military Personnel; Sanabalis, Nobleman; Richard Rennick, Writer
Time period(s): Indeterminate
Locale(s): Alternate Universe

Summary: A natural disaster is blamed on a minority race with psychic powers. Kaylin Neva is one of those brought to the castle to help ease tensions, where a play is about to be performed to soothe the public. Unfortunately, a controversial premise for the play, followed by a murder, makes the situation more volatile than ever.

Other books by the same author:
Cast in Secret, 2007

Cast in Courtlight, 2006
Cast in Shadow, 2005
Children of the Blood, 1992
Into the Dark Lands, 1991

Other books you might like:
Dave Duncan, *The Crooked House*, 2000
Lorna Freeman, *The King's Own*, 2005
Daniel Hood, *King's Cure*, 2000
Mindy L. Klasky, *The Glasswright's Apprentice*, 2000
Melisa Michaels, *Cold Iron*, 1997

▮510▮

BRANDON SANDERSON

The Hero of Ages

(New York: Tor, 2008)

Story type: Sword and Sorcery; Magic Conflict
Series: Mistborn. Book 3
Subject(s): Disasters; Mystery
Major character(s): Elend Venture, Ruler; Vin, Psychic; Sazed, Religious
Time period(s): Indeterminate
Locale(s): Alternate Universe

Summary: The final volume in the trilogy has the protagonists in deep trouble. Vin has been tricked into freeing the evil that was concealed by a faked prophecy, an evil which now makes it deadly to enter the mists that spread through the land. The heroes are divided among themselves and desperate to find a way to undo the harm they've done.

Where it's reviewed:
Booklist, October 1, 2008, page 32
Publishers Weekly, August 18, 2008, page 50

Other books by the same author:
Alcatraz and the Evil Librarians, 2007
The Well of Ascension, 2007
Mistborn, 2006
Elantris, 2005

Other books you might like:
David B. Coe, *Children of Amarid*, 1997
Steven Erikson, *Memories of Ice*, 2005
David Farland, *Brotherhood of the Wolf*, 1999
Barbara Hambly, *The Rainbow Abyss*, 1991
Sheri S. Tepper, *The Awakeners*, 1987

▮511▮

ANDRZEJ SAPKOWSKI

Blood of Elves

(London: Gollancz, 2008)

Story type: Magic Conflict; Legend
Subject(s): Prophecy; War
Major character(s): Ciri, Child, Psychic; Geralt, Wizard; Triss Merigold, Student
Time period(s): Indeterminate
Locale(s): Alternate Universe

Summary: The various races have gone through periods of relative harmony and others of discord. Now elves and dwarves and humans are killing one another again. In the midst of this renewed turmoil, a child is born who possesses unusual abilities and whose role may be to fill an ancient prophecy. To do so, she has to survive the efforts of her enemies to destroy her. This novel was originally published in Poland.

Other books by the same author:
The Last Witch, 2007

Other books you might like:
Kate Elliott, *King's Dragon*, 1997
Jennifer Fallon, *Wolfblade*, 2004
Kate Forsyth, *The Skull of the World*, 2001
Mercedes Lackey, *By the Sword*, 1991
Robin McKinley, *The Hero and the Crown*, 1984

512

PATRICE SARATH

Gordath Wood

(New York: Ace, 2008)

Story type: Magic Conflict; Alternate World
Subject(s): Magic; Quest
Major character(s): Lynn Romano, Horse Trainer; Kate Mossland, Traveller; Crae, Military Personnel
Time period(s): 2000s
Locale(s): New York; Alternate Universe

Summary: Lynn Romano takes a short cut through the forest one day and finds herself in an alternate world where magic works and where women are expected to be subservient to men. There is also a war going on, which leaves little opportunity for her to discover someone who can help her return to her own world. First novel.

Other books you might like:
Lynn Abbey, *The Guardians*, 1982
Barbara Hambly, *Circle of the Moon*, 2005
Mickey Zucker Reichert, *The Beasts of Barakhai*, 2001
Will Shetterly, *NeverNever*, 1993
Tad Williams, *City of Golden Shadow*, 1996

513

STEVEN SAVILE

Curse of the Necrarch

(Nottingham, United Kingdom: Black Library, 2008)

Story type: Sword and Sorcery; Magic Conflict
Series: Warhammer
Subject(s): Magic; Vampires
Major character(s): Reinhardt Metzger, Knight; Radu the Forsaken, Vampire; Kaspar Bohme, Warrior
Time period(s): Indeterminate
Locale(s): Alternate Universe

Summary: A group of vampires has been living in a remote mountain retreat for many years and has been largely ignored by the citizens of the nearby empire. When one of them leaves their refuge and kills a number of people,

an aging knight organizes an expedition to rid the world of their foul presence.

Other books by the same author:
Retribution, 2007
Dominion, 2006
Slaine the Exile, 2006
Inheritance, 2006
Houdini's Last Illusion, 2004

Other books you might like:
Mark Acres, *Dark Divide*, 1991
Steven Brust, *Taltos*, 1988
Christie Golden, *Vampire of the Mists*, 1991
William King, *Vampireslayer*, 2001
Richard A. Knaak, *Ruby Flames*, 1999

514

STEVEN E. SCHEND

Blackstaff Tower

(Renton, WA: Wizards of the Coast, 2008)

Story type: Sword and Sorcery; Magic Conflict
Series: Forgotten Realms
Subject(s): Secrets; Magic
Major character(s): Vajra Safahr, Apprentice; Samark, Wizard; Khondar Naomal, Wizard
Time period(s): Indeterminate
Locale(s): Alternate Universe

Summary: A group of friends led by a wizard and his apprentice/lover investigates forgotten tombs and other dangerous places in order to learn the secrets with which they can protect their city. While doing so they discover a plot against the young heir to the throne and a plan to seize power over all of Waterdeep.

Other books by the same author:
Blackstaff, 2006

Other books you might like:
Lynn Abbey, *The Nether Scroll*, 2000
Jaleigh Johnson, *Mistshore*, 2008
Paul S. Kemp, *Dawn of Night*, 2004
Mel Odom, *Under Fallen Stars*, 1999
R.A. Salvatore, *The Chaos Curse*, 1994

515

ROBERT SCOTT
JAY GORDON , Co-Author

The Larion Senators

(London: Gollancz, 2008)

Story type: Sword and Sorcery; Magic Conflict
Series: Eldarn Sequence. Book 3
Subject(s): Quest; Magic
Major character(s): Steven Taylor, Traveller; Gilmour, Government Official; Garec, Woodsman
Time period(s): Indeterminate
Locale(s): Alternate Universe

Summary: Although the protagonists defeated an evil

sorcerer in the previous book in this series, the evil possessing him has escaped and still threatens the land of Eldarn. They set out on separate courses, each to complete a quest that will provide a weapon against the danger threatening them all. This is the final volume in the series.

Other books by the same author:
Lessek's Key, 2006 (Jay Gordon, co-author)
The Hickory Staff, 2005 (Jay Gordon, co-author)

Other books you might like:
Jennifer Fallon, *Lord of the Shadows*, 2003
Raymond Feist, *Talon of the Silver Hawk*, 2003
Mercedes Lackey, *Alta*, 2004
Janny Wurts, *Fugitive Prince*, 1997

516

SHARON SHINN

Fortune and Fate

(New York: Ace, 2008)

Story type: Magic Conflict; Literary
Series: Twelve Houses. Book 5
Subject(s): Magic; Quest
Major character(s): Wen, Military Personnel; Karryn, Noblewoman; Jasper Paladar, Nobleman
Time period(s): Indeterminate
Locale(s): Alternate Universe

Summary: Wen is disillusioned by the outcome of a war and plans to devote her time to helping others recover during the aftermath. She rescues a young woman who is being kidnapped and finds a place as instructor to the woman's guardian's bodyguards, but she finds herself drawn romantically to her new employer.

Where it's reviewed:
Library Journal, October 15, 2008, page 61
Publishers Weekly, September 15, 2008, page 49

Other books by the same author:
Reader and Raelynx, 2007
Dark Moon Defender, 2006
The Thirteenth House, 2006
Mystic and Rider, 2005
Summers at Castle Auburn, 2001

Other books you might like:
Jacqueline Carey, *Kushiel's Justice*, 2007
Sara Douglass, *Beyond the Hanging Wall*, 2003
Elizabeth Haydon, *Destiny*, 2001
Juliet Marillier, *Heir to Sevenwaters*, 2008
Andre Norton, *The Warding of Witch World*, 1996

517

SHERWOOD SMITH

King's Shield

(New York: DAW, 2008)

Story type: Young Adult; Sword and Sorcery
Series: Inda. Book 3

Subject(s): Coming-of-Age; Magic
Major character(s): Indevan-Dal "Inda", Teenager, Warrior; Evred, Ruler; T'Dor Marth-Davan, Warrior
Time period(s): Indeterminate
Locale(s): Alternate Universe

Summary: Inda went into voluntary exile as a child in order to avoid a situation which would have resulted in either war or dishonor. He returns at the age of 19 to discover that his childhood playmate is on the throne and that his own military skills are required in the service of his country. Unfortunately, his experience is all in naval warfare and it is a land battle that is looming.

Where it's reviewed:
Locus, August 2008, page 27

Other books by the same author:
The Fox, 2007
Inda, 2006
Court Duel, 1998
Crown Duel, 1997
Wren's War, 1995

Other books you might like:
Dave Duncan, *Children of Chaos*, 2006
Mercedes Lackey, *Exile's Honor*, 2002
William Nicholson, *Jango*, 2007
Andre Norton, *Three Against the Witch World*, 1965
Lawrence Watt-Evans, *Dragon Weather*, 1999

518

JERI SMITH-READY

The Reawakened

(Don Mills, Ontario: Luna, 2008)

Story type: Sword and Sorcery; Magic Conflict
Series: Aspect of Crow. Book 3
Subject(s): Magic; Secrets
Major character(s): Rhia, Sorceress; Marek, Warrior; Lycas, Traveller
Time period(s): Indeterminate
Locale(s): Alternate Universe

Summary: The world is torn between the powers of the Descendants and the people led by the Reawakened in a world in which people can enjoy union with animal spirits that transform them and give them magical powers. Rhia is one of the leaders of the Reawakened who risks her life to protect the rest from harm, even though that puts strains on her relations with her husband and friends.

Where it's reviewed:
Publishers Weekly, September 15, 2008, page 50

Other books by the same author:
Wicked Game, 2008
Voice of Crow, 2007
Eyes of Crow, 2006

Other books you might like:
Charles De Lint, *The Dreaming Place*, 1990
Tom Deitz, *Ghostcountry's Wrath*, 1995
Andre Norton, *Trey of Swords*, 1977

Ken Rand, *Pax Dakota*, 2008
Elizabeth Vaughan, *Dagger-Star*, 2007

519

MATTHEW STOVER

Caine Black Knife

(New York: Del Rey, 2008)

Story type: Sword and Sorcery; Magic Conflict
Subject(s): Magic; Quest
Major character(s): Caine Black Knife, Criminal; Orbek Black Knife, Worker; Tyrkilld, Knight
Time period(s): 22nd century
Locale(s): Earth

Summary: Two centuries from now, the world of science and magic are no longer separate. Caine is an assassin, an entertainer, and an enigma. His adventures nearly wipe out an entire tribe in a barbaric alternate reality. High technology and sword and sorcery intersect during his various adventures.

Where it's reviewed:
Publishers Weekly, August 18, 2008, page 49

Other books by the same author:
Shatterpoint, 2003
Blade of Tyshalle, 2001
Heroes Die, 1998
Jericho Moon, 1998
Iron Dawn, 1997

Other books you might like:
Dan Abnett, *Riders of the Dead*, 2003
David Gemmell, *Bloodstone*, 1994
Michael Moorcock, *Blood*, 1994
Andrew J. Offutt, *Chieftain of Andor*, 1976
Karl Edward Wagner, *Night Winds*, 1978

520

HARRY TURTLEDOVE

The Breath of God

(New York: Tor, 2008)

Story type: Historical/Pre-history; Alternate World
Subject(s): Alternate History; Pre-Columbian History
Major character(s): Hamnet Thyssen, Nobleman; Ulric Skazkki, Warrior; Trasamund, Leader
Time period(s): Indeterminate Past
Locale(s): Earth

Summary: In a prehistoric world where magic works, the breakup of the glaciers opens a route to unexplored parts of the landscape. A party of explorers seeks to discover what lies in the outer world, but there are enemies there using mammoths and powerful magic to enforce their rule. This is the sequel to *Beyond the Gap*.

Where it's reviewed:
Publishers Weekly, October 6, 2008, page 39

Other books by the same author:
Bridge of the Separator, 2006

Every Inch a King, 2005
Jaws of Darkness, 2004
Conan of Venarium, 2003
Advance and Retreat, 2002

Other books you might like:
Jean Auel, *Clan of the Cave Bear*, 1980
Lin Carter, *Zanthodon*, 1980
W. Michael Gear, *People of the Moon*, 2005
    Kathleen O'Neal Gear, co-author
Bjorn Kurten, *Singletusk*, 1986
William Sarabande, *The Sacred Stones*, 1991

521

C.L. WERNER

Runefang

(Nottingham, United Kingdom: Black Library, 2008)

Story type: Sword and Sorcery; Magic Conflict
Series: Warhammer
Subject(s): Magic; Quest
Major character(s): Ernst von Rabwald, Nobleman, Warrior; Max Kessler, Warrior; Armin von Starkberg, Nobleman, Warrior
Time period(s): Indeterminate
Locale(s): Alternate Universe

Summary: The royal army is called out when an enemy force invades Wissenland, but the troops are dismayed to discover that their opponents are undead and cannot be easily killed. As their city is placed under siege, a small group of adventurers escape and go on a quest into the wilderness to find a magical sword that can reverse the tide of battle.

Other books by the same author:
Palace of the Plague Lord, 2007
Witch Killer, 2006
Witch Finder, 2005
Blood and Steel, 2003
Blood Money, 2003

Other books you might like:
Lin Carter, *Kellory the Warlock*, 1984
Roland Green, *Conan and the Death Lord of Thanza*, 1997
Graham McNeill, *Heldenhammer*, 2008
Anthony Reynolds, *Knight Errant*, 2008
Brian Ruckley, *Winterbirth*, 2007

522

CAROLE WILKINSON

Dragon Moon

(New York: Hyperion, 2008)

Story type: Young Adult; Historical/Fantasy
Series: Dragon. Book 3
Subject(s): Orphans; Quest
Major character(s): Ping, Child, Orphan; Kai, Mythical Creature (dragon); Jun, Traveller

Time period(s): Indeterminate Past
Locale(s): China

Summary: Ping is an orphan in ancient China who has acquired notoriety because of her position as keeper of the dragon, Kai. But Kai has enemies and Ping decides that they should follow instructions left by an old friend and travel to a remote part of China where humans do not threaten the dragons. Unfortunately, their enemies do not want them to complete their journey.

Where it's reviewed:
Language Arts, September 2008, page 73

Other books by the same author:
Garden of the Purple Dragon, 2007
Dragon Keeper, 2005

Other books you might like:
Leah R. Cutter, *The Paper Mage*, 2003
Kara Dalkey, *Genpei*, 2000
Geraldine Harris, *White Cranes Castle*, 1979
Tim Lukeman, *Rajan*, 1979
Jessica Amanda Salmonson, *Ou Lu Khen and the Beautiful Madwoman*, 1985

523

GENE WOLFE

An Evil Guest

(New York: Tor, 2008)

Story type: Futuristic; Magic Conflict
Subject(s): Magic; Secrets

Major character(s): Gideon Chase, Investigator; Cassie Casey, Actress; William Reis, Diplomat, Magician
Time period(s): Indeterminate Future
Locale(s): United States

Summary: An investigator who is also a sorcerer enlists the aid of an unsuccessful actress in his latest case, which involves the strange activities of an interplanetary diplomat. She gets caught in the middle of a personal battle between the two men, both of whom can draw on scientific and magical resources when required.

Where it's reviewed:
Booklist, September 1, 2008, page 59
Library Journal, August 1, 2008, page 76
Magazine of Fantasy & Science Fiction, October 2008, page 33
Publishers Weekly, July 14, 2008, page 48

Other books by the same author:
Pirate Freedom, 2007
Innocents Aboard, 2004
The Knight, 2004
Castleview, 1990
Free Live Free, 1984

Other books you might like:
C.S. Friedman, *Black Sun Rising*, 1991
Kim Newman, *The Night Mayor*, 1989
Madeline Robins, *The Stone War*, 1999
Brian Stableford, *The Empire of Fear*, 1988
Lawrence Watt-Evans, *The Reign of the Brown Magician*, 1996

Fantasy

The Year in Horror: 2008
by
Don D'Ammassa

There are undoubtedly numerous reasons why readers might enjoy horror fiction, but one frequent suggestion is that supernatural events suggest the possibility that existence does not necessarily have to be entirely rational and logical. If the Devil and evil exist, then so too must God and goodness. If we feel constrained by rules imposed by society or nature, then it is possible in horror fiction to imagine a reality in which those rules can be overthrown. If ghosts exist, then death is not the end of self awareness. The appeal of fiction whose purpose is to generate fear is undeniable. We do not ride roller coasters because they will make us feel safe. The best of supernatural fiction shows us a reality in which what we believe to be absolute truth can be denied, and if that is the case, then anything at all is possible. Perhaps most important of all, if we become truly immersed in a story drenched with strong emotion, even if that emotion is fear or revulsion, then it is much more difficult to set it aside than otherwise.

Although horror fiction has been popular in Europe for centuries, it enjoyed its most successful years in the United States during the 1970s and 1980s. Inevitably, public tastes changed and a surfeit of mass produced, generic tales of possessed children, vengeful ghosts, and small town horrors led to a major downturn during the late 1980s. For more than a decade, horror fiction became increasingly the province of the smaller publishers and until recently none of the major imprints had a designated "horror" line, although they occasionally published supernatural fiction under other guises. The most popular authors who survived the crash continued to write and sell successfully, but Stephen King, Dean R. Koontz, Anne Rice, and a few others were simply best selling authors whose work was perceived as rising above its genre, and in fact all three have written novels outside the horror field. Other, less prominent writers, turned to other subject matter, stopped writing altogether, or saw their work marketed as "thrillers."

Horror fiction has made something of a comeback during the past few years, although it still depends heavily on the small press and the internet. The best known print magazines are *Cemetery Dance* and *Weird Tales*, both published bi-monthly. Much of the most effective horror fiction consists of short stories, and mass market publishers have largely eliminated single author collections because they do not sell as consistently well as do novels. It is not clear whether this reflects a change in attitude of the reading public or whether it has become a self fulfilling prophecy. Whatever the cause, the small press now publishes the vast majority of single author collections. Some of the major publishers have begun to label occasional releases as horror, but as of this writing only Leisure books has a dedicated horror line. They publish primarily newer writers in the field and many of their titles were previously released in small press editions.

One branch of horror fiction has a very strong overlap with contemporary fantasy. Typically these novels feature a highly competent female protagonist in a contemporary urban setting, either our world or one very similar to it. Their opposition is generally some form of supernatural evil, most frequently involving vampires or werewolves and other shape changers, although some of these mythical creatures might actually be allied with the protagonist. These novels are published as dark fantasy, urban fantasy, or paranormal romance. Depending upon how one defines the difference between fantasy and horror, it is possible that this has become the most popular form of modern horror fiction. In some of these series, vampires and other supernatural creatures are accepted by the public as part of everyday life, suggesting that they are fantasy rather than horror, although they often contain classic horror motifs. Others are more clearly set in our reality, with entire cultures of vampires or other mythical beings living secretly among us, sometimes clearly evil although the current trend is to make them as varied in motive and basic nature as are the human characters.

Given the importance of short fiction, it is not surprising that many of the best books in the genre this year were anthologies or collections. *The Year's Best Fantasy and Horror 2008*, edited by Ellen Datlow, Kelly Link, and Gavin J. Grant, continues to be a reliable sampling of the best of literary horror and fantasy. Datlow also edited an excellent original anthology this year, *Inferno*. Stephen Jones has selected a different but no less entertaining sampling for his *The Best New Horror 19*. Peter Straub brought together a talented team of writers for an anthology designed to suggest the future of horror children, *Poe's Children*. Canadian small press publisher Ash-Tree Press continues to turn out interesting collections of new and classic horror stories, but unfortunately these limited editions are not widely available.

Several single-author collections are of particular note in 2008. Stephen King's *Just After Sunset* brings together most of his more recent stories in a collection of stories that vary greatly in theme and which generally avoid the explicit tone of much of his earlier fiction. David Niall Wilson's *Ennui and Other States of Madness*, Stephen Mark Rainey's *Other Gods*, and Brian Lumley's *The Taint and Other Novellas* are all workmanlike collections exploring the various preoccupations of the horror field and each maintains a consistent level of quality. Robert E. Howard, the creator of Conan, was reintroduced to horror readers with *The Horror Stories of Robert E. Howard*.

There were also a few notable novels, the most impressive of which was Stephen King's *Duma Key*. King seems to have gotten his second breath after producing a couple of lackluster novels and last year's *Lisey's Story* and this year's title are both notably better. *Duma Key* is set on an island off the coast of Florida and involves a typical King mix of strange events, deeply drawn characters, and an inevitable rush to a confrontation. Bentley Little has carved out a little niche for himself in which familiar components of contemporary society - department stories, vacation resorts, university campuses - are abstracted from the ordinary and those who stray within their reach are subject to supernatural or sometimes just very strange forces. Part of his formula is isolation from the outside world, to the point where his characters sometimes cease to act rationally, as though they've forgotten how society actually functions. This is the case in *The Academy*, in which a local school suddenly switches from public to charter, apparently at the behest of the principal, who institutes a new set of draconian policies that intimidate students, teachers, and parents alike. Naturally, things are even more worrisome than surface events suggest.

F. Paul Wilson seems to be bringing his Repairman Jack series closer to its conclusion in *By the Sword*. A nefarious cult is trying to breed its own version of the Messiah, but that's only one of the dangers he faces in this very complex twelfth book in the series. Jack's popularity is in part due to his outsider status. He has dropped out of established society and adopted a unilateral libertarian existence in which he pays no taxes and obeys only those laws with which he agrees. Wilson's monsters tend to be non-traditional, sometimes human. Mario Acevedo makes use of more familiar supernatural creatures, but gives them a unique twist.

Vampires were once the best known symbol of evil in horror fiction, but for the last decade they have been just as likely to appear as the hero, or at worst a troubled, contradictory personality. Acevedo introduced his recurring vampire detective, Felix Gomez, in the lightly humorous *The Nymphos of Rocky Flats* back in 2006. This year saw his third outing, *The Undead Karma Sutra*, which has a more serious tone. Gomez is on a quest to find a manuscript that will supposedly increase his paranormal powers in an adventure that involves kidnapping, aliens, and some mildly explicit sex.

Delirium Books, a small press publisher of expensive limited edition hardcovers, has begun a program of more affordable trade paperback reprints of some of its titles. This should make at least some of that imprint's better offerings more widely available. Delirium published two very good novels in 2008. *Dominion* by Greg F. Gifune is a suspenseful psychological thriller whose protagonist has sunk into a deep depression following the death of his wife in an automobile accident. He begins to receive anonymous phone calls and observe things on his computer that do not seem possible. Technology and the supernatural have interfaced and the borders between the living and the dead are no longer absolute. *Daemon* by Harry Shannon bears some similarities. The protagonist is divorced in this case but still has feelings for his ex-wife, who is killed while working as a security officer. His outrage and grief grow even stronger when her corpse is mutilated at the local morgue, and he eventually assembles a team to hunt down the creature that has been despoiling the dead.

There was a veritable flood of paranormal romance/urban fantasy novels this year, at least several dozen different series ranging from obvious fantasy to very dark supernatural tales. One of the best of these was *Lord of Bones* by Justine Musk, second in a series about two people who travel the world tracking down demonically possessed people. Jeanne C. Stein's *Legacy*, fourth in the Anna Strong series, pits a relatively benign vampire against a particularly nasty werewolf in a battle over the estate of a mutual acquaintance. Lilith Saintcrow, having brought her Dante Valentine series to a conclusion, released the first three titles in the Jill Kismet series, starting with *Night Shift*, with a heroine whose vocation is battling supernatural creatures and forces allied with evil. Other writers with notable series in this vein include Kat Richardson, L.A. Banks, Sherrilyn Kenyon, Kelley Armstrong, Kim Harrison, Charlaine Harris, and Karen Marie Moning, most of whom added new titles in 2008.

Young adult horror fiction was dominated by *Breaking Dawn* by Stephenie Meyer, part of her series of vampire romances for teenagers, and the Demonata series by Darren Shan, but horror fiction for younger readers has yet to produce as many interesting writers as has young adult fantasy. The best novel in this category during 2008 was *The Devouring* by Simon Holt, in which a magical book contains the key to preventing disasters when disembodied demons enter the world and begin possessing children. Only a handful of titles were published for younger readers. Although the Goosebumps name has been revived by R.L. Stine, it has not enjoyed the same degree of popularity that it did during the 1990s.

The future of horror fiction as a separate genre seems more problematic than ever. The field has been dominated by the same half dozen writers for more than twenty years, and while some of the newer names such as Brian Keene, Tim Lebbon, and Cherie Priest are undeniably talented, none of them have demonstrated as broad an appeal as have Stephen King, Ramsey Campbell, Brian Lumley, and other established writers. The short fiction market remains healthy but primarily in specialized venues, magazines, and anthologies, which have a limited readership and which receive minimal exposure. The proliferation of dark urban fantasy has diverted some authors into that category and blurred the distinction between the two forms. It is probable that the horror genre will change even more in the years to come.

Recommended Titles

Although short horror fiction is frequently more successful than full length novels, 2008 was particularly weighted in that direction with a large number of excellent collections. Some of the titles listed below are from the first half of the year and are covered in the second volume of *What Do I Read Next? 2008*.

The Undead Karma Sutra by Mario Acevedo

Inferno edited by Ellen Datlow

The Year's Best Fantasy and Horror 2008 edited by Ellen Datlow, Gavin Grant, & Kelly Link

Dominion by Greg F. Gifune

The Devouring by Simon Holt

The Horror Stories of Robert E. Howard by Robert E. Howard

The Best New Horror 19 edited by Stephen Jones

Duma Key by Stephen King

Just After Sunset by Stephen King

The Academy by Bentley Little

The Taint and Other Novellas by Brian Lumley

Lord of Bones by Justine Musk

Other Gods by Stephen Mark Rainey

Underground by Kat Richardson

Night Shift by Lilith Saintcrow

Daemon by Harry Shannon

Legacy by Jeanne C. Stein

Poe's Children edited by Peter Straub

Ennui and Other States of Madness by David Niall Wilson

By the Sword by F. Paul Wilson

Horror Titles

524

MARIO ACEVEDO

The Undead Karma Sutra
(New York: Eos, 2008)

Story type: Vampire Story; Mystery
Series: Felix Gomez. Book 3
Subject(s): Vampires; Secrets
Major character(s): Felix Gomez, Vampire, Detective—
 Private; Carmen Arellano, Vampire; Gilbert Odin,
 Alien
Time period(s): 2000s (2008)
Locale(s): Florida

Summary: Felix Gomez is a vampire turned private detective who manages to survive without taking human life. In addition to dealing with his fellow undead, he is trying to track down the killer of an acquaintance who turned out to be an alien. The need to neutralize his vampire angst makes his job even more difficult.

Where it's reviewed:
Booklist, March 15, 2008, page 38
Library Journal, February 15, 2008, page 96
Publishers Weekly, December 10, 2007, page 39

Other books by the same author:
The Nymphos of Rocky Flats, 2006
X-Rated Bloodsuckers, 2006

Other books you might like:
Vincent Courtney, *The Vampire Beat*, 1991
P.N. Elrod, *Song in the Dark*, 2005
Tanya Huff, *Blood Lines*, 1991
Lee Killough, *Blood Hunt*, 1987
S.A. Swiniarski, *Raven*, 1996

525

DAVIS ANGSTEN

Night of the Furies
(New York: Thomas Dunne, 2008)

Story type: Ancient Evil Unleashed; Legend
Subject(s): Legends; Secrets
Major character(s): Jack Duran, Tourist; Phoebe Auerbach,
Archaeologist; Dan Duran, Tourist
Time period(s): 2000s (2008)
Locale(s): Greece

Summary: Jack and Dan Duran team up with an archaeologist to reproduce one of the ceremonies used to invoke the magical powers of the Oracle in Greece. Disturbing sensations accompany the ceremony, and a short time later Dan disappears. Jack must then figure out what happened to his brother, and whether or not they have disturbed another Greek legend, the Furies.

Other books by the same author:
Dark Gold, 2007

Other books you might like:
Ramsey Campbell, *Ancient Images*, 1989
Katherine Kurtz, *Lammas Night*, 1983
Douglas Preston, *The Wheel of Darkness*, 2007
 Lincoln Child, co-author
James Rollins, *The Last Oracle*, 2008
Manda Scott, *The Crystal Skull*, 2008

526

JENNIFER ARMINTROUT

All Souls' Night
(Don Mills, Ontario: Mira, 2008)

Story type: Vampire Story; Romance
Series: Blood Ties. Book 4
Subject(s): Vampires; Romance
Major character(s): Carrie Ames, Doctor, Vampire; Nathan
 Grant, Vampire; Ziggy, Student
Time period(s): 2000s
Locale(s): Chicago, Illinois

Summary: Dr. Carrie Ames was turned into a vampire, but her personality remains the same and she chooses not to take innocent lives. With other like-minded vampires, she seeks to prevent the emergence of the Soul Eater, a powerful evil whose victory would change the balance of power in the world.

Other books by the same author:
Ashes to Ashes, 2008
Possession, 2007
The Turning, 2006

Other books you might like:
Keri Arthur, *Darkest Kiss*, 2008
Richelle Mead, *Succubus Dreams*, 2008
Adrian Phoenix, *In the Blood*, 2008
Maggie Shayne, *Edge of Twilight*, 2004
Jeanne C. Stein, *Legacy*, 2008

527

KELLEY ARMSTRONG

Living With the Dead

(New York: Bantam, 2008)

Story type: Serial Killer
Subject(s): Secrets; Werewolves
Major character(s): Robyn Peltier, Public Relations; Portia Kane, Celebrity; Hope Adams, Worker
Time period(s): 2000s (2008)
Locale(s): Los Angeles, California

Summary: Robyn Peltier is trying to make a new life for herself as a public relations consultant in Los Angeles when she stumbles into the secret of a hidden society living within our own. When her current client is murdered, she discovers that there is more going on than meets the eye, that supernatural creatures are real and that she is in danger of becoming their next victim.

Where it's reviewed:
Booklist, October 1, 2008, page 32
Library Journal, September 15, 2008, page 50
Publishers Weekly, September 1, 2008, page 37

Other books by the same author:
Personal Demon, 2008
No Humans Involved, 2007
Broken, 2006
Haunted, 2005
Stolen, 2003

Other books you might like:
Karen Chance, *Claimed by Shadow*, 2007
Nancy Collins, *Darkest Heart*, 2002
Yasmine Galenorn, *Changeling*, 2007
Laurell Hamilton, *Bloody Bones*, 1996
Anton Strout, *Dead to Me*, 2008

528

KERI ARTHUR

The Darkest Kiss

(New York: Bantam, 2008)

Story type: Vampire Story; Romance
Series: Riley Jensen. Book 6
Subject(s): Romance; Vampires
Major character(s): Riley Jensen, Werewolf; Quinn O'Connor, Vampire; Shadow, Werewolf
Time period(s): 2000s
Locale(s): Australia

Summary: Riley Jensen is a human, vampire, werewolf hybrid whose job is to track down criminals who use their supernatural powers for evil. Her current assignment is to track down a serial killer who specializes in high profile victims, but her job is hampered when a second killer's activities intersect her investigation, and her vampire ex-lover chooses that moment to come back into her life.

Where it's reviewed:
Publishers Weekly, March 31, 2008, page 44

Other books by the same author:
Dangerous Games, 2007
Tempting Evil, 2007
Embraced by Darkness, 2007
Kissing Sin, 2007
Full Moon Rising, 2006

Other books you might like:
Jaid Black, *One Dark Night*, 2004
Shannon Drake, *Dead by Dusk*, 2004
Laurell Hamilton, *Bloody Bones*, 1996
Marjorie M. Liu, *The Iron Hunt*, 2008
Maggie Shayne, *Edge of Twilight*, 2004

529

KERI ARTHUR

Destiny Kills

(New York: Bantam, 2008)

Story type: Mystery; Magic Conflict
Subject(s): Magic; Coming-of-Age
Major character(s): Destiny McCree, Mythical Creature, Fugitive; Trae Wilson, Thief, Fugitive
Time period(s): 2000s (2008)
Locale(s): Oregon

Summary: A thief and a partial amnesiac become uneasy partners as both are pursued by mysterious forces who seem intent upon killing them. They eventually learn their connection to a clique of evil sorcery, which they defeat because one of them is not entirely human and has supernatural power over the oceans.

Other books by the same author:
The Darkest Kiss, 2008
Dangerous Games, 2007
Kissing Sin, 2007
Embraced by Darkness, 2007
Full Moon Rising, 2006

Other books you might like:
Jenna Black, *Watchers in the Night*, 2006
Nina Kiriki Hoffman, *A Fistful of Sky*, 2002
Sherrilyn Kenyon, *Acheron*, 2008
Maggie Shayne, *Born in Twilight*, 1997
Carrie Vaughn, *Kitty and the Dead Man's Hand*, 2008

530

L.A. BANKS

Bite the Bullet

(New York: St Martins, 2008)

Story type: Werewolf Story; Mystery
Series: Crimson Moon. Book 2

Subject(s): Werewolves; Secrets
Major character(s): Sasha Trudeau, Military Personnel, Werewolf; Max Hunter, Military Personnel; Clarissa McGill, Military Personnel
Time period(s): 2000s (2008)
Locale(s): United States

Summary: A secret government agency has organized a special military unit to battle supernatural enemies. Among the soldiers recruited are some with paranormal powers of their own, including Sasha Trudeau, who is a werewolf. When a group of rogue creatures threatens to upset the balance of power, she and her comrades must track them down.

Other books by the same author:
Bad Blood, 2008
The Bitten, 2008
Cursed, 2007
The Damned, 2006
The Forsaken, 2006

Other books you might like:
Kelley Armstrong, *Bitten*, 2001
Karen Chance, *Touch the Dark*, 2006
Nancy Collins, *Wild Blood*, 1993
Robert R. McCammon, *The Wolf's Hour*, 1989
Carrie Vaughn, *Kitty and the Dead Man's Hand*, 2008

531

TOM BECKER

Lifeblood

(New York: Orchard Books, 2008)

Story type: Young Adult; Mystery
Series: Darkside. Book 2
Subject(s): Secrets
Major character(s): Jonathan Starling, Teenager; Elias Carnegie, Werewolf, Detective—Private; Humphrey Glanville, Criminal
Time period(s): 19th century
Locale(s): London, England

Summary: Jonathan Starling explores more of the Darkside, a part of Victorian London where the supernatural is real, in his quest to find his missing mother. Unfortunately, his plans are disrupted by a series of murders, and the continued interest of two men who don't necessarily wish him the best.

Where it's reviewed:
School Librarian, Summer 2008, page 56

Other books by the same author:
Darkside, 2008
Nighttrap, 2008

Other books you might like:
Nancy Collins, *Sunglasses After Dark*, 1989
Simon R. Green, *Something from the Nightside*, 2003
Laurell Hamilton, *Burnt Offerings*, 1998
Graham Masterton, *The Doorkeepers*, 2001
Stephenie Meyer, *Twilight*, 2005

532

JENNA BLACK

The Devil's Due

(New York: Bantam, 2008)

Story type: Ancient Evil Unleashed; Romance
Series: Morgan Kingsley. Book 2
Subject(s): Demons; Magic
Major character(s): Morgan Kingsley, Psychic; Lugh, Demon; Raphael, Demon
Time period(s): 2000s
Locale(s): Philadelphia, Pennsylvania

Summary: Morgan Kingsley is a professional exorcist in a world where sometimes demons are accepted as guests in the bodies of the living. She faces a terrifying challenge when one of these demonic entities takes a particular interest in her, poisoning her relationship with her boyfriend.

Other books by the same author:
Hungers of the Heart, 2008
The Devil You Know, 2008
Secrets in the Shadows, 2007
Shadows in the Soul, 2007
Watchers in the Night, 2006

Other books you might like:
Lori Herter, *Possession*, 1992
Peter James, *Possession*, 1988
Russ Martin, *The Possession of Jessica Young*, 1982
Richelle Mead, *Storm Born*, 2008
Roger Zelazny, *Lord Demon*, 1999
　　Jane Lindskold, co-author

533

KEALAN PATRICK BURKE

Master of the Moors

(Escanaba, MI: Necessary Evil, 2008)

Story type: Mystery; Ancient Evil Unleashed
Subject(s): Secrets; Coming-of-Age
Major character(s): Kate Mansfield, Teenager; Grady, Servant; Neil Mansfield, Teenager, Handicapped (blind)
Time period(s): 19th century
Locale(s): England

Summary: After a young woman is found dead on the moor, a man named Mansfield falls under the influence of a mysterious illness. His two children are terrified by his condition, and by the sudden outbreak of acts of violence on the moors that suggest an ancient evil has returned to claim new victims.

Other books by the same author:
Currency of Souls, 2007
Vessels, 2006
The Hides, 2005
The Turtle Boy, 2004

Other books you might like:
Les Daniels, *Yellow Fog*, 1988

Horror

Barbara Hambly, *Bride of the Rat God*, 1994
Brian Stableford, *The Werewolves of London*, 1990
Bram Stoker, *Lair of the White Worm*, 1911
Michael Talbot, *The Bog*, 1986

534

JACI BURTON

The Darkest Touch
(New York: Dell, 2008)

Story type: Ancient Evil Unleashed; Mystery
Series: Demon Hunters. Book 3
Subject(s): Demons; Secrets
Major character(s): Angelique Deveraux, Fugitive,
Archaeologist; Isabelle Deveraux, Fugitive,
Archaeologist; Ryder, Hunter
Time period(s): 2000s (2008)
Locale(s): Italy; Australia

Summary: Angelique and Isabelle Deveraux are both
archaeologists. When Isabelle disappears, Angelique is
on the run, protecting a mysterious magical artifact which
is sought after by the powers of good and evil. The
former is represented by Ryder, a professional demon
hunter, while the latter include a number of demonic
creatures intent upon her destruction.

Other books by the same author:
Taken by Sin, 2009
Nothing Personal, 2008
Hunting the Demon, 2007
Wild, Wicked, and Wanton, 2007
Surviving Demon Island, 2006

Other books you might like:
Alex Archer, *Destiny*, 2006
Jenna Black, *The Devil's Due*, 2008
Sherrilyn Kenyon, *One Silent Night*, 2008
Michael Marano, *Dawn Song*, 1998
Lilith Saintcrow, *To Hell and Back*, 2008

535

J.R. CAMPBELL , Editor
CHARLES PREPOLEC , Co-Editor

Gaslight Grimoire
(Calgary, Alberta: Edge, 2008)

Story type: Anthology
Subject(s): Short Stories; Mystery and Detective Stories
Major character(s): Sherlock Holmes, Detective—Private;
John Watson, Doctor

Summary: In each of these 11 original stories, Sherlock
Holmes investigates a case involving the paranormal,
haunted houses, alien creatures, spontaneous human
combustion, and other mysteries. The contributors
include Barbara Hambly, Chico Kidd, Barbara Roden,
Kim Newman, Chris Roberson, and others.

Other books you might like:
Loren D. Estleman, *Sherlock Holmes vs. Dracula*, 1978

Michael Kurland, *The Infernal Device*, 1979
Austin Mitchelson, *Hellbirds*, 1976
Nicholas Utechin, co-author
Ralph Vaughan, *Sherlock Holmes and the Coils of Time*,
2005
Manly Wade Wellman, *Sherlock Holmes' War of the
Worlds*, 1975
Wade Wellman, co-author

536

RAMSEY CAMPBELL

Inconsequential Tales
(New York: Hippocampus, 2008)

Story type: Collection
Subject(s): Short Stories

Summary: The twenty five stories in this collection were
previously published over the three decades of the
author's career. Campbell tends to write quieter horror
stories not dependent on explicit violence. Some of these
stories were later rewritten and published under different
titles.

Other books by the same author:
The Grin of the Dark, 2008
The Darkest Part of the Woods, 2002
Ghosts and Grisly Things, 2000
The Count of Eleven, 1991
Ancient Images, 1989

Other books you might like:
Charles L. Grant, *Tales from the Nightside*, 1981
Stephen King, *Nightmares and Dreamscapes*, 1993
Thomas F. Monteleone, *Fearful Symmetries*, 2004
David Schow, *Zombie Jam*, 2003
F. Paul Wilson, *Aftershock and Others*, 2009

537

ELLEN DATLOW , Editor
KELLY LINK , Co-Editor
GAVIN J. GRANT , Co-Editor

The Year's Best Fantasy and
Horror 2008
(New York: St. Martin's, 2008)

Story type: Anthology
Subject(s): Short Stories

Summary: The 21st volume in this annual collection of
horror and fantasy stories is drawn from major publishers and the small press, and many titles from publications not normally associated with the field. An extensive
list of honorable mentions and a lengthy commentary on
the state of the genre is also included. Contributors
include M. Rickert, Karen Joy Fowler, Elizabeth Hand,
William Browning Spencer, Joyce Carol Oates, and
others.

Where it's reviewed:
Publishers Weekly, August 25, 2008, page 56

Other books by the same author:
Inferno, 2007
The Dark, 2003
Lethal Kisses, 1996
Twists of the Tale, 1996
Blood Is Not Enough, 1989

Other books you might like:
Karen Joy Fowler, *The Sweetheart Season*, 1996
Elizabeth Hand, *Black Light*, 1999
Joyce Carol Oates, *The Museum of Dr. Moses*, 2007
M. Rickert, *Map of Dreams*, 2006
William Browning Spencer, *The Ocean and All Its Devices*, 2006

538

MELISSA DE LA CRUZ

Revelations

(New York: Hyperion, 2008)

Story type: Vampire Story; Young Adult
Series: Blue Bloods. Book 3
Subject(s): Vampires
Major character(s): Schuyler Van Alen, Teenager, Vampire; Mimi Force, Wealthy; Jack Force, Teenager
Time period(s): 2000s (2008)
Locale(s): United States; Argentina

Summary: Schuyler Van Alen is only half vampire and as such is considered suspect by the pure bloods. When a crisis is precipitated in Argentina, the vampires discover that they need her help if they are to win the ensuing battle. At the same time, Schuyler becomes more romantically attached to a young man whom she is supposedly forbidden to bond with.

Other books by the same author:
Masquerade, 2007
Blue Bloods, 2006

Other books you might like:
Carmen Adams, *The Band*, 1994
Amelia Atwater-Rhodes, *Demon in My View*, 2000
P.C. Cast, *Marked*, 2007
   Kristin Cast, co-author
Cameron Dokey, *Eternally Yours*, 1994
L.J. Smith, *The Awakening*, 1991

539

JOCELYN DRAKE

Nightwalker

(New York: Eos, 2008)

Story type: Psychic Powers; Vampire Story
Series: Dark Days. Book 1
Subject(s): Psychic Powers; Secrets
Major character(s): Mira, Psychic; Danaus, Vampire Hunter; Ryan, Warlock

Time period(s): 2000s (2008)
Locale(s): United States

Summary: Mira is a nightwalker, with a psychic ability to control fire which she uses to battle evil supernatural creatures. Centuries old, she is part of a secret organization that looks after the world, but her latest enemy is a human, a vampire hunter. First novel.

Other books you might like:
Rachel Caine, *Chill Factor*, 2004
Karen Chance, *Midnight's Daughter*, 2008
Kat Richardson, *Poltergeist*, 2007
Lilith Saintcrow, *Night Shift*, 2008
Rob Thurman, *Nightlife*, 2006

540

DORANNA DURGIN

Revenge

(New York: Pocket Star, 2008)

Story type: Ghost Story; Mystery
Series: Ghost Whisperer. Book 1
Subject(s): Ghosts; Revenge
Major character(s): Melinda Gordon, Businesswoman, Psychic; Gordon Reese, Spirit; Craig Lusak, Lawyer
Time period(s): 2000s (2008)
Locale(s): Grandview, New York

Summary: Melinda Gordon is one of those rare individuals who can communicate with ghosts. When she sees the ghost of a murdered man haunting someone he believes responsible for his death, she intervenes and must solve the mystery and discover who the real murderer is before a terrible injustice is done.

Other books by the same author:
Dark Debts, 2003
Impressions, 2003
Changespell Legacy, 2002
A Feral Darkness, 2001
Wolverine's Daughter, 2000

Other books you might like:
Owen Brookes, *Deadly Communion*, 1984
Robert C. Dennis, *Conversations with a Corpse*, 1974
Jack Ellis, *Seeing Eye*, 1995
H.B. Gilmour, *The Eyes of Laura Mars*, 1978
Dean R. Koontz, *The Vision*, 1977

541

C.M. EDDY JR.

The Loved Dead and Other Tales

(Narragansett, RI: Fenham, 2008)

Story type: Collection
Subject(s): Short Stories

Summary: This is a collection of reprints of stories published in *Weird Tales* and other pulp magazines from the 1930s. Eddy wrote in a style similar to that of H.P. Lovecraft and other more successful writers of that era. The title story is one of his best tales.

Other books by the same author:
Erased from Exile, 1976
Exit into Eternity, 1973

Other books you might like:
Robert Bloch, *Hell on Earth*, 2000
Robert E. Howard, *Nameless Cults*, 2001
Frank Belknap Long, *The Dark Beasts*, 1964
H.P. Lovecraft, *Waking Up Screaming*, 2003
Howard Wandrei, *The Eerie Mr. Murphy*, 2003

542

PAUL FINCH

Ghost Realm

(Ashcroft, British Columbia: Ash-Tree, 2008)

Story type: Collection
Subject(s): Short Stories

Summary: The author presents nine stories of supernatural horror set in various parts of the British Isles. Each of the stories suggests that some legend may be more than just a fairy tale. The protagonists of the stories discover that the secrets of the past have the power to affect those living in the present.

Other books by the same author:
Stains, 2007
Darker Ages, 2004
Cape Wrath, 2002
Aftershocks, 2001
The Shadows Beneath, 2000

Other books you might like:
Robert Aickman, *Collected Strange Stories*, 1999
Algernon Blackwood, *Ancient Sorceries and Other Stories*, 1927
Robert Bloch, *The Early Fears*, 1993
M.R. James, *Count Magnus and Other Ghost Stories*, 2005
Arthur Machen, *The Bowmen and Other Legends of War*, 2005

543

R. PATRICK GATES

Nowhere to Hide

(New York: Pinnacle, 2008)

Story type: Serial Killer; Coming-of-Age
Subject(s): Serial Killers; Murder
Major character(s): Billy Teags, Child; Donald Desmond, Child; William Teags, Serial Killer
Time period(s): 2000s (2008)
Locale(s): United States

Summary: Billy Teags and his friends are nervous about the existence of the Monster, a serial killer who specializes in murdering children. The home which should provide refuge for Billy is in fact the focus of a terrible danger that will explode in deadly violence.

Other books by the same author:
Grimm Reapings, 2006
The Prison, 2004
Grimm Memorials, 1990
Fear, 1988

Other books you might like:
Thomas Harris, *Red Dragon*, 1981
Edward Lee, *Coven*, 1991
Graham Masterton, *A Terrible Beauty*, 2003
John Saul, *Black Lightning*, 1995
Michael Slade, *Ghoul*, 1989

544

ALISON GAYLIN

Heartless

(New York: Obsidian, 2008)

Story type: Serial Killer; Psychic Powers
Subject(s): Mystery; Psychic Powers
Major character(s): Zoe Greene, Journalist; Warren Clark, Actor; Vanessa St. James, Writer
Time period(s): 2000s
Locale(s): Mexico

Summary: Zoe Greene runs off to Mexico with her charming actor boyfriend, Warren Clark, unaware that he is a member of a bizarre cult led by a man with genuine psychic powers. When she discovers that Warren is connected to a ritual murder and mutilation, Zoe begins to have second thoughts, then learns that he intends to use her to make another ritual sacrifice.

Where it's reviewed:
Library Journal, September 1, 2008, page 116
Publishers Weekly, July 21, 2008, page 140

Other books by the same author:
Trashed, 2007
Hide Your Eyes, 2005
You Kill Me, 2005

Other books you might like:
Charles De Lint, *Mulengro*, 1985
Samuel Key, *From a Whisper to a Scream*, 1992
Mercedes Lackey, *Burning Water*, 1989
John Saul, *Black Lightning*, 1995
Michael Slade, *Cut-Throat*, 1992

545

CHRIS MARIE GREEN

Break of Dawn

(New York: Ace, 2008)

Story type: Vampire Story; Mystery
Series: Vampire Babylon. Book 3
Subject(s): Vampires; Secrets
Major character(s): Dawn Madison, Entertainer, Stuntman; Matt Lonigan, Detective—Private; Eva Claremont, Vampire
Time period(s): 2000s

Locale(s): Los Angeles, California

Summary: Dawn Madison is still determined to discover what happened to her father, who stumbled into the secret world of vampires living among us. With her private detective boyfriend, she finds a fresh layer of mystery that could lead her to the same fate as befell the one she seeks.

Other books by the same author:
Midnight Rising, 2008
Night Rising, 2007

Other books you might like:
Jenna Black, *Shadows on the Soul*, 2007
Shannon Drake, *Deep Midnight*, 2001
Karen Marie Moning, *Darkfever*, 2006
Maggie Shayne, *Edge of Twilight*, 2004
Rob Thurman, *Madhouse*, 2008

546

MARTIN H. GREENBERG, Editor
DANIEL M. HOYT, Co-Editor

Better Off Undead

(New York: DAW, 2008)

Story type: Anthology
Subject(s): Short Stories

Summary: The 18 original stories in this collection all make use of familiar themes from horror and supernatural fiction. In most cases, however, they turn these ideas on their head and invoke humor rather than horror. The contributors include Chelsea Quinn Yarbro, Esther Friesner, Alan Dean Foster, Devon Monk, S.M. Stirling, and others.

Other books by the same author:
Lighthouse Hauntings, 2000 (Charles G. Waugh, co-editor)
Children of the Night, 1999
Black Cats and Broken Mirrors, 1998 (John Helfers, co-editor)
Celebrity Vampires, 1995
Devil Worshippers, 1990 (Charles G. Waugh, co-editor)

Other books you might like:
Esther Friesner, *Demon Blues*, 1989
Craig Shaw Gardner, *Bride of the Slime Monster*, 1990
Andrew Harman, *101 Damnations*, 1995
Terry Pratchett, *Good Omens*, 1990
     Neil Gaiman, co-author
William Mark Simmons, *Habeas Corpses*, 2005

547

ROBERT GREENBERGER

The Golden Army

(Milwaukee, OR: Dark Horse, 2008)

Story type: Magic Conflict; Alternate Universe
Series: Hellboy

Subject(s): Magic; Apocalypse
Major character(s): Hellboy, Mythical Creature; Liz Sherman, Psychic; Abe Sapien, Mythical Creature
Time period(s): 2000s
Locale(s): United States; Alternate Universe

Summary: The arrangement between our world and an alternate reality where mystical creatures exist is breaking down. A new dictator has come to power there and has raised an army with which he plans to suppress both realities, but Hellboy and his friends have other plans. This novel is based on the movie.

Other books by the same author:
Doors into Chaos, 2001
The Romulan Stratagem, 1995

Other books you might like:
Christopher Golden, *The Lost Army*, 1997
Brian Hodge, *On Earth As It Is in Hell*, 2005
Tim Lebbon, *Unnatural Selection*, 2006
Graham Masterton, *Night Wars*, 2006
Yvonne Navarro, *Hellboy*, 2004

548

JAMIE LEIGH HANSEN

Cursed

(New York: Tor, 2009)

Story type: Romance; Psychic Powers
Subject(s): Romance; Psychic Powers
Major character(s): Alex Foster, Worker, Psychic; Beth Ann Raines, Care Giver; Maeve, Mythical Creature
Time period(s): 2000s
Locale(s): Spokane, Washington

Summary: Alex has vivid dreams in which he knows a woman named Beth Ann Raines. Elsewhere, the actual Beth Ann has returned to her family home, where she is threatened by a demonic force. Alex must learn who she is and find a way to protect her from creatures that have no physical bodies.

Other books by the same author:
Betrayed, 2008

Other books you might like:
Robert C. Dennis, *The Sweat of Fear*, 1973
H.B. Gilmour, *The Eyes of Laura Mars*, 1978
Dean R. Koontz, *The Face of Fear*, 1977
John Miglis, *Killing Eyes*, 1984
John Tigges, *Evil Dreams*, 1986

549

KIM HARRISON, Editor

Hotter Than Hell

(New York: Harper, 2008)

Story type: Anthology
Subject(s): Short Stories

Summary: This is a collection of original stories of the supernatural in the contemporary world. The themes tend to be traditional ones including vampires and shape changing creatures and there is a strong element of romance in many of them. The contributors include Keri Arthur, Tanya Huff, Susan Krinard, Lilith Saintcrow, Carrie Vaughn, and others.

Other books by the same author:
For a Few Demons More, 2007
A Fistful of Charms, 2006
Every Which Way But Dead, 2005
Dead Man Walking, 2004
The Good, the Bad, and the Undead, 2004

Other books you might like:
Keri Arthur, *Dangerous Games*, 2007
Tanya Huff, *Blood Lines*, 1991
Susan Krinard, *Chasing Midnight*, 2007
Lilith Saintcrow, *To Hell and Back*, 2008
Carrie Vaughn, *Kitty and the Dead Man's Hand*, 2008

550

RAVEN HART

The Vampire's Betrayal

(New York: Ballantine, 2008)

Story type: Vampire Story; Romance
Series: Savannah Vampire. Book 4
Subject(s): Vampires; Romance
Major character(s): William Cuyler Thorne, Vampire; Jack McShane, Vampire; Connie Jones, Police Officer
Time period(s): 2000s (2008)
Locale(s): Savannah, Georgia

Summary: Jack McShane and William Thorne are members of a group of benevolent vampires who secretly guard the human race against supernatural enemies. The possible return of a violent Mayan goddess to the world is the focus of their efforts in this installment in the series, complicated by the fact that McShane's love interest is a police officer who believes all vampires are evil.

Other books by the same author:
The Vampire's Revenge, 2009
The Vampire's Kiss, 2007
The Vampire's Secret, 2007
The Vampire's Seduction, 2006

Other books you might like:
Laurell Hamilton, *The Lunatic Cafe*, 1995
Angela Knight, *Master of the Night*, 2004
Maggie Shayne, *Demon's Kiss*, 2007
Susan Sizemore, *Masters of Darkness*, 2006
Susan Squires, *One with the Night*, 2007

551

BARB HENDEE

Blood Memories

(New York: Roc, 2008)

Story type: Vampire Story; Mystery
Subject(s): Vampires; Secrets

Major character(s): Eleisha Clevon, Vampire; Margaritte Latour, Vampire; Wade Sheffield, Police Officer, Telepath
Time period(s): 2000s
Locale(s): Portland, Oregon

Summary: Eleisha Clevon is startled when one of her friends, a fellow vampire, commits suicide. She is even more rattled when the police discover a stack of bodies in the dead vampire's basement, and launch a wide-ranging investigation. The situation gets even more dangerous when she finds out that one of the two policemen leading the effort can read minds.

Other books by the same author:
Child of a Dead God, 2008 (J.C. Hendee, co-author)
Rebel Fay, 2007 (J.C. Hendee, co-author)
Sister of the Dead, 2005 (J.C. Hendee, co-author)
Thief of Lives, 2004 (J.C. Hendee, co-author)
Dhampir, 2003 (J.C. Hendee, co-author)

Other books you might like:
L.A. Banks, *The Forsaken*, 2006
Ray Garton, *Lot Lizards*, 1991
Tom Holland, *Slave of My Thirst*, 1996
Anne Rice, *Interview with the Vampire*, 1976
Whitley Strieber, *The Hunger*, 1981

552

MARK P. HENDERSON

Rope Trick: Thirteen Strange Tales

(Ashcroft, British Columbia: Ash-Tree, 2008)

Story type: Collection
Subject(s): Short Stories

Summary: These thirteen original stories tend toward the literary side. Most of the conflict arises out of interactions among the various characters and at times the supernatural content is almost an afterthought. "Rope Trick" and "Disappearing Act" are particularly effective stories.

Other books you might like:
Stephen Dedman, *Never Seen by Waking Eyes*, 2005
Charles L. Grant, *A Glow of Candles and Other Stories*, 1981
Brian Hodge, *Falling Idols*, 1998
Alan Ryan, *Quadriphobia*, 1986
Peter Straub, *Houses Without Doors*, 1990

553

RITA HERRON

Insatiable Desire

(New York: Grand Central, 2008)

Story type: Psychic Powers; Mystery
Series: Demonborn. Book 1
Subject(s): Psychic Powers; Romance
Major character(s): Clarissa King, Psychic; Vincent Valtrez, FBI Agent; Waller, Police Officer

Time period(s): 2000s (2008)
Locale(s): Eerie, Tennessee

Summary: A psychic and a skeptical FBI agent investigate a series of murders of young women in a small town in Tennessee. Their awakening romantic feelings for one another are tempered by his unwillingness to accept her visions of a supernatural force making use of the killer.

Where it's reviewed:
Publishers Weekly, July 14, 2008, page 49

Other books by the same author:
In the Flesh, 2008
Don't Say a Word, 2007
Say You Love Me, 2007
In a Heartbeat, 2006
A Breath Away, 2005

Other books you might like:
Robert C. Dennis, *The Sweat of Fear*, 1973
Stephen Gresham, *Midnight Boy*, 1987
Deborah Leblanc, *Water Witch*, 2008
Richard Matheson, *A Stir of Echoes*, 1958
T.M. Wright, *The Place*, 1990

554

SIMON HOLT

The Devouring

(New York: Little, Brown, 2008)

Story type: Young Adult; Ancient Evil Unleashed
Subject(s): Demons
Major character(s): Regina Halloway, Teenager; Henry Halloway, Child; Aaron Cole, Teenager
Time period(s): 2000s
Locale(s): United States

Summary: A teenaged girl finds a mysterious journal that talks about bodiless creatures called the Vours which can seize control of the bodies of the living. Then some of the children in the neighborhood, including her own brother, begin to act strangely and she realizes that she is the only one who knows the secret. First novel.

Where it's reviewed:
Kliatt, September 28, 2008, page 13

Other books you might like:
Amelia Atwater-Rhodes, *Demon in My View*, 2000
Rachel Caine, *Midnight Eve*, 2007
Steven Charles, *Nightmare Session*, 1986
Simon Lake, *Someone's Watching*, 1993
Joseph Locke, *Kiss of Death*, 1992

555

CHARLIE HUSTON

Every Last Drop

(New York: Del Rey, 2008)

Story type: Vampire Story; Mystery
Series: Joe Pitt. Book 4

Subject(s): Vampires; Secrets
Major character(s): Joe Pitt, Detective—Private, Vampire; Dexter Predo, Vampire, Leader
Time period(s): 2000s
Locale(s): New York, New York

Summary: A relatively benevolent vampire who once worked as a private investigator is now an outcast, caught between the warring clans of vampires that secretly live among human beings. He is offered a chance to be accepted by one clan, but only if he infiltrates the other and derails a plot to "cure" them of their vampiric disease.

Where it's reviewed:
Booklist, September 15, 2008, page 28

Other books by the same author:
Half the Blood of Brooklyn, 2007
No Dominion, 2006
Already Dead, 2005

Other books you might like:
Vincent Courtney, *Harvest of Blood*, 1992
P.N. Elrod, *Cold Streets*, 2003
Tanya Huff, *Blood Debt*, 1997
Lee Killough, *Bloodwalk*, 1997
Adrian Phoenix, *A Rush of Wings*, 2007

556

ANTHONY IZZO

The Dark Ones

(New York: Pinnacle, 2008)

Story type: Ancient Evil Unleashed; Reanimated Dead
Subject(s): Secrets; Coming-of-Age
Major character(s): Laura Pennington, Doctor; David Dresser, Worker; Lars Engel, Reanimated Dead
Time period(s): 2000s
Locale(s): Buffalo, New York

Summary: Lars Engel, a devoted servant of Satan, has returned from the dead. That attracts the attention of the Guardians, a secret group dedicated to fighting evil who can draw upon mystical forces to battle their enemies. The daughter of one of the Guardians is unaware of her heritage until a crisis brings her abilities to the surface.

Where it's reviewed:
Publishers Weekly, May 5, 2008, page 51

Other books by the same author:
Evil Harvest, 2007
Cruel Winter, 2005

Other books you might like:
Clive Barker, *The Damnation Game*, 1985
Stephen King, *Desperation*, 1996
Graham Masterton, *Night Wars*, 2006
Mary SanGiovanni, *Found You*, 2008
Peter Saxon, *The Curse of Rathlaw*, 1968

Horror

557

SIMON JANUS

The Scrubs

(Anaheim, CA: Bad Moon, 2008)

Story type: Science Fiction; Alternate Universe
Subject(s): Scientific Experiments; Prisoners and Prisons
Major character(s): Keeler, Prisoner; O'Keefe, Government Official; Davey, Child
Time period(s): 2000s
Locale(s): United States

Summary: Keeler unwisely agrees to participate in a scientific experiment while imprisoned under the wardenship of O'Keefe, a power hungry man obsessed with the psychic ability of another of his charges, a man who can literally create entranceways into other worlds. The other worlds are horribly dangerous, however, and a young boy is trapped in one of them.

Other books you might like:

Jonathan Carroll, *The Land of Laughs*, 1980
Rick Hautala, *Beyond the Shroud*, 1996
Edward Lee, *House Infernal*, 2007
Graham Masterton, *The Doorkeepers*, 2001
F. Paul Wilson, *Gateways*, 2003

558

CAROLYN JEWEL

My Wicked Enemy

(New York: Forever, 2008)

Story type: Vampire Story; Romance
Subject(s): Vampires; Magic
Major character(s): Carson Philips, Witch; Alvaro Magellan, Sorcerer; Nikodemus, Leader
Time period(s): 2000s
Locale(s): New York, New York

Summary: Carson Philips is a witch who has recently escaped her bondage to Alvaro Magellan, a power-hungry sorcerer whose activities are concealed from the contemporary world. Nikodemus is a man with supernatural powers who might be able to help her avoid recapture, but only if she decides she can trust him.

Other books by the same author:

A Darker Crimson, 2005
Lord Ruin, 2002

Other books you might like:

Cameron Dean, *Eternal Hunger*, 2007
Sherrilyn Kenyon, *Dark Side of the Moon*, 2006
Karen Marie Moning, *Bloodfever*, 2006
Kat Richardson, *Greywalker*, 2006
Maggie Shayne, *Angel's Pain*, 2008

559

STEPHEN JONES , Editor

The Mammoth Book of Best New Horror 19

(Philadelphia: Running Press, 2008)

Story type: Anthology
Subject(s): Short Stories

Summary: This installment in this long running best of the year series covers fiction published in 2007. The editor draws on a variety of sources including several published in England. The contributors include Neil Gaiman, Ramsey Campbell, Christopher Fowler, Joe Hill, Tom Piccirilli, Joe Lansdale, and others.

Other books by the same author:

The Mammoth Book of New Terror, 2004
The Mammoth Book of Vampires, 2004
The Mammoth Book of Vampire Stories by Women, 2001
The Mammoth Book of Frankenstein, 1994
The Mammoth Book of Terror, 1991

Other books you might like:

Ramsey Campbell, *Ghosts and Grisly Things*, 2000
Christopher Fowler, *The Bureau of Lost Souls*, 1989
Joe Hill, *20th Century Ghosts*, 2006
Joe R. Lansdale, *The Gods of the Razor*, 2007
Tom Piccirilli, *Bastards of Alchemy*, 2002

560

STACIA KANE

Personal Demons

(Rockville, MD: Juno, 2008)

Story type: Possession; Mystery
Subject(s): Demons; Monsters
Major character(s): Megan Chase, Psychic, Entertainer; Greyson Dante, Agent; Brian Stone, Journalist
Time period(s): 2000s (2008)
Locale(s): United States

Summary: Megan Chase is a radio therapist with psychic powers who tries to free people from what she thinks are metaphorical personal demons. What she doesn't realize is that she may be the only person on Earth who is not possessed by a genuine personal demon, and that makes her a powerful tool in a hidden battle. First novel.

Other books you might like:

Yasmine Galenorn, *Dragon Wytch*, 2008
Thomas F. Monteleone, *Eyes of the Virgin*, 2002
Dan Simmons, *Carrion Comfort*, 1989
Lisa Tuttle, *Familiar Spirit*, 1983
Roger Zelazny, *Lord Demon*, 1999
    Jane Lindskold, co-author

561

NATE KENYON

The Reach

(New York: Leisure, 2008)

Story type: Psychic Powers; Mystery
Subject(s): Psychic Powers; Scientific Experiments
Major character(s): Jess Chambers, Student; Evan Wasserman, Psychologist; Sarah, Patient
Time period(s): 2000s
Locale(s): Boston, Massachusetts

Summary: Jess Chambers is a psychology student who is asked to help with the diagnosis of a young girl named Sarah, who seems to have extraordinary mental powers. She feels that the child is being mistreated by the institution where she's held, but that's because she is unaware of the danger that Sarah represents.

Other books by the same author:
Bloodstone, 2005

Other books you might like:
John Farris, *The Fury*, 1976
Simon Janus, *The Scrubs*, 2008
Stephen King, *Firestarter*, 1980
Ursula K. Le Guin, *The Lathe of Heaven*, 1971
Frank M. Robinson, *Waiting*, 1999

562

SHERRILYN KENYON

Acheron

(New York: St Martins, 2008)

Story type: Apocalyptic Horror; Ancient Evil Unleashed
Series: Dark Hunter. Book 14
Subject(s): Immortality; Reincarnation
Major character(s): Acheron, Deity; Ryssa, Royalty; Tory Kafieri, Professor
Time period(s): 2000s (2008); Indeterminate Past
Locale(s): Greece; Tennessee

Summary: Acheron was a minor god who was placed in a immortal but human body and charged with protecting the human race from supernatural evil. In the present day, he encounters a woman who may expose his secrets. Most of this novel is actually a prequel to the earlier books in the series, describing Acheron's conversion in ancient Greece.

Other books by the same author:
Devil May Cry, 2007
Dark Side of the Moon, 2006
Unleash the Night, 2006
Kiss of the Night, 2004
Night Pleasures, 2002

Other books you might like:
Nancy Holder, *Measure of a Man*, 1997
Karen Marie Moning, *Darkfever*, 2006
Irene Radford, *Guardian of the Trust*, 2000
Jennifer Roberson, *Scotland the Brave*, 1996

Roger Zelazny, *Lord Demon*, 1999
Jane Lindskold, co-author

563

SHERRILYN KENYON

One Silent Night

(New York: St Martins, 2008)

Story type: Vampire Story; Ancient Evil Unleashed
Series: Dark Hunter. Book 16
Subject(s): Vampires; Secrets
Major character(s): Stryker, Mythical Creature (Demigod); Zephyra, Immortal; Hades, Deity
Time period(s): 2000s (2008)
Locale(s): United States; Mythical Place

Summary: Stryker is a demigod who fancies himself the lord of evil. He has raised an army of vampires and demons with which to confront his enemies and destroy them, including most of the human race. What he doesn't count on is the intervention of his ex-wife, Zephyra, immortal and powerful in her own right.

Other books by the same author:
Acheron, 2008
Devil May Cry, 2007
Dark Side of the Moon, 2006
Unleash the Night, 2006
Kiss of the Night, 2004

Other books you might like:
Jenna Black, *The Devil You Know*, 2008
Jaci Burton, *Hunting the Demon*, 2007
Nancy Holder, *Blood and Fog*, 2003
Marjorie M. Liu, *The Iron Hunt*, 2008
Lilith Saintcrow, *Working for the Devil*, 2006

564

J. ROBERT KING

The Shadow of Reichenbach Falls

(New York: Forge, 2008)

Story type: Possession; Historical/Victorian
Subject(s): Murder; Memory Loss
Major character(s): Sherlock Holmes, Detective—Private, Amnesiac; Thomas Carnacki, Student—College, Detective—Private; James Moriarty, Criminal, Professor
Time period(s): 19th century
Locale(s): England; Switzerland

Summary: Both Sherlock Holmes and Professor Moriarty survived their supposedly fatal fall from Reichenbach Falls. Holmes has amnesia and Moriarty is possessed by a demonic force. A small group of friends including an occult investigator attempt to restore Holmes' memory and deal with the supernatural entity.

Where it's reviewed:
Booklist, June 1, 2008, page 64
Publishers Weekly, May 5, 2008, page 47

Horror

Other books by the same author:
Legions, 2003
Onslaught, 2002
Apocalypse, 2001
Lancelot Du Lethe, 2001
Invasion, 2000

Other books you might like:
Loren D. Estleman, *Sherlock Holmes vs. Dracula*, 1978
Robert Lee Hall, *Exit Sherlock Holmes*, 1977
Michael Kurland, *The Infernal Device*, 1979
Austin Mitchelson, *Hellbirds*, 1976
     Nicholas Utechin, co-author
Ralph Vaughn, *Sherlock Holmes and the Terror Out of Time*, 2002

565

STEPHEN KING

Just After Sunset

(New York: Scribner, 2008)

Story type: Collection
Subject(s): Short Stories

Summary: The fourteen stories in this collection are all previously uncollected and are largely more recent work. King's themes include demonic cats, magical exercise machines, strange hitchhikers, unusual mental powers, and other fantastic elements.

Where it's reviewed:
Booklist, September 15, 2008, page 5
Library Journal, September 15, 2008, page 51
New York Times Book Review, November 23, 2008, page 17

Other books by the same author:
Duma Key, 2008
Cell, 2006
Lisey's Story, 2006
Bag of Bones, 1998
The Shining, 1977

Other books you might like:
Charles Beaumont, *The Howling Man*, 1992
Ray Bradbury, *Bradbury Stories*, 2003
T.E.D. Klein, *Dark Gods*, 1985
Richard Matheson, *Button, Button*, 2008
William F. Nolan, *Nightshadows*, 2008

566

DEBORAH LEBLANC

Water Witch

(New York: Leisure, 2008)

Story type: Child-in-Peril; Mystery
Subject(s): Magic; Psychic Powers
Major character(s): Dunny Pollock, Writer; Angelle Pollock, Teacher; Nicky Strahan, Child
Time period(s): 2000s (2008)

Locale(s): Louisiana

Summary: Dunny Pollock has always hidden her unusual psychic powers, but she is forced to make use of them when her sister calls her to Louisiana to help in the search for some missing children. Dunny senses something more than simple kidnapping or even murder, and uncovers a plot to unleash malevolent supernatural powers into the world.

Other books by the same author:
Morbid Curiosity, 2007
A House Divided, 2006
Grave Intent, 2005
Family Inheritance, 2004

Other books you might like:
Ken Eulo, *Nocturnal*, 1983
Charles L. Grant, *In a Dark Dream*, 1989
Rick Hautala, *Moonbog*, 1982
James Herbert, *Moon*, 1985
Mary Stewart, *Touch Not the Cat*, 1976

567

EDWARD LEE

Brides of the Impaler

(New York: Leisure, 2008)

Story type: Ancient Evil Unleashed; Erotic Horror
Subject(s): Erotica; Supernatural
Major character(s): Cristina Nichols, Artist; Paul Nasher, Lawyer; Jess Franklin, Lawyer
Time period(s): 2000s
Locale(s): New York, New York

Summary: Artifacts related to Vlad Tepes are unearthed and moved to New York City. There two couples fall under the influence of a supernatural, erotic force while around them, a group of homeless women are bound to service with a spectral nun. The situation grows more frightening as impaled bodies begin appearing around the city.

Other books by the same author:
House Infernal, 2007
Flesh Gothic, 2005
The Backwoods, 2005
Messenger, 2004
City Infernal, 2001

Other books you might like:
Don Davis, *Sins of the Flesh*, 1989
     Jay Davis, co-author
Charles L. Grant, *The Hour of the Oxrun Dead*, 1977
Daniel Rhodes, *Next, After Lucifer*, 1987
John Shirley, *Cellars*, 1982
John Skipp, *The Scream*, 1988
     Craig Spector, co-author

568

KIM LENOX

Night Falls Darkly

(New York: Signet, 2008)

Story type: Immortality; Historical/Victorian
Series: Shadow Guards. Book 1
Subject(s): Immortality; Secrets
Major character(s): Elena Whitney, Amnesiac; Archer Black, Immortal; Selene Pavlenko, Noblewoman
Time period(s): 1880s (1887)
Locale(s): London, England

Summary: Elena Whitney is a young woman who has very little memory of her own past. She is the ward of Archer Black, a mysterious nobleman who, unbeknownst to her, is an immortal and a member of the Shadow Guard, which protects humanity from supernatural evil. In their first adventure, they must solve the Jack the Ripper murders. First novel.

Where it's reviewed:
Publishers Weekly, August 18, 2008, page 50

Other books you might like:
Karl Alexander, *Time After Time*, 1979
Virginia Baker, *Jack Knife*, 2007
Robert Bloch, *Night of the Ripper*, 1984
Charles De Lint, *Mulengro*, 1985
Marie Bellow Lowndes, *The Lodger*, 1913

569

BENTLEY LITTLE

The Academy

(New York: Signet, 2008)

Story type: Small Town Horror; Satire
Subject(s): Secrets; Schools
Major character(s): Jody Hawkes, Principal; Linda, Teacher; Brad Becker, Student
Time period(s): 2000s (2008)
Locale(s): United States

Summary: The staff of a public school are startled when their principal announces that they will become a charter school instead. They are dismayed when a new set of rigid rules are put in place, and students begin disappearing. At the same time, a mysterious power influences the actions of some of the staff and parents.

Where it's reviewed:
Publishers Weekly, June 2, 2008, page 34

Other books by the same author:
The Vanishing, 2007
The Burning, 2006
Dispatch, 2005
The Resort, 2004
The Policy, 2003

Other books you might like:
Steven Charles, *Nightmare Session*, 1986
Lee Duigon, *Schoolhouse*, 1988

Ed Kelleher, *The School*, 1988
  Harriet Vidal, co-author
Nicholas Pine, *Night School*, 1994
John Saul, *The Devil's Labyrinth*, 2007

570

MARGARET LUCKE

House of Whispers

(Rockville, MD: Juno, 2008)

Story type: Mystery; Paranormal
Series: Supernatural Properties. Book 1
Subject(s): Mystery; Secrets
Major character(s): Claire Scanlan, Real Estate Agent, Psychic; Ben Grant, Businessman; Avery Collier, Real Estate Agent
Time period(s): 2000s
Locale(s): California

Summary: Claire Scanlan is trying to make a new career for herself as a real estate agent when she is assigned to sell a house where an unsolved murder took place. Shortly after her first visit, she begins to acquire knowledge about the murder supernaturally and realizes that she is being compelled to solve the mystery. Her chief suspect, unfortunately, is a man to whom she is increasingly attracted.

Other books by the same author:
A Relative Stranger, 1991

Other books you might like:
Ken Eulo, *Nocturnal*, 1983
Charles L. Grant, *In a Dark Dream*, 1989
Dean R. Koontz, *Hideaway*, 1992
Richard Matheson, *A Stir of Echoes*, 1958
Mary Stewart, *Touch Not the Cat*, 1976

571

BRIAN LUMLEY

The Taint and Other Novellas

(Nottingham, United Kingdom: Solaris, 2008)

Story type: Collection
Subject(s): Short Stories

Summary: All seven of the novellas in this collection make use of the Cthulhu Mythos backdrop created by Howard Phillips Lovecraft, but the stories are otherwise unrelated. They deal with superhuman creatures inimical to humanity. All have been previously published, most of them early in the author's career.

Where it's reviewed:
Booklist, September 1, 2008, page 67
Publishers Weekly, August 13, 2008, page 49

Other books by the same author:
Brian Lumley's Freaks, 2004
Beneath the Moors and Darker Places, 2002
Necroscope Avengers, 2001
The Whisperer and Other Voices, 2001

Horror

Vamphyri!, 1989

Other books you might like:
Robert Bloch, *Strange Eons*, 1979
Don D'Ammassa, *Servants of Chaos*, 2002
August Derleth, *In Lovecraft's Shadow*, 1998
Frank Belknap Long, *Escape from Tomorrow*, 1995
H.P. Lovecraft, *Necronomicon*, 2008

572

RONALD DAMIEN MALFI

Passenger

(North Webster, IN: Delirium, 2008)

Story type: Mystery
Subject(s): Memory Loss; Identity
Major character(s): Palmer Troy, Amnesiac; Clarence,
    Worker; Eleanor, Religious
Time period(s): 2000s
Locale(s): Baltimore, Maryland

Summary: A man wakes up on a bus with no memory of
his past. When he tries to find out who he is, he discovers that he has had an entire series of identities, each
starting after another bout of amnesia. There is also a
tendency for people in his vicinity to die suddenly, apparently of natural causes.

Other books by the same author:
Via Dolorosa, 2007
The Fall of Never, 2006
The Nature of Monsters, 2006
The Space Between, 2000

Other books you might like:
Rick Hautala, *Cold Whisper*, 1990
Stephen King, *Bag of Bones*, 1998
Dean R. Koontz, *The Bad Place*, 1990
Peter Straub, *In the Night Room*, 2004
Lisa Tuttle, *Lost Futures*, 1992

573

JEFF MARIOTTE

River Runs Red

(New York: Jove, 2008)

Story type: Ancient Evil Unleashed; Legend
Subject(s): Legends; Native Americans
Major character(s): James Livingston Truly, Spy; Molly
    McCall, Journalist; Wade Scheiner, Journalist
Time period(s): 2000s
Locale(s): Texas

Summary: An archaeologist exploring Native American
ruins in Texas inadvertently releases an ancient force
that can control the flow of rivers. Years later several
people are brought together to witness and participate in
a long-standing battle between two supernatural beings
who are essentially forces of nature.

Other books by the same author:
Missing White Girl, 2007

Witch's Canyon, 2007
The Slab, 2003
Haunted, 2002
Close to the Ground, 2000

Other books you might like:
Susan Cooper, *Mandrake*, 1964
Owl Goingback, *Shaman Moon*, 1997
Graham Masterton, *Manitou Blood*, 2005
David Seltzer, *Prophecy*, 1979
Martin Cruz Smith, *Nightwing*, 1979

574

L.H. MAYNARD
M.P.N. SIMS , Co-Author

Black Cathedral

(New York: Leisure, 2008)

Story type: Apocalyptic Horror; Haunted House
Series: Department 18. Book 1
Subject(s): Haunted Houses; Cults
Major character(s): Robert Carter, Psychic; Jane Talbot,
    Investigator; Simon Crozier, Administrator
Time period(s): 2000s (2008)
Locale(s): Scotland

Summary: A party of business executives disappears during a retreat to a remote island. A psychic investigator is
stunned by a supernatural force and wakens to find his
partner missing. Bizarre deaths and other occurrences all
appear to be linked to a cult that once prayed to a forbidden god and waits now to walk the earth again.

Other books by the same author:
Demon Eyes, 2007
The Shelter, 2006
The Seminar, 2003
The Hidden Language of Demons, 2001
Silent Turmoil, 1999

Other books you might like:
Edward Lee, *Coven*, 1991
Graham Masterton, *The House That Jack Built*, 1996
John Skipp, *The Scream*, 1988
    Craig Spector, co-author
J.N. Williamson, *Horror House*, 1981
F. Paul Wilson, *The Haunted Air*, 2002

575

MICHAEL MCCARTY

Liquid Diet

(Effort, PA: Black Death, 2008)

Story type: Vampire Story; Erotic Horror
Subject(s): Vampires; Secrets
Major character(s): Andrew Bloodsworth, Vampire; Bella
    Donna, Radio Personality; Master, Vampire
Time period(s): 2000s
Locale(s): United States

Summary: A woman working as a disc jockey meets a

charming man who turns out to be a vampire, though not of the evil variety. Their steamy romance overlaps with a plot by an older, more powerful, and more vicious vampire known as the Master.

Other books by the same author:
Little Creatures, 2008
Monster Behind the Wheel, 2007 (Mark McLaughlin, co-author)

Other books you might like:
Nina Bangs, *Night Bites*, 2005
Jenna Black, *Watchers in the Night*, 2006
Ray Garton, *Live Girls*, 1987
Nancy Kilpatrick, *Bloodlover*, 2000
William Tedford, *Liquid Diet*, 1992

576

MICHAEL MCCARTY

Little Creatures

(Cedar Rapids, IA: Samsdot, 2008)

Story type: Collection
Subject(s): Short Stories

Summary: The 25 stories in this collection include the Stoker Award-nominated "Night of the Squealer." The themes and settings are very diverse, ranging from humorous variations of standard horror themes to deadly serious stories of horror.

Other books by the same author:
Liquid Diet, 2008
Monster Behind the Wheel, 2007 (Mark McLaughlin, co-author)

Other books you might like:
Clive Barker, *In the Flesh*, 1986
M. John Harrison, *Things That Never Happen*, 2003
John Maclay, *Dreadful Delineations*, 2007
David B. Silva, *A Little White Book of Lies*, 2005
Jeffrey Thomas, *Terra Incognita*, 2000

577

RICHELLE MEAD

Storm Born

(New York: Zebra, 2008)

Story type: Legend; Alternate Universe
Series: Dark Swan. Book 1
Subject(s): Demons; Magic
Major character(s): Eugenie Markham, Shaman; Dorian, Mythical Creature, Ruler; Kiyo, Mythical Creature (shapeshifter)
Time period(s): 2000s
Locale(s): United States; Mythical Place

Summary: Eugenie Markham is a shaman who spends most of her time expelling evil and mischievous spirits from our world. When she discovers that they have abducted a human being and carried him off to the netherworld, she decides to mount a rescue operation.

Other books by the same author:
Frost Bite, 2008
Succubus Dreams, 2008
Succubus on Top, 2008
Succubus Blues, 2007
Vampire Academy, 2007

Other books you might like:
Jim Butcher, *Blood Rites*, 2004
Tanya Huff, *Blood Lines*, 1991
Mercedes Lackey, *Jinx High*, 1991
Karen Marie Moning, *Darkfever*, 2006
Sarban, *Ringstones*, 1961

578

RICHELLE MEAD

Succubus Dreams

(New York: Kensington, 2008)

Story type: Erotic Horror; Mystery
Series: Succubus. Book 3
Subject(s): Erotica; Psychic Powers
Major character(s): Georgina Kincaid, Mythical Creature (succubus); Seth Mortenstern, Writer; Dante, Wizard
Time period(s): 2000s
Locale(s): Seattle, Washington

Summary: Georgina is a succubus who interprets her instructions from the netherworld rather loosely. She's carrying on an awkward romance with a writer whom she has to be careful to avoid killing, the normal outcome of her love affairs. There's also the troublesome problem that someone is stealing her life force while she's sleeping.

Other books by the same author:
Frostbite, 2008
Shadow Kiss, 2008
Succubus on Top, 2008
Storm Born, 2008
Succubus Blues, 2007

Other books you might like:
Mario Acevedo, *The Nymphos of Rocky Flats*, 2006
Ray Garton, *Live Girls*, 1987
Tim Powers, *The Stress of Her Regard*, 1989
Anne Rice, *Queen of the Damned*, 1988
Ray Russell, *Incubus*, 1976

579

WILLIAM MEIKLE

The Sirens

(Effort, PA: Black Death, 2008)

Story type: Legend; Ancient Evil Unleashed
Series: Midnight Eye Files. Book 2
Subject(s): Legends; Secrets
Major character(s): Derek Adams, Detective—Private; Betty Mulholland, Police Officer; Jim Morton, Journalist

Time period(s): 2000s
Locale(s): Scotland
Summary: Detective Derek Adams undertakes to track down a missing man whose mother wants him to be present at a funeral. The search takes him to an island off the coast of Ireland where he discovers the man has fallen under the spell of a kelpie, a sinister version of the mermaid legend.

Other books by the same author:
The Amulet, 2007
Berserker, 2001
Watchers of the Wall, 2001
Island Life, 2001
Millennium Macabre, 2000

Other books you might like:
Robert Aickman, *Cold Hand in Mine*, 1975
Charles De Lint, *Our Lady of the Harbor*, 1991
Mollie Hunter, *The Kelpie's Pearls*, 1964
Sarban, *Ringstones*, 1961
Lisa Tuttle, *Mysteries*, 2005

580

STEPHENIE MEYER

Breaking Dawn

(New York: Little, Brown, 2008)

Story type: Vampire Story; Young Adult
Subject(s): Vampires; Romance
Major character(s): Bella Swan, Teenager; Edward Cullen, Vampire, Teenager; Jacob Black, Werewolf
Time period(s): 2000s
Locale(s): United States
Summary: Bella Swan is a young girl who is caught between two romances, one with a vampire and one with a werewolf. When she finally decides which path to follow in the future, a new crisis arises which could change everything forever.

Where it's reviewed:
Booklist, September 1, 2008, page 88
Entertainment Weekly, August 15, 2008, page 68

Other books by the same author:
Eclipse, 2007
New Moon, 2006
Twilight, 2005

Other books you might like:
Rachel Caine, *Glass Houses*, 2006
Charlaine Harris, *All Together Dead*, 2007
Kimberly Raye, *Just One Bite*, 2007
Darren Shan, *Cirque du Freak*, 2001
L.J. Smith, *The Chosen*, 1997

581

BRIAN MORELAND

Shadows in the Mist

(New York: Berkley, 2008)

Story type: Ancient Evil Unleashed; Apocalyptic Horror
Subject(s): Magic; Demons; Historical

Major character(s): Jack Chambers, Military Personnel; Sean Chambers, Military Personnel; John Mahoney, Military Personnel
Time period(s): 2000s; 1940s (1944)
Locale(s): Germany
Summary: Sean Chambers is mystified by the secret diary of his dying grandfather. He is summoned to Germany to the man's deathbed where he discovers that during World War II, someone used magic to raise demons, supposedly to help the Nazis defeat their enemies. Although they were stopped at the time, it's possible that their evil is still active. First novel.

Other books you might like:
David Bishop, *Fiends of the Eastern Front*, 2007
Katherine Kurtz, *Lammas Night*, 1983
Graham Masterton, *The Devils of D-Day*, 1978
Kim Newman, *The Bloody Red Baron*, 1995
Tim Powers, *Declare*, 2001

582

JUSTINE MUSK

Lord of Bones

(New York: Roc, 2008)

Story type: Possession; Paranormal
Subject(s): Demons; Possessions
Major character(s): Jess Shepard, Artist; Ramsey Doe, Teenager; Soulbreaker, Demon
Time period(s): 2000s
Locale(s): United States

Summary: An artist and a teenaged orphan saved the world from an apocalyptic fate in *Blood Angel*, but they discover that their job isn't complete in this sequel. All over the country, innocent people are becoming possessed by minor demons preparing the way for the greatest of them all, the Soulbreaker.

Other books by the same author:
Uninvited, 2007
Blood Angel, 2005

Other books you might like:
Laurell Hamilton, *The Obsidian Butterfly*, 1999
Graham Masterton, *Manitou Blood*, 2005
Jeffrey Sackett, *The Demon*, 1991
John Shirley, *Demons*, 2002
Roger Zelazny, *Lord Demon*, 1999
    Jane Lindskold, co-author

583

STEVE NILES
JEFF MARIOTTE , Co-Author

Eternal Damnation

(New York: Pocket Star, 2008)

Story type: Vampire Story; Disaster
Series: 30 Days of Night. Book 4
Subject(s): Vampires; Secrets

Major character(s): Forrest Tilden, Security Officer; Stella Olemaun, Celebrity; Eben Olemaun, Police Officer
Time period(s): 2000s (2008)
Locale(s): United States

Summary: An elite group within the American government recognizes not only that vampires exist but that pose a growing threat to the stability of the country. Several innocent people get caught in the middle when violent action is taken against the hidden enemy, a situation which might promote the very chaos that it is intended to prevent.

Other books by the same author:
Immortal Remains, 2007 (Jeff Mariotte, co-author)
30 Days of Night, 2006 (Jeff Mariotte, co-author)
Rumors of the Undead, 2006 (Jeff Mariotte, co-author)
Savage Membrane, 2002

Other books you might like:
David Dvorkin, *Insatiable*, 1993
Ray Garton, *Night Life*, 2005
Brian Lumley, *Necroscope*, 1986
Michael Romkey, *The Vampire Virus*, 1998
Colin Wilson, *The Space Vampires*, 1967

| 584 |

WILLIAM OLLIE

The Damned
(Modesto, CA: Morningstar, 2008)

Story type: Apocalyptic Horror; Ancient Evil Unleashed
Subject(s): Demons; Disasters
Major character(s): Scott Freeman, Salesman; Warren, Entertainer; Dub, Survivor
Time period(s): 2000s (2008)
Locale(s): United States

Summary: Scott Freeman is on his way home from another assignment selling equipment when the world suddenly changes all around him. Most of the population has disappeared and those who survived are being hunted down by the damned, freed from Hell to return and bring terror to the Earth. First novel.

Other books you might like:
Joan Aiken, *The Cockatrice Boys*, 1996
James Blish, *Black Easter*, 1968
Edward Lee, *City Infernal*, 2001
Madeline Robins, *The Stone War*, 1999
John Shirley, *Demons*, 2002

| 585 |

DANEL OLSON , Editor

Exotic Gothic 2
(Ashcroft, British Columbia: Ash-Tree, 2008)

Story type: Anthology
Subject(s): Short Stories

Summary: This collection of 24 original stories is arranged by continent, providing gothic tales of horror from every part of the world. The styles and themes are quite diverse, and generally avoid more explicit forms of horror. The contributors include Nancy Collins, Christopher Fowler, Elizabeth Massie, Nicholas Royle, John Whitbourn, and others.

Other books by the same author:
Exotic Gothic, 2007

Other books you might like:
Nancy Collins, *Cold Turkey*, 1992
Christopher Fowler, *Personal Demons*, 1998
Elizabeth Massie, *The Fear Report*, 2004
Nicholas Royle, *The Matter of the Heart*, 1997
John Whitbourn, *Rollover Night*, 1990

| 586 |

DAVID A. PAGE

Mithras Court
(Renton, WA: Wizards of the Coast, 2008)

Story type: Historical/Victorian; Mystery
Series: Ravenloft
Subject(s): Historical; Secrets
Major character(s): Lewis Wentworth, Investigator, Military Personnel; Robert Drake, Professor; Gregory Crandall, Nobleman
Time period(s): 1890s
Locale(s): London, England

Summary: Lewis Wentworth has spent years searching for the man who murdered his wife. His investigation leads him to a mysterious part of London unknown to the outside world, a place where he might finally have vengeance, but also a place where it is possible for the dead to walk among the living. First novel.

Other books you might like:
Gordon Dahlquist, *The Glass Books of the Dream Eaters*, 2006
Simon R. Green, *Daemons Are Forever*, 2008
Barbara Hambly, *Bride of the Rat God*, 1994
Graham Masterton, *The Doorkeepers*, 2001
S.M. Peters, *Whitechapel Gods*, 2008

| 587 |

VICTOR PELEVIN

The Sacred Book of the Werewolf
(New York: Viking, 2008)

Story type: Werewolf Story; Erotic Horror
Subject(s): Werewolves; Humor
Major character(s): A Hu-Li, Werewolf; Alexander, Government Official, Werewolf; Pavel Ivanovich, Scholar
Time period(s): 2000s
Locale(s): Russia

Summary: A Hu-Li is an oriental werefox who is visiting Russia when she becomes romantically involved with a local official who is a werewolf. Their affair, and their

Horror

lengthy conversations, provide a satirical look at modern Russia and the world around it while revealing a hidden society living within our own. This book was originally published in Russia.

Where it's reviewed:
Booklist, August 1, 2008, page 58
New Statesman, March 3, 2008, page 58
New York Times Book Review, September 28, 2008, page 14
Publishers Weekly, August 4, 2008, page 13
Times Literary Supplement, March 7, 2008, page 21

Other books by the same author:
The Helmet of Horror, 2007
A Werewolf Problem in Central Russia and Other Stories, 2003
Buddha's Little Finger, 2001
Omon Ra, 1998
Yellow Arrow, 1997

Other books you might like:
Patty Brisco, *The Other People*, 1970
P.D. Cacek, *Canyons*, 2000
Michael Cadnum, *Saint Peter's Wolf*, 1991
Caitlin Kiernan, *Low Red Moon*, 2003
Brian Stableford, *The Werewolves of London*, 1990

588

VICKI PETTERSSON

The Touch of Twilight

(New York: Eos, 2008)

Story type: Black Magic; Femme Fatale
Series: Sign of the Zodiac. Book 3
Subject(s): Secrets; Magic
Major character(s): Joanna Archer, Celebrity, Psychic; Xavier Archer, Wealthy; Regan, Psychic
Time period(s): 2000s (2008)
Locale(s): Las Vega, Nevada

Summary: To most of the world, Joanna Archer is just another celebrity. Secretly, she is part of a paranormal league that helps protect the world from the Shadows, an opposing force of evil supernatural creatures. In her third adventure, she is troubled by the presence of a doppelganger and other eerie threats.

Other books by the same author:
The Scent of Shadows, 2007
The Taste of Night, 2007

Other books you might like:
Kelley Armstrong, *Haunted*, 2005
Keri Arthur, *Destiny Kills*, 2008
L.A. Banks, *Bad Blood*, 2008
Charlaine Harris, *Grave Sight*, 2005
Kat Richardson, *Greywalker*, 2006

589

ADRIAN PHOENIX

In the Blood

(New York: Pocket Books, 2009)

Story type: Vampire Story; Mystery
Series: Dante Baptiste. Book 2
Subject(s): Vampires; Conspiracies
Major character(s): Dante Baptiste, Vampire, Musician; Heather Wallace, FBI Agent; Alexander Lyons, FBI Agent
Time period(s): 2000s
Locale(s): Seattle, Washington

Summary: Dante Baptiste, a rock star, is also secretly a vampire, although not an evil one. He is searching for the truth about his past, but the information is confusing thanks to a mysterious government cover up. There are also evil vampires at large, the Fallen, and FBI agents who can both help and hinder his investigation.

Other books by the same author:
A Rush of Wings, 2007

Other books you might like:
Vincent Courtney, *The Vampire Beat*, 1991
P.N. Elrod, *Quincey Morris, Vampire*, 2001
Charlie Huston, *Already Dead*, 2005
Lee Killough, *Blood Hunt*, 1987
S.A. Swiniarski, *Raven*, 1996

590

JOHN LLEWELLYN PROBERT

Coffin Nails

(Ashcroft, British Columbia: Ash-Tree, 2008)

Story type: Collection
Subject(s): Short Stories
Summary: This is a collection of eighteen horror stories, mostly set in the contemporary world. The author explores the worlds of troubled teenagers, ancient curses, supernatural murder, horrors hidden in deserted attics, witchcraft, and other themes.

Other books by the same author:
The Faculty of Terror, 2006

Other books you might like:
Charles Beaumont, *A Touch of the Creature*, 1999
Charles L. Grant, *Nightmare Seasons*, 1982
T.E.D. Klein, *Dark Gods*, 1985
Richard Matheson, *Offbeat*, 2002
Patrick McGrath, *Blood and Water and Other Tales*, 1988

591

KIMBERLY RAYE

Just One Bite

(New York: Ballantine, 2008)

Story type: Vampire Story; Romance
Series: Dead End Dating. Book 4

Subject(s): Vampires; Humor
Major character(s): Lil Marchette, Vampire, Business-woman; Vinnie Balducci, Vampire, Criminal; Evie, Worker
Time period(s): 2000s
Locale(s): New York, New York

Summary: Lil Marchette is a vampire who runs a dating service. Unfortunately, she is forced to accept as a client a prominent criminal, also a vampire, who wants to find a woman who meets very specific qualifications. The only one in sight is Marchette's assistant, Evie, whom she is unwilling to sacrifice. A blend of serious and absurd elements.

Other books by the same author:
Dead and Dateless, 2007
Your Coffin or Mine?, 2007
Dead End Dating, 2006

Other books you might like:
Michelle Bardsley, *Because Your Vampire Said So*, 2008
Dakota Cassidy, *Accidentally Dead*, 2008
MaryJanice Davidson, *Dead and Loving It*, 2006
Lionel Fenn, *Kent Montana and the Moderately Vicious Vampire*, 1992
Kim Harrison, *The Good, the Bad, and the Undead*, 2004

592

TONY RICHARDS

Dark Rain

(New York: Eos, 2008)

Story type: Magic Conflict; Small Town Horror
Subject(s): Magic; Demons
Major character(s): Ross Devries, Investigator; Cassandra Mallory, Investigator; Saul Hobart, Police Officer
Time period(s): 2000s (2008)
Locale(s): Raine's Landing, Massachusetts

Summary: The town of Raine's Landing has always been plagued by magic and the supernatural. The two protagonists have devoted their lives to investigating these incidents and, when necessary, taking steps to combat the evil that periodically emerges. Their challenge now may be too much to overcome, a virtual godling of evil.

Other books by the same author:
Shadows and Other Tales, 2008
Ghost Dance, 2005
The Harvest Bride, 1987

Other books you might like:
Rick Hautala, *Moondeath*, 1980
Stephen King, *Needful Things*, 1991
Dean R. Koontz, *Phantoms*, 1983
Al Sarrantonio, *Horrorween*, 2006
J. Michael Straczynski, *Demon Night*, 1989

593

TONY RICHARDS

Shadows and Other Tales

(Colusa, CA: Dark Regions, 2008)

Story type: Collection
Subject(s): Short Stories

Summary: This is a collection of 21 short stories, most of them previously published between 2000 and 2007. The author addresses a variety of familiar and unfamiliar horror themes including ghosts, monsters, curses, and weird occurrences. One story is original to this collection.

Other books by the same author:
Dark Rain, 2008
Ghost Dance, 2005
The Harvest Bride, 1987

Other books you might like:
Joe R. Lansdale, *Bumper Crop*, 2004
Richard Matheson, *Blood Lines*, 2006
William F. Nolan, *Dark Universe*, 2001
John Shirley, *Black Butterflies*, 1998
David Niall Wilson, *Ennui and Other States of Madness*, 2008

594

NORA ROBERTS

The Hollow

(New York: Jove, 2008)

Story type: Haunted House; Ancient Evil Unleashed
Series: Sign of Seven. Book 2
Subject(s): Haunted Houses; Demons
Major character(s): Layla Darnell, Unemployed; Cal, Worker; Quinn, Psychic
Time period(s): 2000s
Locale(s): Hawkins Falls, Maryland

Summary: A group of children inadvertently awaken an ancient evil force which periodically afflicts the town with sanity-wrenching visions of evil. As adults, those responsible return to face the evil and hopefully to drive it back into its own reality.

Where it's reviewed:
Booklist, May 1, 2008, page 74

Other books by the same author:
Morrigan's Cross, 2006
Blue Dahlia, 2004
Face the Fire, 2002
Midnight Bayou, 2002
Carolina Moon, 2000

Other books you might like:
Joseph A. Citro, *Shadow Child*, 1987
Rick Hautala, *Moondeath*, 1980
Stephen King, *It*, 1986
Michael Paine, *The Night School*, 2006
Dan Simmons, *Summer of Night*, 1991

595

WENDY ROBERTS

Devil May Ride

(New York: Obsidian, 2008)

Story type: Mystery; Ancient Evil Unleashed
Series: Ghost Dusters. Book 2
Subject(s): Secrets; Ghosts
Major character(s): Sadie Novak, Businesswoman, Psychic; Zack Bowman, Worker; Dawn Novak, Young Woman
Time period(s): 2000s (2008)
Locale(s): Washington

Summary: Sadie Novak and her partner clean up crime scenes for a living. Sadie is also able to communicate in a limited fashion with the dead. On their latest job, a large amount of missing cash makes them the target of a violent motorcycle gang that deals with drugs, and if Sadie isn't careful, she may join the ghosts of their earlier victims.

Other books by the same author:
The Remains of the Dead, 2007

Other books you might like:
Doranna Durgin, *Revenge*, 2008
William Hope Hodgson, *Carnacki, the Ghost Finder*, 1913
Brian Lumley, *Necroscope*, 1986
Steven Piziks, *Plague Room*, 2008
Mary Stewart, *Touch Not the Cat*, 1976

596

BARBARA RODEN , Editor
CHRISTOPHER RODEN , Co-Editor

Shades of Darkness

(Ashcroft, British Columbia: Ash-Tree, 2008)

Story type: Anthology
Subject(s): Short Stories

Summary: All 26 stories in this collection appear here for the first time. They tend to be written in emulation of the style of the traditional English ghost story, with a few exceptions. The contributors include Melanie Tem, Paul Finch, Simon Bestwick, Joel Lane, Glen Hirschberg, and others.

Other books by the same author:
Acquaintance with the Night, 2004 (Christopher Roden, co-editor)
Shadows and Silence, 2000 (Christopher Roden, co-editor)

Other books you might like:
Simon Bestwick, *A Hazy Shade of Winter*, 2004
Paul Finch, *Ghost Realm*, 2008
Joel Lane, *The Lost District and Other Stories*, 2006
John Maclay, *Dreadful Delineations*, 2007
Melanie Tem, *The Deceiver*, 2003

597

GORD ROLLO

The Jigsaw Man

(New York: Leisure, 2008)

Story type: Horror; Medical
Subject(s): Medical Thriller
Major character(s): Michael Fox, Prisoner; Alexander Drake, Businessman; Nathan Marshall, Doctor
Time period(s): 2000s
Locale(s): Buffalo, New York

Summary: Michael Fox is so despondent that he is considering taking his own life when he is approached by a mysterious man with a strange offer. He is working for Dr. Nathan Marshall, who will pay a large sum of money for Fox's right arm. Fox reluctantly agrees, but discovers that there is more to the deal than he expected.

Other books by the same author:
Lost in Translation, 2007

Other books you might like:
Brian Keene, *Terminal*, 2005
Richard Laymon, *Resurrection Dreams*, 1988
Tim Lebbon, *Mesmer*, 1997
Graham Masterton, *Feast*, 1988
John Saul, *Cry for the Strangers*, 1979

598

LOIS RUBY

The Secrets of Laurel Oaks

(New York: Starscape, 2008)

Story type: Young Adult; Ghost Story
Subject(s): Ghosts
Major character(s): Lila Barry, Teenager; Gabe Barry, Child; Daphne, Ghost
Time period(s): 2000s
Locale(s): Louisiana

Summary: Lila Barry and her family are visiting a deserted plantation in Louisiana when Lila begins to have strange visions. She sees the ghost of a young girl who was at one time a slave on the plantation. Her ghost is tied to the house because she was unjustly accused of murder when she was alive.

Where it's reviewed:
Kliatt, September 2008, page 20

Other books by the same author:
Shanghai Shadows, 2006
Journey to Jamestown, 2005
Soon Be Free, 2002
Steal Away Home, 1999
Skin Deep, 1996

Other books you might like:
Bruce Coville, *The Ghost Wore Gray*, 1988
Richie Tankersley Cusick, *Walk of the Spirit*, 2008
Mary Downing Hahn, *Wait Till Helen Comes*, 1987

A.M. Jenkins, *Beating Heart*, 2006
Carol Beach York, *Nights in Ghostland*, 1987

599

LILITH SAINTCROW

Hunter's Prayer

(New York: Orbit, 2008)

Story type: Urban; Mystery
Series: Jill Kismet. Book 2
Subject(s): Secrets; Demons
Major character(s): Jill Kismet, FBI Agent; Saul Dustcircle, Mythical Creature; Dominic, FBI Agent, Mythical Creature
Time period(s): 2000s (2008)
Locale(s): United States

Summary: A special group within the FBI that deals with supernatural incursions from the demon world is called in for its second case. Someone, or something, is slaughtering prostitutes and that same party might also be interested in bringing the career of Jill Kismet to a premature end.

Other books by the same author:
Night Shift, 2008
Redemption Alley, 2008
Dead Man Rising, 2006
Working for the Devil, 2006
Dark Watcher, 2004

Other books you might like:
Jocelyn Drake, *Nightwalker*, 2008
Yasmine Galenorn, *Dragon Wytch*, 2008
Laurell Hamilton, *The Killing Dance*, 1987
Anton Strout, *Dead to Me*, 2008
Rob Thurman, *Madhouse*, 2008

600

LILITH SAINTCROW

Night Shift

(New York: Orbit, 2008)

Story type: Magic Conflict; Urban
Series: Jill Kismet. Book 1
Subject(s): Demons; Secrets
Major character(s): Jill Kismet, FBI Agent; Pericles, Demon; Dominic, Mythical Creature
Time period(s): 2000s (2008)
Locale(s): United States

Summary: A woman touched by the mark of a demon works with shapeshifters assigned to a secret division of the FBI to combat the incursions of creatures from the demon world into our own. In her first adventure, she has to track down a pack of inhuman killers.

Other books by the same author:
Hunter's Prayer, 2008
Redemption Alley, 2008
Dead Man Rising, 2006

Working for the Devil, 2006
Dark Watcher, 2004

Other books you might like:
Marie Brennan, *Doppelganger*, 2006
Karen Chance, *Touch the Dark*, 2006
Nancy Collins, *Sunglasses After Dark*, 1989
Kim Harrison, *For a Few Demons More*, 2007
Kat Richardson, *Underground*, 2008

601

LILITH SAINTCROW

To Hell and Back

(New York: Orbit, 2008)

Story type: Legend; Magic Conflict
Series: Dante Valentine. Book 5
Subject(s): Legends; Hell
Major character(s): Dante Valentine, Agent; Japhrimel, Angel; Lucifer, Demon
Time period(s): 2000s (2008)
Locale(s): New Jersey; Mythical Place

Summary: Dante Valentine has been returned from Hell, but her memory is impaired. She does realize that the only way to be free is if she can kill Lucifer himself. Aided by her friend Japhrimel, she discovers a way to alter her very nature and become the instrument by which the lord of Hell can be destroyed.

Other books by the same author:
Hunter's Prayer, 2008
Redemption Alley, 2008
Night Shift, 2008
Dead Man Rising, 2006
Working for the Devil, 2006

Other books you might like:
James Blish, *Black Easter*, 1968
Steven Brust, *To Reign in Hell*, 1984
Alan Ross Schrader, *Satan's Chance*, 1982
David Seltzer, *The Omen*, 1976
Margaret Weis, *Warrior Angel*, 2007
   Liz Weis, co-author

602

MARY SANGIOVANNI

Found You

(New York: Leisure, 2008)

Story type: Small Town Horror; Paranormal
Subject(s): Monsters; Secrets
Major character(s): Steven Corimar, Police Officer; David Kohlar, Businessman; Jake Dylan, Criminal
Time period(s): 2000s
Locale(s): United States

Summary: Sally survived the attentions of a horrible supernatural creature in *The Hollower*, but she succumbs very early in this sequel. Her bereaved brother and a police officer investigate her death and discover that it was not a suicide as it appeared, but rather the result of her encounter with a unique and frightening monster.

Other books by the same author:
The Hollower, 2007

Other books you might like:
Gary Braunbeck, *Coffin County*, 2008
Matthew J. Costello, *Sleep Tight*, 1987
Graham Masterton, *The Devil in Gray*, 2004
Al Sarrantonio, *October*, 1990
John Shirley, *In Darkness Waiting*, 1990

603

DARREN SHAN

Death's Shadow

(New York: Little, Brown, 2008)

Story type: Young Adult; Apocalyptic Horror
Series: Demonata. Book 7
Subject(s): Apocalypse; Demons
Major character(s): Bec, Teenager; Lord Loss, Mythical
    Creature; Beranabus, Wizard
Time period(s): Indeterminate Future
Locale(s): Earth

Summary: After a horde of demons invaded the Earth,
civilization collapsed. The most powerful defender of
the survivors is Bec, who has escaped imprisonment to
oppose the demons once again. Unfortunately, something
else has come with her, an evil force that makes the
demons look like amateurs.

Other books by the same author:
Demon Apocalypse, 2008
Bec, 2006
Demon Thief, 2006
Allies of the Night, 2004
Cirque du Freak, 2001

Other books you might like:
Joan Aiken, *The Cockatrice Boys*, 1996
James Blish, *The Day After Judgment*, 1971
Edward Lee, *House Infernal*, 2007
William Ollie, *The Damned*, 2008
John Shirley, *Demons*, 2002

604

HARRY SHANNON

Daemon

(North Webster, IN: Delirium, 2008)

Story type: Horror; Supernatural Vengeance
Subject(s): Monsters; Mystery
Major character(s): Jeff Lehane, Security Officer; Charlie
    Spinks, Security Officer; Whiz Ligotti, Security Of-
    ficer
Time period(s): 2000s
Locale(s): Las Vegas, Nevada

Summary: Jeff Lehane is outraged and devastated when
his ex-wife is killed while acting as bodyguard to a rock
star. He is even more disturbed when someone or

something breaks into the morgue and devours part of
her body, so he organizes a group of his fellow security
officers to track down whoever or whatever is
responsible.

Other books by the same author:
Dead and Gone, 2008
The Pressure of Darkness, 2006
Eye of the Burning Man, 2005
Night of the Beast, 2002

Other books you might like:
Brian Keene, *The Ghoul*, 2007
Edward Lee, *Ghouls*, 1988
John Passarella, *Ghoul Trouble*, 2000
Mark Ronson, *The Ghoul*, 1980
Robert Tralins, *The Ghoul Lovers*, 1972

605

HARRY SHANNON

Dead and Gone

(North Webster, IN: Delirium, 2008)

Story type: Curse; Ancient Evil Unleashed
Subject(s): Legends; Ghosts
Major character(s): Jack Wade, Actor; Kate Eidson, Police
    Officer; Billy Bob Mercer, Criminal
Time period(s): 2000s
Locale(s): Dry Wells, Nevada

Summary: Unemployed actor Jack Wade moves his
comatose wife to a remote cabin, without realizing that
it is built on a haunted Native American burial ground.
He senses things watching or following him, but the
presence of several living criminals confuses the issue
until he and a policewoman stumble upon a more
frightening truth.

Other books by the same author:
Daemon, 2008
The Pressure of Darkness, 2006
Eye of the Burning Man, 2005
Night of the Beast, 2002

Other books you might like:
Owl Goingback, *Darker than Night*, 1999
Rick Hautala, *Dead Silence*, 1992
Graham Masterton, *The Manitou*, 1975
Michael Paine, *Steel Ghosts*, 2005
Jack Scaparro, *Deathsong*, 1989

606

SHARI SHATTUCK

Speak of the Devil

(New York: Signet, 2008)

Story type: Mystery; Psychic Powers
Subject(s): Psychic Powers; Secrets
Major character(s): Greer Sands, Psychic; Joshua Sands,
    Teenager, Psychic; Leah Falconer, Businesswoman
Time period(s): 2000s

Locale(s): Los Angeles, California

Summary: Greer Sands tries to use her psychic powers to help people, but she has been having visions of horrifying events she seems powerless to avert. Her teenaged son has similar powers and he also tries to make use of them, but without the training and discipline his mother has learned over the years.

Other books by the same author:
Eye of the Beholder, 2007
The Man She Thought She Knew, 2006
Lethal, 2005
Loaded, 2003

Other books you might like:
Owen Brookes, *Deadly Communion*, 1984
Charles L. Grant, *Chariot*, 1998
Richard Grant, *In the Land of Winter*, 1997
James Herbert, *Moon*, 1985
T.M. Wright, *The Ascending*, 1994

607

EVE SILVER

Demon's Hunger

(New York: Grand Central, 2008)

Story type: Romance; Ancient Evil Unleashed
Series: Compact of Sorcerers. Book 2
Subject(s): Romance; Demons
Major character(s): Vivien Cairn, Anthropologist; Dain Hawkins, Sorcerer; Darqun Vane, Sorcerer
Time period(s): 2000s (2008)
Locale(s): New Orleans, Louisiana

Summary: Vivien Cairn thinks she may be losing her mind because she has suddenly become subject to intense erotic feelings. Dain Hawkins is a secret sorcerer, part of a group that protects the world from demonic incursions. He believes that Vivien is being affected by a creature from the other world and falls in love with her in the process of protecting her.

Other books by the same author:
His Wicked Sins, 2008
Dark Prince, 2007
Demon's Kiss, 2007
Driven, 2007 (as Even Kenin)
His Dark Kiss, 2006

Other books you might like:
C.T. Adams, *Captive Moon*, 2006
   Cathy Clamp, co-author
Jenna Black, *The Devil's Due*, 2008
Susan Krinard, *Body and Soul*, 1998
Marjorie M. Liu, *The Iron Hunt*, 2008
Maggie Shayne, *Angel's Pain*, 2008

608

KASSANDRA SIMS

Hellbent and Heartfirst

(New York: Tor, 2008)

Story type: Romance; Paranormal
Subject(s): Demons; Secrets
Major character(s): Jacyn Boaz, Worker; Jimmy Wayne Broadus, Worker, Musician; Amber, Worker
Time period(s): 2000s
Locale(s): New Orleans, Louisiana

Summary: Jacyn Boaz travels to New Orleans to help with the aftermath of Hurricane Katrina, where she meets a man to whom she is attracted. Her life becomes complicated when she discovers that he is engaged in a battle against demonic forces and that associating with him puts her own life in danger.

Where it's reviewed:
Publishers Weekly, February 11, 2008, page 56

Other books by the same author:
Falling Upwards, 2007
The Midnight Work, 2005

Other books you might like:
Jenna Black, *The Devil You Know*, 2008
Marie Brennan, *Warrior and Witch*, 2006
Justine Musk, *Lord of Bones*, 2008
Kat Richardson, *Greywalker*, 2006
Rob Thurman, *Nightlife*, 2006

609

JOHN SKIPP
CORY GOODFELLOW , Co-Author

Jake's Wake

(New York: Leisure, 2008)

Story type: Reanimated Dead; Black Magic
Subject(s): Demons; Secrets
Major character(s): Jacob Connaway, Religious, Reanimated Dead; Esther Echevarria, Housewife; Eddie Echevarria, Worker
Time period(s): 2000s (2008)
Locale(s): California

Summary: Pastor Jake is buried but he has not been laid to rest. He returns from the dead in an apparent miracle, but he is accompanied by demons rather than angels. One family become the focal point for the battle between good and evil for control of the world.

Other books by the same author:
The Long Last Call, 2006
Animals, 1993 (Craig Spector, co-author)
The Bridge, 1991 (Craig Spector, co-author)
Dead Lines, 1989 (Craig Spector, co-author)
The Cleanup, 1987 (Craig Spector, co-author)

Other books you might like:
Gary Brandner, *Carrion*, 1986
Geoffrey Caine, *Legion of the Dead*, 1992

Horror

Brian Hodge, *The Darker Saints*, 1993
Brian Keene, *The Rising*, 2003
Thomas F. Monteleone, *The Resurrectionist*, 1995

610

JERI SMITH-READY

Wicked Game

(New York: Pocket, 2008)

Story type: Vampire Story; Romance
Subject(s): Vampires; Romance
Major character(s): Ciara Griffin, Worker; Shane McAllister, Vampire; Gideon, Vampire
Time period(s): 2000s
Locale(s): United States

Summary: Ciara Griffin has second thoughts about her internship at a radio station when she discovers that all of the disc jockeys are actually more or less harmless vampires. When the station is threatened with a hostile takeover, she hatches a plan to promote them as vampires, which the public will interpret as a harmless hoax. Unfortunately, some nasty vampires object to the publicity. First novel.

Where it's reviewed:
Booklist, April 1, 2008, page 56
Publishers Weekly, January 14, 2008, page 36

Other books by the same author:
The Reawakened, 2008
Voice of Crow, 2007
Eyes of Crow, 2006

Other books you might like:
MaryJanice Davidson, *Undead and Unemployed*, 2004
Andrew Fox, *Fat White Vampire Blues*, 2003
Charlaine Harris, *Club Dead*, 2003
Kerrelyn Sparks, *Vamps and the City*, 2006
Valerie Stivers, *Blood Is the New Black*, 2007

611

JEANNE C. STEIN

Legacy

(New York: Ace, 2008)

Story type: Vampire Story; Werewolf Story
Series: Anna Strong. Book 4
Subject(s): Vampires; Mystery
Major character(s): Anna Strong, Bounty Hunter, Vampire; Gloria Estrella, Actress, Model; Rory O'Sullivan, Businessman
Time period(s): 2000s
Locale(s): San Diego, California

Summary: Anna Strong is slowly adjusting to life as a vampire, the non-evil kind. Her ex-partner, a bounty hunter, is recovering from his wounds and the evil vampire who converted her is dead, having left her his fortune. Or has he? A female werewolf shows up to contest the will, and not just by legal means.

Other books by the same author:
The Watcher, 2007
Blood Drive, 2006
The Becoming, 2006

Other books you might like:
Nina Bangs, *Night Bites*, 2005
Patricia Briggs, *Blood Bound*, 2007
Shannon Drake, *Deep Midnight*, 2001
Laurell Hamilton, *Circus of the Damned*, 1995
Jeri Smith-Ready, *Wicked Game*, 2008

612

PETER STRAUB , Editor

Poe's Children

(New York: Doubleday, 2008)

Story type: Anthology
Subject(s): Short Stories

Summary: One of the leading writers of modern horror fiction edits this collection of original stories by authors including Ramsey Campbell, Joe Hill, Stephen King, Thomas Tessier, Kelly Link, and others. The stories tend toward the literary end of the genre, more dependent on atmosphere and prose style than on explicit horror.

Where it's reviewed:
Booklist, October 1, 2008, page 32
Library Journal, September 15, 2008, page 49
Locus, November 2008, page 17
Publishers Weekly, September 8, 2008, page 36

Other books by the same author:
In the Night Room, 2004
Lost Boy, Lost Girl, 2003
Houses Without Doors, 1990
Shadowland, 1980
Ghost Story, 1979

Other books you might like:
Ramsey Campbell, *Ghosts and Grisly Things*, 2000
Joe Hill, *20th Century Ghosts*, 2006
Stephen King, *Just After Sunset*, 2008
Kelly Link, *Pretty Monsters*, 2008
Thomas Tessier, *Ghost Music*, 2000

613

TRISHA TELEP , Editor

The Mammoth Book of Vampire Romance

(Philadelphia: Running Press, 2008)

Story type: Anthology
Subject(s): Short Stories; Vampires

Summary: The editor has gathered here more than two dozen short stories about romance and vampires, primarily from authors active in that genre. The contributors include Jenna Black, Keri Arthur, Susan Sizemore,

Lilian Saintcrow, Karen Chance, Nancy Holder, and others.

Other books you might like:
Keri Arthur, *The Darkest Kiss*, 2008
Jenna Black, *Hungers of the Heart*, 2008
Karen Chance, *Claimed by Shadow*, 2007
Sherrilyn Kenyon, *Kiss of the Night*, 2004
Maggie Shayne, *Demon' Kiss*, 2007

614

JEFFREY THOMAS

Thirteen Specimens
(North Webster, IN: Delirium, 2008)

Story type: Collection
Subject(s): Short Stories

Summary: This is a collection of 13 stories and prose poems on a variety of unusual themes involving magic and the supernatural. The subjects venture through plagues of centipedes, living cameras, a visit to the Netherworld, Halloween horrors, Korean devils, monsters, and other terrors.

Where it's reviewed:
Booklist, September 15, 2008, page 33

Other books by the same author:
Voices from Hades, 2008
Doomsdays, 2007
The Dream Dealers, 2006
Letters from Hades, 2003
Terra Incognita, 2000

Other books you might like:
Gary Braunbeck, *Destinations Unknown*, 2006
Tim Lebbon, *Fears Unnamed*, 2004
Thomas Ligotti, *Sideshow and Other Stories*, 2003
Lance Olsen, *Hideous Beauties*, 2003
Tim Powers, *Night Moves and Other Stories*, 2001

615

JONATHAN THOMAS

Midnight Call and Other Stories
(New York: Hippocampus, 2008)

Story type: Collection
Subject(s): Short Stories

Summary: Many of the stories in this collection were previously published in a limited small press edition in 1992. The rest are original to this collection. The author sets most of his stories in New England and makes use of traditional horror themes and devices.

Other books by the same author:
Stories from the Big Black House, 1992

Other books you might like:
Algernon Blackwood, *In the Realm of Terror*, 1957
Rick Hautala, *Bedbugs*, 2000
Brian Hodge, *Lies and Ugliness*, 2002

Frank Belknap Long, *Night Fear*, 1979
John Maclay, *Dreadful Delineations*, 2007

616

SCOTT THOMAS

The Garden of Ghosts
(Colusa, CA: Dark Regions, 2008)

Story type: Collection
Subject(s): Short Stories

Summary: This is a collection of ghost stories, all set in the Victorian era. The treatment is very traditional, with vengeful ghosts, trapped souls, haunted houses, and other standard themes of that form. Most of them develop suspense through atmosphere rather than overt violence.

Other books by the same author:
Over the Darkening Fields, 2007
Westermead, 2006
Cobwebs and Whispers, 2001

Other books you might like:
August Derleth, *Not Long for This World*, 1948
M.R. James, *Count Magnus and Other Ghost Stories*, 2005
Oliver Onions, *Tragic Casements*, 2001
Peter Straub, *Ghost Story*, 1979
H. Russell Wakefield, *The Clock Strikes Twelve*, 1939

617

CARRIE VAUGHN

Kitty and the Dead Man's Hand
(New York: Grand Central, 2008)

Story type: Werewolf Story; Mystery
Series: Kitty. Book 5
Subject(s): Magic; Secrets
Major character(s): Kitty Norville, Celebrity, Werewolf; Ben O'Farrell, Werewolf, Lawyer; Odysseus Grant, Entertainer, Magician
Time period(s): 2000s (2008)
Locale(s): Las Vegas, Nevada

Summary: Kitty Norville is a werewolf who has traveled to Las Vegas with her fiance, Ben. What is intended to be a restful visit is complicated by the presence of werewolf hunters in the same hotel, a stage magician whose tricks might be more than they seem, and other dangers including vampires.

Other books by the same author:
Kitty and the Silver Bullet, 2008
Kitty Takes a Holiday, 2007
Kitty Goes to Washington, 2006
Kitty and the Midnight Hour, 2005

Other books you might like:
Keri Arthur, *Full Moon Rising*, 2006
L.A. Banks, *Bite the Bullet*, 2008

Horror

Jim Butcher, *Fool Moon*, 2001
Charlaine Harris, *All Together Dead*, 2007
Robert R. McCammon, *The Wolf's Hour*, 1989

Jenna Black, *Hungers of the Heart*, 2008
Jeaniene Frost, *Halfway to the Grave*, 2007
Susan Sizemore, *A Stirring of Dust*, 1997

618

MICHAEL WALTERS

The Shadow Walker

(New York: Berkley, 2008)

Story type: Serial Killer; Mystery
Subject(s): Serial Killers; Murder
Major character(s): Drew McLeish, Police Officer; Nergui, Government Official; Doripalam, Police Officer
Time period(s): 2000s
Locale(s): Mongolia

Summary: The authorities in Mongolia are troubled by the depredations of a serial killer who slaughters and mutilates his victims in horrible ways. When a visiting Englishman becomes one of the victims, they enlist the aid of a British police officer, who is in danger of becoming the next victim rather than providing the help they seek. First novel.

Other books you might like:
Charles De Lint, *Mulengro*, 1985
Jonathan Maberry, *Ghost Road Blues*, 2006
Jeff Mariotte, *The Slab*, 2003
John Saul, *Black Lightning*, 1995
Michael Slade, *Ghoul*, 1987

619

CHRISTINE WARREN

One Bite with a Stranger

(New York: St Martins, 2008)

Story type: Vampire Story; Romance
Series: Others. Book 1
Subject(s): Vampires; Romance
Major character(s): Dmitri Vidame, Vampire; Regina McNeill, Worker; Ava Markham, Worker
Time period(s): 2000s (2008)
Locale(s): New York, New York

Summary: Regina is the cautious one in her circle of friends, but she agrees to visit a trendy club where she meets Dmitri Vidame, a suave and handsome man. What she doesn't know is that Dmitri is a vampire, in fact one of an elite group whose job is to keep an eye on the more reckless of his kind.

Other books by the same author:
You're So Vein, 2009
Walk on the Wild Side, 2008
Howl at the Moon, 2007
The Demon You Know, 2007
She's No Faerie Princess, 2006

Other books you might like:
Amanda Ashley, *After Sundown*, 2003
Nina Bangs, *Night Bites*, 2005

620

STEVEN E. WEDEL

Little Graveyard on the Prairie

(Anaheim, CA: Bad Moon, 2008)

Story type: Collection
Subject(s): Short Stories

Summary: This is a collection of atmospheric horror stories which avoid explicit gore in favor of mood and situation. The title story involves the manager of a small cemetery who discovers that the dead aren't always at ease and that he can be influenced by their presence.

Other books by the same author:
Murder by Human Wolves, 2008
Ulrik, 2008
Shara, 2006
Call to the Hunt, 2005
Darkscapes, 2002

Other books you might like:
Richard Christian Matheson, *Barking Sands*, 1999
William F. Nolan, *Nightworlds*, 2004
Alan Ryan, *The Bones Wizard and Other Stories*, 1988
David Schow, *Havoc Swims Jaded*, 2006
F. Paul Wilson, *The Soft*, 1989

621

WRATH JAMES WHITE

Succulent Prey

(New York: Leisure, 2008)

Story type: Serial Killer; Mystery
Subject(s): Secrets; Serial Killers
Major character(s): Joseph Miles, Serial Killer; Damon Trent, Patient; Alicia, Young Woman
Time period(s): 2000s (2008)
Locale(s): United States

Summary: When he was a child, Joseph Miles was the only victim to survive the attacks of a serial child killer. As an adult, he starts to have violent urges and realizes that he has been infected by a homicidal disease. He tries to find a cure before it takes control of him and he murders the woman he loves.

Other books by the same author:
Orgy of Souls, 2008 (Maurice Broaddus, co-author)
The Book of a Thousand Sins, 2005

Other books you might like:
Ramsey Campbell, *The Count of Eleven*, 1991
John Farris, *The Axman Cometh*, 1989
Tim Lebbon, *Face*, 2003
Edward Lee, *The Backwoods*, 2005

John Skipp, *The Cleanup*, 1987
Craig Spector, co-author

622

DAVID NIALL WILSON

Ennui and Other States of Madness

(Colusa, CA: Dark Regions, 2008)

Story type: Collection
Subject(s): Short Stories

Summary: Fourteen of the stories in this collection are reprints and three appear for the first time. Wilson demonstrates a wide range in his subject matter, mixing conventional and unconventional themes. Several of the stories take place in or allude to the historical past and most are character-oriented rather than plot-driven.

Other books by the same author:
Ancient Eyes, 2007
Lasombra, 2003
Roll Them Bones, 2003
This Is My Blood, 1999
To Dream of Dreamers Lost, 1998

Other books you might like:
Charles L. Grant, *Nightmare Seasons*, 1982
Brian Hodge, *The Convulsion Factory*, 1996
Tony Richards, *Shadows and Other Tales*, 2008
Thomas Tessier, *Ghost Music*, 2000
F. Paul Wilson, *The Barrens and Others*, 1992

623

DAVID NIALL WILSON

The Not Quite Right Reverend Cletus J. Diggs and the Currently Accepted Habits of Nature

(Anaheim, CA: Bad Moon, 2008)

Story type: Science Fiction; Genetic Manipulation
Subject(s): Scientific Experiments; Horror
Major character(s): Cletus J. Diggs, Religious; Jasper Winslow, Fisherman; Horton Buck, Government Official (coroner)
Time period(s): 2000s
Locale(s): Virginia

Summary: When a casual fisherman finds a strange body in the swamp—half human, half animal—he thinks at first that it's a hoax. When he shares his discovery with others, he learns that the body is real and enlists the aid of a conman minister to track down the people responsible for the abomination.

Other books by the same author:
Lasombra, 2003
Roll Them Bones, 2003
This Is My Blood, 1999
To Dream of Dreamers Lost, 1998
To Sift Through Bitter Ashes, 1997

Other books you might like:
Edgar Rice Burroughs, *The Monster Men*, 1963
Edward Lee, *Creekers*, 1994
Robert R. McCammon, *Boys' Life*, 1991
Manly Wade Wellman, *After Dark*, 1980
H.G. Wells, *The Island of Dr. Moreau*, 1896

Horror

The Year in Science Fiction: 2008
by
Don D'Ammassa

During the 1980s science fiction became more reflective of the present than the future, and has subsequently become increasingly interested in short term extrapolations rather than the future a century or more from now. Although there have been notable exceptions, most writers—particularly newcomers to the field—have shown little interest in galactic civilizations and alien worlds except within the subgenre of military science fiction, where they are simply symbols of human rivals. Instead, writers have concentrated on the consequences of ecological deterioration, global warming, overpopulation, the risks of uncontrolled technological development, and similar themes. As authors and publishers understandably sought for wider audiences, many of the traditional themes and devices of the genre were discarded or modified, and mainstream writing techniques became more and more important. While much of this has proven to be beneficial, at the same time it has resulted in the loss of what made the genre uniquely interesting to many readers.

If you ask a general sample of the population what science fiction is about, they will mention spaceships, other planets, and alien races, even though for the past several years most novels dealing with these themes have been largely tie-ins to movies and television shows. 2008 was the first year in quite some time when space opera—adventures in outer space and on other worlds—has actually been a dominant theme in novels. These are not the same kind of space opera that used to be written by Edward E. Smith, Edmond Hamilton, or even Poul Anderson and Robert A. Heinlein, but they are undeniably close relatives.

Modern space opera encompasses a range of different story types, varying from near future voyages to other planets within our solar system to vast galactic civilizations in which humanity is just one of many intelligent, space traveling races. Although the terms aren't precise and lines of demarcation are vague, there are three main forms of modern space opera. First we have what might be called Other Worlds Adventure, that is, space travel might be peripherally involved, but the focus of the story is a civilization on another world. In most cases, these are human colony worlds although some novels suggest that these colonies might eclipse Earth and become new power bases. Other novels depict the interface between human and alien races. The aliens might be relatively unsophisticated, even primitive, and limited to one planet, or they might be a space faring civilization equal or superior to humanity. Travel from one world to another might be common or extremely rare. This form of space opera is more likely to employ hard science as part of the narrative. The specific subject matter is quite varied, and might include political intrigue, high adventure, scientific or other mysteries, social satire, or explorations of possible variations of social or psychological structures.

The second form of space opera is closer to what the term originally suggested, with plots that resemble the traditional western. Travel among planets is almost invariably a common occurrence and the protagonists might well visit multiple worlds during the course of the story. The existence of alien races is almost always assumed, although in most cases the aliens generally function as human beings and can be viewed simply as foreigners. Emphasis is usually on high adventure, occasionally mixed with hard science. Most of the tie-in novels in the *Star Trek*, *Warhammer*, and *Star Wars* series fall into this category. The third branch of space opera— military SF—has evolved into a separate sub-genre that overlaps to some extent with tie-in novels. The protagonists are almost always military rather than civilian personnel, or the latter caught up in conflicts between military units. Although there have been some excellent examples of military science fiction__notably David Feintuch and Jerry Pournelle—these stories tend to be written to a more specific formula than other space opera and it is less likely that individual novels will stand out.

The outstanding novel this year is technically an Other Worlds adventure, although the treatment and perspective is so different that the label feels inappropriate. Neal Stephenson's *Anathem* takes place on a planet that very closely resembles our own. The inhabitants are human and they have camcorders, cell phones, and other forms of advanced technology, although they have different names. The unique perspective is provided by the fact that the narrator, Erasmas, is living within a cloistered society that constitutes virtually another world of its own. He is part of a community analogous to a monastery and convent combined, except that their order is not dedicated to a particular religion but rather to the accumulation and preservation of knowledge. Civilization has risen and fallen several times in the past, but there is a sense of continuity provided by these sheltered communities. The stability of their culture is challenged, however, when they discover that a manned space vehicle is orbiting their planet and studying them from outer space. It is almost certainly the most impressive accomplishment in science fiction for 2008.

Ben Bova has been mixing hard science with adventure for several years now with his Grand Tour novels, a very loosely related series that examines in very realistic terms the conditions we might expect to encounter on various planets within our own solar system. His latest, *Mars Life*, demonstrates that discoveries on other worlds might have profound effects back on Earth. In this case, a theocratically dominated human government is unbalanced by the discovery of fossils on the planet Mars. Mars was also the setting for Joe Haldeman's *Marsbound*, which reverts to a very traditional genre format. The protagonist is a teenager who is emigrating to the colony on Mars with her family, a decision about which she has understandably mixed emotions. Haldeman's treatment is very realistic and understated, describing the voyage in considerable detail, and suggesting how new colonists might make the transition to life in an unfriendly environment. John Varley continues the sequence begun in *Red Thunder* and continued in *Red Lightning* with *Rolling Thunder*, which describes the habitat on Europa, one of the moons of Jupiter. A musician travels there from Mars to participate in a cultural exchange and gets caught up in local intrigue. Both Varley and Haldeman evoke some of the feel of the young adult novels of Robert A. Heinlein, although both are marketed for adult audiences.

Tobias S. Buckell returns to the universe he introduced in his first two novels in *Sly Mongoose*, although we have skipped forward a few generations and there is only one recurring character. Buckell describes in lavish detail a society created on a hostile but resource rich planet whose population is under further stress because of an alien incursion. Brian Herbert and Kevin J. Anderson have continued their collaborative expansion of the late Frank Herbert's Dune series with *Paul of Dune*, in many ways the most interesting of their efforts. In the original series, there is a noticeable jump from the defeat of the original empire and the aftermath of the Jihad that has destroyed the old order and made Paul Muad'dib the most powerful man in the galaxy. This volume fills in that gap, showing Paul's ambivalent attitude toward the violence that is being carried out in his name and the efforts by various groups to oppose his

rise. On a less grandiose scale, Jack McDevitt continues his series about interstellar antiques collector Alex Benedict in *The Devil's Eye*, the sixth and to date best installment in this series. Benedict receives an unusual communication from a woman who has had her memories erased, which results in a mission to discover what happened to her during the past year that caused her to commit what amounts to suicide. Benedict and his companion visit a remote planet that derives its income from a somewhat bizarre tourist trade, only to uncover a plot to conceal an impending disaster.

Two space based adventure stories were also noteworthy. Michael Flynn revitalizes another classic science fiction theme—the alien artifact—in *The January Dancer*. Captain January and his crew are performing repairs on their ship on an unexplored planet when they discover what appears to be an artifact from an alien civilization embodying a new technology. As word of its unusual potential spreads, the artifact becomes the ultimate treasure in a large scale battle to possess it. Alastair Reynolds carries us into the very distant future in *House of Suns*, a civilization so far in advance of our own that everyday technology often feels like magic. The story involves a clan of effectively immortal clones, all copies of the same original but very much varied after the passage of thousands of years and travel throughout the universe. The clones periodically gather in a great convocation to exchange information, and on the eve of their next meeting, someone springs a trap, killing the vast majority of them, threatening to wipe out their line forever. The balance of the novel is essentially a murder mystery on a grand scale. It was a below average year for military science fiction, however, and the most noteworthy title was *When Duty Calls* by William C. Dietz, the eighth in his Legion of the Damned series. A unit consisting of cyborged soldiers, human bodies augmented with drastic mechanical alterations, gets involved in a combination of military and political struggles during a war against the insectlike Ramanthians. This is one of the author's best books.

One other exceptional novel in 2008 involved other worlds, but not planets reached by ordinary space travel. In Walter John Williams' *Implied Spaces*, Earth has created thirteen pocket universes, in each of which the laws of nature can be altered. The protagonist is one of the original designers who has achieved a form of immortality because his personality can be stored and downloaded into new bodies. In various guises, he visits these artificial realities until his explorations uncover a mysterious plot that could only be possible if one of the godlike artificial intelligences has been subverted. The novel is particularly effective in mixing elements of fantasy and science fiction together in unusual combinations.

Not all of the outstanding novels of the year were set in outer space. Alternate history, which has become a significant subgenre during the past several years, was well represented by *Half a Crown* by Jo Walton, third in her series set in a world where the British reached an accommodation with Hitler. In the concluding volume in the trilogy, a peace conference is the stimulus for an international crisis that could cause turmoil throughout Europe. Walton's series is particularly worthwhile because of the depth of her characterization and the convincing manner in which she depicts a population resigned to authoritarian rule.

The late Arthur C. Clarke and Frederik Pohl are both considered classic masters of the genre, and *The Last Theorem* is their first and only collaboration. The story chronicles the life of a Sir Lankan college student who is obsessed with solving Fermat's last theorem, a puzzle that has fascinated generations of mathematicians. This near future Earth is increasingly subject to local wars and the collapse of authority, a descent into chaos that has attracted the attention of the Great Galactics, an alien race who consider humanity little more than animals. The Galactics decide to dispatch a cleanup crew to scour the planet of life and prevent human violence from spreading to other worlds. Fortunately, a secretive group of humans has harnessed a new technology and uses it to enforce global peacekeeping, just in time to avert the extinction of the human race. The contrast between this latest novel and the earlier work of both authors is indicative of the changes the genre has undergone—an increased concern with social issues, deeper characterization, and careful, precise prose.

Although the return of space opera to a prominent place in science fiction is a welcome sign, the pendulum should not swing too far in the other direction. Science fiction has always encompassed a wide range of settings and story lines. It seems likely that this is a temporary spike and that 2009 will produce a more balanced and varied selection of notable novels. Gardner Dozois' an-

nual *The Year's Best Science Fiction 25* is up to its usual quality standards and provides a good cross section of the best short fiction published during the year.

Recommended Titles

2008 was an unusually good year for novels, particularly adventures in outer space. It was less exceptional for anthologies and short story collections than usual. Some of the titles below are from the first half of the year and are covered in the second volume of

What Do I Read Next? 2008.

Mars Life by Ben Bova

Sly Mongoose by Tobias Buckell

The Last Theorem by Arthur C. Clarke & Frederik Pohl

When Duty Calls by William C. Dietz

The Year's Best Science Fiction 25 edited by Gardner Dozois

The January Dancer by Michael Flynn

Marsbound by Joe Haldeman

The Dreaming Void by Peter Hamilton

Paul of Dune by Brian Herbert and Kevin J. Anderson

The Devil's Eye by Jack McDevitt

House of Suns by Alastair Reynolds

Anathem by Neal Stephenson

Rolling Thunder by John Varley

Half a Crown by Jo Walton

Implied Spaces by Walter John Williams

Science Fiction Titles

624

DAN ABNETT

Titanicus

(Nottingham, United Kingdom: Black Library, 2008)

Story type: Space Opera; Military
Series: Warhammer
Subject(s): Space Travel; Space Colonies
Major character(s): Daric Goland, Military Personnel; Cally Samstag, Military Personnel; Gearheart, Military Personnel
Time period(s): Indeterminate Future
Locale(s): Orestes, Planet—Imaginary

Summary: Interstellar war is conducted by means of enormous armored machines with human operators inside. When the planet Orestes is invaded by enemy forces, a relief mission is launched, but internal problems and lack of numbers hamper their efforts.

Other books by the same author:
Only in Death, 2007
Ravenor Rogue, 2007
The Saint, 2007
Traitor General, 2004
Straight Silver, 2002

Other books you might like:
William H. Keith Jr., *Bolo Brigade*, 2007
R.M. Meluch, *Strength and Honor*, 2008
John Ringo, *Hell's Faire*, 2003
David Sherman, *Wings of Hell*, 2008
    Dan Cragg, co-author
Timothy Zahn, *The Cobra Trilogy*, 2004

625

ANN AGUIRRE

Wanderlust

(New York: Ace, 2008)

Story type: Space Opera; Space Colony
Series: Sirantha Jax. Book 2
Subject(s): Space Travel; Aliens
Major character(s): Sirantha Jax, Diplomat; March, Rebel; Dina, Spacewoman

Time period(s): Indeterminate Future
Locale(s): Ithiss-Tor, Planet—Imaginary

Summary: One time star pilot Sirantha Jax is out of work and desperate when she's offered a position as a diplomat traveling to a remote planet. Her job is to convince the locals to join a trading coalition, but her job is complicated by carnivorous aliens, a group of interplanetary gangsters, a tempestuous romance with one of her crewmates, and other difficulties.

Other books by the same author:
Grimspace, 2007

Other books you might like:
Lois McMaster Bujold, *Cetaganda*, 1996
C.J. Cherryh, *Hammerfall*, 2001
Julie E. Czerneda, *Hidden in Sight*, 2003
Doris Egan, *Two-Bit Heroes*, 1992
S.L. Viehl, *Bio Rescue*, 2004

626

LOU ANDERS , Editor

Fast Forward 2

(Amherst, NY: Pyr, 2008)

Story type: Anthology
Subject(s): Short Stories

Summary: There is no unifying theme in this anthology and none of the 14 stories have been previous published. They range from adventures in outer space to futuristic murder mysteries to examinations of the possible future of technology. The contributors include Cory Doctorow, Nancy Kress, Ian McDonald, Mike Resnick, Jack McDevitt, Tobias Buckell, and others.

Where it's reviewed:
Locus, November 2008, page 54

Other books by the same author:
Sideways in Crime, 2008
Fast Forward 1, 2007
Futureshocks, 2006
Live Without a Net, 2003

Other books you might like:
Tobias S. Buckell, *Sly Mongoose*, 2008
Cory Doctorow, *Overclocked*, 2007
Nancy Kress, *The Aliens from Earth*, 1993

Jack McDevitt, *The Devil's Eye*, 2008
Ian McDonald, *Empire Dreams*, 1988

627

KEVIN J. ANDERSON

The Ashes of Worlds

(New York: Orbit, 2008)

Story type: Space Opera; Military
Series: Saga of Seven Suns. Book 7
Subject(s): Aliens; Space Travel
Major character(s): Jess Tamblyn, Military Personnel; Sullivan Gold, Administrator; Zan'nh, Alien, Government Official
Time period(s): Indeterminate Future
Locale(s): Outer Space

Summary: This is the last of a seven-volume series about an interstellar war that involves a variety of human and alien civilizations, where allegiances frequently change. The author describes the final heroic battles and ties up most of the loose ends, providing a detailed summary of the very confusing events in the first six books. There are few clear villains on either side and many of the characters perform heroically in the final days of the war.

Other books by the same author:
Metal Swarm, 2007
A Forest of Stars, 2003
Captain Nemo, 2002
Hidden Empire, 2002
Dogged Persistence, 2001

Other books you might like:
Greg Egan, *Incandescence*, 2008
Peter Hamilton, *Fallen Dragon*, 2002
Brian Herbert, *The Battle of Corrin*, 2004
    Kevin J. Anderson, co-author
Alastair Reynolds, *Redemption Ark*, 2002
Dan Simmons, *Hyperion*, 1989

628

TAYLOR ANDERSON

Crusade

(New York: Roc, 2008)

Story type: Alternate Universe; Military
Series: Destroyermen. Book 2
Subject(s): War; Alternate History
Major character(s): Matthew Reddy, Military Personnel, Sea Captain; Chack, Alien; Sandra Tucker, Military Personnel, Nurse
Time period(s): 1940s
Locale(s): Alternate Earth

Summary: Two American destroyers and a Japanese cruiser were transported from the middle of World War II into an alternate Earth where humans never evolved. A war is underway between a race of reptiles and the mammalian Lemurians. The Americans side with the Le-

murians, but the reptiles capture the Japanese warship.

Where it's reviewed:
Booklist, September 1, 2008, page 59
Publishers Weekly, August 11, 2008, page 33

Other books by the same author:
Into the Storm, 2007

Other books you might like:
John Birmingham, *Weapons of Choice*, 2004
William R. Forstchen, *Down to the Sea*, 2000
Harry Harrison, *West of Eden*, 1984
John Ringo, *Into the Looking Glass*, 2005
S.M. Stirling, *Conquistador*, 2003

629

CHRISTOPHER ANVIL

War Games

(New York: Baen, 2008)

Story type: Collection
Subject(s): Short Stories

Summary: This retrospective collection contains 17 short stories plus the complete novel, *The Steel, the Mist, and the Blazing Sun*, almost all originally published during the 1950s and 1960s. Anvil specializes in light adventure, often with a humorous twist. The most common theme in this collection is warfare, although not always in conventional forms.

Other books by the same author:
The Trouble with Humans, 2007
The Trouble with Aliens, 2006
Interstellar Patrol II, 2005
Interstellar Patrol, 2003
Pandora's Legions, 2002

Other books you might like:
Poul Anderson, *Dialogue with Darkness*, 1985
Gordon R. Dickson, *The Human Edge*, 2003
Keith Laumer, *Future Imperfect*, 2003
Murray Leinster, *First Contacts*, 1998
Eric Frank Russell, *Major Ingredients*, 2000

630

ELIZABETH BEAR

All the Windwracked Stars

(New York: Tor, 2008)

Story type: Wild Talents; Immortality
Subject(s): Secrets; Immortality
Major character(s): Muire, Immortal; Cathoair, Sports Figure; Gunther Watsen, Student
Time period(s): Indeterminate Future
Locale(s): Earth

Summary: The author blends fantasy elements with science fiction in this story of a future so remote that technology often feels like magic. Muire is the last survivor of a group of immortals created in the distant past, or that's what she believes until she finds evidence that another of her kind exists somewhere in a decadent and dangerous city.

Where it's reviewed:
Booklist, October 15, 2008, page 29
Magazine of Fantasy and Science Fiction, October-November 2008, page 3
Publishers Weekly, September 8, 2008, page 39

Other books by the same author:
Dust, 2007
Undertow, 2007
Carnival, 2006
Hammered, 2005
Scardown, 2005

Other books you might like:
Rene Barjavel, *The Immortals*, 1975
Ben Bova, *Orion Among the Stars*, 1995
Lin Carter, *The Immortal of World's End*, 1976
C.J. Cherryh, *Gate of Ivrel*, 1976
Sheila Finch, *The Garden of the Shaped*, 1987

631

K.A. BEDFORD

Time Machines Repaired While-U-Wait

(Calgary, Alberta: Edge, 2008)

Story type: Humor; Time Travel
Subject(s): Humor; Time Travel; Mystery
Major character(s): Aloysius Webb, Technician; Dickhead McMahon, Businessman; James Rutherford, Widow(er)
Time period(s): Indeterminate Future
Locale(s): Earth

Summary: Spider Webb spends most of his time repairing time machines, until the day he finds a dead body hidden in one of them. When his superiors try to hush things up, this just makes him more suspicious than ever, and hardens his resolve to solve the case. Mystery and humor mix as he uncovers the truth.

Other books by the same author:
Eclipse, 2006
Hydrogen Steel, 2006
Orbital Burn, 2003

Other books you might like:
Poul Anderson, *Shield of Time*, 1990
Kage Baker, *The Graveyard Game*, 2001
Keith Laumer, *The Great Time Machine Hoax*, 1964
Paul Levinson, *The Plot to Save Socrates*, 2006
Barry N. Malzberg, *Chorale*, 1978

632

CHRISTOPHER L. BENNETT

Greater than the Sum

(New York: Pocket, 2008)

Story type: Space Opera; Military
Series: Star Trek: The Next Generation

Subject(s): Aliens; Space Travel
Major character(s): Jean-Luc Picard, Spaceship Captain, Military Personnel; T'Ryssa Chen, Military Personnel; Worf, Alien, Military Personnel
Time period(s): Indeterminate Future
Locale(s): Spaceship; Planet—Imaginary

Summary: An exploratory mission discovers a new technology, but they are almost immediately attacked by the alien Borg. A military starship is dispatched to the scene to prevent the Borg from acquiring the technology, which could make them more powerful than ever before.

Other books by the same author:
Drowned in Thunder, 2007
The Buried Age, 2007
Watchers on the Walls, 2006
Ex Machina, 2005

Other books you might like:
Roger MacBride Allen, *Final Inquiries*, 2008
Peter Hamilton, *Pandora's Star*, 2004
David Mack, *Gods of Night*, 2008
Jack McDevitt, *Odyssey*, 2006
Timothy Zahn, *Night Train to Rigel*, 2005

633

C.F. BENTLEY (Pseudonym of Phyllis Irene Radford Karr)

Harmony

(New York: DAW, 2008)

Story type: Space Opera; Space Colony
Subject(s): Aliens; Space Colonies
Major character(s): Sissy du Maigrie pu Chauncey, Religious; Jake Hannigan, Military Personnel; Gregor da Ivan pa Crystal Temple, Religious
Time period(s): Indeterminate Future
Locale(s): Harmony, Planet—Imaginary; Outer Space

Summary: The planet Harmony and its colonies are reclusive and refuse to deal with either the human or alien civilizations in their vicinity, which are currently involved in an interstellar war. The society of Harmony itself is collapsing, not only because of tensions within its theocratic government but because of physical changes in the home planet itself.

Where it's reviewed:
Library Journal, August 1, 2008, page 74
Publishers Weekly, June 23, 2008, page 41

Other books by the same author:
Enigma, 2009

Other books you might like:
Poul Anderson, *Earthman, Go Home!*, 1960
Michael Bishop, *Stolen Faces*, 1977
Frederik Pohl, *Stopping at Slowyear*, 1991
Bob Shaw, *The Palace of Eternity*, 1969
Timothy Zahn, *The Third Lynx*, 2007

634

SYLVIE BERARD

Of Wind and Sand

(Calgary, Alberta: Edge, 2008)

Story type: Space Colony; First Contact
Subject(s): Space Colonies; Aliens
Major character(s): Rliebkl, Alien; Selm, Settler, Prisoner
Time period(s): Indeterminate Future
Locale(s): Mars II, Planet—Imaginary

Summary: Humans have colonized a planet they call Mars II despite the presence of an intelligent, lizardlike species. At first it appears that the two races will live together peacefully, but eventually tensions cause conflict. Much of the story is reflected in the relationship between individual humans and aliens. First novel.

Other books you might like:
C.J. Cherryh, *Foreigner*, 1994
Alan Dean Foster, *Diuturnity's Dawn*, 2002
Stephen Leigh, *Speaking Stones*, 1999
Andre Norton, *Ordeal in Otherwhere*, 1964
Brian Stableford, *Chimera's Cradle*, 1997

635

SHANE BERRYHILL

Chance Fortune in the Shadow Zone

(New York: Starscape, 2008)

Story type: Young Adult; Coming-of-Age
Series: Chance Fortune. Book 2
Subject(s): Teen Relationships; Secrets
Major character(s): Chance Fortune, Teenager; Gothika, Teenager; Iron Maiden, Teenager
Time period(s): Indeterminate Future
Locale(s): Alternate Universe

Summary: Chance Fortune is the leader of a band of teen-aged superheroes who has no powers himself but who is quick-witted enough to keep his position. When a tele-portation device malfunctions and strands them in the Shadow Zone, a kind of miniature universe, someone begins kidnapping members of the team and Chance must rescue them.

Other books by the same author:
Chance Fortune and the Outlaws, 2006

Other books you might like:
K.A. Applegate, *Destination Unknown*, 2001
Eoin Colfer, *Artemis Fowl*, 2001
Arthur Byron Cover, *Born in Fire*, 2002
Catherine Jinks, *Evil Genius*, 2005
Dean Wesley Smith, *Whodunnit*, 2003

636

BEN BOVA

Laugh Lines

(New York: Baen, 2008)

Story type: Collection
Subject(s): Short Stories; Humor

Summary: This collection includes most of the author's humorous science fiction, including two complete novels. *The Starcrossed* is the story of a conspiracy within the television industry and is based in part on the circum-stances surrounding the short-lived television series *The Star Lost*. *Cyberbooks* is about a revolutionary new publishing technique.

Where it's reviewed:
Publishers Weekly, May 26, 2008, page 43

Other books by the same author:
Mars Life, 2008
The Sam Gunn Omnibus, 2007
The Green Trap, 2006
Mercury, 2005
Powersat, 2005

Other books you might like:
Poul Anderson, *All One Universe*, 1996
Gordon R. Dickson, *In the Bone*, 1987
Joe Haldeman, *None So Blind*, 1996
Keith Laumer, *The Lighter Side*, 2002
Robert Sheckley, *Is That What People Do?*, 1984

637

ERIC BROWN

Necropath

(Nottingham, United Kingdom: Solaris, 2008)

Story type: Mystery; Space Opera
Subject(s): Aliens; Space Colonies
Major character(s): Jeff Vaughan, Security Officer, Tele-path; Jimmy Chandra, Police Officer; Rao, Doctor
Time period(s): Indeterminate Future
Locale(s): Earth

Summary: Jeff Vaughan is working as a security officer on an ocean based spaceport when his telepathic abilities lead to his discovery of a bizarre religious cult among recent arrivals. When he and a police officer attempt to investigate, they discover that someone is willing to kill them to preserve their secrets. Part of this novel was previously published as *Bengal Station*.

Other books by the same author:
Kethani, 2008
Helix, 2007
Threshold Shift, 2006
The Fall of Tartarus, 2005
New York Dreams, 2004

Other books you might like:
Roger MacBride Allen, *Inferno*, 1994
F.M. Busby, *The Singularity Project*, 1993

Paul J. McAuley, *Whole Wide World*, 2002
Mel Odom, *Stalker Analog*, 1993
Robert J. Sawyer, *Illegal Alien*, 1997

638

TOBIAS S. BUCKELL

Sly Mongoose

(New York: Tor, 2008)

Story type: Coming-of-Age; Space Opera
Subject(s): Coming-of-Age; Space Colonies
Major character(s): Timas, Teenager, Worker; Katerina, Diplomat, Teenager; Pepper, Spy
Time period(s): Indeterminate Future
Locale(s): Chilo, Planet—Imaginary

Summary: Timas is a rather mature teenager working on the planet Chilo when a mysterious stranger quite literally falls out of the sky. Then an external force begins to attack the planet, conquering one city after another, searching for mysterious information contained somewhere on Chilo.

Where it's reviewed:
Booklist, July 1, 2008, page 50
Publishers Weekly, June 23, 2008, page 41

Other books by the same author:
Ragamuffin, 2007
Crystal Rain, 2006

Other books you might like:
Poul Anderson, *The Avatar*, 1978
Lois McMaster Bujold, *Barrayar*, 1991
C.J. Cherryh, *Downbelow Station*, 1981
Ursula K. Le Guin, *The Left Hand of Darkness*, 1969
Alastair Reynolds, *Chasm City*, 2000

639

M.M. BUCKNER

Watermind

(New York: Tor, 2008)

Story type: Alternate Intelligence; Hard Science Fiction
Subject(s): Disasters; Computers
Major character(s): C.J. Reilly, Worker; Max Pottevents, Worker; Watermind, Artificial Intelligence
Time period(s): Indeterminate Future
Locale(s): Louisiana

Summary: Two people discover that a fortuitous combination of organic waste matter, functioning computers chips, and microscopic machines have combined to form a kind of artificial life. The watermind is intriguing at first, but then proves to be dangerous, and when it seeks to escape into the ocean, they realize the future of the world is at stake.

Where it's reviewed:
Booklist, October 1, 2008, page 33
Isaac Asimov's Science Fiction, October 2008, page 228
Publishers Weekly, September 15, 2008, page 50

Other books by the same author:
War Surf, 2005
Neurolink, 2004
Hyperthought, 2003

Other books you might like:
Steve Alten, *Goliath*, 2002
Martin Caidin, *The God Machine*, 1968
D.F. Jones, *Colossus*, 1966
Edward M. Lerner, *Fools' Experiment*, 2008
Charles Eric Maine, *B.E.A.S.T.*, 1969

640

ORSON SCOTT CARD

Ender in Exile

(New York: Tor, 2008)

Story type: Space Opera; Coming-of-Age
Series: Ender. Book 9
Subject(s): Aliens; Coming-of-Age
Major character(s): Andrew Wiggin, Government Official, Spaceman; Valentine Wiggin, Writer; Jane, Artificial Intelligence
Time period(s): Indeterminate Future
Locale(s): Planet—Imaginary

Summary: Andrew "Ender" Wiggin has saved the world, but now he finds himself sought after by the various human factions. In order to remain neutral, he immigrates to the colony worlds where he learns more about both the aliens he defeated and the humans among whom he finds himself.

Where it's reviewed:
Booklist, October 1, 2008, page 4

Other books by the same author:
A War of Gifts, 2007
Empire, 2006
Shadow of the Giant, 2005
Shadow Puppets, 2002
Ender's Shadow, 1999

Other books you might like:
Poul Anderson, *Ensign Flandry*, 1966
Joe Haldeman, *Forever Free*, 1999
Keith Laumer, *End as a Hero*, 1985
Frederik Pohl, *Gateway*, 1977
Timothy Zahn, *Angelmass*, 2001

641

JEFF CARLSON

Plague War

(New York: Ace, 2008)

Story type: Disaster; Quest
Subject(s): Disasters; Plague
Major character(s): Ruth Goldman, Scientist; Cam Najarro, Survivor; Newcombe, Survivor
Time period(s): Indeterminate Future
Locale(s): United States

Summary: A plague of nanotechnology, microscopic machines, has killed all humans and animals below ten thousand feet altitude. The survivors are slowly stirring now that Ruth Goldman has found a vaccine that is effective, but as she and her companions make their way across what's left of the United States, they discover that both the remnants of the American government and various foreign powers have reasons for wishing to suppress her discovery. This is the sequel to *Plague Year*.

Other books by the same author:
Plague Year, 2007

Other books you might like:
Michael Crichton, *Prey*, 2002
Don H. DeBrandt, *V.I.*, 2000
Michael Flynn, *The Nanotech Chronicles*, 1991
Steven Piziks, *Corporate Mentality*, 1999
John Shirley, *Crawlers*, 2003

642

PATRICK CARMAN

Rivers of Fire

(New York: Little, Brown, 2008)

Story type: Young Adult; Space Colony
Series: Atherton. Book 2
Subject(s): Space Colonies; Disasters
Major character(s): Edgar, Teenager, Orphan; Samuel, Teenager; Isabel, Teenager
Time period(s): Indeterminate Future
Locale(s): Outer Space

Summary: Atherton was an artificial world built in orbit with three separate environments which were arranged in tiers. A disaster has resulted in the barriers between these regions collapsing, and the inhabitants of each struggle to survive as everything they know begins to change.

Where it's reviewed:
School Library Journal, August 2008, page 116

Other books by the same author:
Into the Mist, 2007
The House of Power, 2007
The Tenth City, 2006
Beyond the Valley of Thorns, 2005
The Dark Hills Divide, 2005

Other books you might like:
Brian W. Aldiss, *Non-Stop*, 1959
Stephen Baxter, *Raft*, 1991
Philip Jose Farmer, *The Maker of Universes*, 1965
Karl Schroeder, *Pirate Sun*, 2008
Bob Shaw, *The Ragged Astronauts*, 1986

643

JEFFREY A. CARVER

Sunborn

(New York: Tor, 2008)

Story type: Hard Science Fiction; Space Opera
Series: Chaos Chronicles. Book 4

Subject(s): Disasters; Space Travel
Major character(s): John Bandicut, Spaceman; Antares, Alien; Napoleon, Robot
Time period(s): Indeterminate Future
Locale(s): Outer Space

Summary: John Bandicut, aided by a variety of aliens and a pair of sentient robots, has a new mission. A space station is menaced by mysterious gravity waves that threaten to tear it apart. Bandicut barely escapes when it is finally destroyed, and in the process he learns that the same force is literally turning stars into novas and wiping out entire civilizations.

Where it's reviewed:
Analog, September 2008, page 136
Publishers Weekly, September 1, 2008, page 40

Other books by the same author:
Eternity's End, 2000
The Infinite Sea, 1996
Strange Attractors, 1995
Neptune Crossing, 1994
Dragon Rigger, 1993

Other books you might like:
Poul Anderson, *Satan's World*, 1968
Ben Bova, *Mars Life*, 2008
Alexander Jablokov, *Deepdrive*, 1998
Jack McDevitt, *Chindi*, 2002
Alastair Reynolds, *House of Suns*, 2008

644

ARTHUR C. CLARKE
FREDERIK POHL , Co-Author

The Last Theorem

(New York: Ballantine, 2008)

Story type: Political; Hard Science Fiction
Subject(s): Aliens; Mathematics
Major character(s): Ranjit Subramanian, Scientist; Gamini Bandara, Political Figure; Myra de Soyza, Scientist
Time period(s): 21st century
Locale(s): Sri Lanka; United States

Summary: A young Sri Lankan who is obsessed with the problem of proving Fermat's last theorem becomes involved in pivotal events as the dominant race in the galaxy decides to exterminate the potentially dangerous human race. His life becomes a reflection of events that will change the future of humanity.

Where it's reviewed:
Publishers Weekly, June 30, 2008, page 166

Other books by the same author:
The Collected Stories of Arthur C. Clarke, 2000
The Hammer of God, 1993
Imperial Earth, 1975
Rendezvous with Rama, 1973
Childhood's End, 1953

Other books you might like:
Poul Anderson, *After Doomsday*, 1962
Gregory Benford, *Eater*, 2000
Fred Hoyle, *The Black Cloud*, 1957

William Tenn, *Of Men and Monsters*, 1968
Robert Charles Wilson, *The Harvest*, 1993

John Darnton, *Neanderthal*, 1969
James Rollins, *Amazonia*, 2002
Charles Wilson, *Direct Descendant*, 1995

645

SUZANNE COLLINS

The Hunger Games
(New York: Scholastic, 2008)

Story type: Young Adult; Coming-of-Age
Subject(s): Teen Relationships; Coming-of-Age
Major character(s): Katniss Everdeen, Teenager; Peeta Mellark, Teenager; Cinna, Worker, Stylist
Time period(s): Indeterminate Future
Locale(s): North America

Summary: Some time in the future, the North American continent has collapsed into a mix of primitive and modern elements. A new country known as Panem has arrived which dominates outlying communities and requires that they send teenagers to engage in duels to the death to be televised across the nation. The protagonist is chosen as one of the latest round of contestants.

Where it's reviewed:
Booklist, September 1, 2008, page 97
Entertainment Weekly, September 12, 2008, page 139
School Library Journal, September 2008, page 176

Other books by the same author:
Gregor and the Code of Law, 2008
Gregor and the Marks of Secret, 2007
Gregor and the Prophecy of Bane, 2005

Other books you might like:
Neal Barrett Jr., *Through Darkest America*, 1988
Suzy McKee Charnas, *Motherlines*, 1978
Suzanne Martel, *The City under Ground*, 1964
Paul O. Williams, *The Breaking of Northwall*, 1980
John Wyndham, *Re-Birth*, 1955

646

CARLOS J. CORTES

Perfect Circle
(New York: Bantam, 2008)

Story type: Techno-Thriller; Mystery
Subject(s): Aliens; Disasters
Major character(s): Paul Reece, Scientist; Mark O'Reilly, Foreman; Owen Deholt, Businessman
Time period(s): 2000s
Locale(s): Republic of the Congo

Summary: A drilling project in Africa makes a startling discovery. Four miles beneath the Earth's surface they encounter the shell of an artificial object constructed of unknown materials. They launch a secret program to explore the artifact while spies, the local government, and guerrilla forces clash around them. First novel.

Other books you might like:
Lincoln Child, *Deep Storm*, 2007
Michael Crichton, *Congo*, 1976

647

BEN COUNTER

Battle for the Abyss
(Nottingham, United Kingdom: Black Library, 2008)

Story type: Space Opera; Military
Series: Warhammer
Subject(s): Space Travel; Quest
Major character(s): Cestus, Military Personnel; Brynngar, Spaceship Captain; Kaminska, Military Personnel
Time period(s): Indeterminate Future
Locale(s): Outer Space

Summary: As civil war threatens to destroy an interstellar empire from within, one faction deploys a fleet for a sneak attack on the home world of the most powerful of the loyalist forces. A small contingent of space marines are dispatched on a desperate mission to head off the attack and prevent disaster.

Other books by the same author:
Hammer of Daemons, 2008
Chapter War, 2007
Galaxy in Flames, 2006
Crimson Tears, 2005
Grey Knights, 2004

Other books you might like:
Dan Abnett, *Legion*, 2008
William C. Dietz, *When Duty Calls*, 2008
Roland Green, *On the Verge*, 1998
Sandy Mitchell, *Scourge the Heretic*, 2008
James Swallow, *Red Fury*, 2008

648

JULIE E. CZERNEDA

Riders of the Storm
(New York: DAW, 2008)

Story type: Space Opera; Psychic Powers
Subject(s): Psychic Powers; Aliens
Major character(s): Aryl Sarc, Psychic, Settler; Enris Mendolar, Settler; Marcus Bowman, Explorer
Time period(s): Indeterminate Future
Locale(s): Planet—Imaginary

Summary: On a planet where three intelligent races co-exist, two exiles are rescued by a human with whom they investigate the mysterious abandonment of a settlement and the apparent disappearance of an entire clan. Control of the abandoned area turns into a three-way power struggle that could affect the stability of the planet's culture.

Where it's reviewed:
Library Journal, September 15, 2008, page 48

Other books by the same author:
Reap the Wild Wind, 2007
Regeneration, 2006
Hidden in Sight, 2003
In the Company of Others, 2001
Changing Vision, 2000

Other books you might like:
Marion Zimmer Bradley, *City of Sorcery*, 1984
C.J. Cherryh, *Rider at the Gate*, 1995
Doris Egan, *Two-Bit Heroes*, 1992
Alan Dean Foster, *Diuturnity's Dawn*, 2002
S.L. Viehl, *Shockball*, 2001

649

JAMES F. DAVID

The Book of Summer
(New York: Tor, 2008)

Story type: Space Colony; Religious
Subject(s): Space Colonies; Slavery
Major character(s): Grandma Jones, Government Official; Summer, Slave; Rey, Slave
Time period(s): Indeterminate Future
Locale(s): America, Planet—Imaginary

Summary: The colony on planet America was founded by fundamentalist Christians but has since been cut off from the home world. Although it has a thriving economy, it is based on slavery. When the ruler of the colony decides to reverse herself and free all the slaves, she runs into opposition from those vested interests who are profiting on the system as it is.

Other books by the same author:
Thunder of Time, 2005
Before the Cradle Falls, 2002
Ship of the Damned, 2000
Footprints of Thunder, 1999
Fragments, 1997

Other books you might like:
Isaac Asimov, *The Currents of Space*, 1952
Sharon Baker, *Journey to Memblar*, 1987
Phyllis Gotlieb, *Flesh and Gold*, 1998
Elizabeth Lynn, *The Sardonyx Net*, 1981
Ann Maxwell, *Fire Dancer*, 1982

650

KEITH R.A. DECANDIDO

A Burning House
(New York: Pocket, 2008)

Story type: Space Opera; Espionage
Series: Star Trek
Subject(s): Aliens; Secrets
Major character(s): Klag, Spaceship Captain, Alien; Goran, Military Personnel, Alien; Rodek, Military Personnel, Alien
Time period(s): Indeterminate Future

Locale(s): Qo'noS, Planet—Imaginary
Summary: Klag is a Klingon starship captain whose return to his homeworld is less restful than he expected. There are various conspiracies and political battles underway and various innocent parties are caught up in the expanding and increasingly dangerous conflict. Klag proves to be the not entirely willing force that resolves some of the difficulties.

Other books by the same author:
Command and Conquer, 2007
Down These Mean Streets, 2006
Articles of the Federastion, 2005
Destruction of Illusions, 2003
The Art of the Impossible, 2003

Other books you might like:
C.J. Cherryh, *Invader*, 1995
John M. Ford, *The Final Reflection*, 1984
Michael Jan Friedman, *Her Klingon Soul*, 1997
Robert E. Vardeman, *The Klingon Gambit*, 1981
Timothy Zahn, *Conqueror's Heritage*, 1995

651

CLAIRE DELACROIX

Fallen
(New York: Tor, 2008)

Story type: Mystery; Dystopian
Subject(s): Secrets; Romance
Major character(s): Lilia Desjardins, Scientist; Adam Montgomery, Alien; Gideon Fitzgerald, Scientist
Time period(s): 2090s (2099)
Locale(s): Earth
Summary: Lilia Desjardins is determined to unearth the truth about a plot against prominent scientist Gideon Fitzgerald. Her investigation takes an unusual turn when she meets Adam Montgomery, a secretive visitor from another world whose body has been surgically altered so that he can pass for human.

Other books by the same author:
The Warrior, 2004
The Scoundrel, 2003
The Beauty, 2001
The Heiress, 1999
The Princess, 1998

Other books you might like:
Catherine Asaro, *The Quantum Rose*, 2000
Lois McMaster Bujold, *A Civil Campaign*, 1999
Jayne Castle, *Ghost Hunter*, 2006
Jayne Ann Krentz, *Soft Focus*, 2000
Anne McCaffrey, *Decision at Doona*, 1969

652

WILLIAM C. DIETZ

When Duty Calls
(New York: Ace, 2008)

Story type: Space Opera; Military
Series: Legion of the Damned. Book 8

Subject(s): Cyborgs; Space Colonies
Major character(s): Antonio Santan, Military Personnel; Liam Quinlan, Military Personnel; Christine Vanderveen, Diplomat
Time period(s): Indeterminate Future
Locale(s): Planet—Imaginary

Summary: A group of cyborg soldiers find themselves in deep trouble on a hostile planet when the officer commanding them considers his own career in preference to their well-being. Elsewhere a diplomat attempts to forge an alliance with a splinter group of humans who have adopted wholesale cloning.

Where it's reviewed:
Booklist, October 1, 2008, page 32

Other books by the same author:
When All Seems Lost, 2007
Logos Run, 2006
For Those Who Fell, 2004
Deathday, 2001
By Force of Arms, 2000

Other books you might like:
David Drake, *The Forlorn Hope*, 1984
Elizabeth Moon, *Once a Hero*, 1997
John Ringo, *When the Devil Dances*, 2002
David Weber, *By Schism Rent Asunder*, 2008
Timothy Zahn, *The Cobra Trilogy*, 2004

653

KAREN DIONNE

Freezing Point

(New York: Jove, 2008)

Story type: Disaster; Medical
Subject(s): Secrets; Animals/Rats
Major character(s): Ben Maki, Businessman, Environmentalist; Zo Zelinski, Scientist; Donald Gillette, Businessman
Time period(s): Indeterminate Future
Locale(s): Antarctica

Summary: In the near future, worldwide water shortages have reached a critical point. An American corporation is experimenting with a plan to melt icebergs using microwaves beamed from orbit but the head of the company is secretly and illegally helping along the calving of glaciers in the Antarctic. Then a large colony of icebound rats emerges carrying a new kind of plague which could affect the entire ocean. First novel.

Where it's reviewed:
Publishers Weekly, August 11, 2008, page 34

Other books you might like:
Stephen Baxter, *Anti-Ice*, 1993
Alan Dean Foster, *The Thing*, 1981
James Herbert, *Lair*, 1979
David C. Poyer, *The White Continent*, 1980
George H. Smith, *The Coming of the Rats*, 1961

654

B.K. EVENSON

No Exit

(Milwaukie, OR: Dark Horse, 2008)

Story type: Space Colony; Mystery
Series: Aliens
Subject(s): Aliens; Secrets
Major character(s): Anders Kramm, Detective—Private; Matthew Darby, Businessman; Bjorn, Spaceman
Time period(s): Indeterminate Future
Locale(s): Outer Space; Planet—Imaginary

Summary: Anders Kramm wakens from suspended animation to discover that the alien infestation of Earth is under control. The aliens were not exterminated, however, and have been re-established on another planet as part of a conspiracy by elements within the human government. First novel.

Other books you might like:
David Bischoff, *Genocide*, 1994
Diane Carey, *Cauldron*, 2007
Michael Jan Friedman, *Original Sin*, 2005
S.D. Perry, *Labyrinth*, 1996
John Shirley, *Forever Midnight*, 2006

655

ERIC FLINT
VIRGINIA DEMARCE , Co-Author

1635: The Dreeson Incident

(New York: Baen, 2008)

Story type: Historical; Time Travel
Series: Ring of Fire
Subject(s): Alternate History; Time Travel
Major character(s): Mike Stearns, Leader, Time Traveler; Gustavus Adolphus, Royalty; Rebecca Stearns, Time Traveler
Time period(s): 17th century
Locale(s): Europe

Summary: The town of Grantville has been displaced in time back to the 17th century. There Mike Stearns leads an effort to create a new nation allied with the King of Sweden. Using highly advanced technology, the new country has a great advantage, but the entrenched interests strike back using assassination and other methods to get their way.

Where it's reviewed:
Booklist, October 1, 2008, page 32

Other books by the same author:
1824: The Arkansas War, 2006
1812: The Rivers of War, 2005
1633, 2002
1632, 2000
Mother of Demons, 1997

Other books you might like:
Michael Bishop, *No Enemy But Time*, 1982
L. Sprague de Camp, *Lest Darkness Fall*, 1941

Kirk Mitchell, *Never the Twain*, 1987
S.M. Stirling, *Island in the Sea of Time*, 1998
Connie Willis, *Doomsday Book*, 1992

656

ERIC FLINT , Editor
MIKE RESNICK , Co-Editor

The Best of Jim Baens Universe 2

(New York: Baen, 2008)

Story type: Anthology
Subject(s): Short Stories

Summary: This is the second volume of selected science fiction and fantasy stories which were previously published on the Internet. The two genres are approximately evenly represented. The contributors include Kevin J. Anderson, John Barnes, James P. Hogan, Nancy Kress, Jack McDevitt, and many others.

Other books by the same author:
1824: The Arkansas War, 2006
1812: The Rivers of War, 2005
1633, 2002
1632, 2000
Mother of Demons, 1997

Other books you might like:
Kevin J. Anderson, *Dogged Persistence*, 2001
John Barnes, *Apostrophes and Apocalypses*, 1998
James P. Hogan, *Catastrophes, Chaos, and Convolutions*, 2005
Nancy Kress, *Beaker's Dozen*, 1998
Jack McDevitt, *Outbound*, 2006

657

ERIC FLINT
DAVE FREER , Co-Author

Slow Train to Arcturus

(New York: Baen, 2008)

Story type: Space Opera; Space Colony
Subject(s): Aliens; Space Travel
Major character(s): Kretz, Alien; Selna, Alien; Howard Dansson, Spaceman, Worker
Time period(s): Indeterminate Future
Locale(s): Outer Space

Summary: The inhabitants of the planet Mira send a spaceship to investigate the approach of an enormous artificial object in space. They discover it is a slow moving ship consisting of separate modules, each with a different human culture designed to survive a journey that will take many generations to complete. Some of the humans are friendly, but others are not.

Where it's reviewed:
Booklist, September 1, 2008, page 60
Library Journal, October 15, 2008, page 60
Publishers Weekly, August 11, 2008, page 33

Other books by the same author:
1824: The Arkansas War, 2006
1812: The Rivers of War, 2005
1633, 2002
1632, 2000
Mother of Demons, 1997

Other books you might like:
Brian W. Aldiss, *Non-Stop*, 1959
Elizabeth Bear, *Dust*, 2007
Ken MacLeod, *Learning the World*, 2005
Robert Reed, *Marrow*, 2000
Richard Paul Russo, *Ship of Fools*, 2001

658

ERIC FLINT , Editor
MIKE RESNICK , Co-Editor

When Diplomacy Fails

(Deerfield, IL: ISFiC Press, 2008)

Story type: Anthology; Military
Subject(s): Short Stories

Summary: This is an anthology of nine military science fiction stories, all previously published. The subject matter ranges from war on other planets to war in space and all are basically adventure stories. The contributors include John Ringo, David Drake, David Weber, Tanya Huff, Harry Turtledove, and others.

Other books by the same author:
1824: The Arkansas War, 2006
1812: The Rivers of War, 2005
1633, 2002
1632, 2000
Mother of Demons, 1997

Other books you might like:
David Drake, *The Butcher's Bill*, 1998
Tanya Huff, *The Heart of Valor*, 2007
John Ringo, *Gust Front*, 2001
Harry Turtledove, *The Man with the Iron Heart*, 2008
David Weber, *By Schism Rent Asunder*, 2008

659

MICHAEL FLYNN

The January Dancer

(New York: Tor, 2008)

Story type: Space Opera; Future Shock
Subject(s): Space Travel; Secrets
Major character(s): Amos January, Spaceship Captain; The Fudir, Criminal; Hugh O'Carroll, Political Figure
Time period(s): Indeterminate Future
Locale(s): Outer Space; Planet—Imaginary

Summary: The crew of a spaceship discover an alien artifact that predates human history, one that is rumored to have extraordinary powers. The lure of the artifact is so powerful that many different parties are determined to control it, which sets off a series of battles, chases, captures, escapes, and other adventures in space and on various planets.

Where it's reviewed:
Booklist, September 15, 2008, page 32
Library Journal, August 1, 2008, page 74
Locus, September 2008, page 23
Publishers Weekly, August 4, 2008, page 48

Other books by the same author:
Eifelheim, 2006
The Wreck of the River of Stars, 2003
Falling Stars, 2001
Lodestar, 2000
The Nanotech Chronicles, 1991

Other books you might like:
Iain Banks, *Inversions*, 1998
C.J. Cherryh, *Downbelow Station*, 1981
Peter Hamilton, *Judas Unchained*, 2006
Alastair Reynolds, *House of Suns*, 2008
Timothy Zahn, *Night Train to Rigel*, 2005

660

MATT FORBECK

Mutant Chronicles

(New York: Del Rey, 2008)

Story type: Dystopian; Military
Subject(s): Prophecy; Monsters
Major character(s): Mitch Hunter, Military Personnel; Nathan Rooker, Military Personnel; Samuel, Religious
Time period(s): 28th century
Locale(s): Earth

Summary: Several centuries from now, Earth is dominated by megacorporations who field private armies against one another. Disaster strikes when a horde of mutant creatures is released from confinement. The mutants can turn fallen enemies into lethal killing machines almost as powerful as themselves. This is based on a movie screenplay.

Other books by the same author:
Prophecy of the Dragons, 2006
The Dragons Revealed, 2006
Blood Bowl, 2005
Dead Ball, 2005
Marked for Death, 2005

Other books you might like:
Robert Lynn Asprin, *The Cold Cash War*, 1977
John Brunner, *Stand on Zanzibar*, 1968
S.N. Lewitt, *Cybernetic Jungle*, 1992
Marta Randall, *Dangerous Games*, 1980
Mack Reynolds, *The Earth War*, 1963

661

ALAN DEAN FOSTER

Quofum

(New York: Del Rey, 2008)

Story type: Space Opera; First Contact
Subject(s): Aliens; Secrets
Major character(s): Esra Tellenberg, Scientist; Valnadireb, Alien, Scientist; Tiare Haviti, Scientist
Time period(s): Indeterminate Future
Locale(s): Quofum, Planet—Imaginary

Summary: A small group of scientists are sent to study a planet that appears to blink in and out of existence. They are puzzled by the profuse variety of species from various different lines of evolution, but their stay is longer than they wanted after one of the crew turns out to be a criminal intent upon marooning them there.

Where it's reviewed:
Booklist, October 1, 2008, page 32
Publishers Weekly, August 25, 2008, page 56

Other books by the same author:
Patrimony, 2007
Lost and Found, 2004
Drowning World, 2003
Flinx's Folly, 2003
Dirge, 2000

Other books you might like:
Gordon R. Dickson, *Mission to Universe*, 1965
Philip Jose Farmer, *Night of Light*, 1966
Larry Niven, *The Legacy of Heorot*, 1987
  Jerry Pournelle, co-author
Andre Norton, *Star Rangers*, 1955
Vernor Vinge, *A Deepness in the Sky*, 1999

662

NICK GEVERS , Editor

Extraordinary Engines

(Nottingham, United Kingdom: Solaris, 2008)

Story type: Anthology
Subject(s): Short Stories; Technology

Summary: The 12 stories in this original anthology are all examples of steampunk, a nebulously defined area of science fiction in which technology during the 19th century took various different courses. The contributors include Jeffrey Ford, Jay Lake, Kage Baker, Robert Reed, James Morrow, and others. Several of the stories verge on fantasy.

Other books you might like:
James P. Blaylock, *The Digging Leviathan*, 1984
Paul Di Filippo, *The Steampunk Trilogy*, 1994
William Gibson, *The Difference Engine*, 1990
  Bruce Sterling, co-author
Ian R. MacLeod, *The Light Ages*, 2003
Neal Stephenson, *The Diamond Age*, 1995

663

JAMES C. GLASS

The Viper of Portello

(Bonney Lake, WA: Fairwood Press, 2008)

Story type: Space Opera; Military
Subject(s): Space Colonies; Secrets
Major character(s): Eduardo Cabral, Military Personnel; Vicente Pinzon, Government Official; Cesario Monsarez, Government Official
Time period(s): Indeterminate Future
Locale(s): Planet—Imaginary

Summary: Eduardo Cabral was a talented and deadly soldier who was also a man sensitive to the arts. When he is betrayed by the government for which he fought, he emigrates to another planet where his plans to remain in exile are ended when a revolution takes place on his home world. He returns and finds himself in a position of power, but also with a terrifying responsibility.

Other books by the same author:
Matrix Dreams and Other Stories, 2004
Empress of Light, 2001
Shanji, 1999

Other books you might like:
Gordon R. Dickson, *Naked to the Stars*, 1961
Joe Haldeman, *Forever Free*, 1999
Stephen Leigh, *Dark Water's Embrace*, 1998
Jerry Pournelle, *West of Honor*, 1976
Timothy Zahn, *Cobra Bargain*, 1988

664

THOMAS GLAVINIC

Night Work

(New York: Canongate, 2008)

Story type: Disaster; End of the World
Subject(s): Disasters; Mystery
Major character(s): Jonas, Survivor
Time period(s): 2000s (2008)
Locale(s): Vienna, Austria

Summary: Jonas wakes up one day to discover that everyone else in the city of Vienna, and perhaps the world, has disappeared without a trace. Some mechanical devices are still working, but no one answers the telephone and the Internet is down. He sets out on a journey to find his girlfriend but instead discovers much he didn't know about himself. This novel was originally published in German.

Where it's reviewed:
Publishers Weekly, September 1, 2008, page 34

Other books you might like:
Richard Grant, *Rumors of Spring*, 1987
Richard Matheson, *I Am Legend*, 1954
Tim Powers, *Earthquake Weather*, 1996
Mary Shelley, *The Last Man*, 1826
James White, *Second Ending*, 1962

665

TONY GONZALES

Eve

(London: Gollancz, 2008)

Story type: Dystopian; Future Shock
Subject(s): Cloning; Space Colonies
Major character(s): Falek Grange, Clone; Vince, Worker; Advent Eturrer, Military Personnel
Time period(s): Indeterminate Future
Locale(s): Outer Space; Planet—Imaginary

Summary: The setting is a distant future where the stars are dominated by humankind although the location of Earth has been lost. The creation of a clone is the trigger for a series of events which will precipitate interstellar conflict and change the very nature of human civilization. First novel.

Other books you might like:
Iain Banks, *Excession*, 1996
Greg Egan, *Incandescence*, 2008
Peter Hamilton, *The Dreaming Void*, 2008
Alastair Reynolds, *House of Suns*, 2008
Dan Simmons, *Endymion*, 1996

666

JOE HALDEMAN

Marsbound

(New York: Ace, 2008)

Story type: Hard Science Fiction; Space Colony
Subject(s): Space Travel; Coming-of-Age
Major character(s): Carmen Dula, Settler; Paul Collins, Spaceman; Fly-in-Amber, Alien
Time period(s): Indeterminate Future
Locale(s): Outer Space; Mars

Summary: Teenager Carmen Dula is having second thoughts about accompanying her family to Mars until she meets a handsome young spaceship pilot. Once arrived, the colonists discover the existence of other visitors, a small group of aliens placed on Mars as a kind of organic early warning system for yet another and more dangerous intelligence.

Where it's reviewed:
Booklist, August 1, 2008, page 51
Publishers Weekly, June 13, 2008, page 37

Other books by the same author:
The Accidental Time Machine, 2007
Peace and War, 2006
Old Twentieth, 2005
Camouflage, 2004
The Coming, 2000

Other books you might like:
Kevin J. Anderson, *Climbing Olympus*, 1994
Ben Bova, *Mars Life*, 2008
John Brunner, *Born under Mars*, 1967

Robert A. Heinlein, *Red Planet*, 1949
Paul J. McAuley, *Red Dust*, 1997

667

WARREN HAMMOND

Ex-Kop

(New York: Tor, 2008)

Story type: Mystery; Future Shock
Series: Kop. Book 2
Subject(s): Secrets; Crime and Criminals
Major character(s): Juno Mazambe, Photographer; Maggie Orzo, Police Officer; Ian Davies, Police Officer
Time period(s): 28th century (2788)
Locale(s): Earth

Summary: Juno Mazambe has lost his job as a police officer and is barely getting by taking photographs and doing odd jobs. When his old partner, Maggie Orzo, asks him to help her prove a condemned girl is innocent of murder, he agrees in order to pay for his wife's medical bills, but the investigation has further ramifications including a serial killer and Maggie's new partner.

Where it's reviewed:
Publishers Weekly, August 18, 2008, page 48

Other books by the same author:
Kop, 2007

Other books you might like:
K.A. Bedford, *Hydrogen Steel*, 2006
Eric Brown, *New York Blues*, 2001
Peter Hamilton, *The Nano Flower*, 1995
Lee Killough, *Dragon's Teeth*, 1990
Richard K. Morgan, *Altered Carbon*, 2002

668

NICK HARKAWAY

The Gone-Away World

(New York: Knopf, 2008)

Story type: Satire; Humor
Subject(s): Humor; Satire
Major character(s): Gonzo Lubitsch, Troubleshooter; Humbert Pestle, Criminal; Elisabeth Soames, Troubleshooter
Time period(s): Indeterminate Future
Locale(s): United States

Summary: Gonzo Lubitsch is one of a group of people who are called upon to save the world whenever it gets into trouble. Their episodic adventures involve mysterious assassins, open conflicts, the threat of war, and a nasty villainous mastermind. The story mixes broad humor with barbed satire. First novel.

Where it's reviewed:
Booklist, August 1, 2008, page 7
Bookseller, May 23, 2008, page 13
Library Journal, September 15, 2008, page 44
Publishers Weekly, July 21, 2008, page 147

Times Literary Supplement, June 27, 2008, page 21
Other books you might like:
Philip K. Dick, *Ubik*, 1969
Daniel F. Galouye, *Simulacron-3*, 1964
Shepherd Mead, *The Carefully Considered Rape of the World*, 1965
Tim Scott, *Love in the Time of Fridges*, 2008
Kurt Vonnegut, *Cat's Cradle*, 1963

669

BRIAN HERBERT
KEVIN J. ANDERSON , Co-Author

Paul of Dune

(New York: Tor, 2008)

Story type: Space Colony; Religious
Series: Dune
Subject(s): Religious Conflict; Space Colonies
Major character(s): Paul Atreides, Ruler; Stilgar, Military Personnel; Gurney Halleck, Bodyguard
Time period(s): Indeterminate Future
Locale(s): Arrakis, Planet—Imaginary; Outer Space

Summary: This novel is meant to fill in gaps in the Dune saga by Frank Herbert. Paul Atreides and his followers have defeated the emperor and launched a jihad that is sweeping across the galaxy. Not only does Paul fear that events have escaped his control, but he also must face furtive enemies within his own camp.

Where it's reviewed:
Booklist, August 1, 2008, page 8
Library Journal, September 15, 2008, page 48
Publishers Weekly, October 27, 2008, page 50

Other books by the same author:
Sandworms of Dune, 2007 (Kevin J. Anderson, co-author)
Hunters of Dune, 2006 (Kevin J. Anderson, co-author)
The Battle of Corrin, 2004 (Kevin J. Anderson, co-author)
The Machine Crusade, 2003 (Kevin J. Anderson, co-author)
The Butlerian Jihad, 2002 (Kevin J. Anderson, co-author)

Other books you might like:
Kevin J. Anderson, *The Ashes of Worlds*, 2008
Peter Hamilton, *The Dreaming Void*, 2008
Paul J. McAuley, *The Quiet War*, 2008
Alastair Reynolds, *Revelation Space*, 2000
Dan Simmons, *Hyperion*, 1989

670

BRIAN HERBERT

Webdancers

(Waterville, ME: Five Star, 2008)

Story type: Time Travel; Space Colony
Series: Timeweb Chronicles. Book 3
Subject(s): Time Travel; Aliens

Major character(s): Noah Watanabe, Scientist; Eshaz, Alien; Doge Anton, Government Official
Time period(s): Indeterminate Future
Locale(s): Outer Space

Summary: The timeweb links all of the galaxy, but it also makes conflict easier. Humans have been battling a race of shapeshifters and now must face another force consisting of hybrids. Just when things begin to look as though they are moving to a conclusion, a fourth force arrives to throw the situation out of balance again.

Other books by the same author:
The Web and the Stars, 2007
Timeweb, 2006
Prisoners of Arionn, 1997
The Race for God, 1990
Sidney's Comet, 1983

Other books you might like:
Kevin J. Anderson, *The Ashes of Worlds*, 2008
Peter Hamilton, *Pandora's Star*, 2004
Frank Herbert, *Dune Messiah*, 1969
Alastair Reynolds, *The Prefect*, 2007
Walter Jon Williams, *The Praxis*, 2002

671

JESSICA INCLAN

Intimate Beings

(New York: Kensington, 2008)

Story type: Psychic Powers; Mystery
Subject(s): Psychic Powers; Aliens
Major character(s): Claire Edwards, Psychic (teleporter), Teacher; Darl James, Psychic (teleporter); Odhran, Alien
Time period(s): 2000s
Locale(s): Earth

Summary: Claire Edwards has the ability to teleport, to mentally transfer herself to any other place on the planet. She thinks that she's unique and undiscovered, but there are others with the same talent, and a group of inhuman creatures who become aware of her existence.

Other books by the same author:
Being with Him, 2008
Reason to Believe, 2008
Believe in Me, 2007
When You Believe, 2007
The Instant When Everything Is Perfect, 2006

Other books you might like:
Jayne Castle, *Ghost Hunter*, 2006
Philip K. Dick, *The Unteleported Man*, 1964
Steven Gould, *Reflex*, 2004
Jacqueline Lichtenberg, *Mahogany Trinrose*, 1981
Anne McCaffrey, *Damia*, 1992

672

STEVEN L. KENT

The Clone Elite

(New York: Ace, 2008)

Story type: Military; Space Colony
Series: Clones. Book 4
Subject(s): Aliens; Cloning
Major character(s): Wayson Harris, Military Personnel, Clone; William Sweetwater, Scientist; Mark Philips, Military Personnel
Time period(s): 26th century (2514)
Locale(s): New Copenhagen, Planet—Imaginary

Summary: Wayson Harris is a clone who successfully gained his freedom during earlier volumes in this series. Now he is drafted into the military again when an alien invasion force threatens to defeat the human race. Harris and a team of soldiers and scientists try to stem the tide of defeat on a remote colony world.

Other books by the same author:
The Clone Alliance, 2007
Rogue Clone, 2006
The Clone Republic, 2006

Other books you might like:
Lois McMaster Bujold, *Brothers in Arms*, 1989
Gordon R. Dickson, *Naked to the Stars*, 1961
R.M. Meluch, *Strength and Honor*, 2008
Mike Shepherd, *Kris Longknife: Intrepid*, 2008
Timothy Zahn, *The Cobra Trilogy*, 2004

673

NICK KYME , Editor
LINDSEY PRIESTLEY , Co-Editor

Planetkill

(Nottingham, United Kingdom: Black Library, 2008)

Story type: Anthology
Series: Warhammer
Subject(s): Short Stories

Summary: This is a collection of seven original stories set in the context of the Warhammer universe, in which highly trained military units battle with religious fervor against one another and against an alien enemy which may have supernatural components. The contributors include Richard Williams, Graham McNeill, Matthew Farrer, Steve Parker, and others.

Other books by the same author:
Oathbreaker, 2008
Back from the Dead, 2006

Other books you might like:
Ben Counter, *Battle for the Abyss*, 2008
Matthew Farrer, *Crossfire*, 2003
Graham McNeill, *The Killing Ground*, 2008
Steven Parker, *Rebel Winter*, 2007
Richard Williams, *Relentless*, 2008

674

CLAUDE LALUMIERE , Editor

Tesseracts Twelve

(Calgary, Alberta: Edge, 2008)

Story type: Anthology
Subject(s): Short Stories

Summary: The 2008 anthology of speculative fiction from Canadian authors includes seven novellas, ranging from traditional science fiction to contemporary fantasy. A recurring theme in this volume is respect for traditions of previous generations. Contributors include David Nickle, Derryl Murphy, and E.L. Chen.

Where it's reviewed:
Locus, November 2008, page 50

Other books by the same author:
Island Dreams, 2003
Open Space, 2003
Witpunk, 2002 (Marty Halpern, co-author)

Other books you might like:
Paul Di Filippo, *Fuzzy Dice*, 2003
Jeffrey Ford, *The Empire of Ice Cream*, 2006
Elizabeth Hand, *Bibliomancy*, 2003
Robert J. Sawyer, *Relativitiy*, 2005
Jeffrey Thomas, *Punktown*, 1999

675

KRIS LANDON

The Cold Minds

(New York: Ace, 2008)

Story type: Space Opera; Mystery
Series: Cold Minds. Book 2
Subject(s): Artificial Intelligence; Secrets
Major character(s): Iain sen Paolo, Spaceman; Linnea Kiaho, Spacewoman; Hakon sen Efrem, Spaceman
Time period(s): Indeterminate Future
Locale(s): Terranova, Planet—Imaginary; Outer Space

Summary: The machine intelligences who destroyed the human population on Earth has located the hidden civilization founded by descendants of the few survivors. The two protagonists know that this is the truth, but the organization that controls space travel among humans is unwilling to publicly admit that the danger has returned and are reluctant to cooperate.

Other books by the same author:
The Hidden Worlds, 2007

Other books you might like:
Philip K. Dick, *Vulcan's Hammer*, 1960
Brian Herbert, *The Machine Crusade*, 2003
    Kevin J. Anderson, co-author
D.F. Jones, *Colossus and the Crab*, 1977
Fred Saberhagen, *Berserker Death*, 2005
Tricia Sullivan, *Dreaming in Smoke*, 1998

676

EDWARD M. LERNER

Fools' Experiment

(New York: Tor, 2008)

Story type: Alternate Intelligence; Mystery
Subject(s): Computers; Secrets
Major character(s): Doug Carey, Scientist; Cheryl Stern, Scientist; Arthur Jason Rosenberg, Scientist
Time period(s): Indeterminate Future
Locale(s): United States

Summary: A group of scientists are experimenting with the possibility of creating an artificial intelligence, but they are unaware of the fact that they have succeeded in creating something that is self-aware and dangerous. At first the entity is confined to their laboratories, but when it escapes into the Internet, it has the potential to affect the entire world.

Where it's reviewed:
Booklist, September 15, 2008, page 29
Library Journal, August 1, 2008, page 75
Publishers Weekly, September 22, 2008, page 43

Other books by the same author:
Moonstruck, 2005
Probe, 1991

Other books you might like:
Greg Bear, *Blood Music*, 1985
John Brunner, *Double, Double*, 1969
M.M. Buckner, *Watermind*, 2008
Philip K. Dick, *Vulcan's Hammer*, 1960
David Gerrold, *When Harlie Was One*, 1972

677

DAVID MACK

Gods of Night

(New York: Pocket, 2008)

Story type: Space Opera; Invasion of Earth
Series: Star Trek: Destiny. Book 1
Subject(s): Aliens; Secrets
Major character(s): Jean-Luc Picard, Spaceship Captain, Military Personnel; William Riker, Spaceship Captain, Military Personnel; Ezri Dax, Spaceship Captain, Military Personnel
Time period(s): 24th century (2373)
Locale(s): Outer Space

Summary: After finally achieving peace, the Federation faces a new threat when the alien Borg return to menace all other forms of life once again. Three starship captains find themselves playing pivotal roles in the defense of humanity against a force that intends total extinction.

Other books by the same author:
Mere Mortals, 2008
Reap the Whirlwind, 2007
Road of Bones, 2006
Warpath, 2006
Harbinger, 2005

Other books you might like:
Kevin J. Anderson, *Hidden Empire*, 2002
Christopher L. Bennett, *Greater than the Sum*, 2008
Gordon R. Dickson, *Hour of the Horde*, 1970
Peter Hamilton, *Judas Unchained*, 2006
Jack McDevitt, *Omega*, 2003

678

DAVID MACK

Mere Mortals

(New York: Pocket, 2008)

Story type: Space Opera; Military
Series: Star Trek: Destiny. Book 2
Subject(s): Space Exploration; Aliens
Major character(s): Nanietta Bacco, Government Official; William Riker, Spaceship Captain, Military Personnel; Ezri Dax, Spaceship Captain, Military Personnel
Time period(s): 24th century (2381)
Locale(s): Outer Space; Earth; Planet—Imaginary

Summary: With the Federation facing defeat in the face of an overpowering invasion, Starfleet prepares its final defenses. Captain Riker and his crew are elsewhere, attempting to gain the assistance of an even more powerful but aloof alien species to avert the catastrophe.

Other books by the same author:
Gods of Night, 2008
Reap the Whirlwind, 2007
Road of Bones, 2006
Warpath, 2006
Harbinger, 2005

Other books you might like:
Roger MacBride Allen, *Allies and Aliens*, 1995
Gregory Benford, *Cosm*, 1998
Christopher L. Bennett, *Greater than the Sum*, 2008
Michael Flynn, *The January Dancer*, 2008
Edmond Hamilton, *Doomstar*, 1966

679

GEORGE R.R. MARTIN , Editor

Busted Flush

(New York: Tor, 2008)

Story type: Anthology
Subject(s): Short Stories

Summary: Several authors contribute inter-related stories in this volume of the popular series. The premise is that an alien virus resulted in mutations, some of which include superpowers similar to comic book superheroes. The contributors include Victor Milan, Melinda Snodgrass, Stephen Leigh, Carrie Vaughn, and others.

Where it's reviewed:
Locus, November 2008, page 21
Publishers Weekly, October 13, 2008, page 41

Other books by the same author:
The Ice Dragon, 2006

A Feast for Crows, 2005
A Storm of Swords, 2000
A Clash of Kings, 1997
A Game of Thrones, 1996

Other books you might like:
Michael Bishop, *Count Geiger's Blues*, 1992
Arthur Byron Cover, *Born in Fire*, 2002
Tom De Haven, *Freaks' Amour*, 1979
Michael Jan Friedman, *The Price of Peace*, 2002
Marjorie M. Liu, *Dark Mirror*, 2005

680

MICHAEL A. MARTIN
ANDY MANGELS , Co-Author

Kobayashi Maru

(New York: Pocket, 2008)

Story type: Space Opera; Military
Series: Star Trek Enterprise
Subject(s): Aliens; Secrets
Major character(s): Jonathan Archer, Spaceship Captain, Military Personnel; T'Pol, Alien, Scientist; Charles Tucker, Engineer, Military Personnel
Time period(s): 22nd century (2155)
Locale(s): Outer Space

Summary: Captain Jonathan Archer and his crew have been assigned to picket duty, checking passing interstellar traffic to watch for anything unusual. Archer suspects that the alien Romulans are behind a series of attacks on commercial ships that threatens to destroy the unity of the various human factions.

Other books by the same author:
Forged in Fire, 2007 (Andy Mangels, co-author)
The Good That Men Do, 2007 (Andy Mangels, co-author)
Last Full Measure, 2006 (Andy Mangels, co-author)
The Red King, 2005 (Andy Mangels, co-author)
Cathedral, 2002 (Andy Mangels, co-author)

Other books you might like:
Poul Anderson, *Harvest of Stars*, 1993
Keith R.A. DeCandido, *A Burning House*, 2008
Gordon R. Dickson, *The Far Call*, 1978
David Gerrold, *Voyage of the Star Wolf*, 1990
Keith Laumer, *The Glory Game*, 1972

681

DAVID MARUSEK

Getting to Know You

(New York: Del Rey, 2008)

Story type: Collection
Subject(s): Short Stories

Summary: Five of the ten stories in this collection of reprints are set in the same universe as the author's first novel, *Counting Heads*. Marusek explores various implications of the development of new technologies and the impact of science on the daily lives of individuals.

Where it's reviewed:
Publishers Weekly, February 12, 2008, page 67

Other books by the same author:
Mind over Ship, 2009
Counting Heads, 2005

Other books you might like:
Ben Bova, *Challenges*, 1993
Cory Doctorow, *Overclocked*, 2007
William Gibson, *Burning Chrome*, 1989
Joe Haldeman, *A Separate War and Other Stories*, 2006
Bruce Sterling, *A Good Old Fashioned Future*, 2001

682

PAUL J. MCAULEY

The Quiet War

(London: Gollancz, 2008)

Story type: Space Opera; Space Colony
Subject(s): Space Travel; Space Colonies
Major character(s): Sri Hong-Owen, Professor; Arvam Peixoto, Military Personnel; Macy Minnot, Worker
Time period(s): Indeterminate Future
Locale(s): Outer Space; Earth

Summary: The human race has begun to split into two separate cultures. Earth has evolved into a repressive planetary dictatorship while its colonies elsewhere in the solar system have developed a freer, more adaptive society. The move toward war seems inevitable as the two cultures clash. First in a series.

Other books by the same author:
Cowboy Angels, 2007
White Devils, 2004
Whole Wide World, 2002
The Secret of Life, 2001
Shrine of Stars, 2000

Other books you might like:
Poul Anderson, *Harvest of Stars*, 1998
Gordon R. Dickson, *The Outposter*, 1972
David Feintuch, *Midshipman's Hope*, 1994
Robert A. Heinlein, *The Moon Is a Harsh Mistress*, 1966
Frederik Pohl, *Man Plus*, 1976

683

TODD MCCAFFREY

Dragonheart

(New York: Del Rey, 2008)

Story type: Space Opera; Space Colony
Series: Pern. Book 21
Subject(s): Space Colonies; Coming-of-Age; Dragons
Major character(s): Fiona, Settler; Karina, Trader; Talenth, Alien
Time period(s): Indeterminate Future

Locale(s): Pern, Planet—Imaginary
Summary: Young Fiona likes the idea of bonding with one of the dragons of Pern, even though this is an activity usually reserved for males. With the opportunity comes great responsibility, however, and she is severely tested when a crisis challenges her resolve. The author is continuing the series created by his mother, Anne McCaffrey.

Other books by the same author:
Dragonsblood, 2005

Other books you might like:
Jeffrey A. Carver, *Dragon Rigger*, 1993
Chris Cymri, *Dragons Can Only Rust*, 1995
Marjorie Kellogg, *The Book of Air*, 2003
Anne McCaffrey, *Dragonseye*, 1997
Irene Radford, *The Dragon's Revenge*, 2005

684

JACK MCDEVITT

The Devil's Eye

(New York: Ace, 2008)

Story type: Mystery; Disaster
Series: Alex Benedict. Book 4
Subject(s): Aliens; Disasters
Major character(s): Alex Benedict, Antiques Dealer; Chase Kolpath, Antiques Dealer; Krestoff, Security Officer
Time period(s): Indeterminate Future
Locale(s): Outer Space; Salud Afar, Planet—Imaginary

Summary: Alex Benedict receives a cryptic message from a writer who had her memory erased. He and Chase Kolpath travel to the remote world of Salud Afar to attempt to discover what caused the woman to essentially commit suicide. There they uncover a conspiracy designed to conceal an imminent disaster.

Where it's reviewed:
Booklist, November 1, 2008, page 30
Publishers Weekly, September 22, 2008, page 42

Other books by the same author:
Cauldron, 2007
Seeker, 2005
Ships in the Night, 2005
Polaris, 2004
Chindi, 2002

Other books you might like:
Poul Anderson, *A Circus of Hells*, 1970
Lois McMaster Bujold, *Diplomatic Immunity*, 2002
Frederik Pohl, *Stopping at Slowyear*, 1991
Robert Silverberg, *Downward to the Earth*, 1970
Timothy Zahn, *Night Train to Rigel*, 2005

685

GRAHAM MCNEILL

The Killing Ground

(Nottingham, United Kingdom: Black Library, 2008)

Story type: Military; Space Opera
Series: Warhammer

Subject(s): Space Travel; Aliens
Major character(s): Uriel Ventris, Military Personnel; Pasanius, Military Personnel; Cawlen Hurq, Criminal
Time period(s): Indeterminate Future
Locale(s): Outer Space

Summary: Uriel Ventris and his companions have defeated their enemies in space and on strange other worlds. Now it is time to go home, but the journey there involves dangerous stopovers and encounters with more of their enemies, both human and inhuman. An episodic journey ensues during which it appears that they will never reach their goal.

Other books by the same author:
Storm of Iron, 2008
False Gods, 2006
Dead Sky, Black Sun, 2004
Warriors of Ultramar, 2003
Nightbringer, 2002

Other books you might like:
Bill Baldwin, *The Defiant*, 1996
Bruce Balfour, *Star Crusader*, 1995
Jack Campbell, *Valiant*, 2008
Sandra McDonald, *The Outback Stars*, 2007
Joel C. Rosenberg, *Hero*, 1990

686

GRAHAM MCNEILL

Mechanicus

(Nottingham, United Kingdom: Black Library, 2008)

Story type: Space Opera; Military
Series: Warhammer
Subject(s): Civil War; Space Colonies
Major character(s): Dalia Cythera, Worker; Rho-mu 31, Military Personnel; Koriel Zeth, Government Official
Time period(s): Indeterminate Future
Locale(s): Mars

Summary: The settlements on Mars are governed with repressive force which has resulted in a simmering revolutionary movement. A young woman with an affinity for machinery is taken from prison and introduced to the rarified world of the government, just as violence begins to erupt all over the planet.

Other books by the same author:
Storm of Iron, 2008
False Gods, 2006
Dead Sky, Black Sun, 2004
Warriors of Ultramar, 2003
Nightbringer, 2002

Other books you might like:
Dan Abnett, *Legion*, 2008
Ben Counter, *Hammer of Daemons*, 2008
Anthony Reynolds, *Dark Apostle*, 2007
James Swallow, *Red Fury*, 2008
Richard Williams, *Relentless*, 2008

687

R.M. MELUCH

Strength and Honor

(New York: DAW, 2008)

Story type: Military; Space Opera
Series: Tour of the Merrimack. Book 4
Subject(s): Aliens; War
Major character(s): John Farragut, Spaceship Captain, Military Personnel; Romulus, Ruler; Augustus, Fugitive
Time period(s): Indeterminate Future
Locale(s): Outer Space; Planet—Imaginary

Summary: The alliance between the empire led by Earth and a breakaway group calling itself the Palatine Empire has broken down following the apparent defeat of their common alien enemy and the assassination of a prominent politician. As the two sides threaten each other's home world, the resurgent alien forces threaten to destroy them both.

Where it's reviewed:
Booklist, November 1, 2008, page 30

Other books by the same author:
The Sagittarius Command, 2007
Wolf Star, 2006
The Myriad, 2004
The Queen's Squadron, 1992
Chicago Red, 1990

Other books you might like:
Roger MacBride Allen, *Allies and Aliens*, 1995
David Feintuch, *Children of Hope*, 2001
Mike Resnick, *Starship: Mercenary*, 2007
Mike Shepherd, *Kris Longknife: Intrepid*, 2008
David Weber, *The Armageddon Inheritance*, 1993

688

JUDITH MERRIL
C.M. KORNBLUTH, Co-Author

Spaced Out

(Framingham, MA: NESFA, 2008)

Story type: Collection
Subject(s): Science Fiction

Summary: This is an omnibus of three novels, two of them collaborations, the third by Merril alone. *Gunner Cade* was published in 1952 and concerns a future soldier who questions what he has been led to believe. A colony on Mars seeks independence in *Outpost Mars*, also from 1952. *Shadow on the Hearth* from 1950 is a story of survival after a nuclear war.

Other books by the same author:
Homecalling and Other Stories, 2005
The Best of Judith Merril, 1976
Daughters of the Earth, 1968
Out of Bounds, 1960
The Tomorrow People, 1960

Science Fiction

Other books you might like:
Robert A. Heinlein, *Beyond This Horizon*, 1948
C.M. Kornbluth, *Not This August*, 1955
Murray Leinster, *Operation Outer Spce*, 1954
Frederik Pohl, *Drunkard's Walk*, 1960
Robert Sheckley, *The Status Civilization*, 1960

689

SANDY MITCHELL

Cain's Last Stand

(Nottingham, United Kingdom: Black Library, 2008)

Story type: Military; Space Opera
Series: Warhammer
Subject(s): Military Life; Space Colonies
Major character(s): Ciaphas Cain, Military Personnel,
  Aged Person; Donal, Student; Varan, Military
  Personnel
Time period(s): Indeterminate Future
Locale(s): Perlia, Planet—Imaginary

Summary: Ciaphas Cain has retired after a distinguished
military career to run a school on the planet Perlia. He is
forced to come out of retirement when an offensive thrust
by an enemy force threatens to conquer Perlia, organizing a resistance force out of students and civilians.

Other books by the same author:
Scourge the Heretic, 2008
Ciaphas Cain: Hero of the Imperium, 2007
Duty Calls, 2007
Caves of Ice, 2004
For the Emperor, 2003

Other books you might like:
Dan Abnett, *The Armour of Contempt*, 2006
David Drake, *Fireships*, 1996
David Feintuch, *Fisherman's Hope*, 1996
Graham McNeill, *Storm of Iron*, 2008
Andre Norton, *Star Guard*, 1955

690

THOMAS NEVINS

The Age of the Conglomerates

(New York: Del Rey, 2008)

Story type: Political; Post-Disaster
Subject(s): Government; Political Crimes and Offenses
Major character(s): George Salter, Aged Person; Christine
  Salter, Scientist; Gabriel Cruz, Scientist
Time period(s): Indeterminate Future
Locale(s): New York, New York

Summary: In the not-too-distant future, the traditional
American government collapses under the weight of the
national debt and other problems. They are replaced by a
party consisting primarily of business managers who
initiate a new system that treats much of the population
as expendable. The consequences are revealed through
the viewpoint of an elderly couple, their successful

granddaughter, and another who has been left to fender
for herself. First novel.

Where it's reviewed:
Publishers Weekly, June 2, 2008, page 30

Other books you might like:
Brian W. Aldiss, *Enemies of the System*, 1978
John Brunner, *Shockwave Rider*, 1875
L. Timmel DuChamp, *Alanya to Alanya*, 2005
James Patrick Kelly, *Burn*, 2005
Frederik Pohl, *Gladiator-at-Law*, 1955

691

S.D. PERRY

Criminal Enterprise

(Milwaukie, OR: Dark Horse, 2008)

Story type: Space Colony; Horror
Series: Aliens
Subject(s): Aliens; Space Colonies
Major character(s): Thomas Chase, Criminal; Peter Chase,
  Criminal; Deirdre Weber, Spacewoman
Time period(s): Indeterminate Future
Locale(s): Fantasia, Planet—Imaginary; Outer Space

Summary: Tommy Chase travels to a remote planet where
his brother is involved in the illegal interplanetary drug
trade. He arrives in time to get caught up in a battle with
a rival criminal organization, but both sides finally have
to unite against a worse enemy, a colony of predatory
aliens.

Other books by the same author:
State of War, 2003
Cloak, 2001
City of the Dead, 1999
Berserker, 1998
Caliban Cove, 1998

Other books you might like:
Nathan Archer, *Cold War*, 1997
David Bischoff, *Hunter's Planet*, 1994
Diane Carey, *Cauldron*, 2007
Robert Sheckley, *Alien Harvest*, 1995
John Shirley, *Forever Midnight*, 2006

692

MICHAEL REAVES

Street of Shadows

(New York: Del Rey, 2008)

Story type: Space Opera; Mystery
Series: Star Wars: Coruscant Nights. Book 1
Subject(s): Secrets; Murder
Major character(s): Jax Pavan, Detective—Private; I-5YQ,
  Robot; Den Dhur, Journalist
Time period(s): Indeterminate
Locale(s): Coruscant, Planet—Imaginary

Summary: Jedi Jax Pavan is a private detective on Coruscant who is hired to find out who murdered a local artist.

Science Fiction

With the help of a robot sidekick, he begins his investigation, only to discover that there are sinister forces who intend to eliminate him if he gets too close to the truth.

Other books by the same author:
Fear Itself, 2007
Hell on Earth, 2001
Shadow Hunter, 2001
Street Magic, 1991
I, Alien, 1978

Other books you might like:
K.A. Bedford, *Hydrogen Steel*, 2006
Eric Brown, *New York Dreams*, 2004
Mick Farren, *The Long Orbit*, 1988
Richard K. Morgan, *Altered Carbon*, 2002
Mack Reynolds, *Chaos in Lagrangia*, 1984

693

KIT REED

Enclave

(New York: Tor, 2008)

Story type: Disaster; Mystery
Subject(s): Disasters; Secrets
Major character(s): Sargent Whitemore, Administrator; Cassie Rivard, Health Care Professional; Benedictus, Religious
Time period(s): Indeterminate Future
Locale(s): Mediterranean

Summary: The world is falling apart thanks to pollution, global warming, overpopulation, and economic collapse. Sarge is an ex-military man who has built what is supposed to be a safe refuge for 100 children in the middle of the Mediterranean, but the refuge is not what it appears to be and one of its residents is a killer.

Other books by the same author:
The Baby Merchant, 2006
Dogs of Truth, 2005
Thinner than Thou, 2004
Seven for the Apocalypse, 1999
Armed Camps, 1969

Other books you might like:
Wilhelmina Baird, *Clipjoint*, 1994
Hal Clement, *Needle*, 1957
Eric James Fullilove, *The Stranger*, 1997
Spider Robinson, *Very Bad Deaths*, 2004
John C. Wright, *Orphans of Chaos*, 2005

694

LAURA E. REEVE

Peacekeeper

(New York: Roc, 2008)

Story type: Military; Space Opera
Series: Ariane Kedros. Book 1
Subject(s): Space Travel; Secrets
Major character(s): Ariane Kedros, Military Personnel;

Matt Journey, Spaceman; Owen Edones, Military Personnel
Time period(s): Indeterminate Future
Locale(s): Outer Space; Planet—Imaginary

Summary: Major Ariane Kedros has assumed a new identity to protect herself from reprisals after a mission which cost countless lives. Now someone is assassinating her former friends and her name is on the list, so she agrees to serve as bait in an effort to capture the people responsible. First novel.

Where it's reviewed:
Publishers Weekly, October 13, 2008, page 41

Other books you might like:
Joe Haldeman, *Forever Peace*, 1997
Mike Resnick, *Starship: Mercenary*, 2007
Mike Shepherd, *Kris Longknife: Intrepid*, 2008
David Weber, *Ashes of Victory*, 2000
Timothy Zahn, *Cobra Bargain*, 1988

695

ANDY REMIC

Biohell

(Nottingham, United Kingdom: Solaris, 2008)

Story type: Disaster; Cyberpunk
Subject(s): Scientific Experiments; Disasters
Major character(s): Franco Haggis, Military Personnel; Slick Guinness, Worker; Keenan, Military Personnel
Time period(s): Indeterminate Future
Locale(s): The City, Planet—Imaginary

Summary: On a planet which has become one gigantic city, the latest fad is biomods, nanotechnology implanted in the human body that allows certain modifications. Something goes wrong with the implants and much of the planet's population is changed into violent creatures resembling zombies who attack those who were not modified.

Other books by the same author:
War Machine, 2007
Warhead, 2005
Quake, 2004
Spiral, 2003

Other books you might like:
Kevin J. Anderson, *Assemblers of Infinity*, 1993
    Douglas Beason, co-author
Greg Bear, *Blood Music*, 1985
Michael Flynn, *The Nanotech Chronicles*, 1991
Steven Piziks, *The Nanotech War*, 2002
John Shirley, *Crawlers*, 2003

696

ANTHONY REYNOLDS

Dark Disciple

(Nottingham, United Kingdom: Black Library, 2008)

Story type: Space Opera; Military
Series: Warhammer

Subject(s): War; Secrets
Major character(s): Marduk, Military Personnel; Magos Darioq, Prisoner; Rutger Augustine, Military Personnel
Time period(s): Indeterminate Future
Locale(s): Outer Space; Planet—Imaginary

Summary: Marduk has become a leader of a splinter faction of the human military in a far-flung interstellar civilization. The discovery of a technological device unknown to his rivals provides him with the opportunity to increase his power, but only if he can master its use before his enemies strike a fatal blow.

Other books by the same author:
Knight of the Realm, 2009
Empire in Chaos, 2008
Knight Errant, 2008
Dark Apostle, 2007
Mark of Chaos, 2006

Other books you might like:
Ben Counter, *Battle for the Abyss*, 2008
Lee Lightner, *Wolf's Honour*, 2008
Steve Lyons, *Death World*, 2006
Graham McNeill, *Mechanicus*, 2008
Sandy Mitchell, *Cain's Last Stand*, 2008

697

JOHN RINGO
TRAVIS S. TAYLOR , Co-Author

Claws That Catch

(New York: Baen, 2008)

Story type: Space Opera; Humor
Series: Vorpal Blade. Book 4
Subject(s): Aliens; Space Travel
Major character(s): William Weaver, Spaceship Captain; Eric Bergstresser, Spaceman; Miriam Moon, Linguist
Time period(s): Indeterminate Future
Locale(s): Outer Space

Summary: The crew of the starship *Vorpal Blade* continue their adventures, this time seeking remnants of an apparently extinct race that may have had the secret of manufacturing faster than light engines. Unfortunately, personality conflicts among the crew make things difficult for the captain to maintain order, let alone complete his mission.

Other books by the same author:
Manxome Foe, 2008 (Travis S. Taylor, co-author)
Vorpal Blade, 2007 (Travis S. Taylor, co-author)
Into the Looking Glass, 2005
Von Neumann's War, 2005 (Travis S. Taylor, co-author)
There Will Be Dragons, 2003

Other books you might like:
Poul Anderson, *The High Crusade*, 1960
Murray Leinster, *The Greks Bring Gifts*, 1964
Frederik Pohl, *Gateway*, 1977
Eric Frank Russell, *Men, Martians, and Machines*, 1956
Steve White, *The Disinherited*, 1993

698

J.D. ROBB

Salvation in Death

(New York: Putnam, 2008)

Story type: Mystery; Religious
Series: Eve Dallas. Book 27
Subject(s): Secrets; Murder
Major character(s): Eve Dallas, Detective—Homicide; Delia Peabody, Detective—Homicide; Roarke, Businessman, Spouse (Eve's Husband)
Time period(s): 2050s
Locale(s): New York, New York

Summary: Eve Dallas and her team are called upon to investigate the poisoning of religious leaders in a futuristic version of New York City. Their efforts uncover evidence that at least one of the victims was leading a secret life and might have had ties to a criminal organization.

Where it's reviewed:
Publishers Weekly, September 29, 2008, page 59

Other books by the same author:
Strangers in Death, 2008
Three in Death, 2007
Origin in Death, 2005
Survivor in Death, 2005

Other books you might like:
Lloyd Biggle, *Silence Is Deadly*, 1977
Eric James Fullilove, *The Stranger*, 1997
Richard K. Morgan, *Altered Carbon*, 2002
Mel Odom, *Lethal Interface*, 1992
Denise Vitola, *Opalite Moon*, 1997

699

CHRIS ROBERSON

End of the Century

(Amherst, NY: Pyr, 2008)

Story type: Mystical; Mystery
Subject(s): Legends; Mystery
Major character(s): Galaad, Knight; Sandford Blank, Detective—Private; Alice Fell, Teenager, Fugitive
Time period(s): 1890s (1897); 1990s (1999)
Locale(s): London, England

Summary: Three separate stories from three different ages are linked by the legend of the Holy Grail. A knight urges King Artor to search for a mystical object, a private detective investigates a series of Jack the Ripper type murders, and a teenager is pursued by inhuman creatures. Although there are elements of fantasy, the Grail is rationalized as a scientific object.

Where it's reviewed:
Publishers Weekly, October 20, 2008, page 40

Other books by the same author:
Dawn of War II, 2009
The Dragon's Nine Sons, 2008

The Line of Dichotomy, 2007
Paragaea, 2006
Here, There, and Everywhere, 2005

Other books you might like:
James P. Blaylock, *The Paper Grail*, 1991
Mary Cochrane, *The Forever King*, 1992
    Warren Murphy, co-author
Kate Mosse, *Labyrinth*, 2005
Lewis Perdue, *The Tesla Bequest*, 1984
James Rollins, *Deep Fathom*, 2001

700

JUSTINA ROBSON

Going Under

(Amherst, NY: Pyr, 2008)

Story type: Disaster; Fantasy
Series: Quantum Gravity. Book 3
Subject(s): Disasters; Legends
Major character(s): Lila Black, Cyborg; Zal Ahriman,
    Mythical Creature; Teazle, Demon
Time period(s): Indeterminate Future
Locale(s): Earth

Summary: Science fiction and fantasy are mixed in this
story of a future in which the fundamental rules of the
universe have been altered by a change in quantum reality, making it possible for people to visit an alternate
universe of mythical creatures. The protagonist is a cyborg who uses her enhanced scientific gifts in a world of
fairies.

Where it's reviewed:
Booklist, August 1, 2008, page 54
Library Journal, July 1, 2008, page 71
Publishers Weekly, July 21, 2008, page 147

Other books by the same author:
Selling Out, 2007
Keeping It Real, 2006
Living Next Door to the God of Love, 2006
Natural History, 2005
Mappa Mundi, 2002

Other books you might like:
Piers Anthony, *Chaos Mode*, 1993
Philip Jose Farmer, *Dark Is the Sun*, 1979
Esther Friesner, *The Sherwood Game*, 1995
Madeline Robins, *The Stone War*, 1999
Lawrence Watt-Evans, *The Cyborg and the Sorcerors*,
    1982

701

JAMES ROLLINS

The Last Oracle

(New York: Morrow, 2008)

Story type: Genetic Manipulation; Child-in-Peril
Series: Sigma. Book 5

Subject(s): Scientific Experiments; Genetic Engineering
Major character(s): Painter Crowe, Spy; Gray Pierce, Spy;
    Elizabeth Polk, Scholar
Time period(s): 2000s (2008)
Locale(s): United States; Russia

Summary: A man dies bringing a cryptic message to
representatives of Sigma, a super-secret counter espionage organization. He has discovered that individuals
inside the former Soviet Union have kidnapped a group
of mutated gypsy children and are using them in a
program designed to create child savants with the power
to see the future.

Where it's reviewed:
Library Journal, May 15, 2008, page 93
Publishers Weekly, August 25, 2008, page 69

Other books by the same author:
The Judas Strain, 2007
Black Order, 2006
Map of Bones, 2005
Sandstorm, 2004
Ice Hunt, 2003

Other books you might like:
Michael Crichton, *The Terminal Man*, 1972
Clive Cussler, *Dragon*, 1990
Tim Powers, *Declare*, 2001
Douglas Preston, *The Ice Limit*, 2000
    Lincoln Child, co-author
Matthew J. Reilly, *Temple*, 2001

702

JOHN SCALZI

Agent to the Stars

(New York: Tor, 2008)

Story type: First Contact; Humor
Subject(s): Aliens; Humor
Major character(s): Thomas Stein, Agent; Joshua, Alien;
    Miranda, Worker
Time period(s): Indeterminate Future
Locale(s): United States

Summary: An alien race decides to open contact with
Earth, but they are so ugly looking and bad smelling that
they decide to hire an agent. Thomas Stein faces the
challenge of his career in making them socially acceptable to the human race. This novel was previously
published in a limited collectors' edition.

Other books by the same author:
Zoe's Tale, 2008
The Last Colony, 2007
The Android's Dream, 2006
The Ghost Brigades, 2006
Old Man's War, 2005

Other books you might like:
Piers Anthony, *The Hard Sell*, 1990
Mark Clifton, *When They Come from Space*, 1961
Joe Clifford Faust, *Boddekker's Demons*, 1997
Frederik Pohl, *The Space Merchants*, 1953

C.M. Kornbluth, co-author
Robert Silverberg, *Invaders from Earth*, 1958

703

JOHN SCALZI

Zoe's Tale
(New York: Tor, 2008)

Story type: Young Adult; Space Opera
Series: Old Man's War. Book 4
Subject(s): Teen Relationships; Space Colonies
Major character(s): Zoe Boutin Perry, Teenager, Settler; Hickory, Alien; Gretchen, Teenager, Settler
Time period(s): Indeterminate Future
Locale(s): Huckleberry, Planet—Imaginary

Summary: Zoe and her family are supposed to be emigrating to the planet Roanoke but something goes wrong and the ship ends up on a new world, Huckleberry. There she makes contact with an unusual alien species who revere her as an almost supernatural creature. This leads to first contact with a much more technologically sophisticasted race.

Where it's reviewed:
Booklist, August 1, 2008, page 54
Magazine of Fantasy & Science Fiction, October 2008, page 36
Publishers Weekly, June 23, 2008, page 42

Other books by the same author:
Agent to the Stars, 2008
The Last Colony, 2007
The Android's Dream, 2006
The Ghost Brigades, 2006
Old Man's War, 2005

Other books you might like:
Alan Dean Foster, *Flinx's Folly*, 2003
Robert A. Heinlein, *Podkayne of Mars*, 1963
Alexei Panshin, *Rite of Passage*, 1968
James H. Schmitz, *Telzey Amberdon*, 2000
Timothy Zahn, *Dragon and Thief*, 2003

704

KEN SCHOLES

Long Walks, Last Flights, and Other Strange Journeys
(Bonney Lake, WA: Fairwood, 2008)

Story type: Collection
Subject(s): Short Stories

Summary: All of the stories in this collection were previously published between 2004 and 2008. Scholes tends toward the literary end of the spectrum and these stories are almost all set in the present or very near future. There are elements of humor and satire as well as speculation about the consequences of current trends.

Other books by the same author:
Lamentation, 2009
Last Flight of the Goddess, 2006
Other books you might like:
Paul Di Filippo, *Neutrino Drag*, 2004
Nancy Kress, *Beaker's Dozen*, 1998
Richard Parks, *Worshipping Small Gods*, 2007
Robert Reed, *The Dragons of Springplace*, 1999
Pamela Sargent, *Thumbprints*, 2004

705

TIM SCOTT

Love in the Time of Fridges
(New York: Bantam, 2008)

Story type: Humor; Satire
Subject(s): Humor; Artificial Intelligence
Major character(s): Huckleberry Lindbergh, Police Officer; Nena, Fugitive; Mendes, Businessman
Time period(s): Indeterminate Future
Locale(s): Seattle, Washington; Mexico

Summary: This comical satire feature a policeman who loses his job and stumbles into a mysterious conspiracy that results in his becoming a fugitive in a future in which common household appliances have personalities and can talk. He is accompanied on his perilous adventures by a handful of refrigerators that have gone feral.

Where it's reviewed:
Publishers Weekly, June 30, 2008, page 166
Other books by the same author:
Outrageous Fortune, 2007
Other books you might like:
Philip K. Dick, *Ubik*, 1969
Thomas M. Disch, *The Brave Little Toaster*, 1986
Isidore Haiblum, *Out of Sync*, 1990
Henry Kuttner, *Robots Have No Tails*, 1952
Shepherd Mead, *The Big Ball of Wax*, 1954

706

WILLIAM SHATNER
GARFIELD REEVES-STEVENS , Co-Author
JUDITH REEVES-STEVENS , Co-Author

Collision Course
(New York: Pocket, 2008)

Story type: Space Opera; Coming-of-Age
Series: Star Trek
Subject(s): Coming-of-Age; Aliens
Major character(s): James T. Kirk, Teenager; Spock, Alien, Student; Elissa Corso, Teenager
Time period(s): 23rd century (2249)
Locale(s): San Francisco, California; Outer Space
Summary: Teenaged James Kirk has no intention of entering Starfleet Academy. Equally young Spock is investigating a mystery inside the Vulcan embassy on Earth. The paths of the two very different young men will cross as they each seek their own destiny.

Science Fiction

Other books by the same author:
Captain's Glory, 2006
Captain's Blood, 2003
Beyond the Stars, 2000
Avenger, 1997
The Ashes of Eden, 1995

Other books you might like:
Diane Carey, *Starfleet Academy*, 1997
Gene DeWeese, *Engines of Destiny*, 2005
Diane Duane, *Honor Blade*, 2000
Vonda N. McIntyre, *The Entropy Effect*, 1981
Kevin Ryan, *The Edge of the Sword*, 2002

707

MIKE SHEPHERD

Kris Longknife: Intrepid

(New York: Ace, 2008)

Story type: Space Opera; Military
Series: Kris Longknife. Book 6
Subject(s): Space Travel; Space Colonies
Major character(s): Kris Longknife, Military Personnel; Victoria Peterwald, Military Personnel; Drago, Spaceship Captain
Time period(s): Indeterminate Future
Locale(s): Outer Space; *Wasp*, Spaceship

Summary: Kris Longknife is only a lieutenant but she has considerable influence with the captain because of her family and her recent experiences. While the ship is hunting space pirates, they stumble upon a plot to assassinate members of an aristocratic family, and Kris has to deal with the issue despite a long-standing feud between that family and her own.

Other books by the same author:
Kris Longknife: Audacious, 2007
Kris Longknife: Resolute, 2006
Kris Longknife: Defiant, 2005
Kris Longknife: Deserter, 2005
Kris Longknife: Mutineer, 2004

Other books you might like:
Lois McMaster Bujold, *Brothers in Arms*, 1989
David Feintuch, *Midshipman's Hope*, 1994
Sandra McDonald, *The Outback Stars*, 2007
Elizabeth Moon, *Against the Odds*, 2000
David Weber, *In Enemy Hands*, 1997

708

DAVID SHERMAN
DAN CRAGG , Co-Author

Wings of Hell

(New York: Del Rey, 2008)

Story type: Space Opera; Military
Series: Starfist. Book 13
Subject(s): Space Colonies; Aliens
Major character(s): Charlie Bass, Military Personnel; Tim

Kerr, Military Personnel; Lupo Ratliff, Military Personnel
Time period(s): Indeterminate Future
Locale(s): Outer Space

Summary: Human civilization is threatened by a powerful alien race and limited conflict along the borders of their respective spheres of influence continues. The human government, however, is poised to declare the threat even greater than it really is, precipitating a war across the galaxy. A complex mixture of military science fiction and political machinations.

Where it's reviewed:
Publishers Weekly, November 10, 2008, page 35

Other books by the same author:
Firestorm, 2007 (Dan Cragg, co-author)
Point Blank, 2006 (Dan Cragg, co-author)
A World of Hurt, 2004 (Dan Cragg, co-author)
Lazarus Rising, 2003 (Dan Cragg, co-author)
Technokill, 2000 (Dan Cragg, co-author)

Other books you might like:
Dan Abnett, *Titanicus*, 2008
R.M. Meluch, *The Myriad*, 2004
John Ringo, *Gust Front*, 2001
David Weber, *Off Armageddon Reef*, 2006
Timothy Zahn, *The Backlash Mission*, 1986

709

LINNEA SINCLAIR

Shades of Dark

(New York: Bantam, 2008)

Story type: Space Opera; Romance
Subject(s): Space Travel; Secrets
Major character(s): Chadisah "Chaz" Bergren, Spaceship Captain; Gabriel Ross Sullivan, Religious, Telepath; Thad Bergren, Prisoner
Time period(s): Indeterminate Future
Locale(s): Outer Space; Planet—Imaginary

Summary: Chaz Bergren has escaped the clutches of a repressive interstellar empire and supports herself and her lover, a telepath, by running cargo from one planet to the next. She is uninterested in returning to the more civilized part of the galaxy until she discovers that her brother has been arrested and faces harsh punishment in her absence.

Where it's reviewed:
Publishers Weekly, June 30, 2008, page 167

Other books by the same author:
Games of Command, 2007
The Down Home Zombie Blues, 2007
The Accidental Goddess, 2006
Finders Keepers, 2005
Gabriel's Ghost, 2005

Other books you might like:
C.J. Cherryh, *The Chanur Saga*, 2005
Doris Lopes Heald, *Mistwalker*, 1994
Andre Norton, *Plague Ship*, 1959

S.L. Viehl, *Beyond Varallan*, 2000
Timothy Zahn, *The Icarus Hunt*, 1999

710

BRIAN FRANCIS SLATTERY

Liberation
(New York: Tor, 2008)

Story type: Satire; Dystopian
Subject(s): Utopia/Dystopia; Humor
Major character(s): Marco Angelo Oliveira, Criminal; Keira Shamu, Criminal; Zeke Hezekiah, Criminal
Time period(s): Indeterminate Future; Multiple Time Periods

Summary: A worldwide economic collapse results in a reversion of civilization to institutions of times long past. In the former America, slavery is re-introduced and Native American tribes begin raiding homes and businesses near their land. A group of criminals embarks on a plan to restore the old world.

Where it's reviewed:
Publishers Weekly, August 25, 2008, page 56

Other books by the same author:
Spaceman Blues, 2007

Other books you might like:
Margaret Atwood, *The Handmaid's Tale*, 1985
J.G. Ballard, *Hello America*, 1981
Neal Barrett Jr., *Dawn's Uncertain Light*, 1989
Paul E. Erdman, *The Last Days of America*, 1981
Alan Seymour, *The Coming Self Destruction of the United States of America*, 1969

711

NEAL STEPHENSON

Anathem
(New York: Morrow, 2008)

Story type: Religious; Literary
Subject(s): Religion; Secrets
Major character(s): Erasmas, Religious, Rebel; Orolo, Religious, Scientist; Cord, Artisan
Time period(s): Indeterminate
Locale(s): Planet—Imaginary

Summary: Erasmas is a young member of a cloistered religious community that has virtually no contact with the secular world on his planet. The expulsion of one of his teachers and other strange events suggest to him that something is going on in the skies of his world that the authorities do not want the public to know about.

Where it's reviewed:
Booklist, July 1, 2008, page 5
Library Journal, August 1, 2008, page 72
New York Times Book Review, October 19, 2008, page 22

Other books by the same author:
Quicksilver, 2004

The Confusion, 2004
The Cryptonomicon, 1999
The Diamond Age, 1995
Snow Crash, 1993

Other books you might like:
Iain Banks, *The Algebraist*, 2004
Ursula K. Le Guin, *The Dispossessed*, 1974
China Mieville, *Perdido Street Station*, 2001
Walter M. Miller Jr., *A Canticle for Leibowitz*, 1959
Dan Simmons, *Hyperion*, 1989

712

S.M. STIRLING

The Scourge of God
(New York: Roc, 2008)

Story type: Disaster; Quest
Series: Sunrise Lands. Book 4
Subject(s): Religious Conflict; Disasters
Major character(s): Rudi Mackenzie, Traveller; Mathilda Arminger, Prisoner; Ingolf, Religious
Time period(s): 2020s (2021)
Locale(s): North America

Summary: A mysterious change in the laws of nature has rendered almost all technology inoperable. In the aftermath, civilization collapses into feudalism and a religious cult that believes God is punishing humanity rises to power. Rudi Mackenzie embarks on a journey across the continent to seek the true cause of the change, unaware that he is being pursued by a killer.

Other books by the same author:
The Sunrise Lands, 2007
A Meeting at Corvallis, 2006
The Sky People, 2006
The Protector's War, 2005
Rising Storm, 2002

Other books you might like:
Poul Anderson, *Orion Shall Rise*, 1983
Theodore Judson, *Fitzpatrick's War*, 2004
Walter M. Miller Jr., *A Canticle for Leibowitz*, 1959
Paul O. Williams, *The Breaking of Northwall*, 1980
Roger Zelazny, *Damnation Alley*, 1969

713

JAMES SWALLOW

Red Fury
(Nottingham, United Kingdom: Black Library, 2008)

Story type: Space Opera; Military
Series: Warhammer
Subject(s): Space Travel; War
Major character(s): Rafen, Military Personnel; Kayne, Military Personnel; Corbulo, Military Personnel
Time period(s): Indeterminate Future
Locale(s): Outer Space

Summary: Schisms within the ranks of a military organization resulted in massive fatalities and now the Blood

Angels are badly depleted. It is essential that they recruit new soldiers to fill their ranks before their enemies discover the truth and move against them to take advantage of their weakened position. Unfortunately, there are other factions that wish to see them destroyed.

Other books by the same author:
Day of the Vipers, 2008
Faith and Fire, 2006
Blood Relative, 2005
Deus Encarmine, 2004
Eclipse, 2004

Other books you might like:
Randall N. Bills, *Pandora's Gambit*, 2007
Ben Counter, *Chapter War*, 2007
William H. Keith, *Bolo Rising*, 1989
Victor Milan, *A Rending of Falcons*, 2007
John Ringo, *Hell's Faire*, 2003

714

KAREN TRAVISS

Aspho Fields

(New York: Del Rey, 2008)

Story type: Space Opera; Military
Subject(s): Aliens; Space Colonies
Major character(s): Marcus Fenix, Military Personnel; Dominic Santiago, Military Personnel; Carlos Santiago, Military Personnel
Time period(s): Indeterminate Future
Locale(s): Outer Space; Sera, Planet—Imaginary

Summary: Three friends enlist in the army to help protect the human race from alien enemies. During the course of the war, they become widely separated, but as a new threat arises, they may be reunited for the ultimate battle. Two of them will become distracted by a startling revelation about the third.

Other books by the same author:
Judge, 2008
Ally, 2007
Blood Lines, 2006
City of Pearl, 2004
Crossing the Line, 2004

Other books you might like:
John Dalmas, *The Regiment*, 1987
William C. Dietz, *For Those Who Fell*, 2004
Walter H. Hunt, *The Dark Wing*, 2001
John Scalzi, *Zoe's Tale*, 2008
David Weber, *The Apocalypse Troll*, 1999

715

KAREN TRAVISS

Judge

(New York: Eos, 2008)

Story type: Space Opera; Disaster
Series: Shan Frankland. Book 6

Subject(s): Aliens; Ecology
Major character(s): Shan Frankland, Spacewoman, Immortal; Eddie Michallat, Spaceman, Expatriate; Aras, Alien
Time period(s): 25th century (2401-2426)
Locale(s): Earth; Outer Space

Summary: Shan Frankland has returned to Earth despite her determination not to expose the planet's population to the parasite which is now resident in her body. Events force her hand, however, when an alien race decides that it is time to reclaim the Earth's ecology, even if that means wiping out millions of people to accomplish.

Where it's reviewed:
Locus, July 2008, page 23

Other books by the same author:
Ally, 2007
Blood Lines, 2006
Matriarch, 2006
City of Pearl, 2004
Hard Contact, 2004

Other books you might like:
Arthur C. Clarke, *The Last Theorem*, 2008
    Frederik Pohl, co-author
Philip K. Dick, *The Zap Gun*, 1967
Frederik Pohl, *The Annals of the Heechee*, 1987
Mack Reynolds, *Space Visitor*, 1977
Robert Silverberg, *Hot Sky at Midnight*, 1994

716

HARRY TURTLEDOVE

The Man with the Iron Heart

(New York: Del Rey, 2008)

Story type: Alternate History; Military
Subject(s): Alternate History; Military Life
Major character(s): Reinhard Heydrich, Historical Figure, Military Personnel; Louis Weissberg, Military Personnel; Vladimir Bokov, Military Personnel
Time period(s): 1940s (1942-1949)
Locale(s): Germany

Summary: An alternate history of World War II features a world in which Reinhard Heydrich is not killed and goes into hiding when the Allies capture Germany. Heydrich organizes an underground resistance and engages in guerilla warfare, surprising an occupation army that is not prepared for unconventional warfare.

Other books by the same author:
The Valley-Westside War, 2008
Beyond the Gap, 2007
The Disunited States of America, 2006
Drive to the East, 2005
Curious Notions, 2004

Other books you might like:
Stephen Baxter, *Weaver*, 2008
Ben Bova, *Triumph*, 1993
Christopher Priest, *The Separation*, 2002
Fred Saberhagen, *A Century of Progress*, 1983
Jo Walton, *Farthing*, 2006

717

HARRY TURTLEDOVE

The United States of Atlantis
(New York: Tor, 2008)

Story type: Alternate World; Historical
Series: Atlantis. Book 2
Subject(s): Alternate History; War
Major character(s): Victor Radcliffe, Revolutionary; Matthew Radcliffe, Revolutionary; Charles Cornwallis, Military Personnel
Time period(s): 18th century
Locale(s): Alternate Earth

Summary: In a version of this world where the continent of Atlantis exists, British colonists hope to rebel against their homeland after the end of the conflict with France. Victor Radcliffe is the leader of a band of revolutionaries whose popularity growing in the face of growing repression by King George.

Where it's reviewed:
Publishers Weekly, October 27, 2008, page 37

Other books by the same author:
Gladiator, 2007
Opening Atlantis, 2007
The Disunited States of America, 2006
Drive to the East, 2005
Days of Infamy, 2004

Other books you might like:
John Barnes, *Kaleidoscope Century*, 1995
Michael Moorcock, *Gloriana*, 1978
Mike Resnick, *Dragon America*, 2005
Keith Roberts, *Pavane*, 1968
Robert Charles Wilson, *Darwinia*, 1998

718

MARK L. VAN NAME

Slanted Jack
(New York: Baen, 2008)

Story type: Space Opera; Quest
Series: Jon and Lobo. Book 2
Subject(s): Space Travel; Aliens
Major character(s): Jon Moore, Cyborg, Mercenary; Lobo, Artificial Intelligence; Maggie Park, Spacewoman
Time period(s): Indeterminate Future
Locale(s): Outer Space; Planet—Imaginary

Summary: Jon Moore is a cyborg who works as a mercenary and general odd jobs man in space. He gets involved with an old friend in a somewhat questionable scheme, which leads to his involuntary rescue of a prisoner. She turns out to have a number of dangerous secrets and their association and a visit to a frontier world add up to trouble and danger.

Where it's reviewed:
Publishers Weekly, May 12, 2008, page 40

Other books by the same author:
One Jump Ahead, 2007

Other books you might like:
Poul Anderson, *A Circus of Hells*, 1970
Alan Dean Foster, *Drowning World*, 2003
Murray Leinster, *The Pirates of Zan*, 1959
Andre Norton, *The Solar Queen*, 2003
Timothy Zahn, *Night Train to Rigel*, 2005

719

S.L. VIEHL

Omega Games
(New York: Roc, 2008)

Story type: Space Opera; Space Colony
Series: Stardoc. Book 8
Subject(s): Space Colonies; Plague
Major character(s): Cherijo Torin, Doctor, Spacewoman; Duncan Reever, Spaceman; Grey Veil, Doctor
Time period(s): Indeterminate Future
Locale(s): Trellus, Planet—Imaginary

Summary: Doctor Cherijo Torin is trying to find a cure for a mysterious new plague that is spreading through the galaxy. Acting on a tip, she and her husband travel to the planet Trellus where they find themselves marooned on a world where violence is inexplicably increasing.

Other books by the same author:
Plague of Memory, 2007
Rebel Ice, 2006
Afterburn, 2005
Bio Rescue, 2004
Blade Dancer, 2003

Other books you might like:
John Brunner, *The Repairmen of Cyclops*, 1965
Simon Lang, *Hopeship*, 1994
Stephen Leigh, *Dark Water's Embrace*, 1998
Murray Leinster, *This World Is Taboo*, 1961
Alan E. Nourse, *Star Surgeon*, 1959

720

JO WALTON

Half a Crown
(New York: Tor, 2008)

Story type: Alternate History; Mystery
Series: Peace with Honor. Book 3
Subject(s): Alternate History; Nazis
Major character(s): Peter Carmichael, Police Officer; Adolf Hitler, Historical Figure, Dictator; Paula Berman, Fugitive
Time period(s): 1960s (1960)
Locale(s): England

Summary: England negotiated peace with Nazi Germany, which allowed the Axis powers to win the war, leaving the British Isles nominally free but actually a fascist state. Peter Carmichael is a police officer who suspects that a plot may exist to overthrow the government on the eve of an international peace conference.

Science Fiction

Where it's reviewed:
Publishers Weekly, August 4, 2008, page 43

Other books by the same author:
Ha'penny, 2007
Farthing, 2006
Tooth and Claw, 2003
The Prize in the Game, 2002
The King's Name, 2001

Other books you might like:
Brian W. Aldiss, *The Year Before Yesterday*, 1987
Stephen Baxter, *Weaver*, 2008
David Dvorkin, *Budspy*, 1987
Ken MacLeod, *The Human Front*, 2002
Christopher Priest, *The Separation*, 2002

721

STEVE WHITE

Saint Antony's Fire

(New York: Baen, 2008)

Story type: Alternate Universe; Historical/Elizabethan
Subject(s): Alternate History; Aliens
Major character(s): Thomas Winslow, Sea Captain; Francis Walsingham, Government Official, Nobleman; Elizabeth, Ruler
Time period(s): 16th century
Locale(s): England; Alternate Universe

Summary: In an alternate version of Elizabethan England, the war with Spain takes a turn for the worse when Spanish explorers discover a cache of alien technology. They use these newfound weapons to turn the tide against the English, threatening to bring Elizabeth's rule to an end.

Where it's reviewed:
Publishers Weekly, September 8, 2008, page 39

Other books by the same author:
Blood of the Heroes, 2006
The Prometheus Project, 2005
Forge of the Titans, 2003
Eagle Against the Stars, 2000
Prince of Sunset, 1998

Other books you might like:
Stephen Baxter, *Anti-Ice*, 1993
Michael Kurland, *The Whenabouts of Burr*, 1975
Mike Resnick, *Dragon America*, 2005
Keith Roberts, *Pavane*, 1968
S.M. Stirling, *The Peshawar Lancers*, 2002

722

WALTER JON WILLIAMS

Implied Spaces

(San Francisco: Night Shade, 2008)

Story type: Space Opera; Alternate Intelligence
Subject(s): Artificial Intelligence; Space Colonies
Major character(s): Aristide, Scientist; Bitsy, Artificial

Intelligence; Daljit, Scientist
Time period(s): Indeterminate Future
Locale(s): Alternate Universe; Outer Space

Summary: In the far future, humans are able to create entire pocket universes in each of which the laws of nature can be altered. Aristide is wandering through one when he uncovers a plot to seize control of the various realities and unite them into a single, insane quest.

Where it's reviewed:
Analog, November 2008, page 135
Booklist, June 1, 2008, page 67
Library Journal, May 15, 2008, page 95
Publishers Weekly, May 5, 2008, page 49

Other books by the same author:
Conventions of War, 2005
The Sundering, 2003
Destiny's Way, 2002
The Praxis, 2002
Frankensteins and Foreign Devils, 1998

Other books you might like:
Philip Jose Farmer, *The Maker of Universes*, 1965
Michael Flynn, *The January Dancer*, 2008
Alastair Reynolds, *The Prefect*, 2007
Karl Schroeder, *Sun of Suns*, 2006
Lawrence Watt-Evans, *Out of This World*, 1994

723

JOHN ZAKOUR

The Flaxen Femme Fatale

(New York: DAW, 2008)

Story type: Humor; Mystery
Series: Zachary Johnson. Book 6
Subject(s): Humor; Secrets
Major character(s): Zachary Nixon Johnson, Detective—Private; Natasha, Clone; HARV, Artificial Intelligence
Time period(s): Indeterminate Future
Locale(s): California

Summary: Zachary Johnson is the last private detective on Earth. His latest job involves the escape of a cloned, enhanced assassin named Natasha from a government project. While tracking her down, Johnson encounters robots, androids, and others, all apparently intent upon injuring him. When he finally does catch up to Natasha, he begins to wonder if she might have been justified in escaping.

Other books by the same author:
The Blue-Haired Bombshell, 2007
The Frost-Haired Vixen, 2006
The Radioactive Redhead, 2005 (Lawrence Ganem, co-author)
The Doomsday Brunette, 2004 (Lawrence Ganem, co-author)
The Platinum Blonde, 2001 (Lawrence Ganem, co-author)

Other books you might like:
Douglas Adams, *Dirk Gently's Holistic Detective
    Agency*, 1987
Ron Goulart, *Brainz, Inc.*, 1985

Isidore Haiblum, *Interworld*, 1977
Keith Hartman, *Gumshoe Gorilla*, 2001
William F. Nolan, *Space for Hire*, 1971

The Year in Historical Fiction
by
Daniel S. Burt

What do a Nobel Prize recipient (Toni Morrison), a country western singer-songwriter icon (Willie Nelson), a Shamus Award winner (Dennis Lehane), and twenty-five first novelists have in common? All have historical novels collected here: a testament to the persistence and attraction of the historical fiction genre. This begs the question, why? One would think that after the countless historical novels that have appeared since Sir Walter Scott first transported his readers back to the historical past in the early nineteenth century there would be little left for a historical novelist to be original about, no historical figures left unexamined or historical era in need of an imaginative makeover. But that is not the case. Collected here are 150 new forays into the historical past, chronicling virtually every era from the Ancient Greeks and Romans, to the Middle Ages, the Tudor and Elizabethan Ages, and through each century from the seventeenth to the early twenty-first, with fresh takes on such familiar historical figures as Alexander the Great (Shan Sa's *Alexander and Alestria*, Mary Queen of Scots (Philippa Gregory's *The Other Queen* and Elisabeth Mc-Neill's *Blood Royal*), and William Shakespeare (Christopher Rush's *Will* and Jess Winfield's *My Name Is Will*). The historical novel remains tempting for writer and reader alike because it is the only effective time machine ever devised. Historical novels have the unique ability to bring the historical past back to life and to explore both the unknown and the historically familiar with revealing intimacy. Good historical novelists bring the past to life; great historical novelists bridge the gap between past eras and our own to uncover commonality and timeless relevance.

Historical fiction persists even though it remains one of the most demanding and contested of fictional genres. Historical novels have drawn criticism both for their errors and falsification of the historical record and for neglecting entertainment for historical detail work. By invading the province of the historian with an intention to elucidate the past as well as to entertain, the historical novelist must serve two opposed masters, satisfying the often contradictory goals of historical and imaginative truth. Not bound by the same restrictions as the historian to report only what is known and verifiable, the historical novelist is free to look beneath the facts of history for insights, to fill in gaps in the historical record with speculation and surmise. The writer of historical fiction must satisfy both the impulses of the historian and the novelist that often diverge.

Despite the challenge of taking us somewhere we haven't yet been or think we know too well already or of finding the right balance between verifiable and imaginative truth, the historical past remains a prime fictional destination. The novels collected here from the second half of 2008 represent what can be done in the form and why the form remains so popular for both writers and readers alike.

Selection Criteria

More so than any other fictional genre, it is necessary to define exactly what constitutes a historical novel. All novels deal with the past, except science fiction that is set in the future, or fantasy novels set in an imagined, alternative world outside historical time. Yet not all novels are truly historical. Central to any workable definition of historical fiction is the degree to which the writer attempts not to recall the past but to recreate it. In some cases the time frame, setting, and customs of a novel's era are merely incidental to its action and characterization. In other cases, period details function as little more than a colorful backdrop for characters and situations that could as easily be played out in a different era with little alteration. So-called historical "costume dramas" could to a greater or lesser degree work as well with a change of costume in a different place and time. The novels that we can identify as truly historical, however, attempt much more than incidental period surface details or interchangeable historical eras. What justifies a designation as a historical novel is the writer's efforts at providing an accurate and believable representation of a particular historical era. The writer of historical fiction shares with the historian a verifiable depiction of past events, lives, and customs. In historical fiction, the past itself becomes as much a subject for the novelist as the characters and action.

Most of us use the phrase "historical novel" casually, never really needing an exact definition to make ourselves understood. We just know it when we see it. This listing, however, requires a set of criteria to determine what's in and what's out. Otherwise the list has no boundaries. If the working definition of historical fiction is too loose, every novel set in a period before the present qualifies, and nearly every novel becomes a historical novel immediately upon publication. If the definition is so strict that only books set in a time before the author's birth, for example, make the cut, then countless works that critics, readers, librarians, and the authors themselves think of as historical novels would be excluded.

The challenge here, therefore, has been to fashion a definition or set of criteria flexible enough to include novels that pass what can be regarded as the litmus test for historical fiction: Did the author use his or her imagination—and often quite a bit of research—to evoke another and earlier time than the author's own? Walter Scott, who is credited with "inventing" the historical novel in English during the early nineteenth century, provides a useful criterion in the subtitle of *Waverley*, his initial historical novel, the story of Scottish life at the time of the Jacobite Rebellion of 1745: "'Tis Sixty Years Since." This supplies a possible formula for separating the created past from the remembered past. What is unique and distinctive about the so-called historical novel is its attempt to imagine a distant period of time before the novelist's lifetime. Scott's sixty-year span between a novel's composition and its imagined era offers an arbitrary but useful means to distinguish between the personal and the historical past. The distance of two generations or nearly a lifetime provides a necessary span for the past to emerge as history and forces the writer to rely on more than recollection to uncover the patterns and textures of the past. I have, therefore, adopted Scott's formula but adjusted it to fifty years, including those books in which the significant portion of their plots is set in a period fifty years or more before the novel was written.

Because a rigid application of this fifty-year rule might disqualify quite a few books intended by their authors and regarded by their readers to be historical novels, another test has been applied to books written about more recent eras: Did the author use actual historical figures and events while setting out to recreate a specific, rather than a general or incidental, historical period? Although it is, of course, risky to speculate about a writer's intention, it is possible by looking at the book's approach, its use of actual historical figures, and its emphasis on a distinctive time and place that enhances the reader's knowledge of past lives, events, and customs to detect when a book conforms to what most would consider a central preoccupation of the historical novel.

I have tried to apply these criteria for the historical novel thoughtfully, and have allowed some exceptions when warranted by special circumstances. I hope I have been able to anticipate what most readers would consider historical novels, but I recognize that I may have overlooked some worthy representations of the past in the interest of dealing with a manageable list of titles. Finally, not every title in the Western, historical mystery, or historical romance genres has been included to avoid unnecessary duplication with the other sections of this book. I have included those novels that share characteristics with another genre—whether fantasy, Western, mystery, or romance—that seem to put the strongest emphasis on historical interest, detail, and accuracy.

Historical Fiction Highlights in the Second Half of 2008

The three famous names mentioned above each supply intriguing historical fictions. Toni Morrison's *A Mercy* about slavery in colonial America serves as a kind of prequel to her masterpiece *Beloved*. Willie Nelson teams with western historical novelist Mike Blakely for an Old West Texas tale (*A Tale Out of Luck*). Dennis Lehane, author of the acclaimed novel *Mystic River*, has produced a massive historical novel, *The Given Day*, about the 1919 Boston Police Strike and the transformation of modern America. Other well-known and celebrated writers are represented here, including Sebastian Barry (*The Secret Scripture*), Ian Buruma (*The China Lover*), Emma Donoghue (*The Sealed Letter*), Amitav Ghosh (*Sea of Poppies*), David Liss (*The Whiskey Rebels*), Philip Roth (*Indignation*), John Vernon (*Lucky Billy*), and A.N. Wilson (*Winnie and Wolf*). Stalwarts of the historical novel genre are also here, such as Gillian Bradshaw (*The Sun's Bride*), Philippa Gregory (*The Other Queen* and *Fallen Skies*), Colleen McCullough (*The Independence of Miss Mary Bennet*), Arturo Perez-Reverte (*The King's Gold*), and Danielle Steel (*A Good Woman*). Among the many first historical novelists collected here, some of the most interesting include David Boling's t *Guernica*, about the Nazi firebombing of the Spanish town that was commemorated in Picasso's famous painting; Ella March Chase's *The Virgin Queen's Daughter*, about a purported daughter of Queen Elizabeth; and Padma Viswanathan's *The Toss of a Lemon*, a family saga set in South India.

Series remain popular ways of presenting historical novels and extending treatment of a historical subject. Examples of additional installments of ongoing series include the nautical sagas of Broos Campbell's *Peter Wicked* and Julian Stockwin's *The Privateer's Revenge*, the espionage/adventure series of C.C. Humphrey's *Absolute Honor*, and Beverly Swerling's documentation of the growth and development of New York City in *City of God*. Admired historical novelist Sharon Kay Penman brings her trilogy set in twelfth-century England to a close with *Devil's Brood*.

Another interesting trend in recent historical fiction is historical fantasy - violations of the historical record with the supernatural and disruption of the space/time continuum. Alternate history remains a popular sub-category of historical fantasy. There are two offerings by the reigning master of the form, Harry Turtledove, who provides an alternative version of World War II in *The Man with the Iron Heart* and the American Revolution in *The United States of Atlantis*. Another intriguing what-if is David Fitz-Enz's re-imagining of the War of 1812 in *Redcoats' Revenge*. Perhaps the longest anticipated historical fantasy sequel is Katherine Neville's *The Fire*, the continuation of her much-admired 1988 debut, *The Eight*.

The other trend that is obvious in this collection is that Jane Austen's life and fiction seems to be rivaling Arthur Conan Doyle's Sherlock Holmes for the number of pastiches, continuations, and makeovers. Holmsiana is represented here by three works: John R. King's *The Shadow of Reichenbach Falls* imagines what really happened when Holmes and his nemesis Moriarty took a plunge in Switzerland; John Gardner's *Moriarty* has even more to say about Holmes' archrival; and Gyles Brandreth's *Oscar Wilde and a Game Called Murder* teams up Wilde, Arthur Conan Doyle, and Bram Stoker in a Victorian-era mystery. But there are no fewer than four novels collected here that draw on Jane Austen's life and works. Carrie Bebris's *The Matters at Mansfield* is a Regency-era mystery that uses Elizabeth Bennet and Darcy from Austen's *Pride and Prejudice* as sleuths. Rebecca Ann Collins's *Netherfield Revisited* is a sequel to *Pride and Prejudice* projected into the Victorian period, while Colleen McCullough's *The Independence of Miss Mary Bennet* centers on Elizabeth Bennet's priggish younger sister for a adventure of her own. Finally, Jill Pitkeathley's *Cassandra and Jane* treats the Austen biography from the perspective of the author's relationship with her beloved sister. Sherlock Holmes, the most popular fictional character of all time, still is the reigning champion, but the Austenites seem to be gaining!

Historical Mysteries

The workhorse sub-genre of historical fiction is indisputably historical mystery, and examples of crime investigation over the centuries are well represented here. Detective work is being done in Ancient Rome (John Maddox Roberts's *SPQR II: Oracle of the Dead*), Medieval Japan (Laura Joh Rowland's *The Fire Kimono*), Medieval England (Priscilla Royal's *Forsaken Soul* and Alys Clare's *The Paths of the Air*), and Medieval Ireland (Cora Harrison's *A Secret and Unlawful Killing*); the nineteenth century (Charles Finch's *The September Society* and Sara Fraser's *The Resurrection Man*); and during and after World War I (Graham Ison's *Hardcastle's Burglar* and Charles Todd's *A Matter of Justice*) and World War II (James R. Benn's *Blood Alone*, Patrick Culhane's *Red Sky in the Morning*, and John Lawton's *Second Violin*).

Among the unusual sleuths at work here are Beatrix Potter in Susan Wittig Albert's *The Tale of Briar Bank*, real-life detective Edward Vidocq in Louis Bayard's *The Black Tower*, and a slave during the American Civil War in David Fuller's *Sweetsmoke*. Real life crimes and criminals are featured in Martin Caparros's *Valfierno*

about the 1911 theft of Da Vinci's Mona Lisa and moonshiners during Prohibition in Matt Bondurant's *The Wettest County in the World*.

Fictional Biographies

One of the richest sub-genre of the historical novel is fictional biography, in which a historical figure's life or a significant portion of that life is depicted, with the novelist able to fill in the gaps in the historical record or speculate when factual evidence is lacking. There are biographical studies of both the famous and the obscure. In the former category, there is the painter Frida Kahlo in Slavenka Drakulic's *Frida's Bed*, Chinggis Khan in Yashushi Inoue's *The Blue Wolf*, Adolf Hitler in A.N. Wilson's *Winnie and Wolf*, writer Daphne DuMaurier in Justine Picardie's *Daphne* , and outlaw Billy the Kid in John Vernon's *Lucky Billy*. Among the lesser known, there is Jean-Jacques Rousseau's older brother, Francois, in Stephan Audequy's *The Only Son*; actress, film star, and journalist Yamaguchi Yoshiko in Ian Buruma's *The China Lover*; photographer Edward S. Curtis in Alan Cheuse's *To Catch the Lightning*; and a trio of royals: the Grand Duchess Tatiana Romanov in Carolly Erickson's *The Tsarina's Daughter*; the daughter of King Ferdinand and Queen Isabella, Princess Juana of Castille, in C.W. Gortner's *The Last Queen*; and Princess Nefertari, the niece of Queen Nefertiti, in Michelle Moran's *The Heretic Queen*. Some of the most exotic biographical profiles are those of A'isha bint Abi Bakr, the wife of Muhammad Sherry Jones's *The Jewel of Medina*; and the thirteenth-century Turkish Sufi mystic known as Rumi in Nahal Tajadod's *Rumi: The Fire of Love* .

Intriguing Events and Oddities

One of the greatest benefits of the historical form are entertaining introductions to unfamiliar aspects of the historical past, and there are several examples of off-the-beaten-track subjects collected here. Pre-Castro Cuba is the scene of Rachel Kushner's *Telex from Cuba* . Charles F. Price's *Nor the Battle to the Strong* focuses on the southern campaign during the Revolutionary War and the important Battle of Eutaw Springs. Mormon life during the nineteenth century is the subject of two novels: David Eberhoff's *The 19th Wife* and Alissa York's *Effigy*. A.N. Wilson looks at the relationship between Adolf Hitler and Richard Wagner's daughter-in-law in *Winnie and Wolf*. Ami Silber's *Early Bright* tackles the Los Angeles music scene during the 1940s. Diana Burg's *Dalliance* is based on an actual divorce case from the 1860s. Kathleen Kent's *The Heretic's Daughter* explores the Salem witchcraft trials from the perspective of an actual family during the time.

Finally, there are also several novels that really offer an eccentric's eye-view. Hannah Tinti's *The Good Thief* is a rousing picaresque adventure of a New England one-armed orphan during the nineteenth century. Andre Behrs's *The Sin Eaters* looks at the unusual custom of literally consuming another's sin, and Steve Thayer's *The Leper* tracks the treatment of leprosy during the twentieth century. Kirsten Menger-Anderson's *Doctor Olaf van Schuler's Brain* chronicles the history of New York City from colonial times based on several doctor's medical obsessions. All of these novels carry out the historical novel's basic appeal: of recreating the past to entertain and illuminate.

Recommendations Titles

Here are my selections of the 30 most accomplished and interesting historical novels for the second half of 2008:

The Secret Scripture by Sebastian Barry

The Black Tower by Louis Bayard

The Sun's Bride by Gillian Bradshaw,

The China Lover by Ian Buruma

To Catch the Lightning by Alan Cheuse

The Four Seasons by Laurel Corona

The Glass of Time by Michael Cox

The Eleventh Man by Ivan Doig

The Sealed Letter by Emma Donoghue

Frida's Bed by Slavenka Drakulic

The 19th Wife by David Ebershoff

The Little Book by Selden Edwards

The Tsarina's Daughter by Carolly Erickson

Sea of Poppies by Amitav Ghosh

The Last Queen by C.W. Gortner

The Other Queen by Philippa Gregory

The Jewel of Medina by Sherry Jones

Telex from Cuba by Rachel Kushner

The Given Day by Dennis Lehane

The Whiskey Road by David Liss

A Quiet Adjustment by Benjamin Markovits

Doctor Olaf von Schuler's Brain by Kirsten Menger-Anderson

A Mercy by Toni Morrison

Devil's Brood by Sharon Kay Penman

The King's Gold by Arturo Perez-Reverte

Nor the Battle to the Strong by Charles F. Price

City of God by Beverly Swerling

The Good Thief by Hannah Tinti

Lucky Billy by John Vernon

Winnie and Wolf by A.N. Wilson

For More Information about Historical Fiction

Printed Sources

Lynda G. Adamson, *American Historical Fiction: An Annotated Guide to Novels for Adults and Young Adults*. Phoenix: Oryx Press, 1999.

Lynda G. Adamson, *World Historical Fiction: An Annotated Guide to Novels for Adults and Young Adults*. Phoenix: Oryx Press, 1999.

Daniel S. Burt, *What Historical Fiction Do I Read Next?* Detroit: Gale, Vols. 1-3, 1997-2003.

Daniel S. Burt, *The Biography Book*. Westport: Oryx/Greenwood Press, 2001.

Mark C. Carnes, *Novel History: Historians and Novelists Confront America's Past (and Each Other)*. New York: Simon & Schuster, 2001.

Donald K Hartman, *Historical Figures in Fiction*. Phoenix: Oryx Press, 1994.

Electronic Sources

The Historical Novel Society (http//www.historicalnovel society.org). Includes articles, interviews, and reviews of historical novels.

Of Ages Past: The Online Magazine of Historical Fiction (http://www.angelfire.com/il/ofagespast/). Includes novel excerpts, short stories, articles, author profiles, and reviews.

Soon's Historical Fiction Site (http://uts.cc.utexas.edu/~soon/histfiction/). A rich source of information on the historical novel genre, including links to more specialized sites on particular authors and types of historical fiction.

Historical Titles

724

JOHN ADDIEGO

The Islands of Divine Music

(Denver: Unbridled Books, 2008)

Story type: Historical/American West Coast; Family Saga
Subject(s): Family Relations; Italian Americans
Major character(s): Rosari Verbicaro, Spouse (of Giuseppe); Giuseppe Verbicaro, Spouse (of Rosari)
Time period(s): 20th century
Locale(s): Italy; San Francisco, California

Summary: Addiego offers a multigenerational Italian family saga in America. Rosari is forced to flee to San Francisco from Italy where she meets Giuseppe Verbicaro, a laborer whom she marries. Their life together is dramatically affected when Giuseppe takes up with a pregnant prostitute. The ramifications are worked out in successive generations of descendants. The novel offers a capsule history of the 20th century as reflected by this Italian family.

Where it's reviewed:
Booklist, October 15, 2008, page 23
Library Journal, October 1, 2008, page 55

Other books you might like:
Emilio Calderon, *The Creator's Map*, 2008
Christopher Castellani, *The Saint of Lost Things*, 2005
Louisa Ermelino, *The Black Madonna*, 2001
Bea Gonzalez, *The Bitter Taste of Time*, 2008
Adriana Tragiani, *The Queen of the Big Time*, 2004

725

SUSAN WITTIG ALBERT

The Tale of Briar Bank

(New York: Berkley Prime Crime, 2008)

Story type: Mystery; Historical/Edwardian
Series: Cottage Tales of Beatrix Potter. Book 5
Subject(s): Mystery and Detective Stories; Authors and Writers; Rural Life
Major character(s): Beatrix Potter, Historical Figure, Writer
Time period(s): 1900s

Locale(s): Sawrey, England

Summary: Albert offers a fifth installment of her cozy mystery series involving Beatrix Potter. Journeying from London to her Hill Top Farm in England's Lake District, Potter learns of the death of a longtime resident of the area who is killed by a falling tree limb. It is suspected that he was a victim of a curse after unearthing an ancient treasure. To learn the truth, Potter turns to her animal assistants in this delightful period mystery.

Where it's reviewed:
Booklist, September 15, 2008, page 31
Publishers Weekly, August 4, 2008, page 47

Other books by the same author:
Nightshade, 2008
The Tale of Hawthorn House, 2007
The Tale of Cuckoo Brow Wood, 2006
The Tale of Holly How, 2005
The Tale of Hill Top Farm, 2004

Other books you might like:
Peter Abrahams, *End of Story*, 2006
Irene Allen, *The Elizabeth Elliot Series*, 1992-
Barbara Rogan, *Suspicion*, 1999
Diane Setherfield, *The Thirteenth Tale*, 2006
Deborah Woodworth, *A Deadly Shaker Spring*, 1998

726

MATILDA ASENSI

Everything under the Sky

(New York: Harper, 2008)

Story type: Historical/Roaring Twenties; Mystery
Subject(s): Artists and Art; China; Treasure
Major character(s): Elvira De Poulain, Artist (painter), Widow(er); Fernanda, Teenager
Time period(s): 1920s
Locale(s): Shanghai, China; China

Summary: In this thriller set in Shanghai in the 1920s, Spanish painter Elvira De Poulain travels to China to deal with the aftermath of her husband's murder and his tangled affairs. She is left an antique chest with clues directing her to a lost treasure buried 2,000 years before by China's first emperor. To find it, Elvira and her teenage niece, Fernanda, set out on a cross-country race against her husband's killers in this atmospheric period thriller.

Where it's reviewed:
Booklist, September 1, 2008, page 46
Publishers Weekly, August 18, 2008, page 39

Other books by the same author:
The Last Cato, 2006

Other books you might like:
Margaret Atwood, *The Blind Assassin*, 2000
Tom Harper, *The Lost Temple*, 2007
Anita Shreve, *The Pilot's Wife*, 1998
Evelyn Smith, *Miss Melville's Revenge*, 1989
Nicholas Sparks, *The Guardian*, 2003

727

STEPHANE AUDEGUY

The Only Son

(Orlando: Harcourt, 2008)

Story type: Historical/French Revolution
Subject(s): Authors and Writers; Biography
Major character(s): Francois Rousseau, Historical Figure; Jean-Jacques Rousseau, Historical Figure, Writer
Time period(s): 18th century
Locale(s): Geneva, Switzerland; Paris, France

Summary: Audeguy resurrects the life and times of writer Jean-Jacques Rousseau's forgotten elder brother, Francois. Born in Geneva in 1705, Francois is trained as a clock maker, is disowned by his family, and makes his way to Paris where he finds work in a brothel and is introduced to the shady world of pre-Revolution Parisian libertines. When the Revolution comes, Francois seeks refuge outside the city. The novel offers his reflections, particularly to his more famous younger brother, Jean-Jacques, in old age, offering a fascinating perspective on 18th-century France.

Where it's reviewed:
Kirkus Reviews, August 15, 2008, page 835
Library Journal, October 1, 2008, page 55
Publishers Weekly, July 21, 2008, page 139

Other books by the same author:
The Theory of Clouds, 2007

Other books you might like:
Jean Echenoz, *Ravel*, 2007
Lion Feuchtwanger, *'Tis Folly to Be Wise*, 1953
Endore S. Guy, *Voltaire, Voltaire!*, 1961
Ron Hansen, *Exiles*, 2008
Francisco Rebolledo, *Rasero*, 1995

728

SEBASTIAN BARRY

The Secret Scripture

(New York: Viking Press, 2008)

Story type: Family Saga
Subject(s): Old Age; Hospitals; Mental Illness

Major character(s): Roseanne McNulty, Patient; Willima Grene, Doctor
Time period(s): 20th century
Locale(s): Sligo, Ireland

Summary: Irish history throughout the 20th century is recollected from the perspective of 100-year-old Roseanne McNulty who secretly records her life in a hidden journal she keeps in the mental asylum where she has been locked up for decades. She reflects on the impact of two world wars, the emergence of the Irish Republic, and the domination of the Catholic Church in the lives of the Irish in general and Roseanne's family in particular. Her recollections alternate with the clinical record kept by psychiatrist William Grene as he determines whether Roseanne can be released.

Where it's reviewed:
Booklist, May 15, 2008, page 20
Kirkus Reviews, April 15, 2008, page 380
Library Journal, June 15, 2008, page 53

Other books by the same author:
Annie Dunne, 2006
A Long Way Home, 2005
Hinterland, 2002
The Whereabouts of Eneas McNulty, 1998

Other books you might like:
Frank Delaney, *Tipperary*, 2007
Roddy Doyle, *A Star Called Henry*, 1999
Thomas Flanagan, *The Tenants of Time*, 1988
Edward Rutherfurd, *The Rebels of Ireland*, 2006
Leon Uris, *Trinity*, 1976

729

LOUIS BAYARD

The Black Tower

(New York: William Morrow, 2008)

Story type: Mystery; Historical/Regency
Subject(s): Mystery and Detective Stories; Detection
Major character(s): Hector Carpentier, Doctor, Student; Eugene Francois Vidocq, Historical Figure, Detective—Police
Time period(s): 1810s
Locale(s): Paris, France

Summary: In Bayard's mystery/thriller master detective (and real-life figure) Eugene Vidodq recruits the assistance of Parisian doctor Hector Carpentier in a murder investigation that leads the pair to the discovery of the whereabouts of Marie Antoinettes son who was thought to have died in prison in 1795. The discovery involves the detective and doctor in a dangerous cover-up and political intrigue.

Where it's reviewed:
Booklist, August 1, 2008, page 43
Kirkus Reviews, August 1, 2008, page 767
Library Journal, August 1, 2008, page 61
New York Times Book Review, August 24, 2008, page 26
Publishers Weekly, July 21, 2008, page 140

Other books by the same author:
The Pale Blue Eye, 2006
Mr. Timothy, 2003
Endangered Species, 2001
Fool's Errand, 1999

Other books you might like:
Claude Izner, *Murder on the Eiffel Tower*, 2008
Manny Meyers, *The Last Mystery of Edgar Allan Poe*, 1978
Josh Russell, *Yellow Jack*, 1999
Harold Schechter, *Nevermore*, 1999
Kay Nolte Smith, *A Tale of the Wind*, 1991

730

ANDREW BEAHRS

The Sin Eaters

(New Milford, CT: Toby Press, 2008)

Story type: Historical/Seventeenth Century
Subject(s): American Colonies
Major character(s): Sarah, Widow(er), Healer; Sam Ridley, Vagrant; Bill Palmer, Outcast
Time period(s): 17th century
Locale(s): England; Virginia, American Colonies

Summary: Set in early 17th-century England, this is a grim tale of widower and herbalist Sarah who provokes the vengeance of vagrant Sam Ridley. She flees from him along with Bill Palmer, a man so desperate that he is compelled to become a sin-eater, devouring the food set on top of corpses to draw off their sins. Bill comes to Sarah's aid before she manages to depart for a new life in colonial Virginia.

Where it's reviewed:
Kirkus Reviews, September 15, 2008, page 967
Library Journal, September 15, 2008, page 43
Publishers Weekly, September 8, 2008, page 35

Other books by the same author:
Strange Saint, 2005

Other books you might like:
Tracy Chevalier, *Falling Angels*, 2001
Philippa Gregory, *Earthly Joys*, 1998
Maria McCann, *As Meat Loves Salt*, 2001
Betsy Tobin, *Bone House*, 2001
Paul West, *The Fifth of November*, 2001

731

CARRIE BEBRIS

The Matters at Mansfield

(New York: Forge, 2008)

Story type: Historical/Regency; Mystery
Series: Mr. and Mrs. Darcy. Book 4
Subject(s): Mystery and Detective Stories; Marriage
Major character(s): Fitzwilliam Darcy, Gentleman, Spouse (of Elizabeth); Elizabeth Bennet Darcy, Gentlewoman, Spouse (of Darcy)

Time period(s): 19th century
Locale(s): England

Summary: Characters from Jane Austen's *Pride and Prejudice* and *Mansfield Park* are united in this entertaining Regency mystery based on the Austen canon. Elizabeth and Darcy pay a visit to Mansfield where they are soon busy sorting out cases of mistaken identities and sudden disappearances. Lady Catherine de Bourgh's daughter runs off with Henry Crawford, and he is found dead shortly thereafter. The Darcys take on the job of finding out who did it.

Where it's reviewed:
Booklist, August 1, 2008, page 44
Kirkus Reviews, July 1, 2008, page 670
Publishers Weekly, July 14, 2008, page 46

Other books by the same author:
North by Northanger, 2006
Suspense and Sensibility, 2005
Pride and Prescience, 2004

Other books you might like:
Pamela Aidan, *These Three Remains*, 2007
Elizabeth Ashton, *Mr. Darcy's Daughters*, 2003
Julia Barrett, *Presumption*, 1993
Stephanie Barron, *The Jane Austen Series*, 1997-
Emma Tennant, *Pemberley, or, Pride and Prejudice Continued*, 1993

732

JAMES R. BENN

Blood Alone

(New York: Soho Press, 2008)

Story type: Mystery; Historical/World War II
Series: Billy Boyle. Book 3
Subject(s): Mystery and Detective Stories; World War II; Crime and Criminals
Major character(s): Billy Boyle, Police Officer, Military Personnel
Time period(s): 1940s (1943)
Locale(s): Sicily, Italy

Summary: Boston cop turned special investigator for General Eisenhower Billy Boyle is dispatched to Sicily during the Allied invasion with a message from Lucky Luciano to the local mafia to cooperate with the Allies. Complications ensue, and Billy's mission proves deadly as he must cope both with threats to his own safety and a case of amnesia that complicates his recollection of his mission and his role in it.

Where it's reviewed:
Booklist, August 1, 2008, page 41
Kirkus Reviews, July 15, 2008, page 721
Publishers Weekly, June 23, 2008, page 40

Other books by the same author:
The First Wave, 2007
Billy Boyle, 2006

Other books you might like:
John Dunning, *Two O'Clock Eastern Wartime*, 2000
Mark Frost, *The Second Objective*, 2007

Historical

Jack Higgins, *Luciano's Luck*, 1982
Jeff Shaara, *The Rising Tide*, 2006
Daniel Silva, *The Secret Servant*, 2007

733

CORDELIA FRANCES BIDDLE

Deception's Daughter

(New York: Thomas Dunne Books, 2008)

Story type: Mystery; Historical/Americana
Series: Martha Beale. Book 2
Subject(s): Mystery and Detective Stories; City and Town Life
Major character(s): Martha Beale, Heiress, Detective—Amateur; Thomas Kelman, Government Official
Time period(s): 1840s (1842)
Locale(s): Philadelphia, Pennsylvania

Summary: Iconoclastic heiress and occasional sleuth Martha Beale investigates with Constable Kelman the disappearance of a young socialite. Their search takes them from the city's upper classes to its mean streets in a mystery packed with authentic and convincing period details.

Where it's reviewed:
Booklist, July 1, 2008, page 42
Kirkus Reviews, June 15, 2008, page 622
Publishers Weekly, May 12, 2008, page 38

Other books by the same author:
The Conjurer, 2007
Murder at San Simeon, 1996 (Patricia Hearst, co-author)
Beneath the Wind, 1993

Other books you might like:
Caleb Carr, *The Angel of Darkness*, 1997
Dianne Day, *Beacon Street Mourning*, 2000
Joel Rose, *The Blackest Bird*, 2007
Harold Schechter, *The Hum Bug*, 2001
Randall Silvis, *On Night's Shore*, 2001

734

DAVE BOLING

Guernica

(New York: Bloomsbury, 2008)

Story type: Historical/World War II; Family Saga
Subject(s): Civil War/Spanish; War; Family Relations
Major character(s): Justo Ansotegui, Farmer; Josepe Ansotegui, Fisherman; Xabier Ansotegui, Fisherman
Time period(s): 19th century; 20th century
Locale(s): Spain

Summary: Boling dramatizes the famous firebombing by the Nazis of Guernica in 1937 during the Spanish Civil War from the perspective of a trio of brothers—Justo, Josepe, and Xabier Ansotegui. Abandoned, they struggle to survive on their family farm, growing to maturity to participate in the events of the Civil War, culminating with the Guernica tragedy. The novel offers a vivid

portrait of the era and events, as well as a depiction of real-life future Basque president Jose Antonio Aguirre and artist Pablo Picasso.

Where it's reviewed:
Booklist, August 1, 2008, page 45
Kirkus Reviews, July 15, 2008, page 715
Publishers Weekly, July 7, 2008, page 37

Other books you might like:
Jose Maria Gironella, *One Million Dead*, 1963
Ernest Hemingway, *For Whom the Bell Tolls*, 1940
David Leavitt, *While England Sleeps*, 1993
Andre Malraux, *Man's Hope*, 1938
Rosie Thomas, *The White Dove*, 1986

735

MATT BONDURANT

The Wettest County in the World

(New York: Scribner, 2008)

Story type: Historical/Depression Era; Historical/Roaring Twenties
Subject(s): Prohibition Era; Rural Life; Authors and Writers
Major character(s): Sherwood Anderson, Historical Figure, Writer; Forrest Bondurant, Bootlegger; Howard Bondurant, Bootlegger
Time period(s): 1920s
Locale(s): Franklin County, Virginia

Summary: Bondurant dramatizes his own family history in this novel set in rural Virginia during the Depression and concerning the area's moonshine business. In the 1930s, writer Sherwood Anderson arrives to research a magazine article on the infamous "Bondurant Boys," including Forrest, Howard, and Jack Bondurant, whose bootlegging business sets them on a dangerous confrontation with corrupt state officials.

Where it's reviewed:
Booklist, September 1, 2008, page 51
Kirkus Reviews, August 15, 2008, page 835
Library Journal, July 1, 2008, page 58
New York Times Book Review, November 9, 2008, page 44

Other books by the same author:
The Third Translation, 2005

Other books you might like:
Dorothy Garlock, *High on a Hill*, 2002
Craig Holden, *The Jazz Bird*, 2002
Lee Irby, *7,000 Clams*, 2004
Elmore Leonard, *The Moonshine War*, 1969
Charles F. Price, *The Cock's Spur*, 2000

736

RHYS BOWEN

A Royal Pain

(New York: Berkley Prime Crime, 2008)

Story type: Historical/Depression Era; Mystery
Series: Lady Georgiana Rannoch. Book 2

Subject(s): Mystery and Detective Stories; Kings, Queens, Rulers, etc.
Major character(s): Lady Georgiana Rannoch, Noblewoman
Time period(s): 1930s
Locale(s): England

Summary: Lady Georgiana Rannoch, a noblewoman who moonlights as a housecleaner in disguise to make ends meet, is given a mission by the queen to help the courtship of a young Bavarian princess and the Prince of Wales, diverting his attentions from his current American love interest. A series of suspicious deaths cause Lady Georgie to shift her focus from royal matchmaker to sleuth.

Where it's reviewed:
Booklist, July 1, 2008, page 43
Kirkus Reviews, May 15, 2008, page 518
Publishers Weekly, May 12, 2008, page 39

Other books by the same author:
Her Royal Spyness, 2007
In Dublin's Fair City, 2007
Oh Danny Boy, 2006
In Like Flynn, 2005
Death of Riley, 2002

Other books you might like:
Tasha Alexander, *A Poisoned Season*, 2007
C.S. Harris, *What Angels Fear*, 2006
Anne Perry, *Buckingham Palace Gardens*, 2008
Deanna Raybourn, *Silent in the Grave*, 2007
Jacqueline Winspear, *An Incomplete Revenge*, 2008

737

GILLIAN BRADSHAW

The Sun's Bride

(Sutton, England: Severn House, 2008)

Story type: Historical/Ancient Greece; Action/Adventure
Subject(s): Ancient History; Pirates
Major character(s): Isokrates, Sea Captain; Dionysia, Captive
Time period(s): 3rd century B.C. (246)
Locale(s): Mediterranean; At Sea

Summary: Bradshaw provides a seafaring adventure set in the third century B.C. Isokrates commands a ship hunting pirates preying on sailing vessels to sell their passengers as slaves. Taking a pirate ship, he rescues Dionysia, a young captive, who was on her way to the Egyptian court to warn King Ptolemy of an impending attack on Cairo. Isokrates falls in love with the beautiful Dionysia and undergoes numerous challenges as he assists her in her mission to prevent an attack on Egypt.

Where it's reviewed:
Booklist, June 1, 2008, page 45
Publishers Weekly, July 7, 2008, page 39

Other books by the same author:
Cleopatra's Heir, 2002
The Wolf Hunt, 2001
The Sand Reckoner, 2000
Island of Ghosts, 1998

Horses of Heaven, 1991

Other books you might like:
Ruth Downie, *Terra Incognita*, 2008
Jo Graham, *Black Ships*, 2008
Ursula K. Le Guin, *Lavinia*, 2008
Ben Pastor, *Water Thief*, 2007
Sa Shan, *Alexander and Alestria*, 2008

738

GYLES BRANDRETH

Oscar Wilde and a Game Called Murder

(New York: Simon & Schuster, 2008)

Story type: Historical/Victorian; Mystery
Series: Oscar Wilde. Book 2
Subject(s): Mystery and Detective Stories; Authors and Writers; Victorian Period
Major character(s): Oscar Wilde, Historical Figure, Writer; Arthur Conan Doyle, Historical Figure, Writer; Bram Stoker, Historical Figure, Writer
Time period(s): 1890s (1892)
Locale(s): London, England

Summary: Brandreth offers a second Victorian mystery featuring Oscar Wilde as sleuth. At a meeting of the Socrates Club that Wilde founded, whose members include Arthur Conan Doyle and Bram Stoker, a game of murder in which players are invited to submit the name of someone they would kill if they could get away with it turns real. Wilde must become a detective in earnest, accompanied by his Watson, Sherlock Holmes creator Doyle. The mystery is full of period elements and details drawn from Wilde's biography.

Where it's reviewed:
Booklist, August 1, 2008, page 46
Kirkus Reviews, July 15, 2008, page 722
Publishers Weekly, July 7, 2008, page 40

Other books by the same author:
Oscar Wilde and a Death of No Importance, 2007

Other books you might like:
Peter Ackroyd, *The Last Testament of Oscar Wilde*, 1983
Russell Brown, *Sherlock Holmes and the Mysterious Friend of Oscar Wilde*, 1988
Louis Edwards, *Oscar Wilde Discovers America*, 2003
James Reese, *The Dracula Dossier*, 2008
Walter Scatterthwait, *Wilde West*, 1991

739

CARINA BURAM

The Streets of Babylon

(New York: Marion Boyars, 2008)

Story type: Historical/Victorian; Mystery
Series: London Mystery

Historical

Subject(s): Mystery and Detective Stories; Victorian Period
Major character(s): Euthanasia Bondeson, Writer; Owain Evans, Detective—Police
Time period(s): 1850s (1851)
Locale(s): London, England

Summary: In this promising debut, Burman offers an intriguing Victorian mystery teaming up Swedish novelist Euthanasia Bondeson and Welsh police detective Owain Evans. In London to visit the Crystal Palace Exhibition of 1851, Euthanasia joins forces with Evans to find her missing companion and later the mystery surrounding a body they discover along the way. The novel offers a knowing tour of period London as well as a refreshing set of sleuths.

Where it's reviewed:
Kirkus Reviews, May 15, 2008, page 518

Other books you might like:
Tasha Alexander, *A Fatal Waltz*, 2008
Gerri Brightwell, *The Dark Lantern*, 2008
Michel Faber, *The Crimson Petal and the White*, 2002
Philip Gooden, *The Salisbury Manuscript*, 2008
Will Thomas, *To Kingdom Come*, 2005

740

DIANA BURG

Dalliance

(Syracuse: Syracuse University Press, 2008)

Story type: Historical/Americana; Historical/American Civil War
Subject(s): Marriage; Divorce; Trials
Major character(s): Mary W. Turner Burch, Spouse (of Isaac); Isaac H. Burch, Spouse (of Mary), Banker; David Stuart, Lawyer
Time period(s): 1860s
Locale(s): Illinois

Summary: Based on an actual Illinois divorce trial of 1860, this first novel details the story of Mary Turner who marries the well-to-do, but dull, banker, Isaac Burch, but prefers the company of Chicago lawyer David Stuart. The scandal concerning their "dalliance" results in a very public divorce trial that exposes the private lives of fashionable society during the period. Told through diary entries, letters, and eyewitness reporting, the novel offers a believable portrait of life during the period.

Other books you might like:
Chris Adrian, *Gob's Grief*, 2000
Patricia O'Brien, *Harriet and Isabella*, 2008
Jacqueline Sheckan, *Truth*, 2003
Jane Smiley, *The All-True Travels and Adventures of Lidie Newton*, 1998
John Vernon, *Peter Doyle*, 1991

741

IAN BURUMA

The China Lover

(New York: Penguin Press, 2008)

Story type: Historical/World War II; Historical/Exotic
Subject(s): Actors and Actresses; Movie Industry; Biography
Major character(s): Yamaguchi Yoshiko, Actress, Historical Figure; Sidney Vanoven, Homosexual; Sato Daisuke, Agent (talent)
Time period(s): 20th century
Locale(s): Japan; China; Beirut, Lebanon

Summary: Buruma inventively reimagines the life of real life actress, film star, and journalist Yamaguchi Yoshiko, a Japanese citizen born in the Chinese province of Manchuria who goes on to film success in Japan and the U.S. Yoshiko's career is refracted from the perspectives of multiple narrators, including American homosexual Sidney Vanoven who provides a detailed portrait of postwar Tokyo, and talent agent Sato Daisuke, who offers a view of the Japanese invasion of Manchuria. Yoshiko provides her own account of her later career as a famous Japanese journalist reporting from Beirut at the height of the Middle East conflict. An excess of riches, the novel's focus is at times dispersed over too many interests.

Where it's reviewed:
Booklist, August 1, 2008, page 33
Kirkus Reviews, August 1, 2008, page 769
Library Journal, August 1, 2008, page 64
New York Times Book Review, October 15, 2008, page 14
Publishers Weekly, June 16, 2008, page 28

Other books by the same author:
Playing the Game, 1991

Other books you might like:
Jennifer Cody Epstein, *The Painter from Shanghai*, 2008
Jeffrey Hantover, *The Jewel Trader of Pegu*, 2008
Kazuo Ishiguro, *An Artist of the Floating World*, 1986
Salman Rushdie, *The Enchantress of Florence*, 2008
John Tolland, *Occupation*, 1987

742

EMILIO CALDERON

The Creator's Map

(New York: Penguin Press, 2008)

Story type: Historical/World War II
Subject(s): Nazis; World War II; Magic
Major character(s): Jose Maria Hurtado de Mendoza, Student—College; Montse, Refugee; Junio Valerio Cima Vivarini, Scholar
Time period(s): 1930s (1937)
Locale(s): Rome, Italy; Germany

Summary: Against the backdrop of the Spanish Civil War, Fascist Italy, Nazi Germany, and the run-up to World

War II, the Nazis and a secret group of antifascists compete to find an ancient map locating the source of black magic. Jose Maria Hurtado is a Spanish architectural student in Rome recruited in the search. He soon finds himself in a love triangle with Montse, a young Spanish refugee, and Junio Vivarini, a Venetian paleographer working with the Nazis. The search for the map takes Jose on a dangerous journey through Italy and Germany.

Where it's reviewed:
Publishers Weekly, May 26, 2008, page 36

Other books you might like:
Lluis-Anton Baulenas, *For a Sack of Bones*, 2008
Juan Eslava Gala, *The Mule*, 2008
Ildefonso Falcones, *Cathedral of the Sea*, 2008
Jose Maria Gironella, *One Million Dead*, 1963
Jose Maria Gironella, *Peace After War*, 1969

743

BROOS CAMPBELL

Peter Wicked

(Ithaca, NY: McBooks Press, 2008)

Story type: Historical/Regency; Adventure
Series: Matty Graves. Book 3
Subject(s): Sea Stories; Pirates
Major character(s): Matty Graves, Military Personnel (naval officer)
Time period(s): 1800s
Locale(s): Washington, District of Columbia; *Tomahawk*, At Sea

Summary: Mixed race naval officer Matty Graves is summoned to Washington to answer questions surrounding the death of his former captain. Given his first command, Graves is then dispatched to capture a former friend and crewmate, Peter Wickett, who has turned pirate. The period details are authentic and much of the book's interest comes from its intriguing central character.

Where it's reviewed:
Booklist, September 1, 2008, page 40
Library Journal, September 1, 2008, page 114
Publishers Weekly, July 21, 2008, page 141

Other books by the same author:
The War of Knives, 2007
No Quarter, 2006

Other books you might like:
Alexander Kent, *The Richard Bolitho Series*, 1968-1986
Dewey Lambdin, *Sea of Grey*, 2002
Patrick O'Brian, *The Aubrey/Maturin Series*, 1968-2004
Dudley Pope, *The Nicholas Ramage Series*, 1965-
Richard Woodman, *The Richard Drinkwater Series*, 1984-

744

MARTIN CAPARROS

Valfierno

(New York: Atria Books, 2008)

Story type: Historical/Edwardian
Subject(s): Crime and Criminals; Art
Major character(s): Eduardo de Valfierno, Historical Figure, Thief
Time period(s): 1910s
Locale(s): Paris, France

Summary: The actual 1911 theft of Leonardo DaVinci's masterpiece, the *Mona Lisa*, is the occasion for this novel by Argentinian author Caparros. Told through multiple voices, the novel centers on the caper's mastermind, Eduardo de Valfierno, who comes from poverty in Argentina and transforms himself into a nobleman and the brains behind one of the most famous art thefts of all time.

Where it's reviewed:
Booklist, April 15, 2008, page 35
Kirkus Reviews, May 1, 2008, page 449
Library Journal, May 15, 2008, page 88
Publishers Weekly, May 5, 2008, page 43

Other books you might like:
Susan M. Dodd, *The Silent Woman*, 2001
Meghan McCarthy, *Steal Back the Mona Lisa*, 2006
Robert Noah, *The Man Who Stole the Mona Lisa*, 1998
Alyson Richman, *The Last Van Gogh*, 2006
Frederick Turner, *Redemption*, 2006

745

MAGGIE CARTER-DEVRIES

Amelia's Secret

(Bloomington, IN: AuthorHouse, 2008)

Story type: Historical/Post-American Civil War
Subject(s): Islands; Small Town Life; Marriage
Major character(s): Katie Eppes, Spouse (of Jeff); T.J. "Jeff" Eppes, Spouse (of Katie)
Time period(s): 19th century
Locale(s): Amelia Island, Florida

Summary: Taking place in the years following the American Civil War on Florida's Amelia Island, this novel dramatizes the arrival of beauty Katie Eppes from the north, newly wed to railroad magnate T.J. "Jeff" Eppes, a descendant of President Thomas Jefferson. Katie's free spirit runs afoul of the island's more conservative social etiquette and leads to tragedy.

Other books you might like:
James Carlos Blake, *Red Grass River*, 1998
Peter Matthiesson, *Bone by Bone*, 1999
Robert Newton Peck, *Hallapoosa*, 1988
Charles F. Price, *The Cock's Spur*, 2000
Judith Richards, *Summer Lightning*, 1968

746

DAVID ALLAN CATES

Freeman Walker

(Denver: Unbridled Books, 2008)

Story type: Historical/American Civil War; Historical/
American West
Subject(s): Slavery; African Americans; Civil War
Major character(s): Jimmy "Freeman Walker" Gates, Slave
(freed)
Time period(s): 19th century
Locale(s): Virginia; England; California
Summary: The novel follows the career of Jimmy Gates,
the son of a slave mother and her master (who later
changes his name to Freeman Walker). Freed by his
father, Jimmy is sent away to a British boarding school.
When his father dies, Jimmy leaves school and finds
work making horse saddles. He returns to the U.S. just
as the Civil War begins and sets off for the gold mines in
the west. Jimmy's mixed race marks him as an outsider,
a perspective that the novel exploits in its various
settings.

Where it's reviewed:
Booklist, October 15, 2008, page 22
Library Journal, October 1, 2008, page 55
Publishers Weekly, August 25, 2008, page 50

Other books by the same author:
X Out of Wonderland, 2005
Hunger in America, 1992

Other books you might like:
Valerie Martin, *Property*, 2003
James McBride, *Song Yet Sung*, 2008
Toni Morrison, *A Mercy*, 2008
Nancy Rawles, *My Jim*, 2005
Michael C. White, *Soul Catcher*, 2007

747

ELLA MARCH CHASE

The Virgin Queen's Daughter

(New York: Crown, 2009)

Story type: Historical/Elizabethan
Subject(s): Kings, Queens, Rulers, etc.; Identity
Major character(s): Elinor "Nelly" de Lacey, Gentle-
woman; Elizabeth I, Historical Figure, Royalty
Time period(s): 16th century
Locale(s): England
Summary: This Elizabethan-era novel concerns Elinor
(Nell) de Lacey, who befriended Princess Elizabeth when
she was a prisoner in the Tower of London, and years
later is called to court when Elizabeth becomes queen.
Nell is the spitting image of Elizabeth, and rumors begin
to spread that she is actually the queen's daughter. The
novel offers a vivid depiction of court life during the
reign of Elizabeth.

Where it's reviewed:
Publishers Weekly, September 29, 2008, page 58

Other books you might like:
Patricia Finney, *Firedrake's Eye*, 1992
Philippa Gregory, *The Virgin Lover*, 2004
Robin Maxwell, *Virgin*, 2001
Rosalind Miles, *I, Elizabeth*, 1994
Alison Weir, *The Lady Elizabeth*, 2008

748

ALAN CHEUSE

To Catch the Lightning

(Naperville, IL: Sourcebooks, 2008)

Story type: Historical/American West
Subject(s): Indians of North America; Photography;
Biography
Major character(s): Edward S. Curtis, Historical Figure,
Photographer; William Myers, Scholar; Jimmy Fly-
Wing, Indian
Time period(s): 20th century
Locale(s): United States
Summary: Cheuse tells the story of actual photographer
Edward S. Curtis who, in 1904, set out to create a picto-
rial record of the remaining Native American tribes. To
help him, he recruits a classical scholar, William Myers,
and Jimmy Fly-Wing, a Plains Indian. The novel
chronicles the challenges to Curtis's personal life he
experiences while embarked on his epic quest of
documenting a rapidly vanishing way of life.

Where it's reviewed:
Booklist, October 1, 2008, page 25
Kirkus Reviews, August 1, 2008, page 770
Library Journal, September 15, 2008, page 44
Publishers Weekly, July 7, 2008, page 34

Other books by the same author:
Lost and Old Rivers, 1998
The Light Possessed, 1990
The Tennessee Waltz, 1990
The Grandmothers' Club, 1986

Other books you might like:
Margaret Coel, *Wife of Moon*, 2004
Louise Erdrich, *The Bingo Palace*, 1994
David Foster, *The Puce Island*, 1985
Charles Frazer, *Thirteen Moons*, 2006
Marianne Wiggins, *The Shadow Catcher*, 2007

749

ALYS CLARE

The Paths of the Air

(Sutton, England: Severn House, 2008)

Story type: Mystery; Historical/Medieval
Series: Helewise of Hawkenlye. Book 11
Subject(s): Mystery and Detective Stories; Middle Ages;
Religious Life
Major character(s): Helewise of Hawkenlye, Religious;
Josse d'Acquin, Mercenary (soldier of fortune)

Time period(s): 12th century (1196)
Locale(s): England

Summary: A stranger arrives at the estate of Sir Josse d'Acquin. He is given shelter before vanishing, and later a body turns up in the nearby woods. Meanwhile, the search is on for a runaway monk who is in possession of treasure. Josse turns to Abbess Helewise of Hawkenlye for assistance on both fronts.

Where it's reviewed:
Booklist, May 1, 2008, page 39
Kirkus Reviews, June 15, 2008, page 623
Publishers Weekly, June 23, 2008, page 41

Other books by the same author:
The Enchanter's Forest, 2008
Heart of Ice, 2006
The Tavern in the Morning, 2002
Ashes of the Elements, 2001
Fortune Like the Moon, 2000

Other books you might like:
P.C. Doherty, *The Matthew Jankyn Series*, 1988-
Margaret Frazer, *The Prioress' Tale*, 1997
Ian Morson, *The William Falconer Series*, 1994-
Ellis Peters, *The Brother Cadfael Series*, 1977-1994
Kate Sedley, *The Midsummer Rose*, 2004

750

BREENA CLARKE

Stand the Storm
(New York: Little, Brown, 2008)

Story type: Historical/American Civil War
Subject(s): African Americans; Sewing; Slavery
Major character(s): Sewing Annie Coats, Slave, Seamstress; Gabriel Coats, Slave; Ellen Coats, Slave
Time period(s): 1860s
Locale(s): Washington, District of Columbia (Georgetown)

Summary: This richly-imagined second novel describes the impact of the Civil War on a family of slaves in Washington, D.C. Sewing Annie Coats trains her two children—Gabriel and Ellen—in sewing skills, which they use to survive in the turmoil that grips the U.S. and Washington during the war. In the Coatses, Clarke provides a vivid portrait of the workings of slavery and its transformation brought about by emancipation.

Where it's reviewed:
Booklist, July 1, 2008, page 38
Kirkus Reviews, June 1, 2008, page 567
Publishers Weekly, May 19, 2008, page 3

Other books by the same author:
River, Cross My Heart, 1999

Other books you might like:
Yvette Christianse, *Unconfessed*, 2006
Valerie Martin, *Property*, 2003
Toni Morrison, *A Mercy*, 2008
Nancy Rawles, *My Jim*, 2005
Margaret Walker, *Jubilee*, 1966

751

BARBARA CLEVERLY

Bright Hair about the Bone
(New York: Delta, 2008)

Story type: Historical/Roaring Twenties; Amateur Detective
Series: Laetitia Talbot Mystery. Book 3
Subject(s): Mystery and Detective Stories; Archaeology
Major character(s): Laetitia Talbot, Archaeologist, Detective—Amateur
Time period(s): 1920s (1926)
Locale(s): Burgundy, France

Summary: This third installment of Cleverly's 1920s-era mystery series featuring British archaeologist and amateur sleuth Laetitia Talbot has the heroine investigating the death of her godfather in Burgundy, France. In disguise, she gets a job on a dig that may hold the clue to his death. Her investigation leads to secrets of a French noble family and Celtic and Christian revelations that could have a profound impact.

Where it's reviewed:
Booklist, September 15, 2008, page 27
Kirkus Reviews, August 1, 2008, page 844
Publishers Weekly, August 4, 2008, page 47

Other books by the same author:
The Tomb of Zeus, 2007
Tug of War, 2007
The Bee's Kiss, 2006
The Damascened Blade, 2004
The Last Kashmiri Rose, 2002

Other books you might like:
Kerry Greenwood, *Death by Water*, 2008
Clare Langley-Hawthorne, *The Serpent and the Scorpion*, 2008
Gillian Linscott, *The Nell Bray Series*, 1991-
Elizabeth Peters, *The Amelia Peabody Series*, 1975-
David Roberts, *Bones of the Buried*, 2001

752

BEATRICE COLIN

The Glimmer Palace
(New York: Riverhead Books, 2008)

Story type: Historical/World War I; Historical/Roaring Twenties
Subject(s): World War I; Orphans; Movie Industry
Major character(s): Lilly Nelly Aphrodite, Orphan; Ilya Yurasov, Director
Time period(s): 1910s; 1920s
Locale(s): Berlin, Germany

Summary: Colin dramatizes the career of German orphan Lilly Nelly Aphrodite, who nearly starves during World War I and after the war finds success acting in the burgeoning German film industry under the direction of Russian Ilya Yurasov. Lilly's love for Yurasov is complicated by the return of her missing-in-action

Historical

husband and Yurasov's long-lost fiancee. Lilly's professional and personal adventures are presented against a vivid backdrop of German history in the first half of the 20th century.

Where it's reviewed:
Booklist, June 1, 2008, page 41
Kirkus Reviews, June 15, 2008, page 611
Library Journal, June 15, 2008, page 54
New York Times Book Review, September 14, 2008, page 22
Publishers Weekly, May 5, 2008, page 42

Other books by the same author:
Disappearing Act, 2002
Nude Untitled, 2000

Other books you might like:
Tessa Barclay, *A Tissue of Lies*, 2008
Jeffrey Deaver, *Garden of Beasts*, 2004
Len Deighton, *Winter*, 1987
Frances McNeil, *Sisters of Fortune*, 2008
Michael Pye, *The Pieces from Berlin*, 2003

753

REBECCA ANN COLLINS

Netherfield Park Revisted

(Naperville, IL: Sourcebooks, 2008)

Story type: Historical/Victorian
Series: Pemberley Chronicles. Book 3
Subject(s): Victorian Period; Family Life; Marriage
Major character(s): Jonathan Bingley, Gentleman, Spouse (of Amanda-Jane); Amanda-Jane Bingley, Spouse (of Jonathan); Anna Faulkner, Gentlewoman
Time period(s): 1850s (1859)
Locale(s): Hertfordshire, England

Summary: This sequel to Jane Austen's *Pride and Prejudice* is set during the mid-Victorian period and concerns Jonathan Bingley, the son of Charles and Jane Bingley (Elizabeth Bennet's sister in *Pride and Prejudice*). Married to Amanda-Jane, the daughter of Elizabeth's friend Charlotte and Mr. Collins, Jonathan purchases Netherfield Hall, the residence that brought his father and Darcy into contact with the Bennets in the first place. Jonathan's marriage is challenged by his attraction to another woman, Anna Faulkner.

Where it's reviewed:
Booklist, September 1, 2008, page 49

Other books by the same author:
Mr. Darcy's Daughter, 2008
The Ladies of Longbourn, 2008
The Pemberley Chronicles, 2008
The Women of Pemberley, 2008
My Cousin Caroline, 2001

Other books you might like:
Pamela Aidan, *These Three Remains*, 2007
Carrie Bebris, *The Matters at Mansfield*, 2008
Colleen McCullough, *The Independence of Miss Mary Bennet*, 2008
Jill Pitkeathley, *Cassandra and Jane*, 2008

Emma Tennant, *Pemberley, or, Pride and Prejudice Continued*, 1993

754

LAUREL CORONA

The Four Seasons

(New York: Voice Hyperion, 2008)

Story type: Historical/Seventeenth Century
Subject(s): Music and Musicians; Biography; Sisters
Major character(s): Antonio Vivaldi, Historical Figure, Composer; Maddalena, Orphan, Musician; Chiaretta, Orphan, Musician
Time period(s): 17th century; 18th century
Locale(s): Venice, Italy

Summary: Corona dramatizes the life and career of composer Antonio Vivaldi in Venice in the 18th century from the perspectives of two orphaned sisters, Maddalena and Chiaretta, who are abandoned at Venice's Pieta foundling hospital and join its renowned music academy. Chiaretta becomes a celebrated soloist and marries well. Maddalena takes up the violin and becomes Vivaldi's pupil. His romantic feelings for her are sublimated into his famous compositions.

Where it's reviewed:
Booklist, October 1, 2008, page 22
Publishers Weekly, September 15, 2008, page 44

Other books you might like:
Stephanie Cowell, *Marrying Mozart*, 2004
Janice Galloway, *Clara*, 2003
James Landis, *Longing*, 2000
Barbara Quick, *Vivaldi's Virgins*, 2007
David Weiss, *Sacred and Profane*, 1968

755

MICHAEL COX

The Glass of Time

(New York: W.W. Norton, 2008)

Story type: Historical/Victorian
Subject(s): Victorian Period; Orphans
Major character(s): Esperanza Gorst, Orphan, Servant; Emily Grace Duport, Noblewoman, Widow(er)
Time period(s): 1870s (1876)
Locale(s): England

Summary: Cox's sequel to *The Meaning of Night*, his pastiche of a Victorian sensation novel, has 19-year-old orphan Esperanza Gorst go undercover as a lady's maid to penetrate the secrets in the household of Emily Duport, Baroness Tansor. The novel's complex intrigue plot depends greatly on details from the first novel, so readers are advised to start there for a full enjoyment of this atmospheric gothic thriller.

Where it's reviewed:
Booklist, August 1, 2008, page 44
Kirkus Reviews, July 15, 2008, page 716
Library Journal, September 1, 2008, page 114

Publishers Weekly, August 18, 2008, page 39

Other books by the same author:
The Meaning of Night, 2006

Other books you might like:
Jonathan Barnes, *The Somnambulist*, 2008
Peter Carey, *Jack Maggs*, 1998
Michel Faber, *The Crimson Petal and the White*, 2002
Anne Perry, *Buckingham Palace Gardens*, 2008
Will Thomas, *The Limehouse Text*, 2006

756

TANIA ANNE CROSSE

Cherrybrook Rose

(Sutton, England: Severn House, 2008)

Story type: Historical/Victorian
Subject(s): Victorian Period; Small Town Life
Major character(s): Henry Maddiford, Businessman (mill manager); Rose Maddiford, Young Woman
Time period(s): 1870s (1875)
Locale(s): Dartmoor, England

Summary: This Victorian era novel is set in the wilds of Dartmoor and concerns Henry Maddiford, manager of the Cherrybrook gunpowder mills, and his daughter Rose, whom he has raised alone since her mother's death in childbirth. Rose is an indulged and independent young woman. When she meets a prisoner on the desolate moors, it starts a chain of events that leads to a mill explosion and a reversal of her fortunes.

Where it's reviewed:
Booklist, June 1, 2008, page 55

Other books by the same author:
A Bouquet of Thorns, 2008
The River Girl, 2006
Morwellham's Child, 2004

Other books you might like:
Caroline Benton, *The Path of the Dead*, 2006
Judith Ivory, *The Indiscretion*, 2001
Robin Paige, *Death at Dartmoor*, 2002
Jennifer St. Giles, *Darkest Dreams*, 2006
Rhonda Thompson, *The Cursed One*, 2006

757

PATRICK CULHANE (Pseudonym of Max Allan Collins)

Red Sky in Morning

(New York: William Morrow, 2008)

Story type: Historical/World War II; Mystery
Subject(s): World War II; Sea Stories; African Americans
Major character(s): Peter Maxwell, Military Personnel (ensign)
Time period(s): 1940s (1943)
Locale(s): San Francisco, California; At Sea (Pacific)

Summary: This World War II-era thriller has Ensign Peter Maxwell serving aboard an ammunition ship with an all African-American crew and a racist captain. When the ship's second-in-command is killed, Maxwell finds himself staving off a potential mutiny as he is forced to investigate the murder as the ship sets out across the Pacific. Culhane skillfully blends period details, military action, and detection.

Where it's reviewed:
Booklist, May 1, 2008, page 40
Kirkus Reviews, July 1, 2008, page 666

Other books by the same author:
Black Hats, 2007

Other books you might like:
Richard Bausch, *Peace*, 2008
James R. Benn, *Blood Alone*, 2008
Mark Frost, *The Second Objective*, 2007
Kathryn Miller Haines, *The Winter of Her Discontent*, 2008
David L. Robbins, *The Assassins Gallery*, 2006

758

ANDREW DAVIDSON

The Gargoyle

(New York: Doubleday, 2008)

Story type: Historical/Medieval
Subject(s): Accidents; Artists and Art; Reincarnation
Major character(s): Marianne Engel, Artist (sculptor)
Time period(s): 2000s; 14th century
Locale(s): Germany

Summary: This unusual first novel intertwines a contemporary story of an unnamed narrator who is horribly disfigured in an auto accident and events that occurred 800 years before. In the hospital he is visited by a sculptress of gargoyles named Marianne Engel who insists that they were once lovers in medieval Germany. At first skeptical, the patient eventually is drawn into Marianne's story of their past life and agrees to live with her after his discharge. Complications follow, including a divine message that comes to Marianne that she only has a few more gargoyles to sculpt before being called from earth. Eerie but compelling, the novel weaves together an intriguing story that spans (and defies) the centuries.

Where it's reviewed:
Booklist, September 1, 2008, page 44
Kirkus Reviews, June 15, 2008, page 612
Library Journal, June 1, 2008, page 90
New York Times Book Review, August 17, 2008, page 11
Publishers Weekly, June 16, 2008, page 30

Other books you might like:
Jonathan Barnes, *The Somnambulist*, 2008
William Golding, *Darkness Visible*, 1979
Lawrence Goldstone, *The Anatomy of Deception*, 2008
David Mitchell, *Cloud Atlas*, 2004
M.J. Rose, *The Reincarnationist*, 2007

Historical

759

DAVID STUART DAVIES

Without Conscience

(New York: St. Martin's Minotaur, 2008)

Story type: Historical/World War II; Mystery
Series: Johnny Hawke. Book 2
Subject(s): World War II; Mystery and Detective Stories
Major character(s): Johnny Hawke, Detective—Private;
Peter Blake, Orphan, Child
Time period(s): 1940s (1942)
Locale(s): London, England

Summary: In the second World War II-era mystery featuring private eye Johnny Hawke, the detective investigates the murder of a cross-dressing husband in 1942 London. At the same time, a manhunt is on for an army deserter on a murderous crime spree, while orphan Peter Blake, beset by bullies, flees to London to find Hawke. The intrigue is set against a vividly described wartime background.

Where it's reviewed:
Booklist, November 1, 2008, page 28
Kirkus Reviews, September 1, 2008, page 917
Publishers Weekly, September 15, 2008, page 48

Other books by the same author:
Forests of the Night, 2007
Comes the Dark, 2006
The Veiled Detective, 2004

Other books you might like:
Bernard Cornwell, *Gallows Thief*, 2002
Charles Finch, *A Beautiful Blue Death*, 2007
David Liss, *A Conspiracy of Paper*, 2000
Anne Perry, *Death of a Stranger*, 2002
Graham Swift, *The Light of Day*, 2003

760

FRANCES DE PONTES PEEBLES

The Seamstress

(New York: HarperCollins, 2008)

Story type: Historical/Depression Era; Historical/Roaring
Twenties
Subject(s): Sisters; Sewing; Orphans
Major character(s): Emilia dos Santos, Orphan,
Seamstress; Luzia dos Santos, Orphan, Seamstress
Time period(s): 1920s; 1930s
Locale(s): Brazil

Summary: This first novel follows two orphaned sisters, Emilia and Luzia dos Santos, whose sewing skills take them in radically different directions. Emilia marries a wealthy doctor and moves to a city where her dressmaking skills are recognized; Luzia, however, takes to crime and gains notoriety as a female outlaw, nicknamed "the Seamstress." The contrasting stories of the sisters help dramatize the turbulent history of Brazil during the period.

Where it's reviewed:

Kirkus Reviews, June 1, 2008, page 568
Library Journal, July 1, 2008, page 63
Publishers Weekly, May 12, 2008, page 31

Other books you might like:
Isabel Allende, *Daughter of Fortune*, 2006
Isabel Allende, *Portrati in Sepia*, 2001
Natasha Bauman, *The Disorder of Longing*, 2008
Emma Donoghue, *The Sealed Letter*, 2008
John Updike, *Brazil*, 1996

761

PABLO DE SANTIS

The Paris Enigma

(New York: HarperCollins, 2008)

Story type: Historical/Victorian; Mystery
Subject(s): Mystery and Detective Stories; Detection
Major character(s): Sigmundo Salvatrio, Detective—
Private; Viktor Arkazy, Detective—Private
Time period(s): 1880s (1889)
Locale(s): Paris, France

Summary: Argentine author De Santis offers a mystery thriller set in Paris at the 1889 World's Fair. Young Sigmundo Salvatrio travels to Paris to attend a meeting of the Justice League of master sleuths. When one falls to his death from the Eiffel Tower, Viktor Arkazy takes Salvatrio on as his apprentice to solve the mystery.

Where it's reviewed:
Kirkus Reviews, September 1, 2008, page 968
New York Times Book Review, November 16, 2008,
page 26
Publishers Weekly, September 15, 2008, page 44

Other books you might like:
Deborah Finerman, *Mademoiselle Victorine*, 2007
Kate Horsley, *Black Elk in Paris*, 2006
Elizabeth Lord, *A Secret Inheritance*, 2008
Mary Pope Osborne, *Night of the New Magicians*, 2006
Caroline Seebohm, *The Innocents*, 2007

762

IVAN DOIG

The Eleventh Man

(Orlando: Harcourt, 2008)

Story type: Historical/American West; Historical/World
War II
Subject(s): World War II; Sports/Football; Friendship
Major character(s): Ben Reinking, Military Personnel,
Journalist; Cass Standish, Military Personnel, Pilot
Time period(s): 1940s
Locale(s): Montana; Europe; Pacific Islands

Summary: Doig dramatizes the experiences of the starting 11 of a championship Montana college football team during World War I. Ben Reinking is commissioned as a war correspondent to cross the globe to document the battle stories of his teammates. Transported by Women's

Airforce Service Pilot Cass Standish, Ben travels from the South Pacific to the European front during the Battle of the Bulge to chronicle what has become of the former football players on the battlefield rather than the gridiron.

Where it's reviewed:
Booklist, July 1, 2008, page 5
Kirkus Reviews, August 1, 2008, page 770
Library Journal, August 1, 2008, page 66
New York Times Book Review, November 23, 2008, page 9
Publishers Weekly, June 16, 2008, page 28

Other books by the same author:
The Whistling Season, 2006
Prairie Nocturne, 2003
Mountain Time, 1999
Ride with Me, Mariah Montana, 1990
Dancing at the Rascal Fair, 1987

Other books you might like:
Ronald Florence, *The Last Season*, 2000
Julie Garwood, *Come the Spring*, 1997
James Reasoner, *Battlelines*, 2001
Larry Watson, *Montana 1948*, 1993
James Welch, *Fools Crow*, 1986

763

EMMA DONOGHUE

The Sealed Letter

(Orlando: Harcourt, 2008)

Story type: Historical/Victorian
Subject(s): Marriage; Divorce; Women's Rights
Major character(s): Emily "Fido" Faithfull, Business-woman; Helen Codrington, Spouse (of Harry); Harry Codrington, Military Personnel (naval officer), Spouse (of Helen)
Time period(s): 1860s (1864)
Locale(s): London, England

Summary: Based in part on an actual notorious Victorian-era divorce case, Donoghue's novel portrays business-woman and feminist pioneer Emily "Fido" Faithfull who reestablishes contact with a former best friend, Helen Codrington, who has returned to London after a posting to Malta with her naval officer husband Harry. The manipulative Helen is Emily's opposite, and her sexual infidelity provokes a scandalous divorce trial while presenting Emily with a conflict between her loyalty to her friend and what she learns about her.

Where it's reviewed:
Booklist, August 1, 2008, page 38
Kirkus Reviews, July 1, 2008, page 666
Library Journal, August 1, 2008, page 66
Publishers Weekly, June 16, 2008, page 29

Other books by the same author:
Longing, 2007
Touching Subjects, 2006
Life Mask, 2004
The Woman Who Gave Birth to Rabbits, 2002
Slammerkin, 2001

Other books you might like:
Malcolm Archibald, *Pryde's Rock*, 2007
Tessa Barclay, *A Tissue of Lies*, 2008
George Macdonald Fraser, *The Reavers*, 2008
Jane Gardam, *The Flight of the Maidens*, 2001
Janice Graham, *The Tailor's Daughter*, 2006

764

SLAVENKA DRAKULIC

Frida's Bed

(New York: Penguin Books, 2008)

Story type: Arts
Subject(s): Biography; Artists and Art; Women
Major character(s): Frida Kahlo, Historical Figure, Artist; Diego Rivera, Historical Figure, Artist
Time period(s): 20th century
Locale(s): Mexico

Summary: On her deathbed in 1954, Mexican painter Frida Kahlo recalls her complex and pain-filled life, from her bout of polio at the age of six to the streetcar accident that caused her addiction to painkillers, to her troubled marriage to Mexican muralist Diego Rivera. Croatian author Drakulic shows how Kahlo's art became her way of coping with her physical and emotional wounds.

Where it's reviewed:
Booklist, August 1, 2008, page 35
Kirkus Reviews, August 1, 2008, page 771
Publishers Weekly, July 28, 2008, page 51

Other books by the same author:
S.: A Novel about the Balkans, 2000
As If I Am Not There, 1999
Marble Skin, 1998
The Taste of a Man, 1997
Holograms of Fear, 1992

Other books you might like:
Kate Braverman, *The Incantations of Frida K.*, 2002
Meaghan Delahunt, *In the Casa Azul*, 2002
Carlos Fuentes, *The Years with Laura Diaz*, 2000
Barbara Mujica, *Frida*, 2001
Elena Poniatowska, *Dear Diego*, 1986

765

CAROLA DUNN

The Black Ship

(New York: St. Martin's Minotaur, 2008)

Story type: Mystery; Historical/Roaring Twenties
Series: Daisy Dalrymple. Book 17
Subject(s): Mystery and Detective Stories
Major character(s): Daisy Dalrymple, Journalist, Detective—Amateur; Alec Fletcher, Detective—Police
Time period(s): 1920s (1925)
Locale(s): London, England

Summary: Husband and wife detectives Daisy Dalrymple and Alec Fletcher take on a new case when they move

Historical

into a large house near London's Hampton Heath. The couple is shocked when a dead body turns up in the garden. An investigation leads to uncovering a complex intrigue involving bootleggers and American gangsters. This is an interesting view of the Prohibition era from the English perspective, animated by the series' forward-thinking central protagonist.

Where it's reviewed:
Booklist, September 1, 2008, page 53
Kirkus Reviews, July 15, 2008, page 724
Publishers Weekly, July 7, 2008, page 40

Other books by the same author:
The Bloody Tower, 2007
Gunpowder Plot, 2006
Fall of a Philanderer, 2005
A Mourning Wedding, 2004
Die Laughing, 2003

Other books you might like:
Jill Churchill, *Who's Sorry Now?*, 2006
Kerry Greenwood, *Queen of the Flowers*, 2008
Faye Kellerman, *Straight into Darkness*, 2005
Gillian Linscott, *The Nell Bray Series*, 1991-
Jacqueline Winspear, *Pardonable Lies*, 2005

766

DAVID EBERSHOFF

The 19th Wife

(New York: Random House, 2008)

Story type: Historical/American West
Subject(s): Mormons; Marriage; Women
Major character(s): Ann Eliza Young, Historical Figure, Spouse (of Brigham Young); Brigham Young, Historical Figure, Political Figure; Jordan Scott, Murderer (accused), Runaway
Time period(s): 19th century; 21st century
Locale(s): Utah; Arizona

Summary: Ebershoff's intriguing novel alternates between an autobiographical account by Ann Eliza Young, the real-life 19th wife of Mormon leader Brigham Young and that of fictional Jordan Scott in the present whose mother was another 19th wife and whose father he is accused of murdering. Ann Eliza broke from the church and wrote a book about her experiences which helped put an end to Mormon polygamy. Both narratives offer intriguing portraits of outsiders and outcasts.

Where it's reviewed:
Booklist, July 1, 2008, page 33
Kirkus Reviews, July 1, 2008, page 667
New York Times Book Review, August 31, 2008, page 17

Other books by the same author:
Pasadena, 2002
The Rose City, 2001
The Danish Girl, 2000

Other books you might like:
Amelia Bean, *The Fancher Train*, 1958
Judith Freeman, *Red Water*, 2002

John Gates, *Sister Wife*, 2001
Marjorie Jarrett, *Wives of the Wind*, 1980
Margaret Blair Young, *Bound for Canaan*, 2002
　　Darius Aidan Gray, co-author

767

CLYDE EDGERTON

The Bible Salesman

(New York: Little, Brown, 2008)

Story type: Historical/World War II
Subject(s): Crime and Criminals
Major character(s): Preston Clearwater, Con Man; Henry Dampier, Salesman (Bible)
Time period(s): 1940s
Locale(s): North Carolina

Summary: Edgerton's witty period piece concerns car thief and con artist Preston Clearwater and his dupe, young Bible salesman Henry Dampier. As Dampier progresses legally in his chosen profession, his unfortunate involvement with Clearwater's nefarious activities complicates matters. Edgerton captures the region and the era with skill in this entertaining odd-couple road buddy novel.

Where it's reviewed:
Booklist, August 1, 2008, page 33
Kirkus Reviews, July 1, 2008, page 677
Library Journal, August 1, 2008, page 66
New York Times Book Review, August 31, 2008, page 13
Publishers Weekly, June 16, 2008, page 32

Other books by the same author:
Where Trouble Sleeps, 1997
Killer Diller, 1991
The Floatplane Notebooks, 1988
Walking Across Egypt, 1987
Raney, 1985

Other books you might like:
Howard Bahr, *Pelican Road*, 2008
James Carlos Blake, *A World of Thieves*, 2002
John Coyne, *The Caddie Who Played with Hickory*, 2008
Elizabeth Gill, *Silver Street*, 2008
Theodore Weesner, *The Car Thief*, 2001

768

SELDEN EDWARDS

The Little Book

(New York: Dutton, 2008)

Story type: Historical/Victorian; Historical/Fantasy
Subject(s): Time Travel
Major character(s): Stan "Wheeler" Burden, Time Traveler; Sigmund Freud, Historical Figure, Doctor; Gustav Mahler, Historical Figure, Composer
Time period(s): 1980s (1988); 1890s (1897)
Locale(s): San Francisco, California; Vienna, Austria

Summary: Edwards' ingenious first novel is a time travel adventure, sending baseball star and famed rock 'n' roller, Stan "Wheeler" Burden to Vienna in the 1890s. He is plunged into the city's rich cultural mix as Freud is discovering the Oedipus complex, Gustav Mahler is writing his symphonies, and anti-Semitism is spreading and catching the attention of a young Adolf Hitler. Vienna of the period is brilliantly animated here, spiced up by cameo appearances by the aforementioned as well as by Mark Twain, Winston Churchill, Buddy Holly, and others.

Where it's reviewed:
Booklist, August 1, 2008, page 36
Kirkus Reviews, June 15, 2008, page 613
Library Journal, August 1, 2008, page 66
Publishers Weekly, June 23, 2008, page 12

Other books you might like:
Carol Hill, *Henry James' Midnight Song*, 1993
Max Phillips, *The Artist's Wife*, 2001
Jody Shields, *The Fig Eater*, 2000
Daniel Silva, *A Death in Vienna*, 2004
Frank Tallis, *A Death in Vienna*, 2005

769

CAROLLY ERICKSON

The Tsarina's Daughter

(New York: St. Martin's Press, 2008)

Story type: Historical/Russian Revolution; Historical/World War I
Subject(s): Russian Empire; Russians; Kings, Queens, Rulers, etc.
Major character(s): Tatiana Romanov, Historical Figure, Royalty; Nicholas II, Historical Figure, Ruler; Alexandra, Historical Figure, Royalty
Time period(s): 1910s; 1980s (1989)
Locale(s): St. Petersburg, Russia; Canada

Summary: The second of Tsar Nicholas II and Empress Alexandra's four daughters, the Grand Duchess Tatiana Romanov, offers her story of how she survived the execution of her family by the Bolsheviks in 1918. Living under an assumed named in Canada in 1989, Tatiana, here Tania, reflects on her life in pre-World War I St. Petersburg, the threat to her father's reign during the war that leads up to the Russian Revolution, and the captivity of her family. Erickson's novel offers an unusual and vivid insider's perspectives on the Romanovs and their demise.

Where it's reviewed:
Kirkus Reviews, August 1, 2008, page 771
Library Journal, July 1, 2008, page 60
Publishers Weekly, June 23, 2008, page 33

Other books by the same author:
The Secret Life of Josephine, 2007
The Hidden Diary of Marie Antoinette, 2005

Other books you might like:
Robert Alexander, *Rasputin's Daughter*, 2006
Robert Alexander, *The Romanov Bride*, 2008
Natasha Borovsky, *A Daughter of Nobility*, 1985

Tom Bradby, *The White Russian*, 2003
James Fleming, *White Blood*, 2007

770

CHARLES FINCH

The September Society

(New York: St. Martin's Minotaur, 2008)

Story type: Historical/Victorian; Mystery
Series: Charles Lenox. Book 2
Subject(s): Mystery and Detective Stories; Victorian Period; Detection
Major character(s): Charles Lenox, Detective—Amateur
Time period(s): 1860s (1866)
Locale(s): Oxford, England; London, England

Summary: In the sequel to the author's *A Beautiful Blue Death*, Victorian amateur detective Charles Lenox investigates a double murder committed in India in 1847 and another committed in London in 1866. Lenox gets involved investigating the disappearance of two young men from Oxford's Lincoln College and their connection to a sinister "September Society." Period elements feature prominently, especially a detailed knowledge of Oxford, in this atmospheric mystery that recalls Dorothy Sayers' Lord Peter Wimsey mysteries.

Where it's reviewed:
Booklist, May 1, 2008, page 41
Kirkus Reviews, June 15, 2008, page 624
Publishers Weekly, June 9, 2008, page 34

Other books by the same author:
A Beautiful Blue Death, 2007

Other books you might like:
Tasha Alexander, *A Fatal Waltz*, 2008
Marjorie Eccles, *The Shape of Sand*, 2006
Anne Perry, *Buckingham Palace Gardens*, 2008
Mariah Stewart, *Mercy Street*, 2008
Stephen White, *Dead Time*, 2008

771

JANE FINNIS

Buried Too Deep

(Scottsdale: Poisoned Pen Press, 2008)

Story type: Mystery; Historical/Ancient Rome
Series: Aurelia Marcella. Book 3
Subject(s): Mystery and Detective Stories; Roman Empire
Major character(s): Aurelia Marcella, Innkeeper; Lucius Marcella, Innkeeper
Time period(s): 1st century (98 A.D.)
Locale(s): Britannia, Roman Empire

Summary: Aurelia Marcella is an innkeeper along with her twin brother Lucius in Roman Britannia during the first century. When a neighboring farmer is killed by Gallic sea raiders, it soon becomes clear that the raids are far from random, and Aurella sets out to discover both the motive for the attacks and those responsible for directing them. This intriguing mystery has both a pleas-

Historical

ing sleuth and a knowledgeable portrait of day-to-day life during the period.

Where it's reviewed:
Kirkus Reviews, May 1, 2008, page 458
Publishers Weekly, April 7, 2008, page 45

Other books by the same author:
A Bitter Chill, 2005
Get Out or Die, 2003

Other books you might like:
Gillian Bradshaw, *Island of Ghosts*, 1998
Lindsey Davis, *A Body in the Bathhouse*, 2002
William Dietrich, *Hadrian's Wall*, 2004
Stanley Kelli, *Nox Dormienda*, 2008
Simon Scarrow, *The Eagle's Conquest*, 2002

772

DAVID FITZ-ENZ

Recoats' Revenge: An Alternate History of 1812

(Washington, D.C.: Potomac Books, 2008)

Story type: Historical/War of 1812; Alternate History
Subject(s): War of 1812; Military Life; Alternate History
Major character(s): Arthur Wellesley, Military Personnel, Historical Figure (Duke of Wellington); James Madison, Historical Figure, Political Figure; Andrew Jackson, Historical Figure, Military Personnel
Time period(s): 1810s (1814)
Locale(s): Washington, District of Columbia

Summary: This intriguing alternate history of the War of 1812 imagines what might have happened if the Duke of Wellington had been dispatched after his victory over Napoleon to North America to engage the Americans. President Madison has no choice but to call on General Andrew Jackson to direct the defense of the country, and the novel speculates what would then have transpired as these two military leaders face off.

Other books you might like:
Geoffrey Edwards, *Fire Bell in the Night*, 1997
Eric Flint, *1812: The Rivers of War*, 2005
David Nevin, *1812*, 1996
Harry Turtledove, *The Man with the Iron Heart*, 2008
Peter G. Ysouras, *Britannia's Fist*, 2008

773

SARA FRASER (Pseudonym of Roy Clews)

The Resurrection Man

(Sutton, England: Severn House, 2008)

Story type: Historical/Regency
Series: Thomas Potts
Subject(s): Mystery and Detective Stories; Small Town Life; Detection
Major character(s): Thomas Potts, Police Officer (parish constable)
Time period(s): 1820s (1826)

Locale(s): Worcestershire, England
Summary: Parish Constable Thomas Potts investigates a series of grisly murders and body snatchings, believed to be the work of a notorious criminal gang known as the Ripping Boys. Potts is not so sure and to get to the truth he resorts to an early use of fingerprint identification.

Where it's reviewed:
Booklist, August 1, 2008, page 47

Other books by the same author:
A Bitter Legacy, 2003
The Surgeon's Apprentice, 2001
The Target, 1998
The Summer of the Fancy Man, 1993

Other books you might like:
Tasha Alexander, *A Fatal Waltz*, 2008
Gerri Brightwell, *The Dark Lantern*, 2008
Tracy Grant, *Daughter of the Game*, 2002
Nicholas Griffin, *The House of Sight and Shadow*, 2001
Ross King, *Ex-Libris*, 2001

774

DAVID FULLER

Sweetsmoke

(New York: Hyperion, 2008)

Story type: Historical/American Civil War; Mystery
Subject(s): Mystery and Detective Stories; Slavery
Major character(s): Cassius, Slave
Time period(s): 1860s
Locale(s): Virginia

Summary: In this intriguing mystery debut, Cassius, a slave on a Virginia tobacco plantation during the Civil War, sets out to discover who is responsible for killing his surrogate mother, a freed black woman. On the road, he must deal with slave traders, operators of the underground railroad, Confederate soldiers, and Union spies.

Where it's reviewed:
Kirkus Reviews, August 1, 2008, page 772
New York Times Book Review, September 21, 2008, page 29
Publishers Weekly, July 14, 2008, page 41

Other books you might like:
Breena Clarke, *Stand the Storm*, 2008
Barbara Hambly, *Sold Down the River*, 2000
James McBride, *The Song Not Yet Sung*, 2008
Miriam Grace Monfredo, *Brothers of Cain*, 2001
Toni Morrison, *A Mercy*, 2008

775

DAVID FULMER

Lost River

(Boston: Houghton Mifflin Harcourt, 2009)

Story type: Historical/Americana; Mystery
Series: Valentin St. Cyr Mystery. Book 4

Subject(s): Mystery and Detective Stories; City and Town Life; Prostitution
Major character(s): Valentin St. Cyr, Detective—Private; Tom Anderson, Businessman
Time period(s): 1910s (1913)
Locale(s): New Orleans, Louisiana

Summary: In this Valentin St. Cyr mystery set in New Orleans in the 1910s, St. Cyr comes to the aid of his former employer Tom Anderson, who rules the legendary red-light district of Storyville, after a corpse is found in one of Anderson's bordellos. More victims follow, and St. Cyr must discover why someone is targeting the male customers of Storyville.

Where it's reviewed:
Booklist, November 15, 2008, page 20
Kirkus Reviews, October 1, 2008, page 1038
Library Journal, Nobember 1, 2008, page 46
Publishers Weekly, October 6, 2008, page 38

Other books by the same author:
The Blue Door, 2008
The Dying Crapshooter's Blues, 2007
Rampart Street, 2006
Jass, 2005
Chasing the Devil's Tail, 2001

Other books you might like:
Kenneth Abel, *Cold Steel Rain*, 2000
James Lee Burke, *The Tin Roof Blowdown*, 2007
Julie Smith, *New Orleans Beat*, 1994
Frederick Turner, *Redemption*, 2006
Penn Williamson, *Mortal Sins*, 2000

776

ALICE FULTON

The Nightingales of Troy
(New York: W.W. Norton, 2008)

Story type: Historical/Roaring Twenties
Subject(s): Women; Marriage; Family Relations
Major character(s): Mamie Flynn Garrahan, Spouse; Annie Garrahan, Nurse; Ruth Garrahan, Young Woman
Time period(s): 20th century
Locale(s): Troy, New York

Summary: In a series of linked stories, Fulton chronicles the lives of four generations of women in Troy, New York. Stories from each decade of the 20th century document the conditions for women and their progress over the century. Beginning in 1908, Mamie Flynn Garrahan has five children before she is 30. Her daughter, Annie, becomes a nurse during the Great Depression, while her daughter Ruth is on hand when the Beatles visit New York. Filled with details that animate a family in every era, this collection is an impressive fictional debut from poet Fulton.

Where it's reviewed:
Booklist, July 1, 2008, page 35
Kirkus Reviews, June 1, 2008, page 567
Library Journal, May 1, 2008, page 55
Publishers Weekly, March 24, 2008, page 49

Other books you might like:
Dorothea Malm, *The Woman Question*, 1957
Dan McCall, *Beecher*, 1979
Patricia O'Brien, *Harriet and Isabella*, 2008
Maura D. Shaw, *The Keeners*, 2004
Jacqueline Sheckan, *Truth*, 2003

777

JOHN GARDNER

Moriarty
(Orlando: Harcourt, 2008)

Story type: Historical/Edwardian; Mystery
Subject(s): Mystery and Detective Stories; Crime and Criminals
Major character(s): James Moriarty, Organized Crime Figure, Professor; Jack "Idle Jack" Idell, Organized Crime Figure, Nobleman
Time period(s): 1900s (1900)
Locale(s): London, England

Summary: Gardner, who died in 2007, supplies a final, third adventure for Sherlock Holmes's nemesis, Professor Moriarty. Having survived the Reichenbach Falls, Moriarty returns in 1900 to London to reassert his control over his underworld empire. Vying for control is Sir Jordan Jack Idell, or "Idle Jack," and Moriarty must overcome this challenge to his crime supremacy.

Where it's reviewed:
Booklist, November 15, 2008, page 21
Publishers Weekly, September 29, 2008, page 62

Other books by the same author:
Seafire, 1994
License Renewed, 1991
Broken Chain, 1990
The Revenge of Moriarty, 1975
The Return of Moriarty, 1974

Other books you might like:
Gyles Brandreth, *Oscar Wilde and a Game Called Murder*, 2008
John R. King, *The Shadow of Reichenbach Falls*, 2008
Laurie R. King, *The Mary Russell/Sherlock Holmes Series*, 1994-
Michael Kurland, *The Empress of India*, 2006
Gerard Williams, *Dr. Mortimer and the Aldgate Mystery*, 2001

778

JOHN GARDNER

No Human Enemy
(New York: Thomas Dunne Books, 2008)

Story type: Historical/World War II; Mystery
Series: Suzie Mountford. Book 5
Subject(s): World War II; Mystery and Detective Stories
Major character(s): Suzie Mountford, Police Officer; Tommy Livermore, Police Officer
Time period(s): 1940s

Historical

Locale(s): London, England

Summary: London under attack from V-1 rockets is the backdrop for this case in which policewoman Mountford and her partner (and lover) Tommy Livermore investigate the bombing of a convent in which one of the nuns killed was apparently murdered before the rocket landed. This is presumably the final volume in the series, following Gardner's death.

Where it's reviewed:
Booklist, August 1, 2008, page 46
Kirkus Reviews, June 15, 2008, page 624
Publishers Weekly, June 16, 2008, page 36

Other books by the same author:
Troubled Night, 2006
Angels Dining at the Ritz, 2004
Scorpius, 1988
Role of Honor, 1984
Icebreaker, 1983

Other books you might like:
James R. Benn, *Blood Alone*, 2008
David Stuart Davies, *Forests of the Night*, 2007
Christopher Nicole, *Angel in Jeopardy*, 2007
David Peace, *Tokyo Year Zero*, 2007
Sally Spencer, *A Long Time Dead*, 2006

779

MARK GATISS

Black Butterfly

(New York: Simon & Schuster, 2008)

Story type: Historical/Roaring Twenties; Mystery
Series: Lucifer Box
Subject(s): Espionage; Mystery and Detective Stories; Detection
Major character(s): Lucifer Box, Spy
Time period(s): 1950s
Locale(s): England; Istanbul, Turkey; Jamaica

Summary: As Queen Elizabeth is crowned, the aging secret agent Lucifer Box takes on a baffling case that takes him from London and Istanbul to Jamaica. He must discover why so many important British peers keep dying in reckless accidents and the secret of the mysterious Black Butterfly. Full of cloak-and-dagger intrigue, the novel features an entertaining protagonist and a colorful period backdrop.

Where it's reviewed:
Publishers Weekly, December 11, 2008, page 49

Other books by the same author:
The Devil in Amber, 2006
The Vesuvius Club, 2004

Other books you might like:
Michael Cox, *The Glass of Time*, 2008
Mark Frost, *The Second Objective*, 2007
Graham Ison, *Hardcastle's Spy*, 2004
John Lawton, *Second Violin*, 2008
James Lear, *The Back Passage*, 2006

780

AMITAV GHOSH

Sea of Poppies

(New York: Farrar, Straus and Giroux, 2008)

Story type: Historical/Victorian; Historical/Exotic
Subject(s): Sea Stories; Servants
Major character(s): Benjamin Burnham, Businessman (opium merchant); Zachary Reid, Sailor; Deeti, Widow(er)
Time period(s): 1830s (1838)
Locale(s): *Ibis*, At Sea; India

Summary: Ghosh's picaresque story chronicles the voyage of the *Ibiz*, a ship transporting Indian coolies to Mauritius in 1838. First detailing how crew and cargo came to the vessel, the novel collects a rich cast of characters, including opium merchant and ship owner Benjamin Burnham, the mulatto second mate Zachary Reid, and a fugitive widow, Deeti. All constitute a microcosm of the Middle East during the 19th century, and the interconnection of their various stories make for a rich and complex narrative.

Where it's reviewed:
Booklist, October 15, 2008, page 23
Kirkus Reviews, September 1, 2008, page 907
Library Journal, October 1, 2008, page 56
Publishers Weekly, August 18, 2008, page 38

Other books by the same author:
The Hungry Tide, 2005
The Glass Palace, 2001
The Calcutta Chromosome, 1995
The Shadow Lines, 1989
The Circle of Reason, 1986

Other books you might like:
Thalassa Ali, *Companions of Paradise*, 2006
Timothy Mo, *An Insular Possession*, 1987
Arundhati Roy, *The God of Small Things*, 1997
Shan Sa, *The Empress*, 2006
Thrity N. Umrigar, *The Space between Us*, 2005

781

ELIZABETH GILL

Sweet Wells

(Sutton, England: Severn House, 2008)

Story type: Historical/Depression Era
Subject(s): Small Town Life; Family Life
Major character(s): Maddy Grant, Young Woman; Jonas Ward, Widow(er)
Time period(s): 1930s
Locale(s): England

Summary: This novel, set in the 1930s in England, shows the vengeance of Jonas Ward after his wife dies in childbirth. He takes out his bitterness on Maddy Grant and her family by claiming title to their ancestral home. Maddy struggles to survive in the tough Depression years preceding World War II.

Where it's reviewed:
Booklist, October 15, 2008, page 24

Other books by the same author:
Silver Street, 2008
Swan Island, 2007
The Secret, 2007
Home to the High Falls, 2006
The Foxglove Tree, 2006

Other books you might like:
Maeve Binchy, *Light a Penny Candle*, 1983
Elaine Crowley, *The Ways of Women*, 1993
Philippa Gregory, *Fallen Skies*, 2008
Owen Madoc, *Keeping Secrets*, 2008
Tom Phelan, *In the Season of Daisies*, 1996

782

BEA GONZALEZ

The Bitter Taste of Time

(New York: St. Martin's Press, 2008)

Story type: Family Saga
Subject(s): Family Relations; Women; Hotels and Motels
Major character(s): Maria Encarna, Hotel Owner; Cecilia Encarna, Hotel Worker; Matilde Encarna, Hotel Worker
Time period(s): 20th century (1920-1997)
Locale(s): Canteira, Spain

Summary: Spanning the history of Spain in the 20th century, Gonzalez's novel traces several generations of Encarna women, led by Maria who opens a hotel in Canteira, a picturesque small town. The novel follows the lives of the Encarnas, including Cecilia, Carmen, Matilde, Asuncion, and Gloria. Their experiences mirror developments in the town during war and from the changes brought on by modernity.

Where it's reviewed:
Library Journal, July 1, 2008, page 60
Publishers Weekly, June 30, 2008, page 158

Other books by the same author:
The Mapmaker's Opera, 2007

Other books you might like:
Lluis-Anton Baulenas, *For a Sack of Bones*, 2008
Dave Boling, *Guernica*, 2008
Emilio Calderon, *The Creator's Map*, 2008
Juan Eslava Gala, *The Mule*, 2008
Ildefonso Falcones, *Cathedral of the Sea*, 2008

783

PHILIP GOODEN

The Salisbury Manuscript

(New York: Soho Constable, 2008)

Story type: Historical/Victorian; Mystery
Subject(s): Mystery and Detective Stories; Victorian Period

Major character(s): Thomas Ansell, Lawyer
Time period(s): 1870s (1873)
Locale(s): Salisbury, England

Summary: Gooden launches a new historical mystery series set during the Victorian period in the cathedral town of Salisbury. London attorney Thomas Ansell arrives to take possession of Canon Felix Slater's father's memoir. When the canon turns up dead, the police suspect Ansell when he is found in the canon's study standing over the corpse, stained in the victim's blood. To prove his innocence, Ansell turns detective to find the real killer.

Where it's reviewed:
Publishers Weekly, May 12, 2008, page 39

Other books by the same author:
An Honorable Murderer, 2005
Mask of Night, 2004
Alms for Oblivion, 2003
The Pale Companion, 2002
Sleep of Death, 2000

Other books you might like:
Tasha Alexander, *A Fatal Waltz*, 2008
Jonathan Barnes, *The Somnambulist*, 2008
David Dickinson, *Death of an Old Master*, 2004
Michel Faber, *The Crimson Petal and the White*, 2002
Will Thomas, *To Kingdom Come*, 2005

784

C.W. GORTNER

The Last Queen

(New York: Ballantine Books, 2008)

Story type: Historical/Renaissance
Subject(s): Kings, Queens, Rulers, etc.; Biography
Major character(s): Juana of Castile, Historical Figure, Royalty; Philip of Flanders, Historical Figure, Royalty
Time period(s): 15th century
Locale(s): Spain

Summary: Gortner provides an autobiographical portrait of Spanish Princess Juana of Castile, daughter of King Ferdinand and Queen Isabella. Married to Philip of Flanders, heir to the Hapsburg Empire, Juana unexpectedly becomes next in line to the Spanish crown, plunging her into a complex balancing act of divided loyalties that lead her to the brink of insanity, giving her the nickname Juana La Loca (the Mad). This is a capable and believable reconstruction of the period and a fascinating historical figure.

Where it's reviewed:
Publishers Weekly, April 14, 2008, page 33

Other books by the same author:
The Secret Lion, 2006

Other books you might like:
Gioconda Belli, *The Scroll of Seduction*, 2006
Carolly Erickson, *The Last Wife of Henry VIII*, 2006
Frances Parkinson Keyes, *I, the King*, 1966

Historical

Robin Maxwell, *Virgin*, 2001
Jan Vlachos Westcott, *The Queen's Grace*, 1959

785

ANN GRANGER

A Mortal Curiosity

(New York: St. Martin's Minotaur, 2008)

Story type: Historical/Victorian; Mystery
Series: Benjamin Ross and Lizzie Martin. Book 2
Subject(s): Mystery and Detective Stories; Victorian Period; Small Town Life
Major character(s): Benjamin Ross, Detective—Police; Lizzie Martin, Companion
Time period(s): 1860s (1864)
Locale(s): Hampshire, England

Summary: Ladies companion and amateur sleuth Lizzie Martin accepts an assignment in Hampshire as the companion of a young woman who recently lost her newborn daughter. When the local rat-catcher is stabbed to death soon after Lizzie's arrival, she investigates alongside her beau, Scotland Yard inspector Benjamin Ross.

Where it's reviewed:
Booklist, July 1, 2008, page 43
Kirkus Reviews, June 15, 2008, page 625
Publishers Weekly, June 23, 2008, page 40

Other books by the same author:
The Companion, 2007
That Way Murder Lies, 2005
A Restless Evil, 2002
Shades of Murder, 2001
Beneath These Stones, 2000

Other books you might like:
Gillian Bray, *The Nell Bray Series*, 1991-
Carola Dunn, *The Daisy Dalrymple Series*, 1994-
Michel Faber, *The Crimson Petal and the White*, 2002
Laurie R. King, *The Mary Russell/Sherlock Holmes Series*, 1994-
Joan Lock, *Dead Letters*, 2003
Gerard Williams, *Dr. Mortimer and the Aldgate Mystery*, 2001

786

KERRY GREENWOOD

Death by Water

(Scottsdale: Poisoned Pen Press, 2009)

Story type: Mystery; Historical/Roaring Twenties
Series: Phryne Fisher Mystery
Subject(s): Mystery and Detective Stories; Crime and Criminals; Cruise Ships
Major character(s): Phryne Fisher, Detective—Amateur
Time period(s): 1920s
Locale(s): Australia; *S.S. Hinemoa*, At Sea

Summary: Aussie flapper Phryne Fisher boards a luxury cruise ship on a voyage to New Zealand to find a jewel thief who is preying on the first-class passengers. As bait, she is carrying the Great Queen of Sapphires, the Maharani. Filled with period details, the mystery is a rollicking cruise among the glamour set.

Other books by the same author:
Heavenly Pleasures, 2008
Earthly Pleasures, 2007
The Green Mill Murder, 2007
Away with the Fairies, 2006
Murder in Montparnasse, 2004

Other books you might like:
Ilene Birkwood, *Deadly Deception*, 2004
Janet Evanovich, *Hot Six*, 2000
James Patterson, *2nd Chance*, 2002
John Sherwood, *A Botanist at Bay*, 1985
Phyllis A. Whitney, *Star Flight*, 1993

787

KERRY GREENWOOD

Queen of the Flowers

(Scottsdale: Poisoned Pen Press, 2008)

Story type: Mystery; Historical/Roaring Twenties
Series: Phryne Fisher Mystery
Subject(s): Mystery and Detective Stories; Crime and Criminals
Major character(s): Phryne Fisher, Detective—Amateur
Time period(s): 1920s (1928)
Locale(s): Australia

Summary: Australian flapper and amateur sleuth Phryne Fisher has been chosen Queen of the Flowers in the annual Flower Parade. Accompanying her is a troubled young woman who vanishes, sending Phryne on a mission to find her.

Where it's reviewed:
Booklist, May 1, 2008, page 40
Kirkus Reviews, April 1, 2008, page 331
Publishers Weekly, March 31, 2008, page 42

Other books by the same author:
Death Before Wicket, 2008
Raisins and Almonds, 2007
Away with the Fairies, 2006
Murder on the Ballarat Train, 2006
Flying too High, 2006

Other books you might like:
Caroline Carver, *Dead Heat*, 2004
Jill Churchill, *Who's Sorry Now?*, 2006
Janet Evanovich, *Hot Six*, 2000
John Sherwood, *A Botanist at Bay*, 1985
Phyllis A. Whitney, *Star Flight*, 1993

788

PHILIPPA GREGORY

Fallen Skies

(New York: Simon & Schuster, 2008)

Story type: Historical/Roaring Twenties
Subject(s): World War I; Marriage; Singing
Major character(s): Lily Pears, Entertainer (chorus girl); Stephen Winters, Veteran (World War I)
Time period(s): 1920s
Locale(s): England

Summary: In this suspenseful period piece, Lily Pears is a working-class girl who seeks success as a chorus girl and performer in this novel set in England in the aftermath of the Great War. Failing to get ahead, Lily accepts a marriage proposal from Stephen Winters, a decorated veteran, but soon learns that all is not well in the Winters family.

Where it's reviewed:
Kirkus Reviews, October 15, 2008, page 1086
Publishers Weekly, September 29, 2008, page 58

Other books by the same author:
The Other Queen, 2008
The Boleyn Inheritance, 2006
The Constant Princess, 2005
The Virgin's Lover, 2004
Meridon, 1990

Other books you might like:
Rennie Airth, *River of Darkness*, 1999
Pat Barker, *Life Class*, 2007
Doris Lessing, *Alfred and Emily*, 2008
Ann Patchett, *Bel Canto*, 2001
Katherine Stone, *Island of Dreams*, 2000

789

PHILIPPA GREGORY

The Other Queen

(New York: Touchstone Book, 2008)

Story type: Historical/Elizabethan
Subject(s): Kings, Queens, Rulers, etc.; Prisoners and Prisons; Biography
Major character(s): Mary Queen of Scots, Historical Figure, Ruler; George Talbot, Historical Figure, Nobleman; Bess of Hardwick, Historical Figure, Spouse (of George)
Time period(s): 16th century
Locale(s): Scotland; England

Summary: Gregory dramatizes the life of Mary, Queen of Scots during the 16 years she was held by the command of her cousin, Elizabeth I, at the estate of George Talbot, earl of Shrewsbury, and his wife, Bess of Hardwick. The novel alternates among all three perspectives, presenting an intriguing domestic triangle as Mary secretly plots to seize the English throne and drives a wedge between husband and wife.

Where it's reviewed:
Booklist, April 15, 2008, page 32
Library Journal, July 1, 2008, page 61
Publishers Weekly, May 5, 2008, page 41

Other books by the same author:
The Constant Princess, 2008
The Boleyn Inheritance, 2006
The Virgin Lover, 2004
Meridon, 1990
The Favored Child, 1989

Other books you might like:
Margaret George, *Mary Queen of Scotland and the Isles*, 1992
Virginia Henley, *A Woman of Passion*, 1999
Jean Plaidy, *The Captive Queen of the Scots*, 1970
Reay Tannahill, *Fatal Majesty*, 1999
Jan Vlachos Westcott, *The Tower and the Dream*, 1974

790

SUSANNA GREGORY

The Butcher of Smithfield

(London: Sphere, 2008)

Story type: Historical/Seventeenth Century; Mystery
Series: Thomas Chaloner. Book 3
Subject(s): Mystery and Detective Stories; Espionage
Major character(s): Thomas Chaloner, Spy, Musician (amateur)
Time period(s): 17th century (1663)
Locale(s): London, England

Summary: This third adventure for spy Thomas Chaloner in Restoration London has him out of favor with his employer, the earl of Clarendon, England's Lord Chancellor. To get back in the earl's good graces, Chaloner must solve the mysterious death of a solicitor and journalist who died after eating cucumber. He is soon launched upon a complex intrigue involving multiple murders, allowing the author to supply an authentic depiction of the period, its customs, and history.

Where it's reviewed:
Kirkus Reviews, July 15, 2008, page 724
Publishers Weekly, July 15, 2008, page NA

Other books by the same author:
Blood on the Strand, 2007
The Mark of a Murderer, 2005
A Killer in Winter, 2003
A Plague on Both Your Houses, 1998
A Bone of Contention, 1997

Other books you might like:
Philip Gooden, *Alms for Oblivion*, 2003
Philip Kerr, *Dark Matter*, 2003
Edward Marston, *The King's Evil*, 2000
Fidelis Morgan, *The Rival Queen*, 2001
Elizabeth Redfern, *Auriel Rising*, 2005

Historical

791

HUGO HAMILTON

Disguise

(New York: Harper, 2008)

Story type: Historical/World War II
Subject(s): Identity; Music and Musicians; Jews
Major character(s): Gregor Liedmann, Musician
Time period(s): 20th century; 21st century
Locale(s): Nuremberg, Germany; Berlin, Germany

Summary: This novel, set in Germany in the aftermath of World War II, concerns Gregor Liedmann, who is raised in Nuremburg and becomes a musician in Berlin. At issue is the question of Gregor's identity. Is he really a Jewish survivor of the Holocaust adopted by a German couple when their infant son was killed? Or is this story merely an invention Gregor has manufactured to deny his past and heritage? The novel explores these questions 60 years after the fact as Gregor deals with the consequences of his past on his individuality and moral make-up.

Where it's reviewed:
Booklist, December 1, 2008, page 21
Kirkus Reviews, October 1, 2008, page 1029
New York Times Book Review, January 18, 2008, page 6
Publishers Weekly, October 6, 2008, page 34

Other books by the same author:
Headbanger, 2001
Sad Bastard, 2001
Dublin Where the Palm Trees Grow, 1996
The Love Test, 1995
The Last Shot, 1992

Other books you might like:
Sebastian Barry, *The Secret Scripture*, 2008
Don DeLillo, *The Body Artist*, 2001
Anna Quindlen, *Black and Blue*, 1998
Marilynne Robinson, *Gilead*, 2004
Angel Wagenstein, *Isaac's Torah*, 2008

792

TOM HARPER

The Lost Temple

(New York: Thomas Dunne Books, 2007)

Story type: Adventure
Subject(s): Adventure and Adventurers; Archaeology; Mythology
Major character(s): C.S. Grant, Adventurer
Time period(s): 1940s (1947)
Locale(s): Greece

Summary: This Indiana Jones-type thriller is set in the aftermath of World War II as the British, Americans, and Russians are all searching for the legendary shield of Achilles, which may contain a powerful chemical element that could be used in a weapon. British adventurer C.S. Grant is sent to Greece to help recover a murdered archaeologist's notebook. As he searches for clues to the whereabouts of the shield, the excitement begins.

Where it's reviewed:
Booklist, November 15, 2008, page 20
Library Journal, November 1, 2008, page 57
Publishers Weekly, September 8, 2008, page 36

Other books by the same author:
Siege of Heaven, 2007
Knights of the Cross, 2006
The Mosaic of Shadows, 2005

Other books you might like:
Rai Aren, *Secret of the Sand*, 2007
Steve Berry, *The Charlemagne Pursuit*, 2008
David Gibbins, *The Lost Tomb*, 2008
Tom Martin, *Pyramid*, 2007
Paul Sussman, *The Lost Army of Cambyses*,

793

C.S. HARRIS

Where Serpents Sleep

(New York: Obsidian, 2008)

Story type: Historical/Regency; Mystery
Series: Sebastian St. Cyr Mystery. Book 4
Subject(s): Mystery and Detective Stories; Detection
Major character(s): Sebastian St. Cyr, Nobleman; Sir William Hadley, Gentleman, Judge; Hero Jarvis, Detective—Amateur
Time period(s): 1810s (1812)
Locale(s): London, England

Summary: Set in Regency London, this installment of Harris's period mystery series featuring gentleman detective Sebastian St. Cyr has him investigating the savage murder of eight prostitutes in a London house of refuge. Suspects range from the girls' pimp to customer Sir William Hadley, a Bow Street magistrate. Assisting St. Cyr is Hero Jarvis, the daughter of his longtime mortal enemy.

Where it's reviewed:
Booklist, November 15, 2008, page 22
Publishers Weekly, October 6, 2008, page 39

Other books by the same author:
Why Mermaids Sing, 2007
When Gods Die, 2006
What Angels Fear, 2005

Other books you might like:
Stephanie Barron, *The Jane Austen Series*, 1996-
Wilder Perkins, *Hoare and the Portsmouth Atrocities*, 1998
Kate Ross, *The Julian Kestrel Series*, 1993-
Rosemary Stevens, *The Tainted Snuff Box*, 2001
Will Thomas, *The Hellfire Conspiracy*, 2007

794

CORA HARRISON

A Secret and Unlawful Killing

(New York: St. Martin's Minotaur, 2008)

Story type: Historical/Medieval; Mystery
Series: Burren Mysteries. Book 2
Subject(s): Mystery and Detective Stories; Middle Ages; Law
Major character(s): Mara, Judge
Time period(s): 16th century (1509)
Locale(s): Burren, Ireland

Summary: In this mystery set in the harsh countryside of the Burren in western Ireland during the 16th century, the investigation of the murder of a tax collector falls to Mara, the sole woman Brehon, or judge, in Ireland. When another body is discovered, apparently a suicide, Mara is convinced that the two deaths are connected. Her search for answers to the mystery provides the reader with an intimate look at Irish law and the customs of the times.

Where it's reviewed:
Booklist, September 1, 2008, page 67
Kirkus Reviews, July 15, 2008, page 725
Publishers Weekly, July 14, 2008, page 46

Other books by the same author:
Michaelmas Tribute, 2008
My Lady Judge, 2007

Other books you might like:
Kate Horsley, *Confessions of a Pagan Nun*, 2001
Michael Jecks, *A Friar's Bloodfeud*, 2005
Edward Rutherfurd, *The Princes of Ireland*, 2004
Ana Seymour, *Maid of Killarney*, 2002
Peter Tremayne, *A Prayer for the Damned*, 2007

795

CHRISTOPH HEIN

Settlement

(New York: Metropolitan Books, 2008)

Story type: Historical/World War II; Coming-of-Age
Subject(s): Small Town Life; Coming-of-Age
Major character(s): Bernhard Haber, Refugee
Time period(s): 1940s
Locale(s): Guldenberg, Germany

Summary: Hein's novel chronicles the experiences of Bernhard Haber, a refugee from Breslau after the 1945 Soviet invasion, in a small East German town. Bernhard's life at school, the attacks that lead to torching his father's workshop and the killing of his dog, through his work as a smuggler, carpenter, and finally as the town big-shot are dramatized. The often enigmatic Bernhard is described from the perspective of five of his acquaintances. The novel offers an interesting portrait of postwar smalltown German life.

Where it's reviewed:
Booklist, August 1, 2008, page 38
Publishers Weekly, July 7, 2008, page 38

Other books by the same author:
Willenbrock, 2003
The Tango Player, 1992
The Distant Lover, 1989

Other books you might like:
Gunter Grass, *Too Far Afield*, 2000
Jack Higgins, *Day of Judgment*, 1979
Henry Porter, *Brandenburg Gate*, 2005
Ingo Schulze, *New Lives*, 2008
Gerald Seymour, *Dead Ground*, 1999

796

C.C. HUMPHREYS

Absolute Honor

(New York: St. Martin's Press, 2008)

Story type: Historical/Georgian; Adventure
Series: Jack Absolute. Book 3
Subject(s): Adventure and Adventurers; Espionage
Major character(s): Jack Absolute, Adventurer, Spy; Red Hugh McClune, Military Personnel; Laetitia Fitzpatrick, Young Woman
Time period(s): 1760s (1761)
Locale(s): Bath, England; Canada; Rome, Italy

Summary: In the further adventures of English spy Jack Absolute, following the Battle of Quebec during the French and Indian War, Absolute returns to England with Irish grenadier Red Hugh McClune. In Bath, Absolute gets involved with McClune's cousin, Laetitia Fitzpatrick. His attachment leads him into a dangerous conspiracy, and the truth about his new friends becomes clear when Jack is sent undercover to Rome.

Where it's reviewed:
Library Journal, October 15, 2008, page 56
Publishers Weekly, August 25, 2008, page 47

Other books by the same author:
The Blooding of Jack Absolute, 2007
Jack Absolute, 2006

Other books you might like:
Rita Cleary, *Spies and Tories*, 1999
Bernard Cornwell, *Redcoat*, 1988
Thomas Fleming, *Liberty Tavern*, 1976
Diana Gabaldon, *Lord John and the Hand of the Devils*, 2008
Richard Woodman, *The Guineaman*, 2000

797

YASUSHI INOUE

The Blue Wolf: A Novel of the Life of Chinggis Khan

(New York: Columbia University Press, 2008)

Story type: Historical/Exotic
Subject(s): Biography; China

Historical

Major character(s): Chinggis Khan, Historical Figure, Military Personnel
Time period(s): 12th century
Locale(s): Asia

Summary: Japanese writer Inoue Yashushi offers a biographical portrait of Chinggis Khan, the great Mongol leader and conqueror of most of Asia. The novel, based on both history and legend, begins in Chinggis's youth and supplies the psychological basis for his grand ambition and obsessions. It goes on to Chinggis's rise to power and the great campaigns that created his empire.

Where it's reviewed:
Library Journal, September 1, 2008, page 117

Other books by the same author:
Confucius, 1992
Wind and Waves, 1989
The Roof Tile of Tempyo, 1975
The Counterfeiter, 1965
The Hunting Gun, 1961

Other books you might like:
Taylor Caldwell, *The Earth Is the Lord's*, 1940
Don Dandrea, *Orlok*, 1986
Conn Iggulden, *Genghis: Birth of an Empire*, 2007
Conn Iggulden, *Genghis: Lord of the Bow*, 2008
Pamela Sargent, *Ruler of the Sky*, 1993

798

GRAHAM ISON

Hardcastle's Burglar

(Sutton, England: Severn House, 2008)

Story type: Historical/World War I; Mystery
Series: Hardcastle
Subject(s): World War I; Mystery and Detective Stories
Major character(s): Ernest Hardcastle, Detective—Police; Charles Marriott, Detective—Police
Time period(s): 1910s
Locale(s): England

Summary: Inspector Hardcastle and Detective Sergeant Marriott investigate the death of Sir Adrian Rivers, of the Surrey Rifles, who has married the working class Muriel, a bookmaker's daughter. The answer to the mystery of who is responsible for Sir Adrian's death may be found in the fact that curios from Rivers estate have been turning up for sale by a local antique dealer.

Where it's reviewed:
Booklist, May 15, 2008, page 24
Kirkus Reviews, July 1, 2008, page 678

Other books by the same author:
Hardcastle's Actress, 2007
Drumfire, 2006
Hardcastle's Airmen, 2006
Hardcastle's Armistice, 2004
Whiplash, 2004

Other books you might like:
Rennie Airth, *River of Darkness*, 1999
Micheal Gilbert, *Into Battle*, 1997
Gillian Linscott, *Absent Friends*, 1999

Anne Perry, *No Graves as Yet*, 2003
Charles Todd, *A False Mirror*, 2006

799

CLAUDE IZNER

Murder on the Eiffel Tower

(New York: St. Martin's Minotaur, 2008)

Story type: Historical/Victorian; Mystery
Series: Victor Legris. Book 1
Subject(s): Mystery and Detective Stories; Detection
Major character(s): Victor Legris, Store Owner (bookseller), Detective—Amateur
Time period(s): 1880s (1889)
Locale(s): Paris, France

Summary: Set during the celebrations marking the unveiling of Gustave Eiffel's famous tower in Paris, this atmospheric period mystery features bookseller and amateur sleuth Victor Legris who investigates a series of baffling murders, apparently due to bee stings. To get to the truth, Legris takes the reader on an impressive and believable tour of Paris during the Belle Epoque.

Where it's reviewed:
Booklist, August 1, 2008, page 44
Kirkus Reviews, July 15, 2008, page 725
Publishers Weekly, June 30, 2008, page 164

Other books by the same author:
The Montmarte Investigation, 2008
The Pere-Lachaise Mystery, 2007

Other books you might like:
Jonathan Barnes, *The Somnambulist*, 2008
Louis Bayard, *The Black Tower*, 2008
Gerri Brightwell, *The Dark Lantern*, 2008
William Dietrich, *The Rosetta Key*, 2008
Yannick Murphy, *Signed, Mata Hari*, 2007

800

SHERRY JONES

The Jewel of Medina

(New York: Ballantine Books, 2008)

Story type: Historical/Exotic
Subject(s): Biography; Marriage
Major character(s): A'isha bint Abi Bakr, Historical Figure, Spouse (of Muhammad); Muhammad, Historical Figure, Religious
Time period(s): 7th century
Locale(s): Arabia

Summary: Jones supplies a biographical portrait of A'isha bint Abi Bakr, the favored wife of the prophet Muhammad. The novel chronicles A'isha's youth and betrothal to Muhammad at age six, when she is confined to her house until her marriage three years later. Forced to leave Mecca for Medina when it becomes unsafe for Muhammad, A'isha is shown growing from a naive child to a savvy, worldly woman whose counsel becomes important to Muhammad.

Where it's reviewed:
New York Times Book Review, December 14, 2008, page 10
Publishers Weekly, October 6, 2008, page 51

Other books you might like:
Driss Chraibi, *Muhammad*, 1998
Eva Etzioni-Halevy, *The Triumph of Deborah*, 2007
Edwin Hoyt, *The Voice of Allah*, 1970
Mohja Kahf, *The Girl in the Tangerine Scarf*, 2006
Hunter Nedjma, *The Almond*, 2005

801

STEPHEN GRAHAM JONES

Ledfeather

(Tuscaloosa, AL: FC2, 2008)

Story type: Historical/American West
Subject(s): Indians of North America; Indian Reservations; Frontier and Pioneer Life
Major character(s): Doby Saxon, Indian
Time period(s): 19th century; 21st century
Locale(s): Montana

Summary: Set on a Montana Blackfeet Indian reservation, Jones's novel tells two stories: that of an Indian boy, Doby Saxon, in the present and an Indian agent on the reservation in 1884. The novel shows how the actions of this agent greatly impact the lives of generations of Blackfeet Indians, including Doby. Jones offers a knowing portrait of reservation life and the historical changes that are played out over the century.

Where it's reviewed:
Booklist, September 1, 2008, page 48

Other books by the same author:
The Long Trial of Nolan Dugatti, 2008
Demon Theory, 2006
Bleed into Me, 2005
The Bird Is Gone, 2005
All the Beautiful Sinners, 2003

Other books you might like:
Alan Cheuse, *To Catch the Lightning*, 2008
April Christofferson, *Clinical Trial*, 2000
Louise Erdrich, *The Bingo Palace*, 1994
Charles Frazer, *Thirteen Moons*, 2006
Thomas King, *Truth and Bright Water*, 1999

802

JANE KAMENSKY , Co-Author
JILL LAPORE , Co-Author

Blindspot: By a Gentleman in Exile and a Lady in Disguise

(New York: Spiegel & Grau, 2008)

Story type: Romance; Amateur Detective
Subject(s): Artists and Art; American Colonies; Slavery

Major character(s): Stewart Jameson, Artist (painter), Detective—Amateur; Fanny "Francis Weston" Easton, Detective—Amateur, Apprentice; Ignatius Alexander, Slave (runaway), Doctor
Time period(s): 1760s (1764)
Locale(s): Scotland; Boston, Massachusetts

Summary: Set in colonial Boston before the Revolution, this novel looks at the relationship between painter Stewart Jameson, who has been chased by debtors from Scotland, and an orphan, Francis Weston, whom he takes on as an apprentice. Francis is eventually revealed as Fanny, the daughter of a prominent Boston family who would rather be in hiding. The pair takes on the investigation of the murder of an abolitionist with the assistance of one of Steward's old friends from Edinburgh, Dr. Ignatius Alexander, a former runaway slave. Period details dominate in this novel that offers an interesting look at racial attitudes in pre-Revolutionary America.

Where it's reviewed:
Kirkus Reviews, October 1, 2008, page 1038
Library Journal, September 1, 2008, page 118
New York Times Book Review, February 1, 2009, page 5
Publishers Weekly, August 4, 2008, page 41

Other books you might like:
Michael Gruber, *The Forgery of Venus*, 2008
Ward Just, *Forgetfulness*, 2006
Rosalind Laker, *The Golden Tulip*, 1991
John Sandford, *The Hanged Man's Song*, 2003
Susan Vreeland, *Life Studies*, 2005

803

LARRY KARP

The King of Ragtime

(Scottsdale: Poisoned Pen Press, 2008)

Story type: Mystery; Historical/Victorian America
Subject(s): Mystery and Detective Stories; Music and Musicians
Major character(s): Scott Joplin, Historical Figure, Musician; Nell Stark, Musician, Detective—Amateur; Martin Niederhoffer, Musician
Time period(s): 1910s (1916)
Locale(s): New York, New York

Summary: In this second period mystery featuring musician Scott Joplin, it is 1916, and Joplin has approached Irving Berlin to produce his musical play. Accompanied by his young musical student, Martin Niederhoffer, a bookkeeper in Berlin's office, Joplin visits Berlin's office only to discover a murder victim. Suspected of the crime, Joplin and Niederhoffer go into hiding, while Joplin's friend, Nell Stark, goes undercover in Berlin's office to solve the mystery and clear her friends.

Where it's reviewed:
Kirkus Reviews, August 1, 2008, page 782

Other books by the same author:
The Ragtime Kid, 2006
First Do No Harm, 2004
The Midnight Special, 2001
Scamming the Birdman, 2000

The Music Box Murders, 1999

Other books you might like:
Eileen Charbonneau, *Waltzing in Ragtime*, 1996
Tananarive Due, *Joplin's Ghost*, 2005
Oakley M. Hall, *Ambrose Bierce and the Death of Kings*, 2001
Daniel Lynch, *Yellow*, 1992
Robert Skinner, *The Wesley Farrell Series*, 1997-

804

STANLEY KELLI

Nox Dormienda

(Waterville, ME: Five Star, 2008)

Story type: Historical/Ancient Rome; Mystery
Series: Arcturus. Book 1
Subject(s): Mystery and Detective Stories; Roman Empire
Major character(s): Arcturus, Doctor; Agricola, Political Figure
Time period(s): 1st century (83 A.D.)
Locale(s): London, Roman Empire

Summary: Stanley debuts with a mystery set in Roman Britain involving Julius Alpinus Classicanus Favonianus, better known as Arcturus, a doctor of mixed Roman and Briton heritage who serves Britannia's governor, Agricola. In first-century London, Arcturus investigates the murder of a Syrian messenger from Roman emperor Domitian in a local temple. The author's research into the period is clearly on display in this promising debut.

Where it's reviewed:
Kirkus Reviews, May 15, 2008, page 521
Publishers Weekly, May 26, 2008, page 42

Other books you might like:
Ruth Downie, *Terra Incognita*, 2008
Jane Finnis, *Buried Too Deep*, 2008
John Maddox Roberts, *The SPQR Series*, 1990-
Steven Saylor, *The Roma Sub Rosa Series*, 1991-
David Wishart, *Parthian Shot*, 2004

805

LINDA KENNEY

Beacon on the Hill

(Marietta, GA: Harper House, 2008)

Story type: Historical/Americana
Subject(s): African Americans; Biography; Medicine
Major character(s): John A. Kenney, Historical Figure, Doctor; Booker T. Washington, Historical Figure, Political Figure
Time period(s): 20th century
Locale(s): United States

Summary: The novel provides a biographical portrait of historical figure John A. Kenney, the personal physician to Booker T. Washington and George Washington Carver. The son of a slave, Kenney traveled with Washington during his Goodwill Tours through the south, founded a hospital for blacks at Tuskegee, and when forced out of Alabama by the Ku Klux Klan, opened a new hospital in Newark, New Jersey. Written by Kenney's granddaughter, the novel dramatizes the challenges and tribulations of a black physician during the 20th century.

Other books you might like:
Beverly Clark, *Yesterday Is Gone*, 1997
Jeffrey Hudson, *A Case of Need*, 1993
John Irving, *A Son of the Circus*, 1994
Norman Rush, *Mortals*, 2003
Neil Shulman, *The Backyard Tribe*, 1994

806

KATHLEEN KENT

The Heretic's Daughter

(New York: Little, Brown, 2008)

Story type: Historical/Seventeenth Century
Subject(s): Family Relations; Witches and Witchcraft; Trials
Major character(s): Martha Carrier, Historical Figure, Housewife; Sarah Carrier, Historical Figure, Child
Time period(s): 17th century (1690s)
Locale(s): Andover, Massachusetts, American Colonies; Salem, Massachusetts, American Colonies

Summary: Based on the author's own family history, the novel, set during the Salem witch trials, treats the Carrier family from the perspective of ten-year-old Sarah, whose mother, Martha, is accused by her neighbors of witchcraft and steadfastly resists capitulating to the hysteria that engulfs her community. The young Sarah offers an eyewitness account of the famous witchcraft trials and the impact on a family caught up in the rush to judgment.

Where it's reviewed:
Booklist, August 1, 2008, page 35
Kirkus Reviews, July 15, 2008, page 715
Library Journal, July 1, 2008, page 61
Publishers Weekly, June 30, 2008, page 160

Other books you might like:
Shirley Barker, *Peace, My Daughters*, 1949
Megan Chance, *Susannah Morrow*, 2004
Maryse Conde, *I, Tituba, Black Witch of Salem*, 1992
Victoria Lincoln, *A Dangerous Innocence*, 1958
Susan Meissner, *The Shape of Mercy*, 2008

807

J. ROBERT KING

The Shadow of Reichenbach Falls

(New York: Forge, 2008)

Story type: Historical/Victorian; Mystery
Subject(s): Mystery and Detective Stories; Detection; Victorian Period
Major character(s): Thomas Carnaki, Student—College, Detective—Private; Sherlock Holmes, Detective—

Private, Amnesiac; James Moriarity, Criminal, Professor
Time period(s): 1890s (1891)
Locale(s): Switzerland

Summary: What could have happened at the Reichenbach Falls, the site of the famous mortal combat between Sherlock Holmes and his nemesis, Professor Moriarity? Arthur Conan Doyle brought Holmes back from certain death for more adventures. Here King offers a different scenario about what occurred at the Falls and afterwards. Holmes becomes linked with another young detective, Thomas Carnaki, and a young woman, related to Holmes adversary. Holmes is soon back on Moriaritys trail in this entertaining Holmesian pastiche.

Where it's reviewed:
Booklist, June 1, 2008, page 54
Kirkus Reviews, June 1, 2008, page 575
Publishers Weekly, May 5, 2008, page 47

Other books by the same author:
Le Morte d'Avalon, 2003
Lancelot du Lethe, 2001
Mad Merlin, 2000

Other books you might like:
Caleb Carr, *The Italian Secretary*, 2005
Michael Chabon, *The Final Solution*, 2004
Mitch Cullin, *A Slight Trick of the Mind*, 2005
Laurie R. King, *The Game*, 2004
Michael Kurland, *The Empress of India*, 2006

808

RACHEL KUSHNER

Telex from Cuba
(New York: Scribner, 2008)

Story type: Family Saga
Subject(s): Business Enterprises; Politics
Major character(s): K.C. Stites, Teenager; Everly Lederer; Rachel K, Dancer
Time period(s): 1950s
Locale(s): Cuba

Summary: Kushner's debut looks at pre-Castro Cuba from the perspective of two young people, K.C. Stites and Everly Lederer, who grow up in privilege among the American colonies of the United Fruit Company's sugar plantation and the Nicaro nickel mines. Their experiences with the growing unrest and revolution is paralleled with happenings in Havana surrounding burlesque dancer Rachel K who gets involved with Castro and his rebels. The novel offers a convincing portrait of the region and the period, as well as appearances by such historical figures as Fidel and Raul Castro, and Ernest Hemingway.

Where it's reviewed:
Booklist, April 15, 2008, page 35
Kirkus Reviews, May 15, 2008, page 512
New York Times Book Review, July 6, 2008, page 1
Publishers Weekly, March 17, 2008, page 43

Other books you might like:
Charles Fleming, *After Havana*, 2004

Oscar Hijuelos, *A Simple Habana Melody*, 2002
Stephen Hunter, *Havana*, 2003
Thomas Sanchez, *King Bongo*, 2003
Zoe Valdes, *I Gave You All I Had*, 1999

809

CLARE LANGLEY-HAWTHORNE

The Serpent and the Scorpion
(New York: Penguin Press, 2008)

Story type: Historical/Edwardian; Amateur Detective
Series: Ursula Marlow. Book 2
Subject(s): Mystery and Detective Stories; Gender Roles
Major character(s): Ursula Marlow, Heiress, Detective— Amateur; Lord Oliver Wrotham, Nobleman, Lawyer
Time period(s): 1910s (1911)
Locale(s): England; Egypt

Summary: In the follow-up to the author's *Consequences of Sin*, Edwardian heiress Ursula Marlow travels on a business trip to Egypt on behalf of the family's textile company. She investigates a new friend's death and a suspicious fire in one of her factories that results in the discovery of the body of a young woman killed before the fire started. Ursula tries to discover the connection. Meanwhile, her romance with Lord Oliver Wrotham is jeopardized when Ursula refuses to accept the expected subservient role of wife.

Where it's reviewed:
Kirkus Reviews, August 1, 2008, page 782
Publishers Weekly, August 11, 2008, page 32

Other books by the same author:
Consequences of Sin, 2007

Other books you might like:
John Boyne, *Crippen*, 2006
Marion Chesney, *Hasty Death*, 2004
Tracy Chevalier, *Falling Angels*, 2001
Rachael King, *The Sound of Butterflies*, 2007
Robin Paige, *Death in Hyde Park*, 2004

810

WARD LARSEN

Stealing Trinity
(Ipswich, MA: Oceanview, 2008)

Story type: Historical/World War II
Subject(s): World War II; Espionage
Major character(s): Michael Thatcher, Military Personnel (British officer); Alexander Braun, Spy; Lydia Cole Murray, Heiress
Time period(s): 1940s
Locale(s): New Mexico; Germany; Guam

Summary: Larsen's World War II thriller is set during the waning days of the war and concerns the attempt by the Nazis, led by spy Alexander Braun, to steal the secrets of the atomic bomb. Braun is pursued by British officer Michael Thatcher, joined by old flame Lydia Cole, in a chase that goes from the South Pacific to the site of the

Historical

Manhattan Project at Los Alamos, New Mexico.

Where it's reviewed:
Booklist, September 1, 2008, page 57
Library Journal, August 1, 2008, page 69
Publishers Weekly, August 18, 2008, page 41

Other books by the same author:
The Perfect Assassin, 2006

Other books you might like:
Millicent Dillon, *Harry Gold*, 2000
Joseph Kanon, *Los Alamos*, 1997
Peter Millar, *Stealing Thunder*, 1999
Richard Rayne, *The Devil's Wind*, 2005
Martin Cruz Smith, *Los Alamos*, 1985

811

JOHN LAWTON

Second Violin

(New York: Atlantic Monthly Press, 2008)

Story type: Historical/World War II; Mystery
Series: Inspector Troy. Book 6
Subject(s): Mystery and Detective Stories; World War II; Anti-Semitism
Major character(s): Frederick Troy, Detective—Police; Winston Churchill, Historical Figure, Political Figure
Time period(s): 1930s; 1940s
Locale(s): London, England; Vienna, Austria

Summary: The sixth installment of Lawton's Inspector Troy mystery series (although chronologically the earliest) is set against the backdrop of the major events leading up to World War II. Troy investigates the murder of London rabbis that becomes connected with other events involving Britain's entry into the war and the opening of the Battle of Britain. Atmospheric in its use of period details, the intrigue is balanced by a knowing sense of the period and its pressures.

Where it's reviewed:
Kirkus Reviews, September 1, 2008, page 909
Publishers Weekly, September 15, 2008, page 43

Other books by the same author:
A Little White Death, 2006
Flesh Wounds, 2005
Bluffing Mr. Churchill, 2004
Old Flames, 2003
Black Out, 1995

Other books you might like:
Ken Follett, *Hornet Flight*, 2002
Mark Gatiss, *Black Butterfly*, 2008
Joel N. Ross, *Double Cross Blind*, 2005
Daniel Silva, *The Unlikely Spy*, 1996
Sarah Waters, *The Night Watch*, 2006

812

DENNIS LEHANE

The Given Day

(New York: William Morrow, 2008)

Story type: Historical/Americana; Historical/World War I
Subject(s): Labor Conditions; City and Town Life; Crime and Criminals
Major character(s): Danny Coughlin, Police Officer; Luther Laurence, Criminal; Babe Ruth, Historical Figure, Sports Figure
Time period(s): 1910s
Locale(s): Boston, Massachusetts

Summary: Boston-based crime novelist Lehane ventures back in time to Boston during World War I and the police strike of 1919 in this richly-imagined ambitious historical novel. It connects the stories of two individuals on different sides of Boston's social unrest—police officer Danny Coughlin and black criminal Luther Laurence. Danny agrees to go undercover to infiltrate the Bolsheviks and anarchists who are recruiting the disaffected in Boston's slums. There he meets Luther and comes to sympathize with the plight of the laboring classes and their connections with the injustice afflicting the police force. The novel recreates both the period and place with skill, including appearances by a young Boston pitcher named Babe Ruth.

Where it's reviewed:
Booklist, August 1, 2008, page 5
Library Journal, August 1, 2008, page 69
Publishers Weekly, July 7, 2008, page 37

Other books by the same author:
Coronado, 2006
Shutter Island, 2003
Mystic River, 2001
Gone, Baby, Gone, 1998
Sacred, 1997

Other books you might like:
John Hart, *Down River*, 2007
Kathleen Kent, *The Heretic's Daughter*, 2008
David Liss, *The Whiskey Rebels*, 2008
Hannah Tinti, *The Good Thief*, 2008
David Wroblewski, *The Story of Edgar Sawtelle*, 2008

813

DAVID LISS

The Whiskey Rebels

(New York: Random House, 2008)

Story type: Historical/Americana; Historical/Post-American Revolution
Subject(s): Business; Suspense; Frontier and Pioneer Life
Major character(s): Ethan Saunders, Veteran, Spy (former); Joan Maycott, Widow(er); Alexander Hamilton, Historical Figure, Political Figure
Time period(s): 1790s
Locale(s): Pennsylvania; New York, New York

Summary: Liss offers a suspense novel set against the backdrop of post-Revolutionary War America and the financial panic of 1792. In two interlinked stories, Ethan Saunders, former captain and spy under George Washington, comes into conflict with Alexander Hamilton's attempt to establish a national bank and reorganize American society along modern capitalistic lines; while Joan Maycott, living in the western Pennsylvania frontier undergoes considerable challenges in her progression from frontierswoman to prosperous whiskey merchant. The novel offers a vivid portrait of early American life as well as such famous figures as Alexander Hamilton and Aaron Burr.

Where it's reviewed:
Booklist, September 1, 2008, page 5
Kirkus Reviews, September 1, 2008, page 910
Library Journal, August 1, 2008, page 69
Publishers Weekly, August 4, 2008, page 44

Other books by the same author:
The Ethical Assassin, 2006
A Spectacle of Corruption, 2004
The Coffee Trader, 2003
A Conspiracy of Paper, 2000

Other books you might like:
Calvin Baker, *Dominion*, 2006
Leland Baldwin, *The Delectable Country*, 1939
Jerome Charyn, *Johnny One-Eye*, 2008
William Dietrich, *The Rosetta Key*, 2008
James McBride, *The Song Not Yet Sung*, 2008

814

OWEN MADOC

Keeping Secrets

(Sutton, England: Severn House, 2008)

Story type: Historical/Depression Era
Subject(s): Small Town Life; Friendship; Family Relations
Major character(s): Gillian Finch, Friend (of Dorothy); Dorothy Prosser, Friend (of Gillian); Ronnie Knox, Businessman
Time period(s): 1930s
Locale(s): Wales

Summary: Set in a tight-knit, small Welsh community during the 1930s, this novel describes the challenges to the friendship of cousins Gillian Finch and Dorothy Prosser who are first separated by a family dispute and then fall for the same man, Ronnie Knox. Family secrets and the conservative customs of the times present obstacles for both girls' search for happiness.

Where it's reviewed:
Booklist, September 1, 2008, page 48

Other books by the same author:
Mothers and Daughters, 2007
Take My Child, 2006
No Child of Mine, 2004
Bad to the Bone, 2003
By Lies Betrayed, 2001

Other books you might like:
Maeve Binchy, *Light a Penny Candle*, 1983
Elaine Crowley, *The Ways of Women*, 1993
Annabel Davis-Goff, *This Cold Country*, 2002
Tom Phelan, *In the Season of Daisies*, 1996
Niall Williams, *The Fall of Light*, 2002

815

KAREN MAITLAND

Company of Liars

(New York: Delacorte, 2008)

Story type: Historical/Medieval
Subject(s): Middle Ages; Plague; Travel
Major character(s): Camelot, Peddler; Zophiel, Magician, Con Man; Rodrigo, Musician
Time period(s): 14th century (1348)
Locale(s): England

Summary: In this first novel, Maitland offers an alternative *Canterbury Tales*. In 1348 as the crops fail in England and plague sweeps the country, a motley group travels across the south of England in search of refuge. Each has a tale to tell, including the half-blind, disfigured peddler, Camelot; magician and con man Zophiel; and Venetian musician Rodrigo. Their stories provide a microcosmic portrait of life during the 14th century.

Where it's reviewed:
Booklist, September 1, 2008, page 41
Kirkus Reviews, September 1, 2008, page 910
Library Journal, August 1, 2008, page 70
Publishers Weekly, August 25, 2008, page 49

Other books you might like:
Bernard Cornwell, *The Archer's Tale*, 2001
P.C. Doherty, *The Death of a King*, 1985
Ken Follett, *World Without End*, 2007
Susanna Gregory, *A Plague on Both Your Houses*, 1998
Judith Merkle Riley, *A Vision of Light*, 1989

816

VALERO MANFREDI

The Lost Army

(London: Macmillan, 2008)

Story type: Action/Adventure
Subject(s): Ancient History; War; Military Life
Major character(s): Xenophon, Historical Figure, Military Personnel; Cyrus the Younger, Historical Figure, Royalty; Artaxerxes II, Historical Figure, Royalty
Time period(s): 4th century B.C.
Locale(s): Syria; Persia

Summary: Set during the 4th century B.C., the novel describes the adventures of an army of Greek mercenaries led by the general Xenophon, employed by Cyrus the Younger to help him seize the throne of Persia from his brother Artaxerxes II. Described from the perspective of the women who accompanied the army on its campaign,

Historical

the novel provides a vivid recreation of one of the most celebrated military marches in history.

Other books by the same author:
Pharoah, 2008
The Last Legion, 2005
Tyrant, 2005
Spartan, 2003
Alexander, 2001

Other books you might like:
Elizabeth Cook, *Achilles*, 2002
Priscilla Galloway, *The Courtesan's Daughter*, 2002
Phillip Parotti, *The Greek Generals Talk*, 1982
Sa Shan, *Alexander and Alestria*, 2008
Barry Unsworth, *The Songs of Kings*, 2003

817

BENJAMIN MARKOVITS

A Quiet Adjustment

(New York: W.W. Norton, 2008)

Story type: Historical/Regency
Subject(s): Marriage; Authors and Writers
Major character(s): Annabella Milbanke, Historical Figure, Spouse (of Byron); George Gordon Byron, Historical Figure, Writer; Augusta Leigh, Historical Figure
Time period(s): 19th century
Locale(s): England

Summary: Markovits continues his fictional study of the life of Romantic poet Byron with a focus on his wife, Annabella Milbanke. Courted by the famous author, the 19-year-old beauty becomes his wife despite his philandering reputation. Once married, Annabella meets Augusta Leigh, Byron's half sister, and learns of her incestuous relationship with Byron. Eventually, the couple separates, and Annabella devotes her efforts to saving Augusta from ruin and revenging herself on her famous husband.

Where it's reviewed:
Booklist, August 1, 2008, page 37
Kirkus Reviews, July 15, 2008, page 718
Publishers Weekly, June 16, 2008, page 28

Other books by the same author:
Imposture, 2007
Fathers and Daughters, 2005
The Syme Papers, 2004
Either Side of Winter, 2003

Other books you might like:
Frederico Andahazi, *The Merciful Women*, 2000
John Crowley, *Lord Byron's Novel*, 2005
Lucille Iremonger, *My Sister, My Love*, 1981
Jude Morgan, *Passion*, 2005
Frederic Prokosch, *The Missolanghi Manuscript*, 1968

818

COLLEEN MCCULLOUGH

The Independence of Miss Mary Bennet

(New York: Simon & Schuster, 2009)

Story type: Historical/Victorian
Subject(s): Marriage; Family Life; Women
Major character(s): Mary Bennet, Gentlewoman; Elizabeth Bennet, Spouse (of Darcy); Fitzwilliam Darcy, Gentleman, Spouse (of Elizabeth)
Time period(s): 1830s
Locale(s): England

Summary: McCullough gives shy, bookish Mary Bennet, Elizabeth's "sensible" sister, her say (and a last word) in this extension of Jane Austen's classic, *Pride and Prejudice*. Twenty years after Austen's novel, Darcy and Elizabeth are trapped in a loveless marriage, and the death of Mrs. Bennet frees Mary to pursue her passion for women's rights and social justice. Setting off to document the plight of England's poor, Mary has an amazing series of adventures, as Darcy tries to keep his in-law's activities quiet to protect his political aspirations.

Where it's reviewed:
Kirkus Reviews, December 1, 2008, page 1222
Publishers Weekly, October 27, 2008, page 32

Other books by the same author:
Anthony and Cleopatra, 2007
The Touch, 2003
The October Horse, 2002
Morgan's Run, 2000
The Ladies of Missalonghi, 1987

Other books you might like:
Elizabeth Ashton, *Mr. Darcy's Daughters*, 2003
Janet Aylmer, *Darcy's Story*, 2006
Julia Barrett, *The Third Sister*, 1996
Amanda Elyot, *By a Lady*, 2006
Jude Morgan, *Indiscretion*, 2006

819

ERIN MCGRAW

The Seamstress of Hollywood Boulevard

(Boston: Houghton Mifflin, 2008)

Story type: Historical/Depression Era; Historical/Roaring Twenties
Subject(s): Movie Industry; Sewing
Major character(s): Nell Plat, Seamstress
Time period(s): 20th century
Locale(s): Kansas; Hollywood, California

Summary: Based on the actual life of the author's grandmother, this novel details the arrival in Los Angeles by Kansan Nell Plat in 1901. She sets up shop as a seamstress for the budding motion picture industry, and she is soon outfitting such Jazz Age icons as the It girl herself, Clara Bow. Nell's career offers a convincing portrait of the early days of the movies from the perspective of one of its down-to-earth laborers.

Where it's reviewed:
Kirkus Reviews, June 1, 2008, page 568
Library Journal, July 1, 2008, page 63
Publishers Weekly, May 12, 2008, page 31

Other books by the same author:
The Good Life, 2006
The Baby Tree, 2002
Lies of the Saints, 1996
Bodies at Sea, 1989

Other books you might like:
Isabel Allende, *Portrait in Sepia*, 2001
Adele Geras, *Facing the Light*, 2004
Larry McMurtry, *Somebody's Darling*, 2002
Jane Smiley, *Ten Days in the Hills*, 2007
Stuart Woods, *The Prince of Beverly Hills*, 2004

820

ELISABETH MCNEILL

Blood Royal

(Sutton, England: Severn House, 2008)

Story type: Historical/Tudor Period
Subject(s): Kings, Queens, Rulers, etc.; Biography
Major character(s): Mary Queen of Scots, Historical Figure, Ruler; Nathan, Peddler
Time period(s): 16th century
Locale(s): Scotland; England; France

Summary: McNeill chronicles the life of Mary Queen of Scots in flashbacks from her execution in 1587 through scenes from her birth, her childhood in France, and her ascendance to the throne of Scotland. Mary's story is intertwined with a parallel fictional story of a peddler named Nathan whose paths crosses the Queen's.

Where it's reviewed:
Booklist, November 1, 2008, page 22

Other books by the same author:
Flodden Field, 2007
The Storm, 2006
Turn of the Tide, 2006
The Last Cocktail Party, 2002
A Bombay Affair, 2000

Other books you might like:
Margaret George, *Mary Queen of Scotland and the Isles*, 1992
Philippa Gregory, *The Other Queen*, 2008
Jean Vlachos Plaidy, *The Captive Queen of the Scots*, 1970
Reay Tannahill, *Fatal Majesty*, 1999
Jan Westcott, *The Tower and the Dream*, 1974

821

LAUREL MEANS

The Long Journey Home

(Chicago: Academy Chicago Publishers, 2008)

Story type: Historical/Post-American Civil War
Subject(s): Small Town Life; Frontier and Pioneer Life
Major character(s): Henry Morton, Veteran (Civil War), Widow(er); Agnes Marie Guyette, Spouse (of Henry)
Time period(s): 1860s
Locale(s): Minnesota

Summary: Set in the aftermath of the Civil War, this melodramatic tale goes from disaster to disaster as Henry Morton returns home to Minnesota from the war only to find his wife dead and his farm in ruin. Striking out for a new life, he unwisely weds a barmaid, and their attempt to settle down goes from bad to worse when his bride walks into a lake and drowns her daughter in grief before being rescued by a passing wagon train, and Henry is charged with her murder.

Where it's reviewed:
Kirkus Reviews, July 1, 2008, page 670

Other books you might like:
David Anthony Durham, *Walk through Darkness*, 2002
Lenore Hart, *Becky*, 2008
Annie Proulx, *Close Range*, 1999
John Sandford, *Winter Prey*, 1993
Stephen Wright, *The Amalgamation Polka*, 2006

822

ROSE MELIKAN

The Blackstone Key

(New York: Simon & Schuster, 2008)

Story type: Historical/Georgian; Espionage
Series: Mary Finch. Book 1
Subject(s): Mystery and Detective Stories; Espionage
Major character(s): Mary Finch, Orphan, Heir; Captain Robert Holland, Military Personnel
Time period(s): 1790s (1795)
Locale(s): Suffolk, England

Summary: In this espionage mystery set in England in 1795, teacher Mary Finch visits her previously estranged uncle on his Suffolk estate. When he dies, leaving Mary his heir, she sets out to decode mysterious papers found in her uncle's library with the help of army officer Robert Holland. The key to the code is Blackstone's Commentaries on the Laws of England, and what is revealed puts Mary and Holland at the center of a treasonous plot. This is the first volume of an intended trilogy.

Where it's reviewed:
Booklist, July 1, 2008, page 41
Publishers Weekly, June 23, 2008, page 37

Other books you might like:
Julia Barrett, *Presumption*, 1993
Stephanie Barron, *The Jane Austen Mystery Series*, 1997-

Benjamin Markavits, *A Quiet Adjustment*, 2008
Jude Morgan, *Passion*, 2005
Sean Russell, *Under Enemy Colors*, 2007

823

KIRSTEN MENGER-ANDERSON

Doctor Olaf van Schuler's Brain

(Chapel Hill, NC: Algonquin Books, 2008)

Story type: Family Saga
Subject(s): Medicine; City and Town Life; Family Relations
Major character(s): Olaf van Schuler, Doctor; Elizabeth Steenwycks, Doctor; Stuart Steenwycks, Doctor
Time period(s): Multiple Time Periods (17th-20th centuries)
Locale(s): New York, New York

Summary: This intriguing debut offers chapters in the history of several generations of doctors in New York City beginning with Dr. Olaf van Schuler who emigrated from Holland to New Amsterdam in 1664 to continue his obsession with dissecting animal brains. Each subsequent generation following, including Dr. Elizabeth Steenwycks and her plastic surgeon father Dr. Stuart Steenwycks, display their medical obsessions against the backdrop of changing times and customs in New York City.

Where it's reviewed:
Booklist, September 1, 2008, page 4
Kirkus Reviews, September 1, 2008, page 911
New York Times Book Review, November 30, 2008, page 13
Publishers Weekly, June 9, 2008, page 27

Other books you might like:
Carrie Brown, *The Hatbox Baby*, 2000
Patricia Duncker, *The Doctor*, 2000
Nicholas Griffin, *The House of Sight and Shadow*, 2001
Michael Pye, *The Drowning Room*, 1995
Beverly Swerling, *City of Dreams*, 2001

824

SIMON MONTEFIORE

Sashenka

(New York: Simon & Schuster, 2008)

Story type: Historical/Russian Revolution
Subject(s): Jews; Russians; Communism
Major character(s): Sashenka Zeitlin, Revolutionary; Katinka Vinsky, Historian
Time period(s): 20th century (1916-1994)
Locale(s): Russia

Summary: Historian Montefiore offers a fictionalized treatment of modern Russian history from the Revolution through the Stalinist years from the perspective of Sashenka Zeitlin, a Russian Jew who becomes an ardent revolutionary in 1916. In 1939, however, she falls from grace and is forced to choose between her lover, her family, and the communist cause. Attempting to answer all of the questions surrounding Sashenka's choices and their consequences is historian Katinka Vinsky in 1994 researching what really happened to Sashenka and her family.

Where it's reviewed:
Booklist, November 1, 2008, page 25
Kirkus Reviews, October 1, 2008, page 1032
Library Journal, November 1, 2008, page 58
Publishers Weekly, September 15, 2008, page 42

Other books by the same author:
My Affair with Stalin, 1997

Other books you might like:
Vassilly Aksyonov, *Generations of Winter*, 1994
Robert Alexander, *The Kitchen Boy*, 2003
Travis Holland, *The Archivist's Story*, 2007
Robert Littell, *The Revolutionist*, 1988
Anatoli Rybakov, *Fear*, 1992

825

MICHELLE MORAN

The Heretic Queen

(New York: Crown, 2008)

Story type: Historical/Ancient Egypt
Subject(s): Kings, Queens, Rulers, etc.; Egyptian Religion; Ancient History
Major character(s): Nefertari, Royalty, Historical Figure; Seti I, Historical Figure, Ruler; Ramesses II, Historical Figure, Ruler
Time period(s): 13th century B.C.
Locale(s): Thebes, Egypt

Summary: Moran continues her account of court life in ancient Egypt, following the career of Princess Nefertari, the niece of the infamous Queen Nefertiti. Raised in the household of Pharaoh Seti I, Nefertari falls in love with his heir, Ramesses II. They marry, and the novel provides a fascinating insider's look at Egyptian court intrigue as well as the events leading up to the release of the Hebrews from slavery and the various internal and external threats to Egyptian rule during the 19th dynasty.

Where it's reviewed:
Booklist, August 1, 2008, page 35
Library Journal, August 1, 2008, page 71
Publishers Weekly, July 7, 2008, page 38

Other books by the same author:
Nefertiti, 2007

Other books you might like:
Gillian Bradshaw, *Cleopatra's Heir*, 2002
Allen Drury, *Return to Thebes*, 1977
Pauline Gedge, *House of Illusions*, 1987
Christian Jacq, *The Lady of Abu Simbel*, 1998
Judith Tarr, *Lord of the Two Lands*, 1993

826

TONI MORRISON

A Mercy

(New York: Knopf, 2008)

Story type: Historical/Seventeenth Century
Subject(s): American Colonies; African Americans;
Slavery
Major character(s): Florens, Slave; Jacob Vaark, Plantation
Owner; Rebekka Vaark, Spouse (of Jacob)
Time period(s): 17th century (1690)
Locale(s): Maryland, American Colonies

Summary: Morrison returns to the impact of slavery previously treated so brilliantly in *Beloved* in this thematic prequel set in the American Colonies in 1690. Florens has been sold by her Maryland master to northern farmer Jacob Vaark. His relationship with his wife Rebekka is detailed as well as the other damaged lives they collect, including a Native American and a mixed-race woman, who collectively form a community of sorts representing the various bitter legacies of slavery and gender oppression in the New World.

Where it's reviewed:
Booklist, September 1, 2008, page 5
Kirkus Reviews, September 1, 2008, page 912
Library Journal, October 15, 2008, page 58
New York Times Book Review, November 30, 2008,
page 1
Publishers Weekly, September 15, 2008, page 42

Other books by the same author:
Love, 2003
Paradise, 1998
Jazz, 1992
Beloved, 1987
Song of Solomon, 1977

Other books you might like:
David Anthony Durham, *Walk through Darkness*, 2002
James McBride, *Song Yet Sung*, 2008
Alice Randall, *The Wind Done Gone*, 2001
Lalita Tademy, *Cane River*, 2001
Michael C. White, *Soul Catcher*, 2007

827

WILLIE NELSON
MICHAEL BLAKELY , Co-Author

A Tale Out of Luck

(New York: Center Street, 2008)

Story type: Historical/American West
Subject(s): Small Town Life; Indians of North America
Major character(s): Hank Tomlinson, Rancher
Time period(s): 19th century
Locale(s): Texas

Summary: Country music icon Nelson and veteran western novelist Blakely team up to produce this western tale in which a murdered rustler outside of Luck, Texas, threatens to provoke an Indian uprising. Rancher Hank

Tomlinson, a former Texas Ranger, is reminded by the circumstances surrounding the killing of others he encountered during his Ranger days, and he sets out to solve the mystery of the death and its possible connection with the past.

Where it's reviewed:
Kirkus Reviews, July 1, 2008, page 670
Library Journal, September 1, 2008, page 120
Publishers Weekly, June 9, 2008, page 23

Other books you might like:
Charles Brashear, *Killing Cynthia Ann*, 1999
Max Crawford, *Lords of the Plain*, 1985
E.L. Doctorow, *Welcome to Hard Times*, 1975
Elmer Kelton, *The Way of the Coyote*, 2001
Larry McMurtry, *Dead Man's Walk*, 1995

828

KATHERINE NEVILLE

The Fire

(New York: Ballantine Books, 2008)

Story type: Historical/Fantasy
Subject(s): Games; Conspiracies
Major character(s): Alexandra Solarin, Sports Figure
(chess master); Charlemagne, Historical Figure,
Royalty; Lord Byron, Historical Figure, Writer
Time period(s): 19th century; 20th century
Locale(s): Colorado; Europe

Summary: In the long anticipated sequal to Neville's debut, *The Eight,* Alexandra Solarin, child chess prodigy, returns to search for the legendary chess set, the Montglane Service, that holds the key to immortality. Her search in the present is juxtaposed with action in the past that involves such historical figures as Charlemagne, Isaac Newton, Lord Byron, and Napoleon. Brilliantly researched with authentic historical details, fans of *The Eight* will not be disappointed by this fantasy thriller.

Where it's reviewed:
Booklist, September 1, 2008, page 53
Kirkus Reviews, September 1, 2008, page 912
Library Journal, September 1, 2008, page 120
Publishers Weekly, August 4, 2008, page 255

Other books by the same author:
The Magic Circle, 1998
A Calculated Risk, 1992
The Eight, 1988

Other books you might like:
Amy Bloom, *Away*, 2007
Stephen King, *The Talisman*, 1984
Sarah Micklem, *Firethorn*, 2004
Christopher Pike, *Alosha*, 2004
Kira Salak, *The White Mary*, 2008

Historical

829

CHARLES O'BRIEN

Assassin's Rage

(Sutton, England: Severn House, 2008)

Story type: Historical/French Revolution; Mystery
Series: French Revolution. Book 7
Subject(s): Mystery and Detective Stories
Major character(s): Anne Cartier, Teacher, Detective—
Amateur; Paul de Saint-Martin, Spouse (of Anne),
Detective—Police
Time period(s): 1780s (1788)
Locale(s): Paris, France

Summary: Amateur sleuth Anne Cartier and her husband,
police detective Paul de Saint-Martin attempt to inden-
tify the person who has been inciting riots that caused
the assassination of two of Paris' most important
officials. Set expertly against a background of the actual
events of the Revolution, OBrien offers a thrilling tour
of Revolutionary-era France.

Where it's reviewed:
Booklist, May 1, 2008, page 17
Kirkus Reviews, June 15, 2008, page 625
Publishers Weekly, June 16, 2008, page 36

Other books by the same author:
Cruel Choices, 2007
Fatal Carnival, 2006
Lethal Beauty, 2005
Noble Blood, 2004
Black Gold, 2002

Other books you might like:
T.F. Banks, *The Thief-Taker*, 2001
Stephanie Barron, *The Jane Austen Series*, 1996-
Kathryn Davis, *Versailles*, 2002
Carolly Erickson, *The Hidden Diary of Marie
Antoinette*, 2005
Rosemary Stevens, *The Beau Brummel Series*, 2000-

830

SHARON KAY PENMAN

Devil's Brood

(New York: G.P. Putnam's Sons, 2008)

Story type: Historical/Medieval
Series: Henry II and Eleanor of Aquitaine Trilogy. Book
3
Subject(s): Middle Ages; Kings, Queens, Rulers, etc.;
Family Relations
Major character(s): Henry II, Historical Figure, Ruler;
Eleanor of Aquitaine, Historical Figure, Royalty
Time period(s): 12th century
Locale(s): England

Summary: Penman brings to a conclusion her trilogy on
England in the 12th century and the reign of King Henry
II and Eleanor of Aquitaine. Opening in 1192, the novel
offers an insider's view of conflict within the royal family as Henry must contend with the backbiting and envy
of his ambitious three eldest sons who join with their
mother in an alliance with their father's bitterest enemy,
King Louis of France. Complex both in its depiction of
the politics of the period and the psychology of the royals, this is a brilliant historical dramatization.

Where it's reviewed:
Booklist, August 1, 2008, page 5
Library Journal, September 15, 2008, page 46

Other books by the same author:
Time and Chance, 2002
The Queen's Man, 1996
The Reckoning, 1991
Falls the Shadow, 1988
Here Be Dragons, 1985

Other books you might like:
Margaret Bell, *Duchess of Aquitaine*, 2006
Judith Koll Healey, *The Canterbury Papers*, 2004
Ellen Jones, *Beloved Enemy*, 1994
Pamela Kaufman, *The Book of Eleanor*, 2002
Jean Plaidy, *The Plantagenet Prelude*, 1980

831

ARTURO PEREZ-REVERTE

The King's Gold

(New York: G.P. Putnam's Sons, 2008)

Story type: Historical/Seventeenth Century; Adventure
Series: Captain Alatriste. Book 4
Subject(s): Adventure and Adventurers
Major character(s): Diego Alatriste y Tenorio, Veteran,
Military Personnel (captain); Inigo Balboa, Ward,
Teenager; Gualterio Malatesta, Veteran, Military
Personnel
Locale(s): Seville, Spain

Summary: In the fourth outing in the author's rousing
Captain Alatriste series, the down-on-his-luck soldier of
fortune and his young ward, Inigo Balboa, are asked to
recruit a dozen swordsmen to intercept a shipment of
contraband gold returning from the West Indies. The
Spanish Crown hangs in the balance, and Alatriste winds
up in a rematch with his old adversary, Gualterio
Malatesta. Perez-Reverte delivers a swashbuckling tale
anchored by convincing period detail.

Where it's reviewed:
Booklist, August 1, 2008, page 7
Kirkus Reviews, July 1, 2008, page 671
Publishers Weekly, June 9, 2008, page 32

Other books by the same author:
The Painter of Battles, 2008
The Sun over Breda, 2007
Purity of Blood, 2006
Captain Alatriste, 2005
The Queen of the South, 2004

Other books you might like:
Francoise d'Aubigne Chandernagor, *The King's Way*,
1984
Nicholas Griffin, *The House of Sight and Shadow*, 2001
Andrew Miller, *Ingenious Pain*, 1997

Jean-Christophe Rufin, *The Abyssinian*, 1999
Wilbur Smith, *Birds of Prey*, 1997

832

CAROLINE PETIT

Deep Night

(New York: Soho, 2009)

Story type: Adventure; Espionage
Subject(s): China; War; Espionage
Major character(s): Leah Kolbe, Fiance(e) (of Jonathan); Jonathan Hawatyne, Fiance(e) (of Leah)
Time period(s): 1930s (1937)
Locale(s): Hong Kong; Macau, China

Summary: Set during the second Sino-Japanese War in 1937, this sequel to Petit's *The Fat Man's Daughter* has fiances Jonathan Hawatyne and Leah Kolbe in Hong Kong as the war begins. Jonathan heads to the front, and Leah, after Hong Kong surrenders, escapes by boat to Macau where she begins work for the British spying on the Japanese. This is a colorful espionage thriller with authentic period details.

Where it's reviewed:
Booklist, November 15, 2008, page 20
Library Journal, December 1, 2008, page 118
Publishers Weekly, October 6, 2008, page 36

Other books by the same author:
The Fat Man's Daughter, 2005

Other books you might like:
Jicai Feng, *The Three-Inch Golden Lotus*, 1994
Lisa Huang Fleischman, *Dream of the Walled City*, 2000
Janice Y.K. Lee, *The Piano Teacher*, 2009
Leslie Li, *Bittersweet*, 1992
Ruthanne Lum McCunn, *God of Luck*, 2007

833

JUSTINE PICARDIE

Daphne

(New York: Bloomsbury, 2008)

Story type: Romantic Suspense
Subject(s): Biography; Authors and Writers
Major character(s): Daphne du Maurier, Historical Figure, Writer; John Alexander Symington, Historical Figure, Scholar
Time period(s): 1950s; 1960s (1957-1960)
Locale(s): England

Summary: This intriguing novel animates the life of popular romantic suspense author Daphne du Maurier. Set when du Mauier is in her 50s, the novel interweaves details of her past life with her current obsession: the lives of the Brontes, particularly the scapegrace son, Branwell. Researching his biography, du Maurier gets involved with a Bronte scholar, J.A. Symington. Du Maurier's life also becomes the obsession of a nameless researcher in the present who tries to draw some conclu-

sions that link du Maurier and the Brontes.

Where it's reviewed:
Booklist, July 1, 2008, page 34
Kirkus Reviews, June 15, 2008, page 618
Library Journal, May 15, 2008, page 93
Publishers Weekly, April 7, 2008, page 38

Other books by the same author:
Wish I May, 2004

Other books you might like:
Lynne Reid Banks, *Path to the Silent Country*, 1977
Brunonia Barry, *The Lace Reader*, 2008
Sebastian Barry, *The Secret Scripture*, 2008
Douglas A. Martin, *Branwell*, 2006
Laura Joh Rowland, *The Secret Adventures of Charlotte Bronte*, 2008

834

JILL PITKEATHLEY

Cassandra and Jane

(New York: Harper, 2008)

Story type: Historical/Regency; Historical/Georgian
Subject(s): Authors and Writers; Biography; Sisters
Major character(s): Jane Austen, Historical Figure, Writer; Cassandra Austen, Historical Figure
Time period(s): 19th century
Locale(s): Hampshire, England

Summary: House of Lords peer Pitkeathley offers a biographical portrait of writer Jane Austen from the perspective of her beloved sister Cassandra who paints a portrait of their family life and her sister's adventures in both love and art. True to the biographical facts, the novel is particularly authentic in rendering the customs of life during the Regency period.

Where it's reviewed:
Booklist, September 15, 2008, page 24
Library Journal, September 15, 2008, page 47
Publishers Weekly, July 28, 2008, page 53

Other books you might like:
Amanda Elyot, *By a Lady*, 2006
Syrie James, *The Lost Memoirs of Jane Austen*, 2007
Nancy Moser, *Just Jane*, 2007
Sally Smith O'Rourke, *The Man Who Loved Jane Austen*, 2006
Barbara Ker Wilson, *Antipodes Jane*, 1985

835

CHARLES F. PRICE

Nor the Battle to the Strong

(Savannah: Frederik C. Beil, 2008)

Story type: Historical/American Revolution; Military
Subject(s): Revolutionary War; Military Life; Biography
Major character(s): Nathanael Greene, Historical Figure,

Military Personnel; James Johnson, Military Personnel

Time period(s): 1780s (1781)
Locale(s): South Carolina; Virginia

Summary: Price treats the American Revolution in the southern colonies from two perspectives: General Nathanael Greene, commander of the Southern Continental Army, and foot soldier James Johnson. Greene is charged with dislodging British forces in South Carolina as Johnson is involved in Virginia with the maneuvering of Lafayette's forces against the British army led by Cornwallis. Johnson eventually travels south in time to join Greene's troops at the Battle of Eutaw Springs, one of the bloodiest in the Revolution.

Other books by the same author:
The Cock's Spur, 2000
Freedom's Altar, 1999
Hiwassee, 1996

Other books you might like:
Gwen Bristow, *Celia Garth*, 1959
Jimmy Carter, *The Hornet's Nest*, 2003
Robert Morgan, *Brave Enemies*, 2003
Shirley Seifert, *Let My Name Stand Fair*, 1957
Jeff Shaara, *The Glorious Cause*, 2002

836

ROBERT J. RANDISI

Hey There (You with the Gun in Your Hand)

(New York: St. Martin's Minotaur, 2009)

Story type: Mystery; Amateur Detective
Series: Rat Pack Mystery. Book 3
Subject(s): Mystery and Detective Stories; Movie Industry
Major character(s): Eddie Gianelli, Detective—Amateur; Jerry Epstein, Organized Crime Figure; Sammy Davis Jr., Historical Figure, Entertainer
Time period(s): 1960s (1961)
Locale(s): Las Vegas, Nevada; Reno, Nevada; Tahoe, Nevada

Summary: In this third Rat Pack mystery, it's 1961, and Vegas pit boss Eddie Gianelli and gunman Jerry Epstein are called upon to save Sammy Davis Jr.'s reputation. Sammy is being blackmailed over an embarrassing photo. Gianelli and Epstein must contend with the blackmailers as well as federal agents assigned to protect the reputation of the new president, John F. Kennedy.

Where it's reviewed:
Booklist, November 15, 2008, page 20
Kirkus Reviews, October 1, 2008, page 1040

Other books by the same author:
Luck Be a Lady, Don't Die, 2007
The Picasso Flop, 2007
Everybody Kills Somebody Sometimes, 2006
Arch Angels, 2004
The Masks of Auntie Laveau, 2002

Other books you might like:
David Baldacci, *Stone Cold*, 2007

Stephen Hunter, *Havana*, 2003
Steve Lopez, *In the Clear*, 2002
Michael McGarrity, *The Big Gamble*, 2002
Harold Robbins, *Sin City*, 2002

837

RON RASH

Serena

(New York: Ecco, 2008)

Story type: Historical/Roaring Twenties
Subject(s): Business Enterprises; Lumber Industry; Marriage
Major character(s): George Pemberton, Spouse (of Serena); Serena Pemberton, Spouse (of George)
Time period(s): 1920s (1929)
Locale(s): North Carolina

Summary: Set during the 1920s, the novel traces the experiences of newlyweds George and Serena Pemberton who travel from Boston into the North Carolina mountains to create a timber business. Serena masters the wilderness but must contend with challenges to her marriage. George has fathered an illegitimate child, and when Serena learns that she cannot have children, her jealousy and vengeance lead to destruction. Very atmospheric, the novel sets this domestic story against a richly described period and regional background.

Where it's reviewed:
Booklist, September 1, 2008, page 48
Kirkus Reviews, August 15, 2008, page 840
Library Journal, June 1, 2008, page 93
Publishers Weekly, May 19, 2008, page 30

Other books by the same author:
The World Made Straight, 2006
Saints at the River, 2004
One Foot in Eden, 2002
Raising the Dead, 2002
Among the Believers, 2000

Other books you might like:
Aaron Roy Evans, *Bloodroot*, 2000
Tim Gautreaux, *The Clearing*, 2003
Jim Harrison, *True North*, 2004
Ken Kesey, *Sometimes a Great Notion*, 1964
Robert Morgan, *This Rock*, 2001

838

JAMES REESE

The Dracula Dossier

(New York: William Morrow, 2008)

Story type: Historical/Victorian; Vampire Story
Subject(s): Vampires; Authors and Writers
Major character(s): Bram Stoker, Historical Figure, Writer; William Butler Yeats, Historical Figure, Writer; Lady Jane Wilde, Historical Figure
Time period(s): 1880s (1888)

Locale(s): London, England

Summary: Set in 1888, a decade before Bram Stoker published *Dracula*, this novel purports to be the journal kept by Stoker describing his adventures that inspired his creation. Attending an initiation ceremony of the Order of the Golden Dawn, at the behest of Lady Jane Wilde (Oscar's mother) and poet William Butler Yeats, Stoker gets involved with Francis Tumblety, a medical supply salesman, who is possessed by an evil Egyptian god and sets out to ritually slaughter Whitechapel prostitutes. Stoker tries to stop him, picking up the details that he will later work into his famous horror novel.

Where it's reviewed:
Booklist, September 15, 2008, page 24
Kirkus Reviews, September 1, 2008, page 913
Library Journal, September 15, 2008, page 47
Publishers Weekly, August 18, 2008, page 38

Other books by the same author:
The Witchery, 2006
The Book of Spirits, 2003
The Book of Shadows, 2002

Other books you might like:
Gyles Brandreth, *Oscar Wilde and a Game Called Murder*, 2008
Richard Gordon, *Jack the Ripper*, 1980
Edward B. Hanna, *The Whitechapel Horrors*, 1993
Tom Holland, *Slave of My Thirst*, 1999
Ann Victoria Roberts, *Moon Rising*, 2001

839

JOHN MADDOX ROBERTS

Oracle of the Dead
(New York: St. Martin's Minotaur, 2008)

Story type: Historical/Ancient Rome; Amateur Detective
Series: SPQR Roman Mysteries. XII
Subject(s): Mystery and Detective Stories; Roman Empire
Major character(s): Decius Caecilius Metellus, Detective—Amateur
Time period(s): 1st century B.C.
Locale(s): Roman Empire

Summary: As civil war threatens between the armies of Julius Caesar and Pompey, in this installment of Roberts's accomplished mystery series, Decius Caecilius Metellus is traveling as a praetor peregrinus, hearing cases outside of Rome. In a southern Italian town, when the hairless body of a priest of Apollo is found outside the Oracle of the Dead, Metellus takes up the investigation which leads to a conspiracy with wide-ranging implications.

Where it's reviewed:
Kirkus Reviews, October 15, 2008, page 1095
Publishers Weekly, October 13, 2008, page 40

Other books by the same author:
Under Vesuvius, 2007
A Point of Law, 2006
The Princess and the Pirates, 2005
The River God's Vengeance, 2004
The Tribune's Curse, 2003

Other books you might like:
Lindsey Davis, *The Marcus Didius Falco Series*, 1989-
Conn Iggulden, *Emperor: The Gates of Rome*, 2002
Steven Saylor, *The Roma Sub Rosa Series*, 1991-
Marilyn Todd, *Second Act*, 2003
David Wishart, *In at the Death*, 2007

840

PHILIP ROTH

Indignation
(Boston: Houghton Mifflin, 2008)

Story type: Historical/Korean War; Coming-of-Age
Subject(s): Universities and Colleges; Anti-Semitism; Jews
Major character(s): Marcus Messner, Student—College; Olivia Hutton, Young Woman
Time period(s): 1950s
Locale(s): Newark, New Jersey; Ohio

Summary: Roth presents a coming-of-age tale set during the Korean War that depicts the progress of Marcus Messner, the son of an overprotective kosher butcher, from Newark to the bucolic campus of Winesburg, Ohio, where he attempts to come to grips with its conservative, WASPish Midwestern values. The conflicts and paradoxes Marcus confronts are embodied by Olivia Hutton, the girl he falls for and whose sexual contradictions typify the period.

Where it's reviewed:
Booklist, May 1, 2008, page 6
Kirkus Reviews, June 1, 2008, page 570
Library Journal, September 1, 2008, page 122
New York Times Book Review, September 21, 2008, page 1
Publishers Weekly, May 12, 2008, page 37

Other books by the same author:
Everyman, 2006
The Plot Against America, 2004
The Human Stain, 2000
Operation Shylock, 1993
Deception, 1990

Other books you might like:
Louis Begley, *Matters of Honor*, 2007
John Grisham, *A Painted House*, 2001
Pete Hamill, *Loving Women*, 1989
Deborah Johnson, *The Air between Us*, 2008
Thomas Mallon, *Fellow Travelers*, 2007

841

LAURA JOH ROWLAND

The Fire Kimono
(New York: St. Martin's Minotaur, 2008)

Story type: Mystery; Historical/Seventeenth Century
Series: Ichiro Sano. Book 13
Subject(s): Mystery and Detective Stories; Samurai

Historical

Major character(s): Sano Ichiro, Detective—Police, Warrior (samurai); Lord Matsudaira, Nobleman
Time period(s): 1700s (1700)
Locale(s): Edo, Japan

Summary: Set in 1700 in Edo (contemporary Tokyo), this installment of Rowland's popular mystery series has Sano Ichiro, now chamberlain warding off war with his chief rival, Lord Matsudaira, investigating the death of a cousin of the shogun whose skeleton is discovered after the fire that leveled Edo. Suspicion falls on Sano's own mother, Etsuko, and he must discover the truth to prevent her execution.

Where it's reviewed:
Booklist, October 1, 2008, page 27
Kirkus Reviews, September 15, 2008, page 971

Other books by the same author:
The Snow Empress, 2007
Red Chrysanthemum, 2006
The Assassin's Touch, 2005
The Pillow Book of Lady Wisteria, 2002
Black Lotus, 2001

Other books you might like:
Alison Fell, *The Pillow Book of Lady Onogoro*, 1994
Dale Furutani, *Kill the Shogun*, 2000
I.J. Parker, *Island of Exiles*, 2007
Lucia St. Clair Robson, *The Tokaido Road*, 1991
Susan Fromberg Schaeffer, *The Snow Fox*, 2004

842

PRISCILLA ROYAL

Forsaken Soul

(Scottsdale: Poisoned Pen Press, 2008)

Story type: Historical/Medieval; Mystery
Series: Eleanor of Tyndal. Book 5
Subject(s): Mystery and Detective Stories; Middle Ages; Religious Life
Major character(s): Eleanor of Tyndal, Religious (prioress)
Time period(s): 13th century (1273)
Locale(s): England

Summary: Prioress Eleanor of Tyndal investigates the death of Martin the Cooper, found in a Tyndal inn with a prostitute, an apparent poisoning victim. More poisoning deaths follow, and Eleanor finds herself in the center of a complex intrigue, set against a vivid period background.

Where it's reviewed:
Kirkus Reviews, June 1, 2008, page 576
Publishers Weekly, June 2, 2008, page 31

Other books by the same author:
Sorrow Without End, 2008
Justice for the Damned, 2007
Tyrant of the Mind, 2007
Wine of Violence, 2005

Other books you might like:
Alys Clare, *Ashes of the Elements*, 2001
Margaret Frazer, *The Widow's Tale*, 2005
Joanne Harris, *Holy Fools*, 2004

Janet Lawrence, *Death at the Table*, 1997
Peter Tremayne, *The Leper's Bell*, 2005

843

JAMES RUNCIE

Canvey Island

(New York: Other Press, 2008)

Story type: Coming-of-Age; Family Saga
Subject(s): Islands; Floods; Guilt
Major character(s): Martin Turner, Young Man
Time period(s): 20th century (1953-1980s)
Locale(s): England

Summary: The impact of a devastating flood on Britain's Canvey Island in 1953 is the subject of this novel. Martin Turner's mother, Lily, drowns in the flood, and Martin struggles with survivor's guilt as he ages as well as resentment toward his father and aunt who begin to live together soon after the flood. Told from various perspectives, the novel looks at the dissolution of a family in the face of tragedy.

Where it's reviewed:
Booklist, October 1, 2008, page 22
Kirkus Reviews, September 15, 2008, page 972
Library Journal, October 1, 2008, page 62
Publishers Weekly, September 15, 2008, page 42

Other books by the same author:
The Colour of Heaven, 2003
The Discovery of Chocolate, 2001

Other books you might like:
Louis Begley, *Matters of Honor*, 2007
Pete Hamill, *Loving Women*, 1989
Thomas Mallon, *Fellow Travelers*, 2007
Katherine Mosby, *The Season of Lillian Dawes*, 2002
Philip Roth, *Indignation*, 2008

844

CHRISTOPHER RUSH

Will

(Woodstock, NY: Overlook Press, 2008)

Story type: Historical/Elizabethan; Historical/Seventeenth Century
Subject(s): Biography; Authors and Writers
Major character(s): William Shakespeare, Historical Figure, Writer
Time period(s): 16th century; 17th century
Locale(s): Stratford-on-Avon, England; London, England

Summary: A bedridden and aging William Shakespeare dictates his will to his lawyer and recounts his experiences from his early days in Stratford through his theatrical success in London. Rush tackles the most contentious aspects of the Bard's career, including his religion, his relationship with poet Christopher Marlowe, and the facts behind his famous sonnets. Utterly convincing as a soliloquy, the novel is a tour de force of biographical and period re-creation.

Where it's reviewed:
Publishers Weekly, June 23, 2008, page 35

Other books by the same author:
Last Lesson of the Afternoon, 1994
Peace Comes Dropping Slow, 1983

Other books you might like:
Carol Goodman, *The Sonnet Lover*, 2007
Robert Nye, *The Late Mr. Shakespeare*, 1999
Grace Tiffany, *Will*, 2004
J.P. Wearing, *The Shakespeare Diaries*, 2007
Jess Winfield, *My Name Is Will*, 2008

845

KEIICHIRO RYU

The Blade of the Courtesans
(New York: Vertical, 2008)

Story type: Historical/Seventeenth Century; Historical/
Exotic
Subject(s): Samurai
Major character(s): Seichiro Matsunaga, Warrior
(samurai); Musashi Miyamoto, Warrior (samurai)
Time period(s): 16th century
Locale(s): Tokyo, Japan

Summary: This Japanese period novel follows the adventures of a young samurai, Seichiro Matsunaga, trained by the legendary swordsman Musashi Miyamoto. Sent to Yoshiwara, the pleasure quarter of old Tokyo, Seichiro comes to the defense of the inhabitants against spies from the Yagyu Clan. Brilliantly imagined, the novel offers a vivid portrait of life during the Edo Period of Japanese history.

Other books you might like:
James Clavell, *Shogun*, 1975
Eleanor Cooney, *Deception*, 1992
  Daniel Altieri, co-author
Takashi Matsuoka, *Cloud of Sparrows*, 2002
Laura Joh Rowland, *The Fire Kimono*, 2008
Susan Fromberg Schaeffer, *The Snow Fox*, 2004

846

ALAN SAVAGE

The Flowing Tide
(Sutton, England: Severn House, 2008)

Story type: Historical/World War II
Subject(s): World War II; Espionage; Sea Stories
Major character(s): Lord Duncan Eversham, Military
Personnel, Nobleman; Rebecca Strong, Spy
Time period(s): 1940s (1941)
Locale(s): At Sea; England

Summary: It's 1941 in Savage's World War II thriller concerning Lieutenant Lord Duncan Eversham who is in command of a flotilla protecting the English coast from raiding German forces. When he rescues the survivors of a sinking merchantman, he is plunged into a complex espionage tangle through involvement with one of the survivors, American Rebecca Strong, who is on an crucial secret mission for the British government.

Other books by the same author:
The Whirlwind, 2007
Blue Yonder, 2006
The Brightest Day, 2006
Stop Rommell, 1998
The Sword and the Jungle, 1976

Other books you might like:
Alexander Fullerton, *Last Lift from Crete*, 2005
Duncan Harding, *Sink the Hood*, 2000
Phillip McCutcheon, *Convoy of Fear*, 1990
Nicholas Monsarrat, *The Cruel Sea*, 1953
Douglas Reeman, *The Destroyers*, 1990

847

KARL H. SCHLESIER

Aurora Crossing
(Lubbock, TX: Texas Tech University Press, 2008)

Story type: Historical/American West; Coming-of-Age
Subject(s): Indians of North America; Coming-of-Age
Major character(s): John Seton, Indian; Chief Joseph,
Historical Figure, Indian
Time period(s): 1870s
Locale(s): West

Summary: Anthropologist Schlesier provides a fictional portrait of the struggles of Chief Joseph and Nez Perce who in 1877 embarked on an epic 1,200 mile march battling their way to seek a final refuge in Canada. Their story is told from the perspective of a mixed-race young man named John Seton who finds himself in conflict between his Indian heritage and the forces of modernity that will transform his world.

Where it's reviewed:
Booklist, October 15, 2008, page 22
Kirkus Reviews, September 15, 2008, page 972

Other books by the same author:
Trail of the Red Butterfly, 2007
Josanie's War, 1998

Other books you might like:
Bill Duggan, *Chief Joseph*, 1992
Frank Borden Hanes, *The Fleet Rabble*, 1961
Will Henry, *From Where the Sun Now Stands*, 1960
Terry C. Johnston, *Lay the Mountain Low*, 2000
John A. Sanford, *Song of the Meadowlark*, 1986

848

KATE SEDLEY

The Green Man
(Sutton, England: Severn House, 2008)

Story type: Historical/Medieval; Mystery
Series: Roger the Chapman

Subject(s): Mystery and Detective Stories; Middle Ages; Detection
Major character(s): Roger the Chapman, Peddler, Detective—Amateur; Richard, Historical Figure, Nobleman (Duke of Gloucester)
Time period(s): 15th century (1482)
Locale(s): Scotland; England

Summary: In this installment of Sedley's acclaimed medieval mystery series, Richard, Duke of Gloucester, recruits Roger the Chapman to serve as the bodyguard to the Duke of Albany, the younger brother of the king, during the invasion of Scotland. On the way, the royal party is attacked and one of Albany's friends is murdered and a series of baffling events follow, giving Roger the opportunity to do what he does best: solve mysteries. Full of convincing period details, the novel makes full use of the political and social realities of the era.

Where it's reviewed:
Booklist, June 1, 2008, page 49
Kirkus Reviews, March 15, 2008, page NA
Publishers Weekly, April 7, 2008, page 46

Other books by the same author:
The Three Kings of Cologne, 2007
The Prodigal Son, 2006
The Burgundian's Tale, 2005
Nine Men Dancing, 2003
The Lammas Feast, 2002
The Saint John's Fern, 2002

Other books you might like:
Alys Clare, *The Paths of the Air*, 2008
Margaret Frazer, *The Sister Frevisse Series*, 1993-
Edward Marston, *The Domesday Books Series*, 1993-
Ian Morson, *The Falconer Series*, 1994-
Leonard Tourney, *The Matthew Stock Series*, 1980-

849

MARY ANN SHAFFER
ANNIE BARROWS , Co-Author

The Guernsey Literary and Potato Peel Pie Society

(New York: The Dial Press, 2008)

Story type: Historical/World War II
Subject(s): World War II; Islands; Authors and Writers
Major character(s): Juliet Ashton, Writer; Dawsey Adams, Farmer
Time period(s): 1940s
Locale(s): Guernsey, England

Summary: A London writer, Juliet Ashton, assembles a collection of letters from Guernsey islanders with the help of farmer Dawsey Adams. The letters describe life on the island under German occupation, including the founding of the Guernsey Literary and Potato Peel Pie Society. What emerges is a colorful group of characters pressed to extremes by the war and the Nazis.

Where it's reviewed:
Booklist, July 1, 2008, page 34
Kirkus Reviews, June 15, 2008, page 620

Library Journal, July 1, 2008, page 67
Publishers Weekly, April 21, 2008, page 30

Other books you might like:
Tim Binding, *Lying with the Enemy*, 1999
Karen Joy Fowler, *The Jane Austen Book Club*, 2004
Elizabeth George, *A Place of Hiding*, 2003
Frances Murray, *Castaway*, 1978
Northcote C. Parkinson, *Devil to Pay*, 1973

850

SA SHAN

Alexander and Alestria

(New York: Harper, 2008)

Story type: Historical/Ancient Greece
Subject(s): Kings, Queens, Rulers, etc.; Biography; Ancient History
Major character(s): Alexander the Great, Historical Figure, Military Personnel; Alestria, Royalty (Amazon queen); Bagoas, Slave
Time period(s): 4th century B.C.
Locale(s): Middle East; Greece; India

Summary: This biographical profile of Alexander the Great explores the relationship between Alexander and an Amazon queen, Alestria. The former combatants become lovers, to the disappointment of Alexander's lover, the slave Bagoas, and Alestria's Amazons. Their unusual relationship is played out against a backdrop of warfare and political intrigue in exotic locales.

Where it's reviewed:
Booklist, July 1, 2008, page 33
Kirkus Reviews, June 1, 2008, page 571
Publishers Weekly, May 12, 2008, page 35

Other books by the same author:
Empress, 2006
The Girl Who Played Go, 2003

Other books you might like:
Steve Barry, *The Venetian Betrayal*, 2007
Harold Lamb, *Alexander of Macedon*, 1946
Steven Pressfield, *The Afghan Campaign*, 2006
Steven Pressfield, *The Last of the Amazons*, 2002
Mary Renault, *Funeral Games*, 1981

851

JOHN SHORS

Beside a Burning Sea

(New York: New American Library, 2008)

Story type: Historical/World War II
Subject(s): World War II; Shipwrecks; Survival
Major character(s): Akira, Military Personnel, Prisoner; Ratu, Stowaway; Jake, Engineer
Time period(s): 1940s (1942)
Locale(s): Pacific Islands

Summary: Shors' wartime drama is the story of survival set in the South Pacific during World War II. After a

U.S. hospital ship is torpedoed and sunk by the Japanese, the survivors seek safety on a remote island. They include a Japanese prisoner, Akira, a Fijian stowaway, Ratu, and the ship's black engineer, Jake. The novel details the challenges they face and the new community that is formed on the island.

Where it's reviewed:
Booklist, August 1, 2008, page 33
Kirkus Reviews, August 1, 2008, page 777

Other books by the same author:
Beneath a Marble Sky, 2004

Other books you might like:
Thomas Fleming, *Time and Tide*, 1987
Homer Hickam, *The Far Reaches*, 2007
Richard Hoyt, *Old Soldiers Sometimes Lie*, 2002
James Reasoner, *Trial by Fire*, 2002
Kathleen Tyau, *Makai*, 1999

852

AMI SILBER

Early Bright

(New Milford, CT: Toby Press, 2008)

Story type: Historical/World War II
Subject(s): Music and Musicians; Crime and Criminals
Major character(s): Louis Greenberg, Musician, Con Artist
Time period(s): 1940s
Locale(s): Los Angeles, California

Summary: Set in the jazz music scene of post-World War II Los Angeles, this atmospheric novel follow the adventures of Jewish musician and conman Louis Greenberg as he is introduced to the bebop scene of Los Angeles' black community while bilking war widows out of their savings. Greenberg is an intriguing antihero whose passion for jazz contrasts with his nefarious activities.

Where it's reviewed:
Kirkus Reviews, August 15, 2008, page 841
Library Journal, August 1, 2008, page 72
Publishers Weekly, July 21, 2008, page 138

Other books you might like:
Bebe Moore Campbell, *Brothers and Sisters*, 1994
Lynn Freed, *House of Women*, 2002
Albert Murray, *Train Whistle Guitar*, 1974
Patrick Neate, *Twelve Bar Blues*, 2001
Nina Revoyr, *Southland*, 2003

853

DANIELLE STEEL

A Good Woman

(New York: Delacorte, 2008)

Story type: Historical/Edwardian; Historical/World War I
Subject(s): World War I; Romance; Marriage
Major character(s): Annabelle Worthington, Socialite, Health Care Professional; Josiah Millbank, Banker

Time period(s): 1910s
Locale(s): New York, New York; Paris, France

Summary: Annabelle Worthington is a daughter of privilege whose father and brother die in the sinking of the *Titanic*. Annabelle marries older banker Josiah Millbank, but their relationship ends disastrously with him sending her off to Paris where she pursues a career as a doctor during World War I. Annabelle is a resourceful heroine even as she is a long-suffering one in this romantic tale of challenge and fortitude.

Where it's reviewed:
Booklist, September 1, 2008, page 5
Kirkus Reviews, September 15, 2008, page 974
Publishers Weekly, August 11, 2008, page 26

Other books by the same author:
Honor Thyself, 2008
Rogue, 2008
Amazing Grace, 2007
Sisters, 2007
Mirror Image, 1998

Other books you might like:
Beatrice Colin, *The Glimmer Palace*, 2008
Marc Dugain, *The Officers' Ward*, 2001
Frances McNeil, *Sisters of Fortune*, 2008
Judith Claire Mitchell, *The Last Day of the War*, 2004
Caroline Seebohm, *The Innocents*, 2007

854

JULIAN STOCKWIN

The Privateer's Revenge

(Ithaca, NY: McBooks Press, 2008)

Story type: Historical/Napoleonic Wars; Action/Adventure
Series: Kydd Sea Adventure. Book 9
Subject(s): Sea Stories; Military Life; War
Major character(s): Thomas Kydd, Military Personnel (British naval officer); Nicholas Renzi, Clerk
Time period(s): 1800s
Locale(s): Channel Islands, England; *HMS Teazer*, At Sea

Summary: In this installment of Stockwin's Napoleonic Era naval adventure series, Captain Thomas Kydd is assigned to the Channel Islands where he is framed for smuggling and dismissed from naval service. He is recruited to captain a privateer and sets about taking prizes, while his friend Nicholas Renzi gets involved in a plot to kidnap Napoleon and restore the Bourbon throne.

Where it's reviewed:
Publishers Weekly, August 25, 2008, page 54

Other books by the same author:
The Admiral's Daughter, 2007
Quarterdeck, 2005
Seaflower, 2003
Artemis, 2002
Kydd, 2001

Other books you might like:
Tom Connery, *A Shred of Honour*, 1999
Dewey Lambdin, *The Alan Lewrie Series*, 1989-

Historical

Jan Needle, *The Spithead Nymph*, 2004
Dudley Pope, *The Nicholas Ramage Series*, 1965-
Jay Worrall, *Sails on the Horizon*, 2006

855

BEVERLY SWERLING

City of God (A Novel of Passion and Wonder in Old New York)

(New York: Simon & Schuster, 2008)

Story type: Family Saga
Series: Old New York City. Book 4
Subject(s): City and Town Life; Family Life
Major character(s): Samuel Devrey, Businessman; Mei-Hua, Spouse (of Samuel); Carolina Randolph, Heiress
Time period(s): 19th century (1830s-1850s)
Locale(s): New York, New York

Summary: Swerling continues her series on the growth and development of New York City in this installment set in the decades preceding the Civil War. Merchant Samuel Devrey marries heiress Mei-Hua in China, but their union is not recognized in New York, allowing him to also marry another heiress, Carolina Randolph, while trying to keep both households. Carolina increasingly is drawn to Samuel's cousin, Dr. Nicholas Turner, who is committed to improving the services and research at Bellevue Hospital. The domestic tangle here is set against a brilliantly reconstructed period New York City.

Where it's reviewed:
Booklist, October 15, 2008, page 4
Kirkus Reviews, October 15, 2008, page 1092
Library Journal, November 15, 2008, page 66
Publishers Weekly, October 27, 2008, page 33

Other books by the same author:
City of Glory, 2007
Shadowbrook, 2004
City of Dreams, 2001

Other books you might like:
Pete Hamill, *Forever*, 2003
Joel Rose, *The Blackest Bird*, 2007
Harold Schechter, *The Hum Bug*, 2001
Randall Silvis, *On Night's Shore*, 2001
Gillen D'Arcy Wood, *Hosack's Folly*, 2005

856

NAHAL TAJADOD

Rumi: The Fire of Love

(Woodstock, NY: Overlook Press, 2008)

Story type: Historical/Medieval
Subject(s): Biography; Religious Life
Major character(s): Djalal al-din Mohammad Balkhi, Historical Figure (aka Rumi), Religious; Shams of Tabriz, Religious; Hesam, Religious
Time period(s): 13th century

Locale(s): Turkey

Summary: Tajadod offers a fictionalized biography of 13th century Turkish Sufi mystic Djalal al-din Mohammad Balkhi, better known as Rumi, who is transformed from a bookish scholar to the person who initiated the *sama*, the spiritual dance that gives his sect its name of whirling dervishes. Rumi's life is described in the context of his various relationships with his lover, Shams of Tabriz, and a disciple, Hesam, who transcribes the many turns in Rumi's fascinating story.

Where it's reviewed:
Booklist, August 1, 2008, page 38
Kirkus Reviews, June 15, 2008, page 621
Library Journal, July 1, 2008, page 68
Publishers Weekly, June 9, 2008, page 33

Other books you might like:
Driss Chraibi, *Muhammad*, 1998
Edwin Hoyt, *The Voice of Allah*, 1970
Sherry Jones, *The Jewel of Medina*, 2008
Mohja Kahf, *The Girl in the Tangerine Scarf*, 2006
Hunter Nedjma, *The Almond*, 2005

857

STEVE THAYER

The Leper

(St. Cloud, MN: North Star Press, 2008)

Story type: Historical/World War I
Subject(s): World War I; Diseases
Major character(s): John Severson, Military Personnel, Teacher
Time period(s): 20th century (1910s-1970s)
Locale(s): France; St. Paul, Minnesota; Louisiana

Summary: In this vivid and compelling novel, John Severson is a Marine captain during World War I who contracts leprosy. Sent to Louisiana's Witch Tree leprosarium, which is described in detail, Severson eventually manages to escape to Hawaii's Molokai leper colony where he serves as sheriff. The novel sheds considerable light on the treatment of leprosy and lepers during the 20th century.

Where it's reviewed:
Booklist, October 1, 2008, page 25
Publishers Weekly, July 28, 2008, page 53

Other books by the same author:
Wolf Pass, 2003
The Wheat Field, 2002
Silent Snow, 1999
The Weatherman, 1995
Saint Mudd, 1988

Other books you might like:
Kiana Davenport, *Song of the Exile*, 1999
Graham Greene, *A Burnt-Out Case*, 1961
Kathy Reichs, *Bones to Ashes*, 2007
Jeff Talarigo, *The Pearl Diver*, 2004
Kathleen Tyau, *Makai*, 1999

858

HANNAH TINTI

The Good Thief

(New York: Dial Press, 2008)

Story type: Action/Adventure
Subject(s): Orphans; Crime and Criminals
Major character(s): Ren, Orphan; Benjamin Nab, Con Man
Time period(s): 19th century
Locale(s): New England

Summary: This picaresque adventure novel concerns a one-handed orphan named Ren. An inmate of a prison-like orphanage, Ren is rescued by Benjamin Nab who claims to be his long-lost brother. Nab is a con man and petty thief who ushers Ren into a nightmarish and violent underworld. At times a brilliant pastiche of the 19th-century novel with several modernist twists, this is a richly imagined debut novel.

Where it's reviewed:
Booklist, June 1, 2008, page 44
Kirkus Reviews, June 1, 2008, page 572
New York Times Book Review, September 28, 2008, page 27
Publishers Weekly, May 5, 2008, page 43

Other books by the same author:
Animal Crackers, 2004

Other books you might like:
Louis Bayard, *The Black Tower*, 2008
David Benioff, *City of Thieves*, 2008
Kathleen Kent, *The Heretic's Daughter*, 2008
Dennis Lehane, *The Given Day*, 2008
David Wroblewski, *The Story of Edgar Sawtelle*, 2008

859

CHARLES TODD

A Matter of Justice

(New York: William Morrow, 2009)

Story type: Historical/World War I; Mystery
Series: Ian Rutledge Mystery. Book 11
Subject(s): World War I; Mystery and Detective Stories
Major character(s): Ian Rutledge, Detective—Police (Scotland Yard inspector), Veteran (World War I); Hamish MacLeod, Spirit, Military Personnel (corporal)
Time period(s): 1920s
Locale(s): Somerset, England

Summary: Inspector Ian Rutledge in Todd's acclaimed World War I-era mystery series investigates the murder of a man who had made his fortune two decades before as a soldier in the Boer War. Universally despised in Somerset where he lived, there are limitless suspects that Rutledge must rule out, aided by his dead spirit assistant, Hamish MacLeod.

Where it's reviewed:
Booklist, December 1, 2008, page 30

Kirkus Reviews, November 1, 2008, page 1141
New York Times Book Review, December 28, 2008, page 22
Publishers Weekly, November 3, 2008, page 41

Other books by the same author:
A Pale Horse, 2008
A False Mirror, 2007
A Long Shadow, 2006
A Cold Treachery, 2005
A Fearsome Doubt, 2002

Other books you might like:
Philippa Gregory, *Fallen Skies*, 2008
Graham Ison, *Hardcastle's Airmen*, 2006
Lilian Nattel, *The Singing Fire*, 2004
Anne Perry, *No Graves As Yet*, 2003
Jacqueline Winspear, *An Incomplete Revenge*, 2008

860

PETER TREMAYNE   (Pseudonym of Peter Berresford Ellis)

Dancing with Demons

(New York: Simon & Schuster, 2008)

Story type: Historical/Medieval; Mystery
Series: Sister Fidelma Mystery. Book 18
Subject(s): Mystery and Detective Stories; Religious Life; Celts
Major character(s): Sister Fidelma, Religious (nun), Detective—Amateur
Time period(s): 7th century
Locale(s): Ireland

Summary: In this installment of Tremayne's mystery series set in 7th-century Ireland, Sister Fidelma investigates the murder of Ireland's High King. A kinsman, Dubh Duin, was found in the king's chamber with the murder weapon. At issue is not who did it, but why, and civil war hangs in the balance of Fidelma's answer to that question. Tremayne is up to his usual standards in providing an authentic portrait of the period and the customs of early Ireland.

Where it's reviewed:
Kirkus Reviews, September 1, 2008, page 919
Publishers Weekly, August 18, 2008, page 47

Other books by the same author:
A Prayer for the Damned, 2007
Master of Souls, 2006
Badger's Moon, 2005
The Leper's Bell, 2004
Our Lady of Darkness, 2000

Other books you might like:
Cora Harrison, *A Secret and Unlawful Killing*, 2008
Michael Jecks, *A Friar's Bloodfeud*, 2005
Morgan Llywellan, *Pride of Lions*, 1996
Edward Rutherfurd, *The Princes of Ireland*, 2004
Joni Sensei, *The Humming of Numbers*, 2008

Historical

861

HARRY TURTLEDOVE

The Man with the Iron Heart

(New York: Del Rey, 2008)

Story type: Alternate History; Historical/World War II
Subject(s): World War II; Alternate History; War
Major character(s): Reinhard Heydrich, Historical Figure, Military Personnel; Harry S. Truman, Historical Figure, Political Figure
Time period(s): 1940s
Locale(s): Germany; United States

Summary: Turtledove, the reigning master of alternate history, imagines what might have happened had Nazi SS leader Reinhardt Heydrich not died in 1942 but survived to lead the resistance movement following Germany's defeat. The fanatics of the German Freedom Front, led by Heydrich, launch a campaign of suicide bombings, kidnapping, and assassination, presenting a major challenge for President Harry S. Truman and the American administration in dealing with modern terrorism.

Other books by the same author:
After the Downfall, 2008
The United States of Atlantis, 2008
Return Engagement, 2005
Walk in Hell, 2000
In the Balance, 1994

Other books you might like:
Robert Conroy, *1945*, 2007
Alison Gold, *The Devil's Mistress*, 1997
Ron Hansen, *Hitler's Niece*, 1999
Philip Kerr, *Hitler's Peace*, 2005
Mitch Silver, *In Secret Service*, 2007

862

HARRY TURTLEDOVE

The United States of Atlantis

(New York: ROC, 2008)

Story type: Alternate History; Historical/Fantasy
Series: Atlantis. Book 2
Subject(s): Revolutions; War; Resistance Movements
Major character(s): Victor Radcliffe, Revolutionary; George Washington, Historical Figure, Military Personnel; Marie-Joseph, marquis de Lafayette, Historical Figure, Military Personnel
Time period(s): 18th century
Locale(s): American Colonies; Atlantis, Atlantic Ocean

Summary: This inventive re-imagination of the American Revolution chronicles the efforts of Victor Radcliffe, leader of the freedom fighters, in resistance of British occupation of the colony of Atlantis. The ensuing war parallels the events of the Revolution and involves recognizable historical figures like George Washington and Lafayette but with intriguing alterations.

Where it's reviewed:
Booklist, November 14, 2008, page 23

Library Journal, December 1, 2008, page 117
Publishers Weekly, October 27, 2008, page 36

Other books by the same author:
In at the Death, 2007
Opening Atlantis, 2007
End of the Beginning, 2005
Ruled Britannia, 2002
How Few Remain, 1997

Other books you might like:
Brendan Du Bois, *Resurrection Day*, 1999
Kathleen Ann Goona, *In Wartimes*, 2007
Robert Harris, *Fatherland*, 1992
Greg Iles, *Black Cross*, 1995
Andre Norton, *The Shadow of Albion*, 1999

863

JOHN VERNON

Lucky Billy

(Boston: Houghton Mifflin, 2008)

Story type: Historical/American West
Subject(s): Crime and Criminals; Biography; Irish Americans
Major character(s): Billy the Kid, Historical Figure, Outlaw; Pat Garrett, Historical Figure, Lawman
Time period(s): 19th century
Locale(s): New Mexico

Summary: Vernon offers this biographical portrait of legendary outlaw Billy the Kid. Beginning with his escape from a New Mexican jail in 1881, the novel flashes back to his capture by his former friend Sheriff Pat Garrett and Billy's earlier experiences during the Lincoln County war. Vernon places the Lincoln County dispute in the context of Anglo-Irish enmity and stays close to the historical record in his treatment of the famous outlaw.

Where it's reviewed:
Booklist, November 15, 2008, page 18
Kirkus Reviews, October 15, 2008, page 1092
New York Times Book Review, November 30, 2008, page 7
Publishers Weekly, October 15, 2008, page 43

Other books by the same author:
The Last Canyon, 2001
All for Love, 1995
Peter Doyle, 1991
Lindbergh's Son, 1987
La Salle, 1986

Other books you might like:
Bill Brooks, *The Stone Garden*, 2001
Loren D. Estleman, *Journey of the Dead*, 1998
Elizabeth Fackler, *Billy the Kid*, 1995
William W. Johnstone, *Song of Eagles*, 1999
Larry McMurtry, *Anything for Billy*, 1988

864

PENNY VICENZI

An Outrageous Affair

(Woodstock, NY: Overlook Press, 2008)

Story type: Historical/World War II
Subject(s): Family Relations; Scandal; Secrets
Major character(s): Lady Caroline Hunterton, Gentle-woman; Magnus Phillips, Journalist
Time period(s): 20th century (1940s-1970s)
Locale(s): England; New York, New York; Hollywood, California

Summary: The novel tells the story of Lady Caroline Hunterton over a span of 30 years, from World War II to the 1970s. Journalist Magnus Phillips plans to publish a tell-all book about Caroline's scandalous past, and the novel details those secrets and the efforts to keep them hidden from Caroline's beloved daughters. The scene shifts from wartime London to Hollywood in the 1950s as Caroline's adventures twist and turn with each era.

Where it's reviewed:
Booklist, August 1, 2008, page 37

Other books by the same author:
Sheer Abandon, 2007
The Dilemma, 2007
Something Dangerous, 2004
No Angel, 2003
Old Sin, 1989

Other books you might like:
Tessa Barclay, *A Tissue of Lies*, 2008
Adele Geras, *Hester's Story*, 2004
Rachel Kushner, *Telex from Cuba*, 2008
Frances McNeil, *Sisters of Fortune*, 2008
Padma Viswanathan, *The Toss of a Lemon*, 2008

865

PADMA VISWANATHAN

The Toss of a Lemon

(Orlando: Harcourt, 2008)

Story type: Historical/Victorian; Family Saga
Subject(s): Marriage; Women; Small Town Life
Major character(s): Sivakami, Spouse (of Hanumarath-nam), Widow(er); Hanumarathnam, Spouse (of Si-vakami)
Time period(s): 19th century; 20th century
Locale(s): India

Summary: This first novel, based on the author's grand-mother's life, explores events in a southern Indian vil-lage beginning in 1896. The novel chronicles the life of a Tamil Brahmin girl, Sivakami, from her marriage at the age of ten through a long widowhood as modern Indian history takes shape and impacts her life and that of her village. The novel looks at the conflict between traditional Indian life and its strict caste rules and the forces of modernization that transformed India.

Where it's reviewed:
Booklist, August 1, 2008, page 40
Kirkus Reviews, July 15, 2008, page 720
Library Journal, August 1, 2008, page 74
Publishers Weekly, July 14, 2008, page 40

Other books you might like:
Linda Holeman, *The Linnet Bird*, 2005
Amulya Malladi, *A Breath of Fresh Air*, 2002
Kamala Markandeya, *Nectar in a Sieve*, 1955
Susanna Moore, *One Last Look*, 2003
Bharati Mukherjee, *The Holder of the World*, 1993

866

ANGEL WAGENSTEIN

Isaac's Torah

(New York: Handsel Books, 2008)

Story type: Historical/World War II
Subject(s): Jews; Holocaust
Major character(s): Isaac Jacob Blumenfeld, Tailor, Prisoner
Time period(s): 20th century
Locale(s): Poland; Russia

Summary: Isaac Jacob Blumenfeld narrates the story of his life and his experiences from birth in the shtetl of Kolodetz, part of the Austro-Hungarian Empire before World War I that is subsequently claimed by Poland. Drafted to serve first in the Austrian army, then in the Polish army, he becomes a prisoner of the Nazis, first as a Pole, then as a Jew. He is then liberated by the Soviets before being sent to Siberia. Through it all, Isaac displays a black humor that becomes part of his survival strategy.

Where it's reviewed:
Booklist, October 15, 2008, page 22
Kirkus Reviews, September 15, 2008, page 975
Publishers Weekly, August 4, 2008, page 41

Other books by the same author:
Farewell, Shanghai, 2007

Other books you might like:
Ahron Appelfeld, *All Whom I Have Loved*, 2007
Amy Bloom, *Away*, 2007
Richard A. Lourie, *Hatred of Tulips*, 2007
Caryl Phillips, *The Nature of Blood*, 1997
Sara Young, *My Enemy's Cradle*, 2008

867

JERI WESTERSON

Veil of Lies

(New York: St. Martin's Minotaur, 2008)

Story type: Historical/Medieval; Mystery
Subject(s): Middle Ages; Mystery and Detective Stories; Knights and Knighthood
Major character(s): Crispin Guest, Knight (former); Nicholas Walcote, Businessman, Spouse (of Phil-ippa); Philippa Walcote, Spouse (of Nicholas)
Time period(s): 14th century (1384)

Historical

Locale(s): London, England

Summary: This medieval mystery debut features Crispin Guest, a former knight stripped of his rank after being implicated in a plot against Richard II, who makes his living as a tracker or crime solver. Nicholas Walcote, a wealthy London merchant, hires him to investigate his young wife, Philippa, whom he suspects of infidelity. When Nicholas is found stabbed to death in a locked room, his widow asks Guest to find his killer. Nicholas's death may be connected with a relic in his possession that is reputed to compel truthtelling. This is a promising start for a proposed series dealing expertly with medieval customs and history.

Where it's reviewed:
Booklist, October 1, 2008, page 30
Kirkus Reviews, September 1, 2008, page 920
Publishers Weekly, September 1, 2008, page 38

Other books you might like:
Alys Clare, *The Paths of the Air*, 2008
Roberta Gellis, *A Personal Devil*, 2001
Philippa Morgan, *Chaucer and the Doctor of Physics*, 2006
Ian Morson, *The William Falconer Series*, 1994-
Ellis Peters, *The Brother Cadfael Series*, 1977-1994

868

A.N. WILSON

Winnie and Wolf

(New York: Farrar, Straus and Giroux, 2008)

Story type: Historical/Roaring Twenties
Subject(s): Biography; Nazis
Major character(s): Adolf Hitler, Historical Figure; Winifred "Winnie" Wagner, Historical Figure
Time period(s): 1920s; 1930s
Locale(s): Germany

Summary: Wilson imagines the relationship between Adolf Hitler and Winifred, the daughter-in-law of composer Richard Wagner. Opening in 1925, the novel explores Hitler's fascination with Wagner's operas that leads him to his involvement with Winnie, who after her husband's death take charge of the Bayreuth Festival. Wilson's knowledge of Hitler and Wagner's music is clear in this attempt to look at the German dictator in a different light.

Where it's reviewed:
Booklist, September 15, 2008, page 26
Kirkus Reviews, September 15, 2008, page 975
Library Journal, December 1, 2008, page 120
New York Times Book Review, November 23, 2008, page 16
Publishers Weekly, July 21, 2008, page 136

Other books by the same author:
A Bottle in the Smoke, 1990
Incline Our Hearts, 1989
Love Unknown, 1987
Gentlemen in England, 1986

Other books you might like:
Beryl Bainbridge, *Young Adolf*, 1979

Stephen Fry, *Making History*, 1997
Ron Hansen, *Hitler's Niece*, 1999
Norman Mailer, *The Castle in the Forest*, 2007
Andrew Nagorski, *Last Stop Vienna*, 2003

869

DARRYL WIMBERLEY

Kaleidoscope

(New Milford, CT: Toby Press, 2008)

Story type: Historical/Roaring Twenties; Mystery
Subject(s): Mystery and Detective Stories; Carnivals; Organized Crime
Major character(s): Jack Romaine, Gambler; Oliver Bladehorn, Organized Crime Figure
Time period(s): 1920s (1929)
Locale(s): Cincinnati, Ohio; Tampa, Florida

Summary: In this mystery set in the 1920s, small-time gambler Jack Romaine is given the chance to pay off his debts to gangster Oliver Bladehorn by picking up a woman being released from prison who is to lead him to a cache of money and stocks. The trail leads to Tampa, Florida, and Kaleidoscope, the winter resting place of traveling carnivals. There Jack goes to work to find the stash while avoiding another searcher who will stop at nothing to gain the treasure. Wimberley vividly depicts the carnival world of the period.

Where it's reviewed:
Kirkus Reviews, August 1, 2008, page 779
Library Journal, August 1, 2008, page 77
Publishers Weekly, July 14, 2008, page 47

Other books by the same author:
Pepperfish Keys, 2007
The King of Colored Town, 2007
Strawman's Hammock, 2001
A Tinker's Damn, 2000
Dead Man's Bay, 2000

Other books you might like:
Matt Bondurant, *The Wettest County in the World*, 2008
Beatrice Colin, *The Glimmer Palace*, 2008
David Fulmer, *Lost River*, 2009
Craig Holden, *The Jazz Bird*, 2002
Jacqueline Winspear, *An Incomplete Revenge*, 2008

870

JESS WINFIELD

My Name Is Will

(New York: Twelve, 2008)

Story type: Historical/Elizabethan
Subject(s): Biography; Authors and Writers
Major character(s): William Shakespeare, Historical Figure, Writer; William Shakespeare Greenberg, Student—Graduate
Time period(s): 16th century; 1980s

Locale(s): Stratford-on-Avon, England; Santa Cruz, California

Summary: Winfield, a founding member of the Reduced Shakespeare Company, has produced this first novel on his favorite subject that alternates between two stories. In 1582, in Stratford, the 18-year-old Shakespeare sows his wild oats and gets involved with a group of secret Catholics. Four centuries later, William Shakespeare Greenberg is working on his master's thesis on Shakespeare and Catholicism. The two stories juxtapose the wild and crazy days of two youths in very different eras.

Where it's reviewed:
Booklist, May 15, 2008, page 22
Kirkus Reviews, May 15, 2008, page 517
New York Times Book Review, July 27, 2008, page 9
Publishers Weekly, April 14, 2008, page 33

Other books you might like:
Anthony Burgess, *Nothing Like the Sun*, 1964
Bruce Cook, *Young Will*, 2004
Stephanie Cowell, *The Players*, 1997
Grace Tiffany, *Will*, 2004
J.P. Wearing, *The Shakespeare Diaries*, 2007

871

SALLY WRIGHT

Code of Silence

(Sutton, England: Severn House, 2008)

Story type: Mystery
Subject(s): Mystery and Detective Stories; Espionage
Major character(s): Ben Reese, Widow(er)
Time period(s): 1950s (1957)
Locale(s): Columbus, Ohio

Summary: Set in the 1950s, this espionage thriller concerns university archivist Ben Reese, who goes to meet a friend who never shows up. A few days later, the friend's body is found, an apparent suicide. Ben is not so sure, and he receives a series of puzzling clues from the dead man that he uses to track down the killer and his motive for murder.

Where it's reviewed:
Booklist, December 1, 2008, page 28
Kirkus Reviews, December 1, 2008, page 1230

Other books by the same author:
Watches of the Night, 2008
Out of the Ruins, 2003
Pursuit and Persuasion, 2000
Pride and Predator, 1998
Publish and Perish, 1997

Other books you might like:
Loren D. Estleman, *Frames*, 2008
Jim Hougan, *The Magdalene Cipher*, 2006
Richard Montanari, *Badlands*, 2008
Katherine Neville, *The Fire*, 2008
Javier Sierra, *The Lady in Blue*, 2007

872

ALISSA YORK

Effigy

(New York: Thomas Dunne Books, 2008)

Story type: Historical/American West
Subject(s): Mormons; Marriage; Women
Major character(s): Erastus Hammer, Rancher; Dorrie Hammer, Spouse (of Erastus); Bendy Drown, Worker
Time period(s): 1860s
Locale(s): Utah

Summary: Set in the Utah frontier of the 1860s, York's novel details the experiences of Dorrie Hammer, the fourth and youngest wife of rancher and game hunter Erastus Hammer. He is most interested in Dorrie's skill in taxidermy, converting his kills into lifelike trophies. Dorrie is befriended by ranchhand Bendy Drown, a relationship that proves dangerous. York's portrait of a Mormon household at the time is inspired in part by the actual events of the Mountain Meadow Massacre of 1857.

Where it's reviewed:
Booklist, September 1, 2008, page 44

Other books by the same author:
Mercy, 2003

Other books you might like:
David Ebershoff, *The 19th Wife*, 2008
Vardis Fisher, *Children of God*, 1939
John Gates, *Sister Wife*, 2001
Leo V. Gordon, *Powder Keg*, 1991
Marjorie Jarrett, *Wives of the Wind*, 1980

873

IMAN HUMAYDAN YOUNES

Wild Mulberries

(Northampton, MA: Interlink Books, 2008)

Story type: Historical/Depression Era; Coming-of-Age
Subject(s): Small Town Life; Coming-of-Age
Major character(s): Sarah, Young Women
Time period(s): 1930s
Locale(s): Lebanon

Summary: Younes's novel is set in a small village in the mountains of Lebanon and follows the coming-of-age drama of Sarah whose mother has abandoned her and whose father is interested only in the silkworms he raises. Connected to Sarah's story is the collective story of the village itself as its traditions give way to the modern world.

Where it's reviewed:
Kirkus Reviews, June 15, 2008, page 622

Other books you might like:
Ellyn Bache, *Safe Passage*, 1988
Philip Caputo, *Delcorso's Gallery*, 1983
Ron Leshem, *Beaufort*, 2008
Amin Maalouf, *The Rock of Tanios*, 1994
Hanan Shaykh, *The Story of Zahra*, 1984

Historical

Inspirational Fiction in 2009

Inspirational fiction is often seen as never changing; however, over the last few years this genre has in fact been evolving. The genre's publishers are more open to unusual or new ideas and the authors are focusing on more realistic and timely themes and characters. The current trend is to see more pirates, a few vampires, and even supernatural thrillers or paranormal-themed stories. More and more readers are finding characters they can relate to and even see themselves in, written within a genre that for years has had to deal with people considering it too preachy.

While readers will still find the traditional storys such as those involving the Amish, Colleen Coble's *Anathema* offers not just the Amish but an outstanding mystery. And the traditional stories such as Karen Kingsbury writes, the stories that follow flawed characters on their journey with Christ, may not all end happily ever after, but all have their characters learning to hold on to their faith above everything else. Karen added to her growing fan base with the recent releases of *Take One*, which once again unites readers with the Baxter Family; and *This Side of Heaven*, which chronicles the struggles of its main character, Josh, to turn his life around, and the effects of his death—just as he is succeeding—on his family, whom he had disappointed up till then, but who must re-evaluate him as they learn more about him. Fans of Inspirational fiction have always adored Karen's writing but an increasing number of non-inspirational or secular readers are finding these titles and learning that while Inspirational fiction will always be faith-based to some extent it is not necessarily preachy.

Inspirational fiction has been opening the door more widely to types of stories that one wouldn't expect to find in the genre, as with Tracey Bateman's *Distant Heart* who's heroine is a former prostitute. Toni has vowed to never allow any man to have control over her again. Sam Two-Feathers, the wagon train's preacher, knows Toni is worthy of love but convincing her of it is another matter. Ms. Bateman's story allows readers to love a character who does not have the perfect past. Life isn't easy for her, but that doesn't mean God doesn't love her, nor does it mean that she's not worthy of a new start and a happily ever after. Stories such as this are attracting more mainstream readers who find favorite authors in a genre that they formerly overlooked.

Inspirational fiction has always dealt with grief and lost spouses, and that has not changed. Jamie Langston Turner has written one such novel that deals with the loss of a spouse and how faith can help the bereaved move beyond the grief. *Sometimes a Light Surprises* deals with Ben Buckley who is still grieving for his wife even years after her death. Ben blames the "religion" she found and feels anger and bewilderment over her death. The story follows Ben's attempts to work through his grief, his questions, and his anger.

Mark Andrew Olson's *Ulterior Motives* follows another direction that inspirational fiction is following. Mr. Olson's story deals with Greg Cahill and his involvement with a terrorist the government is hoping Greg can break. The story is not easy, nor is it simple. The story is complex and readers are given a faith-based story within a world that often is not shown to have any faith at all.

A bona-fide mystery/thriller that deals with the Christian music world has been written by Terri Blackstock, author of the four-volume Restoration series, which she completed last year. Her *Double Minds* centers around Parker James, a singer/songwriter of growing popularity, who appears to have been intended target of a murder when an intern is killed while substituting for her in the studio reception area where she usually works. Though there are biblical references appearing throughout the book, it refrains from being "preachy," yet manages successfully to the challenges of maintaining a true Christian faith against a suspenseful backdrop. Much interesting information about the Christian music industry is imparted as well: recording, touring, photographing a CD cover, publicity, and marketing, as well as relations with the musicians.

There are more and more inspirational fantasies been published now. One of these is George Bryan Polivka's *Blaggard's Moon*, which not only embraces the idea of a fantasy world, but also a growing list of characters who are pirates. Smith Delaney is a pirate who must deal with his own death as well as his faith in God.

Inspirational fiction is continuing to evolve and grow as the publishers allow a greater variety of the changes and challenges that we as readers face in everyday life to be written about within the genre's novels. The future of inspirational fiction is open to even more diversity while it continues the traditional stories that previous fans have always loved. The more the genre opens to wider sub-genres the more it will attract readers to these titles and so many more. There are increasingly new things to read and experience within the inspirational fiction genre and the future looks to be bright.

Recommended Titles

Anathema by Colleen Coble

Take One by Karen Kingsbury

This Side of Heaven by Karen Kingsbury

Distant Heart by Tracey Bateman

Sometimes a Light Surprises by Jamie Langston Turner

Double-Minds by Terri Blackstock

Ulterior Motives by Mark Andrew Olson

Blaggard's Moon by George Bryan Polivka

Inspirational Titles

874

SHELLEY ADINA

Be Strong and Curvaceous

(Boston: Faithwords, 2009)

Story type: Young Adult; Contemporary
Series: All About Us. Book 3
Subject(s): Faith; Teen Relationships; Mystery
Major character(s): Carly Aragon, Teenager; Lindsay MacPhail, Teenager
Time period(s): 2000s
Locale(s): San Francisco, California (Spencer Academy)

Summary: Carly Aragon has enjoyed spring break in Mexico. Now she's returning to Spencer Academy and her best friends. When Carly gets to her dorm, however, she is shocked to learn she is sharing a room with Lady Lindsay MacPhail—and even worse—Lindsay is dating Carly's secret crush. Lindsay and Carly are total opposites who don't get along until Lindsay begins to receive mysterious emails. Carly helps her roommate get to the bottom of the mystery, and the two girls are thrust into a dangerous situation.

Other books by the same author:
Its All About Us: A Novel, 2008 (All About Us. Book 1)
The Fruit of My Lipstick, 2008 (All About Us. Book 2)

Other books you might like:
Jodi Lynn Anderson, *Love and Peaches*, 2008

875

HANNAH ALEXANDER (Pseudonym of Mel Hodde and Cheryl Hodde)

A Killing Frost

(Don Mills, Ontario, Canada: Steeple Hill, 2009)

Story type: Religious; Mystery
Series: River Dance. Book 1
Subject(s): Secrets; Kidnapping
Major character(s): Jama Keith, Doctor; Tyrell Mercer, Fiance(e) (of Jama, former)
Time period(s): 2000s
Locale(s): River Dance, Missouri

Summary: Dr. Jama Keith returns to River Dance, Missouri to open a new clinic. The townspeople were instrumental in helping Jama getting a good education and the doctor is looking forward to repaying them for their kindness. Jama hopes that she can get her work done while avoiding her ex-boyfriend, Tyrell, but she soon runs into him. The brilliant physician is hiding secrets from Tyrell that she'd rather not reveal. The former couple find themselves thrown together when two men on the FBI's Most Wanted list kidnap Tyrell's niece. Soon, Jama is forced to tell Tyrell about her past in order to help save the little girl's life.

Where it's reviewed:
Publishers Weekly, November 24, 2008, page 39

Other books by the same author:
Hidden Motive, 2008 (previously published as Crystal Cavern)
Hideaway Series, 2003-

Other books you might like:
Lori Copeland, *Now and Always*, 2008
Dee Henderson, *Kidnapped*, 2008

876

TAMERA ALEXANDER

Beyond This Moment

(Ada, MI: Bethany House, 2009)

Story type: Historical; Romance
Series: Timber Ridge Reflections. Book 2
Subject(s): Christian Life
Major character(s): Molly Whitcomb, Professor; James McPherson, Lawman (sheriff)
Time period(s): 1870s (post-civil war)
Locale(s): Timber Ridge, Colorado

Summary: Embarrassed by a costly mistake, Dr. Molly Whitcomb accepts a position teaching children in Timber Ridge, Colorado. On the way to Colorado, Molly buys a wedding ring to help her hide her earlier life. In Colorado, Molly meets Sheriff James McPherson, a caring and very perceptive man. Molly repairs her broken faith in God while in Colorado, and she also builds a relationship with the Sheriff. As their relationship grows closer, Sheriff James can't help but notice that Molly is hiding something from him. Her secrets slowly rise to the surface and threaten to destroy the beautiful new life that Molly has constructed.

Other books by the same author:
From a Distance, 2008 (Timber Ridge Reflections. Book 1)
Remembered, 2007
Rekindled, 2006
Revealed, 2006

Other books you might like:
Susan Page Davis, *Wyoming Brides*, 2008
Cathy Marie Hake, *That Certain Spark*, 2009
Tracie Peterson, *A Love to Last Forever*, 2009
Stephanie Grace Whitson, *A Claim of Her Own*, 2009

877

TRACEY BATEMAN

Distant Heart

(New York: Avon Inspire, 2008)

Story type: Religious; Historical
Series: Westward Hearts. Book 2
Subject(s): Faith; Love; Racism
Major character(s): Toni Rodden, Prostitute (former), Friend (of Fannie); Sam Two-Feathers, Indian (Cheyenne), Religious (preacher); Fannie Caldwell, Friend (of Toni), Fiance(e) (of Blake); Blake Tanner, Leader (of wagon train), Fiance(e) (of Fannie)
Time period(s): 1850s (1850)
Locale(s): Oregon

Summary: After years of selling her body, Toni has finally carved out a place for herself on a wagon train headed to Oregon. While most of the women tend to stay away from Toni, Fannie Caldwell and her two siblings have accepted her as a part of their family. As Fannie and wagon master Blake Tanner prepare for their upcoming nuptials, Toni wonders if she will ever find someone who is willing to accept her dark past and love her despite her sins. Sam Two-Feathers, the half-Indian wagon scout and preacher for the train, is sure that Toni is worthy of love. Now, it's up to Sam to show Toni that true love is within her reach.

Other books by the same author:
Dangerous Heart, 2008 (Westward Hearts. Book 2)
Defiant Heart, 2007 (Westward Hearts. Book 1)

Other books you might like:
Rosanne Bittner, *Walk by Faith*, 2008
DiAnn Mills, *Awaken My Heart*, 2008

878

JAMES SCOTT BELL

Deceived

(Grand Rapids, MI: Zondervan, 2009)

Story type: Mystery
Subject(s): Christian Life; Murder; Crime and Criminals
Major character(s): Liz Towne, Spouse; Mac MacDonald, Veteran, Convict; Roxanne Towne, Relative (sister-in-law of Liz)
Time period(s): 2000s (2008)
Locale(s): Pack Canyon, California

Summary: Married couple Liz and Arty Towne make a startling discovery one day while traveling through a canyon on the edge of Los Angeles. They uncover a dead body in possession of a satchel of diamonds. Liz decides that this is her chance to become rich. When Liz's sister-in-law Roxanne suspects that Liz is up to no good, she enlists her friend and Gulf War veteran Mac to help her get to the bottom of the mystery. Liz, Mac, and Roxanne chase each other through Los Angeles and the surrounding canyons, and when the three characters finally meet, the truth is revealed. Then, the characters must make important decisions that will impact the rest of their lives.

Where it's reviewed:
Publisher's Weekly, January 12, 2009, page 31

Other books by the same author:
The Whole Truth, 2008
Try Darkness, 2008
No Legal Grounds, 2007
Try Dying, 2007
Presumed Guilty, 2007

Other books you might like:
Randy Alcorn, *Deception*, 2008
Susan Page Davis, *Finding Marie*, 2007
Paul Robertson, *The Heir*, 2007
Gayle Roper, *Fatal Deduction*, 2008

879

TERRI BLACKSTOCK

Double Minds

(Grand Rapids, MI: Zondervan, 2009)

Story type: Religious; Modern
Subject(s): Music and Musicians; Faith; Mystery
Major character(s): Parker James, Singer (songwriter), Receptionist
Time period(s): 2000s
Locale(s): Nashville, Tennessee

Summary: Parker James is a Christian songwriter who longs to break into the music business. To help pay the bills, Parker works as a receptionist at recording studio. When a young woman is murdered while filling in for Parker, the songwriter can't help but wonder if the wrong girl got killed. With the assistance of her police officer brother, Parker sets out to discover the motivation behind the murder. Parker soon uncovers a deadly conspiracy within the music industry that makes her reassess her plans for the future. In order to discover the truth, Parker must trust in God to lead her in the right direction.

Other books by the same author:
Restoration Series, 2005-2008

Other books you might like:
Brandilyn Collins, *Dark Pursuits*, 2008
Kristin Heitzmann, *The Edge of Recall*, 2008

Lis Wiehl, *Face of Betrayal*, 2009
   April Henry, co-author

880

MAGGIE BRENDAN

No Place for a Lady

(Grand Rapids, MI: Revell, 2009)

Story type: Historical; Romance
Series: Heart of the West. Book 1
Subject(s): Adventure and Adventurers; Romance
Major character(s): Crystal Clark, Southern Belle; Luke Weber, Rancher
Time period(s): 1890s (1892)
Locale(s): Yampa Valley, Colorado

Summary: After her father died, Crystal Clark sold her Georgia plantation and accepted her Aunt Kate's offer to spend some time at her Colorado cattle ranch. Strong-willed Crystal is determined to prove her abilities to Kate's ranch hands, especially handsome foreman Luke Weber. Impressed by the young woman's spirit and her ability to learn, Luke soon finds himself falling for the beautiful Southern belle. Just when Crystal begins to feel as if she belongs on the ranch, tragedy strikes and the young woman begins to question her faith and her place in the world. Now, Crystal must decide is she should try to save the ranch from a greedy neighbor or return to the life she left behind in Georgia.

Other books you might like:
Janet Lee Barton, *Desert Roses*, 2009
Kim Vogel Sawyer, *The Summerfeld Trilogy*, 2007-2008

881

WANDA E. BRUNSTETTER

A Cousin's Promise

(Uhrichsville, OH: Barbour, 2009)

Story type: Religious; Romance
Series: Indiana Cousins. Book 1
Subject(s): Amish; Accidents; Marriage
Major character(s): Wayne Lambright, Farmer, Fiance(e) (of Loraine); Loraine Miller, Fiance(e) (of Wayne); Jake Beechy, Boyfriend (of Loraine, former)
Time period(s): 2000s
Locale(s): Indiana

Summary: When Wayne Lambright is crippled in a horrific traffic accident, he worries that he won't be able to provide for his fiancee Loraine. Though Loraine is ready to stand by Wayne, she feels him growing more distant every day. Suddenly, Loraine's former boyfriend, Jake Beechy, returns to town after spending some time in the English world. Jake is hoping that Loraine will forgive her and take him back, but she remains committed to her fiance. As Wayne continues to isolate himself, Loraine wonders if she should give Jake another chance.

Where it's reviewed:
Publishers Weekly, January 12, 2009, page 31

Other books by the same author:
White Christmas Pie, 2008
Brides of Webster County Series, 2007-
Sisters of Holmes County Series, 2007-
Brides of Lancaster County Series, 2006-

Other books you might like:
Beverly Lewis, *The Courtship of Nellie Fisher Series*, 2007-
Cindy Woodsmall, *Sisters of the Quilt Series*, 2006-

882

LINORE ROSE BURKARD

Before the Season Ends

(Eugene, OR: Harvest House, 2008)

Story type: Historical/Regency; Romance
Subject(s): Interpersonal Relations; Faith
Major character(s): Ariana Forsythe, Young Woman; Phillip Mornay, Rogue, Wealthy
Time period(s): 1810s (1813)
Locale(s): London, England

Summary: While many of her contemporaries are searching for a husband with deep pockets, spirited country beauty Ariana Forsythe is determined to marry a man who is devoted to Christ. In order to avoid an unfortunate match, Ariana's parents send her away to spend some time at her aunt's townhouse in the Mayfair district of London. She soon encounters Phillip Mornay, a bachelor who Ariana dismisses as a godless rogue. Her perception of Phillip changes when a scandal puts Ariana's reputation at risk. Though Ariana admits that she was wrong to judge Phillip so harshly, she has a difficult time reconciling her budding feelings for the handsome gentleman with her oath to only give her heart to a fellow Christian. First novel.

Where it's reviewed:
Publisher's Weekly, October 27, 2008, Page 34

Other books you might like:
Catherine Palmer, *Bachelor's Bargain*, 2006

883

LINORE ROSE BURKARD

The House in Grosvenor Square

(Eugene, OR: Harvest House, 2009)

Story type: Romance; Historical/Regency
Subject(s): Humor; Faith; Love
Major character(s): Ariana Forsythe, Fiance(e) (of Phillip), Crime Victim (kidnapped); Phillip Mornay, Fiance(e) (of Ariana), Wealthy
Time period(s): 19th century
Locale(s): London, England

Summary: Ariana Forsythe is busy planning her wedding to the wealthy Phillip Mornay. The young woman knows that her life will change drastically once she marries Phillip, and she promises to use her new situation to help those less fortunate than herself. As Ariana's friends and family tour her future home, Phillip begins to notice

Inspirational

that various items around the house have gone missing. Each time Ariana visits the house, something else disappears. While Phillip ponders these strange coincidences, he is shocked to learn that his fiancee has been kidnapped. Now, Phillip must unravel the mystery behind Ariana's kidnapping in order to discover what the abductor wants.

Other books by the same author:
Before the Season Ends, 2008

Other books you might like:
Catherine Palmer, *English Ivy*, 2007

884

AMANDA CABOT

Paper Roses

(Grand Rapids, MI: Revell, 2009)

Story type: Historical; Romance
Series: Texas Dreams Trilogy. Book 1
Subject(s): Love; Mail Order Brides; Murder
Major character(s): Sarah Dobbs, Mail Order Bride; Clay Canfield, Rancher
Time period(s): 1850s (1856)
Locale(s): Ladreville, Texas

Summary: The letters Austin Canfield wrote made the emotionally damaged Sarah Dobbs dream of a better life for herself and her young sister under the Texas sky. When the mail order bride arrives in San Antonio to meet her groom, Sarah is devastated when she learns that Austin's been murdered. Austin's brother, Clay, wants nothing more than to find out the truth about how his brother died. Though he offers to pay for the cost of Sarah and her sister's tickets back to Philadelphia, the young woman decides to stay and takes a job in the nearby town. Soon, Sarah becomes involved in the investigation into Austin's death and Clay finds himself falling for the brave and faithful young woman.

Other books you might like:
Lori Copeland, *Brides of the West Series*, 1998-2007
Al Lacy, *Mail Order Bride Series*, 1998-2004

885

JAMIE CARIE

Wind Dancer

(Nashville: B&H Publisher, 2009)

Story type: Historical; Romance
Subject(s): Faith; Love; War
Major character(s): Isabelle Renoir, Frontierswoman; Samuel Holt, Spy
Time period(s): 18th century
Locale(s): North America

Summary: In the British-held territory, Isabelle Renoir is known for being eccentric. The beautiful frontierswoman is famous for dancing in the moonlight as she praises God. Independent and determined to live life on her own terms, Isabelle is comfortable hunting for her own food

and taking care of herself. When she meets American spy Samuel Holt in the woods one day, the attraction is instantaneous. Isabelle, however, does not intend to get involved with any man, let alone a revolutionary. After parting ways, Isabelle is captured by a group of Indians. She is surprised to discover that Samuel has been taken as well. Isabelle and Samuel must stick together if they hope to escape with their lives.

Other books by the same author:
The Duchess and the Dragon, 2008
Snow Angel, 2007

Other books you might like:
Jamie Carie, *Wind Dancer*, 2008
Craig Parshall, *The Thistle and the Cross Series*, 2007-
Janet Parshall, co-author

886

MELODY CARLSON

All I Have to Give

(Grand Rapids, MI: Revell, 2008)

Story type: Family Saga; Contemporary
Subject(s): Christmas; Family Relations; Infertility
Major character(s): Anna, Spouse (of Michael); Michael, Spouse (of Anna)
Time period(s): 2000s
Locale(s): United States

Summary: After several painful miscarriages, Anna and Michael have given up on the idea of ever having children of their own. As Michael makes plans to turn the nursery into a home office, Anna becomes increasingly concerned about a health problem that resembles the disease that took her mother's life. With Christmas fast approaching, Anna and Michael search for the perfect gifts to help cheer them up during these dark times. Anna's Christmas surprise for Michael ends up being a gift he won't soon forget!

Other books by the same author:
An Irish Christmas, 2007

Other books you might like:
Kathleen Morgan, *One Perfect Gift*, 2008
Marlo Schalesky, *If Tomorrow Never Comes*, 2009
Rebeca Seitz, *Scrapping Plans*, 2009
Lauraine Snelling, *One Perfect Day*, 2008

887

MELODY CARLSON

Just Another Girl

(Ada, MI: Revell, 2009)

Story type: Young Adult
Subject(s): Mentally Handicapped; Sisters
Major character(s): Aster Flynn, Teenager; Lily Flynn, Teenager, Mentally Ill Person
Time period(s): 2000s
Locale(s): United States

Summary: Seventeen-year-old Aster Flynn has a lot of responsibility, like caring for her mentally handicapped sister Lily. As she gets older, however, Aster wishes she had more freedom to be "just another girl." When a boy begins to notice Aster, she decides to get her parents and older sister more involved with Lily's care so that Aster can do all the fun things she's only dreamed about. Making this change, however, has consequences Aster never predicted. Aster doesn't want to hurt Lily's feelings, and her family is having a hard time adjusting to the new rules. Will Aster ever win the freedom she wants?

Other books by the same author:
On My Own, 2002
Diary of a Teenage Girl: Becoming Me, 2000

Other books you might like:
Nancy N. Rue, *Lucy's Perfect Summer*, 2009
Debbie Viguie, *The Spring of Candy Apples*, 2009

888

MELODY CARLSON

Spring Broke

(Colorado Springs: David C. Cook, 2009)

Story type: Contemporary; Religious
Series: 86 Bloomberg Place. Book 3
Subject(s): Faith
Major character(s): Kendall, Young Woman; Lelani, Young Woman
Time period(s): 2000s
Locale(s): Maui, Hawaii

Summary: Four women, who each struggles in her own way, help each other solve their problems. Kendall has to face the facts: she is pregnant, bill collectors are calling her apartment, and her three roommates are suffering through difficulties of their own. Lelani, who fled from her home in Maui, gets a call from her parents. They want Lelani and her friends to come to Hawaii for a break, and the girls wonder how they can make it happen. They organize a garage sale to try and raise the funds, and in going through her attic, Kendall gains some insight into her spending problems.

Other books by the same author:
I Heart Bloomberg, 2008 (86 Bloomberg Place. Book 1)
Let Them Eat Fruitcake, 2008 (86 Bloomberg Place. Book 2)
Diary of a Teenage Girl Series, 2000-

Other books you might like:
Neta Jackson, *The Yada Yada Prayer Group Series*, 2003-
Rebeca Seitz, *Sisters, Ink Series*, 2008

889

JULIE CAROBINI

Sweet Waters

(Nashville: B&H Publishing Group, 2009)

Story type: Contemporary; Religious
Subject(s): Faith; Family; Secrets

Major character(s): Tara Sweet, Worker, Sister (of Camille); Camille Sweet, Sister (of Tara); Josh, Fire Fighter
Time period(s): 2000s
Locale(s): Otter Bay, California

Summary: After breaking up with her boyfriend and learning that her mother's about to marry a much younger man, Tara Sweet decides to move back to Otter Bay, California with her younger sister Camille. When she arrives on the West Coast, Tara is flooded with a wave of happy memories from her childhood. She can't remember why her parents even insisted on leaving this magical place. Tara takes a job at a local inn and restaurant where she makes several new friends, including handsome firefighter Josh. As Tara and Camille learn more about why their family left so many years ago, the sisters begin to question everything they once believed in.

Other books by the same author:
Truffles by the Sea, 2008
Chocolate Beach, 2007

Other books you might like:
Deborah Bedford, *Family Matters*, 2008
Denise Hunter, *Sweetwater Gap*, 2008

890

ROBIN CAROLL

Bayou Betrayal

(Don Mills, Ontario: Steeple Hill, 2009)

Story type: Religious; Modern
Subject(s): Murder; Faith; Family
Major character(s): Monique Harris, Widow(er); Gary Anderson, Police Officer
Time period(s): 2000s
Locale(s): Louisiana

Summary: When Monique Harris finally finds her biological father, she's disappointed to learn that he's in prison for murder. Her father's family, however, accepts Monique as one of their own. When Monique loses her husband in a terrible accident, she turns to her newfound relatives for help. Soon, Monique begins to realize that not everyone wants her to stay in the Louisiana Bayou. When someone endangers Monique's life, Deputy Sheriff Gary Anderson promises to keep the young woman safe as he searches for the criminal behind the threats. The two quickly realize the deep connection that they team up to find the person who wants Monique out of the picture.

Other books by the same author:
Bayou Corruption, 2008
Bayou Paradox, 2008
Bayou Judgment, 2008
Bayou Justice, 2007

Other books you might like:
Irene Hannon, *Against All Odds*, 2009
Dee Henderson, *Uncommon Heroes Series*, 2003-2006
Carol Steward, *Shield of Refuge*, 2008

Inspirational

891

MINDY STARNS CLARK

Shadows of Lancaster County

(Eugene, OR: Harvest House, 2009)

Story type: Religious; Modern
Subject(s): Faith; Amish
Major character(s): Anna Bailey, Sister (of Bobby); Bobby Jensen, Brother (of Anna)
Time period(s): 2000s
Locale(s): Lancaster County, Pennsylvania

Summary: Anna Bailey moved to California several years ago to escape a traumatic event from her past. When her sister-in-law calls to tell her that her brother Bobby is missing, Anna returns to Pennsylvania Amish country to try to find him. As she searches for Bobby, she soon discovers a vast conspiracy involving stolen jewels, DNA mapping, and the past that Anna has tried to keep hidden for so long. Anna must put her faith in God to protect her from a team of resolute killers during her determined search for her sibling.

Other books by the same author:
Whispers of the Bayou, 2008

Other books you might like:
Wanda E. Brunstetter, *A Sister's Hope*, 2008
B.J. Hoff, *Rachel's Secret*, 2008

892

COLLEEN COBLE

Cry in the Night

(Nashville: Thomas Nelson, 2009)

Story type: Religious; Mystery
Series: Rock Harbor. Book 4
Subject(s): Faith; Suspense; Missing Persons
Major character(s): Bree Matthews, Rescuer (search-and-rescue worker), Spouse (of Kade); Kade Matthews, Ranger (park ranger), Spouse (of Bree)
Time period(s): 2000s
Locale(s): Rock Harbor, Michigan

Summary: While taking her dog Samson out for a walk one evening, Bree Matthews discovers a baby abandoned in the woods of Rock Harbor, Michigan. Against the objections of her husband Kade, Bree takes the baby girl in and begins to search for the child's mother. Bree desperately wants to have another child with Kade, but the doctors have told her that she should consider adoption. Bree plans to bring the little girl into her family if her parents cannot be located. As she grows more attached to the child, she uncovers a mystery that connects the baby's mother to the mysterious death of Bree's first husband, Anu. The clues quickly lead Bree into a dangerous world of kidnapping and corruption that puts her entire family at risk.

Other books by the same author:
Anathema, 2008
Lonestar Sanctuary, 2008
Abomination, 2007

Fire Dancer, 2006
Aloha Reef Series, 2005-

Other books you might like:
Mindy Starns Clark, *The Buck Stops Here*, 2004
Dee Henderson, *O'Malley Series*, 2000-
Susan Meissner, *Days and Hours*, 2007

893

BRANDILYN COLLINS

Dark Pursuit

(Grand Rapids, MI: Zondervan, 2008)

Story type: Contemporary; Mystery
Subject(s): Mystery; Faith; Family
Major character(s): Darell Brooke, Writer; Kaitlan Sering, Addict (former drug addict)
Time period(s): 2000s
Locale(s): United States

Summary: Kaitlan Sering, a former drug addict, leaves behind her violent boyfriend to move in with her grandfather, who has suffered an accident that left him unable to focus. Her grandfather, novelist Darell Brooke, was a bestselling suspense writer before the accident; now, he has a hard time writing anything. He dreams of writing a suspense thriller that will get him back on top of the fiction world. When a killer sets his sights on Kaitlan, she needs to help her grandfather think clearly so that he can save her from being murdered. Darell, however, can't resist the idea that Kaitlan's story would make a great new novel, and this knowledge clouds his judgment when it comes to saving her.

Other books by the same author:
Kanner Lake Series, 2006-
Hidden Faces Series, 2004-
Chelsea Adams Series, 2001-2002

Other books you might like:
Terri Blackstock, *Double Minds*, 2009
Colleen Coble, *Lonestar Sanctuary*, 2008

894

MARY CONNEALY

Gingham Mountain

(Uhrichsville, OH: Barbour, 2009)

Story type: Romance; Historical/American West
Series: Lassoed in Texas. Book 3
Subject(s): Orphans
Major character(s): Hannah Cartwright, Teacher; Grant Cooper, Cowboy, Rancher; Prudence, Seamstress
Time period(s): 1870s (1870)
Locale(s): Sour Springs, Texas

Summary: Grant Cooper, a Texas rancher, takes care of several orphans and also runs a ranch. Hannah Cartwright, a school teacher, wants to make sure the children Grant adopts are treated right. She doesn't want the innocent orphans forced to do all the hard work on Cooper's ranch. As Grant and Hannah fight over the fate of the orphans and begin to fall in love, another woman named Prudence enters the picture. Prudence, the town seamstress, wants to marry Grant, and she's not above conniving to win his heart. The Lassoed in Texas series focuses on relationships and family life in Texas.

Other books by the same author:
Calico Canyon, 2008 (Lassoed in Texas. Book 2)
Petticoat Ranch, 2007 (Lassoed in Texas. Book 1)

Other books you might like:
Deeanne Gist, *Deep in the Heart of Trouble*, 2008
Marcia Gruver, *Chasing Charity*, 2009
Marcia Gruver, *Diamond Duo*, 2008
Al Lacy, *All My Tomorrows*, 2003
    JoAnna Lacy, co-author
Al Lacy, *The Little Sparrows*, 2003
    JoAnna Lacy, co-author
Al Lacy, *Whispers in the Wind*, 2003
    JoAnna Lacy, co-author

895

LYN COTE

The Desires of Her Heart

(New York, NY: Avon Inspire, February 2009)

Story type: Historical; Religious
Series: Texas: Star of Destiny. Book 1
Subject(s): Faith; Family; Love
Major character(s): Dorritt Mott, Young Woman; Quinn, Scout
Time period(s): 1820s (1821)
Locale(s): Texas

Summary: After watching her stepfather gamble away the family's savings, Dorritt Mott vows never to trap herself in a marriage. In order to avoid repaying his debt, Dorritt's stepfather moves the family from New Orleans to the Texas territory. Leading them through the rugged terrain is Quinn, a half-Cherokee scout. On the journey, Dorritt and Quinn become fast friends. Just as Dorritt begins to question her resolve to stay single, revelations about Quinn's dealings with her stepfather threaten their budding romance. As the two try to understand their feelings for one another, a dangerous plot threatens the entire group.

Other books by the same author:
Her Captain's Heart, 2008
Blessed Assurance, 2007
Women of Ivy Manor Series, 2005-2006

Other books you might like:
Tracey Bateman, *Westward Hearts Series*, 2008-
DiAnn Mills, *Awaken My Heart*, 2008

896

KAYE DACUS

Menu for Romance

(Uhrichsville, OH: Barbour, 2009)

Story type: Contemporary; Romance
Series: Brides of Bonneterre. Book 2

Subject(s): Love; Cooks and Cooking
Major character(s): Meredith Guidry, Planner (party), Caterer; Major O'Hara, Cook
Time period(s): 2000s
Locale(s): Bonneterre, Louisiana

Summary: Meredith Guidry is a party planner, and her company's best chef Major O'Hara has just announced he is leaving to open his own catering company. Without Major's help, Meredith struggles to keep her business afloat until an old college boyfriend calls her out of the blue. He wants her to move to Annapolis with him and leave her business behind. She wonders if this move and this man are her true destiny. When Major learns about Meredith's plans, he questions his motivation for leaving her side, and he vows to stop Meredith from getting involved with another man.

Other books by the same author:
Ransome Trilogy, 2009-
Stand-In Groom, 2009 (Brides of Bonneterre. Book 1)

Other books you might like:
Lois Richer, *Rocky Mountain Legacy*, 2009

897

KAYE DACUS

Ransome's Honor

(Eugene, OR: Harvest House, 2009)

Story type: Historical; Romance
Series: Ransome Trilogy. Book 1
Subject(s): Faith; Romance
Major character(s): Julia Witherington, Young Woman; William Ransome, Military Personnel (captain)
Time period(s): 1810s (1814)
Locale(s): England

Summary: Before leaving to fight in a war, navy captain William Ransome broke Julia Witherington's heart by not proposing to her. In 1814, he is sailing to Portsmouth, England, after fighting in the war with France. Meanwhile, Julia, now 29, learns that she will not earn her dowry unless she marries without delay. Julia and William conspire to act as a married couple for one year so they can split the dowry. As Julia and William struggle to act as a married couple, they develop genuine feelings for each other.

Other books by the same author:
Brides of Bonneterre Series, 2009-

Other books you might like:
Lawana Blackwell, *The Jewel of Gresham Green*, 2008
Lori Wick, *The Proposal*, 2002

898

KAYE DACUS

Stand-In Groom

(Uhrichsville, OH: Barbour, 2009)

Story type: Contemporary; Romance
Series: Brides of Bonneterre. Book 1

Subject(s): Weddings; Christian Life; Love
Major character(s): Anne Hawthorne, Planner (wedding); George Laurence, Bridegroom
Time period(s): 2000s
Locale(s): Bonneterre, Louisiana

Summary: Anne Hawthorne, a single wedding planner, meets George Laurence, the perfect man. She soon learns, however, that she is being hired to plan George's wedding. Anne's strict Christian values keep her in check, but her business and her faith are on the line as she struggles to plan the nuptials of a man she is falling in love with. Meanwhile, George, who is also a devout Christian, seems to be struggling with his own attraction to Anne. Furthermore, George is hiding a very big secret that just might change everything for him and Anne. First novel.

Other books you might like:
Denise Hunter, *The Convenient Groom*, 2008
Trish Perry, *The Guy I'm Not Dating*, 2006
Virginia Smith, *Age Before Beauty*, 2009
Laura Jensen Walker, *Daring Chloe*, 2008

899

SUSAN PAGE DAVIS

Inside Story

(Eugene, OR: Harvest House, 2009)

Story type: Contemporary; Romance
Series: Frasier Island. Book 3
Subject(s): Romance; Faith; Military Life
Major character(s): Claudia Gillette, Journalist; Bill White, Military Personnel
Time period(s): 2000s
Locale(s): United States; Philippines

Summary: This fast-paced romance begins when Claudia and Bill are introduced to one another. Claudia Gillette is a journalist for a ritzy magazine. Bill White is a no-nonsense navy man. When Claudia decides to write a story about Bill's secret missions, she gets clearance from Bill's superior—a move that enrages Bill. He fears for Claudia's life and for the safety of his team, which he feels that she is endangering. Characters from other Frasier Island books also make an appearance in this novel.

Other books by the same author:
Finding Marie, 2007 (Frasier Island. Book 2)
Frasier Island, 2007 (Frasier Island. Book 1)

Other books you might like:
Kristen Heitzmann, *The Edge of Recall*, 2008
Dee Henderson, *Uncommon Heroes Series*, 2003-2005

900

MARY DEMUTH

Daisy Chain

(Grand Rapids, MI: Zondervan, 2009)

Story type: Contemporary; Religious
Series: Defiance Texas Trilogy. Book 1

Subject(s): Guilt; Grief; Faith
Major character(s): Jed Pepper, Abuse Victim, Friend (of Daisy); Daisy Chance, Crime Victim (kidnapped), Friend (of Jed)
Time period(s): 1970s (1973)
Locale(s): Defiance, Texas

Summary: Thirteen-year-old Daisy Chance disappeared shortly after her best friend, Jed Pepper, refused to walk her home from the ruins of an old church. Jed blames himself for the young girl's disappearance and desperately searches for clues to his friend's whereabouts. In the meantime, Jed must protect his mother and sister from his preacher father's increasingly violent behavior. With the help of Daisy's morally questionable mother and several other colorful characters, Jed attempts to set things right before it's too late.

Other books by the same author:
Watching the Tree Limbs, 2006
Wishing on Dandelions, 2006

Other books you might like:
Elizabeth Musser, *Searching for Eternity*, 2007

901

BRANDT DODSON

Daniel's Den

(Eugene, OR: Harvest House, 2009)

Story type: Mystery; Contemporary
Subject(s): Death; Faith; Suspense
Major character(s): Daniel Borden, Accountant; Laura Traynor, Businesswoman (owns a bed and breakfast), Single Parent (of Andy); Andy Traynor, Child (of Laura)
Time period(s): 2000s
Locale(s): Washington, District of Columbia

Summary: After discovering that a recently deceased co-worker was stealing money from the company, Daniel suddenly finds himself blamed for his colleague's death and on the run from a group of assassins. Scared and confused, Daniel finds himself at Laura Traynor's inn. Since the death of her husband, Laura has been struggling to keep the business afloat while caring for her young son Andy. Though Laura and Daniel feel an immediate connection, their budding romance is put on hold when the killers show up at the inn. Now on the run with Laura and Andy, Daniel must put his faith in God to help him unravel the mystery surrounding his company before it's too late.

Other books by the same author:
White Soul, 2008
The Lost Sheep, 2007
The Root of All Evil, 2007

Other books you might like:
Craig Parshall, *Trial by Ordeal*, 2006

902

MEREDITH EFKEN

Play It Again, SAHM

(Buffalo, NY: Steeple Hill Cafe, 2009)

Story type: Contemporary; Religious
Subject(s): Friendship; Faith
Major character(s): Rosalyn Ebberly, Parent; Hannah, Parent; Iona, Parent
Time period(s): 2000s
Locale(s): United States

Summary: *Play it Again, SAHM* is the humorous story of a group of online friends, and stay-at-home moms, who are getting together for their first face-to-face meeting. Aside from the ladies who have been in the group for a long time, two new moms named Iona and Hannah are trying to join the club. Hannah's assertive spirit does not go over well with the rest of the ladies, and one mom in particular is having a hard time staying civil.

Other books by the same author:
Home for the Holidays, 2006
SAHM, I Am, 2005

Other books you might like:
Neta Jackson, *The Yada Yada Prayer Group Series*, 2003-
Karen Kingsbury, *Sunrise Series*, 2008-

903

JERRY S. EICHER

Rebecca's Return

(Eugene, OR; Harvest House, 2009)

Story type: Romance; Religious
Series: Adams County Trilogy. Book 2
Subject(s): Faith; Amish; Love
Major character(s): Rebecca Keim, Fiance(e) (of John), Young Woman; John Miller, Fianc(e) (of Rebecca)
Time period(s): 2000s
Locale(s): Wheat Ridge

Summary: Rebecca Keim is still in love with John Miller and she plans to marry him. When she returns to Wheat Ridge, however, John acts differently toward her. They argue and fail to resolve this issue. In the midst of their fighting, John is suddenly injured and Rebecca is again called to her childhood home to care for her aunt. While in Wheat Ridge, Rebecca is reminded of a love from the past. Now that John does not seem to want Rebecca as his wife, she contemplates giving her former flame a second chance.

Other books by the same author:
Rebecca's Promise, 2009 (Adams County Trilogy. Book 1)
Sarah's Son, 2008
Living Christianity, 2003 (nonfiction)
Transforming the Believer, 2002

Other books you might like:
Wanda E. Brunstetter, *Brides of Webster County Series*, 2006-
Cindy Woodsmall, *Sisters of the Quilt Series*, 2006-

904

JERRY S. EICHER

Rebecca's Promise

(Eugene, OR: Harvest House, 2009)

Story type: Romance; Religious
Series: Adams County Trilogy. Book 1
Subject(s): Faith; Love; Amish
Major character(s): Rebecca Keim, Fiance(e) (of John), Young Woman; John Miller, Fianc(e) (of Rebecca)
Time period(s): 2000s
Locale(s): Milroy

Summary: Rebecca Keim promises to marry John Miller, however, she still wonders about a love from her past. When Rebecca was just a girl, she promised her heart to someone else, and that promise haunts her as she plans to become the wife of John. Soon, Rebecca is called to her childhood home of Milroy to care for her aunt for an extended period. While in her hometown of Milroy, Rebecca decides to search for her lost love and put her worries to rest.

Other books by the same author:
Hannah, 2009
Rebecca's Return, 2009 (Adams County Trilogy. Book 2)
Hannah's Dream, 2008
Sarah, 2007
A Time to Live, 2006

Other books you might like:
Wanda E. Brunstetter, *Brides of Webster County Series*, 2006-
Cindy Woodsmall, *Sisters of the Quilt Series*, 2006-

905

MIRALEE FERRELL

Love Finds You in Last Chance, California

(Bloomington, MN; Summerside Press, 2009)

Story type: Romance; Historical
Series: Love Finds You. Book 6
Subject(s): Love; Ranch Life; Faith
Major character(s): Alexia Travers, Young Woman, Rancher; Justin Phillips, Rancher
Time period(s): 1880s (1889)
Locale(s): Last Chance, California

Summary: Alexia Travers is reeling from the recent loss of her father, and she's struggling to keep up with the work and expenses that come with maintaining her father's horse ranch. Several men are interested in making Alexia their wife, but she doesn't feel a connection to any of them. Resolved to make the ranch work, she

Inspirational

dresses as a man and runs the ranch herself. Soon, Justin Phillips, an old friend of Alexia's father, arrives at the ranch with his young son. Alexia and Justin battle to be the best rancher on the land, and in the process, they fall in love. When disaster strikes, their love is tested.

Other books by the same author:
The Other Daughter, 2007

Other books you might like:
Andrea Boeshaar, *Love Finds You in Miracle, Kansas*, 2008
  Love Finds You. Book 1
Irene Brand, *Love Finds You in Valentine, Nebraska*, 2008
  Love Finds You. Book 3
Sandra D. Bricker, *Love Finds You in Snowball, Alaska*, 2008
  Love Finds You. Book 2
Lori Wick, *Big Sky Dreams Series*, 2007-

906

SIBELLA GIORELLO

The River Runs Dry

(Nashville: Thomas Nelson, 2009)

Story type: Contemporary
Subject(s): Faith
Major character(s): Margaret Harmon, FBI Agent
Time period(s): 2000s
Locale(s): Seattle, Washington

Summary: FBI agent Raleigh Harmon is sent to Seattle because of her inability to follow direct orders. There, Raleigh immediately gets assigned to a case and begins searching for a missing woman. Her unique background makes her the perfect detective for the job. While on the case, Raleigh struggles to deal with her family troubles and still perform at her job, where she feels that she can trust no one. Raleigh tries to keep her emotions in check, but as her personal and professional lives become more and more complicated, Raleigh begins to come apart at the seams.

Where it's reviewed:
Booklist, February 15, 2009, page 39
Publishers Weekly, January 19, 2009, page 39

Other books by the same author:
The Stones Cry Out, 2007

Other books you might like:
Margaret Daly, *What Sarah Saw*, 2009
Amy Wallace, *Healing Promises*, 2008

907

DEEANNE GIST

A Bride in the Bargain

(Ada, MI; Bethany House, 2009)

Story type: Historical; Romance
Subject(s): Faith; Love

Major character(s): Joe Denton, Widow(er); Anna Ivey, Young Woman (Mercer bride)
Time period(s): 1860s (1860)
Locale(s): Seattle, Washington

Summary: When Joe Denton loses his wife, he learns that half of his land is about to be taken away. He decides to purchase a wife from the group of women brought from the east. He is still not over his wife, but he doesn't need to find love, just a cook who will help him keep his land. The wife he chooses, Anna Ivey, has no plans to marry and she refuses to cooperate with Joe's plan. As the day when Joe must give up his land approaches, he tries to convince Anna to become his wife, and in the process, he develops real feelings for her.

Other books by the same author:
Deep in the Heart of Trouble, 2008
Courting Trouble, 2007
The Measure of a Lady, 2006
A Bride Most Begrudging, 2005

Other books you might like:
Cathy Marie Hake, *Fancy Pants*, 2007
Cathy Marie Hake, *Whirlwind*, 2008

908

SHELLEY SHEPHARD GRAY

Wanted

(New York: Avon Inspire, 2009)

Story type: Contemporary; Romance
Series: Sisters of the Heart. Book 2
Subject(s): Amish; Romance; Christian Life
Major character(s): Katie Brenneman, Child-Care Giver; Jonathan Lundy, Widow(er), Parent
Time period(s): 2000s
Locale(s): United States

Summary: Jonathan Lundy asks Katie Brenneman to help him care for his daughters for a short time. Katie has developed feelings for Jonathan, so she happily offers her assistance. They get along very well and Katie believes that they may be falling in love. Suddenly, a mysterious note shows up and threatens to expose the past that Katie has been hiding. While she was experimenting with life outside of the Amish lifestyle, she did some things that she is ashamed of, and now those mistakes are threatening to destroy her new relationship with Jonathan. Books in the Sisters of the Heart series explore relationships in Amish societies.

Other books by the same author:
Hidden, 2008 (Sisters of the Heart. Book 1)

Other books you might like:
Wanda E. Brunstetter, *Brides of Lancaster County Series*, 2007-
Wanda E. Brunstetter, *A Cousin's Promise*, 2009
Jerry S. Eicher, *Rebecca's Promise*, 2009
Mary Ellis, *A Widow's Hope*, 2009
B.J. Hoff, *Rachel's Secret*, 2008
Beverly Lewis, *The Preacher's Daughter*, 2005
Beverly Lewis, *The Parting*, 2007
Beth Wiseman, *Plain Pursuit*, 2009

909

MARCIA GRUVER

Chasing Charity

(Uhrichsville, OH: Barbour Publishing, 2009)

Story type: Historical; Romance
Series: Texas Fortunes Trilogy. Book 2
Subject(s): Oil; Romance
Major character(s): Charity Bloom, Fiance(e); Buddy Pierce, Oil Industry Worker; Daniel Clark, Fiance(e)
Time period(s): 1900s (1905)
Locale(s): Humble, Texas

Summary: In this novel, Charity Bloom is set to marry Daniel Clark, but she and the rest of the people who live in Humble, Texas, learn that Daniel has run away with her best friend. Devastated, Charity tries to forgive them. Soon, a man named Buddy Pierce shows up in town looking to strike oil, and he finds it on Charity Bloom's property. Buddy also develops feelings for Charity. He wonders if he can convince Charity to try love again. Then Daniel returns to town, desperate to win Charity back.

Other books by the same author:
Diamond Duo, 2008 (Texas Fortunes Trilogy. Book 1)

Other books you might like:
Kelly Eileen Hake, *Prairie Promise Series*, 2008-2009
Karen Kingsbury, *Sunrise Series*, 2007-

910

CATHY MARIE HAKE

That Certain Spark

(Ada, MI: Bethany House, 2009)

Story type: Historical; Romance
Subject(s): Faith; Love
Major character(s): Karl Van der Vort, Blacksmith; Taylor Bestman, Doctor, Sister (of Enoch); Enoch Bestman, Veterinarian, Brother (of Taylor)
Time period(s): 1800s
Locale(s): Gooding , Texas

Summary: The residents of Gooding, Texas are excited to hear that a pair of siblings was coming to town to fill the roles of town veterinarian and doctor. The townspeople, however, are shocked and surprised when Enoch and Taylor Bestman arrive in town. No one expected that the new doctor would be a woman, especially blacksmith Karl Van der Vort. The stubborn and traditional Karl becomes Taylor's first unwilling patient when he injuries himself on the job. Determined not to let her gender interfere with her work, Taylor sets out to prove her skills to the citizens of Gooding. Despite his objections, Karl begins to fall for the intelligent doctor, giving Taylor a glimpse of the kind heart that lies behind his rough exterior.

Other books by the same author:
Forevermore, 2008
Whirlwind, 2008
Bittersweet, 2007

Fancy Pants, 2007
Letter Perfect, 2006
Other books you might like:
Deeanne Gist, *Courting Trouble*, 2007
Deeanne Gist, *Deep in the Heart of Trouble*, 2008
Kelly Eileen Hake, *The Bride Bargain*, 2008

911

KELLY EILEEN HAKE

The Bride Backfire

(Uhrichsville, OH: Barbour, 2009)

Story type: Historical/American West; Romance
Series: Prairie Promises. Book 2
Subject(s): Feuds; Family; Love
Major character(s): Adam Grogan, Friend (of Opal); Opal Speck, Friend (of Adam)
Time period(s): 1850s (1857)
Locale(s): Nebraska

Summary: The Specks and the Grogans have been feuding for years. A truce between the two warring families seemed to be on the horizon until Adam Grogan trespassed on Speck land. Knowing that her family will kill Adam for his actions, Opal Speck declares that the young man is the father of her unborn child. Adam now finds himself in an even more difficult situation. If he doesn't go along with Opal's lie and marry someone he barely knows, he runs the risk of starting an all-out war between the two families. Adam and Opal must rely on their faith in God to help them through these troubled times.

Other books by the same author:
The Bride Bargain, 2008 (Prairie Promises. Book 1)

Other books you might like:
Cathy Marie Hake, *Fancy Pants*, 2007
Cathy Marie Hake, *Whirlwind*, 2008

912

KAREN HANCOCK

The Enclave

(Ada, MI; Bethany House, 2009)

Story type: Religious; Mystery
Subject(s): Romance; Suspense; Faith
Major character(s): Lacey McHenry, Researcher (genetics); Cameron Reinhardt, Researcher (genetics)
Time period(s): 2000s
Locale(s): United States

Summary: Lacey McHenry knew that winning a prestigious fellowship to study at the Kendell-Jakes Longevity Institute would change her life in many ways, but she never thought that taking the position could put her life in danger. While working late one evening, Lacey encounters an intruder who believes the institute is involved in a conspiracy. Shaken by the visit, Lacey does a little digging of her own. When she uncovers a plot involving institute administrators, the young researcher is unsure of whom she can trust. Though she's become close to Cameron Reinhardt, Lacey now wonders if he isn't hiding some dangerous secrets of his own.

Other books by the same author:
Legends of the Guardian King Series (2003-)

Other books you might like:
Kristen Heitzmann, *The Edge of Recall*, 2008
Paul Robertson, *According to Their Deeds*, 2008

913

IRENE HANNON

Against All Odds

(Ada, MI: Revell, 2009)

Story type: Romantic Suspense
Series: Heroes of Quantico. Book 1
Subject(s): Terrorism; Faith; Romance
Major character(s): Monica Callahan, Young Woman; Evan Cooper, FBI Agent (Hostage Rescue Team)
Time period(s): 2000s
Locale(s): United States

Summary: Evan Cooper is an FBI agent whose specialty is convincing bad guys to release hostages. He is saddled with the uncomfortable job of keeping Monica Callahan safe. Because of her father, Monica is being threatened by a terrorist group, but she isn't afraid of terrorists, and she doesn't want to follow any of the precautions that Evan insists on. While protecting Monica, Evan begins to fall in love with the striking woman. When Monica's distant father does something to jeopardize her safety, Evan struggles to save Monica from the imminent danger.

Other books by the same author:
Apprentice Father, 2009
When Love Abides, 2008
Rainbow's End, 2007

Other books you might like:
Dee Henderson, *The Negotiator*, 2005
Dee Henderson, *Uncommon Heroes Series*, 2002-2005

914

ROBIN LEE HATCHER

When Love Blooms

(Grand Rapids, MI: Zondervan, 2009)

Story type: Historical; Romance
Subject(s): Cancer; Love
Major character(s): Emily Harris, Governess; Gavin Blake, Rancher
Time period(s): 1880s (1883)
Locale(s): Boise City, Idaho

Summary: Spoiled Emily Harris is taking on a difficult job. She is moving to the high country of Idaho where the local people must perform hard work just to scrape by. She is moving there to be the governess of two needy girls. When Gavin Blake meets Emily, he guesses that she won't be very successful at making a life in Idaho.

His guess is that she won't make it through one winter. Emily, however, wants to show everyone that she can survive the rough Idaho life, and Gavin's skepticism only encourages her to try harder. Emily attempts to make a difference in the world and her determined spirit attracts the attention of two men. Emily must then make important decisions about love and life.

Other books by the same author:
Wagered Heart, 2008
Return to Me, 2007
Catching Kate, 2004

Other books you might like:
Lori Wick, *City Girl*, 2008

915

LAURA HAYDEN

Red, White, and Blue

(Carol Stream, IL: Tyndale, 2009)

Story type: Contemporary; Political
Series: America the Beautiful. Book 2
Subject(s): Presidents; Christian Life; Politics
Major character(s): Kate Rosen, Political Figure (Presidential adviser); Emily Benton, Political Figure (President)
Time period(s): 2000s
Locale(s): Washington, District of Columbia

Summary: Kate Rosen serves as the adviser to her best friend Emily Benton, who also happens to be the first female elected to the presidency of the United States. Kate loves her job, but her Christian beliefs often cause her discomfort in the world of sleazy politics. As Emily prepares to take office, Kate is bothered by some of Emily's decisions and actions. She worries that her best friend is being changed by the power she's been given. When Kate learns that Emily has done something that goes against her Christian beliefs, she has to choose between supporting her friend and acting according to her faith.

Other books by the same author:
America the Beautiful, 2008 (America the Beautiful. Book 1)

Other books you might like:
James Scott Bell, *Deadlock*, 2002
Tim Downs, *Less than Dead*, 2008
Elizabeth White, *Off the Record*, 2007

916

ROXANNE HENKE

On a Someday

(Eugene, OR: Harvest House, 2009)

Story type: Contemporary; Religious
Subject(s): Family; Modern Life; Faith
Major character(s): Claire Westin, Professor, Spouse (of Jim); Jim Westin, Store Owner (grocery store), Spouse (of Claire); Drew Westin, Banker (loan of-

ficer), Relative (son of Claire and Jim)

Time period(s): 2000s

Locale(s): North Dakota

Summary: When Claire and Jim Westin married 25 years ago, they always looked forward to the things that they would do when they retired. Grocery store owner Jim dreams of restoring a classic car, while Claire hopes to finish an abandoned project. As the years pass, the couple keeps putting off their plans in order to raise a family and further their careers. When Claire's mother dies, she decides to finish writing the book she started long ago. Surprisingly, the book becomes a best seller and Claire embarks on a whirlwind press tour. Jim is still looking forward to retirement, but his plans for his grocery store chain are dashed when son Drew decides that he doesn't want to take over the family business. Soon, a health crisis forces all of the family members to reassess their hopes and dreams.

Other books by the same author:

Learning to Fly, 2008

With Love, Libby, 2006

Always Jan, 2005

Other books you might like:

Nicole Bart, *Summer Snow*, 2008

Lori Copeland, *A Perfect Love*, 2008

    Angela Hunt, co-author

917

KATHY HERMAN

The Real Enemy

(Colorado Springs: David C. Cook, 2009)

Story type: Mystery; Contemporary

Series: Sophie Trace Trilogy. Book 1

Subject(s): Mystery; Marriage; Faith

Major character(s): Brill Jessup, Police Officer (chief), Spouse (of Kurt); Kurt Jessup, Spouse (of Brill); Emily Jessup, Relative (daughter of Brill and Kurt)

Time period(s): 2000s

Locale(s): Memphis, Tennessee; Sophie Trace, Tennessee

Summary: Devastated by her husband Kurt's infidelity, Brill Jessup and her family move to Sophie Trace to escape their past. The couple decides to remain together for their daughter Emily, but they have a hard time hiding their true feelings for each other. Soon after the Jessups arrive in Sophie Trace, citizens begin to go missing and Brill dives into an investigation that involves myths, legends, and mysteries. While working on the case, Brill also reflects on her marriage and searches for a way to forgive the husband who has hurt her so badly.

Other books by the same author:

Phantom Hollow Series, 2007-

Baxter Series, 2001-

Other books you might like:

Terri Blackstock, *Double Minds*, 2009

Brandilyn Collins, *Dark Pursuits*, 2008

918

HOMER HICKAM

Red Helmet

(Nashville: Thomas Nelson, 2008)

Story type: Contemporary; Religious

Subject(s): Faith; Miners and Mining

Major character(s): Cable Jordan, Miner; Song Hawkins, Businesswoman, Wealthy

Time period(s): 2000s

Locale(s): Highcoal, West Virginia

Summary: No-nonsense New Yorker Song Hawkins is running her dad's coal company when she falls for a blue-collar mining manager named Cable Jordan. Although the wealthy socialite loves Cable, she has difficulty adjusting to his rural West Virginia life. When Song is called to investigate dwindling profits and other problems at a mine, she goes undercover as a miner and learns the business from the deep inside. She makes friends and witnesses firsthand the trials and tribulations of working in a mine. During her time in the mine, she reflects on her marriage problems and gets involved with a murder investigation.

Where it's reviewed:

Publishers Weekly, September 24, 2007, page 40

Other books by the same author:

The Coalwood Series, 1999-2002

The Josh Thurlow Series, 1996-2007

Other books you might like:

Pamela Binnings Ewen, *The Moon in the Mango Tree*, 2008

Jane Kirkpatrick, *A Land of Sheltered Promise*, 2009

919

DON HOESEL

Elisha's Bones

(Ada, MI: Bethany House, 2009)

Story type: Mystery; Religious

Subject(s): Faith; Suspense

Major character(s): Jack Hawthorne, Professor; Gordon Reese, Wealthy (billionaire)

Time period(s): 2000s

Summary: After leaving behind the exciting world of archeological field work for the classroom, professor Jack Hawthorne looks forward to spending a quiet Christmas break at home in North Carolina. His plans for a relaxing vacation are put on hold when billionaire Gordon Reese invites him on a quest to find the bones of the Biblical prophet Elisha. The dying man is desperate to find the bones that can supposedly bring the dead back to life, and he's willing to pay Jack a great deal of money to help him. As their journey takes them to exotic locations around the world, Jack is forced to confront the tragedy that took him out of the field years ago. First novel.

920

B.J. HOFF

American Anthem

(Eugene, OR; Harvest House, 2009)

Story type: Romance; Religious
Subject(s): Faith; Love
Major character(s): Susanna Fallon, Governess; Michael Emmanuel, Musician
Time period(s): 1870s (1870)
Locale(s): New York, New York

Summary: Susanna Fallon, an Irish governess, seeks revenge on the man who ruined her sister's life, so she sets out to find him. When she locates the musician, she can't believe he is the same man her sister described. A doctor falls in love and struggles with the secret that could destroy his relationship. A poor family worries about how they will survive until an unlikely savior arrives on their doorstep. Each novel revolves around characters who maintain their hope and faith in the face of their crushing circumstances. Previously published as three separate novels.

Other books by the same author:
The Riverhaven Years Series, 2008-
Mountain Song Legacy, 2006-

Other books you might like:
Michael Phillips, *Dream of Love*, 2008

921

ANGELA HUNT

She's in a Better Place

(Carol Stream, IL; Tyndale, 2009)

Story type: Contemporary; Religious
Series: Fairlawn. Book 3
Subject(s): Faith; Family; Forgiveness
Major character(s): Jennifer Graham, Undertaker; Gerald Huffman, Undertaker
Time period(s): 2000s
Locale(s): United States

Summary: Jennifer Graham runs the Fairlawn Funeral Home. She is also raising two kids and preparing for an important national test. As if she didn't have enough to worry about, her assistant Gerald spontaneously announces that he is suffering from a severe disease. Jennifer learns that Gerald no longer speaks to his daughter, and she decides to help them get reacquainted. The reconciliation, however, will not go as simply as Jennifer would like.

Other books by the same author:
Doesn't She Look Natural, 2008 (Fairlawn Series. Book 1)
She Always Wore Red, 2008 (Fairlawn Series. Book 2)

Other books you might like:
Colleen Coble, *Lonestar Secrets*, 2009
Lois Richer, *Rocky Mountain Legacy*, 2009

922

DENISE HUNTER

Sweetwater Gap

(Nashville: Thomas Nelson, 2009)

Story type: Contemporary
Subject(s): Faith; Relationships; Love
Major character(s): Josephine "Josie" Mitchell, Photographer; Laurel, Relative (sister of Josie); Grady McKenzie, Foreman
Time period(s): 2000s
Locale(s): United States

Summary: Josephine Mitchell is dealing with a lot of guilt because of her past—a past that she has never revealed to anyone. Despite the guilt, Josephine comes home to Blue Ridge Orchard to help her sister Laurel during a difficult pregnancy. Laurel wants Josephine to pitch in and help with the hard work. Laurel's husband Nate wants Josephine to convince Laurel to sell the orchard. Grady MacKenzie, who runs the apple orchard, has a real problem with Josephine. As Josephine spends time at the orchard, she develops feelings for Grady, and she faces the past that she has been running away from for years.

Where it's reviewed:
Publishers Weekly, October 13, 2008, page 38

Other books by the same author:
The Convenient Groom, 2008
Surrender Bay, 2007
Finding Faith, 2006
Saving Grace, 2005

Other books you might like:
Julie Carobini, *Sweet Waters*, 2009
Kim Vogel Sawyer, *Where the Heart Leads*, 2008
Lisa Wingate, *Word Gets Around*, 2009

923

NOEL HYND

Midnight in Madrid

(Grand Rapids, MI: Zondervan, 2009)

Story type: Psychological Suspense; Mystery
Series: Russian Trilogy. Book 2
Subject(s): Treasure; Mystery
Major character(s): Alexandra "Alex" LaDuca, Government Official (U.S. Treasury Agent)
Time period(s): 2000s
Locale(s): Madrid, Spain; Europe

Summary: Alexandra LaDuca, a U.S. Treasury agent, and her new partner travel through Europe in search of an artifact that was pilfered from a museum in Madrid. The artifact is associated with many myths and legends, and since the artifact has gone missing, mysterious deaths and strange accidents have been occurring all over Europe. Alexandra's search is complicated by the strange occurrences that seem to follow the artifact wherever it goes and she begins to wonder who she can trust.

Other books by the same author:
Conspiracy in Kiev, 2008 (Russian Trilogy. Book 1)

Other books you might like:
Jill Ellizabeth Nelson, *Reluctant Smuggler*, 2008
John B. Olson, *Fossil Hunter*, 2008

924

ANNIE JONES

Barefoot Brides

(Buffalo, NY; Steeple Hill, 2009)

Story type: Contemporary
Series: Barefoot Believers. Book 2
Subject(s): Faith; Family; Love
Major character(s): Moxie Weatherby, Adoptee, Relative
(sister of Jo and Kate); Jo Cromwell, Religious
(minister), Relative (sister of Moxie and Kate); Kate
Cromwell, Doctor, Relative (sister of Moxie and Jo)
Time period(s): 2000s
Locale(s): Santa Sofia, Florida

Summary: Moxie Weatherby was raised by strangers far
away from the rest of her biological family, including
two sisters she didn't know she had. A chance run-in allows Moxie to meet her sisters in Santa Sofia, Florida.
There, a newspaper editor wants to pen an article about
Moxie's life, so she digs into her past and tells him her
story. Moxie's sister Jo is in the process of opening a
ministry, and a minister is helping her realize her dream.
Meanwhile, Moxie's other sister Kate is preparing for
her dream wedding to a doctor.

Other books by the same author:
The Barefoot Believers, 2008 (The Barefoot Believers.
Book 1)

Other books you might like:
Rebeca Seitz, *Sisters, Ink Series*, 2008-

925

KAREN KINGSBURY

Take One

(Grand Rapids, MI: Zondervan, 2009)

Story type: Contemporary; Religious
Series: Above the Line. Book 1
Subject(s): Faith; Family; Movie Industry
Major character(s): Chase Ryan, Filmmaker, Religious
(former missionary); Keith Ellison, Filmmaker,
Religious (former missionary)
Time period(s): 2000s
Locale(s): Bloomington, Indiana

Summary: Chase Ryan and Keith Ellison are two
missionaries-turned-filmmakers who get the chance of a
lifetime—to make a film that will change the world for
the better. They dive into making their ground-breaking
movie and struggle with reconciling the perils of the
Hollywood movie industry and their Christian beliefs.
As they get deeper into the project, however, they begin
to wonder if they will be a success or if they will fail

and let their investors down. The opportunity that once
seemed sent from God now seems to be a mistake, as
the filmmakers try to remember what is was that first
inspired them to leave their mission and make a movie.

Other books by the same author:
Sunset, 2008
Summer, 2007
Sunrise, 2007
911 Series, 2003-

Other books you might like:
Dee Henderson, *O'Malley Series*, 2001-
Lisa Wingate, *Word Gets Around*, 2009

926

KAREN KINGSBURY

This Side of Heaven

(Nashville: Hachette Book Group, 2009)

Story type: Religious
Subject(s): Faith; Family
Major character(s): Josh Warren, Driver (tow truck
driver); Annie Warren, Parent (mother of Josh); Nate
Warren, Parent (father of Josh)
Time period(s): 2000s
Locale(s): United States

Summary: Nate and Annie Warren worry about their son
Josh. He has had trouble with the law, can't find work,
and lost the love of his life when he couldn't straighten
up his life. When he comes into a large amount of
money, Josh decides to live a Christian life and search
for the daughter whom he has never met. When disaster
strikes Josh's life, his parents and other family members
make an attempt to learn more about their son. In their
search for information, they realize their son had many
secrets, and his true soul is revealed to them for the very
first time.

Where it's reviewed:
Publishers Weekly, November 10, 2008, page 34

Other books by the same author:
Between Sundays, 2008
Like Dandelion Dust, 2006
On Every Side, 2006
Redemption Series, 2002-

Other books you might like:
Deborah Bedford, *Family Matters*, 2008

927

JULIE KLASSEN

The Apothecary's Daughter

(Ada, MI: Bethany House, 2009)

Story type: Historical/Regency; Religious
Subject(s): Faith; Family
Major character(s): Lillian Haswell, Young Woman,
Worker; Francis Baylor, Assistant
Time period(s): 19th century

Inspirational

Locale(s): London, England; Bedsley Priors, England

Summary: Lillian Haswell is known as the apothecary's daughter in Bedsley Priors, the small English town where she grew up. If it was up to Lillian, she would leave Bedsley Priors. When her aunt and uncle invite Lillian to stay at their home in London, she leaves behind her family and everything she knows. In London, Lillian meets several suitors, but she worries that her low rural upbringing could hamper her from finding a suitable match. Suddenly, Lillian learns that her father has become very ill, so she rushes home to run the apothecary shop for him. As a woman, she is not allowed to run the shop on her own, but Francis, her father's assistant, helps her with the work. Will she be able to return to London in time to secure a good husband?

Where it's reviewed:
Booklist, December 15, 2008, page 27
Publishers Weekly, November 24, 2008, page 39

Other books by the same author:
Lady of Milkweed Manor, 2008

Other books you might like:
Siri Mitchell, *Constant Heart*, 2008
Lori Wick, *English Garden Series*, 2002-

928

PATTI LACY

What the Bayou Saw

(Grand Rapids, MI: Kregel Publications, 2009)

Story type: Religious; Mystery
Subject(s): Suspense; Racial Conflict
Major character(s): Sally Stevens, Teacher
Time period(s): 2000s (2005)
Locale(s): Normal, Illinois

Summary: Sally Stevens has almost managed to forget what happened to her all those years ago. Since leaving Louisiana, Sally has kept her childhood secrets to herself. Not even her husband knows about what happened to her. Now a professor at a university, Sally is shocked when one of her students is brutally raped. The terrible crime forces Sally to admit the truth about her past to the people she cares about. After all these years, Sally finally tells the story of what happened to her and her best friend in 1959.

Other books by the same author:
An Irishwoman's Tale, 2008

Other books you might like:
Nancy N. Rue, *Healing Stones*, 2007
    Stephan Arterburn, co-author

929

STEPHEN R. LAWHEAD

Tuck

(Nashville: Thomas Nelson, 2009)

Story type: Historical; Religious
Series: King Raven. Book 3

Subject(s): Faith; Love; Fantasy

Summary: The people of Wales are happy that King Raven has come to help them. Before his arrival, they were tyrannized by Norman oppressors. Friar Tuck has greatly assisted King Raven in his quest to lead the people. In this novel, Abbot Hugo plans to strike out Rhi Bran y Hud and his people for good. After Abbot Hugo's brutal attack, Rhi Bran and his people are disheartened and on the verge of giving up. Suddenly, Tuck, who has always served in the background, steps up with a plan that gives hope to Rhi Bran and his followers.

Other books by the same author:
Hood, 2008 (King Raven Series, book 1)
Scarlet, 2008 (King Raven Series, Book 2)
Dragon King Series, 2007

Other books you might like:
Bernard Cornwell, *Agincourt*, 2009

930

TAMERA LEIGH

Faking Grace

(Colorado Springs: Multnomah Books, 2008)

Story type: Religious; Contemporary
Subject(s): Journalism; Faith; Love
Major character(s): Maizy Grace Stewart, Journalist; Jack Prentiss, Publisher
Time period(s): 2000s
Locale(s): Nashville, Tennessee

Summary: Maizy Grace Stewart wants a job as an investigative journalist, but all she has is a part-time gig at a Nashville newspaper that doesn't quite pay the rent. To supplement her income, Maizy takes a job at Steeple Side Christian Resources, a Nashville newspaper. The problem is that the company only hires Christians. Maizy is sure she can fake her faith, but managing editor Jack Prentiss has his eye on her. He soon makes it his mission to prove that Maizy's a fraud. Things get even more complicated when Maizy's newspaper boss asks her to write an expose on Steeple Side. Maizy must now decide if she's willing to risk the friendships she's made and the faith she's found in order to further her career.

Other books by the same author:
Perfecting Kate, 2007
Splitting Harriet, 2007
Stealing Adda, 2006

Other books you might like:
Robin Lee Hatcher, *Loving Libby*, 2005
Elizabeth White, *Controlling Interest*, 2005
Lori Wick, *A Place Called Home*, 2005

931

ROBERT LIPARULO

Gatekeepers

(Nashville: Thomas Nelson, 2009)

Story type: Young Adult; Fantasy
Series: Dreamhouse Kings. Book 3

Subject(s): Mystery; Faith; Fantasy
Major character(s): Xander King, Teenager; David King, Teenager
Time period(s): 2000s
Locale(s): Pineville

Summary: After David and Xander King move to Pineville, they reside in a scary home that is full of mysteries. In their hallway, they find a portal to other times. Soon after their discovery, their mother is kidnapped and taken to another time. David and Xander promise to find their mother, but a mysterious villain named Taksidian keeps trying to stop them. An elderly man arrives at the door one day and tells David and Xander that the boys are Gatekeepers. He tells them that their responsibility is to guard the portals, and he gives them information that could help them save their mother.

Other books by the same author:
House of Dark Shadows, 2008 (Dreamhouse Kings. Book 1)
Watcher in the Woods, 2008 (Dreamhouse Kings. Book 2)

Other books you might like:
Alexander Key, *Escape to Witch Mountain*, 1968-
Alexander Key, *Return from Witch Mountain*, 1984-
C.S. Lewis, *The Chronicles of Narnia Series*, 1998-

932

CHRISTINE LYNXWILER

Forever Christmas

(Uhrichsville, OH: Barbour, 2007)

Story type: Religious; Romance
Subject(s): Faith; Family; Love
Major character(s): Kristianna Harrington, Store Owner (of Forever Christmas); Shawn, Lawyer (for Summer Valley Outdoors)
Time period(s): 2000s
Locale(s): Jingle Bells, Arkansas

Summary: The residents of Jingle Bells, Arkansas face a difficult decision. Though their town's name has always been a source of great pride, the citizens of Jingle Bells consider changing the moniker in order to bring Summer Valley Outdoors into their community. While Kristianna Harrington believes that the company could bring new jobs to the area, she worries that the name change could spell disaster for her Christmas-themed shop. With two broken engagements under her belt, Kristianna isn't looking forward to walking down the aisle as the maid of honor in her best friend's upcoming wedding. Certain that marriage isn't in her cards, Kristianna has resolved herself to a solitary life as a businesswoman. Now that her livelihood is threatened, Kristianna does everything she can to convince her neighbors to keep the town's name. Her only obstacle is the Shawn, the handsome lawyer working for Summer Valley Outdoors. Though Shawn claims to have feelings for Kristianna, she wonders if he's just trying to trick her in order to get what he wants.

Other books by the same author:
Along Came a Cowboy, 2008

Promise Always, 2006
Other books you might like:
Susan May Warren, *Noble Legacy Series*, 2007-2008

933

CHRISTINE LYNXWILER

The Reluctant Cowgirl

(Uhrichsville, OH: Barbour, 2009)

Story type: Romance; Contemporary
Series: McCord Sisters. Book 1
Subject(s): Love; Faith; Modern Life
Major character(s): Crystal McCord, Actress; Jeremy Buchanan, Rancher
Time period(s): 2000s
Locale(s): Arkansas

Summary: Crystal McCord left her family's Arkansas ranch to try to make it as an actress on Broadway. When her show closes, Crystal returns to her apartment to find her boyfriend in bed with her roommate. Feeling confused and hurt, Crystal decides to return home to organize her thoughts and take a break from life in the big city. After she arrives, Crystal runs into Jeremy Buchanan, the young man who purchased a neighboring ranch. Jeremy is attracted to Crystal, but he is having a hard time letting people into his life. Ever since his ex-wife disappeared with their daughter, Jeremy has found it difficult to trust. By putting their faith in God, Crystal and Jeremy open themselves up to love and discover the strength to reach for their dreams.

Other books by the same author:
Along Came a Cowboy, 2008
Forever Christmas, 2007
Promise Me Always, 2006

Other books you might like:
Yvonne Lehman, *A Bride Idea*, 2007
Debra White Smith, *First Impressions*, 2004

934

DIANN MILLS

Breach of Trust

(Carol Stream, IL: Tyndale House, 2009)

Story type: Romantic Suspense
Series: Call of Duty. Book 1
Subject(s): Secrets; Politics
Major character(s): Paige Rogers, Government Official (former CIA Agent), Librarian; Daniel Keary, Political Figure (candidate for governor)
Time period(s): 2000s
Locale(s): Split Creek, Oklahoma

Summary: Librarian Paige Rogers, a former CIA Agent, is struggling with the knowledge that she is the only survivor of a brutal attack that took place seven years ago. Every day, she wonders if the man who betrayed her—the man she holds responsible for destroying her team—will come back to finish her. A stranger has recently shown up in her small town of Split Creek, Oklahoma, and he's asking questions about Paige. Furthermore, the man Paige blames for attacking her team, Daniel Keary, is running for governor. Paige is the only thing standing in the way of his election. Is she strong enough to reveal to the world the truth about Keary?

Other books by the same author:
Awaken My Heart, 2008
A Texas Legacy Christmas, 2007
When the Nile Runs Red, 2007

Other books you might like:
Dee Henderson, *True Courage*, 2004
Dee Henderson, *True Honor*, 2002

935

SARA MILLS

Miss Match

(Chicago: Moody Publishers, 2009)

Story type: Historical; Mystery
Series: Allie Fortune Mystery. Book 2
Subject(s): Suspense; Faith; Love
Major character(s): Jack O'Connor, FBI Agent; Allie Fortune, Detective—Private
Time period(s): 1940s (1947)
Locale(s): New York, New York; Germany

Summary: Allie Fortune, the only female detective in New York City, friend Jack O'Conner comes to her with a problem. His long-lost love Maggie has sent him a message saying that she needs his help. She and a young girl are being held in Berlin, and the FBI will not help. Maggie is in possession of classified documents that several dangerous criminals want to confiscate. Allie and Jack pose as missionaries and travel to Berlin to rescue Maggie, but they run into danger at every turn.

Other books by the same author:
Miss Fortune, 2009 (Allie Fortune Mystery. Book 1)

Other books you might like:
Noel Hyland, *Conspiracy in Kiev*, 2008
Amy Wallace, *Healing Promises*, 2008
Nicole Young, *Patricia Amble Mystery Series*, 2007-

936

KATHLEEN MORGAN

One Perfect Gift

(Grand Rapids, MI: Revell, 2008)

Story type: Historical; Romance
Series: Culdee Creek. Book 5
Subject(s): Christmas; Faith; Love
Major character(s): Jessica Ashmore, Nurse, Parent (of Emma); Emma Ashmore, Child (Jessica's daughter); Sean MacKay, Military Personnel (former)
Time period(s): 1930s (1933)
Locale(s): Colorado Springs, Colorado

Summary: When her mother-in-law threatens to sue for custody of her six-year-old daughter Emma, widow Jessica Ashmore packs up her few belongings and her child to look for work in Colorado. After a nursing job in Colorado Springs falls through, Jessica finds temporary work caring for a stroke victim. The position is almost perfect, except for the client's angry son, Sean MacKay. The young man doesn't like having strangers at Culdee Creek Ranch, but he eventually warms to Jessica and Emma. Soon, Jessica learns the source of Sean's frustration towards God. The young mother makes it her mission to heal Sean's heart and bring him back to Christ in time for Christmas.

Other books by the same author:
A Fire Within, 2007
Wings of Morning, 2006
Child of Promise, 2002
Lady of Light, 2001

Other books you might like:
Melody Carlson, *All I Have to Give*, 2008

937

MEL ODOM

Blood Lines

(Carol Stream, IL: Tyndale, 2009)

Story type: Religious; Legal
Series: Military NCIS. Book 3
Subject(s): Murder; Faith; Family
Major character(s): Shel McHenry, Military Personnel (NCIS Agent); Bobby Lee Gant, Crime Suspect; Victor Gant, Organized Crime Figure
Time period(s): 2000s
Locale(s): United States

Summary: The NCIS team, a group of agents who investigate military crimes, is looking into a violent crime committed against a marine and his wife. The NCIS agents are sure they've found the culprit when they focus on Bobby Lee Gant; however, Bobby's father, Victor Gant, is determined to have his son freed. Agent Shel McHenry is injured while trying to arrest Bobby. Far away in Texas, Shel's father Tyrel is struggling with realizations about his military past. His deeds come back to haunt him just as his son is trying to recuperate.

Other books by the same author:
Apocalypse Unleashed, 2008
Blood Evidence, 2007 (Military NCIS. Book 2)
Paid in Blood, 2006 (Military NCIS. Book 1)

Other books you might like:
Don Brown, *Black Sea Affair*, 2008
DiAnn Mills, *Breach of Trust*, 2009

938

MARK ANDREW OLSON

Ulterior Motives

(Ada, MI: Bethany House, 2009)

Story type: Mystery; Religious
Subject(s): Faith; War; Suspense

Major character(s): Greg Cahill, FBI Agent (former),
Religious (chaplain); Omar Nirubi, Terrorist,
Scientist
Time period(s): 2000s
Locale(s): United States

Summary: After receiving word of a New Year's Day plot
against the United States, the government hunts down
and captures the terrorist cell's leader. Federal officials
soon discover that the person responsible for organizing
the plan isn't who they expected. The blond-haired, blue-
eyed Omar Nirubi has invented a chemical that could
kill thousands of people in a matter of hours. Though the
English-speaking scientist endures days of forceful
questioning, he refuses to give them any more information on how and where the attack will take place. With
time running out and officials scrambling to find answers,
the FBI brings in ousted agent Greg Cahill to talk with
the terrorist. Greg is a tortured soul who became a prison
chaplain after a mistake on the job left a child dead.
Unsure of how he can help, Greg agrees to speak with
Nirubi. The connection that Greg forges with Nirubi
may be the government's only hope of saving thousands
of lives.

Other books by the same author:
The Warriors, 2008
The Watchers, 2008

Other books you might like:
James Scott Bell, *Try Darkness*, 2008
Jerome Teel, *The Divine Appointment*, 2008

939

CHRISTA PARRISH

Home Another Way

(Bloomington, MN: Bethany House, 2008)

Story type: Contemporary; Religious
Subject(s): Fathers and Daughters; Faith; Forgiveness
Major character(s): Sarah Graham, Young Woman
Time period(s): 2000s
Locale(s): Jonah, New York

Summary: Sarah Graham is a broke 27-year-old with few
prospects for the future. Following the death of his wife,
Sarah's father left his daughter in the care of her
grandmother. Over the years, Sarah used music to escape
her troubled past. Sarah was admitted to Julliard, but
forfeited her seat when she unexpectedly became
pregnant. After Sarah's baby was stillborn, she gave up
hope for having a happy life. Years later, the death of
her father draws the angry and confused Sarah to a
mountain village in New York in the hopes of collecting
an inheritance. Sarah's plans to get the money and leave
are dashed when she learns that her father's will forces
her to stay in the tiny town for six months before she
collects a single dime. Sarah settles in for a long winter
and soon makes some shocking discoveries about her
father and the people who loved him. First novel.

Where it's reviewed:
Publisher's Weekly, July 14, 2008, page 40

Other books you might like:
Tina Forkner, *Ruby Among Us*, 2008
Sally John, *The Remedy for Regret*, 2005

940

CRAIG PARSHALL

The Rose Conspiracy

(Eugene, OR: Harvest House, 2009)

Story type: Contemporary; Mystery
Subject(s): Faith; Forgiveness; Murder
Major character(s): Vinnie Archmont, Artist, Crime
Suspect (murder); J.D. Blackstone, Professor, Lawyer
Time period(s): 2000s
Locale(s): Washington, District of Columbia

Summary: A historic discovery leads to murder and deception in *The Rose Conspiracy*. Soon after uncovering new
information about Abraham Lincoln's death, the president
of the Smithsonian Institute is found dead in his office.
Artist Vinnie Archmont was sculpting the man's likeness
on the day he died, and she was the last person to see
him alive. When Vinnie becomes a suspect in the man's
death, she hires hotshot lawyer J.D. Blackstone to defend
her. What appears to be a simple murder case soon turns
into a vast conspiracy that reaches to the highest levels
of the government. J.D. turns to his religious expert
uncle for help in decoding a puzzle that could not only
lead to the killer, but also expose the inner workings of
one of the country's most powerful secret societies.

Other books by the same author:
Sons of Glory, 2008
Captives and Kings, 2007
Trial by Ordeal, 2006
The Last Judgement, 2005

Other books you might like:
Don Brown, *Defiance*, 2007
Paul Robertson, *According to Their Deeds*, 2009

941

TRACIE PETERSON

A Dream to Call My Own

(Ada, MI: Bethany House, 2009)

Story type: Historical; Romance
Series: Brides of Gallatin County. Book 3
Subject(s): Murder; Love; Grief
Major character(s): Lacy Gallatin, Young Woman; Dave
Shepard, Lawman
Time period(s): 19th century
Locale(s): Gallatin County, Montana

Summary: Devastated by the loss of her father, Lacy has
sworn to find the man responsible for his death and make
him pay. Bent on revenge, Lacy's quest brings her closer
to Deputy Sheriff Dave Shepard. Dave's determined
search for the killer has led nowhere. Lacy believes that
she can help, but Dave thinks that the beautiful and
spirited young woman will only distract him from his
work. As the two argue about how to handle the case,
Dave and Lacy find themselves in the middle of a heated

romance. Though she has feelings for Dave, Lacy needs to make sure that her attraction to the lawman doesn't get in the way of her plans for vengeance.

Other books by the same author:
A Love to Last Forever, 2009 (Brides of Gallatin County. Book 2)
A Promise to Believe In, 2008 (Brides of Gallatin County. Book 1)
Ladies of Liberty Series, 2007-2008

Other books you might like:
Tracey Bateman, *Dangerous Heart*, 2008
Cathy Marie Hake, *Whirlwind*, 2008
Lori Wick, *Big Sky Dreams Series*, 2007-

942

TRACIE PETERSON

A Love to Last Forever

(Ada, MI: Bethany House, 2009)

Story type: Historical; Religious
Series: Brides of Gallatin County. Book 2
Subject(s): Faith; Love
Major character(s): Beth Gallatin, Young Woman, Neighbor (of Nick); Nick Lassiter, Young Man, Neighbor (of Beth)
Time period(s): 19th century
Locale(s): Montana

Summary: After watching her older sister fall in love, all Beth Gallatin wants is a romance of her very own. Neighbor Nick Lassiter has loved Beth from the moment he set eyes on her, but she doesn't see him as anything other than a friend. A life-long reader, Beth's head is filled with romantic visions of how love should be. After a wealthy railroad tycoon comes to town and turns Beth's head, Nick realizes that he'll have to fight for the woman he loves. Beth finally comes to appreciate the love Nick has for her, but a secret from his past could tear the couple apart forever.

Other books by the same author:
A Promise to Believe In, 2008 (Brides of Gallatin County. Book 1)

Other books you might like:
Lori Copeland, *Now and Always*, 2008
Marcia Gruver, *Chasing Charity*, 2009
Susan May Warren, *Finding Stephanie*, 2008

943

GEORGE BRYAN POLIVKA

Blaggard's Moon

(Eugene, OR; Harvest House, 2009)

Story type: Fantasy; Religious
Subject(s): Faith; Death
Major character(s): Smith Delaney, Pirate
Locale(s): Drammun, Fictional Country

Summary: Smith Delaney must make a choice. When he meets an innocent young child who touches his heart, he can either save her and risk his own life, or save himself and kill her. He makes his choice and is sentenced to death. As he waits for his death, he reflects on the events that brought him to this point. He tells the story of his life and analyzes the people he has hurt and admits the reasons for his actions. Most of his decisions were based on his need to satisfy his own greed. Smith judges his own actions before he plans to meet the God who will judge him.

Other books by the same author:
Trophy Case Trilogy, 2007-2008

Other books you might like:
Donita K. Paul, *Dragon Keeper Chronicles Series*, 2004-2008

944

DEBORAH RANEY

Insight

(Buffalo, NY: Steeple Hill, 2009)

Story type: Contemporary; Romance
Subject(s): Death; Transplants; Love
Major character(s): Olivia Cline, Widow(er), Assistant; Reed Vincent, Artist
Time period(s): 2000s
Locale(s): Hanover Falls, Missouri

Summary: Though her husband has been unfaithful, Olivia Cline is committed to making their marriage work. Shortly before leaving her job as an interior designer in Chicago to follow him to Hanover Falls, Missouri, Olivia learns that an explosion has left her husband in serious condition. When she arrives in Missouri, she finds her husband clinging to life on a ventilator. After removing her husband from life support, Olivia discovers that she's pregnant. With no friends, family, or job, the widow wonders how she will support herself and the baby. To help her through the grieving process, Olivia takes a job as an assistant to artist Reed Vincent. The handsome painter has just started working again after receiving a corneal transplant which saved his eyesight. As Reed and Olivia grow closer, she discovers a shocking secret that could tear the two apart forever.

Other books by the same author:
Within this Circle, 2007
Clayburn Series, 2007-
A Vow To Cherish, 2006

Other books you might like:
Cindy Martinusen, *Eventide*, 2008
Jackina Stark, *Tender Grace*, 2009

945

DEBORAH RANEY

Yesterday's Embers

(New York: Simon & Schuster, 2009)

Story type: Contemporary; Religious
Series: Clayburn Novel. Book 3

Subject(s): Faith; Grief; Love
Major character(s): Doug DeVore, Widow(er), Parent;
  Mickey Valdez, Child-Care Giver
Time period(s): 2000s
Locale(s): Clayburn, Kansas

Summary: After losing his beautiful wife Kaye and their
six-year-old daughter Rachel in a terrible accident, Doug
DeVore wonders how he will manage to raise his five
remaining children and keep the family farm running.
Daycare owner Mickey Valdez has watched the DeVore
children grow over the years, and Doug's tragedy tears
at her heart. When Mickey offers to help Doug with the
kids, the last thing she expects is to fall in love with the
haggard father. The two lost souls face many obstacles
as they embark on a tentative relationship that could
bring more heartache into their lives.

Other books by the same author:
Remember to Forget, 2008 (Clayburn Novel. Book 2)
Leaving November, 2007 (Clayburn Novel. Book 1)

Other books you might like:
Carolyne Aarsen, *A Family for Luke*, 2008
Kathryn Springer, *Family Treasures*, 2008

946

PAUL ROBERTSON

According to Their Deeds

(Ada, MI; Bethany House, 2009)

Story type: Mystery; Religious
Subject(s): Suspense
Major character(s): Charles Beale, Store Owner (book
  dealer)
Time period(s): 2000s
Locale(s): Washington, District of Columbia

Summary: Charles Beale lives and works just a stone's
throw away from the heart of Washington, DC. The
owner of a rare bookshop only encounters politicians
inside the walls of his Alexandria, Virginia store. When
a faithful client with ties to the government dies in a
burglary attempt, Charles agrees to buy back the books
he sold the victim. As he completes an inventory of the
new acquisitions, Charles finds documents that implicate
a number of Washington power players in a horrible
conspiracy. When he realizes that these papers may have
led to his client's death, Charles questions his next move.
Soon, the book dealer finds himself the target of a deadly
plot. Charles must then untangle the mystery of his
client's death in order to save his own life.

Other books by the same author:
Road to Nowhere, 2009
The Heir, 2007

Other books you might like:
James Scott Bell, *Try Darkness*, 2008
Karen Hancock, *The Enclave*, 2009

947

LISA SAMSON

The Passion of Mary-Margaret

(Nashville: Thomas Nelson, 2009)

Story type: Contemporary; Religious
Subject(s): Faith; Love
Major character(s): Mary-Margaret Fisher, Religious; Jude
  Keller, Young Man
Time period(s): 2000s
Locale(s): United States

Summary: Mary-Margaret Fisher, a religious sister, talks
to Jesus. She asks for guidance and then she follows the
advice she is given. She is asking Jesus to save her from
a confusing situation. Mary-Margaret met Jude when she
was attending a convent school, and despite her sacred
intentions, she found herself attracted to the young unruly
man. When Jude took off for a secular life in the city,
however, Mary-Margaret went back to her preparations
for sisterhood. When Jude comes back into Mary-
Margaret's life, he is in desperate need of some divine
intervention. Mary-Margaret asks Jesus to tell her what
to do to help the man she holds so dear.

Where it's reviewed:
Publishers Weekly, January 19,2009, page 39

Other books by the same author:
Embrace Me, 2008
Quaker Summer, 2008
Straight Up, 2006

Other books you might like:
Claudia Mair Burney, *Wounded: A Love Story*, 2008
Ann H. Gabhart, *The Outsider*, 2008
Sharlene MacLaren, *Hannah Grace*, 2009

948

KIM VOGEL SAWYER

A Promise for Spring

(Ada, MI: Baker Publishing Group, 2009)

Story type: Religious; Historical
Subject(s): Faith; Romance; Family
Major character(s): Emmaline Bradford, Fiance(e) (of
  Geoffrey); Geoffrey Garrett, Rancher, Fiance(e) (of
  Emmaline)
Time period(s): 1870s (1874)
Locale(s): England; Kansas

Summary: At 17, Emmaline Bradford watched as her
beloved fiance, Geoffrey Garrett, set out to make his
fortune in America. For five years, Emmaline waited in
England for Geoffrey to send word for her to come to
Kansas. During this time, Geoffrey was working hard to
start a successful sheep-herding ranch and prepare a
proper home for his bride. When Geoffrey finally sends
for her, Emmaline is having doubts about their
relationship. After arriving at the ranch, she explains her
fears and asks Geoffrey to release her from their
engagement. Instead, the young man offers her a
compromise: if Emmaline stays with Geoffrey until the

spring and still decides that she wants to return to England, he'll pay for her return home. As the months pass, Emmaline slowly beings to remember the love she once had for her fiance.

Other books by the same author:
My Heart Remembers, 2008
Where the Heart Leads, 2008
Where the Willows Grow, 2007

Other books you might like:
Robin Lee Hatcher, *Patterns of Love*, 2008

949

NICOLE SEITZ

A Hundred Years of Happiness

(Nashville: Thomas Nelson, 2009)

Story type: Contemporary; Religious
Subject(s): Family Relations; Vietnam War; Veterans
Major character(s): John Porter, Carpenter, Veteran (Vietnam War); Lisa Le, Young Woman; Katherine, Relative (daughter of John)
Time period(s): 2000s
Locale(s): South Carolina

Summary: Lisa Le is the daughter of an American soldier who died while fighting in the war. John Porter served in Vietnam and is still haunted by his experiences there. John's daughter arranges for her father to attend a service for veterans in hopes that the experience will help her father deal with his memories. The service leads John to the mother of Lisa Le. They discuss their perspectives of the Vietnam Conflict and help each other form a deeper understanding of the past.

Where it's reviewed:
Booklist, February 15, 2009, page 30
Publishers Weekly, December 15, 2008, page 34

Other books by the same author:
Trouble the Water, 2008
The Spirit of Sweetgrass, 2007

Other books you might like:
Patti Callahan, *When Light Breaks*, 2006
Gilbert Morris, *Pages of Promise*, 2008

950

ANN SHOREY

The Edge of Light

(Grand Rapids, MI: Revell, 2009)

Story type: Historical; Family Saga
Series: At Home in Beldon Grove. Book 1
Subject(s): Widows/Widowers; Frontier and Pioneer Life
Major character(s): Molly McGarvie, Widow(er)
Time period(s): 1830s (1838-1839)
Locale(s): St. Lawrenceville, Missouri

Summary: Molly McGarvie's life changes forever when her husband Samuel dies of cholera and leaves her alone to take care of their children. The young woman's

troubles are further compounded when her brother-in-law steals the family business out from under her, leaving her without an income or a home. Molly knows she must make a new start and that means heading out on her own. During her journey, Molly faces more loss when one of her sons goes missing. In order to survive, Molly must trust in God to protect her family and bring her son back home. First novel.

Other books you might like:
Mary Connealy, *Montana Rose*, 2009
Kathleen Morgan, *Brides of Culdee Creek Series*, 1999-2001

951

JILL EILEEN SMITH

Michal

(Ada, MI; Revell, 2009)

Story type: Historical; Religious
Series: Wives of King David. Book 1
Subject(s): Marriage; History; Biblical Fiction
Major character(s): David, Spouse (of Michal), Musician (harpist); Michal, Spouse (of David), Relative (daughter of Saul); King Saul, Royalty, Parent (father of Michal)
Time period(s): 11th century

Summary: Michal's only respite from her father's terrible rages is the moments she gets to listen to David play his harp. The young princess falls in love with the handsome musician, but King Saul is suspicious of David's relationship with his daughter. After David slays Goliath, Saul agrees to allow the two young lovers to marry. Their happiness, however, is short lived and David must flee the city after the king launches two attacks on his son-in-law's life. Though David promises to return for Michal one day, the young woman must endure years of heartache locked behind the palace walls. First novel.

Other books you might like:
Tommy Tenney, *Hadassah Covenant*, 2005
    Mark Andrew Olsen, co-author

952

VIRGINIA SMITH

Age Before Beauty

(Ada, MI; Revell, 2009)

Story type: Contemporary; Romance
Series: Sister-to-Sister. Book 2
Subject(s): Sisters; Faith; Love
Major character(s): Allie Harrod, Parent, Spouse
Time period(s): 2000s
Locale(s): United States

Summary: Afraid that she might miss the milestones in her new baby's life, Allie Harrod decides to sell makeup to help make ends meet. Though the job was supposed to make things easier, Allie finds her list of problems growing by the minute. Besides the fact that her clothes no longer fit, Allie is dealing with a husband who is disinterested in doing anything but helping his attractive colleague fix her new home. While she worries about her marriage falling apart, Allie must also deal with a mettling mother-in-law who plans to move into her son's home. While her sister assures her that God will help lead the way, Allie is uncertain about the Lord's place in her crazy life.

Other books by the same author:
Stuck in the Middle, 2008 (Sister-to-Sister. Book 1)

Other books you might like:
Lois Richer, *Rocky Mountain Legacy*, 2009

953

JACKINA STARK

Tender Grace

(Ada, MI: Bethany House, 2009)

Story type: Religious; Contemporary
Subject(s): Death; Peace; Grief
Major character(s): Audrey Eaton, Spouse (of Tom), Widow(er)
Time period(s): 2000s
Locale(s): United States

Summary: Audrey Eaton always believed that she and her beloved husband, Tom, had time to do all of the things that they dreamed of when they were newlyweds. Her hopes for the future are shattered when Tom, just shy of 60, passes away in his sleep one evening. Without her partner, Audrey feels lost and confused about her place in the world. Determined to begin healing, Audrey embarks on a journey to a place that she and Tom never had the chance to visit. With her husband's Bible close by, the widow's trip takes her to new places and introduces her to new ways of thinking that help her rediscover her identity. First novel.

Where it's reviewed:
Booklist, February 1, 2009, page 29
Publishers Weekly, December 22, 2008, page 32

Other books by the same author:
Because Love Welcomed Me, 1992 (nonfiction)
Framing a Rainbow: How to Teach Your Children to Love God, 1990 (nonfiction)

Other books you might like:
Davis Bunn, *The Book of Hours*, 2006
Cindy Martinusen, *Eventide*, 2008
Jamie Langston Turner, *No Dark Valley*, 2008

954

ANN TATLOCK

The Returning

(Ada, MI: Bethany House, 2009)

Story type: Religious; Contemporary
Subject(s): Family Relations; Faith; Marriage
Major character(s): Andrea Sheldon, Spouse (of John); John Sheldon, Convict, Spouse (of Andrea)

Time period(s): 2000s
Locale(s): United States

Summary: When Andrea married John Sheldon, she knew he didn't love her. The couple, however, stayed together and had three children before John was sent to prison for a drunk driving accident. Now, John is returning home after a five-year sentence. Excited and nervous about his return, Andrea knows that his presence will drastically alter the life she's carved out for herself and their children. Though John swears that his time in prison has helped him find Jesus, Andrea is unsure if her husband has truly changed. John must now do whatever it takes to show his family that he deserves a second chance.

Other books by the same author:
Every Secret Thing, 2007

Other books you might like:
Denise Hunter, *Sweetwater Gap*, 2008
Beverly LaHaye, *Times and Seasons*, 2008
   Terri Blackstock, co-author
Susan May Warren, *Reclaiming Nick*, 2007

955

DIANA WALLIS TAYLOR

Journey to the Well

(Ada, MI; Revell, 2009)

Story type: Historical; Religious
Subject(s): Faith; History; Biblical Fiction
Major character(s): Marah, Young Woman (13-year-old)
Time period(s): B.C.

Summary: Thirteen-year-old Marah is a young girl who dreams of marrying her childhood friend. Her dreams are crushed when her father forces her to marry an older man. Over the years, Marah's encounters with men harden her to the opposite sex. She wonders if she will ever meet a man who she can believe in. One day, she goes to the well to fetch some water and ends up encountering Jesus. Her meeting with the Messiah changes the course of Marah's life forever.

Other books by the same author:
Wings of the Wind, 2006 (poetry)

Other books you might like:
Lynn Austin, *Chronicles of the Kings Series*, 2005-

956

JAMIE LANGSTON TURNER

Sometimes a Light Surprises

(Ada, MI: Bethany House, 2009)

Story type: Contemporary; Religious
Subject(s): Grief; Faith; Love
Major character(s): Ben Buckley, Widow(er)
Time period(s): 2000s
Locale(s): United States

Summary: After 20 years, Ben Buckley is still grieving for his murdered wife Chloe. There is still no informa-

Inspirational

tion on who murdered the pretty mother of four or why they wanted her dead, but Ben has always suspected that it might have something to do with the changes his wife experienced just weeks before her death. Chloe had met a woman who helped her find God. At the time, Ben couldn't understand Chloe's sudden conversion and the two fought intensely just before her death. Now, after years of guilt and isolation, Ben is forced to open himself up to love and tear walls he constructed around his heart.

Other books by the same author:
Some Wildflower in My Heart, 2006
Winter Birds, 2006
No Dark Valley, 2004

Other books you might like:
William P. Young, *The Shack*, 2008

957

M.L. TYNDALL

The Blue Enchantress
(Uhrichsville, OH: Barbour Publishing, 2009)

Story type: Historical; Romance
Series: Charles Towne Belles. Book 2
Subject(s): Suspense; Faith; Love
Major character(s): Hope Westcott, Slave; Nathaniel Mason, Businessman (owns a shipping business)
Time period(s): 18th century
Locale(s): North America (Charles Towne)

Summary: After a terrible childhood in an unloving home, Hope Westcott planned to marry well and open an orphanage for abandoned children. Hope's search for love brings her to a small island in the Caribbean where she quickly runs into trouble. Nathaniel Mason has ignored his calling to become a preacher and started a small shipping business around the islands. During a business trip, Nathaniel sees a young woman he recognizes from Charles Towne being sold as a slave. To save Hope, Nathaniel agrees to sell one of his boats. Following the rescue, Nathaniel learns that Hope's own actions got her into this dreadful mess. Nathaniel doesn't want anything to do with Hope, but he soon learns that God has other plans for the two of them.

Other books by the same author:
The Red Siren, 2009 (Charles Towne Belles. Book 1)
Legacy of the King's Pirates Series, 2007-2008

Other books you might like:
Kelly Eileen Hake, *The Bride Bargain*, 2008

958

M.L. TYNDALL

The Red Siren
(Uhrichsville, OH: Barbour, 2009)

Story type: Historical; Romance
Series: Charles Towne Belles. Book 1
Subject(s): Pirates; Redemption
Major character(s): Faith Westcott, Noblewoman, Pirate;

Dajon Waite, Military Personnel (captain), Guardian
Time period(s): 18th century (1713)
Locale(s): North America (Charles Towne)

Summary: Faith Wescott becomes a pirate so that she can raise enough money to care for herself and her sisters. She hopes this will stop her father from marrying them off to awful, albeit rich men. By night, Faith acts as a pirate called the Red Siren. One of the first ships she overtakes is run by Dajon Waite. Years later, Faith's father arranges for her to marry a horrible man. In a strange coincidence, her father also arranges for Captain Waite to be his daughters' guardian. After his ship was overtaken by pirates, Dajon has renewed his faith and become a good Christian. Faith recognizes Dajon, but he does not recognize her as the notorious Red Siren. A romance develops between the two lost souls, but Faith fears Dajon will realize her other identity.

Other books by the same author:
The Blue Enchantress, 2008 (Charles Towne Belles. Book 2)
The Restitution, 2008
The Falcon and the Sparrow, 2008
The Redemption, 2007
The Reliance, 2007

Other books you might like:
Gilbert Morris, *The Exiles*, 2003
Kathleen Y'Barbo, *Beloved Castaway*, 2007

959

JENNIFER ERIN VALENT

Fireflies in December
(Carol Stream, IL: Tyndale, 2008)

Story type: Historical; Historical/Depression Era
Subject(s): Depression (Economic); Racism; Christianity
Major character(s): Jessilyn Lassiter, Teenager; Gemma, Orphan, Friend (of Jessilyn)
Time period(s): 1930s (1932)
Locale(s): Virginia

Summary: Jessilyn Lassiter relays a story that took place in 1932, the year she turned 13 years old. Jessilyn decides to help her friend Gemma when her house burns down. Gemma loses both her parents in the fire, and Jessilyn's father offers to take the girl in as his own. The residents of their small Virginia town, however, do not think that an African-American girl should be living with a white family. When the Klu Klux Klan gets involved, Jessilyn learns first-hand about the hate that runs through the people in her small town, especially when they direct some of their most violent threats toward Jessilyn. Will the family support Gemma despite their neighbors? First novel.

Where it's reviewed:
Publisher's Weekly, December 1, 2008, page 31

Other books you might like:
Gilbert Morris, *The Courtship*, 2007
Donna VanLiere, *The Angels of Morgan Hill*, 2007

960

LAURA JENSEN WALKER

Turning the Paige

(Grand Rapids, MI: Zondervan, 2009)

Story type: Religious; Contemporary
Series: Getaway Girls. Book 2
Subject(s): Faith; Family Relations; Friendship
Major character(s): Paige Kelley, Divorced Person, Worker (temp)
Time period(s): 2000s
Locale(s): Sacramento, California; Scotland

Summary: Paige Kelley is in a rut. She is divorced and has been working as a temp for three years. Although she wants to have a family, she spends all of her time caring for her sick mother. Then, the women in Paige's book club suggest she break out of her rut, and she begins to think about how she might be able to go on an adventure. She questions whether putting her own needs above others' needs is a Christian way to act. After searching her soul, Paige ventures out on a trip to Scotland, where she gets a chance to begin the life she's only dreamed of.

Other books by the same author:
Daring Chloe, 2008 (Getaway Girls. Book 1)
Reconstructing Natalie, 2008
Miss Invisible, 2007

Other books you might like:
Robin Jones Gunn, *Sisterchicks in Wooden Shoes*, 2009
Rebeca Seitz, *Scrapping Plans*, 2009

961

SUSAN MAY WARREN

Nothing but Trouble

(Carol Stream, IL: Tyndale, 2009)

Story type: Contemporary; Romance
Series: P.J. Sugar. Book 1
Subject(s): Faith; Love; Murder
Major character(s): P.J. Sugar, Detective—Amateur, Girlfriend (of Boone, former); Boone, Detective—Police, Boyfriend (of PJ, former)
Time period(s): 2000s
Locale(s): United States

Summary: After ten years of drifting about the country, P.J. Sugar decides that it's time to return to her hometown and settle down. Unfortunately, everywhere PJ goes, trouble seems to follow. When a former teacher is murdered, the husband of P.J.'s best friend is accused of the crime. The young woman's determination to clear her friend's name brings her face-to-face with local police detective and ex-boyfriend Boone. As P.J. and Boone attempt to unravel a deadly conspiracy that could endanger both of their lives, sparks begin to fly between the two former lovers.

Other books by the same author:
Noble Legacy Series, 2006-2008
Josey Adventures Series, 2006-

Team Hope Series, 2005-2006
Mission: Russia Series, 2005-2008
Deep Haven Series, 2003-2004

Other books you might like:
Barbara Phinney, *Deadly Homecoming*, 2008
Ramona Richards, *A Murder among Friends*, 2008

962

TIFFANY L. WARREN

The Bishop's Daughter

(Boston: Grand Central, 2009)

Story type: Contemporary
Subject(s): Faith; Love
Major character(s): Darrin Bainbridge, Journalist
Time period(s): 2000s
Locale(s): United States

Summary: Darrin Bainbridge is a reporter in search of a great story. Then, his mother visits him and can't say enough good things about Bishop Kumal Prentiss from Atlanta. Darrin knows that some ministers—the ones who drive expensive cars and live in mansions—are just scamming people, and he wonders if that is the case with Bishop Prentiss. He decides to venture to Atlanta to find out. There, he joins the bishop's church, determined to show his mother that the bishop is a fraud. While there, Darrin also meets the Bishop's daughter. Falling in love with her complicates his perfect plan.

Other books by the same author:
Farther than I Meant to Go, Longer than I Meant to Stay, 2006
What a Sista Should Do, 2005

Other books you might like:
Michele Andrea Bowen, *Holy Ghost Corner*, 2008
Michele Andrea Bowen, *Second Sunday*, 2009
Jacquelin Thomas, *Divine Match-Up*, 2008

963

STEPHANIE GRACE WHITSON

A Claim of Her Own

(Ada, MI: Bethany House, 2009)

Story type: Historical; Romance
Subject(s): Salvation; Gold
Major character(s): Mattie Flynn, Singer
Time period(s): 1870s (1876)
Locale(s): Deadwood, South Dakota

Summary: Mattie Flynn is a 20-year-old woman who works as a singer at a gambling house. Her boss is an awful man, so Mattie ventures on her own to Deadwood, South Dakota, to search for her brother Dillon, who went to Deadwood to find gold and suggests that he may have found enough for the two of them to start a new life. Mattie struggles through some tough experiences in the rough town of Deadwood, but she also makes some good friends. She meets a wonderful preacher and begins to fall in love with him. However, her old boss at the

Inspirational

gambling house is still searching for Mattie, and she worries what will happen to her new friends if he shows up in Deadwood.

Other books by the same author:
Unbridled Dreams, 2008
Jacob's List, 2007
Hilltop in Tuscany, 2006
Garden in Paris, 2005
Watchers on the Hill, 2004
Secrets on the Wind, 2003

Other books you might like:
Robin Lee Hatcher, *Wagered Heart*, 2008
Wick Lori, *Sabrina*, 2007
Allison K. Pittman, *with Endless Sight*, 2008

964

LORI WICK

Jessie

(Eugene, OR: Harvest House, 2008)

Story type: Religious; Historical
Series: Big Sky Dreams. Book 3
Subject(s): Romance; Faith; Abandonment
Major character(s): Jessie Wheeler, Spouse (of Seth), Parent; Seth Redding, Spouse (of Jessie)
Time period(s): 1870s-1890s (1873-1890)
Locale(s): Token Creek, Minnesota

Summary: Set in 19th century Montana, this novel follows Jessie Wheeler through the toughest time of her life. Just as she is preparing for the birth of her second child, Jessie's husband Seth abandons her. He moves away, never to be heard of again. By herself, Jessie continues to operate Token Creek's general store, care for her daughters, and soldier on despite her pain and loneliness. Eight years later, Seth comes back to town with a renewed faith, but Jessie cannot allow herself to trust him. Will she allow him back in to the family that he abandoned?

Other books by the same author:
Sabrina, 2008 (Big Sky Dreams. Book 2)
Cassidy, 2007 (Big Sky Dreams. Book 1)

Other books you might like:
Robin Lee Hatcher, *Wagered Heart*, 2008
Lauraine Snelling, *Daughters of Blessing Series*, 2006-

965

LISA WINGATE

Word Gets Around

(Ada, MI: Bethany House, 2009)

Story type: Romance; Contemporary
Subject(s): Relationships; Healing; Movie Industry
Major character(s): Lauren Eldridge, Horse Trainer; Nate Heath, Writer (screenwriter)
Time period(s): 2000s
Locale(s): Daily, Texas

Summary: After Lauren Eldridge's husband passes away, she returns to Daily to help her father. He might lose his farm if Lauren doesn't come home to help him tame a wild horse. A movie is being filmed in Daily and the horse is slated to be one of film's biggest stars. Laura doesn't want to head home at first, but her father has always been there for her, so she decides to help him. When Lauren returns to Daily, the town is in the throes of producing the movie, and everyone seems to have a role to play. Lauren and sexy screenwriter Nate develop a romance as they take turns narrating this story of a big Hollywood movie being made in a small Texas town.

Where it's reviewed:
Booklist, February 1, 2009, page 35
Publisher's Weekly, December 22, 2008, page 32

Other books by the same author:
A Month of Summer, 2008
Talk of the Town, 2008
A Thousand Voices, 2007

Other books you might like:
Karen Kingsbury, *Take One*, 2009
Christine Lynxwiler, *The Reluctant Cowgirl*, 2009

966

KATHLEEN Y'BARBO

Beloved Counterfeit

(Uhrichsville, OH: Barbour, 2009)

Story type: Romance; Historical
Series: Fairweather Keys. Book 3
Subject(s): Faith; Love; Secrets
Major character(s): Ruby O'Shea, Guardian (of her nieces); Micah Tate, Religious (preacher), Widow(er); Thomas Hawkins, Pirate, Parent
Time period(s): 1830s
Locale(s): Fairweather Key, Florida

Summary: After washing up on the shores of Fairweather Key, Ruby O'Shea and her three nieces are determined to make a new life for themselves. Following the death of her sister, Ruby took the girls away from their pirate father, Thomas Hawkins. While working in the village and passing her nieces off as her daughters, Ruby meets Micah Tate. After the death of his wife, Micah devoted his life to God and decided to become a preacher. Though he feels a strong connection to Ruby, he believes that she is hiding something from him. When Thomas Hawkins comes looking for his daughters, Ruby's secrets come to light. Micah must now decide if he can forgive Ruby for her sins or if he will abandon his love in favor of his faith.

Other books by the same author:
Beloved Captive, 2008 (Fairweather Keys. Book 2)
Beloved Castaway, 2007 (Fairweather Keys. Book 1)

Other books you might like:
Deeanne Gist, *Bride Most Begrudging*, 2005
Deeanne Gist, *Deep in the Heart of Trouble*, 2008
Lori Wick, *Sophie's Heart*, 2004

967

NICOLE YOUNG

Kiss Me If You Dare

(Ada, MI; Revell, 2009)

Story type: Mystery; Religious
Series: Patricia Amble Mystery. Book 3
Subject(s): Death; Faith; Suspense
Major character(s): Patricia "Tish" Amble, Business-woman (home renovator); Denton Braddock, Professor
Time period(s): 2000s
Locale(s): Del Gloria, California

Summary: Forced to leave her wounded boyfriend in Michigan with a group of drug lords, Tish assumes a new identify in Del Gloria, California. Only her boyfriend's friend, Denton Braddock, knows who Tish really is. As she sets about putting her new life in order, Tish wonders what happened in Michigan. Desperate to find out the fate of her boyfriend, Tish must decide if learning the truth is worth risking the life she's built in California. When her work on a set of homes is destroyed, the young woman suspects that someone knows her secret.

Other books by the same author:
Kill Me If You Can, 2008 (Patricia Amble Mystery. Book 2)
Love Me If You Must, 2007 (Patricia Amble Mystery. Book 1)

Other books you might like:
Terri Blackstock, *Restoration Series*, 2005-
Brandilyn Collins, *Kanner Lake Series*, 2006-

Inspirational

Fiction for Hard Times
by
Natalie Danford

Nobody would deny that times are tough. Money is tight, and discretionary spending is falling as quickly as the unemployment rate is rising. The poor economic climate is bound to have an impact on books and publishing—and, more specifically, on fiction—has it does on just about every other aspect of life.

There is some disagreement in the publishing community about whether or not a recession is good or bad for business. On the one hand, books are a relatively cheap form of entertainment and they offer better "bang for the buck" than, say, movies. During the Great Depression, book sales—along with sales of just about every other consumer item under the sun—sank significantly; during less damaging recessions, such as that of the 1980s, books have seemed to benefit.

These days are different, though. Today books don't compete with movie tickets for discretionary spending dollars so much as they compete with "free" media on the Internet. Even in good times, reading is declining. And while the National Endowment for the Arts tried to claim that the decline in readers of literature had reversed itself in January 2009, showing an increase for the first time in twenty-five years, further study of the figures used showed that the NEA had changed its standard of measurement to include reading online material. It is absolutely indisputable that book sales have been slowing in the shadow of blogs, social networking sites, television, and all the other distractions bombarding us daily. (The effect of the new generation of electronic readers, including Amazon's Kindle, on the sale of e-books remains to be seen and may stand as a bright spot in the bleak outlook for books, though e-books, of course, are much less expensive and offer smaller margins than hard copy bound books printed on paper.) Publishers are downsizing and eliminating many of the imprints developed during the flush years. (Imprints are smaller publishing houses within a publishing house.) Overall, the number of books being published is dropping in all categories, and fiction is no exception.

But tough economic times don't have an impact only on book sales and book publishing—they also find their way into the material of popular fiction itself. Will readers of fiction who have been forced to tighten their belts be more likely to reach for a serious tome such as *The Grapes of Wrath*, or dive into fluffy escapism such as *Sex and the City*? Only time will tell.

The books being published at this moment, of course, were not written mere moments ago. The lag time between completing a novel or a collection of stories and seeing it in print ranges from one to three years. But there are certain themes and tropes that find their way into the zeitgeist as bad times approach and certain trends in publishing that can always be counted on to surge when consumers are holding onto their dollars more tightly.

First and foremost, publishers become increasingly risk-averse as the economy sinks. This means debut novels by unknown authors grow more and more rare, while the "sure thing" from a well-known writer—preferably one whose name crops up regularly on best-seller lists—receives top priority. Sequels such as Nelson DeMille's *The Gate House* (Grand Central Publishing, 2008) and Kate Atkinson's *When Will There Be Good News?* (Little Brown, 2008), another of her sly literary mysteries featuring detective Jackson Brodie, will crowd the shelves over the next couple of years. Publishers bank on the familiar drawing repeat readers, and at the same time they save themselves the expense of "launching" unknown authors and trying to build audiences for them.

The actual content of books may also reflect economic woes or simply grant the reader an opportunity to consider them. So-called "social novels" have been with us since the Victorian era and attempt to examine a social ill or trend through fictional characters. (The Charles Dickens tale of poor *Oliver Twist* is a classic example of an early social novel.) It is debatable whether there are more stories of the rich and poor appearing on shelves, or readers tend to take more notice of them during hard economic times, but there certainly is a large flock of new novels of this type hitting bookstores now or arriving in the near future.

While it may seem contradictory, stories of the wealthy and brutal are often enjoyed during bad economic times, especially if the wealthy characters get their comeuppance in the end. Ron Rash's *Serena* (Ecco, 2008) is one such novel. The book harks back to the Great Depression—it is set in 1929—and follows a ruthless couple, Serena and George Pemberton. This married couple runs a timber business in North Carolina. First and foremost, they plan to destroy the beautiful land that they have purchased and strip it of its trees. Along the way, they treat their workers badly, but they are also ruthless with others. Serena discovers that she is infertile, and also that George had a child out of wedlock before he met her. She is subsequently horribly cruel to that child and his mother, Rachel. Rachel is depicted foraging for food in order to survive, while Serena browbeats the loggers she and her husband employ and trains an eagle she keeps as a pet to kill rattlesnakes. (She also shoots and kills a bear and attempts to impress upon her husband that to dominate his workers is the only way to be successful.) *Serena* was a finalist for the PEN/ Faulkner Award.

Same lesson, different era: In Paul Torday's *Bordeaux* (Houghton Mifflin Harcourt, 2009), a man named Frances Wilberforce makes a mint in the computer business, but being rich doesn't help him find happiness. In fact, if anything, he's more unhappy after he makes his fortune. He also develops a serious drinking problem due to his indulgence in fine wine. Eventually he finds himself without friends or any love in his life, because alcohol takes up all his time. He acquires a vast wine collection from an acquaintance and dedicates himself to drinking his way through it. He is not particularly likeable nor is he admirable. Torday avoids sentimentality or reverence for twelve-step programs and other recovery possibilities and instead paints a portrait of a rich man who knows no satisfaction.

Count Steven Stelfox as another among the large number of rich-yet-dissatisfied characters. In *Kill Your Friends* (Harper Perennial, 2008), author John Niven looks back at the days when the record industry was waning. Kill Your Friends follows ruthless and disaffected A&R man Steven Stelfox. Steven does not have enough of a grasp of the big picture to realize that digital music and free downloads are about to kill off the music industry, making him obsolete. He is wholly focused on the moment and on finding the next high-earning act and scoring big.

This is the type of "social novel" that works only because of what the reader knows—i.e., that all of Steven's preoccupations and petty concerns will soon be moot anyway. But this particular type of book has potential appeal during an economic downturn, not only because it depicts the rich as massively unhappy (hinting that it is actually preferable to be penniless), but also because it shows a character surviving something that did not seem surmountable at the time. In an odd way, these unlikable characters who have fallen from grace are an inspiration to anyone going through tough times.

The flip side of these stories of the unhappy rich is the variety of stories of the poor, who are often equally unhappy, but much, much nicer about it. Meant, perhaps, to test the theory that misery loves company and to soothe the battered feelings of those who have watched the value of their homes dip precipitously are titles such as Daphne Uviller's *Super in the City* (Bantam, 2009). If the booming 1990s were represented by books like Candace Bushnell's *Sex and the City* (first a newspaper column, then a book, then a successful HBO series, and, finally, a movie)—frothy confections about women shopping their hearts out and tottering through Manhattan's chic restaurants in stiletto heels—then perhaps this era will be marked by titles such as Uviller's. Obviously with the title of her novel she's playing on that earlier book. Like Bushnell's stand-in, Carrie Bradshaw, Uviller's protagonist, Zephyr Zuckerman, has a loyal group of friends, but they're all down on their luck. One is divorced; another is brilliant but must look for dates on the Internet. Zephyr herself has broken up with her boyfriend and failed to finish graduate school. Her parents own a brownstone in New York City, and when the superintendent there is arrested, Zephyr takes his place, maintaining the building and learning all the secrets of its tenants—and developing her plumbing skills.

Also featuring adult children who return to the bosom of the family—if they ever left it—is *If You Eat You Never Die* by Tony Romano (Harper Perennial, 2008). This novel-in-stories depicts a loving recently immigrated Italian-American family in Chicago in the 1940s. The family deals with problems related to both not having a high income and feeling out of place in the United States. Son Giacomo is ashamed of his Italian background and changes his name to Jim, while mother Lucia fears she'll never understand her new country or its traditions. Here the poor and struggling are gentle and deserving folk piously satisfied with very little. The senior citizen fixed-income set stars in Michael Zadoorian's *The Leisure Seeker* (William Morrow, 2009), about a couple married for almost sixty years. The two set out to follow Route 66 in an RV, making one last trip. Husband John is in the throes of Alzheimer's disease, though he's still well enough to handle the occasional driving stint. Wife Ella can no longer drive and walks with a cane. She has breast cancer, hypertension, and kidney failure. She wears a wig due to chemotherapy-induced hair loss and rides in a motorized scooter. They tootle along, slightly confused, slightly uncomfortable, and always together. They also eat whatever they like: Recognizing that they are toward the end of their lives together, they throw nutritional caution to the winds.

The couple in Valerie Laken's *Dream House* (Harper, 2009) are not married quite as long when they purchase a home, unaware that the place was involved in a crime two decades earlier. Immediately, the purchase causes conflict in their relationship. They've had to borrow money from Kate's parents, and her husband, Stuart, slacks off on the renovations. The house is in disrepair, but located in a rapidly gentrifying neighborhood.

Stephen Amidon's *Security* (Farrar, Straus and Giroux, 2009), too, deals with disparities in wealth. The residents of the same small Massachusetts town inhabit different spots on the social scale. Doyle Cutler is a well-off man who employs Edward Inman to perform security detail for him. Edward is married to a woman who is attempting to climb to a higher station in life by running for mayor. Edward's old girlfriend is struggling to maintain a meaningful relationship with her own sullen son. All of them are trying to remain mobile in a society where their positions seem fixed firmly in place.

More difficult times that have been at least somewhat overcome are depicted in Malla Nunn's *A Beautiful Place to Die* (Atria, 2009), set in Johannesburg, South Africa in the 1950s, with apartheid recently instituted and awkwardly employed. This combination mystery and social novel depicts a white police officer investigating the murder of another white police officer, with the help of his own Zulu assistant, who was one of the few people who appears to have admired the dead man. Because the victim was so unpopular, there is a long list of possible suspects. The strange dance required when white and black people interacted under apartheid is depicted in full, and even the divisions among whites (the dead man was a Boer, while the investigator is an Englishman) are explored in detail.

The characters in Susan Rebecca White's *Bound South* also chafe at the boundaries set by class, with a good dose of racial division tossed into the mix. In the modern American South, Caroline Parker is a spoiled teenager raised as much by her family's housekeeper as she is by her own mother. The housekeeper, Faye, also has a daughter, Missy Meadows, who keenly feels the absence of her biological father. Eventually Caroline leaves town to look for Missy's father. Making her journey, Caroline is just one of a crowd of fictional characters in this season's books who are waiting out the hard times and hoping for something better.

Recommended Titles

The Gate House by Nelson DeMille

When Will There Be Good News? by Kate Atkinson

Serena by Ron Rash

Bordeaux by Paul Torday

Kill Your Friends by John Niven

Super in the City by Daphne Uviller

If You Eat You Never Die by Tony Romano

The Leisure Seeke by Michael Zadoorian

Dream House by Valerie Laken

Security by Stephen Amidon

A Beautiful Place to Die by Malla Nunn

Bound South by Susan Rebecca White

Popular Fiction Titles

H.G. ADLER

The Journey

(New York: Random House, 2008)

Story type: Literary
Subject(s): Holocaust; Family Relations; Historical
Major character(s): Leopold Lustig, Doctor; Caroline Lustig, Spouse
Time period(s): 1940s
Locale(s): Ruhenthal, Germany

Summary: This German novel was originally published in 1962 and was written by a Holocaust survivor who passed away in 1988. Doctor Leopold Lustig and his wife, Caroline, are sent to the walled city of Ruhenthal (probably based on Theresienstadt, where the author was imprisoned.) They are in the work camp along with their adult children, Paul and Zerlina. The situation is described obliquely, or rather from a viewpoint so close in to the characters' minds that it reflects their own disorientation and confusion. Paul survives the experience and returns to his home, where no one wants to discuss what happened. Translated from the German by Peter Filkins.

Where it's reviewed:
Booklist, October 1, 2008, page 22
Publishers Weekly, August 11, 2008, page 25

Other books you might like:
Marguerite Duras, *The War*, 1985
    memoir
Irene Nemirovsky, *Suite Francaise*, 2006
W.G. Sebald, *Austerlitz*, 2002

STEPHEN AMIDON

Security

(New York: Farrar, Straus and Giroux, 2009)

Story type: Literary
Subject(s): Money
Major character(s): Walt Steckl, Widow(er); Doyle Cutler, Wealthy

Time period(s): 2000s
Locale(s): Stoneleigh, Massachusetts

Summary: In a small college town in western Massachusetts, a large cast of characters interacts and faces problems. Security expert Edward Inman disdains his mayoral candidate wife and pines for his ex, Kathryn. Edward is called to help out the town's wealthiest resident Doyle Cutler. Widower Walt Steckl works as an electrician and pops pills; Kathryn's son Conor mopes. Walt's daughter, Mary, is taking a class at the local college, and a classmate is sleeping with the professor. Mary herself accuses Doyle of sexual abuse. Conor knows the truth about what happened. Secrets seem to hide in every house.

Where it's reviewed:
Kirkus Reviews, December 1, 2008, page NA
Publishers Weekly, November 17, 2008, page 38

Other books by the same author:
Human Capital, 2004
The New City, 2000
The Primitive, 1995
Thirst, 1992
Subdivision, 1991

Other books you might like:
James Collins, *Beginner's Greek*, 2008
Tom Perrotta, *Little Children*, 2004

970

MARIE ARANA

Lima Nights

(New York: Dial, 2008)

Story type: Literary
Subject(s): Family Relations; Infidelity
Major character(s): Carlos Bluhm, Spouse; Maria Fernandez, Dancer
Time period(s): 1980s (1986); 2000s (2006)
Locale(s): Lima, Peru

Summary: In 1986, Carlos Bluhm visits a low-rent club in Lima, Peru, and falls in love with a dancer, Maria Fernandez. Carlos is married and has children and sits solidly in Peru's middle class, not because he has a lot of money, but because of his background. His family carefully emphasizes its German heritage and they speak only Spanish at home. Carlos becomes obsessed with Maria, however, and sets up a love nest for her. The story switches back and forth between that moment and a moment 20 years in the future, when their relationship has played out and Maria, who was under-age at the time they met, is trying to hold onto Carlos.

Where it's reviewed:
Booklist, December 1, 2008, page 24
Publishers Weekly, October 20, 2008, page 34

Other books by the same author:
Cellophane, 2006
American Chica, 2001 (memoir)

Other books you might like:
Joseph O'Neill, *Netherland*, 2008
Philip Roth, *Exit Ghost*, 2007

971

KATE ATKINSON

When Will There Be Good News?

(New York: Little, Brown, 2008)

Story type: Literary
Subject(s): Mystery; Detection; Missing Persons
Major character(s): Jackson Brodie, Detective—Private; Joanna, Doctor, Parent
Time period(s): 2000s
Locale(s): Edinburgh, Scotland

Summary: When Joanna was six, she saw her mother and siblings murdered. Now a mother and a doctor living in Edinburgh, Scotland, she is informed by the police that the man who committed the killings is soon to be released from prison. Private detective Jackson Brodie (who also appeared in two earlier Atkinson novels) participated in the search for the missing Joanna at the time of her family's demise and is contacted by Joanna's child's nanny when the woman goes missing shortly after receiving the news. Several different stories appear unrelated, but ultimately they all tie in. These include the past relationship between Jackson and a police officer also working on the case, and some suspicions about Joanna's husband and an insurance investigation.

Where it's reviewed:
Entertainment Weekly, October 3, 2008, page 81
The New York Times Book Review, October 12, 2008, page 15
The New York Times, September 22, 2008, page E1
The Seattle Times, October 15, 2008, page I5

Other books by the same author:
One Good Turn, 2006
Case Histories, 2004
Emotionally Weird, 2000
Human Croquet, 1997
Behind the Scenes at the Museum, 1996

Other books you might like:
Stieg Larsson, *The Girl with the Dragon Tattoo*, 2008
Richard Price, *Lush Life*, 2008

972

STEPHANE AUDEGUY

The Only Son

(Orlando: Harcourt, 2008)

Story type: Literary
Subject(s): Family Relations
Major character(s): Francois Rousseau, Historical Figure; Jean-Jacques Rousseau, Historical Figure, Writer
Time period(s): 18th century
Locale(s): France

Summary: French philosopher and famed memoirist Jean-Jacques Rousseau's older brother gets the spotlight trained on him in this historical novel. Little is known of Francois Rousseau, and his famous brother mentioned him rarely, but the course of his life reflects the course of history in the 18th century. He is born in 1705 and takes to science rather than philosophy, the purview of his brother, Jean-Jacques, who is seven years his junior. After several adventures, including a stint in prison, he heads to Paris, where he lives happily among artists and thinkers until the French Revolution begins to loom on the horizon. The two brothers never spend any time together as adults. Translated from the French by John Cullen.

Where it's reviewed:
The New York Times Book Review, November 2, 2008, page 23
The Seattle Times, October 26, 2008, page 17

Other books by the same author:
The Theory of Clouds, 2007

Other books you might like:
Carolly Erickson, *The Hidden Diary of Marie Antoinette*, 2005
James Tipton, *Annette Vallon*, 2007

973

TIFFANY BAKER

The Little Giant of Aberdeen County

(New York: Grand Central Publishing, 2009)

Story type: Literary
Subject(s): Obesity; Family Relations
Major character(s): Truly Plaice, Teenager; Serena Jane Plaice, Teenager
Time period(s): 1970s
Locale(s): Aberdeen County, New York

Summary: Truly Plaice is obese and seems to grow by the day. Her sister, Serena Jane, is tiny and adorable. When Truly is 12, their father dies, and the sisters are split. Truly is sent to live with a poor farming family in upstate New York, while her sister is taken in by a minister and his wife. But Serena Jane is raped and then marries her rapist when she turns out to be pregnant. The couple goes to live in Buffalo, then returns eight years later. Soon after, Serena dies, and Truly takes over raising her child. At the same time, Serena Jane's cruel husband, now a doctor, thinks he can cure Truly's obesity.

Where it's reviewed:
Publishers Weekly, September 8, 2008, page 33

Other books you might like:
Katie Crouch, *Girls in Trucks*, 2008
Lauren Groff, *The Monsters of Templeton*, 2008
Wally Lamb, *She's Come Undone*, 1992
Elizabeth McCracken, *The Giant's House*, 1996

974

JESSE BALL

The Way through Doors

(New York: Vintage, 2009)

Story type: Literary
Subject(s): Memory
Major character(s): Selah Morse, Writer; Mora Klein, Patient
Time period(s): 2000s
Locale(s): New York, New York

Summary: Selah Morse is a crafter of pamphlets and a petty bureaucrat in New York City. He sees a young woman hit by a taxi and takes her to the hospital, where he makes up a name for her (Mora Klein) and lies and says that he is her boyfriend. The woman has lost her memory, and so the hospital staff instructs Selah to take her home and not to let her sleep. He accomplishes this by telling her an intricate series of stories that relate to each other and often circle back on each other. In the process, he tries to draw out Mora Klein's true identity.

Where it's reviewed:
Publishers Weekly, October 13, 2008, page 34

Other books by the same author:
Samedi the Deafness, 2007

Other books you might like:
Roberto Bolano, *The Savage Detectives*, 2007
David Foster Wallace, *Infinite Jest*, 1996
Colson Whitehead, *The Intuitionist*, 1998

975

RAY BANKS

Sucker Punch

(New York: Houghton Mifflin Harcourt, 2009)

Story type: Literary
Subject(s): Crime and Criminals
Major character(s): Cal Innes, Convict; Liam Wooley, Sports Figure
Time period(s): 2000s
Locale(s): Los Angeles, California; Manchester, England

Summary: Cal Innes is out of prison and working not as a private detective, his previous employment, but cleaning a friend's boxing gym in England. He's assigned to accompany boxer Liam Wooley to Los Angeles, where Liam will be competing in a match. Once there, they get mixed up with some bad seeds, and soon enough Liam is kidnapped and another boxer is dead. Suddenly Cal can't get anyone back home on the phone, and he's virtually abandoned in a foreign country, trying to figure out what happened and trying to deal with the Los Angeles police. He doesn't now who's trustworthy.

Where it's reviewed:
Booklist, December 1, 2008, page 33
Kirkus Reviews, November 15, 2008, page NA
Publishers Weekly, November 17, 2008, page 39

Other books by the same author:
Gun, 2008
Saturday's Child, 2008
No More Heroes, 2008
The Big Blind, 2004
Mill Town, 1995

Other books you might like:
Christa Faust, *Money Shot*, 2008
Stieg Larsson, *The Girl with the Dragon Tattoo*, 2008

976

BRUNONIA BARRY

The Lace Reader

(New York: William Morrow, 2008)

Story type: Literary
Subject(s): Prophecy
Major character(s): Towner Whitney, Narrator; Cal Boynton, Religious
Time period(s): 2000s
Locale(s): Salem, Massachusetts

Summary: Towner Whitney, descended from a long line of fortunetellers and mind readers, can predict the future by looking at pieces of lace. She returns to her hometown of (where else?) Salem, Massachusetts, after an absence of 15 years. She's still bothered by the death of her twin and her great-aunt's recent death. She discovers upon returning that her aunt's once-abusive husband has become a minister and is making a name for himself by railing against witchcraft, in a reference to Salem's past as a witch-hunting center. Towner is an unreliable narrator who refers to herself as a liar right up-front.

Where it's reviewed:
Journal Record, August 15, 2008, page NA
The New York Times, July 24, 2008, page E4
People, August 4, 2008, page 47
The St. Petersburg Times, August 10, 2008, page 7L
USA Today, August 21, 2008, page 13B

Other books you might like:
Chris Bohjalian, *The Double Bind*, 2007
Dennis Lehane, *Shutter Island*, 2003

977

NEIL BARTLETT

Skin Lane

(London: Serpent's Tail, 2008)

Story type: Literary
Subject(s): Sexual Behavior; Homosexuality/Lesbianism

Major character(s): Mr. Freeman, Worker; Ralph, Apprentice
Time period(s): 1960s (1967)
Locale(s): London, England

Summary: Mr. Freeman (his first name is never revealed) is the slow and steady type. He has been working at the same job, treating animal pelts, for 33 years. He lives a solitary existence, until he begins dreaming about the naked body of a young man. When he is assigned to mentor his boss's nephew, Ralph, he recognizes Ralph as the living version of the dead man in his dreams. He also begins to acknowledge his own sexual attraction to Ralph. It is the first time in his life that he has felt attraction of any kind. He soon begins to obsess over the apprentice.

Where it's reviewed:
Publishers Weekly, September 1, 2008, page 37

Other books by the same author:
Mr. Clive and Mr. Page, 1998
The House on Brooke Street, 1997
The Game of Love and Chance, 1992
Ready to Catch Him Should He Fall, 1990

Other books you might like:
Scott Heim, *Mysterious Skin*, 1995
Rose Tremain, *The Road Home*, 2008

978

KYLE BEACHY

The Slide

(New York: Dial, 2009)

Story type: Contemporary
Subject(s): Coming-of-Age; Conduct of Life
Major character(s): Potter Mays, Graduate
Time period(s): 2000s
Locale(s): Missouri

Summary: Potter Mays graduates from college and moves back in with his parents in Missouri. He floats through the days, finding meaningless, underpaid work and trying to decide whether he loves his longtime girlfriend. They have cheated on each other in the past. She's out of town in any case, so Potter spends time with another high school friend. Potter learned a lot of information in college, but he didn't learn how to live life or how to be an adult. He asks a lot of people around him for advice, but seems oblivious to the fact that they have problems, too.

Where it's reviewed:
Kirkus Reviews, December 1, 2008, page NA
Publishers Weekly, November 17, 2008, page 42

Other books you might like:
Adam Davies, *The Frog King*, 2002
Ben Dolnick, *Zoology*, 2007

979

JOHN BERGER

From A to X

(Brooklyn: Verso, 2008)

Story type: Literary
Subject(s): Political Prisoners
Major character(s): Xavier, Political Prisoner; A'ida, Pharmacist
Time period(s): 2000s
Locale(s): Suse, Fictional City

Summary: Subtitled "A Story in Letters," this novel consists of fictional letters reportedly found in an abandoned prison. The letters are found in the cell of Xavier, a political prisoner, and penned by his lover, A'ida. Xavier is suspected of terrorism. Because the two are aware that prison personnel are reading their letters, everything they write to each other is heavily encoded, and the letters range into dreams, poetry, fantasies, and other non-literal forms in order to convey their messages. In her letters, A'ida also describes life in Suse, the town where she lives, but the country where Suse is located is deliberately left open to interpretation, sending the message that this could happen anywhere.

Where it's reviewed:
Booklist, September 15, 2008, page 25
Kirkus Reviews, August 1, 2008, page NA
Publishers Weekly, August 11, 2008, page 31

Other books by the same author:
Hold Everything Dear, 2007 (essays)
The Shape of a Pocket, 2001 (essays)
Sense of Sight, 1993 (essays)
About Looking, 1988 (essays)
Ways of Seeing, 1972 (essays)

Other books you might like:
Richard Flanagan, *The Unknown Terrorist*, 2007
Joseph O'Neill, *Netherland*, 2008

980

ROBERTO BOLANO

2666

(New York: Farrar, Straus & Giroux, 2008)

Story type: Literary
Subject(s): Violence
Major character(s): Benno von Archimboldi, Writer; Quincy Fate Williams, Journalist
Time period(s): 2000s
Locale(s): Santa Teresa, Mexico

Summary: In the first of five sections, four European literary critics travel to a small Mexican town, Santa Teresa, in search of reclusive German novelist Benno von Archimboldi. In the second, a Spanish professor travels to Santa Teresa with his daughter and begins to hear voices. The third section follows Quincy Fate Williams, a journalist from New York who goes to Santa Teresa to report on a boxing match. The fourth section lists the details of the rapes and murders of many women in and around Santa Teresa. The fifth section finally turns up Benno von Archimboldi, the writer sought by literary critics in the first. The Chilean author passed away in 2003. Translated from the Spanish by Natasha Wimmer.

Where it's reviewed:
New York, September 8, 2008, page 94
The New York Times Book Review, November 9, 2008, page 1
The New York Times, November 13, 2008, page C1
O, the Oprah Magazine, November 2008, page 192
Time, November 24, 2008, page 60

Other books by the same author:
The Savage Detectives, 2008
Amulet, 2007
Last Evenings on Earth, 2006
Distant Star, 2004
By Night in Chile, 2003

Other books you might like:
Michael Ondaatje, *Divisadero*, 2007
Laura Restrepo, *Delirium*, 2007

981

MATT BONDURANT

The Wettest County in the World

(New York: Scribner, 2008)

Story type: Literary
Subject(s): Family Problems; Prohibition Era; Historical
Major character(s): Sherwood Anderson, Historical Figure; Forrest Bondurant, Bootlegger
Time period(s): 1920s (1928); 1930s (1934)
Locale(s): Franklin County, Virginia

Summary: The author fictionalizes the true story of his own great-uncle, Forrest Bondurant. Forrest was a bootlegger in rural Virginia during Prohibition, as were many others. Forrest and his brothers got involved in making moonshine in order to survive during a time when money was scarce. The area where he lived had a disproportionate number of murders and violent attacks, similar to a gang war. Forrest once survived having his throat slit and walked miles to the hospital. In 1934, real-life author Sherwood Anderson arrives in town to investigate the story for a newspaper, but no one will talk to him. A local sheriff is trying to use the problems in the area for his own gain.

Where it's reviewed:
Booklist, September 1, 2008, page 51
The New York Times Book Review, November 9, 2008, page 44
Publishers Weekly, June 9, 2008, page 27

Other books by the same author:
The Third Translation, 2005

Other books you might like:
Dennis Lehane, *The Given Day*, 2008
Richard Price, *Lush Life*, 2008
David Wroblewski, *The Story of Edgar Sawtelle*, 2008

982

T.C. BOYLE

The Women

(New York: Viking, 2009)

Story type: Literary
Subject(s): Love
Major character(s): Frank Lloyd Wright, Historical Figure; Sato Tadashi, Student
Time period(s): 1950s
Locale(s): Taliesin, Wisconsin

Summary: This fictionalized account of the life and career of architect Frank Lloyd Wright is narrated by Japanese architecture student Sato Tadashi. Tadashi comes to live with Wright and study at his feet at Taliesin. Also there, sometimes on and off, are Wright's mistress Maude Miriam Noel, another mistress, Mamah, whom Wright considered his soul mate, dancer Olgivanna, and his first wife, Kitty, mother of his six children. A fire wreaks havoc, as does Wright's forceful personality and his insistence on turning women against each other. In Tadashi's telling, Wright is a magnetic personality who commands respect and attention.

Where it's reviewed:
Booklist, November 1, 2008, page 5
Kirkus Reviews, December 15, 2008, page NA
Publishers Weekly, November 17, 2008, page 37

Other books by the same author:
The Inner Circle, 2004
Drop City, 2003
The Road to Wellville, 1993
Water Music, 1981
Descent of Man, 1979 (short stories)

Other books you might like:
Nancy Horan, *Loving Frank*, 2007
Ron Rash, *Serena*, 2008

983

ADAM BRAVER

November 22, 1963

(New York: Tin House Books, 2008)

Story type: Literary
Subject(s): Historical
Major character(s): John Kennedy, Historical Figure; Jackie Kennedy, Historical Figure
Time period(s): 1960s (1963)
Locale(s): Texas; Washington, District of Columbia

Summary: This novel imagines the day of President Kennedy's assassination. The First Lady and the President are tracked closely, but the man who provides the casket for Kennedy's body is also given his say, as are a stranger who gives Jackie Kennedy a cigarette outside the hospital and the mechanic who readies the car for them in Dallas before they arrive. Familiar details, like the pink suit the First Lady wore that day, are woven together with imagined or previously unknown ones.

Popular Fiction

The autopsy is described in detail, and the funeral arrangements are seen from the points-of-view of various White House servants.

Where it's reviewed:
Dallas Morning News, November 16, 2008, page NA
Publishers Weekly, September 15, 2008, page 43

Other books by the same author:
Crows over the Wheatfield, 2006
Divine Sarah, 2004
Mr. Lincoln's Wars, 2004

Other books you might like:
Anonymous, *Primary Colors*, 1996
Zachary Lazar, *Sway*, 2008
Curtis Sittenfeld, *American Wife*, 2008

984

SYLVIA BROWNRIGG

The Delivery Room
(New York: Counterpoint, 2008)

Story type: Literary
Subject(s): Psychology
Major character(s): Mira Braverman, Psychologist; Peter, Spouse
Time period(s): 1990s (1998)
Locale(s): London, England

Summary: Mira Braverman has a therapy practice in London, and many of her patients have problems relating to their children or lack thereof. One is performing long-distance parenting of her sister back in Serbia. An American journalist would like to become a single mother. A wealthy woman can't buy fertility, and another woman is mourning a miscarriage. Mira's husband, Peter, has a son whose existence he didn't know of until recently, and Peter's son has his own child-bearing issues: His wife wants to have a child, but he's unconvinced. Then Peter is diagnosed with lymphoma, and Mira learns empathy for her patients the hard way.

Where it's reviewed:
The New York Times Book Review, November 17, 2008, page 8
Publishers Weekly, September 22, 2008, page 38

Other books by the same author:
Morality Tale, 2008
Pages for You, 2001
The Metaphysical Touch, 1998
Ten Women Who Shook the World, 1997 (short stories)

Other books you might like:
Anne Enright, *The Gathering*, 2007
Valerie Martin, *Trespass*, 2007

985

CHRISTOPHER BUCKLEY

Supreme Courtship
(New York: Hachette/Twelve, 2008)

Story type: Contemporary
Subject(s): Satire; Politics

Major character(s): Pepper Cartwright, Judge
Time period(s): 2000s
Locale(s): Washington, District of Columbia

Summary: Pepper Cartwright is a judge on a television show (think Judge Judy) with a Texas accent and a red pick-up truck when she is appointed to the Supreme Court. She's appointed not because she is capable, but because the president, Donald Vanderdamp, has seen his first two nominees shot down for silly reasons and he appoints Pepper as a kind of poke at his Congressional naysayers after spotting her television show. Eventually there is an election that needs to be decided by the Supreme Court (think Bush v. Gore) and Pepper needs to step up to the plate and act.

Where it's reviewed:
The New York Times Book Review, September 7, 2008, page 4
News-Sentinel, October 18, 2008, page NA
The Seattle Times, September 14, 2008, page 14
USA Today, September 9, 2008, page 4D
The Weekly Standard, September 22, 2008, page NA

Other books by the same author:
Boomsday, 2007
Florence of Arabia, 2004
No Way to Treat a First Lady, 2002
Little Green Men, 1999
Thank You for Smoking, 1994

Other books you might like:
Ana Marie Cox, *Dog Days*, 2006
Jessica Cutler, *The Washingtonienne*, 2005

986

CANDACE BUSHNELL

One Fifth Avenue
(New York: Voice, 2008)

Story type: Contemporary
Subject(s): Real Estate
Major character(s): Mindy Gooch, Editor; Schiffer Diamond, Actress; Philip Oakland, Writer
Time period(s): 2000s (2007)
Locale(s): New York, New York

Summary: In New York City after 9/11 but before the economy goes bust, inhabitants of a fancy building on lower Fifth Avenue's "Gold Coast" sleep together, squabble, and snub each other. The building buzzes like a beehive. Many of the residents are writers and editors. Mindy Gooch is a magazine editor and the co-op board's president. Philip Oakland is a Pulitzer Prize-winning author who has a "friends with benefits" relationship with neighbor Schiffer Diamond, an actress who's growing long in the tooth. A gay man who makes a living as a "society walker" and an 80-something gossip columnist also live in the building. A 7,000-square-foot apartment eventually sells for 20 million dollars.

Where it's reviewed:
Entertainment Weekly, September 29, 2008, page 76
The New York Times Book Review, September 28, 2008, page 8

The New York Times, September 26, 2008, page E29
Time, October 6, 2008, page 80
USA Today, September 25, 2008, page 5D

Other books by the same author:
Lipstick Jungle, 2005
Trading Up, 2003
Four Blondes, 2000
Sex and the City, 1996 (non-fiction)

Other books you might like:
Lauren Weisberger, *The Devil Wears Prada*, 2003
Alex Witchel, *The Spare Wife*, 2008

987

ETHAN CANIN

America America

(New York: Random House, 2008)

Story type: Literary
Subject(s): Politics
Major character(s): Corey Sifter, Editor; Henry Bonwiller, Political Figure
Time period(s): 1970s (1972); 2000s (2006)
Locale(s): New York

Summary: From the vantage point of middle age, small newspaper editor Corey Sifter recalls the campaign in 1972 of Senator Henry Bonwiller's run for the presidency. Sifter lived in a small town outside of Buffalo, New York, at the time, and Bonwiller was a larger-than-life liberal senator from the state whose campaign manager happened to be the richest man in Sifter's small town. In the present time of the book, in 2006, Bonwiller has just passed away, but back then, Sifter was the senator's driver and had an inside look at the daily routine of a political campaign. An accident ruined Bonwiller's chances, and Sifter still wonders what might have been.

Where it's reviewed:
The Houston Chronicle, July 27, 2008, page 11
The Seattle Times, July 20, 2008, page 16
Star Tribune, July 27, 2008, page 15E
USA Today, July 8, 2008, page 5D

Other books by the same author:
Carry Me Across the Water, 2001
For Kings and Planets, 1999
Blue River, 1996
The Palace Thief, 1994 (short stories)
Emperor of the Air, 1987 (short stories)

Other books you might like:
Dominick Dunne, *A Season in Purgatory*, 1993
Sue Miller, *The Senator's Wife*, 2008

988

OTTAVIO CAPPELLANI

Sicilian Tragedee

(New York: Farrar, Straus and Giroux, 2008)

Story type: Literary
Subject(s): Satire; Organized Crime

Major character(s): Alfio Turrisi, Organized Crime Figure; Betty Pirrotta, Actress; Tino Cagnotto, Director
Time period(s): 2000s
Locale(s): San Giovanni la Punta, Italy

Summary: Alfio Turrisi of Catania is a Mafia captain, but he's distracted from the business at hand by actress Betty Pirrotta, the daughter of another big man in the region, Turi Pirrotta. Several other actors and theater people figure prominently in this story of requited and unrequited love. Director Tino Cagnotto is raising a production of *Romeo and Juliet*, but all anyone cares about is whether the lead actor will do something vulgar on stage. The action is madcap and over-the-top. Mafia members and government ministers are equally inept as they operatically battle over the rights to the culture and resources of the small island of Sicily. Translated from the Italian by Frederika Randall.

Where it's reviewed:
Booklist, August 1, 2008, page 39
Kirkus Reviews, September 1, 2008, page NA
Publishers Weekly, May 19, 2008, page 30

Other books by the same author:
Who Is Lou Sciortino?, 2007

Other books you might like:
Amara Lakhous, *Clash of Civilizations over an Elevator in Piazza Vittorio*, 2008
Alessandro Piperno, *The Worst Intentions*, 2007
Roberto Saviano, *Gomorrah*, 2007
    non-fiction

989

JONATHAN CARROLL

The Ghost in Love

(New York: Farrar, Straus and Giroux, 2008)

Story type: Literary
Subject(s): Afterlife
Major character(s): Ling, Spirit; Ben Gould, Survivor
Time period(s): 2000s
Locale(s): Connecticut

Summary: Ben Gould hits his head on the sidewalk in a fall and is, according to the order of things, supposed to die, but he survives. Due to this glitch, his ghost, Ling, has already arrived on Earth and now doesn't know exactly how to handle the situation. Ling begins to have romantic feelings for Ben's very cheerful girlfriend, too. Meanwhile, Ben has been gifted with all sorts of abilities, including time travel and mind-reading. Also, Ben's dog can talk to him now. Ben meets another survivor of a serious accident and discovers that they have a kinship.

Where it's reviewed:
Booklist, July 1, 2008, page 6
Kirkus Reviews, August 15, 2008, page NA
Publishers Weekly, August 4, 2008, page 43

Other books by the same author:
Glass Soup, 2005
The Wooden Sea, 2001
Bones of the Moon, 1988
White Apples, 1987

The Land of Laughs, 1980

Other books you might like:
Audrey Niffenegger, *The Time Traveler's Wife*, 2003
Carolyn Parkhurst, *The Dogs of Babel*, 2003

990

MARISHA CHAMBERLAIN

The Rose Variations

(New York: Soho Press, 2009)

Story type: Literary
Subject(s): Feminism; Music and Musicians
Major character(s): Rose MacGregor, Composer
Time period(s): 1970s (1975)

Summary: Composer Rose MacGregor moves to cold Minnesota in 1975 to teach music at a college. She's the only woman in the department, and the other professors refer to her as "the girl composer." Feminism is just beginning to set down roots in academia, and Rose observes these developments firsthand. Back in New Hampshire, Rose was always defined by her family, and especially by her sister, to whom she served as the serious counterbalance. In Minnesota, though, she begins to blossom and has a series of affairs. Eventually she befriends a cellist who is creating an all-female commune out in the country. Eventually, Rose's troubled sister arrives on the scene.

Where it's reviewed:
Publishers Weekly, November 17, 2008, page 40

Other books by the same author:
Powers, 1983 (poetry)
Shout, Applaud, 1976 (poetry)

Other books you might like:
Emma Donoghue, *Stir-Fry*, 1994
Margot Livesey, *The House on Fortune Street*, 2008

991

CAROLYN CHUTE

The School on Heart's Content Road

(New York: Atlantic Monthly Press, 2008)

Story type: Literary
Subject(s): Rural Life; Militia Movements
Major character(s): Gordon St. Onge, Leader; Richard Rex York, Leader
Time period(s): 1990s
Locale(s): Egypt, Maine

Summary: In rural Maine, Gordon St. Onge leads a commune for poor people who want to live off the land and want the government to butt out of their business. Another local man organizes a militia that claims many of the same members. The viewpoint shifts among a large number of characters, including children. There are problems with drug use and with guns (the characters are wary of attempts to take their guns away), with the local public education system, and with simply getting along. The mother of a couple of young characters is in prison on a drug charge.

Where it's reviewed:
Booklist, October 1, 2008, page 26
Entertainment Weekly, November 7, 2008, page 6
Publishers Weekly, September 8, 2008, page 35

Other books by the same author:
Snow Man, 1999
Merry Men, 1994
Letourneau's Used Auto Parts, 1988
The Beans of Egypt, Maine, 1985

Other books you might like:
Annie Proulx, *The Shipping News*, 1994
Elizabeth Strout, *Olive Kitteredge*, 2008

992

CHRIS CLEAVE

Little Bee

(New York: Simon and Schuster, 2009)

Story type: Literary
Subject(s): Refugees
Major character(s): Andrew, Journalist; Sarah, Journalist; Little Bee, Refugee
Time period(s): 2000s
Locale(s): London, England

Summary: Nigerian refugee Little Bee (known to all by her childhood nickname) shows up on the London doorstep of journalists Andrew and Sarah after meeting them briefly in her home country. She has fled a massacre in her village, and they are the only people she knows in England. Sarah and Andrew met Little Bee when they were in Nigeria on vacation, and Little Bee and her sister were running from soldiers. When Little Bee does appear in London, Andrew has killed himself, leaving Sarah alone to raise their small child. Sarah takes in Little Bee, who has trouble getting over her violent past.

Where it's reviewed:
Booklist, December 15, 2008, page 24
Kirkus Reviews, November 15, 2008, page NA
Publishers Weekly, November 10, 2008, page 30

Other books by the same author:
Incendiary, 2005

Other books you might like:
Uwem Akpan, *Say You're One of Them*, 2008
Yiyun Li, *The Vagrants*, 2009

993

FRANCISCO COLOANE

Tierra del Fuego

(New York: Europa Editions, 2008)

Story type: Literary
Subject(s): Short Stories

Locale(s): Chile

Summary: Rough-edged men live out difficult experiences on Chilean islands in this collection of nine stories by a Chilean author who passed away in 2000. In one story, a murder haunts a man. In another, a group looks for gold and the members double-cross each other. A cook begins to care for a lamb and his demeanor softens; a sailor can't do what his friend has asked. A man building a lighthouse in a remote area doesn't like the way other men are looking at his wife. A young man boards with a married couple and becomes attracted to the wife. Translated from the Spanish by Howard Curtis.

Where it's reviewed:
Publishers Weekly, October 20, 2008, page 34

Other books by the same author:
Cape Horn and Other Stories from the End of the World, 1991

Other books you might like:
Amitav Ghosh, *Sea of Poppies*, 2008
Per Petterson, *To Siberia*, 2008

994

LAUREL CORONA

The Four Seasons

(New York: Voice, 2008)

Story type: Literary
Subject(s): Historical; Music and Musicians
Major character(s): Chiaretta, Musician; Maddalena, Orphan, Musician; Antonio Vivaldi, Historical Figure, Composer
Time period(s): 18th century
Locale(s): Venice, Italy

Summary: Two sisters are abandoned at a foundling hospital in Venice. Fortunately, the hospital, the Ospedale della Pieta, also houses a music academy where the orphans are taught to perform. Each sister develops her own spectacular musical ability, and though their personalities diverge from each other, they remain close throughout their lives. Maddalena, the older sister, learns the violin and studies with composer Antonio Vivaldi, inspiring some of his work. He pours his unexpressed passion for her into his music instead. Chiaretta develops into a talented singer and a classic blonde beauty and marries into a wealthy Venetian family.

Where it's reviewed:
Booklist, October 1, 2008, page 22
Publishers Weekly, September 15, 2008, page 44

Other books by the same author:
Until Our Last Breath, 2008 (non-fiction)

Other books you might like:
Tracy Chevalier, *Girl with a Pearl Earring*, 1999
Sarah Dunant, *The Birth of Venus*, 2004
Rose Tremain, *Music and Silence*, 2000

995

MARTIN CORRICK

By Chance

(New York: Random House, 2008)

Story type: Literary
Subject(s): Fate; Identity
Major character(s): James Watson Bolsover, Writer; Kitty Bolsover, Spouse
Time period(s): 20th century
Locale(s): England

Summary: James Watson Bolsover, a British man who considers himself unremarkable, is on vacation in an unnamed place when a storm keeps him in his hotel room for a long stretch. He looks back at his life and considers his identity and the role of fate in shaping it. Bolsover was a reader and writer and found a career as a technical writer and copywriter. He married Kitty and they had a satisfying relationship, but then Kitty died. In a car accident, Bolsover then killed a child, and he reveals that he is now on the island not vacationing, but in order to avoid contact with the child's father.

Where it's reviewed:
Booklist, September 15, 2008, page 24
Kirkus Reviews, September 1, 2008, page NA
The New York Times Book Review, November 9, 2008, page 44
Publishers Weekly, July 7, 2008, page 34

Other books by the same author:
After Berlin, 2005
The Navigation Log, 2003

Other books you might like:
Ian McEwan, *On Chesil Beach*, 2007
Michael Ondaatje, *Divisadero*, 2007

996

LOUIS DE BERNIERES

A Partisan's Daughter

(New York: Knopf, 2008)

Story type: Literary
Subject(s): Love; Politics
Major character(s): Chris, Widow(er); Roza, Lover
Time period(s): 1970s
Locale(s): London, England

Summary: When Chris first meets Roza, he mistakes her for a call girl, but it turns out she's a hippie instead. She lives in a house with a bunch of other artistic types and appears to lead an exciting life full of free-wheeling sex. She claims she actually once did work as a prostitute, though no longer. Roza is a Bulgarian Serb whose father supported Tito. She tells Chris stories about the old country, including one about a sexual affair with her own father. She reveals a great deal to him about Eastern European politics and the suffering of her people through these stories. Chris is enchanted and very attracted to Roza, but he's also not sure exactly how much of her tale to believe.

Popular Fiction

Where it's reviewed:
Booklist, September 15, 2008, page 26
Kirkus Reviews, August 15, 2008, page NA
Publishers Weekly, August 4, 2008, page 43

Other books by the same author:
Birds Without Wings, 2004
Red Dog, 2001
Corelli's Mandolin, 1995
The Troublesome Offspring of Cardinal Guzman, 1994
The War of Don Emmanuel's Nether Parts, 1992

Other books you might like:
Ian McEwan, *On Chesil Beach*, 2007
Tod Wodicka, *All Shall Be Well; and All Shall Be Well; and All Manner of Things Shall Be Well*, 2008

997

BARBARA DELINSKY

While My Sister Sleeps
(New York: Doubleday, 2009)

Story type: Contemporary
Subject(s): Family Relations; Sports/Running
Major character(s): Robin Snow, Sports Figure; Kathryn Snow, Parent
Time period(s): 2000s
Locale(s): United States

Summary: Potential Olympic runner Robin Snow goes for a run and is found collapsed by the side of the road. Though David, a high school teacher, performs CPR, she remains brain-dead. For one week, Robin's family members and others deal with what to do next. Robin's mother, Kathryn, regrets that she never revealed that her husband was not Robin's father, because Robin's biological father, too, had an enlarged heart. Robin's sister, Molly, feels terribly guilty because she refused to go running with Robin on the day of the incident. Molly also begins to have feelings for David, who discovered Robin. Robin's brother is currently being blackmailed at work and, like Molly, always resented Robin's star status in the family.

Where it's reviewed:
Booklist, December 1, 2008, page 26
Publishers Weekly, November 3, 2008, page 37

Other books by the same author:
The Secret Between Us, 2008
Family Tree, 2007
A Woman's Place, 1997
Together Alone, 1995
Suddenly, 1994

Other books you might like:
Margaret Mazzantini, *Don't Move*, 2004
Jodi Picoult, *Change of Heart*, 2008

998

NELSON DEMILLE

The Gate House
(New York: Grand Central Publishing, 2008)

Story type: Action/Adventure
Subject(s): Marriage; Organized Crime
Major character(s): John Sutter, Lawyer; Susan Sutter, Divorced Person
Time period(s): 2000s (2002)
Locale(s): Long Island, New York

Summary: In a sequel to *The Gold Coast*, John Sutter is reunited with his wealthy ex-wife, Susan, on Long Island's wealthy North Shore. In the previous novel, Susan had an affair with a Mafia don and then killed him. John divorced her and moved to London. Now he's back, and coincidentally living in the gate house on what was previously Susan's family's enormous estate. Post-9/11, however, things aren't what they once were. The estate has been divided into parcels of land and sold off to the nouveau riche, and Susan's family home is now inhabited by a wealthy Iranian. Susan is living in the area, however, and so is the son of her dead lover, who invites John to become his organization's attorney. John and Susan flirt with the idea of getting back together.

Where it's reviewed:
Booklist, September 1, 2008, page 4
The Denver Post, October 26, 2008, page E11
Kirkus Reviews, September 1, 2008, page NA
Newsday, November 5, 2008, page NA
Publishers Weekly, August 18, 2008, page 38

Other books by the same author:
Wild Fire, 2006
Plum Island, 1997
The Gold Coast, 1990
The Charm School, 1988
The Talbot Odyssey, 1987

Other books you might like:
David Baldacci, *Divine Justice*, 2008
Vince Flynn, *Extreme Measures*, 2008

999

LEONARD DOWNIE JR.

The Rules of the Game
(New York: Knopf, 2009)

Story type: Contemporary
Subject(s): Politics; Journalism
Major character(s): Sarah Page, Journalist; Susan Cameron, Political Figure
Time period(s): 2000s
Locale(s): Washington, District of Columbia

Summary: In a fictional scenario with some echoes of the 2008 presidential election, an elderly Democratic president is elected, despite the fact that his running mate, the 41-year-old and charismatic junior senator from California, Susan Cameron, has very little experience. The president dies shortly after taking office, and Cameron is thrust into the driver's seat. Investigative reporter Sarah Page is attempting to redeem herself after an affair with a co-worker. She covers the story with energy and ambition, and along the way she uncovers a conspiracy that seems to be related to murder. The author was executive editor of *The Washington Post* from 1991 until 2008.

Where it's reviewed:
Booklist, November 1, 2008, page 4
Kirkus Reviews, October 15, 2008, page NA
Publishers Weekly, October 20, 2008, page 30

Other books by the same author:
The News about the News: American Journalism in Peril, 2002 (nonfiction)
The New Muckrakers, 1976 (nonfiction)
Mortgage on America: The Real Cost of Real Estate Speculation, 1974 (nonfiction)
Justice Denied: The Case for Reform of the Courts, 1973 (nonfiction)

Other books you might like:
Richard Clarke, *Breakpoint*, 2007
John Grisham, *The Associate*, 2009

1000

GERALD EARLY , Co-Editor
E. LYNN HARRIS , Co-Editor

Best African American Fiction: 2009

(New York: Bantam, 2009)

Story type: Literary; Anthology
Subject(s): African Americans; Short Stories

Summary: Short stories and novel excerpts make up this anthology of work published from 2006 to 2009. Emily Raboteau's "Orb Weaver" steps into metafiction territory. Chimamanda Ngozi Adichie's "Cell One" is set in Nigeria and follows the son of a professor who is infatuated with gangsters. Tiphanie Yanique's contribution covers the generation gap between Caribbean-born immigrants to the United States. Mat Johnson's novel excerpt is set in 18th-century New York and looks at slavery. Helen Lee's "This Kind of Red" depicts a woman trying to ease her mind as she waits to strike back at the husband who batters her.

Where it's reviewed:
Booklist, November 15, 2008, page 17
Kirkus Reviews, December 1, 2008, page NA
Publishers Weekly, November 10, 2008, page 33

Other books you might like:
Laura Furman, *The O. Henry Prize Stories 2008*, 2008
Heidi Pitlor, *The Best American Short Stories 2008*, 2008

1001

DAVID EBERSHOFF

The 19th Wife

(New York: Random House, 2008)

Story type: Literary
Subject(s): Marriage; Religious Life
Major character(s): Brigham Young, Historical Figure, Political Figure; Ann Eliza Young, Historical Figure, Spouse; Jordan Scott, Murderer (accused), Runaway
Time period(s): 2000s; 1890s (1890)
Locale(s): Mesadale, Arizona; Salt Lake City, Utah

Summary: Two stories weave together: in the present, Jordan Scott has been excommunicated from the Mormon Church. He returns to the small Mormon town where he was raised to attempt to clear the name of his mother, who is accused of murdering his father. His mother was his father's 19th wife. This story alternates with a fictionalized version of the story of Ann Eliza Young, the 19th wife of church founder Brigham Young. Ann Eliza left the church herself and published two autobiographies in which she urged the church to stop practicing polygamy. The novel incorporates a wide array of letters, emails, diary entries, and other types of writing.

Where it's reviewed:
The Record, September 14, 2008, page F16
The Seattle Times, August 17, 2008, page 14
The Tampa Tribune, September 7, 2008, page 10

Other books by the same author:
Pasadena, 2002
The Rose City, 2001 (short stories)
The Danish Girl, 2000

Other books you might like:
Jon Krakauer, *Under the Banner of Heaven*, 2003 non-fiction
Curtis Sittenfeld, *American Wife*, 2008

1002

ELISSA ELLIOTT

Eve

(New York: Delacorte, 2009)

Story type: Literary
Subject(s): Bible
Major character(s): Eve, Biblical Figure; Adam, Biblical Figure
Locale(s): Garden of Eden, Fictional Country

Summary: This "novel of the first woman" retells the story of Adam and Eve both in the Garden of Eden and beyond. At first all is well, until Adam can't resist Lucifer's insistence that he eat some forbidden fruit. Years later, they have been fruitful and multiplied and live on an estate with their sons, Cain and Abel, and daughters. Abel herds animals, while Cain raises crops. Adam tries to spread the word about God, but Cain insists on worshipping a Sumerian goddess and lusts after one of his sisters. Sibling rivalry leads to murder.

They're just a typical dysfunctional family, living in Biblical times.

Where it's reviewed:
Kirkus Reviews, December 1, 2008, page NA
Publishers Weekly, November 10, 2008, page 32

Other books you might like:
David Maine, *Fallen*, 2005
Marie Phillips, *Gods Behaving Badly*, 2007

1003

JOSH EMMONS

Prescription for a Superior Existence

(New York: Scribner, 2008)

Story type: Literary
Subject(s): Cults
Major character(s): Montgomery Shoal, Religious; Jack Smith, Cult Member
Time period(s): 2000s
Locale(s): California

Summary: Jack Smith uses a corporate credit card to pay for a visit to a strip club, and his boss gives him an ultimatum: Either quit or join a religious sect similar to Scientology called Prescription for a Superior Existence, or PASE. Jack joins the group and finds himself fascinated by and frightened of its fervent leader, Montgomery Shoal. At first Jack resists the religion, but after kidnapping and reprogramming, he starts to fall into line. PASE dictates a strict no-sex and no-drug policy and obeisance to a deity said to be embodied by Montgomery Shoal. However, a mass suicide may be in the works.

Where it's reviewed:
Booklist, May 1, 2008, page 72
Kirkus Reviews, April 1, 2008, page NA
Publishers Weekly, February 11, 2008, page 47

Other books by the same author:
The Loss of Leon Meed, 2007

Other books you might like:
Amanda Boyden, *Babylon Rolling*, 2008
Chuck Palahniuk, *Fight Club*, 1996

1004

RICHARD PAUL EVANS

Grace

(New York: Simon & Schuster, 2008)

Story type: Contemporary
Subject(s): Love; Charity; Homeless People
Major character(s): Eric, Teenager; Grace, Teenager
Time period(s): 2000s (2006)
Locale(s): Utah

Summary: From many years in the future, Eric, now a grandfather, recalls his family's move from California to Utah the year he entered the ninth grade. The memory is prompted in 2006 by his grandchildren asking him to read them a Christmas story over the holidays. That leads Eric to a book-length reverie about the period after he discovered his classmate Grace eating food out of the garbage. Eric and his younger brother agree to hide her in their fort in the backyard and bring food to her. Everyone in the family is stressed. Their father is sick and their mother working extra-hard, and the Cuban missile crisis is happening to boot.

Where it's reviewed:
The St. Petersburg Times, October 23, 2008, page 4

Other books by the same author:
The Gift, 2007
Finding Noel, 2006
The Sunflower, 2005
The Last Promise, 2002
The Christmas Box, 1993

Other books you might like:
Debbie Macomber, *A Cedar Cove Christmas*, 2008
Nicholas Sparks, *The Lucky One*, 2008

1005

BERNARDINE EVARISTO

Blonde Roots

(New York: Riverhead, 2009)

Story type: Literary
Subject(s): Slavery; Africans
Major character(s): Doris, Slave
Locale(s): Africa

Summary: In this re-imagining of the African slave trade in an alternate universe, it is Africans who come to Europe and take white-skinned people into slavery. Some are brought back to Africa, and others are shipped to a parallel version of the United States. An Englishwoman and cabbage farmer named Doris is taken to work for a man named Bwana, a notorious and cruel slaveholder. The Africans are amused by the provincial traditions and language of their European slaves. Some slaves from Europe (the Africans refer to it as "the Gray Continent" due to the weather) kiss up to their masters; others plot their escape.

Where it's reviewed:
Kirkus Reviews, December 1, 2008, page NA
New Statesman, August 4, 2008, page 51
Publishers Weekly, November 10, 2008, page 31

Other books by the same author:
Soul Tourists, 2005
The Emperor's Babe, 2002

Other books you might like:
Amitav Ghosh, *Sea of Poppies*, 2008
Robert Harris, *Fatherland*, 1992

1006

JON FASMAN

The Unpossessed City

(New York: Penguin Press, 2008)

Story type: Literary
Subject(s): Mystery; History; Historical
Major character(s): Jim Vilatzer, Historian
Time period(s): 2000s
Locale(s): Moscow, Russia; Rockville, Maryland

Summary: Jim Vilatzer is the son of a Russian father who was raised in the Maryland suburbs of Washington, D.C. In his 30s, Jim finds himself in a bind when he gets into debt with gangsters to cover his gambling losses. Also, his girlfriend has just dumped him. Desperate to pay off his debts, Jim, who grew up speaking Russian, takes a job in Moscow interviewing survivors of the gulag for some kind of non-profit group. Soon, he finds himself getting involved with former nuclear scientists in Russia, and American intelligence groups get interested in the work he's doing.

Where it's reviewed:
Booklist, September 15, 2008, page 31
Publishers Weekly, September 1, 2008, page 34

Other books by the same author:
The Geographer's Library, 2005

Other books you might like:
Travis Holland, *The Archivist's Story*, 2007
Tom Rob Smith, *Child 44*, 2008

1007

PATRICIA FERGUSON

Peripheral Vision

(New York: Other Press, 2008)

Story type: Literary
Subject(s): Illness; Mothers and Sons
Major character(s): Ruby, Parent; Iris, Nurse; Sylvia, Doctor
Time period(s): 1950s; 1990s
Locale(s): London, England

Summary: A series of stories set in the 1950s and 1990s interweave and reflect on each other, though they rarely directly intersect. In the 1950s, Ruby begins to receive nasty letters after her son George loses an eye through an accident that may have been her fault. Iris is one of the nurse's caring for George, and she begins a romantic relationship with a medical student, but shes wary of the class differences between them. In the later years, Sylvia, an eye surgeon, reads the notes on George's case while also dealing with her own disturbing lack of maternal instinct after giving birth to her first child. The author has published other novels in England, but this is her first book to be published in the United States.

Where it's reviewed:
Publishers Weekly, August 4, 2008, page 43

Other books you might like:
Carol Shields, *Unless*, 2002
Darin Strauss, *More Than It Hurts You*, 2008

1008

JEFFREY FLEISHMAN

Promised Virgins

(New York: Arcade Publishing, 2009)

Story type: Literary
Subject(s): War
Major character(s): Jay Morgan, Journalist; Alija, Linguist
Time period(s): 1990s
Locale(s): Kosovo, Serbia

Summary: Jay Morgan is on assignment in Kosovo to report on the conflict between the Serbs and the Albanians there. He hires Alija to interpret for him, but Alija turns out to have a personal stake in the war: Her brother, Ardian, a university student, is missing, and she's afraid he may have been killed. Jay, still grieving over the death of his wife, a photographer, investigates on his own time, but doesn't share all of the gruesome details he discovers with Alija. Jay's work takes him into the mountains, where he tracks down a mysterious Muslim leader. The author is an experienced war correspondent; this is his first work of fiction.

Where it's reviewed:
Kirkus Reviews, November 15, 2008, page NA
Publishers Weekly, November 10, 2008, page 31

Other books you might like:
Nadeem Aslam, *The Wasted Vigil*, 2008
Aleksander Hemon, *The Lazarus Project*, 2008

1009

DAVID FRANCIS

Stray Dog Winter

(San Francisco: MacAdam/Cage, 2008)

Story type: Literary
Subject(s): Communism; Homosexuality/Lesbianism
Major character(s): Darcy Bright, Artist; Fin Bright, Artist; Aurelio, Police Officer
Time period(s): 1980s (1984)
Locale(s): Moscow, Union of Soviet Socialist Republics

Summary: In the gloomy days of the Cold War, Australian artist Darcy Bright willingly heeds his artist sister's invitation to join her in Moscow, where she is painting industrial landscapes. Darcy is gay and embarks on an affair with Aurelio, a police officer from Cuba who has been assigned to round up homosexuals. Also, Darcy's sister admits that she used his artwork to obtain her current commission. He suspects she may be up to no good, especially since she's asked him to sneak something through customs for her upon arriving. Darcy is nervous about all this, but also energized. He likes the danger and the subterfuge.

Where it's reviewed:
Booklist, September 1, 2008, page 50

Popular Fiction

Los Angeles Magazine, October 2008, page 88
Publishers Weekly, August 4, 2008, page 46

Other books by the same author:
The Great Inland Sea, 2005

Other books you might like:
David Benioff, *City of Thieves*, 2008
Tom Rob Smith, *Child 44*, 2008

1010

CARLOS FUENTES

Happy Families

(New York: Random House, 2008)

Story type: Literary
Subject(s): Short Stories; Family Relations
Locale(s): Mexico

Summary: The well-known Mexican author offers personal stories that reveal something not only about their characters, but about history as well. As the title indicates, the stories revolve around family relationships. Several consider the father-son bond (or lack thereof), including one about a father who wants to force his sons into the priesthood. Another features a high-ranking politician who cannot control himself, but tries to impose strict rules on his own son. Short poetic sections are included among the more structured stories. Translated from the Spanish by Edith Grossman.

Where it's reviewed:
Booklist, August 1, 2008, page 35
Kirkus Reviews, August 1, 2008, page NA
Publishers Weekly, August 4, 2008, page 44
The Seattle Times, October 5, 2008, page 15

Other books by the same author:
Will and Fortune, 2008 (novel)
The Eagle's Throne, 2006 (novel)
Terra Nostra, 1995 (novel)
A Change of Skin, 1968 (novel)
The Death of Artemio Cruz, 1962 (novel)

Other books you might like:
Anton Chekhov, *The Complete Short Novels*, 2005
Alice Munro, *Carried Away*, 2006

1011

LISA GENOVA

Still Alice

(New York: Pocket Books, 2009)

Story type: Literary
Subject(s): Aging; Diseases
Major character(s): Alice Howland, Professor
Time period(s): 2000s
Locale(s): Cambridge, Massachusetts

Summary: Alice Howland is a busy, competent professor of psychology at Harvard when she notices that little things are slipping her mind. She loses track of her

Blackberry, for example. She goes to the doctor and is diagnosed with Alzheimer's disease. Within two years Alice, who is not yet 50 years old, can't remember the names of her three adult children. Different family members have different reactions to her illness. Her children are afraid they may have inherited it, while her doctors are struggling to treat her. Her husband, also a professor, has difficulty accepting her decline. The author holds a doctorate in neuroscience.

Where it's reviewed:
Booklist, November 15, 2008, page 27
Publishers Weekly, October 20, 2008, page 31

Other books you might like:
John Bayley, *Elegy for Iris*, 1999
    memoir
Sue Miller, *The Senator's Wife*, 2008

1012

MIRIAM GERSHOW

The Local News

(New York: Spiegel & Grau, 2009)

Story type: Literary
Subject(s): Family Relations; Missing Persons
Major character(s): Lydia Pasternak, Teenager; Danny
    Pasternak, Teenager
Time period(s): 1990s; 2000s
Locale(s): United States

Summary: Nerd Lydia and jock Danny are brother and sister and attend high school together, but they hang out with very different crowds. Then Danny disappears. Lydia recalls the earlier Danny, who was awkward and had trouble in school, and his subsequent transformation (after the family moved to a new town) into one of the popular kids. With Danny missing, Danny's friends look after Lydia and pay attention to her for the first time. Their parents hire a private investigator who is also the focus of some of Lydia's attention. Ten years later, at her high school reunion, Lydia comes to terms with all that happened.

Where it's reviewed:
Publishers Weekly, October 27, 2008, page 29

Other books you might like:
Stewart O'Nan, *Songs for the Missing*, 2008
Alice Sebold, *The Lovely Bones*, 2002

1013

AMITAV GHOSH

Sea of Poppies

(New York: Farrar, Straus and Giroux, 2008)

Story type: Literary
Subject(s): Travel; Historical
Major character(s): Paulette, Orphan; Jack Crowle, Sailor;
    Zachary Reid, Sailor
Time period(s): 1830s (1838)
Locale(s): *Ibis*, At Sea

Summary: On the Ibis, a ship sailing from Calcutta to China on an opium-related errand, the forces of colonialism play themselves out in miniature. Biracial second mate Zachary Reid hails from Baltimore. Orphan Paulette has stowed away on the ship and nurses a crush on him. First mate Jack Crowle is a brutal racist, and the captain casts himself in a godlike role. Also on board are a man charged unfairly with forgery and another who rescued a woman from being burned on her husband's funeral pyre. The author includes a glossary to help with some of the unusual historic terms used.

Where it's reviewed:
The Christian Science Monitor, October 29, 2008, page 25
Kirkus Reviews, September 1, 2008, page NA
New York, September 8, 2008, page 92
Publishers Weekly, August 18, 2008, page 38

Other books by the same author:
The Hungry Tide, 2005
The Glass Palace, 2000
The Calcutta Chromosome, 1995
The Shadow Lines, 1988
The Circle of Reason, 1986

Other books you might like:
Aravind Adiga, *The White Tiger*, 2008
Michel Faber, *The Crimson Petal and the White*, 2002

1014

GLORIA GOLDREICH

Open Doors
(New York: Mira, 2008)

Story type: Literary
Subject(s): Family Relations
Major character(s): Elaine Gordon, Artist
Time period(s): 2000s
Locale(s): New York; California; Jerusalem, Israel

Summary: Ceramic artist Elaine Gordon's husband dies suddenly, and as part of her recovery process she leaves her New York state home and goes to visit each of her four adult children, who live in various parts of the world and are dealing with various issues. One daughter, Sarah, lives in Jerusalem and is an Orthodox Jew. Sarah's twin, Lisa, is in Russia, trying to adopt a child on her own. Peter lives in California and has children, but is unhappy in his marriage. Finally, Denis lives in New Mexico with his partner, and Elaine has trouble accepting that he is gay.

Where it's reviewed:
Publishers Weekly, August 4, 2008, page 43

Other books by the same author:
Dinner with Anna Karenina, 2006
Years of Dreams, 1992
Leah's Children, 1985
Four Days, 1980
Leah's Journey, 1978

Other books you might like:
Risa Miller, *Welcome to Heavenly Heights*, 2003
Belva Plain, *Evergreen*, 1978

1015

JANE GREEN

The Beach House
(New York: Viking, 2008)

Story type: Contemporary
Subject(s): Widows/Widowers; Friendship
Major character(s): Nan Powell, Widow(er)
Time period(s): 2000s
Locale(s): Nantucket, Massachusetts

Summary: Nan Powell has been widowed, and she decides to fill her family's large house on Nantucket with boarders to return the house to its previous busy state. She takes in a man who is separated from his wife and coming to terms with his sexuality and a single mother and her difficult teenage daughter. Then Nan's own adult son, Michael, comes to stay. He's had a disastrous affair with his boss back in New York and needs to come home and work things out in his own head. Against the backdrop of luxurious Nantucket, Nan comes to terms with the next phase of her life and steadfastly refuses to sell out to developers.

Where it's reviewed:
Booklist, May 15, 2008, page 20
Kirkus Reviews, May 1, 2008, page NA
Publishers Weekly, April 28, 2008, page 110

Other books by the same author:
Second Chance, 2007
Swapping Lives, 2006
Straight Talking, 2003
Bookends, 2002
Mr. Maybe, 2001

Other books you might like:
Elizabeth Berg, *Open House*, 2000
Elin Hilderbrand, *A Summer Affair*, 2008
Sherri Rivkin, *Lovehampton*, 2008

1016

BARBARA HALL

The Music Teacher
(Chapel Hill, NC: Algonquin Books, 2009)

Story type: Literary
Major character(s): Pearl Swain, Teacher; Hallie Bolaris, Teenager
Time period(s): 2000s
Locale(s): Los Angeles, California

Summary: Pearl Swain has been dumped by her husband, a professor who left her for a student, and she has withdrawn into her trailer and become introverted. She still teaches violin, however, and she is startled one day to be faced with a 14-year-old student with talent. Hallie Bolaris is mourning the death of her mother and has begged her aunt to pay for her violin lessons. Hallie's passion for music makes Pearl look at her own engagement, or lack thereof, with all aspects of her life. Pearl herself had great potential but never lived up to it, and she often doesn't act on her feelings.

Where it's reviewed:
Booklist, December 1, 2008, page 24
Kirkus Reviews, October 15, 2008, page NA
Publishers Weekly, October 6, 2008, page 33

Other books by the same author:
The Noah Confessions, 2007 (young adult)
Dixie Storms, 2005 (young adult)
A Summons to New Orleans, 2000

Other books you might like:
Wally Lamb, *The Hour I First Believed*, 2008
Anita Shreve, *Testimony*, 2008

1017

GAIL HAREVEN

The Confessions of Noa Weber
(Brooklyn: Melville House, 2009)

Story type: Literary
Subject(s): Romance
Major character(s): Noa Weber, Writer; Alek, Journalist
Time period(s): 1970s (1972); 2000s
Locale(s): Israel

Summary: Noa Weber outwardly appears very successful. She's a well-known writer and feminist and the single mother of a 29-year-old daughter. But in her written confessions, addressed to her daughter, she reveals that she has nursed an obsession for a Russian named Alek whom she met at a party when she was 17 in 1972. Noa moved in with Alek and became pregnant, and her strong feelings for him never wavered. Now Alek is a reporter working abroad, but she remains secretly dedicated to him and meets him anywhere he wants, whenever he invites her. Even Noa herself is troubled and puzzled by her feelings for Alek, but she can't shake them. Translated from the Hebrew by Dalya Bilu.

Where it's reviewed:
Publishers Weekly, November 24, 2008, page 37

Other books you might like:
Tana French, *In the Woods*, 2007
A.B. Yehoshua, *Friendly Fire*, 2008

1018

KAREN HARPER

Mistress Shakespeare
(New York: Putnam, 2009)

Story type: Literary
Subject(s): History
Major character(s): Anne Whateley, Historical Figure; William Shakespeare, Historical Figure, Writer
Time period(s): 16th century
Locale(s): London, England

Summary: Anne Whateley is in love with William Shakespeare, and the two apply for a marriage license, but then, Shakespeare marries Anne Hathaway instead, presum-

ably because she is pregnant. Whateley flees to London and begins working in her family's business, but when Shakespeare moves to London shortly afterward, the two former lovers and childhood friends are reunited and find they still have feelings for each other. Shakespeare considers Whateley his muse and writes poetry dedicated to her. Whateley helps him to find a theater for his plays to be produced and she even saves his life during a fire.

Where it's reviewed:
Kirkus Reviews, December 15, 2008, page NA
Publishers Weekly, November 24, 2008, page 36

Other books by the same author:
Below the Surface, 2008
The Hiding Place, 2008
The Hooded Hawke, 2007
The Last Boleyn, 2006
The Poyson Garden, 1999

Other books you might like:
Robin Maxwell, *Signora Da Vinci*, 2009
Anne Easter Smith, *The King's Grace*, 2009

1019

E. LYNN HARRIS

Just Too Good to Be True
(New York: Doubleday, 2008)

Story type: Contemporary
Subject(s): Sports/Football; African Americans
Major character(s): Carmyn Bledsoe, Parent; Brady Bledsoe, Sports Figure
Time period(s): 2000s
Locale(s): Atlanta, Georgia

Summary: Carmyn Bledsoe owns two beauty salons in Atlanta, Georgia, and has expended a lot of effort raising her son, Brady, who was the result of a rape that Carmyn no longer remembers. Brady is now a football player at Central Georgia University, and his mother oversees his career and is working to keep him celibate until he marries. Agents with questionable morals gather around Brady, however, including one who tries to tempt him with sexually available women. The agent also sets up Brady's godfather, a professor who may be gay, for seduction so that he can then blackmail the family.

Where it's reviewed:
Essence, July 2008, page 66
Kirkus Reviews, May 15, 2008, page NA
Publishers Weekly, May 26, 2008, page 38
USA Today, May 22, 2008, page 6D

Other books by the same author:
I Say a Little Prayer, 2006
A Love of My Own, 2002
Any Way the Wind Blows, 2001
If This World Were Mine, 1997
And This Too Shall Pass, 1996

Other books you might like:
Mary B. Morrison, *Who's Loving You*, 2008
Carl Weber, *Something on the Side*, 2008

1020

JIM HARRISON

The English Major

(Toronto: House of Anansi Press, 2008)

Story type: Literary
Subject(s): Travel; Divorce
Major character(s): Cliff, Teacher; Vivian, Spouse
Time period(s): 2000s

Summary: In a moment of mid-life crisis, former teacher and farmer Cliff embarks on a journey to visit all 48 contiguous states. He's not leaving much behind in Michigan. He's lost his family's farm. He's divorced Vivian after 38 years of marriage because she turned out to have been unfaithful. Even his beloved dog has died. As he drives, Cliff considers the events of his life. He also brings along a jigsaw puzzle of the United States and tosses a piece of the puzzle out the window each time he visits a new state. He meets up with a former student in Minnesota and visits his son in San Francisco.

Where it's reviewed:
The Houston Chronicle, November 2, 2008, page 14
Kirkus Reviews, August 15, 2008, page NA
The New York Times Book Review, October 19, 2008, page 12
Publishers Weekly, June 2, 2008, page 25
The Seattle Times, October 5, 2008, page 14

Other books by the same author:
Returning to Earth, 2006
True North, 2005
The Road Home, 1999
The Woman Lit By Fireflies, 1990
Dalva, 1988

Other books you might like:
Julia Glass, *I See You Everywhere*, 2008
David Wroblewski, *The Story of Edgar Sawtelle*, 2008

1021

JOHN HASKELL

Out of My Skin

(New York: Farrar, Straus and Giroux, 2009)

Story type: Literary
Subject(s): Identity
Major character(s): Haskell, Writer
Time period(s): 2000s
Locale(s): Los Angeles, California

Summary: A writer named Haskell, like the author, moves from New York to Los Angeles and accepts an assignment to write about a Steve Martin impersonator. In the process of writing the article, he starts working as an impersonator himself. The writer also impersonates Steve Martin, but he dedicates a great deal of time to thinking about other Hollywood actors and figures as well and their public and private lives. He meditates frequently on what is real and what is false, and he works to keep up an ongoing impersonation of Steve Martin without ever

returning to his own true personality. He also meets a woman, who is frequently confused about whether he is acting as himself or as Steve Martin.

Where it's reviewed:
Kirkus Reviews, December 1, 2008, page NA
Publishers Weekly, November 24, 2008, page 36

Other books by the same author:
American Purgatorio, 2004
I Am Not Jackson Pollock, 2003 (short stories)

Other books you might like:
Benjamin Kunkel, *Indecision*, 2005
Salvatore Scibona, *The End*, 2008

1022

NICOLE HELGET

The Turtle Catcher

(New York: Houghton Mifflin Harcourt, 2009)

Story type: Literary
Subject(s): Family Relations
Major character(s): Liesel Richter, Teenager
Time period(s): 1920s
Locale(s): New Germany, Minnesota

Summary: During World War I, Liesel Richter lives in New Germany, Minnesota, which is populated by a number of German immigrants, including her own parents. What Liesel doesn't know is that her mother, recently emigrated, was already pregnant by her Jewish lover when she married Liesel's father, Wilhelm Richter. Liesel was born a hermaphrodite, which her mother believes was punishment for her indiscretion. As a result, Liesel is rarely allowed off her family's farm. She develops a friendship with a retarded neighbor. The town's residents are divided along many lines, especially with regard to World War I and the strength, or not, of their attachment to Germany.

Where it's reviewed:
Publishers Weekly, October 27, 2008, page 30

Other books by the same author:
The Summer of Ordinary Ways, 2005 (memoir)

Other books you might like:
Jeffrey Eugenides, *Middlesex*, 2002
Mary Ann Shaffer, *The Guernsey Literary and Potato Peel Pie Society*, 2008

1023

BILL HENDERSON , Editor

The Pushcart Prize XXXIII

(Wainscott, NY: Pushcart Press, 2008)

Story type: Literary; Anthology
Subject(s): Short Stories; Anthology

Summary: This prestigious annual anthology, now more than three decades old, collects stories (as well as essays and poetry) from small literary magazines. This year's 60 selections include "Retreat" by Wells Tower, about a property developer living in Maine, and Katie Chase's "Man and Wife," set in a fictional world where very young girls have marriages arranged for them. Other authors of short stories represented here include Beena Kamlani, Jack Livings, and Elizabeth Tallent. The volume also offers a mailing list for the presses represented and an index of previous winners of the prize.

Where it's reviewed:
Booklist, November 15, 2008, page 14
Kirkus Reviews, October 15, 2008, page NA
Publishers Weekly, November 3, 2008, page 41

Other books by the same author:
The Pushcart Prize XXXII, 2008
The Pushcart Prize XXXI, 2007
The Pushcart Prize XXX, 2005
The Pushcart Prize XXIX, 2004
The Pushcart Book of Short Stories, 2002

Other books you might like:
Laura Furman, *The O. Henry Prize Stories 2008*, 2008
Heidi Pitlor, *The Best American Short Stories 2008*, 2008

SARA HOUGHTELING

Pictures at an Exhibition

(New York: Knopf, 2009)

Story type: Literary
Subject(s): War; Art
Major character(s): Max Berenzon, Heir; Rose Clement, Museum Curator
Time period(s): 1940s
Locale(s): Paris, France

Summary: Max Berenzon's father is a respected gallery owner, but he refuses to take Max under his wing. Instead, he hires curator Rose Clement and teaches her the business. Max nurses a crush on Rose. Then the war arrives, and the assimilated Jewish Berenzon family hides in the countryside. Rose tries to keep inventory of all the art that is being looted by Nazis. When the war is over, Max returns, and he finds that many works of art are missing, as are many Jews. His family's gallery has been emptied entirely. He works to track down Rose.

Where it's reviewed:
Kirkus Reviews, December 1, 2008, page NA
Publishers Weekly, November 17, 2008, page 42

Other books you might like:
Geraldine Brooks, *People of the Book*, 2008
Irene Nemirovsky, *Suite Francaise*, 2006

1025

YU HUA

Brothers

(New York: Pantheon, 2009)

Story type: Literary
Subject(s): China; Cultural Conflict

Major character(s): Li Guan, Businessman; Song Gang, Scholar
Time period(s): 1990s
Locale(s): China

Summary: Li Guan and Song Gang are not actually brothers, but stepbrothers. In their small Chinese village, Li Guan's mother marries Song Gang's father. Emblematic of the new versus the old China, the brothers are both allied and at odds during and after the Cultural Revolution. First, they compete for a woman who chooses quiet, thoughtful Song Gang. Li Guan aims to get her attention with all kinds of capitalist schemes, including something called the "National Virgin Beauty Competition." The novel was published in two volumes in Taiwan. Translated from the Chinese by Eileen Cheng-yin Chow and Carlos Roja.

Where it's reviewed:
Kirkus Reviews, December 15, 2008, page NA
Publishers Weekly, November 24, 2008, page 37

Other books by the same author:
Cries in the Drizzle, 2007
Chronicle of a Blood Merchant, 2003
To Live, 2003
The Past and the Punishments, 1996 (short stories)

Other books you might like:
Ma Jian, *Beijing Coma*, 2008
Mo Yan, *Life and Death Are Wearing Me Out*, 2008

1026

NANCY HUSTON

Fault Lines

(New York: Grove/Black Cat, 2008)

Story type: Literary
Subject(s): Family Relations; Judaism
Major character(s): Sol, Child; Randall, Parent
Time period(s): 2000s (2004); 1960s (1962)
Locale(s): California; Canada

Summary: A member of each of four generations of a family is visited at six years of age and then later in life. In 2004, Sol is six and goes to Protestant church services, though, or because, his mother is Catholic and his father is Jewish. When Randall, Sol's father, is six in 1982, he lives with his parents in Israel for a year so his mother, Sadie, can study. Terrible events injure Sadie, however. In 1962, it's Sadie who is six. Her mother marries a Jewish man Sadie hopes will keep them safe. Finally, Sadie's mother is a child and discovers that she may have been adopted. The novel won France's Prix Femina.

Where it's reviewed:
Booklist, August 1, 2008, page 36
Kirkus Reviews, August 15, 2008, page NA
The New York Times Book Review, November 2, 2008, page 7
Publishers Weekly, June 2, 2008, page 25

Other books by the same author:
Dolce Agonia, 2001
Slow Emergencies, 2001
The Mark of the Angel, 1999

The Goldberg Variations, 1996
Plainsong, 1993

Other books you might like:
Natalie Danford, *Inheritance*, 2007
Susan Vreeland, *Girl in Hyacinth Blue*, 1999

1027

M. ANN JACOBY

Life After Genius

(New York: Grand Central Publishing, 2008)

Story type: Literary
Subject(s): Coming-of-Age
Major character(s): Theodore Mead Fegley, Genius,
    Teenager
Time period(s): 2000s
Locale(s): High Grove, Illinois

Summary: Days before he is supposed to graduate from
college, Theodore Mead Fegley goes home, confused
and unsettled. From there, he recalls his years as a teenage math prodigy and his early days in college, when he
was light years ahead of the other students intellectually
but behind them emotionally. His mother overwhelmed
him; his father, who ran a funeral home, was emotionally absent. His popular cousin overshadowed him. He
also reveals that he has hallucinations and recalls his attempts to prove the complex Riemann Hypothesis and
the machinations of another student who tried to sabotage
him.

Where it's reviewed:
Booklist, September 15, 2008, page 26
Kirkus Reviews, September 1, 2008, page NA
Publishers Weekly, August 4, 2008, page 45

Other books you might like:
Mark Haddon, *The Curious Incident of the Dog in the
    Night-Time*, 2003
Marisha Pessl, *Special Topics in Calamity Physics*, 2006

1028

IRIS JOHANSEN

Dark Summer

(New York: St. Martin's Press, 2008)

Story type: Contemporary
Subject(s): Revenge; Animals/Dogs; Mystery
Major character(s): Devon Brady, Veterinarian; Jude Mar-
    rock, Animal Trainer; Ned, Animal
Time period(s): 2000s
Locale(s): Caribbean; Denver, Colorado

Summary: On a Caribbean island, veterinarian Devon
Brady treats Jude Marrock's black lab, Ned, after
someone shoots at the two while they look for earthquake
survivors. Jude specializes in training dogs to have
unique intuitive abilities. Devon is attracted to him,
though she thinks there is something odd about him, too.
Jude seems jittery, and he leaves Ned in Devon's care
and promises to return to pick up the dog later, but never

does. Devon saves Ned's life and heads home to Denver,
Colorado, with the dog, but strange things start to happen and she finds herself the target of international
criminals.

Where it's reviewed:
Booklist, September 1, 2008, page 4
Publishers Weekly, August 11, 2008, page 27

Other books by the same author:
Quicksand, 2008
Silent Thunder, 2008
The Treasure, 2008
Pandora's Daughter, 2007
The Killing Game, 1999

Other books you might like:
Kay Hooper, *Blood Sins*, 2008
Dean R. Koontz, *The Darkest Evening of the Year*, 2007

1029

DIANE JOHNSON

Lulu in Marrakech

(New York: Dutton, 2008)

Story type: Literary
Subject(s): Cultural Conflict; Spies
Major character(s): Lulu Sawyer, Spy; Ian Drumm,
    Wealthy
Time period(s): 2000s
Locale(s): Marrakech, Morocco

Summary: Lulu Sawyer is a CIA employee and delighted
to accept an undercover posting to Morocco, where she
is supposed to be gathering information on various
Islamic groups that may have nefarious aims. What she
spends more time doing, however, is hanging around the
pool at the mansion of her wealthy British boyfriend, Ian
Drumm, and talking to the eccentrics who gather there.
Lulu has plenty of opportunity to observe clashes of
Eastern and Western culture. She also watches warily as
a Saudi woman vies for Ians affections, partly as a way
to escape an unhappy marriage. The whole crowd is very
concerned for a young Muslim girl hiding from her
brother, who wants her killed for casting a black mark
on their family's honor.

Where it's reviewed:
Entertainment Weekly, October 3, 2008, page 79
Kirkus Reviews, August 15, 2008, page NA
Publishers Weekly, July 7, 2008, page 34
The Seattle Times, October 12, 2008, page 16
Vogue, October 2008, page 278

Other books by the same author:
L'Affaire, 2003
Le Mariage, 2000
Le Divorce, 1997
Persian Nights, 1987
The Shadow Knows, 1974

Other books you might like:
Susan Isaacs, *Shining Through*, 1988
Yannick Murphy, *Signed, Mata Hari*, 2007

Popular Fiction

1030

TONI JORDAN

Addition

(New York: Morrow, 2009)

Story type: Literary
Subject(s): Mental Illness
Major character(s): Grace Vandenburg, Teacher; Seamus O'Reilly, Lover
Time period(s): 2000s
Locale(s): Melbourne, Australia

Summary: Grace Vandenburg, a teacher on leave from her job, doesn't see her compulsion to count everything from the miles she drives to the number of times she chews her food as a problem. She finds that her mental illness fills her days. Then she meets Seamus O'Reilly and falls in love. Understandably enough, Seamus wants to help Grace heal and guides her into recovery. The only problem is that Grace finds life dull when she's not counting. Grace and Seamus must work together to find a happy medium between Grace's quirky zone and what society considers normal.

Where it's reviewed:
Publishers Weekly, November 10, 2008, page 29

Other books you might like:
Aimee Bender, *An Invisible Sign of My Own*, 2000
Mark Haddon, *The Curious Incident of the Dog in the Night-Time*, 2003

1031

STEPHANIE KALLOS

Sing Them Home

(New York: Atlantic Monthly Press, 2009)

Story type: Literary
Subject(s): Family Relations
Major character(s): Hope Jones, Parent; Larken Jones, Professor; Gaelan Jones, Television Personality
Time period(s): 1970s (1978); 2000s (2003)
Locale(s): Emlyn Springs, Nebraska

Summary: In 1978, Hope Jones disappears from her small-town Nebraska home and family, presumably the victim of a tornado, leaving behind three children and a husband. The novel then skips forward 25 years to find the children as adults, at a time when their father is struck by lightning while playing golf. One daughter is an art history professor who self-medicates with food. The other daughter goes through people's trash and takes things. The son is a television meteorologist who frequently engages in casual sex. They discover that their father had a long-term relationship with another woman. All three adult children have experienced the lack of their mother over the years in different ways.

Where it's reviewed:
Booklist, November 1, 2008, page 25
Kirkus Reviews, October 15, 2008, page NA
Publishers Weekly, September 1, 2008, page 33

Other books by the same author:
Broken for You, 2004

Other books you might like:
Tiffany Baker, *The Little Giant of Aberdeen County*, 2009
David Wroblewski, *The Story of Edgar Sawtelle*, 2008

1032

JANE KAMENSKY , Co-Author
JILL LEPORE , Co-Author

Blindspot: By a Gentleman in Exile and a Lady in Disguise

(New York: Spiegel & Grau, 2008)

Story type: Historical
Subject(s): Slavery
Major character(s): Stewart Jameson, Artist, Detective—Amateur; Ignatius Alexander, Doctor
Time period(s): 1760s (1764)

Summary: Scottish painter Stewart Jameson has relocated to Boston, Massachusetts, where he creates portraits of the well-off people of the city. He takes on a boy as an apprentice, but the boy turns out to be a woman and a runaway from one of the city's wealthy families. The two of them join forces with Ignatius Alexander, a former slave, to solve the mysterious death of a local abolitionist, who appears to have been murdered. Stewart and his would-be apprentice also undertake a torrid affair. Both co-authors are college professors who have written non-fiction history books.

Where it's reviewed:
Publishers Weekly, August 4, 2008, page 41

Other books you might like:
Emma Donoghue, *Slammerkin*, 2001
Sheri Holman, *The Dress Lodger*, 2000

1033

JONATHON KEATS

The Book of the Unknown: Tales of the Thirty-Six

(New York: Random House, 2009)

Story type: Literary
Subject(s): Short Stories; Folklore; Judaism

Summary: Twelve stories, along with a fictional academic-style foreword and afterword, look at the individuals known in the Talmud as the Lamedh-Vov, 36 righteous people who are responsible for the survival of humanity. Each allegorical story follows one of the righteous. In one, a former circus performer tries to cheer up a ruler. In another, a gambler loses everything all in one shot. A bricklayer must serve as the angel of death. The daughter of a pharmacist doles out placebos, and a widower makes a golem, a mythical monster, out of clay. Each story has a moral, and each character is lifelike, though based on an archetype and living in a fantastical world.

Where it's reviewed:
Booklist, December 1, 2008, page 21
Kirkus Reviews, November 15, 2008, page NA
Publishers Weekly, July 28, 2008, page 64

Other books by the same author:
The Pathology of Lies, 1999

Other books you might like:
Cynthia Ozick, *The Pagan Rabbi and Other Stories*, 1995
Isaac Bashevis Singer, *The Collected Stories of Isaac Bashevis Singer*, 1983

1034

DANIEL KEHLMANN

Me and Kaminski

(New York: Pantheon, 2008)

Story type: Literary
Subject(s): Art; Relationships
Major character(s): Sebastian Zollner, Journalist; Manuel Kaminski, Artist
Time period(s): 2000s
Locale(s): Germany

Summary: Journalist Sebastian Zollner is writing a biography of painter Manuel Kaminski and hoping to outshine a colleague who has recently written a similar book. Sebastian lives alone and is very morose and self-involved, yet he doesn't see his own foibles clearly at all. He's also a terrible journalist. Though Manuel is reclusive, Sebastian manages to work his way into the artist's life and even reunites him with his ex-wife. The two men develop a very strange relationship, but it is one of the few relationships that either has with other people. Manuel was once ranked with Picasso and Chagall, but then he went blind. Translated from the German by Carol Brown Janeway.

Where it's reviewed:
Booklist, October 15, 2008, page 23
Publishers Weekly, August 18, 2008, page 37

Other books by the same author:
Measuring the World, 2006

Other books you might like:
Kate Christensen, *The Great Man*, 2007
Tod Wodicka, *All Shall Be Well; and All Shall Be Well; and All Manner of Things Shall Be Well*, 2008

1035

KATHLEEN KENT

The Heretic's Daughter

(New York: Little, Brown, 2008)

Story type: Literary
Subject(s): Witches and Witchcraft; Historical
Major character(s): Sarah Carrier, Child; Martha Carrier, Parent

Time period(s): 17th century (1692)
Locale(s): Andover, Massachusetts

Summary: The Carriers are outcasts in Andover, Massachusetts. They dont quite fit in with their Puritan community. Narrator Sarah Carrier, who is nine when the novel opens, has the usual issues of a girl her age, including strict parents and an annoying sibling. The community has its problems, too, including a smallpox epidemic and Indian raids. Times are tough, people are going hungry, and when the Salem witch trials start up, Sarah's mother, Martha, is immediately accused of witchcraft and brought to trial. She refuses to buckle and insists on her own innocence, which only makes neighbors and others more suspicious. Sarah and the rest of her family visit Martha in jail. The author is a descendant of the real Martha Carrier.

Where it's reviewed:
The New York Times Book Review, September 7, 2008, page 20

Other books you might like:
Brunonia Barry, *The Lace Reader*, 2008
Lauren Groff, *The Monsters of Templeton*, 2008

1036

NINA KILLHAM

Believe Me

(New York: Plume, 2009)

Story type: Literary
Subject(s): Family Relations; Religion
Major character(s): Nic Delano, Teenager; Lucy Delano, Scientist
Time period(s): 2000s
Locale(s): United States

Summary: Astrophysicist Lucy Delano has to answer tough questions, many of them coming from her 13-year-old son, Nic (named for Nicolaus Copernicus). Nic has questions about everything ranging from sex to the Bible, but his atheist mother is more disturbed about the latter subject than the former. Nic begins hanging around with some religious Christians. At first, he goes for the home-baked cookies, but to his mother's dismay, he begins to develop an interest in the Bible and the Christian lifestyle. Nic has some Jewish relatives and a Muslim babysitter, and he engages all of them in his dialogue about faith.

Where it's reviewed:
Publishers Weekly, November 17, 2008, page 43

Other books by the same author:
Mounting Desire, 2005
How to Cook a Tart, 2002

Other books you might like:
Thomas Rayfiel, *Colony Girl*, 1999
Paula Sharp, *I Loved You All*, 2000

Popular Fiction

1037

NANCI KINCAID

Eat, Drink, and Be from Mississippi

(New York: Little, Brown, 2009)

Story type: Literary
Subject(s): City and Town Life; Family Relations; Brothers and Sisters
Major character(s): Truely Noonan; Courtney Noonan, Rebel
Time period(s): 2000s
Locale(s): San Francisco, California

Summary: Courtney and Truely Noonan are siblings living in small-town Mississippi. Courtney is the first to leave. She takes off for California with a guy she meets at a Grateful Dead concert. Truely follows her to the coast soon afterwards. He goes to college and makes a mint off the Internet. Each sibling marries, then sees that relationship end. Eventually they mutually care for an African-American teenager, tutoring him so that he can get his GED and giving him a place to live. Though the siblings aren't quite estranged, they aren't really close until this teenager brings them back together.

Where it's reviewed:
Kirkus Reviews, November 1, 2008, page NA
Publishers Weekly, November 17, 2008, page 41

Other books by the same author:
As Hot as It Was You Ought to Thank Me, 2005
Verbena, 2002
Balls, 1998
Pretending the Bed Is a Raft, 1997 (short stories)
Crossing Blood, 1992

Other books you might like:
Julia Glass, *I See You Everywhere*, 2008
Marilynne Robinson, *Gilead*, 2006

1038

STEPHEN KING

Just After Sunset

(New York: Scribner, 2008)

Story type: Literary
Subject(s): Short Stories

Summary: Thirteen short stories explore surreal and imaginative scenarios. In one, a man dreams that his daughter has died, then wakes up and finds the dream has impacted his waking life. In another a man gets trapped in a portable toilet stall and there is only one way out. There are references to real-life events: in one story a survivor of 9/11 feels guilty for having lived. A violent cat "from Hell" is featured in one story, while in another a married couple engage in an argument that escalates into violence. Psychological illnesses also crop up in several stories.

Where it's reviewed:
People, November 24, 2008, page 53

USA Today, November 11, 2008, page 6D

Other books by the same author:
Duma Key, 2008 (novel)
Lisey's Story, 2006 (novel)
Everything's Eventual, 2002
Dolores Claiborne, 1992 (novel)
Misery, 1987 (novel)

Other books you might like:
Neil Gaiman, *Fragile Things*, 2006
Alison Lurie, *Women and Ghosts*, 1994

1039

DEAN R. KOONTZ

Your Heart Belongs to Me

(New York: Bantam, 2008)

Story type: Contemporary
Subject(s): Transplants
Major character(s): Ryan Kelly, Businessman
Time period(s): 2000s
Locale(s): Newport Coast, California

Summary: Ryan Kelly is living the high life on the money he has made with his Internet business. He has a beautiful house and is getting ready to marry a beautiful woman. Then he learns, at 34, that he has a defect in his heart and must get a transplant immediately to live. He gets the transplant and still hopes to get married and continue on with his plans. Indeed, his life seems to be good again, but then Ryan begins to be stalked by someone sending heart-shaped gifts, accompanied by increasingly menacing notes. He fears that his heart donor is somehow threatening him.

Where it's reviewed:
Publishers Weekly, October 7, 2008, page 35

Other books by the same author:
Odd Hours, 2008
The Darkest Evening of the Year, 2007
The Good Guy, 2007
Brother Odd, 2006
Odd Thomas, 2003

Other books you might like:
Lisa Gardner, *Say Goodbye*, 2008
Stephen King, *Duma Key*, 2008

1040

AMY KOPPELMAN

I Smile Back

(New York: Two Dollar Radio, 2008)

Story type: Literary
Subject(s): Drugs; Family Problems
Major character(s): Laney Brooks, Parent, Spouse
Time period(s): 2000s
Locale(s): Short Hills, New Jersey

Summary: In the slick suburb of Short Hills, New Jersey,

Laney Brooks appears to have a perfect existence. Her husband is sweet. Her children are normal and healthy. They live in a large house with a pool. But Laney starts drinking and taking drugs to deflect the alienation she feels, and then she begins having sex with other people. Her husband seems boring to her, and soon her self-destructive behavior spirals out of control. In flashback, she reveals that her father once inadvertently taught her to repress her feelings. She also starts to see disturbingly familiar patterns in her young son.

Where it's reviewed:
Publishers Weekly, September 15, 2008, page 41

Other books by the same author:
A Mouthful of Air, 2003

Other books you might like:
Ann Packer, *Songs Without Words*, 2007
Curtis Sittenfeld, *American Wife*, 2008

1041

HANIF KUREISHI

Something to Tell You

(New York: Scribner, 2008)

Story type: Literary
Subject(s): Family Relations
Major character(s): Jamal Khan, Divorced Person
Time period(s): 2000s
Locale(s): London, England

Summary: Jamal Khan's best days are behind him, specifically the 1980s. Back then, if Jamal's memories are to be trusted, he was happy. He was in love with a wonderful woman. London was a hopping multicultural soup. He saw a different movie or concert every night. Today, however, Jamal is the divorced father of a 12-year-old and can't seem to get a relationship off the ground. His sister seems to have lost it and is courting a friend of Jamal's, though she already has multiple children fathered by other men. These events swirl around Jamal, but he never takes the helm of his own life.

Where it's reviewed:
Booklist, April 15, 2008, page 26
The New York Times Book Review, August 24, 2008, page 6
Publishers Weekly, August 11, 2008, page 31
The Seattle Times, August 17, 2008, page 14

Other books by the same author:
The Body, 2004
Intimacy and Midnight All Day, 2001
Intimacy, 1999
Love in a Blue Time, 1997 (short stories)
The Buddha of Suburbia, 1990

Other books you might like:
Jhumpa Lahiri, *The Namesake*, 2003
Joseph O'Neill, *Netherland*, 2008

1042

VALERIE LAKEN

Dream House

(New York: Harper, 2009)

Story type: Literary
Subject(s): Marriage
Major character(s): Kate Kinzler, Spouse; Walker Price, Prisoner
Time period(s): 1980s; 2000s
Locale(s): Ann Arbor, Michigan

Summary: In 1987, someone dies in the home of an African-American family. Almost 20 years later, Kate Kinzler and her wealthy slacker husband, Stuart, buy a house in a rapidly gentrifying neighborhood, and Kate gets to work on the renovations. The house eventually ends Stuart and Kate's relationship, in part because Stuart is horrified to learn that they're living in a place where a murder occurred. Kate goes right on remodeling, however. The book alternates between Caucasian Kate and African-American Walker Price, who has been in prison and whose family used to own the house.

Where it's reviewed:
Booklist, November 15, 2008, page 30
Publishers Weekly, October 27, 2008, page 30

Other books you might like:
Nancy Huston, *Fault Lines*, 2008
Nathan McCall, *Them*, 2007

1043

AMARA LAKHOUS

Clash of Civilizations Over an Elevator in Piazza Vittorio

(New York: Europa Editions, 2008)

Story type: Literary
Subject(s): Cultural Conflict
Major character(s): Parviz Mansoor Samadi, Cook; Benedetta Esposito, Maintenance Worker; Iqbal Amir Allah, Store Owner
Time period(s): 2000s
Locale(s): Rome, Italy

Summary: A murder takes place in the elevator of a residential apartment building in increasingly multicultural Rome. Each of the residents has a turn to offer an opinion on who committed the murder and why. The residents include Iranian chef Parviz Mansoor Samadi; Bangladeshi shopkeeper Iqbal Amir Allah; and Neapolitan Benedetta Esposito. One Italian woman fears that her dog's recent disappearance is related to the arrival of Chinese restaurants in the neighborhood. Amedeo, the prime suspect of the Roman police, shares his diary entries. All reflect the wary relationships between immigrants to modern Rome and Italians. Translated from the Italian by Ann Goldstein.

Where it's reviewed:
Booklist, October 1, 2008, page 26

Philadelphia Enquirer, October 15, 2008, page NA
Publishers Weekly, August 11, 2008, page 29

Other books you might like:
Stieg Larsson, *The Girl with the Dragon Tattoo*, 2008
Alessandro Piperno, *The Worst Intentions*, 2007

1044

WALLY LAMB

The Hour I First Believed

(New York: Harper, 2008)

Story type: Literary
Subject(s): Family Relations; Violence
Major character(s): Caelum Quirk, Teacher; Maureen Quirk, Nurse
Time period(s): 1990s (1999)
Locale(s): Littleton, Colorado; Three Rivers, Connecticut

Summary: Caelum Quirk and his third wife, the younger Maureen, a school nurse, move to Littleton, Colorado, and are pleased to find employment at the same school: Columbine High School. When tragedy strikes in the form of the now-famous school shooting in 1999, Caelum is away, visiting a relative, but Maureen is inside the school and hides in the library. She escapes with her life, but is so deeply marked by the trauma that the couple leaves Colorado and goes to Caelum's family in Connecticut. While there, Maureen struggles to move forward, while Caelum uncovers a terrible secret about his own family.

Where it's reviewed:
Dallas Morning News, November 23, 2008, page NA
Entertainment Weekly, November 14, 2008
The New York Times Book Review, December 14, 2008, page 13
The Seattle Times, November 28, 2008, page G10
USA Today, November 11, 2008, page 6D

Other books by the same author:
I Know This Much Is True, 1998
She's Come Undone, 1992

Other books you might like:
Anita Shreve, *Testimony*, 2008
Lionel Shriver, *We Need to Talk about Kevin*, 2003

1045

JANICE Y.K. LEE

The Piano Teacher

(New York: Viking, 2009)

Story type: Literary
Subject(s): Love; Infidelity
Major character(s): Claire Pendleton, Teacher; Will Truesdale, Chauffeur; Trudy Liang, Socialite
Time period(s): 1950s; 1940s
Locale(s): Hong Kong

Summary: British Will Truesdale works as a chauffeur for a wealthy Chinese couple in Hong Kong and meets Claire Pendleton in 1952, when Claire arrives in Hong Kong with her dull husband and begins giving piano lessons to the daughter of Will's employers. Will and Claire develop an intimate relationship, which sets Will to recalling his last relationship, a passionate romance with socialite Trudy Liang that ended badly in 1942. At that time, Will was sent to an internment camp for foreigners, and Trudy was involved in nefarious events during the Japanese occupation. As Will and Claire's relationship develops, she learns about his past.

Where it's reviewed:
Kirkus Reviews, October 1, 2008, page NA
Publishers Weekly, September 8, 2008, page 34

Other books you might like:
Andrew Sean Greer, *The Story of a Marriage*, 2008
Kate Morton, *The House at Riverton*, 2008

1046

DENNIS LEHANE

The Given Day

(New York: William Morrow, 2008)

Story type: Literary
Subject(s): Historical; Mystery
Major character(s): Danny Coughlin, Police Officer; Emma Goldman, Historical Figure; Babe Ruth, Historical Figure, Sports Figure
Time period(s): 1910s (1919)
Locale(s): Boston, Massachusetts

Summary: In the period after World War I life is rough for Danny Coughlin, a beat cop in Boston's North End neighborhood. Some police officers are attempting to organize, but unionization is seen very negatively at the time. Organizers are suspected of Bolshevism. Historical figures like Babe Ruth and Emma Goldman make appearances, but it is the hardscrabble existence of Danny himself that serves as the focus for this novel. Eventually he is drawn into a police strike (which did actually occur in Boston in 1919) and the bloody riots that stem from it. He also befriends an African-American man on the run from the law.

Where it's reviewed:
The Houston Chronicle, October 12, 2008, page 15
The New York Times, September 18, 2008, page E1
The Seattle Times, September 21, 2008, page 14
USA Today, September 23, 2008, page 4D

Other books by the same author:
Mystic River, 2001
Prayers for Rain, 1999
Gone, Baby, Gone, 1998
Darkness, Take My Hand, 1996
A Drink Before the War, 1994

Other books you might like:
Nancy Horan, *Loving Frank*, 2007
Michael Lowenthal, *Charity Girl*, 2007
Mark Winegardner, *Crooked River Burning*, 2000

1047

JULIA LEIGH

Disquiet

(New York: Penguin, 2008)

Story type: Literary; Gothic
Subject(s): Marriage; Family Relations; Mental Illness
Major character(s): Olivia, Parent; Sophie, Mentally Ill Person
Time period(s): 2000s
Locale(s): France

Summary: Olivia appears outside a large house in the French countryside with her two young children. At first her key doesn't work in the gate, but eventually the group gains entry, and it turns out that this is the home of Olivia's mother, though the two haven't seen each other in a very long time. Soon after Olivia arrives and announces that she's left the husband who beat her, her brother and his wife, Sophie, show up as well. Sophie carries with her always the body of their stillborn baby. When the group goes on a picnic, for example, she brings the dead baby and pretends to feed it.

Where it's reviewed:
Entertainment Weekly, November 28, 2008, page 77
Kirkus Reviews, September 15, 2008, page NA
Publishers Weekly, August 4, 2008, page 41

Other books by the same author:
The Hunter, 2001

Other books you might like:
Stewart O'Nan, *Songs for the Missing*, 2008
Roxana Robinson, *Cost*, 2008

1048

JEFFREY LENT

After You've Gone

(New York: Atlantic Monthly Press, 2009)

Story type: Literary
Major character(s): Henry Dorn, Widow(er); Lydia Pearce, Wealthy
Time period(s): 1920s (1922)
Locale(s): Amsterdam, Netherlands

Summary: After Henry Dorn's wife and son die in an accident, he leaves the United States to escape painful memories and visits Holland. Henry goes to Amsterdam with the idea of doing some genealogical research, but on the boat on the way over he meets Lydia Pearce, the descendant of sawmill owners who doesn't need to work for a living, and the two have an affair in Amsterdam. Descriptions of their relationship alternate with Henry's memories of his wife, his son's addiction to morphine, and Henry's own difficult and impoverished childhood in Nova Scotia. Lydia, too, reveals a somewhat troubled past.

Where it's reviewed:
Kirkus Reviews, October 15, 2008, page NA
Publishers Weekly, September 15, 2008, page 40

Other books by the same author:
A Peculiar Grace, 2007
Lost Nation, 2002
In the Fall, 2000

Other books you might like:
Richard Paul Russo, *Bridge of Sighs*, 2007
David Wroblewski, *The Story of Edgar Sawtelle*, 2008

1049

LAURA LIPPMAN

Hardly Knew Her

(New York: William Morrow, 2008)

Story type: Literary; Collection
Subject(s): Short Stories

Summary: The author, known for her mysteries, offers 17 stories of women in various difficult situations. In one, a first-time drug buyer nervously figures out the system. In another, disappointed romantics fill a bar in Dublin, Ireland. Well-off women reveal a dark underbelly as they participate in scams and murders. Many of them act out of a desire for revenge. The Tess Monaghan character who stars in many of the author's mysteries makes an appearance, as does a madam in Washington, D.C., who has a high-class clientele. An older woman makes a career as a porn star. In general, sexist men get their just desserts.

Where it's reviewed:
Booklist, September 1, 2008, page 55
Kirkus Reviews, August 15, 2008, page NA
Publishers Weekly, August 25, 2008, page 50
The Seattle Times, October 12, 2008, page 17

Other books by the same author:
Another Thing to Fall, 2008
What the Dead Know, 2007
Butchers Hill, 2005
In Big Trouble, 1999
Baltimore Blues, 1997

Other books you might like:
Shirley Ann Grau, *Nine Women*, 1986
Alison Lurie, *Women and Ghosts*, 1994

1050

ALAN LITTELL

Courage

(New York: Thomas Dunne Books, 2008)

Story type: Literary
Subject(s): Ships
Major character(s): John Driscoll, Sailor
Time period(s): 1950s (1950)
Locale(s): At Sea

Summary: The crew of a ship is sent to rescue five survivors aboard a foundering ship that is in trouble 150 miles off the coast of Ireland in the North Atlantic in 1950. It's winter, and the conditions are rough. Fourth mate John Driscoll is part of the crew, and he describes both conditions on the ship and the natural and difficult conditions surrounding it. He also describes his own personal route from someone who feared the water to someone who makes his living on it. He wants to prove something with this rescue. This book was originally published in England in 1962.

Where it's reviewed:
Booklist, November 1, 2008, page 22
Publishers Weekly, September 1, 2008, page 33

Other books you might like:
Nicholas Monsarrat, *The Cruel Sea*, 1951
Dani Shapiro, *Picturing the Wreck*, 1995

1051

JOAN LONDON

The Good Parents

(New York: Black Cat/Grove, 2009)

Story type: Literary
Subject(s): Missing Persons
Major character(s): Maya, Young Woman; Toni, Parent; Jacob, Parent
Time period(s): 2000s
Locale(s): Melbourne, Australia

Summary: At 18, Maya leaves her family's home in the country and moves to Melbourne for a new job. She embarks on an affair with her boss, and then her parents, Toni and Jacob, come to visit, only to discover that Maya has vanished. Toni and Jacob wait for news of her, and meanwhile they examine their own relationship and their role as parents. Toni was influenced by an earlier marriage; Jacob was influenced by his own absent father. Maya continues to leave telephone messages with her brother, so they know she is alive. Maya's landlady and her boss's son also have their say.

Where it's reviewed:
Kirkus Reviews, October 15, 2008, page NA
Publishers Weekly, September 22, 2008, page 35

Other books by the same author:
Gilgamesh, 2003

Other books you might like:
Laura Lippman, *What the Dead Know*, 2007
Stewart O'Nan, *Songs for the Missing*, 2008

1052

STEPHEN LOVELY

Irreplaceable

(New York: Voice, 2009)

Story type: Literary
Subject(s): Death
Major character(s): Isabel, Scientist; Bernice, Parent; Janet, Patient
Time period(s): 2000s
Locale(s): Iowa; Chicago, Illinois

Summary: Isabel is a young, healthy botanist when she has an accident on her bicycle and is killed. Her organs are harvested, and a patient in Chicago, Janet, is designated to receive Isabel's heart. The novel follows the various players and the repercussions of Isabel's death. Isabel's mother has mixed feelings about the organ donation. Janet goes back to teaching after she recovers, but her marriage is on shaky ground. She reaches out to Isabel's parents and tries to befriend them, but they are unsure how to react. Meanwhile, the driver who hit Isabel stands trial and is acquitted, but he lives with a guilty secret.

Where it's reviewed:
Kirkus Reviews, December 15, 2008, page NA
Publishers Weekly, October 13, 2008, page 34

Other books you might like:
Chris Bohjalian, *Before You Know Kindness*, 2004
Elin Hilderbrand, *Barefoot*, 2007

1053

BRIAN LYNCH

The Winner of Sorrow

(Urbana-Champaign: IL: Dalkey Archive Press)

Story type: Literary
Subject(s): Historical
Major character(s): William Cowper, Historical Figure
Time period(s): 18th century
Locale(s): England

Summary: This fictionalized autobiography is based on the life of poet William Cowper. At the start, Cowper is old and ill. He casts an eye backward and goes over his mother's death and his love for words, which started early in his life and continued to grow. He also considers the minister who inspired him and the woman he never stopped loving. Eventually, Cowper goes crazy and begins to have hallucinations. Cowper himself inspired later poets such as Wordsworth and Burns, but he is not much celebrated today. The narrative is rather non-linear; this is a novel about voice.

Where it's reviewed:
Publishers Weekly, November 24, 2008, page 37

Other books you might like:
Sara Gruen, *Water for Elephants*, 2006
Nancy Horan, *Loving Frank*, 2007

1054

JANET NICHOLS LYNCH

Chest Pains

(Bridgehampton, NY: Bridge Works, 2009)

Story type: Literary
Subject(s): Music and Musicians
Major character(s): Gordon Clay, Professor
Time period(s): 2000s
Locale(s): California

Summary: Gordon Clay teaches music at a community

college. He's an unhappy, somewhat solitary man who is going through a period of restlessness when he's awakened by a late-night phone call. In what seems like an incredible coincidence, the woman calling is looking for her ex, also named Gordon Clay, and she shares a name with Gordon's ex. But she's looking for her son, and Gordon doesn't have a son. He soon finds himself thinking about the parallel couple, however, and wondering what happened to the young man who was missing. He also deals with a tone-deaf student and recurring chest pains.

Where it's reviewed:
Publishers Weekly, September 8, 2008, page 33

Other books by the same author:
Messed Up, 2009 (young adult)
Peace Is a Four-Letter Word, 2005 (young adult)

Other books you might like:
Michael Dahlie, *A Gentleman's Guide to Graceful Living*, 2008
Philip Roth, *Exit Ghost*, 2007

1055

DEBBIE MACOMBER

A Cedar Cove Christmas

(Don Mills, Ontario: Mira, 2008)

Story type: Contemporary
Series: Cedar Cove. Book 9
Subject(s): Christmas
Major character(s): Mary Jo Wyse, Parent; David, Parent
Time period(s): 2000s
Locale(s): Cedar Cove, Washington

Summary: A very pregnant Mary Jo Wyse arrives in quaint Cedar Cove on Christmas Eve. She's trying to track down her baby's father, David, but she doesn't find him. She can't find a hotel room, either, so she stays in a room above someone's barn. The owners of the barn would like to let her sleep in the house, but they have a house full of guests for the holiday, so that's impossible. That night she delivers her child with the animals looking on. The animals include a donkey and a camel, who are going to participate in the town's Christmas pageant.

Where it's reviewed:
Publishers Weekly, August 18, 2008, page 40

Other books by the same author:
8 Sandpiper Way, 2008 (Cedar Cove Series)
Twenty Wishes, 2008 (Blossom Street Series)
50 Harbor Street, 2004 (Cedar Cove Series)
311 Pelican Court, 2003 (Cedar Cove Series)
16 Lighthouse Road, 2001 (Cedar Cove Series)

Other books you might like:
Jan Karon, *Home to Holly Springs*, 2007
Nicholas Sparks, *The Lucky One*, 2008

1056

GREGORY MAGUIRE

A Lion Among Men

(New York: Morrow, 2008)

Story type: Fantasy
Series: The Wicked Years. Volume 3
Subject(s): Courage
Major character(s): Brrr, Animal (Cowardly Lion)
Locale(s): Oz, Fictional City

Summary: Brrr, the Cowardly Lion of L. Frank Baum's *The Wonderful Wizard of Oz,* has a chance to tell his version of events. As a cub he was yanked from his family and used in medical experiments. He became famous after traveling the Yellow Brick Road with Dorothy and the gang. Now he is working as a spy in order to avoid the impact of laws against talking animals such as himself. Meanwhile, a war is brewing between Munchkinland and Oz. Oz is ruled by an emperor who has been manipulated by evil advisors and is a bit of a bumbler.

Where it's reviewed:
The Christian Science Monitor, October 21, 2008, page 25
Kirkus Reviews, November 1, 2008, page NA
Times Union, October 12, 2008, page NA

Other books by the same author:
What-the-Dickens, 2007
Son of a Witch, 2005 (The Wicked Years, Volume 2)
Mirror, Mirror, 2003
Confessions of an Ugly Stepsister, 1999
Wicked, 1995 (The Wicked Years, Volume 1)

Other books you might like:
Margaret Atwood, *Good Bones and Simple Murders*, 1994
Keith Donohue, *The Stolen Child*, 2006

1057

KARAN MAHAJAN

Family Planning

(New York: Harper Perennial, 2008)

Story type: Literary
Subject(s): Family Relations; Cultures and Customs
Major character(s): Rakesh Ahuja, Spouse, Parent; Arjun Ahuja, Musician
Time period(s): 2000s
Locale(s): New Delhi, India

Summary: Rakesh Ahuja works as a minister of urban development in New Delhi, India. His job is in jeopardy, so he is stressed at the office trying to save his own skin, but his home life is no better. Rakesh has 13 children who are all very needy. His wife is addicted to soap operas and doesn't do much during the day. She is currently upset because an actor she liked has died. Arjun, the eldest of their children, would like to become a rock star and is trying to find a way to be an individual and not just a member of his large family.

Where it's reviewed:
Booklist, November 1, 2008, page 24
Publishers Weekly, August 4, 2008, page 41

Other books you might like:
Aravind Adiga, *The White Tiger*, 2008
Jhumpa Lahiri, *The Namesake*, 2003

1058

LOUIS MAISTROS

The Sound of Building Coffins

(New Milford, CT: The Toby Press, 2009)

Story type: Literary
Subject(s): Floods
Major character(s): Noonday Morningstar, Religious
Time period(s): 19th century (1891)
Locale(s): New Orleans, Louisiana

Summary: In 1891 in New Orleans, African-American preacher Noonday Morningstar performs an exorcism of a one-year-old boy that will have repercussions for years and generations. Noonday's son, Typhus, seems to feel its effects the most. He falls in love with a girl he's seen only in a photograph. An abortion performer, a prison guard, and a horn player are also present for the exorcism and they also find the experience hard to shake. Eventually a flood hits New Orleans, and in some ways it gives these characters a chance at a fresh start. Spirits are as present as live people in this vision of New Orleans, and voodoo has surprising effects.

Where it's reviewed:
Kirkus Reviews, December 15, 2008, page NA
Publishers Weekly, November 17, 2008, page 40

Other books by the same author:
The Big Punch, 2000

Other books you might like:
Sara Gruen, *Water for Elephants*, 2006
Shirley Hazzard, *The Great Fire*, 2003

1059

KAREN MAITLAND

Company of Liars

(New York: Delacorte, 2008)

Story type: Literary; Historical
Subject(s): Diseases; Voyages and Travels
Major character(s): Zophiel, Traveller; Adela, Traveller; Rodrigo, Traveller
Time period(s): 14th century (1348)
Locale(s): England

Summary: A ragtag group meets randomly and travels together through England in 1348, trying to reach the seashore and stay ahead of the Black Plague. Each member of the group will turn out to have a secret. Osmond and Adela have been banished by their families due to Adela's pregnancy. Rodrigo is a performer traveling with his apprentice, Jofre. Cygnus claims to be half-man and half-swan. Zophiel is a con man; Camelot sells

fake articles of faith. Healer Pleasance turns out to be Jewish. A young albino girl shadows them, casting fear into their hearts, and at night they hear the mysterious howling of an animal that appears to be stalking them and following them from place to place.

Where it's reviewed:
Booklist, September 1, 2008, page 41
Kirkus Reviews, September 1, 2008, page NA
New Statesman, February 18, 2008, page 60
Publishers Weekly, August 25, 2008, page 49

Other books by the same author:
The White Room, 1996

Other books you might like:
Ken Follett, *The Pillars of the Earth*, 1989
Katherine Neville, *The Fire*, 2008

1060

SANDOR MARAI

Esther's Inheritance

(New York: Knopf, 2008)

Story type: Literary
Subject(s): Love
Major character(s): Esther, Farmer; Lajos, Con Man
Time period(s): 2000s
Locale(s): Hungary

Summary: Esther lives a quiet and regret-filled life with a cousin out in the country. The two of them grow almonds to make a living. More than two decades earlier, though, Esther knew great love. She was quite enamored of Lajos, who was her brother's roommate and very dashing. Lajos loved her back, or so he said, but then he married her sister Vilma and disappeared. Now Vilma is dead, and Lajos sends Esther a telegram, then shows up with his children. Esther has always known that Lajos is a con man, but she still finds him difficult to resist. Translated from the Hungarian by George Szirtes. The author passed away in 1989.

Where it's reviewed:
Publishers Weekly, August 25, 2008, page 47

Other books by the same author:
The Rebels, 2007
Casanova in Bolzano, 2004
Embers, 2001
Memoir of Hungary, 1944-48, 1996 (non-fiction)

Other books you might like:
William Boyd, *Restless*, 2006
Peter Esterhazy, *Celestial Harmonies*, 2004

1061

MERRILL MARKOE

Nose Down, Eyes Up

(New York: Villard, 2008)

Story type: Contemporary
Subject(s): Animals/Dogs; Psychology

Major character(s): Jimmy, Animal; Gil, Handyman
Time period(s): 2000s
Locale(s): Malibu, California

Summary: Gil is the handyman on a fancy estate in California. He's lacking in ambition and engages in casual relationships. Then Gil discovers he can communicate with dogs. He finds advice from Jimmy the dog especially helpful. It seems Jimmy runs Dr. Phil-style seminars for dogs, helping them to get what they want by manipulating their owners and explaining human emotion to his canine colleagues. (The title expresses Jimmy's most basic advice.) Then Jimmy realizes that Gil is not his biological parent and starts a search for his birth mother, who, it turns out, lives with Gil's ex-wife.

Where it's reviewed:
Publishers Weekly, October 13, 2008, page 38

Other books by the same author:
Walking in Circles Before Lying Down, 2006
The Psycho Ex Game, 2004
It's My F-ing Birthday, 2002
How to Be Hap-Hap-Happy Like Me!, 1994 (satire)
What the Dogs Have Taught Me, 1992 (essays)

Other books you might like:
Garth Stein, *The Art of Racing in the Rain*, 2008
David Wroblewski, *The Story of Edgar Sawtelle*, 2008

`1062`

KIRSTEN MENGER-ANDERSON

Doctor Olaf van Schuler's Brain

(Chapel Hill, NC: Algonquin Books, 2008)

Story type: Literary; Collection
Subject(s): Short Stories; Medicine
Major character(s): Olaf van Schuler, Doctor
Time period(s): Multiple Time Periods
Locale(s): Amsterdam, Netherlands; New Amsterdam, New York, American Colonies

Summary: The short stories in this collection follow various generations of experimental doctors. The family saga begins in the 17th century, when the doctor of the title is influenced by a recent change in common wisdom: mental illness, long believed to be a kind of immorality, is now accepted as a medical disorder. Olaf eventually emigrates from Amsterdam to New Amsterdam, which would become New York City, and the following generations of doctors inherit his interest in the brain and experimentation. The stories spotlight medical issues over the years, such as a belief in phrenology and the use of hypnosis, right up to a leaky breast implant in the 1970s.

Where it's reviewed:
Booklist, September 1, 2008, page 4
Kirkus Reviews, September 1, 2008, page NA
The New York Times Book Review, November 30, 2008, page 13
Publishers Weekly, June 9, 2008, page 27
Sun Sentinel, October 29, 2008, page NA

Other books you might like:
Kirsten Bakis, *Lives of the Monster Dogs*, 1997 novel
Ethan Canin, *The Palace Thief*, 1994

`1063`

TONI MORRISON

A Mercy

(New York: Knopf, 2008)

Story type: Literary
Subject(s): Slavery
Major character(s): Jacob Vaark, Plantation Owner; Rebekka Vaark, Spouse; Florens, Slave
Time period(s): 17th century (1680s)
Locale(s): American Colonies

Summary: Each of the women on Jacob Vaark's isolated farm offers a different perspective. There is Jacob's wife, Rebekka, who has seen several children die. Florens is a slave given to Jacob by her own mother as repayment of a debt that her mother's slave-owner owed him. Native American Lina has survived smallpox and rape to work as a servant to Jacob and Rebekka, though she feels a strange discomfort around the house's other servant, Sorrow, who survived a shipwreck. Jacob himself has risen quickly from poor Dutch orphan to well-off landowner. When a free African blacksmith arrives on the scene, each character sees him differently.

Where it's reviewed:
Dallas Morning News, November 16, 2008, page NA
The New York Times, November 4, 2008, page C1
People, November 17, 2008, page 49
Philadelphia Inquirer, November 12, 2008, page NA
USA Today, November 13, 2008, page 3D

Other books by the same author:
Love, 2003
Jazz, 1992
Beloved, 1987
Song of Solomon, 1986
The Bluest Eye, 1970

Other books you might like:
Joseph O'Neill, *Netherland*, 2008
Marilynne Robinson, *Gilead*, 2004

`1064`

DANIYAL MUEENUDDIN

In Other Rooms, Other Wonders

(New York: W.W. Norton, 2009)

Story type: Literary; Collection
Subject(s): Short Stories
Major character(s): K.K. Harouni, Wealthy
Time period(s): 2000s
Locale(s): Lahore, Pakistan

Summary: Eight stories deal with wealthy Pakistani man K.K. Harouni and his family members and servants. In one story, Harouni's impoverished handyman raises a family of 12 daughters and one son on very little money, but with a strict moral code. In another, a woman leaves her husband for a well-placed servant in the Harouni household, but when he is forced to return to his wife, she is left to raise his baby alone. In another story, a woman becomes Harouni's mistress and gains social standing and financial security, then loses it all upon his death. In each story, a small misstep risks upsetting the entire apple cart.

Where it's reviewed:
Kirkus Reviews, December 1, 2008, page NA
Publishers Weekly, November 17, 2008, page 39

Other books you might like:
Aravind Adiga, *The White Tiger*, 2008
Samrat Upadhyay, *The Guru of Love*, 2003

NAMI MUN

Miles from Nowhere

(New York: Riverhead, 2008)

Story type: Literary
Subject(s): Runaways; Drugs
Major character(s): Joon Mee, Runaway
Time period(s): 1980s
Locale(s): New York, New York

Summary: Korean-American Joon Mee is only 13 when she runs away from her family in the Bronx and starts living on the streets of New York City. She finds a room in a homeless shelter and finds work as a prostitute. Drug addiction drags Joon down, and she struggles to salvage herself. Joon narrates her own story, which lasts for six years. Many characters come in and out of her field of vision, including junkies, prostitutes, and all sorts of criminals, who school Joon in the ways of the streets. She tries to get out and even attends a meeting of Narcotics Anonymous but is not always successful.

Where it's reviewed:
Booklist, November 15, 2008, page 30
Kirkus Reviews, October 1, 2008, page NA
Publishers Weekly, September 1, 2008, page 33

Other books you might like:
Heather Lewis, *House Rules*, 1994
Roxana Robinson, *Cost*, 2008
Sapphire, *Push*, 1996

1066

ARTHUR NERSESIAN

The Sacrificial Circumcision of the Bronx

(New York: Akashic Books, 2008)

Story type: Literary; Historical
Subject(s): City and Town Life
Major character(s): Robert Moses, Historical Figure; Paul Moses, Historical Figure

Time period(s): 1950s; Indeterminate Future
Locale(s): New York, New York; Mexico

Summary: In this historical novel, the second a series, Robert Moses begins to work to become a prominent figure in New York City, where he eventually attempts to remake the topography of the city with a system of highways. Meanwhile, his brother, Paul, is attracted to a woman who eventually leads him to Mexico. He becomes involved in radical movements that will prove his undoing and ends up back in New York, destitute. Another portion of the book takes place in a post-apocalyptic future, when an FBI agent has the memories and thoughts of Robert Moses running unbidden through his brain.

Where it's reviewed:
Publishers Weekly, September 15, 2008, page 45

Other books by the same author:
The Swing Voter of Staten Island, 2007
Suicide Casanova, 2002
Dogrun, 2000
Manhattan Loverboy, 2000
The Fuck-Up, 1999

Other books you might like:
Roberto Bolano, *The Savage Detectives*, 2007
Robert Caro, *The Power Broker*, 1974
    non-fiction
David Foster Wallace, *Infinite Jest*, 1996

1067

ELLE NEWMARK

The Book of Unholy Mischief

(New York: Atria, 2008)

Story type: Literary; Historical
Subject(s): Historical; Magic; Poverty
Major character(s): Luciano, Orphan
Time period(s): 15th century (1498)
Locale(s): Venice, Italy

Summary: In Renaissance Venice, orphan Luciano snags a spot as the apprentice to the chef of the doge, the city-state's leader. Rumors run rampant about the existence of a book that can teach people how to perform alchemy and other magic. The chef in the palace kitchen teaches Luciano not just how to cook, but how to get by in the storm of intrigue that is brewing in the city. Luciano remains connected to his poor friends who live on the street and still nurses a crush on one girl, but more and more he is caught between the two worlds.

Where it's reviewed:
Publishers Weekly, September 22, 2008, page 37

Other books you might like:
Sarah Dunant, *In the Company of the Courtesan*, 2006
Philippa Gregory, *The Queen's Fool*, 2004

1068

JOHN NIVEN

Kill Your Friends

(New York: Harper Perennial, 2008)

Story type: Contemporary
Subject(s): Music and Musicians; Drugs
Major character(s): Steven Stelfox, Businessman
Time period(s): 1990s (1997)
Locale(s): London, England

Summary: As the record industry dies off due to digital recordings and free downloads, A&R man Steven Stelfox is still looking for the next big thing. He considers a black rapper, but passes him up in favor of a trashy female group reminiscent of the Spice Girls. Steven drinks and takes lots of drugs and has no regard at all for the music of the artists he courts; he simply wants to discover a hit and become head of his division at a large record company. A rival is hired to be his boss, however, and Steven sees his dreams beginning to fade.

Where it's reviewed:
Booklist, October 15, 2008, page 23
Kirkus Reviews, October 1, 2008, page NA
Publishers Weekly, September 15, 2008, page 41

Other books by the same author:
Music from Big Pink, 2005

Other books you might like:
Bill Flanagan, *A&R*, 2000
Pagan Kennedy, *The Exes*, 1998

1069

AMELIE NOTHOMB

Tokyo Fiancee

(New York: Europa Editions, 2009)

Story type: Literary
Subject(s): Love
Major character(s): Amelie, Student; Rinri, Student
Time period(s): 1990s
Locale(s): Tokyo, Japan

Summary: Belgian Amelie is studying Japanese in Tokyo. She studies, but she also teaches, tutoring Rinri, a wealthy young Japanese man, in French. Rinri falls in love with Amelie, but his feelings are not returned. Amelie needs her independence and resists his advances. No matter how much time they spend together, she cannot develop feelings for him, though they do have sex. Though they are not in love, or perhaps because they are not in love, they engage in lengthy and meaningful conversations; much of the novel consists of dialogue between the two. Translated from the French by Alison Anderson.

Where it's reviewed:
Kirkus Reviews, November 15, 2008, page NA
Publishers Weekly, November 17, 2008, page 42

Other books by the same author:
The Book of Proper Names, 2005

The Character of Rain, 2002
Fear and Trembling, 2001
Loving Sabotage, 2000
The Stranger Next Door, 1998

Other books you might like:
Muriel Barbery, *The Elegance of the Hedgehog*, 2008
Alessandro Piperno, *The Worst Intentions*, 2007

1070

MALLA NUNN

A Beautiful Place to Die

(New York: Atria, 2009)

Story type: Literary
Subject(s): Apartheid; Murder
Major character(s): Emmanuel Cooper, Detective—Police
Time period(s): 1950s (1952)
Locale(s): Johannesburg, South Africa

Summary: Shortly after the introduction of apartheid, Emmanuel Cooper, a white police detective of English descent, investigates the murder of another white officer. The victim turns out not to have been a particularly nice person, especially in dealing with his wife and son. He did have a fan in Cooper's Zulu assistant, however. The victim's family and colleagues try to block the investigation. Possible murderers begin to comprise a long list, as the man was so unpopular, but several parties do not want any white suspects investigated. The indirect methods required when black and white people interact are painstakingly explored.

Where it's reviewed:
Booklist, December 1, 2008, page 27
Kirkus Reviews, October 15, 2008, page NA
Publishers Weekly, October 27, 2008, page 32

Other books you might like:
Greg Iles, *The Devil's Punchbowl*, 2009
Charles Todd, *A Matter of Justice*, 2009

1071

STEWART O'NAN

Songs for the Missing

(New York: Viking, 2008)

Story type: Literary
Subject(s): Small Town Life; Missing Persons
Major character(s): Kim Larsen, Teenager; Ed Larsen, Parent; Fran Larsen, Parent
Time period(s): 2000s
Locale(s): Kingsville, Ohio

Summary: Kim Larsen, a popular, seemingly normal 18-year-old in the small town of Kingsville, Ohio, disappears on her way to work one afternoon just before she is going to leave for college. Her parents and her 15-year-old sister search everywhere for her. Kim's car shows up in Sandusky. Her father goes to that area to help look for her, while her mother stays home in case there is word from her. As time passes, Kim's family wonders how long they should keep looking for her and whether they should move on with their lives.

Where it's reviewed:
Booklist, October 1, 2008, page 25
Entertainment Weekly, November 7, 2008, page 95
Kirkus Reviews, August 15, 2008, page NA
Milwaukee Journal Sentinel, November 9, 2008, page NA
Publishers Weekly, September 22, 2008, page 37

Other books by the same author:
Last Night at the Lobster, 2007
The Good Wife, 2005
A Prayer for the Dying, 1999
The Names of the Dead, 1996
Snow Angels, 1994

Other books you might like:
Laura Lippman, *What the Dead Know*, 2007
Anita Shreve, *Testimony*, 2008

1072

TONY O'NEILL

Down and Out on Murder Mile

(New York: Harper Perennial, 2008)

Story type: Literary
Subject(s): Drugs
Major character(s): Unnamed Character, Narrator
Time period(s): 2000s
Locale(s): Los Angeles, California; London, England

Summary: An unnamed narrator is developing a bad heroin habit. The situation is not helped by his marriage (his second) to a junkie. They live in filth in Los Angeles, and then move to London, but they cannot clean up their act. The narrator has a rather fuzzy background as a musician, but he's too stoned to work now. His days consist of selling his belongings and doing other more nefarious things in order to obtain drugs. Finally, he manages to get into a methadone program and begins to rehabilitate, after a period of attempting to work the system.

Where it's reviewed:
Booklist, September 1, 2008, page 44
Kirkus Reviews, September 1, 2008, page NA
Publishers Weekly, August 18, 2008, page 37

Other books by the same author:
Songs from the Shooting Gallery, 2007 (poetry)
Digging the Vein, 2006
Seizure Wet Dreams, 2000 (poetry)

Other books you might like:
Albyn Leah Hall, *Deliria*, 1994
Irvine Welsh, *Trainspotting*, 1996

1073

ALLY O'BRIEN

The Agency

(New York: St. Martin's Press, 2009)

Story type: Contemporary
Subject(s): Writing; Publishing
Major character(s): Tess Drake, Agent
Time period(s): 2000s
Locale(s): London, England

Summary: When Tess Drake's boss dies in a compromising position, she takes over his literary agency and immediately sets out to bring in a stable of new writers. She makes plenty of friends and enemies in the process. First, Tess sets out to stake a claim to an American children's book writer, but then someone begins to blackmail her over it. The police contact Tess and tell her there may be evidence linking her to the death of her boss. Also, Tess has been having an affair with the husband of the woman who manages the office, and she has a former friend who is gunning for her.

Where it's reviewed:
Kirkus Reviews, December 1, 2008, page NA
Publishers Weekly, November 24, 2008, page 36

Other books you might like:
Debra Ginsberg, *Blind Submission*, 2006
Olivia Goldsmith, *The Bestseller*, 1996

1074

DAVID N. ODHIAMBO

The Reverend's Apprentice

(Vancouver: Arsenal Pulp Press, 2008)

Story type: Literary
Subject(s): Cultures and Customs
Major character(s): Jonah Ayot, Student—Graduate
Time period(s): 2000s
Locale(s): Pennsylvania

Summary: Jonah Ayot hails from the fictional African country of Liwani. He's the son of a minister and travels to (also fictional) Dingham University in Pennsylvania to complete his graduate work. Once there, he begins to misbehave and has a series of affairs. Jonah lives with a minister who tries to fix him up with an upstanding young woman from his church, but Jonah has the hots for an exotic dancer. Of course, he only wants to help the exotic dancer out of her difficult circumstances and into a better life. Unfortunately for Jonah, his minister landlord also holds the power of attorney over his inheritance and therefore has great control over him.

Where it's reviewed:
Publishers Weekly, August 11, 2008, page 29

Other books by the same author:
Kipligat's Chance, 2004
Diss/Ed Banded Nation, 2000

Other books you might like:
Cris Mazza, *Waterbaby*, 2007
Matthew Sharpe, *The Sleeping Father*, 2003

1075

YOKO OGAWA

The Housekeeper and the Professor
(New York: Picador, 2009)

Story type: Literary
Subject(s): Aging
Major character(s): Unnamed Character, Housekeeper;
    Unnamed Character, Professor
Time period(s): 2000s
Locale(s): Japan

Summary: An unnamed woman is the ninth in a series of housekeepers sent to tend to the home of a professor living out in the country. She is the first one he finds even minimally acceptable, so she and her young son visit the professor daily. The professor was in a car accident, however, and his memory is ruined, so she must reintroduce herself every day when she arrives. The professor can remember all kinds of mathematical theorems, but little else. He also remembers a lot about baseball, an interest he shares with the child. Translated from the Japanese by Stephen Snyder.

Where it's reviewed:
Kirkus Reviews, December 1, 2008, page NA
Publishers Weekly, November 17, 2008, page 40

Other books by the same author:
The Diving Pool, 2008

Other books you might like:
Muriel Barbery, *The Elegance of the Hedgehog*, 2008
Ma Jian, *Beijing Coma*, 2008

1076

LUCIA ORTH

Baby Jesus Pawn Shop
(Sag Harbor, NY: Permanent Press, 2008)

Story type: Literary
Subject(s): Political Crimes and Offenses
Major character(s): Doming Aquinaldo, Driver; Trace
    Caldwell, Diplomat
Time period(s): 1980s
Locale(s): Manila, Philippines

Summary: In the final days of the brutal regime of Ferdinand Marcos, Doming Aquinaldo is working as a driver for a diplomat representing the United States, Trace Caldwell. Caldwell is a Marcos supporter and part of a government that has ignored the escalating brutality, though his wife is turning against the Marcos regime as she witnesses violent acts. Aquinaldo, too, has seen his friends beaten and his own father was murdered by the Marcos forces. As a result, Aquinaldo cannot go home to the village where he grew up. Both men are waiting out the end of a political era.

Where it's reviewed:
Booklist, November 1, 2008, page 22
Publishers Weekly, September 8, 2008, page 37

Other books you might like:
Jessica Hagedorn, *Dogeaters*, 1990
Cormac McCarthy, *No Country for Old Men*, 2005

1077

ARTO PAASILINNA

The Howling Miller
(New York: Canongate U.S., 2008)

Story type: Literary
Subject(s): Mental Illness
Major character(s): Gunnar Huttunen, Mentally Ill Person
Time period(s): 1940s
Locale(s): Finland

Summary: Wacky Gunnar purchases a mill in northern Finland after World War II and begins to run the mill successfully. At first the locals don't mind that he mimics animals, impersonates people, and tells improbable stories. But eventually he begins to howl at the moon, and this is too weird for the villagers, who have him committed to a mental institution. He goes on to escape, along with a fellow patient who has been pretending to be crazy to avoid serving in the military. On the outside, he lives like a hermit to avoid being recaptured.

Where it's reviewed:
Publishers Weekly, August 4, 2008, page 42

Other books by the same author:
The Year of the Hare, 2006

Other books you might like:
Greg Hollingshead, *Bedlam*, 2006
Mikael Niemi, *Popular Music from Vittula*, 2004

1078

CHE PARKER

The Precious Life
(New York: Strebor Books, 2008)

Story type: Contemporary
Subject(s): African Americans; Marriage
Major character(s): Joshua, Spouse; Kathryn, Spouse
Time period(s): 2000s
Locale(s): Washington, District of Columbia

Summary: Kathryn and Joshua have been together for more than a decade, since they met in college, and they have a young son. Their marriage appears to be unraveling, however. Kathryn is still reeling from having survived the 9/11 attack on the Pentagon. Soon after that, her family is involved in a car accident. Then she discovers that Joshua has cheated on her. Joshua, too, is discovering things about Kathryn that make him unhappy, namely that she was promiscuous in college. He is also haunted by memories of his best friend, who was stabbed. Both have trouble juggling work and rearing their child.

Where it's reviewed:
Publishers Weekly, October 6, 2008, page 36

Other books by the same author:
The Tragic Flaw, 2007

Other books you might like:
Treasure E. Blue, *Keyshia and Clyde*, 2008
E. Lynn Harris, *I Say a Little Prayer*, 2006

1079

JAYNE ANN PHILLIPS

Lark and Termite

(New York: Knopf, 2009)

Story type: Literary
Subject(s): Coming-of-Age
Major character(s): Lark, Teenager; Termite, Relative; Robert Leavitt, Military Personnel
Time period(s): 1950s (1950); 1950s (1959)
Locale(s): West Virginia

Summary: Robert Leavitt is stationed in Korea during the war there, and he has left his wife and son, Termite, back in the United States. Leavitt dies in the conflict. The story picks up again nine years after Robert's death, when Termite's half-sister, 17-year-old Lark, is raising Termite and the two are living with an aunt in West Virginia. Termite is disabled and does not speak. Lark does not remember her mother, who left for Atlanta many years earlier, though unbeknownst to her, her aunt and her mother were involved in a love triangle before her mother married Robert Leavitt. Bits and pieces of this history are slowly revealed.

Where it's reviewed:
Booklist, October 15, 2008, page 5
Kirkus Reviews, October 15, 2008, page NA
Publishers Weekly, October 27, 2008, page 30

Other books by the same author:
MotherKind, 2000
Shelter, 1994
Fast Lanes, 1987 (short stories)
Machine Dreams, 1986
Black Tickets, 1979 (short stories)

Other books you might like:
Jim Harrison, *Returning to Earth*, 2006
Marilynne Robinson, *Gilead*, 2004

1080

MORTEN RAMSLAND

Doghead

(New York: Thomas Dunne, 2009)

Story type: Literary
Subject(s): Family Relations
Major character(s): Askild Erikkson, Architect; Asger Erikkson, Narrator
Time period(s): 2000s
Locale(s): Denmark

Summary: Asger Erikkson is summoned home to Denmark because his grandmother, Bjork, is dying. While he visits, he passes back over several generations' worth of family history, beginning with story of his grandfather, Askild, a Norwegian naval architect who survived a Nazi concentration camp and the moved to Denmark to find work after he couldn't shake an obsession with cubism well enough to draw practical designs. The family experiences many zany events: One family member is born in an outhouse, while another believes in ghosts and prophecies. Against a tragic historical backdrop, their wacky superstitions and beliefs unfold. Translated from the Danish by Tiina Nunnally.

Where it's reviewed:
Booklist, December 1, 2008, page 21
Kirkus Reviews, November 15, 2008, page NA
Publishers Weekly, October 6, 2008, page 33

Other books you might like:
Michael Chabon, *The Yiddish Policemen's Union*, 2007
Rivka Galchen, *Atmospheric Disturbances*, 2008
David Wroblewski, *The Story of Edgar Sawtelle*, 2008

1081

RON RASH

Serena

(New York: Ecco, 2008)

Story type: Literary
Subject(s): Marriage
Major character(s): Serena Pemberton, Spouse; George Pemberton, Businessman
Time period(s): 1920s (1929)
Locale(s): North Carolina

Summary: At the start of the depression, newly married George and Serena Pemberton move to the North Carolina mountains, where they have purchased 34,000 acres of land that they plan to harvest for timber. Both spouses are tough as nails and will stop at nothing to build an empire. Serena attempts to have George's child, but finds she cannot, and then she sets out to destroy the woman who had George's child before they were married. She also dominates the local lumberjacks. George and Serena are in a race against the Secretary of the Interior, who is trying to buy up land for national parks.

Where it's reviewed:
The Christian Science Monitor, November 13, 2008, page 25
The New York Times, October 6, 2008, page C6
The New Yorker, December 1, 2008, page 81
People, October 20, 2008, page 51
The Seattle Times, November 23, 2008, page I5

Other books by the same author:
Chemistry and Other Stories, 2007 (short stories)
The World Made Straight, 2006
Saints at the River, 2004
One Foot in Eden, 2002
Casualties, 2000 (short stories)

Other books you might like:
Cormac McCarthy, *The Crossing*, 1994
Annie Proulx, *Postcards*, 1992

1082

JON RAYMOND

Livability

(New York: Bloomsbury USA, 2008)

Story type: Literary; Collection
Subject(s): Short Stories
Locale(s): Pacific Northwest

Summary: Nine stories set in the Pacific Northwest show characters testing the boundaries of morality. In one, a recent widower meets someone from his past. In another story, a boy engages in a fight due to peer pressure, even as his grandfather is dying. One story follows a strange dinner party as it unfolds, after the host invites two men working on his yard to stay as guests; another features two co-workers who end up locked in a mall after the store that employs them closes. A longer story features a woman who is planning to go to Alaska to earn money working in a cannery, but is nabbed stealing dog food before her trip gets underway.

Where it's reviewed:
Kirkus Reviews, November 15, 2008, page NA
Publishers Weekly, October 13, 2008, page 37

Other books by the same author:
The Half-Life, 2004

Other books you might like:
Miranda July, *No One Belongs Here More Than You*, 2007
Jim Shepard, *Like You'd Understand, Anyway*, 2007

1083

SHERI REYNOLDS

The Sweet In-Between

(New York: Shaye Areheart Books, 2008)

Story type: Literary
Subject(s): Family Relations; Gender Roles
Major character(s): Kendra "Kenny" Lugo, Teenager
Time period(s): 2000s
Locale(s): Virginia

Summary: Kendra Lugo goes by the name "Kenny" and dresses like a boy, binding her breasts and cutting her hair very short. Her father is in prison and her mother is dead, so she lives with her father's girlfriend and her children in an area that is threatened by gentrification. A young woman in the house next door is shot and killed, and Kendra tries to deal with the nearby death and her own confusion. She is attracted to a woman, but still not certain of her own identity. She's concerned that when she turns 18 she'll no longer be able to stay with the only adult she trusts.

Where it's reviewed:
Booklist, October 1, 2008, page 25

Publishers Weekly, August 25, 2008, page 47

Other books by the same author:
Firefly Cloak, 2006
A Gracious Plenty, 1997
The Rapture of Canaan, 1996
Bitterroot Landing, 1994

Other books you might like:
Chris Bohjalian, *Trans-Sister Radio*, 2000
Anita Shreve, *Testimony*, 2008

1084

CHERYL ROBINSON

In Love with a Younger Man

(New York: NAL, 2009)

Story type: Contemporary
Subject(s): Romance
Major character(s): Olena Day, Businesswoman; Matthew Harper, Salesman
Time period(s): 2000s
Locale(s): United States

Summary: Olena Day is stubborn, and she's been burned by love in the past. Her first love killed himself when they were teenagers. Another man insisted she have an abortion, then left her for another woman he had impregnated. Now 43-year-old Olena is successful and well-off, but lonely. While taking a break from her job, she meets a man named Matthew Harper, who works at a car dealership and who is 18 years her junior, but also financially stable. Olena and Matthew are intensely attracted to each other, but also wary of getting involved because of the age difference.

Where it's reviewed:
Publishers Weekly, November 24, 2008, page 37

Other books by the same author:
Sweet Georgia Brown, 2008
It's Like That, 2006
If It Ain't One Thing, 2005
When I Get Free, 2003
Memories of Yesterday, 2002

Other books you might like:
Terry McMillan, *How Stella Got Her Groove Back*, 1996
Kayla Perrin, *Single Mama's Got More Drama*, 2009

1085

MARILYNNE ROBINSON

Home

(New York: Farrar, Straus and Giroux, 2008)

Story type: Literary
Subject(s): Family Relations
Major character(s): Jack Boughton, Unemployed; Glory Boughton, Care Giver; Robert Boughton, Parent (of Glory)
Time period(s): 1950s (1957)

Popular Fiction

Locale(s): Gilead, Iowa

Summary: In a companion to *Gilead*, the author revisits previously seen characters. In that novel, the narrator's best friend was the Reverend Robert Boughton. Here, Boughton is aging and being cared for by his 38-year-old daughter, Glory. Then Glory's brother, Jack, comes back to town. He's been away for 20 years and doesn't seem to have accomplished much. Glory narrates her brother's replaying of the parable of the prodigal son. Their small Iowa town still remembers the scandal that drove her brother away and is slow to forgive his impregnating a teenager all those years ago. Family secrets bob to the surface.

Where it's reviewed:
Entertainment Weekly, September 12, 2008, page 141
Newsweek, September 22, 2008, page 73
O, the Oprah Magazine, September 2008, page 218
People, September 22, 2008, page 63
Vogue, September 2008, page 662

Other books by the same author:
Gilead, 2004
The Death of Adam, 1998 (essays)
Housekeeping, 1997
Mother Country, 1989 (essays)

Other books you might like:
Julia Glass, *I See You Everywhere*, 2008
Marina Lewycka, *A Brief History of Tractors in Ukrainian*, 2005

1086

TONY ROMANO

If You Eat You Never Die: Chicago Tales

(New York: Harper Perennial, 2008)

Story type: Collection
Subject(s): Short Stories; Emigration and Immigration
Major character(s): Fabio Comingo, Hairdresser; Lucia Comingo, Spouse
Time period(s): 1940s
Locale(s): Chicago, Illinois

Summary: Eight short stories all feature members of the Italian-American Comingo family in Chicago following their post-war immigration to the United States. Father Fabio works as a barber, but not very hard. Mother Lucia is puzzled by most American traditions and ways. Of the two sons, one is ashamed of his Italian heritage (he changes his name from Giacomo to Jim), while the other, Michelino, vaunts it. Each family member has a chance to speak in first person. Lucia and Fabio both recall their courtship back in Italy. Jim grows from boyhood to adulthood and has children of his own.

Where it's reviewed:
Kirkus Reviews, October 15, 2008, page NA
Publishers Weekly, October 20, 2008, page 33

Other books by the same author:
When the World Was Young, 2007 (novel)

Other books you might like:
Helen Barolini, *Umbertina*, 1999
  novel
Stuart Dybek, *The Coast of Chicago*, 1990

1087

M.J. ROSE

The Memorist

(New York: Mira, 2008)

Story type: Literary
Subject(s): Reincarnation; Crime and Criminals
Major character(s): Ludwig Van Beethoven, Historical Figure; Meer Logan, Traveller
Time period(s): 2000s
Locale(s): Vienna, Austria

Summary: Since childhood, Meer Logan has been haunted by dreams that seem to belong to someone else's life, a life lived in the 1800s. The dreams always included unfamiliar music. When a series of events involving a box, a flute, and a letter seem to indicate that the memories that have been haunting her are really those of famed composer Beethoven, she heads to Vienna to investigate. In doing so, she unwittingly becomes involved in an international arts and antiques theft. In Austria, she meets up with both an FBI agent and all kinds of criminals.

Where it's reviewed:
Booklist, October 1, 2008, page 28
Kirkus Reviews, October 15, 2008, page NA
People, November 10, 2008, page 51
Publishers Weekly, September 15, 2008, page 43

Other books by the same author:
The Reincarnationist, 2008
The Venus Fix, 2007
Lying in Bed, 2006
The Delilah Complex, 2006
The Halo Effect, 2005

Other books you might like:
Ron Rash, *Serena*, 2008
Lisa Tucker, *The Song Reader*, 2003

1088

PHILIP ROTH

Indignation

(New York: Houghton Mifflin, 2008)

Story type: Literary
Subject(s): Coming-of-Age
Major character(s): Marcus Messner, Student—College
Time period(s): 1950s (1951)
Locale(s): Newark, New Jersey; Winesburg, Ohio

Summary: In 1951, Marcus Messner transfers from a college near his hometown of Newark, New Jersey, to Winesburg College in Ohio to get out from under the thumb of his father. His father is a butcher and has been tracking every move Marcus makes. Marcus takes up with a beautiful but troubled girl who admits that she has attempted suicide. He is shocked at the midwestern culture of football players and fraternities that he encounters on the new campus. At one point he reveals that he is telling the story from beyond the grave, and then he continues to recount how he died.

Where it's reviewed:
The New York Times Book Review, September 28, 2008, page 30
The New York Times, September 17, 2008, page E1
Newsweek, September 22, 2008, page 73
The Seattle Times, September 14, 2008, page 14
USA Today, September 16, 2008, page 1D

Other books by the same author:
Exit Ghost, 2007
The Plot Against America, 2004
The Human Stain, 2000
I Married a Communist, 1998
American Pastoral, 1997

Other books you might like:
Saul Bellow, *Herzog*, 1964
Joseph O'Neill, *Netherland*, 2008
Richard Paul Russo, *Empire Falls*, 2001

1089

SALMAN RUSHDIE

The Enchantress of Florence

(New York: Random House, 2008)

Story type: Literary
Subject(s): Historical
Major character(s): Qara Koz, Royalty; Nino Argalia, Military Personnel
Time period(s): 16th century
Locale(s): Florence, Italy; Sikri, India

Summary: Characters from the Emperor Akbar's court in India and Renaissance Florence get together. Qara Koz is a princess rumored to be so beautiful that the mere sight of her face causes men to fall over in shock. She keeps her face covered at all times. Also part of the court is Nino Argalia, an Italian who has converted to Islam and serves as general. These and other characters tell long and intricate stories that sometimes intertwine with each other, revealing the connections and parallels between East and West. Argalia talks at length about his native city of Florence and the political machinations taking place there.

Where it's reviewed:
The Denver Post, July 6, 2008, page E9
The New York Times, June 3, 2008, page E7
Philadelphia Inquirer, June 26, 2008, page NA
The Seattle Times, August 17, 2008, page 14
USA Today, June 5, 2008, page 5D

Other books by the same author:
Shalimar the Clown, 2005
The Moor's Last Sigh, 1996
The Satanic Verses, 1989
Shame, 1983

Midnight's Children, 1981

Other books you might like:
Aravind Adiga, *The White Tiger*, 2008
Sarah Dunant, *The Birth of Venus*, 2004
John Speed, *The Temple Dancer*, 2006

1090

DANNY SCHEINMANN

Random Acts of Heroic Love

(New York: Thomas Dunne Books, 2009)

Story type: Literary
Subject(s): Love; Fathers and Sons
Major character(s): Leo Deakin, Professor; Moritz Daniecki, Military Personnel
Time period(s): 1990s (1992); 1910s (1917)
Locale(s): Ecuador; England; Europe

Summary: Professor Leo Deakin is brokenhearted when his beloved girlfriend dies in a bus accident while they are vacationing in Ecuador. He returns to England, but he cannot seem to get over his loss. In an attempt to soothe Leo's pain, Leo's father recounts the story of his own father, Leo's grandfather, Moritz Daniecki. Moritz was a prisoner of war in World War I who escaped and trekked across Siberia to get back to Poland and the woman he'd left behind. Moritz told this story to Leo's father in the 1930s. The narratives intersect and mirror each other in many different ways, large and small.

Where it's reviewed:
Booklist, November 15, 2008, page 27
Kirkus Reviews, October 15, 2008, page NA
Publishers Weekly, November 3, 2008, page 40

Other books you might like:
Michael Ondaatje, *Divisadero*, 2007
Mark Slouka, *The Visible World*, 2007

1091

INGO SCHULZE

New Lives

(New York: Knopf, 2008)

Story type: Literary
Subject(s): Communism
Major character(s): Enrico Turmer, Journalist
Time period(s): 1990s (1990)
Locale(s): German Democratic Republic

Summary: Enrico Turmer has always considered himself an artist. He dabbles in theater and fiction. But then in 1990 he takes a job as a journalist and starts to focus on the real world, and he finds the work liberating. Enrico's turn from deep thinker to someone more focused on reality is mirrored by the changes to East Germany. Enrico becomes more crass and more concerned with material things than ideas, and so does his country. The novel is told mostly through a fictional cache of found letters that Enrico wrote to his sister, who fled to the West, to his best friend, and to a woman he doesn't know well.

Popular Fiction

Translated from the German by John E. Woods.

Where it's reviewed:
Booklist, October 15, 2008, page 24
Kirkus Reviews, September 15, 2008, page NA
The New York Times, October 29, 2008, page C6
Newsweek International, November 28, 2005, page 52

Other books by the same author:
Simple Stories, 2000
33 Moments of Happiness, 1998 (short stories)

Other books you might like:
Nancy Lukens, *Daughters of Eve*, 1993
Bernhard Schlink, *Self's Deception*, 2007
Michael Wallner, *April in Paris*, 2007

1092

WILL SELF

The Butt

(New York: Bloomsbury, 2008)

Story type: Satire
Subject(s): Crime and Criminals; Smoking
Major character(s): Tom Brodzinski, Criminal; Reggie Lincoln, Crime Victim; Brian Prentice, Criminal
Time period(s): 2000s
Locale(s): Feltham Islands, Fictional City

Summary: Tom Brodzinski, on vacation in the Feltham Islands, steps out onto the balcony of his hotel to smoke a cigarette. When he's done, he flips the butt over the side, and it lands on Reggie Lincoln. As a result, Reggie is hospitalized, and Tom is charged with a crime and found guilty. According to the laws of the Feltham Islands, once a colonized set of islands and now a vacation paradise, Tom must venture into the outback to make restitution. His companion on this trip is Brian Prentice, also convicted of a crime, though Tom doesn't know what that crime is. The two struggle to stay alive in the wilderness and to reach their destination.

Where it's reviewed:
Publishers Weekly, August 4, 2008, page 46

Other books by the same author:
The Book of Dave, 2006
Dorian, 2002
Tough, Tough Toys for Tough, Tough Boys, 1999 (short stories)
Great Apes, 1997
Cock and Bull, 1993

Other books you might like:
Christopher Buckley, *Thank You for Smoking*, 1994
Matthew Sharpe, *Jamestown*, 2007

1093

MARIA SEMPLE

This One Is Mine

(New York: Little, Brown, 2008)

Story type: Contemporary
Subject(s): Marriage; Drugs

Major character(s): Violet Parry, Spouse; Teddy Reyes, Musician
Time period(s): 2000s
Locale(s): Los Angeles, California

Summary: Violet Parry is married to a music company executive and has a young daughter. She has quit her job as a television writer to stay home and take care of her daughter, and she feels trapped. Then she meets a musician, Teddy Reyes, who entertains her, even though (or maybe because) he's a former addict. Violet grows more and more distant from her husband and daughter as she gets more involved with Teddy. She and Teddy begin an affair. She sends her husband away to practice yoga in order to get him out of the house. Meanwhile, Teddy gets interested in drugs again. The author was a television producer and writer.

Where it's reviewed:
Booklist, November 1, 2008, page 26
Kirkus Reviews, October 1, 2008, page NA
Publishers Weekly, September 15, 2008, page 41

Other books you might like:
Candace Bushnell, *One Fifth Avenue*, 2008
Wendy Walker, *Four Wives*, 2008

1094

MARY ANN SHAFFER , Co-Author
ANNIE BARROWS , Co-Author

The Guernsey Literary and Potato Peel Pie Society

(New York: The Dial Press, 2008)

Story type: Contemporary
Subject(s): Friendship; War
Major character(s): Juliet Ashton, Writer; Dawsey Adams, Farmer
Time period(s): 1940s (1946)
Locale(s): Guernsey, United Kingdom

Summary: Juliet Ashton is a journalist who has grown tired of her work while covering the war. She is the focus of this epistolary novel, which includes letters to and from Juliet and her friends in which Juliet, in her thirties, reveals that she would like to settle down. She also corresponds with Dawsey Adams, a farmer on Guernsey, one of the Channel Islands. He reveals to her the history of the few inhabitants of the island during the war, when Guernsey was occupied by the Germans. Dawsey and Juliet have never met, but he bought a used book with her name written on the inside flap, and he tracked her down. Mary Ann Shaffer began writing this novel but passed away before she could finish it; Annie Barrows, her niece, completed it.

Where it's reviewed:
The Denver Post, August 10, 2008, page E11
Entertainment Weekly, September 5, 2008, page 81
Newsday, August 17, 2008, page NA
Time, August 4, 2008, page 76
USA Today, August 14, 2008, page 11B

Other books you might like:
Dave Boling, *Guernica*, 2008
Helene Hanff, *84, Charing Cross Road*, 1970

1095

SANDI KAHN SHELTON

Kissing Games of the World

(New York: Shaye Areheart Books, 2008)

Story type: Literary
Subject(s): Family Relations; Single Parent Families
Major character(s): Jamie McClintock, Parent; Arley McClintock, Child; Christopher Goddard, Child
Time period(s): 2000s
Locale(s): Chester, Connecticut

Summary: Single mother Jamie McClintock moves into an older man's house with her son, Arley. The man she is living with also has a child living with him, his grandson, Christopher. Their small Connecticut town gossips about them, though both adults insist that theirs is not a romantic relationship. Then the man dies in Jamie's bed. Soon his adult son, the father of Christopher, comes to town and wants to know what Jamie was doing with his father. He also wants to sell the house and take Christopher away with him. As the two argue over these circumstances, Jamie learns more about the background of her late friend.

Where it's reviewed:
Publishers Weekly, September 15, 2008, page 44

Other books by the same author:
A Piece of Normal, 2007
What Comes After Crazy, 2006

Other books you might like:
Julia Glass, *I See You Everywhere*, 2008
Francine Prose, *Goldengrove*, 2008

1096

MICHAEL SHILLING

Rock Bottom

(New York: Little, Brown, 2009)

Story type: Literary
Subject(s): Music and Musicians
Major character(s): Dario Cox, Musician; Bobby, Musician; Adam, Musician
Time period(s): 1990s
Locale(s): Amsterdam, Netherlands

Summary: Dario Cox starts his punk band, Blood Orphans, as a joke he concocts with Joey Fredericks, who becomes the band's manager. Still, they go on to a certain amount of success. The other band members have issues, too. Base guitarist Bobby struggles with eczema; guitarist Adam is actually talented but unsure how to harness those talents; and singer Shane is a former Christian rocker. The band falls apart during the course of the novel, which takes place during one day in Amsterdam, where they've gone to play a gig. A music journalist,

however, tags their hit song as racist, and it's all downhill from there. Each of the characters tells about the events from his own point of view.

Where it's reviewed:
Kirkus Reviews, November 15, 2008, page NA
Publishers Weekly, October 20, 2008, page 31

Other books you might like:
Bill Flanagan, *A&R*, 2000
Pagan Kennedy, *The Exes*, 1998

1097

ANITA SHREVE

Testimony

(New York: Little, Brown, 2008)

Story type: Literary
Subject(s): Scandal
Major character(s): Mike Bordwin, Principal; Silas, Student—High School; Rob, Student—High School
Time period(s): 2000s
Locale(s): New England

Summary: Mike Bordwin is headmaster at an upper-crust New England prep school, the Avery School. Scandal erupts at the school when three male basketball players are discovered to have been videotaped performing sexual acts with a female freshman. But the numerous narrators reveal the undercurrents running below this shocking event. Silas, a scholarship student, caught his mother in bed with Mike Bordwin the morning that it all went down. The victim is the one who calls the police and makes the scandal public. Rob sees his early admission to Brown yanked away. Parents of students have their say as well.

Where it's reviewed:
Booklist, September 1, 2008, page 6
Entertainment Weekly, October 31, 2008, page 66
Kirkus Reviews, September 1, 2008, page NA
Publishers Weekly, August 11, 2008, page 25
Star Tribune, October 19, 2008, page 14E

Other books by the same author:
Body Surfing, 2007
A Wedding in December, 2005
Sea Glass, 2002
Fortune's Rocks, 1999
The Weight of Water, 1997

Other books you might like:
Jodi Picoult, *Nineteen Minutes*, 2007
Cornelia Read, *The Crazy School*, 2008

1098

ANNE RIVERS SIDDONS

Off Season

(New York: Grand Central Publishing, 2008)

Story type: Contemporary
Subject(s): Friendship; Marriage

Major character(s): Lilly McCall, Widow(er)
Time period(s): 2000s; 1960s (1962)
Locale(s): Edgewater, Maine

Summary: When Lilly McCall's husband dies, she travels to their beach house in Maine to spread his ashes there. What Lilly doesn't know, however, is that her husband frequently went to the house without her in the off season but lied and claimed he was traveling. While at the house, Lilly recalls the summer of 1962, when 11-year-old Lilly led a gang of kids and fell in love with a boy who returned her affections. The two shared a first kiss. When Lilly's parents learned the boy's family was Jewish, she was forbidden to see him anymore. The boy, too, was shocked to learn that he was Jewish, and his surprise led to his untimely death.

Where it's reviewed:
Booklist, May 15, 2008, page 23
Publishers Weekly, April 7, 2008, page 38

Other books by the same author:
Colony, 1992
Outer Banks, 1991
Peachtree Road, 1991
Homeplace, 1987
The House Next Door, 1978

Other books you might like:
Jane Green, *The Beach House*, 2008
Elin Hilderbrand, *Barefoot*, 2007

1099

DAN SIMMONS

Drood

(New York: Little, Brown, 2009)

Story type: Literary
Subject(s): Competition
Major character(s): Wilkie Collins, Historical Figure; Charles Dickens, Historical Figure
Time period(s): 1860s
Locale(s): London, England

Summary: The author imagines the events that might have inspired the last novel written by Charles Dickens, as seen through the eyes of fellow writer and competitor Wilkie Collins. Collins is with Dickens on the scene of a train crash, where Dickens first encounters the creepy Drood, who apparently has been making the trip inside a coffin. Dickens becomes obsessed with the mystery of who Drood is, and Collins follows along, though he disdains Dickens for writing too easily and quickly. Dickens has been much more successful than Collins, and Collins is sullen about it. Despite their various ailments, the two men in their fifties trail Drood and discover that he is involved in necromancy.

Where it's reviewed:
Kirkus Reviews, December 1, 2008, page NA
Publishers Weekly, November 24, 2008, page 35

Other books by the same author:
Muse of Fire, 2008
The Terror, 2007
Ilium, 2003

Endymion, 1995
The Fall of Hyperion, 1990

Other books you might like:
Kurt Andersen, *Heyday*, 2007
Arthur Phillips, *Angelica*, 2007

1100

CURTIS SITTENFELD

American Wife

(New York: Random House, 2008)

Story type: Literary
Subject(s): Politics; Marriage
Major character(s): Alice Blackwell, Spouse; Charles Blackwell, Spouse, Political Figure
Time period(s): 2000s
Locale(s): Washington, District of Columbia

Summary: This novel fictionalizes the life of Laura Bush, wife of the president of the United States. Alice Blackwell (nee Lindgren) is the stand-in for Laura Bush. She comes from Wisconsin rather than Texas. She is a librarian who is both smitten with a brash man she meets named Charlie and repulsed by his staunchly right-wing WASP family. Alice had an abortion when she was younger and has voted for Democrats. She is defensive of Charlie when his family thinks he won't amount to much, but she's unhappy with his prosecution of a long and illegal war once he is president.

Where it's reviewed:
New York, September 15, 2008, page 83
The New York Times, August 29, 2008, page E2
The Seattle Times, September 7, 2008, page 14
Time, September 15, 2008, page 59
USA Today, August 28, 2008, page 1D

Other books by the same author:
The Man of My Dreams, 2006
Prep, 2005

Other books you might like:
Elizabeth Dewberry, *His Lovely Wife*, 2006
Dominick Dunne, *A Season in Purgatory*, 1993
Sue Miller, *The Senator's Wife*, 2008

1101

ALI SMITH

The First Person and Other Stories

(New York: Pantheon, 2009)

Story type: Literary; Collection
Subject(s): Short Stories

Summary: Twelve stories depict small moments in daily life. In one story, the narrator spins a panicked reaction to an exit sign in a movie theater. In another story, an eavesdropper internally responds to a heated discussion about novels versus short stories. Yet another narrator considers issues of fashion as it relates to beheadings. In one story, a woman finds a child who isn't hers in her shopping cart and the child turns out to be unpleasant; in another, a boy suffers from a disease that cannot be identified. A woman is granted the chance to talk to her younger self.

Where it's reviewed:
The Financial Times, October 11, 2008, page 19
Kirkus Reviews, November 15, 2008, page NA
Publishers Weekly, November 10, 2008, page 33

Other books by the same author:
The Book Lover, 2008 (non-fiction)
The Accidental, 2006 (novel)
The Whole Story and Other Stories, 2004
Hotel World, 2002 (novel)
Like, 1998 (novel)

Other books you might like:
Aimee Bender, *The Girl in the Flammable Skirt*, 1998
Judy Budnitz, *Nice Big American Baby*, 2005

1102

GUO SONGFEN

Running Mother and Other Stories

(New York: Columbia University Press, 2009)

Story type: Literary; Collection
Subject(s): Short Stories
Locale(s): Taiwan

Summary: In six short stories, the late author (who passed away in 2005) presents the history of Taiwan and its troubles. In one story, a newly married couple struggles to maintain balance when it turns out that the wife will need to be a caretaker for her tuberculosis-stricken husband rather than simply his spouse. In another story, a widow and her husband's ghost sit together and recall their long personal history as it reflects the history of Taiwan. The title story features a man who has recurring and strange dreams about his mother and enlists a psychiatrist friend to help interpret them.

Where it's reviewed:
Publishers Weekly, October 20, 2008, page 33

Other books you might like:
Jhumpa Lahiri, *Unaccustomed Earth*, 2008
Yiyun Li, *A Thousand Years of Good Prayers*, 2005

1103

SISTER SOULJAH

Midnight

(New York: Atria, 2008)

Story type: Contemporary
Subject(s): Emigration and Immigration; Multicultural; Muslims
Major character(s): Midnight, Teenager; Akemi, Artist
Time period(s): 2000s
Locale(s): New York, New York (Brooklyn)

Summary: Midnight is a Sudanese child who comes to the United States to live with his mother when he is eight.

He learns English more quickly than she does and serves as her interpreter, and he also learns his way around the streets. His mother starts her own business, and Midnight falls in love with Akemi, who is Japanese. Her father is unhappy with the match, and Akemi doesn't speak English. Despite this multicultural romance, Midnight works to maintain his heritage and his Muslim religious traditions. He lives in a dangerous neighborhood, however, and must deal with drugs and crime.

Where it's reviewed:
Booklist, October 1, 2008, page 24
Essence, November 2008, page 79
Kirkus Reviews, September 15, 2008, page NA
Publishers Weekly, August 25, 2008, page 52

Other books by the same author:
The Coldest Winter Ever, 1999
No Disrespect, 1994

Other books you might like:
Jiro Adachi, *The Island of Bicycle Dancers*, 2004
K'wan, *Gangsta*, 2002

1104

NICHOLAS SPARKS

The Lucky One

(New York: Grand Central Publishing, 2008)

Story type: Contemporary
Subject(s): Fate
Major character(s): Logan Thibault, Military Personnel
Time period(s): 2000s
Locale(s): Iraq; Hampton, North Carolina

Summary: On his third tour of duty in Iraq, Marine Logan Thibault finds a picture of a woman and keeps it with him. When he survives to go back to the United States, he believes it is the picture that has kept him safe. He also believes it gives him luck, as he begins winning card games. No one at the base where he was stationed in Iraq knows who the woman is, so Logan walks across a good part of the United States attempting to locate her. Finally he finds her in North Carolina, but he doesn't want her to be put off by the strange story of how she has served as his lucky charm, so he doesn't tell her right away.

Where it's reviewed:
Entertainment Weekly, October 31, 2008, page 67
Publishers Weekly, October 27, 2008, page 49

Other books by the same author:
The Choice, 2007
Dear John, 2006
Nights in Rodanthe, 2002
A Bend in the Road, 2001
The Notebook, 1996

Other books you might like:
Richard Paul Evans, *The Gift*, 2007
Danielle Steel, *Amazing Grace*, 2007
Robert James Waller, *The Bridges of Madison County*, 1992

Popular Fiction

1105

NANCY SPILLER

Entertaining Disasters
(New York: Counterpoint, 2009)

Story type: Literary
Subject(s): Phobias; Mental Illness
Major character(s): Unnamed Character, Journalist;
    Richard Cronenberg, Editor; Lenore, Parent
Time period(s): 2000s
Locale(s): Los Angeles, California

Summary: An unnamed and neurotic journalist who writes advice about entertaining at home is ordered to entertain an editor in her own home and promptly panics. The woman has a phobia about having people in her home. Her husband is dull, and memories of her mother, Lenore, a single mother and mental patient, haunt her. Her mother, too, was terrified of failure and once buried a Thanksgiving turkey in the ground rather than serve it. Slowly, the plans for the dinner unravel. Guests back out with unbelievable last-minute excuses, and the unnamed journalist is frozen with fear. Each chapter features a recipe, most of them intentionally unworkable.

Where it's reviewed:
Booklist, November 15, 2008, page 27
Kirkus Reviews, December 1, 2008, page NA
Publishers Weekly, November 17, 2008, page 42

Other books you might like:
James Hamilton-Paterson, *Cooking with Fernet Branca*,
    2005
Nina Killham, *How to Cook a Tart*, 2002

1106

ILANA STANGER-ROSS

Sima's Undergarments for Women
(New York: Overlook Press, 2009)

Story type: Literary
Subject(s): Friendship
Major character(s): Sima Goldner, Store Owner; Timna,
    Seamstress
Time period(s): 2000s
Locale(s): New York, New York (Brooklyn)

Summary: In the Borough Park neighborhood of Brooklyn, Sima sells lingerie out of her home and feels her annoyance with her husband and her quiet life increasing daily. Then Israeli immigrant Timna comes to work for Sima as a seamstress, and the two develop a friendship, and Sima grows to admire Timna for her adventurous nature. Timna is in some ways the child Sima never had, because she was rendered infertile due to venereal disease, something that has weighed heavily on her for years. Sima also suspects that Timna herself is pregnant. Other neighborhood women are involved in other subplots.

Where it's reviewed:
Booklist, December 1, 208, page 24
Kirkus Reviews, November 1, 2008, page NA
Publishers Weekly, September 29, 2008, page 57

Other books you might like:
Ellen Litman, *The Last Chicken in America*, 2007
Risa Miller, *Welcome to Heavenly Heights*, 2003

1107

DANIELLE STEEL

A Good Woman
(New York: Delacorte, 2008)

Story type: Historical/World War I
Subject(s): Love
Major character(s): Annabelle Worthington, Wealthy
Time period(s): 1910s
Locale(s): France; New York, New York

Summary: Heiress Annabelle Worthington looks set to live a life of privilege in New York City as her mother and her mother's mother and so on did before her. Then the *Titanic* goes down and her father and brother drown in the accident, and World War I erupts. Annabelle's mother marries her off to a gay man for the sake of appearances. Eventually they divorce. Annabelle, who has long volunteered as a nurse, heads to France to study medicine. She becomes an ambulance driver in the war and eventually a doctor. She is also raped by a soldier and gives birth to a daughter.

Where it's reviewed:
Booklist, September 1, 2008, page 5
Publishers Weekly, August 11, 2008, page 26

Other books by the same author:
Rogue, 2008
Amazing Grace, 2007
Coming Out, 2006
H.R.H., 2006
The House, 2006

Other books you might like:
Jayne Ann Krentz, *Twist of Fate*, 1991
Nicholas Sparks, *The Lucky One*, 2008

1108

INDU SUNDARESAN

In the Convent of Little Flowers
(New York: Atria, 2008)

Story type: Literary
Subject(s): Short Stories; Cultures and Customs
Time period(s): 2000s
Locale(s): India; United States

Summary: A collection of short stories examines modern India and the people who populate it. In one story, a city reporter visits her small hometown, where a 12-year-old widow is to be burned on her husband's funeral pyre. In another, when a family moves to the city from the country, the changes are hard on their son, who becomes overly materialistic and violent. A woman of Indian origin adopted by Americans and raised in Seattle is spurred by a letter from a biological relative to recall the early days of her existence. Another woman returns from the United States to India after her sister has died there.

Where it's reviewed:
Publishers Weekly, October 20, 2008, page 33

Other books by the same author:
The Splendor of Silence, 2007
The Feast of Roses, 2003
The Twentieth Wife, 2002

Other books you might like:
Kiran Desai, *The Inheritance of Loss*, 2005
Jhumpa Lahiri, *Unaccustomed Earth*, 2008

1109

MATTILDA BERNSTEIN SYCAMORE

So Many Ways to Sleep Badly

(San Francisco: City Lights, 2008)

Story type: Literary
Subject(s): Drugs; Sexual Behavior
Major character(s): Unnamed Character, Narrator
Time period(s): 2000s
Locale(s): San Francisco, California

Summary: An unnamed insomniac narrator runs wild and romps from bed to bed in modern-day San Francisco. The narrator may or may not be a biological female, though she lives as one now. She has sex with strangers and turns tricks for money. She takes copious amounts of drugs. She riffs on the more bourgeois aspects of San Francisco life, such as NPR and occasionally participates in yoga. She also laments the high rents in the city and the roaches that infest her apartment. Other topics include Internet sex and surfing for partners, herbal medicine, vegan restaurants, and tweakers.

Where it's reviewed:
Publishers Weekly, August 18, 2008, page 42

Other books by the same author:
Pulling Taffy, 2003

Other books you might like:
Leslie Feinberg, *Stone Butch Blues*, 2004
Jeanette Winterson, *Oranges Are Not the Only Fruit*, 1991

1110

AHMET HAMDI TANPINAR

A Mind at Peace

(Brooklyn: Archipelago Books, 2008)

Story type: Literary
Subject(s): Love
Major character(s): Mumtaz, Student; Nuran, Lover; Ihsan, Teacher
Time period(s): 1930s
Locale(s): Turkey

Summary: The author of this 1949 novel is a well-known Turkish novelist who passed away in 1962. After his parents die, Mumtaz devotes himself to the study of Turkish literature and history under the tutelage of his cousin Ihsan. He hopes to preserve the past by learning more about it, but there's no stopping progress, and in the background of Mumtaz's personal story, Turkey is being transformed into a more modern country. At the same time, he falls in love with Nuran, whose own family history makes things between them extremely complicated. Mumtaz, however, believes that love can make all things right. Translated from the Turkish by Erdag Goknar.

Where it's reviewed:
Publishers Weekly, September 8, 2008, page 37

Other books by the same author:
The Time Regulation Institute, 2002

Other books you might like:
Kiran Desai, *The Inheritance of Loss*, 2005
Orhan Pamuk, *My Name Is Red*, 2001
Orhan Pamuk, *Snow*, 2004

1111

PAUL TORDAY

Bordeaux

(New York: Houghton Mifflin Harcourt, 2009)

Story type: Literary
Subject(s): Money; Alcoholism
Major character(s): Frances Wilberforce, Wealthy
Time period(s): 2000s
Locale(s): England

Summary: Frances Wilberforce has sold his software company for a mint, and now he spends his days enjoying himself. Most days, that means he downs four bottles of wine all on his own. His friends eventually confront him, prodding him to seek treatment for alcoholism. But Frances insists that wine is simply a hobby, and he enjoys learning more about it. He begins to hang out at a wine store and even meets a woman who becomes a love interest. The owner of the wine store pleads with Frances to take over his business. The story moves backward through four different "vintages," i.e., periods in the main character's life.

Where it's reviewed:
Publishers Weekly, November 10, 2008, page 32

Other books by the same author:
Salmon Fishing in the Yemen, 2007

Other books you might like:
Kate Christensen, *The Epicure's Lament*, 2004
Marina Lewycka, *A Short History of Tractors in Ukrainian*, 2005

1112

ADRIANA TRAGIANI

Very Valentine

(New York: Harper, 2009)

Story type: Contemporary
Subject(s): Family Relations

Popular Fiction

Major character(s): Valentine Roncalli, Artisan; Teodora, Aged Person
Time period(s): 2000s
Locale(s): New York, New York; Capri, Italy

Summary: Valentine Roncalli leaves her job as a teacher and moves to New York City's Greenwich Village, where she lives with her grandmother and takes over Angelini Shoe Company. Valentine loves working as a cobbler and learns a lot from her grandmother. Unfortunately, the business is in bad shape financially, and Valentine's home and business are both at risk. Valentine also becomes involved with an Italian chef, who invites her to meet him on the island of Capri. Valentine travels to Italy with her grandmother and they look up one of the grandmother's old flames, who also has an attractive son.

Where it's reviewed:
Publishers Weekly, November 3, 2008, page 37

Other books by the same author:
Home to Big Stone Gap, 2006
Lucia, Lucia, 2003
Milk Glass Moon, 2002
Big Cherry Holler, 2001
Big Stone Gap, 2000

Other books you might like:
Maeve Binchy, *Whitethorn Woods*, 2007
Kate Jacobs, *The Friday Night Knitting Club*, 2007

1113

YASUTAKA TSUTSUI

Salmonella Men on Planet Porno

(New York: Pantheon, 2008)

Story type: Literary
Subject(s): Short Stories

Summary: In surreal short stories, very strange things happen, yet no one seems to find them out of the ordinary. In one, a character journeys for the first time to a city where people speak only in nonsensical syllables. In another, a tree causes two people to have sexual dreams about others. The paparazzi follow an office worker, snapping his picture and reporting his every move, in another. A man committed to smoking is determined to kill himself rather than have his cigarettes taken from him. The title story imagines a planet with wild sexual activity. Translated from the Japanese by Andrew Driver.

Where it's reviewed:
Entertainment Weekly, November 14, 2008, page 77
Kirkus Reviews, September 15, 2008, page NA
Publishers Weekly, August 4, 2008, page 42

Other books by the same author:
What the Maid Saw, 1990

Other books you might like:
Roberto Bolano, *2666*, 2008
Haruki Murakami, *The Elephant Vanishes*, 1993

1114

JOHN UPDIKE

The Widows of Eastwick

(New York: Knopf, 2008)

Story type: Literary
Subject(s): Aging
Major character(s): Alexandra, Widow(er); Jane, Widow(er); Sukie, Widow(er)
Time period(s): 2000s
Locale(s): Eastwick, Rhode Island

Summary: In a sequel to *The Witches of Eastwick*, the witches are now aged and less sassy. They've married and been widowed. Sexy Sukie writes romance novels; Jane inherited money from her husband, but Alexandra is just getting by. They've traveled as far as India and China, but now all have returned to the idyllic coastal town of Eastwick. They are no longer capable of casting spells. When they do manage to summon some of their old supernatural powers, they accidentally cause a death. They spend the summer trying to make up for past sins, but the people of Eastwick are not happy to have them back.

Where it's reviewed:
Entertainment Weekly, October 24, 2008, page 75
Kansas City Star, October 29, 2008, page NA
Kirkus Reviews, August 15, 2008, page NA
The New York Times Book Review, October 26, 2008, page 1
Publishers Weekly, July 28, 2008, page 48

Other books by the same author:
Terrorist, 2006
Rabbit at Rest, 1990
The Witches of Eastwick, 1984
Rabbit Run, 1969
Couples, 1968

Other books you might like:
Elizabeth Buchan, *Revenge of the Middle-Aged Woman*, 2003
Philip Roth, *Indignation*, 2008

1115

DAPHNE UVILLER

Super in the City

(New York: Bantam, 2009)

Story type: Literary
Subject(s): Work; Mystery
Major character(s): Zephyr Zuckerman, Maintenance Worker
Time period(s): 2000s
Locale(s): New York, New York

Summary: Zephyr Zuckerman has broken up with her boyfriend and dropped out of graduate school multiple times. When the superintendent of the New York City apartment building her parents own is arrested, she takes over the job. She uncovers an art theft ring and some mysterious containers in the super's apartment. She also nurses a crush on the building's exterminator. Like all supers, she learns a lot of secrets about the tenants. Zephyr also has a pack of friends who are trying to find themselves and help her solve the crime. One is a social worker; the other is a divorced scientist.

Where it's reviewed:
Kirkus Reviews, December 1, 2008, page NA
Publishers Weekly, November 17, 2008, page 41

Other books you might like:
Laurie Gwen Shapiro, *The Matzo Ball Heiress*, 2006
Lauren Weisberger, *Chasing Harry Winston*, 2008

1116

DAVID VANN

Legend of a Suicide

(Amherst, MA: University of Massachusetts Press, 2008)

Story type: Literary
Subject(s): Short Stories; Suicide; Fathers and Sons
Major character(s): Roy, Teenager
Time period(s): 2000s
Locale(s): Alaska

Summary: In five stories and a novella, a boy experiences and then considers from new viewpoints and angles the suicide of his own father, both before and after the fact. Roy's father shoots himself on his fishing boat when Roy is still young. Additional stories examine Roy's relationship with his stepmother and his angry fantasies about the men who attempt to date his mother. The longest story shows Roy and his father living in the Alaska wilderness on an island for four months when Roy is 13. Each story reveals a new aspect of the father-son relationship. This collection won the AWP Award in Short Fiction.

Where it's reviewed:
Publishers Weekly, October 6, 2008, page 37

Other books by the same author:
A Mile Down, 2005 (memoir)

Other books you might like:
Jim Harrison, *The English Major*, 2008
Susan Minot, *Monkeys*, 1986

1117

TONY VIGORITO

Nine Kinds of Naked

(New York: Harcourt/Harvest, 2008)

Story type: Contemporary
Subject(s): Time Travel
Major character(s): Diablo, Drifter; Bridget Snapdragon, Spouse; Clovis, Time Traveler
Time period(s): 2000s
Locale(s): Normal, Illinois

Summary: This over-the-top novel is an exercise in absurdity. Diablo stumbles into the misnamed Normal,

Illinois, where nothing is normal, and is soon arrested for watching Bridget Snapdragon as she goes skinny-dipping. In jail, Diablo manages to balance a playing card on the back of a bee, causing a violent storm to erupt. Clovis arrives in town from the ninth century, where he escaped a stoning. Another man can only speak in the present tense. An obstetrician is fascinated by a stripper. A priest is driven mad by celibacy. All these characters and many more intersect in an ever-widening example of chaos theory.

Where it's reviewed:
Booklist, September 1, 2008, page 49
Kirkus Reviews, August 1, 2008, page NA
Publishers Weekly, August 4, 2008, page 45
Texas Monthly, October 2008, page 64

Other books by the same author:
Just a Couple of Days, 2007 (self-published)

Other books you might like:
Christopher Moore, *The Lust Lizard of Melancholy Cove*, 1999
Robert Rankin, *The Hollow Chocolate Bunnies of the Apocalypse*, 2003

1118

ANGEL WAGENSTEIN

Isaac's Torah

(New York: Other Press, 2008)

Story type: Literary
Subject(s): Humor; Judaism
Major character(s): Isaac Jacob Blumenfeld, Tailor, Prisoner; Shmuel Ben-David, Religious
Time period(s): 1940s
Locale(s): Kolodetz, Europe

Summary: Isaac is a tailor in the town of Kolodetz, which is part of the Austro-Hungarian empire, then becomes part of Poland, is absorbed into Russia, then is invaded by Germans, and finally turns Soviet. Isaac, who is Jewish, pretends to be crazy in order to avoid the punishment inflicted on local Jewish people by the various political forces. He and the local rabbi trade jokes and folklore. Isaac survives both Siberia and a concentration camp, as well as being drafted to serve in the military forces of the various conquerors. Translated from the Bulgarian by Elizabeth Frank and Deliana Simeonova.

Where it's reviewed:
Booklist, October 15, 2008, page 22
Publishers Weekly, August 4, 2008, page 41

Other books by the same author:
Farewell, Shanghai, 2007

Other books you might like:
Amy Bloom, *Away*, 2007
Geraldine Brooks, *People of the Book*, 2008
Meir Shalev, *A Pigeon and a Boy*, 2007

Popular Fiction

1119

LAUREN WEISBERGER

Chasing Harry Winston

(New York: Simon & Schuster, 2008)

Story type: Literary; Contemporary
Subject(s): Friendship; Careers
Major character(s): Adriana, Wealthy; Emmy, Cook; Leigh, Editor
Time period(s): 2000s
Locale(s): New York, New York

Summary: Three women in their late twenties are working to establish their careers and love lives in New York City. Emmy is a good cook who works scouting restaurant locations and whose longtime boyfriend has just dumped her. Leigh is an editor and has a steady boyfriend, but she's not sure he's the one. Adriana doesn't really work. She's supported by her rich Brazilian parents and spends a lot of time getting waxed and having her nails done. She doesn't have a steady guy, either, but dates a lot of different men. Emmy and Adriana make a pact to sleep with as many men as possible over the course of a year.

Where it's reviewed:
Buffalo News, May 27, 2008, page NA
Cosmopolitan, August 2008, page 30
Entertainment Weekly, May 30, 2008, page 90
People, June 9, 2008, page 55
USA Today, May 28, 2008, page 1D

Other books by the same author:
Everyone Worth Knowing, 2005
The Devil Wears Prada, 2003

Other books you might like:
Candace Bushnell, *One Fifth Avenue*, 2008
Emily Giffin, *Something Borrowed*, 2004

1120

PATRICIA WEITZ

College Girl

(New York: Riverhead, 2008)

Story type: Literary
Subject(s): College Life
Major character(s): Natalie Bloom, Student—College
Time period(s): 2000s
Locale(s): Connecticut

Summary: Natalie Bloom has a working-class background. She is 20 and a student in her last year at the University of Connecticut. She gets good grades, but to her dismay she is still a virgin. Natalie is the youngest of seven children and the first in her family to attend college, so she feels a lot of pressure and takes her major in Russian history very seriously. She gets distracted, however, once she meets a rich boy who sleeps with her, then ignores her. Natalie begins to obsess about him and her grades drop; she changes her physical appearance. She also begins to deal with the suicide of her older brother.

Where it's reviewed:
Kirkus Reviews, October 1, 2008, page NA
Publishers Weekly, September 8, 2008, page 34

Other books you might like:
Junot Diaz, *The Brief Wondrous Life of Oscar Wao*, 2007
Curtis Sittenfeld, *Prep*, 2005

1121

SUSAN REBECCA WHITE

Bound South

(New York: Touchstone, 2009)

Story type: Literary
Subject(s): Race Relations
Major character(s): Louise Parker, Spouse; Caroline Parker, Teenager; Missy Meadows, Teenager
Time period(s): 2000s
Locale(s): Atlanta, Georgia

Summary: Spoiled housewife Louise Parker lives in a big house in a fancy Atlanta neighborhood with her equally spoiled teenage daughter, Caroline, who rebels at every opportunity. Their housekeeper, Faye, also has a daughter, Missy Meadows, who is searching for her absent father. Her father has become a minister and stars in a Christian soap opera. Caroline has an affair with a high school teacher and runs off, and Missy runs off, too, with Charles, Louise's son, in search of Missy's father. The relationships between the characters draw a portrait of the modern American South and the divides between its inhabitants.

Where it's reviewed:
Publishers Weekly, November 24, 2008, page 36

Other books you might like:
Sue Monk Kidd, *The Secret Life of Bees*, 2007
Lee Smith, *The Last Girls*, 2002

1122

ELIE WIESEL

A Mad Desire to Dance

(New York: Knopf, 2009)

Story type: Literary
Subject(s): Mental Health
Major character(s): Doriel Waldman, Patient
Time period(s): 1990s
Locale(s): New York

Summary: A novel composed mainly of notes from therapy sessions follows the story of Doriel, the patient. Doriel grew up in Brooklyn, the son of immigrant Jewish parents. His mother was a member of the Resistance. Doriel also had two siblings who died in the war, and his parents died soon after. Doriel was passed along to relatives and made his fortune, but his female therapist suspects that he's never had intimate relations with anyone, either psychologically or physically. He lives under tremendous pressure and anxiety. Doriel and his therapist consider issues such as whether madness actually exists and grapple with his survivor's guilt. Translated from the French by Catherine Temerson.

Where it's reviewed:
Booklist, November 15, 2008, page 5
Kirkus Reviews, January 1, 2009, page NA
Publishers Weekly, November 24, 2008, page 35

Other books by the same author:
The Time of the Uprooted, 2005
Twilight, 1988
The Gates of the Forest, 1966
The Town Beyond the Wall, 1964
Night, 1960 (memoir)

Other books you might like:
Geraldine Brooks, *People of the Book*, 2008
A.B. Yehoshua, *Friendly Fire*, 2008

1123

CAROL WINDLEY

Home Schooling
(New York: Atlantic, 2009)

Story type: Literary; Collection
Subject(s): Short Stories

Summary: The eight short stories in this collection look at situations teetering on the edge. Several stories focus on broken marriages or those going swiftly downhill. In one, a single father's girlfriend wonders how others see her fraught relationship with his child. In another, a woman marries her friend's ex-husband, and in a third a woman becomes involved with a much older man. Other tenuous and difficult relationships are featured. A teenager's father loses his job as headmaster at a boarding school when a student dies. A friend accompanies a mother on vacation, only to find herself saddled with the friend's child.

Where it's reviewed:
Booklist, December 1, 2008, page 22
Kirkus Reviews, November 1, 2008, page NA
Publishers Weekly, September 8, 2008, page 33

Other books by the same author:
Breathing Underwater, 1998
Visible Light, 1993

Other books you might like:
Elizabeth Hay, *Small Change*, 2001
Alice Munro, *Hateship, Friendship, Courtship, Loveship, Marriage*, 2001

1124

DAVID WROBLEWSKI

The Story of Edgar Sawtelle
(New York: Ecco, 2008)

Story type: Literary
Subject(s): Animals/Dogs; Mutism

Major character(s): Edgar Sawtelle, Animal Trainer; Almondine, Dog
Time period(s): 1970s
Locale(s): Wisconsin

Summary: Edgar Sawtelle grows up in rural Wisconsin using only sign language. Though there is no physical reason for it, he has never spoken. His parents are dog breeders, and Edgar, too, communes with dogs and speaks to them in sign language. The family develops a unique dog breed, and Edgar is particularly close to a dog named Almondine. When Edgar is a teenager, his father dies under mysterious circumstances. When his uncle then begins to come around and show interest in Edgar's mother, Edgar grows even more suspicious. Occasionally a dog speaks directly to the reader. At one point, Edgar and three dogs are lost in the woods and roam for days before finding a cabin for shelter.

Where it's reviewed:
The Christian Science Monitor, June 13, 2008, page 25
The Houston Chronicle, July 13, 2008, page 16
The New York Times Book Review, August 3, 2008, page 6
The New Yorker, June 30, 2008, page 77
USA Today, June 19, 2008, page 4D

Other books you might like:
Sara Gruen, *Water for Elephants*, 2006
Yann Martell, *Life of Pi*, 2002
Audrey Niffenegger, *The Time Traveler's Wife*, 2003
Carolyn Parkhurst, *The Dogs of Babel*, 2003

1125

A.B. YEHOSHUA

Friendly Fire
(New York: Harcourt, 2008)

Story type: Literary
Subject(s): Marriage; Family Relations
Major character(s): Amotz Ya'ari, Engineer; Daniela Ya'ari, Spouse
Time period(s): 2000s
Locale(s): Tanzania; Tel Aviv, Israel

Summary: Daniela decides to take a weeklong trip to Africa without her husband of 37 years, Amotz, after her sister, a diplomat in Tanzania, dies. In Tanzania, Daniela discovers that her brother-in-law has been growing increasingly troubled since his son died in a friendly fire incident in a Palestinian town. The book alternates between Daniela's discoveries in Tanzania and Amotz's experiences back home in Tel Aviv without her. He is tending to his aging father and their children and grandchildren. Translated from the Hebrew by Stuart Schoffman.

Where it's reviewed:
Publishers Weekly, August 11, 2008, page 25

Other books by the same author:
A Woman in Jerusalem, 2006
The Liberated Bride, 2003
A Journey to the End of the Millennium, 1999
Mr. Mani, 1992

The Lover, 1978

Other books you might like:
Carol Shields, *Happenstance*, 1994
Amy Wilentz, *Martyrs' Crossing*, 2001

1126

MICHAEL ZADOORIAN

The Leisure Seeker

(New York: William Morrow, 2009)

Story type: Literary
Subject(s): Marriage
Major character(s): Ella Robina, Traveller; John Robina, Traveller
Time period(s): 2000s
Locale(s): United States

Summary: John and Ella, both in their golden years, defy their son and daughter and take a long trip in an RV across Route 66 to Disneyland. Ella has cancer, and John has Alzheimer's disease. They start out from Detroit, and Ella drives and recalls important and minor events in their lives and observes that with their various failings, the two of them add up to one competent human being. She also identifies with the tumbledown tourist attractions where they stop along the way, and they both eat as much unhealthy food as they like. Despite the bleak subject matter, Ella is a buoyant and observant character.

Where it's reviewed:
Booklist, December 15, 2008, page 24
Publishers Weekly, October 27, 2008, page 30

Other books by the same author:
Second Hand, 2000

Other books you might like:

Louis Begley, *About Schmidt*, 1996
Lisa Genova, *Still Alice*, 2009

1127

GWENDOLYN ZEPEDA

Houston, We Have a Problema

(New York: Grand Central Publishing, 2009)

Story type: Contemporary
Subject(s): Superstition
Major character(s): Jessica Luna, Insurance Agent; Madame Hortensia, Psychic
Time period(s): 2000s
Locale(s): Houston, Texas

Summary: Jessica Luna is stuck. In her mid-twenties, she works at a job she doesn't enjoy and is torn between two men, an artist and a businessman. Because Jessica's overbearing family has always made decisions for her, she finds herself unable to function as an adult. She begins visiting a psychic, Madame Hortensia, and consulting all kinds of signs and oracles and obeying the messages that she receives from them, or believes that she receives from them. Jessica "reads" everything from her daily horoscope to the image of the Virgin of Guadalupe that hangs from her car's rearview mirror.

Where it's reviewed:
Publishers Weekly, September 22, 2008, page 36

Other books by the same author:
To the Last Man I Slept With and All The Jerks Just Like Him, 2004 (short stories)

Other books you might like:
Mary Castillo, *In Between Men*, 2006
Alisa Valdes-Rodriguez, *The Dirty Girls Social Club*, 2003

Series Index

This index alphabetically lists series to which books featured in the entries belong. Beneath each series name, book titles are listed alphabetically with author names and genre codes. The genre codes are as follows: *c* Popular Fiction, *f* Fantasy, *h* Horror, *i* Inspirational, *m* Mystery, *r* Romance, *s* Science Fiction, *t* Historical, and *w* Western. Numbers refer to the entries that feature each title.

Time Period Index

This index chronologically lists the time settings in which the featured books take place. Main headings refer to a century; where no specific time is given, the headings MULTIPLE TIME PERIODS, INDETERMINATE PAST, INDETERMINATE FUTURE, and INDETERMINATE are used. The 18th through 21st centuries are broken down into decades when possible. (Note: 1800s, for example, refers to the first decade of the 19th century.) Featured titles are listed alphabetically beneath time headings, with author names and genre codes. The genre codes are as follows: *c* Popular Fiction, *f* Fantasy, *h* Horror, *i* Inspirational, *m* Mystery, *r* Romance, *s* Science Fiction, *t* Historical, and *w* Western. Numbers refer to the entries that feature each title.

INDETERMINATE FUTURE

INDETERMINATE

Geographic Index

This index provides access to all featured books by geographic settings—such as countries, continents, oceans, and planets. States and provinces are indicated for the United States and Canada. Also interfiled are headings for fictional place names (Spaceships, Imaginary Planets, etc.). Sections are further broken down by city or the specific name of the imaginary locale. Book titles are listed alphabetically under headings, with author names and genre codes. The genre codes are as follows: *c* Popular Fiction, *f* Fantasy, *h* Horror, *i* Inspirational, *m* Mystery, *r* Romance, *s* Science Fiction, *t* Historical, and *w* Western. Numbers refer to the entries that feature each title.

AFRICA

Blonde Roots - Bernardine Evaristo   *c*   1005
The Gaudí Key - Esteban Martin   *m*   137
Heart and Soul - Sarah A. Hoyt   *f*   461

ALBANIA

The Fire - Katherine Neville   *m*   149

ALTERNATE EARTH

Crusade - Taylor Anderson   *s*   628
The United States of Atlantis - Harry Turtledove   *s*   717

ALTERNATE UNIVERSE

The Bell at Sealey Head - Patricia A. McKillip   *f*   485
The Black Ship - Diana Pharaoh Francis   *f*   450
Blackstaff Tower - Steven E. Schend   *f*   514
Blood of Elves - Andrzej Sapkowski   *f*   511
Bloodheir - Brian Ruckley   *f*   508
Cast in Fury - Michelle Sagara   *f*   509
Chance Fortune in the Shadow Zone - Shane Berryhill   *s*   635
City of Jade - Dennis L. McKiernan   *f*   484
The Crown - Deborah Chester   *f*   438
Curse of the Necrarch - Steven Savile   *f*   513
Dark Vengeance - Ed Greenwood   *f*   457
Dark Whispers - Bruce Coville   *f*   441
A Darkness Forged in Fire - Chris Evans   *f*   445
Dead Reign - T.A. Pratt   *f*   498
Dragonforge - James Maxey   *f*   483
Elfslayer - Nathan Long   *f*   478
The Engine's Child - Holly Phillips   *f*   496
Eon: Dragoneye Reborn - Alison Goodman   *f*   455
The Flame and the Shadow - Denise Rossetti   *f*   507
Fortune and Fate - Sharon Shinn   *f*   516
Foundation - Mercedes Lackey   *f*   467
The Gods Return - David Drake   *f*   442
The Golden Army - Robert Greenberger   *h*   547
The Golden Tower - Fiona Patton   *f*   495
Gordath Wood - Patrice Sarath   *f*   512
Graceling - Kristin Cashore   *f*   436
The Gypsy Morph - Terry Brooks   *f*   432
Heart and Soul - Sarah A. Hoyt   *f*   461

Heir to Sevenwaters - Juliet Marillier   *f*   481
Heldenhammer - Graham McNeill   *f*   487
The Hero of Ages - Brandon Sanderson   *f*   510
The Horseman's Gambit - David B. Coe   *f*   439
The House of the Stag - Kage Baker   *f*   427
Ill Met in the Arena - Dave Duncan   *f*   443
Implied Spaces - Walter Jon Williams   *s*   722
Inkdeath - Cornelia Funke   *f*   452
King's Shield - Sherwood Smith   *f*   517
Knight Errant - Anthony Reynolds   *f*   502
The Knight of the Red Beard - Andre Norton   *f*   493
Lamplighter - D.M. Cornish   *f*   440
The Larion Senators - Robert Scott   *f*   515
The Long Look - Richard Parks   *f*   494
The Lord Protector's Daughter - L.E. Modesitt Jr.   *f*   488
Lord Tophet - Gregory Frost   *f*   451
Magic to the Bone - Devon Monk   *f*   489
The Magicians and Mrs. Quent - Galen Beckett   *f*   429
The Melting Stones - Tamora Pierce   *f*   497
Mistshore - Jaleigh Johnson   *f*   463
Morningtide - Cory J. Herndon   *f*   459
Nagash the Sorcerer - Mike Lee   *f*   471
The Night Bird - Catherine Asaro   *f*   426
The Phoenix Endangered - Mercedes Lackey   *f*   468
Princeps' Fury - Jim Butcher   *f*   433
The Reawakened - Jeri Smith-Ready   *f*   518
The Red Country - Sylvia Kelso   *f*   465
Runefang - C.L. Werner   *f*   521
Saint Antony's Fire - Steve White   *s*   721
Shadows Return - Lynn Flewelling   *f*   448
The Snow Queen - Mercedes Lackey   *f*   469
The Soldier King - Violette Malan   *f*   479
Soul of Fire - Sarah A. Hoyt   *f*   462
Stalking the Vampire - Mike Resnick   *f*   501
The Steel Remains - Richard K. Morgan   *f*   492
Swallowing Darkness - Laurell Hamilton   *f*   458
The Ten Thousand - Paul Kearney   *f*   464
Tender Morsels - Margo Lanagan   *f*   470
Thunderer - Felix Gilman   *f*   454
Toll the Hounds - Steven Erikson   *f*   444
Too Many Curses - A. Lee Martinez   *f*   482
Two to the Fifth - Piers Anthony   *f*   425
Undead - Richard Lee Byers   *f*   434
The Wyrmling Horde - David Farland   *f*   446

AMERICAN COLONIES

A Mercy - Toni Morrison   *c*   1063
The United States of Atlantis - Harry Turtledove   *t*   862

MARYLAND

A Mercy - Toni Morrison   *t*   826

MASSACHUSETTS

Andover
The Heretic's Daughter - Kathleen Kent   *t*   806

Salem
The Heretic's Daughter - Kathleen Kent   *t*   806

NEW YORK

New Amsterdam
Doctor Olaf van Schuler's Brain - Kirsten Menger-Anderson   *c*   1062

VIRGINIA

The Sin Eaters - Andrew Beahrs   *t*   730

ANTARCTICA

Freezing Point - Karen Dionne   *s*   653

ARABIA

The Jewel of Medina - Sherry Jones   *t*   800

ARCTIC

Hidden - Eve Kenin   *r*   317

ARGENTINA

Revelations - Melissa de la Cruz   *h*   538

Buenos Aires
The Book of Murder - Guillermo Martinez   *m*   138
The Paris Enigma - Pablo De Santis   *m*   63

A Good Woman - Danielle Steel *r* 401
The Leper - Steve Thayer *t* 857
The Only Son - Stephane Audeguy *c* 972
Traitor's Kiss - Mary Blayney *r* 219

Burgundy
Bright Hair about the Bone - Barbara
  Cleverly *t* 751

Fontigny Sainte-Reine
Bright Hair about the Bone - Barbara
  Cleverly *m* 49

Paris
Assassin's Rage - Charles O'Brien *t* 829
The Black Tower - Louis Bayard *m* 15
The Black Tower - Louis Bayard *t* 729
Folly Du Jour - Barbara Cleverly *m* 50
The Glass of Time - Michael Cox *m* 55
A Good Woman - Danielle Steel *t* 853
Illegal Action - Stella Rimington *m* 164
Murder on the Eiffel Tower - Claude
  Izner *t* 799
Murder on the Eiffel Tower - Claude
  Izner *m* 99
Mystic Rider - Patricia Rice *r* 376
The Only Son - Stephane Audeguy *t* 727
The Paris Enigma - Pablo De Santis *m* 63
The Paris Enigma - Pablo De Santis *t* 761
Pictures at an Exhibition - Sara
  Houghteling *c* 1024
The Shadow of Reichenbach Falls - John R.
  King *m* 109
Sherlock Holmes Was Wrong - Pierre
  Bayard *m* 16
Ultimate Weapon - Shannon McKenna *r* 349
Valfierno - Martin Caparros *t* 744

Saint-Cloud
The Black Tower - Louis Bayard *m* 15

Saint-Denis
The Black Tower - Louis Bayard *m* 15

Saint-Tropez
Moscow Rules - Daniel Silva *m* 175

GERMANY

The Creator's Map - Emilio Calderon *t* 742
The Gargoyle - Andrew Davidson *t* 758
The Man with the Iron Heart - Harry
  Turtledove *s* 716
The Man with the Iron Heart - Harry
  Turtledove *t* 861
Me and Kaminski - Daniel Kehlmann *c* 1034
Miss Match - Sara Mills *i* 935
Shadows in the Mist - Brian Moreland *h* 581
Stealing Trinity - Ward Larsen *t* 810
Winnie and Wolf - A.N. Wilson *t* 868

Berlin
Disguise - Hugo Hamilton *t* 791
The Glimmer Palace - Beatrice Colin *t* 752
Stealing Trinity - Ward Larsen *m* 116

Guldenberg
Settlement - Christoph Hein *t* 795

Munich
The Laughter of Dead Kings - Elizabeth
  Peters *m* 155

Nuremberg
Disguise - Hugo Hamilton *t* 791

Ruhenthal
The Journey - H.G. Adler *c* 968

Wolfach
The Daughters Grimm - Minda Webber *r* 414

GERMAN DEMOCRATIC REPUBLIC

New Lives - Ingo Schulze *c* 1091

GREECE

Acheron - Sherrilyn Kenyon *h* 562
Alexander and Alestria - Sa Shan *t* 850
The Lost Temple - Tom Harper *t* 792
Night of the Furies - Davis Angsten *h* 525
A Seduction at Christmas - Cathy
  Maxwell *r* 347

Delos
Murder in Mykonos - Jeffrey M. Siger *m* 174

Mykonos
Murder in Mykonos - Jeffrey M. Siger *m* 174

Syros
Murder in Mykonos - Jeffrey M. Siger *m* 174

GUAM

Stealing Trinity - Ward Larsen *t* 810

HELL

Immortals: The Crossing - Joy Nash *r* 359

HONG KONG

Deep Night - Caroline Petit *t* 832
The Piano Teacher - Janice Y.K. Lee *c* 1045

HUNGARY

Esther's Inheritance - Sandor Marai *c* 1060

Budapest
Ultimate Weapon - Shannon McKenna *r* 349

INDIA

Alexander and Alestria - Sa Shan *t* 850
Dark Whispers - Bruce Coville *f* 441
In the Convent of Little Flowers - Indu
  Sundaresan *c* 1108
Sea of Poppies - Amitav Ghosh *t* 780
Soul of Fire - Sarah A. Hoyt *f* 462
The Toss of a Lemon - Padma
  Viswanathan *t* 865

New Delhi
Family Planning - Karan Mahajan *c* 1057

Sikri
The Enchantress of Florence - Salman
  Rushdie *c* 1089

IRAQ

The Lucky One - Nicholas Sparks *c* 1104

IRELAND

Borderlands - Brian McGilloway *m* 142
Dancing with Demons - Peter Tremayne *t* 860

Burren
A Secret and Unlawful Killing - Cora
  Harrison *t* 794

Cork
Illegal Action - Stella Rimington *m* 164

Dublin
Deadly Gift - Heather Graham *r* 285

Glenskahey
The Likeness - Tana French *m* 69

Kingdom of the Burren
A Secret and Unlawful Killing - Cora
  Harrison *m* 86

Sligo
The Secret Scripture - Sebastian Barry *t* 728

IRELAND, NORTHERN

Borderlands - Brian McGilloway *m* 142

ISRAEL

The Confessions of Noa Weber - Gail
  Hareven *c* 1017

Jerusalem
Moscow Rules - Daniel Silva *m* 175
Open Doors - Gloria Goldreich *c* 1014

Tel Aviv
Friendly Fire - A.B. Yehoshua *c* 1125

ITALY

The Darkest Touch - Jaci Burton *h* 534
The Islands of Divine Music - John
  Addiego *t* 724

Agrigento
Blood Alone - James R. Benn *m* 20

Capri
Very Valentine - Adriana Tragiani *c* 1112

Florence
The Enchantress of Florence - Salman
  Rushdie *c* 1089

Gela
Blood Alone - James R. Benn *m* 20

Lake Como
The Edge of Impropriety - Pam
  Rosenthal *r* 380

Rome
The 731 Legacy - Lynn Sholes *m* 173
Absolute Honor - C.C. Humphreys *t* 796
Black Market Truth - Sharon Kaye *m* 106

Clash of Civilizations Over an Elevator in Piazza Vittorio - Amara Lakhous *c* 1043
Conspiracy in Kiev - Noel Hynd *m* 97
The Creator's Map - Emilio Calderon *t* 742
Daughter of Egypt - Constance O'Banyon *r* 362

San Giovanni la Punta
Sicilian Tragedee - Ottavio Cappellani *c* 988

Sicily
Blood Alone - James R. Benn *t* 732

Venice
The Book of Unholy Mischief - Elle Newmark *c* 1067
The Four Seasons - Laurel Corona *c* 994
The Four Seasons - Laurel Corona *t* 754

Vittoria
Blood Alone - James R. Benn *m* 20

JAMAICA

Black Butterfly - Mark Gatiss *t* 779

Montego Bay
Anchors Aweigh - Kathleen Bacus *m* 5

JAPAN

The China Lover - Ian Buruma *t* 741
The Housekeeper and the Professor - Yoko Ogawa *c* 1075

Edo
The Fire Kimono - Laura Joh Rowland *t* 841

Karuizawa
Real World - Natsuo Kirino *m* 110

Tokyo
The Blade of the Courtesans - Keiichiro Ryu *t* 845
Deadly Beautiful - Sam Baker *m* 7
Real World - Natsuo Kirino *m* 110
Tokyo Fiancee - Amelie Nothomb *c* 1069

KOREA, NORTH

Pyongyang
The 731 Legacy - Lynn Sholes *m* 173

LAOS

Curse of the Pogo Stick - Colin Cotterill *m* 54

LEBANON

Wild Mulberries - Iman Humaydan Younes *t* 873

Beirut
The China Lover - Ian Buruma *t* 741

MACAO

Deep Night - Caroline Petit *m* 156

MARS

Marsbound - Joe Haldeman *s* 666

Mechanicus - Graham McNeill *s* 686

MEDITERRANEAN

Enclave - Kit Reed *s* 693
The Sun's Bride - Gillian Bradshaw *t* 737

MEXICO

Frida's Bed - Slavenka Drakulic *t* 764
Happy Families - Carlos Fuentes *c* 1010
Heartless - Alison Gaylin *h* 544
Love in the Time of Fridges - Tim Scott *s* 705
The Sacrificial Circumcision of the Bronx - Arthur Nersesian *c* 1066

Mexico City
Night Kills - John Lutz *m* 128

Puerto Vallarta
Greasing the Pinata - Tim Maleeny *m* 133

Santa Teresa
2666 - Roberto Bolano *c* 980

Tijuana
Crash Into Me - Jill Sorenson *m* 180

MIDDLE EAST

Alexander and Alestria - Sa Shan *t* 850
The Treasure - Iris Johansen *r* 307

MONGOLIA

The Shadow Walker - Michael Walters *h* 618

Dalanzadgad
The Shadow Walker - Michael Walters *m* 194

Ulan Baatar
The Shadow Walker - Michael Walters *m* 194

MOROCCO

The Fire - Katherine Neville *m* 149

Marrakech
Lulu in Marrakech - Diane Johnson *c* 1029

MYTHICAL PLACE

The Battle of the Labyrinth - Rick Riordan *f* 504
Hell and Earth - Elizabeth Bear *f* 428
King of Sword and Sky - C.L. Wilson *r* 419
Knight's Fork - Rowena Cherry *r* 242
One Silent Night - Sherrilyn Kenyon *h* 563
Storm Born - Richelle Mead *h* 577
To Hell and Back - Lilith Saintcrow *h* 601
Up in Smoke - Katie MacAlister *r* 333

Corvo City
Phenomenal Girl 5 - A.J. Menden *r* 351

Otherworld
Bedeviled - Maureen Child *r* 243

Stephensgate
Ransom My Heart - Mia Thermopolis *r* 406

NEPAL

Into the Shadow - Christina Dodd *r* 257

NETHERLANDS

Amsterdam
After You've Gone - Jeffrey Lent *c* 1048
Doctor Olaf van Schuler's Brain - Kirsten Menger-Anderson *c* 1062
Rock Bottom - Michael Shilling *c* 1096

NORTH AMERICA

The Blue Enchantress - M.L. Tyndall *i* 957
The Hunger Games - Suzanne Collins *s* 645
The Red Siren - M.L. Tyndall *i* 958
The Scourge of God - S.M. Stirling *s* 712
Wind Dancer - Jamie Carie *i* 885

OUTER SPACE

The Ashes of Worlds - Kevin J. Anderson *s* 627
Aspho Fields - Karen Traviss *s* 714
Battle for the Abyss - Ben Counter *s* 647
Claws That Catch - John Ringo *s* 697
The Cold Minds - Kris Landon *s* 675
Collision Course - William Shatner *s* 706
Criminal Enterprise - S.D. Perry *s* 691
Dark Disciple - Anthony Reynolds *s* 696
The Devil's Eye - Jack McDevitt *s* 684
Eve - Tony Gonzales *s* 665
Gods of Night - David Mack *s* 677
Harmony - C.F. Bentley *s* 633
Implied Spaces - Walter Jon Williams *s* 722
The January Dancer - Michael Flynn *s* 659
Judge - Karen Traviss *s* 715
The Killing Ground - Graham McNeill *s* 685
Kobayashi Maru - Michael A. Martin *s* 680
Kris Longknife: Intrepid - Mike Shepherd *s* 707
Marsbound - Joe Haldeman *s* 666
Mere Mortals - David Mack *s* 678
No Exit - B.K. Evenson *s* 654
Paul of Dune - Brian Herbert *s* 669
Peacekeeper - Laura E. Reeve *s* 694
The Quiet War - Paul J. McAuley *s* 682
Red Fury - James Swallow *s* 713
Rivers of Fire - Patrick Carman *s* 642
Shades of Dark - Linnea Sinclair *s* 709
Slanted Jack - Mark L. Van Name *s* 718
Slow Train to Arcturus - Eric Flint *s* 657
Strength and Honor - R.M. Meluch *s* 687
Sunborn - Jeffrey A. Carver *s* 643
Webdancers - Brian Herbert *s* 670
Wings of Hell - David Sherman *s* 708

PACIFIC ISLANDS

Beside a Burning Sea - John Shors *t* 851
The Eleventh Man - Ivan Doig *t* 762

PAKISTAN

Lahore
In Other Rooms, Other Wonders - Daniyal Mueenuddin *c* 1064

The Sacrificial Circumcision of the Bronx - Arthur
Nersesian *c* 1066
Salvation in Death - J.D. Robb *s* 698
Scarpetta - Patricia Cornwell *m* 53
Sima's Undergarments for Women - Ilana
Stanger-Ross *c* 1106
The Sour Cherry Surprise - David
Handler *m* 84
Super in the City - Daphne Uviller *c* 1115
Third Strike - Zoe Sharp *m* 171
Very Valentine - Adriana Tragiani *c* 1112
The Way through Doors - Jesse Ball *c* 974
The Whiskey Rebels - David Liss *t* 813
The Winter of Her Discontent - Kathryn Miller
Haines *m* 83
Worth Fighting For - Molly O'Keefe *r* 363
Year of the Dog - Henry Chang *m* 44

Promise Falls
Too Close to Home - Linwood Barclay *m* 11

Seaside
Old Flame - Ira Berkowitz *m* 21

Southampton
The Water's Edge - Daniel Judson *m* 103

Troy
The Nightingales of Troy - Alice Fulton *t* 776

NORTH CAROLINA
The Bible Salesman - Clyde Edgerton *t* 767
On the Move - Pamela Britton *r* 227
Serena - Ron Rash *t* 837
Serena - Ron Rash *c* 1081

Charlotte
At First Sight - Stephen J. Cannell *m* 40
The Last Day - John Ramsey Miller *m* 145

Concord
The Last Day - John Ramsey Miller *m* 145

Dewell Hill
In a Dark Season - Vicki Lane *m* 115

Dillworth
The Last Day - John Ramsey Miller *m* 145

Dobbs
Death's Half Acre - Margaret Maron *m* 135

Durham
Death's Half Acre - Margaret Maron *m* 135
A Killer Workout - Kathryn Lilley *m* 122

Glory
Talk of the Town - Karen Hawkins *r* 293

Hampton
The Lucky One - Nicholas Sparks *c* 1104

Hot Springs
In a Dark Season - Vicki Lane *m* 115

Maggie Hollow
A Killer Workout - Kathryn Lilley *m* 122

Raleigh
Talk of the Town - Karen Hawkins *r* 293

Ransom
In a Dark Season - Vicki Lane *m* 115

Wilmington
The Telltale Turtle - Joyce Lavene *m* 119

NORTH DAKOTA
On a Someday - Roxanne Henke *i* 916

OHIO
Indignation - Philip Roth *t* 840

Cincinnati
Kaleidoscope - Darryl Wimberley *m* 198
Kaleidoscope - Darryl Wimberley *t* 869

Cleveland
Nemesis: The Final Case of Eliot Ness - William
Bernhardt *m* 22
Takeover - Lisa Black *m* 24

Columbus
Code of Silence - Sally Wright *t* 871

Kingsville
Songs for the Missing - Stewart
O'Nan *c* 1071

Newburgh Heights
Nemesis: The Final Case of Eliot Ness - William
Bernhardt *m* 22

Winesburg
Indignation - Philip Roth *c* 1088

OKLAHOMA

Adelaide
Ghost at Work - Carolyn Hart *m* 87

Boynton
The Sky Took Him - Donis Casey *m* 42

Eden
His Small-Town Girl - Arlene James *r* 303

Enid
The Sky Took Him - Donis Casey *m* 42

Garber
The Sky Took Him - Donis Casey *m* 42

Split Creek
Breach of Trust - DiAnn Mills *i* 934

OREGON
Destiny Kills - Keri Arthur *h* 529
Distant Heart - Tracey Bateman *i* 877

Maiden's Bay
Sinister Sudoku - Kaye Morgan *m* 146

Otis
Sinister Sudoku - Kaye Morgan *m* 146

Portland
Blood Memories - Barb Hendee *h* 551
Chasing Smoke - Bill Cameron *m* 39
Magic to the Bone - Devon Monk *f* 489

Night Kill - Ann Littlewood *m* 124
Sinister Sudoku - Kaye Morgan *m* 146
Sweetheart - Chelsea Cain *m* 38
Ultimate Weapon - Shannon McKenna *r* 349

Redmond
Devil May Ride - Wendy Roberts *m* 165

Salem
Sweetheart - Chelsea Cain *m* 38

PACIFIC NORTHWEST
Livability - Jon Raymond *c* 1082

PENNSYLVANIA
The Reverend's Apprentice - David N.
Odhiambo *c* 1074
The Whiskey Rebels - David Liss *t* 813

Coudersport
Nemesis: The Final Case of Eliot Ness - William
Bernhardt *m* 22

Erie
Everything but a Bride - Holly Jacobs *r* 300
Once upon a Christmas - Holly Jacobs *r* 301
Once upon a Thanksgiving - Holly
Jacobs *r* 302

Gilbeytown
The Man for Me - Gemma Bruce *r* 229

Lancaster County
Shadows of Lancaster County - Mindy Starns
Clark *i* 891

Philadelphia
Deception's Daughter - Cordelia Frances
Biddle *m* 23
Deception's Daughter - Cordelia Frances
Biddle *t* 733
The Devil's Due - Jenna Black *h* 532

RHODE ISLAND

Eastwick
The Widows of Eastwick - John
Updike *c* 1114

Millstone
The Ghost and the Haunted Mansion - Alice
Kimberly *m* 108

Newport
Deadly Gift - Heather Graham *r* 285
A Good Woman - Danielle Steel *r* 401
Marry Christmas - Jane Goodger *r* 281
Stealing Trinity - Ward Larsen *m* 116

Providence
Teaser - Jan Brogan *m* 31

Quindicott
The Ghost and the Haunted Mansion - Alice
Kimberly *m* 108

Wickford
A Veiled Deception - Annette Blair *m* 25

Geographic Index

URUGUAY

VENEZUELA

WALES

Genre Index

This index lists the books featured as main entries in *What Do I Read Next?* by genre and story type within each genre. Beneath each of the nine genres, the story types appear alphabetically, and titles appear alphabetically under story type headings. The name of the primary author, genre code and the book entry number also appear with each title. The genre codes are as follows: *c* Popular Fiction, *f* Fantasy, *h* Horror, *i* Inspirational, *m* Mystery, *r* Romance, *s* Science Fiction, *t* Historical, and *w* Western. For definitions of the story types, see the "Key to Genre Terms" following the Introduction.

FANTASY

Alternate History

And Less than Kind - Mercedes Lackey *f* 466

Alternate World

The Breath of God - Harry Turtledove *f* 520
The Engine's Child - Holly Phillips *f* 496
Gordath Wood - Patrice Sarath *f* 512
Heart and Soul - Sarah A. Hoyt *f* 461
The Magicians and Mrs. Quent - Galen Beckett *f* 429
Thirteen Orphans - Jane Lindskold *f* 473

Anthology

Catopolis - Martin H. Greenberg *f* 456
Enchantment Place - Denise Little *f* 474
Imaginary Friends - John Marco *f* 480
Witch High - Denise Little *f* 475

Collection

Deltora Quest - Emily Rodda *f* 506
Elric: The Sleeping Sorceress - Michael Moorcock *f* 490
Elric: To Rescue Tanelorn - Michael Moorcock *f* 491
Guinevere's Truth and Other Stories - Jennifer Roberson *f* 505
The Serial Garden - Joan Aiken *f* 424

Coming-of-Age

Eon: Dragoneye Reborn - Alison Goodman *f* 455
Foundation - Mercedes Lackey *f* 467
The Golden Tower - Fiona Patton *f* 495
Ill Met in the Arena - Dave Duncan *f* 443

Contemporary

The Burning Man - Mark Chadbourn *f* 437
Dragon Wytch - Yasmine Galenorn *f* 453
Gale Force - Rachel Caine *f* 435
Gentleman Takes a Chance - Sarah A. Hoyt *f* 460
The Iron Hunt - Marjorie M. Liu *f* 477
Ironhand - Charlie Fletcher *f* 447

The Knights of the Cornerstone - James P. Blaylock *f* 430
Magic to the Bone - Devon Monk *f* 489
New Tricks - John Levitt *f* 472
The Sweet Scent of Blood - Suzanne McLeod *f* 486
Thirteen Orphans - Jane Lindskold *f* 473
Underground - Kat Richardson *f* 503

Disaster

The Gypsy Morph - Terry Brooks *f* 432
The Melting Stones - Tamora Pierce *f* 497

Futuristic

An Evil Guest - Gene Wolfe *f* 523

Historical

The Gypsy Crown - Kate Forsyth *f* 449
Hell and Earth - Elizabeth Bear *f* 428
Soul of Fire - Sarah A. Hoyt *f* 462

Historical/Fantasy

Dragon Moon - Carole Wilkinson *f* 522

Historical/Pre-history

The Breath of God - Harry Turtledove *f* 520

Humor

Dead Reign - T.A. Pratt *f* 498
Stalking the Vampire - Mike Resnick *f* 501
Too Many Curses - A. Lee Martinez *f* 482
Two to the Fifth - Piers Anthony *f* 425

Legend

The Battle of the Labyrinth - Rick Riordan *f* 504
The Bell at Sealey Head - Patricia A. McKillip *f* 485
Blood of Elves - Andrzej Sapkowski *f* 511
Gentleman Takes a Chance - Sarah A. Hoyt *f* 460
Here Lies Arthur - Philip Reeve *f* 500
The Snow Queen - Mercedes Lackey *f* 469

Light Fantasy

The Bell at Sealey Head - Patricia A. McKillip *f* 485

Literary

Fortune and Fate - Sharon Shinn *f* 516
Miranda - John R. Little *f* 476

Magic Conflict

And Less than Kind - Mercedes Lackey *f* 466
The Black Ship - Diana Pharaoh Francis *f* 450
Blackstaff Tower - Steven E. Schend *f* 514
Blood of Elves - Andrzej Sapkowski *f* 511
Bloodheir - Brian Ruckley *f* 508
The Burning Man - Mark Chadbourn *f* 437
Caine Black Knife - Matthew Stover *f* 519
The Crown - Deborah Chester *f* 438
Curse of the Necrarch - Steven Savile *f* 513
Dark Vengeance - Ed Greenwood *f* 457
A Darkness Forged in Fire - Chris Evans *f* 445
Dead Reign - T.A. Pratt *f* 498
Dragon Wytch - Yasmine Galenorn *f* 453
Dragonforge - James Maxey *f* 483
Elfslayer - Nathan Long *f* 478
Eon: Dragoneye Reborn - Alison Goodman *f* 455
An Evil Guest - Gene Wolfe *f* 523
The Flame and the Shadow - Denise Rossetti *f* 507
Fortune and Fate - Sharon Shinn *f* 516
Gale Force - Rachel Caine *f* 435
The Gods Return - David Drake *f* 442
Gordath Wood - Patrice Sarath *f* 512
Graceling - Kristin Cashore *f* 436
The Gypsy Morph - Terry Brooks *f* 432
Heldenhammer - Graham McNeill *f* 487
Hell and Earth - Elizabeth Bear *f* 428
The Hero of Ages - Brandon Sanderson *f* 510
The Horseman's Gambit - David B. Coe *f* 439
The House of the Stag - Kage Baker *f* 427
Inkdeath - Cornelia Funke *f* 452
The Iron Hunt - Marjorie M. Liu *f* 477
Knight Errant - Anthony Reynolds *f* 502
The Knight of the Red Beard - Andre Norton *f* 493
The Knights of the Cornerstone - James P. Blaylock *f* 430

HISTORICAL

INSPIRATIONAL

Satire

ROMANCE

Adventure

Alternate History

Amateur Detective

Americana

Anthology

Contemporary

SCIENCE FICTION

Subject Index

This index lists subjects which are covered in the featured titles. Beneath each subject heading, titles are arranged alphabetically with the author names, genre codes, and entry numbers also indicated. The genre codes are as follows: *c* Popular Fiction, *f* Fantasy, *h* Horror, *i* Inspirational, *m* Mystery, *r* Romance, *s* Science Fiction, *t* Historical, and *w* Western.

Biological Warfare

The 731 Legacy - Lynn Sholes   *m*   173

Biotechnology

A Patent Lie - Paul Goldstein   *m*   76

Blackmail

After the Kiss - Suzanne Enoch   *r*   262
Green Monster - Rick Shefchik   *m*   172
Rainstone Fall - Peter Helton   *m*   92
White Nights - Ann Cleeves   *m*   48

Boats and Boating

Precious Cargo - Clyde Ford   *m*   67

Books and Reading

Murder on the Eiffel Tower - Claude
Izner   *m*   99
Risque Business - Tawny Weber   *r*   415

Brainwashing

Irreversible - Liz Maverick   *r*   346

Brothers

The Bridesmaid's Turn - Nicole Foster   *r*   273
The Decadent Duke - Virginia Henley   *r*   296

Brothers and Sisters

Eat, Drink, and Be from Mississippi - Nanci
Kincaid   *c*   1037

Business

Body Copy - Michael Craven   *m*   58
A Most Unconventional Match - Julia
Justiss   *r*   312
Ready and Willing - Elizabeth Bevarly   *r*   216
Trigger City - Sean Chercover   *m*   45
The Whiskey Rebels - David Liss   *t*   813

Business Enterprises

Serena - Ron Rash   *t*   837
Telex from Cuba - Rachel Kushner   *t*   808

Cancer

Chasing Smoke - Bill Cameron   *m*   39
When Love Blooms - Robin Lee
Hatcher   *i*   914

Careers

Chasing Harry Winston - Lauren
Weisberger   *c*   1119

Carnivals

The Chocolate Snowman Murders - JoAnna
Carl   *m*   41
Kaleidoscope - Darryl Wimberley   *m*   198
Kaleidoscope - Darryl Wimberley   *t*   869

Castles

Newlyweds of Convenience - Jessica
Hart   *r*   292
Shadow Rider - Kathrynn Dennis   *r*   254

Catering Business

Stuff Dreams Are Made Of - Don Bruns   *m*   35

Celts

Dancing with Demons - Peter Tremayne   *t*   860

Change

Coming Home - Elisabeth Rose   *r*   379
The Hiding Place - Karen Harper   *r*   291
His Captive Lady - Anne Gracie   *r*   284
Home for the Holidays - Lisa Plumley   *r*   370
Marry Christmas - Jane Goodger   *r*   281
Snowbound in Dry Creek - Janet
Tronstad   *r*   412

Charity

Grace - Richard Paul Evans   *c*   1004

Cheating

Blackbird, Farewell - Robert Greer   *m*   82

Child Custody

Sweet Trouble - Susan Mallery   *r*   340

Children

The Hiding Place - Karen Harper   *r*   291
The Inherited Twins - Cathy Gillen
Thacker   *r*   404

China

*The Blue Wolf: A Novel of the Life of Chinggis
Khan* - Yasushi Inoue   *t*   797
Brothers - Yu Hua   *c*   1025
Deep Night - Caroline Petit   *t*   832
Deep Night - Caroline Petit   *m*   156
Everything under the Sky - Matilda
Asensi   *t*   726

Chinese Americans

Year of the Dog - Henry Chang   *m*   44

Christian Life

Beyond This Moment - Tamera
Alexander   *i*   876
Deceived - James Scott Bell   *i*   878
Red, White, and Blue - Laura Hayden   *i*   915
Stand-In Groom - Kaye Dacus   *i*   898
Wanted - Shelley Shephard Gray   *i*   908

Christianity

Fireflies in December - Jennifer Erin
Valent   *i*   959
The Gaudi Key - Esteban Martin   *m*   137

Christmas

All I Have to Give - Melody Carlson   *i*   886
All I Want for Christmas Is a Vampire - Kerrelyn
Sparks   *r*   397
Angel Unaware - Elizabeth Sinclair   *r*   389
Calico Christmas at Dry Creek - Janet
Tronstad   *r*   411
A Cedar Cove Christmas - Debbie
Macomber   *r*   336

A Cedar Cove Christmas - Debbie
Macomber   *c*   1055
Christmas Getaway - Anne Stuart   *r*   403
Christmas Is Murder - C.S. Challinor   *m*   43
Holiday with a Vampire II - Merline
Lovelace   *r*   332
Home for the Holidays - Lisa Plumley   *r*   370
Indigo Christmas - Jeanne M. Dams   *m*   60
The Magical Christmas Cat - Lora
Leigh   *r*   327
Marry-Me Christmas - Shirley Jump   *r*   310
A McKettrick Christmas - Linda Lael
Miller   *r*   355
The Mistletoe Wager - Christine Merrill   *r*   352
No Peeking - Stephanie Bond   *r*   221
One Candlelight Christmas - Julia
Justiss   *r*   313
One Perfect Gift - Kathleen Morgan   *i*   936
Searching for Santa - Janet Dailey   *r*   248
Silver Bells - Fern Michaels   *r*   353
Six Geese A-Slaying - Donna Andrews   *m*   2
Snowy Night with a Stranger - Jane
Feather   *r*   265
To All a Good Night - Donna Kauffman   *r*   316
A Virgin River Christmas - Robyn Carr   *r*   236
A Wallflower Christmas - Lisa Kleypas   *r*   320
Welcome to Serenity - Sherryl Woods   *r*   421
Yuletide Treasure - Lauraine Snelling   *r*   395

City and Town Life

*City of God (A Novel of Passion and Wonder in
Old New York)* - Beverly Swerling   *t*   855
Deception's Daughter - Cordelia Frances
Biddle   *t*   733
Doctor Olaf van Schuler's Brain - Kirsten
Menger-Anderson   *t*   823
Eat, Drink, and Be from Mississippi - Nanci
Kincaid   *c*   1037
The Given Day - Dennis Lehane   *t*   812
Lost River - David Fulmer   *t*   775
The Sacrificial Circumcision of the Bronx - Arthur
Nersesian   *c*   1066

Civil War

Freeman Walker - David Allan Cates   *t*   746
Mechanicus - Graham McNeill   *s*   686
Stranger Room - Frederick Ramsay   *m*   161

Civil War/Spanish

Guernica - Dave Boling   *t*   734

Cloning

The Clone Elite - Steven L. Kent   *s*   672
Eve - Tony Gonzales   *s*   665

College Life

College Girl - Patricia Weitz   *c*   1120
The Likeness - Tana French   *m*   69

Comedians

It Happened One Knife - Jeffrey Cohen   *m*   51

Coming-of-Age

Aurora Crossing - Karl H. Schlesier   *t*   847
Collision Course - William Shatner   *s*   706
The Dark Ones - Anthony Izzo   *h*   556
Destiny Kills - Keri Arthur   *h*   529
Dragonheart - Todd McCaffrey   *s*   683

Family

Family Life

Family Problems

Family Relations

Subject Index

Subject Index

Mysticism

Mythology

Native Americans

Nazis

Neo-Nazis

Newspapers

Obesity

Oil

Old Age

Organized Crime

Orphans

Paranormal

Parapsychology

Parent and Child

Parenthood

Peace

Philosophy

Phobias

Photography

Physically Handicapped

Pirates

Plague

Police Procedural

Political Crimes and Offenses

Political Movements

Political Prisoners

Political Thriller

Politics

Subject Index

Subject Index

Character Name Index

This index alphabetically lists the major characters in each featured title. Each character name is followed by a description of the character. Citations also provide titles of the books featuring the character, listed alphabetically if there is more than one title; author names and genre codes. The genre codes are as follows: *c* Popular Fiction, *f* Fantasy, *h* Horror, *i* Inspirational, *m* Mystery, *r* Romance, *s* Science Fiction, *t* Historical, and *w* Western. Numbers refer to the entries that feature each title.

A

Aal Masood, Kamal (Royalty)
The Desert King - Olivia Gates   *r*   278

Abbott, Kathleen (Friend; Spouse)
Ghost at Work - Carolyn Hart   *m*   87

Absolute, Jack (Adventurer; Spy)
Absolute Honor - C.C. Humphreys   *t*   796

Acheron (Deity)
Acheron - Sherrilyn Kenyon   *h*   562

Adam (Biblical Figure)
Eve - Elissa Elliott   *c*   1002

Adam (Musician)
Rock Bottom - Michael Shilling   *c*   1096

Adams, Dara (Gypsy; Royalty)
To Protect a Princess - Gail Barrett   *r*   214

Adams, Dawsey (Farmer)
The Guernsey Literary and Potato Peel Pie Society - Mary Ann Shaffer   *t*   849
The Guernsey Literary and Potato Peel Pie Society - Mary Ann Shaffer   *c*   1094

Adams, Derek (Detective—Private)
The Sirens - William Meikle   *h*   579

Adams, Hope (Worker)
Living With the Dead - Kelley Armstrong   *h*   527

Adderhead (Ruler)
Inkdeath - Cornelia Funke   *f*   452

Adela (Traveller)
Company of Liars - Karen Maitland   *c*   1059

Adolphus, Gustavus (Royalty)
1635: The Dreeson Incident - Eric Flint   *s*   655

Adriana (Wealthy)
Chasing Harry Winston - Lauren Weisberger   *c*   1119

Agricola (Political Figure)
Nox Dormienda - Stanley Kelli   *t*   804

Ahern, Hallie (Journalist; Detective—Amateur)
Teaser - Jan Brogan   *m*   31

Ahriman, Zal (Mythical Creature)
Going Under - Justina Robson   *s*   700

Ahuja, Arjun (Musician)
Family Planning - Karan Mahajan   *c*   1057

Ahuja, Rakesh (Spouse; Parent)
Family Planning - Karan Mahajan   *c*   1057

A'ida (Pharmacist)
From A to X - John Berger   *c*   979

A'isha bint Abi Bakr (Historical Figure; Spouse)
The Jewel of Medina - Sherry Jones   *t*   800

Akemi (Artist)
Midnight - Sister Souljah   *c*   1103

Akira (Military Personnel; Prisoner)
Beside a Burning Sea - John Shors   *t*   851

Alatriste y Tenorio, Diego (Veteran; Military Personnel)
The King's Gold - Arturo Perez-Reverte   *t*   831

Albemarle, Stephen (Diplomat; Spy)
Deep Night - Caroline Petit   *m*   156

Albright, Matt (Detective—Police; Divorced Person)
Ding Dong Dead - Deb Baker   *m*   6

Aldeen, Nina (Professor)
Body Copy - Michael Craven   *m*   58

Alden, Esme (Investigator—Private)
Loose and Easy - Tara Janzen   *r*   305

Alden, Lindy (Nurse)
A Common Ordinary Murder - Donald Pfarrer   *m*   157

Aldrich, Tyler (Wealthy; Businessman)
His Small-Town Girl - Arlene James   *r*   303

Alec (Spy)
Shadows Return - Lynn Flewelling   *f*   448

Alek (Journalist)
The Confessions of Noa Weber - Gail Hareven   *c*   1017

Aleksia (Sorceress)
The Snow Queen - Mercedes Lackey   *f*   469

Alestria (Royalty)
Alexander and Alestria - Sa Shan   *t*   850

Alexander (Government Official; Werewolf)
The Sacred Book of the Werewolf - Victor Pelevin   *h*   587

Alexander, Ignatius (Doctor)
Blindspot: By a Gentleman in Exile and a Lady in Disguise - Jane Kamensky   *c*   1032

Alexander, Ignatius (Slave; Doctor)
Blindspot: By a Gentleman in Exile and a Lady in Disguise - Jane Kamensky   *t*   802

Alexander, James "Jax" (Spy)
The Archangel Project - C.S. Graham   *m*   79

Alexander, Logan Tyler (Lawyer; Mythical Creature)
Fiance at Her Fingertips - Kathleen Bacus   *r*   211

Alexander the Great (Historical Figure; Military Personnel)
Alexander and Alestria - Sa Shan   *t*   850

Alexandra (Historical Figure; Royalty)
The Tsarina's Daughter - Carolly Erickson   *t*   769

Alexandra (Widow(er))
The Widows of Eastwick - John Updike   *c*   1114

Alicia (Young Woman)
Succulent Prey - Wrath James White   *h*   621

Alija (Linguist)
Promised Virgins - Jeffrey Fleishman   *c*   1008

Allah, Iqbal Amir (Store Owner)
Clash of Civilizations Over an Elevator in Piazza Vittorio - Amara Lakhous   *c*   1043

Allardyce, Christian Michael (Nobleman)
The Edge of Desire - Stephanie Laurens   *r*   324

Allegra (Prisoner)
The Night Bird - Catherine Asaro   *f*   426

Allegro, Matteo "Matt" (Businessman; Bridegroom)
Espresso Shot - Cleo Coyle   *m*   56

Alley, Parker (Fisherman)
Fisherman's Bend - Linda Greenlaw   *m*   81

Allon, Gabriel (Spy; Artist)
Moscow Rules - Daniel Silva   *m*   175

Almondine (Dog)
The Story of Edgar Sawtelle - David Wroblewski   *c*   1124

Amber (Worker)
Hellbent and Heartfirst - Kassandra Sims   *h*   608

Amble, Patricia "Tish" (Businesswoman)
Kiss Me If You Dare - Nicole Young   *i*   967

Amelie (Student)
Tokyo Fiancee - Amelie Nothomb   *c*   1069

Ames, Carrie (Doctor; Vampire)
All Souls' Night - Jennifer Armintrout   *h*   526

Anderson, Annie (Journalist; Detective—Amateur)
Deadly Beautiful - Sam Baker   *m*   7

Anderson, Gary (Police Officer)
Bayou Betrayal - Robin Caroll   *i*   890

Anderson, Jaycee (Sports Figure; Businesswoman)
Slippery When Wet - Kimberly Raye   *r*   375

Anderson, Molly (Survivor; Heroine)
Razor Girl - Marianne Mancusi   *r*   342

Anderson, Sherwood (Historical Figure; Writer)
The Wettest County in the World - Matt
    Bondurant   *t*   735

Anderson, Sherwood (Historical Figure)
The Wettest County in the World - Matt
    Bondurant   *c*   981

Anderson, Tom (Businessman)
Lost River - David Fulmer   *t*   775

Andrei (Organized Crime Figure)
The Spy Who Came for Christmas - David
    Morrell   *m*   147

Andrew (Journalist)
Little Bee - Chris Cleave   *c*   992

Angel, Nick (Writer)
Risque Business - Tawny Weber   *r*   415

Angel, Shay (Hunter)
Red Fire - Deidre Knight   *r*   321

Anna (Spouse)
All I Have to Give - Melody Carlson   *i*   886

Ansell, Thomas (Lawyer)
The Salisbury Manuscript - Philip
    Gooden   *t*   783

Ansotegui, Josepe (Fisherman)
Guernica - Dave Boling   *t*   734

Ansotegui, Justo (Farmer)
Guernica - Dave Boling   *t*   734

Ansotegui, Xabier (Fisherman)
Guernica - Dave Boling   *t*   734

Antares (Alien)
Sunborn - Jeffrey A. Carver   *s*   643

Anton, Doge (Government Official)
Webdancers - Brian Herbert   *s*   670

ap Daffyd, Rhodri (Warrior; Minstrel)
Magic in His Kiss - Shari Anton   *r*   207

Aphrodite, Lilly Nelly (Orphan)
The Glimmer Palace - Beatrice Colin   *t*   752

Appleton, Hannah (Companion)
A Wallflower Christmas - Lisa Kleypas   *r*   320

Aquinaldo, Doming (Driver)
Baby Jesus Pawn Shop - Lucia Orth   *c*   1076

Aragon, Carly (Teenager)
Be Strong and Curvaceous - Shelley
    Adina   *i*   874

Aras (Alien)
Judge - Karen Traviss   *s*   715

Aravan (Sea Captain; Explorer)
City of Jade - Dennis L. McKiernan   *f*   484

Archer, Joanna (Celebrity; Psychic)
The Touch of Twilight - Vicki
    Pettersson   *h*   588

Archer, Jonathan (Spaceship Captain; Military
Personnel)
Kobayashi Maru - Michael A. Martin   *s*   680

Archer, Xavier (Wealthy)
The Touch of Twilight - Vicki
    Pettersson   *h*   588

Archeth (Government Official)
The Steel Remains - Richard K. Morgan   *f*   492

Archmont, Vinnie (Artist; Crime Suspect)
The Rose Conspiracy - Craig Parshall   *i*   940

Arcturus (Doctor)
Nox Dormienda - Stanley Kelli   *t*   804

Arellano, Carmen (Vampire)
The Undead Karma Sutra - Mario
    Acevedo   *h*   524

Argalia, Nino (Military Personnel)
The Enchantress of Florence - Salman
    Rushdie   *c*   1089

Aristide (Scientist)
Implied Spaces - Walter Jon Williams   *s*   722

Arjun (Traveller)
Thunderer - Felix Gilman   *f*   454

Arkazy, Viktor (Detective—Private)
The Paris Enigma - Pablo De Santis   *t*   761

Arkhorn, Yimt (Royalty)
A Darkness Forged in Fire - Chris
    Evans   *f*   445

Arminger, Mathilda (Prisoner)
The Scourge of God - S.M. Stirling   *s*   712

Artaxerxes II (Historical Figure; Royalty)
The Lost Army - Valero Manfredi   *t*   816

Arthur (Nobleman)
Here Lies Arthur - Philip Reeve   *f*   500

Arzaky, Viktor (Detective—Private)
The Paris Enigma - Pablo De Santis   *m*   63

Ashburn, Winter (Gentlewoman; Thief)
Passion and Pleasure in London - Melody
    Thomas   *r*   408

Ashen (Ruler)
The Knight of the Red Beard - Andre
    Norton   *f*   493

Ashling (Religious)
Morningtide - Cory J. Herndon   *f*   459

Ashmore, Emma (Child)
One Perfect Gift - Kathleen Morgan   *i*   936

Ashmore, Jessica (Nurse; Parent)
One Perfect Gift - Kathleen Morgan   *i*   936

Ashton, Juliet (Writer)
*The Guernsey Literary and Potato Peel Pie Soci-
ety* - Mary Ann Shaffer   *t*   849
*The Guernsey Literary and Potato Peel Pie Soci-
ety* - Mary Ann Shaffer   *c*   1094

Ashtyn (Nobleman; Military Personnel)
Daughter of Egypt - Constance
    O'Banyon   *r*   362

Ashwin, Holly (Mythical Creature; Professor)
Dark Desires after Dusk - Kresley Cole   *r*   246

Astrid (Noblewoman)
Surrender to Me - Sophie Jordan   *r*   309

Atarus, Ryven (Military Personnel; Nobleman)
No Words Alone - Autumn Dawn   *r*   252

Athesa (Noblewoman)
The Long Look - Richard Parks   *f*   494

Atreides, Paul (Ruler)
Paul of Dune - Brian Herbert   *s*   669

Auerbach, Phoebe (Archaeologist)
Night of the Furies - Davis Angsten   *h*   525

Augustine, Rutger (Military Personnel)
Dark Disciple - Anthony Reynolds   *s*   696

Augustus (Fugitive)
Strength and Honor - R.M. Meluch   *s*   687

Aurelio (Police Officer)
Stray Dog Winter - David Francis   *c*   1009

Austen, Cassandra (Historical Figure)
Cassandra and Jane - Jill Pitkeathley   *t*   834

Austen, Jane (Historical Figure; Writer)
Cassandra and Jane - Jill Pitkeathley   *t*   834

Axiom (Deity)
Between Light and Dark - Elissa Wilds   *r*   418

Aylis (Explorer; Psychic)
City of Jade - Dennis L. McKiernan   *f*   484

Ayot, Jonah (Student—Graduate)
The Reverend's Apprentice - David N.
    Odhiambo   *c*   1074

B

B., Luciana (Secretary)
The Book of Murder - Guillermo
    Martinez   *m*   138

Babcock, Edgar (Detective—Homicide)
Death Swatch - Laura Childs   *m*   46

Bacco, Nanietta (Government Official)
Mere Mortals - David Mack   *s*   678

Bagoas (Slave)
Alexander and Alestria - Sa Shan   *t*   850

Bailey, Anna (Sister)
Shadows of Lancaster County - Mindy Starns
    Clark   *i*   891

Bainbridge, Darrin (Journalist)
The Bishop's Daughter - Tiffany L.
    Warren   *i*   962

Bainbridge, Tommy (Sports Figure; Philanthropist)
The Man for Me - Gemma Bruce   *r*   229

Baines, Tommy (Convict)
Ritual - Mo Hayder   *m*   91

Balboa, Inigo (Ward; Teenager)
The King's Gold - Arturo Perez-Reverte   *t*   831

Balducci, Vinnie (Vampire; Criminal)
Just One Bite - Kimberly Raye   *h*   591

Baldwin, Joanne (Sorceress)
Gale Force - Rachel Caine   *f*   435

Balkhi, Djalal al-din Mohammad (Historical Figure; Religious)
Rumi: The Fire of Love - Nahal Tajadod   *t*   856

Bandara, Gamini (Political Figure)
The Last Theorem - Arthur C. Clarke   *s*   644

Bandicut, John (Spaceman)
Sunborn - Jeffrey A. Carver   *s*   643

Bane, Oscar (Crime Suspect)
Scarpetta - Patricia Cornwell   *m*   53

Baptiste, Dante (Vampire; Musician)
In the Blood - Adrian Phoenix   *h*   589

Barclay, Ben (Lawyer)
The Daddy Verdict - Karen Rose Smith   *r*   393

Bareris (Warrior)
Undead - Richard Lee Byers   *f*   434

Baristani, Ellysetta (Healer; Royalty)
King of Sword and Sky - C.L. Wilson   *r*   419

Barker, Cyrus (Detective—Private)
The Black Hand - Will Thomas   *m*   190

Barnes, Natalie (Innkeeper; Detective—Amateur)
Murder Most Maine - Karen
    MacInerney   *m*   130

Barnett, Samantha (Baker; Businesswoman)
Marry-Me Christmas - Shirley Jump   *r*   310

Barone, Regina (Caterer; Single Parent)
Sea Fever - Virginia Kantra   *r*   314

Barrett, Nola (Aged Person)
In a Dark Season - Vicki Lane   *m*   115

Blake, Peter (Orphan; Child)
Without Conscience - David Stuart
    Davies   *m*   62
Without Conscience - David Stuart
    Davies   *t*   759

Blandford, Natalie (Noblewoman)
A Wallflower Christmas - Lisa Kleypas   *r*   320

Blank, Sandford (Detective—Private)
End of the Century - Chris Roberson   *s*   699

Bledsoe, Brady (Sports Figure)
Just Too Good to Be True - E. Lynn
    Harris   *c*   1019

Bledsoe, Carmyn (Parent)
Just Too Good to Be True - E. Lynn
    Harris   *c*   1019

Bledsoe, Paul (Detective—Homicide)
The 7th Victim - Alan Jacobson   *m*   100

Bleifert, Tereska (Student—College)
Shoot the Lawyer Twice - Michael
    Bowen   *m*   29

Bligh, Conor (Mythical Creature; Warrior)
Lost in You - Alix Rickloff   *r*   377

Bliss, Vicky (Art Historian; Detective—Amateur)
The Laughter of Dead Kings - Elizabeth
    Peters   *m*   155

Blomkvist, Carl Mikael (Journalist;
Detective—Amateur)
The Girl with the Dragon Tattoo - Stieg
    Larsson   *m*   118

Bloodsworth, Andrew (Vampire)
Liquid Diet - Michael McCarty   *h*   575

Bloom, Charity (Fiance(e))
Chasing Charity - Marcia Gruver   *i*   909

Bloom, Natalie (Student—College)
College Girl - Patricia Weitz   *c*   1120

Bluhm, Carlos (Spouse)
Lima Nights - Marie Arana   *c*   970

Blumenfeld, Isaac Jacob (Tailor; Prisoner)
Isaac's Torah - Angel Wagenstein   *c*   1118
Isaac's Torah - Angel Wagenstein   *t*   866

Boaz, Jacyn (Worker)
Hellbent and Heartfirst - Kassandra
    Sims   *h*   608

Bobby (Musician)
Rock Bottom - Michael Shilling   *c*   1096

Bohme, Kaspar (Warrior)
Curse of the Necrarch - Steven Savile   *f*   513

Bokov, Vladimir (Military Personnel)
The Man with the Iron Heart - Harry
    Turtledove   *s*   716

Bolaris, Hallie (Teenager)
The Music Teacher - Barbara Hall   *c*   1016

Bollingsworth, Priscilla (Detective—Homicide;
Divorced Person)
Black and White and Dead All Over - John
    Darnton   *m*   61

Bolsover, James Watson (Writer)
By Chance - Martin Corrick   *c*   995

Bolsover, Kitty (Spouse)
By Chance - Martin Corrick   *c*   995

Bombay, Mississippi "Missi" (Criminal; Inventor)
Stand by Your Hitman - Leslie Langtry   *r*   323

Bondeson, Euthanasia (Writer)
The Streets of Babylon - Carina Buram   *t*   739

Bondurant, Forrest (Bootlegger)
The Wettest County in the World - Matt
    Bondurant   *c*   981

The Wettest County in the World - Matt
    Bondurant   *t*   735

Bondurant, Howard (Bootlegger)
The Wettest County in the World - Matt
    Bondurant   *t*   735

Bonwiller, Henry (Political Figure)
America America - Ethan Canin   *c*   987

Bookchild, Rossamunde (Child; Orphan)
Lamplighter - D.M. Cornish   *f*   440

Boone (Detective—Police; Boyfriend)
Nothing but Trouble - Susan May
    Warren   *i*   961

Borden, Daniel (Accountant)
Daniel's Den - Brandt Dodson   *i*   901

Bordwin, Mike (Principal)
Testimony - Anita Shreve   *c*   1097

Bosch, Harry (Detective—Homicide)
The Brass Verdict - Michael Connelly   *m*   52

Boughton, Glory (Care Giver)
Home - Marilynne Robinson   *c*   1085

Boughton, Jack (Unemployed)
Home - Marilynne Robinson   *c*   1085

Boughton, Robert (Parent)
Home - Marilynne Robinson   *c*   1085

Bowman, Marcus (Explorer)
Riders of the Storm - Julie E. Czerneda   *s*   648

Bowman, Rafe (Businessman)
A Wallflower Christmas - Lisa Kleypas   *r*   320

Bowman, Stephen (Journalist)
Murder at Deviation Junction - Andrew
    Martin   *m*   136

Bowman, Zack (Worker)
Devil May Ride - Wendy Roberts   *m*   165
Devil May Ride - Wendy Roberts   *h*   595

Box, Lucifer (Spy)
Black Butterfly - Mark Gatiss   *t*   779

Boyer, August "Augie" (Detective—Private; Drug
Addict)
The Man in the Blizzard - Bart
    Schneider   *m*   169

Boyle, Billy (Police Officer; Military Personnel)
Blood Alone - James R. Benn   *m*   20
Blood Alone - James R. Benn   *t*   732

Boyle, Danny (Police Officer)
Hell Hole - Chris Grabenstein   *m*   78

Boynton, Cal (Religious)
The Lace Reader - Brunonia Barry   *c*   976

Braddock, Denton (Professor)
Kiss Me If You Dare - Nicole Young   *i*   967

Bradford, Emmaline (Fiance(e))
A Promise for Spring - Kim Vogel
    Sawyer   *i*   948

Brady, Devon (Veterinarian)
Dark Summer - Iris Johansen   *c*   1028

Brannigan, Ryan (Landlord; Fisherman)
Destiny Bay - Sarah Abbot   *r*   200

Branza (Child)
Tender Morsels - Margo Lanagan   *f*   470

Braun, Alexander (Spy)
Stealing Trinity - Ward Larsen   *t*   810

Braun, Alexander (Military Personnel; Spy)
Stealing Trinity - Ward Larsen   *m*   116

Braverman, Mira (Psychologist)
The Delivery Room - Sylvia Brownrigg   *c*   984

Brax (Warrior)
The Golden Tower - Fiona Patton   *f*   495

Brenneman, Katie (Child-Care Giver)
Wanted - Shelley Shephard Gray   *i*   908

Brewster, Sky Eyes (Indian; Widow(er))
Pale Moon Stalker - Shirl Henke   *r*   295

Briar (Vampire)
Angel's Pain - Maggie Shayne   *r*   386

Briec the Mighty (Mythical Creature)
About a Dragon - G.A. Aiken   *r*   202

Bright, Darcy (Artist)
Stray Dog Winter - David Francis   *c*   1009

Bright, Fin (Artist)
Stray Dog Winter - David Francis   *c*   1009

Bright, Pearl (Expatriate; Orphan)
Thirteen Orphans - Jane Lindskold   *f*   473

Brightly, Cynthia (Gentlewoman)
Like No Other Lover - Julie Anne Long   *r*   331

Brioche, Jeanette (Businesswoman)
Welcome to Serenity - Sherryl Woods   *r*   421

Broadus, Jimmy Wayne (Worker; Musician)
Hellbent and Heartfirst - Kassandra
    Sims   *h*   608

Brodie, Jackson (Detective—Private)
When Will There Be Good News? - Kate
    Atkinson   *c*   971

Brody, Meredith (Abuse Victim)
The Spy Who Came for Christmas - David
    Morrell   *m*   147

Brodzinski, Tom (Criminal)
The Butt - Will Self   *c*   1092

Brogan, Ray (Kidnapper; Artist)
The Big O - Declan Burke   *m*   36

Bromley, Phineas (Military Personnel; Highwayman)
Before the Scandal - Suzanne Enoch   *r*   263

Brooke, Darell (Writer)
Dark Pursuit - Brandilyn Collins   *i*   893

Brooke, Maxwell (Nobleman)
The Dangerous Duke - Christine Wells   *r*   416

Brooks, Laney (Parent; Spouse)
I Smile Back - Amy Koppelman   *c*   1040

Brown, Lizzie (Witch; Warrior)
The Accidental Demon Slayer - Angie
    Fox   *r*   274

Brrr (Animal)
A Lion Among Men - Gregory
    Maguire   *c*   1056

Brunovsky, Nikita (Businessman)
Illegal Action - Stella Rimington   *m*   164

Bryant, Arthur (Detective—Police)
The Victoria Vanishes - Christopher
    Fowler   *m*   68

Bryant, Dwight (Police Officer)
Death's Half Acre - Margaret Maron   *m*   135

Bryant, Michael (Journalist)
Christmas Spirit - Rebecca York   *r*   422

Brynngar (Spaceship Captain)
Battle for the Abyss - Ben Counter   *s*   647

Bryson, Calvin (Wealthy)
The Knights of the Cornerstone - James P.
    Blaylock   *f*   430

Buchanan, Ian (Military Personnel; Recluse)
A Virgin River Christmas - Robyn Carr   *r*   236

Buchanan, Jeremy (Rancher)
The Reluctant Cowgirl - Christine
    Lynxwiler   *i*   933

Character Name Index

Corbuc, Sybilla (Servant; Midwife)
Shadow Rider - Kathrynn Dennis *r* 254

Corbulo (Military Personnel)
Red Fury - James Swallow *s* 713

Cord (Artisan)
Anathem - Neal Stephenson *s* 711

Corimar, Steven (Police Officer)
Found You - Mary SanGiovanni *h* 602

Cornick, Bran (Leader)
Cry Wolf - Patricia Briggs *f* 431

Cornick, Charles (Werewolf)
Cry Wolf - Patricia Briggs *f* 431

Cornwallis, Charles (Military Personnel)
The United States of Atlantis - Harry
    Turtledove *s* 717

Corrington, Janelle (Doctor; Guardian)
The Druid Made Me Do It - Natale
    Stenzel *r* 402

Corso, Elissa (Teenager)
Collision Course - William Shatner *s* 706

Corydonais (Immortal; Royalty)
Crate and Peril - J.D. Warren *r* 413

Cosi, Clare (Businesswoman)
Espresso Shot - Cleo Coyle *m* 56

Costa, Hector (Detective—Police)
Buried Strangers - Leighton Gage *m* 71

Coughlin, Danny (Police Officer)
The Given Day - Dennis Lehane *t* 812
The Given Day - Dennis Lehane *c* 1046

Covington, Rebecca (Journalist)
Talk of the Town - Sherrill Bodine *r* 220

Cowper, William (Historical Figure)
The Winner of Sorrow - Brian Lynch *c* 1053

Cox, Dario (Musician)
Rock Bottom - Michael Shilling *c* 1096

Coy, Flora (Aged Person)
Dead Dancing Women - Elizabeth Kane
    Buzzelli *m* 37

Coyne, Mara (Lawyer)
The Map Thief - Heather Terrell *m* 187

Crabbel (Sailor)
The Black Ship - Diana Pharaoh Francis *f* 450

Crae (Military Personnel)
Gordath Wood - Patrice Sarath *f* 512

Craft, Cooper (Doctor)
3 Men and a Body - Stephanie Bond *m* 28

Craig, Renato (Detective—Private)
The Paris Enigma - Pablo De Santis *m* 63

Crais, Finnula (Kidnapper; Outlaw)
Ransom My Heart - Mia Thermopolis *r* 406

Crandall, Gregory (Nobleman)
Mithras Court - David A. Page *h* 586

Craven, Melanie (Spouse)
No Rest for the Wiccan - Madelyn Alt *m* 1

Crenshaw, Anthony (Nobleman)
Miss Delacorte Speaks Her Mind - Heidi
    Ashworth *r* 209

Cromwell, Jo (Religious; Relative)
Barefoot Brides - Annie Jones *i* 924

Cromwell, Kate (Doctor; Relative)
Barefoot Brides - Annie Jones *i* 924

Cronenberg, Richard (Editor)
Entertaining Disasters - Nancy Spiller *c* 1105

Cross, Luther (Detective—Police)
Servant: The Acceptance - L.L. Foster *r* 271

Crowe, Painter (Spy)
The Last Oracle - James Rollins *s* 701

Crowle, Jack (Sailor)
Sea of Poppies - Amitav Ghosh *c* 1013

Crowther, Georgine (Parent)
Deception's Daughter - Cordelia Frances
    Biddle *m* 23

Crozier, Simon (Administrator)
Black Cathedral - L.H. Maynard *h* 574

Cruz, Gabriel (Scientist)
The Age of the Conglomerates - Thomas
    Nevins *s* 690

Culhane (Mythical Creature; Warrior)
Bedeviled - Maureen Child *r* 243

Cullen, Edward (Vampire; Teenager)
Breaking Dawn - Stephenie Meyer *h* 580

Cummings, Elizabeth (Heiress; Socialite)
Marry Christmas - Jane Goodger *r* 281

Curtis, Edward S. (Historical Figure; Photographer)
To Catch the Lightning - Alan Cheuse *t* 748

Cuthwin (Teenager)
Heldenhammer - Graham McNeill *f* 487

Cutler, Doyle (Wealthy)
Security - Stephen Amidon *c* 969

Cutler, Madeira "Maddie" (Designer;
    Detective—Amateur)
A Veiled Deception - Annette Blair *m* 25

Cutter, Derek (Teenager; Crime Suspect)
Too Close to Home - Linwood Barclay *m* 11

Cutter, Jim (Businessman; Detective—Amateur)
Too Close to Home - Linwood Barclay *m* 11

Cyrus (Cyborg)
Two to the Fifth - Piers Anthony *f* 425

Cyrus the Younger (Historical Figure; Royalty)
The Lost Army - Valero Manfredi *t* 816

Cythera, Dalia (Worker)
Mechanicus - Graham McNeill *s* 686

D

da Ivan pa Crystal Temple, Gregor (Religious)
Harmony - C.F. Bentley *s* 633

d'Acquin, Josse (Mercenary)
The Paths of the Air - Alys Clare *t* 749

Daisuke, Sato (Agent)
The China Lover - Ian Buruma *t* 741

Dalgliesh, Adam (Detective—Police; Writer)
The Private Patient - P.D. James *m* 101

Daljit (Scientist)
Implied Spaces - Walter Jon Williams *s* 722

Dallas, Eve (Detective—Homicide)
Salvation in Death - J.D. Robb *s* 698

Dallen (Mythical Creature)
Foundation - Mercedes Lackey *f* 467

Dallencort, Evelyne (Socialite)
Lost River - David Fulmer *m* 70

Dalrymple, Daisy (Journalist;
    Detective—Amateur)
The Black Ship - Carola Dunn *t* 765

Dalziel, Andrew "Andy" (Detective—Police)
The Price of Butcher's Meat - Reginald
    Hill *m* 94

Dampier, Henry (Salesman)
The Bible Salesman - Clyde Edgerton *t* 767

Danaus (Vampire Hunter)
Nightwalker - Jocelyn Drake *h* 539

Danby, Lex (Saloon Keeper/Owner; Widow(er))
Stand by Your Hitman - Leslie Langtry *r* 323

Daniecki, Moritz (Military Personnel)
Random Acts of Heroic Love - Danny
    Scheinmann *c* 1090

Daniels, Debra (Counselor)
Fiance at Her Fingertips - Kathleen
    Bacus *r* 211

Dansson, Howard (Spaceman; Worker)
Slow Train to Arcturus - Eric Flint *s* 657

Dante (Wizard)
Succubus Dreams - Richelle Mead *h* 578

Dante, Greyson (Agent)
Personal Demons - Stacia Kane *h* 560

Daphne (Ghost)
The Secrets of Laurel Oaks - Lois Ruby *h* 598

Dara, Mac (Royalty)
Heir to Sevenwaters - Juliet Marillier *f* 481

Darby, Matthew (Businessman)
No Exit - B.K. Evenson *s* 654

Darcy, Elizabeth Bennet (Gentlewoman; Spouse)
The Matters at Mansfield - Carrie
    Bebris *t* 731

Darcy, Fitzwilliam (Gentleman; Spouse)
The Independence of Miss Mary Bennet - Colleen
    McCullough *t* 818
The Matters at Mansfield - Carrie
    Bebris *t* 731

D'Arcy, Helen (Counselor)
Christmas Is Murder - C.S. Challinor *m* 43

Darioq, Magos (Prisoner)
Dark Disciple - Anthony Reynolds *s* 696

Dark Sky, Frances (Teenager; Indian)
Dead Hot Shot - Victoria Houston *m* 95

Darnell, Layla (Unemployed)
The Hollow - Nora Roberts *h* 594

Darnshof, Greta (Editor)
Illegal Action - Stella Rimington *m* 164

D'Artigo, Camille (Witch)
Dragon Wytch - Yasmine Galenorn *f* 453

D'Artigo, Delilah (Mythical Creature)
Dragon Wytch - Yasmine Galenorn *f* 453

D'Artigo, Menolly (Vampire)
Dragon Wytch - Yasmine Galenorn *f* 453

d'Aubec, Edmond (Nobleman; Businessman)
Bright Hair about the Bone - Barbara
    Cleverly *m* 49

Davey (Child)
The Scrubs - Simon Janus *h* 557

David (Parent)
A Cedar Cove Christmas - Debbie
    Macomber *c* 1055

David (Mythical Creature)
Gale Force - Rachel Caine *f* 435

David (Spouse; Musician)
Michal - Jill Eileen Smith *i* 951

Davidsson, Gerlof (Aged Person)
Echoes from the Dead - Johan Theorin *m* 189

Davidsson, Julia (Nurse; Detective—Amateur)
Echoes from the Dead - Johan Theorin *m* 189

Davies, Ian (Police Officer)
Ex-Kop - Warren Hammond *s* 667

Evvy (Apprentice)
The Melting Stones - Tamora Pierce *f* 497

F

Fairchild, Kate (Gentlewoman; Widow(er))
The Dangerous Duke - Christine Wells *r* 416

Fairfax, Griffin (Gentleman; Single Parent)
His Wicked Sins - Eve Silver *r* 388

Faithfull, Emily "Fido" (Businesswoman)
The Sealed Letter - Emma Donoghue *t* 763

Falcone, Tony (Guardian; Businessman)
Angel Unaware - Elizabeth Sinclair *r* 389

Falconer, Leah (Businesswoman)
Speak of the Devil - Shari Shattuck *h* 606

Fallon, Rick (Security Officer; Divorced Person)
The Other Side of Silence - Bill Pronzini *m* 159

Fallon, Susanna (Governess)
American Anthem - B.J. Hoff *i* 920

Farewell, Peter (Mythical Creature; Explorer)
Soul of Fire - Sarah A. Hoyt *f* 462

Farragut, John (Spaceship Captain; Military Personnel)
Strength and Honor - R.M. Meluch *s* 687

Faulkner, Anna (Gentlewoman)
Netherfield Park Revisited - Rebecca Ann Collins *t* 753

Faulkner, Sam (Teenager; Time Traveler)
The Gate of Days - Guillaume Prevost *f* 499

Federov, Yuri (Organized Crime Figure; Businessman)
Conspiracy in Kiev - Noel Hynd *m* 97

Fegley, Theodore Mead (Genius; Teenager)
Life After Genius - M. Ann Jacoby *c* 1027

Fell, Alice (Teenager; Fugitive)
End of the Century - Chris Roberson *s* 699

Fenix, Marcus (Military Personnel)
Aspho Fields - Karen Traviss *s* 714

Fenner, Matthew (Businessman; Computer Expert)
Sweet Trouble - Susan Mallery *r* 340

Fernanda (Teenager)
Everything under the Sky - Matilda Asensi *t* 726

Fernandez, Maria (Dancer)
Lima Nights - Marie Arana *c* 970

Ferrell, Devlin (Bastard Son; Businessman)
Unlacing Lilly - Gail Ranstrom *r* 374

Ferris, Julie (Real Estate Agent)
Season of Strangers - Kat Martin *r* 345

Ferris, Lewellyn "Lew" (Police Officer)
Dead Hot Shot - Victoria Houston *m* 95

Finch, Emilia (Teenager; Gypsy)
The Gypsy Crown - Kate Forsyth *f* 449

Finch, Gillian (Friend)
Keeping Secrets - Owen Madoc *t* 814

Finch, Mary (Orphan; Heir)
The Blackstone Key - Rose Melikan *t* 822

Finch, Mary (Teacher; Detective—Amateur)
The Blackstone Key - Rose Melikan *m* 143

Finley, Randall (Government Official)
Too Close to Home - Linwood Barclay *m* 11

Fiona (Settler)
Dragonheart - Todd McCaffrey *s* 683

Firefist, Orivon (Slave)
Dark Vengeance - Ed Greenwood *f* 457

Fisher, Mary-Margaret (Religious)
The Passion of Mary-Margaret - Lisa Samson *i* 947

Fisher, Phryne (Detective—Amateur)
Death by Water - Kerry Greenwood *t* 786
Queen of the Flowers - Kerry Greenwood *t* 787

Fitzgerald, Gideon (Scientist)
Fallen - Claire Delacroix *s* 651

Fitzpatrick, Laetitia (Young Woman)
Absolute Honor - C.C. Humphreys *t* 796

Fitzstephen, Hugo (Nobleman; Captive)
Ransom My Heart - Mia Thermopolis *r* 406

Flanagan, Marty (Police Officer)
Dirty Water - Mary-Ann Tirone Smith *m* 178

Fleming, Melisande (Gentlewoman)
To Seduce a Sinner - Elizabeth Hoyt *r* 299

Flemming, Dave (Religious)
8 Sandpiper Way - Debbie Macomber *r* 335

Flemming, Emily (Housewife)
8 Sandpiper Way - Debbie Macomber *r* 335

Fletcher, Alec (Detective—Police)
The Black Ship - Carola Dunn *t* 765

Fletcher, Kieran (Divorced Person; Bully)
Hold My Hand - Serena Mackesy *m* 131

Florens (Slave)
A Mercy - Toni Morrison *c* 1063
A Mercy - Toni Morrison *t* 826

Floyd, C.J. (Detective—Private)
Blackbird, Farewell - Robert Greer *m* 82

Fly-in-Amber (Alien)
Marsbound - Joe Haldeman *s* 666

Fly-Wing, Jimmy (Indian)
To Catch the Lightning - Alan Cheuse *t* 748

Flynn, Aidan (Detective—Private; Heir)
Deadly Night - Heather Graham *r* 287

Flynn, Aster (Teenager)
Just Another Girl - Melody Carlson *i* 887

Flynn, Jeremy (Detective—Private; Musician)
Deadly Harvest - Heather Graham *r* 286

Flynn, Lily (Teenager; Mentally Ill Person)
Just Another Girl - Melody Carlson *i* 887

Flynn, Mattie (Singer)
A Claim of Her Own - Stephanie Grace Whitson *i* 963

Flynn, Zach (Detective—Private)
Deadly Gift - Heather Graham *r* 285

Folchart, Meggie (Child)
Inkdeath - Cornelia Funke *f* 452

Folchart, Mortimer (Artisan)
Inkdeath - Cornelia Funke *f* 452

Fontana, John (Psychic; Businessman)
Dark Light - Jayne Castle *r* 240

Force, Jack (Teenager)
Revelations - Melissa de la Cruz *h* 538

Force, Mimi (Wealthy)
Revelations - Melissa de la Cruz *h* 538

Forester, Bryan (Contractor; Crime Suspect)
Cruel Intent - J.A. Jance *m* 102

Forsyth, Aiden (Nobleman; Military Personnel)
Phantom's Touch - Julie Leto *r* 329

Forsythe, Ariana (Young Woman)
Before the Season Ends - Linore Rose Burkard *i* 882

Forsythe, Ariana (Fiance(e); Crime Victim)
The House in Grosvenor Square - Linore Rose Burkard *i* 883

Fortune, Allie (Detective—Private)
Miss Match - Sara Mills *i* 935

Fortune, Benjamin (Sports Figure; Crime Suspect)
Crash Into Me - Jill Sorenson *m* 180

Fortune, Chance (Teenager)
Chance Fortune in the Shadow Zone - Shane Berryhill *s* 635

Foster, Alex (Worker; Psychic)
Cursed - Jamie Leigh Hansen *h* 548

Foster, Vivienne "Vivi" (Psychic)
Ace Is Wild - Penny McCall *r* 348

Fox, Charlie (Bodyguard)
Third Strike - Zoe Sharp *m* 171

Fox, Michael (Prisoner)
The Jigsaw Man - Gord Rollo *h* 597

Foxcroft, Richard (Doctor)
Third Strike - Zoe Sharp *m* 171

Frankland, Shan (Spacewoman; Immortal)
Judge - Karen Traviss *s* 715

Franklin, Jess (Lawyer)
Brides of the Impaler - Edward Lee *h* 567

Freed, Elliot (Businessman; Detective—Amateur)
It Happened One Knife - Jeffrey Cohen *m* 51

Freeman (Worker)
Skin Lane - Neil Bartlett *c* 977

Freeman, Scott (Salesman)
The Damned - William Ollie *h* 584

French, Mozelle (Volunteer)
The Chocolate Snowman Murders - JoAnna Carl *m* 41

Freud, Sigmund (Historical Figure; Doctor)
The Little Book - Selden Edwards *t* 768

Freymore, Helen "Nell" (Noblewoman)
His Captive Lady - Anne Gracie *r* 284

Frye, Joe (Police Officer)
South of Hell - P.J. Parrish *m* 152

Fudir (Criminal)
The January Dancer - Michael Flynn *s* 659

Fulton, Annalise (Real Estate Agent)
Parents in Training - Barbara McMahon *r* 350

Fulton, Dominic (Computer Expert)
Parents in Training - Barbara McMahon *r* 350

G

Gabriel (Mythical Creature)
Up in Smoke - Katie MacAlister *r* 333

Galaad (Knight)
End of the Century - Chris Roberson *s* 699

Gallagher, Kate (Journalist; Detective—Amateur)
A Killer Workout - Kathryn Lilley *m* 122

Gallatin, Beth (Young Woman; Neighbor)
A Love to Last Forever - Tracie Peterson *i* 942

Gallatin, Gwen (Innkeeper; Orphan)
A Promise to Believe In - Tracie Peterson *r* 368

Gallatin, Lacy (Young Woman)
A Dream to Call My Own - Tracie Peterson *i* 941

Gang, Song (Scholar)
Brothers - Yu Hua *c* 1025

Gant, Bobby Lee (Crime Suspect)
Blood Lines - Mel Odom *i* 937

Gant, Victor (Organized Crime Figure)
Blood Lines - Mel Odom *i* 937

Garcia, Oscar (Detective—Police)
Greasing the Pinata - Tim Maleeny *m* 133

Gard (Mythical Creature; Slave)
The House of the Stag - Kage Baker *f* 427

Gardella Grantworth de Lacy, Victoria (Noblewoman; Vampire Hunter)
When Twilight Burns - Colleen Gleason *r* 280

Garec (Woodsman)
The Larion Senators - Robert Scott *f* 515

Garibaldi, Katerina Pavlova (Noblewoman; Jeweler)
Enticing the Prince - Patricia Grasso *r* 288

Garnett, Nick (Security Officer)
Stalking Susan - Julie Kramer *m* 113

Garrahan, Annie (Nurse)
The Nightingales of Troy - Alice Fulton *t* 776

Garrahan, Mamie Flynn (Spouse)
The Nightingales of Troy - Alice Fulton *t* 776

Garrahan, Ruth (Young Woman)
The Nightingales of Troy - Alice Fulton *t* 776

Garrett, Geoffrey (Rancher; Fiance(e))
A Promise for Spring - Kim Vogel Sawyer *i* 948

Garrett, Michael (Military Personnel)
Lover's Kiss - Mary Blayney *r* 218

Garrett, Pat (Historical Figure; Lawman)
Lucky Billy - John Vernon *t* 863

Garrett, Toni (Waiter/Waitress)
Eggs in Purgatory - Laura Childs *m* 47

Garric (Ruler)
The Gods Return - David Drake *f* 442

Garritt, Eldyn (Businessman)
The Magicians and Mrs. Quent - Galen Beckett *f* 429

Garvaggio, Vinnie (Criminal)
The Winter of Her Discontent - Kathryn Miller Haines *m* 83

Gastner, Bill (Police Officer)
The Fourth Time Is Murder - Steven F. Havill *m* 90

Gates, Jimmy "Freeman Walker" (Slave)
Freeman Walker - David Allan Cates *t* 746

Gavin, Olivia (Vampire)
Let the Night Begin - Kathryn Smith *r* 394

Gavin, Reign (Vampire)
Let the Night Begin - Kathryn Smith *r* 394

Gearheart (Military Personnel)
Titanicus - Dan Abnett *s* 624

Geary, Monica (Actress)
Power Play - Deirdre Martin *r* 344

Gemma (Orphan; Friend)
Fireflies in December - Jennifer Erin Valent *i* 959

Gentry, Meredith (Royalty)
Swallowing Darkness - Laurell Hamilton *f* 458

Geralt (Wizard)
Blood of Elves - Andrzej Sapkowski *f* 511

Ghar (Nobleman)
The Engine's Child - Holly Phillips *f* 496

Gianelli, Eddie (Detective—Amateur)
Hey There (You with the Gun in Your Hand) - Robert J. Randisi *t* 836

Gianelli, Sam (Boyfriend)
Lie Down with the Devil - Linda Barnes *m* 12

Gibbs, Katherine "Kitty" (Captive; Amnesiac)
Irreversible - Liz Maverick *r* 346

Gideon (Vampire)
Wicked Game - Jeri Smith-Ready *h* 610

Gifford, Jessica (Governess)
The Shocking Lord Standon - Louise Allen *r* 205

Gil (Handyman)
Nose Down, Eyes Up - Merrill Markoe *c* 1061

Gillette, Claudia (Journalist)
Inside Story - Susan Page Davis *i* 899

Gillette, Donald (Businessman)
Freezing Point - Karen Dionne *s* 653

Gilmore, Casey (Rancher)
Searching for Santa - Janet Dailey *r* 248

Gilmour (Government Official)
The Larion Senators - Robert Scott *f* 515

Gilmour, Toni (Assistant)
A Spoonful of Poison - M.C. Beaton *m* 17

Giordano, Annabelle (Teenager)
Written in Blood - Sheila Lowe *m* 127

Girard, Sierra (Store Owner)
The Daddy Verdict - Karen Rose Smith *r* 393

Givell, Maria (Art Historian)
The Gaudi Key - Esteban Martin *m* 137

Glanville, Humphrey (Criminal)
Lifeblood - Tom Becker *h* 531

Goddard, Christopher (Child)
Kissing Games of the World - Sandi Kahn Shelton *c* 1095

Goland, Daric (Military Personnel)
Titanicus - Dan Abnett *s* 624

Gold, Sullivan (Administrator)
The Ashes of Worlds - Kevin J. Anderson *s* 627

Goldfarb, Emmanuel "Manny" (Lawyer)
Salvation Boulevard - Larry Beinhart *m* 18

Goldman, Emma (Historical Figure)
The Given Day - Dennis Lehane *c* 1046

Goldman, Ruth (Scientist)
Plague War - Jeff Carlson *s* 641

Goldner, Sima (Store Owner)
Sima's Undergarments for Women - Ilana Stanger-Ross *c* 1106

Gomez, Felix (Vampire; Detective—Private)
The Undead Karma Sutra - Mario Acevedo *h* 524

Gonzalez, Vicente (Police Officer)
Blood Wedding - P.J. Brooke *m* 32

Gooch, Mindy (Editor)
One Fifth Avenue - Candace Bushnell *c* 986

Goodfellow, Robin "Kane" (Mythical Creature)
The Druid Made Me Do It - Natale Stenzel *r* 402

Goodluck, Justine (Detective—Police)
Coyote's Wife - Aimee Thurlo *m* 191

Goodweather, Elizabeth (Farmer; Widow(er))
In a Dark Season - Vicki Lane *m* 115

Goran (Military Personnel; Alien)
A Burning House - Keith R.A. DeCandido *s* 650

Gordon, Elaine (Artist)
Open Doors - Gloria Goldreich *c* 1014

Gordon, Georgina (Noblewoman)
The Decadent Duke - Virginia Henley *r* 296

Gordon, Melinda (Businesswoman; Psychic)
Revenge - Doranna Durgin *h* 540

Gorst, Esperanza (Orphan; Servant)
The Glass of Time - Michael Cox *t* 755
The Glass of Time - Michael Cox *m* 55

Gothika (Teenager)
Chance Fortune in the Shadow Zone - Shane Berryhill *s* 635

Gotrek (Mythical Creature; Warrior)
Elfslayer - Nathan Long *f* 478

Gould, Ben (Survivor)
The Ghost in Love - Jonathan Carroll *c* 989

Grace (Teenager)
Grace - Richard Paul Evans *c* 1004

Grady (Servant)
Master of the Moors - Kealan Patrick Burke *h* 533

Graham, Jennifer (Undertaker)
She's in a Better Place - Angela Hunt *i* 921

Graham, Sarah (Young Woman)
Home Another Way - Christa Parrish *i* 939

Graize (Teenager)
The Golden Tower - Fiona Patton *f* 495

Grange, Falek (Clone)
Eve - Tony Gonzales *s* 665

Granger, Cain (Government Official)
Watch Me - Brenda Novak *r* 361

Grant, Ben (Businessman)
House of Whispers - Margaret Lucke *h* 570

Grant, C.S. (Adventurer)
The Lost Temple - Tom Harper *t* 792

Grant, Maddy (Young Woman)
Sweet Wells - Elizabeth Gill *t* 781

Grant, Nathan (Vampire)
All Souls' Night - Jennifer Armintrout *h* 526

Grant, Odysseus (Entertainer; Magician)
Kitty and the Dead Man's Hand - Carrie Vaughn *h* 617

Graves, Matty (Military Personnel)
Peter Wicked - Broos Campbell *t* 743

Graves, Reginald "Rex" (Lawyer; Widow(er))
Christmas Is Murder - C.S. Challinor *m* 43

Graxen (Mythical Creature)
Dragonforge - James Maxey *f* 483

Grayson (Mercenary; Sorcerer)
The Flame and the Shadow - Denise Rossetti *f* 507

Green, Jess (Young Woman; Journalist)
The Man for Me - Gemma Bruce *r* 229

Greenberg, Louis (Musician; Con Artist)
Early Bright - Ami Silber *t* 852

Greenberg, William Shakespeare (Student—Graduate)
My Name Is Will - Jess Winfield *t* 870

I

Kydd, Thomas (Military Personnel)
The Privateer's Revenge - Julian
    Stockwin   *t*   854

L

Lachlan, Fiona (Gentlewoman; Orphan)
A Seduction at Christmas - Cathy
    Maxwell   *r*   347

LaDuca, Alexandra "Alex" (Government Official)
Conspiracy in Kiev - Noel Hynd   *m*   97
Midnight in Madrid - Noel Hynd   *i*   923

Laemmel, Edie (Child)
Ironhand - Charlie Fletcher   *f*   447

Lafayette, Marie-Joseph, marquis de (Historical
    Figure; Military Personnel)
The United States of Atlantis - Harry
    Turtledove   *t*   862

Lajos (Con Man)
Esther's Inheritance - Sandor Marai   *c*   1060

Lalita (Servant)
Soul of Fire - Sarah A. Hoyt   *f*   462

Lambright, Wayne (Farmer; Fiance(e))
A Cousin's Promise - Wanda E.
    Brunstetter   *i*   881

Lancaster, Abrielle (Television Personality)
Destiny Bay - Sarah Abbot   *r*   200

Landon, Chase (Lawman; Parent)
Texas Ranger Takes a Bride - Patricia
    Thayer   *r*   405

Landry, Michaela (Professor)
For All We Know - Sandra Kitt   *r*   319

Langdon, Lucian (Nobleman)
In Bed with the Devil - Lorraine Heath   *r*   294

Langslow, Meg (Artisan; Detective—Amateur)
Six Geese A-Slaying - Donna Andrews   *m*   2

Lanister, Dane (Criminal)
Magic to the Bone - Devon Monk   *f*   489

Lark (Teenager)
Lark and Termite - Jayne Ann Phillips   *c*   1079

Lark, Kristen (Police Officer)
Burn Out - Marcia Muller   *m*   148

Larsen, Ed (Parent)
Songs for the Missing - Stewart
    O'Nan   *c*   1071

Larsen, Fran (Parent)
Songs for the Missing - Stewart
    O'Nan   *c*   1071

Larsen, Kim (Teenager)
Songs for the Missing - Stewart
    O'Nan   *c*   1071

Larson, Daphne (Gardener; Divorced Person)
Worth Fighting For - Molly O'Keefe   *r*   363

Lassiter, Jessilyn (Teenager)
Fireflies in December - Jennifer Erin
    Valent   *i*   959

Lassiter, Nick (Young Man; Neighbor)
A Love to Last Forever - Tracie
    Peterson   *i*   942

Latham, Anna (Werewolf)
Cry Wolf - Patricia Briggs   *f*   431

Latimer, Chione (Gentlewoman; Writer)
An Improper Aristocrat - Deb Marlowe   *r*   343

Latour, Margaritte (Vampire)
Blood Memories - Barb Hendee   *h*   551

Laurel (Relative)
Sweetwater Gap - Denise Hunter   *i*   922

Laurence, George (Bridegroom)
Stand-In Groom - Kaye Dacus   *i*   898

Laurence, Luther (Criminal)
The Given Day - Dennis Lehane   *t*   812

Laveau, Bleu (Teacher)
Cypress Nights - Stella Cameron   *r*   233

Lawson, Chloe (Baker; Divorced Person)
All That Matters - Stef Ann Holm   *r*   297

Le, Lisa (Young Woman)
A Hundred Years of Happiness - Nicole
    Seitz   *i*   949

Leavitt, Robert (Military Personnel)
Lark and Termite - Jayne Ann Phillips   *c*   1079

Leck (Ruler)
Graceling - Kristin Cashore   *f*   436

Lederer, Everly
Telex from Cuba - Rachel Kushner   *t*   808

Legris, Victor (Store Owner; Detective—Amateur)
Murder on the Eiffel Tower - Claude
    Izner   *t*   799
Murder on the Eiffel Tower - Claude
    Izner   *m*   99

Lehane, Jeff (Security Officer)
Daemon - Harry Shannon   *h*   604

Leigh (Editor)
Chasing Harry Winston - Lauren
    Weisberger   *c*   1119

Leigh, Augusta (Historical Figure)
A Quiet Adjustment - Benjamin
    Markovits   *t*   817

Leighton, Oliver (Nobleman)
Seduction of a Proper Gentleman - Victoria
    Alexander   *r*   204

Lelani (Young Woman)
Spring Broke - Melody Carlson   *i*   888

Lenore (Parent)
Entertaining Disasters - Nancy Spiller   *c*   1105

Lenox, Charles (Detective—Amateur)
The September Society - Charles Finch   *t*   770

Leodora (Entertainer)
Lord Tophet - Gregory Frost   *f*   451

LeRoy, Thomas (Businessman; Criminal)
Stuff Dreams Are Made Of - Don Bruns   *m*   35

Lessor, James (Detective—Amateur; Businessman)
Stuff Dreams Are Made Of - Don Bruns   *m*   35

Leukonovich, Zhenya (Agent)
Death Roe - Joseph Heywood   *m*   93

Levin, Rachel (Teacher)
Marriage 101 - Deborah Shelley   *r*   387

Liane (Royalty)
The Gods Return - David Drake   *f*   442

Liang, Trudy (Socialite)
The Piano Teacher - Janice Y.K. Lee   *c*   1045

Libby, Jewel (Single Parent; Unemployed)
The Jewel of Gresham Green - Lawana
    Blackwell   *r*   217

Liedmann, Gregor (Musician)
Disguise - Hugo Hamilton   *t*   791

Liga (Teenager)
Tender Morsels - Margo Lanagan   *f*   470

Lightfoot (Mythical Creature)
Dark Whispers - Bruce Coville   *f*   441

Ligotti, Whiz (Security Officer)
Daemon - Harry Shannon   *h*   604

Lillis, Harry (Actor)
It Happened One Knife - Jeffrey Cohen   *m*   51

Lily (Teenager)
The Gate of Days - Guillaume Prevost   *f*   499

Lincoln, Reggie (Crime Victim)
The Butt - Will Self   *c*   1092

Linda (Teacher)
The Academy - Bentley Little   *h*   569

Lindbergh, Huckleberry (Police Officer)
Love in the Time of Fridges - Tim Scott   *s*   705

Ling (Spirit)
The Ghost in Love - Jonathan Carroll   *c*   989

Lionsmane, Parno (Military Personnel)
The Soldier King - Violette Malan   *f*   479

Little Bee (Refugee)
Little Bee - Chris Cleave   *c*   992

Livermore, Tommy (Police Officer)
No Human Enemy - John Gardner   *t*   778

Livingston, Lainey (Apprentice; Sorceress)
Phenomenal Girl 5 - A.J. Menden   *r*   351

Llewelyn, Thomas (Detective—Private)
The Black Hand - Will Thomas   *m*   190

Lobo (Artificial Intelligence)
Slanted Jack - Mark L. Van Name   *s*   718

Lockhart, Leila (Widow(er); Businesswoman)
A Dead Man in Barcelona - Michael
    Pearce   *m*   153

Lockwell, Ivy (Worker)
The Magicians and Mrs. Quent - Galen
    Beckett   *f*   429

Logan, Katy Lynn (Saloon Keeper/Owner)
The Dove - Carolyn Brown   *r*   228

Logan, Meer (Traveller)
The Memorist - M.J. Rose   *c*   1087

Longbright, Janice (Detective—Police)
The Victoria Vanishes - Christopher
    Fowler   *m*   68

Longknife, Kris (Military Personnel)
Kris Longknife: Intrepid - Mike
    Shepherd   *s*   707

Lonigan, Matt (Detective—Private)
Break of Dawn - Chris Marie Green   *h*   545

Lopez, John (Police Officer)
Body Copy - Michael Craven   *m*   58

Lord Loss (Mythical Creature)
Death's Shadow - Darren Shan   *h*   603

Louie (Animal)
New Tricks - John Levitt   *f*   472

Louie, Tat (Gang Member)
Year of the Dog - Henry Chang   *m*   44

Lowell, Gretchen (Serial Killer)
Sweetheart - Chelsea Cain   *m*   38

Lowell, Julia (Advertising; Hotel Worker)
Five Star Cowboy - Charlene Sands   *r*   382

Lowenstein, Kiki (Artisan)
Paper, Scissors, Death - Joanna Campbell
    Slan   *m*   177

Lowery, Elizabeth (Artist; Widow(er))
A Most Unconventional Match - Julia
    Justiss   *r*   312

Lubitsch, Gonzo (Troubleshooter)
The Gone-Away World - Nick
    Harkaway   *s*   668

Lucas, Zach "Lightning" (Rodeo Rider; Postal Worker)
Snowbound in Dry Creek - Janet Tronstad   *r*   412

Luciano (Orphan)
The Book of Unholy Mischief - Elle Newmark   *c*   1067

Lucifer (Demon)
To Hell and Back - Lilith Saintcrow   *h*   601

Luelldar (Mythical Creature)
Dark Vengeance - Ed Greenwood   *f*   457

Lugh (Demon)
The Devil's Due - Jenna Black   *h*   532

Lugo, Kendra "Kenny" (Teenager)
The Sweet In-Between - Sheri Reynolds   *c*   1083

Luka (Teenager; Gypsy)
The Gypsy Crown - Kate Forsyth   *f*   449

Luna, Jessica (Insurance Agent)
Houston, We Have a Problema - Gwendolyn Zepeda   *c*   1127

Lundgren, Matt (Police Officer; Boyfriend)
Pane of Death - Sarah Atwell   *m*   4

Lundy, Jonathan (Widow(er); Parent)
Wanted - Shelley Shephard Gray   *i*   908

Lusak, Craig (Lawyer)
Revenge - Doranna Durgin   *h*   540

Lustig, Caroline (Spouse)
The Journey - H.G. Adler   *c*   968

Lustig, Leopold (Doctor)
The Journey - H.G. Adler   *c*   968

Luvo (Mythical Creature)
The Melting Stones - Tamora Pierce   *f*   497

Lycas (Traveller)
The Reawakened - Jeri Smith-Ready   *f*   518

Lydell, Jonathan IV (Writer)
Stranger Room - Frederick Ramsay   *m*   161

Lymon, Al (Aged Person; Knight)
The Knights of the Cornerstone - James P. Blaylock   *f*   430

Lynsted, Dominic (Nobleman)
A Seduction at Christmas - Cathy Maxwell   *r*   347

Lyons, Alexander (FBI Agent)
In the Blood - Adrian Phoenix   *h*   589

M

Mabry, Catherine (Noblewoman)
In Bed with the Devil - Lorraine Heath   *r*   294

Mac Lir, Manannan (Royalty; Deity)
Immortals: The Crossing - Joy Nash   *r*   359

MacDavid, Kathleen MacDav (Gentlewoman; Amnesiac)
Seduction of a Proper Gentleman - Victoria Alexander   *r*   204

MacDonald, Jim (Restaurateur; Boyfriend)
Blackbird, Farewell - Robert Greer   *m*   82

MacDonald, Mac (Veteran; Convict)
Deceived - James Scott Bell   *i*   878

MacGregor, Flynn (Journalist)
Marry-Me Christmas - Shirley Jump   *r*   310

MacGregor, Rose (Composer)
The Rose Variations - Marisha Chamberlain   *c*   990

Macinnes, Nell (Art Historian; Mountaineer)
To Catch a Thief - Christina Skye   *r*   391

MacKay, Sean (Military Personnel)
One Perfect Gift - Kathleen Morgan   *i*   936

MacKenzie, Luke (Detective—Police)
Casting Spells - Barbara Bretton   *r*   225

Mackenzie, Rudi (Traveller)
The Scourge of God - S.M. Stirling   *s*   712

Mackey, Frank (Detective—Police)
The Likeness - Tana French   *m*   69

MacKinnon, Morgan (Military Personnel)
Untamed - Pamela Clare   *r*   245

MacLean, Theresa (Scientist; Fiance(e))
Takeover - Lisa Black   *m*   24

MacLeod, Hamish (Spirit; Military Personnel)
A Matter of Justice - Charles Todd   *t*   859

MacLerie, Duncan (Diplomat; Nobleman)
Possessed by the Highlander - Terri Brisbin   *r*   226

MacMahon, Nick (Guardian; Animal Trainer)
The Hiding Place - Karen Harper   *r*   291

MacNeil, Connor (Doctor; Rebel)
The Rebel Doctor's Bride - Sarah Morgan   *r*   358

MacPhail, Lindsay (Teenager)
Be Strong and Curvaceous - Shelley Adina   *i*   874

MacPhie, Ian (Vampire)
All I Want for Christmas Is a Vampire - Kerrelyn Sparks   *r*   397

Maddalena (Orphan; Musician)
The Four Seasons - Laurel Corona   *t*   754
The Four Seasons - Laurel Corona   *c*   994

Maddiford, Henry (Businessman)
Cherrybrook Rose - Tania Anne Crosse   *t*   756

Maddiford, Rose (Young Woman)
Cherrybrook Rose - Tania Anne Crosse   *t*   756

Maddox, Cassie (Detective—Police)
The Likeness - Tana French   *m*   69

Madison, Dawn (Entertainer; Stuntman)
Break of Dawn - Chris Marie Green   *h*   545

Madison, James (Historical Figure; Political Figure)
Recoats' Revenge: An Alternate History of 1812 - David Fitz-Enz   *t*   772

Madrid, Damion (Friend)
Blackbird, Farewell - Robert Greer   *m*   82

Maeve (Mythical Creature)
Cursed - Jamie Leigh Hansen   *h*   548

Magellan, Alvaro (Sorcerer)
My Wicked Enemy - Carolyn Jewel   *h*   558

Magill, Audrey Fine (Designer)
Ready and Willing - Elizabeth Bevarly   *r*   216

Mags (Apprentice; Slave)
Foundation - Mercedes Lackey   *f*   467

Mahler, Gustav (Historical Figure; Composer)
The Little Book - Selden Edwards   *t*   768

Mahoney, John (Military Personnel)
Shadows in the Mist - Brian Moreland   *h*   581

Mahoney, Rick (Landlord; Businessman)
Holiday Dreams - Annette Mahon   *r*   338

Maitland, Gillian (Werewolf)
Come the Night - Susan Krinard   *r*   322

Maki, Ben (Businessman; Environmentalist)
Freezing Point - Karen Dionne   *s*   653

Mal (Teacher)
Good Luck - Whitney Gaskell   *r*   276

Malatesta, Gualterio (Veteran; Military Personnel)
The King's Gold - Arturo Perez-Reverte   *t*   831

Mallory, Cassandra (Investigator)
Dark Rain - Tony Richards   *h*   592

Mallory, John Justin (Detective—Private)
Stalking the Vampire - Mike Resnick   *f*   501

Maloy, Kelly (Student—Graduate)
Eternal Pleasure - Nina Bangs   *r*   212

Mancarre, Justine (Model; Girlfriend)
Lost River - David Fulmer   *m*   70

Manchester, Vern (Real Estate Agent)
Eggs in Purgatory - Laura Childs   *m*   47

Manhattan, Chase (Lawyer; Consultant)
Wicked Weaves - Joyce Lavene   *m*   120

Manoso, Carlos "Ranger" (Bounty Hunter)
Fearless Fourteen - Janet Evanovich   *r*   264

Mansfield, Kate (Teenager)
Master of the Moors - Kealan Patrick Burke   *h*   533

Mansfield, Neil (Teenager; Handicapped)
Master of the Moors - Kealan Patrick Burke   *h*   533

Mara (Judge)
A Secret and Unlawful Killing - Cora Harrison   *t*   794
A Secret and Unlawful Killing - Cora Harrison   *m*   86

Marah (Young Woman)
Journey to the Well - Diana Wallis Taylor   *i*   955

Maralen (Mythical Creature)
Morningtide - Cory J. Herndon   *f*   459

Marcella, Aurelia (Innkeeper)
Buried Too Deep - Jane Finnis   *t*   771

Marcella, Lucius (Innkeeper)
Buried Too Deep - Jane Finnis   *t*   771

March (Rebel)
Wanderlust - Ann Aguirre   *s*   625

Marchand, Camille (Noblewoman; Bastard Daughter)
Never Romance a Rake - Liz Carlyle   *r*   235

Marchand, Ross (Producer)
Phantom's Touch - Julie Leto   *r*   329

Marchette, Lil (Vampire; Businesswoman)
Just One Bite - Kimberly Raye   *h*   591

Marcus, Josie (Detective—Amateur; Consultant)
Murder with All the Trimmings - Elaine Viets   *m*   193

Marduk (Military Personnel)
Dark Disciple - Anthony Reynolds   *s*   696

Marek (Warrior)
The Reawakened - Jeri Smith-Ready   *f*   518

Margle (Wizard)
Too Many Curses - A. Lee Martinez   *f*   482

Margred (Mythical Creature)
Sea Witch - Virginia Kantra   *r*   315

Markham, Ava (Worker)
One Bite with a Stranger - Christine Warren   *h*   619

Markham, Devon (Assistant; Homosexual)
Cold Hearted - Beverly Barton   *m*   14

Markham, Eugenie (Shaman)
Storm Born - Richelle Mead   *h*   577

Picard, Jean-Luc (Spaceship Captain; Military Personnel)
Gods of Night - David Mack   *s*   677
Greater than the Sum - Christopher L. Bennett   *s*   632

Pierce, Buddy (Oil Industry Worker)
Chasing Charity - Marcia Gruver   *i*   909

Pierce, Daniel "Ace" (Lawyer; FBI Agent)
Ace Is Wild - Penny McCall   *r*   348

Pierce, Gray (Spy)
The Last Oracle - James Rollins   *s*   701

Pieters, Cole (Businessman)
Foundation - Mercedes Lackey   *f*   467

Pike, Joe (Detective—Private)
Chasing Darkness - Robert Crais   *m*   57

Pike, Zeke (Artisan; Recluse)
Triple Exposure - Colleen Thompson   *r*   410

Pims, Sarah (Noblewoman)
The Bride Price - Anne Mallory   *r*   341

Ping (Child; Orphan)
Dragon Moon - Carole Wilkinson   *f*   522

Pinzon, Vicente (Government Official)
The Viper of Portello - James C. Glass   *s*   663

Pirrotta, Betty (Actress)
Sicilian Tragedee - Ottavio Cappellani   *c*   988

Pitt, Joe (Detective—Private; Vampire)
Every Last Drop - Charlie Huston   *h*   555
Every Last Drop - Charlie Huston   *m*   96

Pittman, Laurell (Witch)
Between Light and Dark - Elissa Wilds   *r*   418

Plaice, Serena Jane (Teenager)
The Little Giant of Aberdeen County - Tiffany Baker   *c*   973

Plaice, Truly (Teenager)
The Little Giant of Aberdeen County - Tiffany Baker   *c*   973

Plat, Nell (Seamstress)
The Seamstress of Hollywood Boulevard - Erin McGraw   *t*   819

Platt, Benjamin (Doctor; Military Personnel)
Exposed - Alex Kava   *m*   105

Pleasant, Dan (Police Officer)
Small Crimes - Dave Zeltserman   *m*   199

Plowright, Paul (Religious)
Salvation Boulevard - Larry Beinhart   *m*   18

Plum, Stephanie (Bounty Hunter; Detective—Amateur)
Fearless Fourteen - Janet Evanovich   *r*   264
Plum Spooky - Janet Evanovich   *m*   66

Plusby (Sailor)
The Black Ship - Diana Pharaoh Francis   *f*   450

Po (Royalty)
Graceling - Kristin Cashore   *f*   436

Polk, Elizabeth (Scholar)
The Last Oracle - James Rollins   *s*   701

Pollock, Angelle (Teacher)
Water Witch - Deborah Leblanc   *h*   566

Pollock, Dunny (Writer)
Water Witch - Deborah Leblanc   *h*   566

Pomroy, Adrian (Nobleman)
Scandalizing the Ton - Diane Gaston   *r*   277

Por, Ah (Psychic)
Year of the Dog - Henry Chang   *m*   44

Porter, John (Carpenter; Veteran)
A Hundred Years of Happiness - Nicole Seitz   *i*   949

Porter, Rachel (Unemployed)
Home for the Holidays - Lisa Plumley   *r*   370

Postum, Bob (Aged Person; Criminal)
The Knights of the Cornerstone - James P. Blaylock   *f*   430

Potter, Beatrix (Historical Figure; Writer)
The Tale of Briar Bank - Susan Wittig Albert   *t*   725

Pottevents, Max (Worker)
Watermind - M.M. Buckner   *s*   639

Potts, Thomas (Police Officer)
The Resurrection Man - Sara Fraser   *t*   773

Powell, Nan (Widow(er))
The Beach House - Jane Green   *c*   1015

Prakenskii, Ilya (Bodyguard)
Turbulent Sea - Christine Feehan   *r*   266

Predo, Dexter (Vampire; Leader)
Every Last Drop - Charlie Huston   *h*   555

Predo, Dexter (Vampire)
Every Last Drop - Charlie Huston   *m*   96

Prentice, Brian (Criminal)
The Butt - Will Self   *c*   1092

Prentice, Clare (Journalist; Adoptee)
Conspiracy of Silence - Martha Powers   *m*   158

Prentice, Julia (Wealthy; Socialite)
High-Society Secret Pregnancy - Maureen Child   *r*   244

Prentiss, Jack (Publisher)
Faking Grace - Tamera Leigh   *i*   930

Preston, Brent (Equestrian; Businessman)
A Lady's Luck - Ken Casper   *r*   238

Price, Jordan (Widow(er))
Cold Hearted - Beverly Barton   *m*   14

Price, Walker (Prisoner)
Dream House - Valerie Laken   *c*   1042

Proctor, Molly (Child)
The Sour Cherry Surprise - David Handler   *m*   84

Prosser, Dorothy (Friend)
Keeping Secrets - Owen Madoc   *t*   814

Prudence (Seamstress)
Gingham Mountain - Mary Connealy   *i*   894

Pust, Iskaral (Religious)
Toll the Hounds - Steven Erikson   *f*   444

Q

Q'Daer (Sorcerer)
The Horseman's Gambit - David B. Coe   *f*   439

Quickfire (Businessman)
The House of the Stag - Kage Baker   *f*   427

Quinlan, Liam (Military Personnel)
When Duty Calls - William C. Dietz   *s*   652

Quinn (Scout)
The Desires of Her Heart - Lyn Cote   *i*   895

Quinn (Psychic)
The Hollow - Nora Roberts   *h*   594

Quinn, Frank (Detective—Homicide; Aged Person)
Night Kills - John Lutz   *m*   128

Quinn, Mike (Detective—Police)
Espresso Shot - Cleo Coyle   *m*   56

Quintana, Gabriel (Health Care Professional; Student)
The Dirty Secrets Club - Meg Gardiner   *m*   73

Quinton (Investigator)
Underground - Kat Richardson   *f*   503

Quinton, John (Police Officer)
Murder Most Maine - Karen MacInerney   *m*   130

Quirk, Caelum (Teacher)
The Hour I First Believed - Wally Lamb   *c*   1044

Quirk, Maureen (Nurse)
The Hour I First Believed - Wally Lamb   *c*   1044

Quirt (Nobleman; Sports Figure)
Ill Met in the Arena - Dave Duncan   *f*   443

R

Rachel K (Dancer)
Telex from Cuba - Rachel Kushner   *t*   808

Rachylana (Noblewoman)
The Lord Protector's Daughter - L.E. Modesitt Jr.   *f*   488

Radcliffe, Matthew (Revolutionary)
The United States of Atlantis - Harry Turtledove   *s*   717

Radcliffe, Victor (Revolutionary)
The United States of Atlantis - Harry Turtledove   *t*   862
The United States of Atlantis - Harry Turtledove   *s*   717

Radu the Forsaken (Vampire)
Curse of the Necrarch - Steven Savile   *f*   513

Raeburn, Bailey Ruth (Spirit; Detective—Amateur)
Ghost at Work - Carolyn Hart   *m*   87

Rafen (Military Personnel)
Red Fury - James Swallow   *s*   713

Rafferdy, Dashton (Government Official)
The Magicians and Mrs. Quent - Galen Beckett   *f*   429

Rahel (Mythical Creature)
Gale Force - Rachel Caine   *f*   435

Rain Tairen Soul (Immortal; Royalty)
King of Sword and Sky - C.L. Wilson   *r*   419

Raines, Beth Ann (Care Giver)
Cursed - Jamie Leigh Hansen   *h*   548

Raisin, Agatha (Detective—Private)
A Spoonful of Poison - M.C. Beaton   *m*   17

Rake, Anomander (Ruler)
Toll the Hounds - Steven Erikson   *f*   444

Rakh-amn-Hotep (Ruler; Religious)
Nagash the Sorcerer - Mike Lee   *f*   471

Ralf (Government Official)
Forsaken Soul - Priscilla Royal   *m*   166

Ralph (Apprentice)
Skin Lane - Neil Bartlett   *c*   977

Ramesses II (Historical Figure; Ruler)
The Heretic Queen - Michelle Moran   *t*   825

Ramos, Johnny (Military Personnel; Government Official)
Loose and Easy - Tara Janzen   *r*   305

Randall (Parent)
Fault Lines - Nancy Huston   *c*   1026

Snow, Kathryn (Parent)
While My Sister Sleeps - Barbara
  Delinsky   *c*   997

Snow, Robin (Sports Figure)
While My Sister Sleeps - Barbara
  Delinsky   *c*   997

Soames, Elisabeth (Troubleshooter)
The Gone-Away World - Nick
  Harkaway   *s*   668

Sofia (Spy; Imposter)
The Scarlet Spy - Andrea Pickens   *r*   369

Sofya (Entertainer)
The Kiss Murder - Mehmet Murat
  Somer   *m*   179

Sol (Child)
Fault Lines - Nancy Huston   *c*   1026

Solarin, Alexandra (Genius; Sports Figure)
The Fire - Katherine Neville   *m*   149

Solarin, Alexandra (Sports Figure)
The Fire - Katherine Neville   *t*   828

Somerset, Stuart (Political Figure; Heir)
Delicious - Sherry Thomas   *r*   409

Sonnet, Karen (Businesswoman)
Into the Shadow - Christina Dodd   *r*   257

Sophie (Mentally Ill Person)
Disquiet - Julia Leigh   *c*   1047

Sorensen, Paige (Widow(er))
Written in Blood - Sheila Lowe   *m*   127

Soter (Businessman)
Lord Tophet - Gregory Frost   *f*   451

Soulbreaker (Demon)
Lord of Bones - Justine Musk   *h*   582

Spar (Psychic)
The Golden Tower - Fiona Patton   *f*   495

Spartz, Riley (Journalist; Detective—Amateur)
Stalking Susan - Julie Kramer   *m*   113

Speck, Opal (Friend)
The Bride Backfire - Kelly Eileen Hake   *i*   911

Spinks, Charlie (Security Officer)
Daemon - Harry Shannon   *h*   604

Spock (Alien; Student)
Collision Course - William Shatner   *s*   706

Sproule, Raven (Farmer)
The Bell at Sealey Head - Patricia A.
  McKillip   *f*   485

Spurgeon (Religious)
The Gypsy Crown - Kate Forsyth   *f*   449

Stafford, Mackenzie (Actress)
Flashback - Jill Shalvis   *r*   385

Stafford, Niall "Trey" (Nobleman)
An Improper Aristocrat - Deb Marlowe   *r*   343

Stafford, Nora (Mechanic)
Envy the Night - Michael Koryta   *m*   112

Stamatos, Tassos (Detective—Homicide)
Murder in Mykonos - Jeffrey M. Siger   *m*   174

Standish, Cass (Military Personnel; Pilot)
The Eleventh Man - Ivan Doig   *t*   762

Stanhope, Maxwell (Bounty Hunter; Nobleman)
Pale Moon Stalker - Shirl Henke   *r*   295

Stanhope, Sabrina (Madam)
Dial Me for Murder - Amanda
  Matetsky   *m*   139

Stanley, Eleanor Stark "Nell" (Musician)
The King of Ragtime - Larry Karp   *m*   104

Stanton, Arthur (Veteran; Crime Suspect)
Mad about the Boy? - Dolores
  Gordon-Smith   *m*   77

Stanton, Evelyn (Gentlewoman)
The Dragon Earl - Jade Lee   *r*   326

Stark, Nell (Musician; Detective—Amateur)
The King of Ragtime - Larry Karp   *t*   803

Starling, Jonathan (Teenager)
Lifeblood - Tom Becker   *h*   531

Stearns, Mike (Leader; Time Traveler)
1635: The Dreeson Incident - Eric Flint   *s*   655

Stearns, Rebecca (Time Traveler)
1635: The Dreeson Incident - Eric Flint   *s*   655

Steckl, Walt (Widow(er))
Security - Stephen Amidon   *c*   969

Steeg, Jackson (Detective—Homicide)
Old Flame - Ira Berkowitz   *m*   21

Steele, Tamara (Artisan; Single Parent)
Ultimate Weapon - Shannon McKenna   *r*   349

Steenwycks, Elizabeth (Doctor)
Doctor Olaf van Schuler's Brain - Kirsten
  Menger-Anderson   *t*   823

Steenwycks, Stuart (Doctor)
Doctor Olaf van Schuler's Brain - Kirsten
  Menger-Anderson   *t*   823

Stein, Thomas (Agent)
Agent to the Stars - John Scalzi   *s*   702

Stelfox, Steven (Businessman)
Kill Your Friends - John Niven   *c*   1068

Stellar, Denny (Zoo Keeper)
Night Kill - Ann Littlewood   *m*   124

Sterling, Velda (Secretary; Fiance(e))
The Goliath Bone - Mickey Spillane   *m*   181

Stern, Cheryl (Scientist)
Fools' Experiment - Edward M. Lerner   *s*   676

Stevens, Sally (Teacher)
What the Bayou Saw - Patti Lacy   *i*   928

Stewart, Maizy Grace (Journalist)
Faking Grace - Tamera Leigh   *i*   930

Stilgar (Military Personnel)
Paul of Dune - Brian Herbert   *s*   669

Stites, K.C. (Teenager)
Telex from Cuba - Rachel Kushner   *t*   808

Stoker, Bram (Writer; Businessman)
The Dracula Dossier - James Reese   *m*   163

Stoker, Bram (Historical Figure; Writer)
The Dracula Dossier - James Reese   *t*   838
Oscar Wilde and a Game Called Murder - Gyles
  Brandreth   *t*   738

Stone, Alex (Spy; Psychic)
Night Shadow - Cherry Adair   *r*   201

Stone, Alexis "Lexi" (Spy; Psychic)
Night Shadow - Cherry Adair   *r*   201

Stone, Brian (Journalist)
Personal Demons - Stacia Kane   *h*   560

Stone, Cotten (Journalist)
The 731 Legacy - Lynn Sholes   *m*   173

Strahan, Nicky (Child)
Water Witch - Deborah Leblanc   *h*   566

Street, Dan (Detective—Homicide)
Dial Me for Murder - Amanda
  Matetsky   *m*   139

Striker, Gabriel (Detective—Private)
Defending Angels - Mary Stanton   *m*   184

Stringer, Jim (Detective—Police)
Murder at Deviation Junction - Andrew
  Martin   *m*   136

Strong, Anna (Bounty Hunter; Vampire)
Legacy - Jeanne C. Stein   *h*   611

Strong, Rebecca (Spy)
The Flowing Tide - Alan Savage   *t*   846

Stryker (Mythical Creature)
One Silent Night - Sherrilyn Kenyon   *h*   563

Stuart, Alexa (Businesswoman)
Hot as Hell - HelenKay Dimon   *r*   255

Stuart, David (Lawyer)
Dalliance - Diana Burg   *t*   740

Sturgis, Milo (Detective—Homicide)
Bones - Jonathan Kellerman   *m*   107

Subramanian, Ranjit (Scientist)
The Last Theorem - Arthur C. Clarke   *s*   644

Sugar, P.J. (Detective—Amateur; Girlfriend)
Nothing but Trouble - Susan May
  Warren   *i*   961

Sukie (Widow(er))
The Widows of Eastwick - John
  Updike   *c*   1114

Sullivan, Cooper (Doctor)
Winning the Single Mom's Heart - Linda
  Goodnight   *r*   283

Sullivan, Gabriel Ross (Religious; Telepath)
Shades of Dark - Linnea Sinclair   *s*   709

Sullivan, Marcie (Widow(er))
A Virgin River Christmas - Robyn Carr   *r*   236

Summer (Slave)
The Book of Summer - James F. David   *s*   649

Summerfield, Nathaniel (Businessman)
Ready and Willing - Elizabeth Bevarly   *r*   216

Summerfield, Silas Leyton (Sea Captain)
Ready and Willing - Elizabeth Bevarly   *r*   216

Summerlin, Violet (Consultant; Businesswoman)
No Peeking - Stephanie Bond   *r*   221

Sumner, David (Businessman)
Talk of the Town - Sherrill Bodine   *r*   220

Sutherland, Eliza Jane (Gentlewoman; Care Giver)
Her Montana Man - Cheryl St. John   *r*   399

Sutter, John (Lawyer)
The Gate House - Nelson DeMille   *c*   998

Sutter, Susan (Divorced Person)
The Gate House - Nelson DeMille   *c*   998

Swain, Pearl (Teacher)
The Music Teacher - Barbara Hall   *c*   1016

Swan, Bella (Teenager)
Breaking Dawn - Stephenie Meyer   *h*   580

Sweeney, Francis (Doctor)
Nemesis: The Final Case of Eliot Ness - William
  Bernhardt   *m*   22

Sweeny, Bridget (Housekeeper; Single Parent)
Hold My Hand - Serena Mackesy   *m*   131

Sweet, Camille (Sister)
Sweet Waters - Julie Carobini   *i*   889

Sweet, Tara (Worker; Sister)
Sweet Waters - Julie Carobini   *i*   889

Sweetwater, William (Scientist)
The Clone Elite - Steven L. Kent   *s*   672

Swift Dragon, Konowa (Military Personnel;
  Mythical Creature)
A Darkness Forged in Fire - Chris
  Evans   *f*   445

Sylvia (Doctor)
Peripheral Vision - Patricia Ferguson *c* 1007

Symington, John Alexander (Historical Figure; Scholar)
Daphne - Justine Picardie *t* 833

T

Tadashi, Sato (Student)
The Women - T.C. Boyle *c* 982

Taerel (Mythical Creature)
Dark Vengeance - Ed Greenwood *f* 457

Tain (Police Officer)
The Frailty of Flesh - Sandra Ruttan *m* 167

Tain (Immortal; Supernatural Being)
Immortals: The Redeeming - Jennifer Ashley *r* 208

Talaith (Witch)
About a Dragon - G.A. Aiken *r* 202

Talbot, George (Historical Figure; Nobleman)
The Other Queen - Philippa Gregory *t* 789

Talbot, Jane (Investigator)
Black Cathedral - L.H. Maynard *h* 574

Talbot, Laetitia (Archaeologist; Detective—Amateur)
Bright Hair about the Bone - Barbara Cleverly *t* 751

Talbot, Laetitia (Archaeologist)
Bright Hair about the Bone - Barbara Cleverly *m* 49

Talenth (Alien)
Dragonheart - Todd McCaffrey *s* 683

Talon (Orphan)
The Wyrmling Horde - David Farland *f* 446

Tam, Szass (Sorcerer)
Undead - Richard Lee Byers *f* 434

Tamblyn, Jess (Military Personnel)
The Ashes of Worlds - Kevin J. Anderson *s* 627

Tammith (Vampire)
Undead - Richard Lee Byers *f* 434

Tang, Amy (Police Officer)
The Dirty Secrets Club - Meg Gardiner *m* 73

Tanner, Blake (Leader; Fiance(e))
Distant Heart - Tracey Bateman *i* 877

Taranis (Mythical Creature)
Swallowing Darkness - Laurell Hamilton *f* 458

Tarnish, Seymour (Postal Worker)
The Ghost and the Haunted Mansion - Alice Kimberly *m* 108

Tate, Micah (Religious; Widow(er))
Beloved Counterfeit - Kathleen Y'Barbo *i* 966

Tatiana (Thief)
Hidden - Eve Kenin *r* 317

Tavi (Ruler)
Princeps' Fury - Jim Butcher *f* 433

Taylor, Genevieve (Mythical Creature)
The Sweet Scent of Blood - Suzanne McLeod *f* 486

Taylor, Jack (Veterinarian)
Broken Pieces - Carla Cassidy *r* 239

Taylor, Steven (Traveller)
The Larion Senators - Robert Scott *f* 515

Teags, Billy (Child)
Nowhere to Hide - R. Patrick Gates *h* 543

Teags, William (Serial Killer)
Nowhere to Hide - R. Patrick Gates *h* 543

Teazle (Demon)
Going Under - Justina Robson *s* 700

Tekoy, Visyna (Noblewoman)
A Darkness Forged in Fire - Chris Evans *f* 445

Tellenberg, Esra (Scientist)
Quofum - Alan Dean Foster *s* 661

Temple, Frank III (Student—College)
Envy the Night - Michael Koryta *m* 112

Templeton, Ethan (Vampire)
Bond of Darkness - Diane Whiteside *r* 417

Tenney, Mitch (Doctor; Divorced Person)
Expecting the Doctor's Baby - Teresa Southwick *r* 396

Teodora (Aged Person)
Very Valentine - Adriana Tragiani *c* 1112

Tepes, Vlad (Nobleman)
The Gate of Days - Guillaume Prevost *f* 499

Termite (Relative)
Lark and Termite - Jayne Ann Phillips *c* 1079

Thalia (Orphan; Royalty)
Daughter of Egypt - Constance O'Banyon *r* 362

Thatcher, Michael (Military Personnel; Widow(er))
Stealing Trinity - Ward Larsen *m* 116

Thatcher, Michael (Military Personnel)
Stealing Trinity - Ward Larsen *t* 810

Thedeus (Knight)
Too Many Curses - A. Lee Martinez *f* 482

Thero (Wizard)
Shadows Return - Lynn Flewelling *f* 448

Thibault, Logan (Military Personnel)
The Lucky One - Nicholas Sparks *c* 1104

Thomas (Religious)
Forsaken Soul - Priscilla Royal *m* 166

Thompson, Natalie (Baker; Single Parent)
Winning the Single Mom's Heart - Linda Goodnight *r* 283

Thomson, Kenny (Farmer)
White Nights - Ann Cleeves *m* 48

Thorn (Slave; Sailor)
The Black Ship - Diana Pharaoh Francis *f* 450

Thorn, Sterling (Nobleman; Sorcerer)
Double Enchantment - Kathryne Kennedy *r* 318

Thorne, Jake (Wealthy; Heir)
Wed to the Texan - Sara Orwig *r* 364

Thorne, William Cuyler (Vampire)
The Vampire's Betrayal - Raven Hart *h* 550

Thornton-McClure, Penelope "Pen" (Store Owner; Detective—Amateur)
The Ghost and the Haunted Mansion - Alice Kimberly *m* 108

Thorsen, Maggy (Store Owner; Detective—Amateur)
Bean There, Done That - Sandra Balzo *m* 8

Thrall, Rafiel (Police Officer; Mythical Creature)
Gentleman Takes a Chance - Sarah A. Hoyt *f* 460

Threnody (Child; Student)
Lamplighter - D.M. Cornish *f* 440

Thyssen, Hamnet (Nobleman)
The Breath of God - Harry Turtledove *f* 520

Tichnor, Carol (Store Owner)
Buffalo Bill's Defunct - Shelia Simonson *m* 176

Tiercel (Wizard)
The Phoenix Endangered - Mercedes Lackey *f* 468

Tilden, Forrest (Security Officer)
Eternal Damnation - Steve Niles *h* 583

Timas (Teenager; Worker)
Sly Mongoose - Tobias S. Buckell *s* 638

Timna (Seamstress)
Sima's Undergarments for Women - Ilana Stanger-Ross *c* 1106

Tiptree, Jacobia "Jake" (Carpenter; Detective—Amateur)
A Face at the Window - Sarah Graves *m* 80

Toal, Pete (Detective—Homocide)
Old Flame - Ira Berkowitz *m* 21

Tomlinson, Hank (Rancher)
A Tale Out of Luck - Willie Nelson *t* 827

Toni (Parent)
The Good Parents - Joan London *c* 1051

Torelli, Giuseppe (Religious)
Black Market Truth - Sharon Kaye *m* 106

Torin, Cherijo (Doctor; Spacewoman)
Omega Games - S.L. Viehl *s* 719

Torrez, Robert (Police Officer)
The Fourth Time Is Murder - Steven F. Havill *m* 90

Torrez, Victoria (Noblewoman; Patriot)
The Rebel and the Lady - Kathryn Albright *r* 203

Towne, Liz (Spouse)
Deceived - James Scott Bell *i* 878

Towne, Roxanne (Relative)
Deceived - James Scott Bell *i* 878

Townsend, Cooper "Smith" (Religious; Contractor)
For All We Know - Sandra Kitt *r* 319

Townsend, Rick (Ranger)
Anchors Aweigh - Kathleen Bacus *m* 5
Anchors Aweigh - Kathleen Bacus *r* 210

T'Pol (Alien; Scientist)
Kobayashi Maru - Michael A. Martin *s* 680

Trasamund (Leader)
The Breath of God - Harry Turtledove *f* 520

Trask, Keir (Alien; Police Officer)
Electra Galaxy's Mr. Interstellar Feller - Candace Sams *r* 381

Travers, Alexia (Young Woman; Rancher)
Love Finds You in Last Chance, California - Miralee Ferrell *i* 905

Traynor, Andy (Child)
Daniel's Den - Brandt Dodson *i* 901

Traynor, Laura (Businesswoman; Single Parent)
Daniel's Den - Brandt Dodson *i* 901

Tregarth, John (Antiques Dealer)
The Laughter of Dead Kings - Elizabeth Peters *m* 155

Tremaine, Donald (Detective—Private)
Body Copy - Michael Craven *m* 58

Tremaine, Nicholas (Lover)
The Mistletoe Wager - Christine Merrill *r* 352

Trent, Damon (Patient)
Succulent Prey - Wrath James White *h* 621

Character Name Index

X

Y

Z

Character Description Index

This index alphabetically lists descriptions of the major characters in featured titles. The descriptions may be occupations (police officer, lawyer, etc.) or may describe persona (amnesiac, runaway, teenager, etc.). For each description, character names are listed alphabetically. Also provided are book titles, author names, genre codes and entry numbers. The genre codes are as follows: *c* Popular Fiction, *f* Fantasy, *h* Horror, *i* Inspirational, *m* Mystery, *r* Romance, *s* Science Fiction, *t* Historical, and *w* Western.

ABUSE VICTIM

Brody, Meredith
The Spy Who Came for Christmas - David Morrell *m* 147

Copeland, Rachel
Triple Exposure - Colleen Thompson *r* 410

Kellerman, Skye
Trust Me - Brenda Novak *r* 360

Pepper, Jed
Daisy Chain - Mary DeMuth *i* 900

Woods, Janet
The Fifth Floor - Michael Harvey *m* 89

ACCOUNTANT

Borden, Daniel
Daniel's Den - Brandt Dodson *i* 901

Niederhoffer, Martin
The King of Ragtime - Larry Karp *m* 104

ACTIVIST

Delarosa, Maria
Precious Cargo - Clyde Ford *m* 67

ACTOR

Belzer, Richard
I Am Not a Cop! - Richard Belzer *m* 19

Clark, Warren
Heartless - Alison Gaylin *h* 544

Lillis, Harry
It Happened One Knife - Jeffrey Cohen *m* 51

Wade, Jack
Dead and Gone - Harry Shannon *h* 605

ACTRESS

Casey, Cassie
An Evil Guest - Gene Wolfe *f* 523

Cole, Lauren
Phantom's Touch - Julie Leto *r* 329

Diamond, Schiffer
One Fifth Avenue - Candace Bushnell *c* 986

Estrella, Gloria
Legacy - Jeanne C. Stein *h* 611

Geary, Monica
Power Play - Deirdre Martin *r* 344

Hamilton, Jayne
The Winter of Her Discontent - Kathryn Miller Haines *m* 83

McCord, Crystal
The Reluctant Cowgirl - Christine Lynxwiler *i* 933

Pirrotta, Betty
Sicilian Tragedee - Ottavio Cappellani *c* 988

Stafford, Mackenzie
Flashback - Jill Shalvis *r* 385

Winter, Rosie
The Winter of Her Discontent - Kathryn Miller Haines *m* 83

Yoshiko, Yamaguchi
The China Lover - Ian Buruma *t* 741

ADDICT

Denton, Joe
Small Crimes - Dave Zeltserman *m* 199

Donovan, Patrick
Season of Strangers - Kat Martin *r* 345

Sering, Kaitlan
Dark Pursuit - Brandilyn Collins *i* 893

ADMINISTRATOR

Crozier, Simon
Black Cathedral - L.H. Maynard *h* 574

Gold, Sullivan
The Ashes of Worlds - Kevin J. Anderson *s* 627

Whitemore, Sargent
Enclave - Kit Reed *s* 693

ADOPTEE

McCarter, Dana
Black Market Truth - Sharon Kaye *m* 106

Prentice, Clare
Conspiracy of Silence - Martha Powers *m* 158

Ryan, Samantha
Expecting the Doctor's Baby - Teresa Southwick *r* 396

Weatherby, Moxie
Barefoot Brides - Annie Jones *i* 924

ADVENTURER

Absolute, Jack
Absolute Honor - C.C. Humphreys *t* 796

Grant, C.S.
The Lost Temple - Tom Harper *t* 792

Oldhall, Nigel
Heart and Soul - Sarah A. Hoyt *f* 461

Pearson, Matt
Daredevil's Run - Kathleen Creighton *r* 247

ADVERTISING

Lowell, Julia
Five Star Cowboy - Charlene Sands *r* 382

AGED PERSON

Barrett, Nola
In a Dark Season - Vicki Lane *m* 115

Cain, Ciaphas
Cain's Last Stand - Sandy Mitchell *s* 689

Coy, Flora
Dead Dancing Women - Elizabeth Kane Buzzelli *m* 37

Davidsson, Gerlof
Echoes from the Dead - Johan Theorin *m* 189

Johnston, Gussie
Old Maid's Puzzle - Terri Thayer *m* 188

Knott, Kezzie
Death's Half Acre - Margaret Maron *m* 135

Lymon, Al
The Knights of the Cornerstone - James P. Blaylock *f* 430

Postum, Bob
The Knights of the Cornerstone - James P. Blaylock *f* 430

Quinn, Frank
Night Kills - John Lutz *m* 128

Salter, George
The Age of the Conglomerates - Thomas Nevins *s* 690

Teodora
Very Valentine - Adriana Tragiani *c* 1112

Vanger, Henrik
The Girl with the Dragon Tattoo - Stieg Larsson *m* 118

Wraxall, Montagu
The Glass of Time - Michael Cox *m* 55

AGENT

Daisuke, Sato
The China Lover - Ian Buruma *t* 741

HARV

The Flaxen Femme Fatale - John Zakour *s* 723

Jane

Ender in Exile - Orson Scott Card *s* 640

Lobo

Slanted Jack - Mark L. Van Name *s* 718

Watermind

Watermind - M.M. Buckner *s* 639

ARTISAN

Binkton

City of Jade - Dennis L. McKiernan *f* 484

Cord

Anathem - Neal Stephenson *s* 711

Folchart, Mortimer

Inkdeath - Cornelia Funke *f* 452

Langslow, Meg

Six Geese A-Slaying - Donna Andrews *m* 2

Lowenstein, Kiki

Paper, Scissors, Death - Joanna Campbell Slan *m* 177

Pike, Zeke

Triple Exposure - Colleen Thompson *r* 410

Roncalli, Valentine

Very Valentine - Adriana Tragiani *c* 1112

Shift, Mary

Wicked Weaves - Joyce Lavene *m* 120

Steele, Tamara

Ultimate Weapon - Shannon McKenna *r* 349

Washington, Dan Ravenheart "Raven"

Precious Cargo - Clyde Ford *m* 67

ARTIST

Akemi

Midnight - Sister Souljah *c* 1103

Allon, Gabriel

Moscow Rules - Daniel Silva *m* 175

Archmont, Vinnie

The Rose Conspiracy - Craig Parshall *i* 940

Birch, Gretchen

Ding Dong Dead - Deb Baker *m* 6

Bright, Darcy

Stray Dog Winter - David Francis *c* 1009

Bright, Fin

Stray Dog Winter - David Francis *c* 1009

Brogan, Ray

The Big O - Declan Burke *m* 36

Caldwell, Chelsea

Christmas Spirit - Rebecca York *r* 422

De Poulain, Elvira

Everything under the Sky - Matilda Asensi *t* 726

Donovan, Maggie

Bedeviled - Maureen Child *r* 243

Ellis, Paige

At First Sight - Stephen J. Cannell *m* 40

Engel, Marianne

The Gargoyle - Andrew Davidson *t* 758

Gordon, Elaine

Open Doors - Gloria Goldreich *c* 1014

Honeysett, Chris

Rainstone Fall - Peter Helton *m* 92

Hunter, Fran

White Nights - Ann Cleeves *m* 48

Jameson, Stewart

Blindspot: By a Gentleman in Exile and a Lady in Disguise - Jane Kamensky *t* 802

Blindspot: By a Gentleman in Exile and a Lady in Disguise - Jane Kamensky *c* 1032

Jordan, Annis

Rainstone Fall - Peter Helton *m* 92

Jorgenson, Jake

Conspiracy of Silence - Martha Powers *m* 158

Kahlo, Frida

Frida's Bed - Slavenka Drakulic *t* 764

Kaminski, Manuel

Me and Kaminski - Daniel Kehlmann *c* 1034

Kherson, Tasha

Murder on the Eiffel Tower - Claude Izner *m* 99

Lowery, Elizabeth

A Most Unconventional Match - Julia Justiss *r* 312

Nichols, Cristina

Brides of the Impaler - Edward Lee *h* 567

Osmond

Company of Liars - Karen Maitland *m* 132

Rivera, Diego

Frida's Bed - Slavenka Drakulic *t* 764

Ruthven, Nell

Adopted: Outback Baby - Barbara Hannay *r* 290

Sanders, Julia

Fresh Kills - Bill Loehfelm *m* 125

Shepard, Jess

Lord of Bones - Justine Musk *h* 582

Vincent, Reed

Insight - Deborah Raney *i* 944

ASSISTANT

Baylor, Francis

The Apothecary's Daughter - Julie Klassen *i* 927

Canby, Heather

Green Monster - Rick Shefchik *m* 172

Cline, Olivia

Insight - Deborah Raney *i* 944

Gilmour, Toni

A Spoonful of Poison - M.C. Beaton *m* 17

Khan, Hassan

Blood Wedding - P.J. Brooke *m* 32

Markham, Devon

Cold Hearted - Beverly Barton *m* 14

Salvatrio, Sigmundo

The Paris Enigma - Pablo De Santis *m* 63

AVENGER

Charles, Wesley

Phenomenal Girl 5 - A.J. Menden *r* 351

Guy of Warwick

Shadow Rider - Kathrynn Dennis *r* 254

Janos, Valery

Ultimate Weapon - Shannon McKenna *r* 349

BABYSITTER

Nevelson, Helen

A Face at the Window - Sarah Graves *m* 80

BAKER

Barnett, Samantha

Marry-Me Christmas - Shirley Jump *r* 310

Keyes, Jesse

Sweet Trouble - Susan Mallery *r* 340

Keyes, Nicole

Sweet Spot - Susan Mallery *r* 339

Lawson, Chloe

All That Matters - Stef Ann Holm *r* 297

Thompson, Natalie

Winning the Single Mom's Heart - Linda Goodnight *r* 283

BANKER

Burch, Isaac H.

Dalliance - Diana Burg *t* 740

McPherson, Heath

The Inherited Twins - Cathy Gillen Thacker *r* 404

Millbank, Josiah

A Good Woman - Danielle Steel *t* 853

Smith-Fennimore, Malcolm

Mad about the Boy? - Dolores Gordon-Smith *m* 77

Westin, Drew

On a Someday - Roxanne Henke *i* 916

BASTARD DAUGHTER

Marchand, Camille

Never Romance a Rake - Liz Carlyle *r* 235

BASTARD SON

Barrow, Devlin

Montana Royalty - B.J. Daniels *r* 249

Deville, Sebastien

The Bride Price - Anne Mallory *r* 341

Ferrell, Devlin

Unlacing Lilly - Gail Ranstrom *r* 374

Morant, Harry

His Captive Lady - Anne Gracie *r* 284

BIBLICAL FIGURE

Adam

Eve - Elissa Elliott *c* 1002

Eve

Eve - Elissa Elliott *c* 1002

BIKER

DeMarco, Manny

Anchors Aweigh - Kathleen Bacus *r* 210

Anchors Aweigh - Kathleen Bacus *m* 5

BLACKSMITH

Van der Vort, Karl

That Certain Spark - Cathy Marie Hake *i* 910

BODYGUARD

Blackhawk, Nicholas

Immortals: The Haunting - Robin T. Popp *r* 371

Cathal

Heir to Sevenwaters - Juliet Marillier *f* 481

Davis, Toni

All I Want for Christmas Is a Vampire - Kerrelyn Sparks *r* 397

Evans, Lucie

Dying for You - Beverly Barton *r* 215

Fox, Charlie

Third Strike - Zoe Sharp *m* 171

Perry, Ryan
Your Heart Belongs to Me - Dean R.
Koontz m 111

Pieters, Cole
Foundation - Mercedes Lackey f 467

Preston, Brent
A Lady's Luck - Ken Casper r 238

Quickfire
The House of the Stag - Kage Baker f 427

Roarke
Salvation in Death - J.D. Robb s 698

Salo, Noah
Everything but a Bride - Holly Jacobs r 300

Siegel, Mitchell
The Book of Lies - Brad Meltzer m 144

Sinclair, Sam
The Man Must Marry - Janet Chapman r 241

Soter
Lord Tophet - Gregory Frost f 451

Stelfox, Steven
Kill Your Friends - John Niven c 1068

Stoker, Bram
The Dracula Dossier - James Reese m 163

Summerfield, Nathaniel
Ready and Willing - Elizabeth Bevarly r 216

Sumner, David
Talk of the Town - Sherrill Bodine r 220

Walcote, Nicholas
Veil of Lies - Jeri Westerson t 867

Wright-Jones, Griffin
The Price of Desire - Jo Goodman r 282

Zoukas, Viktor
Cold in Hand - John Harvey m 88

BUSINESSWOMAN

Amble, Patricia "Tish"
Kiss Me If You Dare - Nicole Young i 967

Anderson, Jaycee
Slippery When Wet - Kimberly Raye r 375

Barnett, Samantha
Marry-Me Christmas - Shirley Jump r 310

Bertrand, Carmela
Death Swatch - Laura Childs m 46

Blair, Gwyneth
The Bell at Sealey Head - Patricia A.
McKillip f 485

Brioche, Jeanette
Welcome to Serenity - Sherryl Woods r 421

Chandler, Lane
The Private Concierge - Suzanne Forster r 270

Cosi, Clare
Espresso Shot - Cleo Coyle m 56

Day, Olena
In Love with a Younger Man - Cheryl
Robinson c 1084

Deitz, Suzanne
Eggs in Purgatory - Laura Childs m 47

Doreen
Murder with All the Trimmings - Elaine
Viets m 193

DuBonnet, Marie "Marisa"
The Prince's Secret Bride - Raye Morgan r 357

Faithfull, Emily "Fido"
The Sealed Letter - Emma Donoghue t 763

Falconer, Leah
Speak of the Devil - Shari Shattuck h 606

Gordon, Melinda
Revenge - Doranna Durgin h 540

Grieux, Ava
Death Swatch - Laura Childs m 46

Hagan, Mallory Kendrick
Texas Ranger Takes a Bride - Patricia
Thayer r 405

Hawkins, Song
Red Helmet - Homer Hickam i 918

Hobbs, Chloe
Casting Spells - Barbara Bretton r 225

Jenkins, Naomi
Hurting Distance - Sophie Hannah m 85

Kellerman, Skye
Trust Me - Brenda Novak r 360

Kent, Willamina
The Man Must Marry - Janet Chapman r 241

Kolbe, Leah
Deep Night - Caroline Petit m 156

Lockhart, Leila
A Dead Man in Barcelona - Michael
Pearce m 153

Marchette, Lil
Just One Bite - Kimberly Raye h 591

McCone, Sharon
Burn Out - Marcia Muller m 148

Mckerney, Catherine
The Case of the Deceiving Don - Carl
Brookins m 33

Montgomery, Kendall
Deadly Night - Heather Graham r 287

Novak, Sadie
Devil May Ride - Wendy Roberts m 165
Devil May Ride - Wendy Roberts h 595

Olander, Claire
The Inherited Twins - Cathy Gillen
Thacker r 404

O'Malley, Gillian
Stiffs and Swine - J.B. Stanley m 183

Penny, Alex
Daredevil's Run - Kathleen Creighton r 247

Shift, Mary
Wicked Weaves - Joyce Lavene m 120

Smith, Callie
Everything but a Bride - Holly Jacobs r 300

Sonnet, Karen
Into the Shadow - Christina Dodd r 257

Stuart, Alexa
Hot as Hell - HelenKay Dimon r 255

Summerlin, Violet
No Peeking - Stephanie Bond r 221

Traynor, Laura
Daniel's Den - Brandt Dodson i 901

Vaughn, Riley
Slippery When Wet - Kimberly Raye r 375

Whitby, Jess
My Lord and Spymaster - Joanna Bourne r 222

Woodyard, Lee McKinney
The Chocolate Snowman Murders - JoAnna
Carl m 41

CAPTIVE

Collins, Mia
Savage Abandon - Cassie Edwards r 261

Dionysia
The Sun's Bride - Gillian Bradshaw t 737

Fitzstephen, Hugo
Ransom My Heart - Mia Thermopolis r 406

Gibbs, Katherine "Kitty"
Irreversible - Liz Maverick r 346

CARE GIVER

Boughton, Glory
Home - Marilynne Robinson c 1085

Raines, Beth Ann
Cursed - Jamie Leigh Hansen h 548

Sutherland, Eliza Jane
Her Montana Man - Cheryl St. John r 399

CARPENTER

Douglas, Mack
Simply the Best - Shirley Jump r 311

McLean, Daniel
Once upon a Christmas - Holly Jacobs r 301

Porter, John
A Hundred Years of Happiness - Nicole
Seitz i 949

Tiptree, Jacobia "Jake"
A Face at the Window - Sarah Graves m 80

CARTOGRAPHER

Zhi, Ma
The Map Thief - Heather Terrell m 187

CATERER

Barone, Regina
Sea Fever - Virginia Kantra r 314

Guidry, Meredith
Menu for Romance - Kaye Dacus i 896

CELEBRITY

Archer, Joanna
The Touch of Twilight - Vicki Pettersson h 588

Kane, Portia
Living With the Dead - Kelley Armstrong h 527

Norville, Kitty
Kitty and the Dead Man's Hand - Carrie
Vaughn h 617

Olemaun, Stella
Eternal Damnation - Steve Niles h 583

CHAUFFEUR

Truesdale, Will
The Piano Teacher - Janice Y.K. Lee c 1045

CHIEFTAN

Wolf Hawk
Savage Abandon - Cassie Edwards r 261

CHILD

Ashmore, Emma
One Perfect Gift - Kathleen Morgan i 936

Barry, Gabe
The Secrets of Laurel Oaks - Lois Ruby h 598

Blake, Peter
Without Conscience - David Stuart Davies t 759
Without Conscience - David Stuart Davies m 62

Bookchild, Rossamunde
Lamplighter - D.M. Cornish f 440

DETECTIVE—PRIVATE

DICTATOR

DIPLOMAT

DIRECTOR

DIVER

Ya'ari, Amotz
Friendly Fire - A.B. Yehoshua   *c* 1125

ENTERTAINER

Chase, Megan
Personal Demons - Stacia Kane   *h* 560

Davis, Sammy Jr.
Hey There (You with the Gun in Your Hand) - Robert J. Randisi   *t* 836

Diverus
Lord Tophet - Gregory Frost   *f* 451

Grant, Odysseus
Kitty and the Dead Man's Hand - Carrie Vaughn   *h* 617

Leodora
Lord Tophet - Gregory Frost   *f* 451

Madison, Dawn
Break of Dawn - Chris Marie Green   *h* 545

Pears, Lily
Fallen Skies - Philippa Gregory   *t* 788

Sofya
The Kiss Murder - Mehmet Murat Somer   *m* 179

Warren
The Damned - William Ollie   *h* 584

ENVIRONMENTALIST

Maki, Ben
Freezing Point - Karen Dionne   *s* 653

EQUESTRIAN

Barrow, Devlin
Montana Royalty - B.J. Daniels   *r* 249

Preston, Brent
A Lady's Luck - Ken Casper   *r* 238

EXPATRIATE

Bright, Pearl
Thirteen Orphans - Jane Lindskold   *f* 473

Michallat, Eddie
Judge - Karen Traviss   *s* 715

EXPLORER

Aravan
City of Jade - Dennis L. McKiernan   *f* 484

Aylis
City of Jade - Dennis L. McKiernan   *f* 484

Bowman, Marcus
Riders of the Storm - Julie E. Czerneda   *s* 648

Farewell, Peter
Soul of Fire - Sarah A. Hoyt   *f* 462

Oldhall, Nigel
Heart and Soul - Sarah A. Hoyt   *f* 461

FARMER

Adams, Dawsey
The Guernsey Literary and Potato Peel Pie Society - Mary Ann Shaffer   *c* 1094
The Guernsey Literary and Potato Peel Pie Society - Mary Ann Shaffer   *t* 849

Ansotegui, Justo
Guernica - Dave Boling   *t* 734

Esther
Esther's Inheritance - Sandor Marai   *c* 1060

Goodweather, Elizabeth
In a Dark Season - Vicki Lane   *m* 115

Haggard, Rich
Point No Point - Mary Logue   *m* 126

Haristeen, Mary Minor "Harry"
Santa Clawed - Rita Mae Brown   *m* 34

Lambright, Wayne
A Cousin's Promise - Wanda E. Brunstetter   *i* 881

Sproule, Raven
The Bell at Sealey Head - Patricia A. McKillip   *f* 485

Thomson, Kenny
White Nights - Ann Cleeves   *m* 48

Tucker, Alafair
The Sky Took Him - Donis Casey   *m* 42

FBI AGENT

Cahill, Greg
Ulterior Motives - Mark Andrew Olson   *i* 938

Cooper, Evan
Against All Odds - Irene Hannon   *i* 913

Dominic
Hunter's Prayer - Lilith Saintcrow   *h* 599

Harmon, Margaret
The River Runs Dry - Sibella Giorello   *i* 906

Hedrick, Karl
Stranger Room - Frederick Ramsay   *m* 161

Jaconetti, Nick
A Veiled Deception - Annette Blair   *m* 25

Kismet, Jill
Hunter's Prayer - Lilith Saintcrow   *h* 599
Night Shift - Lilith Saintcrow   *h* 600

Lyons, Alexander
In the Blood - Adrian Phoenix   *h* 589

Morgan, Grady
Envy the Night - Michael Koryta   *m* 112

O'Connor, Jack
Miss Match - Sara Mills   *i* 935

O'Dell, Maggie
Exposed - Alex Kava   *m* 105

Pierce, Daniel "Ace"
Ace Is Wild - Penny McCall   *r* 348

Tully, R.J.
Exposed - Alex Kava   *m* 105

Vail, Karen
The 7th Victim - Alan Jacobson   *m* 100

Valtrez, Vincent
Insatiable Desire - Rita Herron   *h* 553

Vasquez, Sonora "Sonny"
Crash Into Me - Jill Sorenson   *m* 180

Wallace, Heather
In the Blood - Adrian Phoenix   *h* 589

FIANCE(E)

Miller, John
Rebecca's Promise - Jerry S. Eicher   *i* 904
Rebecca's Return - Jerry S. Eicher   *i* 903

Bloom, Charity
Chasing Charity - Marcia Gruver   *i* 909

Bradford, Emmaline
A Promise for Spring - Kim Vogel Sawyer   *i* 948

Caldwell, Fannie
Distant Heart - Tracey Bateman   *i* 877

Clark, Daniel
Chasing Charity - Marcia Gruver   *i* 909

Cleary, Paul
Takeover - Lisa Black   *m* 24

Forsythe, Ariana
The House in Grosvenor Square - Linore Rose Burkard   *i* 883

Garrett, Geoffrey
A Promise for Spring - Kim Vogel Sawyer   *i* 948

Hammer, Mike
The Goliath Bone - Mickey Spillane   *m* 181

Hawatyne, Jonathan
Deep Night - Caroline Petit   *t* 832

Hutch
Dead Man Dancing - Marcia Talley   *m* 186

Keim, Rebecca
Rebecca's Promise - Jerry S. Eicher   *i* 904
Rebecca's Return - Jerry S. Eicher   *i* 903

Kolbe, Leah
Deep Night - Caroline Petit   *t* 832

Lambright, Wayne
A Cousin's Promise - Wanda E. Brunstetter   *i* 881

MacLean, Theresa
Takeover - Lisa Black   *m* 24

Mercer, Tyrell
A Killing Frost - Hannah Alexander   *i* 875

Miller, Loraine
A Cousin's Promise - Wanda E. Brunstetter   *i* 881

Mornay, Phillip
The House in Grosvenor Square - Linore Rose Burkard   *i* 883

Ruth
Dead Man Dancing - Marcia Talley   *m* 186

Sterling, Velda
The Goliath Bone - Mickey Spillane   *m* 181

Tanner, Blake
Distant Heart - Tracey Bateman   *i* 877

FILMMAKER

Ellison, Keith
Take One - Karen Kingsbury   *i* 925

Ryan, Chase
Take One - Karen Kingsbury   *i* 925

FINANCIER

Shaw, Owen
For Her Eyes Only - Cait London   *r* 330

FIRE FIGHTER

Donnelly, Aidan
Flashback - Jill Shalvis   *r* 385

Josh
Sweet Waters - Julie Carobini   *i* 889

Sneed, Aretha
The Clinch Knot - John Galligan   *m* 72

FISHERMAN

Alley, Parker
Fisherman's Bend - Linda Greenlaw   *m* 81

Ansotegui, Josepe
Guernica - Dave Boling   *t* 734

Ansotegui, Xabier
Guernica - Dave Boling   *t* 734

Brannigan, Ryan
Destiny Bay - Sarah Abbot   *r* 200

Dunham, Cal
Fisherman's Bend - Linda Greenlaw   *m* 81

Oglivie, Ned "Dog"
The Clinch Knot - John Galligan   *m* 72

Winslow, Jasper
The Not Quite Right Reverend Cletus J. Diggs and the Currently Accepted Habits of Nature - David Niall Wilson   *h* 623

FOREMAN

McKenzie, Grady
Sweetwater Gap - Denise Hunter   *i* 922

O'Reilly, Mark
Perfect Circle - Carlos J. Cortes   *s* 646

FRIEND

Abbott, Kathleen
Ghost at Work - Carolyn Hart   *m* 87

Barton, Kay
The Water's Edge - Daniel Judson   *m* 103

Caldwell, Fannie
Distant Heart - Tracey Bateman   *i* 877

Chance, Daisy
Daisy Chain - Mary DeMuth   *i* 900

DeCateur, Eve
Blackbird, Farewell - Robert Greer   *m* 82

Finch, Gillian
Keeping Secrets - Owen Madoc   *t* 814

Gemma
Fireflies in December - Jennifer Erin Valent   *i* 959

Grogan, Adam
The Bride Backfire - Kelly Eileen Hake   *i* 911

Madrid, Damion
Blackbird, Farewell - Robert Greer   *m* 82

Markovich, Rudy
I Am Not a Cop! - Richard Belzer   *m* 19

O'Neill, Norah
Indigo Christmas - Jeanne M. Dams   *m* 60

Pepper, Jed
Daisy Chain - Mary DeMuth   *i* 900

Prosser, Dorothy
Keeping Secrets - Owen Madoc   *t* 814

Rodden, Toni
Distant Heart - Tracey Bateman   *i* 877

Sneed, D'Ontario
The Clinch Knot - John Galligan   *m* 72

Speck, Opal
The Bride Backfire - Kelly Eileen Hake   *i* 911

FRONTIERSWOMAN

Renoir, Isabelle
Wind Dancer - Jamie Carie   *i* 885

FUGITIVE

Augustus
Strength and Honor - R.M. Meluch   *s* 687

Berman, Paula
Half a Crown - Jo Walton   *s* 720

Deveraux, Angelique
The Darkest Touch - Jaci Burton   *h* 534

Deveraux, Isabelle
The Darkest Touch - Jaci Burton   *h* 534

Fell, Alice
End of the Century - Chris Roberson   *s* 699

McCree, Destiny
Destiny Kills - Keri Arthur   *h* 529

Nena
Love in the Time of Fridges - Tim Scott   *s* 705

Warington, Sofie
Soul of Fire - Sarah A. Hoyt   *f* 462

Wilson, Trae
Destiny Kills - Keri Arthur   *h* 529

GAMBLER

Romaine, Jack
Kaleidoscope - Darryl Wimberley   *t* 869
Kaleidoscope - Darryl Wimberley   *m* 198

Wren, Wesley
3 Men and a Body - Stephanie Bond   *m* 28

GAME WARDEN

Denninger, Dani
Death Roe - Joseph Heywood   *m* 93

Service, Grady
Death Roe - Joseph Heywood   *m* 93

GANG MEMBER

Louie, Tat
Year of the Dog - Henry Chang   *m* 44

GARDENER

Larson, Daphne
Worth Fighting For - Molly O'Keefe   *r* 363

Parker, Bella
The Way Home - Jean Brashear   *r* 224

Rapskeller, Charles
The Black Tower - Louis Bayard   *m* 15

GENEALOGIST

Murray, Katharine
Daughter of Deceit - Patricia Sprinkle   *m* 182

GENIUS

Fegley, Theodore Mead
Life After Genius - M. Ann Jacoby   *c* 1027

Solarin, Alexandra
The Fire - Katherine Neville   *m* 149

GENTLEMAN

Bingley, Jonathan
Netherfield Park Revisted - Rebecca Ann Collins   *t* 753

Darcy, Fitzwilliam
The Independence of Miss Mary Bennet - Colleen McCullough   *t* 818
The Matters at Mansfield - Carrie Bebris   *t* 731

Fairfax, Griffin
His Wicked Sins - Eve Silver   *r* 388

Hadley, William
Where Serpents Sleep - C.S. Harris   *t* 793

Jameson, Rory
Passion and Pleasure in London - Melody Thomas   *r* 408

Waterman, Hal
A Most Unconventional Match - Julia Justiss   *r* 312

GENTLEWOMAN

Ashburn, Winter
Passion and Pleasure in London - Melody Thomas   *r* 408

Beaumont, Daphne
Seduction Becomes Her - Shirlee Busbee   *r* 231

Bennet, Mary
The Independence of Miss Mary Bennet - Colleen McCullough   *t* 818

Brightly, Cynthia
Like No Other Lover - Julie Anne Long   *r* 331

Carington, Isobel
To Sin with a Stranger - Kathryn Caskie   *r* 237

Chavenet, Amalie
Untamed - Pamela Clare   *r* 245

Cole, Olivia
The Price of Desire - Jo Goodman   *r* 282

Darcy, Elizabeth Bennet
The Matters at Mansfield - Carrie Bebris   *t* 731

de Lacey, Elinor "Nelly"
The Virgin Queen's Daughter - Ella March Chase   *t* 747

Delacorte, Ginerva "Ginny"
Miss Delacorte Speaks Her Mind - Heidi Ashworth   *r* 209

Everton, Sophie
As Luck Would Have It - Alissa Johnson   *r* 308

Fairchild, Kate
The Dangerous Duke - Christine Wells   *r* 416

Faulkner, Anna
Netherfield Park Revisted - Rebecca Ann Collins   *t* 753

Fleming, Melisande
To Seduce a Sinner - Elizabeth Hoyt   *r* 299

Hunterton, Caroline
An Outrageous Affair - Penny Vicenzi   *t* 864

Lachlan, Fiona
A Seduction at Christmas - Cathy Maxwell   *r* 347

Latimer, Chione
An Improper Aristocrat - Deb Marlowe   *r* 343

MacDavid, Kathleen MacDav
Seduction of a Proper Gentleman - Victoria Alexander   *r* 204

Marlowe, Hermoine
Tempted by the Night - Elizabeth Boyle   *r* 223

Martin, Carolyn
The Bride Price - Anne Mallory   *r* 341

Pennistan, Olivia
Lover's Kiss - Mary Blayney   *r* 218

Randall, Letitia
The Edge of Desire - Stephanie Laurens   *r* 324

Reskeen, Ellery
Lost in You - Alix Rickloff   *r* 377

Stanton, Evelyn
The Dragon Earl - Jade Lee   *r* 326

Sutherland, Eliza Jane
Her Montana Man - Cheryl St. John   *r* 399

GHOST

Daphne
The Secrets of Laurel Oaks - Lois Ruby   *h* 598

GIRLFRIEND

de Lissac, Chantale
A Dead Man in Barcelona - Michael Pearce   *m* 153

Mara
A Secret and Unlawful Killing - Cora
Harrison   *t* 794
A Secret and Unlawful Killing - Cora
Harrison   *m* 86

KIDNAPPER

Brogan, Ray
The Big O - Declan Burke   *m* 36
Crais, Finnula
Ransom My Heart - Mia Thermopolis   *r* 406
Kaysar, Leonardo
Irreversible - Liz Maverick   *r* 346

KNIGHT

de Marins, Bascot
Death of a Squire - Maureen Ash   *m* 3
Djames, Djarrhett Raven Perseus Pendra
Knight's Fork - Rowena Cherry   *r* 242
Galaad
End of the Century - Chris Roberson   *s* 699
Guest, Crispin
Veil of Lies - Jeri Westerson   *m* 197
Veil of Lies - Jeri Westerson   *t* 867
Guy of Warwick
Shadow Rider - Kathrynn Dennis   *r* 254
Lymon, Al
The Knights of the Cornerstone - James P.
Blaylock   *f* 430
Metzger, Reinhardt
Curse of the Necrarch - Steven Savile   *f* 513
Napier, Garth
Border Lass - Amanda Scott   *r* 384
Perez, Angel
The Gypsy Morph - Terry Brooks   *f* 432
Thedeus
Too Many Curses - A. Lee Martinez   *f* 482
Tyrkilld
Caine Black Knife - Matthew Stover   *f* 519
Vulgnash
The Wyrmling Horde - David Farland   *f* 446

LAIRD

Haggerty, Logan
The Pirate Bride - Shannon Drake   *r* 258

LANDLORD

Brannigan, Ryan
Destiny Bay - Sarah Abbot   *r* 200
Mahoney, Rick
Holiday Dreams - Annette Mahon   *r* 338
Miller, Tommy
The Water's Edge - Daniel Judson   *m* 103

LANDOWNER

Shaw, Griffin
Surrender to Me - Sophie Jordan   *r* 309

LAWMAN

Garrett, Pat
Lucky Billy - John Vernon   *t* 863
Landon, Chase
Texas Ranger Takes a Bride - Patricia
Thayer   *r* 405

McPherson, James
Beyond This Moment - Tamera Alexander   *i* 876
Shepard, Dave
A Dream to Call My Own - Tracie
Peterson   *i* 941

LAWYER

Alexander, Logan Tyler
Fiance at Her Fingertips - Kathleen
Bacus   *r* 211
Ansell, Thomas
The Salisbury Manuscript - Philip Gooden   *t* 783
Barclay, Ben
The Daddy Verdict - Karen Rose Smith   *r* 393
Blackstone, J.D.
The Rose Conspiracy - Craig Parshall   *i* 940
Cavanaugh, Matt
Teaser - Jan Brogan   *m* 31
Coyne, Mara
The Map Thief - Heather Terrell   *m* 187
Drury, Douglas
A Lover's Kiss - Margaret Moore   *r* 356
Franklin, Jess
Brides of the Impaler - Edward Lee   *h* 567
Goldfarb, Emmanuel "Manny"
Salvation Boulevard - Larry Beinhart   *m* 18
Graves, Reginald "Rex"
Christmas Is Murder - C.S. Challinor   *m* 43
Haller, Mickey
The Brass Verdict - Michael Connelly   *m* 52
Lusak, Craig
Revenge - Doranna Durgin   *h* 540
Manhattan, Chase
Wicked Weaves - Joyce Lavene   *m* 120
Martinsson, Rebecka
The Black Path - Asa Larsson   *m* 117
Moretti, John
All That Matters - Stef Ann Holm   *r* 297
Munroe, Jamie
Intimate Enemy - Marilyn Pappano   *r* 367
Nasher, Paul
Brides of the Impaler - Edward Lee   *h* 567
O'Farrell, Ben
Kitty and the Dead Man's Hand - Carrie
Vaughn   *h* 617
Payton, Max
Behind the Shadows - Patricia Potter   *r* 372
Pennyworth, Rep
Shoot the Lawyer Twice - Michael Bowen   *m* 29
Pierce, Daniel "Ace"
Ace Is Wild - Penny McCall   *r* 348
Rollins, Jerrold "Jerry"
Murder Inside the Beltway - Margaret
Truman   *m* 192
Seeley, Michael
A Patent Lie - Paul Goldstein   *m* 76
Shawn
Forever Christmas - Christine Lynxwiler   *i* 932
Stuart, David
Dalliance - Diana Burg   *t* 740
Sutter, John
The Gate House - Nelson DeMille   *c* 998
Willan, Samantha
The Rogue Hunter - Lynsay Sands   *r* 383

Winston-Beaufort, Brianna
Defending Angels - Mary Stanton   *m* 184
Woodyard, Joe
The Chocolate Snowman Murders - JoAnna
Carl   *m* 41
Wraxall, Montagu
The Glass of Time - Michael Cox   *m* 55
Wrotham, Oliver
The Serpent and the Scorpion - Clare
Langley-Hawthorne   *t* 809

LEADER

Bisochim
The Phoenix Endangered - Mercedes
Lackey   *f* 468
Cornick, Bran
Cry Wolf - Patricia Briggs   *f* 431
Egar
The Steel Remains - Richard K. Morgan   *f* 492
Nikodemus
My Wicked Enemy - Carolyn Jewel   *h* 558
oc Horin-Gyre, Kanin
Bloodheir - Brian Ruckley   *f* 508
oc Lannis-Haig, Orisian
Bloodheir - Brian Ruckley   *f* 508
Predo, Dexter
Every Last Drop - Charlie Huston   *h* 555
St. Onge, Gordon
The School on Heart's Content Road - Carolyn
Chute   *c* 991
Shaiara
The Phoenix Endangered - Mercedes
Lackey   *f* 468
Stearns, Mike
1635: The Dreeson Incident - Eric Flint   *s* 655
Tanner, Blake
Distant Heart - Tracey Bateman   *i* 877
Trasamund
The Breath of God - Harry Turtledove   *f* 520
York, Richard Rex
The School on Heart's Content Road - Carolyn
Chute   *c* 991

LESBIAN

Kaibara, Kiyomi "Yuzan"
Real World - Natsuo Kirino   *m* 110
Sanders, Julia
Fresh Kills - Bill Loehfelm   *m* 125

LIBRARIAN

Henry, James
Stiffs and Swine - J.B. Stanley   *m* 183
Kanahele, Momi
Holiday Dreams - Annette Mahon   *r* 338
McLean, Margaret "Meg"
Buffalo Bill's Defunct - Shelia Simonson   *m* 176
Rogers, Paige
Breach of Trust - DiAnn Mills   *i* 934

LINGUIST

Alija
Promised Virgins - Jeffrey Fleishman   *c* 1008
Guinness, October "Tobie"
The Archangel Project - C.S. Graham   *m* 79
Harrisdaughter, Xera
No Words Alone - Autumn Dawn   *r* 252

MOUNTAINEER

Macinnes, Nell
To Catch a Thief - Christina Skye *r* 391

MURDERER

Becker, Arno
Kaleidoscope - Darryl Wimberley *m* 198

Best, Charles "Chick" Jr.
At First Sight - Stephen J. Cannell *m* 40

Campbell, Ozzie
A Face at the Window - Sarah Graves *m* 80

Ellis, Rogan
Countdown - Michelle Maddox *r* 337

Ryo
Real World - Natsuo Kirino *m* 110

Scott, Jordan
The 19th Wife - David Ebershoff *t* 766
The 19th Wife - David Ebershoff *c* 1001

MUSEUM CURATOR

Clement, Rose
Pictures at an Exhibition - Sara
  Houghteling *c* 1024

Schmidt, Anton Z.
The Laughter of Dead Kings - Elizabeth
  Peters *m* 155

MUSICIAN

Adam
Rock Bottom - Michael Shilling *c* 1096

Ahuja, Arjun
Family Planning - Karan Mahajan *c* 1057

Baptiste, Dante
In the Blood - Adrian Phoenix *h* 589

Bobby
Rock Bottom - Michael Shilling *c* 1096

Broadus, Jimmy Wayne
Hellbent and Heartfirst - Kassandra Sims *h* 608

Chaloner, Thomas
The Butcher of Smithfield - Susanna
  Gregory *t* 790

Chiaretta
The Four Seasons - Laurel Corona *c* 994
The Four Seasons - Laurel Corona *t* 754

Clayton, Greg
Her Best Christmas Ever - Judy Duarte *r* 260

Cox, Dario
Rock Bottom - Michael Shilling *c* 1096

David
Michal - Jill Eileen Smith *i* 951

Deveau, Chantal
Mystic Rider - Patricia Rice *r* 376

Diverus
Lord Tophet - Gregory Frost *f* 451

Emmanuel, Michael
American Anthem - B.J. Hoff *i* 920

Flynn, Jeremy
Deadly Harvest - Heather Graham *r* 286

Greenberg, Louis
Early Bright - Ami Silber *t* 852

Joplin, Scott
The King of Ragtime - Larry Karp *t* 803
The King of Ragtime - Larry Karp *m* 104

Liedmann, Gregor
Disguise - Hugo Hamilton *t* 791

Maddalena
The Four Seasons - Laurel Corona *t* 754
The Four Seasons - Laurel Corona *c* 994

McNeill, Libby
Coming Home - Elisabeth Rose *r* 379

Myrrdin
Here Lies Arthur - Philip Reeve *f* 500

Niederhoffer, Martin
The King of Ragtime - Larry Karp *m* 104
The King of Ragtime - Larry Karp *t* 803

Odegard, Elizabeth
The Man in the Blizzard - Bart Schneider *m* 169

Reyes, Teddy
This One Is Mine - Maria Semple *c* 1093

Ricucci, Danny
Marriage 101 - Deborah Shelley *r* 387

Rodrigo
Company of Liars - Karen Maitland *t* 815

Stanley, Eleanor Stark "Nell"
The King of Ragtime - Larry Karp *m* 104

Stark, Nell
The King of Ragtime - Larry Karp *t* 803

MYTHICAL CREATURE

Ahriman, Zal
Going Under - Justina Robson *s* 700

Alexander, Logan Tyler
Fiance at Her Fingertips - Kathleen
  Bacus *r* 211

Ashwin, Holly
Dark Desires after Dusk - Kresley Cole *r* 246

Bellorus, Kirisin
The Gypsy Morph - Terry Brooks *f* 432

Bimm, Fredrika
Fish out of Water - MaryJanice Davidson *r* 250

Blackhawk, Nicholas
Immortals: The Haunting - Robin T. Popp *r* 371

Bligh, Conor
Lost in You - Alix Rickloff *r* 377

Briec the Mighty
About a Dragon - G.A. Aiken *r* 202

Cavannaugh, Caer
Deadly Gift - Heather Graham *r* 285

Culhane
Bedeviled - Maureen Child *r* 243

Dallen
Foundation - Mercedes Lackey *f* 467

D'Artigo, Delilah
Dragon Wytch - Yasmine Galenorn *f* 453

David
Gale Force - Rachel Caine *f* 435

Deacon
Dancing with the Devil - Laura Drewry *r* 259

Death
Dead Reign - T.A. Pratt *f* 498

Denoriel
And Less than Kind - Mercedes Lackey *f* 466

Dhu, Vidal
And Less than Kind - Mercedes Lackey *f* 466

Dominic
Hunter's Prayer - Lilith Saintcrow *h* 599
Night Shift - Lilith Saintcrow *h* 600

Dorian
Storm Born - Richelle Mead *h* 577

Doyle
Swallowing Darkness - Laurell Hamilton *f* 458

Dustcircle, Saul
Hunter's Prayer - Lilith Saintcrow *h* 599

Farewell, Peter
Soul of Fire - Sarah A. Hoyt *f* 462

Gabriel
Up in Smoke - Katie MacAlister *r* 333

Gard
The House of the Stag - Kage Baker *f* 427

Goodfellow, Robin "Kane"
The Druid Made Me Do It - Natale
  Stenzel *r* 402

Gotrek
Elfslayer - Nathan Long *f* 478

Graxen
Dragonforge - James Maxey *f* 483

Groves, Mia
Immortals: The Haunting - Robin T. Popp *r* 371

Gunner
Ironhand - Charlie Fletcher *f* 447

Hellboy
The Golden Army - Robert Greenberger *h* 547

Hunter, Dylan
Sea Fever - Virginia Kantra *r* 314

Icehart
The Snow Queen - Mercedes Lackey *f* 469

Kai
Dragon Moon - Carole Wilkinson *f* 522

Kallinikos, Dimitri
The Accidental Demon Slayer - Angie Fox *r* 274

Kincaid, Georgina
Succubus Dreams - Richelle Mead *h* 578

Kiyo
Storm Born - Richelle Mead *h* 577

Lightfoot
Dark Whispers - Bruce Coville *f* 441

Lord Loss
Death's Shadow - Darren Shan *h* 603

Luelldar
Dark Vengeance - Ed Greenwood *f* 457

Luvo
The Melting Stones - Tamora Pierce *f* 497

Maeve
Cursed - Jamie Leigh Hansen *h* 548

Maralen
Morningtide - Cory J. Herndon *f* 459

Margred
Sea Witch - Virginia Kantra *r* 315

Mayling
Up in Smoke - Katie MacAlister *r* 333

McCree, Destiny
Destiny Kills - Keri Arthur *h* 529

Ormson, Tom
Gentleman Takes a Chance - Sarah A.
  Hoyt *f* 460

Rahel
Gale Force - Rachel Caine *f* 435

Rhys
Morningtide - Cory J. Herndon *f* 459

Roc, Ragna
Two to the Fifth - Piers Anthony *f* 425

Sapien, Abe
The Golden Army - Robert Greenberger *h* 547

OUTCAST

Palmer, Bill
The Sin Eaters - Andrew Beahrs   *t* 730

OUTLAW

Billy the Kid
Lucky Billy - John Vernon   *t* 863

Crais, Finnula
Ransom My Heart - Mia Thermopolis   *r* 406

McClain, Waco
To Seduce a Texan - Georgina Gentry   *r* 279

PARALEGAL

Kepler, Michelle Alison
The Bodies Left Behind - Jeffery Deaver   *m* 64

PARENT

Ahuja, Rakesh
Family Planning - Karan Mahajan   *c* 1057

Ashmore, Jessica
One Perfect Gift - Kathleen Morgan   *i* 936

Benson, Flora Jean
Blackbird, Farewell - Robert Greer   *m* 82

Bernice
Irreplaceable - Stephen Lovely   *c* 1052

Bledsoe, Carmyn
Just Too Good to Be True - E. Lynn
   Harris   *c* 1019

Boughton, Robert
Home - Marilynne Robinson   *c* 1085

Brooks, Laney
I Smile Back - Amy Koppelman   *c* 1040

Carrier, Martha
The Heretic's Daughter - Kathleen Kent   *c* 1035

Crowther, Georgine
Deception's Daughter - Cordelia Frances
   Biddle   *m* 23

David
A Cedar Cove Christmas - Debbie
   Macomber   *c* 1055

DeVore, Doug
Yesterday's Embers - Deborah Raney   *i* 945

Dunbar, Casey
The Other Side of Silence - Bill Pronzini   *m* 159

Ebberly, Rosalyn
Play It Again, SAHM - Meredith Efken   *i* 902

Hannah
Play It Again, SAHM - Meredith Efken   *i* 902

Harrod, Allie
Age Before Beauty - Virginia Smith   *i* 952

Hawkins, Thomas
Beloved Counterfeit - Kathleen Y'Barbo   *i* 966

Iona
Play It Again, SAHM - Meredith Efken   *i* 902

Jacob
The Good Parents - Joan London   *c* 1051

Joanna
When Will There Be Good News? - Kate
   Atkinson   *c* 971

Jones, Hope
Sing Them Home - Stephanie Kallos   *c* 1031

Landon, Chase
Texas Ranger Takes a Bride - Patricia
   Thayer   *r* 405

Larsen, Ed
Songs for the Missing - Stewart O'Nan   *c* 1071

Larsen, Fran
Songs for the Missing - Stewart O'Nan   *c* 1071

Lenore
Entertaining Disasters - Nancy Spiller   *c* 1105

Lundy, Jonathan
Wanted - Shelley Shephard Gray   *i* 908

McClintock, Jamie
Kissing Games of the World - Sandi Kahn
   Shelton   *c* 1095

Montoya, Connie
Her Best Christmas Ever - Judy Duarte   *r* 260

Olivia
Disquiet - Julia Leigh   *c* 1047

Randall
Fault Lines - Nancy Huston   *c* 1026

Ruby
Peripheral Vision - Patricia Ferguson   *c* 1007

Saul
Michal - Jill Eileen Smith   *i* 951

Snow, Kathryn
While My Sister Sleeps - Barbara
   Delinsky   *c* 997

Toni
The Good Parents - Joan London   *c* 1051

Warren, Annie
This Side of Heaven - Karen Kingsbury   *i* 926

Warren, Nate
This Side of Heaven - Karen Kingsbury   *i* 926

Wheeler, Jessie
Jessie - Lori Wick   *i* 964

Wyse, Mary Jo
A Cedar Cove Christmas - Debbie
   Macomber   *c* 1055

PATIENT

Janet
Irreplaceable - Stephen Lovely   *c* 1052

Klein, Mora
The Way through Doors - Jesse Ball   *c* 974

McNulty, Roseanne
The Secret Scripture - Sebastian Barry   *t* 728

Sarah
The Reach - Nate Kenyon   *h* 561

Trent, Damon
Succulent Prey - Wrath James White   *h* 621

Waldman, Doriel
A Mad Desire to Dance - Elie Wiesel   *c* 1122

PATRIOT

Torrez, Victoria
The Rebel and the Lady - Kathryn
   Albright   *r* 203

PEDDLER

Camelot
Company of Liars - Karen Maitland   *t* 815
Company of Liars - Karen Maitland   *m* 132

Nathan
Blood Royal - Elisabeth McNeill   *t* 820

Roger the Chapman
The Green Man - Kate Sedley   *t* 848

PHARMACIST

A'ida
From A to X - John Berger   *c* 979

PHILANTHROPIST

Bainbridge, Tommy
The Man for Me - Gemma Bruce   *r* 229

James, Mallory
Billionaire's Marriage Bargain - Leanne
   Banks   *r* 213

PHOTOGRAPHER

Copeland, Rachel
Triple Exposure - Colleen Thompson   *r* 410

Curtis, Edward S.
To Catch the Lightning - Alan Cheuse   *t* 748

Mazambe, Juno
Ex-Kop - Warren Hammond   *s* 667

Mitchell, Josephine "Josie"
Sweetwater Gap - Denise Hunter   *i* 922

PILOT

Standish, Cass
The Eleventh Man - Ivan Doig   *t* 762

PIRATE

Delaney, Smith
Blaggard's Moon - George Bryan Polivka   *i* 943

Drake, Gabriel "Cornish Dragon"
Pleasuring the Pirate - Emily Bryant   *r* 230

Hawkins, Thomas
Beloved Counterfeit - Kathleen Y'Barbo   *i* 966

Red Robert
The Pirate Bride - Shannon Drake   *r* 258

Westcott, Faith
The Red Siren - M.L. Tyndall   *i* 958

PLANNER

Guidry, Meredith
Menu for Romance - Kaye Dacus   *i* 896

Hawthorne, Anne
Stand-In Groom - Kaye Dacus   *i* 898

PLANTATION OWNER

Vaark, Jacob
A Mercy - Toni Morrison   *t* 826
A Mercy - Toni Morrison   *c* 1063

POLICE OFFICER

Anderson, Gary
Bayou Betrayal - Robin Caroll   *i* 890

Aurelio
Stray Dog Winter - David Francis   *c* 1009

Bayless, Rick
The Private Concierge - Suzanne Forster   *r* 270

Black, Doug
Into the Flame - Christina Dodd   *r* 256

Boyle, Billy
Blood Alone - James R. Benn   *m* 20
Blood Alone - James R. Benn   *t* 732

Boyle, Danny
Hell Hole - Chris Grabenstein   *m* 78

Bryant, Dwight
Death's Half Acre - Margaret Maron   *m* 135

POSTAL WORKER

Lucas, Zach "Lightning"
Snowbound in Dry Creek - Janet Tronstad *r* 412

Tarnish, Seymour
The Ghost and the Haunted Mansion - Alice Kimberly *m* 108

PRINCIPAL

Bordwin, Mike
Testimony - Anita Shreve *c* 1097

Hawkes, Jody
The Academy - Bentley Little *h* 569

Remington, Harry
Once upon a Thanksgiving - Holly Jacobs *r* 302

PRISONER

Akira
Beside a Burning Sea - John Shors *t* 851

Allegra
The Night Bird - Catherine Asaro *f* 426

Arminger, Mathilda
The Scourge of God - S.M. Stirling *s* 712

Bergren, Thad
Shades of Dark - Linnea Sinclair *s* 709

Blumenfeld, Isaac Jacob
Isaac's Torah - Angel Wagenstein *c* 1118
Isaac's Torah - Angel Wagenstein *t* 866

Darioq, Magos
Dark Disciple - Anthony Reynolds *s* 696

Fox, Michael
The Jigsaw Man - Gord Rollo *h* 597

Grimes, Abb
The Night Stalker - James Swain *m* 185

Keeler
The Scrubs - Simon Janus *h* 557

Orden, Fallion
The Wyrmling Horde - David Farland *f* 446

Price, Walker
Dream House - Valerie Laken *c* 1042

Selm
Of Wind and Sand - Sylvie Berard *s* 634

PRODUCER

Elliot, Walter
The Brass Verdict - Michael Connelly *m* 52

Marchand, Ross
Phantom's Touch - Julie Leto *r* 329

PROFESSOR

Aldeen, Nina
Body Copy - Michael Craven *m* 58

Ashwin, Holly
Dark Desires after Dusk - Kresley Cole *r* 246

Bayard, Pierre
Sherlock Holmes Was Wrong - Pierre Bayard *m* 16

Blackstone, J.D.
The Rose Conspiracy - Craig Parshall *i* 940

Braddock, Denton
Kiss Me If You Dare - Nicole Young *i* 967

Clay, Gordon
Chest Pains - Janet Nichols Lynch *c* 1054

Conner, Delaney Madison "D.M."
Risque Business - Tawny Weber *r* 415

Deakin, Leo
Random Acts of Heroic Love - Danny Scheinmann *c* 1090

Drake, Robert
Mithras Court - David A. Page *h* 586

Hague, Patricia
The Ruffian on the Stair - Gary Newman *m* 150

Hawthorne, Jack
Elisha's Bones - Don Hoesel *i* 919

Hong-Owen, Sri
The Quiet War - Paul J. McAuley *s* 682

Howland, Alice
Still Alice - Lisa Genova *c* 1011

Hurley, Charlene
The Goliath Bone - Mickey Spillane *m* 181

Jones, Larken
Sing Them Home - Stephanie Kallos *c* 1031

Kafieri, Tory
Acheron - Sherrilyn Kenyon *h* 562

Landry, Michaela
For All We Know - Sandra Kitt *r* 319

Mendez, Felipe
Snakehead - Peter May *m* 140

Miguel
The Gaudi Key - Esteban Martin *m* 137

Moriarity, James
The Shadow of Reichenbach Falls - J. Robert King *t* 807

Moriarty, James
Moriarty - John Gardner *m* 74
Moriarty - John Gardner *t* 777
The Shadow of Reichenbach Falls - J. Robert King *h* 564

Morton, Jessie
Wicked Weaves - Joyce Lavene *m* 120

Pennyworth, Melissa
Shoot the Lawyer Twice - Michael Bowen *m* 29

Rooney, Leah
The Ruffian on the Stair - Gary Newman *m* 150

Unnamed Character
The Housekeeper and the Professor - Yoko Ogawa *c* 1075

Westin, Claire
On a Someday - Roxanne Henke *i* 916

Whitcomb, Molly
Beyond This Moment - Tamera Alexander *i* 876

PROSTITUTE

Bennett, Yvonne
Chasing Darkness - Robert Crais *m* 57

Rodden, Toni
Distant Heart - Tracey Bateman *i* 877

PSYCHIC

Archer, Joanna
The Touch of Twilight - Vicki Pettersson *h* 588

Aylis
City of Jade - Dennis L. McKiernan *f* 484

Caldwell, Chelsea
Christmas Spirit - Rebecca York *r* 422

Carter, Robert
Black Cathedral - L.H. Maynard *h* 574

Cavanaugh, Rowenna
Deadly Harvest - Heather Graham *r* 286

Chablis, Leona Aisling
For Her Eyes Only - Cait London *r* 330

Chase, Megan
Personal Demons - Stacia Kane *h* 560

Ciri
Blood of Elves - Andrzej Sapkowski *f* 511

Cody, Gabrielle
Servant: The Acceptance - L.L. Foster *r* 271

de Leon, Nicole
Magic in His Kiss - Shari Anton *r* 207

Edwards, Claire
Intimate Beings - Jessica Inclan *s* 671

Fontana, John
Dark Light - Jayne Castle *r* 240

Foster, Alex
Cursed - Jamie Leigh Hansen *h* 548

Foster, Vivienne "Vivi"
Ace Is Wild - Penny McCall *r* 348

Gordon, Melinda
Revenge - Doranna Durgin *h* 540

Hortensia
Houston, We Have a Problema - Gwendolyn Zepeda *c* 1127

Hyla
Ill Met in the Arena - Dave Duncan *f* 443

James, Darl
Intimate Beings - Jessica Inclan *s* 671

King, Clarissa
Insatiable Desire - Rita Herron *h* 553

Kingsley, Morgan
The Devil's Due - Jenna Black *h* 532

McIntyre, Sierra
Dark Light - Jayne Castle *r* 240

Mira
Nightwalker - Jocelyn Drake *h* 539

Montgomery, Kendall
Deadly Night - Heather Graham *r* 287

Narigorm
Company of Liars - Karen Maitland *m* 132

Novak, Sadie
Devil May Ride - Wendy Roberts *m* 165
Devil May Ride - Wendy Roberts *h* 595

Por, Ah
Year of the Dog - Henry Chang *m* 44

Quinn
The Hollow - Nora Roberts *h* 594

Regan
The Touch of Twilight - Vicki Pettersson *h* 588

Roberts, Mary Catherine
The Telltale Turtle - Joyce Lavene *m* 119

Sands, Greer
Speak of the Devil - Shari Shattuck *h* 606

Sands, Joshua
Speak of the Devil - Shari Shattuck *h* 606

Sarc, Aryl
Riders of the Storm - Julie E. Czerneda *s* 648

Scanlan, Claire
House of Whispers - Margaret Lucke *h* 570

Sherman, Liz
The Golden Army - Robert Greenberger *h* 547

Spar
The Golden Tower - Fiona Patton *f* 495

Stone, Alex
Night Shadow - Cherry Adair *r* 201

Stone, Alexis "Lexi"
Night Shadow - Cherry Adair   *r* 201
Vin
The Hero of Ages - Brandon Sanderson   *f* 510

PSYCHOLOGIST

Braverman, Mira
The Delivery Room - Sylvia Brownrigg   *c* 984
Delaware, Alex
Bones - Jonathan Kellerman   *m* 107
Wasserman, Evan
The Reach - Nate Kenyon   *h* 561
Wesley, Benton
Scarpetta - Patricia Cornwell   *m* 53

PUBLIC RELATIONS

Peltier, Robyn
Living With the Dead - Kelley Armstrong   *h* 527
VanCleef, Vicki
On the Move - Pamela Britton   *r* 227

PUBLISHER

Prentiss, Jack
Faking Grace - Tamera Leigh   *i* 930

RADIO PERSONALITY

Donna, Bella
Liquid Diet - Michael McCarty   *h* 575
Jamison, Colin
The Telltale Turtle - Joyce Lavene   *m* 119
Roberts, Mary Catherine
The Telltale Turtle - Joyce Lavene   *m* 119

RAKE

Deville, Sebastien
The Bride Price - Anne Mallory   *r* 341
Neville, Kieran
Never Romance a Rake - Liz Carlyle   *r* 235
Sinclair, Vincent
The Mistress Diaries - Julianne MacLean   *r* 334

RANCHER

Blake, Gavin
When Love Blooms - Robin Lee Hatcher   *i* 914
Buchanan, Jeremy
The Reluctant Cowgirl - Christine Lynxwiler   *i* 933
Buchanan, Rory
Montana Royalty - B.J. Daniels   *r* 249
Canfield, Clay
Paper Roses - Amanda Cabot   *i* 884
Cooper, Grant
Gingham Mountain - Mary Connealy   *i* 894
Garrett, Geoffrey
A Promise for Spring - Kim Vogel Sawyer   *i* 948
Gilmore, Casey
Searching for Santa - Janet Dailey   *r* 248
Hammer, Erastus
Effigy - Alissa York   *t* 872
McAllister, Flint
Searching for Santa - Janet Dailey   *r* 248
McCabe, Jarrett
Montana Star - DeAnn Smallwood   *r* 392
McMurray, Teagen
Tall, Dark, and Texan - Jodi Thomas   *r* 407

Moon, Charlie
Snake Dreams - James D. Doss   *m* 65
Morgan, Eli
Leaving Whiskey Bend - Dorothy Garlock   *r* 275
Phillips, Justin
Love Finds You in Last Chance, California - Miralee Ferrell   *i* 905
Tomlinson, Hank
A Tale Out of Luck - Willie Nelson   *t* 827
Travers, Alexia
Love Finds You in Last Chance, California - Miralee Ferrell   *i* 905
Tucker, Jacob
Adopted: Outback Baby - Barbara Hannay   *r* 290
Weber, Luke
No Place for a Lady - Maggie Brendan   *i* 880

RANGER

Matthews, Kade
Cry in the Night - Colleen Coble   *i* 892
Townsend, Rick
Anchors Aweigh - Kathleen Bacus   *r* 210
Anchors Aweigh - Kathleen Bacus   *m* 5

REAL ESTATE AGENT

Collier, Avery
House of Whispers - Margaret Lucke   *h* 570
Ferris, Julie
Season of Strangers - Kat Martin   *r* 345
Fulton, Annalise
Parents in Training - Barbara McMahon   *r* 350
Kingston, Sarah
Bean There, Done That - Sandra Balzo   *m* 8
Manchester, Vern
Eggs in Purgatory - Laura Childs   *m* 47
Sanchez, George
Dirty Water - Mary-Ann Tirone Smith   *m* 178
Scanlan, Claire
House of Whispers - Margaret Lucke   *h* 570

REANIMATED DEAD

Connaway, Jacob
Jake's Wake - John Skipp   *h* 609
Engel, Lars
The Dark Ones - Anthony Izzo   *h* 556

REBEL

Erasmas
Anathem - Neal Stephenson   *s* 711
MacNeil, Connor
The Rebel Doctor's Bride - Sarah Morgan   *r* 358
March
Wanderlust - Ann Aguirre   *s* 625
Noonan, Courtney
Eat, Drink, and Be from Mississippi - Nanci Kincaid   *c* 1037
Pet
Dragonforge - James Maxey   *f* 483

RECEPTIONIST

James, Parker
Double Minds - Terri Blackstock   *i* 879
King, Karen
The Big O - Declan Burke   *m* 36

Valentine, Emma Jean
Mama Does Time - Deborah Sharp   *m* 170

RECLUSE

Buchanan, Ian
A Virgin River Christmas - Robyn Carr   *r* 236
Pike, Zeke
Triple Exposure - Colleen Thompson   *r* 410

REFUGEE

Haber, Bernhard
Settlement - Christoph Hein   *t* 795
Little Bee
Little Bee - Chris Cleave   *c* 992
Montse
The Creator's Map - Emilio Calderon   *t* 742

REINCARNATED PERSON

Charles, Wesley
Phenomenal Girl 5 - A.J. Menden   *r* 351
Elliot, Robert
Phenomenal Girl 5 - A.J. Menden   *r* 351

RELATIVE

Cromwell, Jo
Barefoot Brides - Annie Jones   *i* 924
Cromwell, Kate
Barefoot Brides - Annie Jones   *i* 924
Holt, Stephen
The Dangerous Duke - Christine Wells   *r* 416
Jessup, Emily
The Real Enemy - Kathy Herman   *i* 917
Katherine
A Hundred Years of Happiness - Nicole Seitz   *i* 949
Laurel
Sweetwater Gap - Denise Hunter   *i* 922
Michal
Michal - Jill Eileen Smith   *i* 951
Perika, Daisy
Snake Dreams - James D. Doss   *m* 65
Ruth
Dead Man Dancing - Marcia Talley   *m* 186
Termite
Lark and Termite - Jayne Ann Phillips   *c* 1079
Towne, Roxanne
Deceived - James Scott Bell   *i* 878
Weatherby, Moxie
Barefoot Brides - Annie Jones   *i* 924
Westin, Drew
On a Someday - Roxanne Henke   *i* 916

RELIGIOUS

Ashling
Morningtide - Cory J. Herndon   *f* 459
Balkhi, Djalal al-din Mohammad
Rumi: The Fire of Love - Nahal Tajadod   *t* 856
Ben-David, Shmuel
Isaac's Torah - Angel Wagenstein   *c* 1118
Benedictus
Enclave - Kit Reed   *s* 693
Boynton, Cal
The Lace Reader - Brunonia Barry   *c* 976
Cahill, Greg
Ulterior Motives - Mark Andrew Olson   *i* 938

Carter, Joshua
The Dove - Carolyn Brown *r* 228

Cato, Jacob
The Dragon Earl - Jade Lee *r* 326

Connaway, Jacob
Jake's Wake - John Skipp *h* 609

Cromwell, Jo
Barefoot Brides - Annie Jones *i* 924

da Ivan pa Crystal Temple, Gregor
Harmony - C.F. Bentley *s* 633

Diggs, Cletus J.
The Not Quite Right Reverend Cletus J. Diggs and the Currently Accepted Habits of Nature - David Niall Wilson *h* 623

du Maigrie pu Chauncey, Sissy
Harmony - C.F. Bentley *s* 633

Eleanor
Passenger - Ronald Damien Malfi *h* 572

Eleanor of Tyndal
Forsaken Soul - Priscilla Royal *t* 842

Ellison, Keith
Take One - Karen Kingsbury *i* 925

Erasmas
Anathem - Neal Stephenson *s* 711

Fisher, Mary-Margaret
The Passion of Mary-Margaret - Lisa Samson *i* 947

Flemming, Dave
8 Sandpiper Way - Debbie Macomber *r* 335

Helewise of Hawkenlye
The Paths of the Air - Alys Clare *t* 749

Hesam
Rumi: The Fire of Love - Nahal Tajadod *t* 856

Ingolf
The Scourge of God - S.M. Stirling *s* 712

Morningstar, Noonday
The Sound of Building Coffins - Louis Maistros *c* 1058

Muhammad
The Jewel of Medina - Sherry Jones *t* 800

Nagash
Nagash the Sorcerer - Mike Lee *f* 471

Orolo
Anathem - Neal Stephenson *s* 711

Plowright, Paul
Salvation Boulevard - Larry Beinhart *m* 18

Pust, Iskaral
Toll the Hounds - Steven Erikson *f* 444

Rakh-amn-Hotep
Nagash the Sorcerer - Mike Lee *f* 471

Ryan, Chase
Take One - Karen Kingsbury *i* 925

Samuel
Mutant Chronicles - Matt Forbeck *s* 660

Sazed
The Hero of Ages - Brandon Sanderson *f* 510

Selby, George
A Spoonful of Poison - M.C. Beaton *m* 17

Shams of Tabriz
Rumi: The Fire of Love - Nahal Tajadod *t* 856

Shoal, Montgomery
Prescription for a Superior Existence - Josh Emmons *c* 1003

Sister Fidelma
Dancing with Demons - Peter Tremayne *t* 860

Spurgeon
The Gypsy Crown - Kate Forsyth *f* 449

Sullivan, Gabriel Ross
Shades of Dark - Linnea Sinclair *s* 709

Tate, Micah
Beloved Counterfeit - Kathleen Y'Barbo *i* 966

Thomas
Forsaken Soul - Priscilla Royal *m* 166

Torelli, Giuseppe
Black Market Truth - Sharon Kaye *m* 106

Townsend, Cooper "Smith"
For All We Know - Sandra Kitt *r* 319

Two-Feathers, Sam
Distant Heart - Tracey Bateman *i* 877

Tyler, John
The 731 Legacy - Lynn Sholes *m* 173

RESCUER

Hunter, Ian
Dark Whispers - Bruce Coville *f* 441

Matthews, Bree
Cry in the Night - Colleen Coble *i* 892

Whitefield, Jane
Runner - Thomas Perry *m* 154

RESEARCHER

McHenry, Lacey
The Enclave - Karen Hancock *i* 912

Reinhardt, Cameron
The Enclave - Karen Hancock *i* 912

Salander, Lisbeth
The Girl with the Dragon Tattoo - Stieg Larsson *m* 118

RESTAURATEUR

MacDonald, Jim
Blackbird, Farewell - Robert Greer *m* 82

REVOLUTIONARY

Radcliffe, Matthew
The United States of Atlantis - Harry Turtledove *s* 717

Radcliffe, Victor
The United States of Atlantis - Harry Turtledove *s* 717
The United States of Atlantis - Harry Turtledove *t* 862

Zeitlin, Sashenka
Sashenka - Simon Montefiore *t* 824

ROBOT

Don
Two to the Fifth - Piers Anthony *f* 425

I-5YQ
Street of Shadows - Michael Reaves *s* 692

Napoleon
Sunborn - Jeffrey A. Carver *s* 643

RODEO RIDER

Lucas, Zach "Lightning"
Snowbound in Dry Creek - Janet Tronstad *r* 412

ROGUE

Mornay, Phillip
Before the Season Ends - Linore Rose Burkard *i* 882

ROYALTY

Aal Masood, Kamal
The Desert King - Olivia Gates *r* 278

Adams, Dara
To Protect a Princess - Gail Barrett *r* 214

Adolphus, Gustavus
1635: The Dreeson Incident - Eric Flint *s* 655

Alestria
Alexander and Alestria - Sa Shan *t* 850

Alexandra
The Tsarina's Daughter - Carolly Erickson *t* 769

Arkhorn, Yimt
A Darkness Forged in Fire - Chris Evans *f* 445

Artaxerxes II
The Lost Army - Valero Manfredi *t* 816

Baristani, Ellysetta
King of Sword and Sky - C.L. Wilson *r* 419

Charlemagne
The Fire - Katherine Neville *t* 828

Corydonais
Crate and Peril - J.D. Warren *r* 413

Cyrus the Younger
The Lost Army - Valero Manfredi *t* 816

Dara, Mac
Heir to Sevenwaters - Juliet Marillier *f* 481

Djames, Djarrhett Raven Perseus Pendra
Knight's Fork - Rowena Cherry *r* 242

Djerroldina, Electra
Knight's Fork - Rowena Cherry *r* 242

Eleanor of Aquitaine
Devil's Brood - Sharon Kay Penman *t* 830

Elizabeth I
The Virgin Queen's Daughter - Ella March Chase *t* 747

E'non, Lea
The Crown - Deborah Chester *f* 438

Gentry, Meredith
Swallowing Darkness - Laurell Hamilton *f* 458

Heldenhammer, Sigmar
Heldenhammer - Graham McNeill *f* 487

Juana of Castile
The Last Queen - C.W. Gortner *t* 784

Kazanov, Drako
Enticing the Prince - Patricia Grasso *r* 288

Koz, Qara
The Enchantress of Florence - Salman Rushdie *c* 1089

Liane
The Gods Return - David Drake *f* 442

Mac Lir, Manannan
Immortals: The Crossing - Joy Nash *r* 359

Montenevada, Nico
The Prince's Secret Bride - Raye Morgan *r* 357

Morgan, Aliyah
The Desert King - Olivia Gates *r* 278

Nefertari
The Heretic Queen - Michelle Moran *t* 825

Philip of Flanders
The Last Queen - C.W. Gortner *t* 784

Po
Graceling - Kristin Cashore *f* 436

Rain Tairen Soul
King of Sword and Sky - C.L. Wilson *r* 419

Sweetwater, William
The Clone Elite - Steven L. Kent   *s* 672

Tellenberg, Esra
Quofum - Alan Dean Foster   *s* 661

T'Pol
Kobayashi Maru - Michael A. Martin   *s* 680

Tristan
Hidden - Eve Kenin   *r* 317

Valnadireb
Quofum - Alan Dean Foster   *s* 661

Warren, Lily
A Patent Lie - Paul Goldstein   *m* 76

Watanabe, Noah
Webdancers - Brian Herbert   *s* 670

Zarkazian, Valenden
Season of Strangers - Kat Martin   *r* 345

Zelinski, Zo
Freezing Point - Karen Dionne   *s* 653

SCOUT

Quinn
The Desires of Her Heart - Lyn Cote   *i* 895

SEA CAPTAIN

Aravan
City of Jade - Dennis L. McKiernan   *f* 484

Haggerty, Logan
The Pirate Bride - Shannon Drake   *r* 258

Isokrates
The Sun's Bride - Gillian Bradshaw   *t* 737

Kennett, Sebastian
My Lord and Spymaster - Joanna Bourne   *r* 222

Reddy, Matthew
Crusade - Taylor Anderson   *s* 628

Summerfield, Silas Leyton
Ready and Willing - Elizabeth Bevarly   *r* 216

Winslow, Thomas
Saint Antony's Fire - Steve White   *s* 721

SEAMSTRESS

Bergerine, Juliette
A Lover's Kiss - Margaret Moore   *r* 356

Coats, Sewing Annie
Stand the Storm - Breena Clarke   *t* 750

Plat, Nell
The Seamstress of Hollywood Boulevard - Erin McGraw   *t* 819

Prudence
Gingham Mountain - Mary Connealy   *i* 894

Santos, Emilia dos
The Seamstress - Frances de Pontes Peebles   *t* 760

Santos, Luzia dos
The Seamstress - Frances de Pontes Peebles   *t* 760

Timna
Sima's Undergarments for Women - Ilana Stanger-Ross   *c* 1106

SECRETARY

B., Luciana
The Book of Murder - Guillermo Martinez   *m* 138

Carlisle, Emily
Wed to the Texan - Sara Orwig   *r* 364

Sterling, Velda
The Goliath Bone - Mickey Spillane   *m* 181

Tucker, Martha
The Sky Took Him - Donis Casey   *m* 42

SECURITY OFFICER

Evans, Lucie
Dying for You - Beverly Barton   *r* 215

Fallon, Rick
The Other Side of Silence - Bill Pronzini   *m* 159

Garnett, Nick
Stalking Susan - Julie Kramer   *m* 113

Krestoff
The Devil's Eye - Jack McDevitt   *s* 684

Lehane, Jeff
Daemon - Harry Shannon   *h* 604

Ligotti, Whiz
Daemon - Harry Shannon   *h* 604

McNamara, Sawyer
Dying for You - Beverly Barton   *r* 215

Paxton, Noah
Hot as Hell - HelenKay Dimon   *r* 255

Spinks, Charlie
Daemon - Harry Shannon   *h* 604

Tilden, Forrest
Eternal Damnation - Steve Niles   *h* 583

Vaughan, Jeff
Necropath - Eric Brown   *s* 637

SERIAL KILLER

Lowell, Gretchen
Sweetheart - Chelsea Cain   *m* 38

Miles, Joseph
Succulent Prey - Wrath James White   *h* 621

Teags, William
Nowhere to Hide - R. Patrick Gates   *h* 543

SERVANT

Corbuc, Sybilla
Shadow Rider - Kathryn Dennis   *r* 254

Gorst, Esperanza
The Glass of Time - Michael Cox   *t* 755
The Glass of Time - Michael Cox   *m* 55

Grady
Master of the Moors - Kealan Patrick Burke   *h* 533

Lalita
Soul of Fire - Sarah A. Hoyt   *f* 462

O'Neill, Norah
Indigo Christmas - Jeanne M. Dams   *m* 60

SETTLER

Dula, Carmen
Marsbound - Joe Haldeman   *s* 666

Fiona
Dragonheart - Todd McCaffrey   *s* 683

Gretchen
Zoe's Tale - John Scalzi   *s* 703

Mendolar, Enris
Riders of the Storm - Julie E. Czerneda   *s* 648

Perry, Zoe Boutin
Zoe's Tale - John Scalzi   *s* 703

Sarc, Aryl
Riders of the Storm - Julie E. Czerneda   *s* 648

Selm
Of Wind and Sand - Sylvie Berard   *s* 634

SHAMAN

Markham, Eugenie
Storm Born - Richelle Mead   *h* 577

Perika, Daisy
Snake Dreams - James D. Doss   *m* 65

SINGER

Drake, Joley
Turbulent Sea - Christine Feehan   *r* 266

Flynn, Mattie
A Claim of Her Own - Stephanie Grace Whitson   *i* 963

James, Parker
Double Minds - Terri Blackstock   *i* 879

SINGLE PARENT

Barone, Regina
Sea Fever - Virginia Kantra   *r* 314

Barton, Jessica Anne
Tall, Dark, and Texan - Jodi Thomas   *r* 407

Collins, Jenny
Snowbound in Dry Creek - Janet Tronstad   *r* 412

Colton, Georgeann Grady
Colton's Secret Service - Marie Ferrarella   *r* 267

Fairfax, Griffin
His Wicked Sins - Eve Silver   *r* 388

Hunter, Fran
White Nights - Ann Cleeves   *m* 48

Keyes, Jesse
Sweet Trouble - Susan Mallery   *r* 340

Libby, Jewel
The Jewel of Gresham Green - Lawana Blackwell   *r* 217

Moretti, John
All That Matters - Stef Ann Holm   *r* 297

Sayers, Mariah
Broken Pieces - Carla Cassidy   *r* 239

Shortz, Fen
The Daughters Grimm - Minda Webber   *r* 414

Steele, Tamara
Ultimate Weapon - Shannon McKenna   *r* 349

Sweeny, Bridget
Hold My Hand - Serena Mackesy   *m* 131

Thompson, Natalie
Winning the Single Mom's Heart - Linda Goodnight   *r* 283

Traynor, Laura
Daniel's Den - Brandt Dodson   *i* 901

Wilder, Firebird
Into the Flame - Christina Dodd   *r* 256

Williams, Samantha
Once upon a Thanksgiving - Holly Jacobs   *r* 302

SISTER

Bailey, Anna
Shadows of Lancaster County - Mindy Starns Clark   *i* 891

Bestman, Taylor
That Certain Spark - Cathy Marie Hake   *i* 910

Sweet, Camille
Sweet Waters - Julie Carobini   *i* 889

Burns, Dominick
No Peeking - Stephanie Bond *r* 221

Canyon, Rory
Slippery When Wet - Kimberly Raye *r* 375

Cathoair
All the Windwracked Stars - Elizabeth Bear *s* 630

Fortune, Benjamin
Crash Into Me - Jill Sorenson *m* 180

Humate
Ill Met in the Arena - Dave Duncan *f* 443

Mitchell, Eric
Power Play - Deirdre Martin *r* 344

Quirt
Ill Met in the Arena - Dave Duncan *f* 443

Ruth, Babe
The Given Day - Dennis Lehane *c* 1046
The Given Day - Dennis Lehane *t* 812

Sanderson, Ryan
Line of Scrimmage - Marie Force *r* 269

Snow, Robin
While My Sister Sleeps - Barbara Delinsky *c* 997

Solarin, Alexandra
The Fire - Katherine Neville *m* 149
The Fire - Katherine Neville *t* 828

Wooley, Liam
Sucker Punch - Ray Banks *c* 975
Sucker Punch - Ray Banks *m* 9

Wright, Reno
Home for the Holidays - Lisa Plumley *r* 370

SPOUSE

Abbott, Kathleen
Ghost at Work - Carolyn Hart *m* 87

Ahuja, Rakesh
Family Planning - Karan Mahajan *c* 1057

A'isha bint Abi Bakr
The Jewel of Medina - Sherry Jones *t* 800

Anna
All I Have to Give - Melody Carlson *i* 886

Bennet, Elizabeth
The Independence of Miss Mary Bennet - Colleen McCullough *t* 818

Bess of Hardwick
The Other Queen - Philippa Gregory *t* 789

Bingley, Amanda-Jane
Netherfield Park Revisited - Rebecca Ann Collins *t* 753

Bingley, Jonathan
Netherfield Park Revisited - Rebecca Ann Collins *t* 753

Blackwell, Alice
American Wife - Curtis Sittenfeld *c* 1100

Blackwell, Charles
American Wife - Curtis Sittenfeld *c* 1100

Bluhm, Carlos
Lima Nights - Marie Arana *c* 970

Bolsover, Kitty
By Chance - Martin Corrick *c* 995

Brooks, Laney
I Smile Back - Amy Koppelman *c* 1040

Burch, Isaac H.
Dalliance - Diana Burg *t* 740

Burch, Mary W. Turner
Dalliance - Diana Burg *t* 740

Cavanaugh, Patrick
Indigo Christmas - Jeanne M. Dams *m* 60

Codrington, Harry
The Sealed Letter - Emma Donoghue *t* 763

Codrington, Helen
The Sealed Letter - Emma Donoghue *t* 763

Comingo, Lucia
If You Eat You Never Die: Chicago Tales - Tony Romano *c* 1086

Craven, Melanie
No Rest for the Wiccan - Madelyn Alt *m* 1

Darcy, Elizabeth Bennet
The Matters at Mansfield - Carrie Bebris *t* 731

Darcy, Fitzwilliam
The Independence of Miss Mary Bennet - Colleen McCullough *t* 818
The Matters at Mansfield - Carrie Bebris *t* 731

David
Michal - Jill Eileen Smith *i* 951

Eaton, Audrey
Tender Grace - Jackina Stark *i* 953

Eppes, Katie
Amelia's Secret - Maggie Carter-deVries *t* 745

Eppes, T.J. "Jeff"
Amelia's Secret - Maggie Carter-deVries *t* 745

Garrahan, Mamie Flynn
The Nightingales of Troy - Alice Fulton *t* 776

Guyette, Agnes Marie
The Long Journey Home - Laurel Means *t* 821

Hammer, Dorrie
Effigy - Alissa York *t* 872

Hanumarathnam
The Toss of a Lemon - Padma Viswanathan *t* 865

Harrod, Allie
Age Before Beauty - Virginia Smith *i* 952

Jessup, Brill
The Real Enemy - Kathy Herman *i* 917

Jessup, Kurt
The Real Enemy - Kathy Herman *i* 917

Joshua
The Precious Life - Che Parker *c* 1078

Kathryn
The Precious Life - Che Parker *c* 1078

Kharkov, Elena
Moscow Rules - Daniel Silva *m* 175

Kinzler, Kate
Dream House - Valerie Laken *c* 1042

Lustig, Caroline
The Journey - H.G. Adler *c* 968

Matthews, Bree
Cry in the Night - Colleen Coble *i* 892

Matthews, Kade
Cry in the Night - Colleen Coble *i* 892

Mei-Hua
City of God (A Novel of Passion and Wonder in Old New York) - Beverly Swerling *t* 855

Michael
All I Have to Give - Melody Carlson *i* 886

Michal
Michal - Jill Eileen Smith *i* 951

Milbanke, Annabella
A Quiet Adjustment - Benjamin Markovits *t* 817

Parker, James
The Way Home - Jean Brashear *r* 224

Parker, Louise
Bound South - Susan Rebecca White *c* 1121

Parry, Violet
This One Is Mine - Maria Semple *c* 1093

Pemberton, George
Serena - Ron Rash *t* 837

Pemberton, Serena
Serena - Ron Rash *t* 837
Serena - Ron Rash *c* 1081

Peter
The Delivery Room - Sylvia Brownrigg *c* 984

Redding, Seth
Jessie - Lori Wick *i* 964

Reed, Anna
Good People - Marcus Sakey *m* 168

Reed, Tom
Good People - Marcus Sakey *m* 168

Roarke
Salvation in Death - J.D. Robb *s* 698

Saint-Martin, Paul de
Assassin's Rage - Charles O'Brien *t* 829

Sanderson, Susannah
Line of Scrimmage - Marie Force *r* 269

Sheldon, Andrea
The Returning - Ann Tatlock *i* 954

Sheldon, John
The Returning - Ann Tatlock *i* 954

Sivakami
The Toss of a Lemon - Padma Viswanathan *t* 865

Snapdragon, Bridget
Nine Kinds of Naked - Tony Vigorito *c* 1117

Towne, Liz
Deceived - James Scott Bell *i* 878

Vaark, Rebekka
A Mercy - Toni Morrison *c* 1063
A Mercy - Toni Morrison *t* 826

Verbicaro, Giuseppe
The Islands of Divine Music - John Addiego *t* 724

Verbicaro, Rosari
The Islands of Divine Music - John Addiego *t* 724

Vivian
The English Major - Jim Harrison *c* 1020

Walcote, Nicholas
Veil of Lies - Jeri Westerson *t* 867

Walcote, Philippa
Veil of Lies - Jeri Westerson *t* 867

Westin, Claire
On a Someday - Roxanne Henke *i* 916

Westin, Jim
On a Someday - Roxanne Henke *i* 916

Wheeler, Jessie
Jessie - Lori Wick *i* 964

Woods, Janet
The Fifth Floor - Michael Harvey *m* 89

Woods, Johnny
The Fifth Floor - Michael Harvey *m* 89

Woodyard, Joe
The Chocolate Snowman Murders - JoAnna Carl *m* 41

Ya'ari, Daniela
Friendly Fire - A.B. Yehoshua *c* 1125

Young, Ann Eliza
The 19th Wife - David Ebershoff   *t* 766
The 19th Wife - David Ebershoff   *c* 1001

SPY

Absolute, Jack
Absolute Honor - C.C. Humphreys   *t* 796

Albemarle, Stephen
Deep Night - Caroline Petit   *m* 156

Alec
Shadows Return - Lynn Flewelling   *f* 448

Alexander, James "Jax"
The Archangel Project - C.S. Graham   *m* 79

Allon, Gabriel
Moscow Rules - Daniel Silva   *m* 175

Beck, Jordon
A Bodyguard for Christmas - Donna
   Young   *r* 423

Box, Lucifer
Black Butterfly - Mark Gatiss   *t* 779

Braun, Alexander
Stealing Trinity - Ward Larsen   *t* 810
Stealing Trinity - Ward Larsen   *m* 116

Carlyle, Elizabeth
Illegal Action - Stella Rimington   *m* 164

Carmichael, Devlin
Lord of Shadows - Mary Lennox   *r* 328

Chaloner, Thomas
The Butcher of Smithfield - Susanna
   Gregory   *t* 790

Crowe, Painter
The Last Oracle - James Rollins   *s* 701

Deprez, Paul
The Blackstone Key - Rose Melikan   *m* 143

Doskeav, Anna Katrina
I Am Not a Cop! - Richard Belzer   *m* 19

Durmant, Alexander
As Luck Would Have It - Alissa Johnson   *r* 308

Everton, Sophie
As Luck Would Have It - Alissa Johnson   *r* 308

Holt, Samuel
Wind Dancer - Jamie Carie   *i* 885

Kagan, Paul
The Spy Who Came for Christmas - David
   Morrell   *m* 147

Kennett, Sebastian
My Lord and Spymaster - Joanna Bourne   *r* 222

Kolbe, Leah
Deep Night - Caroline Petit   *m* 156

Nergui
The Shadow Walker - Michael Walters   *m* 194

Pepper
Sly Mongoose - Tobias S. Buckell   *s* 638

Pierce, Gray
The Last Oracle - James Rollins   *s* 701

Saunders, Ethan
The Whiskey Rebels - David Liss   *t* 813

Sawyer, Lulu
Lulu in Marrakech - Diane Johnson   *c* 1029

Seregil
Shadows Return - Lynn Flewelling   *f* 448

Sofia
The Scarlet Spy - Andrea Pickens   *r* 369

Stone, Alex
Night Shadow - Cherry Adair   *r* 201

Stone, Alexis "Lexi"
Night Shadow - Cherry Adair   *r* 201

Strong, Rebecca
The Flowing Tide - Alan Savage   *t* 846

Truly, James Livingston
River Runs Red - Jeff Mariotte   *h* 573

Violet
Your Heart Belongs to Me - Dean R.
   Koontz   *m* 111

STEWARD

Huck, Travis
Bones - Jonathan Kellerman   *m* 107

Wren, Jacquelyn "Mistress Jack"
Pleasuring the Pirate - Emily Bryant   *r* 230

STORE OWNER

Allah, Iqbal Amir
*Clash of Civilizations Over an Elevator in Piazza
   Vittorio* - Amara Lakhous   *c* 1043

Beale, Charles
According to Their Deeds - Paul
   Robertson   *i* 946

Chablis, Leona Aisling
For Her Eyes Only - Cait London   *r* 330

Dow, Felicity "Liss"
No Rest for the Wiccan - Madelyn Alt   *m* 1

Girard, Sierra
The Daddy Verdict - Karen Rose Smith   *r* 393

Goldner, Sima
Sima's Undergarments for Women - Ilana
   Stanger-Ross   *c* 1106

Harrington, Kristianna
Forever Christmas - Christine Lynxwiler   *i* 932

Hobbs, Chloe
Casting Spells - Barbara Bretton   *r* 225

Legris, Victor
Murder on the Eiffel Tower - Claude Izner   *t* 799
Murder on the Eiffel Tower - Claude Izner   *m* 99

Menlow, Regina
A Bodyguard for Christmas - Donna
   Young   *r* 423

Pellicano, Dewey
Old Maid's Puzzle - Terri Thayer   *m* 188

Thornton-McClure, Penelope "Pen"
The Ghost and the Haunted Mansion - Alice
   Kimberly   *m* 108

Thorsen, Maggy
Bean There, Done That - Sandra Balzo   *m* 8

Tichnor, Carol
Buffalo Bill's Defunct - Shelia Simonson   *m* 176

Westin, Jim
On a Someday - Roxanne Henke   *i* 916

Wright, Reno
Home for the Holidays - Lisa Plumley   *r* 370

STOWAWAY

Ratu
Beside a Burning Sea - John Shors   *t* 851

STUDENT

Amelie
Tokyo Fiancee - Amelie Nothomb   *c* 1069

Becker, Brad
The Academy - Bentley Little   *h* 569

Carpentier, Hector
The Black Tower - Louis Bayard   *m* 15
The Black Tower - Louis Bayard   *t* 729

Chambers, Jess
The Reach - Nate Kenyon   *h* 561

Donal
Cain's Last Stand - Sandy Mitchell   *s* 689

Eona
Eon: Dragoneye Reborn - Alison
   Goodman   *f* 455

Khan, Hassan
Blood Wedding - P.J. Brooke   *m* 32

Merigold, Triss
Blood of Elves - Andrzej Sapkowski   *f* 511

Morris, Brenda
Thirteen Orphans - Jane Lindskold   *f* 473

Mumtaz
A Mind at Peace - Ahmet Hamdi
   Tanpinar   *c* 1110

Quintana, Gabriel
The Dirty Secrets Club - Meg Gardiner   *m* 73

Rinri
Tokyo Fiancee - Amelie Nothomb   *c* 1069

Spock
Collision Course - William Shatner   *s* 706

Tadashi, Sato
The Women - T.C. Boyle   *c* 982

Threnody
Lamplighter - D.M. Cornish   *f* 440

Watsen, Gunther
All the Windwracked Stars - Elizabeth
   Bear   *s* 630

Ziggy
All Souls' Night - Jennifer Armintrout   *h* 526

STUDENT—COLLEGE

Bleifert, Tereska
Shoot the Lawyer Twice - Michael Bowen   *m* 29

Bloom, Natalie
College Girl - Patricia Weitz   *c* 1120

Carnacki, Thomas
The Shadow of Reichenbach Falls - J. Robert
   King   *h* 564
The Shadow of Reichenbach Falls - John R.
   King   *m* 109

Carnaki, Thomas
The Shadow of Reichenbach Falls - J. Robert
   King   *t* 807

Heywood, Charlotte
The Price of Butcher's Meat - Reginald
   Hill   *m* 94

Mendoza, Jose Maria Hurtado de
The Creator's Map - Emilio Calderon   *t* 742

Messner, Marcus
Indignation - Philip Roth   *c* 1088
Indignation - Philip Roth   *t* 840

Palmer, Alice
The Last Day - John Ramsey Miller   *m* 145

Temple, Frank III
Envy the Night - Michael Koryta   *m* 112

Winston-Beaufort, Antonia
Defending Angels - Mary Stanton   *m* 184

STUDENT—GRADUATE

Ayot, Jonah
The Reverend's Apprentice - David N.
   Odhiambo   *c* 1074

TRADER

Karina
Dragonheart - Todd McCaffrey   *s* 683

TRAPPER

Hargrove, Jake
Calico Christmas at Dry Creek - Janet
  Tronstad   *r* 411

TRAVELLER

Adela
Company of Liars - Karen Maitland   *c* 1059
Arjun
Thunderer - Felix Gilman   *f* 454
Jun
Dragon Moon - Carole Wilkinson   *f* 522
Logan, Meer
The Memorist - M.J. Rose   *c* 1087
Lycas
The Reawakened - Jeri Smith-Ready   *f* 518
Mackenzie, Rudi
The Scourge of God - S.M. Stirling   *s* 712
Mossland, Kate
Gordath Wood - Patrice Sarath   *f* 512
Robina, Ella
The Leisure Seeker - Michael Zadoorian   *c* 1126
Robina, John
The Leisure Seeker - Michael Zadoorian   *c* 1126
Rodrigo
Company of Liars - Karen Maitland   *c* 1059
Taylor, Steven
The Larion Senators - Robert Scott   *f* 515
Zophiel
Company of Liars - Karen Maitland   *c* 1059

TROUBLESHOOTER

Lubitsch, Gonzo
The Gone-Away World - Nick Harkaway   *s* 668
Soames, Elisabeth
The Gone-Away World - Nick Harkaway   *s* 668

UNDERTAKER

Graham, Jennifer
She's in a Better Place - Angela Hunt   *i* 921
Huffman, Gerald
She's in a Better Place - Angela Hunt   *i* 921

UNEMPLOYED

Boughton, Jack
Home - Marilynne Robinson   *c* 1085
Clark, Jill
Night Kills - John Lutz   *m* 128
Darnell, Layla
The Hollow - Nora Roberts   *h* 594
Libby, Jewel
The Jewel of Gresham Green - Lawana
  Blackwell   *r* 217
Porter, Rachel
Home for the Holidays - Lisa Plumley   *r* 370

VACATIONER

Willan, Samantha
The Rogue Hunter - Lynsay Sands   *r* 383

VAGRANT

Ridley, Sam
The Sin Eaters - Andrew Beahrs   *t* 730

VAMPIRE

Ames, Carrie
All Souls' Night - Jennifer Armintrout   *h* 526
Arellano, Carmen
The Undead Karma Sutra - Mario
  Acevedo   *h* 524
Balducci, Vinnie
Just One Bite - Kimberly Raye   *h* 591
Baptiste, Dante
In the Blood - Adrian Phoenix   *h* 589
Bloodsworth, Andrew
Liquid Diet - Michael McCarty   *h* 575
Briar
Angel's Pain - Maggie Shayne   *r* 386
Claremont, Eva
Break of Dawn - Chris Marie Green   *h* 545
Clevon, Eleisha
Blood Memories - Barb Hendee   *h* 551
Cullen, Edward
Breaking Dawn - Stephenie Meyer   *h* 580
D'Artigo, Menolly
Dragon Wytch - Yasmine Galenorn   *f* 453
Draconis, Aristotle
Stalking the Vampire - Mike Resnick   *f* 501
Gavin, Olivia
Let the Night Begin - Kathryn Smith   *r* 394
Gavin, Reign
Let the Night Begin - Kathryn Smith   *r* 394
Gideon
Wicked Game - Jeri Smith-Ready   *h* 610
Gomez, Felix
The Undead Karma Sutra - Mario
  Acevedo   *h* 524
Grant, Nathan
All Souls' Night - Jennifer Armintrout   *h* 526
Latour, Margaritte
Blood Memories - Barb Hendee   *h* 551
MacPhie, Ian
All I Want for Christmas Is a Vampire - Kerrelyn
  Sparks   *r* 397
Marchette, Lil
Just One Bite - Kimberly Raye   *h* 591
Master
Liquid Diet - Michael McCarty   *h* 575
McAllister, Shane
Wicked Game - Jeri Smith-Ready   *h* 610
McShane, Jack
The Vampire's Betrayal - Raven Hart   *h* 550
Mortimer, Garrett
The Rogue Hunter - Lynsay Sands   *r* 383
O'Connor, Quinn
The Darkest Kiss - Keri Arthur   *h* 528
October
The Sweet Scent of Blood - Suzanne
  McLeod   *f* 486
Pitt, Joe
Every Last Drop - Charlie Huston   *h* 555
Every Last Drop - Charlie Huston   *m* 96
Predo, Dexter
Every Last Drop - Charlie Huston   *m* 96
Every Last Drop - Charlie Huston   *h* 555

Radu the Forsaken
Curse of the Necrarch - Steven Savile   *f* 513
Reaper
Angel's Pain - Maggie Shayne   *r* 386
Strong, Anna
Legacy - Jeanne C. Stein   *h* 611
Tammith
Undead - Richard Lee Byers   *f* 434
Templeton, Ethan
Bond of Darkness - Diane Whiteside   *r* 417
Thorne, William Cuyler
The Vampire's Betrayal - Raven Hart   *h* 550
Van Alen, Schuyler
Revelations - Melissa de la Cruz   *h* 538
Vidame, Dmitri
One Bite with a Stranger - Christine
  Warren   *h* 619

VAMPIRE HUNTER

Danaus
Nightwalker - Jocelyn Drake   *h* 539
Gardella Grantworth de Lacy, Victoria
When Twilight Burns - Colleen Gleason   *r* 280
Mortimer, Garrett
The Rogue Hunter - Lynsay Sands   *r* 383
Pesaro, Max
When Twilight Burns - Colleen Gleason   *r* 280
Vioget, Sebastian
When Twilight Burns - Colleen Gleason   *r* 280

VETERAN

Alatriste y Tenorio, Diego
The King's Gold - Arturo Perez-Reverte   *t* 831
Guinness, October "Tobie"
The Archangel Project - C.S. Graham   *m* 79
Gunning, William
Bright Hair about the Bone - Barbara
  Cleverly   *m* 49
Haldean, Jack
Mad about the Boy? - Dolores
  Gordon-Smith   *m* 77
Hawkins, Phillip
In a Dark Season - Vicki Lane   *m* 115
MacDonald, Mac
Deceived - James Scott Bell   *i* 878
Malatesta, Gualterio
The King's Gold - Arturo Perez-Reverte   *t* 831
McCord, Steven
A Common Ordinary Murder - Donald
  Pfarrer   *m* 157
Morton, Henry
The Long Journey Home - Laurel Means   *t* 821
Palmer, Lance
The Archangel Project - C.S. Graham   *m* 79
Porter, John
A Hundred Years of Happiness - Nicole
  Seitz   *i* 949
Rutledge, Ian
A Matter of Justice - Charles Todd   *t* 859
Saunders, Ethan
The Whiskey Rebels - David Liss   *t* 813
Smith-Fennimore, Malcolm
Mad about the Boy? - Dolores
  Gordon-Smith   *m* 77

Carnegie, Elias
Lifeblood - Tom Becker *h* 531

Cornick, Charles
Cry Wolf - Patricia Briggs *f* 431

Hu-Li, A
The Sacred Book of the Werewolf - Victor
   Pelevin *h* 587

Jensen, Riley
The Darkest Kiss - Keri Arthur *h* 528

Kavanaugh, Ross
Come the Night - Susan Krinard *r* 322

Latham, Anna
Cry Wolf - Patricia Briggs *f* 431

Maitland, Gillian
Come the Night - Susan Krinard *r* 322

Norville, Kitty
Kitty and the Dead Man's Hand - Carrie
   Vaughn *h* 617

O'Farrell, Ben
Kitty and the Dead Man's Hand - Carrie
   Vaughn *h* 617

Shadow
The Darkest Kiss - Keri Arthur *h* 528

Trudeau, Sasha
Bite the Bullet - L.A. Banks *h* 530

WIDOW(ER)

Alexandra
The Widows of Eastwick - John Updike *c* 1114

Barton, Jessica Anne
Tall, Dark, and Texan - Jodi Thomas *r* 407

Beckett, Johanna "Jo"
The Dirty Secrets Club - Meg Gardiner *m* 73

Brewster, Sky Eyes
Pale Moon Stalker - Shirl Henke *r* 295

Buckley, Ben
Sometimes a Light Surprises - Jamie Langston
   Turner *i* 956

Chris
A Partisan's Daughter - Louis de
   Bernieres *c* 996

Cline, Olivia
Insight - Deborah Raney *i* 944

Collins, Jenny
Snowbound in Dry Creek - Janet Tronstad *r* 412

Danby, Lex
Stand by Your Hitman - Leslie Langtry *r* 323

De Poulain, Elvira
Everything under the Sky - Matilda Asensi *t* 726

Deeti
Sea of Poppies - Amitav Ghosh *t* 780

Denton, Joe
A Bride in the Bargain - Deeanne Gist *i* 907

DeVore, Doug
Yesterday's Embers - Deborah Raney *i* 945

Dorn, Henry
After You've Gone - Jeffrey Lent *c* 1048

Duport, Emily Grace
The Glass of Time - Michael Cox *m* 55
The Glass of Time - Michael Cox *t* 755

Eaton, Audrey
Tender Grace - Jackina Stark *i* 953

Fairchild, Kate
The Dangerous Duke - Christine Wells *r* 416

Goodweather, Elizabeth
In a Dark Season - Vicki Lane *m* 115

Graves, Reginald "Rex"
Christmas Is Murder - C.S. Challinor *m* 43

Gunn-Harrill, Jeanette
The Anteater of Death - Betty Webb *m* 195

Hagan, Mallory Kendrick
Texas Ranger Takes a Bride - Patricia
   Thayer *r* 405

Hanssen, Nathan
Conspiracy of Silence - Martha Powers *m* 158

Harris, Monique
Bayou Betrayal - Robin Caroll *i* 890

Jane
The Widows of Eastwick - John Updike *c* 1114

Johnston, Gussie
Old Maid's Puzzle - Terri Thayer *m* 188

Lockhart, Leila
A Dead Man in Barcelona - Michael
   Pearce *m* 153

Lowery, Elizabeth
A Most Unconventional Match - Julia
   Justiss *r* 312

Lundy, Jonathan
Wanted - Shelley Shephard Gray *i* 908

Martinez, Carlos
Mama Does Time - Deborah Sharp *m* 170

Maycott, Joan
The Whiskey Rebels - David Liss *t* 813

McCall, Lilly
Off Season - Anne Rivers Siddons *c* 1098

McGarvie, Molly
The Edge of Light - Ann Shorey *i* 950

Mildenhall Winthrop, Violet
Death of a Cozy Writer - G.M. Malliet *m* 134

Montrose, Cassandra
The Mistress Diaries - Julianne MacLean *r* 334

Morton, Henry
The Long Journey Home - Laurel Means *t* 821

Noble, Charles
Precious Cargo - Clyde Ford *m* 67

O'Brien, Elizabeth
Calico Christmas at Dry Creek - Janet
   Tronstad *r* 411

O'Malley, Gillian
Stiffs and Swine - J.B. Stanley *m* 183

Osborne, Paul
Dead Hot Shot - Victoria Houston *m* 95

Parnell, Charlotte
Traitor's Kiss - Mary Blayney *r* 219

Powell, Nan
The Beach House - Jane Green *c* 1015

Price, Jordan
Cold Hearted - Beverly Barton *m* 14

Randall, Letitia
The Edge of Desire - Stephanie Laurens *r* 324

Redding, Brent
Stalking Susan - Julie Kramer *m* 113

Reese, Ben
Code of Silence - Sally Wright *t* 871

Rejas, Joe
The Anteater of Death - Betty Webb *m* 195

Rhea
Dancing with the Devil - Laura Drewry *r* 259

Romaine, Jack
Kaleidoscope - Darryl Wimberley *m* 198

Rutherford, James
Time Machines Repaired While-U-Wait - K.A.
   Bedford *s* 631

Sarah
The Sin Eaters - Andrew Beahrs *t* 730

Sivakami
The Toss of a Lemon - Padma
   Viswanathan *t* 865

Sorensen, Paige
Written in Blood - Sheila Lowe *m* 127

Steckl, Walt
Security - Stephen Amidon *c* 969

Sukie
The Widows of Eastwick - John Updike *c* 1114

Sullivan, Marcie
A Virgin River Christmas - Robyn Carr *r* 236

Tate, Micah
Beloved Counterfeit - Kathleen Y'Barbo *i* 966

Thatcher, Michael
Stealing Trinity - Ward Larsen *m* 116

Ward, Jonas
Sweet Wells - Elizabeth Gill *t* 781

Wexin, Lydia
Scandalizing the Ton - Diane Gaston *r* 277

WITCH

Black, Artemis
Immortals: The Crossing - Joy Nash *r* 359

Brown, Lizzie
The Accidental Demon Slayer - Angie Fox *r* 274

Cenda
The Flame and the Shadow - Denise
   Rossetti *f* 507

D'Artigo, Camille
Dragon Wytch - Yasmine Galenorn *f* 453

Dow, Felicity "Liss"
No Rest for the Wiccan - Madelyn Alt *m* 1

Drake, Joley
Turbulent Sea - Christine Feehan *r* 266

Philips, Carson
My Wicked Enemy - Carolyn Jewel *r* 306
My Wicked Enemy - Carolyn Jewel *h* 558

Pittman, Laurell
Between Light and Dark - Elissa Wilds *r* 418

Raynham, Stella
The Sweet Scent of Blood - Suzanne
   McLeod *f* 486

Talaith
About a Dragon - G.A. Aiken *r* 202

WIZARD

Beranabus
Death's Shadow - Darren Shan *h* 603

Bisochim
The Phoenix Endangered - Mercedes
   Lackey *f* 468

Dante
Succubus Dreams - Richelle Mead *h* 578

Geralt
Blood of Elves - Andrzej Sapkowski *f* 511

Jones, Zayvion
Magic to the Bone - Devon Monk *f* 489

Turner, Paige
Dial Me for Murder - Amanda Matetsky   *m* 139

von Archimboldi, Benno
2666 - Roberto Bolano   *c* 980

Ward, Susan
Sweetheart - Chelsea Cain   *m* 38

Weber, Noa
The Confessions of Noa Weber - Gail Hareven   *c* 1017

Whitmore, Angela
The Killing Circle - Andrew Pyper   *m* 160

Wiggin, Valentine
Ender in Exile - Orson Scott Card   *s* 640

Wilde, Oscar
Oscar Wilde and a Game Called Murder - Gyles Brandreth   *m* 30
Oscar Wilde and a Game Called Murder - Gyles Brandreth   *t* 738

Wyatt, Marina
The Edge of Impropriety - Pam Rosenthal   *r* 380

Yeats, William Butler
The Dracula Dossier - James Reese   *t* 838

YOUNG MAN

Keller, Jude
The Passion of Mary-Margaret - Lisa Samson   *i* 947

Lassiter, Nick
A Love to Last Forever - Tracie Peterson   *i* 942

Turner, Martin
Canvey Island - James Runcie   *t* 843

YOUNG WOMAN

Alicia
Succulent Prey - Wrath James White   *h* 621

Callahan, Monica
Against All Odds - Irene Hannon   *i* 913

Charez, Aria
The Bridesmaid's Turn - Nicole Foster   *r* 273

Fitzpatrick, Laetitia
Absolute Honor - C.C. Humphreys   *t* 796

Forsythe, Ariana
Before the Season Ends - Linore Rose Burkard   *i* 882

Gallatin, Beth
A Love to Last Forever - Tracie Peterson   *i* 942

Gallatin, Lacy
A Dream to Call My Own - Tracie Peterson   *i* 941

Garrahan, Ruth
The Nightingales of Troy - Alice Fulton   *t* 776

Graham, Sarah
Home Another Way - Christa Parrish   *i* 939

Grant, Maddy
Sweet Wells - Elizabeth Gill   *t* 781

Green, Jess
The Man for Me - Gemma Bruce   *r* 229

Grimm, Greta
The Daughters Grimm - Minda Webber   *r* 414

Grimm, Rae
The Daughters Grimm - Minda Webber   *r* 414

Haswell, Lillian
The Apothecary's Daughter - Julie Klassen   *i* 927

Hutton, Olivia
Indignation - Philip Roth   *t* 840

Ivey, Anna
A Bride in the Bargain - Deeanne Gist   *i* 907

Keim, Rebecca
Rebecca's Promise - Jerry S. Eicher   *i* 904
Rebecca's Return - Jerry S. Eicher   *i* 903

Kendall
Spring Broke - Melody Carlson   *i* 888

Le, Lisa
A Hundred Years of Happiness - Nicole Seitz   *i* 949

Lelani
Spring Broke - Melody Carlson   *i* 888

Maddiford, Rose
Cherrybrook Rose - Tania Anne Crosse   *t* 756

Marah
Journey to the Well - Diana Wallis Taylor   *i* 955

Maya
The Good Parents - Joan London   *c* 1051

McGinn, Autumn
Dark Deceiver - Pamela Palmer   *r* 366

Miranda
Miranda - John R. Little   *f* 476

Monahan, Christine
Runner - Thomas Perry   *m* 154

Mott, Dorritt
The Desires of Her Heart - Lyn Cote   *i* 895

Novak, Dawn
Devil May Ride - Wendy Roberts   *h* 595

O'Roarke, Lillian
Unlacing Lilly - Gail Ranstrom   *r* 374

Schmidt, Anna
The Shadow of Reichenbach Falls - John R. King   *m* 109

Travers, Alexia
Love Finds You in Last Chance, California - Miralee Ferrell   *i* 905

Vicknair, Nanette
Live and Yearn - Kelley St. John   *r* 400

Witherington, Julia
Ransome's Honor - Kaye Dacus   *i* 897

Wren, Jacquelyn "Mistress Jack"
Pleasuring the Pirate - Emily Bryant   *r* 230

Wyse, Mary Jo
A Cedar Cove Christmas - Debbie Macomber   *r* 336

YOUNG WOMEN

Sarah
Wild Mulberries - Iman Humaydan Younes   *t* 873

ZOO KEEPER

Bentley, Theodora "Teddy"
The Anteater of Death - Betty Webb   *m* 195

Oakley, Iris
Night Kill - Ann Littlewood   *m* 124

Stellar, Denny
Night Kill - Ann Littlewood   *m* 124

Author Index

This index is an alphabetical listing of the authors of books featured in entries and those listed within entries under the rubrics "Other books by the same author" and "Other books you might like." For each author, the titles of books described or listed in this edition and their entry numbers appear. Bold numbers indicate a featured main entry; light-face numbers refer to books recommended for further reading.

Author Index

Author Index

Author Index

Author Index

Author Index

Author Index

Author Index

Author Index

Author Index

Author Index

Title Index

This index alphabetically lists all titles featured in entries and those listed within entries under "Other books by the same author" and "Other books you might like." Each title is followed by the author's name and the number of the entry where the book is described or listed. Bold numbers indicate featured main entries; light-face numbers refer to books recommended for further reading.

Title Index

Title Index

Title Index

Title Index

Title Index

Title Index

Title Index

Title Index

Title Index

Title Index

Title Index

Title Index

Title Index

Title Index

Title Index

Title Index

Title Index